Key to atlas pages 18-143

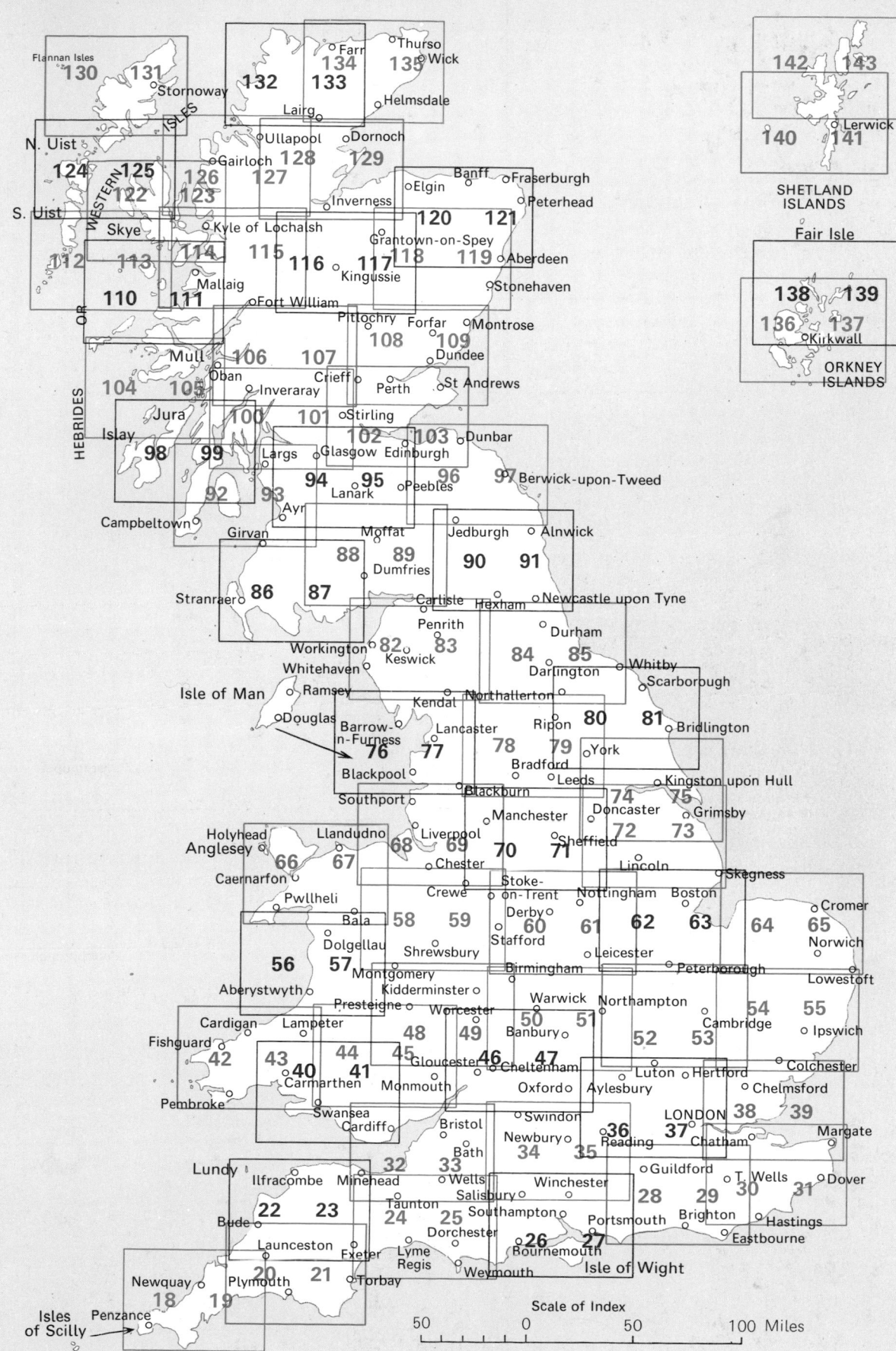

SHETLAND
ISLANDS

Fair Isle

ORKNEY
ISLANDS

Scale of Index

50   0   50   100 Miles

The Ordnance Survey
ATLAS
of Great Britain

The Ordnance Survey
ATLAS
of Great Britain

Book Club Associates

London

1:250 000 maps and index made by the Ordnance Survey, Southampton

Maps on endpapers, pages 14-143, 180-224 © Crown Copyright 1982

Arrangement and all other material © The Hamlyn Publishing Group Ltd. 1982

This edition published 1982 by Book Club Associates
By arrangement with

Ordnance Survey   and   Country Life Books
                         a division of
                         The Hamlyn Publishing Group Limited
                         London · New York · Sydney · Toronto

First published 1982

Printed in Great Britain

Contents

Page 6   **Introduction**   *M J Wise*
Page 8   Great Britain – Physical
Page 9   Great Britain – Geological
Page 11   Great Britain – Climate

Page 14   **A Short History of the Ordnance Survey**
Page 15   **Ordnance Survey Products**

Page 17   Legend for Ordnance Survey 1:250 000 Scale Maps

Pages 18-143   # ORDNANCE SURVEY 1:250 000 Maps

For key see the front and back endpapers of this Atlas

Page 144 **The Historical Geography of Britain**   *R A Butlin*
Page 145 Prehistory to the Romans
Page 147 The Dark Ages
Page 150 Britain to 1350
Page 151 Late Medieval Britain
Page 153 The Agricultural Revolution
Page 155 The Early Industrial Revolution
Page 157 Britain in the Late Nineteenth Century

Page 158 **Modern Britain**   *M J Wise*
Page 159 The Crisis of the 1930s
Page 161 Mineral Resources
Page 162 Industry and Energy
Page 166 The Transport System
Page 168 Agriculture and Fisheries
Page 169 Farming Types
Page 172 Planning for Leisure
Page 173 Planning for Industry
Page 174 Population Patterns
Page 175 Cultural Diversity
Page 178 County Boundaries before 1974
Page 179 County Boundaries since 1974

Page 177 *Acknowledgements and Bibliography*
Page 180 **Index**
Front endpaper   The National Grid
                 Key to atlas pages 18-143
Back endpaper   Key to atlas pages 18-143
                 Key to Ordnance Survey 1:50 000 Scale Maps

Introduction

William Somerville, writing in 1735, described Britain as a 'highly favoured isle'. Today, we may still agree that, while there are many problems of a man-made kind, in most respects Britain is indeed a fortunate country geographically. Its island position near to but separate from Western Europe, its temperate climate, generally plentiful rainfall, great variety of rock types, land forms and soils, its resources of coal and iron, clays and limestones, natural gas and oil, provide a great range of opportunities.

Few areas in the world of similar size offer so great a diversity both of physical and of human characteristics as does Britain. Contrast the remote hamlets of the Scottish Highlands with the thronging streets of Glasgow or London, the open arable lands of East Anglia with the upland grazings of the hills, the industrial landscapes of the Black Country or West Yorkshire with the rural areas that surround them, the New Towns of today with cities, like York, which preserve the fabric of medieval times. The traveller, using this atlas, will be aware, every few miles, of change in the landscape around him. Each observation, each view provokes questions about the evaluations of environment that have been made by people in the past and about the origins of the present use of land. How can we make the best use of the land of Britain today, using it and all its resources fully yet wisely, matching the desire to exploit with the need to conserve?

Diversity of Physical Conditions

Even a swift glance at the relief map shows clear evidence of variety in the contrast between the generally high relief of western and northern Britain and the lower lands of the east and south. Geographers have drawn a broad division between the Highland Zone and the Lowland Zone, separated by an imaginary line drawn across the country from the estuary of the River Tees to that of the Exe. The distinction is not complete for west of the Tees-Exe line there are areas of Lowland, for example in Cheshire and Lancashire and in the Midland Valley of Scotland, while in the Lowland Zone there are uplands and sharp ridges which at points rise to above or near to 305 m (1000 ft). But land over that height dominates in the Highland Zone; there are outstanding mountains such as Ben Nevis (1343 m 4406 ft) and Snowdon (1085 m 3560 ft) and the plains and valleys interrupt or break the generally highland character of the relief.

To a large extent this division reflects geological characteristics. The Highlands are composed mainly of old rocks, primarily of Pre-Cambrian and Palaeozoic ages, which have been folded and fractured in the great Caledonian and Hercynian (Armorican) earth movements and heavily eroded over very long periods of time. The rocks of the Lowland Zone are mainly sedimentary rocks of Mesozoic or Tertiary ages and have been folded into scarplands. The Lowlands have been likened to 'a grained surface' of sawn timber, alternating belts with varied powers to resist denudation – 'grained wood, worn with age'. Even in a nearly continuous outcrop there are many differences in the height and form of the scarps; the local

geological structures vary as do the soils. A full understanding of the land forms in much of Britain must also embrace a knowledge of events subsequent to the deposition and folding of the rocks, especially the effects of the Ice Age, changes in levels of land and sea and erosional processes. Having been the locations of ice caps during the Ice Age, the Highlands bear the clearest signs of glacial erosion: corries or cwms in the mountains, characteristically U-shaped valleys, *roches moutonnées*, hanging valleys. The effects of deposition of materials by ice may also be seen in the Highlands, but these are still more widely exhibited in the Lowlands, by the widespread glacial drifts of the Midlands and East Anglia where deposits of boulder clay smooth the relief and obscure the underlying rocks. The ice sheets and their deposits also altered patterns of drainage and the present courses of rivers such as the Thames, Severn and Warwickshire Avon are, in part, the products of the Ice Age. Even in the areas south of the Thames which were not covered by ice sheets, the effects of near-glacial conditions may be discerned.

The idea of a division into Highland and Lowland Zones is thus a useful way to begin the study of the geography of Britain. Yet there are great differences within the Highland Zone itself, between areas such as Snowdonia or the Scottish Highlands with summits rising to over 1000 m (3300 ft) where sharp relief is a product of geological fracturing and glaciation, and many other extensive areas of the Zone with smoother relief and high-level plateau-like land forms. We may instance the Southern Uplands of Scotland, many parts of the Pennines or the plateau of mid-Wales. For such areas B. W. Sparks has suggested the term Upland Britain, so giving a threefold regional division: Highland, Upland and Lowland.

Regional Contrasts in Climate

Our climate may be a source of both humour and annoyance but, despite occasional extreme events, it is another aspect of the favourability of Britain's physical geography. It is greatly influenced by Britain's maritime situation just off the western edge of the Eurasian land mass. It has been said that, climatically, 'Britain is a battleground', invaded and conquered by one air mass itself soon to be re-conquered by another. The four chief, but not the only, types of air mass are Tropical Maritime, Tropical Continental, Polar Maritime and Polar Continental. Each brings its own type of weather and the battles join along 'fronts', bringing a sequence of sometimes frequent and possibly stormy changes in the weather. There is much variability of weather from day to day and place to place, providing a constant topic of conversation and, according to one's point of view on particular occasions, delight or frustration.

In terms of a world classification of climates the whole island lies within the cool temperate type. Nevertheless notable differences may be discerned within Britain itself. Regional and local differences derive from many factors, including latitude, proximity to the sea, altitude, the relief of the land, aspect, exposure to wind and degree of urban development. Generalising, in winter the west is warmer than the east, while in summer the south is warmer than the north. Precipitation, though, varies from one place to

another more than temperature. The west has more rainfall than the east, with areas of over 1500 mm (60 in) of annual rainfall on the Highland and Upland areas mostly in winter. The east is much drier, with annual totals of less than 750 mm (30 in) over much of the English Lowlands and with the greater proportion falling in the latter six months and, in some areas, in the summer.

Many attempts have been made to divide Britain into climatic regions and to characterise the differences from place to place. One of the simplest attempts superimposes the isotherms for January which run broadly north-south, and for July, which have an east-west trend, to produce four quadrants. The north-west quadrant has cool summers and mild winters, the south-west quadrant has warm summers and mild winters. The north-east quadrant is epitomised by cool summers and cold winters and the south-east, which shows the greatest contrasts in temperature, by warm summers and cold winters. When the general difference in rainfall between west and east is also recalled, a broad regional picture emerges.

A rather more complex pattern of regional climates has been suggested, by S. Gregory. He employs three sets of indicators, the length of the growing season, the magnitude of rainfall and the seasonality of rainfall (*see map page 11*). The growing season of nine or more months of the south-western coasts falls to eight or seven months in Lowland Britain, to six or five months in the Uplands and to four or less in the Grampians and the Western Highlands of Scotland.

Under the heading of rainfall magnitude, Gregory distinguishes those areas that receive at least 1250 mm (50 in) of rain a year with a high probability of its occurrence each year, from those that receive less than 750 mm (30 in) a year with a much lower probability of regularity, with an area of moderate rainfall lying between the two. In terms of rainfall seasonality, he distinguishes the areas of maximum rainfall in the winter half of the year (western Britain and a part of southern England south of the Thames) from the areas of maximum rainfall in the second half of the year. These comprise most of the rest of the country, except for the area between the Thames and the Wash where there is a weakly developed summer maximum.

But yet another distinction should be introduced. About 80% of the population lives in towns and about 11% of the surface area of England and Wales is built upon. Cities, especially large ones, tend to modify the climate. Buildings interrupt air flow and reduce wind speeds; air pollution is higher. The warm air which, particularly by night, covers cities produces what have been termed 'heat islands'. Most towns with high central building densities average 1°-2°C warmer than surrounding countrysides; and on occasions much higher differences are recorded.

It must also be remembered that, even in a temperate climate, departures from the 'norm' and extreme events do occur. A recent example is that of the great drought of 1975-76 which followed a tendency to low rainfall totals in the early 1970s. And, though we do not fully understand the causes, climates do change over time. There have certainly been notable fluctuations in the climatic record of the last 1000 years and it should not be assumed that present climatic conditions will continue unchanged indefinitely.

Climate is one of the factors that influence soil and, broadly speaking, it is possible to draw a distinction between the acidic podsolic soils of the cooler and wetter north and west where high winter rainfall leaches out the soluble salts to leave an impoverished grey soil beneath a black humus layer, and the less leached brown forest soils of the Lowland Zone. But soils also depend upon the parent material, be that solid rock or glacial drift. As we travel from one part of the country to another we notice the rapidity with which changes in the solid rocks occur, very noticeably for example in the scarplands of the Lowland Zone, and soil types reflect such changes. The distribution of glacial drift has been a particularly important factor. We may distinguish between sandy soils, loamy and usually very fertile soils, clay soils often heavy to work, and calcareous soils derived from limestone. A third factor which influences soil type is vegetation, and some soils have a very high content of organic matter. Such soils include the black, fenland soils and peaty and moorland soils. Local elements of geology and relief influence soil type: some areas of hard rock are bare of soil, and the degree of slope may also be important, particularly influencing drainage. It must also be remembered that many of our soils have been tilled, drained and fertilised for centuries, so that they are no longer in a completely natural state.

Atlantic Britain, Highland Britain and Lowland Britain

The concept of Highland and Lowland Zones has also been employed in interpreting the distribution of early settlements. Pioneers in this work were Sir Cyril Fox and Dr L. F. Chitty who in 1932 published a remarkable book, *The Personality of Britain*. They used detailed mapping of archaeological evidence, to examine the distribution of prehistoric settlements in terms both of the physical conditions and what was known of the organisation and technology of each wave of incoming peoples. They recognised two principal sets of embarkation areas for those moving from Europe to Britain. These were the coasts of northwest Europe from Brittany to the Rhine with routes across the narrow seas, and, for those to whom the sea was a highway, the coasts from Spain to Brittany and from the Rhine to the Norwegian fjords.

In Megalithic and early Bronze Age times the Atlantic seaways from Spain were much in use and Britain was in the van of western European progress. But in the middle Bronze Age, land routes across Europe sapped the importance of the Atlantic routes. Britain tended, therefore, to become 'a country on the edge of the known world, the last to receive and absorb cultures moving from east to west'. The Lowland Zone, adjacent to the Continent, was easily invaded and new cultures from the Continent were imposed.

Although later writers have cast doubts upon Fox's ideas, many agree that from about 1000 BC the contrast between Highland and Lowland was very significant. Peoples of the later Bronze and Iron Ages were better equipped than their predecessors to tackle the clearance of the woodlands and to till the heavier soils in the vales. The Romans, it is true, overstepped into the Highland Zone but the boundary

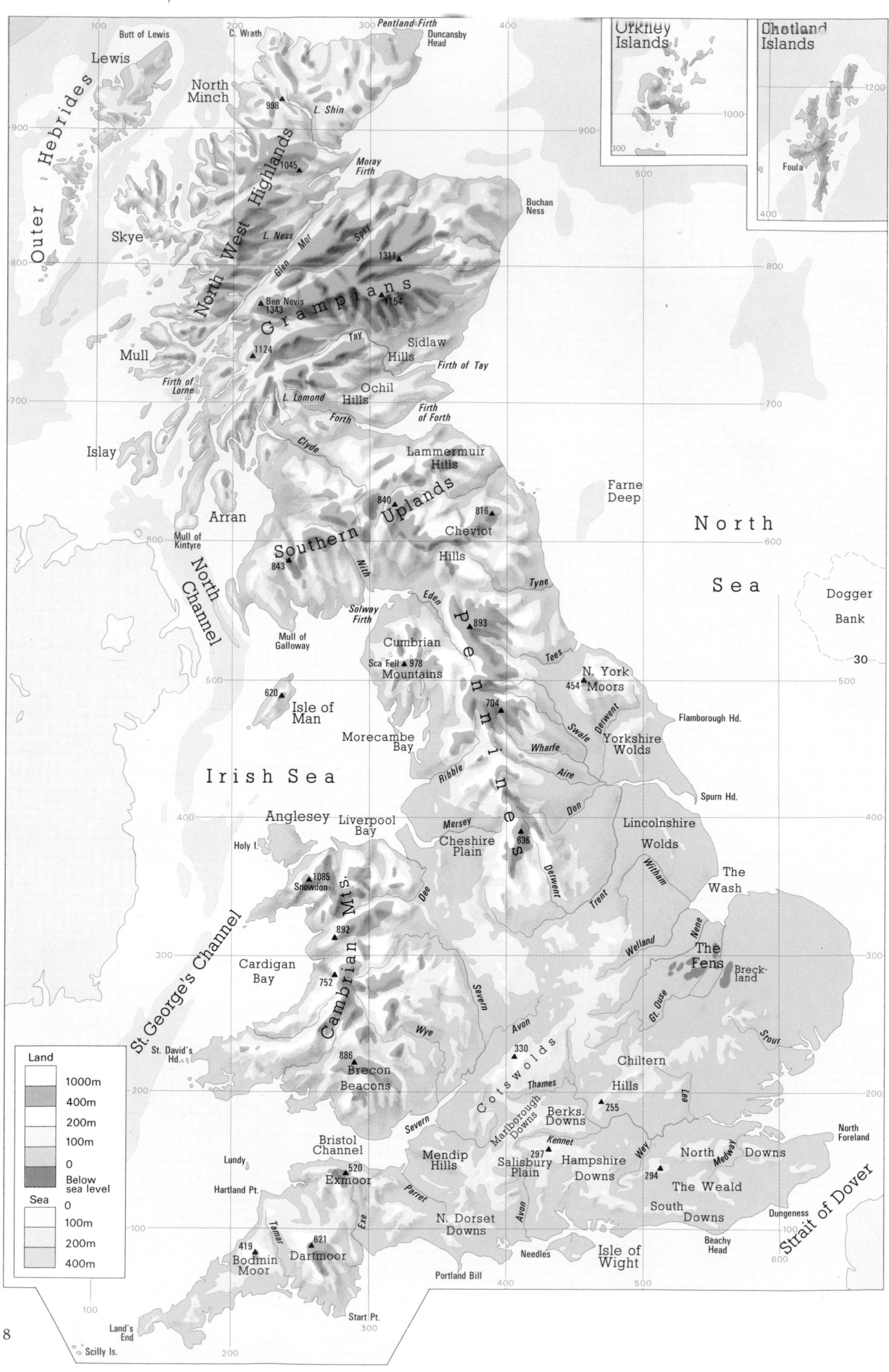

Outer Hebrides
Lewis
Butt of Lewis
C. Wrath
Pentland Firth
Duncansby Head
Orkney Islands
Shetland Islands
1200
300
1000
400
500

North Minch
998
L. Shin
North West Highlands
Moray Firth
Buchan Ness
Skye
L. Ness
Glen Mor
Spey
1045
Mull
Grampians
1311
Ben Nevis 1343
1154
1124
Tay
Sidlaw Hills
Firth of Tay
Firth of Lorne
L. Lomond
Ochil Hills
Firth of Forth
Forth
Islay
Clyde
Lammermuir Hills
Arran
Southern Uplands
840
Cheviot Hills
816
Farne Deep
Mull of Kintyre
843
Nith
Tyne
North Channel
Solway Firth
Eden
Pennines
893
North Sea
Mull of Galloway
Cumbrian Mountains
Sca Fell 978
Tees
Dogger Bank
30
620
Isle of Man
704
N. York Moors
454
Morecambe Bay
Swale
Flamborough Hd.
Irish Sea
Ribble
Wharfe
Yorkshire Wolds
Aire
Spurn Hd.
Anglesey
Liverpool Bay
Mersey
Don
Lincolnshire Wolds
Holy I.
Cheshire Plain
636
Witham
The Wash
1085
Snowdon
Dee
Derwent
Trent
Nene
The Fens
Breck-land
892
Cambrian Mts.
St. George's Channel
Cardigan Bay
752
Severn
Welland
Gt. Ouse
St. David's Hd.
Wye
Avon
Stour
886
Brecon Beacons
330
Cotswolds
Chiltern Hills
Lea
Severn
Thames
Marlborough Downs
Berks. Downs
255
North Foreland
Bristol Channel
Lundy
Mendip Hills
297
Kennet
Hampshire Downs
North Downs
Medway
Wey
Hartland Pt.
520
Exmoor
Salisbury Plain
294
The Weald
Dungeness
Parret
Avon
South Downs
Strait of Dover
Exe
N. Dorset Downs
Beachy Head
419
Tamar
621
Dartmoor
Bodmin Moor
Needles
Isle of Wight
600
Portland Bill
Start Pt.
Land's End
Scilly Is.

Foula

Land
1000m
400m
200m
100m
0
Below sea level
Sea
0
100m
200m
400m

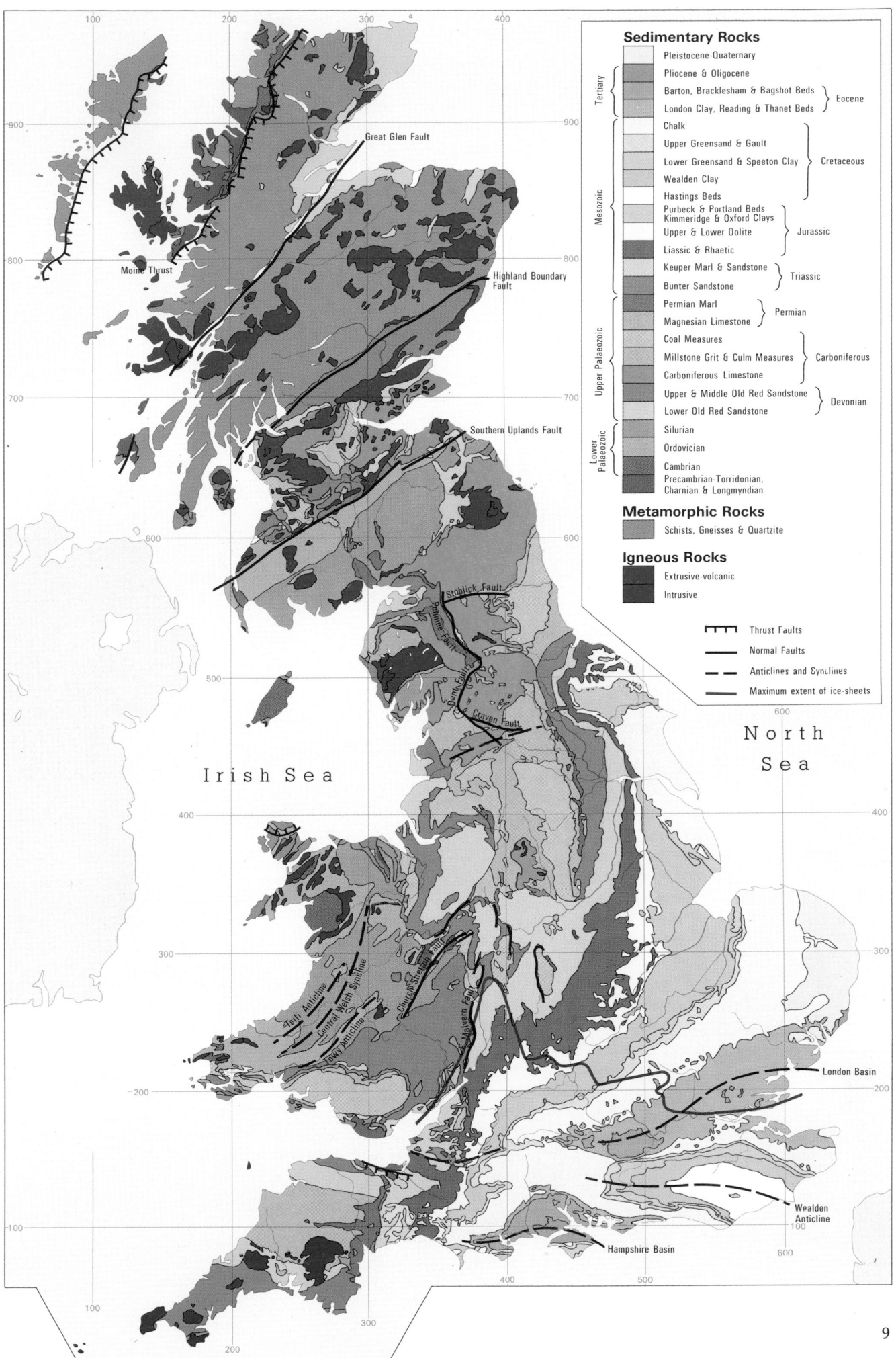

Great Glen Fault

Moine Thrust

Highland Boundary
Fault

Southern Uplands Fault

Stublick Fault

Pennine Fault

Dent Fault

Craven Fault

Irish Sea

North
Sea

Teifi Anticline

Central Welsh Syncline

Towy Anticline

Church Stretton Fault

Malvern Fault

London Basin

Wealden
Anticline

Hampshire Basin

Sedimentary Rocks

Tertiary	Pleistocene-Quaternary
	Pliocene & Oligocene
	Barton, Bracklesham & Bagshot Beds } Eocene
	London Clay, Reading & Thanet Beds }
Mesozoic	Chalk
	Upper Greensand & Gault
	Lower Greensand & Speeton Clay } Cretaceous
	Wealden Clay
	Hastings Beds
	Purbeck & Portland Beds
	Kimmeridge & Oxford Clays } Jurassic
	Upper & Lower Oolite
	Liassic & Rhaetic
	Keuper Marl & Sandstone } Triassic
	Bunter Sandstone
Upper Palaeozoic	Permian Marl } Permian
	Magnesian Limestone
	Coal Measures
	Millstone Grit & Culm Measures } Carboniferous
	Carboniferous Limestone
	Upper & Middle Old Red Sandstone } Devonian
	Lower Old Red Sandstone
Lower Palaeozoic	Silurian
	Ordovician
	Cambrian
	Precambrian-Torridonian, Charnian & Longmyndian

Metamorphic Rocks

Schists, Gneisses & Quartzite

Igneous Rocks

Extrusive-volcanic

Intrusive

Thrust Faults

Normal Faults

Anticlines and Synclines

Maximum extent of ice-sheets

9

between the civil and military zones was approximately that between Highland and Lowland Britain (*see map page 115*). Even in Anglo-Saxon times, the western frontier of their influence at the end of the 6th century was aligned along the outcrop of the Palaeozoic rocks (*see map page 147*).

Such observations led Fox to the proposition that historically the Lowland Zone had nourished 'richer cultures might precariously survive. There were subtler observed, 'the most important centres of any culture or civilisation are likely to be in the south-east of the islands.' Such circumstances, he went on, had led to the 'tragedy' of the early history of Britain. Fresh invasions from the east had, on the one hand, paralysed older cultures by largely destroying them where they were most flourishing and on the other, had tended to cut off the survivals of those cultures in the west from the stimuli of continued contact with Europe.

But the Highland Zone was not simply a barrier to cultural advance nor a region where outliers of former Lowland cultures might precariously survive. There were subtler and more positive influences. Whereas in the Lowland Zone newer cultures were successively imposed on earlier, in Highland Britain they tended to be absorbed by the older cultures. Historically Lowland Britain was characterised by replacement, Highland Britain by fusion and continuity. The power of absorption of the Highland Zone had indeed provided it with a distinctive cultural character of its own. The survival of Celtic languages and traditions was the clearest example.

Later writers have tended to place increased emphasis on one aspect of the geography of the Highland Zone which Fox noted but did not develop, namely the tendency for the shores of the Irish Sea (and its northern and southern approaches) to form a 'culture pool'. R. H. Kinvig (1958), for example, while accepting the value of the idea of a Highland Zone, argued that a better understanding may be gained by subdividing the Highlands into an 'Atlantic Zone' and a 'Moorland Area' lying inland from it.

His Atlantic Zone included the coastal belt of plains and low plateaux along the western and northern coasts and also the islands of Man, the Hebrides, the Shetlands and the Orkneys. He and others distinguished 'Atlantic Britain' on grounds of both physical and historical geography. Historically, the zone had played an active rather than a passive role in that, open southwards to influences *via* sea routes from France, Iberia and the Mediterranean and northwards to influences from Scandinavia, it had been a receiving zone for peoples and cultures. In prehistoric times there was south-north traffic and the builders of the megalithic tombs came by sea. From the 4th century AD onwards contacts between the various parts of Atlantic Britain, and with Gaul and beyond, intensified. Many of the ideas associated with Celtic Christianity came by these routes. By about AD 800 Norse settlers had begun to penetrate and to settle. Eventually the Isle of Man became the capital of an island realm consisting of all the Hebrides. In the 12th century a separate diocese, the Episcopal See of the Isles, was established based on St Patrick's Isle at Peel (*see map page 150*).

E. Estyn Evans (1958) has carried this argument forward into the present day, suggesting a number of aspects of

modern social and folk life in the coastlands of western and northwestern Europe which link what he refers to as the 'Atlantic Ends of Europe'. The thesis is that 'these western lands have a cultural heritage which is rich and varied, and signs are not lacking at the present day that some of these areas are once again going to play a more active part than they have done in the immediate past'. Those words remind us of the rise of national pressures and demands for the devolution of government from London, the route centre of the Lowland Zone.

Thus the simple Highland Zone-Lowland Zone concept requires modification. The case for the existence of an Atlantic Britain is strong and the difference between the true Highlands and the Uplands must also be kept in mind. Such broad divisions as have been indicated form a useful starting-point for more detailed studies of the great variety of regional conditions in Britain.

Land and People

The land of Britain, varied in its landscape and in the resources that it offers, is small in area in relation to the demands of its population of 54,129,000 (1981). The total land area of England, Wales and Scotland is about 22,752,000 hectares (56,200,000 acres), allowing only 0·42 HA (1·04 acres) per head of population, and for England and Wales only about 0·3 HA (0·75 acres) per head. The needs are many and include housing, industry, mineral extraction, transport, agriculture, water supply, recreation and defence. Agriculture accounts in England and Wales for more than three-quarters of land use, with woodland covering about 7% and urban, industrial and associated development about 11%. There is great variation in the quality of agricultural land: about 13% of the land area is under rough grazing and only 3% is truly of first-class quality (*see maps pages 168 and 169*). In 1900 only about 5% of the land surface was in urban uses, but the proportion has increased more rapidly than has population, and land has been much in demand as cities have spread outwards. In the inter-war years losses of farmland to urban uses amounted at times to over 25,000 HA (60,000 acres) a year. The concern aroused led to the improvement of planning control, and since 1945 about 15,700 HA (38,800 acres) a year or about 0·1% of the total land surface of England and Wales has been transferred from agricultural to urban uses. It is not surprising that land use conflicts have arisen over development proposals, for example for the extension of urban land, motorway construction, the creation of reservoirs, the sinking of new coal mines, the building of new power stations, the enlargement of airports or the improvement for agricultural use of heath or wetlands.

Urban and Industrial Britain

The dominant feature of the human geography of Britain is the existence of a great urban system, the product mainly of the rapid industrial and urban growth of the last 200 years. In 1801 some nine million people lived in England and Wales, and one in three lived in towns. By 1851 the population had grown to 18 million and just over a half were urban dwellers. By the beginning of the 20th century, out of 32·5 million people 78% were urban dwellers. Since that

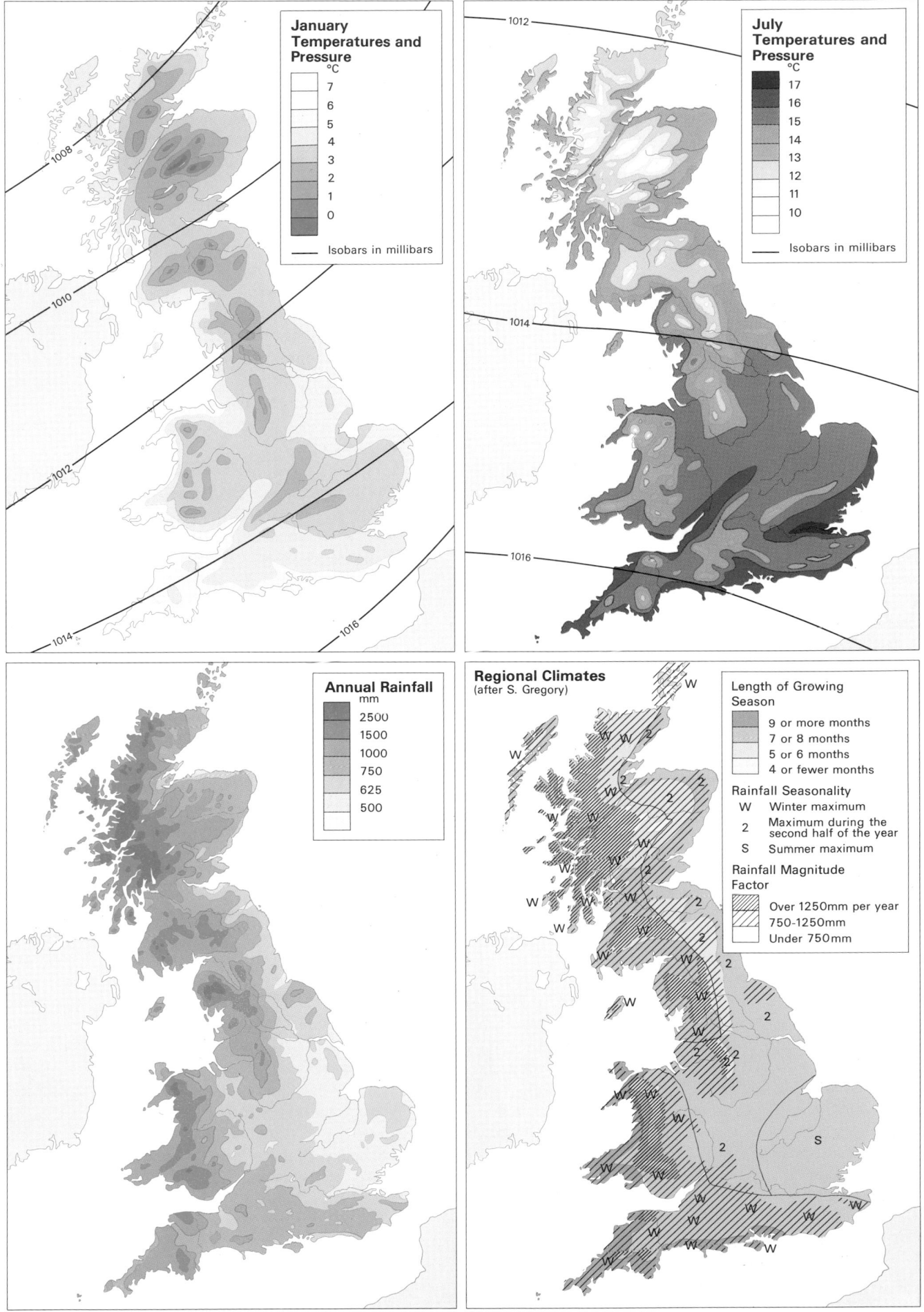

January Temperatures and Pressure
°C
7
6
5
4
3
2
1
0

—— Isobars in millibars

1008
1010
1012
1014
1016

July Temperatures and Pressure
°C
17
16
15
14
13
12
11
10

—— Isobars in millibars

1012
1014
1016

Annual Rainfall
mm
2500
1500
1000
750
625
500

Regional Climates
(after S. Gregory)

Length of Growing Season
9 or more months
7 or 8 months
5 or 6 months
4 or fewer months

Rainfall Seasonality
W   Winter maximum
2   Maximum during the second half of the year
S   Summer maximum

Rainfall Magnitude Factor
Over 1250mm per year
750–1250mm
Under 750mm

time, although the proportion living in towns and cities has not grown greatly, the actual number has and the character and shapes of the urban areas have greatly changed.

Look first at what some call the Central Urban Region, others the British megalopolis (*see map page 173*). A band of dense population stretches northwestwards from the English Channel across the Thames, through the Midlands, dividing on each side of the Pennines and continuing into Lancashire and Yorkshire. The southern part of this megalopolis is focused around London, the midland and northern parts contain a number of urban groups around, for example, Birmingham, Manchester and Leeds. The urban areas do not actually join together; there are breaks of green land between them. But the whole area is closely bound together by main railway lines and motorways that reflect the strength of the economic links between the cities and their activities in the zone.

Outside this English megalopolis some other important urban and industrial zones occur. Indeed the eye may take another line, starting with the South Wales industrial region and Bristol, continuing to the northeast through the West and East Midlands and terminating on Humberside. Traversing northwards there is the industrial region of northeast England with Newcastle-upon-Tyne as its main centre. The central industrial belt of Scotland with Glasgow and Edinburgh as the principal cities provides homes for about three-quarters of Scotland's population of 5·25 million.

The appearance, character and prosperity of the cities and industrial districts in these strongly urbanised zones vary widely. Some of the cities, Edinburgh, Durham, York, Coventry, above all London, were important in medieval times. But supreme significance must be given to the Industrial Revolution of the 18th and 19th centuries. For this was also a geographical revolution. As new methods for smelting iron using coke were introduced the coalfields became important, and mining and industrial towns began to spring up where none had existed before. Developments in industry, including the introduction of the factory system in the metal-using and textile industries, brought people into rapidly-growing industrial cities such as Birmingham and Manchester. Commercial activities intensified. Canals and, after 1830, railways linked the industrial districts together. External trade prospered and new ports were required: estuaries were deepened, channels constructed, dock systems developed on the Thames, Mersey and Clyde. The Clyde, Tyne, Wear and, for a time, the Thames also built the ships which imported food and commodities for conversion into manufactured products and carried away the finished products and the export coal for the bunkers of the great merchant fleets. London grew as port, manufacturing region, chief centre of commerce, and as the location of government and as the biggest centre of wholesale and retail trade (*see maps pages 155 and 157*).

These great developments of what has been described as the palaeotechnic phase of industrial development and which underlie present patterns must be seen in terms of Britain's position as the leading industrial power at a time when the world market was expanding. In time it was to be overtaken, but much of the physical fabric constructed at that time remains. Each industrial region developed its own group of specialised activities. The West Midlands was the home of the metal industries, Lancashire of cotton and the West Riding of woollen textiles. South Wales had its iron and steel, coal, tinplate and non-ferrous metal industries. The northeast and Scotland had coal, iron and steel, shipbuilding and marine engineering. Such a system of specialised industrial regions worked well while the market was strong, but in the Great Depression of 1929-31 those areas that had rather narrowly-based industrial structures and were dependent on industries that were declining nationally fared badly. Unemployment soared and poverty struck. South Wales, Clydeside, northeast England, West Cumberland are examples of what for a time were termed Depressed Areas. By contrast, areas such as the West Midlands and Greater London where the industries were more diversified and which possessed strong shares in such industries as electrical engineering and electrical goods, motor vehicles, the food and drink trades and the service industries, which were expanding nationally, remained relatively prosperous.

The contrast in conditions between the regions and the movement of people away from the hard-hit areas to the more prosperous districts raised new questions. To what extent did the nation possess a responsibility towards areas that had contributed greatly to the national wealth but now, for no fault of their own, found themselves in hard straits? If a responsibility existed, how should it be exercised and what methods could be found to rectify the disparities between areas? Preliminary steps to devise remedies were introduced by 1939 but it is since 1945 that 'regional' policies have been developed and more will be said about these in a later section of this atlas.

The 19th-century industrial districts developed their own distinctive landscapes. Mrs Gaskell writing in 1857 described the Yorkshire landscape between Keighley and Haworth: 'what with villas, great worsted factories, with here and there an old fashioned farm-house . . . it can hardly be called "country" any part of the way'. But those who lived there were perhaps more fortunate than those in the slums of inner Manchester or those in the Black Country, 'black by day and red by night' as the flames from the open blast furnaces were reflected from the clouds. The industrial towns threw out branching lines of houses along the roads joining them and by the end of the century a number of great conurbations, areas in which the built-up areas had become contiguous, had been formed. We now find seven major conurbations, each different from the others. London, by far the largest, grew outwards from its central core to engulf land in Middlesex, Hertfordshire, Essex, Kent and Surrey. Its population in 1981 was 6,696,000 (though, like all the major conurbations, population has been declining recently). The other major conurbations are West Midland, Greater Manchester, Merseyside, Tyneside, West Yorkshire and Clydeside. These conurbations hold about 32% of the population of Great Britain. Outside the conurbations there grew railway towns like Crewe and Swindon, ports such as Southampton, fishing ports such as Grimsby, resort towns like Bournemouth and Blackpool. And many smaller manufacturing towns developed.

Problems of Adaptation and Modernisation

The Great Industrial Age thus contributed vastly to the establishment of the basic pattern of modern urban settlement. Much of its physical structure remains with us; some of it is mean, like the slum houses of the inner areas of the big cities which have been the subject of vigorous clearance, especially since 1945. The street patterns of cities built in the Victorian period were not designed for modern traffic conditions and adapting them to the needs of road transport without damage to the environment poses acute problems. The great railway termini such as St Pancras, Liverpool Street or Waverley remind us of the role of the railway. Some at least of the canals are still at work carrying freight. Although much of the derelict land created by the mines, furnaces and brickworks has been cleared, some still remains: indeed now that the Industrial Age has passed into history a number of industrial museums serve as reminders of the need to create new industries and fresh environments of which we can be proud.

Such changes are symptomatic of the modernisation of the geography of Britain which has been proceeding since the end of the 1939-45 war and especially in the last two decades.

Coal is king no longer. Though still important in the economy, coal production is only about two-fifths of the maximum reached in 1913. For power, we now have a choice of coal, oil, natural gas, or electricity (produced from coal, oil, natural gas, nuclear fuels or, mainly in Scotland, from water power). The period 1965-75 has been described as that of 'a revolution in the UK fuel and power industries unmatched since British coalfields were first developed'. Oil is now more important to the economy than coal and this revolution which began on a basis of imported oil and gas can now draw on the resources of the North Sea. The exploitation of the oil and gas fields has itself produced a revolution in the geography of the North Sea.

The transport system has changed equally radically in the 20th century. The railway system has been reduced in length of rail and transformed technically by electrification and diesel haulage. But except for services such as high speed inter-city trains, commuter traffic and specialised freight, rail has given place to road. Some 2400 km (1500 miles) of motorway have been built in twenty years and the number of motor cars in use has multiplied by six since 1951. There is also the choice of travelling between cities by air and the development of international air traffic has had major consequences for ocean shipping. In freight transport, containerisation in turn has had its effect on 19th-century dock systems, while hovercraft and hydrofoil provide additional types of ferries across the English Channel.

Dramatic changes have also befallen our cities. No longer after 1961 did the population of major conurbations (with one exception) continue to grow. Out-migration exceeded growth by natural increase and in-migration. Decentralisation has provided the key-note. Post-war regional plans, such as that prepared for Greater London by Sir Patrick Abercrombie in 1944, recognised the need to re-create the environment of the inner areas of the industrial conurbations and advocated the delineation of Green Belts to prevent continuing outward sprawl and the creation of New Towns to house 'overspill' population. Later, other towns beyond the conurbations were designated as 'expanded' towns for the same purpose. To the decentralisation created by planning policies has been added the movement away from the conurbations by families who prefer to live in medium-sized or small towns. Possession of the motorcar has given more freedom of choice in deciding where to live. Thus a new urban form, the 'city region', has been brought into existence. The London city region, for example, has a radius of up to about 65 km (40 miles) comprising a region of towns functionally linked together. It extends to Ashford, Basingstoke, Swindon, Milton Keynes, Bedford and Chelmsford. Many of the industrial enterprises formerly located in the Victorian inner areas have moved out to the towns expanding beyond the conurbation edge, leaving gaps behind in the employment structure of the inner city. Indeed the trend to decentralisation has brought about a degree of polarisation between the more prosperous conditions of life in the outer parts of the city regions and the unemployment, poor social facilities and dreary environments of some parts of the inner cities. In such areas lies one of the great challenges for an age of modernisation and a central problem for the 1980s.

The other lies in the adaptation of industry and the provision of new forms of employment. Economic recession in the last years of the 1970s accelerated the speed at which the older industries have drastically slimmed down their labour forces. Unemployment in 1981 has a different distribution from that of 1931 and is no longer localised only in the coalfield-based industrial areas of the north and Wales.

But while most of the people live in towns and cities, and urban land uses are encroaching on the countryside, agricultural land still makes up over three-quarters of the land use of Britain. The distinction between cities and countryside is less clear than it was. City regions extend their influence and their connecting roads and power lines stamp an artificial pattern on the countryside. City dwellers look to the countryside for recreation. Agriculture too has become more intensive. In the 1960s and early 1970s its production increased at an average rate of 2·5% per year while manpower fell dramatically. It now takes only 2·7% of the labour force to grow or rear the crops and livestock that supply 65% of the temperate foodstuffs consumed in Britain. City and countryside have become more inter-related. Agriculture supplies milk, meat, cereals, fruit and vegetables for consumption in the cities which, in turn, produce agricultural machinery, farm requisites and fertilisers for the farm. Meanwhile the appearance of the countryside itself changes especially in those areas where hedgerows have been removed in the interests of mechanised farming, where Dutch elm disease has been prevalent, or where farming takes over hillsides and heathlands. Concern for the countryside and its wildlife has recently been loudly expressed on such issues. Despite such changes there is a rich and diverse countryside to be studied, valued and cared for. It is hoped that the maps of the chapters on historical geography and modern Britain—sketchy though they inevitably are on such a scale—will add to the awareness of these changes and this diversity.

A Short History of the Ordnance Survey

The Ordnance Survey is nearly 200 years old and was formally founded in 1791 under the Board of Ordnance, from which its name is derived. By that time the Survey had already fixed scientifically the relative positions of the Greenwich and Paris observatories by means of a triangulation which formed the basis of later maps.

The Ordnance Survey in the 19th Century

The first production of the one inch to one mile map of Southern England was to satisfy military needs during the Napoleonic Wars. However, after the peace of 1815, maps came to be valued for land transfer, civil engineering and the improvements in drainage and sanitation necessitated by urban growth in early Victorian Britain. Geological outcrops and archaeological sites were also recorded and by the mid-19th century the Ordnance Survey provided a national mapping service for scientific, military and governmental needs. The authority for many of its activities is the Ordnance Survey Act of 1841. As a result of growing governmental requirements for more detailed larger scale maps, Ireland was surveyed at six inches to the mile and the same scale was used in 1840 for maps of northern England and Scotland. After a controversy about the largest 'basic' scales at which Britain should be surveyed, it was decided in 1858 to adopt a scale of 1:2500 (or 25 inches to the mile) for cultivated areas and 1:10 560 (or six inches to the mile) with contours for uncultivated areas of mountain and moorland. Towns of more than 4000 population were to be surveyed at 1:500 or 10 feet to the mile.

Smaller scale maps were derived from the large-scale mapping. The one-inch map continued and a quarter-inch to one mile series was completed in 1888. At the end of the century a smaller scale topographical map at ten miles to the inch or 1:625 000 was authorised.

The first 1:2500 large scale survey was finished in 1896 and by 1914 the first revision had been completed. Methods of map production had changed with the introduction of colour printing and photography but the cost of revising them caused town plans at the scale of 1:500 to be abandoned in 1893 except where locally funded.

The Ordnance Survey Between the Wars

Government economies were intensified by the First World War so that in 1922 Ordnance Survey manpower was drastically reduced and only revision of large-scale maps covering areas of rapid change could be continued. However, increased government legislation in the inter-war years required accurate maps for implementation of official action in land registration, town planning and slum clearance. By the early 1930s it was becoming clear that the Ordnance Survey had been left ill-equipped to supply sufficiently accurate maps. A Departmental Committee under the chairmanship of Sir J. C. Davidson was set up in 1935 to consider how to restore the effectiveness of the national survey. Its Report published in 1938 could not be implemented systematically until after the 1939-45 war but it formed the framework upon which the present-day Ordnance Survey has developed.

The Ordnance Survey Since 1945

The major innovation of the Davidson Report was to introduce the metric National Grid as a reference system, and a single projection to cover the whole country. Previous 1:2500 large scale maps had been produced on separate county projections and this led to a loss of accuracy along county boundaries.

Large-scale maps were to be continuously revised so that they should never become so outdated as in pre-war days. A larger scale of 1:1250 (50 inches to the mile) was to be investigated and if suitable used to map more densely populated urban areas. The 1:25 000 ($2\frac{1}{2}$ inches to one mile) medium-scale map was to be tried, and if successful extended to cover the whole country in a national series.

After the war additional staff were recruited and the large-scale survey, metric conversions and revisions proceeded at the basic scales of 1:1250, 1:2500 and 1:10 000. Smaller-scale maps of one inch to one mile, 1:25 000 scale, 1:250 000 scale or a quarter-inch to one mile and the 1:625 000 scale development of the late Victorian ten-mile map were all published after derivation from large-scale surveys. The One-inch National Series was converted to 1:50 000 scale by the early 1970s.

A Retriangulation was completed in 1962 and forms the basis of present mapping, which also uses the results of a third geodetic levelling when the heights of Ordnance Survey Bench Marks were revised.

In the 1960s the compilation of a computer data base began and the first large-scale maps became available on magnetic tape. Demand for quickly available survey revision information also led to the publication of maps on microfilm and the development of the supply of un-published survey information. During this period the Ordnance Survey has been establishing close contact with map users of all kinds in order to keep abreast of modern mapping needs.

The headquarters of the Ordnance Survey are in Southampton, which has been its home since 1841. Here the large-scale maps are drawn and printed using Master Survey documents maintained in field offices scattered all over Great Britain. Retail customers may obtain Ordnance Survey large scales maps through a countrywide Agency Network and small scales maps through a large number of stockists.

As the resurvey task nears completion much greater emphasis is being given to the swift revision and supply of mapping information. The growing computer data base and the development of new survey and production methods have an increasingly important role in the provision of a rapid and comprehensive service which is of great value to the general public and all sectors of industry and commerce for many purposes.

Ordnance Survey Products

The Ordnance Survey produces maps in many forms and for various specialities which are described below, beginning with the large-scale maps from which the more popular small-scale maps are derived.

LARGE-SCALE MAPS

Maps at 1:1250 scale
(1 cm to 12·5 metres or 50 inches to 1 mile)

Maps at 1:2500 scale
(1 cm to 25 metres or 25 inches to 1 mile)

These are the largest-scale maps produced by the Ordnance Survey. The 1:1250 maps cover urban districts in Great Britain where the population is more than 20,000 per 1000 HA (2471 acres). Each one shows (in black and white) an area of 500 m by 500 m. 1:2500 maps cover less densely populated urban land and normally show areas of 2 km east to west by 1 km north to south.

House numbers and street names, administrative boundaries and heights are shown on both scales of map together with 100 m national grid lines. Acreages are shown on 1:2500-scale maps.

These maps may be bought printed on paper, as transparencies, or more cheaply as printouts from microfilm negatives. This microfilm service is known as the Ordnance Survey SIM (Survey Information on Microfilm) service. Maps can also be obtained on magnetic tape from the Southampton Office as a special service. Lists of large-scale maps on tape are available on request.

The maps are regularly updated and copies of updates may be obtained through the SIM service. The most recent large-scale mapping information may be seen at Ordnance Survey local offices (listed in the Telephone Directory) and all offices can supply copies of the latest survey documents under the SUSI (Supply of Unpublished Survey Information) service.

1:10 000 scale maps
(1 cm to 100 m or approximately 6 inches to 1 mile)

These maps cover the whole country and are the largest-scale of map produced for mountain and moorland areas. Each sheet covers an area of 5 km by 5 km and shows contours in brown on a monochrome base which includes most street names. 1:10 560 scale maps will remain available until they are replaced by 1:10 000 scale sheets.

Town and City Maps
Scale 1:10 000

Town and city maps have been published of four cities and it is intended to extend this series. They are colourful street maps with larger-scale insets of the centre with a street index and items of interest conspicuously shown. Another such map is of Central London which folds to a small size and is coloured with highlighted tourist information.

1:25 000 SCALE MAPS
(4 cm to 1 km or 2 inches to 1 mile)

Pathfinders
(1:25 000 Second Series)

These maps are the Ordnance Survey walker and rambler maps showing the countryside in great detail including rights of way in England and Wales and field boundaries. They are coloured and cover areas of 20 km ($12\frac{1}{2}$ miles) from east to west by 10 km ($6\frac{1}{4}$ miles) from north to south. Pathfinders are gradually replacing the smaller First Series maps at the same scale showing areas of 10 km square. The whole of Great Britain is covered by Pathfinder or First Series 1:25 000 maps.

Outdoor Leisure Maps

These maps of popular recreational areas generally cover some 200 square miles. They are based on Pathfinders or First Series 1:25 000 scale maps but give much additional information about available leisure activity.

SMALL-SCALE MAPS

Landranger Maps
1:50 000 scale (2 cm to 1 km or about $1\frac{1}{4}$ inches to 1 mile)

This is the successor of the old 'One-inch' map and it has become the Ordnance Survey's most popular series. At first, one-inch maps were in monochrome with hachuring to indicate relief. Colours with contours appeared at the end of the 19th century.

The Landranger scale of 1:50 000 was introduced in the early 1970s and the maps are readily recognised by their magenta covers. Each sheet depicts an area of about 620 square miles. Many show tourist information and this is being added to the others when revision takes place. Rights-of-way are marked on maps of England and Wales so that the series can be used for walking as well as for exploring by car.

ROUTE MAPS

The history of the Ordnance Survey popular maps of a smaller scale than 1:50 000 shows a tendency to focus on the needs of the motorist. Two are published at present and are described below.

Routemaster Series of Great Britain
1:250 000 scale (1 cm to 2·5 km or approximately 1 inch to 4 miles)

These maps are the modern successors of the late Victorian Quarter-inch (1:253 440 scale) regional sheets, of which two series had been published by 1928. They were then superseded by a third series designed as a map for motorists in 21 sheets. A fourth series was published in the early 1930s with sheetlines redesigned to reduce the number to 19.

After the war, a fifth series was published in 1957 with a new specification which included hill shading and a rationalised metric scale of 1:250 000 to conform with European standards and a national projection. This series was a combination of a regional physical map with motoring

information. During 1978-79 the 1:250 000 series was again redesigned to cover Britain in nine sheets to give prominence to information of use to tourists and all travellers.

Routeplanner of Great Britain
1:625 000 scale (1 cm to 6·25 km or approximately 1 inch to 10 miles)
The ten miles to the inch scale has been used for Ordnance Survey maps since 1820 when it was first engraved as an index to show the sheetlines of the first one-inch maps. A topographical map of Great Britain at this scale was not published until 1904 when it was issued in twelve sheets. By the 1930s edition the sheet lines had been redesigned so that only three and later two sheets were necessary to cover Britain and the needs of motorists were recognised by showing Ministry of Transport Class A and B roads and AA and RAC telephone boxes.

After the war the scale was enlarged slightly to 1:625 000 and when it was published in 1946 it became known as *The Road Map* with a larger-scale inset for the area covered by London.

In 1964 the map was redesigned and an annually revised Route Planning map was published in two sheets with insets of road networks, a mileage chart and information about British Rail motorail services. National Parks, Forest Parks and areas of outstanding natural beauty were also shown. The newly designed map was immediately successful and since then modifications have been added to make it more useful to motorists. It is now published on one sheet printed both sides to show the whole of Great Britain with the title *Routeplanner*.

ARCHAEOLOGICAL MAPS
Notable archaeological sites have long been included in Ordnance Survey large and small scale maps. More comprehensive period or thematic maps are also available and are described below.

Map of Roman London
Scale 1:2500 (1 cm to 25 metres or 25 inches to 1 mile)
This is a coloured large-scale map of part of the City of London which highlights and describes Roman sites. Roman finds are displayed in over 40 attractive pictures and the sheet also includes a brief history of the Roman occupation of England with seven smaller maps and an illustrated chronology of finds.

Hadrian's Wall
Scale 1:31 680 (1 cm to 0·32 km or 2 inches to 1 mile)
This is an attractively coloured strip map and list of features of Hadrian's Wall, one of the best preserved Roman walls in Europe. It also contains a bibliography.

The Antonine Wall
Scale 1:25 000 (4 cm to 1 km or 2½ inches to 1 mile)
This is a companion strip map of the Scottish Roman wall with identifiable remains and sites highlighted and with a brief description of the wall.

Roman Britain
Scale 1:625 000 (1 cm to 6·25 km or 1 inch to 10 miles)
This map is available in two sheets, North and South, separately or folded in a hard cover with an explanatory text. The map shows Britain between AD 43 and 410. The text includes supplementary maps and lists of sites in various categories.

Britain in the Dark Ages
Scale 1:1 000 000 (1 cm to 10 km or 1 inch to 16 miles)
This map is available with or without an explanatory text and depicts Celtic, pagan and Christian Anglo-Saxon features between AD 410 and 871. The Roman road system is also shown and the text includes a bibliography and gazetteer.

Monastic Britain
Scale 1:625 000 (1 cm to 6·25 km or 1 inch to 10 miles)
The North and South sheets are available with or without a bound text. The maps and text show the geographical distribution and historical development of monastic houses between the Norman Conquest and their suppression in the 16th century.

Britain Before the Norman Conquest
Scale 1:625 000 (1 cm to 6·25 km or 1 inch to 10 miles)
This map is published in two sheets which are available separately with or without a bound text. The map shows Anglo-Saxon, Scandinavian and Celtic forces in Britain from the accession of Alfred the Great to the Norman Conquest. The text introduces and summarises the period and includes useful indexes of names and features.

REPRODUCTIONS OF OLD MAPS
The Ordnance Survey publishes three reproductions of old maps from the 14th to 19th centuries. They are a strip map known as the Bodleian Map of Great Britain from 1360, Symonson's 1596 map of Kent and an 1840 edition one-inch map of Southampton.

EDUCATIONAL MAPS
As well as map extracts published especially for schools, the Ordnance Survey has two publications for all students. They are Student Map Packs each of which contains photographs and maps at different scales as well as one map from the early 19th century. Study notes, geological and land use maps are included for detailed study of a particular area of geographical interest. The areas are Maesteg in South Wales and Washington New Town near Sunderland.

ADMINISTRATIVE MAPS
A number of Ordnance Survey Maps are available which feature administrative, parliamentary or judicial boundaries highlighted on a grey base. They include maps of Greater London at 1:63 360 scale, of the Counties of England and Central Lowlands of Scotland at 1:100 000 scale, the Regions of Scotland at 1:250 000 scale, and of the whole of Britain at 1:625 000 scale.

ORDNANCE SURVEY 1:250 000 Maps

Legend

Primary Routes. These form a national network of recommended through routes which complement the motorway system. Selected places of major traffic importance are known as Primary Route Destinations and are shown on this map thus EXETER. Distances and directions to such destinations are repeated on traffic signs which,

on primary routes, have a green background or, on motorways, have a blue background.
To continue on a primary route through or past a place which has appeared as a destination on previous signs, follow the directions to the next primary destination shown on the green-backed signs.

ROADS
Not necessarily rights of way

M 8	Motorway with service area, service area (limited access) and junction with junction number
M 8	Motorway junction with limited interchange
	Motorway and junction under construction with proposed opening date where known
A 9 (T) Dual carriageway	Trunk road
A 86	Main road
A 86	Roundabout or multiple level junction
B 9163	Secondary road
	Road under construction
Toll	Toll Road tunnel
A 851 B 8056	Narrow road with passing places
	Other tarred road Other minor road
	Gradient 1 in 7 and steeper
18 23	Distances in miles between markers

The representation on this map of a road is no evidence of the existence of a right of way

WATER FEATURES

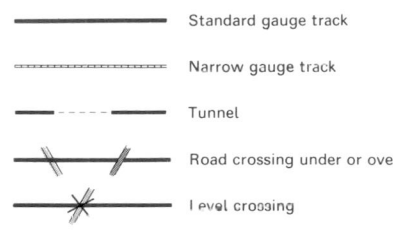

Canal, Lake, Marsh, Bridge, Ferry, Short ferry routes for vehicles, Transport (lift on), for vehicles (drive on), Slopes, Cliff, Flat rock, Low water mark, Foreshore, High water mark, Dunes

ANTIQUITIES

CANOVIVM •	Roman antiquity	⚔	Site of battle (with date)
Castle •	Other antiquities	------	Roman road (course of)

𝔪 Ancient Monuments and Historic Buildings in the care of the Secretaries of State for the Environment, for Scotland and for Wales and that are open to the public

GENERAL FEATURES

⊕ Civil aerodrome { with Customs facilities
+ Civil aerodrome { without Customs facilities

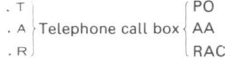
Ⓗ Heliport

. T
. A Telephone call box { PO / AA / RAC
. R

Buildings

Wood

Light-vessel		₽	Windmill
Lighthouse		Λ	Radio or TV mast
▲ Youth hostel			

+ Intersection, latitude longitude at 30' intervals (not shown where it confuses important detail)

RAILWAYS

	Standard gauge track
	Narrow gauge track
	Tunnel
	Road crossing under or over
	Level crossing
	Station

RELIEF

Feet	Metres	
		·274 Heights in feet above mean sea level
3000	914	
2000	610	
1400	427	
1000	305	Contours at 200ft intervals
600	183	
200	61	
0	0	To convert feet to metres multiply by 0·3048

BOUNDARIES

—+—+—	National
- - - -	County, Region or Islands Area

1:250 000 Scale

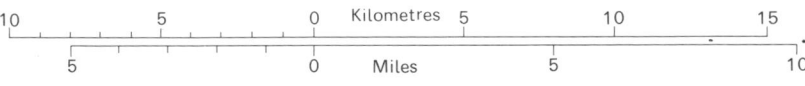

Kilometres 10 5 0 5 10 15

Miles 5 0 5 10

4 centimetres to 10 kilometres (one grid square)

1 kilometre = 0·6214 mile   1 mile = 1·61 kilometres

17

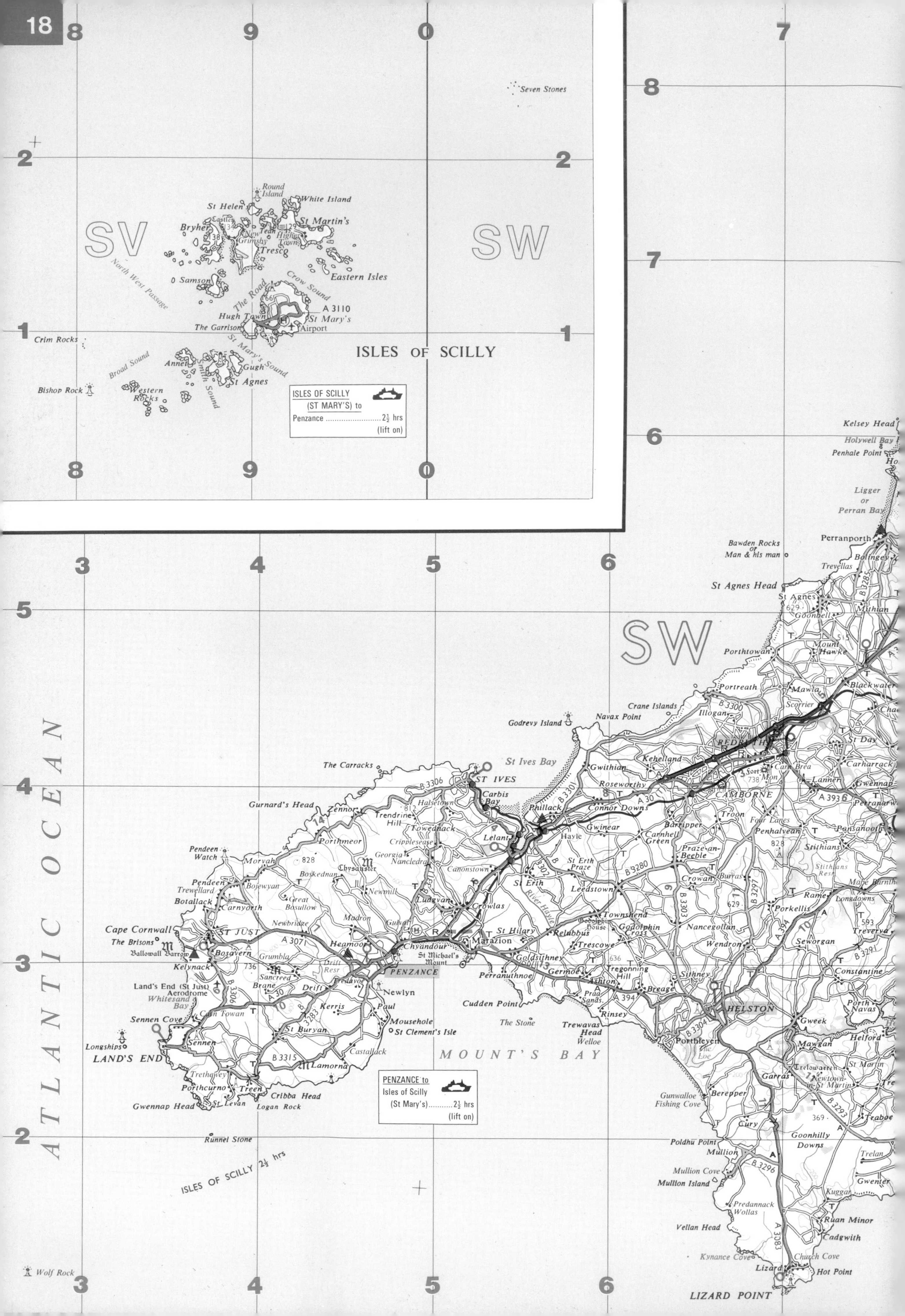

8 9 0 7

8

2 2

7

1 1

ISLES OF SCILLY

3 4 5 6

5

4 4

SW

3 3

2

3 4 5 6

Seven Stones

SV SW

Round Island
St Helen White Island
Bryher St Martin's
Castles Teän Higher
New Grimsby Town
Tresco
Samson Eastern Isles
Crow Sound
The Road
A 3110
Hugh Town St Mary's
The Garrison Airport
Crim Rocks
North West Passage
St Mary's Sound
Anne Gugh
Broad Sound Western Rocks St Agnes
Bishop Rock South Sound

Kelsey Head
Holywell Bay
Penhale Point
Ho

Ligger
or
Perran Bay

Bawden Rocks
or
Man & his man
Perranporth
Trevellas
Bolingey

St Agnes Head
St Agnes
629
Goonbell
Mithian
B 3285

Porthtowan
Mount
Hawke
Portreath
Mawla
Scorrier
Blackwater
Cha

SW

Crane Islands
Navax Point
Godrevy Island
Illogan
B 3300
REDRUTH
St Day
Cam Brea
Lanner
Gwennap
Carharrack
B 3300
CAMBORNE
A 393
Perranarw

St Ives Bay
The Carracks
St Ives
Carbis
Bay
B 3306
Gwithian
Kehelland
Roseworthy
Gwinear
Connor Downs
A 30
Barripper
Troon
Four Lanes
Penhalvean
Stithians
Carnhell
Green
Praze-an-
Beeble
Burras
Stithians
Resr
B 3280
Crowan
629
B 3297
Rame
Longdowns
Stithians
Treverva

ATLANTIC OCEAN

Gurnard's Head
Zennor
Trendrine
Hill
Towednack
Cripplesease
Georgia
Nancledra
Newmill
Ludgvan
Gulval
PENZANCE
Newlyn
Paul
Mousehole
St Clement's Isle

Pendeen
Watch
Morvah
Boskednan
Chysauster
Great
Bosullow
Newbridge
Madron
Heamoor

Canonstown
St Erth
Praze
St Erth
River Hayle
Leedstown
Relubbus
Goldsithney
Perranuthnoe
Germoe
Ashton
Breage

Hayle
Phillack
Lelant

Townshend
Godolphin
Cross
Nancegollan
Wendron
Seworgan

593
Treverva
B 3291
Constantine

Halsetown

St Michael's
Mount
Marazion
St Hilary
Trescowe
Goldolphin
House
Tregonning
Hill

Sithney
Wendron

Cape Cornwall
St JUST
The Brisons
Bosavern
Ballowall Barrow
Kelynack
Grumbla
736

Drift Resr
Pensance
Chyandour

Cudden Point
The Stone

Trewavas
Head
Welloe
Rinsey

HELSTON
Gweek
Helford

Porth
Navas

Land's End (St Just)
Aerodrome
Whitesand
Bay
Sennen Cove

Brane
Sancreed
A 30
Drift
Kerris
St Buryan

Praa
Sands
A 394

Portleven
The
Loe

Gunwalloe
Fishing Cove
Berepper
Mawgan

Garras
Trelowarren
Newtown-
in-St Martin
B 3293

St Martin
Tre

Longships
LAND'S END
Trethewey
Porthcurno
Treen
Cribba Head
Gwennap Head
St Levan
Logan Rock
Lamorna

Castallack
MOUNT'S BAY

Cury
Goonhilly
Downs
Trelan

Poldhu Point
Mullion
B 3296
Mullion Cove
Mullion Island
Predannack
Wollas
Vellan Head

Gwenter
Kuggar
Ruan Minor
Cadgwith
A 3083

Runnel Stone

ISLES OF SCILLY 2½ hrs

Kynance Cove
Church Cove
Lizard
Hot Point

Wolf Rock

LIZARD POINT

ISLES OF SCILLY
(ST MARY'S) to
Penzance .... 2½ hrs
(lift on)

PENZANCE to
Isles of Scilly
(St Mary's)........... 2½ hrs
(lift on)

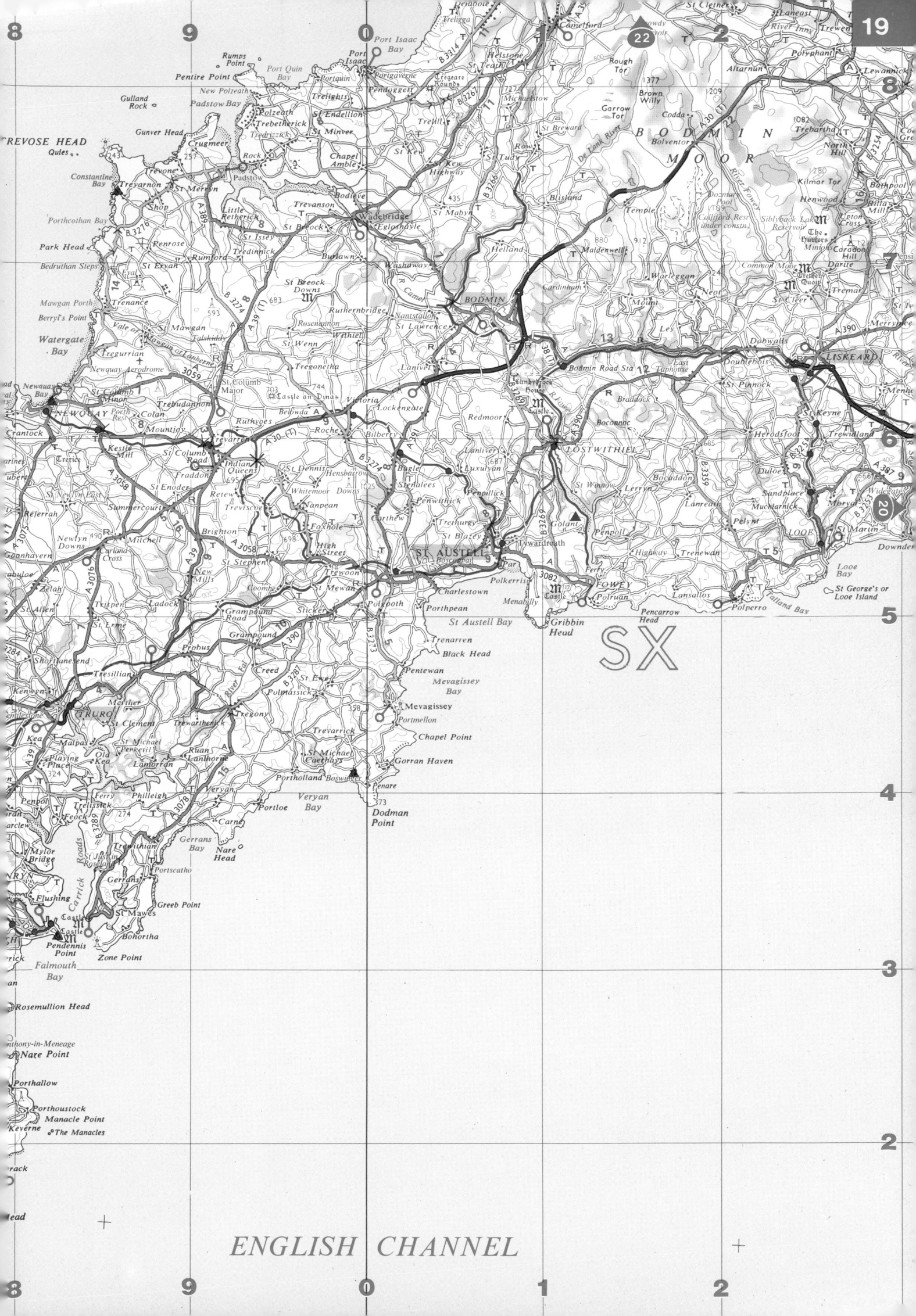

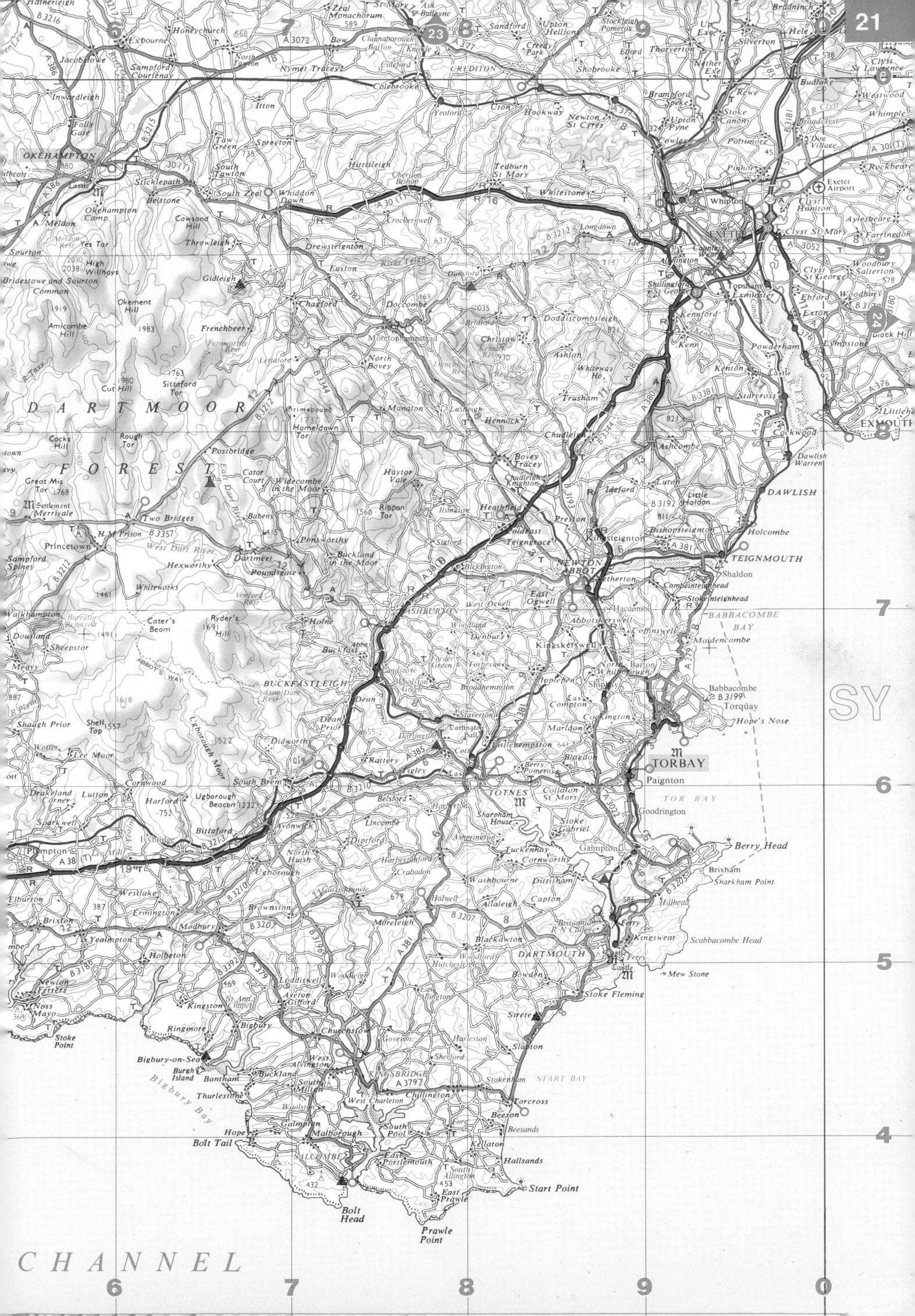

BRISTOL CHANNEL

ILFRAC

LUNDY

North West Point

466

Great Shutter Rock   Rat Island

Bull Point
Rockham Bay   Lee
Morte Point 450 Mortehoe
Woolacombe
Morte Bay   654 688

North Buckland
Baggy Point   Pickwell
Croyde   Georgeham
Bay   Croyde   518
Saunton

Braunton

Braunton
Burrows

BARNSTAPLE

OR

Bideford
Bar

Freming

Appledore

BIDEFORD BAY   Westward Ho!   ORTAM   Tapeley
Westleigh

HARTLAND POINT   Windbury   Abbotsham   B 3236   BIDEFORD
Titchberry   Point
Stoke   Hartland   564   Clovelly   A 39 (T)   343   Wooll
Hartland   Dyke   Clovelly Dykes   Buck's-Mills   Fairy Cross   Land Cross   Alve
Quay   710 A   Buck's Cross   547   10   Littleham   Weare
Philham   710   R   Parkham   Gifford

Elmscott   Woolfardisworthy   T   Parkham   Buckland
South   Ash   Brewer   Monkleigh
Hole   Welcombe   771   Melbury   709   Frithelstock
Knaps   East Putford
Longpeak   Meddon   Ashmansworthy   B 322   Lang
Gooseham   512   Eastcott   Dinworthy   708   West Putford   Stibb Cross   Langtree
Morwenstow   Youlstone   Abbots   Newton
Higher Sharpnose   514   Bradworthy   Bickington   St Petrock   Peters
Point   Shop   656   A 388   616   Marland
Woodford   Upper Tamar   Sutcombe   T   Milton Damerel   560
Lower Sharpnose   Lake Res   Lower Tamar   R Weldon   Shebbear   Buckland
Point   Coombe   Kilkhampton   Alfardisworthy   Lake   Soldon   Holsworthy   Thornbury   Filleigh
Stibb   Cross   Beacon   635   Bradford   400
A 39 (T)   B 3254   Crookbury
B U D E   571   Chilsworthy   Sheep
Poughill   Grimscott   Holsworthy   Black
STRATTON   Launcells   10   Pancrasweek   HOLSWORTHY   Torrington   574
Bude Haven   A 3072   A   663   A   13   High
BUDE   Marhamchurch   Bridgerule   Pyworthy   531   Hollacombe   Graddon
B A Y   216   Hallacombe   632   Moor   400
Widemouth Bay   440   R Deer   Halwill   Beaworthy
Coppathorne   Junction
Dizzard Point   River Tamar   449   Clawton   632   Whitstone
Poundstock   Week   North Tamerton   River Claw   Quodich   917
Tregole   544   St Mary   Tetcott   Lana   Ashwater   Eworthy
Cambeak   St Gennys   Trewint   18   A 388   Germansweek
Crackington   Jacobstow   B 3254   Luffincott   14   Virginstow
Haven   West   598   Northcott   T   Bratton
Wainhouse   852   South   Curry   Boyton   East   Broadwoodwidger   Clovelly
Corner   Wheatley   Bennacott   Panson   Thrushelton
543   Braacott   St Giles   Polapit   Cross Green   Stowford   Lewdown   360
Fire Beacon Point   on the Heath   Tamar   Lifton
Marshgate   841   North   469   Werrington   464   Portgate   Lew trenchard
Boscastle   Warbstow   Petherwin   Broadwoodwidger   Coryton
Castle   Lesnewth   Otterham   641   Yeolmbridge   Carey
Tintagel Head   Trevalga   Tremaine   Egloskerry   Langore   Stowford   Marystow
Bossiney   Hallworthy   Tresmeer   Castle   Lifton   Chillaton
Tintagel   1009   Trewarsa   Davidstow   Treneglos   Red Down   St Stephens   Lawhitton   North
Treknow   Tremail   Tregeare   A 395   LAUNCESTON   930
Start Point   B 3266   Tregadillett   Trewen   South   Kellys
Delabole   St Clether   Laneast   Petherwin   Bradstone
Treligga   Camelford   Trewen   Polyphant   Lezant
Port Isaac   Crowdy   River Inny   Milton Abbot
Bay   Reservoir   Lewannick   Dunterton
B 3314   Helstone   Rough   Altarnun   Codda
St Teath   Tor   800   1082   Brown   20   Garrow
Treglff   722   Michaelstow   1377   Willy   Tor
Boggett   Tregeare   11   Codda   30
Rounds   B 3261

SHEPPEY

Warden Point
Warden
204
Leysdown on Sea
Isle of Hafty
Shell Ness
WHITSTABLE
Seasalter
The Swale
Uplees
Oare
FAVERSHAM
Goodnestone
299
134
Ospringe
Sheldwich
A 251
Selling
Throwley
Badlesmere
Shottenden
Leaveland
Chilham
Molash
Godmersham
Challock
Boughton
Aluph
Eastwell
Park
Westwell
Boughton
Lees
Kennington
-FORD
Hinxhill
Willesborough
Sevington
A 2020
Mersham
Cheeseman's
Green
adoxhurst
Bannington
Orlestone
Bilsington
Ruckinge
amstreet
Warehorne
Snave
ROMNEY
Newchurch
MARSH
Snargate
Ivychurch
Brenzett
LAND MARSH
Brookland
Old
Romney
NEW
ROMNEY
LYDD
Denge
Marsh
Denge Beach
DUNGENESS

West Road

HERNE BAY
REGVLBIVM
Reculver
Swalecliffe
Chestfield
Hillborough
Broomfield
Herne
Hoath
Broadoak
Honey Hill
Tyler Hill
Blean
Rough Common
Hales Place
CANTERBURY
DVROVERNVM
Harbledown
Chartham Hatch
Old Wives Lees
Thannington
Nackington
Chartham
Bridge
Petham
Lower Hardres
Bishopsbourne
Kingston
Upper Hardres Court
Barham
Sole Street
Waltham
Crundale
Olantigh
Hassell Street
Wye
583
Stelling Minnis
Elmsted Court
Derringstone
Woolage Green
B 2068
Hastingleigh
Brook
Lymbridge Green
Lyminge Forest
Denton
590
Rhodes Minnis
Acrise Place
Elham
Swingfield Minnis
Densole
Brabourne
Smeeth
Stowting
Lyminge
Sellinge
Postling
Etchinghill
629
Stanford
A 20
Newington
Beachborough
Hawkinge
Capel-le-Ferne
Westenhanger
Aldington
B 2067
338
Lympne
Castle
Saltwood
Sandgate
Tolls
HYTHE
Burmarsh
Dymchurch
St Mary in the Marsh
St Mary's Bay
Littlestone-on-Sea
Romney Sands
Greatstone-on-Sea
Lydd Airport
Lydd-on-Sea

Birchington
St Nicholas at Wade
Sarre
Marshside
Chislet
Upstreet
West Stourmouth
Hersden
Westbere
Sturry
Stodmarsh
Fordwich
Wickhambreaux
Littlebourne
Ickham
Zoo
A 257
Bekesbourne
Patrixbourne
Adisham
Aylesham
Chillenden
Nonington
Bossingham
Shepherdswell or Sibertswold
Coldred
Wootton
Lydden
Temple Ewell
Fwell Minnis
Alkham
Buckland
West Hougham
A 20
River Stour
ROMAN
East Stourmouth
Westmarsh
Preston
Grove
Elmstone
Hoaden
RVTVPIAE
Great Stonar
Ash
Marshborough
Staple
Wingham
Goodnestone
Knowlton
Easole Street
Elvington
Barfreston
Eythorne
Waldershare Park
A 256
58
Whitfield
St Radegund's Abbey
WEST Hougham
Capel-le-Ferne

SOUTH Channel
MARGATE
Westgate on Sea
B 2049
Acol
St Peter's
BROADSTAIRS
Manston Aerodrome
Minster
RAMSGATE
Cliffs End
Pegwell Bay
SANDWICH
Toll
Woodnesborough
Worth
Eastry
Ham
Belteshanger
Tilmanstone
Great Mongeham
East Studdal
Sutton
Ripple
Ringwould
West Langdon
East Langdon
Guston
West Cliffe
St Margaret's at Cliffe
St Margaret's Bay
Royal Military School
DEAL Castle
Walmer Castle
Kippsdown
Sholden
Northbourne

Long Nose Spit
Foreness Point
White Ness
NORTH FORELAND
2052
Sandwich Flats
Sandwich Bay
THE SMALL DOWNS
Good
THE DOWNS
SOUTH FORELAND
South Goodwin

STRAIT OF DOVER

Varne

RAMSGATE to [ferry] Dunkirk (West)..........2 hrs (seasonal)

DOVER DVBRIS

DOVER to
Calais............1¼-1½ hrs
Boulogne............1¾ hrs
Dunkirk............2½ hrs
Ostend............3½-4 hrs
Zeebrugge............4 hrs
Calais................35 mins
Boulogne............45 mins

FOLKESTONE

FOLKESTONE to
Boulogne............1¾ hrs
Calais................1½ hrs
Ostend............4¼ hrs

East Wear Bay

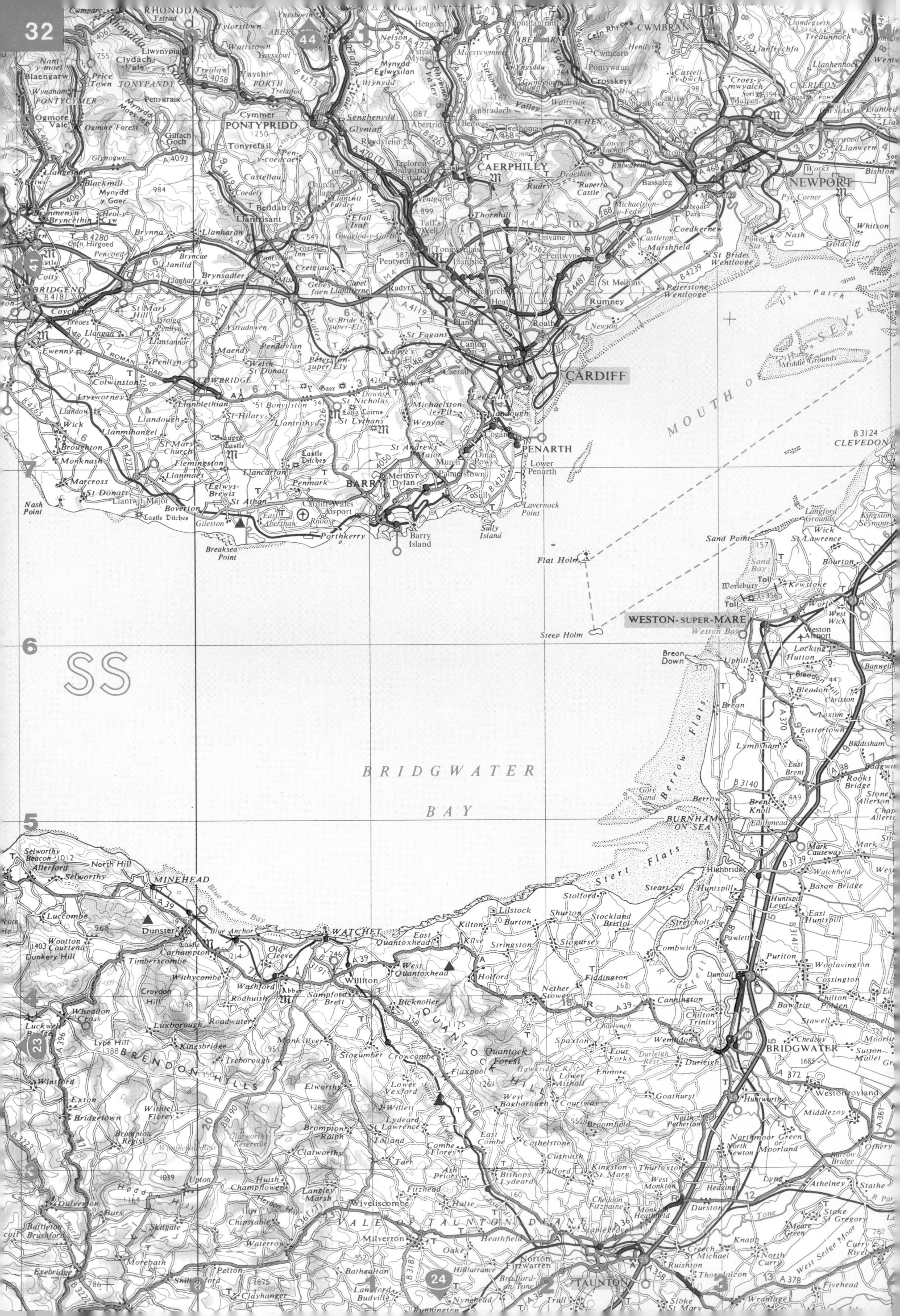
RHONDDA
Tylorstown
ABERCYNON
Hengoed
Pontllanfraith
CWMBRAN
Llanfrechfa
Treaunnock
Nelson
Ystrad Mynach
Mynydd Eglwysilan
Maesycwmmer
Cefn Rhyswg
Cwmcarn
Henllys
Llanhennock
Wattstown
Ynysybwl
Llwynypia
Clydach Vale
TONYPANDY
Trealaw
Ynyshir
PORTH
Trehafod
Nant-y-moel
Blaengarw
Price Town
Wyndham
PONTYCYMER
Penygraig
Cymmer
PONTYPRIDD
Senghenydd
Abertridwr
Glyntaff
Llanbradach
Bedwas
Trethomas
MACHEN
Crosskeys
Pontywaun
Castell-y-bwch
Croes-y-mwyalch
CAERLEON
Pontymister
Ogmore Vale
Ogmore Forest
Gilfach Goch
Tonyrefail
Pen-y-coedcae
Rhydyfelin
Treforest Industrial Estate
CAERPHILLY
Rudry
Draethen
Lower Machen
Rogerstone
Rhiwderin
Bassaleg
NEWPORT
Llanwern
Bishton
Langstone
Pye Corner
Glynogwr
Llangeinor
Blackmill
Mynydd y Gaer
Castellau
Tonteg
Church Village
Llantwit Fardre
Efail Isaf
Beddau
Llantrisant
Nantgarw
Taff's Well
Thornhill
Ruperra Castle
Michaelston-y-Fedw
Tredegar Park
Coedkernew
Marshfield
Castleton
St Brides Wentlooge
Whitson
Goldcliff
Nash
Brynmenyn
Bryncethin
Heol-y-Cyw
Betws
Brynna
Llanharan
Gwaelod-y-Garth
Creigiau
Pentyrch
Tongwynlais
Lisvane
Pentwyn
St Mellons
Peterstone Wentlooge
Rumney
Sarn
Cefn Hirgoed
Pencoed
Bryncae
Llanilid
Brynsadler
Llanharry
Pontyclun
Cross Inn
Miskin
Groes-faen
Capel Llanilltern
Radyr
Whitchurch
Heath
Llandaff
Roath
Coity
BRIDGEND
Coychurch
Treoes
Llangan
St Mary Hill
Graig Penllyn
Llansannor
Ystradowen
St Bride's-super-Ely
St Fagans
Canton
Ewenny
Pendoylan
Welsh St Donats
Maendy
Peterston-super-Ely
St George's
Ely
Caerau
CARDIFF
Penllyn
Colwinston
COWBRIDGE
Gaer
St Nicholas
Downs
Llanblethian
Bonvilston
Michaelston-le-Pit
Leckwith
Llandough
Llysworney
Llandow
Wick
Llanmihangel
St Hilary
Llantrithyd
St Lythans
Long Cairns
Wenvoe
Cogan
PENARTH
Lower Penarth
Broughton
Monknash
St Mary Church
Beaupre Castle
Flemingston
Castle Ditches
St Andrews Major
Dinas Powys
Murch
Palmerstown
Merthyr Dyfan
Marcross
St Donats
Llanmaes
Llantwit Major
Eglwys-Brewis
Llancarfan
Penmark
BARRY
Sully
Lavernock Point
Sully Island
Nash Point
Boverton
St Athan
Gileston
East Aberthaw
Rhoose
Cardiff-Wales Airport
Porthkerry
Barry Island
Breaksea Point
Flat Holm
Steep Holm
MOUTH OF THE SEVERN
Usk Patch
Middle Grounds
CLEVEDON
Kingston Seymour
Langford Grounds
Wick St Lawrence
Sand Point
Sand Bay
Worlebury
Kewstoke
Bourton
Toll
Worle
West Wick
WESTON-SUPER-MARE
Weston Bay
Weston Airport
Locking
Hutton
Banwell
Uphill
Brean Down
Bleadon
Bleadon Hill
Christon
Loxton
Brean
Eastertown
Lympsham
Biddisham
Badgworth
East Brent
Rooks Bridge
Stone Allerton
Brent Knoll
Edithmead
Berrow
Gore Sand
Berrow Flats
BURNHAM-ON-SEA
Highbridge
Mark Causeway
Mark
Watchfield
Bason Bridge
Stert Flats
Steart
Huntspill
Huntspill Level
East Huntspill
SS
BRIDGWATER BAY
Selworthy Beacon
Allerford
Selworthy
North Hill
MINEHEAD
Blue Anchor Bay
Luccombe
Dunster
Blue Anchor
Wootton Courtenay
Dunkery Hill
Carhampton
Timberscombe
WATCHET
Old Cleeve
East Quantoxhead
Kilton
Lilstock
Burton
Stolford
Shurton
Stockland Bristol
Stretcholt
Kilve
Stringston
Stogursey
Combwich
Pawlett
Puriton
Woolavington
Withycombe
Washford
Williton
West Quantoxhead
Holford
Fiddington
Dunball
Cossington
Croydon Hill
Rodhuish
Sampford Brett
Bicknoller
Nether Stowey
Cannington
Chilton Polden
Bawdrip
Wheddon Cross
Luxborough
Roadwater
QUANTOCK HILLS
Charlynch
Chilton Trinity
Stawell
Luckwell Bridge
Lype Hill
Kingsbridge
Monksilver
Stogumber
Crowcombe
Quantock Forest
Spaxton
Four Forks
Durleigh Resr
Wembdon
BRIDGWATER
Chedzoy
Sutton Mallet
Moorlinch
BRENDON HILLS
Treborough
Flaxpool
Hawkridge Resr
Lower Aisholt
Enmore
Durleigh
Winsford
Exton
Elworthy
Lower Vexford
West Bagborough
Courtway
Goathurst
Huntworth
Westonzoyland
Middlezoy
Othery
Bridgetown
Withiel Florey
Willett
Lydeard St Lawrence
Broomfield
North Petherton
Brompton Regis
Wimbleball Resr
Clatworthy Reservoir
Brompton Ralph
Tolland
Combe Florey
East Combe
Cothelstone
Northmoor Green or Moorland
North Newton
Burrow Bridge
Clatworthy
Tarr
Ash Priors
Bishops Lydeard
Fulford
Kingston St Mary
Thurloxton
West Monkton
Lyng
Athelney
Stathe
Haddon Hill
Upton
Huish Champflower
Langley Marsh
Fitzhead
Halse
Cheddon Fitzpaine
Monkton Heathfield
Durston
Hedging
Stoke St Gregory
Meare Green
Dulverton
Bury
Skilgate
Chipstable
Wiveliscombe
VALE OF TAUNTON DEANE
Staplegrove
Creech St Michael
Knapp
North Curry
West Sedge Moor
Curry Rivel
Battleton
Brushford
Waterrow
Milverton
Oake
Heathfield
Norton Fitzwarren
Ruishton
Thornfalcon
Morebath
Exebridge
Petton
Shillingford
Bathealton
Hillfarrance
Bradford-on-Tone
TAUNTON
Fivehead
Clayhanger
Langford Budville
Nynehead
Trull
Stoke St Mary
Wrantage
Runnington

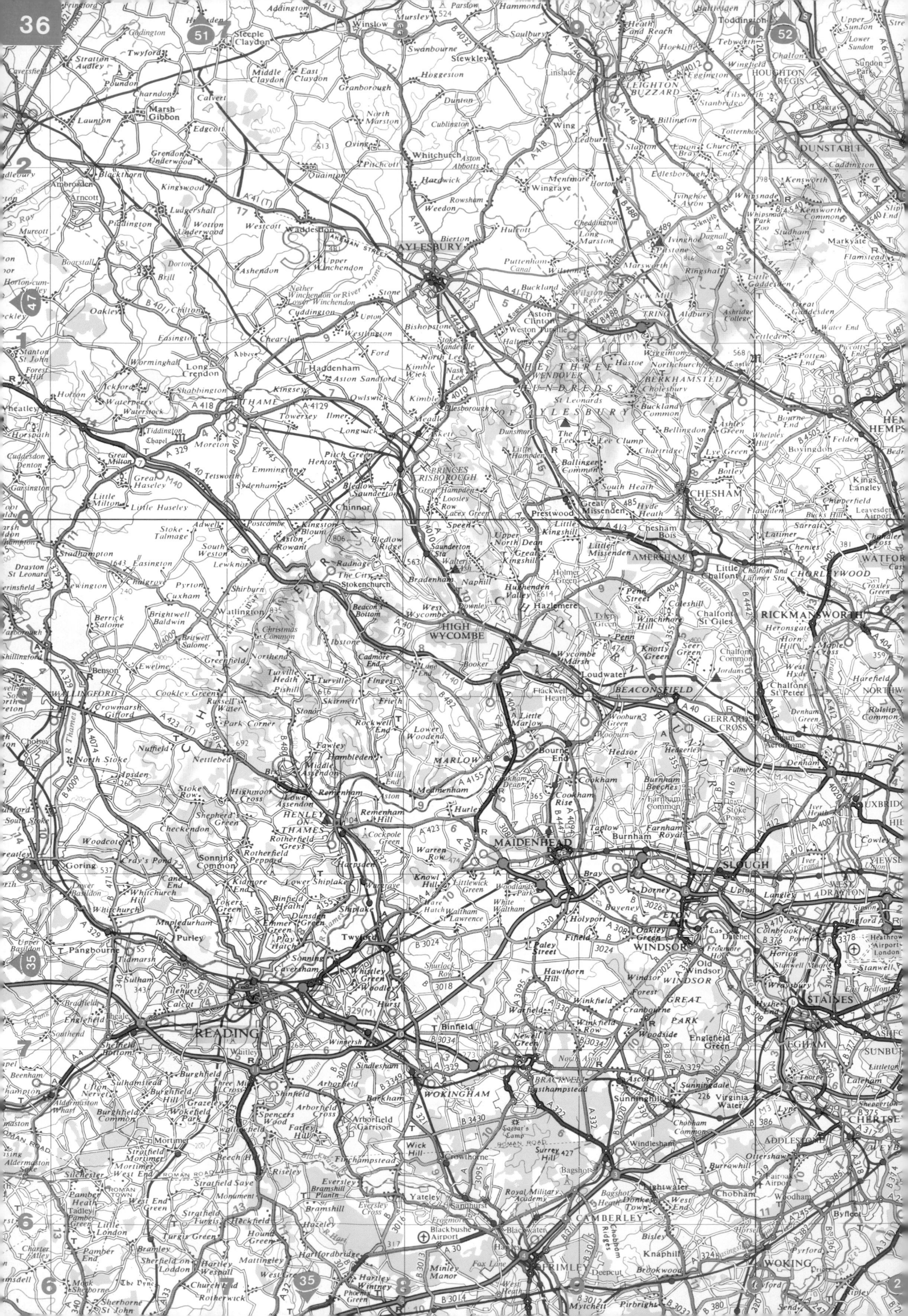

NORTH SEA

TM

TR

Colchester area labels: Mile End, Ardleigh Resr, Crockleford Heath, Great Bromley, Little Bromley, Horsleycross Street, Horsley Cross, Wix, Great Oakley, Little Oakley, A 604, A 120, Elmstead Market, Wivenhoe, Old Heath, Blackheath, Rowhedge, Roman R, Fingringhoe, Alresford, Thorrington, Frating Green, Great Bentley, Aingers Green, Tendring, Beaumont, Little Bentley, Weeley, Weeley Heath, Thorpe-le-Soken, Kirby-le-Soken, Kirby Cross, Horsey Island, The Naze, WALTON-ON-THE-NAZE, FRINTON-ON-SEA, Great Holland, Little Clacton, Great Clacton, BRIGHTLINGSEA, Point Clear, Priory, St Osyth, St Osyth Marsh, Jaywick, Holland-on-Sea, CLACTON-ON-SEA, Colne Point

MERSEA ISLAND, WEST MERSEA, East Mersea, Mersea Flats, The Nass, Virley Channel, Langenhoe, Abberton, Abberton Resr, Peldon, Great Wigborough, TUMULUS

BRADWELL, Bradwell Waterside, Bradwell-on-Sea, Sales Point, St Peter's Flat, OTHONA, Dengie Flat, Tillingham, Dengie, Asheldham, Southminster, Old Montsale, Deal Hall, BLACKWATER, Buxey Sand, Ray Sand, Gunfleet Sand, (disused)

Barrow Deep, Sunk Sand, Sunk

RIVER CROUCH, Foulness Sands, Holliwell Point, Foulness Point, Courtsend, Churchend, FOULNESS ISLAND, MAPLIN SANDS, Mid Barrow, Potton Island, Wakering

Tongue

South Channel, Long Nose Spit, Foreness Point, MARGATE, Westgate on Sea, White Ness, NORTH FORELAND, BROADSTAIRS, RAMSGATE

Warden Point, Warden, Leysdown on Sea, SHEPPEY, Isle of Harty, Shell Ness, The Swale, WHITSTABLE, Seasalter, Swalecliffe, Tankerton, HERNE BAY, Reculver, REGVLBIVM, Hampton, Hillborough, Birchington, St Nicholas at Wade, Sarre, Acol, ISLE OF THANET, St Peter's, Manston, Manston Aerodrome, Minster, Pegwell Bay

FAVERSHAM, Goodnestone, Graveney, Oare, Uplees, Luddenham Court, Ospringe, Sheldwich, Selling, Dunkirk, Boughton Street, Hernhill, Dargate, Yorkletts, Chestfield, Broad Oak, Honey Hill, Tyler Hill, Blean, Rough Common, Hales Place, Sturry, Hoath, Herne, Chislet, Upstreet, Marshside, Hersden, Westbere, Fordwich, Stodmarsh, Wickhambreaux, Grove, Preston, West Stourmouth, East Stourmouth, River Stour, Monkton, Elmstone, Westmarsh, Hoaden, RVTVPIAE, Ash, Marshborough, CANTERBURY, DVROVERNVM, Harbledown, Thannington, Chartham, Chartham Hatch, Old Wives Lees, Bekesbourne, Littlebourne, Wingham, Staple, Eastry, Worth, SANDWICH, Sandwich Bay, Sandwich Flats, Toll, THE SMALL DOWNS, Goodnestone

55
31

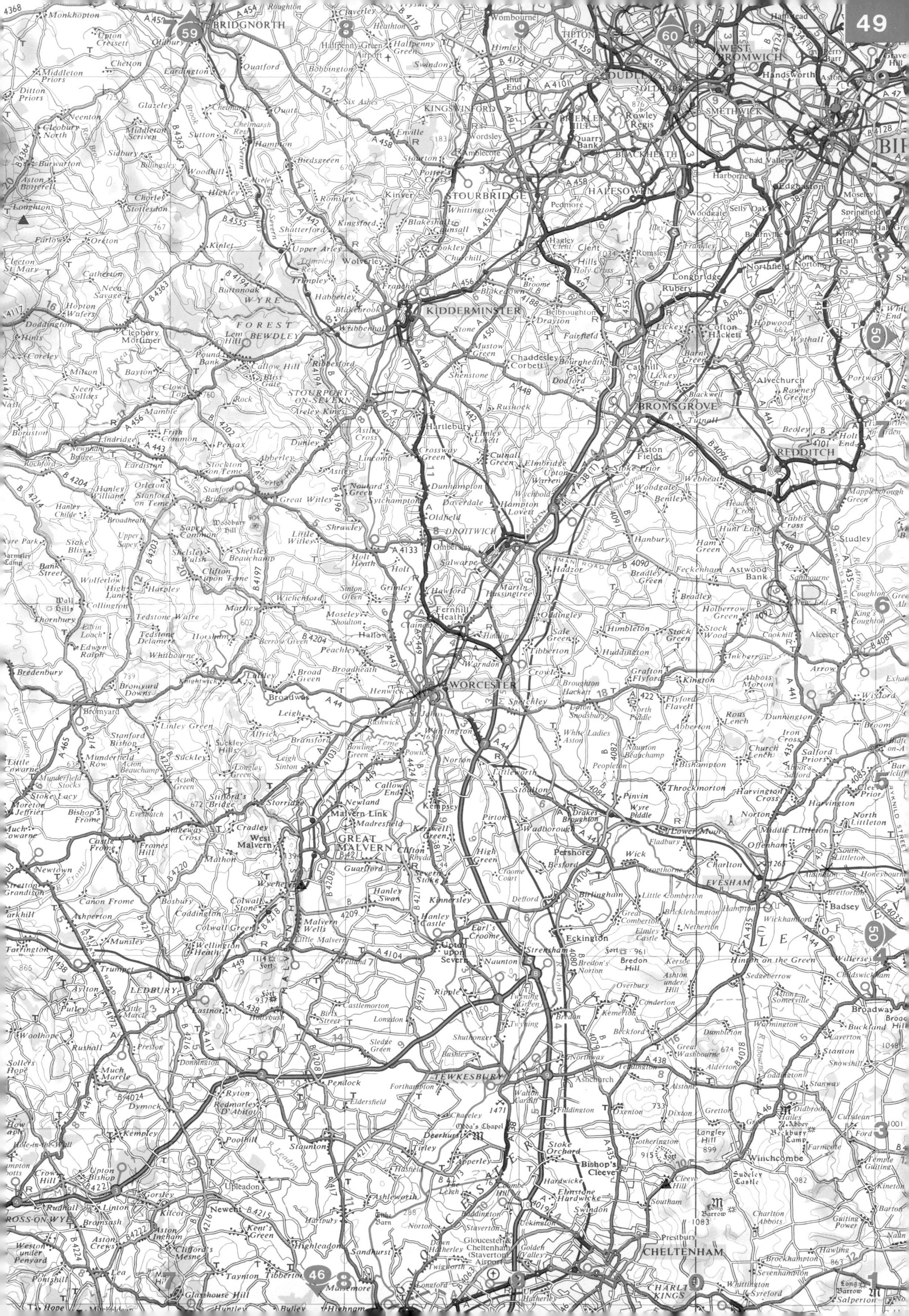

BRIDGNORTH
59
60
WEST BROMWICH
DUDLEY
SMETHWICK
BIRMINGHAM
KINGSWINFORD
STOURBRIDGE
HALESOWEN
BLACKHEATH
KIDDERMINSTER
BROMSGROVE
REDDITCH
BEWDLEY
WYRE FOREST
STOURPORT-ON-SEVERN
DROITWICH
WORCESTER
GREAT MALVERN
MALVERN WELLS
PERSHORE
EVESHAM
LEDBURY
TEWKESBURY
UPTON UPON SEVERN
ROSS-ON-WYE
CHELTENHAM
50
46

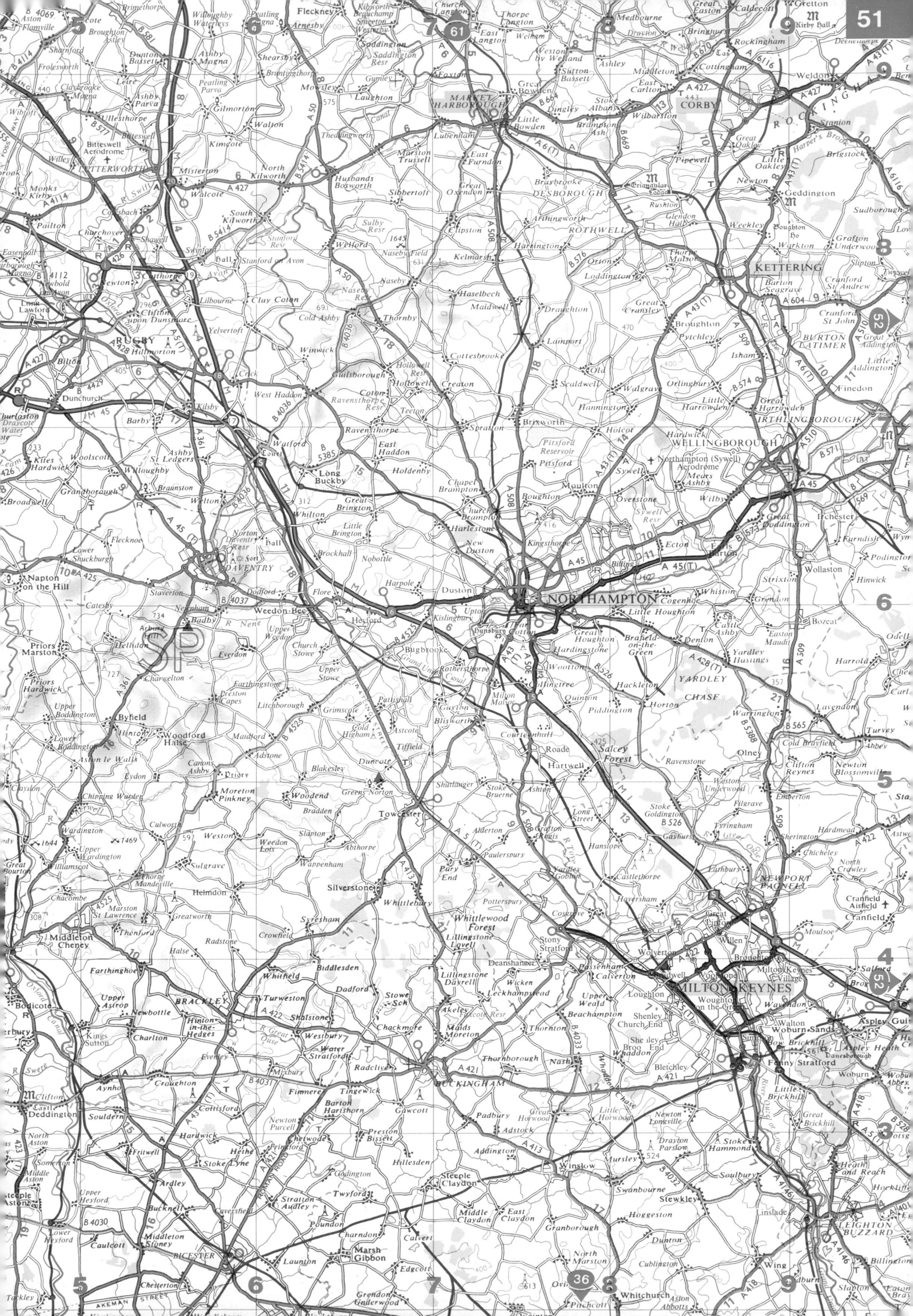

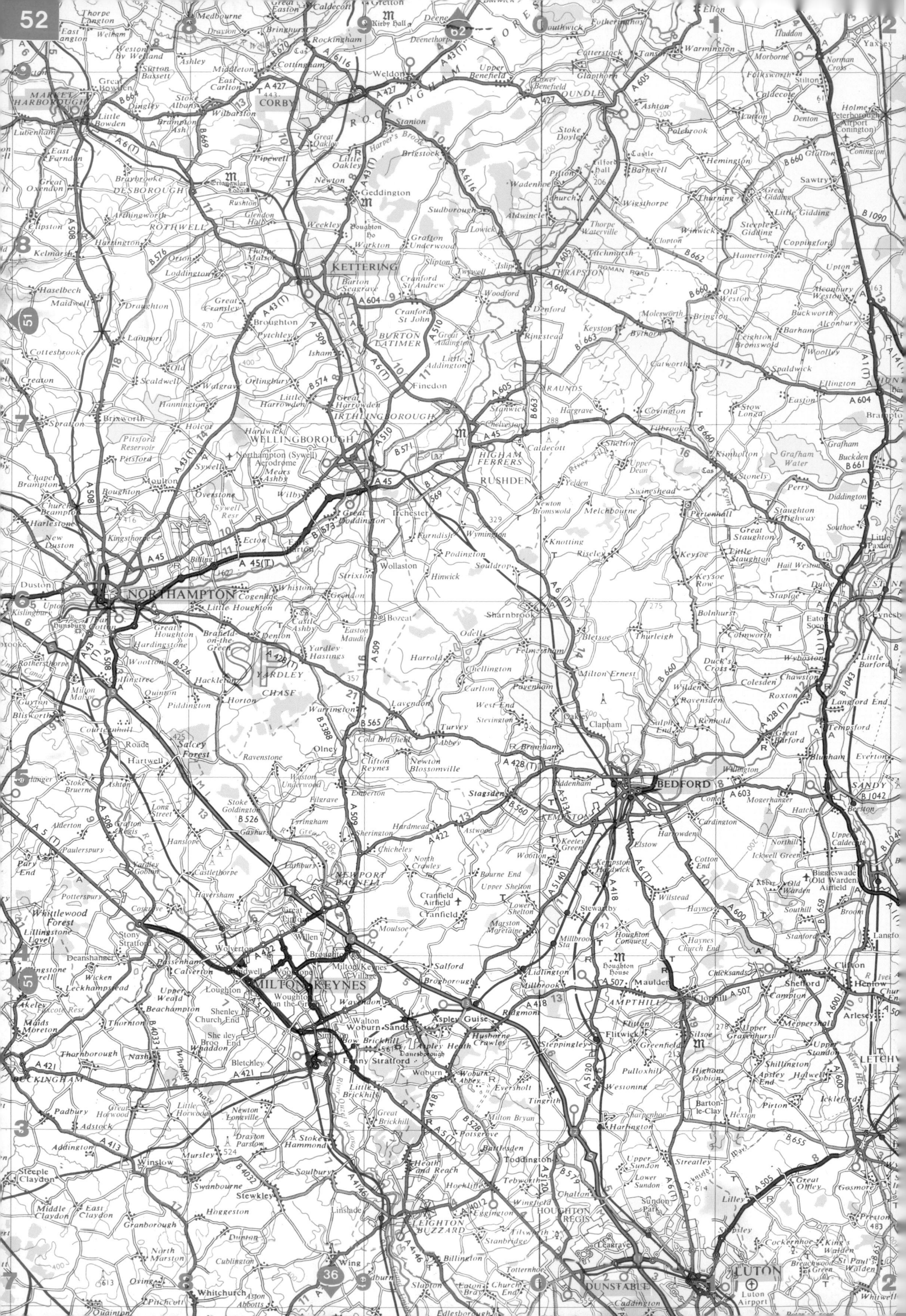

Map

Grid numbers (top): 6 7 8 64 9 0

Grid numbers (left, top to bottom): 9 8 53 7 6 5 53 4 3

Major towns and places:

THETFORD, BURY ST EDMUNDS, NEWMARKET, HAVERHILL, SUDBURY, HALSTEAD, BRAINTREE, COLCHESTER, HADLEIGH, Mildenhall, Brandon, Soham, Lakenheath, Feltwell, Mundford

Mundford, Great Hockham, Puddledock, Eccles Road, Wilby, East Wretham, East Harling, Larling, Hurling Road Sta., Quidenham, Kenninghall, Bridgham, Brettenham, North Lopham, South Lopham, Garboldisham, Blo' Norton, Hopton, Market Weston, Thelnetham, Hinderclay, Redgrave, Coney Weston, Barningham, Hepworth, Rickinghall, Wattisfield, Botesdale

Southery Fens, Methwold Fens, Queen's Ground, Brandon Creek, Brandon Bank, Burnt Fen, Feltwell Anchor, Hockwold Fens, Hockwold cum Wilton, Weeting, Grime's Graves, Santon Downham, Croxton, Brandon Park, Thetford Warren, Priory, Rushford, Gasthorpe, Thorpe

SOUTH LEVEL, Middle Fen, Stuntney, Great Fen, Broad Hill, Isleham Fen, Mildenhall Fen, Beck Row, Holywell Row, West Row, Eriswell, Elveden, Barnham, Euston, Little Fakenham, Honington, Sapiston, Bardwell, Stanton, Walsham le Willows, Gislingham, Westhorpe, Wyverstone

Queen Adelaide, Prickwillow, Kenny Hill, The Delph, Lakenheath Warren, Wangford Fen, Wangford Warren, Shippea Hill Sta., Thistley Green, Isleham, Worlington, Barton Mills, Icklingham, West Stow, Culford, Ingham, Ampton, Great Livermere, Timworth Green, Ixworth Thorpe, Troston, Ixworth, Stowlangtoft, Langham, Four Ashes, Badwell Ash, Great Ashfield, Earl's Green, Hunston, Wyverstone Street

Soham, Wicken, Fordham, Freckenham, Tuddenham, Herringswell, Cavenham, Flempton, Lackford, Hengrave, Fornham All Saints, Fornham St Martin, Great Barton, Pakenham, Thurston, Norton, Stanton Street, Haughley Green, Ward, Old Newton, Little Fen, Fordham Abbey, Chippenham, Kennett, Kentford, Higham, Risby, Westley, Thurston, Elmswell, Tostock, Haughley, Wetherden, Stowupland

Swaffham Prior, Exning, Newmarket Heath, Snailwell, Moulton, Gazeley, Dalham, Denham, Dunstall Green, Chevington, Barrow, Great Saxham, Little Saxham, Horringer, Blackthorpe, Beyton, Woolpit, Drinkstone, Hessett, Drinkstone Green, Rougham Green, Rushbrooke, Sicklesmere, Bradfield St George, Felsham, Rattlesden, Gedding, Poystreet Green, Buxhall, Great Finborough, Combs Ford, Combs

Burwell, Stetchworth, Wooditton, Cheveley, Ashley, Saxon Street, Ousden, Lidgate, Hargrave, Chedburgh, Rede, Hawstead, Whepstead, Great Welnetham, Little Welnetham, Bradfield St Clare, Bradfield Combust, Cockfield, Thorpe Green, Brettenham, Preston St Mary, Hitcham, Thorpe Morieux, Cross Green, Charles Tye, Ringshall, Wattisham, Battisford Tye, Ringshall Stocks, Nedging Tye, Offton

Six Mile Bottom, Westley Waterless, Dullingham, Ditton Green, Upend, Kirtling, Kirtling Green, Brinkley, Burrough Green, Carlton, Great Bradley, Cowlinge, Depden Green, Thorns, Wickhambrook, Clopton Green, Wickham Street, Denston, Hawkedon, Brockley Green, Lawshall, Shimpling Street, Alpheton, Shimpling, Stanstead, Bridge Street, Lavenham, Bildeston, Naughton, Chelsworth, Monks Eleigh, Brent Eleigh, Milden, Semer, Whatfield, Kettlebaston

West Wratting, Weston Colville, Weston Green, Little Bradley, Stradishall, Stansfield, Boxted, Hartest, Glemsford, Monks Eleigh, Semer, Kersey, Lindsey

Balsham, Horseheath, Withersfield, West Wickham, Great Wratting, Hundon, Barnardiston, Poslingford, Chilton Street, Kedington, Cavendish, Clare, Stoke by Clare, Pentlow Hall, Long Melford, Acton, Little Waldingfield, Great Waldingfield, Chelsworth, Kersey

Linton, Bartlow, Shudy Camps, Castle Camps, Haverhill, Sturmer, Wixoe, Ashen, Ovington, Belchamp St Paul, Belchamp Otten, Borley, Sudbury, Foxearth, Belchamp Walter, Bulmer, Middleton, Newton, Great Cornard, Edwardstone, Groton, Boxford, Assington, Layham, Raydon, Polstead, Stoke-by-Nayland, Holton St Mary, Higham, Thorington Street, Stratford St Mary

Ashdon, Church End, Radwinter, Sewards End, Hempstead, Wimbish, Wimbish Green, Steeple Bumpstead, Helions Bumpstead, Birdbrook, Ridgewell, Little Yeldham, Great Yeldham, Stambourne, Toppesfield, Gestingthorpe, Great Henny, Twinstead, Lamarsh, Alphamstone, Bures, Wormingford, Great Horkesley, Little Horkesley, Mount Bures, Nayland, Langham

Debden, Debden Green, Thaxted, Howlett End, Wimbish Green, Little Bardfield, Great Bardfield, Cornish Hall End, Gainsford End, Howe Street, Finchingfield, Wethersfield, Blackmore End, Sible Hedingham, Castle Hedingham, Great Maplestead, Little Maplestead, Wickham St Paul, Pebmarsh, Colne Engaine, Earls Colne, Wakes Colne, Chappel, Fordham, West Bergholt, Mile End, Crockleford Heath, Ardleigh

Takeley, Great Dunmow, Little Dunmow, Lindsell, Duton Hill, Great Easton, Little Easton, Bran End, Stebbing, Rayne, Shalford, Shalford Green, Beazley End, Panfield, Bocking, Bocking Churchstreet, Gosfield, Greenstead Green, High Garrett, Halstead, Colne Valley, Coggeshall, Great Tey, Aldham, Fordstreet, Eight Ash Green, Stanway, Copford Green, Marks Tey, Colchester, Camulodunum

Molehill Green, Churchend, Stisted, Braintree, Bradwell, Black Notley, White Notley, Rivenhall, Silver End, Feering, Messing, Easthorpe, Layer Marney, Birch, Heckfordbridge, Shrub End, Old Heath, Rowhedge, Wivenhoe, Fingringhoe

Rivers/features: R. Great Ouse, R. Lark, River Lark, Little Ouse River, R. Kennett, Icknield Way, R. Stour, R. Colne, R. Brett, R. Pant, R. Chelmer, R. Thet, R. Blackwater, Roman Road, Pedders Way, Devil's Ditch

Roads: A10(T), A1101, A1065, A134, A11(T), A1066, A1088, A143, A45(T), A14, A1302, A1304, A1303, A604, A142, A1092, A1141, A1071, A1017, A1058, A1064, A1024, A130, A12(T), A120, A133, A137, A12, A1232, A1308, A1022

B1386, B1112, B1382, B1104, B1102, B1103, B1085, B1063, B1061, B1052, B1057, B1054, B1053, B1055, B1184, B1057, B1078, B1115, B1508, B1029, B1087, B1066, B1070, B1111, B1113, B1114, B1135, B1126, B1506, B1107, B1106

Mereside: Soham Mere

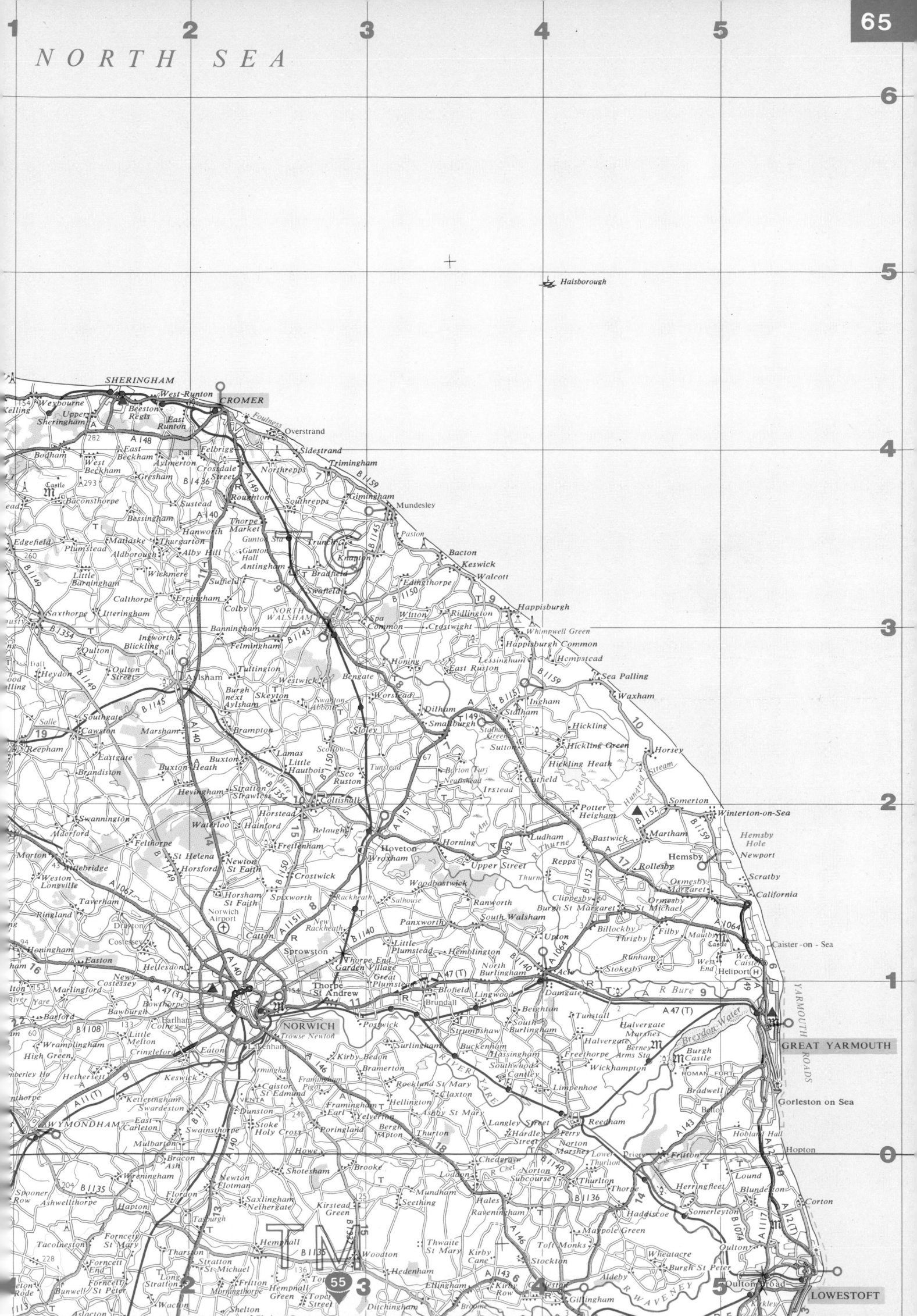

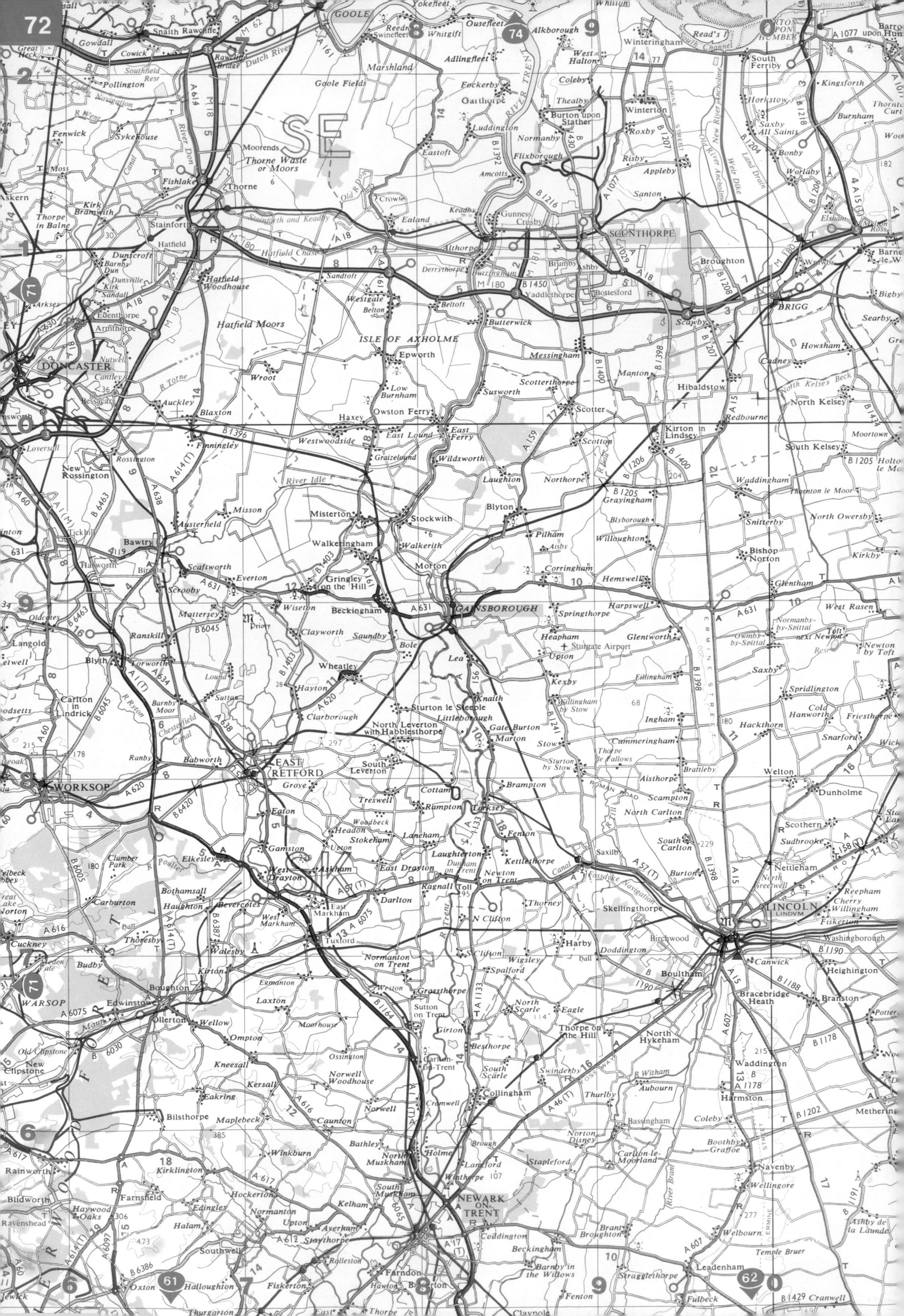

NORTH SEA

RIVER HUMBER

MOUTH OF THE HUMBER

SPURN HEAD

GRIMSBY

CLEETHORPES

MARKET RASEN

LOUTH

MABLETHORPE

Trusthorpe

Sutton on Sea

Sandilands

ALFORD

Chapel St Leonards

Ingoldmells

Ingoldmells Point

Skegness (Ingoldmells) Aerodrome

HORNCASTLE

WOODHALL SPA

SKEGNESS

Wainfleet All Saints

Wainfleet Bank

Gibraltar

Wainfleet Sand

East Halton Skitter

Paull Holme Sands

Goxhill

East Halton

Killingholme

Habrough

Immingham

Ottringham

Patrington

Welwick

Out Newton

Holmpton

Skeffling

Easington

Kilnsea

Bull

Spurn

Humber

Sunk Island

Sunk Island Sands

The Old Hall

Salthaugh Grange

Cherry Cobb Sands

Foulholme Sands

Old Refinery

Kirmington

Brocklesby

Great Limber

Keelby

Stallingborough

Healing

Great Coates

Riby

Laceby

Bradley

Aylesby

Scartho

Humberston

New Waltham

Holton le Clay

Waltham

Cabourne

Swallow

Irby upon Humber

Barnoldby le Beck

Beelsby

Brigsley

Ashby cum Fenby

Cuxwold

Hatcliffe

Grainsby

Tetney Lock

Tetney

North Cotes

Marshchapel

Donna Nook

Nettleton

Rothwell

East Ravendale

North Thoresby

Fulstow

Grainthorpe

North Somercotes

Thoresway

Normanby le Wold

Thorganby

Wold Newton

Ludborough

Covenham Res.

Covenham St Bartholomew

Covenham St Mary

Conisholme

South Somercotes

Saltfleet

Stainton le Vale

Swinhope

Binbrook

North Ormsby

Utterby

Yarburgh

Skidbrooke

Saltfleetby St Clement

Walesby

Kirmond le Mire

North Elkington

Fotherby

Alvingham

Saltfleetby All Saints

Saltfleetby St Peter

Theddlethorpe St Helen

Teulby

Kelstern

Cockerington

Grimoldby

Theddlethorpe All Saints

Gas Terminal

North Willingham

Ludford

South Elkington

Keddington

Manby

Sixhills

A Burgh on Bain

Welton le Wold

Stewton

Little Carlton

Great Carlton

Linwood

Legsby

Hainton

Raithby

Little Cawthorpe

Legbourne

Gayton le Marsh

West Torrington

East Torrington

South Willingham

Donington on Bain

Tathwell

Haugham

Muckton

South Reston

Withern

Strubby

Maltby le Marsh

Thorpe

Holton cum Beckering

Barkwith

Benniworth

Market Stainton

Authorpe

Beesby

Markby

Wragby

Panton

Sotby

Goulceby

Scamblesby

Ruckland

Burwell

Belleau

Aby

Saleby

Bilsby

Huttoft

Langton by Wragby

Hatton

Great Sturton

Swaby

South Thoresby

Anderby Creek

ROMAN ROAD

Belchford

Tetford

South Ormsby

Farlesthorpe

Anderby

Mumby

Baumber

Hemingby

Salmonby

Brinkhill

Driby

Well

Cumberworth

Authorpe Row

Minting

Wispington

Fulletby

West Ashby

Somersby

Ulceby

Hogsthorpe

Gautby

Edlington

Greetham

Ball Harrington

Claxby

Willoughby

Sloothby

High Toynton

Hagworthingham

Aswardby

Langton

Thimbleby

Langton Thornton

Mareham on the Hill

Hameringham

Asgarby

Lusby

Raithby

Sausthorpe

Skendleby

Welton le Marsh

Addlethorpe

Bardney

Bucknall

Horsington

Partney

Scremby

Orby

Orby Marsh

Winthorpe

Seathorne

Southrey

Stixwould

Dalderby

Mavis Enderby

Hareby

Hundleby

Spilsby

Ashby by Partney

Candlesby

Halton Holegate

Burgh le Marsh

Bratoft

Irby in the Marsh

Martin

Martin Dales

Roughton

Wood Enderby

Moorby

Old Bolingbroke

Keal

Toynton All Saints

Great Steeping

Sots Hole

Kirkby on Bain

Haltham

Miningsby

Keal Cotes

Toynton St Peter

Little Steeping

Firsby

Thorpe St Peter

Croft

Tattershall Thorpe

Tumby

Revesby

Toynton Fen Side

Croft Marsh

Seacroft

Tattershall

Coningsby

Mareham le Fen

East Kirkby

Fendike Corner

Havenhouse Sta.

Tattershall Bridge

Castle

New Bolingbroke

Stickford

Timberland

Walcott

Tumby Woodside

New York

Stickney

New Leake

Eastville

Havenhouse

Dogdyke

Chapel Hill

Scrub Hill

Midville

Friskney

Billinghay

Wildmore Fen

Carrington

Lade Bank

Wainfleet Sand

North Kyme

West Fen

East Fen

Friskney Flats

Gipsey Bridge

Frithville

Sibsey

Northlands

Leake Common Side

Old Leake

Wrangle

DEEPS

THE WOLDS

THE FENS

81

2

3 +

4

5

5

Lissett A9
Great Kelk
Ulrom
B1242
Beeford
B1249
North Frodingham
Castle
Skipsea
Dunnington
Bewholme
Atwick
16
B1244
HORNSEA
Brandesburton
Seaton
Hornsea Mere
Rolston
Catwick
Sigglesthorne
Mappleton
Leven
Goxhill
Great Hatfield
Long Riston
Rise
Withernwick
New Ellerby
B1243
Meaux
South Skirlaugh
West Newton
Aldbrough
4
Swine
Old Ellerby Hall
Burton Constable
Flinton
Garton
Coniston
Sproatley
Humbleton
Ganstead
Owstwick
Bilton
Sutton-on-Hull
Lelley
Elstronwick
Tunstall
B1240
Preston
Burton Pidsea
Roos
3
Marfleet
A1033
Waxholme
HEDON
B1362
Rimswell
B1242
Thorngumbald
Burstwick
WITHERNSEA
TON UPON HULL
Halsham
Paull
Keyingham
Hollym
Ottringham
Winestead
A1033
2
East Halton Skitter
Paull Holme Sands
Patrington
Holmpton
Goxhill
Cherry Cobb Sands
Saltaugh Grange
B1445
Out Newton
Welwick
East Halton
Sunk Island
Skeffling
Killingholme
Oil Refinery
The Old Hall
Easington
A160
Sunk Island Sands
Kilnsea
Habrough
Immingham
SPURN HEAD
B1210
Stallingborough
Kirmington
Brocklesby
GRIMSBY
Bull
Healing
Great Coates
A1098
CLEETHORPES
Keelby
Aylesby
Great Limber
Riby
Laceby
Bradley
A18
Scartho
Swallow
Irby upon Humber
Barnoldby le Beck
Humberston
Cabourne
Waltham
New Waltham
Holton le Clay
A1031
A46
Beelsby
Brigsley
Tetney Lock
Cuxwold
Hatcliffe
Ashby cum Fenby
Tetney
North Cotes
Nettleton
Rothwell
East Ravendale
Grainsby
Marshchapel
Donna Nook
Thoresway
Wold Newton
North Thoresby
Fulstow
Grainthorpe
North Somercotes
Swinhope
Ludborough
Covenham St Bartholomew
Conisholme
Normanby le Wold
Stainton le Vale
Covenham St Mary
South Somercotes
Saltfleet
Binbrook
North Ormsby
Utterby
Yarburgh
Skidbrooke
Walesby
Kirmond le Mire
Fotherby
Alvingham
Saltfleetby St Clement
B1203
Tealby
North Elkington
Cockerington
Saltfleetby All Saints
MARKET RASEN
Kelstern
Keddington
Saltfleetby St Peter
Ludford
South Elkington
LOUTH
Grimoldby
Theddlethorpe St Helen
North Willingham
Welton le Wold
Stewton
Manby
Theddlethorpe All Saints
Linwood
Sixhills
A Burgh on Bain
Little Carlton
Great Carlton
Gas Terminal
Legsby
Legbourne
MABLETHORPE

NORTH SEA

Humber

MOUTH OF THE HUMBER

RIVER HUMBER

KINGSTON UPON HULL to
Rotterdam (Europoort)............14 hrs
Zeebrugge...........................15 hrs

73

2

3

4

5

6

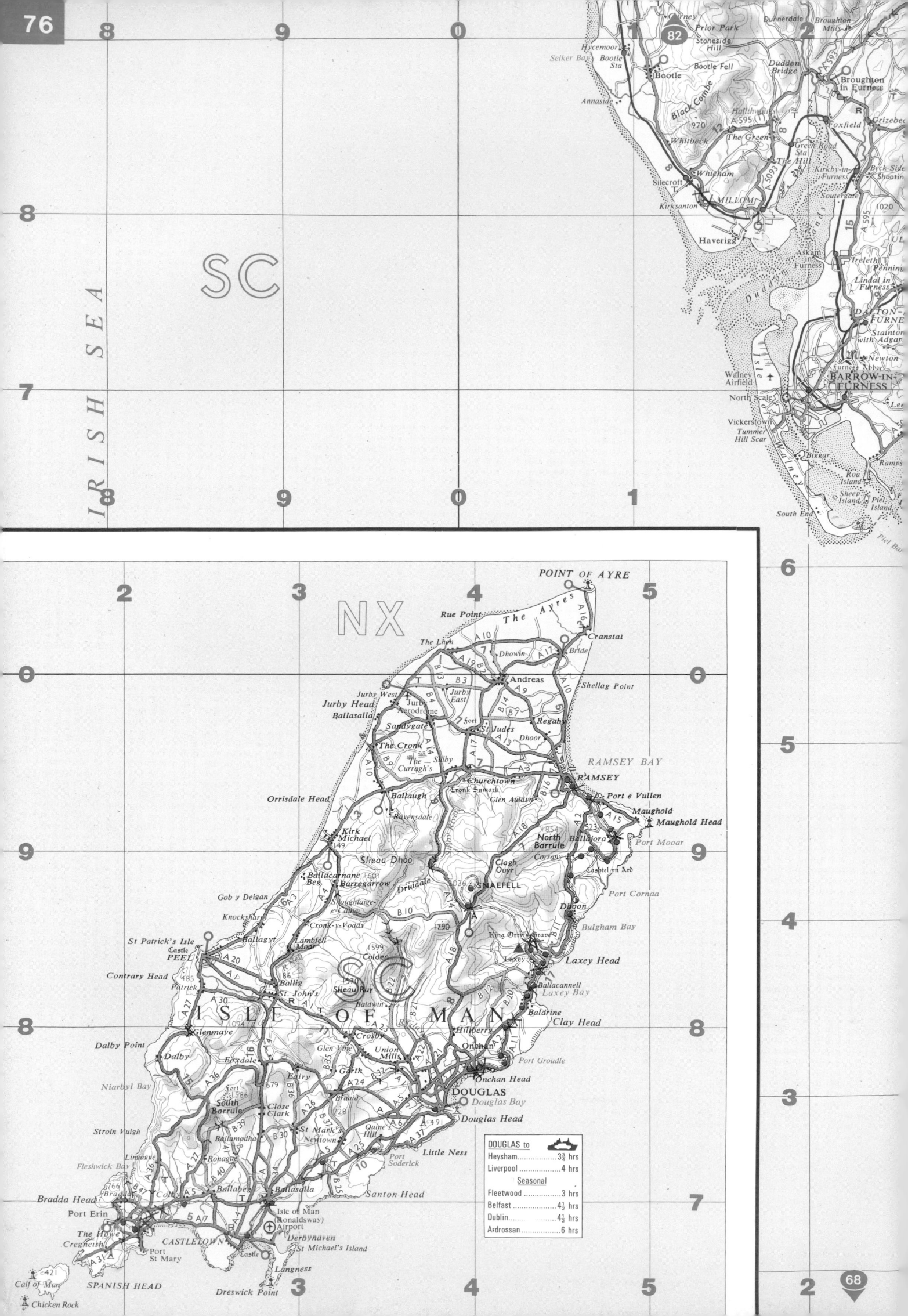

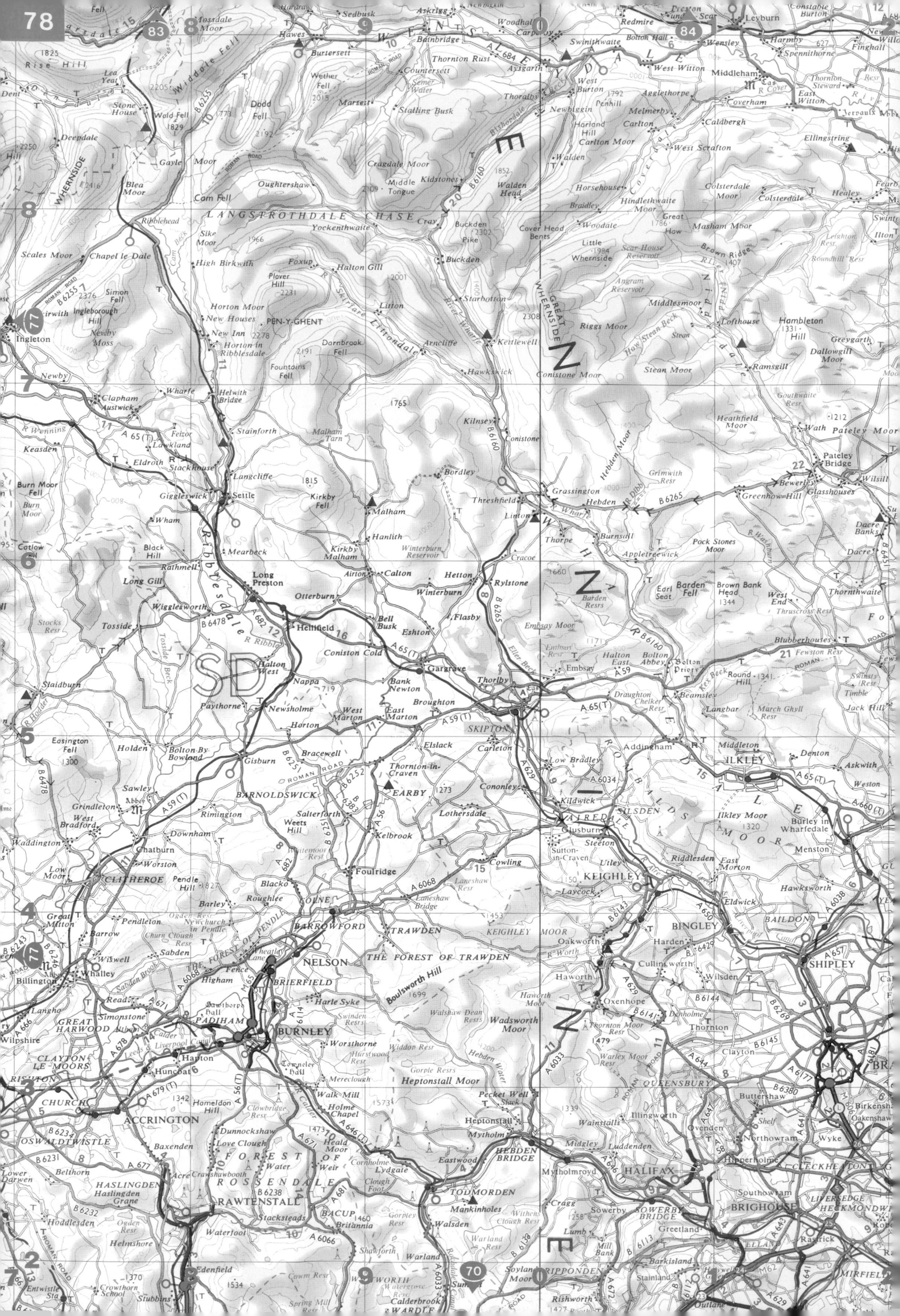

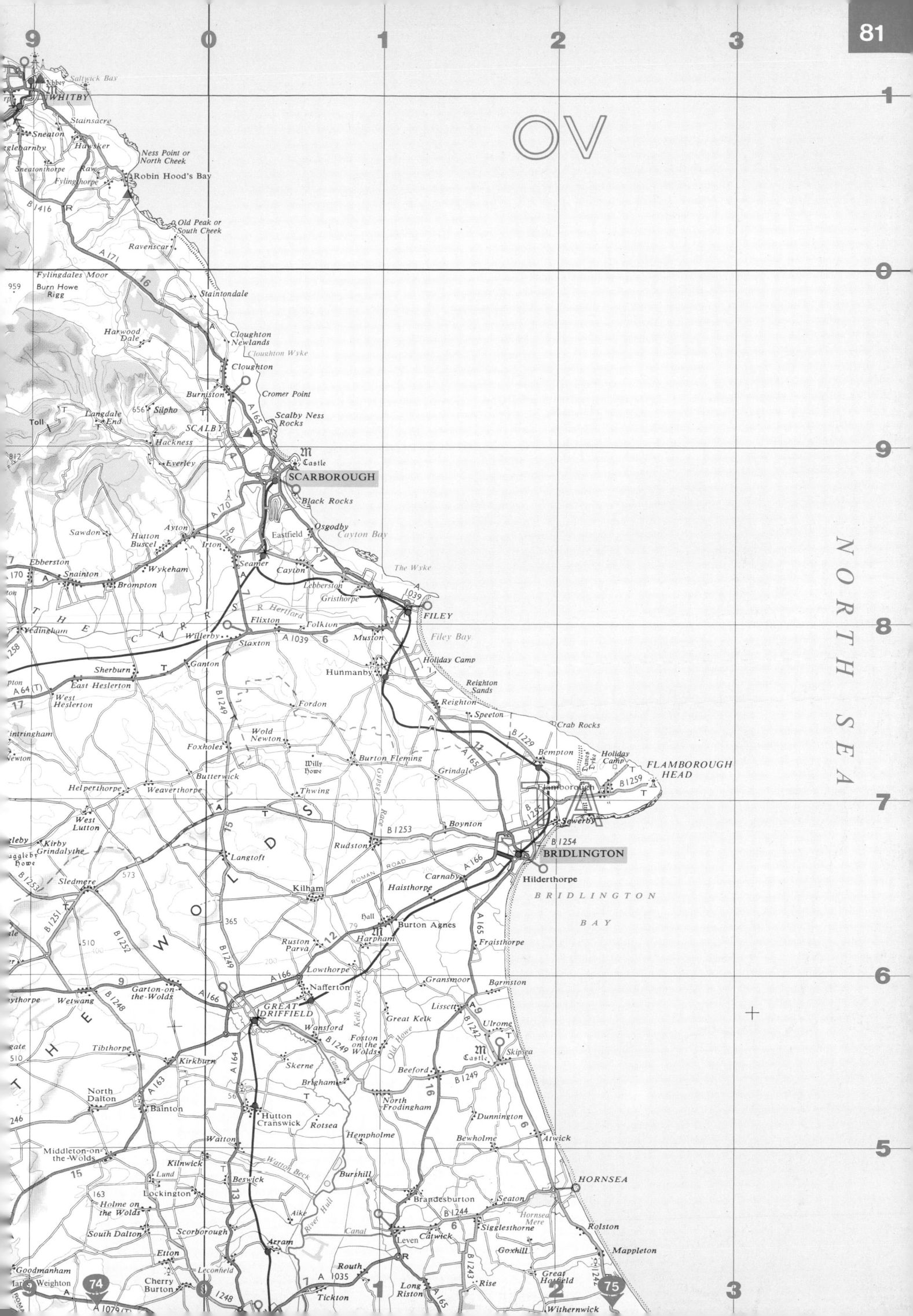

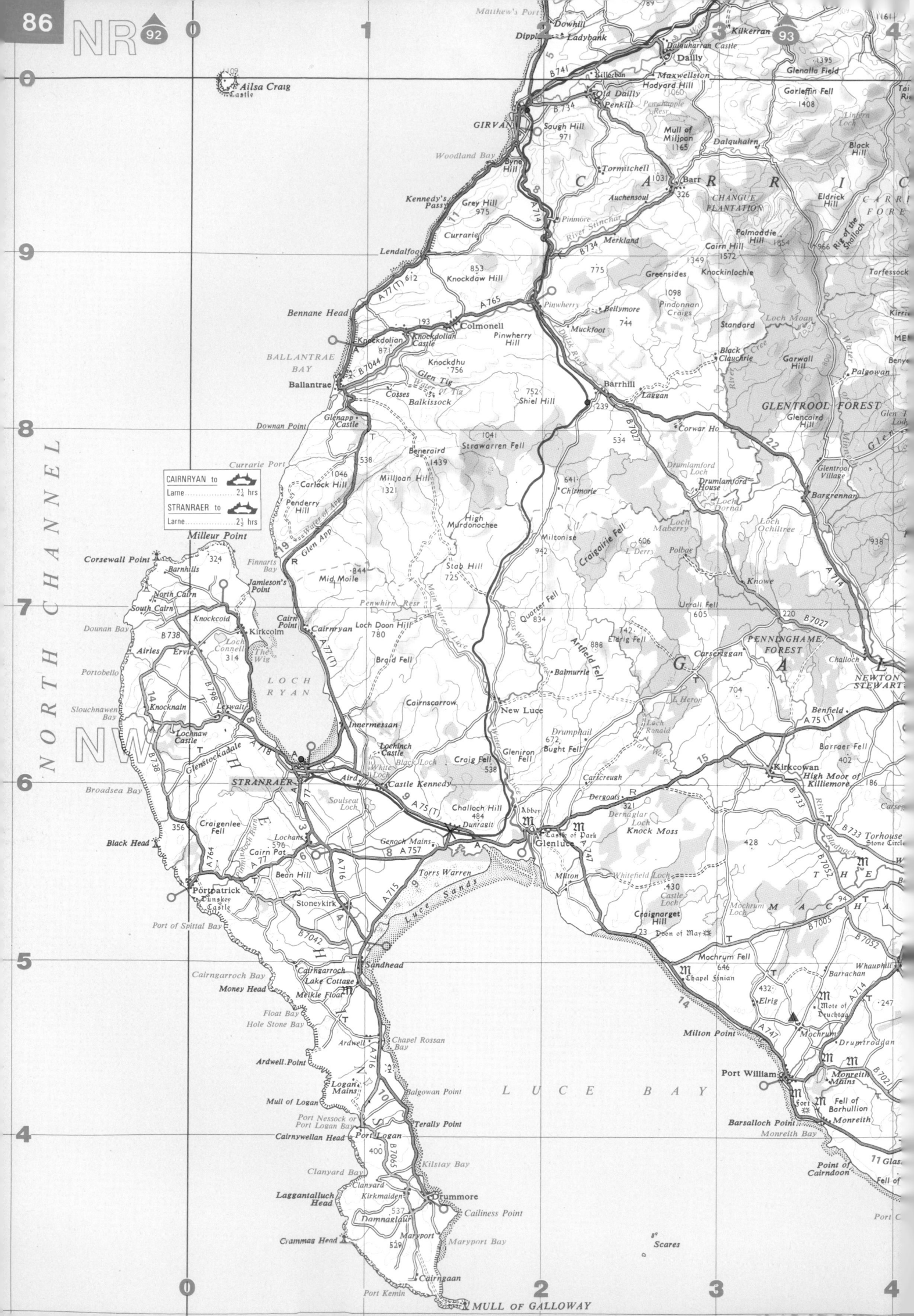

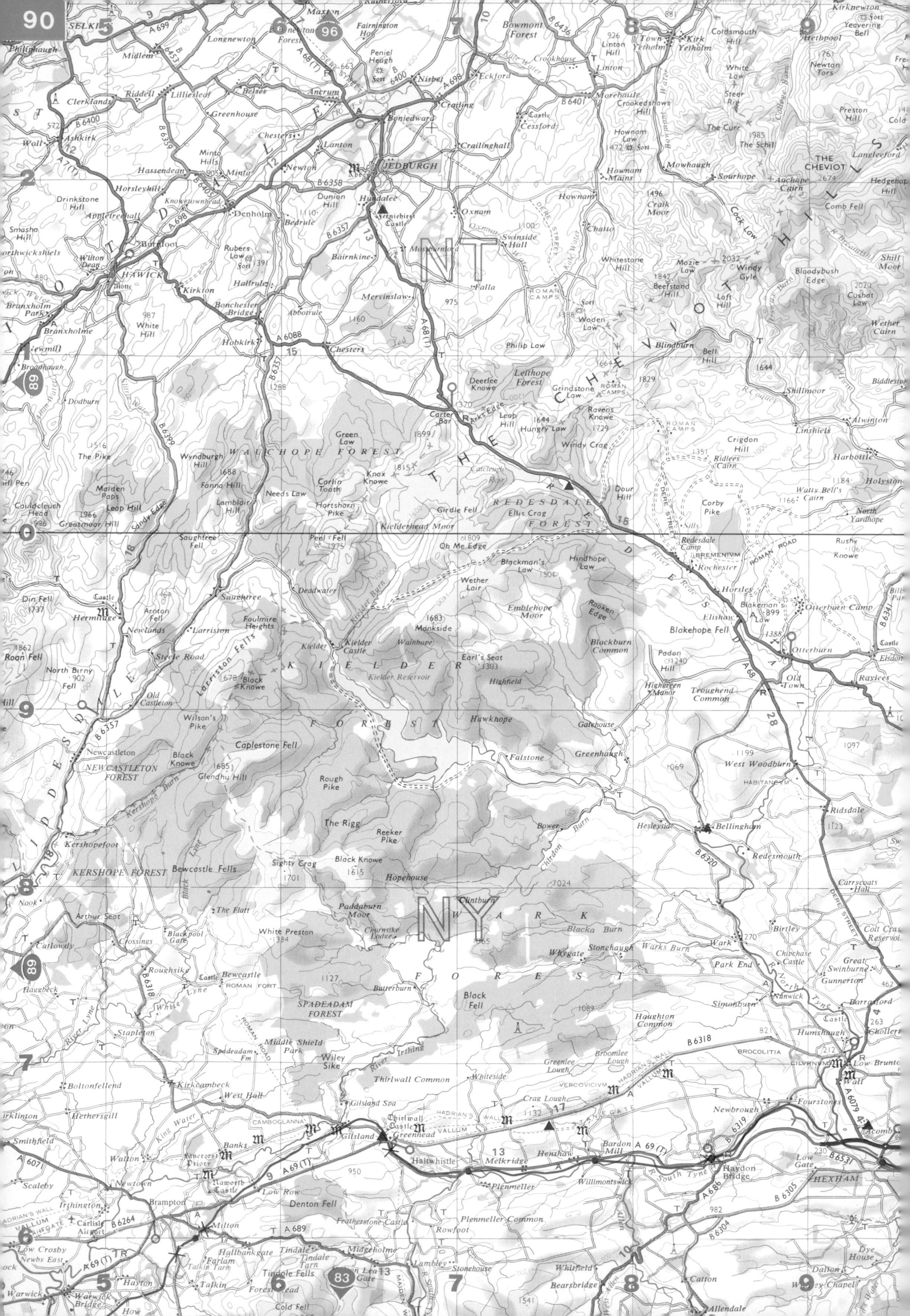

FIRTH OF CLYDE

ROTHESAY
Ascog
Kerrycroy
Scoulag Point
Mountstuart
Bogany Point
Port Bannatyne
Toward Point
Toward
Castle Toward
Innellan
Knock 100
Dunure
Wemyss Bay
Inverkip
Power Sta
Upper Skelmorlie
Skelmorlie
Leap Moor
Garvock
Creuch Hill 1448
North Burnt Hill 1408
Duchal Moor
Cader Dam
Queenside Muir
Hill of Stake 1712
Heathfield
Kilmacolm
Quarrier's Homes Bridge of Weir
Houston
Ranfurly
Brookfield
Bishopton
Rossland Bishopton Sta
Erskine Toll
BEARSDEN
Drumchapel
CLYDEBANK
Yoker
Temple
Partick
Govan
PAISLEY
Glasgow Airport
RENFREW
JOHNSTONE
Elderslie
Millikenpark
Kilbarchan
Lochwinnoch
Howwood
Neilston
BARRHEAD
Clarkston
Newton Mearns
Busby
Thornliebank
Waterfoot
Eaglesham
GREAT CUMBRAE ISLAND
MILLPORT
Kilchattan
Tomont End
Largs Bay
LARGS
1263
Routenburn
Girtley Hill
Kelburn
Whitelee Forest
Ladyland Moor
Burnt Hill 1084
Irish Law 1586
Mistylaw Muir
Waterhead Moor
Blackhouse Moor
Knock Castle
Portrye
Fairlie
Fairlie Terminal
Hunterston Ho
Campbeltown
Little Cumbrae Island
Gull Point
Portencross
Farland Head
Seamill
West Kilbride
Crosbie
Dalry
Kilbirnie
Glengarnock
Beith
Gateside
Barrmill
Burnhouse
The Den
Highfield
Drakemyre
Dalgarven
Baidland Hill
Munnoch Resr
Busbie Muir Resr
CUNNINGHAME
Auchentiber
Dunlop
Lugton
Halket
Gabroc Hill
Fullwood
STEWARTON
Fenwick
Rowallan Castle
Kilmaurs
Crawfurdland Castle
Moscow
Waterside
Rough Hill
Whitelee Hill
Craigendunton Resr
Corse Hill
KILWINNING
Montgreenan
Cunninghamhead
Springside
Knockentiber
Crosshouse
Dreghorn
KILMARNOCK
NEWMILNS
DARVEL
GALSTON
GREENHOLM
Hurlford
Riccarton
Earlston
Shortlees
Sornhill
Middleyard
Craigie
Carnell
Auchmillan
Mossgiel
ARDROSSAN
Horse Isle
SALTCOATS
STEVENSTON
IRVINE
Irvine Bay
Drybridge
Gatehead
Dundonald
Loans
Symington
Bogend
TROON
Lady Isle
Meikle Craig
Barassie
Rosemount
Millburn
Tarbolton
Fallford
Mauchline
Catrine
Sorn
Shawwood
MONKTON
PRESTWICK
New Prestwick
Prestwick Scotland Airport
St Quivox
Annbank Station
Annbank
Stair
Trabboch
Auchinleck
Ochiltree
HOLMHEAD
CUMNOCK
AYR
Wallacetown
Whitletts
Belston
Coylton
Hillhead
Drongan
Sinclairston
DOONFOOT
Burns Cott
Alloway
Doonholm
Martnaham Loch
Littlemill
Rankinston
Carsgailoch Hill
Dalgig
Heads of Ayr
Fisherton
Newark Castle
Dalrymple
Hollybush
Cairntable
Stannery Knowe
NS
Dunure
Brown Carrick Hill
Sauchrie
Culroy
Minishant
Cairnhill
Polnessan
Kilmein Hill
Waterhead
Drumshang
Knoweside
Patna
KYLE FOREST
Benbeoch
Dalmellington
Prickeny Hill
Milroy Hill
Culzean Bay
Culzean Castle
Maidenhead Bay
MAYBOLE
Kirkmichael
Loch Spallander Resr
Bogton Loch
Bellsbank
Enoch Hill
Craignane
Windy Standard
CARSPHAIRN
Maidens
Crossraguel Abbey
Kirkoswald
Crosshill
Turnberry Bay
Turnberry
Brest Rocks
Matthew's Port
Dowhill
Dipple
Ladybank
Kirkmichael
Kilkerran
Dailly
Old Dailly
Maxwellston
Hadyard Hill
Penkill
Garleffin Fell
Tairlaw Ring
Loch Finlas
Big Hill of Glenmount
Glenalla Field
Dersalloch Hill
KYLE
CARRICK

100 101 94 88 86 87

ARDROSSAN to [ferry]
Douglas .... 6 hrs
(seasonal)

1 hr

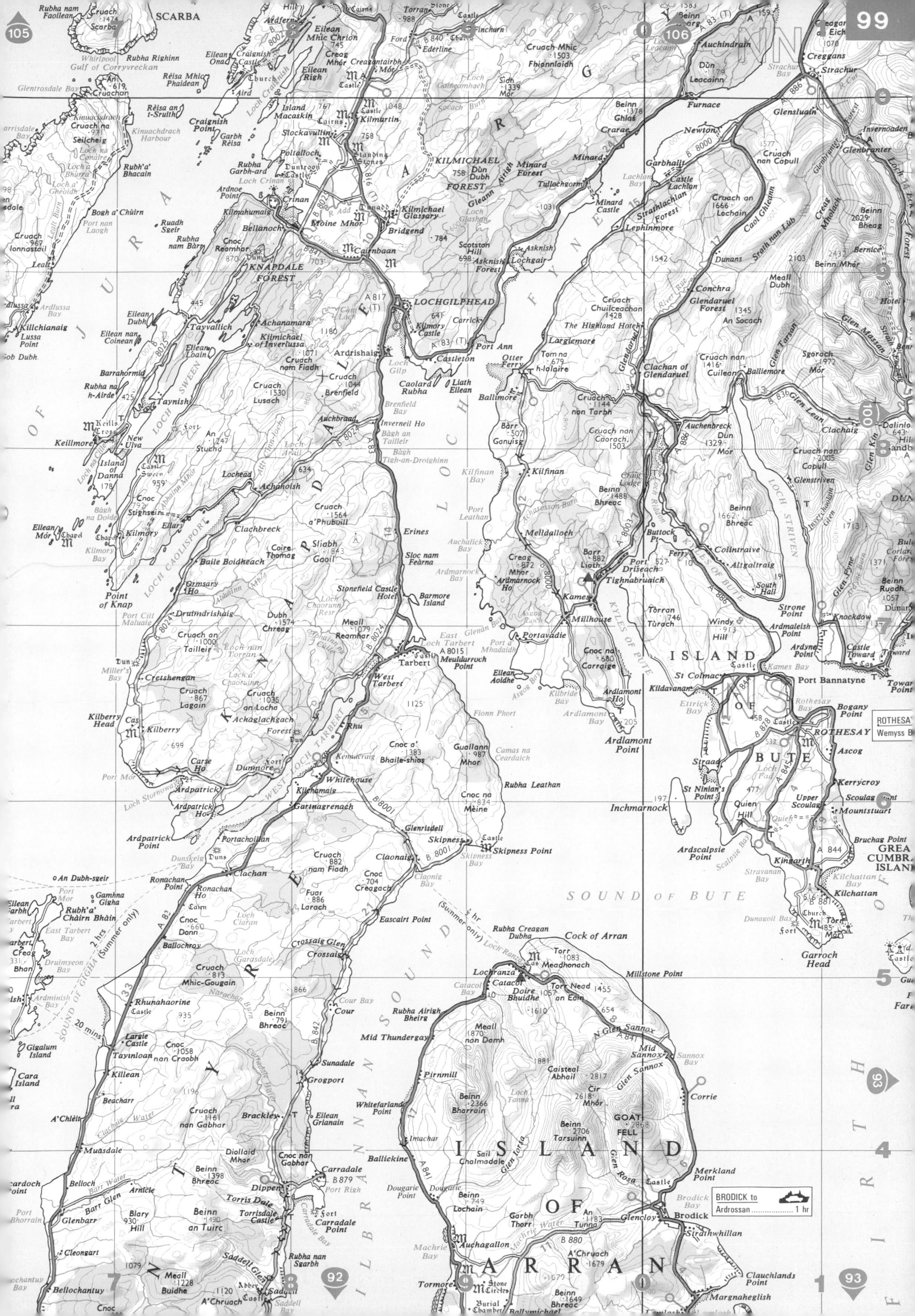

Port Bhiosd
Vaul
Caoles
Rubha Dubh
Point
Hough
Skerries
Clachan Mòr
Balephetrish
Ruaig
B 8069
Haunn
708
Rubh'
a' Chaoil
Rubha
Bay
Balevullin
Gott Bay
Soa
Nead a' Uncoidh
Burg
Rubh'
Cairn na
an
Rubha
Chràiginis
389
B 8068
B 8065
Burgh Beg
t-Suibhein
Stròi
Kenovay
Tiree
B 8068
Treshnish Isles
Fladda
Eilean
Kilkenneith
Aerodrome
Scarinish
Rubha na
TIREE
337
Dloghlum
509
Moss
Seann Charraige
Lunga
Gometra
Middleton 2 Heylipol
Crossapol
TIREE to
Port Mòr
HYNISH
Coll .... ¾ hr
Maisgeir
Port Bharrapol
Barrapol
Rubha
BAY
Oban .... 4½ hrs
Bac Mòr or
B 8065
Loch a'
Tràigh an Dùin
Dutchman's Cap
Eilean
Phuill
Bac Beag
na Creic
Little
Balephuil
8067
Balemartine
Colonsay
Rinn
Carnan
Mannal
Thorbhais
462
Staffa
Balephuil
Mòr
Fingal's Cave
Bay
Hynish
Port Snoig

NL

Rèidh
Eilean
Eilean
Annraidh
Rubha nan
Cearc
Garbh Phort
333
IONA
Abbey
Baile
Mòr
Creich
Aridhglas
265
Stac an Aoineidh
Fionnphort
Loch Poit
na h-I
Eilean na h-
Aon Chaorach
Fidden
Beinn a'
369
Ghlinne Mhòir
ROSS
Greave
Erraid
246
Ardalanish
Soa
Eilean
Beinn a'
Island
nam Muc
Chaol-airigh
411
Arda
Eileah
a' Chalmain
Rubha nam
Maol Mòra
Rubh'
Ardalan
West Reef
Torran Rocks
Sgeir Dhoirbh

Dubh
Artach

NQ

Caillea
Uraga
Be
A 870
Kilchattan
An Rubha
COLONSAY
Scala
Eilean a'
Chladaich
Eilean
Ardskenish
Ca
Leathann
Dubh
304
Eilean
Priory
ORO
Eilean
Caolas Mòr
nan Roh
Gh
Ceann
Riobha

Rubh
Bholse
98
Nave
Island
Ardnave
Point
Eilean Beag
Sgairrail
Sgarb

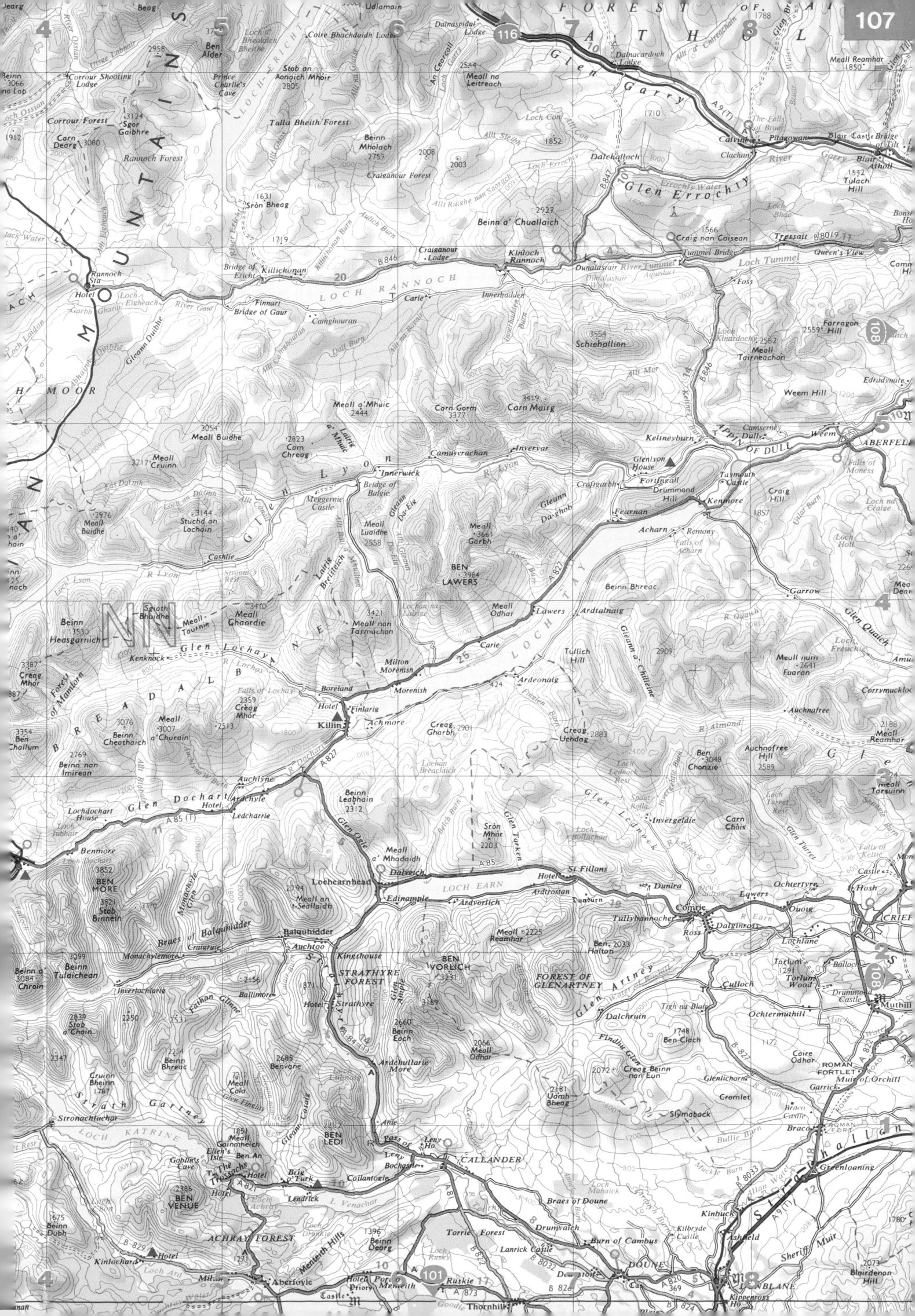

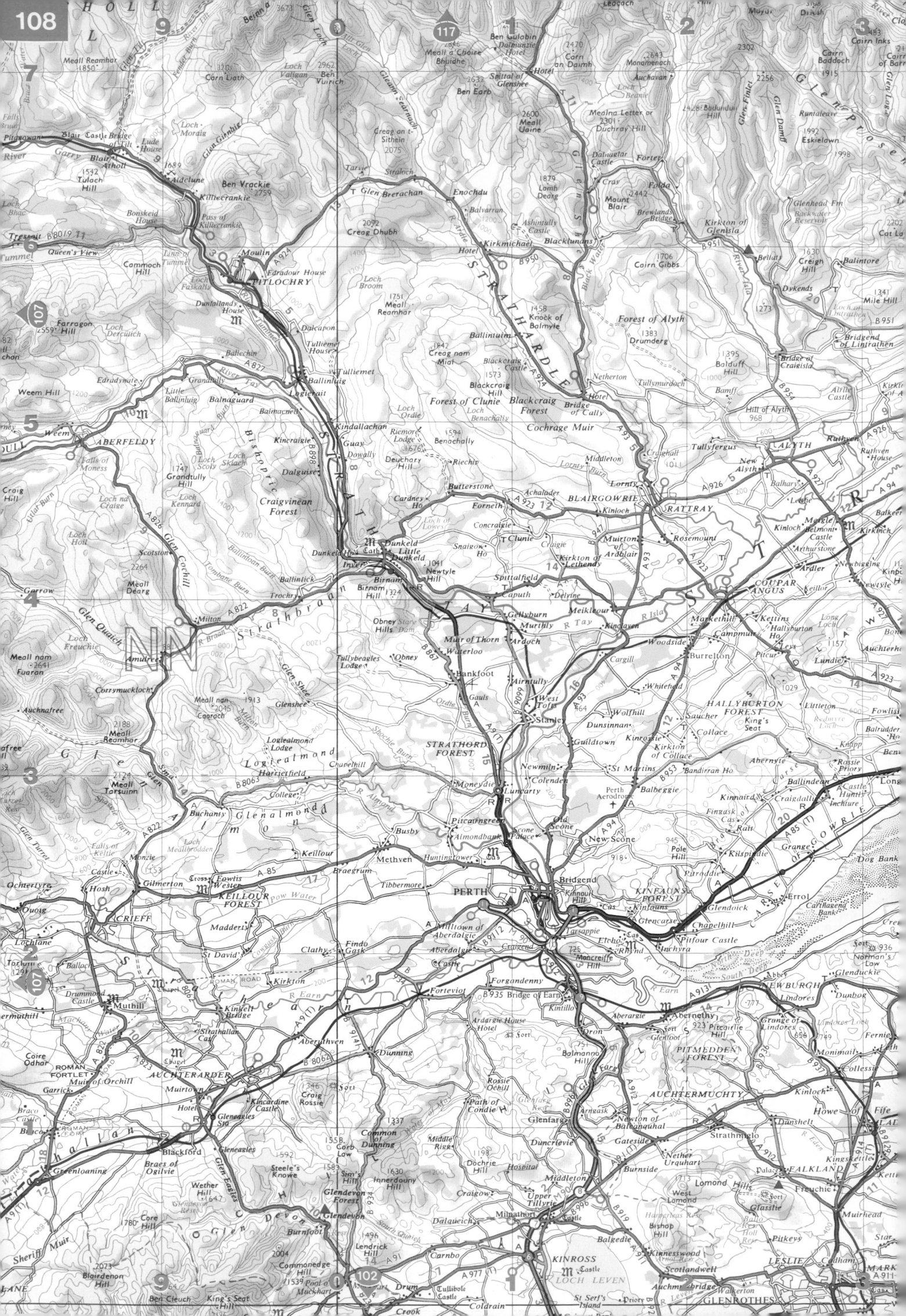

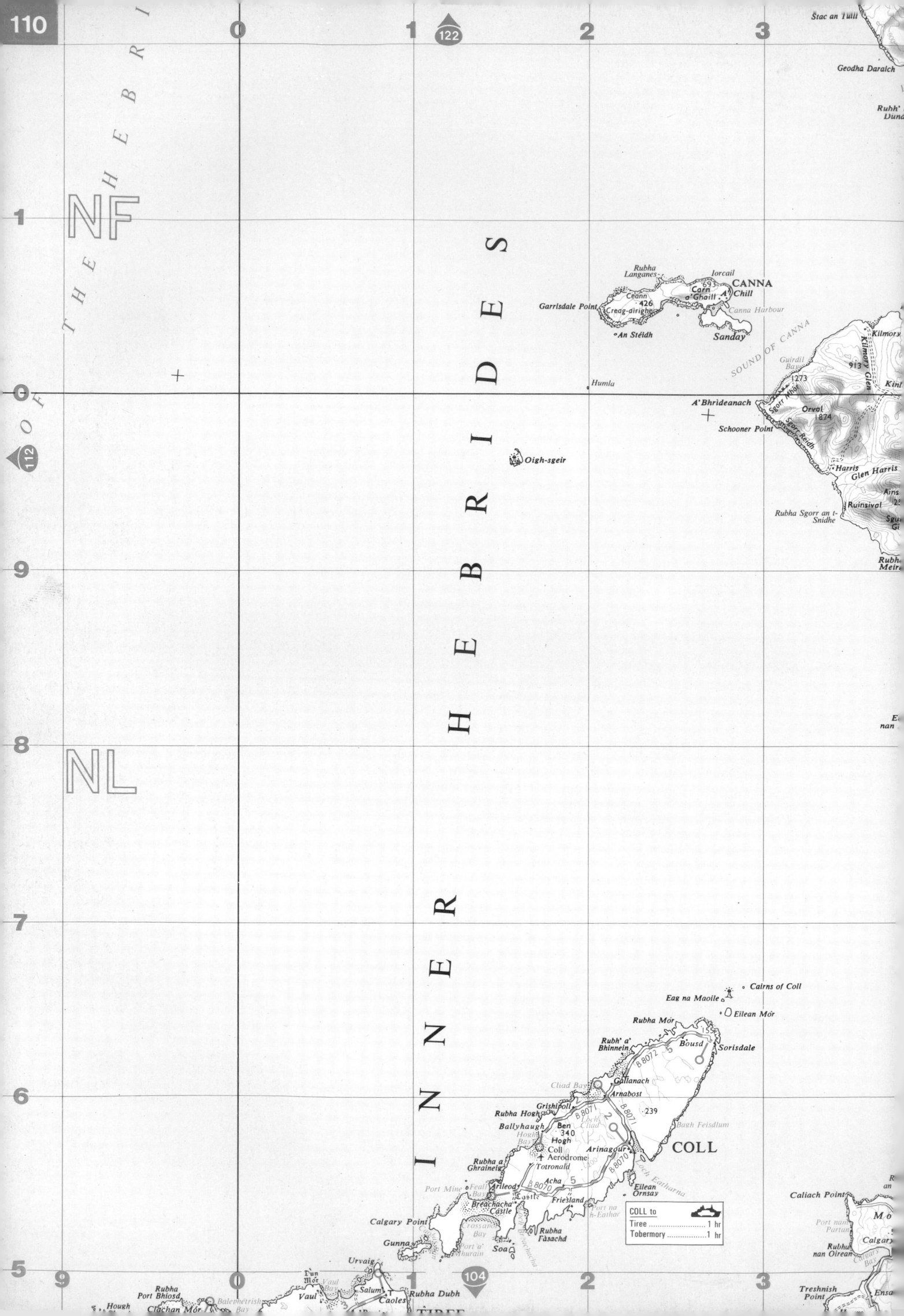

ISLES

WESTERN

OR

HEBRIDES

THE

OF

SEA

ATLANTIC OCEAN

OUTER HEBRIDES

SOUTH UIST

NF

NL

124

West Gerinish
Stilligarry
Howmore
Verran Island
Rubh' Aird-mhicheil
Stoneybridge
Snishival
Ormiclate Castle
Loch Ollay
Rubha Ardvule
Loch Kildonan
Mingary
730 Sheaval
Askernish House
412
Daliburgh
Crossdougal
Kilpheder
Boisdale
Orosay
Garrynamonie
Smerclate
Pollachar
Kilbride
Ludag

Loch Bee
Loch
865
285
Lochskipport
4
Loch Druidibeg
Hecla 1988
Ushinish
1723
Corodale
BEINN MHOR 2033
Buail' a' Ghoill
Loch Eynort
822
Loch Snittisdale
Stulaval
Layaval
Triuirebheinn 1168
Lochboisdale
902
South Lochboisdale
Easaval
Roneval 661

Steisay
Gasay
Sandwick
Cärnan
Caltinish
Glas-elleanan
Luirsay Dubh
551
Skipport
208
Ornish Island
Acairseid Falaich
Mol a' Tuath
200
576 Rubha Rossel
Rubha Bhilidh
Prince's Cave
Rubha Hellisdale
Rubha Bolum
Calvay
Stuley
Rubha na Creige Móire
Calvay
Rubha Meall na Hoe
200
356 Rubha na h-Ordaig
400

Sound of Eriskay
Sgeir a' Mhill

LOCHBOISDALE to
Oban..................5½ hrs

Lingay
Balla
ERISKAY
Ben 610 Screen
Hartamul
Stack Islands
403
14 hrs

Fiaray
Sound of Fiaray
Scurrival Point
Hornish
Eilean Dallaig
Eoligarry
338
Orosay
Traigh Mhór
Greian Head
Ben 680 Cliad
Sgeir Liath
Cuier
Bruernish
Borve Point
Borve
Balnabodach
309
Hotel Tangasdale
Doirlinn Head
Heaval Earsary 1260 1888
Ben Tangaval 1090
BARRA
Brevig
Kiessimul Castle
Castlebay
Rubha Mór
Caolis
Biruastlum
Heishival Mór 624
Uinessan
VATERSAY
Vatersay 279
327
Sound of Sandray
Floddav
Cairn Galtar 678
Sandray
504 Muldoanich

291 Fuday
Rubha nan Eun
Greanamul
Gighay
242 311
Hellisay
Floddav
Fuiay
Bruernish Point
352

Sound of Fuday
Oitir Mhór
North Bay
Sound of Hellisay
SOUND OF BARRA

CASTLEBAY to
Oban..................5½ hrs

Lingay 269
Greanamul
Sound of Pabbay
Pabbay 561
Heiskers
Rosinish
Sound of Mingulay
735 MINGULAY
896 Carnan
Mingulay Bay
Sound of Berneray
Berneray
Barra Head

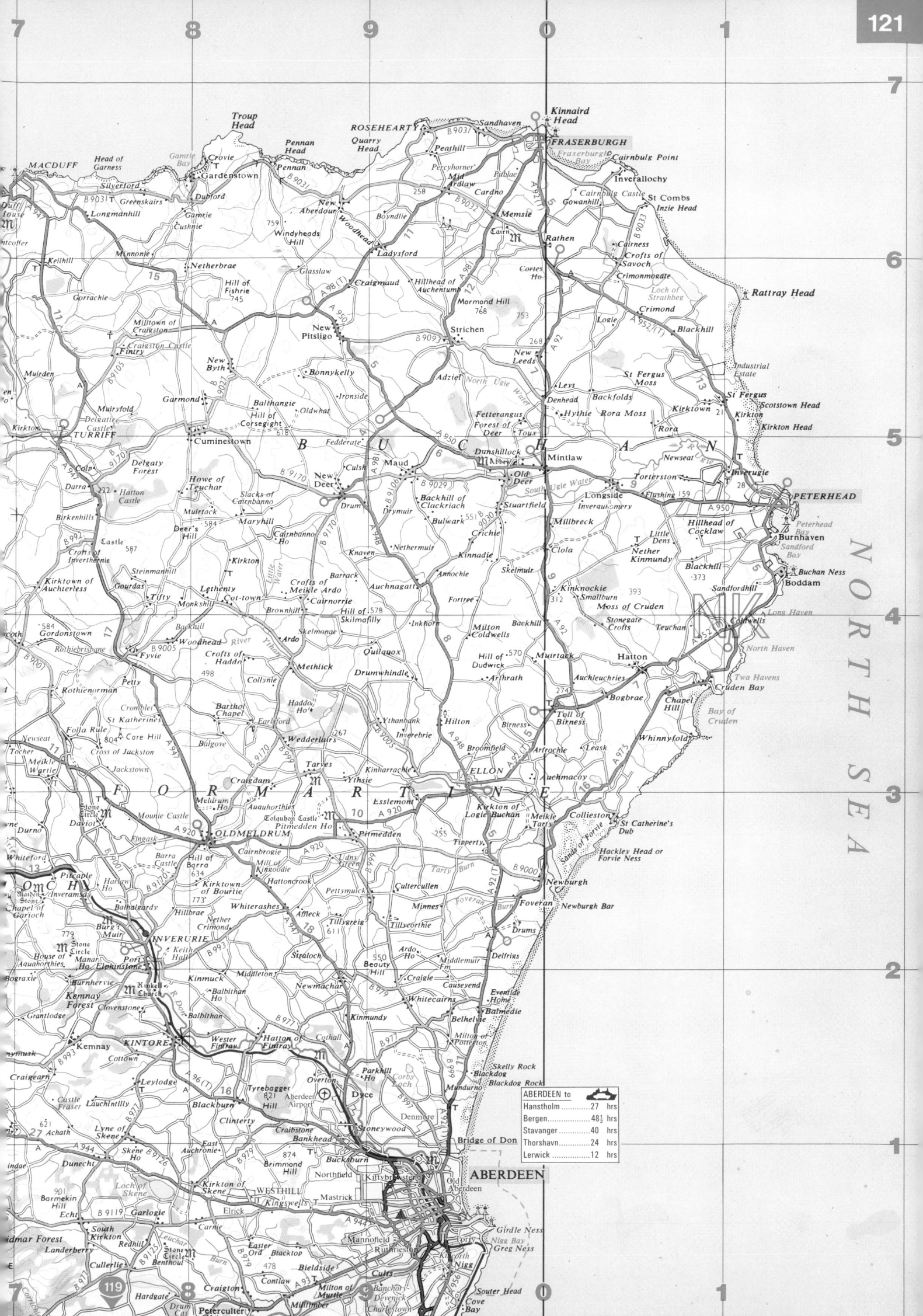

HARRIS

0   1   2   3

T H E   L I T T L E   M I N C H

LOCHMADDY to
Tarbert .... 2½ hrs

2 hrs

TARBERT to
Uig .... 2 hrs

Newton
Newtonferr
B 893
Beinn
Mhòr
Trumisgarry
·588
Torogay
Sgeir a' Chàil
Aird Thormaid
Scotait Mhic Neacail
Sursay
Opsay
Groays
Lingay
Scaravay
Gilsay
of Berneras
Tahay
Sealbhag Anlasary
Hermetray
Groatay
Crogary na Hoe
·504
Rubha an Duine
An t-Iasg
Camas Mòr
Cairidh nan Ob

Trumpan

T   7
11   8
Loch
Fada
Loch
Skealtar
Loch
Maddy
Hotel
Lochmaddy
Weaver's Point
Rubha nam Plèac
·824
North Lee
920
South Lee
An t-Algeach
Madadh Gruamach

Loch Scadday
Loch Eport
Sidinish
Rubha Mhic Gille-mhìcheil
Eigneig Mhór
Eigneig Bheag

WATERNISH
POINT
An Càmastac
Healaval
Eilean Iosal
Eilean Creagach
Ascrib Islands
Ru Chorachan
Kilbride Point
Tots
Balgo
Idrigill
Uig B

1,139
EAVAL
Llernish
124
Floddaybeg
Floddaymore
·379
Ronay
·325
Rubha na Rodagrich
Maragay Mór

Ben ·931
Geary
Geary
Ard Beag
Trumpan
Ardmore Point
Halistra
Hallin
Mingay
Score Horan
Blod nan Laogh
Beinn Charnach Bheag
Lusta
LOCH SNIZORT
Eilean Mór
Lynde
Poll na h-Ealaidh
Greshornish Point
Lyndale
Ho

NF

OUTER   HEBRIDES   OR   WESTERN   ISLES

HEBRIDES

Maaey Riabhach
Greanamul Deas
Rubha Cam nan Gall
·334
Wiay
Isay
Glas-elleanan
Luirsay Dubh
D
Ornish Island
airseid Falaich
I' Tuath
·76
Rubha Rossel
ubha Bhilidh
ve
isdale

DUNVEGAN
HEAD
Geodha nan Each
Blod an Uathair
·1031
Galtrigill
Borreraig
Ben Ettow
Uig
Gob na Hoe
An Ceannalch
Milovaig
Oisgill Bay
Lephin
Neist
Waterstein Head
Moonen Bay
 Feriniquarrie
Totaig
Colbost
Skinidin
Ben Corkeval
Ramasaig
Glen Dale
HEALABHAL MHOR
·1538
Macleod's Tables
HEALABHAL BHEAG
·2160
Ben ·799
Connon
Hoe Rape
·759
The Hoe
Hoe Point
Am Bi-bogha Beag
Am Bi-bogha Mór
Geodha Mór
An Dubh Sgeir
Ollisdal Geo
Flossnan
Macleod's Maidens
IDRIGILL POINT

Isay Island
Claigan
·1074
Beinn Bhreac
·866
Dunvegan
Kilmuir
Lonmore
Roskhill
Roag
Orbost
Vatten
·872
Cruachan Beinn a' Chearcaill
Greshornish
A 850
Flashader
Edinbane
Ben ·800
Uigshad
ISLA

Loch Bharcasaig
Ben Idrigill
·1207
Beinn na Boineid
Harlosh Island
Wiay
Loch BRACADALE
Harlosh Point
Colbost Point
Tarner Island
Bracadale
Struan
Ullinish
Oronsay
Portnalong
Ardtreck Point
Coillore
Loch Har

Hoe
na h-Ordaig
Il

THE   HEBRIDES

INNER   HEBRIDES

Gob na h-Oa
Rubha nan Clach
Fiskavaig
Fernilea
B 8009
·1210
Arnaval
McFarlane's Rock
Gleann Oraid
Talisker Bay
Talisker
Broch
Beinn nan Cuithean
Beinn Bhreac
·1468
Carbost
Merk
Eyne
Stac a' Mheadais
MI
Loch Eyno
An Dubh-sgeir
Stac an Tuill
Geodha Daralch
Rub
Di

112

110

9   0   1   2   3

Rubha Langanes
Rubha Iorcail
CANNA
Carn A' Chill

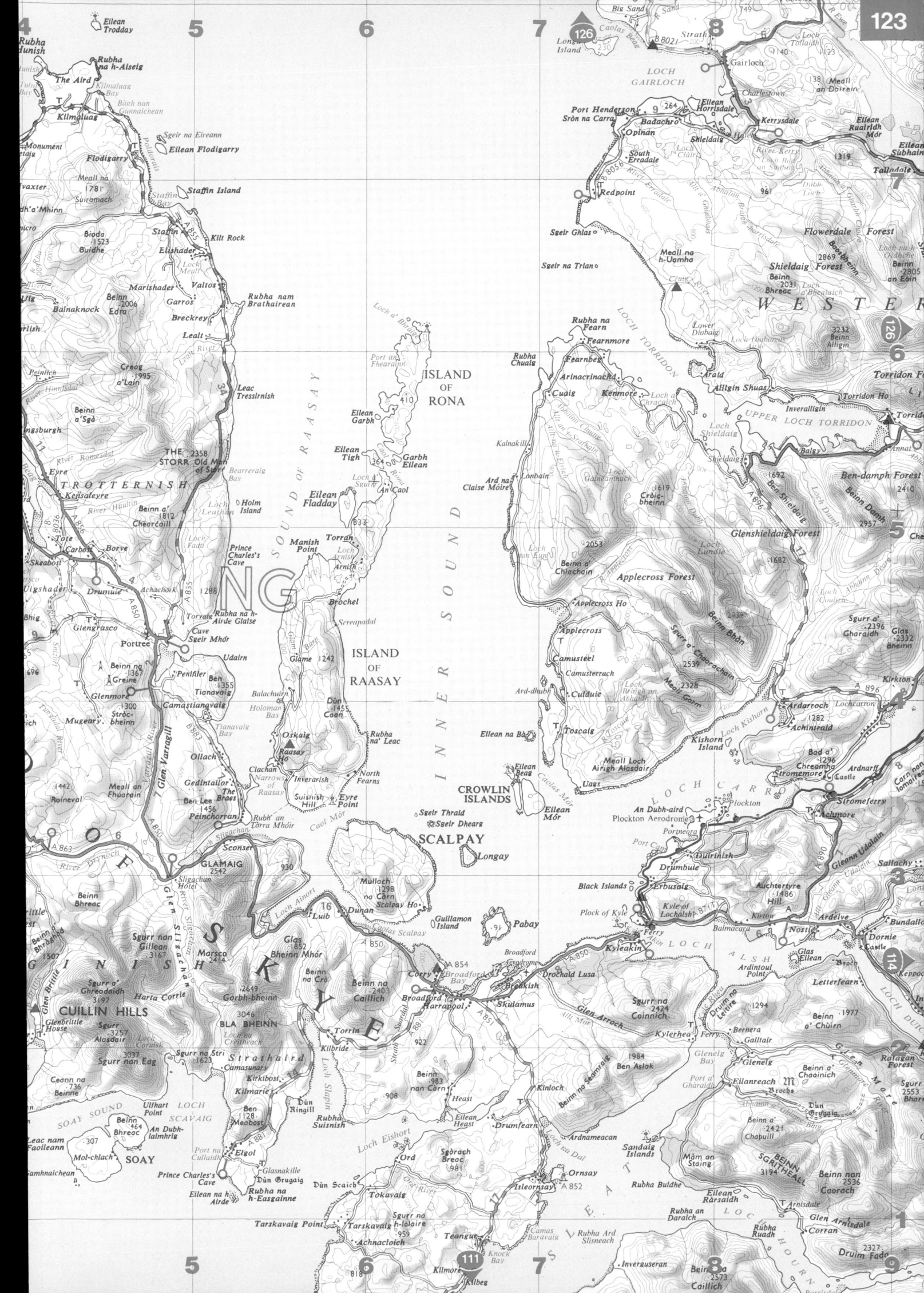

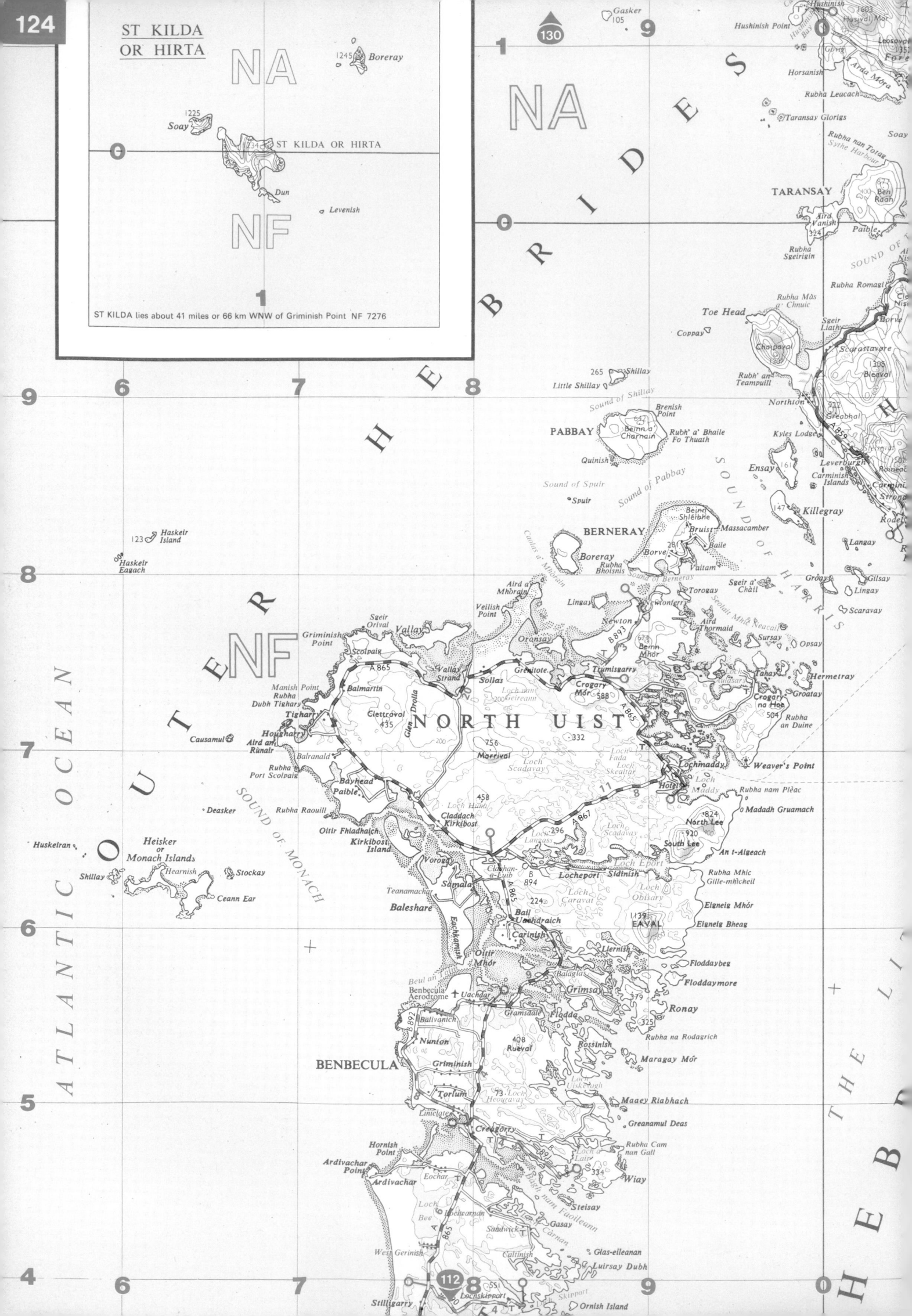

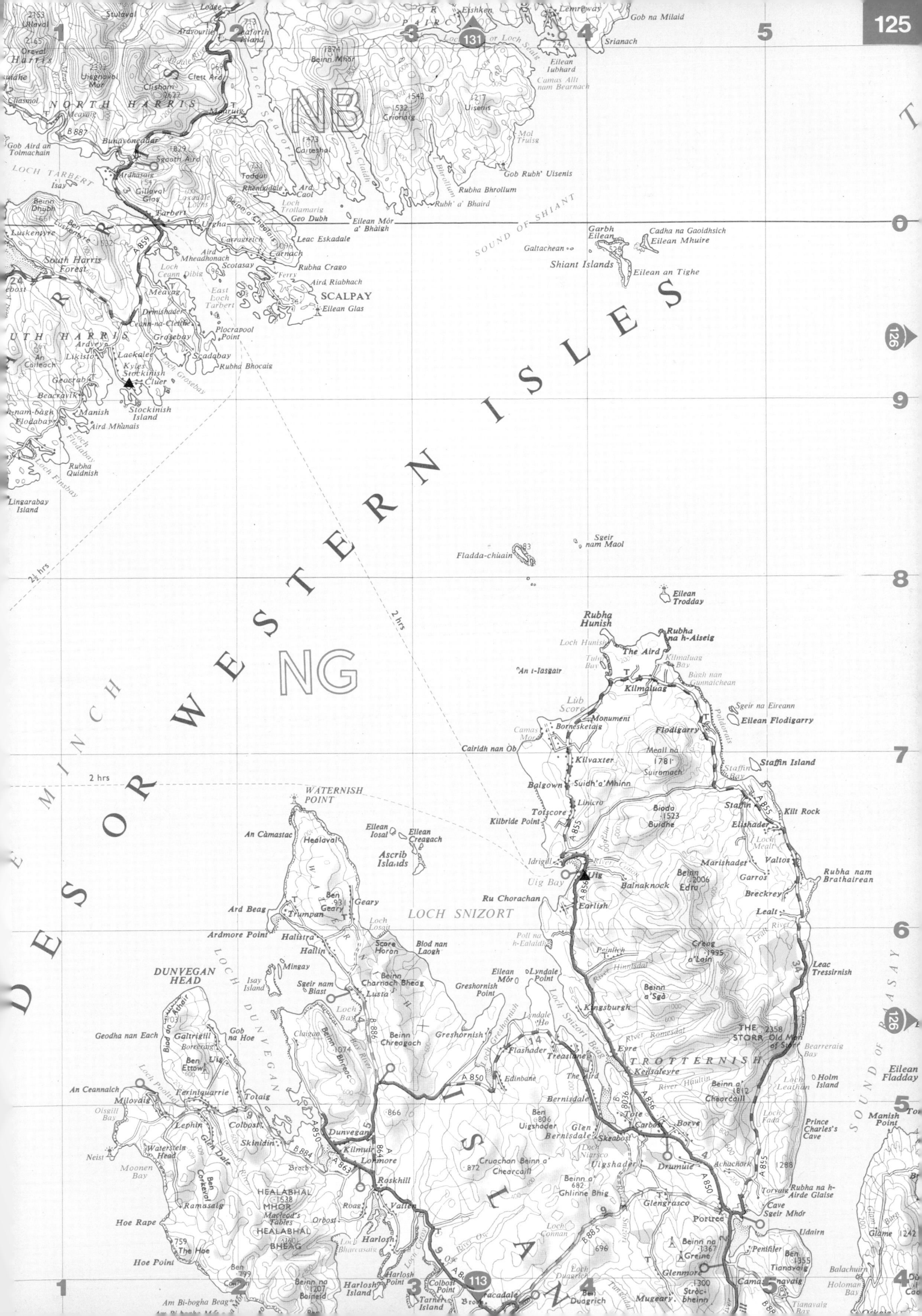

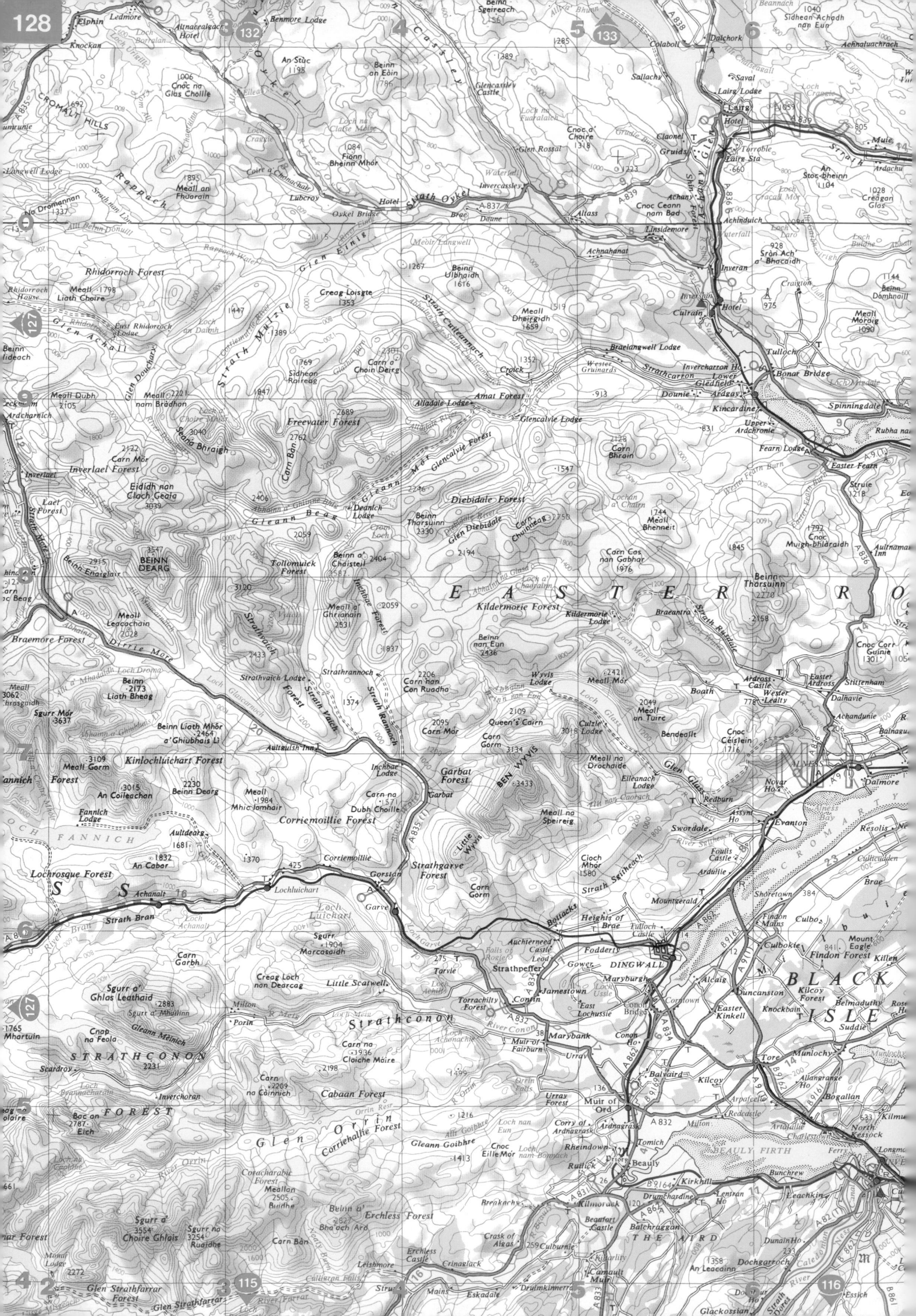

ND

NJ

NH

ATLANTIC OCEAN

6 7 8 9 0

6

5

Flannan Isles

RONA AND SULA SGEIR

HW

Lisgear Mhór
Rona
Lòba Sgeir
o *Gealldruig Mhór*

Sula
Sgeir

3

7 8

RONA lies about 44 miles or 70 km NNE of the BUTT OF LEWIS NB 5166

4

3

R

2

NA

1

Gasker
105

T E

U

0

NF

8 124

Gallan Head
Camas Geodhachan an Duiliss
Aird Uig
Geodha Nasavig
Fiavig Bàgh
670 Forsna
Sgeir Fiavig Tarras
Crowlista
Tim
Ard More Mangersta
Camas Uig
Ardroil
Mangersta
Aird Fenish
Cleite Leathann
Staca Leathann
Islivig
Mealisval
Taraia
Aird Brenish
Brenish
Camas a' Mhoil
625 Laival a Tuath
Caolas an Eilein
Mealasta
Griomaval
Mealasta Island

H E B R

R

E

Kearstay
Gob na h-Airde Móire
Braigh Mòr
Loch Resort
SCARP
Sron Romul
800
Tatan Mòr
Manish
Hushinish
1603 Husival Mòr
Tirga Mòr
Hushinish Point
Leosaval
1352
Forest
Gobig
Arda Mòra
Amhuinn
Horsanish
Rubha Leacach
Taransay Glorigs
Rubha nan Totar
Soay Mòr
Sythe Harbour
WEST
TARANSAY
677 Ben Raah
Aird Vanish
324 Paible
SOUND OF TARANSAY
Rubha Sgeirigin
Aird Nisabost
Rubha Romagi
Toe Head
Rubha Màs a' Chnuic
Clett Nisabost
Sgeir Liath
Borve
Coppay

STACK SKERRY
& SULE SKERRY

HX

o Sule Skerry

o Stack Skerry

+

Stack Skerry lies about 32 miles or 50 km N of WHITEN HEAD NC5068

NB

THE MINCH

EDDRACHILLIS BAY

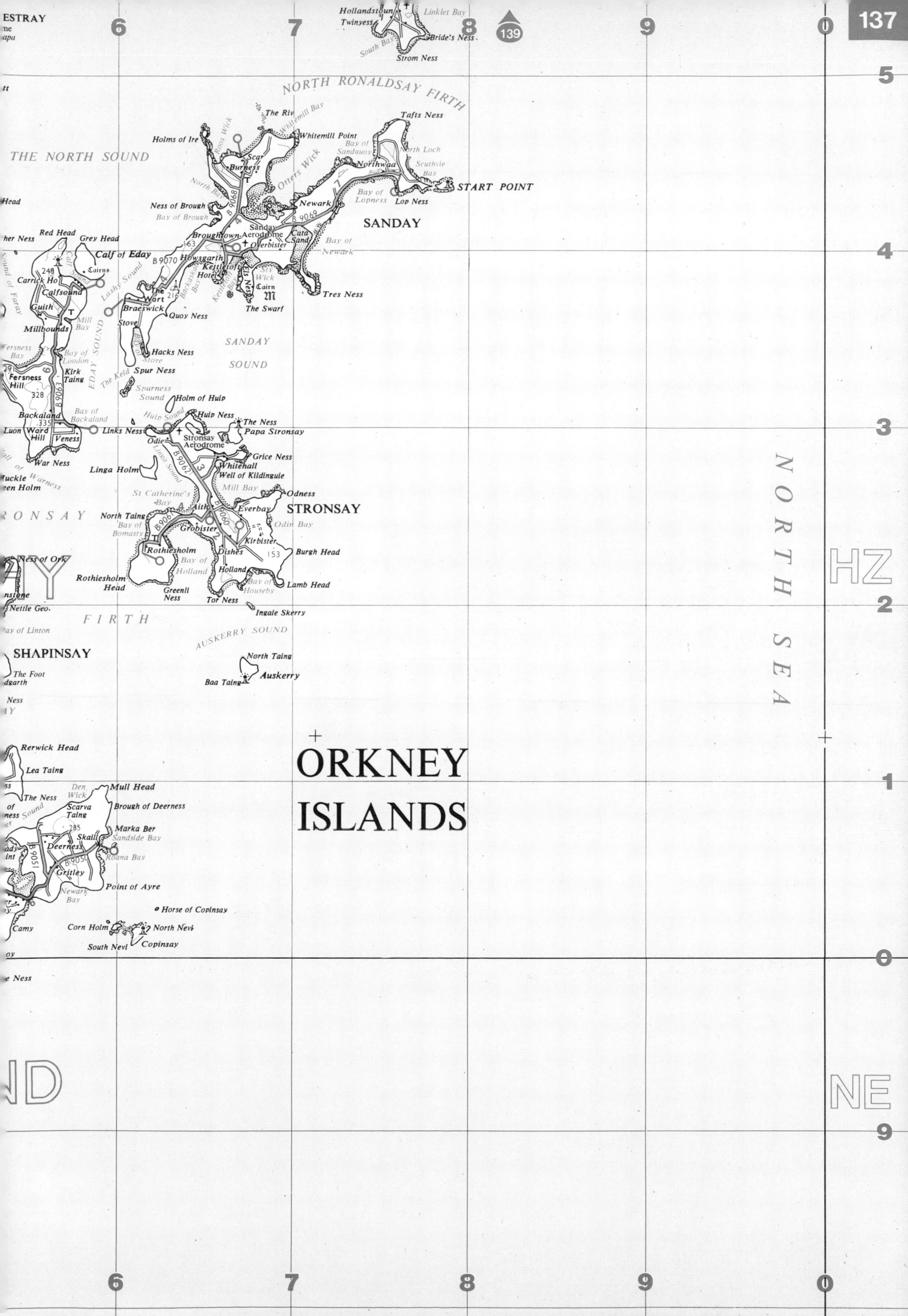

ESTRAY

THE NORTH SOUND

NORTH RONALDSAY FIRTH

Hollandstoun
Twinyess
Linklet Bay
Bride's Ness
South Bay
Strom Ness

139

The Riv
Holms of Ire
Whitemill Point
Whitemill Bay
Tafts Ness
Bay of
Sandauoy
North Loch
Scuthvie
Bay

Scar
Burness
T
Roos Wick
Otters Wick
Newark
Northwaa
Bay of
Lopness
Lop Ness
START POINT

Ness of Brough
North Ba
Bay of Brough
B 9068
Broughtown-Aerodrome
Overbister
SANDAY
Sanday
B 9069
Cata
Sand
Bay of
Newark

Red Head
Grey Head
Calf of Eday
Howsgarth
B 9070
Kettletoft
Hotel
63
Sty
Wick
Cairn
Bay of
Newark

Head
her Ness
Carrick Ho
248
Calfsound
Cairns
The
Wart
216
Backaskeo
Kettletoft Ness
The Swarf
Tres Ness

Guith
T
Braeswick
Store
Quoy Ness
Lashy Sound

Millbounds
Stove
Hacks Ness
SANDAY
SOUND

Fersness
Bay
Kirk
Taing
Bay of
London
Spur Ness

Fersness
Hill
328
Spurness
Sound
Holm of Huip

Backaland
335
Bay of
Backaland
Huip Sound
Huip Ness
The Ness

Luon
Ward
Hill
Veness
Links Ness
Odie
Stronsay
Aerodrome
Papa Stronsay

War Ness
Linga Holm
Grice Ness
Whitehall
Well of Kildinguie

RONSAY
Muckle
Warness
een Holm
St Catherine's
Bay
B 9063
Aith
Everbay
Mill Bay
Odness

AY
Ness of Ork
nstone
North Taing
B 9061
Grobister
B 9060
Kirbister
Odin Bay
STRONSAY

Nettle Geo.
Rothiesholm
Dishes
153
Burgh Head
Bay of
Holland
Holland

ay of Linton
FIRTH
Rothiesholm
Head
Greenli
Ness
Tor Ness
Lamb Head
Bay of
Houseby

Ingale Skerry

AUSKERRY SOUND

SHAPINSAY
The Foot
dgarth
North Taing
Baa Taing
Auskerry

Ness
4Y

NORTH SEA

HZ

Rerwick Head
Lea Taing

Den
Wick
Mull Head
Brough of Deerness

The Ness
of
ness Sound
Scarva
Taing
285
Marka Ber
Skaill
Sandside Bay

Deerness
B 9050
Roana Bay

ady
int
B 905
Gritley

Newark
Bay
Point of Ayre

Horse of Copinsay

ORKNEY
ISLANDS

Camy
Corn Holm
North Nevi
South Nevi
Copinsay

oy
e Ness

ND
NE

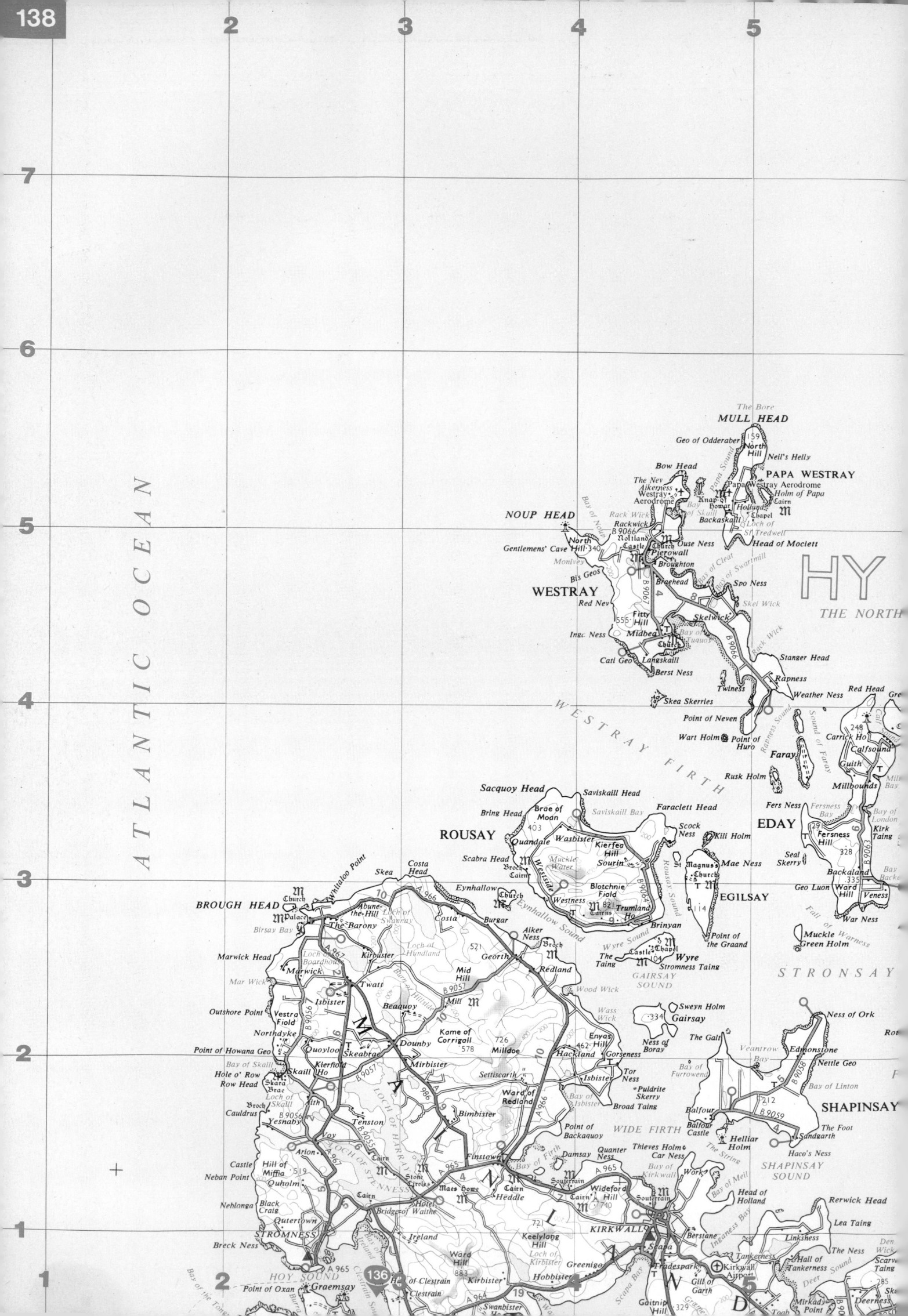

2   **3**   **4**   **5**

7

6

A T L A N T I C   O C E A N

The Bore

MULL HEAD

Geo of Odderaber · 159
North
Hill   Neil's Helly

Bow Head

PAPA WESTRAY

The Nev
Aikerness   Papa Westray Aerodrome
Westray   Knap of   Holm of Papa
Aerodrome   Howar   Holland
NOUP HEAD   Rack Wick   Backaskaill   Chapel   Loch of
Rackwick   Backaskaill   St Tredwell
North   B 9066   Noltland   Ouse Ness   Head of Moclett
Gentlemens' Cave   Hill · 340   Castle   Church
Monivey   Pierowall
  Broughton   Bay of Cleat   Bay of Swartmill
Bi's Geos   Braehead   Spo Ness
WESTRAY   B 9067   Skel Wick
Red Nev   Skelwick
  555   Fitty   8   Rack Wick
  Hill   Midbea   B 9066
Inga Ness   Church   Stanger Head
Cati Geo   Langskaill   Quoug
  Berst Ness   Rapness
  Twiness   Weather Ness   Red Head   Gre
Skea Skerries
  Point of Neven

5

HY
THE NORTH

W E S T R A Y   F I R T H

Wart Holm ● Point of
  Huro   · 248
  Faray   Carrick Ho
  Rusk Holm   Calfsound
  Guith
  Millbounds   Bay of
  London
Sacquoy Head   Saviskaill Head
Bring Head   Brae of   Faraclett Head   Fers Ness   Fersness
  Moan   Saviskaill Bay   Bay
  403   Scock   **EDAY**   Fersness
ROUSAY   Quandale   Wasbister   Ness   Kili Holm   Hill
  Kierfea   Seal   Backaland
Scabra Head   Hill   Mae Ness   Skerry   · 335
  Broch   Sourin   St Magnus   Geo Luon   Ward
Whitaloo Point   Cairn   Muckle   Church   Hill   Veness
Skea   Costa   Water   Blotchnie   · 114   War Ness
  Head   Eynhallow   Fiold   **EGILSAY**   Fall of Warness
BROUGH HEAD   Church   Westness   821   Muckle
  Church   Abune-   Loch of   Church   Trumland   Cairns   Green Holm
  Palace   the-Hill   Swannay   Ho   Brinyan   Point of
  The Barony   Costa   Burgar   the Graand
Birsay Bay   Aiker   Wyre   Sound   *S T R O N S A Y*
Marwick Head   Kirbister   Ness   Castle   Chapel
  521   Georth   Broch   The   **Wyre**
  Marwick   Redland   Taing   104
Mar Wick   Mid   Stromness Taing
  Hill   Wood Wick   *GAIRSAY*
  Twatt   B 9057   Mill   *SOUND*
  Isbister   Wass   Sweyn Holm   Ness of Ork
Outshore Point   Beaquoy   Wick   · 334   **Gairsay**
  Vestra   The Galt   Edmonstone
  Field   Kame of   Enyas   Veantrow   Nettle Geo
Northdyke   Quoyloo   Corrigall   462 Hill   Ness of   Bay   Bay of Linton
Point of Howana Geo   Skeabrae   Dounby   578   Milldoe   Gorseness   Boray
Bay of Skaill   Kierfiold   Mirbister   Hackland   Bay of   B 9058
Hole o' Row   Skaill Ho   Settiscarth   Isbister   Tor   Furrowend   Bay of
Row Head   Skara   Ward of   Isbister   Ness   **SHAPINSAY**
  Brae   Redland   Puldrite   Balfour   212
  Broch   Bimbister   Skerry   Balfour   B 9059
Cauldrus   B 9056   Broad Taing   Castle   The Foot
  Yesnaby   Tenston   Point of   *WIDE FIRTH*   Helliar   Sandgarth
  Backaquoy   Holm   Haco's Ness
  Finstown   Quanter   Thieves Holm
Castle   Arion   Hill of   519   Bay of Firth   Ness   Car Ness   *SHAPINSAY*
  Miffia   Stone   Damsay   Bay of   *SOUND*
Neban Point   Quholm   Circles   Cairn   A 965   Kirkwall   Work   Head of
Nehlonga   Black   Maes Howe   Wideford   Holland   Rerwick Head
  Craig   Cairn   Heddle   Hill · 740   Souterrain   Lea Taing
  Outertown   Hotel   721   **KIRKWALL**   Linksness
STROMNESS   Bridge of Waithe   Scapa   The Ness   Den
Breck Ness   Ireland   Keelylong   Berstane   Wick
  Hill   Greenigoe   Scarva
  Loch of   Tankerness   Taing
HOY SOUND   **136**   Ward   Kirbister   Hobbister   Tradespark   Kirkwall Airport   Hall of
Point of Oxan ●   Hill · 883   Gill of   Tankerness
  Graemsay   of Clestrain   Garth   Mirkady
  Clestrain   A 964   19   Swanbister   Goltnip   Point
  Hill · 329   Toab   Deerness

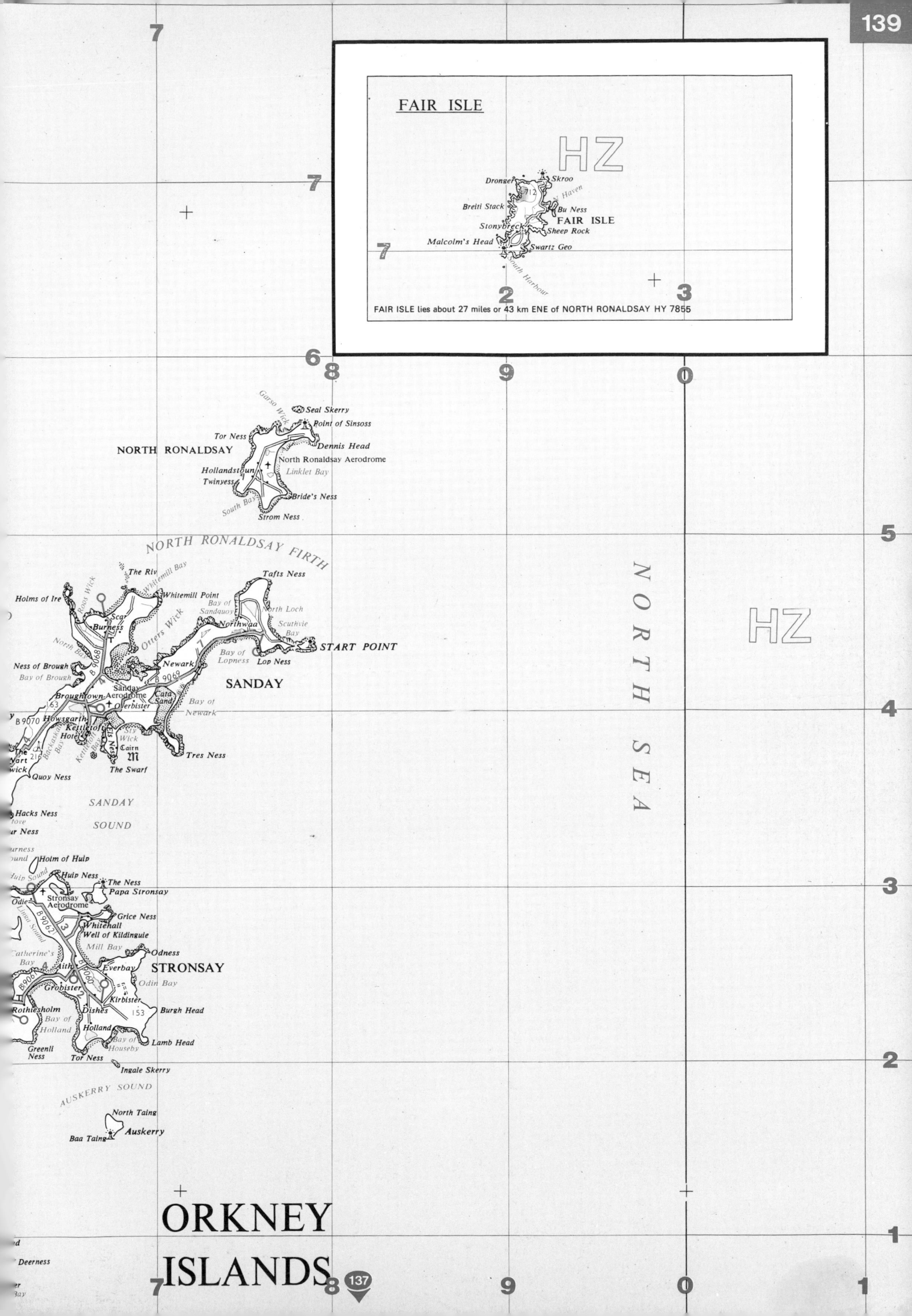

FAIR ISLE

HZ

Dronger • Skroo
North Haven
Breiti Stack
Bu Ness
Stonybreck • FAIR ISLE
Sheep Rock
Malcolm's Head
Swartz Geo
South Harbour

FAIR ISLE lies about 27 miles or 43 km ENE of NORTH RONALDSAY HY 7855

Seal Skerry
Point of Sinsoss
Tor Ness
Dennis Head
NORTH RONALDSAY
North Ronaldsay Aerodrome
Hollandstoun
Linklet Bay
Twinyess
Bride's Ness
South Bay
Strom Ness

NORTH RONALDSAY FIRTH

NORTH SEA

HZ

The Riv
Whitemill Bay
Tafts Ness
Holms of Ire
Whitemill Point
Bay of
Sandauoy
North Loch
Scar
Northwaa
Scuthvie
Burness
Bay
Ness of Brough
Northwaa
START POINT
Newark
Bay of
Lopness • Lop Ness
Bay of Brough
SANDAY
B 9069
Broughtown Aerodrome
Overbister
Bay of
Newark
Howsgarth
Kettletoft Hotel
Wick
Cairn
Tres Ness
The Swarf
Quoy Ness

SANDAY
SOUND

Hacks Ness
Holm of Huip
Huip Ness
The Ness
Papa Stronsay
Stronsay Aerodrome
Grice Ness
Whitehall
Well of Kildinguie
Mill Bay
Odness
Catherine's Bay
Everbay
STRONSAY
Odin Bay
Grobister
Kirbister
Rothiesholm
Dishes
Burgh Head
Bay of Holland
Holland
Bay of Houseby
Lamb Head
Greenli Ness
Tor Ness
Ingale Skerry

AUSKERRY SOUND

North Taing
Baa Taing • Auskerry

ORKNEY
ISLANDS

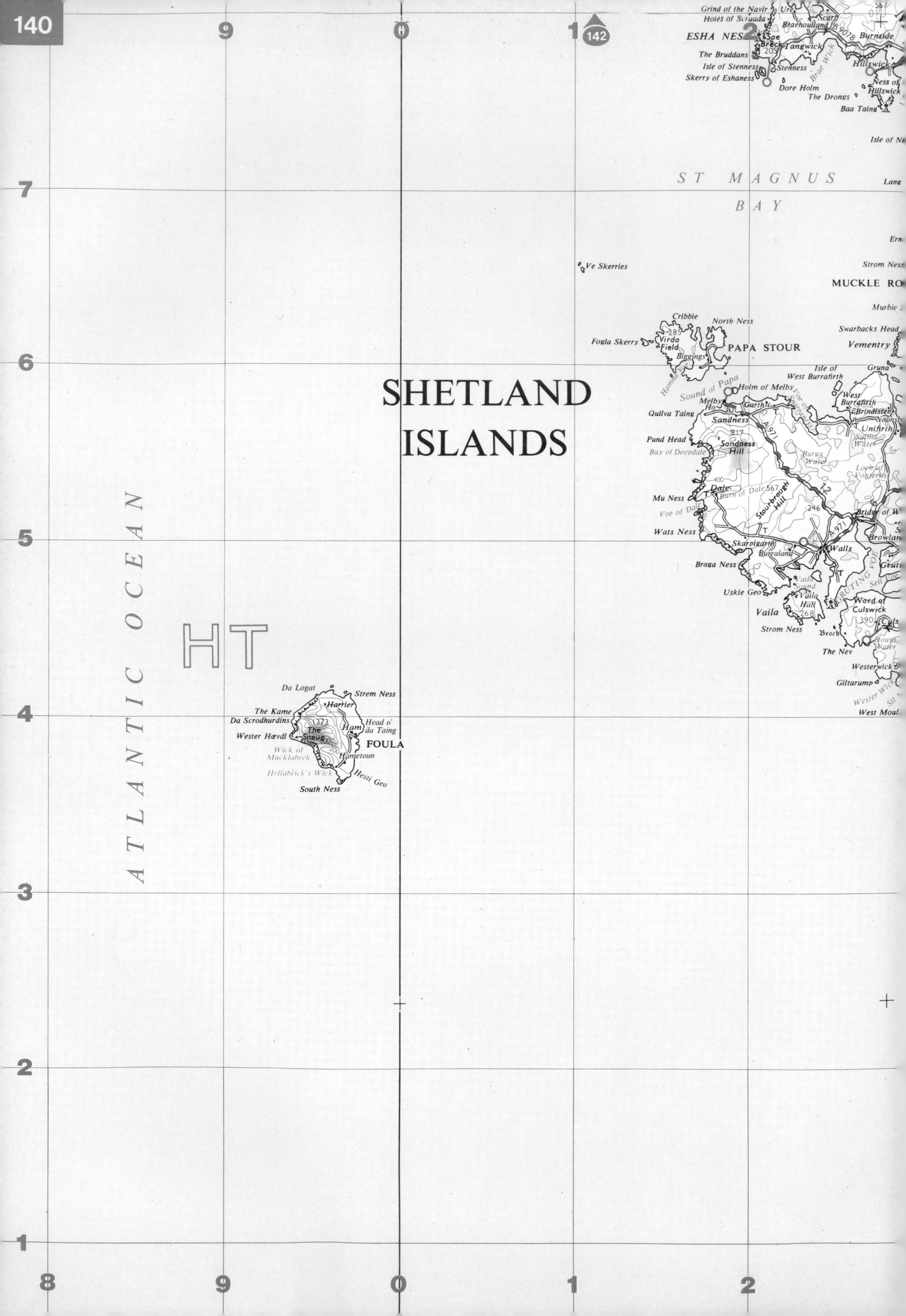

142

Grind of the Navir Ure · Scarff
Holes of Scruada Braehoullland 207 8 Burnside
ESHA NESS Sae Breck · Tangwick
The Bruddans Brae Wick
205 Hillswick
Isle of Stenness Stenness Ness of
Skerry of Eshaness Hillswick
Dore Holm
The Drongs
Baa Taing

Isle of N

ST MAGNUS Lang

BAY

Ern

Strom Ness

Ve Skerries **MUCKLE RO**

Murbie

Cribbie North Ness Swarbacks Head
283 Vementry
Fogla Skerry Virda **PAPA STOUR** Isle of Gruna
Field West Burrafirth West
Biggings Burrafirth
Homla Holm of Melby Brindister
Sound of Papa Melby Garth Naonst
Ho Unifirth
SHETLAND Quilva Taing Sandness Suma
817 Water
Pund Head Sandness Burga Loch of
Hill Water Voxters
ISLANDS Bay of Deepdale 12
400 Dale Burn of Dale 567
Mu Ness Stourbrough 246
A T Voe of Dale Hill Bridge of W
L A N Wats Ness 971
T I Skarpigarth Walls S
A T L A N T I C O C E A N C Burraland Browlan
Braga Ness T Grut
O Watis Sell Voe
C Uskie Geo Sound Vaila WAARD VOE
E Hall Ward of
A Vaila 268 Culswick Cults
N Strom Ness 390
Broch Hous
Water
The Nev Westerwick
Giltarump
Westeri Wick
West Moul

Da Logat Strem Ness
The Kame Harrier
Da Scrodhurdins 373 Head o'
Ham da Taing
Wester Hævdi The **FOULA**
Sneug
Wick of 200 Hametoun
Mucklabrek
Hellabrick's Wick Hesti Geo
South Ness

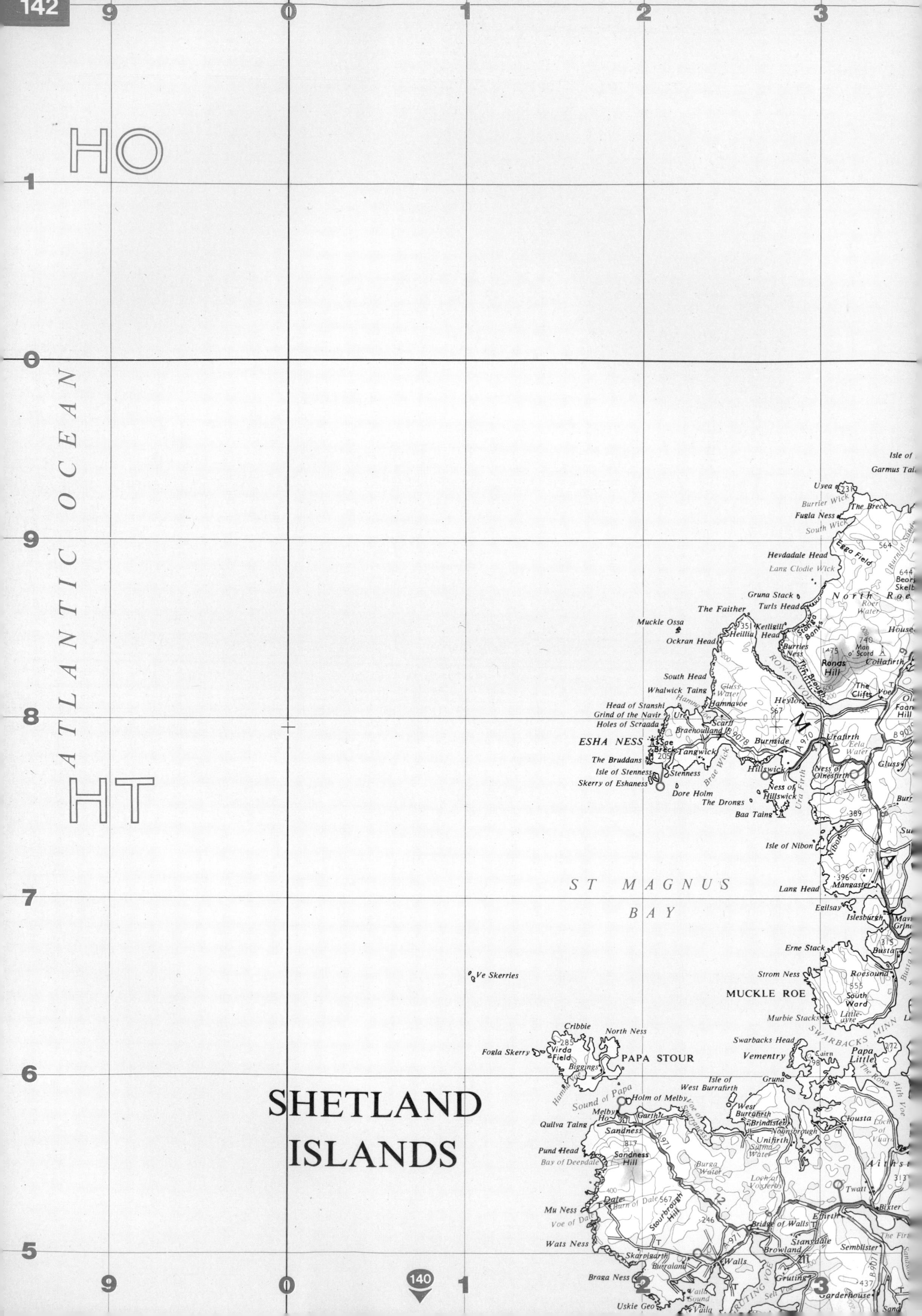

HO

ATLANTIC OCEAN

SHETLAND ISLANDS

St MAGNUS BAY

HT

Isle of Garmus Tai

Uyea **231**
Burrier Wick
The Breck
Fugla Ness
South Wick
Esga Field **564**

Hevdadale Head
Lang Clodie Wick

North Roe
644 Beori Skelb
Gruna Stack
Turls Head
Roer Water
The Faither
Muckle Ossa
351 Kettlgill
Heilliu Head **740 Mai o' Scord**
Ockran Head
Burriies Ness
75
Ronas Hill
Collafirth

South Head
Gluss Water
Whalwick Taing
Heylor
The Clifts
Head of Stanshi
Hamnavoe
567
Faan
Grind of the Navir
Ure
Scarf
Holes of Scraada
Braehoulland
Burnside
Urafirth
Eela Water
ESHA NESS
Breck **203**
Tangwick
Gluss
The Bruddans
Isle of Stenness
Stenness
Ness of Olnesfirth
Skerry of Eshaness
Dore Holm
Hillswick
Ness of Hillswick
389
Baa Taing
The Drongs

Isle of Nibon
Cairn
396 Mangaster

Lang Head
Egilsay
Islesburgh
Mavis
315
Erne Stack
Busta
Strom Ness
Roesound
555
Ve Skerries
MUCKLE ROE
South Ward
Murbie Stacks
Little
ayre
SWARBACKS MINN
Cribbie
North Ness
Swarbacks Head
Papa
Little
Fogla Skerry
Virda Field
Biggings
PAPA STOUR
Vementry
98
Isle of
West Burrafirth
Gruna
Sound of Papa
Holm of Melby
West
Burrafirth
Clousta
Melby
Garth
Brindister
Quilva Taing
Sandness
Unifirth
Sumna
Water
Pund Head
Sandness Hill
817
Burga
Water
Loch of
Voxterby
Twatt
Bay of Deepdale
Dale
Burn of Dale **567**
Stourbrough Hill
Efirth
Bixter
Mu Ness
246
Bridge of Walls
Voe of Dale
Stanydale
Semblister
Wats Ness
Skarpigarth
Walls
Browland
Braga Ness
Burraland
Gruting
437
Uskie Geo
Gardethouse

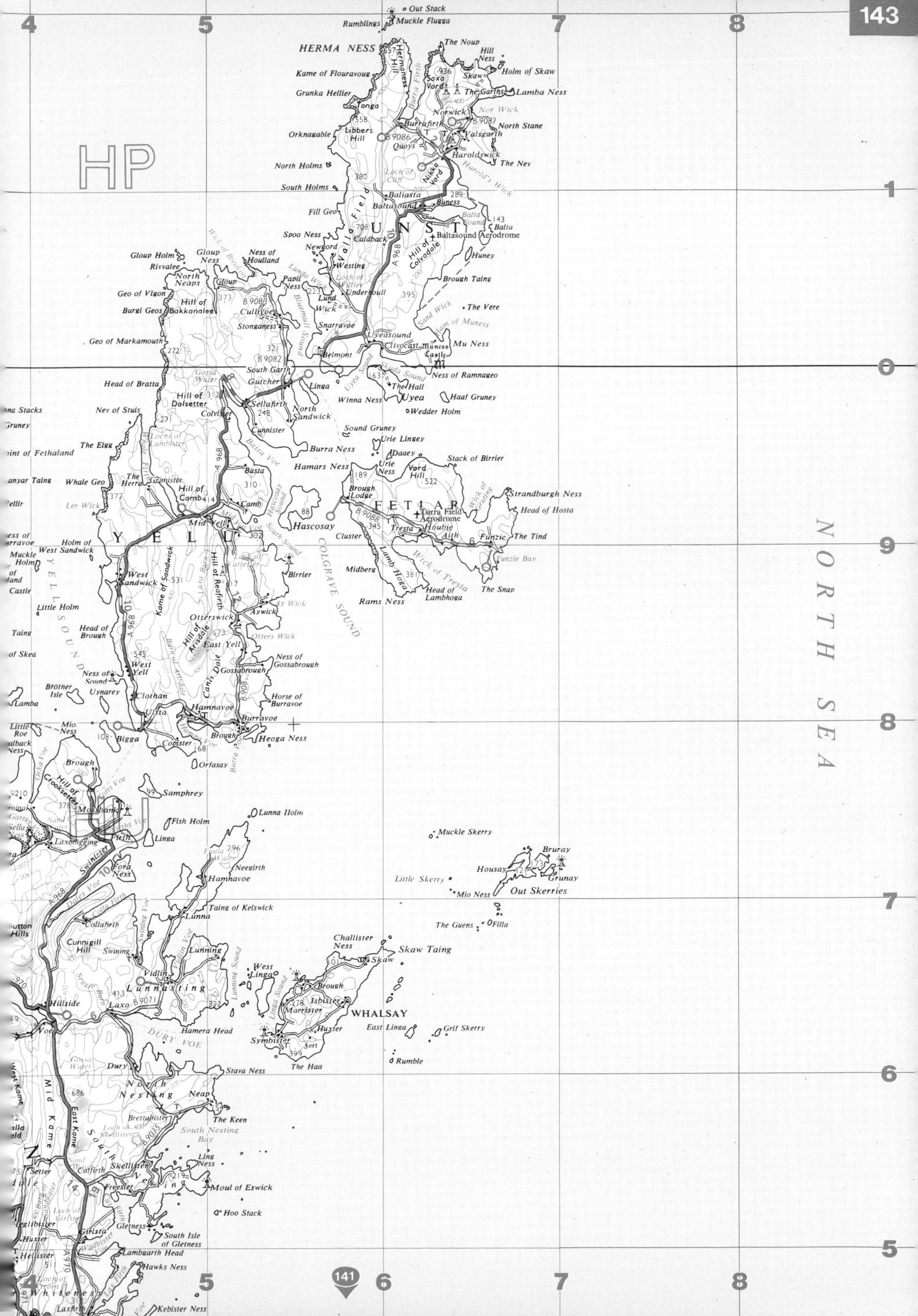

HP

HU

NORTH SEA

HERMA NESS

Out Stack
Rumblings • Muckle Flugga
The Noup
Hill Ness
Hermaness Hill 657
Kame of Flouravoug
936 Skaw • Holm of Skaw
Saxa Vord
Grunka Hellier
The Garths • Lamba Ness
Tonga
Norwick • Nor Wick
558
Burrafirth B 9087 • North Stane
Orknagable
Libbers Hill
B 9086 Valsgarth
Quoys
North Holms
Haroldswick • The Nev
Nikka Vord
Loch of Cliff
South Holms
Baliasta
Fill Geo
Baltasound 289
Buness
U N S T
708 143 Balta
Caldback Baltasound Aerodrome
Spoo Ness
Newgord • Huney
Westing A 968 Hill of Colvadale
Ness of
Houlland Brough Taing
Gloup Holm Gloup
Rivvalee Ness
North Neaps Gloup Papil Ness 395
Geo of Vigon Hill of Burgi Geos Bakkanalee
Cullivoe
Lund Wick Uyeasound
Stonganess
Clivocast Muness Castle
Mu Ness
Geo of Markamouth 272
B 9082 321
Belmont
Head of Bratta Gossa Water South Garth
Gutcher
Linga
Ness of Stuis Hill of Dolsetter 312 Sellafirth
Colvister 248 North Sandwick
Cunnister Winna Ness The Hall
Uyea
Haaf Gruney
Wedder Holm
Lochs of Lumbister 271
Sound Gruney
Urie Lingey
The Eigg Burra Ness
Daaey
Whale Geo Grimister Hamars Ness Urie Ness Stack of Birrier
The Herra 377 Basta 189 Vord Hill 522
Hill of Camb 414 310 Brough Lodge
Camb
FETLAR
88 Turra Field Aerodrome
Hascosay B 9088 345 Tresta Strandburgh Ness
Mid Yell 302 Houbie Head of Hosta
Birrier Cluster Aith Funzie The Tind
West Sandwick Midberg
Holm of Sandwick Funzie Bay
Kame of Sandwick 531 Hill of Redfirth Lamb Hoga The Snap
West Sandwick
Y E L L Rams Ness Head of Lambhoga
Little Holm
Head of Aywick
Brough Hill of Arisdale 673 Ness of Gossabrough
West Yell East Yell
Taing of Skea 545 Otters Wick
Carls Dale Horse of Burravoe
Brother Isle Uynarey Gossabrough
Clothan
Ulsta Hamnavoe
Burravoe
Little Roe Mio Ness Bigga Copister Heoga Ness
Orfasay

COLGRAVE SOUND
YELL SOUND

Brough
Hill of Crooksetter
99 Samphrey
378 Mossbank
Muckle Skerry
Bruray
Lunna Holm Housay
Laxo Wigging Linga Fish Holm Little Skerry Grunay
Fora Ness Mio Ness **Out Skerries**
Neesgirth
Hamnavoe The Guens Filla
Collafirth
Taing of Kelswick
Lunna
Cunnigill Hill Challister Ness
Swining Lunning Skaw Taing
Vidlin West Skaw
Lunnasting West Linga
Brough
Hillside Laxo Isbister
Marrister
Voe Hamera Head Symbister **WHALSAY**
Huxter East Linga Grif Skerry
Dury Sort
Stava Ness The Haa Rumble
North Nesting 686
Neap
Brettabister The Keen
The Keen
South Nesting Bay
Ling Ness
Hoo Stack

The Historical Geography of Britain

Prehistory

The physical environment in which the early cultures of Britain developed at the end of the Ice Age was very different from our contemporary environment, though the principal structure of this island, the disposition of mountain and lowland, remain much the same. The main changes have occurred in the nature and distribution of vegetation types and the extent of woodland and forest cover, in the reduction of undrained land, and in climate.

The early prehistoric cultures of Britain in the Palaeolithic and Mesolithic periods made very little impact on the landscape, although their cave sites and excavated open sites provide an accurate picture of their essential economic character and artefacts. The basis of the economy was the hunting of wild animals and the collecting of wild plants, but this was eventually replaced during the Neolithic (or New Stone) Age by a food-producing economy. The dating of the beginnings of this new culture is only approximate, but it appears that settlement by farmers in Britain occurred before 4400 BC. The Neolithic period terminated about 2000 years later. The initial phase of cultural development, the 'early' Neolithic, took place in the earlier part of the fourth millennium BC, and is associated with stock-breeding, cereal cultivation, flint- and stone-working industries, and distinctive pottery types. The early Neolithic site at Windmill Hill in Wiltshire has revealed a predominance of bones of 'domesticated' animals rather than wild animals, and of the emmer type of wheat – a cultivated crop. The evidence for early Neolithic settlement is not extensive, but it has been inferred that isolated farmsteads predominated.

Flint was extensively used for axes and other implements, including leaf-shaped arrowheads, and there were important flint mines in Sussex, at Findon, for example. Flint-mining also occurred in Cornwall and in Westmorland, and at a later date the famous mine at Grimes Graves in Norfolk came into operation. Distinctive pottery types included the Grimston type, mainly found in Yorkshire and the North, and the more southern Hembury type. In the later Neolithic, material evidence changes: new forms of pottery appear, with decorations and round bases, such as Peterborough ware and grooved ware, and the use of the older, harder rocks for axes intensifies. The economy seems to have to become more pastoral.

A distinctive and notable feature of the Neolithic is the wide range of burial monuments. The main categories of burial monument are the ubiquitous chambered and unchambered tombs, sometimes covered with earth (such as earthen long barrows), sometimes with stones (cairns). The best-known sites are the 'henge' monuments with large standing stones, the most spectacular of which are sites such as Stonehenge and Avebury in Wiltshire. The dominant relic feature of the Neolithic in Scotland is the chambered tomb and long mound, found extensively in the Clyde region and in the extreme north, and the Orkney and Shetland Islands.

The succeeding culture–the Bronze Age–lasted from 2500 to 900 BC, and whereas there is evidence that the Neolithic culture was strong, spontaneous and regional, the initiation of the Bronze Age apparently occurred through colonisation. The evidence for this occurs in the form of the material culture of a group of people known as the Beaker folk (named for the type of pottery with which they are associated), who began the change from Neolithic to Bronze culture. There was no overall and sharp break between these two phases of British prehistory, for change was rapid in the Lowland Zone of the south and east and slower in the Highland Zone of the north and west. The Bronze Age also brought a change to a warmer and drier climate although a marked deterioration began again about 1100 BC.

The most important innovation of the Bronze Age was the introduction of metal tools–initially in the form of thin copper blades of knives and daggers. The early Bronze Age witnessed a series of stages of copper-working, with main production centres in northwest England, Renfrewshire in Scotland, Wessex, Wales and the Welsh border. Flint exploitation continued in the early Bronze Age, but then declined. Settlements seem to have been small clusters of dwellings; barley became a more important crop than wheat. With the climatic deterioration of the end of the early Bronze Age there was more intensive use of river valleys and watery lowlands–an indication, too, of a changing religious focus. The upper (altitudinal) margins of cultivation declined and new regions of power developed, including north Wales and the Thames valley. The settlements of the middle and later Bronze Age included enclosed farmsteads with associated enclosed fields, and so-called 'Celtic' field systems, and large numbers of stone settlements on the uplands of the southwest. Some hilltop forts and enclosures date from this period, but the most characteristic feature is the round burial barrow or cairn, of which very large numbers survive. Other important features of the Bronze Age are the extensive trade in copper products, the decorative personal bronze ornaments, the continued construction and reconstruction of henge monuments (including work at Stonehenge), and the remarkable settlements at Skara Brae in the Orkneys.

The Iron Age culture was first seen about 900 BC, lasting to the Roman invasion of AD 43, and left its mark extensively in the landscape. Initiated by small groups of continental settlers, the first phase of the Iron Age in Britain continued the traditions of the Bronze Age, using small settlements and the first enclosures of old tribal centres with ramparts. Major innovations began in the 8th century BC, including hillforts, new metallurgy and pottery. The period immediately before the Roman invasion saw strong continental influence from Belgic invaders in the south and east (the north and west undergoing very little change), the emergence of strong regional tribal cultures (such as the Thames region, Arras culture in Yorkshire, Cornwall) and widespread trade with the Roman Empire. The Iron Age invaders were Celtic-speaking; they introduced new crops

Prehistory to the Romans The distribution and types of chambered cairns, chambered tombs and long barrows reflect the diversity of Neolithic Britain, very different from the settlement patterns of Roman Britain.

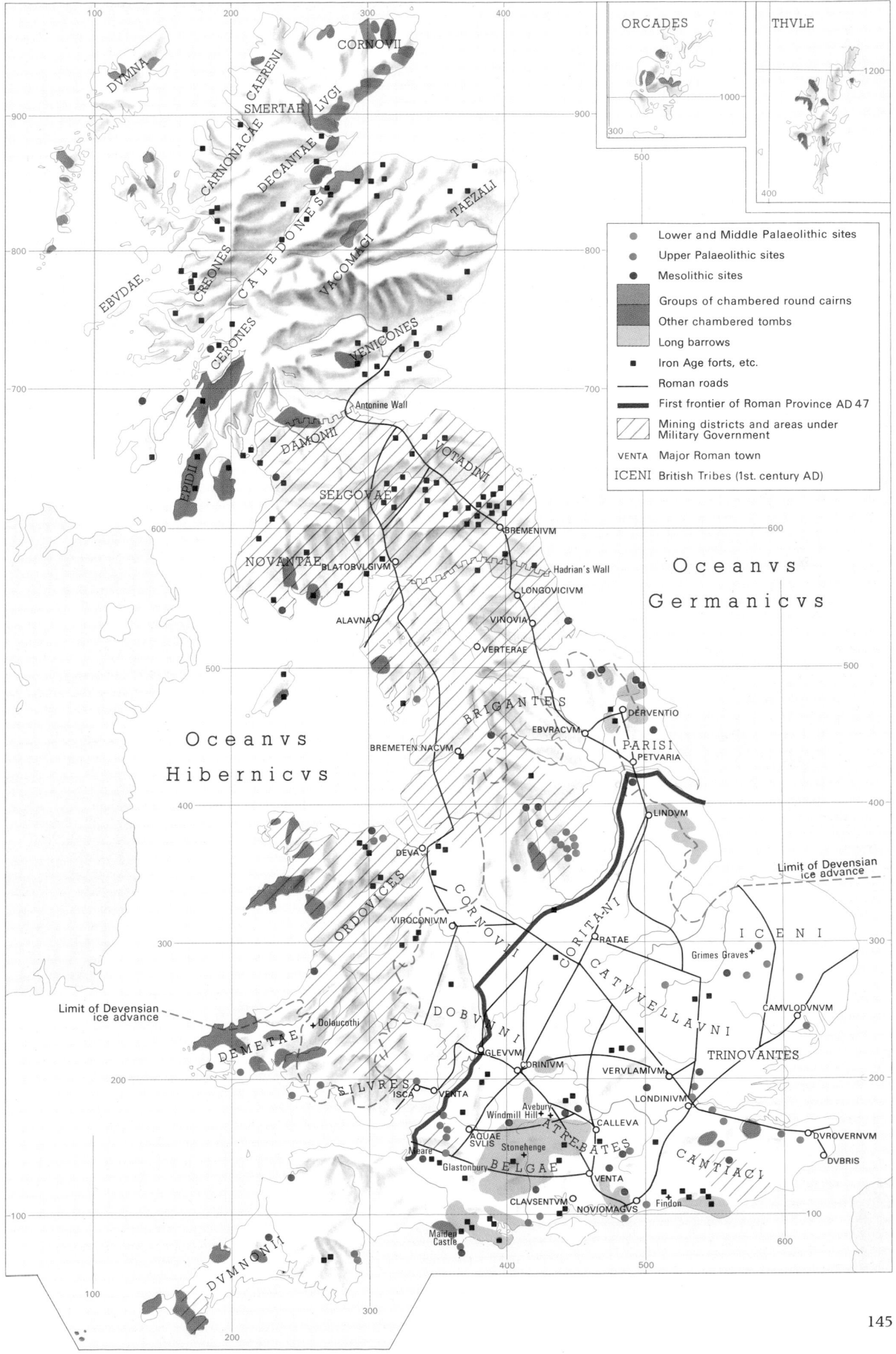

ORCADES

THVLE

Lower and Middle Palaeolithic sites
Upper Palaeolithic sites
Mesolithic sites
Groups of chambered round cairns
Other chambered tombs
Long barrows
Iron Age forts, etc.
Roman roads
First frontier of Roman Province AD 47
Mining districts and areas under Military Government
VENTA Major Roman town
ICENI British Tribes (1st. century AD)

DVMNA

CORNOVII

CAERENI

CARNONACAE

SMERTAE LVGI

DECANTAE

TAEZALI

CREONES

EBVDAE

VACOMAGI

CALEDONES

CERONES

VENICONES

EPIDII

Antonine Wall

DAMONII

VOTADINI

SELGOVAE

Oceanvs
Germanicvs

NOVANTAE
BLATOBVLGIVM

BREMENIVM

Hadrian's Wall

LONGOVICIVM

ALAVNA

VINOVIA

VERTERAE

BRIGANTES

DERVENTIO

Oceanvs
Hibernicvs

BREMETEN NACVM

EBVRACVM

PARISI
PETVARIA

LINDVM

DEVA

Limit of Devensian
ice advance

ORDOVICES

CORNOVII

VIROCONIVM

CORITANI

RATAE

ICENI

Grimes Graves

CAMVLODVNVM

Limit of Devensian
ice advance

Dolaucothi

DEMETAE

DOBVNNI

CATVVELLAVNI

TRINOVANTES

GLEVVM

CORINIVM

VERVLAMIVM

LONDINIVM

SILVRES

VENTA

ISCA

Avebury

Windmill Hill

CALLEVA

ATREBATES

DVROVERNVM

AQVAE
SVLIS

Stonehenge

VENTA

CANTIACI

DVBRIS

Meare

Glastonbury

BELGAE

CLAVSENTVM

NOVIOMAGVS

Findon

Maiden
Castle

DVMNONII

145

such as rye and oats, and used horse-drawn chariots. The major evidence of the Iron Age in the landscape are the hillfort settlements of England (such as Maiden Castle in Dorset), Wales and Scotland. In addition to the walled hillforts are the lake-villages of the southwest, notably Glastonbury and Meare in Somerset. In the late Iron Age tribal capitals or *oppida* developed, such as St Albans and Colchester, and the heavier soils of the Lowland areas were cultivated by use of the new heavy ploughs. Coinage was introduced, as were new processes for corn-grinding and pottery production.

The Claudian invasion of Britain in AD 43 did not end the Iron Age, nor did it completely 'Romanise' Britain. The Roman cultural influence is mainly to be found in the south and east, partly because of the existence there of indigenous political groups, and was least in the north and west which were primarily zones of military occupation. The whole of Britain was, however, only a frontier province of the Roman Empire and one occupied at a very late stage of that Empire's development; it did not reach the same cultural levels as the more central regions of the continental Empire. Christianity reached Britain in the 4th century, and perhaps helped to accelerate the change away from Celtic Iron Age culture, for Christianity had Roman characteristics. There was therefore both continuity and change between Iron Age and Early Christian-Roman culture. The cultural continuity is best seen at the peasant level in the Highland Zone of the north and west. The cultural provinces of Scotland (Atlantic, Western Isles, Southwest and South) remained much the same, to judge by the distinctive types of settlement, pottery and burial monument. Change was more obvious in the south and east of Britain, but it was rarely total and all-embracing, for 'native' settlements continued to exist, even in the Lowland Zone.

The political map of Roman Britain shortly after the conquest (c. AD 47), indicates a frontier zone which includes most of north England, Wales and Scotland. The construction of Hadrian's Wall in c. AD 123-128 and the Antonine Wall in AD 142 are further testimony to the status of these regions, which remained under military rule.

The major landscape features associated with Roman Britain are towns, roads, mining, and various types of agricultural and rural settlement, notably villas, though there was also continuity of settlement in addition to the more obvious Roman innovations.

Under the Roman system of civic administration, each unit or *civitas* had a capital—in the southeast this was usually a pre-Roman site or *oppidum*, elsewhere a *colonia* or colony town, initially populated by Roman citizens and soldiers. At a lower level in the 'urban' hierarchy were small settlements called *vici*, some of which were walled and built on the site of earlier fortified settlements. The total population of Roman Britain was probably under one million, and there were about 60 towns, which varied considerably in size, though none compared with the larger towns and cities of 20th-century Britain. The dimensions of Roman London, for example, were about 1600 metres by 800 metres (1 mile by $\frac{1}{2}$ mile); this was also about the size of the larger towns such as Verulamium (St Albans), Corinium (Cirencester) and Viriconium (Wroxeter). The other Roman towns were very

much smaller. The larger towns had a planned layout, with the forum at the centre, surrounded by a grid-iron street plan. The public buildings included baths, temples and basilicas, hotels (*mansio*), theatres and amphitheatres. Town defences were constructed in some of the towns at the end of the 2nd century AD.

One of the attractions of Britain to the Romans was its mineral resources—silver, gold and other metals were described as the 'price of victory'. Expectations of gold were high, but the only known Roman mine was at Dolaucothi in Carmarthenshire, where advanced mining techniques were used and an eleven-kilometre (seven-mile) aqueduct channel constructed to convey water to the site. Copper resources were exploited in North Wales and Anglesey, but the most extensively-worked mineral was lead, principally in the Mendips, and also in the Matlock area of Derbyshire, Shropshire, Cheshire, Flintshire, Yorkshire and Cumberland. Lead was a major export. Iron was worked in Sussex and the Forest of Dean.

The network of Roman roads in Britain is impressive and extensive, both in terms of its density and the technological achievement that it represents. Some of the major Roman roads remain as trunk roads to the present day, though others have lost their former status. The Fosse Way and Watling Street are two well-known surviving examples of this network. The best-known farm buildings of Roman Britain are the villas (although this term really refers to a whole rural estate). Villas have been described as 'farms with Romanised buildings'; they were most common in Lowland Britain and parts of South Wales. They were less numerous, however, than non-Roman native settlements in the countryside of Roman Britain. Some were built on the sites of Iron Age farms. The villas themselves changed during the period of the Roman occupation. Most Romanised villas had principal farmsteads constructed to a regular (usually rectangular) plan, but this dates from a rebuilding period of the 2nd century. The largest and most luxurious of the villas are quite late in date, and in a minority.

There were some improvements in agricultural techniques in the Roman period, including corn-drying and threshing and perhaps ploughing, though we know little of the size and shape of fields or of the systems of cultivation.

Britain in the Dark Ages

There was no sharp discontinuity between the Roman and Saxon phases of colonisation of Britain: we know, for example, that Anglo-Saxons were used as mercenaries by the Romans in Britain to assist with town defences at the time of the withdrawal of the Roman administration around AD 400. The period of most intense settlement by the Anglo-Saxons was c.400-800. These people were of Germanic origin and their culture was very different from the Roman; they took control of parts of eastern England in the period 400-450, when it seems that Kent and Sussex may have been settled by these rebellious mercenaries. Other pockets of

The Dark Ages The earliest Saxon settlement is denoted by areas in which pagan burials have been found, followed by places with names ending in *-ingas*. The burhs are of later date. Place-names in *-by* indicate Scandinavian settlements, and 'maerdref' sites named *llys-* are sites of royal courts in Wales.

The Dark Ages

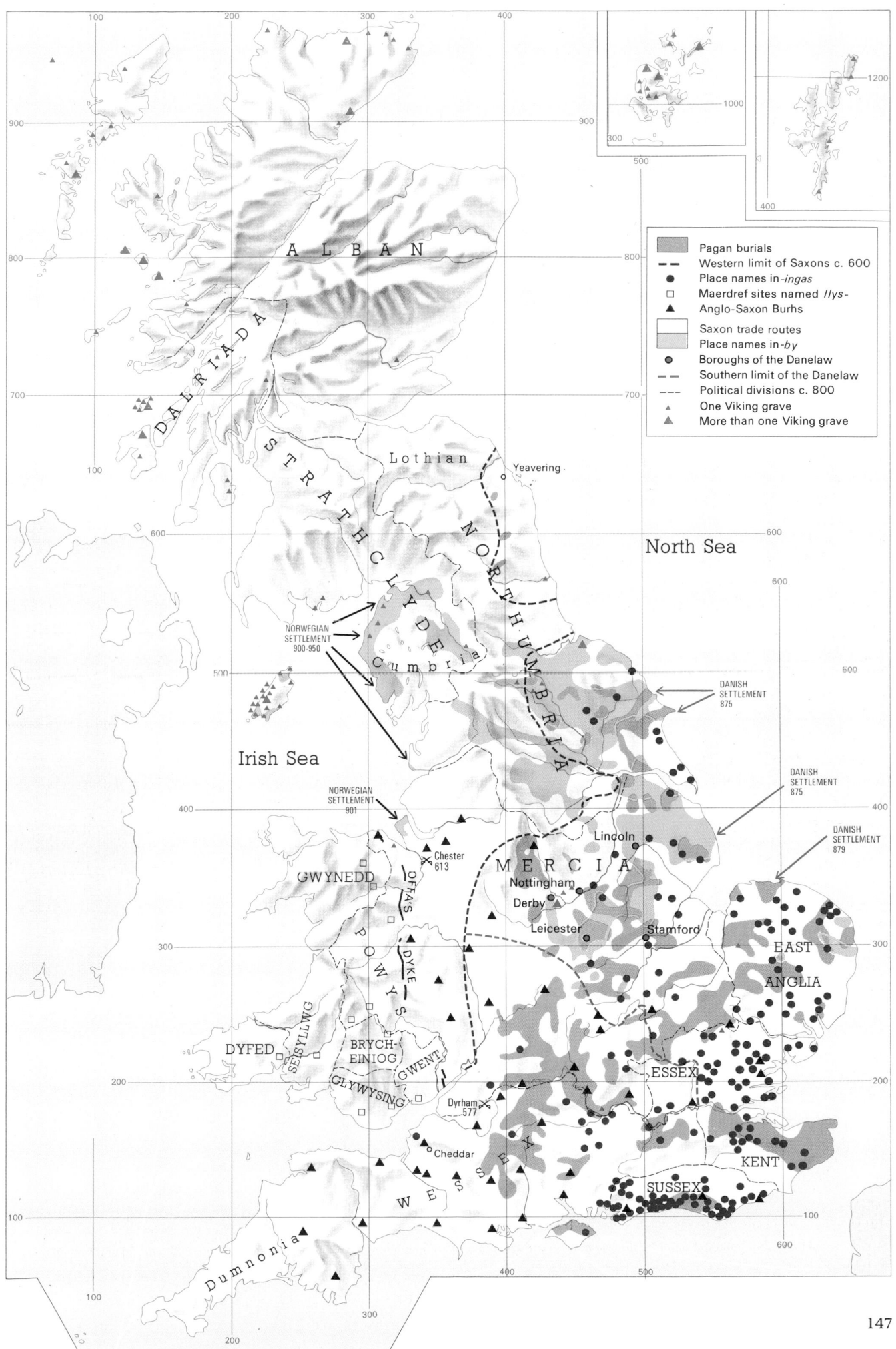

Legend:
- Pagan burials
- Western limit of Saxons c. 600
- Place names in -*ingas*
- Maerdref sites named *llys*-
- Anglo-Saxon Burhs
- Saxon trade routes
- Place names in -*by*
- Boroughs of the Danelaw
- Southern limit of the Danelaw
- Political divisions c. 800
- One Viking grave
- More than one Viking grave

ALBAN

DALRIADA

STRATHCLYDE

Lothian

Yeavering

NORTHUMBRIA

North Sea

NORWEGIAN SETTLEMENT 900-950

Cumbria

Irish Sea

DANISH SETTLEMENT 875

NORWEGIAN SETTLEMENT 901

DANISH SETTLEMENT 875

Lincoln

MERCIA

DANISH SETTLEMENT 879

Chester 613

GWYNEDD

Nottingham

OFFA'S DYKE

Derby

Leicester

Stamford

EAST ANGLIA

POWYS

DYFED

SEISYLLWG

BRYCH-EINIOG

GWENT

GLYWYSING

Dyrham 577

ESSEX

S S E X

Cheddar

KENT

SUSSEX

W E S S E X

Dumnonia

147

settlement were established along the east and south coasts, and, in spite of resistance from the Britons to the Anglo-Saxons, by the mid-6th century the earliest kingdoms had emerged in the south and east. The more powerful kingdoms were those which emerged in the southwest (Wessex), midlands (Mercia) and north (Northumbria). These were involved in struggles not only with each other but also the Britons of the Highland Zone. The early Anglo-Saxon period was one of pagan belief – the distribution of pagan burials is a good indicator of early settlement patterns, as is the distribution of place-names ending in -ingas – but the mission of St Augustine in 597 led to the conversion of the Saxons to Christianity by 670. Evidence of territorial struggle, particularly against the Welsh, survives in the dramatic form of Offa's Dyke, a 192-kilometre (120-mile) earthwork, built in the late 8th century. The general trend of territorial control towards the 10th century involved a reduction in the number and the control of the English kingdoms as Wessex became dominant, the emergence of a major territory – Gwynedd, centred in Snowdonia – in Wales, and the beginnings of a national identity for Scotland.

The effect of the Anglo-Saxon colonisation on the economy and life of Britain, especially Lowland Britain, was profound. A new language was introduced and a new colonisation initiated which changed the intensity of settlement. Much of our evidence for these activities comes from the place-names of the period and from archaeology. The Saxon settlements were not all in virgin territory, for in southern England there was already a fairly dense pattern of Roman-British settlement. There is evidence of Saxon settlement being influenced by pre-existing patterns. The earliest evidence (in the 'mercenary' phase before the Roman withdrawal) is of settlement in Roman towns, villas and forts, but the evidence for later periods also reflects the class structure of society. Two royal palaces have been identified, one at Yeavering in Northumberland, dating from the 7th century, the other at Cheddar in Somerset – a rural palace of the kings of Wessex. At the other end of the scale were the dwellings and farmsteads of yeomen and peasant farmers. It has been suggested that the poorer peasants lived in villages with large numbers of small huts with sunken floors, the best example of which is at Mucking in Essex. The German long-house seems not to have been used widely.

The agricultural mix obviously varied from region to region. Generally the commonest cereals were oats, barley and wheat. Ploughing of the possibly 'open' fields may have been done with a heavy plough pulled by oxen or horses. Animal husbandry was more important in the Highland Zone, and associated with migration to summer pastures.

The early Saxons were not accustomed to town life and it is difficult to assess the degree of continuity of occupation of the Roman towns. Some Roman towns were immediately deserted on the Roman withdrawal, and it is clear that the urban system as a whole declined and decayed. The question of the continued occupation of Roman British town sites is complex, but there is evidence to suggest that life continued in many of these towns, albeit under changed circumstances, and, as Martin Biddle says, 'far from there being a complete break between Roman Britain and Anglo-

Saxon England, the new evidence shows that the roots of the English settlements were planted while Britain was still part of the empire and were strengthened for as long as the civitates remained in being' (Archaeology of Anglo-Saxon England, ed D M Wilson). Roman defence lines were followed by the walls of some medieval towns – London, Lincoln, Canterbury and Chichester, for example. In towns such as Colchester and Winchester continuity was initially preserved by the construction of Saxon royal palaces on the Roman sites. From the late 7th century, however, there were signs of a new town growth, and these early Anglo-Saxon towns were mainly trading and industrial centres, frequently coastal or riverine in location, such as Hamwih (Southampton), Dover, Sandwich, Ipswich. The major commercial centres were London and York. By 880 there were about ten English towns, but by the early 10th century there were about 50, with some of the newer towns built for military rather than commercial reasons. By the end of the Anglo-Saxon period it is thought that there were about 100 places that might be described as towns, in which lived about 10% of the population. Much of this later urban growth came in the form of burhs, fortified against the Danish invaders.

During the course of the 9th century a new element entered Britain's social, cultural and political mix in the form of Scandinavian attacks and settlements. The first recorded raid on England took place in 793 – on the monastery at Lindisfarne; the raids intensified in the 9th century, and in 851 the Vikings first wintered in England. In midland and eastern England the primary influence was that of the Danes, who had previously attacked the coastal lowlands of northwestern continental Europe, and moved inland along the major rivers. From 860 to 880, notwithstanding the strength of the Wessex army of King Alfred, the Danes took eastern Mercia, East Anglia and most of Northumbria. This Danish-held and settled area became the Danelaw, at the centre of which were a group of five fortified towns in the East Midlands: Lincoln, Stamford, Nottingham, Leicester and Derby. A different wave of attacks and settlement occurred in the northwest of England, where from the early 10th century the Norwegians, mainly from the Dublin kingdom, occupied the region west of the Pennines up to the Solway Firth. Attempts were made to found a Norse kingdom east of the Pennines, at York, but a renewed campaign by the Mercian and Wessex kings reduced the area of the Danelaw. Danish raids on England were renewed early in the 10th century, resulting in the conquest and unification of the whole country except for the southwest, under Canute.

The largest area of Scandinavian settlement in England was the Danelaw, which was formally recognised in 886 by Alfred of Wessex and Guthrum. Its four principal regions were Northumbria, East Anglia, the southeast Midlands and the Five Boroughs. The laws and customs of the Danelaw differed from those of Anglo-Saxon England.

The Scandinavians also exercised powerful influence in Scotland, though Wales was less affected. In the 9th century Norwegians (Vikings) took the Orkneys and Shetlands and moved south from Caithness to the Moray Firth. They settled the Western Islands and founded kingdoms in Ireland and

the Isle of Man. There were frequent attacks by the Vikings from Dublin and the Isle of Man on the Welsh coast, and though no permanent settlements resulted the Scandinavian influence is seen in Norse topographical names of coastal features. The Scandinavian settlement affected both rural and urban life, producing an extension of arable cultivation and a stimulus to urban growth.

Against the background of conquest and war, the conversion of Britain to Christianity proceeded at varying pace and with development of different institutions. At the end of the 10th century a revival of monastic life in England occurred, mainly in the south and east, but the main extension of monasticism occurred after the Norman conquest. In Wales early monastic sites had been established by the 'Celtic' saints in the period from the 5th to the 7th century, and these monasteries were of great importance in Welsh religious life for a long period. There were bishops in Wales, but no division into sees, whereas in England the dioceses dated from the 7th-century Augustinian conversion, even though the territories of the sees changed rapidly during troubled times. In Scotland territorial bishoprics are evident by the 11th century, together with a crude parochial system (*see map page 150*). In England the development of a parochial system was well under way, though not complete by 1066.

Medieval Britain

On 14 October 1066, the Anglo-Saxon kingdom ended with the defeat in battle of Harold Godwinson by William, Duke of Normandy (a Norman duchy which had developed in the 10th century). The Conquest represents, however, less of a dramatic change in life in Britain than is sometimes thought, for many of the innovations with which the Normans are associated, including the feudal and manorial systems, were pre-Norman in origin. The administrative geography of Britain before and after the Norman Conquest was varied and complex. There existed in 1066 a number of earldoms—heritages from the Anglo-Saxon administrative system—including Northumbria, East Anglia and Wessex, which comprised groupings of shires. After the Conquest the existing administrative and judicial system of England was used, and co-operation envisaged with the existing officials such as sheriffs, bishops and abbots. The principal innovations of the new regime were a more rigid social structure and a greater emphasis on military skill and defensive systems. The latter was represented in the construction of a national system of royal and baronial castles, many in the larger towns and others constructed along the Welsh Marches and the Scots border.

From the end of the 10th century there began a period of economic expansion in Britain which had a profound effect on regional economies and on landscapes. This expansion began from a small population, a low-technology and predominantly rural economy, a limited urban and commercial base, and a pyramidal social structure. The population of England at the end of the 11th century was about two million, and by 1347 had reached between six and seven million. Little can be known of the equivalent figures for Wales, although one estimate for 1300 is of a population of less than 250,000. Estimates for Scotland suggest a population of c.250,000 for the late 11th century, reaching c.450,000 by the late 14th century. On the whole, what is postulated is a relatively general rapid increase in population in the 12th and 13th centuries, followed by a period of decline, though the rates of increase obviously varied locally and regionally. The population of 11th-century England had a highly uneven distribution, with the highest densities in the Lowlands, notably East Anglia, and the lowest in the Uplands, waste and forest areas. In the Lincolnshire fenland, for example, there were dramatic increases in the village populations in the 12th and 13th centuries. As there was still much under-used space, an inevitable consequence of the rising population was colonisation on a large scale. The major expansion of settlement in England took place in woodland areas, such as the Forest of Arden. Another indication of the advance of settlement and cultivation can be seen in the attempts at disafforestation of royal forest, that is to release some of the legal restraints on 'assarting' (or clearance) in them. Examples of this occurred in the 12th and 13th centuries in Surrey, Devon, Essex, Hampshire and the Southern Uplands of Scotland. Reclamation of marshland was another important feature of colonisation, with major drainage and settlement activity in the Somerset Levels, the Pevensey levels in Sussex, Holderness, the Romney and Walland marshes in Kent. Inroads were also made into the margins of the high moorland areas, including the Pennines, Dartmoor, Exmoor, and the uplands of Southern Scotland and central and north Wales. Much of the land reclamation of early medieval Britain was carried out by the initiative and under the control of the monastic orders, notably the Cistercians. The pace of colonisation was uneven, and in some areas there was already a shortage of land by the 14th century.

The nature of the rural economy in Britain in the 11th, 12th and 13th centuries is impossible to describe in detail, for local and regional variance was considerable. In those areas where arable cultivation was possible on a relatively large scale, much of the land was arranged and managed in 'open' or sub-divided fields (fields divided into tenurial strips), as in parts of the south and east Midlands, but in other areas, such as southwestern England and west Wales, much land was enclosed and held in severalty rather than in common. In many areas there was a mixture of 'open' and 'enclosed' land. The system of farming the open fields, particularly in heavy soil areas, involved the ploughing-up of substantial cultivation ridges, separated by drainage furrows, and these can still be seen, notably in Midland England, as 'ridge-and-furrow' topography. The most mature form of field-system was the two-and-three-field system, found in a broad belt of territory running from northeast England through the Midlands to south central England and with outliers in South Wales, and involving the

Britain to 1350 The Domesday survey of 1086 produced an unparalleled wealth of information about 11th-century England. Steady inroads were made by 1350 on the areas of unfarmed land covered by forest and marsh.

Late Medieval Britain The indication of farming regions at this date are only tentative, but the enclosures of the 15th and 16th centuries were primarily concentrated in regions of arable farming, converting them to sheep-rearing.

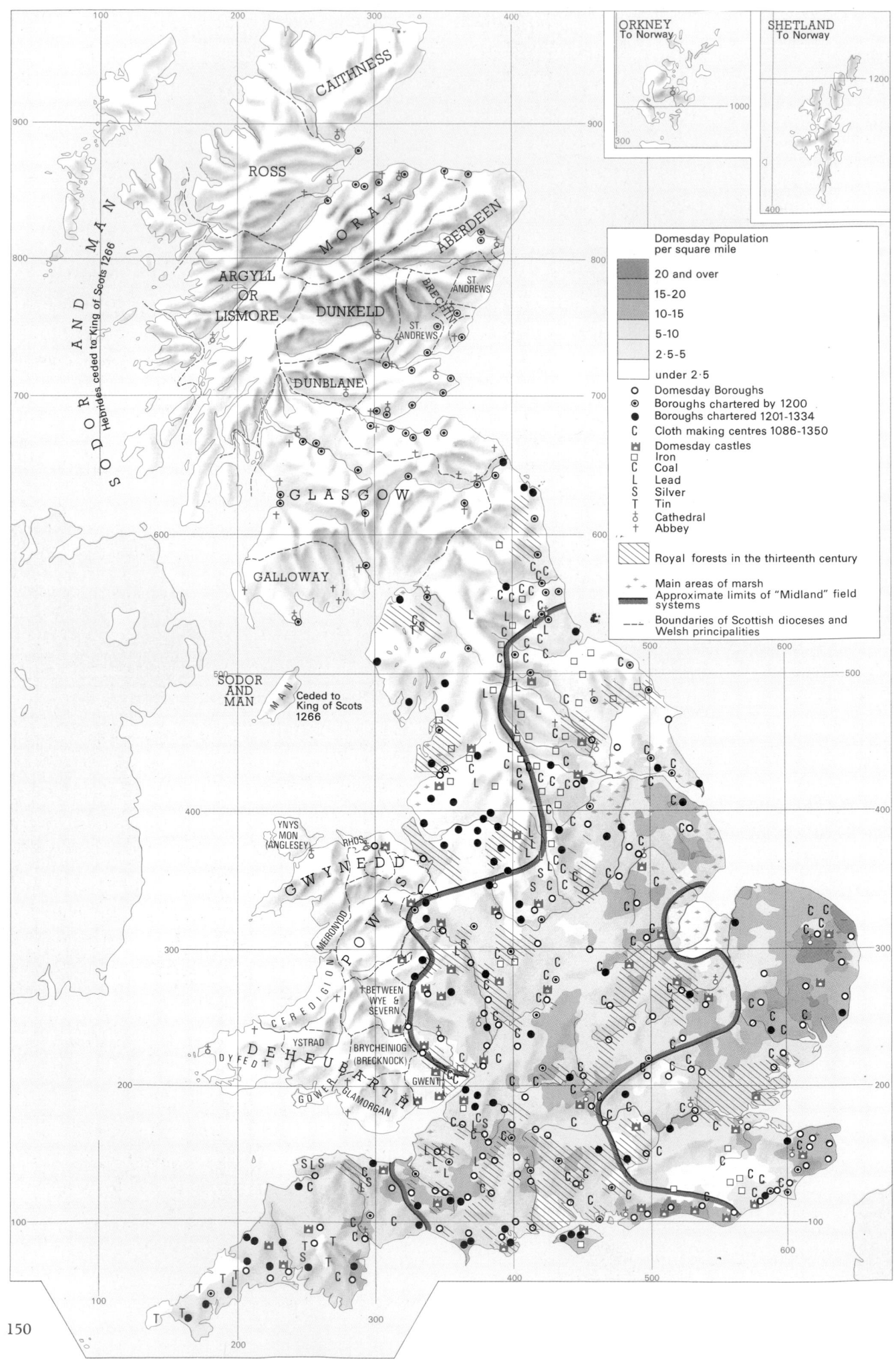

ORKNEY
To Norway

SHETLAND
To Norway

Domesday Population
per square mile

20 and over
15-20
10-15
5-10
2·5-5
under 2·5

○ Domesday Boroughs
◉ Boroughs chartered by 1200
● Boroughs chartered 1201-1334
C Cloth making centres 1086-1350
⌂ Domesday castles
□ Iron
C Coal
L Lead
S Silver
T Tin
✠ Cathedral
✝ Abbey

Royal forests in the thirteenth century

Main areas of marsh
Approximate limits of "Midland" field
systems
Boundaries of Scottish dioceses and
Welsh principalities

CAITHNESS

ROSS

MORAY

ARGYLL
OR
LISMORE

DUNKELD

ABERDEEN

BRECHIN

ST
ANDREWS

ST
ANDREWS

DUNBLANE

SODOR AND MAN
Hebrides ceded to King of Scots 1266

GLASGOW

GALLOWAY

SODOR
AND
MAN

Ceded to
King of Scots
1266

MAN

YNYS
MON
(ANGLESEY)

RHOS

GWYNEDD

POWYS

MEIRONYDD

CEREDIGION

DYFED

YSTRAD

DEHEUBARTH

BETWEEN
WYE &
SEVERN

BRYCHEINIOG
(BRECKNOCK)

GWENT

GOWER

GLAMORGAN

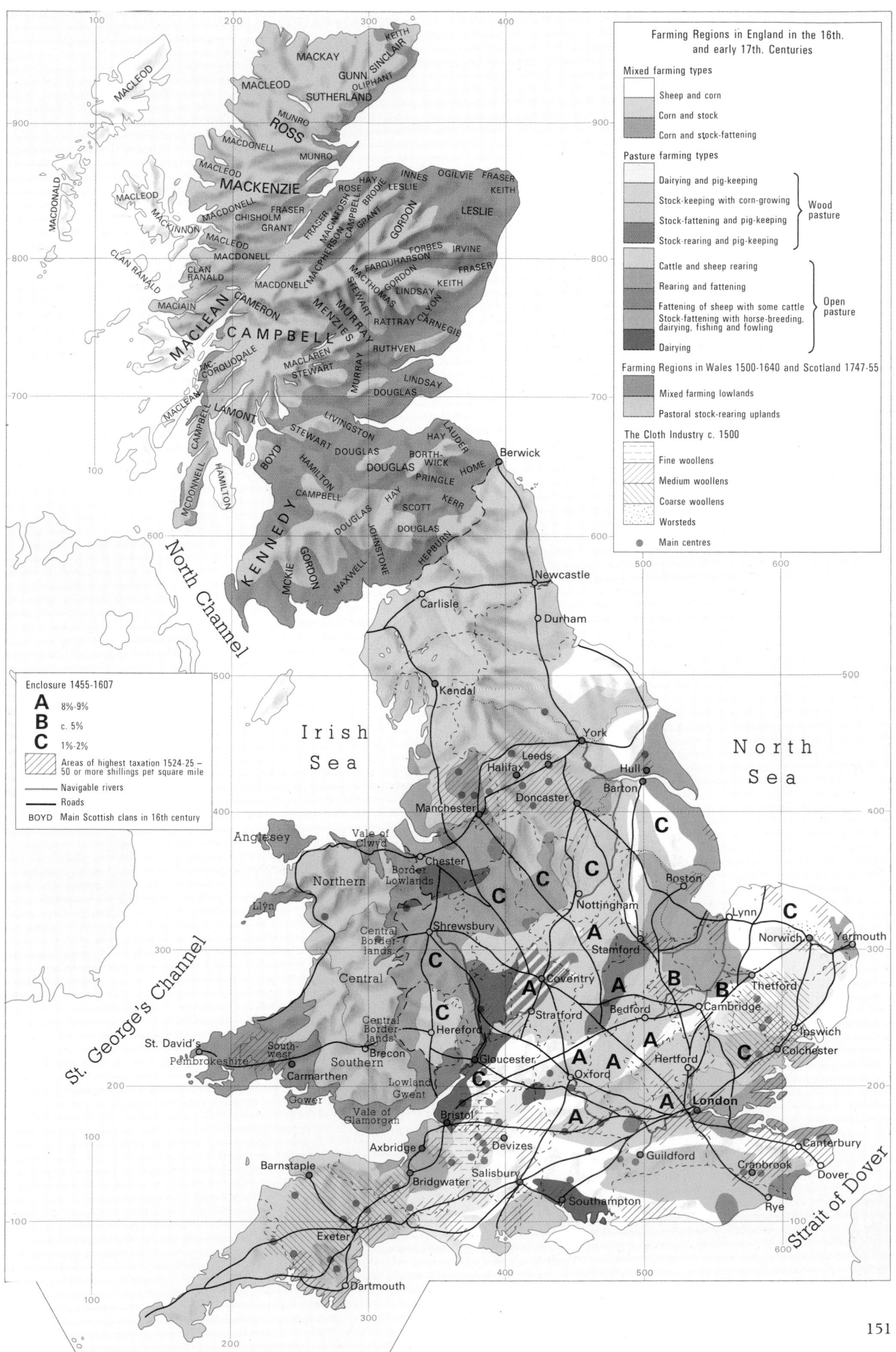

Farming Regions in England in the 16th. and early 17th. Centuries

Mixed farming types
Sheep and corn
Corn and stock
Corn and stock-fattening

Pasture farming types
Dairying and pig-keeping
Stock-keeping with corn-growing
Stock-fattening and pig-keeping
Stock-rearing and pig-keeping
} Wood pasture

Cattle and sheep rearing
Rearing and fattening
Fattening of sheep with some cattle
Stock-fattening with horse-breeding, dairying, fishing and fowling
Dairying
} Open pasture

Farming Regions in Wales 1500-1640 and Scotland 1747-55
Mixed farming lowlands
Pastoral stock-rearing uplands

The Cloth Industry c. 1500
Fine woollens
Medium woollens
Coarse woollens
Worsteds
● Main centres

Enclosure 1455-1607
A 8%-9%
B c. 5%
C 1%-2%
Areas of highest taxation 1524-25 – 50 or more shillings per square mile
Navigable rivers
Roads
BOYD Main Scottish clans in 16th century

North Channel
Irish Sea
North Sea
St. George's Channel
Strait of Dover

MACLEOD
MACDONALD
MACLEOD
MACKINNON
MACDONELL
MACLEAN
MACIAIN
MC CORQUODALE
MACLEAN
MCDONNELL
HAMILTON
LAMONT
KENNEDY
MCKIE
GORDON
MAXWELL
JOHNSTONE
HEPBURN
DOUGLAS
CAMPBELL
HAY
SCOTT
KERR
PRINGLE
HOME
BORTH-WICK
DOUGLAS
LAUDER
HAY
HAMILTON
LIVINGSTON
STEWART
BOYD
DOUGLAS
MACLAREN
STEWART
CAMPBELL
MENZIES
MURRAY
RUTHVEN
CARNEGIE
LINDSAY
DOUGLAS
LINDSAY
RATTRAY
MACTHOMAS
GORDON
LYON
STEWART
KEITH
CAMERON
CLAN RANALD
CLAN RANALD
MACDONELL
MACDONELL
MACPHERSON
CAMPBELL
GRANT
FRASER
CHISHOLM
GRANT
FRASER
MACLEOD
MACDONELL
FARQUHARSON
FORBES
IRVINE
FRASER
MACKAY
GUNN
OLIPHANT
SINCLAIR
KEITH
SUTHERLAND
MACLEOD
ROSS
MUNRO
MUNRO
MACKENZIE
ROSE
HAY
MACINTOSH
BRODIE
LESLIE
INNES
OGILVIE
FRASER
KEITH
LESLIE

Berwick
Newcastle
Carlisle
Durham
Kendal
York
Leeds
Halifax
Hull
Barton
Manchester
Doncaster
Boston
Nottingham
Lynn
Norwich
Yarmouth
Shrewsbury
Stamford
Chester
Thetford
Coventry
Bedford
Cambridge
Stratford
Ipswich
Hereford
Hertford
Colchester
Gloucester
Oxford
London
Bristol
Canterbury
Axbridge
Devizes
Guildford
Cranbrook
Dover
Barnstaple
Salisbury
Bridgwater
Southampton
Rye
Carmarthen
Brecon
St. David's
Pembrokeshire
Exeter
Dartmouth

Anglesey
Vale of Clwyd
Northern
Llŷn
Border Lowlands
Central Borderlands
Central
Central Borderlands
South-west
Southern
Gower
Lowland Gwent
Vale of Glamorgan

sub-division of the two or three major arable fields into furlongs, and the division of the arable area usually into three cropping zones, one of which was normally left fallow. Elsewhere, particularly in upland and heavy woodland areas, there were smaller fields and less regular cropping systems. In many of the upland and marshland areas there was no arable cultivation, except perhaps for very isolated pockets, and the rural economy was essentially pastoral, the main activity being the rearing of sheep and cattle. The large sheep flocks of the lowland coastal marshes, of Kent and Essex, for example, were paralleled by the 'vaccaries' of the Pennines and central Wales. Natural habitats, including woods and marshes, provided fodder and habitat for both domesticated animals and for wild game. An important feature of the medieval landscape was the royal forest and its diminutive form, the deer park. The rural settlements of medieval Britain varied widely in size and form from the undoubtedly large villages of parts of Midland England and East Anglia to the more isolated hamlets and farmsteads of many of the uplands and recently-colonised areas of the west and north of Britain.

The increase in monastic orders in Britain after the Conquest was a significant feature of medieval life. It is estimated that in 1066 there were about 280 religious houses in England and Wales, a figure that had increased to over 1,300 by the end of the 12th century (largely by the establishment of houses of monks, regular canons and nuns, military orders and hospitals). By the 14th century the number had increased to over 2,000, mainly with the addition of mendicant orders of friars after 1221, but the total had declined by 1500. The larger monastic houses were very substantial landowners, and are epitomised best by the relics of the spectacular Cistercian abbeys at Fountains, Rievaulx, Tintern and Melrose. In Scotland 'innovative' monasteries came later, beginning in the 12th century and including the founding of houses by the Augustinians and the Cistercians.

The towns of medieval Britain were small in comparison with their modern counterparts. According to the data of the Domesday Book of 1086, there were 111 boroughs in England, some of which were very small indeed. London was the largest, with a population of about 10,000. There was only one borough in Wales at this time—Rhuddlan. The period of economic expansion, however, witnessed a growth in the number of boroughs in England, which numbered 480 by the beginning of the 14th century. There was an increase in the towns in Wales consequent on the Norman Conquest, notably in south Wales and, in the late 13th century, in northwest Wales. In Scotland, urbanisation appears to have begun during the Norman period and notably after 1124 when David I became King of Scots. Prior to this date he had given burgh charters to Roxburgh and Berwick, and between 1124 and 1153 created eleven royal burghs, including Edinburgh, Stirling and Dunfermline. Burghs were also given charters by the Church, and the early ecclesiastical burghs include Glasgow and Aberdeen.

Industrial activity in medieval Britain was generally not highly location-specific, for the major industries were those that supplied the everyday needs of the populace—food, drink, clothing and materials for building—and were relatively ubiquitous. The towns were important centres of a wide variety of industries, though in the 13th century there are signs that some industries, notably textiles, moved away from the towns to the countryside. By the late Middle Ages the major textile regions of England included Wiltshire and Gloucestershire (producing broad cloth), the West Riding of Yorkshire (low-grade cloth), the Norwich worsted region and the cloth regions of Suffolk and Essex (which became progressively more specialised in production), and the cloth regions of Somerset and Devon. These developments reflected a general change from the export of wool to the export of cloth.

The principal areas of iron production were the Weald of Sussex and Kent, the Forest of Dean and the Cleveland Hills. The efficiency of production was increased by the introduction of a form of blast furnace. In the later Middle Ages there was also an increase in the production of coal, encouraged by a growing timber shortage. The main mining areas were the Tyne valley, south Nottinghamshire, west Yorkshire, south Wales and around the Forth and in Fife in Scotland. Lead, together with silver, was produced in Derbyshire, the Pennine valleys of Yorkshire and Durham, in Cumberland, and north and south Wales. Tin production took place in Cornwall, and copper ore was extracted in Devonshire, Cumberland and Wales. The products of the agriculture and industries of medieval Britain were mainly consumed and used within the mainland, but trade was nevertheless an important feature of economic activity. The largest ports were London, Southampton and Bristol. Much of the trade of the western ports, including Southampton, was with the Gascony wine area. Southampton and Bristol imported wine and exported wool and cloth. The east-coast ports mainly traded with the Baltic and the Low Countries, while London had trading connections with most parts of continental Europe.

The dynamic character and the vicissitudes of life in medieval Britain should be stressed, for the economic and human geographies of regions and settlements were continually changing. There was a decline in the population of England from six or seven million in 1348 to about 2·75 million in the early 16th century, with changes of a similar order in Wales and Scotland. This was mainly due to the effects of epidemic and infectious diseases. The best-known epidemic was the Black Death, which affected Britain from 1348 to 1350, though there were many other epidemics including tuberculosis, measles and smallpox. In some respects the decrease of population which began in the late 14th century was related to a weakening of a feudal mode of production, and paved the way for the early advent of rural and urban capitalism, culminating in the Agricultural and Industrial Revolutions. It has been suggested that in 1509, when Henry VIII succeeded to the throne of England, Britain was still medieval in many aspects: by the end of the Tudor dynasty this medievalism was rapidly disappearing, and nearly all traces of it had vanished by 1700.

The Agricultural Revolution Enclosures at this period affected both the commons and the open-fields that had been communally cultivated since medieval times. Agricultural societies formed an important channel for the spreading of new farming ideas and techniques.

The Agricultural Revolution

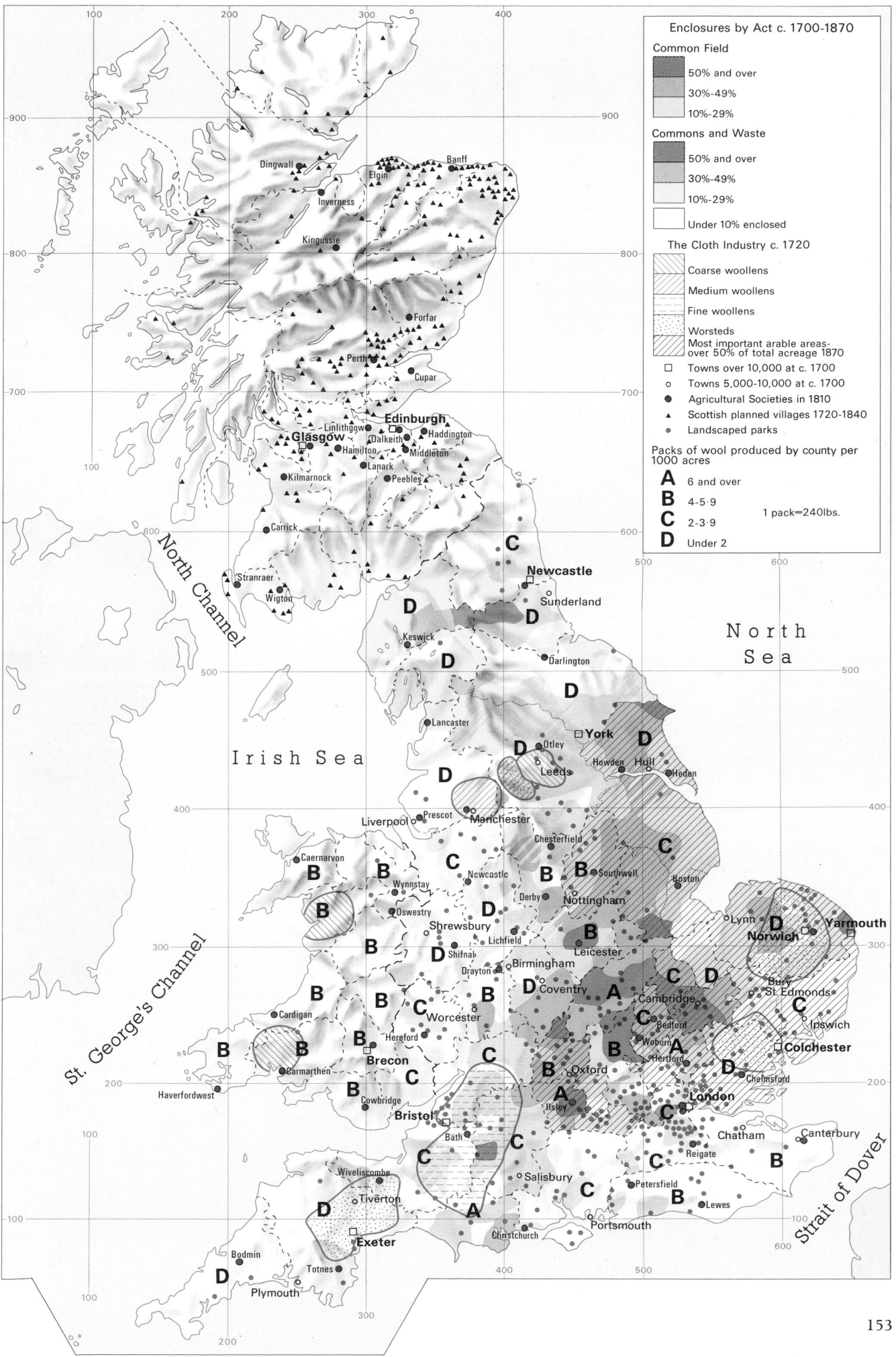

Map legend:

Enclosures by Act c. 1700-1870

Common Field
- 50% and over
- 30%-49%
- 10%-29%

Commons and Waste
- 50% and over
- 30%-49%
- 10%-29%

Under 10% enclosed

The Cloth Industry c. 1720
- Coarse woollens
- Medium woollens
- Fine woollens
- Worsteds
- Most important arable areas- over 50% of total acreage 1870

- □ Towns over 10,000 at c. 1700
- ○ Towns 5,000-10,000 at c. 1700
- ● Agricultural Societies in 1810
- ▲ Scottish planned villages 1720-1840
- • Landscaped parks

Packs of wool produced by county per 1000 acres
- **A** 6 and over
- **B** 4-5.9
- **C** 2-3.9
- **D** Under 2

1 pack=240lbs.

North Sea

North Channel

Irish Sea

St. George's Channel

Strait of Dover

153

The Agricultural Revolution

The 16th and 17th centuries witnessed widespread change of an economic and political nature. In England population trends saw a continuing recovery, probably beginning after about 1470; in 1541 the total was about three million, increasing to four million by 1600, to 5·5 million by 1651, followed by a slight decline before further increase in the 18th century. Estimates for Scotland put the population at 550-800,000 for the late 16th century, and at between 800,000 and one million for 1700.

These population increases mirror the beginning of major changes in the sectoral and space-economies of the regions of Britain. Generally labelled the Agricultural and Industrial Revolutions, the phenomena thus classified were extremely complex and extending over quite a long period of time.

In the rural and agricultural sectors the main indices of change are well known, although their local and regional manifestations require further investigation. Enclosure and technical innovations are the best-known features. Enclosure had been a continuous process over a very long period of time, but accelerated in the 16th and 17th centuries prior to the major burst of 'Parliamentary' enclosure in the 18th and 19th centuries. In the late 15th and the 16th century the conversion of arable land to pasture, on account of the relative profitability of sheep farming, led to a 'de-populating' form of enclosure and the desertion of settlements, particularly in the Midlands. The amount of land enclosed in this fashion was quite small, although more 'silent' forms of enclosure also occurred. By 1600 there were regions which had few or no open fields (though these were mainly peripheral to the great central swathe of open fields), and during the 17th century various methods of enclosure, including enclosure 'by agreement', were used to continue the elimination of the open fields. Enclosure by private Act of Parliament was the major mechanism in the 18th and 19th centuries, and quantitatively was the most important method. In this period there were some 5286 Enclosure Acts, of which 3105 effected the enclosure of open-field arable. The total effect was the enclosure in England of nearly 2·8 million HA (seven million acres) or 21% of the total surface area. The counties most affected were Lincolnshire, West Yorkshire, Norfolk, Northamptonshire and East Yorkshire, and those least affected were Middlesex, Essex, Devon, Rutland, Sussex, Hereford, Cheshire, Monmouth, Cornwall and Kent. The degree of enclosure varied in time, but the periods of greatest intensity were 1760-80 and 1793-1815, the latter being the period of the Napoleonic wars. The acreage for Parliamentary enclosure in Wales is estimated to be 167,000 HA (414,000 acres), with the greatest intensity in the period 1793-1815.

The legal system of enclosure in Scotland differed from that of England and Wales, and landowners were not as constrained from enclosing. Acts of the late 16th century facilitated changes in land tenure, and the Act against Lands Lying in Run-rig of 1695 gave power for division of commons. In the Lowlands, arable enclosure was mainly completed by 1770 in Berwickshire and the Lothians, but had only just begun in Ayrshire and Perthshire. In addition, about 200,000 HA (500,000 acres) of common were enclosed in the Lowlands between 1720 and 1850. The pattern of enclosure in the Scottish Highlands was different, particularly after 1745 with the 'clearance' and amalgamation of Highland farms, which were subsequently let to Lowland sheep graziers. This process initially affected the Central Highlands, and later the northwest Highlands and Islands, leading to large-scale emigration.

The landscape effects of enclosure at this time are plain to see–in the form of regular, usually square or rectangular fields, mainly bounded by hedgerows or stone walls. The economic effects of enclosure in the shorter term are more difficult to measure, for in spite of its association with agricultural improvement it is difficult to prove direct causal relationships. The social consequences of enclosures have tended to be neglected, though opinions tend to polarise around the 'improvement' effects and the 'depopulation' effects.

Enclosure was but one of several manifestations of the advent of a capitalist system of production in the rural economy. We associate the Agricultural Revolution with technical improvements in farming, and usually with improvers, such as Thomas Coke of Norfolk, Robert Bakewell of Leicestershire, the Culleys of Northumberland, Jethro Tull and 'Turnip' Townshend. While it is more accurate to describe some of these as popularisers rather than direct innovators, it is certainly the case that many of the technical improvements of this period are associated with large estates, such as Coke's Norfolk estate, and the estates of innovating landlords in East Lothian. The technical innovations included the introduction of short leys with improved grasses (known as convertible husbandry), new crops (clover, turnips, the potato, ryegrass, sainfoin), new rotations (especially the Norfolk system), the application of fertilisers and the new implements such as Tull's seed drill. The area of improved land was increased by major reclamation schemes (notably the Fenland and of areas of moorland and heathland). The regional chronologies of adoption are very complex, and there is no overall pattern or 'national' picture. Incentives for improving and intensifying agricultural production included the rapidly growing population and the increase in the proportion of the population living in towns, particularly London and the towns of the industrial areas. Improvement is also seen in the newer residences, planned estate villages and the landscaped gardens and parks. What has been described as the flowering or re-building of rural England commenced in the late 17th century, but the architectural expression of the Agricultural Revolution is usually associated with the great buildings of the 18th century and the classical Palladian styles. Landscape gardening also reached its peak in the 18th century, the major practitioners being William Kent, Lancelot Brown and Humphrey Repton.

Agricultural change did not stop in the early 19th century, although progress and advancement were not always universal in rural areas. In the 19th century the legislative context of farming continued to change with

The Early Industrial Revolution The geography of early industrialisation depended on the availability of coal or water for power, and on canals for communications. The concentration of industry into relatively small areas was fed by a dramatic movement of people from rural areas to the towns.

154

The Early Industrial Revolution

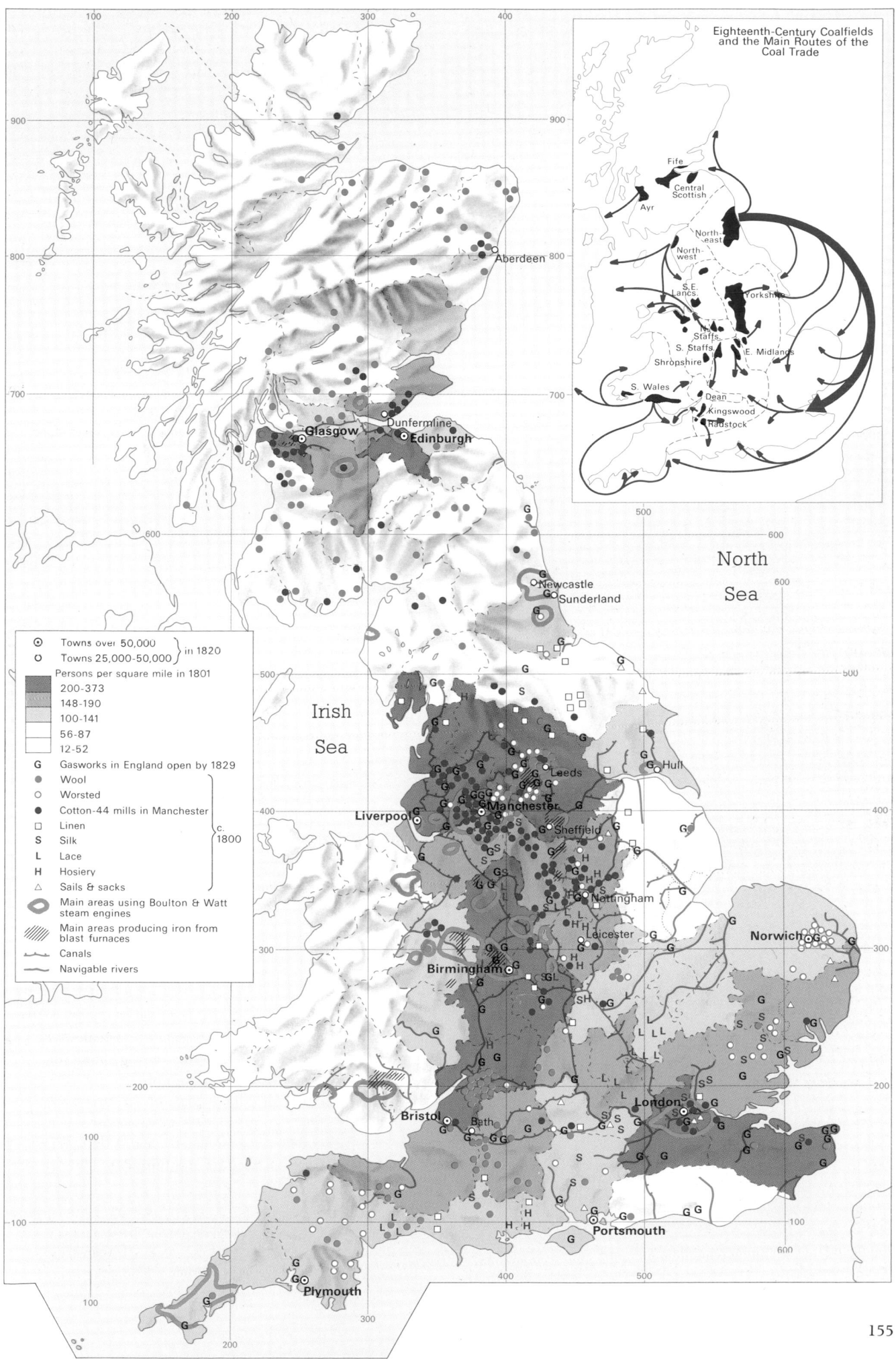

Eighteenth-Century Coalfields and the Main Routes of the Coal Trade

Fife
Central Scottish
Ayr
North-east
North-west
S.E. Lancs.
Yorkshire
N. Staffs.
S. Staffs.
E. Midlands
Shropshire
S. Wales
Dean
Kingswood
Radstock

North Sea

Aberdeen

Glasgow
Dunfermline
Edinburgh

Newcastle
Sunderland

Irish Sea

Leeds
Hull
Liverpool
Manchester
Sheffield
Nottingham
Leicester
Norwich
Birmingham

Bristol
Bath
London

Plymouth
Portsmouth

Legend

⊙ Towns over 50,000
○ Towns 25,000–50,000 } in 1820

Persons per square mile in 1801
  200–373
  148–190
  100–141
  56–87
  12–52

G   Gasworks in England open by 1829
●   Wool
○   Worsted
●   Cotton-44 mills in Manchester
□   Linen
S   Silk   } c.
L   Lace   } 1800
H   Hosiery
△   Sails & sacks
⬭   Main areas using Boulton & Watt steam engines
▨   Main areas producing iron from blast furnaces
〜 Canals
—   Navigable rivers

more Enclosure Acts and the repeal of the Corn Laws (ending the artificial maintenance of prices), the subsidy of land drainage by the Public Money Drainage Act of 1846, and the strengthening of the rights of tenants by the Agricultural Holdings Acts. Farming became a more and more capitally-intensive commercial enterprise, responding to the demands of a rapidly growing population for cheaper food. This process, assisted by new technology (including under-draining, chemical fertilisers and better transport to markets), resulted in improved productivity. It also produced a massive decline in the rural labour force in the course of the 19th century. High investment at the time of high farming could be very profitable, but at other times, particularly the 1880s and 1890s, low prices produced considerable depression and widespread bankruptcy, notably in eastern England.

The Industrial Revolution

The other 'revolution' of the 18th and 19th centuries was 'industrial', a term which has associations not merely with manufacturing and extractional industries but also with rapid urbanisation, rapid population increase and major changes in the transport system. In the mid-18th century the population of Britain was about eleven million, and this figure had risen spectacularly to 45 million by 1911 (of whom less than 10% were engaged in agriculture). The increase was most rapid in mid-century. In the late 18th century, a decline in the death-rate and rise in birth rate because of earlier age at marriage gave a national increase in population of about 40%. The overall figures do, however, mask regional and local variations: in the mid-19th century rural areas of Wales, Scotland and (to a lesser extent) England experienced population decline. Immigration from Ireland was important, though offset by overseas emigration from Britain, giving a net loss of over one million people in the period 1801 to 1911. For the 19th century population growth varied between 11% and 14% a decade, falling, however, to 10% in the first decade of the 20th century. Population growth was highest in the rapidly industrialising and urbanising regions of north and midland England, London, Clydeside and South Wales.

The Industrial Revolution did not start from a totally new base. The textile industries which had developed in the 16th and 17th centuries retained regional distinctiveness. Until the mid-18th century the woollen industry provided about 33% of Britain's industrial output. The wool textile regions changed balance, however, with the decline of the Somerset and Devon and Suffolk producers, and a greater concentration in Gloucestershire, Wiltshire, Norwich and the West Riding (see map page 153). The cotton industry experienced a rapid rise in the 18th century, particularly with the increased demand from the home market after 1750, and the technical advances after 1770. The major areas of production were Lancashire, the East Midlands and the Glasgow region. Coal output also increased rapidly in the 18th century: the total for 1700 was about 2·5 million tons, which increased to 10 million by 1800. The turning point for expansion in coal production was about 1770, with the beginning of the canal era providing a cheaper means of distribution. The largest coalfield was that of northeast England, much of whose output was shipped down the east coast to London. Other smaller areas of production included the coalfields of the Midlands, Yorkshire, Lancashire, the Forest of Dean, the Rhondda and the Firth of Forth. Iron production was mainly concentrated in South Wales, Shropshire, Staffordshire, Yorkshire, and the Central valley of Scotland. Other major industries of the 18th century included silk textiles, glassmaking, and shipbuilding.

Changes in the form of power (especially steam) allied to technological changes—the smelting of iron using coal in the early 18th century, the advent of a wide range of machines and of the factory systems—accelerated industrial activity, particularly in the regions on the developing coalfields. By the mid-19th century the Industrial Revolution had reached its peak. Deeper mining and greater demand led to increased production—from 21 million tons in 1826 to 154 million tons in 1880, with the Northumberland and Durham field the major producer, followed by Lancashire, South Wales and Yorkshire. The iron industry was tied to coal production, and of the mid-century total of 2·7 million tons of pig-iron, the largest producers were Staffordshire, Scotland and South Wales. The working of the iron was not so tied, and metal industries were located in Sheffield and the Black Country, with different locations for shipbuilding and locomotive engineering. The textile industries experienced further concentration, with Lancashire dominating cotton pro-duction. There was less regional dominance by a single region in the woollen industry, although the major concentration was in West Yorkshire.

The railway age (from 1825 onwards) brought massive change in population distribution, with the increasing concentration in the towns of the coalfield and industrial regions. Over 50% of the English population were urban-dwellers in 1851, and 70% by 1881. Urban development was marked in Yorkshire, Lancashire, the Black Country and Birmingham, Tyneside, Central Scotland, London, South Wales and, later in the century, along the coast of southeast England.

As with agriculture, so there was also depression in industry in late-Victorian Britain, especially in the period 1873-1896, when industrial productivity fell, though new industries developed and partly offset decline elsewhere. These included the chemical and electrical engineering industries, food processing, and steel. On the eve of World War I the main trends of the Industrial Revolution had changed, as some of the older industrial areas began to lose population with a drift of population towards the south-east. These trends have continued to dominate throughout the 20th century.

Britain in the Late Nineteenth Century Between 1835 and 1900 the country was covered by a network of railways, often to the detriment of competing canals and roads. London's role as capital of the Empire helped to attract immigrants sufficient to make it one of the world's largest cities, despite a higher-than-normal mortality rate.

Britain in the Late Nineteenth Century

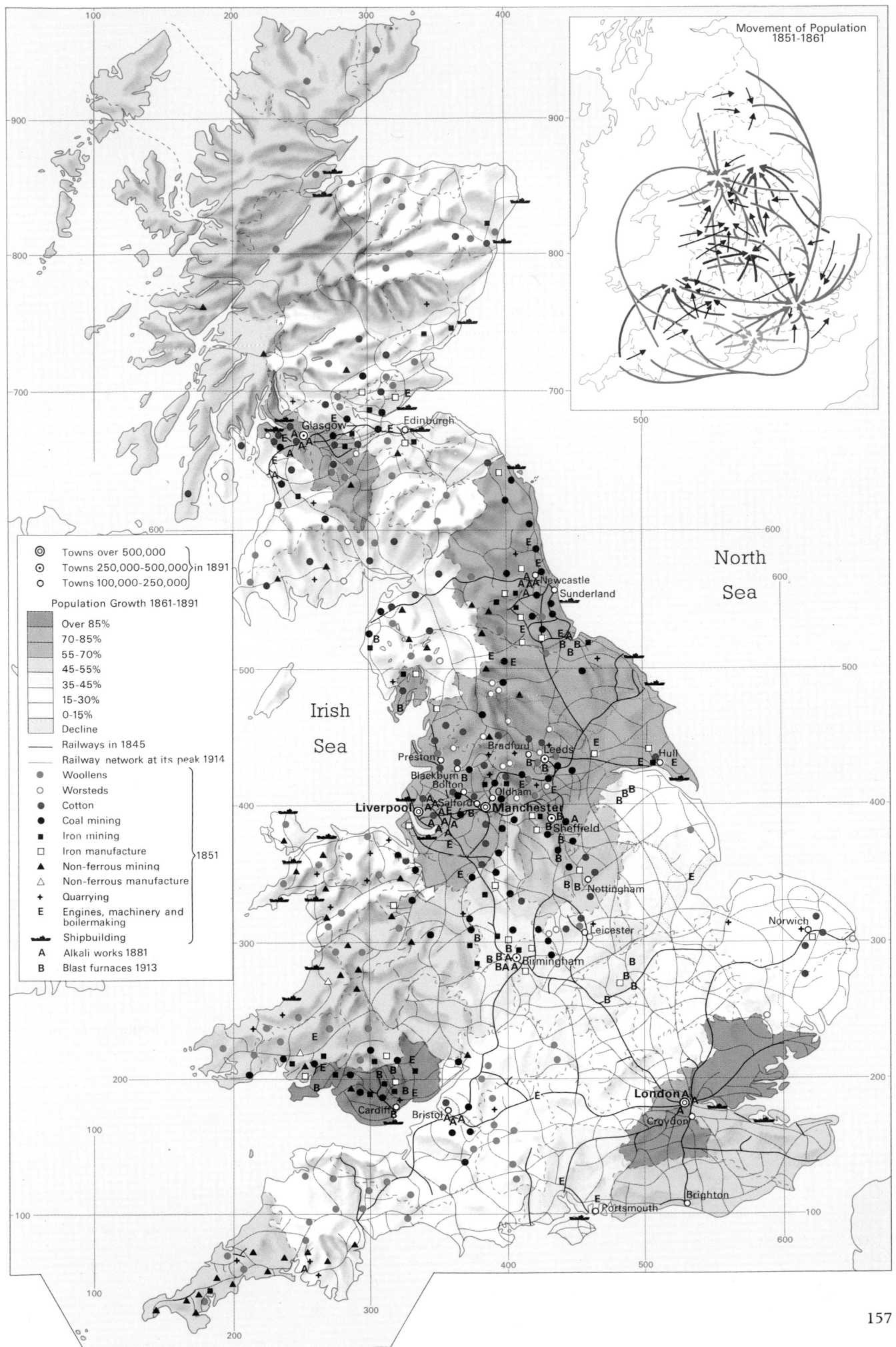

Movement of Population 1851-1861

North Sea

Irish Sea

Legend

- ◎ Towns over 500,000
- ◉ Towns 250,000-500,000 } in 1891
- ○ Towns 100,000-250,000

Population Growth 1861-1891
- Over 85%
- 70-85%
- 55-70%
- 45-55%
- 35-45%
- 15-30%
- 0-15%
- Decline

— Railways in 1845
— Railway network at its peak 1914

- ● Woollens
- ○ Worsteds
- ● Cotton
- ● Coal mining
- ■ Iron mining
- □ Iron manufacture
- ▲ Non-ferrous mining
- △ Non-ferrous manufacture
- + Quarrying
- E Engines, machinery and boilermaking
- ⛴ Shipbuilding

} 1851

- A Alkali works 1881
- B Blast furnaces 1913

Glasgow · Edinburgh · Newcastle · Sunderland · Preston · Bradford · Leeds · Hull · Blackburn · Bolton · Oldham · Liverpool · Salford · Manchester · Sheffield · Nottingham · Leicester · Norwich · Birmingham · Cardiff · Bristol · London · Croydon · Brighton · Portsmouth

Modern Britain

The Legacy of the 1930s

Contrasts between the north and south of Britain are often made in the spirit of rivalry and jest. The Scottish people have their own history and pride. The people of the north of England, it has been remarked, offer 'the backbone of the country' and the superior robustness of the north is contrasted with the agility of intellect, but softer character, of the south. Behind the sometimes provocative jesting about the differences between Yorkshiremen and Londoners, Geordies and Brummies, there lay in the 1930s very great differences in the prosperity and ways of life of the 'two Britains'. Although there were exceptions to the rule, it was in the north that depression was concentrated, in the south that new industries were developing and the cities growing rapidly. Many northerners were moving away seeking the wider opportunities of London and the West Midlands. There was a 'drift' of population to the south of about 1,160,000 between 1923 and 1936. Wales, in this respect, was to be linked with the north rather than the south. Between 1923 and 1937 the insured population of the three southern divisions of the Ministry of Labour increased by 1,396,000 or 41% and the Midlands by 445,000 (27%). The insured population of the rest of Britain increased by only 576,000 or 10%. In terms of actual jobs, the three southern divisions increased by 47%, the Midlands by 32% and the North, Scotland and Wales by only 4%.

This situation was a product of the localisation of industries which had grown before 1914 but were now declining. There were falls in employment in cotton, coal, shipbuilding and some sectors of the iron and steel industries. The industrial districts of the north and Wales were heavily dependent on such industries. To pick out some extremes, unemployment rates in 1932 reached 60·9% in Merthyr Tydfil, 48·9% in Port Talbot, 46·7% in Sunderland, 44·6% in Barnsley, 44% in West Cumberland, 35% in Dundee. The Birmingham rate was 15·3%, Brighton's was 11·4%. Even East Ham in London was no more than 24·1%. And the unemployment rates fell more quickly in the south and the Midlands as economic recovery from the Great Depression began.

For it was in the southern part of Britain that the growing industries were concentrated. Here were the trades manufacturing for the home market and here could be found employment in the service and constructional industries. Motor-car manufacturing was well established in Dagenham, Luton, Oxford, Coventry and Birmingham. Industries linked to the assembly lines, like electrical engineering and the manufacture of components, tyres, car bodies and gear boxes, were in the south. The Birmingham metal trades prospered and the West Midlands, with its closely knit system of 'linkages' between trades, offered jobs to migrants from Wales and the North. Coventry was one of the fastest-growing cities, with an increase of population of 20% between 1931 and 1938 as against 3% for the country as a whole. Jobs were to be found in motor-car and cycle factories, electrical engineering, firms making components, machine-tool industries and in the rayon industry. With about one-fifth of the population of Great Britain, 'Greater London obtained five-sixths of the net increase in the number of factories between 1932 and 1937, two-fifths of all the employment in new factories and one-third of all the factory extensions'. New factories sprang up in the southeast, south, west and north of Greater London, many of them on speculatively built industrial estates along the main roads and railways out of London. Such estates can still be seen in Acton, Perivale, Park Royal and Wembley. Radio and electrical industries, automobile and aircraft engineering, pharmaceuticals, the food and drink trades, paper and printing, scientific instruments, and furniture, all nationally expanding industries, figured prominently.

While such development was in train the Clyde was in the grip of one of the worst concentrations of persistent unemployment lasting for almost all the inter-war period. Conditions on the Tyne were little, if any, better. The demand for action could not be resisted. The Special Areas Act of 1934 was the first of a series of Acts which gave limited powers to Commissioners for the Special Areas to take action to relieve unemployment in South Wales, northeast England, Cumberland and Clydeside. Industrial trading estates were set up, for example at Treforest (near Cardiff), Team Valley (Gateshead) and Hillington (Glasgow). Local authorities began to muster their resources. The Bank of England made available funds for the building of new blast furnaces, steel works and a continuous strip mill at Ebbw Vale: the original plan had been to build the plant on an iron-ore based location in Lincolnshire. Government plants making war materials were sited in the Special Areas. Government contracts, many for naval vessels, helped to bring life to the Clyde, the Tyne and to Barrow. Some of the depressed regions, eastern South Wales for example, profited more than others. Re-armament and the up-swing of trade achieved more than government policy. In 1938 the Royal Commission on the Distribution of the Industrial Population (the 'Barlow Commission') was established and its report was to influence post-war policy for regional development and industrial location.

The circumstances of regional contrast in employment had further consequences in terms of differences in personal incomes, quality of housing, access to medical and social services, opportunities for advancement. The Beveridge Report's recommendation of 1942 of a plan for 'Social Security as part of a general programme of social policy' must be viewed against this background.

The 1930s must not be seen wholly in terms of regional contrast. There was concern for example that the Axial Belt or 'Coffin' stretching from northwest to southeast from Lancashire to London was coming to house too great a share of the country's population (see map page 173). It was an age of technical change: the 'talkies' replaced the silent cinema, almost everybody could afford a radio, and the BBC under Sir John Reith's Directorship had a firm policy from which many young people benefited. New secondary schools were

The Crisis of the 1930s A study carried out in the late 1930s revealed the excessive dependence of many towns on a single industry as a structural problem exacerbating the impact of the depression. This map compares the distribution of these industries with the incidence of unemployment.

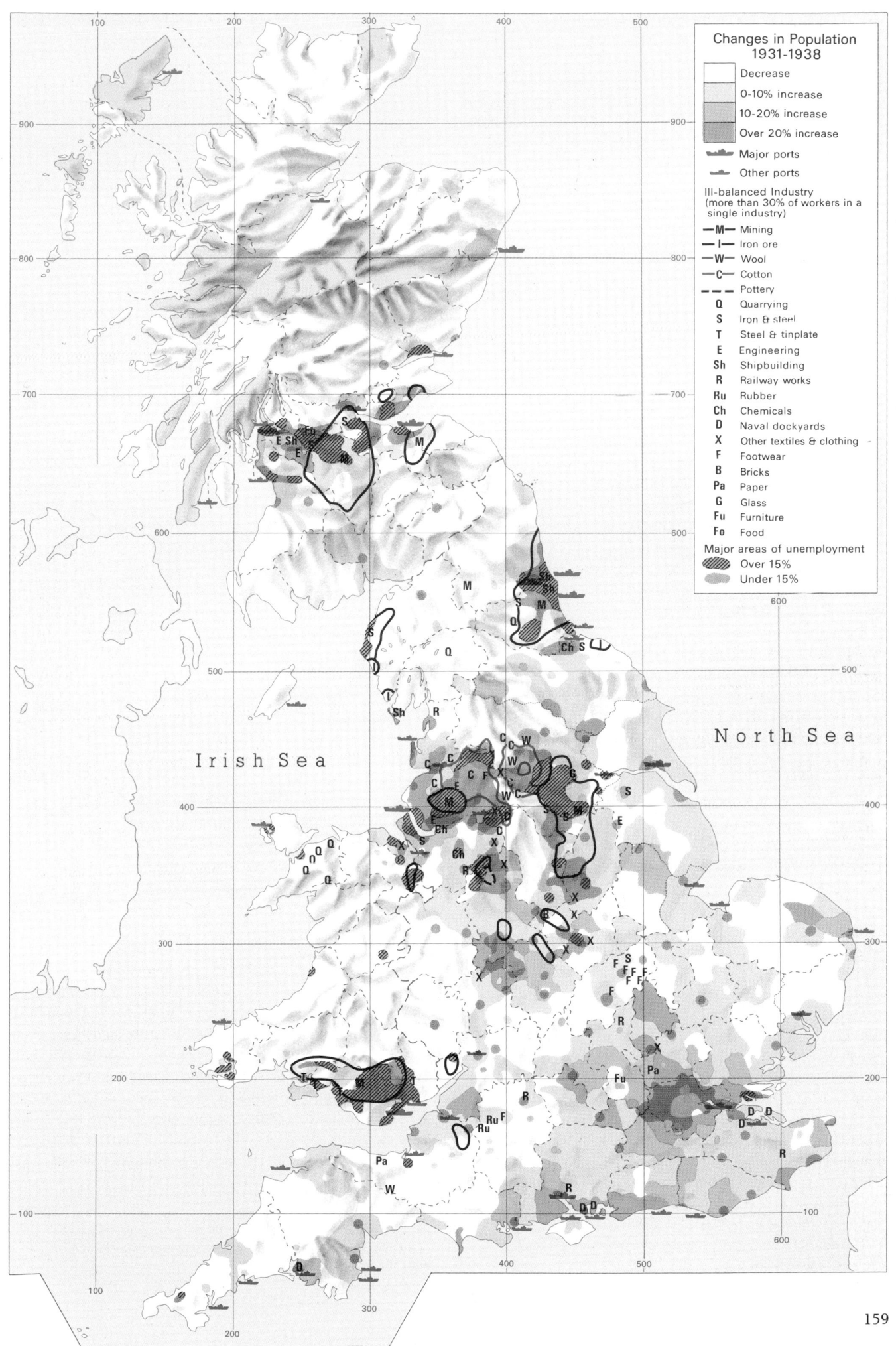

Changes in Population
1931-1938

Decrease
0-10% increase
10-20% increase
Over 20% increase

Major ports
Other ports

Ill-balanced Industry
(more than 30% of workers in a
single industry)

—M— Mining
—I— Iron ore
—W— Wool
—C— Cotton
- - - Pottery
Q   Quarrying
S   Iron & steel
T   Steel & tinplate
E   Engineering
Sh   Shipbuilding
R   Railway works
Ru   Rubber
Ch   Chemicals
D   Naval dockyards
X   Other textiles & clothing
F   Footwear
B   Bricks
Pa   Paper
G   Glass
Fu   Furniture
Fo   Food

Major areas of unemployment
Over 15%
Under 15%

North Sea

Irish Sea

159

established. Motor-car ownership was extending as the Baby Austin and Morris Minor found ready markets. Some new roads were built, among them the Wolverhampton New Road across the derelict land of the Black Country and the North Circular Road linking the industrial areas of north London.

Competition between the railway companies, especially on the routes from London to Scotland, led to the introduction of new and more efficient steam locomotives and reductions in travel times. Air services to the Continent, notably from Croydon, grew in frequency and a network of internal air services was introduced. British passenger liners registered success in the competition for the Atlantic 'Blue Riband'. An Electricity Grid was built, helping, with the rise of road transport and the growth of light industries, to free industry from coal-based locations.

It was the age of suburbia. More than four million houses were built in Britain between the wars, most of them in the suburbs. The better council housing estates attempted to embody Garden City lines with curving, geometrically designed, tree-lined avenues and nearby playing fields and schools. It was a day for the speculative builder and the semi-detached home, increasingly with garage space or garage. There was some ribbon development but more building of estates with local shops and cinema.

Much of this often-criticised housing remains in the 1980s and commands high prices. As cities expanded outwards, trolley-buses and motor-buses began to supplement and then to supersede the electric tram. In Greater London underground lines were extended and Metroland grew in the northwest, backed by the Metropolitan Railway. Such urban sprawl aroused alarm on many counts. These included concern at the growing size and costs of urban growth, concern at the loss for ever of good agricultural land and, under the shadow of Guernica, forebodings about aerial bombardment. And, as the 1930s drew on, the news from the Continent, the increasing pressure of refugees from Nazi Germany and their stories of persecution led increasingly to the conviction that, at least for a time, domestic problems would have to take second place. But even at the worst times of the war preparation for the future of Britain was in progress and the Barlow Report and the Scott Report, together with the Beveridge Report, laid foundations for the planning of the post-war society.

Fuel and Energy Resources

King Coal provided the heat and energy for Britain's Industrial Revolution of the 18th and 19th centuries. Britain's coals are of Carboniferous age: the formerly-wide extent of the Carboniferous rocks has been broken into a number of separate coalfields by subsequent earth movements and by denudation. Except for the anthracite of the western part of the South Wales Coalfield, the coals in Britain are bituminous in type. Considerable variation in coal types exists, from the steam coals of South Wales (formerly so important in the export trade), to the coking coals such as those of Durham, to the general industrial coals which are widespread but best illustrated in the Yorkshire, Nottinghamshire and Derbyshire coalfields (*see maps pages 161 and 162*).

The Northumberland and Durham coalfields were the first to be developed on a large scale, having the advantages of river and sea transport. As demand increased, mining moved from the shallow pits sunk near the outcrops of the main coal seams to deeper pits working seams at depth and through the overlying later rocks on the 'concealed' coalfields. Coal production increased during the 19th century and reached 230 million tons by 1900 and its maximum of 287 million tons in 1913. Of that total about one-third was exported. South Wales produced 57 million tons, Northumberland and Durham 56 million, Yorkshire 44 million, Scotland 42 million, and Nottinghamshire, Derbyshire and Leicestershire 34 million tons.

Production never again rose to such levels. By 1938 total production had fallen to 227 million tons partly as a result of declining exports. Steamships were replaced by oil-fired vessels; production from South Wales was down to 35 million tons (partly due to the decline in steam-coal production), and from Northumberland and Durham to 33 million, though the East Midlands coalfields held stable.

The industry was nationalised in 1947 and the National Coal Board inherited many problems. Geological problems were increasingly encountered and too little investment in new methods and equipment had taken place. There were complex problems of labour relations, arising in part from the diverse local conditions of mining and the past history of management and of variable demand. Nine hundred and fifty collieries existed of which, according to the *Plan for Coal* of 1950, 250 were to be selected for modernisation and reconstruction to yield about 70% of a planned output of 240 million tons. There was now a high demand for coal, in the phase of economic reconstruction after 1945, and before oil began to invade the general market for industrial, railway and household coal. New mines were sunk, mechanical equipment installed and schemes for improved productivity developed. Open-cast working was introduced. The costs of coal production varied widely, being highest in Kent, South Wales, Lancashire, Durham and Scotland and lowest in the East Midlands and Yorkshire. Despite progress there remained until about 1957 a coal 'gap': the industry could not supply enough to meet the country's needs. Of the 221 million tons produced in that year the main users were power stations (46·5 million), industry (37·5 million), domestic users (35·1 million), coke ovens (30·7 million), gas works (26·4 million), and railways (11·4 million).

The change in the industry's position after this date was dramatic. Competition from other sources of energy and improvements in the efficiency of fuel-burning equipment led to declining demand for coal. By 1967 production had fallen to 174 million tons and by 1977 to 120 million. By 1977 the main users were power stations (77·7 million), coke ovens (19·3 million), domestic (10·4 million), industry (9·1 million); the railways had turned to oil and the gas industry had converted to natural gas. Great changes occurred in the geography of coal production as mines in the high-cost coalfields were closed. Now the coalfields of Yorkshire and

Mineral Resources The mining of metals is carried on commercially in a number of locations. The widespread availability of sand and gravel is vital to the construction industry, as is chalk and limestone.

Mineral Resources

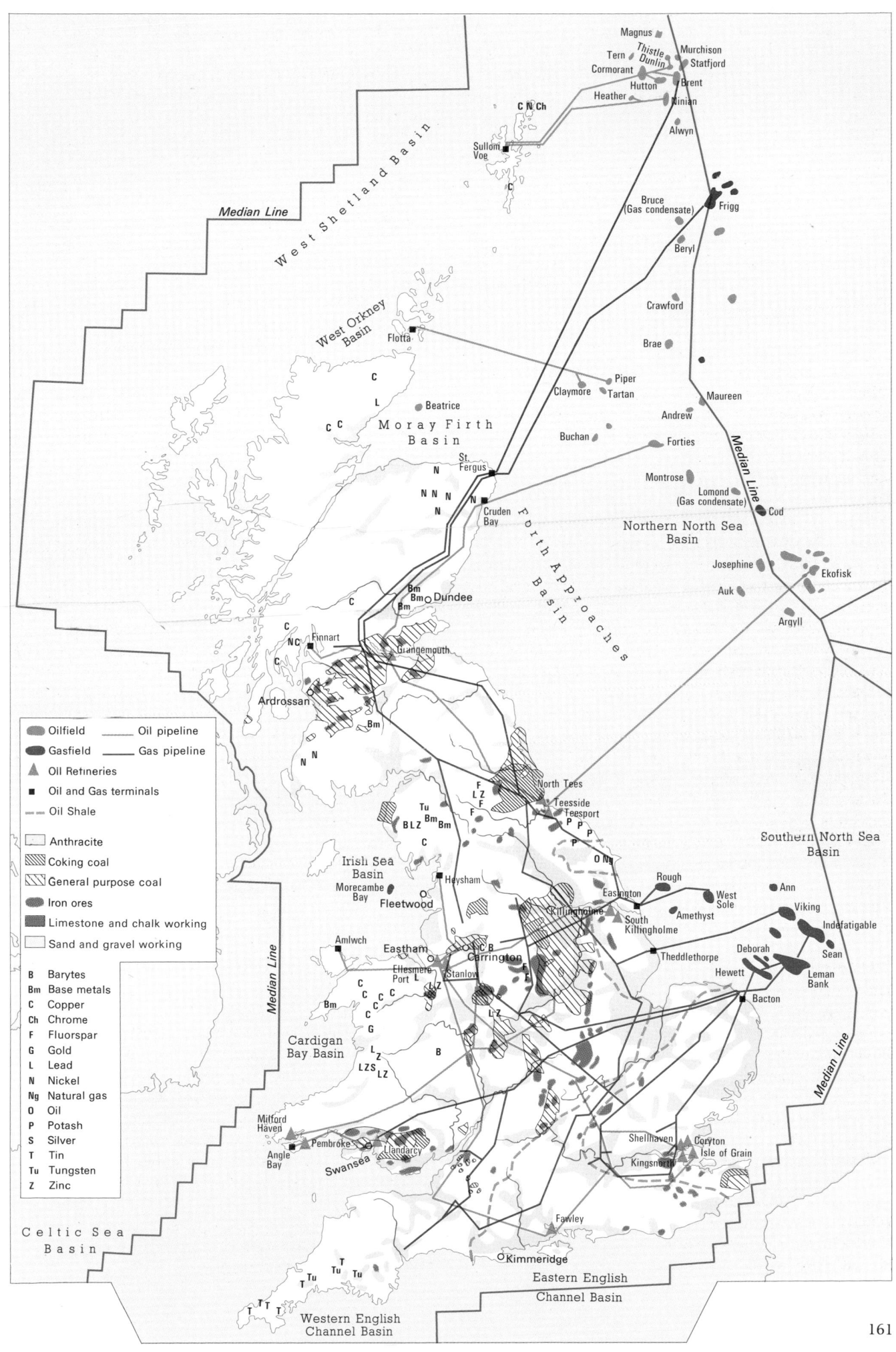

Legend:

- Oilfield
- Gasfield
- Oil Refineries
- Oil and Gas terminals
- Oil Shale
- Oil pipeline
- Gas pipeline

- Anthracite
- Coking coal
- General purpose coal
- Iron ores
- Limestone and chalk working
- Sand and gravel working

B	Barytes
Bm	Base metals
C	Copper
Ch	Chrome
F	Fluorspar
G	Gold
L	Lead
N	Nickel
Ng	Natural gas
O	Oil
P	Potash
S	Silver
T	Tin
Tu	Tungsten
Z	Zinc

West Shetland Basin
Median Line
West Orkney Basin
Moray Firth Basin
Forth Approaches Basin
Northern North Sea Basin
Southern North Sea Basin
Irish Sea Basin
Cardigan Bay Basin
Celtic Sea Basin
Eastern English Channel Basin
Western English Channel Basin

Magnus, Murchison, Statfjord, Thistle, Dunlin, Tern, Cormorant, Hutton, Brent, Heather, Ninian, Alwyn, Bruce (Gas condensate), Frigg, Beryl, Crawford, Brae, Maureen, Piper, Claymore, Tartan, Andrew, Buchan, Forties, Montrose, Lomond (Gas condensate), Cod, Josephine, Ekofisk, Auk, Argyll

Sullom Voe, Flotta, Beatrice, St. Fergus, Cruden Bay, Dundee, Finnart, Grangemouth, Ardrossan, North Tees, Teesside, Teesport, Easington, Rough, West Sole, Ann, Viking, Amethyst, Indefatigable, Sean, Deborah, Leman Bank, Hewett, South Killingholme, Killingholme, Theddlethorpe, Bacton, Heysham, Morecambe Bay, Fleetwood, Amlwch, Eastham, Ellesmere Port, Stanlow, Carrington, Milford Haven, Pembroke, Angle Bay, Swansea, Llandarcy, Shellhaven, Coryton, Isle of Grain, Kingsnorth, Fawley, Kimmeridge

Industry and Energy

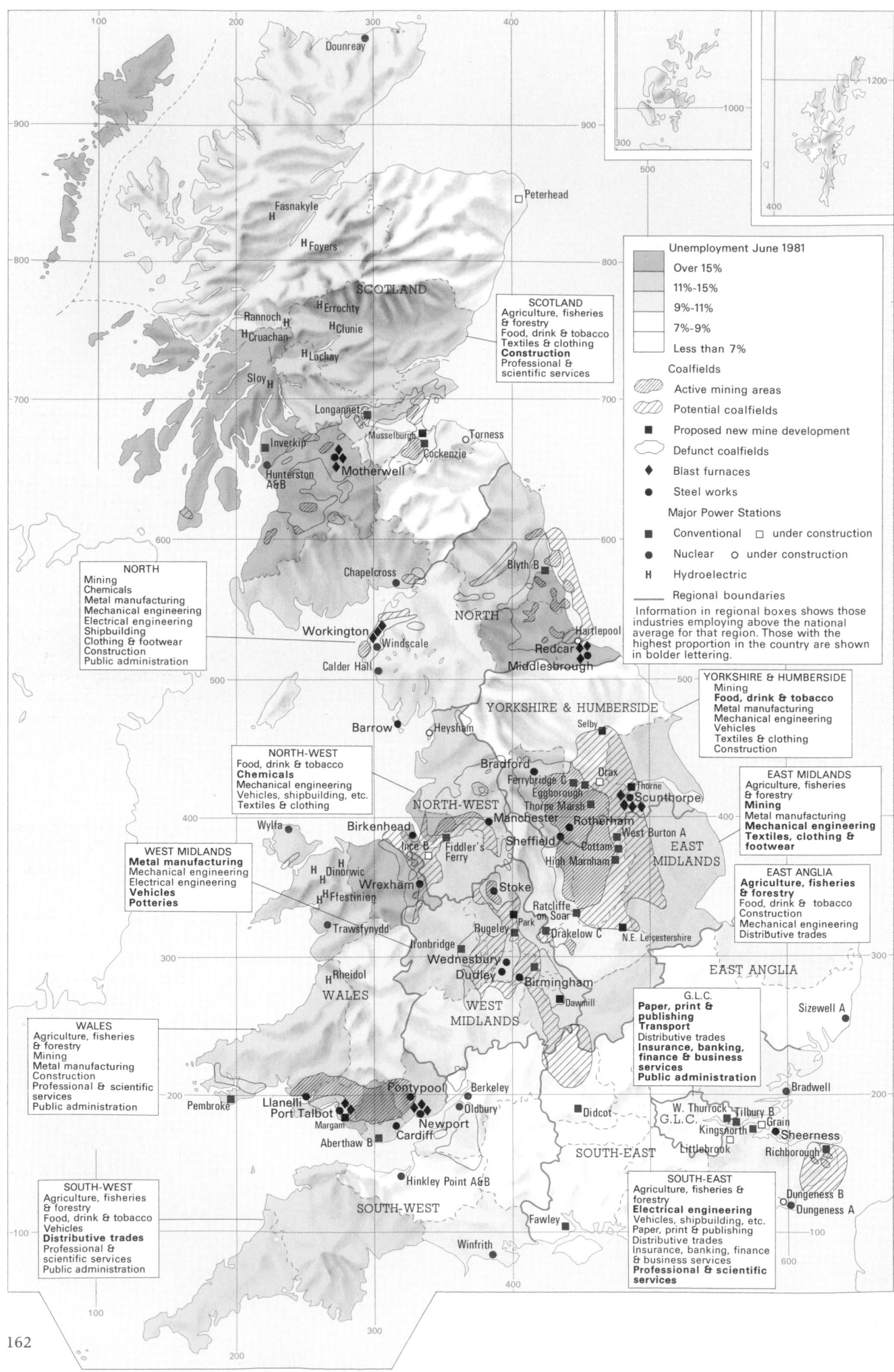

Unemployment June 1981
- Over 15%
- 11%-15%
- 9%-11%
- 7%-9%
- Less than 7%

Coalfields
- Active mining areas
- Potential coalfields
- ■ Proposed new mine development
- Defunct coalfields
- ◆ Blast furnaces
- ● Steel works

Major Power Stations
- ■ Conventional   □ under construction
- ● Nuclear   ○ under construction
- H Hydroelectric
- ── Regional boundaries

Information in regional boxes shows those industries employing above the national average for that region. Those with the highest proportion in the country are shown in bolder lettering.

SCOTLAND
Agriculture, fisheries & forestry
Food, drink & tobacco
Textiles & clothing
Construction
Professional & scientific services

NORTH
Mining
Chemicals
Metal manufacturing
Mechanical engineering
Electrical engineering
Shipbuilding
Clothing & footwear
Construction
Public administration

YORKSHIRE & HUMBERSIDE
Mining
Food, drink & tobacco
Metal manufacturing
Mechanical engineering
Vehicles
Textiles & clothing
Construction

NORTH-WEST
Food, drink & tobacco
Chemicals
Mechanical engineering
Vehicles, shipbuilding, etc.
Textiles & clothing

EAST MIDLANDS
Agriculture, fisheries & forestry
Mining
Metal manufacturing
Mechanical engineering
Textiles, clothing & footwear

WEST MIDLANDS
Metal manufacturing
Mechanical engineering
Electrical engineering
Vehicles
Potteries

EAST ANGLIA
Agriculture, fisheries & forestry
Food, drink & tobacco
Construction
Mechanical engineering
Distributive trades

WALES
Agriculture, fisheries & forestry
Mining
Metal manufacturing
Construction
Professional & scientific services
Public administration

G.L.C.
Paper, print & publishing
Transport
Distributive trades
Insurance, banking, finance & business services
Public administration

SOUTH-WEST
Agriculture, fisheries & forestry
Food, drink & tobacco
Vehicles
Distributive trades
Professional & scientific services
Public administration

SOUTH-EAST
Agriculture, fisheries & forestry
Electrical engineering
Vehicles, shipbuilding, etc.
Paper, print & publishing
Distributive trades
Insurance, banking, finance & business services
Professional & scientific services

162

the East Midlands where costs were lowest and productivity highest produced over one-half of the total. A great local market existed in the thermal electricity generating stations which the Central Electricity Generating Board had erected along the River Trent and the rivers of Yorkshire (*see map page 162*). New reserves have been proved, for example at Selby in Yorkshire, where development is currently in progress, in North-East Leicestershire, where plans for development in the Vale of Belvoir have aroused controversy on environmental grounds, and elsewhere. However, the problem is not so much one of reserves (for there is enough coal for 400-500 years at present rates of production), but of price and convenience. Government strategies for fuel and energy propose an increase in production to about 165 million tons by the end of the century, but doubts have been expressed as to the existence of potential markets for that amount.

The ten years after 1965 saw a revolution in the geography of the UK fuel and power industries. The decline of coal was matched by the rise in importance of natural gas, first imported and then extracted from beneath the North Sea, the development of North Sea oil and the emergence of nuclear power.

The West Sole gas field was found in 1964 and offshore gas production began in 1967. By the early 1970s four major fields Leman, Indefatigable, Hewett and Viking were also in production. Since then, Frigg and Rough have been tapped and natural gas is also produced in association with oil in other fields in the northern North Sea. Four North Sea terminals, Bacton, Theddlethorpe, Easington and St Fergus are linked to the 5600-km (3500-mile) national high-pressure pipe-line system. North Sea gas meets some 81% of total natural gas supplies. Liquefied Natural Gas (LNG) is imported from Algeria to Canvey Island and has higher calorific value than North Sea gas. Further discoveries of natural gas, including the Morecambe field in the Irish Sea, ensure that indigenous production will continue to meet the major part of home needs for the next 30 years at least.

For many years small amounts of oil have been extracted from on-shore fields, notably from Eakring in Nottinghamshire. The discovery of oil in the North Sea in 1969 changed Britain's oil position dramatically, and the first oil flowed ashore in 1975. The scale of investment is indicated by the fact that by the end of 1979, 859 exploration or appraisal wells and 586 development wells had been drilled or begun. The North Sea provides a difficult environment for drilling, with high winds and steep waves, and costs are high. However, the oil is light and of low sulphur content and production is profitable. Among the largest fields in production and reserve are Forties, Brent, Piper and Ninian. Major investments have been made in 1200 km (750 miles) of pipeline and in terminal facilities, notably at Sullom Voe in Shetland. Although Britain still needs to import heavy grades of crude oil these have been

Industry and Energy The listing of major industries derives from regional employment statistics; as industries such as steel become confined to a very few locations, the provision of a wide range of employment regionally becomes important. The areas of potential coalfields shown on the map are exploratory; by no means all are likely to be exploited.

declining and exports have been increasing so that the country has become a net oil exporter.

Our picture of fuel and energy resources must be completed by references to nuclear energy and hydro-electricity (*see map page 162*). Electricity from a nuclear power station (Calder Hall) first entered the Grid in 1956. The commissioning of Berkeley and Bradwell in 1962 marked an important stage in the development of a civil nuclear power programme and 16 stations are now in operation (eleven of which are controlled by the electricity authorities). The government view nuclear energy as a major contributor to the future energy needs of the country and, in addition to the completion of the present construction programme, the search for sites for new stations has now begun. Controversy exists over the scale of the programme required and the best type of system. According to one projection nuclear power stations may provide nearly 20% of electricity generated in Britain by the end of the century.

The contribution of hydro-electricity is mainly in the more remote areas, especially in Scotland. Hydro-electric power supplies only 2% of electricity requirements overall. Most potential sites for other than very small stations have been employed already. Pumped storage schemes have been developed to increase the scale of power stations.

More will be heard of the search for alternative sources of energy. Studies of the possibilities of tidal energy from the Severn estuary have been made. Experiments with wave energy methods have been begun. Investigations into geo-thermal possibilities are in progress. There are advocates of the greater use of wind power. Unfortunately, Britain's climate does not encourage the large-scale development of solar energy even though solar water-heating systems do offer some promise. It will be many years yet before such alternative systems provide other than minor contributions to Britain's needs. Meanwhile there is much to be done in the field of energy conservation.

Industry

Since the end of World War II persistent efforts have been made to influence the location of Britain's industry. The Barlow Commission's Report of 1940 had drawn attention to the problems created by what was regarded as ill-balanced industrial growth in the southeast and the West Midlands, and the narrow industrial structures, declining industries and unemployment in South Wales, Tyneside, Clydeside and the northeast. Measures to remedy the lack of balance and to improve the diversity and the resilience of industries in the Development Areas, as they came to be called, were taken after the war. What has come to be called 'regional policy' developed. There have been, from time to time, changes in the boundaries of the areas delimited as requiring special help; the measures adopted have also varied in kind and in degree. Different governments have given more or less emphasis to regional policy, but the theme has remained a consistent one. Broadly, industrial firms seeking to expand their premises or to build new plant in the southeast and the West Midlands have been subject to control through the need to seek Industrial Development Certificates. Those expanding or establishing themselves in Development Areas have been eligible for various forms of financial assistance.

Industrial estates were built in Development Areas and some factories were constructed in advance of need as a further incentive. The original concept of Development Areas was amended over time, and new designations were introduced. These included Special Development Areas where acute problems, such as the rapid decline in coalmining employment, were judged to merit higher levels of assistance, and Intermediate Areas where lesser benefits were made available after 1969 for areas where employment levels or other signs of sluggish economic performance as well as environment problems such as derelict land, a legacy of previous industry, gave rise to concern.

The assisted areas, taken together, came in the 1970s to include about 40% of the country's employed population; too large a share, in the eyes of some, for regional policy to be really effective. Many attempts have been made to evaluate the economic results, especially in terms of employment creation, of a policy which, despite some variations in practice, carried for a long time a strong political consensus. But policy evaluations of this kind are difficult exercises, even employing sophisticated statistical techniques, for it is impossible to know exactly what would have happened in the absence of such policies. Many studies have made favourable assessments of the effects of the measures taken to encourage job creation. One such study estimates that about 241,000 jobs were created in four large development areas (Scotland, Wales, Northern Ireland, Northern England) in the years 1960-76. By contrast, another suggests that we cannot be absolutely certain that regional policy measures have had any serious effect on the national distribution of industrial activity. The balance of view appears to be that without a regional policy matters would have been considerably worse in the assisted areas.

During the later 1970s, years of increasing unemployment, critical voices have been raised. The high cost of the financial assistance (projected for 1982-83 in the 1978 White Paper as £609 million at 1979 price levels) was pointed out. It was argued that high levels of unemployment were appearing also in certain parts of the so-called growth regions, eg. in Birmingham and east London. The problem, therefore, was to encourage industrial growth and industrial location wherever it could be located. Industrial growth in the southeast should no longer be restricted for here, where scientific research was strongly located, were possibilities for developing science-based industries. And the southeast was well placed in relation to trade with the EEC.

At the time the Barlow Commission reported in 1940, manufacturing industry was, among the various sectors, the major employer of labour. The location of manufacturing industry was thus seen as the key to the location of employment and hence to the distribution of population. But times have changed and employment in manufacturing industry has declined both relatively and actually. By 1980 only 30·4% of Britain's employed workers were engaged in manufacturing, compared with 59·3% in the services group. And location policy had had only a limited effect on the distribution of the servicing industries. Between 1965 and 1980 manufacturing industries shed 1,730,000 workers or 21% of its workforce while jobs in the servicing group went up by 1,950,000.

Some writers refer to this change as a process of 'de-industrialisation', others refer to the 'de-skilling' that has arisen from the decline of jobs in the traditional industries located in the assisted areas. The location of manufacturing industry is no longer such an important factor in the general distribution of population as it once was. And, it is argued, the growth of multi-national corporations has placed decisions affecting important British industries in inter-national, rather than national, hands.

A re-interpretation of regional policy in 1979 was intended to lead to substantial savings in expenditure in 1982-83. To achieve this, the plan was to reduce the areas eligible for assistance to include only about 25% of the employed population. Changes have been made in the status of some areas, for example, Wrexham, Kilmarnock and Ayr which assume Special Development Area status. Between 1980 and 1982 the map shows a significant reduction of the intermediate areas (*see map page 173*). Levels of financial assistance show a similar reduction. The new policy rests also on generating local enterprise, and the establishment of 'enterprise zones' in Tyneside, Clydeside, Merseyside, Manchester, Swansea, Dudley and London has been announced. Certain controls are relaxed and financial assistance given.

The emphasis so far has been on the effects of regional policy to influence industrial location. But there are many other ways in which governments influence industrial location. Some basic industries, like steel, are nationalised: the re-organisation of the steel industry in the late 1970s led to the closure of many plants (eg. Consett, Shelton, Bilston and Corby) and to substantial reductions in the labour force (*see map page 162*). Other industries such as cotton textiles and tinplate have been re-organised with help provided under Acts of Parliament. Since 1966 government bodies (currently the National Enterprise Board) have assisted rationalisation plans, have promoted new ventures and have held share-holdings in many companies. The list of industries in which the government has become involved is long. In addition to those already mentioned it includes shipbuilding, the motor-car industry, machine tools, the aerospace industries, not to mention oil, gas and electricity. Government decisions are also potent influences on the defence industries and on employment in the construction industry.

In recent years the trend towards an economy based on 'service industry' has continued. It has become clear that the 'regional problem', already discussed, is only one aspect of the changes in progress. There has also been a strong de-centralisation of employment from most of the major conurbations to the outer parts of the city regions and to medium and small towns and some rural areas. In the period 1971-77, for example, employment in the Greater London Conurbation declined by 6·6% or 282,000 persons, that in Merseyside by 8·7%, Clydeside by 3·1% and the West Midlands by 2·6%. By contrast, rates of growth in many medium-sized and small cities and towns were of the order of 10 to 13%.

Behind such changes lies the general problem of the decline in the total number of jobs, especially those for men. Male full-time employment declined by over 445,000 in the

years 1971-77, and although there has been a substantial growth in the number of part-time jobs for women, unemployment has become a major issue. In 1965 the general unemployment level was of the order of 1·5%: in 1982 it was over 11%. Some writers have given a picture, in this unhappy situation, of growing regional economic convergence with a more even distribution of employment than in 1965 (*see map page 162*). 'Big industrial areas such as the South-east, North West and West Midlands,' writes one, 'have declined rapidly relative to small rural or peripheral regions such as East Anglia, the South West, Wales and Northern England.' The appearance of unemployment rates in the West Midlands at levels almost as high as in some development areas has certainly come as an unwelcome shock to an area long renowned for its growth.

So the problems have become more complex than was formerly assumed. To the continuing problem of the development areas created by structural decline of employment in basic and long established industries must be added the changes created by declining employment in other manufacturing industries such as the motor-car and related industries. There have been, too, shifts from big cities to smaller ones, a large-scale decentralisation which has left behind problems of regenerating employment in inner cities. Particular local problems, such as that in East London arising from the closure of the docks, add to the complexity.

What will happen when the industrial recession, which has adversely affected industry and employment since 1974, fades and growth begins again? Probably large-scale unemployment will not disappear quickly. Those industries will benefit that have improved their productivity and international competitiveness. Science- and high-level engineering-based industries, many of which have survived and made progress, should grow further, but they are not mass employers of labour. Those service industries which are often termed 'quaternary industries', demanding high skills and providing international services, have also done well and should strengthen their position. There is great skill and much experience available and the development of imaginative education and re-training schemes could maximise the exploitation of future possibilities for the expansion of the economy.

Transport

'Good roads, canals and navigable rivers by diminishing the expenses of carriage put the remote parts of the country more nearly on a level with those in the neighbourhood of the town. They are upon that account the greatest of all improvements.' So wrote the great economist Adam Smith at the time of the Transport Revolution of the 18th century. However, it may be questioned whether the re-shaping of the British transport system in the past 30 years has had the same effect. It is arguable that recent improvements have emphasised the accessibility of places within the main inter-city network to the relative detriment of the more remote areas, and have worked to the advantage of some, and the disadvantage of other, groups of people.

The British economy depends upon an intensively developed efficient transport network for the rapid movement of people and goods between the principal industrial regions. About 60% of freight traffic is generated by or received in the 'axial belt' extending from Kent to Lancashire. The transport industries are themselves major employers with some 2·75 million people employed in transport and in industries like the manufacture and repair of motor-cars, railway vehicles and aircraft.

Changes in the use of the different modes of transport and technical changes have, at least over the most densely populated parts of the country, made for speed of transport and communication between cities. In terms of inland transport, road transport is now of the first importance. About 80% of all passenger travel is made by private car: there are some 14·3 million motor-cars in Britain. Over 80% of inland freight, by tonnage (two-thirds of tonne-kilometres), is carried by road. To meet the problems of congestion on roads that are among the most crowded in the world a major improvement programme was initiated in 1955 and the motorway and improved trunk road network is the product of this. About 2400 km (1500 miles) of motorway have been constructed. Many motorways, together with the improved A1(M), focus on London, around which the M25 is now under construction. From the M1/M6 junction in the east Midlands motorways extend northwards on both sides of the Pennines. The system extends into south Wales and southwest to Exeter. The midland valley of Scotland has its own network. Except for the M25 and the extension of the M40 towards Birmingham, few new major motorways are now planned; attention in road improvement will be given to congested roads to ports and to new roads, including by-passes, that will improve the environment of towns and villages. For much of the existing road network originated in the 18th and early 19th centuries. Towns grew around roads: now we are trying to take traffic around towns. But despite the introduction of traffic management schemes, problems of traffic congestion remain in the main cities, especially London. Birmingham's Inner Ring Road is one successful example of a major new road development within a major city.

About 11% of passenger transport is accounted for by buses and coaches. This is a significant decline since 1960. Much however has been done to improve the organisation of public transport services in the metropolitan counties and express bus services ply busily between the main cities.

The railway map exhibits a most dramatic re-shaping. A modernisation scheme of 1955 was overtaken by the Beeching Report of 1963 which brought subsequent closure of lines and stations and withdrawal of stopping train and local services on many other lines. The railway network has been reduced by about one-third to 17,973 km (11,168 miles) by the end of the 1970s. In 1962 there were 4347 stations open; ten years later this number had fallen to 2362. The emphasis has been on improving the inter-city services. The main-line permanent way has been re-laid and 3767 km (2341 miles) of line is electrified. The Inter-City 125 services, first introduced in 1976, are the world's fastest diesel rail services, amid other notable improvements (the Advanced Passenger Train came into service in late 1981). Less has been done to improve suburban services although, notably, the Tyne and Wear Metro was opened in 1980. Policy for freight has concentrated on long-distance and bulk traffic.

The Transport System

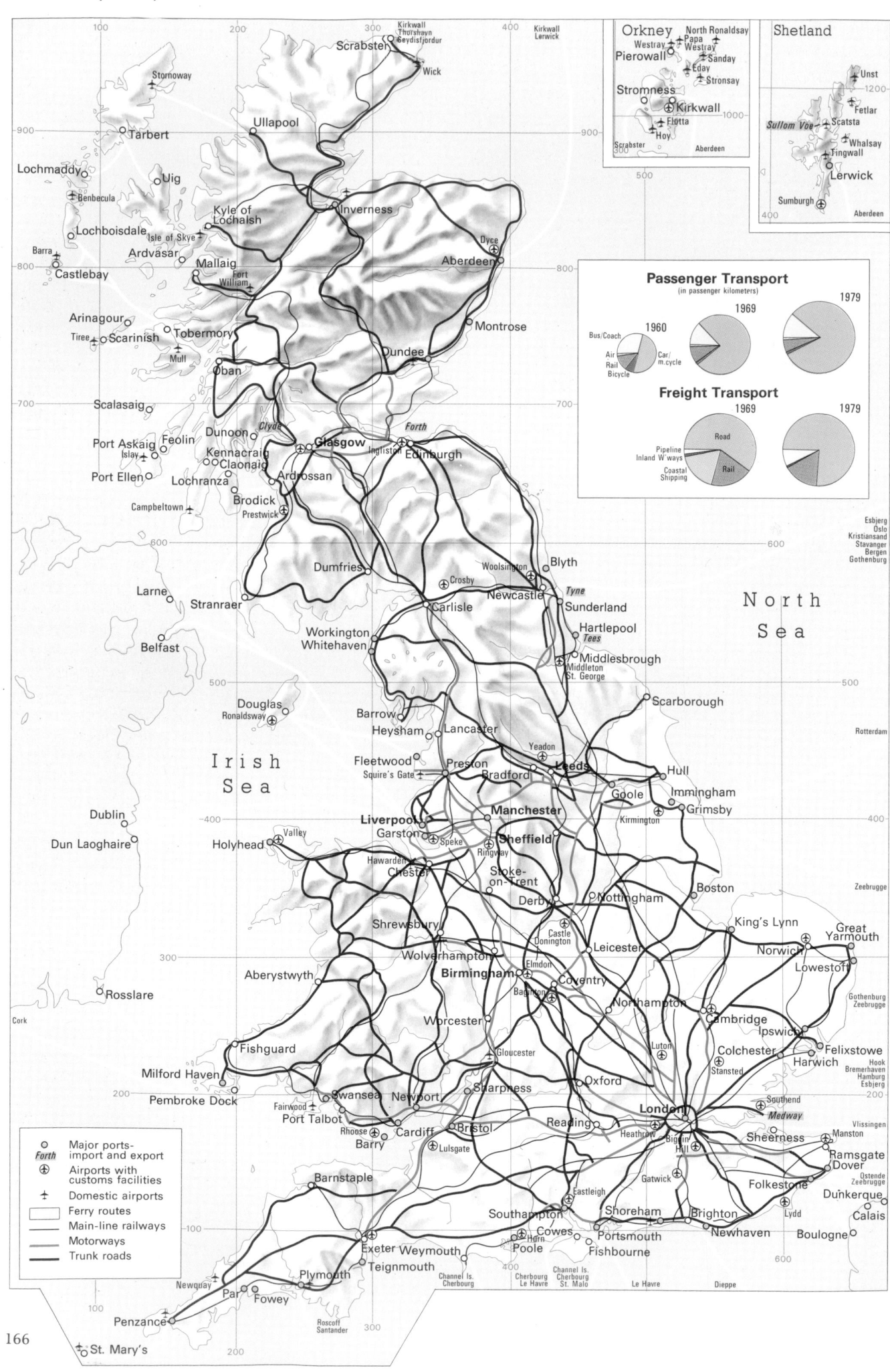

Passenger Transport
(in passenger kilometers)

1960   1969   1979

Bus/Coach
Air
Rail
Bicycle
Car/m.cycle

Freight Transport

1969   1979

Pipeline
Inland W'ways
Coastal Shipping
Road
Rail

Legend

- ○ Major ports–import and export
- *Forth* Airports with customs facilities
- ⊕ Airports with customs facilities
- ✝ Domestic airports
- Ferry routes
- Main-line railways
- Motorways
- Trunk roads

Orkney

Westray, North Ronaldsay, Papa Westray, Sanday, Eday, Stronsay, Pierowall, Stromness, Kirkwall, Flotta, Hoy, Scrabster, Aberdeen

Shetland

Unst, Fetlar, Scatsta, Whalsay, Sullom Voe, Tingwall, Lerwick, Sumburgh, Aberdeen

Esbjerg
Oslo
Kristiansand
Stavanger
Bergen
Gothenburg

North Sea

Rotterdam

Zeebrugge

Gothenburg
Zeebrugge

Hook
Bremerhaven
Hamburg
Esbjerg

Vlissingen

Ostende
Zeebrugge

Irish Sea

Place names

Kirkwall, Thorshavn, Seydisfjordur, Scrabster, Wick, Stornoway, Ullapool, Tarbert, Lochmaddy, Uig, Benbecula, Kyle of Lochalsh, Inverness, Dyce, Aberdeen, Lochboisdale, Isle of Skye, Ardvasar, Barra, Mallaig, Fort William, Castlebay, Montrose, Arinagour, Tobermory, Tiree, Scarinish, Mull, Dundee, Oban, Scalasaig, Dunoon, Clyde, Forth, Glasgow, Inglinston, Edinburgh, Port Askaig, Feolin, Islay, Kennacraig, Claonaig, Ardrossan, Port Ellen, Lochranza, Brodick, Prestwick, Campbeltown, Larne, Dumfries, Woolsington, Blyth, Stranraer, Crosby, Newcastle, Tyne, Carlisle, Sunderland, Belfast, Workington, Whitehaven, Hartlepool, Tees, Middlesbrough, Middleton St. George, Scarborough, Douglas, Ronaldsway, Barrow, Heysham, Lancaster, Yeadon, Dublin, Fleetwood, Preston, Leeds, Hull, Dun Laoghaire, Squire's Gate, Bradford, Holyhead, Valley, Manchester, Goole, Immingham, Liverpool, Garston, Speke, Kirmington, Grimsby, Hawarden, Ringway, Sheffield, Chester, Stoke-on-Trent, Boston, Derby, Nottingham, Shrewsbury, Castle Donington, King's Lynn, Great Yarmouth, Aberystwyth, Wolverhampton, Leicester, Norwich, Lowestoft, Elmdon, Birmingham, Coventry, Baginton, Northampton, Cambridge, Ipswich, Worcester, Luton, Colchester, Felixstowe, Gloucester, Harwich, Fishguard, Milford Haven, Sharpness, Oxford, Stansted, Pembroke Dock, Swansea, Newport, Fairwood, Port Talbot, Bristol, Reading, London, Southend, Medway, Rhoose, Cardiff, Heathrow, Sheerness, Manston, Barry, Lulsgate, Biggin Hill, Ramsgate, Dover, Barnstaple, Gatwick, Folkestone, Dunkerque, Eastleigh, Shoreham, Brighton, Lydd, Calais, Southampton, Cowes, Newhaven, Boulogne, Horn, Portsmouth, Exeter, Weymouth, Poole, Fishbourne, Teignmouth, Channel Is. Cherbourg, Plymouth, Le Havre, St. Malo, Dieppe, Newquay, Par, Fowey, Roscoff, Santander, Penzance, St. Mary's

166

Coal and coke, iron and steel and petroleum products are the most important commodities carried.

Britain's seaports have always played a crucial role in its economic development handling imported materials for manufacture and the exported manufactures. The scale of British seaborne trade, as measured by tonne-kilometres, has declined since 1973, partly because of the economic recession, and partly through the decrease in crude oil imports and the increasing share of European (that is, short-distance) trade. London remains the leading sea-port though many of its older docks have now closed and much traffic is handled at Tilbury. Milford Haven has been the leading oil port but is being overtaken by Sullom Voe in Shetland. The handling of North Sea oil has increased the trade of Tees, Forth and Flotta, in Orkney. Tees, Immingham, Port Talbot and Clyde handle imported ores. Recent developments include the growth of container and roll-on traffic which has more than trebled since 1969, especially at Dover, Felix-stowe, Tilbury, Southampton and Hull.

Inland waterways are much less important to the economy than in the days of the Industrial Revolution. Some of the old narrow canals have been closed; others are used by recreational craft. But the wider and deeper canals of Yorkshire and Humberside remain important and development of certain canals, such as that between Doncaster and Rotherham, and their re-equipment with push-tow barge trains are significant recent developments. The 58-km long (36-mile) Manchester Ship Canal remains important for ocean-going vessels.

Not the least important of recent changes in the transport network has been the construction of pipelines for the carriage of crude oil, petroleum products and natural gas (see map page 161). More than 570 km (350 miles) of submarine pipeline link the North Sea oilfields with the refineries and oil ports. Pipeline systems also carry refined products and natural gas to inland markets: one of the longest is the 500-km (300-mile) pipeline from Milford Haven to the Midlands and Manchester.

Of all the developments that illustrate the impact of technical change that of air transport stands out. The siting of Britain's airports reflects many circumstances, including the needs of the RAF in the face of threats from continental Europe, decisions by local authorities and the location of the markets for air traffic. Except for London, there has been little co-ordination in airport development. Plans for new airports such as the Third London Airport arouse high controversy especially on environmental grounds. A hierarchy of airports may be discerned ranging from major international (Heathrow) through those operating medium- and short-haul international and domestic services, those operating charter services, to the small airports with limited facilities mainly serving regional needs. Although much discussion of air transport is in terms of passenger movements, its contribution to freight transport should not be overlooked. Only about 1% of Britain's overseas trade measured by weight is carried by air but this amounts to more than 15% by value. This is heavily concentrated at London, which in terms of the value of freight handled is now Britain's leading port.

Many tasks remain, for example the Channel Tunnel, but the modernisation of the transport system has been a remarkable achievement. The Severn, Forth and Humber bridges, the High Speed Train, the Advanced Passenger Train, the Victoria and Jubilee Lines of London Transport, the North Sea pipelines are symbols of the change. But many argue that the changes which have been designed to link the major industrial areas and to promote resource development and trade have left many rural areas relatively worse off than before, bereft of railway services and with reduced bus services. Also relatively worse off are those like the poor and the elderly who do not own private transport and have been affected by reduced public transport services. But the problem in part reflects the shape of Britain and the concentration of its population. It is theoretically possible to devise a basic route network for a road or railway system of only 1550 km (970 miles) which would reach to within 9 km of half the population and a more extended network of 2800 km (1750 miles) to reach 70%. But to serve the most remote 30% an additional network of over 6000 km (3750 miles) would be required.

Planning for Land

One of the most fruitful aspects of planning since the 1939-45 war has been the care that has been taken over the use of the land of Britain. Although cities and urban life styles have spread outwards, our countryside, though not unchanged, retains its variety and its beauty, even though it provides more and more for the food, water and leisure of the urban population. The Committee on Land Utilisation in Rural Areas (the Scott Committee) in 1942 had expressed concern at the spread of cities over the countryside, and its recommendations provided pathways for fresh thinking and eventual legislation. Such a pathway led, after much discussion, to the National Parks and Access to the Countryside Act of 1949, applying to England and Wales (see map page 172). The National Parks protect some of the most exceptionally beautiful areas of the countryside: they also provide for access and enjoyment by the general public. In so highly developed a country as Britain, it was impossible to draw boundaries around such areas without also including large numbers of towns and villages—and so the National Parks also include the working environments of the communities within them. Out of this situation, many conflicts have developed on such questions as the emphasis that should be given to the preservation of scenery and wild life and how far development such as new limestone quarries in the Peak District, a new trunk road through the Lake District, minerals exploration in Snowdonia, should be permitted. In Scotland a different scheme was adopted, with the establishment of Forest Parks, and the Forestry Commission there as well as in some English forests has done much to improve the compatibility of tree production and the growing demand for recreation. The problems that exist over the objectives of National Parks should not be allowed to cloud the great benefits which the public have gained from the measures taken both to protect the parks and to display their individually distinctive characteristics.

It is not only in National Parks that special care is taken over new development. There are also 33 Areas of Outstanding Natural Beauty in England and Wales (9% of

Agriculture and Fisheries

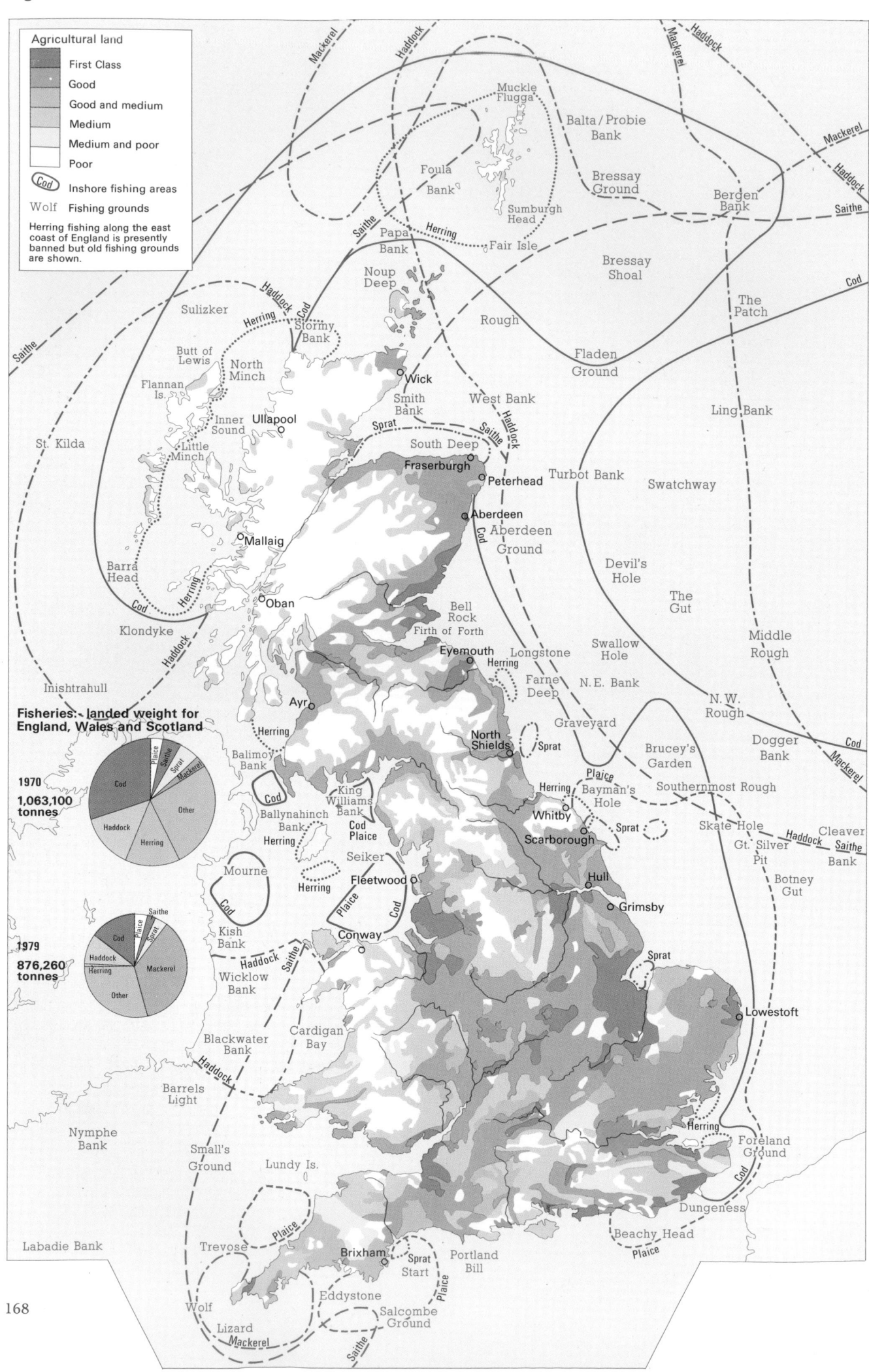

Agricultural land
- First Class
- Good
- Good and medium
- Medium
- Medium and poor
- Poor

(Cod) Inshore fishing areas
Wolf Fishing grounds

Herring fishing along the east coast of England is presently banned but old fishing grounds are shown.

Fisheries: landed weight for England, Wales and Scotland

1970 — 1,063,100 tonnes

1979 — 876,260 tonnes

Mackerel • Haddock • Mackerel • Haddock • Mackerel • Haddock • Saithe • Cod

Mackerel • Mackerel
Saithe • Saithe

Saithe

Haddock • Cod • Noup Deep

Sulizker • Herring • Stormy Bank • West Bank • Rough • The Patch

Balta / Probie Bank
Bressay Ground
Bergen Bank
Bressay Shoal
Foula Bank
Muckle Flugga
Sumburgh Head
Fair Isle
Papa Bank
Herring

Fladen Ground
Ling Bank

Butt of Lewis • North Minch • Smith Bank
Flannan Is. • Inner Sound • Ullapool • Wick
St. Kilda • Little Minch • South Deep • Turbot Bank • Swatchway
Fraserburgh • Peterhead • Aberdeen • Aberdeen Ground
Devil's Hole • The Gut
Mallaig • Oban • Bell Rock • Firth of Forth
Barra Head • Eyemouth • Longstone • Swallow Hole • Middle Rough
Klondyke • Haddock • Herring • Farne Deep • N.E. Bank • N. W. Rough
Inishtrahull • Graveyard • Dogger Bank
Ayr • Herring • North Shields • Sprat • Brucey's Garden • Southernmost Rough
Balimoy Bank • Plaice • Bayman's Hole • Skate Hole • Cleaver Bank
King Williams Bank • Herring • Whitby • Sprat • Gt. Silver Pit • Saithe
Ballynahinch Bank • Cod Plaice • Scarborough • Botney Gut
Herring • Seiker • Hull
Mourne • Herring • Fleetwood • Grimsby
Plaice • Cod
Kish Bank • Conway • Sprat
Haddock • Saithe
Wicklow Bank
Blackwater Bank • Cardigan Bay • Lowestoft
Barrels Light • Haddock
Nymphe Bank • Lundy Is. • Herring • Foreland Ground
Small's Ground
Labadie Bank • Trevose • Plaice • Brixham • Sprat Start • Portland Bill • Beachy Head • Plaice
Wolf • Eddystone • Salcombe Ground • Cod • Dungeness
Lizard • Mackerel • Saithe

168

Farming Types

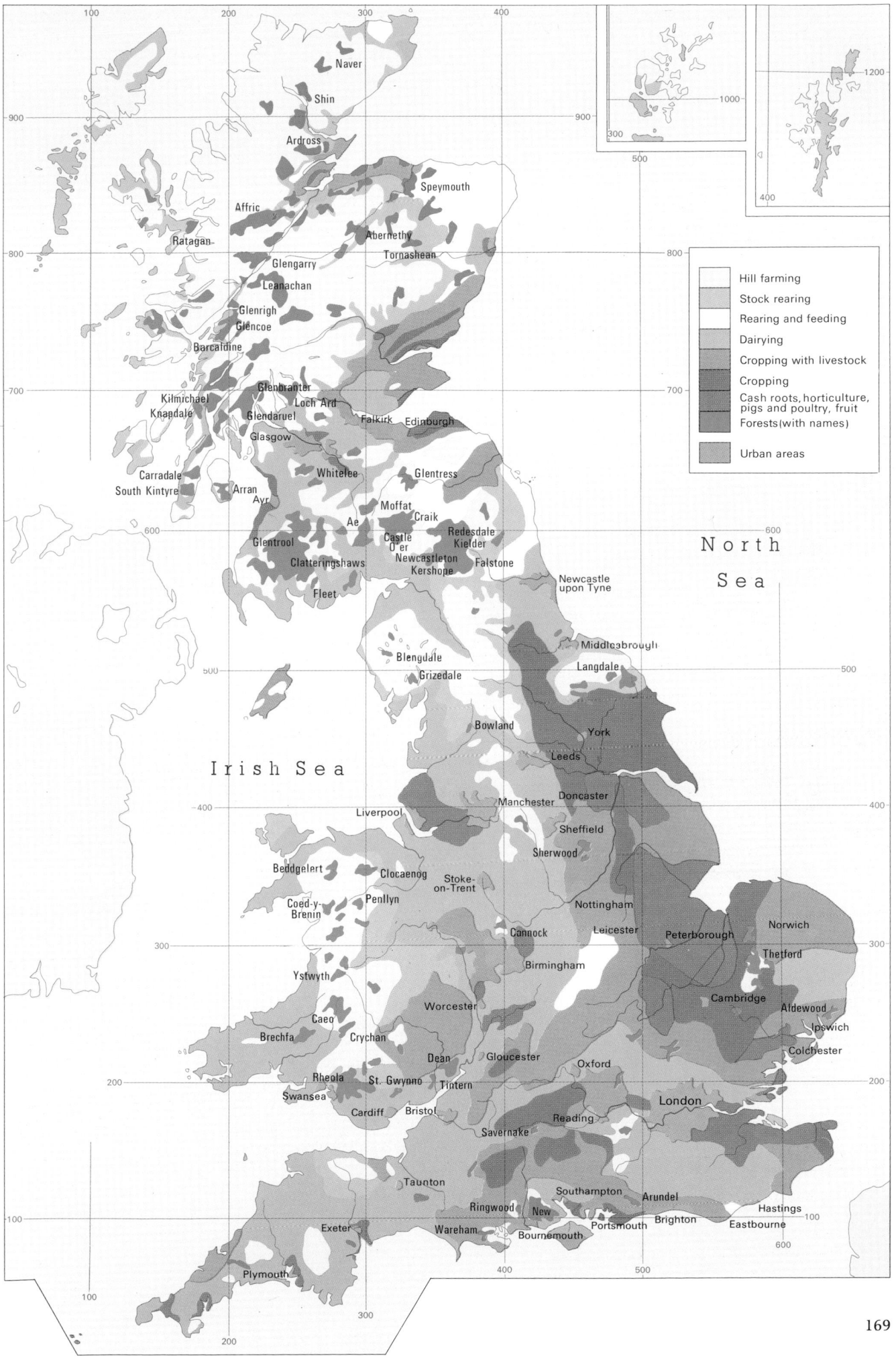

Legend:
- Hill farming
- Stock rearing
- Rearing and feeding
- Dairying
- Cropping with livestock
- Cropping
- Cash roots, horticulture, pigs and poultry, fruit
- Forests (with names)
- Urban areas

North Sea

Irish Sea

Naver
Shin
Ardross
Speymouth
Affric
Abernethy
Ratagan
Tornashean
Glengarry
Leanachan
Glenrigh
Glencoe
Barcaldine
Glenbranter
Kilmichael
Loch Ard
Knapdale
Glendaruel
Glasgow
Falkirk
Edinburgh
Whitelee
Glentress
Carradale
South Kintyre
Arran
Ayr
Moffat
Ae
Craik
Glentrool
Castle O'er
Redesdale
Kielder
Clatteringshaws
Newcastleton
Kershope
Falstone
Fleet
Newcastle upon Tyne
Middlesbrough
Langdale
Blengdale
Grizedale
Bowland
York
Leeds
Doncaster
Liverpool
Manchester
Sheffield
Sherwood
Beddgelert
Clocaenog
Stoke-on-Trent
Coed-y-Brenin
Penllyn
Nottingham
Leicester
Cannock
Peterborough
Norwich
Birmingham
Thetford
Ystwyth
Worcester
Cambridge
Aldewood
Caeo
Ipswich
Brechfa
Crychan
Colchester
Dean
Gloucester
Oxford
Rheola
St. Gwynno
Tintern
London
Swansea
Cardiff
Bristol
Reading
Savernake
Taunton
Southampton
Arundel
Ringwood
New
Hastings
Exeter
Wareham
Portsmouth
Brighton
Eastbourne
Bournemouth
Plymouth

the area) including areas such as the Shropshire hills, the Cotswolds, the Chilterns and the North and South Downs (*see map page 172*). Great progress has also been made in delimiting Heritage Coasts where development is carefully controlled by local authorities. Long-distance footpaths have been signposted and offer splendid opportunities alike for the serious walker and for the gentle stroller.

The need was later seen, and provided for in the Countryside Act of 1968, for recreational access to the smaller but often very lovely areas near to the main cities. By 1977 over 140 Country Parks and 180 Picnic Sites had been established, mainly by local authorities, with the aid of grants from the Countryside Commission for England and Wales. There is a similar, but separate, Commission for Scotland and its plans, based on the distinct landscape characteristics of Scotland and embodying a somewhat different approach from that adopted south of the border, also deserve careful study.

The Scott Committee also argued that good-quality agricultural land should not be used for urban development when land of lesser quality was available. In order to define the extent of the areas of good-, medium- and low-quality farmland a number of land classification schemes have been produced (*see map page 168*). Generally these gradings take account principally of physical conditions such as aspect, height, climate, soil type and drainage conditions but the quality of management is also an important consideration. At present the Ministry of Agriculture recognises five main grades of land and these gradings are used in planning decisions, such as those about urban growth or the lines selected for trunk roads. The amount of truly first-class land is small, about 3% of the total for England and Wales. Grade 2 land, which has minor limitations of soil texture, soil depth or drainage, accounts for about 15%. Including the better areas of Grade 3 (land with moderate limitations) it may be reckoned that about one-third of the agricultural area of England and Wales is of reasonably good quality. Grade 3 land is in fact of diverse qualities ranging from quite good to rather poor and the whole category includes 49% of the total land area. Grades 4 and 5 (poor land) account for a further one-third of England and Wales.

Taken with what has been written in the Introduction about climatic conditions, it will be seen that farming in Britain has to contend with a very diverse range of conditions. Generally speaking the farming patterns that result (*see map page 169*) represent a sophisticated adjustment to physical conditions, to market demands and to changing agricultural technology. Taken overall Britain is a country of mixed farming: the main arable areas are found mainly in the east and some parts of the Midlands and southern England. By contrast, in the west, where rainfall and relief make arable cropping difficult, grassland for livestock production predominates. The hill areas are very valuable for the production of young livestock.

There are about 270,000 farming units in the United Kingdom. However, many of these are part-time holdings and a recent estimate of the number of *bona fide* farm businesses puts the number at about 166,000, with an average overall size of 101 HA (250 acres). Less than a quarter employ more than four farm workers and the

number of regular farm workers has dropped from about 700,000 in 1946 to about 200,000 today. Of all the countries of Western Europe, Britain has the smallest percentage of its population engaged in agriculture. Output per man is high. Some 2·7% of the country's labour force produce two-thirds of the country's needs of temperate foodstuffs.

In part this happy situation is the product of greatly improved technology. The 350,000 horses who worked on farms in 1950 have almost all been replaced by machines. Farming has become capital- and energy-related. About one million tonnes of nitrogen fertilisers are applied to the land each year. Chemical pesticides have played their part. The farming industry has become much more closely related to manufacturing industry and rural-urban interdependence has, in this respect, been intensified.

A second factor behind this position is the support received from the State. After World War II the Government declared its intention to foster a healthy, prosperous and efficient agriculture and under the Agriculture Act of 1948 the Minister of Agriculture supported farmers by deficiency payments on certain commodities, as well as by grants and subsidies of various kinds. The system changed when Britain entered the EEC. Under the Common Agricultural Policy the farmers' prices are maintained by EEC intervention in the marketplace. Argument exists over the Common Agricultural Policy and its effects and it is probably in British interests to obtain changes in its operation. Nevertheless, the general climate of political support for farming in the post-war period has created a climate in agriculture in which 'the catalogue of achievement has grown by the day'.

While many rejoice in the achievements of the industry, others count the cost of change. Many small farms have been amalgamated into larger holdings. In many parts of the country woodlands and hedgerows have been removed, downland and moorland have been ploughed up, and the loss of wild landscape and wildlife is the result. Some complain that too much continuous cropping may eventually affect adversely the quality of the land, others attack factory farming and the over-use of fertilisers. The controversies were well brought out in Parliamentary debates on the Wildlife and Countryside Act (1981).

The argument may be extended to the fate of villages and rural communities. Some have lost population; churches and shops have closed and public transport services have been reduced or withdrawn. Others, nearer the great cities, have been overwhelmed by the influx of newcomers with urban ways of life, jobs in the city and homes in the countryside. The nature of change varies from area to area. But while the agricultural industry has its critics and while not all that has been done in its name may have been wise, it must be admitted that it has contributed greatly to the maintenance of the British countryside and to the improvement of the British economy.

Planning for the Environment and Regional Change

Several schemes for the future welfare and development of Britain were produced during and immediately after World War II. These included plans for the re-development of cities, many of which had been badly damaged by war-time

bombing and where inherited housing problems existed, plans for the more equitable distribution of industry and employment between the regions, and plans for the rural environment, including conservation of the scenic environment and the future prosperity of agriculture.

The Greater London Plan (1944) by Sir Patrick Abercrombie is a leading example of post-war planning. As was generally thought at the time, it assumed that population would not greatly increase: the problem was the re-distribution of people rather than of growth. It embodied the desire to prevent urban sprawl and to contain the growth of cities and employed the idea of a Green Belt on to which the London conurbation would not expand. The re-building of the bomb-damaged and the poor-quality housing of inner London was a priority. However, to accomplish lower densities and with more open space, it would be necessary to move large numbers of families and jobs out of London and New Towns were to be built for this purpose. The problems of the great city had to be solved on a regional scale. Abercrombie's ideas were applied for Greater London with modifications in detail and the eight New Towns which were begun, Crawley, Bracknell, Hemel Hempstead, Hatfield, Welwyn Garden City, Stevenage, Harlow and Basildon provided exciting opportunities for architects and town planners (*see map page 173*). Not all the New Towns built then and later have been equally successful and criticisms can be made with hindsight. Nevertheless the post-war New Towns are widely regarded as an achievement for British town planning.

Such ideas of regional-scale planning were not at first adopted so readily in other urban regions, such as in Manchester and Birmingham. However, much was done, especially in Birmingham, to demolish slums and to build a new inner-urban environment with an inner ring road, new housing areas and more green spaces. New Towns were begun also at Corby (Northamptonshire), Newton Aycliffe and Peterlee in the northeast, Cwmbran (south Wales) and East Kilbride, Glenrothes and Cumbernauld in Scotland.

The Town and Country Planning Act (1947) provided powers for local authorities on development control and land-use change. Green Belts were delimited around the conurbations and other cities of special quality.

The 1950s brought a changed situation. Population grew by 5% between 1951 and 1961 and the extra numbers had to be provided for. While, for the time being at least, employment remained concentrated in cities, people began to move their houses to towns and villages beyond the Green Belts. Widespread ownership of motor cars brought more flexibility in movements to work. Supplementary schemes were needed. Around London, 'expanded' towns like Ashford, Thetford and Bletchley were added to the New Towns programme. Cities like Birmingham, constrained by local authority boundaries, had to look outside their boundaries for housing land, and found themselves in conflict with the surrounding county councils. The decentralisation of population from major cities became a still more obvious phenomenon in the 1960s, accompanied now by a relative decentralisation of jobs. The older urban pattern of compact cities was changing into a pattern of 'city regions'. A second wave of New Town construction was

embarked upon involving the building, usually on a larger scale than in the first wave, of New Towns in the east Midlands (Peterborough, Northampton), the west Midlands (Redditch, Telford), the northwest (Skelmersdale, Runcorn, Warrington, Central Lancashire), the northeast (Washington), Wales (Newtown) and Scotland (Livingston, Irvine). Population grew by a further 5% between 1961 and 1971, and the expectations of a continued growth in numbers, coupled with the desire better to relate plans for town and country with those for transport, the provision of services, and employment, led to an important phase of re-thinking for planning on a regional scale in the mid- and later 1960s. Regional Economic Planning Councils (since discontinued) were established for this task and produced a series of interesting and useful reports. Broad 'structure' planning replaced detailed land-use based planning.

Meanwhile the larger cities continued to lose population and jobs, not only from the inner areas but also from suburban areas. The tendency for dispersion involving the growth of towns of medium and small sizes produced an extension of urban Britain, confirming the tendency towards 'megalopolis', the functionally-linked zone of city regions and high population densities extending from the Channel coast to Lancashire and Yorkshire. But the 1970s did not bring the expected continued growth in population (an increase of only 0·3% in Great Britain 1971-81), and, as one report put it, 'Britain's main cities are losing population in a big rush to the countryside'. The population of Greater London fell by 10·1% to 6·7 million, or below the 1901 population of the same area, with the inner London boroughs losing between 12% and 26% of their populations. In 1961 Southwark had 313,000 people; in 1981, 212,000. Manchester (−17%), Liverpool (−16%), Salford (−13%), Newcastle-upon-Tyne (−10%), Nottingham (−10%), Birmingham (−8%) also demonstrate the trend (*see map page 174*).

By contrast, population has been increasing in the outer rings around conurbations. There is a crescent of increase in the southeast from Norfolk to the Solent, and smaller but similar areas of increase around the west Midland conurbation, south of Manchester, in the east Midlands and beyond Glasgow and Edinburgh. Northeast Scotland has increased its population, mainly, no doubt, the result of oil and oil-related developments. So has the southwest peninsula to which many retired people have moved. The patterns of decentralisation and dispersion noted for the 1950s and 1960s have intensified and extended in the 1970s.

Thus, dynamic urban changes are in progress. Not all these changes are the direct results of town planning, though the policies of containing the outward spread of the

Planning for Leisure Preservation of the countryside for leisure purposes has involved planning both nationally—with the establishment of the National Parks, areas of outstanding natural beauty and long-distance footpaths—and regionally, by the tourist boards and county councils.

Planning for Industry Post-war planning has attempted to break out of the 'industrial coffin' by the encouragement of Development Areas and New Towns. Green belts and areas of outstanding natural beauty are subject to rigorous development constraints, whereas sites of scientific, landscape and historic interest are given varying degrees of protection.

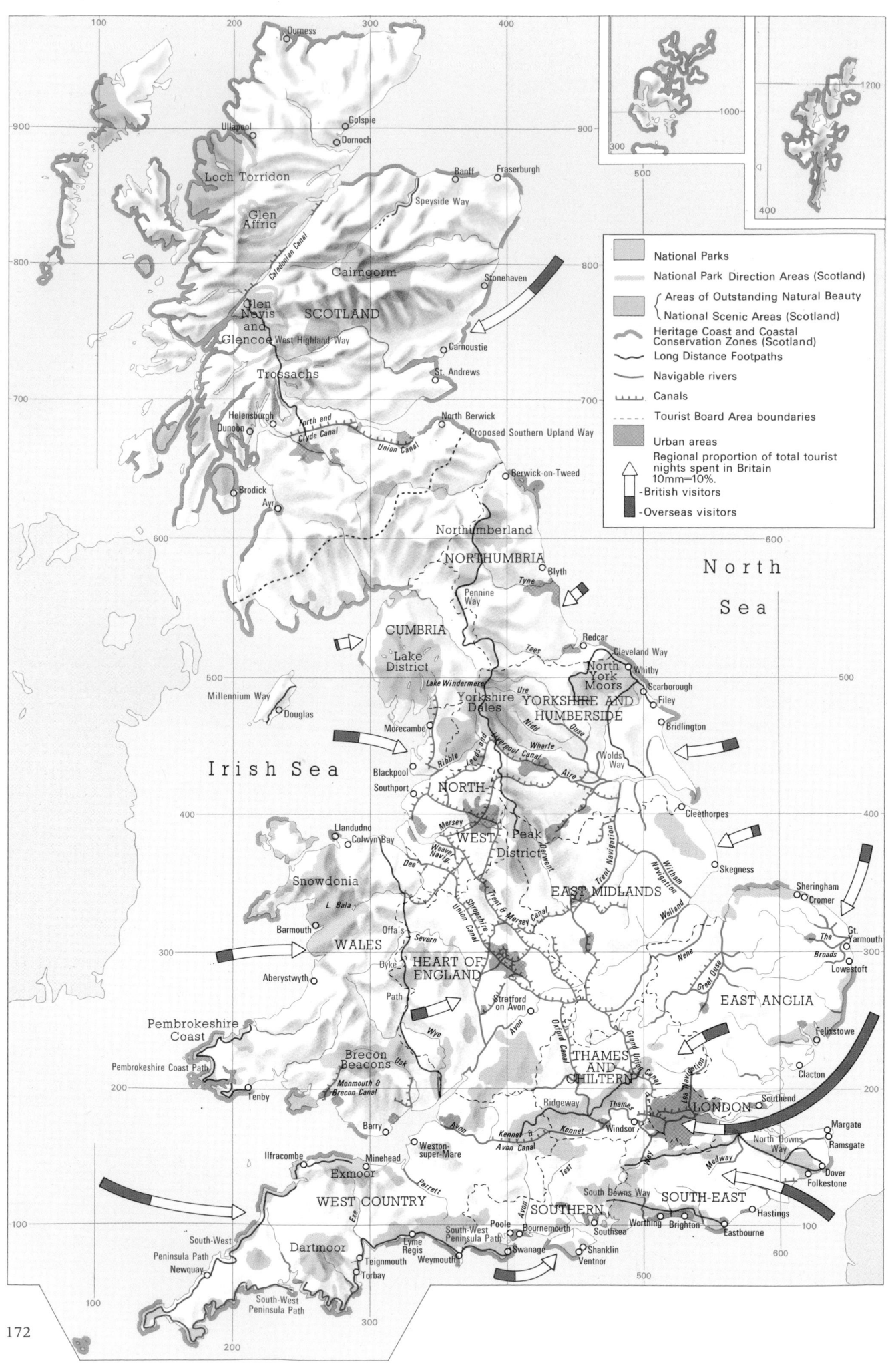

Legend:

- National Parks
- National Park Direction Areas (Scotland)
- { Areas of Outstanding Natural Beauty
- { National Scenic Areas (Scotland)
- Heritage Coast and Coastal Conservation Zones (Scotland)
- Long Distance Footpaths
- Navigable rivers
- Canals
- Tourist Board Area boundaries
- Urban areas
- Regional proportion of total tourist nights spent in Britain 10mm=10%.
  - -British visitors
  - -Overseas visitors

Map labels:

Durness, Golspie, Dornoch, Ullapool, Loch Torridon, Glen Affric, Banff, Fraserburgh, Speyside Way, Cairngorm, Stonehaven, Glen Nevis and Glencoe, SCOTLAND, Carnoustie, West Highland Way, St. Andrews, Trossachs, Helensburgh, Dunoon, North Berwick, Forth and Clyde Canal, Proposed Southern Upland Way, Union Canal, Brodick, Ayr, Berwick-on-Tweed, Northumberland, NORTHUMBRIA, Blyth, Tyne, Pennine Way, CUMBRIA, Redcar, Cleveland Way, Lake District, Tees, Whitby, North York Moors, Scarborough, Lake Windermere, Ure, Filey, Millennium Way, Yorkshire Dales, YORKSHIRE AND HUMBERSIDE, Douglas, Nidd, Bridlington, Morecambe, Wharfe, Leeds and Liverpool Canal, Wolds Way, Irish Sea, Ribble, Aire, Blackpool, Ouse, Southport, NORTH-, Cleethorpes, Llandudno, Mersey, Colwyn Bay, WEST, Peak District, Weaver Navn., Derwent, Skegness, Dee, Sheringham, Snowdonia, Trent Navigation, Cromer, EAST MIDLANDS, Witham Navigation, L. Bala, Trent & Mersey Canal, Welland, The Broads, Gt. Yarmouth, Barmouth, Offa's, Shropshire Union Canal, Severn, WALES, Nene, Lowestoft, Dyke, HEART OF ENGLAND, Great Ouse, Aberystwyth, Path, Stratford on Avon, EAST ANGLIA, Wye, Avon, Felixstowe, Pembrokeshire Coast, Oxford Canal, Brecon Beacons, Usk, Grand Union Canal, THAMES AND CHILTERN, Clacton, Pembrokeshire Coast Path, Monmouth & Brecon Canal, LONDON, Southend, Lee Navigation, Tenby, Ridgeway, Thame, Windsor, Margate, Barry, Avon, Kennet & Avon Canal, Kennet, North Downs Way, Ramsgate, Weston-super-Mare, Medway, Dover, Ilfracombe, Minehead, Test, Wey, Folkestone, Exmoor, Parrett, South Downs Way, SOUTH-EAST, Exe, SOUTHERN, Hastings, WEST COUNTRY, Avon, Worthing, Brighton, Eastbourne, South-West Peninsula Path, Poole, Bournemouth, Southsea, South-West Peninsula Path, Dartmoor, Lyme Regis, Weymouth, Swanage, Shanklin, Ventnor, Newquay, Teignmouth, Torbay, South-West Peninsula Path

North Sea, Irish Sea

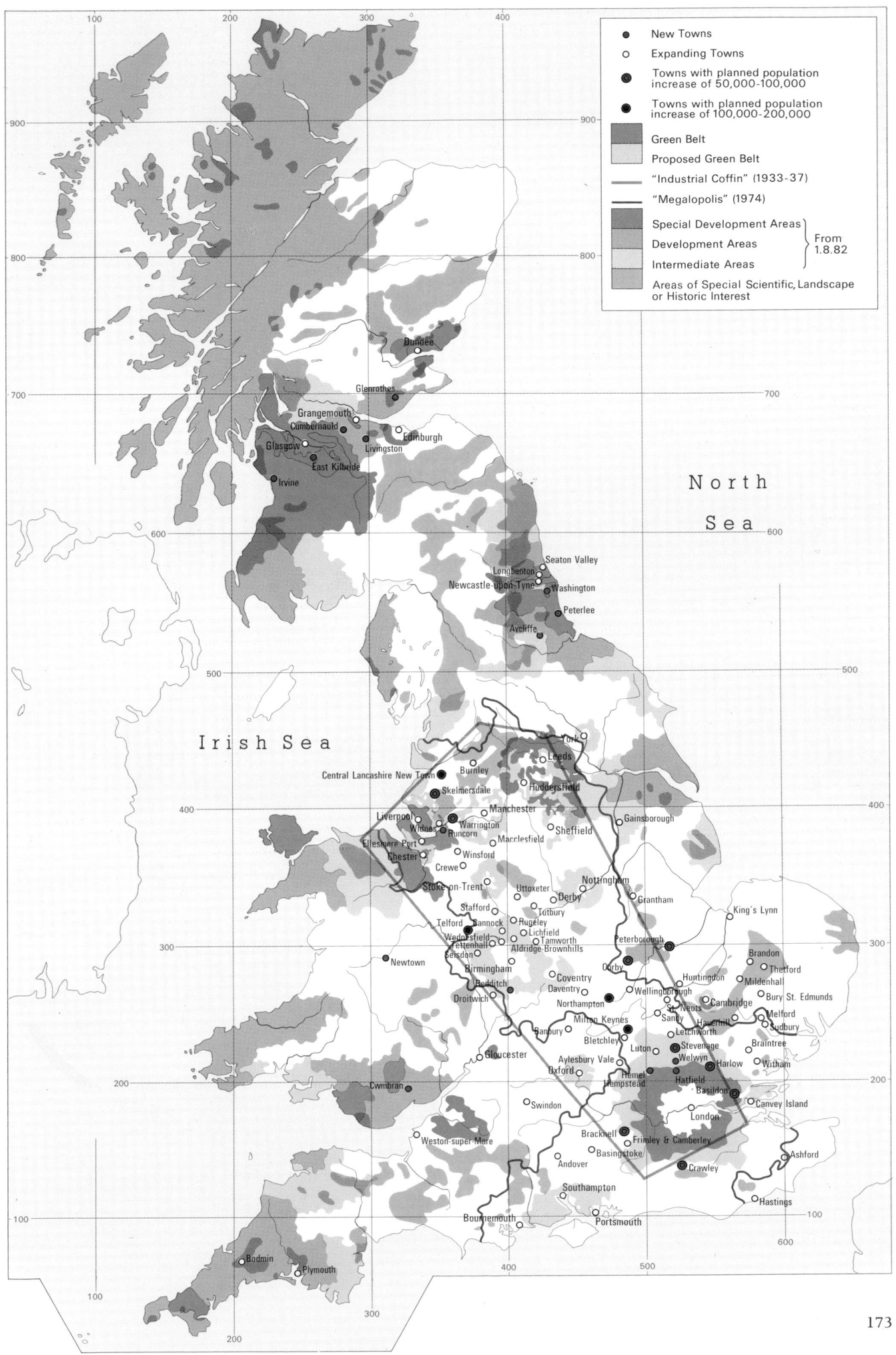

Legend:
- ● New Towns
- ○ Expanding Towns
- ◉ Towns with planned population increase of 50,000-100,000
- ◉ Towns with planned population increase of 100,000-200,000
- Green Belt
- Proposed Green Belt
- "Industrial Coffin" (1933-37)
- "Megalopolis" (1974)
- Special Development Areas ⎫
- Development Areas ⎬ From 1.8.82
- Intermediate Areas ⎭
- Areas of Special Scientific, Landscape or Historic Interest

North Sea

Irish Sea

Dundee
Glenrothes
Grangemouth
Cumbernauld
Glasgow
Livingston
Edinburgh
East Kilbride
Irvine

Seaton Valley
Longbenton
Newcastle-upon-Tyne
Washington
Peterlee
Aycliffe

York
Burnley
Central Lancashire New Town
Leeds
Skelmersdale
Huddersfield
Manchester
Liverpool
Widnes
Warrington
Sheffield
Gainsborough
Ellesmere Port
Runcorn
Macclesfield
Chester
Winsford
Crewe
Nottingham
Stoke-on-Trent
Uttoxeter
Derby
Grantham
King's Lynn
Stafford
Tutbury
Bannock
Rugeley
Telford
Lichfield
Peterborough
Brandon
Wednesfield
Tamworth
Thetford
Fettenhall
Aldridge-Brownhills
Mildenhall
Seisdon
Corby
Newtown
Huntingdon
Bury St. Edmunds
Birmingham
Coventry
Wellingborough
Cambridge
Melford
Redditch
Daventry
Northampton
St. Neots
Haverhill
Sudbury
Droitwich
Santly
Letchworth
Banbury
Milton Keynes
Braintree
Bletchley
Luton
Stevenage
Gloucester
Aylesbury Vale
Welwyn
Harlow
Witham
Oxford
Hemel Hempstead
Hatfield
Basildon
Cwmbran
Swindon
London
Canvey Island
Bracknell
Frimley & Camberley
Basingstoke
Ashford
Andover
Crawley
Weston-super-Mare
Southampton
Hastings
Bournemouth
Portsmouth
Bodmin
Plymouth

Population Patterns

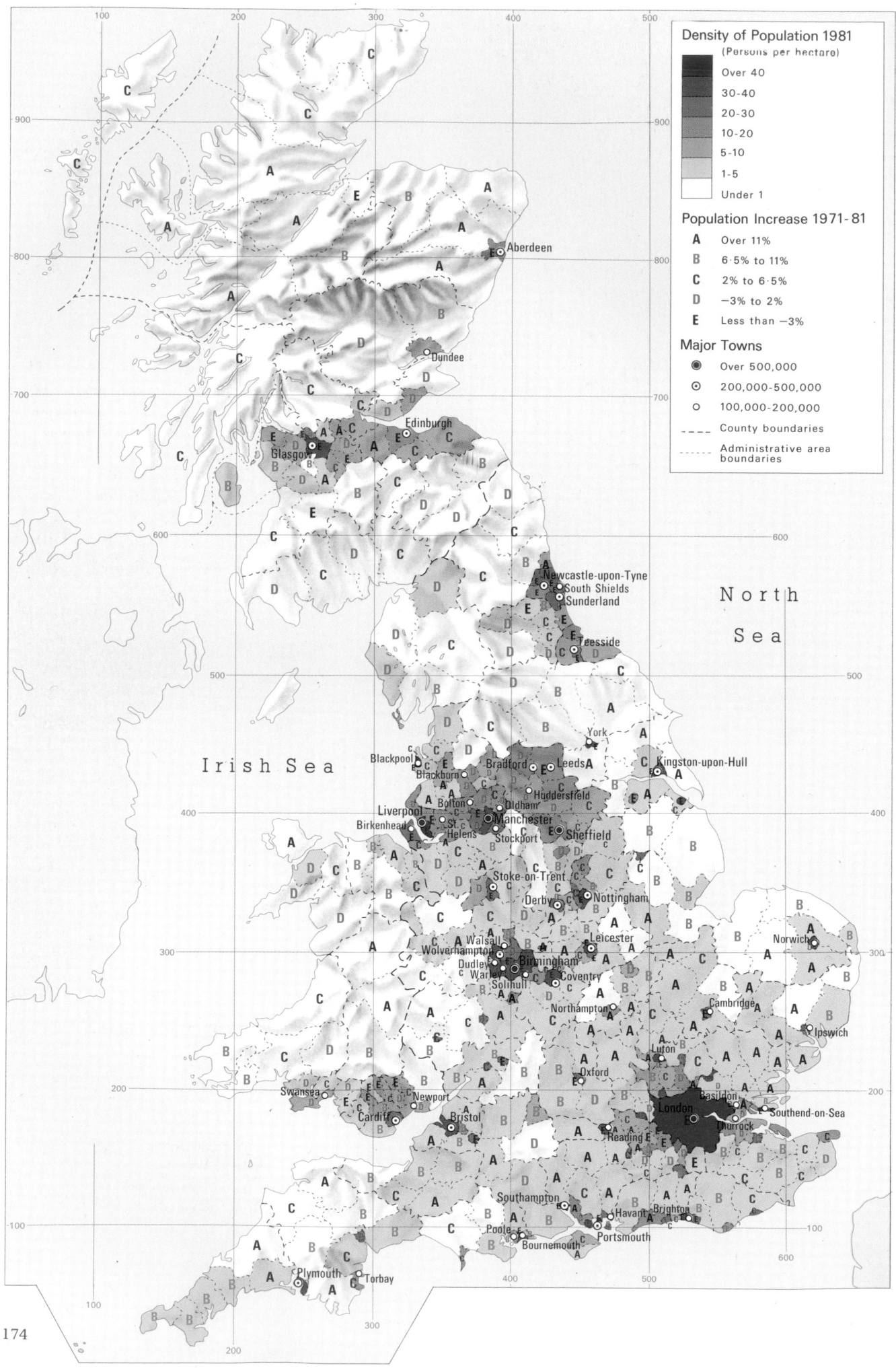

Density of Population 1981
(Persons per hectare)

	Over 40
	30-40
	20-30
	10-20
	5-10
	1-5
	Under 1

Population Increase 1971-81

A Over 11%
B 6·5% to 11%
C 2% to 6·5%
D −3% to 2%
E Less than −3%

Major Towns

⊙ Over 500,000
⊙ 200,000-500,000
○ 100,000-200,000
– – – County boundaries
.... Administrative area boundaries

North Sea

Irish Sea

Aberdeen

Dundee

Edinburgh
Glasgow

Newcastle-upon-Tyne
South Shields
Sunderland
Teesside

York

Blackpool
Blackburn
Bradford   Leeds   Kingston-upon-Hull
Bolton   Huddersfield
Liverpool   Oldham
Birkenhead   St.   Manchester
Helens   Stockport   Sheffield

Stoke-on-Trent

Derby   Nottingham

Walsall   Leicester   Norwich
Wolverhampton
Dudley   Birmingham   Cambridge
Warley   Coventry
Solihull   Ipswich
Northampton
Luton
Oxford   Basildon
Swansea   Newport   London   Southend-on-Sea
Cardiff   Bristol   Thurrock
Reading

Southampton
Havant   Brighton
Poole   Portsmouth
Bournemouth

Plymouth   Torbay

Cultural Diversity

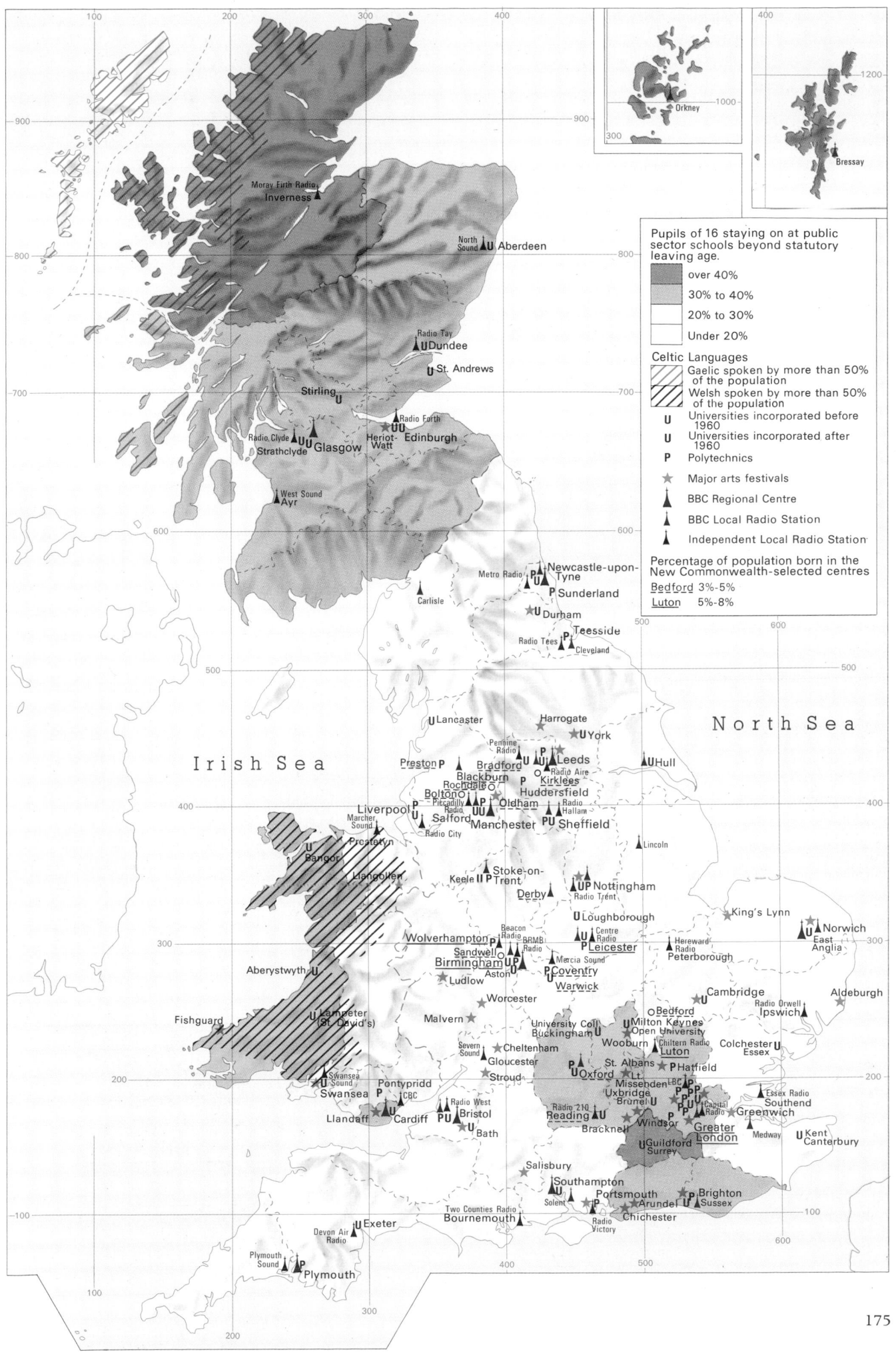

Pupils of 16 staying on at public sector schools beyond statutory leaving age.

- over 40%
- 30% to 40%
- 20% to 30%
- Under 20%

Celtic Languages

- Gaelic spoken by more than 50% of the population
- Welsh spoken by more than 50% of the population
- U Universities incorporated before 1960
- U Universities incorporated after 1960
- P Polytechnics
- ★ Major arts festivals
- ▲ BBC Regional Centre
- ▲ BBC Local Radio Station
- ▲ Independent Local Radio Station

Percentage of population born in the New Commonwealth-selected centres

- Bedford 3%-5%
- Luton 5%-8%

Orkney

Bressay

Moray Firth Radio
Inverness

North Sound U Aberdeen

Radio Tay
U Dundee
U St. Andrews

Stirling U

Radio Forth
Heriot-Watt U U Edinburgh

Radio Clyde U U
Strathclyde Glasgow

West Sound
Ayr

Carlisle

Metro Radio
P U Newcastle-upon-Tyne
P Sunderland
★ U Durham

Radio Tees P Teesside
Cleveland

U Lancaster   Harrogate ★
                    ★ U York

Pennine Radio
Preston P   P U Leeds
Blackburn P Bradford U ★
Rochdale O   Radio Aire Kirklees
Bolton O   U U Huddersfield
Piccadilly A P Oldham Radio Hallam
Radio U U Salford P U Sheffield
Manchester
Radio City

Liverpool
Marcher Sound
U
Bangor Prestatyn
Llangollen

Irish Sea

North Sea

Lincoln

Keele U P Stoke-on-Trent
Derby U   U P Nottingham
            Radio Trent
        U Loughborough

Beacon Radio   Centre Radio
Wolverhampton P   U A Leicester
BRMB Hereward Radio   King's Lynn ★
Sandwell   P A   Peterborough   U Norwich
Birmingham U P   Mercia Sound   East Anglia
Aston U U   P Coventry
★ Ludlow   Warwick

Aberystwyth U

Worcester ★   University Coll   U Cambridge   Aldeburgh ★
              Buckingham   Radio Orwell
Malvern ★   Milton Keynes   Ipswich
U Lampeter   Severn   Open University   Chiltern Radio   Colchester U
(St. David's)   Sound ★ Cheltenham   Wooburn   Essex
Fishguard   Gloucester   St. Albans   Lt Luton
        Stroud   P A   P Hatfield   LBC P
                    Missenden   P A P   Essex Radio
Swansea   P A Oxford   Uxbridge P U P P   Southend
U Sound   Pontypridd   Radio 210   Brunel U P U U P   U
Swansea   P   Reading U A   Capital   Greenwich
        CBC   Windsor ★ Radio
Llandaff   U   Radio West   Greater   U Kent
        U A Bristol   London   Canterbury
Cardiff   P U A   Bracknell   Medway
        U Bath   U Guildford
                Surrey

Salisbury ★

Southampton
Solent A   Portsmouth   P A Brighton
Two Counties Radio   Arundel U ★ Sussex
Bournemouth   Chichester

Devon Air   U Exeter
Radio

Plymouth Sound
A P Plymouth

175

conurbations and decentralisation have set the general pattern. It is the consequences of these changes for the inner city that now cause concern. There is the contrast between the outer parts of the city regions peopled by young, middle-class families and many of the older parts of the inner city with older, poorer and less skilled workers living in pre-1914 houses or more recently-built high-rise blocks and council estates. Industries have moved out or have died. In some areas there are high proportions of immigrant families. The inner-city problem has been the most recent major town planning task. But while there is a general problem, each inner-city area presents its own distinctive problems. The London Docklands are very different from Lambeth and Brixton. The tasks of renewal in Inner Birmingham are not the same as in Liverpool or Glasgow. So planning for urban deprivation has taken precedence in the 1970s with many special studies and the emergence of special grants, programmes and partnership schemes between local and central government. The urban riots of 1981 drew further attention to the problem, especially in south London, Manchester and Liverpool. There are signs of progress but the re-creation of the environments of the inner cities continues to be a major task for the 1980s.

Local Government

The reforms of local government of 1888 and 1894, intended to produce a pattern adapted to the age of the industrial city, also confirmed the existence of units such as the county whose origins lay in early medieval times (*see map page 178*). By the late 1950s and 1960s it had become widely recognised that further major reforms were necessary in the wake of the changes in population distribution, changes in city size, shape and needs and the greater responsibilities, including housing and town planning, which local government had assumed. Royal Commissions on local government in London, England, Wales and Scotland were established. The first result was the establishment in 1963 of the Greater London Council responsible for certain functions for the whole of the London conurbation with a second tier of London Boroughs. The Report of the 'Maud' Royal Commission on Local Government in England in 1969, which included two possible sets of proposals, was hotly argued. The new pattern was set up in 1974 (*see map page 179*). It was based on a smaller number of counties (achieved, for instance, through the amalgamation of Herefordshire and Worcestershire) and county districts, but with metropolitan authorities for major conurbations (such as West Midlands, Merseyside, West Yorkshire, South Yorkshire, and Tyne and Wear). The boundaries of the metropolitan counties were tightly drawn and criticisms were made of the failure to establish regional authorities.

Population Patterns Although the 1981 census showed overall little growth since 1971, it gave evidence of considerable movement of people, especially from the old cities into the countryside around. Some inner city areas lost more than a quarter of their population.

Cultural Diversity The 1960s and 1970s saw a general growth in cultural activity outside the largest towns, sometimes spontaneous and sometimes deliberately fostered. The revival of Celtic traditions and new ethnic minorities in many towns have brought a new cultural mix to Britain.

Wales now has eight county councils (five with historic Welsh names) and 36 district councils; these replace 13 counties, four county boroughs and 164 district councils.

For Scotland, the 'Wheatley' Royal Commission reported in 1969. Its general principles were accepted with amendments and the pattern established by the Local Government (Scotland) Act 1973, by contrast with that in England, accepted the regional principle. It represents a more logical attempt to establish economic and social entities for cities and countryside. There are nine regions, 53 districts and three all-purpose island councils. Local government responsibilities in Scotland differ in certain respects from those in England.

Meanwhile the wider problems of the devolution of political and administrative responsibilities from Westminster were under study by the Kilbrandon Royal Commission on the Constitution, whose report appeared in 1973. Ever since the Union of Scotland and England in 1707 the arrangements for the government of Scotland have differed in some important respects from those in England. Scotland has its own systems of law and education. In 1885 the office of Secretary of State for Scotland was created, and he discharges functions that for England are exercised by the Home Office, the Departments of the Environment, Education and Science, some aspects of the Department of Health and Social Security, and the Ministry of Agriculture. A separate Welsh Ministry was established in 1951 and strengthened in 1964 but its responsibilities, while wide, are less than those of the Scottish Office.

The re-emergence of national feeling at the political level was channelled in the 1960s and early 1970s into campaigns for devolution. Proposals for devolution were brought forward by the government in 1974 and 1975 based on the preservation of the unity of the UK and rejecting federal solutions. Assemblies were proposed for Scotland and Wales, although that for Scotland was to have much the stronger set of powers. After extensive Parliamentary debates from 1976 the referenda required under the Acts failed to secure the necessary majorities and the issue died away, at least temporarily. But the issue of how to reconcile, in a parliamentary democracy, the need for centralised services with the aspiration of regional feeling, remains for further debate. This central question has a wider application than to Scotland and Wales. Cornishmen claim their own right to political expression, and if, say some, there is devolution to Wales and Cornwall, what of Yorkshire with its own rugged traditions? Too little is still known of the economic aspects of regionalism. And there is a long history of discussion, going back to the time of World War I, on how responsibilities for the government of the regions of England can best be arranged. Arguments on this question could gain strength from the recent trend towards the development of city regions.

Currently the relations between central and local government are under strain. Local governments see their powers diminishing and more power attaching to the centre: the centre is concerned at the levels of public expenditure incurred by local government. Local governments differ greatly in their ability to generate current income through the rating system (itself now requiring modification or

reform), and, even though a system of income equalisation exists through funds made available by central government under the Rate Support Grant (recently revised), considerable differences exist in the levels of expenditure and of services provided by local governments. What you may get from the social services depends to an extent on where you live. The suggestion is made, for example, that educational attainment is much influenced by the levels of expenditure of Local Education Authorities: some Welsh authorities where education has been highly valued come out well in this respect (*see map page 175*).

Maps which show variations in levels of service provision by local and national authorities tend to show the south and southeast as the best provided regions with a gradation downwards to Wales, to the industrial districts of Northern England and to Scotland. But at a more detailed level the pattern has to be modified to show the contrast between the poorly-provided inner cities and the better-off suburbs.

The issue of how exactly Britain should be governed at national, regional and local levels will not easily be resolved. Differences between central and local government must be seen in the context of a picture in which government has now become a main influence on the geography of life in Britain. Employment in the civil service, local government, nationalised industries and other government established bodies in itself a strong factor. Governments at different levels influence the geography of Britain through planning decisions, industrial location policies, decisions on the provision of basic services such as transport, energy, water and housing as well as the social services like health, welfare and education. There is still much room for argument on who should make which decisions and for what areas, how the money should be raised and how it should be disbursed.

Acknowledgements and Bibliography

The thematic maps in the Introduction and sections on historical geography and modern Britain were researched by Peter Furtado and made and drawn by Clyde Surveys Ltd., of Maidenhead.

The authors and publishers would like to acknowledge the following as some major sources for these maps:

Great Britain–Geology: Tectonic Map of Great Britain, the Institute of Geological Sciences 1966; and Oxford University Press.

Great Britain–Climate: *The Climate of the British Isles*, T J Chandler and S Gregory, Longman 1976.

The Dark Ages: *The Archaeology of Anglo-Saxon England* ed D M Wilson, Methuen 1976.

Britain to 1350: *A New Historical Geography of England* ed H C Darby, Cambridge University Press 1973. *Feudal Britain* G W S Barrow, Edward Arnold 1956.

Late Medieval Britain: *The Agrarian History of England and Wales IV* ed Joan Thirsk, Cambridge University Press 1967.

The Agricultural Revolution: *An Historical Geography of England and Wales* ed R A Dodgshon and R A Butlin, Academic Press 1978. *Man Made the Land* Alan R H Baker and J B Harley, David & Charles 1973

The Early Industrial Revolution: *The Early Industrial Revolution* E Pawson, Batsford 1979.

Britain in the Late Nineteenth Century: *The Movement of Population* C T Smith, Geographical Journal vol 117, 1951.

Mineral Resources: *The Mineral Resources of Britain* John Blunden, Hutchinson 1975. *A Geography of Energy in the UK* John Fernie, Longman 1981.

Industry and Energy: *Britain 1981* HMSO 1981.

Agriculture and Fisheries: *Fish from the Sea* The White Fish Authority. Fishing grounds–The Watt Committee on Energy, University of Glasgow 1979.

Farming Types: *Types of Farming in Britain* K Buchanan and D J Sinclair, Association of Agriculture 1966.

Planning for Industry: *The Containment of Urban England* Peter Hall, George Allen & Unwin 1974.

Countless books have been written about the history, geography and countryside of Britain. The following titles (as well as those mentioned above) might be of interest about the geography of Britain:

The Personality of Britain Sir Cyril Fox and L F Chitty, National Museum of Wales 1932.

The UK Space ed J W House, Weidenfeld and Nicolson 1977.

The British Isles: A Systematic Geography J W Watson and J B Sissons, Nelson 1964.

An Agricultural Atlas of Great Britain J T Coppock, Faber and Faber 1976.

Countryside Conservation Bryn Green, George Allen & Unwin 1981.

National Parks: Conservation or Cosmetics Ann and Malcolm McEwen, George Allen & Unwin 1982.

Britain's Structure and Scenery L D Stamp, Collins 1974.

Urban and Regional Planning Peter Hall, Penguin 1974.

Airport Strategy and Planning K R Sealy. Oxford University Press 1976.

Land Use and Living Space R H Best, Methuen 1981.

A Living History of the British Isles ed W G V Balchin, Country Life 1981.

A Natural History of the British Isles ed Pat Morris, Country Life 1979.

The Making of the English Landscape W G Hoskins, Penguin 1970.

Wales F V Emery, Longman 1969.

The Making of the Scottish Landscape R N Millman, Batsford 1975.

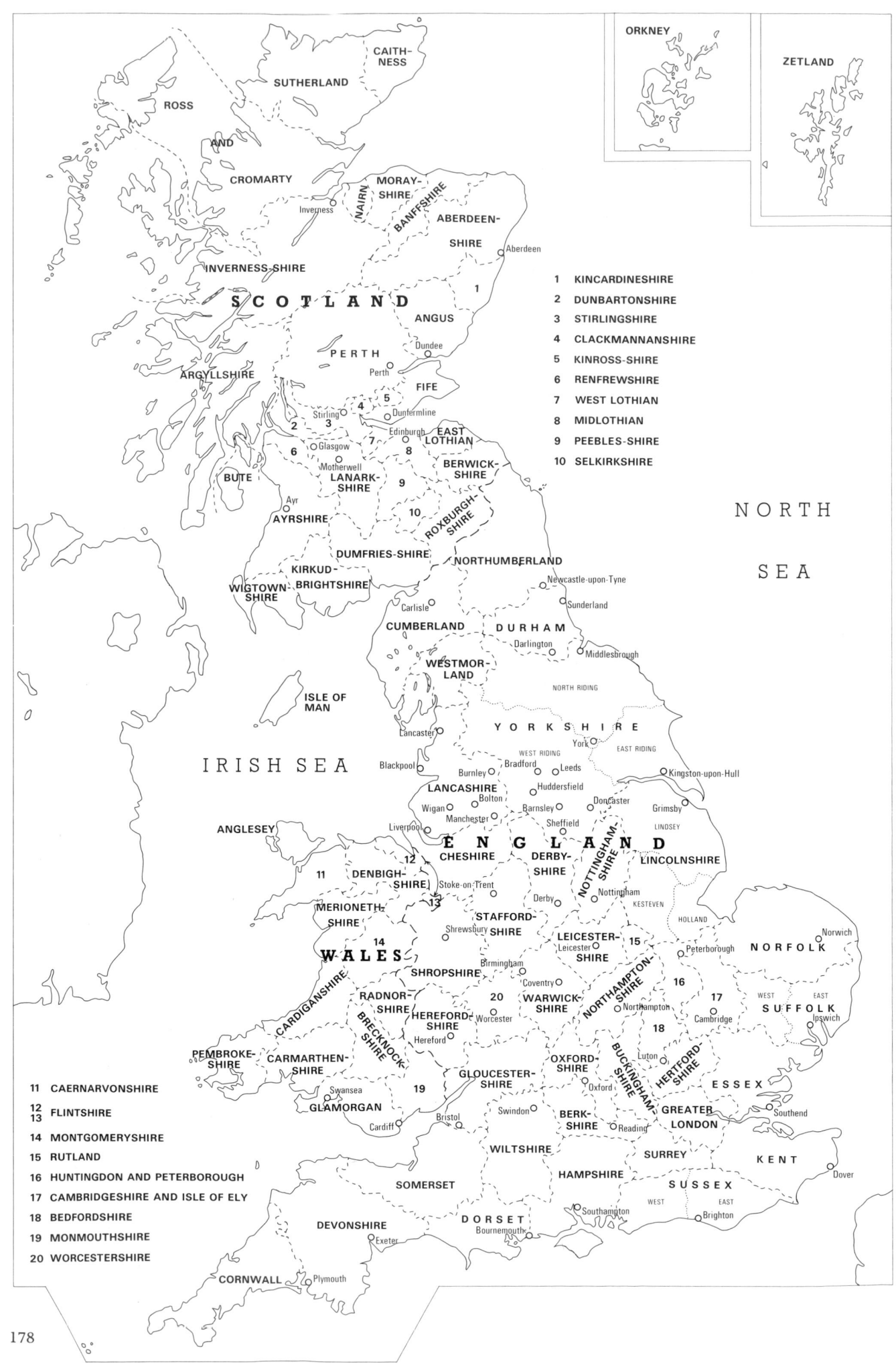

ORKNEY

ZETLAND

SUTHERLAND

CAITH-NESS

ROSS

AND

CROMARTY

Inverness

NAIRN

MORAY-SHIRE

BANFFSHIRE

ABERDEEN-SHIRE

Aberdeen

INVERNESS-SHIRE

S C O T L A N D

1   KINCARDINESHIRE

2   DUNBARTONSHIRE

3   STIRLINGSHIRE

4   CLACKMANNANSHIRE

5   KINROSS-SHIRE

6   RENFREWSHIRE

7   WEST LOTHIAN

8   MIDLOTHIAN

9   PEEBLES-SHIRE

10   SELKIRKSHIRE

ANGUS

PERTH

Dundee

Perth

1

FIFE

ARGYLLSHIRE

4

5

Dunfermline

Stirling

3

Edinburgh

EAST LOTHIAN

2

7

8

BERWICK-SHIRE

6

Glasgow

Motherwell

LANARK-SHIRE

9

BUTE

Ayr

AYRSHIRE

10

ROXBURGH-SHIRE

DUMFRIES-SHIRE

NORTHUMBERLAND

NORTH

KIRKUD-BRIGHTSHIRE

Newcastle-upon-Tyne

WIGTOWN-SHIRE

Carlisle

Sunderland

SEA

CUMBERLAND

DURHAM

Darlington

Middlesbrough

WESTMOR-LAND

NORTH RIDING

ISLE OF MAN

Y O R K S H I R E

Lancaster

York

EAST RIDING

IRISH SEA

Blackpool

WEST RIDING

Bradford

Leeds

Kingston-upon-Hull

Burnley

Huddersfield

LINDSEY

LANCASHIRE

Bolton

Doncaster

Grimsby

ANGLESEY

Wigan

Barnsley

Sheffield

Manchester

Liverpool

E N G L A N D

NOTTINGHAM-SHIRE

12

CHESHIRE

DERBY-SHIRE

LINCOLNSHIRE

11

DENBIGH-SHIRE

Stoke-on-Trent

Derby

Nottingham

KESTEVEN

13

MERIONETH-SHIRE

STAFFORD-SHIRE

HOLLAND

14

Shrewsbury

LEICESTER-SHIRE

15

Norwich

W A L E S

Leicester

Peterborough

N O R F O L K

Birmingham

NORTHAMPTON-SHIRE

16

SHROPSHIRE

Coventry

WEST

EAST

CARDIGANSHIRE

RADNOR-SHIRE

20

WARWICK-SHIRE

Northampton

17

S U F F O L K

HEREFORD-SHIRE

Worcester

Cambridge

Ipswich

BRECKNOCK-SHIRE

18

PEMBROKE-SHIRE

Hereford

Luton

HERTFORD-SHIRE

CARMARTHEN-SHIRE

OXFORD-SHIRE

BUCKINGHAM-SHIRE

ESSEX

19

GLOUCESTER-SHIRE

Oxford

Swansea

GLAMORGAN

Bristol

Swindon

BERK-SHIRE

GREATER LONDON

Southend

Cardiff

Reading

K E N T

WILTSHIRE

SURREY

Dover

HAMPSHIRE

S U S S E X

SOMERSET

WEST

EAST

DORSET

Southampton

Brighton

DEVONSHIRE

Bournemouth

Exeter

CORNWALL

Plymouth

11   CAERNARVONSHIRE

12   FLINTSHIRE

13

14   MONTGOMERYSHIRE

15   RUTLAND

16   HUNTINGDON AND PETERBOROUGH

17   CAMBRIDGESHIRE AND ISLE OF ELY

18   BEDFORDSHIRE

19   MONMOUTHSHIRE

20   WORCESTERSHIRE

County Boundaries since 1974

ORKNEY

SHETLAND

WESTERN

ISLES

HIGHLAND

GRAMPIAN

Inverness

Aberdeen

S C O T L A N D

TAYSIDE

Dundee

Perth

FIFE

CENTRAL

Stirling

Dunfermline

Edinburgh

Glasgow

LOTHIAN

Motherwell

STRATHCLYDE

BORDERS

N O R T H

Ayr

DUMFRIES
AND
GALLOWAY

NORTHUMBERLAND

S E A

Carlisle

Newcastle-upon-Tyne

1

Sunderland

1	TYNE AND WEAR
2	CLEVELAND
3	WEST YORKSHIRE
4	SOUTH YORKSHIRE
5	GREATER MANCHESTER
6	MERSEYSIDE

DURHAM

Darlington

2

Middlesbrough

CUMBRIA

NORTH YORKSHIRE

ISLE OF
MAN

Lancaster

York

IRISH SEA

LANCASHIRE

HUMBERSIDE

Blackpool

Bradford

Leeds

Kingston-upon-Hull

Burnley

3

Huddersfield

Wigan

Bolton

Barnsley

Doncaster

Grimsby

Liverpool

5

Manchester

4

6

Sheffield

E N G L A N D

CHESHIRE

DERBY-

NOTTINGHAM-

LINCOLNSHIRE

G
W
Y
N
E
D
D

CLWYD

SHIRE

SHIRE

Stoke-on-Trent

Derby

Nottingham

STAFFORD-
SHIRE

Shrewsbury

LEICESTERSHIRE

NORFOLK

Norwich

SHROPSHIRE

Leicester

7

Birmingham

Peterborough

WALES

Coventry

NORTHAMPTON-
SHIRE

CAMBRIDGE-
SHIRE

SUFFOLK

POWYS

HEREFORD
AND
WORCESTER

Worcester

WARWICK-
SHIRE

Northampton

8

Cambridge

Ipswich

Hereford

Luton

HERTFORD-
SHIRE

ESSEX

DYFED

GLOUCESTER-
SHIRE

OXFORD-
SHIRE

Oxford

B
U
C
K
I
N
G
H
A
M
-
SHIRE

10

GWENT

Swindon

GREATER

Swansea

11

9

Reading

LONDON

12

Cardiff

Bristol

Southend

AVON

WILTSHIRE

SURREY

K E N T

7	WEST MIDLANDS
8	BEDFORDSHIRE
9	BERKSHIRE
10	WEST GLAMORGAN
11	MID GLAMORGAN
12	SOUTH GLAMORGAN

HAMPSHIRE

Dover

SOMERSET

WEST
SUSSEX

EAST
SUSSEX

DEVON

DORSET

Southampton

Brighton

Exeter

Bournemouth

ISLE OF
WIGHT

CORNWALL

Plymouth

Index

Content
The Index lists all the definitive names shown in the map section of the Atlas. For each entry the Atlas page number is listed and the National Grid map reference is given to the nearest kilometre of the feature to which the name applies.

For long linear features, such as the River Thames, more than one reference is given. For these multiple entries and where a name applies to more than one feature the County, Region or Island Area name is also given.

Abbreviations used in the Index to identify the nature of certain named features and abbreviations for Counties used in the Index are also listed.

Method of Listing Names
Names are listed alphabetically in the Index as they appear on the map. For example, 'Ashdown Forest' appears under 'A', while 'Forest of Bere' is under 'F'. Similarly, 'Beaulieu River' appears under 'B' but 'River Thames' is under 'R'. When the definite article precedes a name, the name appears first. Thus, 'The Wash' becomes 'Wash, The' and is listed under 'W'. An exception to this rule is made in the case of Gaelic and Welsh place names. These are listed under the initial letter of the Gaelic or Welsh definite article. For example, 'An Ceannaich' is listed under 'A', and 'Y Llethr' is listed under 'Y'.

Example Use of Index
To find Dorking refer to the name in the index and read off the reference 28TQ 1649. The first number indicates that Dorking is shown on page 28. The remaining two letters and four figures signify that the town lies within the 100 kilometre square TQ (see diagram on front endpaper) and is 16 kilometres east and 49 kilometres north of the south west corner of the square. The 10 kilometre grid numbers '1' and '4' are shown on the edges of page 28 and the exact location of Dorking is found by estimating '6' tenths eastward from the grid line '1' and '9' tenths northwards from the grid line '4'. In the National Grid Reference system the Eastings (16 for Dorking) are always stated before the Northings (49 for Dorking).

Features can thus be located on the Atlas pages by referring to the page number and grid number only; the two letters are required for the full grid reference to locate a feature on any map which shows the National Grid.

List of County Names Showing Abbreviations Used in this Index

England
Avon	Avon
Bedfordshire	Beds.
Berkshire	Berks.
Buckinghamshire	Bucks.
Cambridgeshire	Cambs.
Cheshire	Ches.
Cleveland	Cleve.
Cornwall	Corn.
Cumbria	Cumbr.
Derbyshire	Derby.
Devon	Devon
Dorset	Dorset
Durham	Durham
East Sussex	E Susx
Essex	Essex
Gloucestershire	Glos.
Greater London	Gtr London
Greater Manchester	Gtr Mches.
Hampshire	Hants.
Hereford and Worcester	Here. and Worc.
Hertfordshire	Herts.
Humberside	Humbs.
Isle of Wight	I. of W.
Kent	Kent
Lancashire	Lancs.
Leicestershire	Leic.
Lincolnshire	Lincs.
Merseyside	Mers.
Norfolk	Norf.
North Yorkshire	N Yorks.
Northamptonshire	Northants.
Northumberland	Northum.
Nottinghamshire	Notts.
Oxfordshire	Oxon.
Shropshire	Shrops.
Somerset	Somer.
South Yorkshire	S Yorks.
Staffordshire	Staffs.
Suffolk	Suff.
Surrey	Surrey
Tyne and Wear	Tyne and Wear
Warwickshire	Warw.
West Midlands	W Mids
West Sussex	W Susx
West Yorkshire	W Yorks.
Wiltshire	Wilts.

Wales
Clwyd	Clwyd
Dyfed	Dyfed
Gwent	Gwent
Gwynedd	Gwyn.
Mid Glamorgan	Mid Glam.
Powys	Powys
South Glamorgan	S Glam.
West Glamorgan	W Glam.

Other Areas
Isle of Man	I. of M.
Isles of Scilly	Is. of Sc.

Region and Islands Area Names
Scotland
Regions
Borders	Borders
Central	Central
Dumfries and Galloway	Dumf. and Galwy.
Fife	Fife
Grampian	Grampn.
Highland	Highld.
Lothian	Lothian
Strathclyde	Strath.
Tayside	Tays.

Islands areas
Orkney	Orkney
Shetland	Shetld.
Western Isles	W Isles

Abbreviations which are used in this Index to identify the nature of certain named features
ant.	Antiquity
chan.	Channel or arm of the sea
dist.	District or name of an area
is.	Island
mt.	Mountain, mount or hill
pt.	Point or headland on coast
sbk.	Sandbank

A

Abbas Combe	25	ST 7022
Abberley	49	SO 7567
Abberley Hill	49	SO 7566
Abberton (Essex)	39	TM 0019
Abberton (Here. and Worc.)	50	SO 9953
Abberton Reservoir	39	TL 9818
Abberwick	91	NU 1213
Abbess Roding	37	TL 5711
Abbey	24	ST 1410
Abbey Brook	70	SK 1892
Abbey Burn	95	NS 9353
Abbeycwmhir	57	SO 0571
Abbey Dore	45	SO 3830
Abbey Head	87	NX 7343
Abbey Hulton	59	SJ 9148
Abbey St. Bathans	96	NT 7662
Abbeystead	77	SD 5654
Abbeytown	82	NY 1750
Abbey Wood	37	TQ 4779
Abbotrule	90	NT 6112
Abbots Bickington	22	SS 3813
Abbots Bromley	60	SK 0824
Abbotsbury	25	SY 5785
Abbotsford	96	NT 5034
Abbotsham	22	SS 4226
Abbotside Common	83	SD 8196
Abbotskerswell	21	SX 8569
Abbots Langley	36	TL 0902
Abbots Leigh	33	ST 5473
Abbotsley	53	TL 2256
Abbots Morton	50	SP 0255
Abbots Ripton	53	TL 2377
Abbot's Salford	50	SP 0650
Abbot's Way (ant.)	21	SX 6266
Abbotswood	26	SU 3722
Abbotts Ann	34	SU 3243
Abdon	48	SO 5786
Aber (Dyfed)	43	SN 4748
Aber (Gwyn.)	67	SH 6572
Aberaeron	56	SN 4562
Aberaman	41	SO 0101
Aberangell	57	SH 8409
Aberarder	116	NH 6225
Aberarder Forest	116	NN 4888
Aberargie	108	NO 1615
Aberarth	56	SN 4763
Aber-banc	43	SN 3541
Aberbargoed	41	SO 1500
Aberbeeg	41	SO 2102
Abercanaid	41	SO 0503
Abercarn	41	ST 2195
Abercegir	57	SH 8001
Aberchalder	115	NH 3403
Aberchalder Burn	116	NH 5618
Aberchalder Forest	115	NN 3499
Aberchirder	121	NJ 6252
Abercraf	41	SN 8212
Abercrombie	103	NO 5102
Abercych	43	SN 2441
Abercynon	41	ST 0894
Aberdalgie	108	NO 0720
Aberdare	41	SO 0002
Aberdaron	56	SH 1726
Aberdeen	119	NJ 9305
Aberdeen Airport	119	NJ 8712
Aberdour	102	NT 1885
Aberdovey Bar	56	SN 5994
Aberdulais	41	SS 7799
Aberdyfi	56	SN 6196
Aber Dysynni	56	SH 5603
Aberedw	44	SO 0747
Abereiddy	42	SM 7931
Abererch	66	SH 3936
Aber Falls	67	SH 6669
Aberfan	41	SO 0700
Aberfeldy	108	NN 8549
Aberffraw	66	SH 3568
Aberffrwd	57	SN 6878
Aberford	79	SE 4336
Aberfoyle	101	NN 5200
Abergavenny	45	SO 2914
Abergeldie Castle	117	NO 2895
Abergele	67	SH 9477
Abergele Roads	67	SH 9379
Abergorlech	43	SN 5833
Abergwesyn	44	SN 8552
Abergwili	43	SN 4421
Abergwynant	57	SH 6717
Abergwynfi	41	SS 8996
Abergynolwyn	57	SH 6706
Aberhosan	57	SN 8197
Aberkenfig	41	SS 8983
Aberlady	103	NT 4679
Aberlady Bay	103	NT 4581
Aberlemno	109	NO 5255
Aberllefenni	57	SH 7609
Abermenai Point	66	SH 4461
Abermeurig	43	SN 5655
Abermule	58	SO 1694
Abernaint	58	SJ 1221
Abernant (Dyfed)	43	SN 3423
Aber-nant (Mid Glam.)	41	SO 0103
Abernethy	108	NO 1816
Abernethy Forest	117	NH 9918
Abernyte	108	NO 2531
Aberporth	43	SN 2651
Aberporth Airfield	43	SN 2549
Aberscross	129	NC 7600
Abersoch	56	SH 3128
Abersychan	45	SO 2704
Abertillery	41	SO 2104
Abertridwr (Mid Glam.)	41	ST 1289
Abertridwr (Powys)	57	SJ 0319
Abertysswg	41	SO 1305
Aberuthven	108	NN 9715
Aberyscir	41	SN 9929
Aberystwyth	56	SN 5881
Abhainn a'Bhealaich	100	NM 9506
Abhainn a' Chadh' Bhuidhe	127	NH 1367
Abhainn a' Choilich	115	NH 0824
Abhainn a' Choire	132	NC 3526
Abhainn a' Gharbh Choire	123	NG 8769
Abhainn a' Ghiubhais Li	127	NH 2471
Abhainn a' Ghlinne Bhig	123	NG 8217
Abhainn a' Ghlinne Bhig	127	NH 3484
Abhainn an Fhasaigh	126	NH 0267
Abhainn an Loin	132	NC 3241
Abhainn an t-Sratha' Chàrnaig	129	NH 7198
Abhainn an t-Srathain	132	NC 2362
Abhainn an t-Srath Chuileannaich	128	NH 4393
Abhainn Bearraray	130	NB 0514
Abhainn Beinn nan Eun	128	NH 4673
Abhainn Bràigh-horrisdale	123	NG 8167
Abhainn Bruachaig	127	NH 0763
Abhainn Cam Linne	106	NM 9723
Abhainn Chòsaidh	114	NG 9201
Abhainn Chuaig	123	NG 7256
Abhainn Crò Chlach	116	NH 6205
Abhainn Cuileig	127	NH 1776
Abhainn Dalach	106	NN 0341
Abhainn Deabhag	115	NH 2724
Abhainn Dearg	126	NG 8847
Abhainn Droma	127	NH 2276
Abhainn Dubh (Highld.)	123	NG 7851
Abhainn Dubh (Highld.)	127	NH 0657
Abhainn Duibhe	107	NN 4253
Abhainn Fionain	106	NM 9518
Abhainn Geiraha	131	NB 5150
Abhainn Ghlas	98	NR 3166
Abhainn Ghleann Iubharnadeal	98	NR 4570
Abhainn Mhòr (Strath.)	99	NR 7377
Abhainn Mhòr (Strath.)	99	NR 7571
Abhainn na Clach Airigh	132	NC 1420
Abhainn na Cuile	99	NR 8269
Abhainn na Frithe	134	NC 8226
Abhainn na Glasa	128	NH 4579
Abhainn Rath	106	NN 2868
Abhainn Sgeamhaidh	133	NC 5616
Abhainn Sithidh	115	NH 0624
Abhainn Srath na Sealga	127	NH 0780
Abhainn Thràil	126	NG 9153
A'Bhrideanach (pt.)	110	NM 2999
A' Bhuidheanach Bheag	116	NN 6677
Abingdon	47	SU 4997
Abinger Common	28	TQ 1145
Abington	95	NS 9323
Abington Pigotts	53	TL 3044
Ab Kettleby	61	SK 7223
Ablington	46	SP 1007
Abney	70	SK 1979
Aboyne	119	NO 5298
Abram	69	SD 6001
Abriachan	116	NH 5535
Abridge	37	TQ 4696
Abthorpe	51	SP 6446
Abune-the-Hill	136	HY 2928
Aby	73	TF 4178
Acairseid Falaich	112	NF 8537
Acarsaid	111	NM 5871
Acaster Malbis	79	SE 5845
Acaster Selby	79	SE 5741
Accrington	78	SD 7528
Acha	110	NM 1854
Achachork	123	NG 4746
Achaglachgach Forest	99	NR 8064
Achahoish	99	NR 7877
A' Chailleach (Highld.) (mt.)	127	NH 1371
A' Chailleach (Highld.) (mt.)	116	NH 6804
A' Chailleach Am Bodach (pt.)	132	NC 2473
Achairn Burn	135	ND 2949
Achalader (Tays.)	108	NO 1245
Achallader (Strath.)	106	NN 3244
Achaluachrach	133	NC 6709
Achanalt	127	NH 2561
Achanamara	99	NR 7887
Achandunie	128	NH 6472
Ach' an Todhair	106	NN 0972
Achany	128	NC 5601
Achany Glen	128	NC 5704
Achaphubuil	115	NN 0875
Acharacle	111	NM 6767
Acharn (Highld.)	111	NM 7050
Acharn (Tays.)	107	NN 7543
Acharosson Burn	100	NR 9376
Achath	119	NJ 7311
Achavanich	135	ND 1742
Achduart	127	NC 0403
Achentoul	134	NC 8733
Achentoul Forest	134	NC 8638
Achfary	132	NC 2939
Achgarve	126	NG 8893
Achiemore (Highld.)	132	NC 3667
Achiemore (Highld.)	134	NC 8958
A' Chill	110	NG 2705
Achiltibuie	126	NC 0208
Achina	133	NC 7060
Achinduich	128	NC 5800
Achingills	135	ND 1663
Achinhoan Head	92	NR 7617
Achintee (Highld.)	126	NG 9441
Achintraid	123	NG 8438
Achintree House	115	NN 1273
Achleck	105	NM 4145
A'Chleit (Highld.) (is.)	132	NC 0320
A'Chlèit (Island of Mull)	105	NM 4118
A'Chlèit (Strath.) (pt.)	92	NR 6841
Achlyness	132	NC 2452
Achmelvich	132	NC 0524
Achmelvich Bay	132	NC 0525
Achmore (Central)	107	NN 5832
Achmore (Highld.)	123	NG 8533
Achmore (Isle of Lewis)	131	NB 3129
Achnaba	106	NM 9436
Achnacarnin	132	NC 0431
Achnacarry	115	NN 1787
Achnacloish	111	NG 5908
Achnacroish	105	NM 8541
Achnadrish	111	NM 4551
Achnagarron	128	NH 6870
Achnaha	111	NM 4668
Achnahanat	128	NH 5198
Achnahannet	117	NH 9727
Achnasaul	115	NN 1589
Achnasheen	127	NH 1658
Achnashellach Forest	126	NH 0247
Achnastank	117	NJ 2733
Achosnich	111	NM 4467
A' Chràlaig	115	NH 0914
Achranich	106	NM 7047
Achray Forest	101	NN 5103
Achreamie	135	ND 0166
Achriabhach	106	NN 1468
Achriesgill	132	NC 2554
A'Chruach (Isle of Arran)	92	NR 9633
A'Chruach (Strath.)	106	NM 9021
A'Chruach (Strath.)	92	NR 6110
A'Chruach (Strath.)	92	NR 7630
A Chruach (Tays.)	107	NN 3756
Achurch	52	TL 0283
Achuvoldrach	133	NC 5659
Achvaich	129	NH 7194
Achvarasdal	134	NC 9864
Achvarasdal Burn	134	NC 9862
Ackergill	135	ND 3553
Ackergill Tower	135	ND 3554
Acklam (Cleve.)	85	NZ 4817
Acklam (N Yorks.)	80	SE 7861
Ackleton	59	SO 7798
Acklington	91	NU 2201
Ackton	79	SE 4121
Ackworth Moor Top	71	SE 4316
Acle	65	TG 3910
Acock's Green	50	SP 1383
Acol	31	TR 3067
Acomb	90	NY 9366
Aconbury	45	SO 5133
Acre	78	SD 7824
Acrefair	58	SJ 2743
Acrise Place	31	TR 1942
Acton (Ches.)	59	SJ 6253
Acton (Gtr London)	37	TQ 2080
Acton (Shrops.)	48	SO 3184
Acton (Suff.)	54	TL 8945
Acton Beauchamp	49	SO 6750
Acton Bridge	69	SJ 5975
Acton Burnell	59	SJ 5301
Acton Green	49	SO 6950
Acton Pigott	59	SJ 5402
Acton Round	59	SO 6395
Acton Scott	48	SO 4589
Acton Trussell	59	SJ 9317
Acton Turville	33	ST 8080
Adbaston	59	SJ 7627
Adber	25	ST 5920
Adderbury	47	SP 4635
Adderley	59	SJ 6639
Adderstone	97	NU 1330
Addiewell	102	NS 9962
Addingham	78	SE 0749
Addington (Bucks.)	51	SP 7428
Addington (Kent)	30	TQ 6659
Addlestone	36	TQ 0464
Addlethorpe	73	TF 5469
Adeney	59	SJ 6918
Adfa	57	SJ 0501
Adforton	48	SO 4071
Adisham	31	TR 2253
Adlestrop	47	SP 2427
Adlingfleet	74	SE 8421
Adlington (Ches.)	69	SJ 9180
Adlington (Lancs)	69	SD 6013
Admaston (Shrops.)	59	SJ 6313
Admaston (Staffs.)	60	SK 0423
Admington	50	SP 1945
Adstock	51	SP 7329
Adstone	51	SP 5951
Adventurers' Fen	53	TL 5668
Advie	117	NJ 1234
Adwell	36	SU 6899
Adwick le Street	71	SE 5308
Adwick upon Dearne	71	SE 4601
Adziel	121	NJ 9453
Ae Village	88	NX 9889
Affleck	121	NJ 8623
Affleck Castle (ant.)	109	NO 4938
Affpuddle	25	SY 8093
Afon Aeron	43	SN 5757
Afon Afan	41	SS 8195
Afon Aled	67	SH 9570
Afon Alwen	67	SJ 0244
Afon Banwy neu Einion	58	SJ 1307
Afon Bidno	57	SN 8584
Afon Biga	57	SN 8589
Afon Cain	58	SJ 1618
Afon Cefni	66	SH 4370
Afon Ceirw	67	SH 9247
Afon Cennen	43	SN 6318
Afon Cerist	57	SH 8416
Afon Claerwen	57	SN 8664
Afon Cledwen	67	SH 8762
Afon Clywedog	57	SN 8890
Afon Cothi	43	SN 6033
Afon Cynin	43	SN 2621
Afon Cywyn	43	SN 3114
Afon Ddu	67	SH 7464
Afon Duad	43	SN 3729
Afon Dugoed	57	SH 9012
Afon Dulas (Gwyn.)	57	SH 7508
Afon Dulas (Powys)	57	SN 7699
Afon Dulyn	67	SH 7267
Afon Dwyfach	66	SH 4746
Afon Dwyfor	66	SH 4941
Afon Dyfi	57	SH 8715
Afon Dysynni	57	SH 6206
Afon Eden	67	SH 7029
Afon Gamlan	57	SH 6924
Afon Glaslyn	66	SH 5941
Afon Gronw	43	SN 2119
Afon Gwy	45	ST 5398
Afon Gwydderig	41	SN 8431
Afon Honddu	45	SO 2925
Afon Leri	57	SN 6588
Afon Llafar	67	SH 8535
Afon Lliw	40	SS 5999
Afon Llugwy	67	SH 6860
Afon Llwchwr	40	SS 4996
Afon Llynfi	41	SO 1331
Afon Lwyd	57	SN 8590
Afon Machno	67	SH 7748
Afon Marteg	57	SN 9974
Afon Mawddach	57	SH 7220
Afon Mellte	41	SN 9209
Afon Mynwy	45	SO 4717
Afon Nyfer	42	SN 1237
Afon Porth-llwyd	67	SH 7365
Afon Rheidol	57	SN 6778
Afon Rhiw	57	SJ 0200
Afon Senni	41	SN 9224
Afon Syfynwy	42	SN 0324
Afon Taf	43	SN 2116
Afon Tanat	58	SJ 1424
Afon Teifi	43	SN 5346
Afon Trannon	57	SN 9890
Afon Troddi (River Trothy)	46	SO 4314
Afon Tryweryn	67	SH 8839
Afon Twrch (Dyfed)	43	SN 6445
Afon Twrch (Dyfed)	41	SN 7715
Afon Twrch (Powys)	57	SH 9714
Afon Twymyn	57	SN 8797
Afon Tywi	43	SN 6624
Afon Vyrnwy	58	SJ 1614
Afon Wnion	57	SH 8021
Afon Yscir	41	SN 9934
Afon Ystrad	67	SJ 0162
Afon Ystwyth	57	SN 6276
Afton Bridgend	88	NS 6212
Afton Resr.	88	NS 6304
Afton Water	88	NS 6307
Agden Resr.	71	SK 2592
Agglethorpe	78	SE 0886
A' Chairbhe	120	NH 0158
A' Ghlas-bheinn	114	NH 0023
A' Ghoil	132	NC 3571
Aigas Forest	128	NH 4341
Aignish	131	NB 4832
Aike	74	TA 0445
Aiker Ness (Orkney)	136	HY 3826
Aikerness (Westray)	138	HY 4552
Aikers	136	ND 4590
Aiketgate	83	NY 4846
Aikton	82	NY 2753
Ailey	45	SO 3348
Ailsa Craig	86	NX 0199
Ailsworth	62	TL 1199
Ainderby Quernhow	79	SE 3480
Ainderby Steeple	84	SE 3392
Aingers Green	39	TM 1120
Ainsdale	68	SD 3111
Ainshval (mt.)	110	NM 3794
Ainstable	83	NY 5346
Ainsworth	69	SD 7610
Aintree	68	SJ 3798
Aira Force	83	NY 3920
Aird (Dumf. and Galwy.)	86	NX 0960
Aird (Isle of Lewis)	131	NB 5635
Aird (Strath.)	99	NM 7600
Aird a' Mhòrain	124	NF 8379
Aird an Rùnair	124	NF 6970
Aird an Troim	131	NB 2316
Aird Barvas	131	NB 3553
Aird Brenish	130	NA 9727
Aird Dell	131	NB 4761
Aird-dhubh	123	NG 7040
Aird Dhubh	126	NG 9382
Airde, The	133	NC 5313
Aird Fada	105	NM 4424
Aird Fenish	130	NA 9929
Aird Luing	105	NM 7406
Aird Mhànais	125	NG 1188
Aird Mheadhonach	125	NG 1998
Aird Nisabost	124	NG 0497
Aird of Coigach	132	NC 0711
Aird of Kinloch	105	NM 5228
Aird of Sleat	111	NG 5900
Aird Riabhach	125	NG 2396
Airdrie	101	NS 7665
Airdriehill	101	NS 7867
Airds Bay	106	NN 0032
Airds Moss	94	NS 5724
Aird, The (Highld.) (dist)	128	NH 5241
Aird, The, (Island of Skye)	123	NG 4052
Aird, The, (Island of Skye)	123	NG 4375
Aird Thormaid	124	NF 9276
Aird Uig	130	NB 0437
Aird Vanish	124	NF 9999
Aire and Calder Navigation (N Yorks.)	71	SE 5820
Aire and Calder Navigation (N Yorks.)	71	SE 6119
Airedale	78	SE 0345
Airie Hill	88	NX 6268
Airies	86	NW 9767
Airlie Castle	108	NO 2952
Airmyn	74	SE 7224
Airntully	108	NO 0935
Airor	111	NG 7205
Airth	102	NS 8987
Airton	78	SD 9059
Aisby (Lincs.)	72	SK 8792
Aisby (Lincs.)	62	TF 0138
Aiskew	79	SE 2788
Aislaby (Cleve)	85	NZ 4012
Aislaby (N Yorks.)	80	NZ 8508
Aislaby (N Yorks.)	80	SE 7785
Aisthorpe	72	SK 9479
Aith (Fetlar)	143	HU 6390
Aith (Orkney)	136	HY 2417
Aith (Shetld.)	141	HU 3455
Aith (Stronsay)	137	HY 6525
Aith Hope	136	ND 2989
Aith Ness	141	HU 5144
Aithsting (dist.)	141	HU 3455
Aith Voe (Shetld.)	141	HU 3458
Aith Voe (Shetld.)	141	HU 4328
Aith Wick	141	HU 4429
Aitnoch	117	NH 9839
Akeld	97	NT 9529
Akeley	51	SP 7037
Akeman Street (Bucks.) (ant.)	36	SP 7316
Akeman Street (Oxon.) (ant.)	47	SP 3213
Akenham	55	TM 1448
Akermoor Loch	89	NT 4020
Alavna Roman Fort (ant.)	82	NY 0437
Albaston	20	SX 4270
Alberbury	58	SJ 3514
Albourne	28	TQ 2616
Albrighton (Shrops.)	59	SJ 4918
Albrighton (Shrops.)	59	SJ 8103
Alburgh	55	TM 2786
Albury (Herts.)	37	TL 4324
Albury (Surrey)	28	TQ 0547
Alby Hill	65	TG 1934
Alcaig	128	NH 5657
Alcaston	48	SO 4587
Alcester	50	SP 0857
Alciston	29	TQ 5005
Alconbury	52	TL 1875
Alconbury Weston	52	TL 1777
Aldbar Castle (ant.)	109	NO 5757
Aldborough (Norf.)	65	TG 1834
Aldborough (N Yorks.)	79	SE 4065
Aldbourne	34	SU 2675
Aldbrough (Humbs.)	75	TA 2338
Aldbrough St. John	84	NZ 2011
Aldbury	36	SP 9612
Aldclune	108	NN 9064
Aldeburgh	55	TM 4656
Aldeburgh Bay	55	TM 4755
Aldeby	65	TM 4593
Aldenham	37	TQ 1198
Alderbury	26	SU 1827
Alderford	65	TG 1218
Alderholt	26	SU 1212
Alderley	33	ST 7690
Alderley Edge	69	SJ 8478
Aldermaston	35	SU 5965
Aldermaston Soke	36	SU 6263
Aldermaston Wharf	35	SU 6067
Alderminster	50	SP 2248
Aldershot	35	SU 8650
Alderton (Glos.)	46	SP 0033
Alderton (Northants.)	51	SP 7346
Alderton (Shrops.)	59	SJ 4923
Alderton (Suff.)	55	TM 3441
Alderton (Wilts.)	33	ST 8382
Alderwasley	60	SK 3153
Aldfield	79	SE 2669
Aldford	68	SJ 4159
Aldham	54	TL 9125
Aldingbourne	28	SU 9205
Aldingham	77	SD 2871
Aldington (Here. and Worc.)	50	SP 0644
Aldington (Kent)	31	TR 0736
Aldochlay	100	NS 3591
Aldreth	53	TL 4473
Aldridge	60	SK 0500
Aldringham	55	TM 4460
Aldsworth	47	SP 1509
Aldunie	121	NJ 3626
Aldwark (Derby.)	71	SK 2257
Aldwark (N Yorks.)	79	SE 4663
Aldwick	28	SZ 9199
Aldwincle	52	TL 0081
Aldworth	35	SU 5579
Aled Isat Resr.	67	SH 9159
Alemoor Loch	89	NT 4015
Ale Water (Borders)	89	NT 4317
Ale Water (Borders)	97	NT 8764
Alexandria	101	NS 3979
Alfardisworthy	22	SS 2911
Alfington	24	SY 1197
Alfold	28	TQ 0333
Alford (Grampn.)	119	NJ 5715
Alford (Lincs.)	73	TF 4575
Alford (Somer.)	25	ST 6032
Alfred's Tower	25	ST 7435
Alfreton	60	SK 4155
Alfrick	49	SO 7453
Alfriston	29	TQ 5103
Alhampton	25	ST 6234
Alhang (mt.)	88	NS 6400
Aline Lodge	131	NB 1911
Alkborough	74	SE 8721
Alkerton	50	SP 3743
Alkham	31	TR 2441
Alkington	59	SJ 5239
Alkmonton	60	SK 1838
Alladale Lodge	128	NH 4389
Alladale River	128	NH 4188
Allaleigh	21	SX 8053
Allanaquoich	117	NO 1191
Allangrange House	128	NH 6251
Allanton (Borders)	97	NT 8654
Allanton (Strath.)	95	NS 8457
Allan Water (Borders)	89	NT 4606
Allan Water (Central)	101	NN 7802
Allardice	119	NO 8174
All Cannings	34	SU 0661
Allendale Common	84	NY 8651
Allendale Town	83	NY 8455
Allenheads	84	NY 8645
Allensmore	45	SO 4635
Aller	24	ST 4029
Allerby	82	NY 0839
Aller Dean	97	NT 9847
Allerford	23	SS 9047
Allermuir Hill	103	NT 2266
Allerston	81	SE 8782
Allerthorpe	74	SE 7847
Allerton	68	SJ 3986
Allerton Bywater	79	SE 4127
Allestree	60	SK 3439
Allexton	62	SK 8100
Allgreave	70	SJ 9767
Allhallows	30	TQ 8377
Alligin Shuas	123	NG 8358
Allimore Green	59	SJ 8519
Allington (Lincs.)	62	SK 8540
Allington (Wilts.)	34	SU 0663
Allington (Wilts.)	34	SU 2039
Allithwaite	77	SD 3876
Allnabad	133	NC 4641
Alloa	102	NS 8893
Allonby	82	NY 0842
Allonby Bay	82	NY 0541
Alloway	93	NS 3318
All Saints South Elmham	55	TM 3482
All Stretton	58	SO 4395
Allt a'Bhunn	133	NC 4812
Allt Ach' a' Bhàthàich	134	NC 8116
Allt a' Chaoil-réidhe	116	NN 5175
Allt a' Chaorainn	114	NM 9587
Allt a' Chaoruinn (Highld.)	127	NC 2703
Allt a' Chireachain	107	NN 7872
Allt a' Choire Mhóir	127	NH 1968
Allt a' Chonais	127	NH 0548
Allt a'Choromaig	106	NM 9120
Allt a' Chraois	133	NC 4438
Allt à Gheallaidh	117	NJ 1238
Allt a' Ghiubhais	123	NG 7968
Allt Airigh-dhamh	134	NC 8238
Allt a' Mhadaidh	127	NH 2274
Allt a' Mhuilinn (Highld.)	134	NC 8312
Allt a' Mhuilinn (Tays.)	116	NN 7675
Alltan Dearg	133	NC 6359
Allt an Dùin	134	NC 8125
Allt an Ealaidh	133	NC 7027
Allt an Stacain	106	NN 1220
Allt an Tairbh	98	NR 5488
Allt an Tiaghaich	132	NC 1623
Allt an t-Srathain	123	NG 7155
Allt Arnan	106	NN 2918
Allt Bail 'a' Mhuilinn	107	NN 5743
Allt Beinn Dònuill	127	NH 2399
Allt Beitheach	111	NM 7551
Allt Beochlich	106	NN 0115
Allt Bhlàraidh	115	NH 3518
Allt Bhran	116	NN 7889
Allt Braglenmore	106	NM 9119
Allt Breinag	116	NH 4707
Allt Càm (Highld.)	116	NN 4477
Allt Càm (Highld.)	116	NN 5178
Allt Càm Ban	116	NH 5606
Allt Camgharaidh	114	NM 9788
Allt Camghouran	107	NN 5253
Allt Car	133	NC 4317
Allt Chaiseagail	133	NC 5810
Alltchaorunn	106	NN 1950
Allt Choire a' Bhalachain	115	NN 0995
Allt Chomhraig	116	NN 8197
Allt Chonoghlais	106	NN 3336
Allt Cinn-locha	99	NR 7879
Allt Coire a'Chaolain	106	NN 2048
Allt Coire an Eoin	106	NN 2172
Allt Coire Lain Oig	116	NN 5198
Allt Coire na Saigh Duibhe	133	NC 4736
Allt Con	107	NN 6967
Allt Conait	107	NN 5245
Allt Connie	117	NO 0786
Allt Crunachdain	116	NN 5291
Allt Cuaich	116	NN 6686
Allt Darrarie	118	NO 3181
Allt Dearg	129	NH 8246
Allt Dochard	106	NN 2045
Allt Doe	116	NH 4107
Allt Easach	106	NN 0642
Allt Eigheach	107	NN 4360
Allt Eileag	127	NC 3107
Allt Fearna	106	NN 1222
Allt Féith Thuill	107	NN 3872
Allt Fionn Ghlinne	106	NN 3122
Alltforgan	57	SH 9624
Allt Forsiescye	135	ND 0158
Allt Garbh	115	NH 1619
Allt Garbh-airigh	128	NH 6399
Allt Garbh Buidhe	117	NN 9981
Allt Gharbh Ghaig	116	NN 7682
Allt Ghlas	107	NN 5364
Allt Glas Choire	116	NN 7378
Allt Glas Dhoire	115	NN 3084
Allt Gleann Da-Eig	107	NN 5944
Allt Gleann nam Meann	101	NN 5114
Allt Gleann Udalain	123	NG 8629
Allt Glen Loch	108	NO 0071
Allt Goibhre	128	NH 4148
Allt Hallater	106	NN 1338
Allt Làire	115	NN 3175
Allt Lon a' Chuil	134	NC 7240
Allt Loraich	115	NN 3878
Allt Lorgy	117	NH 8716
Allt Lundie	115	NH 2807
Allt Madagain	116	NN 6298
Alltmawr	44	SO 0647
Allt Mhoille	106	NN 1031
Allt Mhucarnaich	127	NH 2678
Allt Mór (Highld.)	116	NH 7404
Allt Mór (Highld.)	117	NN 8295
Allt Mór (Island of Skye)	123	NG 7221
Allt Mór (Tays.)	107	NN 7453
Allt na Bogair	107	NN 5954
Alltnacaillich	133	NC 4645
Allt na Caim	107	NN 3763
Allt na Doire Gairbhe	114	NH 0328
Allt na Gile	98	NR 4778
Allt na Glaise	107	NN 5769
Allt na h-Airbhe	127	NH 1193
Allt na h-Eirigh	123	NG 7054
Allt na Lairige (Highld.)	106	NN 2872
Allt na Lairige (Strath.)	106	NN 2316
Allt na Lairige Móire	106	NN 1163
Allt na Lùibe	133	NC 6410
Allt na Muic	115	NH 2515
Allt nan Achaidhean	134	NC 7729
Allt nan Airighèan	98	NR 3650
Allt nan Caorach	128	NH 5267
Allt nan Ramh	132	NC 2237
Allt Odhar	116	NH 5104
Allt Phocaichain	115	NH 3009
Allt Riabhach	115	NH 2219
Allt Riobain	107	NN 4530
Allt Ruighe nan Saorach	107	NN 6463
Allt Sleibh	107	NN 6566
Allt Smeòrail	134	NC 8511
Allt Srath a'Ghlinne	107	NN 6719
Allt Tolaghan	106	NN 2440
Allt Tuileach	117	NJ 2208
Allt Uisg an t-Sithein	116	NH 5921
Alltwalis	43	SN 4431
Alltwen	40	SN 7303
Allweston	25	ST 6614
Almeley	45	SO 3351
Almer	25	SY 9098
Almington	59	SJ 7034
Almondbank	108	NO 0626
Almondbury	70	SE 1614
Almondsbury	33	ST 6083
Alne	79	SE 4965
Alness	128	NH 6569
Alness Bay	128	NH 6367
Alnham	91	NT 9910
Alnmouth	91	NU 2410
Alnmouth Bay	91	NU 2510
Alnwick	91	NU 1912
Alphamstone	54	TL 8735
Alpheton	54	TL 8850
Alphington	21	SX 9190

Name	Page	Grid	Ref
Alport	70	SK	2164
Alpraham	69	SJ	5859
Alresford	39	TM	0621
Alrewas	60	SK	1715
Alsager	59	SJ	7955
Alsagers Bank	59	SJ	8048
Alsop en le Dale	60	SK	1655
Alston	83	NY	7146
Alstone	46	SO	9832
Alstonefield	60	SK	1355
Alston Moor	83	NY	7338
Alswear	23	SS	7222
Altandhu	132	NB	9812
Altandiun	74	NC	8025
Altarnun	19,20	SX	2281
Altass	133	NC	5000
Alterwall	135	ND	2865
Altgaltraig	100	NS	0473
Altham	78	SD	7632
Althorne	38	TQ	9098
Althorpe	74	SE	8309
Altnabreac Station	135	ND	0045
Altnacealgach Hotel	132	NC	2610
Altnafeadh	106	NN	2256
Altnaharra	133	NC	5635
Altofts	79	SE	3723
Alton (Derby.)	71	SK	3664
Alton (Hants.)	35	NY	7139
Alton (Staffs.)	60	SK	0742
Alton Pancras	25	ST	6902
Alton Priors	34	SU	1062
Alton Water Reservoir	55	TM	1536
Altrincham	69	SJ	7687
Altt Ddu	41	SO	0224
Alturlie Point	129	NH	7149
Altyre House	129	NJ	0254
Altyre Woods	129	NJ	0353
Alum Bay	26	SZ	3085
Alva	102	NS	8897
Alvanley	69	SJ	4973
Alvaston	45	SK	3933
Alvechurch	50	SP	0272
Alvecote	60	SK	2404
Alvediston	26	ST	9723
Alveley	49	SO	7584
Alverdiscott	23	SS	5225
Alverstoke	27	SZ	5998
Alverstone	27	SZ	5785
Alverton	61	SK	7942
Alves	129	NJ	1362
Alvescot	47	SP	2704
Alveston (Avon)	57	ST	6388
Alveston (Warw.)	50	SP	2256
Alvie	117	NH	8609
Alvingham	73	TF	3691
Alvington	45	SO	6000
Alwalton	62	TL	1395
Alwen Resr.	67	SH	9454
Alwinton	90	NT	9206
Alyth	108	NO	2448
Amat Forest	128	NH	4690
Am Balg (is.)	132	NC	1866
Ambergate	60	SK	3451
Amber Hill	63	TF	2346
Amberley (Glos.)	46	SO	8401
Amberley (W Susx)	28	TQ	0313
Am Bi-bogha Beag	122	NG	1938
Am Bi-bogha Mòr	122	NG	1838
Amble-by-the-Sea	91	NU	2604
Amblecote	49	SO	8885
Ambleside	83	NY	3704
Ambleston	42	SN	0026
Ambrosden	47	SP	6019
Am Buachaille	100	NN	0507
Amcotts	74	SE	8514
Amersham	36	SU	9597
Amesbury	34	SU	1541
Am Fraoch Eilean	98	NR	4662
Amhainn na Clach Airigh	132	NC	1321
A' Mhoine	133	NC	5160
Amhuinnsuidhe	124	NB	0408
Amicombe Hill	21	SX	5687
Amington	60	SK	2304
Amisfield Town	88	NY	0082
Amlwch	66	SH	4392
Amlwch Port	66	SH	4593
Ammanford	43	SN	6212
Amotherby	80	SE	7473
Ampfield	26	SU	3923
Ampleforth	79	SE	5878
Ampleforth College	79	SE	5978
Ampney Crucis	46	SP	0602
Ampney St. Mary	46	SP	0802
Ampney St. Peter	46	SP	0701
Amport	34	SU	2944
Ampthill	52	TL	0337
Ampton	54	TL	8671
Amroth	42	SN	1607
Amulree	108	NN	8936
An Acairseid	111	NM	4363
Anaheilt	111	NM	8162
An Cabar (mt.)	127	NH	2564
An Càmastac	122	NG	2365
An Caol	123	NG	6152
Ancaster	62	SK	9843
An Ceannaich	122	NG	1350
An Ceann Geal or Whiten Head	133	NC	4968
An Cearcall	107	NN	6270
Anchor	48	SO	1785
An Clachan	98	NR	2171
An Coileach (mt.)	125	NG	0892
An Coileachan (mt.)	127	NH	2468
An Coire	105	NM	8014
Ancroft	97	NT	9945
An Cruachan (Highld.)	115	NH	0935
An Cruachan (Jura)	99	NR	6900
Ancrum	96	NT	6224
Ancton	28	SU	9800
An Cuaidh	126	NG	7689
Anderby	73	TF	5275
Anderby Creek	73	TF	5575
Anderson	25	SY	8797
Anderton	69	SJ	6475
Andover	34	SU	3645
Andover Down	34	SU	3946
Andoversford	46	SP	0219
Andreas	76	SC	4199
An Dubh-aird	123	NG	7833
An Dubh-laimhrig	123	NG	4715
An Dubh Sgeir (Island of Skye)	122	NG	1936
An Dubh-sgeir (Island of Skye)	122	NG	3422
An Dubh-sgeir (Strath.)	92	NR	6655
An Dùn (pt.)	135	NQ	1425
An Dùnan	98	NS	5773
An Fhaochag	111	NG	6903
An Garbh-eilean (is.)	132	NC	3373
An Gead Loch	115	NH	1038
Angersleigh	24	ST	1918
Angle	42	SM	8603
Angle Bay	42	SM	8802
Anglesey	66	SH	4279
Angle Tarn	83	NY	4114
Anglezarke Moor	77	SD	6317
Angmering	28	TQ	0704
Angram	79	SE	5148
Angram Common	83	SD	8499
Angram Reservoir	78	SE	0476
Angry Brow (sbk.)	68	SD	3019
An Iola	106	NM	9747
Ankerville	129	NH	8174
Anlaby	74	TA	0328
An Lairig	116	NN	4977
An Leacainn	116	NH	5740
An Leàn-chàrn (mt.)	132	NC	4152
An Liathanach	127	NH	1257
Anmer	64	TF	7429
Annan	89	NY	1966
Annandale	89	NY	1292
Annaside	76	SD	098b
Annat (Highld.)	126	NG	8954
Annat (Strath.)	106	NN	0322
Annat Bay	126	NH	0397
Annathill	101	NS	7270
Anna Valley	34	SU	3444
Annbank	93	NS	4022
Annbank Station	93	NS	4024
Annesley	61	SK	5153
Annesley Woodhouse	61	SK	4953
Annet	18	SV	8608
Annet Burn	101	NN	6907
Anfield Plain	84	NZ	1551
Annick Water	93	NS	3843
Annie	101	NN	5810
Annochie	121	NJ	9342
Annscroft	58	SJ	4407
An Riabhachan (mt.)	115	NH	1133
An Rubha	98	NR	3594
An Sgarsoch (mt.)	117	NN	9383
An Sgurr	111	NM	4684
An Sleaghach	105	NM	7643
Ansley	50	SP	2991
Anslow	60	SK	2125
Anslow Gate	60	SK	2024
An Socach (Grampn.) (mt.)	117	NO	0980
An Socach (Highld.) (mt.)	132	NC	2558
An Socach (Strath.)	100	NS	0587
An Stac	111	NM	8689
An Stèidh (is.)	110	NG	2103
Anstey (Herts.)	53	TL	4032
Anstey (Leic.)	61	SK	5408
Anstiebury (ant.)	28	TQ	1543
An Stoc-bheinn	128	NC	6402
Anston	71	SK	5184
Anstruther	103	NO	5603
An Stùc (mt.)	132	NC	3409
An Stuchd	99	NR	7580
Ansty (Warw.)	50	SP	3983
Ansty (Wilts.)	26	ST	9526
Ansty (W Susx)	29	TQ	2923
An Suidhe (Highld.)	116	NH	8107
An Suidhe (Strath.)	100	NN	0007
An t-Aigeach (pt.)	124	NF	9364
An t-Teallach (mt.)	127	NH	0684
Anthill Common	27	SU	6412
Anthorn	89	NY	1958
An t-lasgair (is.)	122	NG	3574
Antingham	65	TG	2533
Antonine Wall (Strath.) (ant.)	101	NS	5972
Antonine Wall (Strath.) (ant.)	101	NS	7677
Antony	20	SX	3954
An Torc or Boar of Badenoch	116	NN	6276
Antrobus	69	SJ	6479
An t-Sùileag	114	NN	0282
An Tunna	92	NR	9736
An Uidh	128	NH	6396
Anwick	62	TF	1150
Anwoth	87	NX	5856
Aonach Mór	105	NM	4919
Aonach Beag (Highld.)	106	NN	1971
Aonach Beag (Highld.)	106	NN	4574
Aonach Buidhe	115	NH	0532
Aonach Eagach (mt.)	106	NN	1557
Aonach Mòr (Highld.)	115	NN	1973
Aonach Mòr (Strath.)	116	NN	2148
Aonach Shasuinn	115	NH	1718
Ape Dale	48	SO	4789
Apes Hall	53	TL	5590
Apethorpe	62	TL	0295
Apley	73	TF	1075
Apperknowle	71	SK	3878
Apperley	46	SO	8628
Appin House	106	NM	9349
Appin of Dull	107	NN	7948
Appleby (Humbs.)	74	SE	9414
Appleby in Westmorland	83	NY	6820
Appleby Magna	60	SK	3110
Appleby Parva	60	SK	3109
Applecross	123	NG	7144
Applecross Forest	123	NG	7647
Applecross House	123	NG	7145
Appledore (Devon)	22	SS	4630
Appledore (Devon)	24	ST	0614
Appledore (Kent)	30	TQ	9529
Appleford	47	SU	5293
Appleshaw	34	SU	3048
Appleton	47	SP	4401
Appleton-le-Moors	80	SE	7387
Appleton-le-Street	80	SE	7373
Appleton Roebuck	79	SE	5542
Appleton Thorn	69	SJ	6484
Appleton Wiske	85	NZ	3904
Appletreehall	90	NT	5117
Appletreewick	78	SE	0560
Appley	24	ST	0721
Appley Bridge	69	SD	5209
Appuldurcombe House (ant.)	27	SZ	5579
Apse Heath	27	SZ	5682
Apsley End	52	TL	1232
Apuldram	27	SU	8403
Aquae Sulis (ant.)	33	ST	7464
Aqualate Hall	59	SJ	7719
Aqualate Mere	59	SJ	7720
Araid	123	NG	7958
Aran Benllyn	57	SH	8523
Aran Fawddwy	57	SH	8422
Arbeadie	119	NO	6996
Arbirlot	109	NO	6040
Arboll	129	NH	8781
Arborfield	36	SU	7567
Arborfield Cross	36	SU	7666
Arborfield Garrison	36	SU	7665
Arbor Low (ant.)	70	SK	1663
Arbroath	109	NO	6340
Arbury Hill	51	SP	5358
Arbuthnott	119	NO	8074
Archiestown	120	NJ	2344
Arclid Green	59	SJ	7962
Ardachu	128	NC	6703
Ardalanish	104	NM	3618
Ardalanish Bay	104	NM	3717
Arda Mòra	124	NB	0208
Ardanaiseig	106	NN	0824
Ardargie House Hotel	108	NO	0715
Ardarroch	123	NG	8339
Ard Beag	122	NG	2161
Ardbeg	98	NR	4146
Ard Caol	125	NB	2301
Ardcharnich	127	NH	1788
Ardchattan Priory (ant.)	106	NM	9734
Ardchiavaig	104	NM	3818
Ardchullarie More	101	NN	5813
Ardchyle	101	NN	5229
Ardclach	129	NH	9545
Ard-dhubh	123	NG	7040
Ardd-lin	58	SJ	2516
Ardechive	115	NN	1490
Ardeley	53	TL	3127
Ardelve	123	NG	8727
Arden	101	NS	3684
Ardencaple House	105	NM	7619
Arden Great Moor	85	SE	5193
Ardens Grafton	50	SP	1154
Ardentallan House	105	NM	8323
Ardentinny	100	NS	1887
Ardeonaig	107	NN	6635
Ardersier	129	NH	7854
Ardery	111	NM	7562
Ardessie	127	NH	0589
Ardfern	105	NM	8004
Ardgartan	100	NN	2702
Ardgay	128	NH	5990
Ardgay Station	128	NH	6090
Ardgoil Estate	100	NN	2200
Ardgoil Forest	100	NS	2198
Ardgour (dist.)	106	NM	9467
Argask	102	NO	1310
Arcicle	97	NT	7138
Ardindrean	127	NH	1588
Ardingly	29	TQ	3330
Ardingly Resr.	29	TQ	3429
Ardington	34	SU	4388
Ardintoul Point	123	NG	8324
Ardivachar	124	NF	7445
Ardivachar Point	124	NF	7446
Ardkinglas House	100	NN	1710
Ardlair	121	NJ	5528
Ardlamont Bay	100	NR	9764
Ardlamont House	100	NR	9865
Ardlamont Point	100	NR	9963
Ardleigh	54	TM	0529
Ardleigh Reservoir	54	TM	0328
Ardler	108	NO	2641
Ardley	47	SP	5427
Ardlui	106	NN	3115
Ardlussa	99	NR	6487
Ardlussa Bay	99	NR	6588
Ardmaddy Castle	105	NM	7816
Ardmair	127	NH	1198
Ardmaleish Point	100	NS	0769
Ardmarnock Bay	100	NR	9072
Ardmarnock House	100	NR	9172
Ardmay	100	NN	2802
Ardmeanach (dist.)	104	NM	4327
Ardminish	92	NR	6448
Ardminish Bay	92	NR	6548
Ardmolich	111	NM	7172
Ardmore	132	NC	2051
Ardmore (Islay)	98	NR	4650
Ardmore (Strath.)	100	NS	3178
Ardmore Bay	111	NM	4659
Ard More Mangersta	130	NB	0032
Ardmore Point (Highld.)	132	NC	1651
Ardmore Point (Highld.)	134	NC	7666
Ardmore Point (Island of Mull)	111	NM	4759
Ardmore Point (Island of Skye)	122	NG	2159
Ardmore Point (Islay)	98	NR	4750
Ardmucknish Bay	106	NM	8837
Ard na Claise Mòire	123	NG	6852
Ardnacross	111	NM	5449
Ardnacross Bay	92	NR	7625
Ardnadam	100	NS	1580
Ardnagrask	128	NH	5149
Ardnameacan	123	NG	7114
Ardnamurchan (dist.)	111	NM	5766
Ardnarff	114	NG	8935
Ardnastang	111	NM	8061
Ardnave	98	NR	2873
Ardnave Point	98	NR	2975
Ardneil Bay	93	NS	1847
Ardnish (dist.)	111	NM	7281
Ardno	100	NN	1408
Ardnoe Point	99	NR	7794
Ardo	121	NJ	8538
Ardoch	108	NO	0937
Ardoch Burn	101	NN	7405
Ardochy House	115	NH	2102
Ardo House	121	NJ	9221
Ardoyne	121	NJ	6527
Ardpatrick	99	NR	7560
Ardpatrick House	99	NR	7559
Ardpatrick Point	92	NR	7357
Ardpeaton	100	NS	2185
Ardrishaig	99	NR	8585
Ardroil	130	NB	0432
Ardrossan	93	NS	2342
Ardross Castle	128	NH	6174
Ardscalpsie Point	92	NS	0457
Ardshealach	111	NM	6967
Ardskenish	98	NR	3491
Ardsley	71	SE	3805
Ardsley East	79	SE	3024
Ardslignish	111	NM	5661
Ardtalla	98	NR	4654
Ardtalnaig	107	NN	7039
Ard Thurinish	111	NM	5999
Ardtoe	111	NM	6270
Ardtornish Point	105	NM	6942
Ardtreck Point	122	NG	3336
Ardtrostan	107	NN	6723
Ardtun	105	NM	4022
Arduaine	105	NM	7910
Ardullie	128	NH	5863
Ardvasar	111	NG	6303
Ardverikie Forest	116	NN	5081
Ardvey	125	NG	1292
Ardvorlich	107	NN	6322
Ardvourlie	131	NB	1810
Ardwell	86	NX	1045
Ardwell Point	86	NX	0644
Ardyne Burn	100	NS	1172
Ardyne Point	100	NS	0968
Areley Kings	49	SO	8070
Arenig Fach	57	SH	8241
Arenig Fawr	67	SH	8237
Argoed Mill	57	SN	9962
Argyll (dist.)	100	NM	9903
Aridhglas	104	NM	3123
Arileod	110	NM	1654
Arinacrinachd	123	NG	7458
Arinagour	110	NM	2257
Arion	136	HY	2514
Arisaig (Highld.)	111	NM	6686
Arisaig (Highld.) (dist.)	111	NM	6687
Arisaig House	111	NM	6984
Arivruaich	131	NB	2417
Arkendale	79	SE	3860
Arkengarthdale	84	NZ	0001
Arkengarthdale Moor	84	NY	9405
Arkesden	53	TL	4834
Ark Hill	109	NO	3542
Arkholme	77	SD	5871
Arkle (mt.)	132	NC	3046
Arkley	37	TQ	2296
Arks Edge	90	NT	7106
Arksey	71	SE	5706
Arkwright Town	71	SK	4270
Arlecdon	82	NY	0419
Arlesey	52	TL	1935
Arleston	59	SJ	6410
Arley (Ches.)	69	SJ	6780
Arley (Warw.)	50	SP	2890
Arlingham	46	SO	7010
Arlington (Devon)	23	SS	6140
Arlington (E Susx)	29	TQ	5407
Arlington (Glos.)	46	SP	1006
Armadale (Highld.)	134	NC	7864
Armadale (Lothian)	102	NS	9368
Armadale Bay (Highld.)	134	NC	7965
Armadale Bay (Island of Skye)	111	NG	6404
Armadale Burn	134	NC	7859
Armadale Castle	111	NG	6304
Armathwaite	83	NY	5046
Arminghall	65	TG	2504
Armitage	60	SK	0816
Armscote	50	SP	2444
Armthorpe	71	SE	6105
Arnabost	110	NM	2060
Arnaval (mt.)	122	NG	3431
Arncliffe	78	SD	9371
Arncliffe Cote	78	SD	9470
Arncott	36	SP	6117
Arncroach	103	NO	5105
Arndilly House	120	NJ	2946
Arne	26	SY	9788
Arnesby	51	SP	6192
Arnfield Brook	70	SK	0298
Arngask	102	NO	1310
Arnicle	92	NR	7138
Arnisdale	123	NG	8410
Arnish	123	NG	5948
Arnish Moor	131	NB	4030
Arniston Engine	103	NT	3462
Arnol	131	NB	3148
Arnold	61	SK	5745
Arnot Resr.	103	NO	2002
Arnprior	101	NS	6194
Arnside	77	SD	4578
Arnton Fell	90	NY	5295
Aros (dist.)	111	NM	5249
Aros Bay	98	NR	4652
Aros Mains	105	NM	5645
Aros River	105	NM	5145
Arpafeelie	128	NH	6150
Arrad Foot	77	SD	3080
Arram	74	TA	0344
Arrathorne	84	SE	2093
Arreton	27	SZ	5386
Arrington	53	TL	3250
Arrochar	100	NN	2904
Arrow	50	SP	0856
Arscaig	133	NC	5014
Artafallie	128	NH	6249
Artfield Fell	86	NX	2367
Arthington	79	SE	2644
Arthingworth	51	SP	7581
Arthog	57	SH	6414
Arthrath	121	NJ	9636
Arthur Seat (Cumbr.)	89	NY	4978
Arthur's Seat (Lothian)	103	NT	2872
Arthurstone	108	NO	2642
Artrochie	121	NK	0032
Arundel	28	TQ	0107
Arundel Park	28	TQ	0108
Arvhoulan	106	NN	0188
Asby	82	NY	0620
Ascog	100	NS	1063
Ascot	36	SU	9168
Ascott-under-Wychwood	47	SP	2918
Ascrib Islands	122	NG	3064
Asenby	79	SE	3975
Asfordby	61	SK	7018
Asfordby Hill	61	SK	7219
Asgarby (Lincs.)	62	TF	1145
Asgarby (Lincs.)	73	TF	3366
Asgog Bay	100	NR	9366
Asgog Loch	100	NR	9570
Ash (Kent)	30	TQ	5964
Ash (Kent)	31	TR	2958
Ash (Somer.)	25	ST	4720
Ash (Surrey)	35	SU	8950
Ashampstead	35	SU	5676
Ashbocking	55	TM	1654
Ashbourne	60	SK	1846
Ashbrittle	24	ST	0521
Ash Bullayne	23	SS	7704
Ashburnham Place	29	TQ	6914
Ashburton	21	SX	7569
Ashbury (Devon)	20	SX	5097
Ashbury (Oxon.)	34	SU	2685
Ashby	74	SE	9009
Ashby by Partney	73	TF	4266
Ashby Canal (Leic.)	60	SK	3801
Ashby Canal (Warw.)	50	SP	4191
Ashby cum Fenby	75	TA	2500
Ashby de la Launde	62	TF	0455
Ashby-de-la-Zouch	60	SK	3516
Ashby Folville	61	SK	7012
Ashby Magna	51	SP	5690
Ashby Parva	51	SP	5288
Ashby St. Ledgers	51	SP	5768
Ashby St. Mary	65	TG	3202
Ashchurch	46	SO	9233
Ashcombe	21	SX	9179
Ashcott	25	ST	4336
Ashdon	53	TL	5842
Ashdown Forest	29	TQ	4530
Asheldham	39	TL	9701
Ashen	54	TL	7442
Ashendon	36	SP	7014
Ash Fell	83	NY	7404
Ashfield (Central)	101	NN	7803
Ashfield (Suff.)	55	TM	2062
Ashfield Green	55	TM	2673
Ashford (Devon)	23	SS	5335
Ashford (Kent)	31	TR	0142
Ashford (Surrey)	36	TQ	0671
Ashford Bowdler	48	SO	5170
Ashford Carbonel	48	SO	5270
Ashford Hill	35	SU	5562
Ashford in the Water	70	SK	1969
Ashgill	94	NS	7849
Ashie Moor	116	NH	5931
Ashiestiel Hill	96	NT	4134
Ashill (Devon)	24	ST	0811
Ashill (Norf.)	64	TF	8804
Ashill (Somer.)	24	ST	3217
Ashingdon	38	TQ	8693
Ashington (Northum.)	91	NZ	2687
Ashington (W Susx)	28	TQ	1315
Ashintully Castle	108	NO	1061
Ashkirk	96	NT	4722
Ashleworth	46	SO	8125
Ashley (Cambs.)	54	TL	6961
Ashley (Ches.)	69	SJ	7784
Ashley (Devon)	23	SS	6411
Ashley (Glos.)	46	ST	9394
Ashley (Hants.)	34	SU	3831
Ashley (Northants.)	51	SP	7991
Ashley (Staffs.)	59	SJ	7536
Ashley Green	36	SP	9705
Ashley Heath	26	SU	1105
Ash Magna	59	SJ	5739
Ashmansworth	34	SU	4156
Ashmansworthy	22	SS	3317
Ash Mill	23	SS	7823
Ashmore	25	ST	9117
Ashmore Park	60	SJ	9602
Ashorne	50	SP	3057
Ashover	71	SK	3463
Ashow	50	SP	3170
Ashperton	49	SO	6441
Ashprington	21	SX	8157
Ash Priors	24	ST	1529
Ashreigney	23	SS	6213
Ashridge College	36	SP	9912
Ashstead	23	SO	0010
Ash Thomas	23	ST	0010
Ashton (Ches.)	69	SJ	5069
Ashton (Corn.)	18	SW	6028
Ashton (Devon)	21	SX	8584
Ashton (Here. and Worc.)	48	SO	5164
Ashton (Northants.)	51	SP	7649
Ashton (Northants.)	52	TL	0588
Ashton Common	33	ST	8958
Ashton-in-Makerfield	69	SJ	5799
Ashton Keynes	46	SU	0494
Ashton under Hill	50	SO	9938
Ashton-under-Lyne	69	SJ	9399
Ashton upon Mersey	69	SJ	7792
Ashurst (Hants.)	26	SU	3310
Ashurst (Kent)	29	TQ	5038
Ashurst (W Susx)	28	TQ	1716
Ashurstwood	29	TQ	4236
Ashury (Oxon.)	34	SU	2685
Ashwater	20	SX	3895
Ashwell (Herts.)	53	TL	2639
Ashwell (Leic.)	62	SK	8613
Ashwellthorpe	65	TM	1397
Ashwick	33	ST	6447
Ashwicken	64	TF	7018
Ashworth Moor Resr.	69	SD	8315
Askam in Furness	76	SD	2177
Askern	71	SE	5613
Askernish House	112	NF	7323
Askerswell	25	SY	5292
Askett	36	SP	8105
Askham (Cumbr.)	83	NY	5123
Askham (Notts.)	72	SK	7374
Askham Bryan	79	SE	5548
Askham Richard	79	SE	5347
Askival (mt.)	111	NM	3995
Asknish	100	NR	9291
Asknish Forest	100	NR	9191
Askrigg	84	SD	9491
Askrigg Common	84	SD	9493
Askwith	78	SE	1648
Aslackby	62	TF	0830
Aslacton	55	TM	1591
Aslockton	61	SK	7440
Asloun	119	NJ	5414
Aspatria	82	NY	1442
Aspenden	53	TL	3528
Aspley Guise	52	SP	9436
Aspley Heath	52	SP	9334
Aspull	69	SD	6108
Asselby	74	SE	7127
Assich Forest	129	NH	8146
Assington	54	TL	9338
Assynt House	128	NH	5967
Astbury	69	SJ	8461
Astcote	51	SP	6753
Asterley	58	SJ	3707
Asterton	48	SO	3991
Asthall	47	SP	2811
Asthall Leigh	47	SP	3013
Astley (Here. and Worc.)	49	SO	7867
Astley (Shrops.)	59	SJ	5218
Astley (Warw.)	50	SP	3189
Astley Abbotts	59	SO	7096
Astley Cross	49	SO	8069
Astley Green	69	SJ	7099
Astley Hall (ant.)	69	SD	5718
Aston (Berks.)	36	SU	7884
Aston (Ches.)	59	SJ	6046
Aston (Ches.)	59	SJ	5678
Aston (Derby.)	70	SK	1883
Aston (Here. and Worc.)	48	SO	4571
Aston (Herts.)	53	TL	2722
Aston (Oxon.)	47	SP	3302
Aston (Shrops.)	59	SJ	5228
Aston (Shrops.)	59	SJ	6109
Aston (Somer.)	59	SJ	7540
Aston (S Yorks.)	71	SK	4685
Aston (W Mids)	50	SP	0789
Aston Abbotts	36	SP	8420
Aston Botterell	49	SO	6384
Aston-by-Stone	59	SJ	9131
Aston Cantlow	50	SP	1359
Aston Clinton	36	SP	8812
Aston Crews	46	SO	6723
Aston Eyre	59	SO	6594
Aston Fields	50	SO	9669
Aston Flamville	51	SP	4692
Aston Ingham	46	SO	6823
Aston juxta Mondrum	59	SJ	6556
Aston le Walls	51	SP	4950
Aston Magna	47	SP	1935
Aston Munslow	48	SO	5186
Aston on Clun	48	SO	3981
Aston-on-Trent	61	SK	4129
Aston Resrs.	77	SD	6036
Aston Rogers	58	SJ	3406
Aston Rowant	36	SU	7299
Aston Sandford	36	SP	7507
Aston Somerville	50	SP	0438
Aston Subedge	50	SP	1441
Aston Tirrold	35	SU	5586
Aston Upthorpe	35	SU	5586
Astwick	52	TL	2138
Astwood	52	SP	9547
Astwood Bank	50	SP	0462
Aswarby (Lincs.)	62	TF	0639
Aswardby (Lincs.)	73	TF	3770
Atcham	59	SJ	5409
Athelington	55	TM	2170
Athelney	24	ST	3428
Athelstaneford	103	NT	5377
Atherfield Point	27	SZ	4478
Atherington	23	SS	5923
Atherstone	60	SP	3097
Atherstone on Stour	50	SP	2050
Atherton	69	SD	6703
Atlow (dist.)	107	NN	7872
Atlow	60	SK	2248
Attadale Forest	114	NG	9935
Attadale House	114	NG	9239
Attenborough	61	SK	5134
Attingham	59	SJ	5409
Attleborough (Norf.)	64	TM	0495
Attleborough (Warw.)	50	SP	3790
Attlebridge	65	TG	1216
Atwick	81	TA	1850
Atworth	33	ST	8565
Auborn	72	SK	9262
Auchagallon	92	NR	8934
Auchalick Bay	100	NR	9074
Auchallater	117	NO	1588
Aucharnie	121	NJ	6341
Auchattie	119	NO	6994
Auchavan	108	NO	1969
Auchbraad	99	NR	8381
Auchenblae	119	NO	7279
Auchenbrack	88	NX	7696
Auchencairn	87	NX	7951
Auchencairn Bay	87	NX	8251
Auchencarroch	101	NS	4182
Auchencrow	97	NT	8560
Auchendinny	103	NT	2561
Auchendores Resr.	100	NS	3573
Auchengray	102	NS	9953
Auchengruith	88	NS	8009
Auchenhalrig	121	NJ	3861
Auchenheath	95	NS	8043
Auchenhew	92	NS	0225
Auchenhove	119	NJ	5604
Auchenreoch Loch	87	NX	8171
Auchensaugh Hill	95	NS	8527
Auchentiber	93	NS	3647
Auchgourish	117	NH	9315
Auchindoun Castle (ant.)	121	NJ	3437
Auchindrean	127	NH	1980
Auchineden Hill	101	NS	4980

Auchingilloch (mt.) 94 NS 7035
Auchininna 121 NJ 6446
Auchinleck (Dumf. and Galwy.) 87 NX 4570
Auchinleck (Strath.) 93 NS 5422
Auchinloch 101 NS 6670
Auchintoul 119 NJ 5316
Auchleuchries 121 NK 0136
Auchleven 121 NJ 6224
Auchlochan 95 NS 8037
Auchlossan 119 NJ 5701
Auchlunies 119 NO 8999
Auchlyne 107 NN 5129
Auchlyne West Burn 107 NN 4830
Auchmacoy 121 NJ 9930
Auchmillan 93 NS 5129
Auchmithie 109 NO 6744
Auchmuirbridge 103 NO 2101
Auchmull 119 NO 5874
Auchnacloich 106 NM 9533
Auchnacree 109 NO 4663
Auchnafree 107 NN 8133
Auchnafree Hill 107 NN 8030
Auchnagallin 117 NJ 0533
Auchnagatt 121 NJ 9341
Aucholzie 118 NO 3490
Auchope Cairn 90 NT 8819
Auchronie 118 NO 4480
Auchterarder 107 NN 9312
Auchterderran 103 NT 2195
Auchterhouse 108 NO 3337
Auchtermuchty 103 NO 2311
Auchterneed 128 NH 4959
Auchtertool 103 NT 2190
Auchtertyre Hill 123 NG 8329
Auchter Water 95 NS 8754
Auchtitench Hill 88 NS 7118
Auchtoo 107 NN 5620
Auckengill 135 ND 3764
Auckley 71 SE 6501
Audenshaw 69 SJ 9196
Audlem 59 SJ 6543
Audley 59 SJ 7950
Audley End (ant.) 53 TL 5237
Audley End Station 53 TL 5136
Auds 121 NJ 6564
Aughton (Humbs.) 74 SE 7038
Aughton (Lancs.) 68 SD 3804
Aughton (Lancs.) 77 SD 5467
Aughton (S Yorks.) 71 SK 4586
Aughton Park 68 SD 4106
Auld Darkney (mt.) 109 NO 4266
Auldearn 129 NH 9155
Aulden 45 SO 4654
Auldhame 103 NT 5984
Auldhouse 94 NS 6250
Auldton Fell 89 NT 1108
Aulich Burn 107 NN 5961
Auliston Point 111 NM 5457
Ault a' chruinn 114 NG 9420
Aultanrynie 132 NC 3436
Aultbea 126 NG 8789
Aultdearg 127 NH 2865
Aultgrishan 126 NG 7485
Aultguish Inn 127 NH 3570
Aultibea 135 ND 0423
Aultiphurst 134 NC 8065
Aultmore (Grampn.) 121 NJ 4053
Aultmore (Grampn.) (dist.) 121 NJ 4557
Ault-na-goire 116 NH 5423
Aultnamain Inn 128 NH 6681
Aulton 121 NJ 6028
Aundorach 117 NH 9716
Aunsby 62 TF 0438
Auquhorthies 121 NJ 8329
Auskerry (is.) 137 HY 6716
Auskerry Sound 137 HY 6618
Aust 33 ST 5789
Austerfield 71 SK 6594
Austrey 60 SK 2906
Austwick 77 SD 7668
Authorpe 73 TF 3980
Authorpe Row 73 TF 5373
Avebury 34 SU 0969
Avebury (ant.) 34 SU 1070
Aveley 37 TQ 5680
Avening 46 ST 8797
Averham 61 SK 7654
Aveton Gifford 21 SX 6947
Avielochan 117 NH 9016
Aviemore 117 NH 8912
Avington 34 SU 3767
Avoch 128 NH 6955
Avoch Bay 129 NH 7054
Avon 26 SZ 1498
Avonbridge 102 NS 9072
Avon Castle 26 SU 1303
Avon Dam Resr. 21 SX 6765
Avon Dassett 50 SP 4150
Avonmouth 33 ST 5177
Avon Water 94 NS 7143
Avon Wick 21 SX 7158
Awbridge 26 SU 3323
Awkley 33 ST 5885
Awliscombe 24 ST 1301
Awre 46 SO 7008
Awsworth 61 SK 4843
Axbridge 33 ST 4254
Axe Edge 70 SK 0370
Axford (Hants.) 35 SU 6043
Axford (Wilts.) 34 SU 2369
Axminster 24 SY 2998
Axmouth 24 SY 2591
Aylburton 45 SO 6101
Ayle 83 NY 7149
Aylesbeare 24 SY 0391
Aylesbury 36 SP 8213
Aylesby 75 TA 2007
Aylesford 30 TQ 7359
Aylesham 31 TR 2352
Aylestone 61 SK 5701
Aylmerton 65 TG 1839
Aylsham 65 TG 1926
Aylton 49 SO 6537
Aymestrey 48 SO 4265
Aynho 47 SP 5133
Ayot St. Lawrence 37 TL 1916
Ayot St. Peter 37 TL 2115
Ayr 93 NS 3321
Ayres, The 76 NX 4303
Aysgarth 78 SE 0088
Ayside 77 SD 3983
Ayston 62 SK 8601
Aythorpe Roding 37 TL 5815
Ayton (Borders) 97 NT 9260
Ayton (N Yorks.) 81 SE 9884
Aywick (Yell) 143 HU 5386
Ay Wick (Yell) 143 HU 5486
Azerley 79 SE 2574

B

Baa Taing (Auskerry) 137 HY 6715
Baa Taing (Shetld.) 142 HU 2774
Babbacombe 21 SX 9365
Babbacombe Bay 21 SX 9568
Babbet Ness 103 NO 5914
Babbinswood 58 SJ 3329
Babcary 25 ST 5628
Babel 41 SN 8235
Babell 68 SJ 1574
Babeny 21 SX 6775
Babingley River 64 TF 6825
Babraham 53 TL 5150
Babworth 72 SK 6880
Bac an Eich 127 NH 2249
Bac Beag (is.) 104 NM 2337
Bach Camp (ant.) 45 SO 5460
Bache Hill 48 SO 2163
Bach Island 105 NM 7726
Bachlaig 98 NR 4175
Back 131 NB 4840
Backaland 138 HY 5630
Backaskail Bay 139 HY 6438
Backaskaill 138 HY 4850
Backbarrow 77 SD 3584
Backfolds 121 NK 0252
Backford 68 SJ 3971
Backhill (Grampn.) 121 NJ 7939
Backhill (Grampn.) 121 NK 0039
Backhill of Clackriach 121 NJ 9246
Backhill of Trustach 119 NO 6397
Backies 129 NC 8302
Backlass 135 ND 2053
Backmuir of New Gilston 103 NO 4308
Back of Keppoch 111 NM 6587
Backstane Hill 95 NS 9127
Backwater Reservoir 108 NO 2560
Backwell 33 ST 4868
Backworth 91 NZ 2972
Bac Mór or Dutchman's Cap 104 NM 2438
Bacon End 38 TL 6018
Baconsthorpe 65 TG 1237
Bacton (Here. and Worc.) 45 SO 3732
Bacton (Norf.) 65 TG 3434
Bacton (Suff.) 54 TM 0466
Bacup 78 SD 8622
Bad a'Chreamha 123 NG 8536
Badachro 123 NG 7873
Badandun HiLL 108 NO 2067
Badanloch Forest 134 NC 7935
Badanloch Lodge 134 NC 7933
Badavanich 127 NH 1058
Bad Bog 126 NG 9281
Badbury 34 SU 1980
Badbury Hill 47 SU 2694
Badbury Rings (ant.) 26 ST 9602
Badby 51 SP 5559
Badcall (Highld.) 132 NC 1541
Badcall (Highld.) 132 NC 2355
Badcall Bay 132 NC 1541
Badcaul 126 NH 0191
Baddeley Green 59 SJ 9250
Baddesley Ensor 60 SP 2798
Baddidarach 132 NC 0923
Baddinsgill Reservoir 95 NT 1255
Baddoch 117 NO 1382
Baddoch (mt.) 117 NJ 0719
Badenoch (dist.) 116 NN 7091
Badenscoth 121 NJ 7038
Badentarbat Bay 126 NC 0008
Badenyon 118 NJ 3419
Badger 59 SO 7699
Badgers Mount 37 TQ 5061
Badgeworth (Glos.) 46 SO 9019
Badgworth (Somer.) 32 ST 3952
Badingham 55 TM 3067
Badlesmere 31 TR 0154
Badlipster 135 ND 2049
Badluarach 126 NG 9994
Badminton 33 ST 8082
Badminton House 33 ST 8082
Badmondisfield Hall (ant.) 54 TL 7457
Badninish 129 NH 7694
Badrallach 127 NH 0691
Badsey 50 SP 0743
Badsworth 71 SE 4614
Badwell Ash 54 TL 9969
Bagby 79 SE 4680
Bagendon 46 SP 0006
Bage, The 45 SO 2943
Baggrave Hall 61 SK 6909
Baggy Point 22 SS 4140
Bagh an Tailleir (pt.) 99 NR 8481
Bagh Feisdlum 110 NM 2458
Bàgh Loch an Ròin 132 NC 1954
Bàgh na Doide 99 NR 6976
Bàgh nam Faoileann 124 NF 8444
Bàgh nan Gunnaichean 123 NG 4574
Bàgh Tigh-an-Droighinn 99 NR 8579
Bagillt 68 SJ 2175
Bagillt Bank (sbk.) 68 SJ 2376
Baginton 50 SP 3474
Baglan 41 SS 7493
Bagley 58 SJ 4027
Bagnall 59 SJ 9250
Bagshot (Surrey) 36 SU 9163
Bagshot (Wilts.) 34 SU 3165
Bagshot Heath 36 SU 9061
Bagthorpe (Norf.) 64 TF 7932
Bagthorpe (Notts.) 61 SK 4751
Bagworth 61 SK 4408
Bagwy Llydiart 45 SO 4427
Baidland Hill 93 NS 2552
Baildon 78 SE 1539
Baile 124 NF 9381
Bailebeag 116 NH 5018
Baile Boidheach 99 NR 7473
Baile Mór 104 NM 2824
Bailey Hill 48 SO 2472
Bailiesward 121 NJ 4737
Baillieston 101 NS 6764
Bail Uachdraich 124 NF 8160
Bainbridge 84 SD 9390
Bainton (Cambs.) 62 TF 0906
Bainton (Humbs.) 81 SE 9652
Bairnkine 90 NT 6515
Bait or St. Mary's Island 91 NZ 3575
Bakers End 37 TL 3917
Baker Street 38 TQ 6381
Bakewell 70 SK 2168
Bala 67 SH 9236
Balachuirn 123 NG 5540
Balaglas 124 NF 8457
Bala Lake or Llyn Tegid 67 SH 9033
Balallan 131 NB 2920
Balbeg 116 NH 4924
Balbeggie 108 NO 1629
Balbegno Castle 109 NO 6372
Balbithan 119 NJ 7917
Balbithan House 119 NJ 8018
Balblair 129 NH 7066
Balcary Point 87 NX 8249
Balcherry 129 NH 8182
Balchladich 132 NC 0330
Balchraggan 128 NH 5343
Balchrick 132 NC 1960
Balcombe 29 TQ 3130
Balcomie 103 NO 6209
Balcurvie 103 NO 3400
Balderhead Resr. 84 NY 9118
Baldersby 79 SE 3578
Balderstone 77 SD 6332
Balderton 62 SK 8151
Baldhu 18 SW 7743
Baldinnie 103 NO 4311
Baldock 53 TL 2434
Baldoon Sands 87 NX 4552
Baldrine 76 SC 4281
Balduff Hill 108 NO 2253
Baldwin 76 SC 3581
Baldwinholme 82 NY 3351
Baldwin's Gate 59 SJ 7939
Bale 64 TG 0136
Balemartine 104 NL 9841
Balephetrish Bay 104 NM 0047
Balephuil 104 NL 9640
Balephuil Bay 104 NL 9440
Balerno 102 NT 1666
Baleshare (is.) 124 NF 7861
Balevullin 104 NL 9546
Balfield 109 NO 5468
Balfour 136 HY 4716
Balfour Castle 136 HY 4716
Balfron 101 NS 5488
Balgaveny 121 NJ 6640
Balgavies 109 NO 5351
Balgedie 102 NO 1603
Balgonar 102 NT 0293
Balgove 121 NJ 8133
Balgowan 116 NN 6394
Balgowan Point 86 NX 1242
Balgown 122 NG 3868
Balgray 109 NO 4138
Balgray Reservoir 93 NS 5157
Balgrochan 101 NS 6278
Balgy 123 NG 8454
Balhalgardy 121 NJ 7623
Balhary 108 NO 2646
Baliasta 143 HP 6009
Baligill 134 NC 8566
Balintore (Highld.) 129 NH 8675
Balintore (Tays.) 108 NO 2859
Balintraid 129 NH 7370
Balivanich 124 NF 7755
Balkeerie 108 NO 3244
Balkholme 74 SE 7828
Balkissock 86 NX 1381
Ball 58 SJ 3026
Balla 112 NF 7811
Ballabeg 76 SC 2470
Ballacannell 76 SC 4382
Ballacarnane Beg 76 SC 3088
Ballachulish 106 NN 0857
Ballageich Hill 93 NS 5350
Ballagyr 76 SC 2685
Ballajora 76 SC 4790
Ballamodha 76 SC 2773
Ballantrae 86 NX 0882
Ballantrae Bay 86 NX 0783
Ballantrushal 131 NB 3753
Ballard Point 26 SZ 0481
Ballasalla (I. of M.) 76 SC 2870
Ballasalla (I. of M.) 76 SC 3497
Ballater 118 NO 3695
Ballaugh 76 SC 3493
Ballechin 108 NN 9353
Ballencleuch Law 88 NS 9304
Ballencrieff 103 NT 4878
Ball Hill 34 SU 4263
Balliekine 92 NR 8739
Balliemore (Strath.) 105 NM 8228
Balliemore (Strath.) 100 NS 0584
Ballig 76 SC 2882
Ballikinrain Castle 101 NS 5687
Ballimore (Central) 107 NN 5217
Ballimore (Strath.) 100 NR 9283
Ballinaby 98 NR 2267
Ballindean 108 NO 2529
Ballinger Common 36 SP 9103
Ballingham 45 SO 5731
Ballingry 102 NT 1797
Ballinlick 108 NN 9840
Ballinloan Burn 108 NN 9442
Ballinluig 108 NN 9852
Ballintuim 108 NO 1054
Balloch (Highld.) 129 NH 7346
Balloch (Strath.) 101 NS 3981
Balloch (Tays.) 107 NN 8419
Balloch (Tays.) 109 NO 3557
Ballochan 119 NO 5290
Ballochbuie Forest 117 NO 1989
Balloch Castle 101 NS 3983
Ballochroy 92 NR 7252
Balloch, The (mt.) 121 NJ 4648
Ballo Resr. 103 NO 2204
Balls Cross 28 SU 9826
Ballygown 105 NM 4343
Ballygrant 98 NR 3966
Ballyhaugh 110 NM 1758
Ballymichael 92 NR 9231
Balmacaan Forest 115 NH 3925
Balmacara 123 NG 8127
Balmaclellan 88 NX 6578
Balmacneil 108 NN 9850
Balmae 87 NX 6845
Balmaha 101 NS 4290
Balmalcolm 103 NO 3108
Balmanno Hill 103 NO 1410
Balmartin 124 NF 7273
Balmedie 119 NJ 9617
Balmerino 109 NO 3524
Balmerlawn 26 SU 3003
Balmoral Castle 117 NO 2595
Balmoral Forest 117 NO 2587
Balmore 101 NS 6073
Balmore Forest 115 NH 3333
Balmullo 109 NO 4220
Balmungie 129 NH 7459
Balmurrie 86 NX 2066
Balnabodach 112 NF 7101
Balnacoil 134 NC 8011
Balnacra 126 NG 9746
Balnafoich 116 NH 6835
Balnaglaic 116 NH 4430
Balnagown Castle 129 NH 7675
Balnaguard 108 NN 9451
Balnaguard Burn 108 NN 9249
Balnaguisich 128 NH 6771
Balnahara 105 NM 4534
Balnahard 98 NR 4199
Balnakeil 132 NC 3968
Balnakeil Bay 132 NC 3869
Balnaknock 123 NG 4162
Balnamoon 109 NO 5463
Balnapaling 129 NH 7969
Balquhidder 107 NN 5320
Balranald 124 NF 7169
Balsall Common 50 SP 2377
Balscote 50 SP 3841
Balsham 53 TL 5850
Balta (is.) 143 HP 6608
Baltasound (Unst) 143 HP 6208
Balta Sound (Unst) 143 HP 6508
Baltasound Aerodrome 143 HP 6207
Balterley 59 SJ 7550
Balthangie 121 NJ 8351
Baltonsborough 25 ST 5434
Balvaird 128 NH 5452
Balvarran 108 NO 0762
Balvenie Castle (ant.) 121 NJ 3240
Balvicar 105 NM 7616
Balvraid 117 NH 8231
Bamber Bridge 77 SD 5626
Bamburgh 97 NU 1834
Bamff 108 NO 2251
Bamford 70 SK 2083
Bampton (Cumbr.) 83 NY 5118
Bampton (Devon) 23 SS 9522
Bampton (Oxon.) 47 SP 3103
Bampton Common 83 NY 4716
Banavie 115 NN 1177
Banbury 51 SP 4540
Banc Cwmhelen 40 SN 6811
Banchory 119 NO 6995
Banchory-Devenick 119 NJ 9002
Banc Nant Rhys 57 SN 8279
Bancyfelin 43 SN 3218
Banc-y-ffordd 43 SN 4037
Bandirran House 108 NO 1930
Banff 121 NJ 6863
Bangor 66 SH 5872
Bangor-Is-coed 58 SJ 3945
Banham 54 TM 0688
Bank 26 SU 2807
Bankend (Dumf. and Galwy.) 88 NY 0268
Bankend (Strath.) 95 NS 8033
Bankfoot 108 NO 0635
Bankglen 88 NS 5912
Bankhead (Grampn.) 119 NJ 6608
Bankhead (Grampn.) 119 NJ 8910
Bank Newton 78 SD 9152
Banknock 101 NS 7779
Banks (Cumbr.) 90 NY 5664
Banks (Lancs.) 68 SD 3820
Bankshill 89 NY 1981
Banks Sands 77 SD 3724
Bank Street 49 SO 6362
Banningham 65 TG 2129
Banniskirk House 135 ND 1657
Bannister Green 38 TL 6920
Bannockburn 101 NS 8190
Ban Rubha 105 NM 7106
Banstead 37 TQ 2559
Bantham 21 SX 6643
Banton 101 NS 7479
Banwell 32 ST 3959
Baosbheinn (mt.) 123 NG 8765
Bapchild 30 TQ 9363
Baramore 111 NM 6474
Barassie 93 NS 3232
Barbaraville 129 NH 7472
Barber Booth 70 SK 1184
Barbon 77 SD 6282
Barbreck House 105 NM 8306
Barbreck River 105 NM 8306
Barbrook 23 SS 7147
Barbrook Reservoir 71 SK 2777
Barbury Castle (ant.) 34 SU 1476
Barby 51 SP 5470
Barcaldine Castle (ant.) 106 NM 9140
Barcaldine Forest 106 NM 9741
Barcaldine House 106 NM 9641
Barcheston 50 SP 2639
Barcloy Hill 87 NX 7552
Barcombe 29 TQ 4214
Barcombe Cross 29 TQ 4216
Barcraigs Resr. 93 NS 3857
Barden 84 SE 1493
Barden Fell 78 SE 0858
Barden Resrs. 78 SE 0257
Bardfield Saling 54 TL 6826
Bard Head 141 HU 5135
Bardister 142 HU 3577
Bardney 73 TF 1169
Bardon Mill 90 NY 7764
Bardowie 101 NS 5873
Bardrainney 100 NS 3372
Bardsea 77 SD 3074
Bardsey 78 SE 3643
Bardsey Island (Ynys Enlli) 56 SH 1221
Bardsey Sound 56 SH 1323
Bardsley 69 SD 9201
Bardwell 54 TL 9473
Barewood 45 SO 3856
Barford (Norf.) 65 TG 1007
Barford (Warw.) 50 SP 2660
Barford St. Martin 26 SU 0531
Barford St. Michael 47 SP 4332
Barfrestone 31 TR 2650
Bargatton Loch 88 NX 6962
Bargoed 41 SO 1500
Bargrennan 86 NX 3476
Barham (Cambs.) 52 TL 1375
Barham (Kent) 31 TR 2050
Barham (Suff.) 55 TM 1451
Bar Hill 53 TL 3863
Barholm 62 TF 0811
Barkby 61 SK 6309
Barkestone-le-Vale 61 SK 7734
Barkham 36 SU 7866
Barking 37 TQ 4785
Barking (Suff.) 54 TM 0653
Barkingside 37 TQ 4489
Barking Isles 131 NB 4023
Barkisland 70 SE 0419
Barkston (Lincs.) 62 SK 9241
Barkston (N Yorks.) 79 SE 4936
BarkwAY 53 TL 3835
Barkwith 73 TF 1681
Barlaston 59 SJ 8938
Barlavington 28 SU 9716
Barlborough 71 SK 4777
Barlby 79 SE 6334
Barlestone 60 SK 4205
Barley (Herts.) 53 TL 4038
Barley (Lancs.) 78 SD 8240
Barleythorpe 62 SK 8409
Barling 38 TQ 9289
Barlow (Derby.) 71 SK 3474
Barlow (N Yorks.) 79 SE 6428
Barlow (Tyne and Wear) 91 NZ 1560
Barmby Moor 80 SE 7748
Barmby on the Marsh 79 SE 6828
Barmekin Hill 119 NJ 7207
Barmer 64 TF 8133
Barmoor Castle 97 NT 9939
Barmore Island 99 NR 8771
Barmouth 56 SH 6115
Barmouth Bay 56 SH 5612
Barmpton 84 NZ 3118
Barmston 81 TA 1659
Barnack 62 TF 0705
Barnacle 50 SP 3884
Barnard Castle 84 NZ 0516
Barnard Gate 47 SP 4010
Barnardiston 54 TL 7148
Barnbougle Castle (ant.) 102 NT 1678
Barnburgh 71 SE 4803
Barnby 55 TM 4789
Barnby Dun 71 SE 6109
Barnby IN THE Willows 62 SK 8552
Barnby Moor 71 SK 6684
Barnes 37 TQ 2276
Barnet 37 TQ 3395
Barnetby le Wold 74 TA 0509
Barney 64 TF 9932
Barnham (Suff.) 54 TL 8779
Barnham (W Susx) 28 SU 9604
Barnham Broom 65 TG 0807
Barnhead 109 NO 6657
Barnhill 129 NJ 1457
Barnhills 86 NW 9871
Barnhourie (sbk.) 88 NX 9350
Barningham (Durham) 84 NZ 0810
Barningham (Suff.) 54 TL 9676
Barnoldby le Beck 75 TA 2303
Barnoldswick 78 SD 8746
Barns Green 28 TQ 1227
Barnsley (Glos.) 46 SP 0705
Barnsley (S Yorks.) 71 SE 3406
Barns Ness 96 NT 7277
Barnstaple 23 SS 5533
Barnstaple or Bideford Bay 22 SS 3432
Barnston (Essex) 38 TL 6519
Barnston (Mers.) 68 SJ 2783
Barnt Green 50 SP 0073
Barnton 69 SJ 6374
Barnwell 52 TL 0485
Barnwood 46 SO 8518
Barochan House (ant.) 101 NS 4168
Barons Point 100 NS 2280
Barony, The 136 HY 2527
Barr 86 NX 2794
Barra (is.) 112 NF 6801
Barra Castle 121 NJ 7925
Barrachan 86 NX 3649
Barrack 121 NJ 8942
Barraer Fell 86 NX 3761
Barraglom 131 NB 1634
Barra Head 112 NL 5579
Barrahormid 99 NR 7184
Barrapol 104 NL 9542
Barras 119 NO 8580
Barrasford 90 NY 9273
Barravullin 105 NM 7907
Barr Castle (ant.) 100 NS 3458
Barregarrow 76 SC 3288
Barrel of Butter (is.) 136 HY 3500
Barr Ganuisg 100 NR 9280
Barr Glen 92 NR 6936
Barrhead 101 NS 5068
Barr Hill (Dumf. and Galwy.) 88 NX 7781
Barrhill (Strath.) 86 NX 2382
Barrington (Cambs.) 53 TL 3949
Barrington (Somer.) 24 ST 3918
Barripper 18 SW 6338
Barrisdale Bay 111 NG 8605
Barr Liath 100 NR 9673
Barrmill 93 NS 3651
Barr Mór (Strath.) 105 NM 8138
Barr Mór (Strath.) 100 NN 1312
Barrock 135 ND 2571
Barrock House 135 ND 2862
Barrow (Lancs.) 77 SD 7338
Barrow (Leic.) 62 SK 8815
Barrow (Shrops.) 59 SJ 6500
Barrow (Somer.) 25 ST 7231
Barrow (Suff.) 54 TL 7663
Barroway Drove 63 TF 5703
Barrowby 62 SK 8736
Barrow Deep (lightship) 39 TM 3004
Barrowden 62 SK 9400
Barrowford 78 SD 8538
Barrow Gurney 33 ST 5267
Barrow-in-Furness 76 SD 1969
Barrow Street 25 ST 8330
Barrow upon Humber 75 TA 0721
Barrow upon Soar 61 SK 5717
Barrow upon Trent 60 SK 3528
Barr Water 92 NR 6836
Barry (S Glam.) 41 ST 1168
Barry (Tays.) 109 NO 5334
Barry Island 41 ST 1166
Barry Links 109 NO 5431
Barry Links Station 109 NO 5433
Barsalloch Point 86 NX 3441
Barsby 61 SK 6911
Barsham 55 TM 3989
Barston 50 SP 2078
Bartestree 45 SO 5641
Bar, The (Dyfed) 56 SN 5780
Bar, The (Gwyn.) 66 SH 4161
Bar, The (Gwyn.) 56 SH 6014
Barth Head 136 ND 4285
Barthol Chapel 121 NJ 8134
Barthomley 59 SJ 7652
Bartley 26 SU 3012
Bartlow 53 TL 5845
Barton (Cambs.) 53 TL 4055
Barton (Ches.) 58 SJ 4454
Barton (Devon) 21 SX 9067
Barton (Glos.) 46 SP 0925
Barton (Lancs.) 77 SD 5136
Barton (N Yorks.) 84 NZ 2208
Barton (Warw.) 50 SP 1051
Barton Aerodrome 69 SJ 7397
Barton Bendish 64 TF 7105
Barton Hartshorn 47 SP 6431
Barton in Fabis 61 SK 5232
Barton in the Beans 60 SK 3906
Barton-le-Clay 52 TL 0831
Barton-le-Street 80 SE 7274
Barton-le-Willows 80 SE 7163
Barton Mills 54 TL 7273
Barton Moss 69 SJ 7397
Barton on Sea 26 SZ 2493
Barton-on-the-Heath 47 SP 2532
Barton Seagrave 52 SP 8877
Barton Stacey 34 SU 4340
Barton Stacey Camp 34 SU 4342
Barton St. David 25 ST 5431
Barton Turf 65 TG 3522
Barton-under-Needwood 60 SK 1818
Barton-Upon-Humber 74 TA 0222
Barvas 131 NB 3649
Barway 53 TL 5475
Barwell 61 SP 4496
Barwick 25 ST 5513
Barwick in Elmet 79 SE 3937
Baschurch 58 SJ 4222
Bascote 50 SP 4063
Basford Green 60 SJ 9951
Bashall Eaves 77 SD 6943
Bashley 26 SZ 2496
Basildon 38 TQ 7189
Basing 35 SU 6652
Basingstoke 35 SU 6351
Basingstoke Canal 35 SU 8453
Baslow 71 SK 2572
Bason Bridge 32 ST 3445
Bassaleg 41 ST 2787
Bassenthwaite 82 NY 2332
Bassenthwaite Lake 82 NY 2129
Bassett 26 SU 4116
Bassingbourn 53 TL 3344
Bassingfield 61 SK 6137
Bassingham 72 SK 9059
Bassingthorpe 62 SK 9628
Bass Rock 103 NT 6087
Basta 143 HU 5294
Basta Voe 143 HU 5296
Baston 62 TF 1114
Bastwick 65 TG 4217
Batcombe (Dorset.) 25 ST 6104
Batcombe (Somer.) 25 ST 6838
Bate Heath 69 SJ 6879
Bath 33 ST 7464
Bathampton 33 ST 7765
Bathealton 24 ST 0724
Batheaston 33 ST 7767
Bathford 33 ST 7866
Bathgate 102 NS 9768
Bathley 72 SK 7759
Bathpool 20 SX 2874
Batley 79 SE 2424
Batsford 47 SP 1834
Battersby 85 NZ 5908
Battersea 37 TQ 2876
Battery Point 33 ST 4677
Battisford 54 TM 0554
Battisford Tye 54 TM 0254
Battle (E Susx.) 29 TQ 7416
Battle (Powys) 41 SO 0031
Battlefield 59 SJ 5117
Battlesbridge 38 TQ 7794
Battlesbury (ant.) 33 ST 8945
Battlesden 52 SP 9628
Battleton 23 SS 9127

Battramsley 26 SZ 3099
Bauds of Cullen 121 NJ 4766
Baugh Fell 83 SD 7493
Baughurst 35 SU 5859
Baulking 34 SU 3190
Baumber 73 TF 2174
Baunton 46 SP 0204
Bavelaw Castle (ant.) 102 NT 1662
Baverstock 26 SU 0231
Bawburgh 65 TG 1508
Bawden Rocks or Man and his man 18 SW 6953
Bawdeswell 64 TG 0420
Bawdrip 32 ST 3339
Bawdsey 55 TM 3440
Bawtry 71 SK 6592
Baxenden 78 SD 7726
Baxterley 60 SP 2796
Bayble 131 NB 5231
Bayble Bay 131 NB 5330
Bayble Hill 131 NB 5030
Baycliff 77 SD 2872
Baydon 34 SU 2877
Bayford 37 TL 3108
Bayham Abbey 29 TQ 6436
Bayhead 124 NF 7468
Bayles 83 NY 7044
Baylham 55 TM 1051
Bay of Backaland 138 HY 5730
Bay of Bomasty 137 HY 6123
Bay of Brough 139 HY 6541
Bay of Cleat 138 HY 4646
Bay of Cruden 121 NK 0934
Bay of Deepdale 140 HU 1754
Bay of Firth 136 HY 3814
Bay of Fladdabister 141 HU 4332
Bay of Furrowend 136 HY 4719
Bay of Holland 137 HY 6422
Bay of Houseby 137 HY 6821
Bay of Ireland 136 HY 2809
Bay of Isbister 136 HY 4018
Bay of Keisgaig 132 NC 2469
Bay of Kirkwall 136 HY 4413
Bay of Laig 111 NM 4688
Bay of Linton 137 HY 5318
Bay of London 138 HY 5634
Bay of Lopness 139 HY 7443
Bay of Meil 136 HY 4812
Bay of Newark 139 HY 7139
Bay of Noup 138 HY 4149
Bay of Quendale 141 HU 3712
Bay of Sandoyne 136 HY 4602
Bay of Sandquoy 139 HY 7345
Bay of Skaill (Orkney) 136 HY 2319
Bay of Skaill (Papa Westray) 138 HY 4651
Bay of Stoer 132 NC 0328
Bay of Stove 139 HY 6134
Bay of Swartmill 138 HY 4846
Bay of the Tongue 136 HY 2004
Bay of Tuquoy 138 HY 4644
Bay River 122 NG 2752
Baysdale Beck 85 NZ 6207
Bayston Hill 59 SJ 4809
Bayton 49 SO 6973
Beachampton 51 SP 7737
Beachamwell 64 TF 7505
Beachamwell Warren 64 TF 7607
Beachans 129 NJ 0246
Beacharr 92 NR 6943
Beachborough 31 TR 1638
Beachley 33 ST 5591
Beach River 105 NM 4623
Beachy Head 29 TV 5895
Beacon 24 ST 1705
Beacon End 38 TL 9524
Beacon Fell 77 SD 5642
Beacon Hill (Dorset) 26 SY 9794
Beacon Hill (Hants.) (ant.) 35 SU 4557
Beacon Hill (Powys) 48 SO 1677
Beacon Hill (Wilts.) 34 SU 2043
Beacon Point (Durham) 85 NZ 4445
Beacon Point (Northum.) 91 NZ 3189
Beacon's Bottom 36 SU 7895
Beaconsfield 36 SU 9490
Beacons Reservoir 41 SN 9818
Beacontree 37 TQ 4886
Beacravik 125 NG 1190
Beadlam 79 SE 6584
Beadnell 97 NU 2329
Beadnell Bay 97 NU 2327
Beaford 23 SS 5514
Beal (Northum.) 97 NU 0642
Beal (N Yorks.) 79 SE 5325
Bealings 55 TM 2348
Beaminster 25 ST 4801
Beamish 84 NZ 2253
Beamsley 78 SE 0752
Bean 30 TQ 5972
Beanacre 33 ST 9066
Bean Hill 86 NX 0554
Beanley 91 NU 0818
Beaquoy 136 HY 3022
Beare Green 28 TQ 1842
Bearley 50 SP 1760
Bearneas 126 NH 0242
Bearpark 84 NZ 2343
Bearreraig Bay 123 NG 5153
Bearsbridge 83 NY 7857
Bearsden 101 NS 5471
Bearsted 30 TQ 8055
Bearwood 26 SZ 0496
Beatshach 117 NJ 2737
Beattock 89 NT 0702
Beauchamp Roding 37 TL 5809
Beauchief 71 SK 3381
Beaufort 41 SO 1611
Beaufort Castle 128 NH 5042
Beaulieu 26 SU 3801
Beaulieu Heath (Hants.) 26 SU 3400
Beaulieu Heath (Hants.) 26 SU 4104
Beaulieu River 26 SU 3901
Beaulieu Road Station 26 SU 3405
Beauly 128 NH 5246
Beauly Firth 128 NH 6147
Beaumaris 66 SH 6076
Beaumont (Cumbr.) 89 NY 3459
Beaumont (Essex) 55 TM 1725
Beauport Park 30 TQ 7813
Beaupre Castle (ant) 41 ST 0071
Beausale 50 SP 2470
Beauty Hill 121 NJ 9020
Beaver Dyke Resrs. 79 SE 2254
Beaworthy 20 SX 4699
Beazley End 54 TL 7428
Bebington 68 SJ 3384
Bebside 91 NZ 2881
Beccles 55 TM 4290
Becconsall 77 SD 4422
Beckbury 59 SJ 7601
Beckbury Camp (ant.) 46 SP 0629
Beckenham 37 TQ 3769
Beckermet 82 NY 0206
Beckfoot (Cumbr.) 82 NY 0949
Beckfoot (Cumbr.) 82 NY 1600
Beck Foot (Cumbr.) 83 SD 6196
Beckford 46 SO 9735
Beckhampton 34 SU 0868
Beck Hole 80 NZ 8102
Beckingham (Lincs.) 62 SK 8753
Beckingham (Notts.) 72 SK 7790
Beckington 33 ST 7951
Beckley (E Susx.) 30 TQ 8423
Beckley (Oxon) 47 SP 5611
Beck Row 54 TL 6977
Beck Side 76 SD 2382
Beckton 37 TQ 4381
Beckwithshaw 79 SE 2653
Beda Fell 83 NY 4216
Bedale 79 SE 2688
Bedburn 84 NZ 1031
Beddau 41 ST 0585
Beddgelert 66 SH 5848
Beddingham 29 TQ 4408
Beddington 37 TQ 3165
Bedfield 55 TM 2266
Bedford 52 TL 0449
Bedford Level (Middle Level) (dist.) 63 TL 3393
Bedford Level (North Level) (dist.) 63 TF 2404
Bedford Level (South Level) (dist.) 54 TL 5985
Bedgebury Forest 29 TQ 7233
Bedhampton 27 SU 6906
Bedingfield 55 TM 1768
Bedlington 91 NZ 2581
Bedlinog 41 SO 0901
Bedmond 36 TL 0903
Bednall 60 SJ 9517
Bedrule 90 NT 6017
Bedruthan Steps 19 SW 8569
Bedstone 48 SO 3675
Bedwas 41 ST 1689
Bedworth 50 SP 3587
Beeby 61 SK 6608
Beech (Hants.) 35 SU 6938
Beech (Staffs.) 59 SJ 8538
Beech Hill 36 SU 6964
Beechingstoke 34 SU 0859
Beedon 35 SU 4877
Beeford 81 TA 1254
Beefstand Hill 90 NT 8214
Beeley 71 SK 2667
Beelsby 75 TA 2001
Beenham 35 SU 5868
Beer 24 SY 2289
Beercrocombe 24 ST 3220
Beer Hackett 25 ST 5911
Bee Head 24 SY 2287
Beesands 21 SX 8140
Beesby 73 TF 4680
Beeson 21 SX 8140
Beeston (Beds.) 52 TL 1648
Beeston (Ches.) 69 SJ 5358
Beeston (Norf.) 64 TF 9015
Beeston (Notts.) 61 SK 5336
Beeston (W Yorks.) 79 SE 2930
Beeston Regis 65 TG 1742
Beeswing 88 NX 8969
Beetham 77 SD 4979
Beetley 64 TF 9718
Begbroke 47 SP 4613
Begelly 42 SN 1107
Beguildy 48 SO 1979
Begwns, The 44 SO 1544
Beich Burn 107 NN 6228
Beighton (Norf.) 65 TG 3808
Beighton (S Yorks.) 71 SK 4483
Beinn a' Bha'ach Ard 127 NH 3643
Beinn a' Bheithir 106 NN 0455
Beinn a' Bhoth 131 NB 1316
Beinn a' Bhragaidh 129 NC 8100
Beinn a' Bhràghad 123 NG 4125
Beinn a' Bhuird 117 NO 0898
Beinn a'Bhùiridh 106 NN 0928
Beinn a' Bhùtha 132 NC 2934
Beinn a' Chàisgein Beag 126 NG 9682
Beinn a'Chàisgein Mòr 126 NG 9878
Beinn a Chaisil 105 NM 7847
Beinn a' Chaisteil 127 NH 3781
Beinn Achaladair 106 NN 3443
Beinn a' Chaoinich 123 NG 8618
Beinn a'Chaol-airigh 104 NM 3517
Beinn a' Chaolais 125 NG 2199
Beinn a' Chaorainn (Grampn.) 117 NJ 0401
Beinn a' Chaorrainn (Highld.) 115 NN 3884
Beinn a' Chapuill 123 NG 8215
Beinn a' Charnain 124 NF 6988
Beinn a' Chearcaill 123 NG 4650
Beinn a' Chlachain 123 NG 7147
Beinn a' Chlachair 116 NN 4778
Beinn a' Chlaidheimh 127 NH 0677
Beinn a'Choin 100 NN 3512
Beinn a'Chreachain 107 NN 3743
Beinn a'Chroin 107 NN 3918
Beinn a'Chrùlaiste 106 NN 2456
Beinn a'Chuallaich 107 NN 6861
Beinn a' Chùirn 123 NG 8621
Beinn a'Ghlinne Bhig 123 NG 3945
Beinn a' Ghlinne Mhòir 104 NM 3421
Beinn a' Ghlo 117 NN 9673
Beinn a' Ghràig 105 NM 5437
Beinn Aird da Loch 132 NC 2831
Beinn Airein 111 NM 4079
Beinn Airigh Charr 126 NG 9376
Beinn Alligin 123 NG 8661
Beinn a'Mhanaich 100 NS 2694
Beinn a' Mhùinidh 126 NH 0366
Beinn an Amair 132 NC 3565
Beinn an Dòthaidh 106 NN 3240
Beinn an Eòin (Highld.) 127 NC 3808
Beinn an Eòin (Highld.) 126 NG 9064
Beinn an Lochain 100 NN 2107
Beinn an Oir 98 NR 4974
Beinn an t-Sneachda 114 NM 9880
Beinn an Tuirc 92 NR 7536
Beinn a'Sgà 123 NG 4356
Beinn Bhalgairean 106 NN 2023
Beinn Bhàn (Highld.) 123 NG 8044
Beinn Bhàn (Highld.) 115 NN 1285
Beinn Bhàn (Islay) 98 NR 4056
Beinn Bharrain 92 NR 8942
Beinn Bheag (Highld.) 115 NH 0800
Beinn Bheag (Strath.) 100 NS 1293
Beinn Bheigeir 98 NR 4356
Beinn Bheula 100 NS 1598
Beinn Bhreac (Central) 107 NN 4713
Beinn Bhreac (Central) 107 NN 4196
Beinn Bhreac (Colonsay) 98 NR 3796
Beinn Bhreac (Grampn.) 117 NO 0596
Beinn Bhreac (Highld.) 133 NC 6056
Beinn Bhreac (Highld.) 123 NG 8363
Beinn Bhreac (Highld.) 116 NH 7527
Beinn Bhreac (Highld.) 116 NH 7837
Beinn Bhreac (Highld.) 111 NM 5969
Beinn Bhreac (Island of Arran) 92 NR 9531
Beinn Bhreac (Island of Skye) 122 NG 2553
Beinn Bhreac (Island of Skye) 122 NG 3426
Beinn Bhreac (Island of Skye) 123 NG 4328
Beinn Bhreac (Islay) 98 NR 3571
Beinn Bhreac (Jura) 98 NR 5377
Beinn Bhreac (Jura) 98 NR 5990
Beinn Bhreac (Soay, Island of Skye) 123 NG 4615
Beinn Bhreac (Strath.) 106 NM 9940
Beinn Bhreac (Strath.) 100 NN 0210
Beinn Bhreac (Strath.) 92 NR 7538
Beinn Bhreac (Strath.) 92 NR 7847
Beinn Bhreac (Strath.) 98 NR 9877
Beinn Bhreac (Strath.) 100 NS 0576
Beinn Bhreac (Strath.) 100 NS 3299
Beinn Bhreac (Tays.) 107 NN 7340
Beinn Bhreac (Tays.) 117 NN 8682
Beinn Bhreac-liath 106 NN 3033
Beinn Bhreac Mhòr 116 NH 6719
Beinn Bhrotain 117 NN 9592
Beinn Bhuidhe (Highld.) 111 NM 6053
Beinn Bhuidhe (Highld.) 111 NM 8296
Beinn Bhuidhe (Strath.) 105 NM 5940
Beinn Bhuidhe (Strath.) 106 NN 2018
Beinn Bhuidhe Mhòr 116 NH 7840
Beinn Bragar 131 NB 2643
Beinn Ceannabeinne 133 NC 4264
Beinn Chàiteag 135 ND 1347
Beinn Chaorach 100 NS 2892
Beinn Chapull 106 NM 9319
Beinn Charnach Bheag 122 NG 2757
Beinn Cheathaich 107 NN 4432
Beinn Chlaonleud 111 NM 7352
Beinn Chlianaig 115 NN 2978
Beinn Chreagach (Island of Mull) 105 NM 5121
Beinn Chreagach (Island of Skye) 122 NG 2853
Beinn Chreagach (Ulva) 105 NM 4040
Beinn Chreagach Mhòr 105 NM 6339
Beinn Churalain 106 NM 9846
Beinn Damh 126 NG 8851
Beinn Dearg (Central) 101 NN 5803
Beinn Dearg (Highld.) 132 NC 2765
Beinn Dearg (Highld.) 127 NH 2581
Beinn Dearg (Highld.) 127 NH 2868
Beinn Dearg (Strath.) 100 NN 0204
Beinn Dearg (Tays.) 117 NN 8577
Beinn Dearg Bad Chailleach 126 NG 9187
Beinn Dearg Mhòr 126 NG 8692
Beinn Dearg Mòr 126 NH 0379
Beinn Dhorain 134 NC 9215
Beinn Dhubh 125 NB 0800
Beinn Domhnaill 128 NH 6796
Beinn Donachain 106 NN 1931
Beinn Donn 106 NM 9647
Beinn Dòrain 106 NN 3238
Beinn Dronaig 114 NH 0237
Beinn Dubh (Central) 101 NN 4004
Beinn Dubh (Islay) 98 NR 4263
Beinn Dubhain 134 NC 9320
Beinn Dubhchraig 106 NN 3025
Beinn Each 107 NN 6015
Beinn Edra 123 NG 4562
Beinn Eich 100 NS 3094
Beinn Eighe 126 NG 9659
Beinn Eighe National Nature Reserve 126 NG 9861
Beinn Eilde 116 NN 5684
Beinn Eilideach 127 NH 1692
Beinn Enaiglair 127 NH 2280
Beinn Eunaich 106 NN 1332
Beinneun Forest 115 NH 2207
Beinn Fhada or Ben Attow 114 NH 0118
Beinn Fhionnlaidh 106 NN 0949
Beinn Gàire 111 NM 7874
Beinn Gharbh 132 NC 2122
Beinn Ghlas (Strath.) 106 NM 9525
Beinn Ghlas (Strath.) 100 NN 1318
Beinn Ghlas (Strath.) 100 NR 9899
Beinn Ghobhlach 127 NH 0594
Beinn Ghuilbin 117 NH 8917
Beinn Ghuilean 92 NR 7217
Beinn Heasgarnich 107 NN 4138
Beinn Iadain 111 NM 6955
Beinn Iaruinn 115 NN 2989
Beinn Ime 100 NN 2508
Beinn Inverveigh 106 NN 2738
Beinn Iutharn Mhòr 117 NO 0479
Beinn Làir 126 NG 9873
Beinn Leabhain 107 NN 5728
Beinn Leòid 132 NC 3229
Beinn Liath Bheag 127 NH 2473
Beinn Liath Mhòr a'Ghiubhais Li 127 NH 2871
Beinn Lochain (Strath.) 100 NN 1500
Beinn Lochain (Strath.) 92 NR 9037
Beinn Loinne 115 NH 1507
Beinn Lunndaidh 129 NC 7802
Beinn Maol Chaluim 106 NN 1351
Beinn Mhanach 107 NN 3741
Beinn Mheadhoin (Highld.) 111 NM 7951
Beinn Mheadhoin (Highld.) 106 NM 8869
Beinn Mheadhonach (Isle of Lewis) 131 NB 0923
Beinn Mheadhonach (Strath.) 106 NN 0236
Beinn Mhic-Mhonaidh 106 NN 2034
Beinn Mholach (Isle of Lewis) 131 NB 3538
Beinn Mholach (Tays.) 107 NN 5865
Beinn Mhòr (Grampn.) 117 NH 9928
Beinn Mhòr (Islay) 98 NR 2940
Beinn Mhòr (Isle of Lewis) 131 NB 2509
Beinn Mhòr (North Uist) 124 NF 8976
Beinn Mhòr (South Uist) 112 NF 8031
Beinn Mhòr (Strath.) 105 NM 7921
Beinn Mhòr (Strath.) 100 NS 1090
Beinn na Boineid 122 NG 2339
Beinn na Caillich (Highld.) 111 NG 7906
Beinn na Caillich (Island of Skye) 123 NG 6023
Beinn Na Cille 111 NM 8554
Beinn na Crò 123 NG 5623
Beinn na Croise 105 NM 5625
Beinn na Drise 105 NM 4742
Beinn na Greine 123 NG 4541
Beinn na Gucaig 106 NN 0665
Beinn na h-Uamha 111 NM 6853
Beinn na Lap 107 NN 3769
Beinn na Lice 92 NR 6008
Beinn nam Bad Mòr 134 NC 9955
Beinn nam Beathrach 111 NM 7556
Beinn nam Bò 134 NC 7858
Beinn nan Aighenan 106 NN 1440
Beinn nan Cabar 111 NM 7686
Beinn nan Caorach 123 NG 8712
Beinn nan Càrn 123 NG 6318
Beinn nan Cuithean 122 NG 3129
Beinn nan Eun 128 NH 4475
Beinn nan Imirean 107 NN 4130
Beinn nan Losgann 111 NM 5365
Beinn nan Lus 106 NN 1337
Beinn nan Ramh 127 NH 1466
Beinn na Seamraig 123 NG 7318
Beinn na Sreine 105 NM 4564
Beinn na Srèine 105 NM 4530
Beinn na Sròine 106 NN 2328
Beinn Odhar 106 NN 3333
Beinn Odhar Bheag 111 NM 8477
Beinn Ràtha 134 NC 9561
Beinn Resipol 111 NM 7665
Beinn Rifa-gil 134 NC 7448
Beinn Ruadh (Highld.) 134 NC 8459
Beinn Ruadh (Strath.) 100 NS 1371
Beinn Ruadh (Strath.) 100 NS 1588
Beinn Ruisg 100 NS 3291
Beinn Sgaillinish 98 NR 6184
Beinn Sgeireach 133 NC 4511
Beinn Sgreamhaidh 133 NC 4415
Beinn Sgritheall 123 NG 8312
Beinn Sgulaird 106 NN 0545
Beinn Shlèibhe 124 NF 9283
Beinn Sholum 98 NR 3949
Beinn Spionnaidh 132 NC 3657
Beinn Stumanadh 133 NC 6449
Beinn Suidhe 106 NN 2139
Beinn Talaidh 105 NM 6234
Beinn Tarsuinn 92 NR 9541
Beinn Tart a'Mhill 98 NR 2056
Beinn Teallach 115 NN 3686
Beinn Tharsuinn (Highld.) 127 NH 0543
Beinn Tharsuinn (Highld.) 128 NH 4182
Beinn Tharsuinn (Highld.) 128 NH 6079
Beinn Trilleachan 106 NN 0843
Beinn Tulaichean 107 NN 4119
Beinn Udlaidh 106 NN 2732
Beinn Udlamain 116 NN 5874
Beinn Uidhe 132 NC 2825
Beinn Uird 101 NS 3998
Beinn Ulbhaidh 128 NH 4396
Beinn Uraraidh 98 NR 4054
Beith 93 NS 3454
Bekesbourne 31 TR 1955
Belaugh 65 TG 2818
Belbroughton 49 SO 9177
Belchamp Otten 54 TL 8041
Belchamp St. Paul 54 TL 7942
Belchamp Walter 54 TL 8240
Belchford 73 TF 2975
Belford 97 NU 1033
Belhelvie 119 NJ 9417
Bellabeg 118 NJ 3513
Bellanoch 99 NR 7992
Bellaty 108 NO 2459
Bell Busk 78 SD 9056
Bell Craig 89 NT 1812
Belleau 73 TF 4078
Bellehiglash 117 NJ 1837
Belle Isle 83 SD 3996
Bellerby 84 SE 1192
Bell Hill 90 NT 8409
Belliehill 109 NO 5663
Bellingdon 36 SP 9405
Bellingham 90 NY 8383
Belloch 92 NR 6737
Bellochantuy 92 NR 6632
Bellochantuy Bay 92 NR 6432
Bell Rock or Inchcape 109 NO 7626
Bellsbank 93 NS 4804
Bellshill (Northum.) 97 NU 1230
Bellshill (Strath.) 101 NS 7360
Bellsmyre 101 NS 4076
Bellspool 95 NT 1635
Bellsquarry 102 NT 0465
Bells Yew Green 29 TQ 6136
Bellybought Hill 88 NX 9099
Bellymore 86 NX 2386
Belmaduthy 128 NH 6556
Belmesthorpe 62 TF 0410
Belmont (Lancs.) 69 SD 6715
Belmont (Unst) 143 HP 5600
Belmont Castle 108 NO 2843
Belmont Resr. 69 SD 6717
Belnacraig 118 NJ 3716
Belnahua Fladda 105 NM 7112
Belowda 19 SW 9661
Belper 60 SK 3447
Belsay 91 NZ 1078
Belses 96 NT 5725
Belsford 21 SX 7659
Belstead 55 TM 1341
Belston 93 NS 3820
Belstone 21 SX 6193
Belthorn 77 SD 7124
Beltoft 74 SE 8006
Belton (Humbs.) 74 SE 7806
Belton (Leic.) 61 SK 4420
Belton (Leic.) 62 SK 8101
Belton (Lincs.) 62 SK 9239
Belton (Norf.) 65 TG 4802
Belvedere 37 TQ 4978
Belvide Resr. 59 SJ 8610
Belvoir 62 SK 8133
Bembridge 27 SZ 6488
Bembridge Airport 27 SZ 6387
Bembridge Point 27 SZ 6488
Bemersyde 96 NT 5933
Bempton 81 TA 1972
Benachally 108 NO 0649
Benachie Forest 121 NJ 6820
Benacre 55 TM 5184
Ben Aigan 120 NJ 3048
Ben Alder 116 NN 4971
Ben Alder Forest 116 NN 5375
Ben Alder Lodge 116 NN 5778
Ben Alisky 135 ND 0438
Ben An 101 NN 5008
Benaquhallie 119 NJ 6008
Ben Armine 133 NC 6828
Ben Armine Forest 133 NC 6621
Ben Armine Lodge 133 NC 7019
Ben Arnaboll 133 NC 4559
Ben Arthur 100 NN 2505
Benarty Hill 102 NT 1597
Ben Aslak 123 NG 7519
Ben Attow or Beinn Fhada 114 NH 0118
Ben Auskaird 132 NC 2140
Ben Avon 117 NJ 1401
Benbecula (is.) 124 NF 8251
Benbecula Aerodrome 124 NF 7856
Benbeoch 93 NS 4908
Benbrack (Dumf. and Galwy.) 87 NS 5300
Benbrack (Dumf. and Galwy.) 88 NX 5975
Benbrack (Dumf. and Galwy.) 88 NX 6796
Benbrack (Strath.) 93 NS 5305
Ben Buie 105 NM 6027
Benbuie 88 NX 7196
Ben Casgro 131 NB 4126
Ben Challum 107 NN 3832
Ben Chonzie 107 NN 7730
Ben Clach 107 NN 7515
Ben Cleuch 102 NN 9000
Ben Cliad 112 NF 6704
Ben Connan 122 NG 1940
Ben Corkeval 122 NG 1844
Ben Cruachan 106 NN 0730
Ben-damph Forest 126 NG 8852
Bendealt (mt.) 128 NH 5570
Bendeallt 128 NH 5570
Ben Dell 131 NB 5056
Benderloch 106 NM 9038
Benderloch (dist.) 106 NM 9139
Ben Donich 100 NN 2104
Bendronaig Lodge 114 NH 0138
Ben Duagrich 123 NG 3938
Ben Earb 108 NO 0769
Benenden 30 TQ 8033
Beneraird 86 NX 1378
Ben Ettow 122 NG 1752
Benfield 86 NX 3764
Bengairn 87 NX 7654
Ben Garrisdale 99 NR 6394
Bengate 65 TG 3027
Ben Geary 122 NG 2561
Ben Glas 106 NN 3419
Ben Glas Burn 106 NN 3218
Bengray 88 NX 6259
Ben Griam Beg 134 NC 8341
Ben Griam Mòr 134 NC 8039
Ben Gulabin 108 NO 1072
Ben Halton 107 NN 7220
Ben Hee 133 NC 4234
Ben Hiant 111 NM 5363
Ben Hogh 110 NM 1858
Benholm 109 NO 8069
Ben Hope 133 NC 4749
Ben Horn 129 NC 8006
Ben Hutig 133 NC 5365
Ben Idrigill 122 NG 2338
Beningbrough 79 SE 5257
Benington (Herts.) 37 TL 3023
Benington (Lincs.) 63 TF 3946
Beninner 88 NX 6096
Ben Klibreck 133 NC 6131
Ben Laga 111 NM 6462
Ben Lawers 107 NN 6341
Ben Ledi 101 NN 5609
Ben Lee 123 NG 5033
Benllech 66 SH 5182
Ben Lomond 101 NN 3602
Ben Loyal 133 NC 5748
Ben Lui 106 NN 2626
Ben Luskentyre 125 NG 0999
Ben Macdui (Beinn MacDuibh) 117 NN 9898
Ben Meabost 123 NG 5316
Ben Mòr Coigach 127 NC 0904
Benmore (Central) 107 NN 4125
Ben More (Central) 107 NN 4324
Ben More (Island of Mull) 105 NM 5233
Benmore (Strath.) 100 NS 1385
Ben More Assynt 132 NC 3120
Benmore Forest (Highld.) 132 NC 3216
Benmore Forest (Strath.) 100 NS 1682
Benmore Lodge 132 NC 3211
Bennachie 121 NJ 6522
Bennacott 20 SX 2991
Bennan (Dumf. and Galwy.) 88 NX 5679
Bennan (Dumf. and Galwy.) 88 NX 7995
Bennan (Island of Arran) 92 NR 9821
Bennane Head 86 NX 0986
Bennan Head 92 NR 9920
Bennecarrigan 92 NR 9423
Ben Nevis 106 NN 1671
Benniworth 73 TF 2081
Benover 29 TQ 7048
Ben Raah 124 NB 0301
Ben Rinnes 117 NJ 2435
Ben Scrien 112 NF 7911
Ben Shieldaig 123 NG 8451
Benson 36 SU 6191
Ben Stack 132 NC 2642
Ben Starav 106 NN 1242
Ben Strome 132 NC 2436
Ben Tangaval 112 NL 6399
Ben Tee 115 NN 2497
Benthall (Northum.) 97 NU 2328
Benthall (Shrops.) 59 SJ 6602
Bentham 46 SO 9116
Benthoul 119 NJ 8003
Ben Tianavaig 123 NG 5140
Ben Tirran 118 NO 3774
Bentley (Hants.) 35 SU 7844
Bentley (Here. and Worc.) 50 SO 9966
Bentley (Humbs.) 74 TA 0135
Bentley (S Yorks.) 71 SE 5605
Bentley (Warw.) 60 SP 2895
Bentley Heath 50 SP 1676
Benton 23 SS 6536
Bentpath 89 NY 3190
Bentworth 35 SU 6640
Benty Cowan Hill 88 NS 5808
Ben Uigshader 122 NG 3649
Benvane (Central) 101 NN 5313
Benvane (Strath.) 100 NN 2709
Ben Venue 101 NN 4706
Benvie 108 NO 3231
Ben Vorlich (Strath.) 100 NN 2912
Ben Vorlich (Tays.) 107 NN 6319
Ben Vrackie 108 NN 9563
Ben Vuirich 108 NN 9969
Benwick 53 TL 3490
Ben Wyvis 128 NH 4668
Benyellary 86 NX 4183
Beoley 50 SP 0669
Beoraidbeg 111 NM 6793
Beorgs of Skelberry 142 HU 3588
Bepton 27 SU 8518
Berden 53 TL 4629
Berea 42 SM 7929
Bere Alston 20 SX 4466
Bere Ferrers 20 SX 4563
Berepper 18 SW 6522
Bere Regis 25 SY 8494
Bergh Apton 65 TG 3000
Berinsfield 47 SU 5696
Berkeley 46 ST 6899
Berkhamsted 36 SP 9907
Berkley 33 ST 8049
Berkswell 50 SP 2479
Bermondsey 37 TQ 3579
Bernard Wharf (sbk.) 27 SO 3550
Bernera 123 NG 8020
Bernera Island 105 NM 7939
Berneray (North Uist) 124 NF 9182
Berneray (W Isles) 112 NL 5680
Berney Arms Station 65 TG 4505
Bernice 100 NS 1391
Bernisdale 123 NG 4050
Berrick Salome 36 SU 6293
Berriedale 135 ND 1223
Berriedale Water 135 ND 0630
Berrier 83 NY 3929
Berriew 58 SJ 1801
Berrington (Northum.) 97 NU 0043
Berrington (Shrops.) 59 SJ 5206
Berrow 32 ST 2952
Berrow Flats (sbk.) 32 ST 2854
Berrow Green 49 SO 7458
Berry Head 21 SX 9456
Berry Hill 45 SO 5712
Berryhillock 121 NJ 5060
Berryl's Point 19 SW 8467
Berrynarbor 23 SS 5546
Berry Pomeroy 21 SX 8261
Berry, The (mt.) 136 ND 2490
Berry Top (mt.) 119 NO 8695
Bersham 58 SJ 3048
Berstane 136 HY 4610
Bersted 28 SU 9300
Berst Ness 138 HY 4441
Berth, The (ant.) 58 SJ 4323
Bervie Bay 109 NO 8372
Bervie Water 119 NO 7774
Berwick 29 TQ 5105
Berwick Bassett 34 SU 0973
Berwick Hill 91 NZ 1775
Berwick St. James 34 SU 0739
Berwick St. John 26 ST 9421
Berwick St. Leonard 25 ST 9233
Berwick-upon-Tweed 97 NT 9953
Berwyn (mt.) 67 SJ 0632
Bescar Lane Station 68 SD 3914
Besford 49 SO 9144
Bessacarr 71 SE 6101
Bessels Leigh 47 SP 4501
Bessingham 65 TG 1636
Besthorpe (Norf.) 64 TM 0695
Besthorpe (Notts.) 72 SK 8264
Beswick 81 TA 0148
Betchworth 28 TQ 2149
Bethel 66 SH 5265
Bethersden 30 TQ 9240
Bethesda (Dyfed) 42 SN 0918
Bethesda (Gwyn.) 67 SH 6266
Bethlehem 43 SN 6825
Bethnal Green 37 TQ 3583
Betley 59 SJ 7548
Betsham 30 TQ 6071
Betteshanger 31 TR 3152
Bettiscombe 24 SY 3999
Bettisfield 58 SJ 4535
Betton (Shrops.) 59 SJ 3102
Betton (Shrops.) 59 SJ 6836
Bettws 45 SO 2919

Bettws (Gwent) 32 ST 2991
Bettws (Mid Glam.) 41 SS 9086
Bettws Bledrws 43 SN 5952
Bettws Cedewain 58 SO 1296
Bettws Evan 43 SN 3047
Bettws Gwerfil Goch 67 SJ 0346
Bettws Malpas 32 ST 3090
Bettws-Newydd 45 SO 3606
Bettyhill 133 NC 7061
Betws 43 SN 6311
Betws Garmon 66 SH 5357
Betws-y-coed 67 SH 7956
Betws-yn-Rhos 67 SH 9073
Beulah (Dyfed) 43 SN 2846
Beulah (Powys) 44 SN 9251
Beul an Toim 124 NF 7957
Bevendean 29 TQ 3406
Bevercotes 72 SK 6972
Beverley 74 TA 0339
Beverston 46 ST 8693
Bevington 46 ST 6596
Bewaldeth 82 NY 2134
Bewcastle 90 NY 5674
Bewcastle Fells 90 NY 5681
Bewdley 49 SO 7875
Bewerley 78 SE 1564
Bewholme 81 TA 1650
Bewl Bridge Resr. 29 TQ 6832
Bexhill 29 TQ 7407
Bexley 37 TQ 4973
Bexwell 64 TF 6303
Beyton 54 TL 9363
Biargar (pt.) 141 HU 3635
Bibblon Hill 94 NS 6632
Bibury 46 SP 1106
Bicester 47 SP 5822
Bickenhall 24 ST 2818
Bickenhill 50 SP 1882
Bicker 63 TF 2237
Bicker Haven 63 TF 2534
Bickerstaffe 68 SD 4404
Bickerton (Ches.) 59 SJ 5052
Bickerton (N Yorks.) 79 SE 4450
Bickington (Devon) 23 SS 5332
Bickington (Devon) 21 SX 7972
Bickleigh (Devon) 23 SS 9407
Bickleigh (Devon) 21 SX 5262
Bickleton 22 SS 5031
Bickley 37 TQ 4268
Bickley Moss 59 SJ 5448
Bicknacre 38 TL 7802
Bicknoller 32 ST 1039
Bicknor 30 TQ 8658
Bickton 26 SU 1412
Bicton (Shrops.) 58 SJ 4415
Bicton (Shrops.) 48 SO 2882
Bidborough 29 TQ 5643
Biddenden 30 TQ 8538
Biddenham 52 TL 0250
Biddestone 33 ST 8673
Biddisham 32 ST 3853
Biddlesden 51 SP 6340
Biddlestone 90 NT 9508
Biddulph 69 SJ 8857
Biddulph Moor 69 SJ 9057
Bidean Nam Bian (mt.) 106 NN 1454
Bideford 22 SS 4526
Bideford Bar 22 SS 4333
Bideford or Barnstaple Bay 22 SS 3432
Bidford-on-Avon 50 SP 1052
Bielby 74 SE 7843
Bieldside 119 NJ 8702
Biel Water 103 NT 6476
Bierley 27 SZ 5077
Bierton 36 SP 8415
Bigbury 21 SX 6646
Bigbury Bay 21 SX 6342
Bigbury-on-Sea 21 SX 6544
Bigby 74 TA 0507
Big Corlae 88 NX 6597
Bigga (is.) 143 HU 4479
Biggar (Cumbr.) 76 SD 1966
Biggar (Strath.) 95 NT 0437
Big Garvoun (mt.) 117 NJ 1408
Bigges' Pillar (mt.) 91 NU 1207
Biggin (Derby.) 70 SK 1559
Biggin (Derby.) 60 SK 2548
Biggin (N Yorks.) 79 SE 5434
Biggings 140 HU 1760
Biggin Hill 37 TQ 4159
Biggin Hill Airport 37 TQ 4160
Biggins 77 SD 6078
Biggleswade 52 TL 1944
Biggleswade (Old Warden) Airfield 52 TL 1544
Big Hill of Glenmount 87 NS 4500
Bighouse 134 NC 8964
Bighton 27 SU 6134
Bignor 28 SU 9814
Big Sand 126 NG 7579
Big Water of Fleet 88 NX 5761
Bilberry 10 SX 0150
Bilborough 61 SK 5241
Bilbrook 59 SJ 8703
Bilbrough 79 SE 5246
Bilbster 135 ND 2852
Bildeston 54 TL 9949
Billericay 38 TQ 6794
Billesdon 61 SK 7103
Billesley 50 SP 1456
Billia Field (mt.) 143 HU 3786
Billingborough 62 TF 1134
Billinge 69 SD 5300
Billingford (Norf.) 64 TG 0120
Billingford (Norf.) 55 TM 1678
Billingham 85 NZ 4624
Billinghay 62 TF 1554
Billingley 71 SE 4304
Billingshurst 28 TQ 0825
Billingsley 49 SO 7085
Billington (Beds.) 36 SP 9422
Billington (Lancs.) 77 SD 7235
Billockby 65 TG 4213
Bill of Portland (pt.) 25 SY 6768
Billsmoor Park 90 NY 9496
Billy Row 84 NZ 1637
Bilsborrow 77 SD 5140
Bilsby 73 TF 4776
Bilsington 31 TR 0434
Bilsthorpe 71 SK 6560
Bilston (Lothian) 103 NT 2664
Bilston (W Mids) 50 SO 9496
Bilstone 60 SK 3606
Bilting 31 TR 0549
Bilton (Humbs.) 75 TA 1532
Bilton (Northum.) 91 NU 2210
Bilton (N Yorks.) 79 SE 4750
Bilton (Warw.) 51 SP 4873
Bimbister 136 HY 3216
Binbrook 73 TF 2093
Bincombe 25 SY 6884
Binegar 33 ST 6149
Binfield 35 SU 8471
Binfield Heath 36 SU 7478
Bin Forest, The (Grampn.) 121 NJ 4748
Bin Forest, The (Grampn.) 121 NJ 5143
Bingfield 91 NY 9772
Bingham 61 SK 7039
Bingham's Melcombe 25 ST 7701
Bingley 78 SE 1039
Binham 64 TF 9839
Binley (Hants.) 34 SU 4153
Binley (W Mids) 50 SP 3778
Binnein an Fhidhleir 100 NN 2110
Binnein Mór 106 NN 2166
Binnein Shuas 116 NN 4682
Binniehill 102 NS 8572
Binnimoor Fen 63 TL 4597
Binns, The (ant.) 102 NT 0578
Bin of Cullen (mt.) 121 NJ 4764
Binsey (Cumbld.) (mt.) 82 NY 2235
Binstead (I. of W.) 27 SZ 5792
Binsted (Hants.) 35 SU 7741
Bin, The (mt.) 121 NJ 5043
Binton 50 SP 1454
Bintree 64 TG 0123
Binweston 58 SJ 3004
Bioda Buidhe (mt.) 123 NG 4366
Biod an Athair 122 NG 1554
Biod nan Laogh 122 NG 2958
Birch (Essex) 38 TL 9419
Birch (Gtr Mches.) 69 SD 8507
Bircham Newton 64 TF 7633
Bircham Tofts 64 TF 7732
Birchanger 37 TL 5122
Bircher 48 SO 4765
Birch Green 38 TL 9418
Birchgrove 40 SS 7098
Birchington 31 TR 3069
Birchover 71 SK 2462
Birch Vale 70 SK 0286
Birchwood 72 SK 9370
Bircotes 71 SK 6391
Birdbrook 54 TL 7041
Birdham 27 SU 8200
Birdingbury 50 SP 4368
Birdlip 46 SO 9214
Birdsgreen 49 SO 7685
Birdston 101 NS 6575
Birdwell 71 SE 3401
Birdwood 46 SO 7318
Birgham 97 NT 7939
Birk Beck 83 NY 5907
Birkdale 68 SD 3214
Birkdale Common 83 NY 8302
Birkenburn Resr. 101 NS 6780
Birkenhead 68 SJ 3188
Birkenhills 121 NJ 7445
Birkenshaw (Strath.) 101 NS 6962
Birkenshaw (W Yorks.) 78 SE 2028
Birker Force 82 SD 1999
Birkhall 118 NO 3493
Birkhill 109 NO 3433
Birkin 79 SE 5226
Birley 45 SO 4553
Birling (Kent) 30 TQ 6860
Birling (Northum.) 91 NU 2406
Birlingham 49 SO 9343
Birmingham 50 SP 0787
Birmingham Airport 50 SP 1783
Birnam 108 NO 0341
Birnam Hill 108 NO 0340
Birness 121 NJ 9933
Birnock Water 89 NT 1008
Birns Water 103 NT 4666
Birrier (pt.) 143 HU 5488
Birsay Bay 136 HY 2327
Birse 119 NO 5596
Birsemohr 119 NO 5297
Birstall 61 SK 5809
Birstall Smithies 79 SE 2226
Birstwith 79 SE 2459
Birtley (Here. and Worc.) 48 SO 3669
Birtley (Northum.) 90 NY 8778
Birtley (Tyne and Wear) 84 NZ 2755
Birts Street 49 SO 7836
Biruaslum (is.) 112 NL 6096
Bisbrooke 62 SP 8899
Bis Geos 138 HY 4147
Bishampton 50 SO 9851
Bishop Auckland 84 NZ 2029
Bishopbriggs 101 NS 6070
Bishop Burton 74 SE 9839
Bishopdale Beck 78 SD 9885
Bishop Hill 102 NO 1803
Bishop Middleham 84 NZ 3231
Bishop Monkton 79 SE 3266
Bishop Norton 72 SK 9892
Bishopric (dist.) 108 NN 9647
Bishop Rock 18 SV 8006
Bishops and Clerks (is.) 42 SM 6725
Bishopsbourne 31 TR 1852
Bishops Cannings 34 SU 0364
Bishop's Castle 48 SO 3288
Bishop's Caundle 25 ST 6912
Bishop's Cleeve 46 SO 9527
Bishop's Frome 49 SO 6648
Bishop's Itchington 50 SP 3857
Bishops Lydeard 24 ST 1629
Bishop's Nympton 23 SS 7523
Bishops Offley 59 SJ 7729
Bishop's Stortford 37 TL 4821
Bishop's Sutton 35 SU 6031
Bishop's Tachbrook 50 SP 3161
Bishop's Tawton 23 SS 5630
Bishopsteignton 21 SX 9173
Bishopstoke 27 SU 4619
Bishopston 40 SS 5889
Bishopstone (Bucks.) 36 SP 8010
Bishopstone (E Susx) 29 TQ 4701
Bishopstone (Here. and Worc.) 45 SO 4143
Bishopstone (Wilts.) 26 SU 0625
Bishopstone (Wilts.) 34 SU 2483
Bishop Sutton 33 ST 5859
Bishop's Waltham 27 SU 5517
Bishopswood (Somer.) 24 ST 2512
Bishop's Wood (Staffs.) 59 SJ 8309
Bishopsworth 33 ST 5768
Bishop Thornton 79 SE 2663
Bishopthorpe 79 SE 5947
Bishopton (Durham) 85 NZ 3621
Bishopton (Strath.) 101 NS 4371
Bishopton Station 101 NS 4370
Bishop Wilton 80 SE 7955
Bishton 32 ST 3887
Bisley (Glos.) 46 SO 9005
Bisley (Surrey) 36 SU 9559
Bispham 77 SD 3139
Bissoe 18 SW 7741
Bisterne Close 26 SU 2202
Bitchfield 62 SK 9828
Bittadon 23 SS 5441
Bittaford 21 SX 6557
Bittering 64 TF 9317
Bitterley 48 SO 5577
Bitterne 27 SU 4513
Bitteswell 51 SP 5385
Bitteswell Aerodrome 51 SP 5185
Bitton 33 ST 6769
Bix 36 SU 7285
Bixter 141 HU 3352
Bla Bheinn 123 NG 5221
Blaby 61 SP 5697
Blacka Burn 90 NY 7777
Blackacre 89 NY 0490
Blackadder 97 NT 8452
Blackadder Water 96 NT 7749
Blackawton 21 SX 8050
Black Bay 92 NR 7726
Black Beck 84 SE 1093
Blackborough 24 ST 0909
Blackborough End 64 TF 6614
Black Bourton 47 SP 2804
Blackboys 29 TQ 5220
Blackbrook 59 SJ 7639
Blackbrook Resr. 61 SK 4617
Black Buoy Sand 63 TF 4138
Black Burn (Cumbr.) 83 NY 6841
Black Burn (Grampn.) 129 NJ 1054
Black Burn (Grampn.) 119 NJ 8212
Blackburn (Lancs.) 77 SD 6827
Blackburn (Lothian) 102 NS 9865
Blackburn Common 90 NY 8191
Blackburn Rig 97 NT 7865
Blackbushe Airport 36 SU 8159
Black Callerton 91 NZ 1769
Black Clauchrie 86 NX 2984
Black Combe 76 SD 1385
Black Corries Lodge 106 NN 2956
Black Craig (Dumf. & Galwy.) 87 NX 5095
Black Craig (Grampn.) 118 NO 4394
Black Craig (Orkney) 136 HY 2111
Blackcraig Castle 108 NO 1053
Blackcraig Forest 108 NO 1151
Blackcraig Hill (Dumf. and Galwy.) 88 NX 6982
Blackcraig Hill (Strath.) 88 NS 7401
Blackcraig Hill (Tays.) 108 NO 0952
Black Crofts 106 NM 9234
Blackden Heath 69 SJ 7871
Black Devon 102 NS 9393
Black Dog (Devon) 23 SS 8009
Blackdog (Grampn.) 119 NJ 9514
Blackdog Rock 119 NJ 9613
Black Down (Devon) 24 ST 0907
Black Down (Devon) 20 SX 5081
Black Down (Dorset) 25 SY 6087
Black Down Hills 24 ST 1616
Black Edge 89 NY 4288
Black Esk 89 NY 2193
Black Esk Resr. 89 NY 2096
Black Fell (Northum.) 90 NY 7073
Blackfield 27 SU 4402
Blackford (Cumbr.) 89 NY 3962
Blackford (Somer.) 32 ST 4147
Blackford (Somer.) 25 ST 6526
Blackford (Tays.) 102 NN 8908
Blackfordby 60 SK 3318
Blackgang 27 SZ 4876
Blackgang Chine 27 SZ 4876
Blackhall 85 NZ 4539
Blackhall Forest 119 NO 6694
Blackhalls Rocks 85 NZ 4739
Blackham 29 TQ 4839
Blackhaugh 96 NT 4238
Black Head (Corn.) 18 SW 7716
Black Head (Corn.) 19 SX 0348
Blackhead (Dumf. and Galwy.) 86 NW 9856
Blackheath (Essex) 39 TM 0021
Blackheath (Surrey) 28 TQ 0346
Blackheath (Warw.) 50 SO 9886
Black Heath (Wilts.) 34 SU 0751
Black Hill (Ches.) 70 SJ 9882
Black Hill (Devon) 24 SY 0285
Black Hill (Dumf. and Galwy.) 89 NT 1500
Black Hill (Grampn.) 119 NJ 6712
Blackhill (Grampn.) 121 NK 0756
Blackhill (Grampn.) 121 NK 0843
Black Hill (Lothian) 102 NT 1863
Black Hill (N Yorks.) 78 SD 7561
Black Hill (Shrops.) 48 SO 3279
Black Hill (Strath.) 94 NS 7029
Black Hill (Strath.) 86 NX 3895
Black Hill (W Yorks. - Derby) 70 SE 0704
Black Hill of Mark 118 NO 3281
Blackhills 120 NJ 2757
Blackhope Burn 89 NT 1212
Blackhope Scar 96 NT 3148
Blackhouse Moor 100 NS 2064
Black Islands 123 NG 7529
Black Isle (dist.) 128 NH 6557
Black Knowe (Borders) 89 NT 2210
Black Knowe (Borders) 89 NT 2807
Black Knowe (Borders) 89 NY 5387
Black Knowe (Northum.) 90 NY 5891
Black Knowe (Northum.) 90 NY 6481
Black Knowe Head 96 NT 3121
Blackland 34 SU 0168
Black Law (Borders) 95 NT 2227
Black Law (Borders) 96 NT 3041
Blackley 69 SD 8503
Black Loch (Central) 102 NS 8670
Black Loch (Dumf. and Galwy.) 86 NX 1161
Black Lochs (Strath.) 106 NM 9231
Blacklorg Hill 88 NS 6504
Blacklunans 108 NO 1560
Black Lyne 90 NY 5478
Blackman's Law 90 NY 7497
Black Marsh 58 SJ 3100
Black Meldon 95 NT 2042
Blackmill 41 SS 9386
Blackmoor 27 SU 7833
Blackmoor Gate 23 SS 6443
Blackmoor Vale 25 ST 7315
Blackmore 38 TL 6001
Blackmore End 54 TL 7430
Black Mount (Strath.) 106 NN 2842
Black Mount (Strath.) 106 NN 2947
Black Mount (Strath.) 95 NT 0745
Black Mountain (Dyfed) 41 SN 7418
Black Mountain (Powys) 48 SO 1677
Black Mountain (Shrops.) 48 SO 1983
Black Mountains (Powys) 45 SO 2427
Blackness 102 NT 0579
Blacknest 35 SU 7941
Black Notley 38 TL 7620
Blacko 78 SD 8541
Black Pill 40 SS 6290
Black Point 92 NR 7104
Blackpool 77 SD 3035
Blackpool Airport 77 SD 3131
Blackpool Gate 90 NY 5377
Blackridge 102 NS 8967
Blackrock (Gwent) 41 SO 2112
Blackrock (Islay) 98 NR 3063
Black Rocks (Lothian) 103 NT 2777
Black Rocks (N Yorks.) 81 TA 0587
Blackrod 69 SD 6110
Black Sail Pass 82 NY 1811
Blackshaw 89 NY 0465
Blackshaw Bank (sbk.) 89 NY 0563
Blackside 94 NS 5830
Black's Memorial Lighthouse 105 NM 7534
Blacksmith's Corner 54 TM 0131
Blackstone 28 TQ 2416
Blackthorn 36 SP 6219
Blackthorpe 54 TL 9063
Blacktoft 74 SE 8424
Blackton Resr. 84 NY 9418
Blacktop 119 NJ 8604
Black Torrington 22 SS 4605
Blackwater (Corn.) 18 SW 7346
Black Water (Grampn.) 121 NJ 3328
Black Water (Grampn.) 108 NO 1357
Blackwater (Hants.) 36 SU 8559
Black Water (Highld.) 134 NC 7715
Black Water (Highld.) 127 NH 4066
Black Water (Highld.) 128 NH 5776
Black Water (Highld.) 107 NN 3761
Blackwater (I. of W.) 27 SZ 5086
Blackwater (Suff.) 55 TM 5077
Blackwaterfoot 92 NR 8928
Blackwater Forest 117 NJ 3026
Black Water of Dee or River Dee 88 NX 5973
Blackwater Reservoir 106 NN 3059
Blackwater River 36 SU 7364
Blackwell (Derby.) 70 SK 1272
Blackwell (Durham.) 84 NZ 2712
Blackwell (Here. and Worc.) 50 SO 9972
Blackwood (Gwent) 41 ST 1797
Blackwood (Strath.) 94 NS 7943
Blackwood Hill 59 SJ 9255
Blacon 68 SJ 3767
Bladnoch 87 NX 4254
Bladon 47 SP 4414
Blaeberry Hill 89 NT 2800
Blaenannerch 43 SN 2449
Blaenau Ffestiniog 67 SH 7045
Blaenavon 45 SO 2509
Blaen Dyryn 44 SN 9336
Blaenffos 43 SN 1937
Blaengarw 41 SS 9092
Blaengwrach 41 SN 8605
Blaengwynfi 41 SS 8996
Blaenhafren Source of River Severn 57 SN 8290
Blaenpennal 57 SN 6365
Blaenplwyf 56 SN 5775
Blaenporth 43 SN 2648
Blaenrhondda 41 SS 9299
Blaenwaun 43 SN 2327
Blagdon 21 SX 8561
Blagdon Hill 24 ST 2118
Blagdon Lake 33 ST 5159
Blaich 115 NN 0476
Blaina 41 SO 2008
Blairadam Forest 102 NT 1693
Blair Atholl 108 NN 8765
Blair Castle (Fife) 102 NS 9685
Blair Castle (Tays.) (ant.) 108 NN 8666
Blairdenon Hill 102 NN 8601
Blair Drummond 101 NS 7398
Blairdrummond Moss 101 NS 7297
Blairgowrie 108 NO 1745
Blairhall 102 NT 0089
Blairingone 102 NS 9896
Blairlogie 101 NS 8396
Blairmore 100 NS 1982
Blairnamarrow 117 NJ 2015
Blairskaith 101 NS 5975
Blaisdon 46 SO 7016
Blakebrook 49 SO 8077
Blakedown 49 SO 8778
Blake Hall (ant.) 37 TL 5305
Blakehope Fell 90 NY 8394
Blakehope Head 96 NT 1030
Blakelaw 96 NT 7730
Blakeman's Law 90 NY 8795
Blakemere 45 SO 3641
Blake Muir 96 NT 3030
Blakeney (Glos.) 46 SO 6707
Blakeney (Norf.) 64 TG 0243
Blakeney Point 64 TG 0046
Blakenhall (Ches.) 59 SJ 7247
Blakenhall (W Mids) 50 SO 9297
Blakeshall 49 SO 8381
Blakesley 51 SP 6250
Blakey Ridge 80 SE 6896
Blanch Fell 77 SD 5760
Blanchland 84 NY 9650
Blanchland Moor 84 NY 9552
Blandford Forum 25 ST 8806
Blandford St. Mary 25 ST 8805
Bland Hill 78 SE 2053
Blanefield 101 NS 5579
Blane Water 101 NS 5183
Blankney 72 TF 0660
Blàr a' Chaorainn 106 NN 1066
Blàr Dearg (dist.) 135 ND 0453
Blarghour 100 NM 9913
Blarmachfoldach 106 NN 0969
Blarnalearoch 127 NH 1490
Blary Hill 92 NR 7136
Blashford 26 SU 1406
Blaston 61 SP 8095
Blatherwycke 62 SP 9795
Blatobulgium Roman Fort (ant.) 89 NY 2175
Blawith 77 SD 2888
Blaxhall 55 TM 3657
Blaxton 71 SE 6600
Blaydon 91 NZ 1863
Bleadon 32 ST 3456
Bleadon Hill 32 ST 3557
Bleak Law 95 NT 0651
Bleaklow Hill 70 SK 1096
Blea Moor 78 SD 7781
Blean 31 TR 1260
Bleasby 71 SK 7149
Blea Tarn 82 NY 2914
Bleaval (mt.) 124 NG 0391
Blebocraigs 103 NO 4214
Bleddfa 48 SO 2068
Bledington 47 SP 2422
Bledlow 36 SP 7802
Bledlow Ridge 36 SU 7898
Blegbie 103 NT 4861
Blencarn 83 NY 6331
Blencathra or Saddleback (ant.) 82 NY 3227
Blencogo 82 NY 1947
Blencow 83 NY 4532
Blendworth 27 SU 7113
Blenheim Palace (ant.) 47 SP 4416
Blennerhasset 82 NY 1741
Blervie Castle 129 NJ 0757
Bletchingdon 47 SP 5017
Bletchingley 29 TQ 3250
Bletchley (Bucks.) 52 SP 8733
Bletchley (Shrops.) 59 SJ 6233
Bletherston 42 SN 0721
Bletsoe 52 TL 0258
Blewbury 35 SU 5385
Blickling 65 TG 1728
Blidworth 71 SK 5855
Blindburn 90 NT 8310
Blindcrake 82 NY 1434
Blindley Heath 29 TQ 3645
Blisland 19 SX 0973
Blissford 26 SU 1713
Bliss Gate 49 SO 7472
Blisworth 51 SP 7253
Blithfield Reservoir 60 SK 0524
Blockley 47 SP 1634
Blofield 65 TG 3309
Blo Norton 54 TM 0179
Bloody Bay 111 NM 4858
Bloodybush Edge 90 NT 9014
Blore 60 SK 1349
Blorenge (mt.) 45 SO 2612
Blotchnie Fiold (mt.) 136 HY 4129
Blovid (pt.) 141 HU 4119
Bloxham 47 SP 4235
Bloxwich 60 SJ 9902
Bloxworth 25 SY 8894
Blubberhouses 78 SE 1655
Blue Anchor 32 ST 0343
Blue Anchor Bay 32 ST 0245
Blue Bell Hill 30 TQ 7462
Blue Head 129 NH 8166
Bluemull Sound 143 HP 5503
Blundeston 65 TM 5197
Blunham 52 TL 1551
Blunsdon St. Andrew 34 SU 1389
Bluntisham 53 TL 3674
Blyborough 72 SK 9394
Blyford 55 TM 4276
Blymhill 59 SJ 8112
Blyth (Northum.) 91 NZ 3181
Blyth (Notts.) 71 SK 6287
Blyth Bridge 95 NT 1345
Blythburgh 55 TM 4575
Blythe Bridge 60 SJ 9541
Blythe Edge 96 NT 6056
Blythe Sands 38 TQ 7779
Blyton 72 SK 8594
Boarhills 103 NO 5614
Boarhunt 27 SU 6008
Boar of Badenoch or An Torc 116 NN 6276
Boarshead 29 TQ 5332
Boar's Head Rock 120 NJ 2967
Boars of Duncansby (pt.) 135 ND 3875
Boarstall 36 SP 6214
Boasley Cross 20 SX 5093
Boath 128 NH 5774
Boat of Garten 117 NH 9419
Bobbing 30 TQ 8865
Bobbington 49 SO 8090
Bobbingworth 37 TL 5305
Boblainy Forest 116 NH 4837
Bocaddon 19 SX 1758
Boch-ailean (pt.) 135 ND 1020
Bochastle 101 NN 6107
Bocking 38 TL 7623
Bocking Churchstreet 54 TL 7525
Boconnoc 19 SX 1460
Boddam (Grampn.) 121 NK 1342
Boddam (Shetld.) 141 HU 3915
Boddington 46 SO 8925
Boddin Point 109 NO 7153
Bodedern 66 SH 3380
Bodelwyddan 67 SJ 0075
Bodenham (Here. and Worc.) 45 SO 5251
Bodenham (Wilts.) 26 SU 1626
Bodesbeck Law 89 NT 1610
Bodewryd 66 SH 3990
Bodfach Hall 58 SJ 1320
Bodfari 67 SJ 0970
Bodffordd 66 SH 4276
Bodfuan 66 SH 3237
Bodham 65 TG 1240
Bodiam 30 TQ 7826
Bodicote 51 SP 4537
Bodieve 19 SW 9973
Bodior 66 SH 2876
Bodle Street Green 29 TQ 6514
Bodmin 19 SX 0767
Bodmin Moor 19 SX 1876
Bodmin Road Station 19 SX 1164
Bodney 64 TL 8398
Bodorgan 66 SH 3867
Bodorgan Station 66 SH 3870
Bogallan 128 NH 6350
Bogany Point 100 NS 1065
Bogbrae 121 NK 0335
Bogend 93 NS 3932
Bogh a'Chùirn 99 NR 6893
Boghall 102 NS 9968
Boghole Farm 129 NH 9655
Bogmoor 121 NJ 3562
Bogniebrae 121 NJ 5945
Bognor Regis 28 SZ 9399
Bognor Regis Airfield 28 SU 9400
Bograxie 119 NJ 7119
Bogrie Hill 88 NX 7885
Bogside 95 NS 8353
Bog, The 58 SO 3597
Bogton 121 NJ 6751
Bogton Loch 93 NS 4605
Bogue 88 NX 6481
Bohortha 19 SW 8632
Bohuntine 115 NN 2882
Boisdale 112 NF 7417
Bojewyan 18 SW 3934
Bolam 84 NZ 1922
Bolam Lake 91 NZ 0881
Bold Heath 69 SJ 5389
Boldon 91 NZ 3661
Boldon Colliery 91 NZ 3462
Boldre 26 SZ 3198
Boldron 84 NZ 0314
Bole 72 SK 7987
Bolehill 60 SK 2955
Boleside 96 NT 4933
Bolham Water 24 ST 1612
Bolingey 18 SW 7653
Bollihope Common 84 NY 9733
Bollington (Ches.) 69 SJ 7286
Bollington (Ches.) 69 SJ 9377
Bolney 28 TQ 2622
Bolnhurst 52 TL 0859
Bolshan 109 NO 6252
Bolsover 71 SK 4770
Bolsterstone 71 SK 2696
Bolstone 45 SO 5532
Boltby 79 SE 4886
Bolt Head 21 SX 7236
Bolton (Cumbr.) 83 NY 6323
Bolton (Gtr Mches.) 69 SD 7108
Bolton (Humbs.) 80 SE 7752
Bolton (Lothian) 103 NT 5070
Bolton (Northum.) 91 NU 1013
Bolton Abbey 78 SE 0754
Bolton-By-Bowland 78 SD 7849
Boltonfellend 89 NY 4768
Boltongate 82 NY 2340
Bolto Hall (ant.) 84 SE 0789
Bolton le Sands 77 SD 4867
Bolton-on-Swale 84 SE 2599
Bolton Percy 79 SE 5341
Bolton Priory (ant.) 78 SE 0754
Bolton Upon Dearne 71 SE 4502
Bolt's Law 84 NY 9545
Bolt Tail (pt.) 21 SX 6639
Bolventor 19 SX 1876
Bomere Heath 59 SJ 4719
Bonar Bridge 128 NH 6191
Bonawe Quarries 106 NN 0133
Bonby 74 TA 0015
Boncath 43 SN 2038
Bonchester Bridge 90 NT 5811
Bondleigh 23 SS 6504
Bonehill 60 SK 1902
Bo'Ness 102 NS 9981
Bonhill 101 NS 3979
Boningale 59 SJ 8102
Bonjedward 96 NT 6523
Bonkle 95 NS 8356
Bonnington (Kent) 31 TR 0536
Bonnington (Lothian) 102 NT 1269
Bonnington Smiddy 109 NO 5739
Bonnybank 103 NO 3503
Bonnybridge 101 NS 8280
Bonnykelly 121 NJ 8553
Bonnyrigg and Lasswade 103 NT 3065
Bonnyton (Tays.) 108 NO 3338
Bonnyton (Tays.) 109 NO 6655
Bonsall 71 SK 2758
Bonskeid House 108 NN 8961
Bont 45 SO 3819
Bontddu 57 SH 6618
Bont-dolgadfan 57 SH 8800
Bontgoch Elerch 57 SN 6886
Bontnewydd (Gwyn.) 66 SH 4859
Bont Newydd (Gwyn.) 57 SH 7720
Bontuchel 67 SJ 0857
Bonvilston 41 ST 0674
Booker 36 SU 8491
Booley 59 SJ 5725
Boosbeck 85 NZ 6516

Boot	82	NY 1700
Boothby Graffoe	72	SK 9859
Boothby Pagnell	62	SK 9730
Boothstown	69	SD 7200
Booth Wood Resr	70	SE 0215
Bootle (Cumbr.)	76	SD 1088
Bootle (Mers.)	68	SJ 3394
Bootle Fell	76	SD 1488
Bootle Station	82	SD 0989
Boquhan	101	NS 5387
Boraston	49	SO 6170
Borden	30	TQ 8863
Bordley	78	SD 9465
Bordon Camp	27	SU 7935
Boreham (Essex)	38	TL 7509
Boreham (Wilts.)	33	ST 8944
Boreham Street	29	TQ 6611
Borehamwood	37	TQ 1996
Boreland (Central)	107	NN 5534
Boreland (Dumf. and Galwy.)	89	NY 1790
Boreland Hill	88	NX 9460
Boreray (North Uist)	124	NF 8581
Boreray (St. Kilda or Hirta)	124	NA 1505
Bore Stane	102	NT 1459
Bore, The	138	HY 4956
Borgie	133	NC 6759
Borgie Forest	133	NC 6655
Borgue (Dumf. and Galwy.)	87	NX 6248
Borgue (Highld.)	135	ND 1325
Borle Brook	49	SO 7087
Borley	54	TL 8442
Bornesketaig	122	NG 3771
Borness	87	NX 6145
Borness Point	87	NX 6144
Boroughbridge	79	SE 3966
Borough Green	29	TQ 6057
Borras Head	58	SJ 3653
Borreraig	122	NG 1853
Borrobol Forest	134	NC 7726
Borrobol Lodge	134	NC 8626
Borrodale Burn	111	NM 7086
Borrowash	60	SK 4134
Borrow Beck	83	NY 5205
Borrowby	85	SE 4289
Borrowdale (Cumbr.)	82	NY 2416
Borrowdale (Cumbr.)	82	NY 2514
Borrowdale (Cumbr.)	83	NY 5703
Borrowdale Fells	82	NY 2512
Borrowfield	119	NO 8293
Borth	56	SN 6089
Borthwickbrae	89	NT 4113
Borthwickshiels	89	NT 4315
Borthwick Water	89	NT 4112
Borve (Barra)	112	NF 6501
Borve (Berneray, North Uist)	124	NF 9181
Borve (Harris, W Isles)	124	NG 0294
Borve (Island of Skye)	123	NG 4448
Borve Point	112	NF 6402
Borve River	131	NB 4254
Borwick	77	SD 5273
Bosavern	18	SW 3730
Bosbury	49	SO 6943
Boscastle	20	SX 0990
Boscobel House (ant.)	59	SJ 8308
Boscombe (Dorset)	26	SZ 1191
Boscombe (Wilts.)	34	SU 2038
Boscoppa	19	SX 0353
Bosham	27	SU 8004
Bosherston	42	SR 9694
Boskednan	18	SW 4434
Bosley	69	SJ 9165
Bossall	80	SE 7160
Bossiney	20	SX 0688
Bossingham	31	TR 1549
Bostock Green	69	SJ 6769
Boston	63	TF 3244
Boston Aerodrome	63	TF 2943
Boston Deeps (chan.)	63	TF 4947
Boston Spa	79	SE 4245
Boswinger	19	SW 9941
Botallack	18	SW 3632
Botany Bay	37	TQ 2999
Botcheston	61	SK 4804
Botesdale	54	TM 0475
Bothal	91	NZ 2386
Bothamsall	71	SK 6773
Bothel	82	NY 1838
Bothenhampton	25	SY 4791
Bothwell	101	NS 7058
Bothwell Water	103	NT 6666
Botley (Bucks.)	36	SP 9802
Botley (Hants.)	27	SU 5112
Botley (Oxon.)	47	SP 4806
Botolphs	28	TQ 1909
Bottacks	128	NH 4860
Bottesford (Humbs.)	74	SE 9107
Bottesford (Leic.)	61	SK 8038
Bottisham	53	TL 5460
Bottle Island	126	NB 9502
Bottomcraig	109	NO 3724
Bottoms	78	SD 9321
Botton Head	77	SD 6661
Botusfleming	20	SX 4061
Botwnnog	66	SH 2631
Boughrood	44	SO 1239
Boughspring	45	ST 5597
Boughton (Norf.)	64	TF 7002
Boughton (Northants.)	51	SP 7565
Boughton (Notts.)	71	SK 6768
Boughton Aluph	31	TR 0348
Boughton Green	29	TQ 7651
Boughton House (ant.)	52	SP 9081
Boughton Lees	31	TR 0247
Boughton Malherbe	30	TQ 8849
Boughton Street	31	TR 0559
Boulby	85	NZ 7519
Bouldon	48	SO 5485
Boulmer	91	NU 2614
Boulmer Haven	91	NU 2613
Boulston	42	SM 9812
Boulsworth Hill	78	SD 9335
Boultenstone	118	NJ 4110
Boultham	72	SK 9568
Bourn	53	TL 3256
Bourne	62	TF 0920
Bourne End (Beds.)	52	SP 9644
Bourne End (Bucks.)	36	SU 8987
Bourne End (Herts.)	36	TL 0206
Bournemouth	26	SZ 0991
Bournemouth (Hurn) Airport	26	SZ 1198
Bournes Green	46	SO 9104
Bournheath	49	SO 9474
Bournmoor	84	NZ 3051
Bournville	50	SP 0480
Bourton (Avon)	32	ST 3864
Bourton (Dorset)	25	ST 7630
Bourton (Oxon.)	34	SU 2387
Bourton (Shrops.)	59	SO 5996
Bourton on Dunsmore	50	SP 4370
Bourton-on-the-Hill	47	SP 1732
Bourton-on-the-Water	47	SP 1620
Bousd	110	NM 2563
Boveney	36	SU 9377
Boverton	41	SS 9868
Bovey Tracey	21	SX 8178
Bovingdon	36	TL 0103
Bovington Camp	25	SY 8389
Bow	37	TQ 3783
Bow (Devon)	23	SS 7201
Bow (Flotta, Orkney)	136	ND 3693
Bowbank	84	NY 9423
Bow Brickhill	52	SP 9034
Bowburn	84	NZ 3038
Bowcombe	27	SZ 4786
Bowd	24	SY 1190
Bowden (Borders)	96	NT 5530
Bowden (Devon)	21	SX 8448
Bowden Hill	34	ST 9367
Bowdon	69	SJ 7586
Bower	90	NY 7583
Bowerchalke	26	SU 0122
Bowermadden	135	ND 2364
Bowers Gifford	38	TQ 7588
Bowershall	102	NT 0991
Bowertower	135	ND 2362
Bowes	84	NY 9913
Bowes Moor	84	NY 9311
Bow Fell	82	NY 2406
Bow Head	138	HY 4553
Bowhill	96	NT 4227
Bowland	96	NT 4540
Bowland Bridge	83	SD 4189
Bowley	45	SO 5352
Bowlhead Green	28	SU 9138
Bowling	101	NS 4473
Bowling Bank	58	SJ 3948
Bowling Green	49	SO 8151
Bowmanstead	82	SD 3096
Bowmont Forest	96	NT 7328
Bowmont Water	97	NT 8125
Bowmore	98	NR 3159
Bowness-on-Solway	89	NY 2262
Bowness-on-Windermere	83	SD 4097
Bow of Fife	103	NO 3112
Bowood House	34	ST 9769
Bowsden	97	NT 9941
Bowside Lodge	134	NC 8261
Bow Street	57	SN 6284
Bowthorpe	65	TG 1709
Box (Glos.)	46	SO 8600
Box (Wilts.)	33	ST 8268
Boxbush	46	SO 7412
Boxford (Berks.)	34	SU 4271
Boxford (Suff.)	54	TL 9640
Boxgrove	27	SU 9007
Boxley	30	TQ 7759
Boxted (Essex)	54	TM 0033
Boxted (Suff.)	54	TL 8250
Boxworth	53	TL 3464
Boylestone	60	SK 1835
Boyndie	121	NJ 6463
Boyndie Bay	121	NJ 6765
Boyndlie	121	NJ 9162
Boyne Bay	121	NJ 6166
Boynton	81	TA 1368
Boysack	109	NO 6249
Boyton (Corn.)	20	SX 3192
Boyton (Suff.)	55	TM 3747
Boyton (Wilts.)	34	ST 9539
Bozeat	52	SP 9059
Braaid	76	SC 3176
Braal Castle	135	ND 1360
Brabling Green	55	TM 2964
Brabourne	31	TR 1041
Brabourne Lees	31	TR 0840
Brabster	135	ND 3269
Bracadale	122	NG 3538
Braceborough	62	TF 0713
Bracebridge Heath	72	SK 9767
Braceby	62	TF 0135
Bracewell	78	SD 8648
Brackenfield	71	SK 3759
Brackenthwaite	82	NY 1522
Bracklesham Bay	36	SU 8095
Brackletter	115	NN 1882
Brackley (Northants.)	51	SP 5837
Brackley (Strath.)	92	NR 7941
Bracknell	36	SU 8769
Brack, The	100	NN 2403
Braco	101	NN 8309
Bracobrae	121	NJ 5053
Braco Castle (ant.)	101	NN 8211
Bracon Ash	65	TM 1899
Bracora	111	NM 7192
Bracorina	111	NM 7292
Bradbourne	60	SK 2052
Bradbury	84	NZ 3128
Bradda	76	SC 1970
Bradda Head	76	SC 1870
Bradden	51	SP 6448
Braddock	19	SX 1662
Bradenham	36	SU 8297
Bradenham	64	TF 9208
Bradenstoke	34	SU 0079
Bradfield (Berks.)	35	SU 6072
Bradfield (Essex)	55	TM 1430
Bradfield (Norf.)	65	TG 2633
Bradfield Combust	54	TL 8957
Bradfield Green	69	SJ 6859
Bradfield Moors	71	SK 2292
Bradfield St. Clare	54	TL 9057
Bradfield St. George	54	TL 9059
Bradford (Devon)	22	SS 4207
Bradford (Northum.)	97	NU 1532
Bradford (W Yorks.)	78	SE 1633
Bradford Abbas	25	ST 5814
Bradford Leigh	33	ST 8362
Bradford-on-Avon	33	ST 8260
Bradford-on-Tone	24	ST 1722
Bradford Peverell	25	SY 6592
Brading	27	SZ 6087
Bradley (Derby.)	60	SK 2145
Bradley (Hants.)	35	SU 6341
Bradley (Here. and Worc.)	50	SO 9860
Bradley (Humbs.)	75	TA 2406
Bradley (Staffs.)	59	SJ 8717
Bradley Green	50	SO 9861
Bradley in the Moors	60	SK 0541
Bradmore	61	SK 5831
Bradninch	23	SS 9903
Bradnop	60	SK 0155
Bradpole	25	SY 4794
Bradshaw	69	SD 7312
Bradstone	20	SX 3880
Bradwell (Bucks.)	52	SP 8339
Bradwell (Derby.)	70	SK 1781
Bradwell (Essex)	38	TL 8023
Bradwell (Norf.)	65	TG 5003
Bradwell Green	69	SJ 7563
Bradwell Grove	47	SP 2308
Bradwell-on-Sea	39	TM 0006
Bradwell Waterside	39	TL 9907
Bradworthy	22	SS 3213
Brae (Highld.)	128	NC 4300
Brae (Highld.)	126	NG 8185
Brae (Highld.)	128	NH 6663
Brae (Shetld.)	141	HU 3567
Braeantra	128	NH 5678
Braedownie	117	NO 2875
Braefield	116	NH 4130
Braegrum	108	NO 0024
Braehead (Orkney)	136	HY 5101
Braehead (Strath.)	95	NS 8134
Braehead (Strath.)	95	NS 9550
Braehead (Tays.)	109	NO 6852
Braehead (Westray)	138	HY 4447
Braehead (Wigtown.)	87	NX 4252
Braehoulland	142	HU 2479
Braelangwell Lodge	128	NH 5192
Braemar (Grampn.)	117	NO 1591
Braemar (Grampn.) (dist.)	117	NO 1493
Braemore	135	ND 0630
Braemore Forest	127	NH 2076
Brae of Achnahaird	132	NC 0013
Brae of Glenbervie	119	NO 7684
Brae of Moan	138	HY 3733
Braeriach (Braigh Riabhach)	117	NN 9599
Braeroy Forest	115	NN 3791
Brae Roy Lodge	115	NN 3391
Braeside	100	NS 2375
Braes of Abernethy	117	NJ 0715
Braes of Balquhidder	107	NN 4921
Braes of Doune	101	NN 7005
Braes of Glenlivet	117	NJ 2522
Braes of Lorn	105	NM 8717
Braes of Ogilvie	102	NN 8907
Braes of the Carse	108	NO 2530
Braes o' Lochaber	115	NN 3280
Braes, The	123	NG 5234
Braeswick	139	HY 6037
Brae Wick	142	HU 2477
Brafferton (Durham)	84	NZ 2921
Brafferton (N Yorks.)	79	SE 4370
Brafield-on-the-Green	52	SP 8158
Braga Ness	140	HU 1948
Bragar	131	NB 2947
Bragbury End	37	TL 2621
Bragleenmore	106	NM 9020
Braich Anelog	56	SH 1427
Braich y Pwll	56	SH 1325
Braides	77	SD 4350
Braid Fell	86	NX 1166
Braid Hills	103	NT 2569
Braidley	78	SE 0380
Braidon Bay	119	NO 8777
Braidwood	95	NS 8448
Bràigh Mór	130	NA 9916
Bràigh-nam-bàgh	125	NG 0889
Braigh Riabhach	117	NN 9599
Braigh Sròn Ghorm	117	NN 9078
Braigo	98	NR 2369
Brailes	50	SP 3139
Brailsford	60	SK 2541
Braintree	38	TL 7622
Braiseworth	55	TM 1371
Braishfield	26	SU 3725
Braithwaite	82	NY 2323
Braithwell	71	SK 5394
Bramber	28	TQ 1810
Bramcote	61	SK 5037
Bramdean	27	SU 6127
Bramerton	65	TG 2904
Bramfield (Herts.)	37	TL 2915
Bramfield (Suff.)	55	TM 4073
Bramford	55	TM 1246
Bramhall	69	SJ 8984
Bramham	79	SE 4242
Bramhope	79	SE 2443
Bramley (Hants.)	36	SU 6358
Bramley (Surrey)	28	TQ 0044
Bramley (S Yorks.)	71	SK 4892
Brampford Speke	21	SX 9298
Brampton (Cambs.)	52	TL 2170
Brampton (Cumbr.)	90	NY 5361
Brampton (Cumbr.)	83	NY 6723
Brampton (Lincs.)	72	SK 8479
Brampton (Norf.)	65	TG 2224
Brampton (Suff.)	55	TM 4381
Brampton (S Yorks.)	71	SE 4101
Brampton Abbotts	45	SO 6026
Brampton Ash	51	SP 7887
Brampton Bryan	48	SO 3672
Brampton Station	55	TM 4183
Bramshall	60	SK 0633
Bramshaw	26	SU 2615
Bramshill	36	SU 7461
Bramshill Plantation	36	SU 7562
Bramshott	27	SU 8432
Brancaster	64	TF 7743
Brancaster Bay	64	TF 7546
Brancaster Roads	64	TF 8049
Brancepeth	84	NZ 2238
Branchill	129	NJ 0852
Branderburgh	120	NJ 2371
Brandesburton	75	TA 1147
Brandeston	55	TM 2460
Brandiston	65	TG 1321
Brandon (Durham)	84	NZ 2439
Brandon (Lincs.)	62	SK 9048
Brandon (Northum.)	91	NU 0417
Brandon (Suff.)	54	TL 7886
Brandon (Warw.)	50	SP 4076
Brandon Bank	54	TL 6289
Brandon Creek	54	TL 6091
Brandon Park	54	TL 7784
Brandon Parva	64	TG 0708
Brandsby	79	SE 5872
Brands Hatch	37	TQ 5764
Brand Side	70	SK 0468
Brane	18	SW 4028
Bran End	54	TL 6525
Branksome Park	26	SZ 0490
Brannie Burn	106	NN 1616
Branscombe	24	SY 1988
Bransdale	85	SE 6296
Bransford	49	SO 7952
Bransgore	26	SZ 1897
Bransly Hill	103	NT 6770
Branston (Leic.)	61	SK 8029
Branston (Lincs.)	72	TF 0167
Branston (Staffs.)	60	SK 2221
Branstone	27	SZ 5583
Brant Broughton	62	SK 9154
Brant Fell	83	SD 6595
Brantham	55	TM 1034
Branthwaite	82	NY 0525
Brantingham	74	SE 9429
Branton	91	NU 0416
Branton	71	SE 6501
Branxholme	89	NT 4611
Branxholm Park	89	NT 4612
Branxton	97	NT 8937
Brassington	60	SK 2354
Brasted	29	TQ 4755
Brasted Chart	29	TQ 4653
Brat Bheinn	98	NR 4966
Brathens	119	NO 6798
Bratoft	73	TF 4765
Brattleby	72	SK 9480
Bratton	33	ST 9152
Bratton Castle (ant.)	33	ST 9051
Bratton Clovelly	20	SX 4691
Bratton Fleming	23	SS 6437
Bratton Seymour	25	ST 6729
Braughing	53	TL 3925
Braunston (Leic.)	62	SK 8306
Braunston (Northants.)	51	SP 5366
Braunstone	61	SK 5502
Braunton	22	SS 4836
Braunton Burrows	22	SS 4535
Brawby	80	SE 7378
Brawl	134	NC 8066
Brawlbin	135	ND 0757
Bray	36	SU 9079
Braybrooke	51	SP 7684
Brayford	23	SS 6834
Bray Shop	20	SX 3374
Braystones	82	NY 0006
Brayton	79	SE 6030
Brazacott	20	SX 2691
Breabag (mt.)	132	NC 2917
Breachacha Castle	110	NM 1553
Breachwood Green	37	TL 1522
Breackerie Water	92	NR 6413
Breaclete	131	NB 1538
Breadalbane (dist.)	107	NN 4735
Breadsall	60	SK 3639
Breadstone	46	SO 7000
Breagach Hill	118	NJ 3313
Breage	18	SW 6128
Breakachy	128	NH 4644
Breakish	123	NG 6723
Breaksea Point	41	ST 0265
Bream	45	SO 6005
Breamore	26	SU 1517
Brean	32	ST 2955
Brean Down	32	ST 2858
Brearton	79	SE 3260
Breasclete	131	NB 2135
Breaston	61	SK 4533
Breast Sand	63	TF 5427
Brechfa	43	SN 5230
Brechin	109	NO 5960
Breckles	64	TL 9594
Breck Ness	136	HY 2209
Breckrey	123	NG 5162
Breck, The	142	HU 3292
Brecon	41	SO 0428
Brecon and Abergavenny Canal	41	SO 1122
Brecon Beacons (mt.)	41	SO 0121
Bredbury	69	SJ 9292
Brede	30	TQ 8218
Bredenbury	45	SO 6056
Bredfield	55	TM 2653
Bredgar	30	TQ 8860
Bredhurst	30	TQ 7962
Bredon	49	SO 9236
Bredon Hill	50	SO 9640
Bredon's Norton	49	SO 9339
Bredwardine	45	SO 3344
Breedon on the Hill	60	SK 4022
Breich	102	NS 9560
Breighton	74	SE 7033
Breinton	45	SO 4739
Breiti Stack	139	HZ 2072
Brei Wick	141	HU 4740
Bremenium (ant.)	90	NY 8398
Bremhill	34	ST 9873
Bremia (ant.)	43	SN 6456
Brenchley	29	TQ 6741
Brendon	23	SS 7648
Brendon Common	23	SS 7645
Brendon Hills	24	ST 0135
Brenfield Bay	99	NR 8582
Brenig Resr.	67	SH 9857
Brenish	130	NA 9926
Brenish Point	124	NF 9089
Brent Eleigh	54	TL 9447
Brentford	37	TQ 1778
Brent Knoll	32	ST 3350
Brent Pelham	53	TL 4330
Brentwood	38	TQ 5993
Brenzett	31	TR 0027
Brereton	60	SK 0516
Brereton Green	69	SJ 7764
Brereton Heath	69	SJ 8064
Bressay	141	HU 5040
Bressay Sound	141	HU 4841
Bressingham	54	TM 0780
Brest Rocks	93	NS 1904
Brest Twrch	41	SN 8120
Bretby	60	SK 2923
Bretford	50	SP 4277
Bretforton	50	SP 0943
Bretherdale Head	83	NY 5705
Bretherton	69	SD 4720
Brettabister	141	HU 4857
Brettenham (Norf.)	54	TL 9383
Brettenham (Suff.)	54	TL 9653
Bretton	68	SJ 3563
Brevig	112	NL 6998
Brewham	25	ST 7136
Brewlands Bridge	108	NO 1961
Brewood	59	SJ 8808
Breydon Water	65	TG 4907
Briantspuddle	25	SY 8193
Brickendon	37	TL 3208
Bricket Wood	37	TL 1301
Bricklehampton	50	SO 9842
Bride	76	NX 4501
Bridekirk	82	NY 1133
Bridell	42	SN 1742
Bride's Ness	139	HY 7752
Bridestowe	20	SX 5189
Bridestowe and Sourton Common	21	SX 5688
Brideswell	121	NJ 5739
Bridford	21	SX 8186
Bridge	31	TR 1854
Bridge End (Lincs.)	62	TF 1436
Bridgefoot	82	NY 0529
Bridge Green	53	TL 4636
Bridgemary	27	SU 5702
Bridgend (Cumbr.)	83	NY 3914
Bridgend (Dumf. and Galwy.)	89	NT 0708
Bridgend (Fife)	103	NO 3911
Bridgend (Grampn.)	121	NJ 3731
Bridgend (Grampn.)	121	NJ 5135
Bridgend (Islay)	98	NR 3362
Bridgend (Lothian)	102	NT 0475
Bridgend (Mid Glam.)	41	SS 9079
Bridgend (Strath.)	99	NR 8592
Bridgend (Strath.)	101	NS 6970
Bridgend (Tays.)	108	NO 1224
Bridgend (Tays.)	109	NO 5368
Bridgend of Lintrathen	108	NO 2854
Bridge of Alford	119	NJ 5617
Bridge of Allan	101	NS 7897
Bridge of Avon	117	NJ 1835
Bridge of Balgie	107	NN 5746
Bridge of Brown	117	NJ 1220
Bridge of Buchat	118	NJ 3915
Bridge of Cally	108	NO 1351
Bridge of Canny	119	NO 6597
Bridge of Craigisla	108	NO 2553
Bridge of Dee	88	NX 7360
Bridge of Don	119	NJ 9409
Bridge of Dun	109	NO 6658
Bridge of Dye	119	NO 6585
Bridge of Earn	108	NO 1318
Bridge of Ericht	107	NN 5258
Bridge of Feugh	119	NO 7094
Bridge of Forss	135	ND 0368
Bridge of Gairn	118	NO 3597
Bridge of Gaur	107	NN 5056
Bridge of Muchalls	119	NO 8991
Bridge of Orchy	106	NN 2939
Bridge of Tilt	108	NN 8765
Bridge of Waithe	136	HY 2811
Bridge of Walls	140	HU 2651
Bridge of Weir	101	NS 3865
Bridgerule	22	SS 2803
Bridges	58	SO 3996
Bridge Sollers	45	SO 4142
Bridge Street	54	TL 8749
Bridgetown	23	SS 9233
Bridge Trafford	68	SJ 4471
Bridgewater Canal	69	SJ 7186
Bridgeyate	33	ST 6873
Bridgham	54	TL 9686
Bridgnorth	59	SO 7193
Bridgtown	60	SJ 9808
Bridgwater	24	ST 3037
Bridgwater Bay	32	ST 1852
Bridlington	81	TA 1766
Bridlington Bay	81	TA 1964
Bridport	26	SY 4692
Bridstow	45	SO 5824
Brierfield	78	SD 8436
Brierley (Glos.)	45	SO 6215
Brierley (Here. and Worc.)	45	SO 4956
Brierley (S Yorks.)	71	SE 4011
Brierley Hill	49	SO 9187
Briga Head	135	ND 1875
Brigg	74	TA 0007
Brigham (Cumbr.)	82	NY 0830
Brigham (Humbs.)	81	TA 0753
Brighouse	78	SE 1423
Brighstone	26	SZ 4282
Brighstone Bay	26	SZ 4180
Brighstone Forest	26	SZ 4285
Brightgate	71	SK 2659
Brighthampton	47	SP 3803
Brightling	29	TQ 6821
Brightlingsea	39	TM 0816
Brighton (Corn.)	19	SW 9054
Brighton (E Susx)	29	TQ 3105
Brighton, Hove & Worthing Municipal Airport	28	TQ 2005
Brightons	102	NS 9277
Brightwalton	34	SU 4278
Brightwell	55	TM 2543
Brightwell Baldwin	36	SU 6594
Brightwell-cum-Sotwell	35	SU 5790
Brignall	84	NZ 0712
Brig o'Turk	101	NN 5306
Brigsley	75	TA 2501
Brigsteer	83	SD 4889
Brigstock	52	SP 9485
Brill	36	SP 6513
Brilley	45	SO 2549
Brimfield	48	SO 5267
Brimington	71	SK 4073
Brimmond Hill	119	NJ 8509
Brimpsfield	46	SO 9312
Brimpton	35	SU 5564
Brims	136	ND 2888
Brims Ness (Highld.)	135	ND 0471
Brims Ness (Hoy, Orkney)	136	ND 2988
Brind	74	SE 7430
Brindister (Shetld.)	140	HU 2757
Brindister (Shetld.)	141	HU 4337
Brindle	77	SD 5924
Brindley Ford	59	SJ 8754
Brindley Heath	60	SJ 9914
Brineton	59	SJ 8013
Bring Deeps (chan.)	136	HY 2902
Bringewood Chase	48	SO 4573
Bring Head (Hoy, Shetld.)	136	HY 2702
Bring Head (Rousay)	138	HY 3733
Bringhurst	52	SP 8492
Brington	52	TL 0875
Briningham	64	TG 0334
Brinkburn Priory (ant.)	91	NZ 1198
Brinkhill	73	TF 3773
Brinkley	54	TL 6254
Brinklow	50	SP 4379
Brinkworth	34	SU 0184
Brinscall	77	SD 6321
Brinsley	61	SK 4548
Brinsop	45	SO 4344
Brinsworth	71	SK 4190
Brinton	64	TG 0335
Brinyan	136	HY 4327
Brisley	64	TF 9421
Brislington	33	ST 6170
Brisons, The	18	SW 3331
Bristol	33	ST 5872
Bristol Airport	33	ST 5064
Bristol Channel	40	SS 4267
Briston	64	TG 0632
Britannia	78	SD 8821
Britford	26	SU 1528
Briton Ferry	40	SS 7394
Britwell Salome	36	SU 6792
Brixham	21	SX 9255
Brixton	21	SX 5452
Brixton	37	TQ 3175
Brixton Deverill	33	ST 8638
Brixworth	51	SP 7470
Brize Norton	47	SP 2907
Broad Bay or Loch a Tuath	131	NB 5037
Broad Bench (pt.)	25	SY 8978
Broad Blunsdon	34	SU 1490
Broadbottom	70	SJ 9993
Broadbridge	27	SU 8105
Broadbridge Heath	28	TQ 1431
Broadbury (dist.)	20	SX 4596
Broad Cairn	117	NO 2481
Broad Campden	50	SP 1537
Broad Chalke	26	SU 0325
Broadclyst	21	SX 9897
Broad Clyst Station	21	SX 9995
Broad Down	24	SY 1793
Broadford	123	NG 6423
Broadford Aerodrome	123	NG 6925
Broadford Bay	123	NG 6524
Broad Green	49	SO 7656
Broadhaugh	89	NT 4509
Broad Haven	42	SM 8613
Broad Head	89	NY 3394
Broadheath (Gtr Mches.)	69	SJ 7689
Broadheath (Here. and Worc.)	49	SO 6665
Broadheath (Here. and Worc.)	49	SO 8156
Broadhembury	24	ST 1004
Broadhempston	21	SX 8066
Broad Hill (Cambs.)	54	TL 5976
Broadhill (Strath.)	95	NT 0029
Broad Hinton	34	SU 1076
Broadlands House	26	SU 3520
Broad Law	95	NT 1423
Broad Laying	34	SU 4362
Broadley (Grampn.)	121	NJ 4161
Broadley (Gtr Mches.)	69	SD 8716
Broadley Common	37	TL 4207
Broad Marston	50	SP 1346
Broadmayne	25	SY 7286
Broadmeadows	96	NT 4130
Broadmere	35	SU 6247
Broad Oak (Cumbr.)	82	SD 1194
Broadoak (Dorset)	25	SY 4496
Broadoak (E Susx)	29	TQ 6022
Broad Oak (E Susx)	30	TQ 8320
Broad Oak (Here. and Worc.)	45	SO 4721
Broadoak (Kent)	31	TR 1661
Broadrashes	121	NJ 4354
Broadsea Bay	86	NW 9659
Broad Sound (Dyfed)	42	SM 7307
Broad Sound (Is. of Sc.)	18	SV 8309
Broadstairs	31	TR 3967
Broadstone (Dorset)	26	SZ 0095
Broadstone (Shrops.)	48	SO 5389
Broad Street	30	TQ 8356
Broad Taing	136	HY 4217
Broad Town	34	SU 0977
Broadwas	49	SO 7555
Broadwater	28	TQ 1504
Broadway (Here. and Worc.)	50	SP 0937
Broadway (Somer.)	24	ST 3215
Broadway Hill	50	SP 1136
Broadwell (Glos.)	47	SP 2027
Broadwell (Oxon.)	47	SP 2503
Broadwell (Warw.)	51	SP 4565
Broadwell House	84	NY 9153
Broadwell Lane End	45	SO 5811
Broadwey	25	SY 6683
Broadwindsor	25	ST 4302
Broadwood-Kelly	23	SS 6105
Broadwoodwidger	20	SX 4089
Brobury	45	SU 3444

Brochel 123 NG 5846
Brockbridge 27 SU 6018
Brockdam 97 NU 1624
Brockdish 55 TM 2179
Brockenhurst 26 SU 2902
Brocketsbrae 95 NS 8239
Brockford Street 55 TM 1166
Brockhall 51 SP 6362
Brockham 28 TQ 2049
Brockhampton 45 SO 5932
Brockholes 70 SE 1411
Brocklesby 75 TA 1311
Brockley 33 ST 4666
Brockley Green 54 TL 8254
Brockloch Hill (Dumf. and Galwy.) 87 NX 5173
Brockloch Hill (Dumf. and Galwy.) 88 NX 8179
Brockloch Rig 88 NS 5801
Brockton (Shrops.) 58 SJ 3104
Brockton (Shrops.) 59 SJ 7103
Brockton (Shrops.) 48 SO 3285
Brockton (Shrops.) 59 SO 5793
Brockweir 45 SO 5301
Brockwood Park 27 SU 6226
Brockworth 46 SO 8916
Brocolitia (ant.) 90 NY 8570
Brocton 60 SJ 9619
Brodick 92 NS 0136
Brodick Bay 92 NS 0237
Brodie Castle 129 NH 9757
Brodsworth 71 SE 5007
Brogborough 52 SP 9638
Brokenborough 33 ST 9189
Broken Cross (Ches.) 69 SJ 6872
Broken Cross (Ches.) 69 SJ 8973
Broken Cross Muir (mt.) 95 NS 8436
Brolass (dist.) 105 NM 4923
Bromborough 68 SJ 3582
Brome 55 TM 1376
Brome Street 55 TM 1576
Bromeswell 55 TM 3050
Bromfield (Cumbr.) 82 NY 1746
Bromfield (Salop) 48 SO 4876
Bromham (Beds.) 52 TL 0051
Bromham (Wilts.) 34 ST 9665
Bromley (Gtr London) 37 TQ 4069
Bromley Common 37 TQ 4266
Brompton (Kent) 30 TQ 7668
Brompton (N Yorks.) 79 SE 3796
Brompton (N Yorks.) 81 SE 9482
Brompton-on-Swale 84 SE 2199
Brompton Ralph 24 ST 0832
Brompton Regis 23 SS 9531
Bromsash 46 SO 6424
Bromsgrove 50 SO 9570
Bromyard 49 SO 6554
Bromyard Downs 49 SO 6655
Bronaber 67 SH 7131
Bronant 57 SN 6467
Bronington 59 SJ 4839
Bronllys 41 SO 1435
Bronygarth 58 SJ 2636
Brook (Hants.) 26 SU 2713
Brook (Hants.) 26 SU 3428
Brook (I. of W.) 26 SZ 3983
Brook (Kent) 31 TR 0644
Brook (Surrey) 28 SU 9338
Brooke (Leic.) 62 SK 8405
Brooke (Norf.) 65 TM 2999
Brookfield 101 NS 4164
Brookhouse 77 SD 5464
Brookhouse Green 69 SJ 8061
Brookland 31 TQ 9825
Brookmans Park 37 TL 2404
Brooks 58 SO 1499
Brook Street 37 TQ 5792
Brookthorpe 46 SO 8312
Brookwood 28 SU 9557
Broom (Beds.) 52 TL 1743
Broom (Warw.) 50 SP 0953
Broome (Here. and Worc.) 49 SO 9078
Broome (Norf.) 55 TM 3591
Broome (Shrops.) 48 SO 3981
Broome Park 91 NU 1112
Broomer's Corners 28 TQ 1221
Broomfield (Essex) 38 TL 7009
Broomfield (Grampn.) 121 NJ 9532
Broomfield (Kent) 30 TQ 8452
Broomfield (Kent) 31 TR 2066
Broomfield (Somer.) 24 ST 2231
Broomfleet 74 SE 8727
Broom Hall Airfield 66 SH 4137
Broomhead Resr. 71 SK 2695
Broom Hill (Dorset) 26 SU 0302
Broomhill (Northum.) 91 NU 2400
Broomlee Lough 90 NY 7969
Broomy Law 96 NT 4131
Broomy Lodge 26 SU 2111
Brora 129 NC 9003
Brosdale Island 98 NR 4962
Broseley 59 SJ 6701
Brother Isle 143 HU 4281
Brothers Water 83 NY 4012
Brothertoft 63 TF 2746
Brotherton 79 SE 4825
Brotton 85 NZ 6819
Broubster 135 ND 0360
Brough (Bressay) 141 HU 5141
Brough (Cumbr.) 83 NY 7914
Brough (Derby.) 70 SK 1882
Brough (Highld.) 135 ND 2273
Brough (Humbs.) 74 SE 9326
Brough (Notts.) 72 SK 8358
Brough (Shetld.) 143 HU 4377
Brough (Whalsay) 141 HU 5564
Brough (Yell) 143 HU 5179
Broughall 59 SJ 5641
Brough Head (Highld.) 135 ND 3663
Brough Head (Orkney) 136 HY 2328
Brough Lodge 143 HU 5892
Brough Ness 136 ND 4482
Brough of Deerness (pt.) 137 HY 5908
Brough Sowerby 83 NY 7912
Brough Taing 143 HP 6304
Brough, The 142 HU 2982
Broughton (Borders) 95 NT 1136
Broughton (Bucks.) 52 SP 8940
Broughton (Cambs.) 53 TL 2878
Broughton (Clwyd) 68 SJ 3363
Broughton (Cumbr.) 82 NY 0731
Broughton (Gtr Mches.) 69 SD 8201
Broughton (Hants.) 26 SU 3132
Broughton (Humbs.) 74 SE 9508
Broughton (Lancs.) 77 SD 5234
Broughton (Mid Glam.) 41 SS 9271
Broughton (Northants.) 52 SP 8375
Broughton (N Yorks.) 78 SD 9451
Broughton (N Yorks.) 80 SE 7673
Broughton (Oxon.) 50 SP 4238
Broughton (Westray) 138 HY 4448
Broughton Astley 51 SP 5292
Broughton Beck 76 SD 2882
Broughton Gifford 33 ST 8763
Broughton Hackett 49 SO 9254
Broughton Heights 95 NT 1241
Broughton in Furness 76 SD 2087
Broughton Mills 82 SD 2290
Broughton Moor 82 NY 0533
Broughton Poggs 47 SP 2303
Broughtown 139 HY 6540
Broughty Ferry 109 NO 4630
Browland 140 HU 2750
Brown Bank Head (mt.) 78 SE 1057
Brown Candover 35 SU 5839
Brown Carrick Hill 93 NS 2815
Brown Caterthun (mt.) 109 NO 5566
Brown Clee Hill 49 SO 5985
Brown Cow Hill 117 NJ 2204
Brown Edge 59 SJ 9053
Brown Head 92 NR 8925
Brownhill (Grampn.) 121 NJ 8640
Brownhills (W Mids) 60 SK 0405
Brownlow Heath 69 SJ 8360
Brownmoor Hill 88 NX 9991
Brownmuir 119 NO 7477
Brown Ridge 78 SE 1077
Brownsea Island 26 SZ 0187
Brownston 21 SX 6952
Brown Willy (mt.) 19 SX 1579
Browsholme Hall (ant.) 77 SD 6845
Broxbourne 37 TL 3707
Broxburn (Lothian) 102 NT 0872
Broxburn (Lothian) 96 NT 6977
Broxted 53 TL 5727
Broxwood 45 SO 3654
Bruach, The (mt.) 117 NJ 1105
Bruan 135 ND 3039
Bruar Lodge 117 NN 8376
Bruar Water (Tays.) 107 NN 8269
Bruar Water (Tays.) 117 NN 8375
Bruchag Point 93 NS 1157
Bruddans, The 142 HU 2077
Brue 131 NB 3349
Bruera 68 SJ 4360
Bruern Abbey 47 SP 2620
Bruernish 112 NF 7102
Bruernish Point 112 NF 7300
Bruichladdich 98 NR 2661
Bruisyard 55 TM 3266
Bruisyard Street 55 TM 3365
Brumby 74 SE 8809
Brund 70 SK 1061
Brundall 65 TG 3208
Brundish 55 TM 2669
Brundish Street 55 TM 2671
Brunerican Bay 92 NR 7007
Brunt Hill 96 NT 6874
Bruntingthorpe 51 SP 6090
Brunton (Fife) 108 NO 3220
Brunton (Northum.) 97 NU 2024
Bruntshiel Hill 89 NY 4182
Bruray 143 HU 6972
Brushford 23 SS 9225
Brushford Barton 23 SS 6707
Bruton 25 ST 6834
Bruton Forest 33 ST 7438
Bruxie Hill 119 NO 8280
Bryanston 25 ST 8706
Brydekirk 89 NY 1870
Bryher (is.) 18 SV 8714
Brymbo 58 SJ 2953
Bryn (Gtr Mches.) 69 SD 5701
Bryn (Powys) 44 SN 9055
Bryn (Shrops.) 48 SO 2985
Bryn (W Glam.) 41 SS 8192
Brynamlwg 57 SN 9297
Brynamman 40 SN 7114
Brynberian 42 SN 1035
Bryn Brawd 44 SN 6951
Bryncae 41 SS 9983
Bryn-celli-ddu (ant.) 66 SH 5070
Bryncethin 41 SS 9184
Bryncir 66 SH 4641
Bryn-côch 41 SS 7499
Bryncroes 66 SH 2231
Bryncrug 56 SH 6003
Bryn Crwn 44 SN 8258
Bryn-du (Clwyd) 58 SJ 1435
Bryn-du (Powys) 56 SN 9342
Bryneglwys 58 SJ 1447
Brynford 68 SJ 1774
Bryn Garw (Dyfed) 57 SN 8077
Bryn Garw (Powys) 57 SN 8361
Bryn Gates 69 SD 5901
Brynglas Station 57 SH 6203
Bryngwran 66 SH 3477
Bryngwyn (Gwent) 45 SO 3909
Bryngwyn (Powys) 45 SO 1849
Bryn-henllan 42 SN 0139
Brynhoffnant 43 SN 3351
Brynmawr 41 SO 1911
Brynmenyn 41 SS 9084
Brynna 41 SS 9883
Bryn Nicol 44 SN 8243
Brynrefail 66 SH 4786
Brynsadler 41 ST 0380
Brynsiencyn 66 SH 4867
Brynteg 66 SH 4982
Bryn, The 45 SO 3309
Bryntitley 57 SN 9375
Bryn Trillyn 67 SH 9459
Bryn y Castell 57 SH 0704
Bryn-y-maen (Clwyd) 67 SH 8376
Bryn-y-maen (Powys) 45 SO 1657
Buachaille Etive Beag 106 NN 1854
Buachaille Etive Mór 106 NN 2254
Buail' a' Ghoill 112 NF 8130
Bualintur 123 NG 4020
Bubbenhall 50 SP 3672
Bubwith 74 SE 7136
Buccleuch 89 NT 3214
Buchan (dist.) 121 NJ 9749
Buchanan Smithy 101 NS 4689
Buchan Burn 86 NX 4181
Buchan Hill 87 NX 4281
Buchan Ness 121 NK 1342
Buchanty 107 NN 9328
Buchlyvie 101 NS 5793
Buckabank 83 NY 3749
Buckden (Cambs.) 52 TL 1967
Buckden (N Yorks.) 78 SD 9477
Buckden Pike 78 SD 9678
Buckenham 65 TG 3505
Buckerell 24 ST 1200
Buckfast 21 SX 7367
Buckfastleigh 21 SX 7466
Buckhaven 103 NT 3598
Buckholm 96 NT 4838
Buckhorn Weston 25 ST 7524
Buckhurst Hill 37 TQ 4193
Buckie 121 NJ 4265
Buckies 135 ND 1063
Buckingham 51 SP 6933
Buckland (Bucks.) 36 SP 8812
Buckland (Devon) 21 SX 6743
Buckland (Glos.) 50 SP 0836
Buckland (Herts.) 53 TL 3533
Buckland (Kent) 31 TR 2942
Buckland (Oxon.) 47 SU 3497
Buckland (Surrey) 28 TQ 2250
Buckland Abbey (ant.) 20 SX 4866
Buckland Brewer 22 SS 4120
Buckland Common 36 SP 9306
Buckland Dinham 33 ST 7550
Buckland Filleigh 22 SS 4609
Buckland in the Moor 21 SX 7273
Buckland Monachorum 20 SX 4868
Buckland Newton 25 ST 6905
Buckland St. Mary 24 ST 2713
Buckland-Tout-Saints 21 SX 7546
Bucklebury 35 SU 5570
Bucklerheads 109 NO 4636
Bucklers Hard 26 SZ 4099
Bucklesham 55 TM 2442
Buckley 68 SJ 2764
Buckminster 62 SK 8722
Bucknall (Lincs.) 73 TF 1668
Bucknall (Staffs.) 59 SJ 9147
Bucknell (Oxon.) 47 SP 5525
Bucknell (Shrops.) 48 SO 3574
Bucksburn 119 NJ 8909
Buck's Cross 22 SS 3422
Bucks Green 28 TQ 0732
Bucks Hill 36 TL 0500
Bucks Horn Oak 35 SU 8142
Buck's Mills 22 SS 3523
Buck, The (mt.) 121 NJ 4123
Buckton (Here. and Worc.) 48 SO 3873
Buckton (Northum.) 97 NU 0838
Buckworth 52 TL 1476
Budbrooke 50 SP 2565
Budby 71 SK 6169
Buddo Ness 109 NO 5515
Buddon Ness 109 NO 5530
Bude 22 SS 2006
Bude Bay 22 SS 1706
Bude Haven 22 SS 2006
Budlake 21 SS 9700
Budle 97 NU 1534
Budle Bay 97 NU 1535
Budleigh Salterton 24 SY 0682
Budock Water 19 SW 7832
Buerton 59 SJ 6843
Bugbrooke 51 SP 6757
Bugeilyn 57 SN 8292
Bught Fell 86 NX 2062
Bugle 19 SX 0158
Bugthorpe 80 SE 7757
Buidhe Bheinn 114 NG 9508
Builg Burn 119 NO 6687
Builth Road 44 SO 0253
Builth Wells 44 SO 0351
Bulbarrow Hill 25 ST 7705
Bulby 62 TF 0526
Buldoo 134 NC 9967
Bulford 34 SU 1643
Bulg (mt.) 119 NO 5476
Bulgham Bay 76 SC 4685
Bulkeley 59 SJ 5254
Bulkington (Warw.) 50 SP 3986
Bulkington (Wilts.) 34 ST 9458
Bulkworthy 22 SS 3914
Bull (lightship) 75 TA 3809
Bull Bay (Gwyn.) 66 SH 4294
Bull Bay (Gwyn.) 66 SH 4394
Bulldog Sand 64 TF 6027
Bulley 46 SO 7519
Bullie Burn 101 NN 7809
Bull Point 22 SS 4646
Bullpot Farm 77 SD 6681
Bullwood 100 NS 1674
Bulmer (Essex) 54 TL 8440
Bulmer (N Yorks.) 80 SE 6967
Bulmer Tye 54 TL 8438
Bulphan 38 TQ 6385
Bulverhythe 30 TQ 7809
Bulwark 121 NJ 9345
Bulwell 61 SK 5345
Bulwick 62 SP 9694
Bumble's Green 37 TL 4005
Bunacaimb 111 NM 6588
Bun Allt na Criche 106 NM 9256
Bun an Leoib (chan.) 105 NM 4023
Bunarkaig 115 NN 1887
Bunavoneadar 125 NB 1304
Bunbury 69 SJ 5658
Bunchrew 128 NH 6145
Buncton 28 TQ 1413
Bundalloch 114 NG 8927
Bu Ness (Fair Isle) 139 HZ 2272
Buness (Unst) 143 HP 6209
Bunessan 104 NM 3821
Bungay 55 TM 3389
Bunloinn Forest 115 NH 1608
Bunnahabhainn 98 NR 4173
Bunny 61 SK 5829
Buntait 115 NH 3930
Buntingford 53 TL 3629
Bunwell 65 TM 1293
Burach 115 NH 3814
Burbage (Derby.) 70 SK 0472
Burbage (Leic.) 51 SP 4492
Burbage (Wilts.) 34 SU 2261
Burcombe (Somer.) (dist.) 23 SS 7538
Burcombe (Wilts.) 26 SU 0630
Burcot 47 SU 5595
Burdale 81 SE 8762
Bures 54 TL 9034
Burfa Camp (ant.) 48 SO 2861
Burford 47 SP 2512
Burg 104 NM 3745
Burgar 136 HY 3427
Burga Water 140 HU 2354
Burgess Hill 29 TQ 3118
Burgh (Island of Mull) 105 NM 4226
Burgh (Suff.) 55 TM 2251
Burgh by Sands 89 NY 3259
Burgh Castle 65 TG 4805
Burghclere 35 SU 4660
Burghead 129 NJ 1168
Burghead Bay 129 NJ 0767
Burghfield 36 SU 6668
Burghfield Common 36 SU 6466
Burghfield Hill 36 SU 6567
Burgh Head 137 HY 6923
Burgh Heath 37 TQ 2458
Burghill 45 SO 4744
Burgh Island 21 SX 6443
Burgh Le Marsh 73 TF 5065
Burghley House (ant.) 62 TF 0406
Burgh Muir 121 NJ 7622
Burgh next Aylsham 65 TG 2125
Burgh on Bain 73 TF 2186
Burgh St. Margaret 65 TG 4413
Burgh St. Peter 65 TM 4693
Burghwallis 71 SE 5312
Burgi Geos 143 HP 4703
Burham 30 TQ 7262
Burifa Hill 135 ND 2075
Buriton 27 SU 7319
Burland 59 SJ 6153
Burlawn 19 SW 9970
Burlescombe 24 ST 0716
Burleston 25 SY 7794
Burley (Hants.) 26 SU 2103
Burley (Leic.) 62 SK 8810
Burleydam 59 SJ 6042
Burley Gate 45 SO 5947
Burley in Wharfedale 78 SE 1646
Burley Lodge 26 SU 2305
Burley Street 26 SU 2004
Burlingjobb 45 SO 2558
Burlton 58 SJ 4526
Burmarsh 31 TR 1032
Burmington 50 SP 2637
Burn 79 SE 5928
Burnage 69 SJ 8692
Burnaston 60 SK 2832
Burnby 74 SE 8346
Burncrooks Resr. 101 NS 4879
Burneside 83 SD 5095
Burness 139 HY 6644
Burneston 79 SE 3084
Burnett 33 ST 6665
Burn Farm, The 109 NO 6072
Burnfoot (Borders) 89 NT 4113
Burnfoot (Borders) 90 NT 5116
Burnfoot (Tays.) 102 NN 9804
Burnfoot Resr. 93 NS 4544
Burnham (Berks. - Bucks.) 36 SU 9382
Burnham (Humbs.) 74 TA 0517
Burnham Beeches 36 SU 9585
Burnham Deepdale 64 TF 8044
Burnham Green 37 TL 2616
Burnham Market 64 TF 8342
Burnham Norton 64 TF 8243
Burnham-on-Crouch 38 TQ 9496
Burnham-on-Sea 32 ST 3049
Burnham Overy Staithe 64 TF 8444
Burnham Overy Town 64 TF 8442
Burnham Thorpe 64 TF 8541
Burnhaven 121 NK 1244
Burnhead 88 NX 8595
Burnhervie 119 NJ 7319
Burnhill Green 59 SJ 7800
Burnhope 84 NZ 1948
Burnhope Reservoir 83 NY 8328
Burnhope Seat (mt.) 83 NY 7837
Burnhouse 93 NS 3850
Burn Howe Rigg (mt.) 81 SE 9099
Burniston 81 TA 0193
Burnley 78 SD 8332
Burn Moor 77 SD 7064
Burn Moor Fell 77 SD 7064
Burnmoor Tarn 82 NY 1804
Burnmouth 97 NT 9560
Burnock Water 93 NS 5017
Burn of Acharole 135 ND 2351
Burn of Agie 115 NN 3691
Burn of Arisdale 143 HU 4783
Burn of Aultmore 121 NJ 4556
Burn of Boyne 121 NJ 5858
Burn of Branny 118 NO 4484
Burn of Calletar 119 NO 4769
Burn of Cambus 101 NN 7003
Burn of Cattie 119 NO 5795
Burn of Corrichie 119 NJ 7002
Burn of Dale 140 HU 2053
Burn of Hillside 136 HY 3023
Burn of Houstry 135 ND 1436
Burn of Laxdale 141 HU 4131
Burn of Lochy 117 NJ 1221
Burn of Loin 117 NJ 1409
Burn of Lyth 135 ND 2961
Burn of Ore 136 ND 2893
Burn of Rothes 120 NJ 2248
Burn of Sandvoe 142 HU 3590
Burn of Sandwater 141 HU 4153
Burn of Sheeoch 119 NO 7389
Burn of Tennet 118 NO 5082
Burn of Tulchan 117 NJ 0838
Burn of Turret 119 NO 5480
Burnopfield 84 NZ 1756
Burnsall 78 SE 0361
Burns Cottage 93 NS 3318
Burnside (Fife) 102 NO 1607
Burnside (Lothian) 102 NT 0971
Burnside (Shetld.) 142 HU 2778
Burnside (Strath.) 88 NS 5811
Burnside (Tays.) 109 NO 4259
Burnside (Tays.) 109 NO 5050
Burnside of Duntrune 109 NO 4434
Burnswark 89 NY 1878
Burnt Fen 54 TL 6085
Burn, The 109 NO 5971
Burnt Hill 100 NS 3058
Burntisland 103 NT 2385
Burntwood 60 SK 0609
Burnt Yates 79 SE 2461
Burpham (Surrey) 28 TQ 0151
Burpham (W Susx) 28 TQ 0408
Burrach Mòr 116 NH 5808
Burradon (Northum.) 91 NT 9806
Burradon (Tyne and Wear) 91 NZ 2772
Burrafirth (Unst) 143 HP 6113
Burra Firth (Unst) 143 HP 6116
Burraland (Shetld.) 140 HU 2249
Burraland (Shetld.) 142 HU 3475
Burra Ness 143 HU 5595
Burras 18 SW 6835
Burra Sound 136 HY 2404
Burrator Resr. 21 SX 5568
Burravoe (Shetld.) 141 HU 3667
Burra Voe (Shetld.) 142 HU 3689
Burra Voe (Yell) 143 HU 5279
Burravoe (Yell) 143 HU 5280
Burray 136 ND 4796
Burray Haas 136 ND 4998
Burray Ness 136 ND 5096
Burrelton 108 NO 1936
Burridge 27 SU 5110
Burrier Wick 142 HU 3192
Burries Ness 142 HU 2783
Burrill 79 SE 2387
Burringham 74 SE 8309
Burrington (Avon) 33 ST 4759
Burrington (Devon) 23 SS 6316
Burrington (Here. and Worc.) 48 SO 4472
Burrough Green 54 TL 6355
Burrough on the Hill 61 SK 7510
Burrow Bridge 24 ST 3530
Burrow Head 87 NX 4534
Burrowhill 36 SU 9763
Burrows Hole 97 NU 1340
Burry Holms 40 SS 3992
Burry Port 40 SN 4400
Burscough 68 SD 4310
Burscough Bridge 68 SD 4411
Bursea 74 SE 8033
Burshill 81 TA 0948
Bursledon 27 SU 4809
Burslem 59 SJ 8749
Burstall 55 TM 0944
Burstock 25 ST 4202
Burston (Norf.) 55 TM 1383
Burston (Staffs.) 59 SJ 9330
Burstow 29 TQ 3141
Burstwick 75 TA 2228
Burtersett 84 SD 8989
Burtle 32 ST 3943
Burton (Ches.) 68 SJ 3174
Burton (Ches.) 69 SJ 5063
Burton (Dorset) 26 SZ 1794
Burton (Dyfed) 42 SM 9805
Burton (Lincs.) 72 SK 9574
Burton (Northum.) 97 NU 1732
Burton (Somer.) 32 ST 1944
Burton (Wilts.) 33 ST 8179
Burton Agnes 81 TA 1063
Burton Bradstock 25 SY 4889
Burton Constable 75 TA 1836
Burton Fleming 81 TA 0872
Burton Green (Clwyd) 68 SJ 3458
Burton Green (Warw.) 50 SP 2675
Burton Hastings 50 SP 4189
Burton-in-Kendal 77 SD 5376
Burton in Lonsdale 77 SD 6572
Burton Joyce 61 SK 6443
Burton Latimer 52 SP 9074
Burton Lazars 61 SK 7716
Burton-Le-Coggles 62 SK 9725
Burton Leonard 79 SE 3263
Burton on the Wolds 61 SK 5821
Burton Overy 61 SP 6798
Burton Pedwardine 62 TF 1142
Burton Pidsea 75 TA 2431
Burton Salmon 79 SE 4827
Burton upon Stather 74 SE 8617
Burton upon Trent 60 SK 2423
Burtonwood 69 SJ 5692
Burwardsley 59 SJ 5156
Burwarton 49 SO 6185
Burwash 29 TQ 6724
Burwash Common 29 TQ 6423
Burwell (Cambs.) 53 TL 5866
Burwell (Lincs.) 73 TF 3579
Bur Wick (Shetld.) 141 HU 3840
Burwick (Shetld.) 141 HU 3940
Burwick (S. Ronaldsay) 136 ND 4384
Bury (Cambs.) 53 TL 2883
Bury (Gtr Mches.) 69 SD 8010
Bury (Somer.) 23 SS 9427
Bury (W Susx) 28 TQ 0113
Bury Ditches (ant.) 48 SO 3283
Bury Green 37 TL 4521
Bury Hill 34 SU 3443
Bury St. Edmunds 54 TL 8564
Burythorpe 80 SE 7964
Bury Walls (ant.) 59 SJ 5727
Busbie Muir Resr. 93 NS 2446
Busbridge 28 SU 9842
Busby (Strath.) 94 NS 5856
Busby (Tays.) 108 NO 0327
Buscot 47 SU 2297
Bushbury 59 SJ 9202
Bush Crathie 117 NO 2596
Bushey 37 TQ 1395
Bushey Heath 37 TQ 1594
Bush Green 55 TM 2187
Bushley 46 SO 8734
Bushton 34 SU 0677
Bushy Park 37 TQ 1569
Buss Craig 97 NT 9464
Busta 141 HU 3466
Busta Voe 141 HU 3566
Butcher's Pasture 38 TL 6024
Butcombe 33 ST 5161
Butleigh 25 ST 5233
Butleigh Wootton 25 ST 5034
Butlers Marston 50 SP 3150
Butley 55 TM 3651
Butser Hill 27 SU 7120
Butsfield 84 NZ 1044
Butterburn 90 NY 6774
Buttercrambe 80 SE 7358
Butterknowle 84 NZ 1025
Butterleigh 23 SS 9708
Butterley Reservoir 70 SE 0514
Buttermere (Cumbr.) 82 NY 1717
Buttermere (Cumbr.) 82 NY 1815
Buttermere (Wilts.) 34 SU 3361
Buttershaw 78 SE 1329
Butterstone 108 NO 0646
Butterton 60 SK 0756
Butterwick (Humbs.) 74 SE 8305
Butterwick (Lincs.) 63 TF 3845
Butterwick (N Yorks.) 80 SE 7377
Butterwick (N Yorks.) 81 SE 9971
Butterwick Low (sbk.) 63 TF 4243
Butt Green 59 SJ 6651
Buttington 58 SJ 2408
Buttock Point 100 NS 0074
Butt of Lewis 131 NB 5166
Button Hills 143 HU 3968
Buttonoak 49 SO 7578
Buxey Sand 39 TM 1103
Buxhall 54 TM 0057
Buxted 29 TQ 4923
Buxton (Derby.) 70 SK 0673
Buxton (Norf.) 65 TG 2222
Buxton Heath 65 TG 1821
Bwlch 41 SO 1422
Bwlchgwyn 58 SJ 2653
Bwlchllan 43 SN 5758
Bwlch Mawr (mt.) 66 SH 4247
Bwlchtocyn 56 SH 3126
Bwlch-y-cibau 58 SJ 1717
Bwlch-y-ffridd 57 SO 0695
Bwlch-y-groes (Dyfed) 43 SN 2436
Bwlch-y-groes (Gwyn.) 57 SH 9023
Bwlch-y-sarnau 57 SO 0274
Byerhope Resr 83 NY 8546
Byers Green 84 NZ 2234
Byfield 51 SP 5153
Byfleet 36 TQ 0461
Byford 45 SO 3943
Bygrave 53 TL 2636
Byker 91 NZ 2763
Byland Abbey (ant.) 79 SE 5478
Bylchau 67 SH 9762
Bylchau Rhos-faen 41 SN 7416
Byley 69 SJ 7269
Bynack Burn 117 NN 9704
Bynack More 117 NJ 0406
Byne Hill 86 NX 1794
Byrehope Mount 95 NT 1054
Bythorn 52 TL 0575
Byton 48 SO 3664
Byworth 28 SU 9921

C

Caaf Resr. 93 NS 2450
Caar Bheinn 114 NM 9986
Cabaan Forest 127 NH 3650
Caban Coch Resr. 57 SN 9163
Cabourne 75 TA 1301
Cabrach (Grampn.) 121 NJ 3826
Cabrach (Jura) 98 NR 4964
Cadbury 23 SS 9105
Cadbury Barton 23 SS 6917
Cadbury Camp 33 ST 4572
Cadbury Castle 25 ST 6225
Cadder 101 NS 6172
Caddington 36 TL 0619
Caddonfoot 96 NT 4534
Caddon Water 96 NT 4041
Cadeby (Leic.) 60 SK 4202
Cadeby (S Yorks.) 71 SE 5100
Cadeleigh 23 SS 9107
Cademuir Hill 95 NT 2437
Cader Fawr 41 SN 9712
Cader Idris 57 SH 7013
Cade Street 29 TQ 6021
Cadgwith 18 SW 7214
Cadham 103 NO 2701
Cadha na Gaoidhsich (pt.) 125 NG 4399
Cadishead 69 SJ 7091
Cadle 40 SS 6297
Cadley 34 SU 2066
Cadmore End 36 SU 7892
Cadnam 26 SU 2913
Cadney 74 TA 0103
Cadole 68 SJ 2062
Cadzow Resr. 94 NS 6951
Cae Afon 57 SH 8114
Caeathro 66 SH 5061
Caehopkin 41 SN 8212
Caenlochan Forest 117 NO 1875
Caeo 44 SN 6739
Caerau (Mid Glam.) 41 SS 8594
Caerau (S Glam.) 41 ST 1375
Caer Caradoc (ant.) 48 SO 3075
Caer Caradoc (ant.) 59 SO 4795
Caerdeon 57 SH 6418
Caergeiliog 66 SH 3178
Caergwrle 68 SJ 3057

Caergybi (ant.) 66 SH 2682
Caerlaverock Castle (ant.) 88 NY 0265
Caerleon 32 ST 3390
Caer Llan 45 SO 4908
Caernarfon 66 SH 4862
Caernarfon Bay 66 SH 3055
Caerphilly 41 ST 1587
Caersws 57 SO 0392
Caerwent 33 ST 4790
Caerwys 68 SJ 1272
Caesar's Camp (Berks.) (ant.) 36 SU 8665
Caesar's Camp (Hants.) (ant.) 35 SU 8350
Caethle 56 SN 6099
Cagar Feosaig 129 NC 8404
Cailiness Point 86 NX 1535
Cailleach Head 126 NG 9898
Cailleach Uragaig 98 NR 3898
Cairidh nan Ob 122 NG 3570
Cairnacay 117 NJ 2032
Cairn Avel (ant.) 88 NX 5692
Cairnbaan 99 NR 8390
Cairn Baddoch 108 NO 2770
Cairn Bannoch 117 NO 2282
Cairnbanno House 121 NJ 8444
Cairnborrow 121 NJ 4640
Cairnbrallan 121 NJ 3324
Cairnbrogie 121 NJ 8527
Cairnbulg Castle 121 NK 0164
Cairnbulg Point 121 NK 0365
Cairn Cattoch 120 NJ 2247
Cairncross 118 NO 4979
Cairncross 97 NT 8963
Cairndow 100 NN 1810
Cairn Edward Forest 88 NX 6171
Cairness 121 NK 0360
Cairneyhill 102 NT 0486
Cairnfield House 121 NJ 4162
Cairngaan 86 NX 1232
Cairn Galtar 112 NL 6491
Cairngarroch (Dumf. and Galwy.) 86 NX 0649
Cairngarroch (Dumf. and Galwy.) 87 NX 4977
Cairngarroch Bay 86 NX 0449
Cairn Geldie 117 NN 9988
Cairn Gibbs 108 NO 1859
Cairn Gorm 117 NJ 0004
Cairngorm Mountains 117 NJ 0103
Cairngorms Nature Reserve 117 NN 9598
Cairnharrow 87 NX 5356
Cairn Head 87 NX 4838
Cairnhill (Dumf. and Galwy.) 88 NS 8506
Cairnhill (Grampn.) 121 NJ 6732
Cairn Hill (Strath.) 86 NX 3090
Cairn Holy (ant.) 87 NX 5154
Cairnie 121 NJ 4945
Cairn Inks 108 NO 3072
Cairnkinna Hill 88 NS 7901
Cairn Kinny 94 NS 7821
Cairn Leuchan 118 NO 3791
Cairn Mona Gowan 118 NJ 3305
Cairn-mon-earn 119 NO 7891
Cairn Muldonich 117 NJ 2326
Cairn na Burgh Beg 104 NM 3044
Cairnoch Hill 101 NS 6985
Cairn of Barns 108 NO 3171
Cairn o'Mount 119 NO 6480
Cairnorrie 121 NJ 8640
Cairnpapple (ant.) 102 NS 9871
Cairn Pat 86 NX 0456
Cairn Point 86 NX 0668
Cairnryan 86 NX 0668
Cairnscarrow 86 NX 1364
Cairnsmore of Corsphairn 88 NX 5997
Cairnsmore of Fleet 87 NX 5066
Cairns of Coll (is.) 110 NM 2866
Cairntable (Strath.) 93 NS 4313
Cairn Table (Strath.) 94 NS 7224
Cairn Toul (Carn ant-Sabhail) 117 NN 9697
Cairn Uish 129 NJ 1750
Cairn Water 88 NX 8681
Cairnwell, The (mt.) 117 NO 1377
Cairn William 119 NJ 6516
Cairnywellan Head 86 NX 0940
Caisteal Abhail 92 NR 9644
Caister-on-Sea 65 TG 5212
Caistor 75 TA 1101
Caistor St.Edmund 65 TG 2303
Caistron 91 NT 9901
Caiteshal (mt.) 125 NB 2404
Calair Burn 107 NN 5317
Calback Ness 143 HU 3977
Calbha Beag (is.) 132 NC 1536
Calbha Mór (is.) 132 NC 1636
Calbost 131 NB 4117
Calbourne 26 SZ 4286
Calcot 36 SU 6672
Caldback 143 HP 6006
Caldbeck 82 NY 3239
Caldbergh 78 SE 0984
Caldecote (Cambs.) 52 TL 1488
Caldecote (Cambs.) 53 TL 3456
Caldecote (Herts.) 53 TL 2338
Caldecott (Leic.) 62 SP 8693
Caldecott (Northants.) 52 SP 9968
Calderbank 101 NS 7662
Calder Bridge 82 NY 0405
Calderbrook 69 SD 9418
Calder Burn 115 NN 3399
Caldercruix 101 NS 8167
Calder Dam 100 NS 2965
Calder Fell 77 SD 5648
Calder Mains 135 ND 0959
Caldermill 94 NS 6641
Calder Vale 77 SD 5345
Calder Water 94 NS 6041
Caldey Island 42 SS 1496
Caldey Sound 42 SS 1297
Caldhame 109 NO 4748
Caldicot 33 ST 4888
Caldicot Level 33 ST 4285
Caldon Canal (Staffs.) 59 SJ 9453
Caldon Canal (Staffs.) 60 SJ 9949
Caldwell 84 NZ 1613
Caldwell (Derby.) 60 SK 2517
Caldy 68 SJ 2285
Caledonian Canal (Highld.) 127 NH 1380
Caledonian Canal (Highld.) 115 NH 3405
Caledonian Canal (Highld.) 116 NH 6240
Caledrhydiau 43 SN 4753
Calf of Eday 138 HY 5839
Calf of Flotta 136 ND 3896
Calf of Man 76 SC 1565
Calfsound (Eday) 138 HY 5738
Calf Sound (Eday) 138 HY 5739
Calf, The (mt.) 83 SD 6696
Calf Top 77 SD 6585
Calgary 110 NM 3751
Calgary Bay 110 NM 3550
Calgary Point 110 NM 1052
Caliach Point 110 NM 3454
Califer 129 NJ 0857
California (Central) 102 NS 9076
California (Norf.) 65 TG 5114
Calke 60 SK 3722
Calkin Rig 89 NY 2987
Callaly 91 NU 0509
Callander 101 NN 6208
Callanish 131 NB 2133
Callater Burn 117 NO 1687
Callestick 18 SW 7750
Calligarry 111 NG 6202
Callington 20 SX 3669
Callop River 114 NM 9180
Callow 45 SO 4934
Callow End 49 SO 8349
Callow Hill (Here. and Worc.) 49 SO 7473
Callow Hill (Wilts.) 34 SU 0385
Callows Grave 49 SO 5966
Calmore 26 SU 3314
Calmsden 46 SP 0408
Calne 34 ST 9971
Calow 71 SK 4071
Calpa Mór 116 NH 6710
Calshot 27 SU 4701
Calshot Castle (ant.) 27 SU 4802
Calshot Spit (lightship) 27 SU 4901
Calstock 20 SX 4368
Calstone Wellington 34 SU 0268
Calthorpe 65 TG 1831
Calthwaite 83 NY 4640
Caltinish 124 NF 8341
Calton (N Yorks.) 78 SD 9059
Calton (Staffs.) 60 SK 1050
Calvay (South Uist) 112 NF 7728
Calvay (South Uist) 112 NF 8218
Calve Island 111 NM 5254
Calveley 69 SJ 5958
Calver 71 SK 2374
Calverhall 59 SJ 6037
Calver Hill 45 SO 3748
Calverleigh 23 SS 9214
Calverley 78 SE 2036
Calvert 36 SP 6824
Calverton (Bucks.) 51 SP 7938
Calverton (Notts.) 61 SK 6149
Calvine 107 NN 8066
Cam 46 ST 7599
Cama Choire 116 NN 6879
Camas Airigh Shamhraidh 105 NM 8448
Camas Allt nam Bearnach 125 NB 3608
Camas a' Mhoil 130 NA 9825
Camas Baravaig 123 NG 6909
Camas chil Mhalieu 106 NM 9055
Camas Coille 132 NC 0016
Camas Eilean Ghlais 132 NB 9615
Camas Geodhachan an Duilisg 130 NB 0438
Camas Ghaoideil 111 NM 6683
Camas Gorm 105 NM 7742
Camas-luinie 114 NG 9128
Camas Mór (Highld.) 127 NC 1000
Camas Mór (Highld.) 126 NG 7592
Camas Mór (Island of Skye) 122 NG 3770
Camas na Ceardaich 100 NR 9162
Camas Nathais 105 NM 8737
Camas Pliasgaig 111 NG 4002
Camastianavaig 123 NG 5039
Camas Uig 130 NB 0233
Camasunary 123 NG 5118
Camault Muir 116 NH 5040
Camb 143 HU 5192
Cambeak (pt.) 20 SX 1296
Cam Beck 78 SD 7978
Camber 31 TQ 9619
Camber Castle (ant.) 30 TQ 9218
Camberley 36 SU 8760
Camberwell 37 TQ 3376
Camblesforth 79 SE 6425
Cambo 91 NZ 0285
Camboglanna (ant.) 90 NY 6166
Cambois 91 NZ 3083
Cambo Ness 103 NO 6011
Camborne 18 SW 6440
Cambrian Mountains 57 SH 8809
Cambridge 53 TL 4658
Cambridge Airport 53 TL 4858
Cambus 102 NS 8593
Cambusavie 129 NH 7796
Cambusbarron 101 NS 7792
Cambuscurrie Bay 129 NH 7285
Cambuskenneth 101 NS 8094
Cambuslang 101 NS 6459
Cambusmore Lodge 129 NH 7697
Cam Chreag 107 NN 5349
Camddwr 44 SN 7755
Camden Town 37 TQ 2784
Camelford 20 SX 1083
Camelon 102 NS 8680
Cameron Burn 103 NO 4912
Cameron Resr. 103 NO 4711
Camerory 117 NJ 0231
Camerton (Avon) 33 ST 6857
Camerton (Cumbr.) 82 NY 0330
Camesdale 27 SU 8932
Cam Fell 78 SD 8080
Camghouran 107 NN 5556
Cam Loch (Highld.) 132 NC 2113
Càm Loch (Strath.) 99 NR 8187
Camlo Hill 57 SO 0370
Cammachmore 119 NO 9295
Cammachmore Bay 119 NO 9295
Cammeringham 72 SK 9482
Cammoch Hill 108 NN 8959
Campay 131 NB 1442
Campbells Hill 93 NS 5201
Campbelton 93 NS 1950
Campbeltown 92 NR 7120
Campbeltown Loch 92 NR 7420
Camperdown House 109 NO 3532
Camphill Resr. 93 NS 2655
Campmuir 108 NO 2137
Campsall 71 SE 5313
Campsey Ash 55 TM 3356
Campsie Fells 101 NS 6082
Camps Resr. 95 NT 0022
Camps Water 95 NS 9622
Camp, The 46 SO 9109
Campton 52 TL 1238
Camrose 42 SM 9220
Camserney 107 NN 8149
Camster 135 ND 2641
Camster Burn 135 ND 2348
Camulodunum (ant.) 54 TM 0025
Camus Geodhachan an Duilisg 130 NB 0438
Camus-luinie 114 NG 9428
Camusnagaul (Highld.) 127 NH 0689
Camusnagaul (Highld.) 115 NN 0975
Camusrory 111 NM 8595
Camusteel 123 NG 7042
Camusterrach 123 NG 7141
Camusvrachan 107 NN 6248
Camy (pt.) 137 HY 5401
Canada 26 SU 2817
Canal Foot 77 SD 3177
Canaston Bridge 42 SN 0515
Candacraig House 118 NJ 3411
Candlesby 73 TF 4567
Candy Mill 95 NT 0741
Cane End 36 SU 6779
Canewdon 38 TQ 8994
Canford Bottom 26 SU 0300
Canford Cliffs 26 SZ 0689
Canford Heath 26 SZ 0294
Canisbay 135 ND 3472
Canis Dale 143 HU 5082
Canisp (mt.) 132 NC 2018
Cann 25 ST 8620
Canna (is.) 110 NG 2405
Canna Harbour 110 NG 2804
Cann Common 25 ST 8920
Cannich 115 NH 3331
Cannington 32 ST 2539
Cannock 60 SJ 9710
Cannock Chase 60 SJ 9816
Cannock Wood 60 SK 0412
Cannon Street Station 37 TQ 3280
Canonbie 89 NY 3976
Canon Bridge 45 SO 4341
Canon Frome 49 SO 6543
Canon Pyon 45 SO 4549
Canons Ashby 51 SP 5750
Canonstown 18 SW 5335
Canterbury 31 TR 1557
Cantick Head 136 ND 3489
Cantley (Norf.) 65 TG 3704
Cantley (S Yorks.) 71 SE 6202
Cantlop 59 SJ 5205
Canton 41 ST 1577
Cantraydoune 129 NH 7946
Cantraywood 129 NH 7847
Cantref Resr. 41 SN 9915
Cantsfield 77 SD 6172
Canvey Island 38 TQ 7783
Canwell Hall 60 SK 1400
Canwick 72 SK 9869
Canworthy Water 20 SX 2291
Caol 115 NN 1175
Caolard Rubha 99 NR 8783
Caolas a' Mhòrain 124 NF 8480
Caolas an Eilein 130 NA 9821
Caolas an Scarp 130 NA 9913
Caolas Bàn 110 NM 1151
Caolas Beag 126 NG 7478
Caolas Mór (Highld.) 123 NG 7135
Caolas Mór (Strath.) 98 NR 3586
Caolas Scalpay 123 NG 6127
Caoles 104 NM 0848
Caol Ghleann 100 NS 0693
Caolis 112 NL 6397
Caol Lairig 115 NN 2783
Caol Mór 123 NG 5733
Caol Raineach (chan.) 133 NC 6364
Caol Rona 123 NG 6153
Cape Cornwall 18 SW 3431
Capel 28 TQ 1740
Cape Law 89 NT 1314
Capel Bangor 57 SN 6580
Capel Betws Lleucu 43 SN 6058
Capel Carmel 56 SH 1628
Capel Coch 66 SH 4582
Capel Curig 67 SH 7258
Capel Cynon 43 SN 3849
Capel Dewi 43 SN 4542
Capel Fell 89 NT 1607
Capel Garmon 67 SH 8155
Capel Gwyn (Dyfed) 433 SN 4622
Capel Gwyn (Gwyn.) 66 SH 3575
Capel Gwynfe 40 SN 7222
Capel Hendre 43 SN 5911
Capel Isaac 43 SN 5927
Capel Iwan 43 SN 2836
Capel-le-Ferne 31 TR 2439
Capel Llanilterne 41 ST 0979
Capel Parc 66 SH 4486
Capel St. Mary 55 TM 0838
Capel-y-ffin 45 SO 2531
Capenhurst 68 SJ 3673
Capernwray 77 SD 5372
Cape Wrath 132 NC 2574
Capheaton 91 NZ 0380
Capler Camp (ant.) 45 SO 5932
Caplestone Fell 90 NY 5888
Cappercleuch 95 NT 2423
Capstone 30 TQ 7865
Capton 21 SX 8353
Caputh 108 NO 0940
Caradon Hill 20 SX 2770
Cara Island 92 NR 6444
Carbh-Bheinn 123 NG 5323
Carbis Bay 18 SW 5339
Carbost (Island of Skye) 122 NG 3731
Carbost (Island of Skye) 123 NG 4248
Carbrooke 64 TF 9402
Carburton 71 SK 6173
Carcary 109 NO 6455
Carclew 19 SW 7838
Car Colston 61 SK 7142
Carcroft 71 SE 5409
Cardenden 103 NT 2195
Carden Hall (ant.) 58 SJ 4553
Cardeston 58 SJ 3912
Cardiff 41 ST 1877
Cardiff-Wales Airport 41 ST 0667
Cardigan 43 SN 1846
Cardigan Bay 44 SN 4080
Cardigan Island 42 SN 1651
Cardington (Beds.) 52 TL 0847
Cardington (Shrops.) 59 SO 5095
Cardinham 19 SX 1268
Cardney House 108 NO 0545
Cardno 121 NJ 9663
Cardoness Castle (ant.) 87 NX 5955
Cardow 120 NJ 1942
Cardrona 96 NT 3038
Cardrona Forest 96 NT 3036
Cardross (Central) (ant.) 101 NS 6097
Cardross (Strath.) 100 NS 3477
Cardurnock 89 NY 1758
Car Dyke (Cambs.) (ant.) 53 TL 4769
Car Dyke (Lincs.) (ant.) 62 TF 1437
Car Dyke (Northants.) (ant.) 62 TF 1508
Careby 62 TF 0216
Careston 109 NO 5260
Carew 42 SN 0403
Carew Cheriton 42 SN 0402
Carew Newton 42 SN 0404
Carey 45 SO 5631
Carfrae 103 NT 5769
Cargen 88 NX 9672
Cargenbridge 88 NX 9474
Cargill 108 NO 1536
Cargo 89 NY 3659
Cargreen 20 SX 4262
Carham 97 NT 7938
Carhampton 23 ST 0042
Carharrack 18 SW 7241
Carie (Tays.) 107 NN 6157
Carie (Tays.) 107 NN 6437
Carines 19 SW 7959
Carinish 124 NF 8159
Carisbrooke 27 SZ 4888
Cark 77 SD 3676
Carland Cross 19 SW 8554
Carlby 62 TF 0414
Carleatheran 101 NS 6892
Carlecotes 70 SE 1703
Carleton (Cumbr.) 83 NY 4253
Carleton (Lancs.) 77 SD 3339
Carleton (N Yorks.) 78 SD 9749
Carleton Forehoe 65 TG 0805
Carleton Rode 55 TM 1192
Carlingcott 33 ST 6958
Carlingwark Loch 88 NX 7661
Carlin Tooth 90 NT 6302
Carlisle 83 NY 3955
Carlisle Airport 89 NY 4860
Carlock Hill 86 NX 0877
Carlops 95 NT 1656
Carloway 131 NB 2042
Carlton (Beds.) 52 SP 9555
Carlton (Cambs.) 54 TL 6453
Carlton (Cleve.) 85 NZ 3921
Carlton (Leic.) 60 SK 3905
Carlton (Notts.) 61 SK 6141
Carlton (N Yorks.) 78 SE 0684
Carlton (N Yorks.) 79 SE 6086
Carlton (N Yorks.) 79 SE 6423
Carlton (Suff.) 55 TM 3864
Carlton (S Yorks.) 71 SE 3610
Carlton (W Yorks.) 79 SE 3327
Carlton Colville 55 TM 5190
Carlton Curlieu 61 SP 6997
Carlton Husthwaite 79 SE 4976
Carlton in Cleveland 85 NZ 5004
Carlton in Lindrick 71 SK 5984
Carlton-le-Moorland 72 SK 9058
Carlton Miniott 79 SE 3980
Carlton Moor 78 SE 0383
Carlton-on-Trent 72 SK 7963
Carlton Scroop 62 SK 9445
Carluke 95 NS 8450
Carl Wark (ant.) 71 SK 2681
Carmacoup 94 NS 7927
Carmarthen 43 SN 4120
Carmarthen Bay 40 SN 2400
Carmel (Clwyd) 68 SJ 1676
Carmel (Dyfed) 43 SN 5816
Carmel (Gwyn.) 66 SH 3882
Carmel (Gwyn.) 66 SH 4954
Carmel Head 66 SH 2992
Carminish 124 NG 0284
Carminish Islands 124 NG 0185
Carmont 119 NO 8084
Carmunnock 94 NS 5957
Carmyle 101 NS 6461
Carmyllie 109 NO 5542
Carna 111 NM 6259
Carn a' Bhiorain 127 NH 1483
Carn a Bhodaich 116 NH 5637
Carnaby 81 TA 1465
Carnach (Harris) 125 NG 2297
Carnach (Highld.) 114 NH 0228
Carn a' Chaochain 115 NH 2317
Carn a' Choin Deirg 127 NH 3992
Carn a' Choire Mhòir 117 NH 8428
Carn a' Chrasgie 129 NH 8642
Carn a' Chuilinn 116 NH 4103
Carn a' Ghaill 110 NG 2606
Carn a' Gheòidh 117 NO 1076
Carn a' Ghlinne 127 NH 0660
Carn a' Mhaim 117 NN 9995
Carnan (mt.) 112 NL 5582
Carn an Daimh 106 NN 1371
Carnan Eoin 98 NR 4098
Carn an Fhidhleir or Carn Ealar 117 NN 9084
Carn an Fhreiceadain 116 NH 7207
Carnan Mòr 104 NL 9640
Carn an Righ 117 NO 0277
Carn an t-Sabhail 117 NN 9697
Carn an t-Sean liathanaich 117 NH 8632
Carn an t-Suidhe 117 NJ 2726
Carn an Tuire 117 NO 1780
Carn Bàn (Highld.) 127 NH 3341
Carn Bàn (Highld.) 127 NH 3387
Carn Bàn (Highld.) 116 NH 6303
Carn Ban (Island of Mull) 105 NM 7229
Carn Bàn Mór 117 NN 8896
Carn Beag 127 NH 1055
Carnbee 103 NO 5306
Carn Bhac 117 NO 0482
Carn Bheadhair 117 NJ 0511
Carn Bhrain 128 NH 5287
Carnbo 102 NO 0503
Carn Brea 18 SW 6741
Carn Breac 127 NH 0452
Carn Breac Beag 127 NH 1879
Carn Breugach 105 NM 8127
Carn Cas nan Gabhar 128 NH 5280
Carn Chòis 107 NN 7927
Carn Chuinneag 128 NH 4883
Carn Coire na Creiche 116 NH 6208
Carn Coire na h-Easgainn 116 NH 7313
Carn Daimh 117 NJ 1824
Càrn Dearg 116 NN 5076
Carn Dearg (Highld.) 116 NH 6202
Carn Dearg (Highld.) 115 NN 3488
Carn Dearg (Highld.) 115 NN 3596
Carn Dearg (Highld.-Tays.) 107 NN 4166
Carn Dearg (Strath.) 106 NM 8918
Carn Dearg Mór 117 NN 8291
Carn Dubh'Ic an Deòir 116 NH 7719
Carn Duchara 100 NM 8910
Carnduncan 98 NR 2467
Carne 19 SW 9138
Carn Ealar or Carn an Fhidhleir 117 NN 9084
Carn Ealasaid 117 NJ 2211
Carn Eàs 117 NO 1298
Carn Easgann Bàna 116 NH 4806
Carneddau (mt.) 44 SO 0654
Carnedd Dafydd 67 SH 6663
Carnedd Iago 67 SH 7840
Carnedd Llewelyn 67 SH 6864
Carnedd Moel-siabod 67 SH 7054
Carn Eige 115 NH 1226
Carn Eilrig 117 NH 9305
Carnell 93 NS 4632
Car Ness 136 HY 4614
Carn fadrun (ant.) 66 SH 2835
Carnferg 119 NO 5293
Carnforth 77 SD 4970
Carn Garbh 127 NH 2858
Carn Geuradainn 114 NG 9839
Carn Ghriogair 116 NH 6520
Carn Glas-choire 117 NH 8929
Carn Gorm (Highld.) 127 NH 1349
Carn Gorm (Highld.) 115 NH 3235
Carn Gorm (Highld.) 128 NH 4362
Carn Gorm (Highld.) 128 NH 4570
Carn Gorm (Tays.) 107 NN 6350
Carnhell Green 18 SW 6137
Carnie 119 NJ 8105
Carn Kitty 129 NJ 0942
Carn Leac 115 NN 4097
Carn Leac Saighdeir 117 NJ 2706
Carn Liath (Grampn.) 117 NJ 1827
Carn Liath (Grampn.) 117 NJ 2515
Carn Liath (Grampn.) 117 NO 0386
Carn Liath (Highld.) 116 NN 4790
Carn Liath (Tays.) 108 NN 9369
Carn Mairg 107 NN 6851
Carn Meadhonach 117 NJ 1317
Carn Mhartuin 127 NH 1754
Carn Mór (Grampn.) 117 NJ 2618
Carn Mór (Highld.) 127 NH 2487
Carn Mór (Highld.) 128 NH 4271
Carn Mór (Highld.) 116 NH 4334
Carn Mór (Highld.) 114 NM 9090
Carn Mór (Island of Mull) 105 NM 3948
Carn na Cailliche 129 NJ 1847
Carn na Caim 116 NN 6782
Carn na Cloiche Móire 127 NH 3753
Carn na Còinnich 127 NH 3251
Carn na Drochaide 117 NO 1293
Carn na Dubh Choille 127 NH 3867
Carn na Farraidh 117 NJ 1114
Carn na Feannaige 117 NJ 0908
Carn na h-Easgainn 116 NH 7432
Carn na Làraiche Maoile 116 NH 5811
Carn na Lòine 117 NJ 0636
Carn nam Bad 115 NH 4033
Carn nam Bain-tighearna 117 NH 8425
Carn nam Buailtean 126 NH 0087
Carn nan Con Ruadha 128 NH 4174
Carn nan Iomairean 114 NG 9135
Carn nan Sgeir (is.) 126 NC 0101
Carn nan Tri-tighearnan 117 NH 8239
Carn na Saobhaidh 116 NH 6724
Carn na Saobhaidhe 116 NH 5914
Carn na Sean-lùibe 114 NH 0235
Carno 57 SN 9696
Carnock 102 NT 0489
Carn Odhar 116 NH 6317
Carnon Downs 19 SW 7940
Carnousie 121 NJ 6650
Carnoustie 109 NO 5634
Càrn Phris Mhóir 116 NH 8021
Carn Ruigh Chorrach 117 NH 9834
Carn Sgùlain 116 NH 6909
Carn Sgùmain 117 NH 8740
Carn Sleamhuinn 117 NH 8516
Carn Towan 18 SW 3626
Carnwath 95 NS 9746
Carnyorth 18 SW 3733
Carperby 84 SE 0089
Carracks, The 18 SW 4640
Carradale 92 NR 8138
Carradale Bay 92 NR 8137
Carradale Point 92 NR 8136
Carradale Water 92 NR 7843
Carragreich 125 NG 1998
Carraig Bhàn 98 NR 2572
Carraig Dhubh 98 NR 3062
Carraig Fhada 98 NR 3444
Carraig Mhór 98 NR 4656
Carrbridge 117 NH 9022
Carr Brigs (pt.) 103 NO 6411
Carreg Ddu 66 SH 2742
Carreg-gwylan-fach 42 SM 7730
Carreglefn 66 SH 3889
Carreg-lem 41 SN 8017
Carreg-lwyd 41 SN 8615
Carreg Ti-pw 56 SN 5370
Carregwastad Point 42 SM 9340
Carreg yr Imbill 66 SH 3834
Carr End (pt.) 97 NU 2232
Carrick (Fife) 109 NO 4422
Carrick (Strath.) 100 NR 9087
Carrick (Strath.) 100 NS 1994
Carrick (Strath.) (dist.) 86 NX 3394
Carrick Forest 86 NX 4093
Carrick House 138 HY 5638
Carrick Roads 19 SW 8335
Carriden 102 NT 0181
Carrine 92 NR 6709
Carrington (Gtr Mches.) 69 SJ 7492
Carrington (Lincs.) 63 TF 3155
Carrington (Lothian) 103 NT 3160
Carrington Moss 69 SJ 7491
Carrog 67 SJ 1043
Carron (Central) 102 NS 8882
Carron (Grampn.) 120 NJ 2241
Carron Bridge (Central) 101 NS 7483
Carronbridge (Dumf. and Galwy.) 88 NX 8697
Carronshore 102 NS 8983
Carron Valley Forest 101 NS 6982
Carron Valley Resr. 101 NS 6983
Carrot Hill 109 NO 4540
Carr Shield 83 NY 8047
Carrs, The 81 SE 9678
Carrutherstown 89 NY 1071
Carruth House 100 NS 3566
Carr Vale 71 SK 4669
Carrville 84 NZ 3043
Carrycoats Hall 90 NY 9279
Carsaig 105 NM 5421
Carsaig Bay 105 NM 5320
Carscreugh 86 NX 2260
Carsegowan 87 NX 4258
Carse Gray 109 NO 4653
Carse House 99 NR 7461
Carse of Gowrie (dist.) 108 NO 2726
Carseriggan 86 NX 3167
Carsethorn 88 NX 9959
Carsgailoch Hill 93 NS 5414
Carshalton 37 TQ 2764
Carsington 60 SK 2553
Carsington Reservoir 60 SK 2652
Carskiey 92 NR 6508
Carsluith 87 NX 4854
Carsphairn 88 NX 5693
Carsphairn Forest 88 NS 5701
Caarstairs 95 NS 9345
Carstairs Junction 95 NS 9545
Carswell Marsh 47 SU 3198
Carter Bar 90 NT 6906
Carter's Clay 26 SU 3024
Carterton 47 SP 2706
Carterway Heads 84 NZ 0451
Carthagena Bank (sbk.) 108 NO 2722
Carthew 19 SX 0055
Carthorpe 79 SE 3083
Cartington 91 NU 0304
Cartland 95 NS 8646
Cartmel 77 SD 3778
Cartmel Fell 77 SD 4188
Cartmel Sands 77 SD 3375
Cartmel Wharf (sbk.) 77 SD 3668
Carway 43 SN 4606
Cas 99 NR 7064
Casfad Loch 88 NX 6086
Cashel Dhu 133 NC 4450
Cashlie 107 NN 4942
Cashmoor 26 ST 9813
Cashtel yn Ard (ant.) 76 SC 4689
Cassington 47 SP 4510
Cassiobury Park 36 TQ 0897
Casswell's Bridge 62 TF 1627
Castallack 18 SW 4525
Castellau 41 ST 0586
Castell Dinas (ant.) 41 SO 1730
Castell Howell 43 SN 4448
Castell Odo (ant.) 56 SH 1828
Castell y Bere (ant.) 57 SH 6708
Castell-y-bŵch 32 ST 2792
Castell-y-geifr 41 SN 8216
Casterley Camp (ant.) 34 SU 1153
Casterton 77 SD 6279
Castle 136 HY 2113
Castle Acre 64 TF 8115
Castle-an-Dinas (ant.) 19 SW 9462
Castle Ashby 52 SP 8659
Castlebay 112 NL 6698
Castle Bolton 84 SE 0391
Castle Bromwich 50 SP 1489
Castle Bytham 62 SK 9818
Castlebythe 42 SN 0229
Castle Caereinion 58 SJ 1605
Castle Campbell (ant.) 102 NS 9699
Castle Camps 54 TL 6343
Castle Carrock 83 NY 5455
Castle Cary (Somer.) 25 ST 6332
Castlecary (Strath.) 101 NS 7878
Castle Combe 33 ST 8477
Castlecraig (Borders) 95 NT 1344
Castlecraig (Highld.) 129 NH 8169
Castle Ditches (Hants.) (ant.) 26 SU 1219
Castle Ditches (S Glam.) (ant.) 41 ST 0570
Castle Ditches (W Glam.) (ant.) 41 SS 9667
Castle Donington 61 SK 4427
Castle Douglas 88 NX 7662
Castle Eaton 47 SU 1495
Castle Eden 85 NZ 4338
Castle Forbes 119 NJ 6219
Castleford 79 SE 4225
Castle Fraser 119 NJ 7212
Castle Frome 49 SO 6645
Castle Gresley 60 SK 2718
Castle Haven 119 NO 8884
Castle Heaton 97 NT 9041

Castle Hedingham 54 TL 7835
Castlehill (Highld.) 135 ND 1968
Castle Hill (Highld.) 117 NH 9505
Castlehill (Strath.) 95 NS 8452
Castle Hill (Suff.) 55 TM 1646
Castlehill Point 87 NX 8552
Castle Howard 80 SE 7170
Castle Huntly 108 NO 3029
Castle Kennedy 86 NX 1059
Castle Lachlan 100 NS 0195
Castle Leod 128 NH 4858
Castle Loch (Dumf. and Galwy.) 86 NX 2853
Castle Loch (Dumf. and Galwy.) 89 NY 0881
Castlemaddy 87 NX 5589
Castlemartin 42 SR 9198
Castlemilk 89 NY 1577
Castle Morris 42 SM 9031
Castlemorton 49 SO 7937
Castle O'er 89 NY 2492
Castle O'er Forest 89 NY 2493
Castle of Mey 135 ND 2973
Castle of Old Wick (ant.) 135 ND 3648
Castle of Park (ant.) 86 NX 2057
Castle Point 97 NU 1441
Castle Ring (ant.) 60 SK 0412
Castle Rising 64 TF 6624
Castleshaw Moor 70 SE 0111
Castleside 84 NZ 0748
Castle Stuart 129 NH 7449
Castle Sween 99 NR 7178
Castle, The (pt.) 143 HU 3787
Castlethorpe 51 SP 7944
Castleton (Derby.) 70 SK 1582
Castleton (Gwent) 32 ST 2583
Castleton (N Yorks.) 80 NZ 6808
Castleton (Strath.) 100 NR 8884
Castle Toward 100 NS 1168
Castletown (Highld.) 135 ND 1967
Castletown (I. of M.) 76 SC 2667
Castletown (Tyne and Wear) 91 NZ 3558
Caston 64 TL 9598
Castor 62 TL 1298
Catacol 92 NR 9149
Catacol Bay 92 NR 9049
Cat and Fiddle 70 SK 0071
Cata Sand 139 HY 7040
Catbrain 33 ST 5580
Catcleugh Resr. 90 NT 7303
Catcliffe 71 SK 4288
Catcott 32 ST 3939
Cateran Hill 97 NU 1023
Caterham 29 TQ 3455
Cater's Beam 21 SX 6369
Catesby 51 SP 5159
Catfield 65 TG 3821
Catfirth (Shetld.) 141 HU 4354
Cat Firth (Shetld.) 141 HU 4552
Catford 37 TQ 3872
Catforth 77 SD 4735
Cath 42 SM 7525
Cathcart 101 NS 5960
Cathedine 41 SO 1425
Catherington 27 SU 6914
Catherton 49 SO 6578
Cati Geo 138 HY 4342
Cat Law (mt.) 108 NO 3160
Catlodge 116 NN 6392
Catlowdy 89 NY 4676
Catlow Fell 77 SD 7060
Catmore 35 SU 4579
Caton 77 SD 5364
Caton Moor 77 SD 5763
Cator Court 21 SX 6877
Catrine 93 NS 5225
Cat's Ash 32 ST 3790
Catsfield 29 TQ 7213
Catshill 50 SO 9674
Cattal 79 SE 4454
Cattawade 55 TM 1033
Catterall 77 SD 4942
Catterick 84 SE 2397
Catterick Bridge 84 SE 2299
Catterick Garrison 84 SE 1897
Catterlen 83 NY 4833
Catterline 119 NO 8678
Catterton 79 SE 5045
Catthorpe 51 SP 5578
Cattistock 25 SY 5999
Catton (Norf.) 65 TG 2312
Catton (Northum.) 83 NY 8257
Catton (N Yorks.) 79 SE 3778
Catton Hall 60 SK 2015
Catwick 75 TA 1245
Catworth 52 TL 0873
Caulcott 47 SP 5024
Cauldcleuch Head 89 NT 4600
Cauldcots 109 NO 6547
Cauldhame 101 NS 6494
Cauldon 60 SK 0749
Cauldron Snout 83 NY 8228
Cauldrus (pt.) 136 HY 2116
Cauldshiels Hill 96 NT 5131
Caulkerbush 82 NX 9257
Caulside 89 NY 4480
Caunsall 49 SO 8481
Caunton 72 SK 7460
Causamul (is.) 124 NF 6670
Caus Castle (ant.) 58 SJ 3308
Causeway Grain Head 89 NY 3598
Causewayhead 101 NS 8195
Causeyend 119 NJ 9419
Causey Park 91 NZ 1794
Causey Pike 82 NY 2120
Cautley 83 SD 6994
Cava (is.) 136 ND 3299
Cavendish 54 TL 8046
Cavenham 54 TL 7669
Caversfield 47 SP 5824
Caversham 36 SU 7274
Caver's Hill 96 NT 3921
Caversta 131 NB 3619
Caverswall 59 SJ 9442
Caw (mt.) 82 SD 2294
Cawdor 129 NH 8449
Caw Fell 82 NY 1210
Cawood 79 SE 5737
Cawsand 20 SX 4350
Cawsand Hill 21 SX 6391
Cawston 65 TG 1324
Cawthorne 71 SE 2807
Cawton 79 SE 6476
Caxton 53 TL 3058
Caynham 48 SO 5473
Caynham Camp (ant.) 48 SO 5473
Caythorpe (Lincs.) 62 SK 9348
Caythorpe (Notts.) 61 SK 6845
Cayton 81 TA 0583
Cayton Bay 81 TA 0784
Ceannacroc Forest 115 NH 1613
Ceanna Mór 111 NM 8551
Ceann Creag-arighe 110 NG 2205
Ceann Ear (is.) 124 NF 6461
Ceann Leathad nam Bò (pt.) 135 ND 1323
Ceann na Beinne 123 NG 4217
Ceann-na-Cleithe 125 NG 1794
Ceann Riobha 98 NR 3585
Ceathramh Garbh (dist.) 132 NC 2252
Cedig 57 SH 9922
Cefn-brîth 67 SH 9350
Cefn Bryn 40 SS 5089
Cefn Carnedd (ant.) 57 SO 0189
Cefn Carn-Fadog 41 SN 7617
Cefncennarth 57 SN 9776
Cefn Coch (Clwyd-Gwyn.) 67 SJ 0035
Cefn Coch (Powys) 57 SJ 1026
Cefn-coch (Powys) 44 SN 8254
Cefn-coed-y-cymmer 41 SO 0307
Cefn Cribwr 41 SS 8582
Cefn-crin 57 SO 0272
Cefn Cross 41 SS 8682
Cefn-ddwysarn 67 SH 9638
Cefndeuddwr 57 SH 7226
Cefn Drum 43 SN 6205
Cefn Du 67 SJ 0354
Cefn-Einion 48 SO 2886
Cefn Fannog 44 SN 8251
Cefn Grug 41 SN 8802
Cefn Gwrhyd 40 SN 7208
Cefn Hirgoed 41 SS 9383
Cefni Resr. 66 SH 4477
Cefn Llwydlo 44 SN 8642
Cefn-mawr (Clywd) 58 SJ 2842
Cefn Mawr (Powys) 41 SN 7915
Cefn Merthyr 41 ST 0899
Cefn Morfudd 41 SS 7997
Cefn Onneu 41 SO 1716
Cefn Padrig 40 SN 4800
Cefn Pyllau-duon 41 SO 1111
Cefn Rhyswg 45 ST 2395
Cefn Sidan Sands 40 SN 3702
Cefn-y-bedd 58 SJ 3156
Cefn-y-coed 58 SO 2093
Cefn-y-pant 43 SN 1925
Cefn yr Arail 41 SO 1905
Cefnyresgair 57 SN 7489
Ceidio 66 SH 4085
Ceidio Fawr 66 SH 2838
Ceint 66 SH 4874
Cellan 43 SN 6149
Cellar Head (Isle of Lewis) 131 NB 5656
Cellarhead (Staffs.) 60 SJ 9547
Celtic or Deil's Dike (ant.) 88 NS 7011
Cemaes 66 SH 3793
Cemaes Bay 66 SH 3694
Cemaes Head 42 SN 1350
Cemlyn Bay 66 SH 3393
Cemmaes 57 SH 8306
Cemmaes Road 57 SH 8204
Cenarth 43 SN 2641
Cennin 66 SH 4645
Ceol na mara 111 NM 7561
Ceres 103 NO 4011
Cerne Abbas 25 ST 6601
Cerney Wick 46 SU 0796
Cerrigceinwen 66 SH 4273
Cerrigydrudion 67 SH 9548
Cessford 96 NT 7323
Cessnock Water 93 NS 5028
Chaceley 46 SO 8530
Chacewater 18 SW 7444
Chackmore 51 SP 6835
Chacombe 51 SP 4943
Chadderton 69 SD 9005
Chaddesden 60 SK 3737
Chaddesley Corbett 49 SO 8973
Chaddleworth 34 SU 4177
Chadlington 47 SP 3221
Chadshunt 50 SP 3453
Chad Valley 50 SP 0385
Chadwell St. Mary 38 TQ 6478
Chadwick End 50 SP 2073
Chaffcombe 24 ST 3510
Chagford 21 SX 7087
Chailey 29 TQ 3919
Chainhurst 29 TQ 7347
Chaipaval (is.) 124 NF 9792
Chalbury Common 26 SU 0206
Chaldon 29 TQ 3155
Chaldon Down 25 SY 7881
Chaldon Herring or East Chaldon 25 SY 7983
Chale 27 SZ 4877
Chale Bay 27 SZ 4777
Chale Green 27 SZ 4879
Chalfont and Latimer Station 36 SU 9997
Chalfont Common 36 SU 9892
Chalfont St. Giles 36 SU 9993
Chalfont St. Peter 36 SU 9990
Chalford 46 SO 8902
Chalgrove 36 SU 6396
Chalk 30 TQ 6772
Challacombe 23 SS 6941
Challister Ness 141 HU 5766
Challoch 86 NX 3867
Challoch Hill 86 NX 1658
Challock 31 TR 0050
Chalton (Beds.) 52 TL 0326
Chalton (Hants.) 27 SU 7316
Chalvington 29 TQ 5109
Champany 102 NT 0278
Chancellor, The (mt.) 106 NN 1957
Chandler's Cross 36 TQ 0698
Chandler's Ford 28 SU 4320
Changue Plantation 86 NX 3193
Chanlockfoot 88 NS 7900
Channerwick 141 HU 4023
Chanonry Point 129 NH 7555
Chantry (Somer.) 33 ST 7146
Chantry (Suff.) 55 TM 1443
Chapel 103 NT 2593
Chapel Allerton (Somer.) 32 ST 4050
Chapel Allerton (W Yorks.) 79 SE 2936
Chapel Amble 19 SW 9975
Chapel Brampton 51 SP 7266
Chapel Chorlton 59 SJ 8037
Chapelend Way 54 TL 7039
Chapel-en-le-Frith 70 SK 0580
Chapelfell Top 84 NY 8734
Chapel Finian (ant.) 86 NX 2849
Chapelgate 63 TF 4124
Chapel Haddlesey 79 SE 5826
Chapelhall 101 NS 7862
Chapel Hill (Grampn.) 121 NK 0635
Chapel Hill (Gwent) 45 SO 5200
Chapelhill (Highld.) 129 NH 8273
Chapel Hill (Lincs.) 62 TF 2054
Chapelhill (Tays.) 108 NO 0030
Chapel Hill (Tays.) 108 NO 2021
Chapelknowe 89 NY 3173
Chapel Lawn 48 SO 3176
Chapel Le Dale 77 SD 7377
Chapel Ness 103 NT 4799
Chapel of Garioch 121 NJ 7124
Chapel Point (Corn.) 19 SX 0243
Chapel Point (Dyfed) 42 SS 1495
Chapel Rossan Bay 86 NX 1145
Chapel Row 35 SU 5669
Chapel Stile 82 NY 3205
Chapel St. Leonards 73 TF 5572
Chapelton (Devon) 23 SS 5826
Chapelton (Strath.) 94 NS 6848
Chapelton (Tays.) 109 NO 6247
Chapeltown (Grampn.) 117 NJ 2421
Chapeltown (Lancs.) 69 SD 7315
Chapeltown (S Yorks.) 71 SK 3596
Chapman Sands 38 TQ 8383
Chapmanslade 33 ST 8247
Chappel 54 TL 8928
Chard 24 ST 3208
Chardstock 24 ST 3004
Charfield 33 ST 7292
Charing 30 TQ 9549
Charing Cross Station 37 TQ 3080
Charing Heath 30 TQ 9148
Charingworth 50 SP 1939
Charlbury 47 SP 3519
Charlcombe 33 ST 7467
Charlecote 50 SP 2656
Charlecote Park (ant.) 50 SP 2656
Charles 23 SS 6832
Charleston 109 NO 3845
Charlestown (Corn.) 19 SX 0351
Charlestown (Dorset) 25 SY 6579
Charlestown (Fife.) 102 NT 0683
Charlestown (Grampn.) 119 NJ 9300
Charlestown (Highld.) 123 NG 8175
Charlestown (Highld.) 128 NH 6448
Charlestown of Aberlour 120 NJ 2642
Charles Tye 54 TM 0252
Charlesworth 70 SK 0092
Charleton House 103 NO 4603
Charlton (Gtr London) 37 TQ 4278
Charlton (Here. and Worc.) 50 SP 0045
Charlton (Northants.) 51 SP 5236
Charlton (Wilts.) 25 ST 9021
Charlton (Wilts.) 34 ST 9689
Charlton (Wilts.) 34 SU 1155
Charlton (Wilts.) 26 SU 1723
Charlton (W Susx) 27 SU 8812
Charlton Abbots 46 SP 0324
Charlton Adam 25 ST 5328
Charlton Down 25 ST 8700
Charlton Horethorne 25 ST 6623
Charlton Kings 46 SO 9620
Charlton Mackrell 25 ST 5228
Charlton Marshall 25 ST 8903
Charlton Musgrove 25 ST 7229
Charlton-on-Otmoor 47 SP 5615
Charlwood 28 TQ 2441
Charlynch 24 ST 2337
Charminster 25 SY 6792
Charmouth 24 SY 3693
Charndon 36 SP 6724
Charney Bassett 47 SU 3894
Charnock Richard 69 SD 5415
Charnwood Forest 61 SK 4914
Charsfield 55 TM 2556
Charter Alley 35 SU 5957
Charterhouse 33 ST 4955
Chartershall 101 NS 7990
Charterville Allotments 47 SP 3110
Chartham 31 TR 1054
Chartham Hatch 31 TR 1056
Chartridge 36 SP 9303
Chart Sutton 30 TQ 8049
Charwelton 51 SP 5355
Chase Terrace 60 SK 0409
Chasetown 60 SK 0408
Chasewater 60 SK 0307
Chastleton 47 SP 2429
Chatburn 78 SD 7644
Chatcull 59 SJ 7934
Chatham 30 TQ 7567
Chathill 97 NU 1826
Chat Moss 69 SJ 7095
Chatsworth House (ant.) 71 SK 2670
Chattenden 30 TQ 7672
Chatteris 53 TL 3986
Chatteris Fen 53 TL 3979
Chattisham 55 TM 0942
Chatto 90 NT 7717
Chatton 97 NU 0528
Chawleigh 23 SS 7112
Chawston 52 TL 1556
Chawton 27 SU 7037
Cheadle (Gtr Mches.) 69 SJ 8788
Cheadle (Staffs.) 60 SK 0043
Cheadle Hulme 69 SJ 8686
Cheam 37 TQ 2463
Chearsley 36 SP 7110
Chebsey 59 SJ 8528
Checkendon 36 SU 6682
Checkley (Ches.) 59 SJ 7245
Checkley (Staffs.) 60 SK 0237
Chedburgh 54 TL 7957
Cheddar 33 ST 4553
Cheddar Gorge 33 ST 4653
Cheddar Reservoir 33 ST 4463
Cheddington 36 SP 9217
Cheddleton 60 SJ 9651
Cheddon Fitzpaine 24 ST 2427
Chedgrave 65 TM 3699
Chedington 25 ST 4805
Chediston 55 TM 3577
Chedworth 46 SP 0511
Chedzoy 24 ST 3337
Cheeseman's Green 31 TR 0338
Cheetham Hill 69 SD 8401
Cheldon 23 SS 7313
Chelford 69 SJ 8174
Chelker Resr. 78 SE 0551
Chellaston 60 SK 3830
Chellington 52 SP 9656
Chelmarsh 49 SO 7187
Chelmarsh Resr 49 SO 7387
Chelmondiston 55 TM 2037
Chelmorton 70 SK 1169
Chelmsford 38 TL 7006
Chelsea 37 TQ 2778
Chelsfield 37 TQ 4864
Chelsworth 54 TL 9748
Cheltenham 46 SO 9422
Chelveston 52 SP 9969
Chelvey 33 ST 4668
Chelwood 33 ST 6361
Chelwood Gate 29 TQ 4130
Cheney Longville 48 SO 4184
Chenies 36 TQ 0198
Chepstow 45 ST 5393
Chepstow Park Wood 45 ST 4897
Cherhill 34 SU 0370
Cherington (Glos.) 46 ST 9098
Cherington (Warw.) 50 SP 2936
Cheriton (Devon) 23 SS 7346
Cheriton (Devon) 24 ST 1001
Cheriton (Hants.) 27 SU 5828
Cheriton (Somer.) 25 ST 6825
Cheriton (W Glam.) 40 SS 4593
Cheriton Bishop 21 SX 7793
Cheriton Fitzpaine 23 SS 8606
Cherrington 59 SJ 6619
Cherry Burton 74 SE 9842
Cherry Cobb Sands 75 TA 2121
Cherry Hinton 53 TL 4857
Cherry Willingham 72 TF 0173
Chertsey 36 TQ 0466
Cheselbourne 25 SY 7699
Chesham 36 SP 9601
Chesham Bois 36 SU 9698
Cheshunt 37 TL 3502
Chesil Beach 25 SY 5882
Cheslyn Hay 60 SJ 9707
Chessington 37 TQ 1863
Chester 68 SJ 4066
Chesterblade 33 ST 6641
Chesterfield (Derby.) 71 SK 3871
Chesterfield (Staffs.) 60 SK 1005
Chesterfield Canal (Notts.) 71 SK 6582
Chesterfield Canal (Notts.) 72 SK 7284
Chester-le-Street 84 NZ 2751
Chesters (Borders) 96 NT 6022
Chesters (Borders) 90 NT 6210
Chesterton (Cambs.) 62 TL 1295
Chesterton (Cambs.) 53 TL 4560
Chesterton (Oxon.) 47 SP 5621
Chesterton (Staffs.) 59 SJ 8249
Chesterton Green 50 SP 3558
Chestfield 31 TR 1365
Cheswardine 59 SJ 7129
Cheswick 97 NU 0346
Cheswick Black Rocks 97 NU 0347
Cheswick Green 50 SP 1275
Chetney Marshes 30 TQ 8871
Chetnole 25 ST 6008
Chettiscombe 23 SS 9614
Chettisham 53 TL 5483
Chettle 26 ST 9513
Chetton 49 SO 6690
Chetwode 51 SP 6429
Chetwynd Aston 59 SJ 7517
Cheveley 54 TL 6760
Chevening 29 TQ 4857
Chevington 54 TL 7859
Chevington Drift 91 NZ 2699
Cheviot Hills, The 90 NT 8211
Cheviot, The (mt.) 90 NT 9020
Chevithorne 23 SS 9715
Chew Magna 33 ST 5763
Chew Reservoir 70 SE 0301
Chew Stoke 33 ST 5561
Chewton Mendip 33 ST 5952
Chew Valley Lake 33 ST 5659
Cheynies (is.) 141 HU 3438
Chicheley 52 SP 9046
Chichester 27 SU 8605
Chichester (Goodwood) Airfield 27 SU 8707
Chichester Harbour 27 SU 7703
Chicken Head 131 NB 5029
Chicken Rock 76 SC 1464
Chickerell 25 SY 6480
Chicklade 25 ST 9134
Chicksands 52 TL 1239
Chidden 27 SU 6517
Chiddingfold 28 SU 9635
Chiddingly 29 TQ 5414
Chiddingstone 29 TQ 5045
Chiddingstone Causeway 29 TQ 5147
Chideock 25 SY 4292
Chidham 27 SU 7803
Chieveley 35 SU 4773
Chignall Smealy 38 TL 6611
Chignall St. James 38 TL 6709
Chigwell 37 TQ 4493
Chigwell Row 37 TQ 4693
Chilbolton 34 SU 3939
Chilcomb (Hants.) 27 SU 5028
Chilcombe (Dorset) 25 SY 5291
Chilcompton 33 ST 6452
Chilcote 60 SK 2811
Childer Thornton 68 SJ 3677
Child Okeford 25 ST 8312
Childrey 34 SU 3687
Child's Ercall 59 SJ 6625
Childswickham 50 SP 0738
Childwall 68 SJ 4089
Chilfrome 25 SY 5898
Chilgrove 27 SU 8314
Chilham 31 TR 0753
Chillaton 20 SX 4381
Chillenden 31 TR 2753
Chillerton 27 SZ 4883
Chillesford 55 TM 3852
Chillingham 97 NU 0625
Chillington (Devon) 21 SX 7942
Chillington (Somer.) 24 ST 3811
Chillington Hall 59 SJ 8606
Chilmark 26 ST 9632
Chilson 47 SP 3119
Chilsworthy (Corn.) 20 SX 4172
Chilsworthy (Devon) 22 SS 3206
Chiltern Hills 36 SU 7799
Chiltern Hundreds (dist.) 36 SU 9390
Chilthorne Domer 25 ST 5219
Chilton (Bucks.) 36 SP 6811
Chilton (Durham) 84 NZ 2929
Chilton (Oxon) 35 SU 4885
Chilton Cantelo 25 ST 5621
Chilton Chine 26 SZ 4181
Chilton Foliat 34 SU 3170
Chilton Lane 84 NZ 3031
Chilton Polden 32 ST 3739
Chilton Street 54 TL 7547
Chilton Trinity 32 ST 2939
Chilworth 26 SU 4018
Chimney 47 SP 3500
Chineham 35 SU 6554
Chingford 37 TQ 3893
Chinley 70 SK 0382
Chinley Head 70 SK 0484
Chinnock 25 ST 4613
Chinnor 36 SP 7500
Chipchase Castle 90 NY 8876
Chipnall 59 SJ 7231
Chippenham (Cambs.) 54 TL 6669
Chippenham (Wilts.) 33 ST 9173
Chipperfield 36 TL 0401
Chipping (Herts.) 53 TL 3532
Chipping (Lancs.) 77 SD 6243
Chipping Campden 50 SP 1539
Chipping Hill 38 TL 8215
Chipping Norton 47 SP 3127
Chipping Ongar 37 TL 5502
Chipping Sodbury 33 ST 7282
Chipping Warden 51 SP 4948
Chipstable 24 ST 0427
Chipstead (Kent) 29 TQ 5056
Chipstead (Surrey) 28 TQ 2756
Chirbury 58 SO 2598
Chirdon Burn 90 NY 7481
Chirk 58 SJ 2937
Chirk Castle 58 SJ 2638
Chirmorie 86 NX 2076
Chirnside 97 NT 8756
Chirnsidebridge 97 NT 8556
Chirton 34 SU 0757
Chisbury 34 SU 2766
Chiselborough 25 ST 4614
Chiselbury (ant.) 26 SU 0127
Chiselhampton 47 SU 5999
Chisledon 34 SU 1879
Chislehurst 37 TQ 4470
Chislet 31 TR 2264
Chiswell Green 37 TL 1303
Chiswick 37 TQ 2077
Chisworth 70 SJ 9991
Chithurst 27 SU 8423
Chittering 53 TL 4970
Chitterne 34 ST 9843
Chittlehamholt 23 SS 6420
Chittlehampton 23 SS 6325
Chittoe 34 ST 9666
Chivelstone 21 SX 7838
Chno Dearg 115 NN 3774
Chobham 36 SU 9761
Chobham Common 36 SU 9665
Chobham Ridges 36 SU 9159
Cholderton 34 SU 2242
Cholesbury 36 SP 9307
Chollerton 90 NY 9372
Cholmondeley Castle 59 SJ 5351
Cholsey 35 SU 5886
Cholstrey 45 SO 4659
Choppington 91 NZ 2583
Chopwell 91 NZ 1158
Chorley (Ches.) 59 SJ 5650
Chorley (Lancs.) 69 SD 5817
Chorley (Shrops.) 49 SO 6983
Chorley (Staffs.) 60 SK 0711
Chorleywood 36 TQ 0396
Chorlton 59 SJ 7250
Chorlton-cum-Hardy 69 SJ 8093
Chorlton Lane 58 SJ 4547
Chowley 59 SJ 4756
Chrishall 53 TL 4439
Christchurch (Cambs.) 63 TL 4996
Christchurch (Dorset) 26 SZ 1593
Christchurch (Glos.) 45 SO 5713
Christchurch Bay 26 SZ 2291
Christian Malford 34 ST 9678
Christleton 68 SJ 4365
Christmas Common 36 SU 7193
Christon 32 ST 3956
Christon Bank 97 NU 2122
Christow 21 SX 8385
Christ's Hospital 28 TQ 1428
Chudleigh 21 SX 8679
Chudleigh Knighton 21 SX 8477
Chulmleigh 23 SS 6814
Chunal 70 SK 0391
Church 77 SD 7428
Churcham 46 SO 7618
Church Aston 59 SJ 7317
Church Bay 66 SH 2989
Church Brampton 51 SP 7165
Church Broughton 60 SK 2033
Church Cove 18 SW 7112
Church Crookham 35 SU 8152
Churchdown 46 SO 8819
Church Eaton 59 SJ 8417
Church End (Beds.) 36 SP 9921
Church End (Beds.) 52 TL 1937
Church End (Cambs.) 63 TF 3909
Church End (Cambs.) 53 TL 4857
Church End (Essex) 53 TL 5841
Churchend (Essex) 38 TL 6323
Churchend (Essex) 39 TR 0092
Church End (Hants.) 35 SU 6756
Church End (Warw.) 50 SP 2892
Church End (Wilts.) 34 SU 0278
Church Fenton 79 SE 5136
Church Gresley 60 SK 2918
Church Handborough 47 SP 4212
Church Houses 85 SE 6697
Churchill (Avon) 33 ST 4359
Churchill (Here. and Worc.) 49 SO 8779
Churchill (Oxon.) 47 SP 2824
Churchingford 24 ST 2112
Church Knowle 26 SY 9481
Church Langton 61 SP 7293
Church Lawford 51 SP 4476
Church Lawton 59 SJ 8255
Church Leigh 60 SK 0235
Church Lench 50 SP 0251
Church Minshull 69 SJ 6660
Church Norton 27 SZ 8695
Churchover 51 SP 5080
Church Preen 59 SO 5398
Church Pulverbatch 58 SJ 4303
Churchstanton 24 ST 1914
Church Stoke 58 SO 2694
Churchstow (Devon) 21 SX 7145
Church Stowe (Northants.) 51 SP 6357
Church Street 30 TQ 7174
Church Stretton 58 SO 4593
Churchtown (I. of M.) 76 SC 4294
Churchtown (Lancs.) 77 SD 4842
Churchtown (Mers.) 68 SD 3618
Church Village 41 ST 0886
Church Warsop 71 SK 5668
Churn Clough Resr. 78 SD 7838
Churnsike Lodge 90 NY 6677
Churt 35 SU 8538
Churton 58 SJ 4156
Churwell 79 SE 2729
Chute Causeway (ant.) 34 SU 2856
Chwefru 44 SN 9854
Chwilog 66 SH 4338
Chyandour 18 SW 4731
Ciaran Water 106 NN 2861
Cilan Uchaf 56 SH 2923
Cilcain 68 SJ 1765
Cilcennin 43 SN 5160
Cilfaesty Hill 48 SO 1384
Cilfor 67 SH 6237
Cilfrew 41 SN 7600
Cilfynydd 41 ST 0892
Cilgerran 43 SN 1943
Cilgwyn 41 SN 7430
Ciliau-Aeron 43 SN 5058
Cilieni 41 SN 9035
Cilmery 44 SO 0051
Cilrhedyn 43 SN 2734
Ciltalgarth 67 SH 8840
Cilurnum (ant.) 90 NY 9170
Cilwendeg 43 SN 2238
Cilybebyll 41 SN 7404
Cilycwm 44 SN 7540
Cinderford 46 SO 6513
Cloch Mhòr 128 NH 5003
Cirean Geardail 132 NC 0134
Cirencester 46 SP 0201
Cir Mhòr 92 NR 9743
Cissbury Ring (ant.) 28 TQ 1408
Ciste Dhubh 115 NH 0616
City Dulas 66 SH 4687
City of London 37 TQ 3281
City, The 36 SU 7896
Clachaig 100 NS 1181
Clachaig Water 92 NR 6940
Clachan (Island of Raasay) 123 NG 5436
Clachan (Lismore Island) 105 NM 8543
Clachan (Strath.) 105 NM 7819
Clachan (Strath.) 100 NN 1812
Clachan (Strath.) 92 NR 7656
Clachan (Tays.) 107 NN 8065
Clachan-a-Luib 124 NF 8163
Clachan Burn 134 NC 7261
Clachan Hill 106 NN 1915
Clachan Mòr 104 NL 9847
Clachan of Campsie 101 NS 6179
Clachan of Glendaruel 100 NR 9984
Clachan-Seil 105 NM 7718
Clachan Yell (mt.) 118 NO 4491
Clach Bheinn 100 NS 2195
Clachbreck 99 NR 7675
Clach Leathad 106 NN 2449
Clachtoll 132 NC 0427
Clackmannan 102 NS 9191
Clacton-on-Sea 39 TM 1715
Cladach an Eilein 131 NB 5365
Cladach Cuiashader 131 NB 5558
Cladach Dibadale 131 NB 5554
Claddach Kirkibost 124 NF 7865
Cladich 106 NN 0921
Cladich River 106 NN 0921
Claerwen Resr. 57 SN 8565
Claggain Bay 98 NR 4653
Claggain River 98 NR 4255
Claggan 111 NM 7049
Clagh Ouyr 76 SC 4189
Claife Heights 83 SD 3798
Claigan 122 NG 2353
Claig Castle 98 NR 4762
Claines 49 SO 8559
Clandown 33 ST 6955
Clanfield (Hants.) 27 SU 6916
Clanfield (Oxon.) 47 SP 2801
Clannaborough Barton 23 SS 7402
Clanville 34 SU 3148
Clanyard 86 NX 1037

Clanyard Bay 86 NX 0938
Claonaig 92 NR 8656
Claonaig Bay 92 NR 8755
Claonel 128 NC 5604
Clapgate 26 SU 0102
Clapham (Beds.) 52 TL 0252
Clapham (Gtr London) 37 TQ 2875
Clapham (N Yorks.) 77 SD 7469
Clapham (W Susx) 28 TQ 0906
Clappers 97 NT 9455
Clappersgate 82 NY 3603
Clapton (Somer.) 24 ST 4106
Clapton-in-Gordano 33 ST 4774
Clapton-on-the-Hill 47 SP 1617
Clapworthy 23 SS 6724
Clarbeston 42 SN 0421
Clarbeston Road 42 SN 0121
Clarborough 72 SK 7383
Clardon 135 ND 1468
Clardon Head 135 ND 1570
Clare 54 TL 7645
Clarebrand 88 NX 7666
Claremont Park 37 TQ 1363
Clarencefield 89 NY 0968
Clarkston 94 NS 5757
Clashindarroch 121 NJ 4831
Clashindarroch Forest 121 NJ 4633
Clashmach Hill 121 NJ 4938
Clashmore 132 NC 0331
Clashmore Wood 129 NH 7390
Clashnessie 132 NC 0530
Clashnessie Bay 132 NC 0631
Clashnoir 117 NJ 2222
Clathy 108 NN 9919
Clatt 121 NJ 5426
Clatter 57 SN 9994
Clattering Brig 119 NO 6678
Clatteringshaws Loch 87 NX 5477
Clatto Hill 103 NO 3506
Clatto Resr. 103 NO 3607
Clatworthy 24 ST 0530
Clatworthy Reservoir 24 ST 0431
Clauchlands Point 92 NS 0533
Claughton (Lancs.) 77 SD 5242
Claughton (Lancs.) 77 SD 5666
Clava Cairns (ant.) 129 NH 7544
Claverdon 50 SP 1964
Claverham 33 ST 4566
Clavering 53 TL 4832
Claverley 59 SO 7993
Claverton 33 ST 7864
Clawdd-du-bach 57 SN 8770
Clawdd-newydd 67 SJ 0852
Clawton 20 SX 3599
Claxby (Lincs.) 73 TF 1194
Claxby (Lincs.) 73 TF 4571
Claxton (Norf.) 65 TG 3303
Claxton (N Yorks.) 80 SE 6960
Clay 108 NO 1463
Claybokie 117 NO 0989
Claybrooke Magna 51 SP 4988
Clay Common 55 TM 4781
Clay Coton 51 SP 5977
Clay Cross 71 SK 3963
Claydon (Oxon.) 51 SP 4550
Claydon (Suff.) 55 TM 1350
Claygate 37 TQ 1563
Claygate Cross 29 TQ 6155
Clayhanger (Devon) 24 ST 0223
Clayhanger (W Mids) 60 SK 0404
Clay Head 76 SC 4480
Clayhidon 24 ST 1615
Claybock 135 ND 1659
Clay of Allan 129 NH 8276
Claypole 62 SK 8449
Clayton (Staffs.) 59 SJ 8443
Clayton (S Yorks.) 71 SE 4507
Clayton (W Susx) 29 TQ 3014
Clayton (W Yorks.) 78 SE 1131
Clayton-le-Moors 77 SD 7431
Clayton-le-Woods 77 SD 5722
Clayton West 71 SE 2511
Clayworth 72 SK 7288
Cleadale 111 NM 4788
Cleadon 91 NZ 3862
Cleann Tanagaidh 127 NH 0868
Clearbury Ring (ant.) 26 SU 1524
Clearwell 45 SO 5708
Cleasby 84 NZ 2713
Cleasby Hill 84 NY 9707
Cleat (Barra) 112 NF 6604
Cleat (S. Ronaldsay) 136 ND 4584
Cleatlam 84 NZ 1118
Cleator 82 NY 0113
Cleator Moor 82 NY 0214
Cleckheaton 78 SE 1825
Cledan 48 SN 8644
Cleedownton 48 SO 5880
Cleehill 49 SO 5975
Clee St. Margaret 48 SO 5684
Cleethorpes 75 TA 3008
Cleeton St. Mary 49 SO 6178
Cleeve 33 ST 4566
Cleeve Hill 46 SO 9827
Cleeve Prior 50 SP 0849
Clehonger 45 SO 4637
Cleigh 105 NM 8725
Cleish 102 NT 0998
Cleish Hills 102 NT 0796
Cleite Leathann (mt.) 130 NB 0428
Cleland 101 NS 7958
Clench Common 34 SU 1765
Clenchwarton 63 TF 5820
Clent 49 SO 9179
Clent Hills 49 SO 9380
Cleobury Mortimer 49 SO 6775
Cleobury North 49 SO 6187
Cleongart 92 NR 6734
Clephanton 129 NH 8150
Clerklands 96 NT 5024
Clestrain 136 HY 3006
Clestrain Sound 136 HY 2806
Clett 135 ND 1071
Clett Ard 125 NB 1808
Clett Nisabost 124 NG 0495
Clettraval 124 NF 7471
Cleughbrae 89 NY 0673
Clevancy 34 SU 0475
Clevedon 32 ST 4071
Clevedon Court 33 ST 4271
Cleveland 85 NZ 6213
Cleveland Hills 85 SE 5899
Cleveleys 77 SD 3142
Cleverton 34 ST 9785
Clewer 33 ST 4350
Cley Hill 33 ST 8344
Cley next the Sea 64 TG 0444
Cliad Bay 110 NM 1960
Cliasmol 125 NB 0706
Cliburn 83 NY 5824
Cliddesden 35 SU 6349
Cliffe (Kent) 30 TQ 7376
Cliffe (N Yorks.) 79 SE 6631
Cliffe Hill 29 TQ 4310
Cliff End 30 TQ 8813
Cliffe Woods 30 TQ 7373
Clifford (Here. and Worc.) 45 SO 2445
Clifford (W Yorks.) 79 SE 4244
Clifford Chambers 50 SP 1952
Clifford's Mesne 46 SO 7023
Cliffs End 31 TR 3464
Clift Hills 141 HU 3931
Clifton (Avon) 33 ST 5673
Clifton (Beds.) 52 TL 1739
Clifton (Central) 106 NN 3230
Clifton (Cumbr.) 82 NY 0429
Clifton (Cumbr.) 83 NY 5326
Clifton (Derby.) 60 SK 1644
Clifton (Here. and Worc.) 49 SO 8446
Clifton (Lancs.) 77 SD 4630
Clifton (Northum.) 91 NZ 2082
Clifton (Notts.) 61 SK 5434
Clifton (Oxon.) 47 SP 4831
Clifton Campville 60 SK 2510
Clifton Hampden 47 SU 5495
Clifton Reynes 52 SP 9051
Clifton upon Dunsmore 51 SP 5276
Clifton upon Teme 49 SO 7161
Clift Sound 141 HU 3933
Clifts, The 142 HU 3281
Climping 28 TQ 0002
Clint 79 SE 2559
Clintburn 90 NY 7279
Clinterty 119 NJ 8311
Clint Green 64 TG 0210
Clintmains 96 NT 6132
Clints Dod 103 NT 6268
Clints of Dromore (mt.) 87 NX 5464
Clippesby 65 TG 4214
Clipsham 62 SK 9616
Clipston (Northants.) 51 SP 7181
Clipston (Notts.) 61 SK 6333
Clisham (mt.) 125 NB 1507
Clitheroe 77 SD 7441
Clive 59 SJ 5124
Clivocast 143 HP 6000
Clocaenog 67 SJ 0854
Clocaenog Forest 67 SJ 0152
Clochan 121 NJ 4060
Cloch Point 100 NS 2075
Clock Face 69 SJ 5291
Cloddymoss 129 NH 9859
Clodock 45 SO 3227
Clola 121 NK 0043
Clophill 52 TL 0838
Clopton 52 TL 0680
Clopton Green 54 TL 7654
Closeburn 88 NX 8992
Close Clark 76 SC 2775
Clothall 53 TL 2732
Clothan 143 HU 4581
Clotton 69 SJ 5263
Clougha Pike 77 SD 5559
Clough Foot 78 SD 9123
Cloughton 81 TA 0094
Cloughton Newlands 81 TA 0096
Cloughton Wyke (pt.) 81 TA 0295
Clousta 141 HU 3157
Clova (Grampn.) 121 NJ 4522
Clova (Tays.) 118 NO 3273
Clovelly 22 SS 3124
Clovelly Dykes (ant.) 22 SS 3123
Clove Lodge 84 NY 9317
Clovenfords 96 NT 4436
Clovenstone 119 NJ 7717
Clovullin 106 NN 0063
Clowbridge Resr. 78 SD 8328
Clowne 71 SK 4975
Clows Top 49 SO 7171
Cluanie Forest 115 NH 0409
Cluanie Lodge 115 NH 0910
Cluas Deas 132 NC 0032
Cluer 125 NG 1490
Clumber Park 71 SK 6274
Clun 48 SO 3081
Clunas 129 NH 8846
Clunas Reservoir 129 NH 8545
Clunbury 48 SO 3780
Clunes 115 NN 2088
Clunes Forest 115 NN 2290
Clun Forest 48 SO 2286
Clungunford 48 SO 3978
Clunie (Grampn.) 121 NJ 6350
Clunie (Tays.) 108 NO 1043
Clunie Water 117 NO 1486
Clunton 48 SO 3381
Cluny 103 NT 2495
Cluny Castle (Grampn.) 119 NJ 6812
Cluny Castle (Highld.) 116 NN 6494
Cluster 143 HU 5890
Clutton (Avon) 33 ST 6159
Clutton (Ches.) 58 SJ 4654
Clwt-y-bont 66 SH 5763
Clwydian Range 68 SJ 1464
Clydach (Gwent) 41 SO 2213
Clydach (W Glam.) 40 SN 6801
Clydach Vale 41 SS 9793
Clydebank 101 NS 5069
Clyde Law 88 NT 0217
Clydesdale (dist.) 95 NS 8347
Clydey 43 SN 2535
Clyffe Pypard 34 SU 0776
Clynder 100 NS 2484
Clynderwen 42 SN 1219
Clynelish 129 NC 8905
Clynnog-fawr 66 SH 4149
Clyro 45 SO 2143
Clyro Hill 45 SO 2046
Clyst Honiton 21 SX 9893
Clyst Hydon 24 ST 0301
Clyst St. George 21 SX 9888
Clyst St. Lawrence 24 ST 0200
Clyst St. Mary 21 SX 9890
Clyth 135 ND 2937
Cnap Chaochan Aitinn 117 NJ 1409
Cnap na Feola (mt.) 127 NH 2253
Cnicht 67 SH 6446
Cnoc a'Bhaile-shios 99 NR 8662
Cnoc a'Chapuill 92 NR 9730
Cnoc a'Choire 128 NC 5004
Cnoc a' Ghiubhais (Highld.) 132 NC 2670
Cnoc a' Ghiubhais (Highld.) 133 NC 5423
Cnoc a' Ghriama 132 NC 4026
Cnoc a'Mhadaidh 133 NC 1684
Cnoc an Alaskie 133 NC 4827
Cnocan Conachreag 135 NC 1136
Cnoc an dà Chinn 105 NM 4444
Cnoc an Earrannaiche 135 ND 2441
Cnoc an Eireannaich 134 NC 9527
Cnoc an Fhuarain Bhàin 134 NC 9553
Cnoc an Ime 98 NR 5880
Cnoc an Liath-bhaid Mhóir 134 NC 7529
Cnoc an t-Sabhail 128 NH 6978
Cnoc Badaireach na Gaoithe 134 NC 8452
Cnoc Bad Mhairtein 134 NC 9354
Cnoc Breac 126 NG 7884
Cnoc Buidhe 92 NR 6930
Cnoc Ceann nam Bad 128 NC 5500
Cnoc Céislein 128 NH 5870
Cnoc Coinnich 100 NN 2300
Cnoc Coire na Feàrna 134 NC 9329
Cnoc Corr Guinie 128 NH 6775
Cnoc Craggie 133 NC 6052
Cnoc Creagach 92 NR 8455
Cnoc Donn 92 NR 7452
Cnoc Dubh 98 NR 2262
Cnoc Eille Mòr 92 NR 4547
Cnoc Fraing 116 NH 8014
Cnoc Leamhnachd 134 NC 7511
Cnoc Loch Mhadadh 134 NC 9932
Cnoc Meadhonach 134 NC 8417
Cnoc Mór 92 NR 6800
Cnoc Mór na Claigin 98 NR 4553
Cnoc Moy 92 NR 6115
Cnoc Muigh-bhlàraidh 128 NH 6382
Cnoc na Breun-choille 134 NC 7824
Cnoc na Carraige 100 NR 9768
Cnoc na Glas Choille 127 NC 2708
Cnoc na h'Airighe 100 NS 2290
Cnoc na Maoile 135 ND 0021
Cnoc na Meine 100 NR 9060
Cnoc nan Craobh 92 NR 7345
Cnoc nan Cùilean 133 NC 5946
Cnoc nan Gabhar 92 NR 8039
Cnoc nan Tri-chlach 134 NC 7943
Cnoc Odhar 92 NR 6613
Cnoc Preas a'Mhadaidh 134 NC 9848
Cnoc Reamhar (Island of Arran) 92 NR 9224
Cnoc Reamhar (Strath.) 99 NR 7690
Cnoc Stighseir 99 NR 7176
Cnwch Coch 57 SN 6775
Coad's Green 20 SX 2976
Coal Aston 71 SK 3679
Coalbrookdale 59 SJ 6604
Coalburn 95 NS 8034
Coalcleugh 83 NY 8045
Coaley 46 SO 7701
Coall Head 141 HU 4433
Coalpit Heath 33 ST 6780
Coalport 59 SJ 6902
Coalsnaughton 102 NS 9195
Coaltown of Balgonie 103 NT 2999
Coaltown of Wemyss 103 NT 3295
Coalville 60 SK 4214
Coast 126 NG 9290
Coatbridge 101 NS 7265
Coatdyke 101 NS 7464
Coate 34 SU 0361
Coates (Cambs.) 63 TL 3097
Coates (Glos.) 46 SO 9700
Cotham 85 NZ 5925
Cotham Mundeville 84 NZ 2919
Coatsgate 89 NT 0605
Cobbaton 23 SS 6127
Cobbin's Brook 37 TL 4001
Cobbinshaw Resr. 95 NT 0157
Cobbler, The (mt.) 100 NN 2505
Coberley 46 SO 9615
Cobham (Kent) 30 TQ 6768
Cobham (Surrey) 37 TQ 1060
Cobnash 45 SO 4560
Cochno Loch 101 NS 4976
Cochrage Muir 108 NO 1349
Cockayne 85 SE 6298
Cockayne Hatley 53 TL 2549
Cockayne Ridge 85 NZ 6000
Cock Beck 79 SE 4738
Cock Bridge 117 NJ 2509
Cockburnspath 96 NT 7770
Cock Cairn 118 NO 4688
Cock Clarks 38 TL 8102
Cockenzie and Port Seton 103 NT 4075
Cockerham 77 SD 4651
Cockerington 73 TF 3789
Cockermouth 82 NY 1230
Cockernhoe 37 TL 1223
Cockfield (Durham) 84 NZ 1224
Cockfield (Suff.) 54 TL 9054
Cockfosters 37 TQ 2896
Cock Hill 119 NO 5387
Cocking 27 SU 8717
Cockington 21 SX 8964
Cocklake 33 ST 4349
Cock Law 90 NT 8616
Cocklaw Hill 96 NT 7271
Cockley Beck 82 NY 2401
Cockley Cley 64 TF 7904
Cock of Arran 92 NR 9552
Cockpole Green 36 SU 7981
Cocks Hill 21 SX 5679
Cockshutt 58 SJ 4329
Cockthorpe 64 TF 9842
Cockwood 21 SX 9780
Cod Beck 79 SE 4277
Codda 19 SX 1878
Coddenham 55 TM 1354
Coddington (Ches.) 58 SJ 4455
Coddington (Here. and Worc.) 49 SO 7142
Coddington (Notts.) 62 SK 8354
Codford St. Mary 34 ST 9739
Codford St. Peter 34 ST 9640
Codicote 37 TL 2118
Codnor 60 SK 4149
Codrington 33 ST 7278
Codsall 59 SJ 8603
Codsall Wood 59 SJ 8405
Coedely 41 ST 0285
Coedkernew 32 ST 2783
Coedpoeth 58 SJ 2850
Coed-y-gaer 57 SO 0084
Coed-y-paen 45 ST 3398
Coelbren 41 SN 8411
Coffinswell 21 SX 8968
Cofton Hackett 50 SP 0075
Cogan 41 ST 1772
Cogenhoe 52 SP 8360
Coggeshall 38 TL 8522
Cogra Moss 82 NY 0919
Coigach (dist.) 127 NC 1103
Coignafearn Forest 116 NH 6412
Coignafearn Lodge 116 NH 6815
Coilacriech 118 NO 3287
Coilantogle 101 NN 5906
Coillaig 106 NN 0120
Coille Mhorgil 115 NH 1001
Coillore 122 NG 3537
Coirc Bheinn 105 NM 4832
Coire a' Chonachair 127 NC 3302
Coire Bhachdaidh Lodge 107 NN 5471
Coirefrois Burn 133 NC 7015
Coire na Beinne 135 ND 1440
Coire Odhar (Highld.) 116 NH 5006
Coire Odhar (Tays.) 101 NN 8213
Coire Thomag 99 NR 7974
Coity 41 SS 9281
Coity Mountain 45 SO 2308
Coker 25 ST 5312
Colaboll 133 NC 5610
Coladoir River 105 NM 5529
Colan 19 SW 8661
Colaton Raleigh 24 SY 0787
Col-bheinn 134 NC 8810
Colbost 122 NG 2148
Colbost Point 122 NG 3039
Colby (Cumbr.) 83 NY 6620
Colby (I. of M.) 76 SC 2370
Colby (Norf.) 65 TG 2131
Colchester 54 TM 0025
Cold Ash 35 SU 5169
Cold Ashby 51 SP 6576
Cold Ashton 33 ST 7472
Cold Aston 47 SP 1219
Coldbackie 133 NC 6160
Coldblow 31 TQ 5173
Cold Brayfield 52 SP 9252
Coldean 29 TQ 3408
Coldeast 21 SX 8274
Colden (mt.) 76 SC 3484
Colden Common 27 SU 4822
Coldfair Green 55 TM 4361
Cold Fell 83 NY 6055
Cold Hanworth 72 TF 0383
Coldharbour 28 TQ 1443
Cold Hesledon 85 NZ 4147
Cold Higham 51 SP 6653
Coldingham 97 NT 9065
Coldingham Bay 97 NT 9266
Coldingham Moor 97 NT 8666
Cold Kirby 79 SE 5384
Cold Law 97 NT 9523
Cold Newton 61 SK 7106
Cold Norton 38 TL 8500
Cold Overton 62 SK 8110
Coldrain 102 NO 0700
Coldred 31 TR 2747
Coldridge 23 SS 6907
Coldsmouth Hill 97 NT 8528
Coldstream 97 NT 8439
Coldwaltham 28 TQ 0216
Coldwells 121 NK 1039
Coldwells Croft 121 NJ 5722
Cole 25 ST 6633
Colebatch 48 SO 3187
Colebrook 23 ST 0006
Colebrooke 21 SX 7799
Coleburn 84 SE 2098
Coleby (Humbs.) 74 SE 8919
Coleby (Lincs.) 72 SK 9760
Coleford (Devon) 23 SS 7701
Coleford (Glos.) 45 SO 5710
Coleford (Somer.) 33 ST 6848
Colehill 26 SU 0300
Coleman's Hatch 29 TQ 4533
Colemere 58 SJ 4232
Colenden 108 NO 1029
Coleorton 60 SK 3917
Colerne 33 ST 8171
Colesbourne 46 SO 9913
Colesden 52 TL 1255
Coleshill (Bucks.) 36 SU 9495
Coleshill (Oxon.) 47 SU 2393
Coleshill (Warw.) 50 SP 1989
Colgate 28 TQ 2332
Colgrain 100 NS 3280
Colgrave Sound 143 HU 5789
Colinsburgh 103 NO 4703
Colinton 103 NT 2169
Colintraive 100 NS 0374
Colkirk 64 TF 9126
Coll (Isle of Lewis) 131 NB 4739
Coll (Strath.) (is.) 110 NM 1957
Collace 108 NO 2032
Coll Aerodrome 110 NM 1756
Collafirth (Shetld.) 142 HU 3583
Collafirth (Shetld.) 142 HU 3683
Collafirth (Shetld.) 143 HU 4368
Colla Firth (Shetld.) 143 HU 4469
Collaton St. Mary 21 SX 8660
College Burn 97 NT 8824
Collessie 103 NO 2813
Collie Law 96 NT 4850
Collier Law 84 NZ 0141
Collier Row 37 TQ 4991
Colliers End 37 TL 3720
Collier Street 29 TQ 7145
Colliery Row 85 NZ 3449
Collieston 121 NK 0328
Colliford Reservoir 19 SX 1772
Collin 88 NY 0276
Collingbourne Ducis 34 SU 2453
Collingbourne Kingston 34 SU 2355
Collingham (Notts.) 72 SK 8261
Collingham (W Yorks.) 79 SE 3845
Collington 49 SO 6460
Collingtree 51 SP 7555
Colliston 109 NO 6045
Coll Sands 131 NB 4638
Collynie 121 NJ 8436
Collyweston 62 SK 9903
Colmonell 86 NX 1586
Colmworth 52 TL 1058
Colnabaichin 117 NJ 2908
Colnbrook 36 TQ 0277
Colne (Cambs.) 53 TL 3776
Colne (Lancs.) 78 SD 8839
Colne Engaine 54 TL 8530
Colne Point 39 TM 1012
Colne Valley 54 TL 8529
Colney 65 TG 1808
Colney Heath 37 TL 2005
Colney Street 37 TL 1502
Coln Rogers 46 SP 0809
Coln St. Aldwyns 47 SP 1405
Coln St. Dennis 46 SP 0810
Colonel's Bed, The (mt.) 117 NO 1086
Colonsay (is.) 98 NR 3794
Colp 121 NJ 7448
Colpy 121 NJ 6432
Colsay 141 HU 3618
Colsterdale 78 SE 1280
Colsterdale Moor 78 SE 1181
Colsterworth 62 SK 9224
Colston Bassett 61 SK 7033
Colt Crag Resr. 90 NY 9378
Coltfield 129 NJ 1163
Colt Hill 88 NX 6998
Coltishall 65 TG 2619
Colton (Cumbr.) 77 SD 3186
Colton (Norf.) 65 TG 1009
Colton (N Yorks.) 79 SE 5444
Colton (Staffs.) 60 SK 0520
Colvend 87 NX 8654
Colvister 143 HU 5197
Colwall Green 49 SO 7541
Colwall Stone 49 SO 7542
Colwell 90 NY 9575
Colwell Bay 26 SZ 3288
Colwich 60 SK 0121
Colwinston 41 SS 9475
Colworth 28 SU 9102
Colwyn Bay 67 SH 8478
Colyford 24 SY 2492
Colyton 24 SY 2493
Combe (Berks.) 34 SU 3760
Combe (Here. and Worc.) 48 SO 3463
Combe (Oxon.) 47 SP 4115
Combe Florey 24 ST 1531
Combe Hay 33 ST 7359
Combeinteignhead 21 SX 9071
Combe Martin 23 SS 5846
Combe Martin Bay 23 SS 5748
Combe Moor 48 SO 3663
Combe Raleigh 24 ST 1502
Comberbach 69 SJ 6477
Comberton 53 TL 3856
Combe St. Nicholas 24 ST 3011
Comb Fell 90 NT 9118
Comb Hill 89 NT 3900
Comb Law 88 NS 9407
Combrook 50 SP 3051
Combs (Derby.) 70 SK 0478
Combs (Suff.) 54 TM 0456
Combs Ford 54 TM 0457
Combs Reservoir 70 SK 0379
Combwich 32 ST 2542
Comers 119 NJ 6707
Comlongon Castle (ant.) 89 NY 0868
Commins Coch 57 SH 8403
Commondale 85 NZ 6610
Common Edge 77 SD 3232
Commonedge Hill 102 NN 9701
Common Hill 95 NS 8222
Common Law 95 NT 0732
Common Moor 19 SX 2369
Common of Dunning 102 NO 0109
Common Side 71 SK 3376
Common, The 26 SU 2432
Compstall 70 SJ 9690
Compton (Berks.) 35 SU 5279
Compton (Devon) 21 SX 8664
Compton (Hants.) 27 SU 4625
Compton (Surrey) 28 SU 9547
Compton (Wilts.) 34 SU 1352
Compton (W Susx) 27 SU 7714
Compton Abbas 25 ST 8718
Compton Abbas Airfield 25 ST 8918
Compton Abdale 46 SP 0516
Compton Bassett 34 SU 0372
Compton Bay 26 SZ 3684
Compton Beauchamp 34 SU 2887
Compton Bishop 32 ST 3955
Compton Chamberlayne 26 SU 0229
Compton Dando 33 ST 6464
Compton Down 34 SU 1050
Compton Dundon 25 ST 4933
Compton Martin 33 ST 5456
Compton Pauncefoot 25 ST 6425
Compton Valence 25 SY 5993
Compton Wynyates (ant.) 50 SP 3342
Comrie 107 NN 7722
Conachcraig 117 NO 2786
Cona Glen 106 NM 9471
Conaglen House 106 NN 0268
Conan House 128 NH 5353
Cona River 106 NM 9372
Conchra 100 NS 0288
Concraigie 108 NO 1044
Conderton 50 SO 9637
Condicote 47 SP 1528
Condorrat 101 NS 7373
Condover 59 SJ 4906
Coneyhurst 28 TQ 1024
Coneysthorpe 80 SE 7171
Coney Weston 54 TL 9578
Congerstone 60 SK 3605
Congham 64 TF 7123
Conglass Water 117 NJ 1818
Congleton 69 SJ 8562
Congresbury 33 ST 4363
Conicavel 129 NH 9953
Conic Hill 101 NS 4392
Conie Glen 92 NR 6912
Conieglen Water 92 NR 6914
Coningsby 73 TF 2258
Conington (Cambs.) 52 TL 1785
Conington (Cambs.) 53 TL 3266
Conisbrough 71 SK 5098
Conisby 98 NR 2661
Conisholme 73 TF 3995
Coniston (Cumbr.) 82 SD 3097
Coniston (Humbs.) 75 TA 1535
Coniston Cold 78 SD 9054
Conistone 78 SD 9867
Conistone Moor 78 SE 0270
Coniston Water 82 SD 3094
Connah's Quay 68 SJ 2869
Connel 106 NM 9134
Connel Airfield 106 NM 9035
Connel Park 88 NS 6012
Connor Downs 18 SW 5939
Conon Bridge 128 NH 5455
Cononley 78 SD 9846
Conrig Hill 88 NS 8112
Consall 60 SJ 9748
Consett 84 NZ 1150
Constable Burton 84 SE 1690
Constantine 18 SW 7229
Constantine Bay 19 SW 8574
Contin 128 NH 4555
Contlaw 119 NJ 8402
Contrary Head 76 SC 2282
Conwy 67 SH 7777
Conwy Bay 67 SH 7180
Conwy Falls 67 SH 8053
Conwy Sands 67 SH 7679
Conyer 31 TQ 9664
Cookbury 22 SS 4005
Cookham 36 SU 8985
Cookham Dean 36 SU 8785
Cookham Rise 36 SU 8884
Cookhill 50 SP 0558
Cookley (Here. and Worc.) 49 SO 8480
Cookley (Suff.) 55 TM 3475
Cookley Green 36 SU 6990
Cookney 119 NO 8793
Cooksbridge 29 TQ 4013
Cooksmill Green 38 TL 6306
Coolham 28 TQ 1222
Cooling 30 TQ 7575
Coombe (Corn.) 22 SS 2011
Coombe (Corn.) 19 SW 9551
Coombe Abbey (ant.) 50 SP 4080
Coombe Bissett 26 SU 1026
Coombe Hill 46 SO 8827
Coombe Keynes 25 SY 8484
Coombes 28 TQ 1908
Coopersale Common 37 TL 4702
Cooran Lane 87 NX 4782
Copdock 55 TM 1141
Copeland Forest 82 NY 1507
Copford Green 38 TL 9222
Copinsay 137 HY 6101
Copister 143 HU 4878
Cople 52 TL 1048
Copley 84 NZ 0825
Coplow Dale 70 SK 1679
Copmanthorpe 79 SE 5646
Coppathorne 22 SS 2000
Coppay 124 NF 9393
Coppenhall 59 SJ 9019
Coppingford 52 TL 1680
Copplestone 23 SS 7702
Coppull 69 SD 5613
Copsale 28 TQ 1724
Copster Green 77 SD 6734
Copt Heath 50 SP 1778
Copt Hewick 79 SE 3371
Copthorne 29 TQ 3139
Copt Oak 61 SK 4812
Copythorne 26 SU 3014
Coquetdale 91 NZ 0999
Coquet Island 91 NU 2904
Corachie 127 NH 3246
Corb Law 102 NO 0009
Corbridge 90 NY 9964
Corby 52 SP 8988
Corby Glen 62 SK 9925
Corby Loch 119 NJ 9214
Corby Pike 90 NT 8401
Core Hill (Grampn.) 121 NJ 7632
Core Hill (Tays.) 102 NN 8804
Coreley 49 SO 6173
Corfe 24 ST 2319
Corfe Castle 25 SY 9681
Corfe Mullen 26 SY 9798
Corfton 48 SO 4985
Corgarff 117 NJ 2708
Corhampton 27 SU 6120
Corinium (ant.) 46 SP 0201
Corkickle Station 82 NX 9717
Corlan-fraith 57 SH 6300
Corlarach Forest 100 NS 1573
Corley 50 SP 3085
Corley Ash 50 SP 2886
Corley Moor 50 SP 2884
Cornabus 98 NR 3346
Cornal Burn 89 NT 1104
Cornden Hill 68 SO 2096
Cornelly 41 SS 8281
Corney 82 SD 1191

Cornforth 84 NZ 3034
Corngafallt 57 SN 9464
Cornhill 121 NJ 5858
Cornhill-on-Tweed 97 NT 8639
Corn Holm (Copinsay) 137 HY 5901
Cornholme (W Yorks.) 78 SD 9025
Cornish Hall End 54 TL 6836
Cornquoy 137 ND 5299
Cornriggs 83 NY 8441
Cornsay 84 NZ 1443
Corntown 128 NH 5555
Cornwell 47 SP 2727
Cornwood 21 SX 6059
Cornworthy 21 SX 8255
Corpach 115 NN 0976
Corpach Bay 98 NR 5691
Corpusty 65 TG 1129
Corra-bheinn 105 NM 5732
Corran (Highld.) 123 NG 8509
Corran (Highld.) 106 NN 0163
Corran Narrows 106 NN 0163
Corran River 98 NR 5373
Corrany 76 SC 4589
Correen Hills 121 NJ 5222
Correnie Forest 119 NJ 6410
Correnie Moor 119 NJ 6110
Corrie 92 NS 0243
Corrie Common 89 NY 2085
Corriehallie Forest 127 NH 3748
Corriekinloch 132 NC 3625
Corriemoillie 127 NH 3563
Corriemoillie Forest 127 NH 3566
Corriemulzie River 127 NH 3194
Corrievorrie 116 NH 7724
Corrieyairack Forest 116 NN 4497
Corrieyairack Hill 116 NN 4299
Corrieyairack Pass 116 NN 4298
Corrimony 115 NH 3830
Corringham (Essex) 38 TQ 7183
Corringham (Lincs.) 72 SK 8691
Corris Uchaf 57 SH 7408
Corrour Forest 107 NN 4167
Corrour Shooting Lodge 107 NN 4169
Corrour Station 106 NN 3566
Corrow 100 NN 1800
Corry 123 NG 6424
Corryhabbie Hill 117 NJ 2829
Corrymuckloch 108 NN 8934
Corrynachenchy 105 NM 6441
Corry of Ardnagrask 128 NH 5048
Corscombe 25 ST 5105
Corse 121 NJ 6040
Corse Hill (Dumf. and Galwy.) 88 NS 6803
Corse Hill (Strath.) 94 NS 5946
Corse House 119 NJ 5407
Corsehouse Resr. 93 NS 4850
Corse of Kinnoir 121 NJ 5443
Corserine (mt.) 87 NX 4987
Corsewall Point 86 NW 9872
Cors-goch Glan Teifi 57 SN 6863
Corsham 33 ST 8669
Corsindae 119 NJ 6808
Corsley 33 ST 8246
Corsley Heath 33 ST 8245
Corsock 88 NX 7576
Corston (Avon) 33 ST 6965
Corston (Wilts.) 33 ST 9284
Corstopitum (ant.) 91 NY 9864
Corstorphine 103 NT 1972
Cortachy 109 NO 3959
Cortes House 121 NJ 9959
Corton (Suff.) 65 TM 5497
Corton (Wilts.) 34 ST 9340
Corton Denham 25 ST 6322
Coruanan Lodge 106 NN 0668
Corve Dale 48 SO 5488
Corwar House 86 NX 2780
Corwen 67 SJ 0743
Coryton (Devon) 20 SX 4583
Coryton (Essex) 38 TQ 7482
Cosby 61 SP 5495
Coseley 59 SO 9494
Cosford Station 59 SJ 7905
Cosgrove 51 SP 7942
Cosham 27 SU 6605
Cosheston 42 SN 0003
Cossall 61 SK 4842
Cosses 86 NX 1182
Cossington (Leic.) 61 SK 6013
Cossington (Somer.) 32 ST 3540
Costa 136 HY 3328
Costa Beck 80 SE 7682
Costa Head 138 HY 3130
Costessey 65 TG 1712
Costock 61 SK 5726
Coston 62 SK 8422
Cotebrook 69 SJ 5765
Cotehele House (ant.) 20 SX 4268
Cotehill 83 NY 4750
Cotes (Cumbr.) 77 SD 4886
Cotes (Leic.) 61 SK 5620
Cotes (Staffs.) 59 SJ 8434
Cotesbach 51 SP 5382
Cotgrave 61 SK 6435
Cothall 119 NJ 8716
Cotham 61 SK 7947
Cothelstone 24 ST 1831
Cotherstone 84 NZ 0119
Cotherstone Moor 84 NY 9316
Cothill 47 SU 4699
Cotleigh 24 ST 2002
Coton (Cambs.) 53 TL 4158
Coton (Northants.) 51 SP 6771
Coton (Staffs.) 60 SJ 9832
Coton Clanford 59 SJ 8723
Coton in the Elms 60 SK 2415
Cotswold Hills 46 SO 9302
Cott 21 SX 7861
Cottam (Lancs.) 77 SD 4932
Cottam (Notts.) 72 SK 8179
Cottartown 117 NJ 0331
Cottenham 53 TL 4567
Cotterdale 83 SD 8393
Cottered 53 TL 3129
Cotterstock 52 TL 0490
Cottesbrooke 51 SP 7073
Cottesmore 62 SK 9013
Cottingham (Humbs.) 74 TA 0532
Cottingham (Northants.) 52 SP 8490
Cottisford 47 SP 5831
Cotton 54 TM 0667
Cotton End 52 TL 0845
Cot-town (Grampn.) 121 NJ 5026
Cottown (Grampn.) 119 NJ 7715
Cot-town (Grampn.) 121 NJ 8140
Cotwalton 59 SJ 9234
Coughton 50 SP 0760
Coul 98 NR 2064
Coulags 126 NG 9645
Coulin Forest 126 NG 9954
Coulin Lodge 126 NH 0056
Coull 118 NJ 5102
Coul Point 98 NR 1864
Coulport 100 NS 2087
Coulsdon 37 TQ 3059
Coulter 95 NT 0233
Coulton 79 SE 6374
Cound 59 SJ 5504
Cound Brook 59 SJ 5206
Coundon 84 NZ 2329
Coundon Grange 84 NZ 2327
Countam (Dumf. and Galwy.) (mt.) 88 NS 7101
Countam (Dumf. and Galwy.) (mt.) 88 NX 7698
Countersett 78 SD 9287
Countess Wear 21 SX 9489
Countesthorpe 61 SP 5895
Countisbury 23 SS 7449
Coupar Angus 108 NO 2139
Coupland 97 NT 9331
Cour 92 NR 8248
Cour Bay 92 NR 8248
Courteachan 111 NM 6897
Courteenhall 51 SP 7653
Cour, The 115 NN 2276
Court Henry 43 SN 5522
Courtsend 39 TR 0293
Courtway 24 ST 2033
Cousland 103 NT 3768
Cousley Wood 29 TQ 6533
Cove (Devon) 23 SS 9519
Cove (Hants.) 35 SU 8555
Cove (Highld.) 126 NG 8090
Cove (Strath.) 100 NS 2281
Cove Bay (Grampn.) 119 NJ 9500
Cove Bay (Strath.) 100 NS 2182
Covehithe 55 TM 5281
Coven 59 SJ 9006
Coveney 53 TL 4882
Covenham Resr. 73 TF 3496
Covenham St. Bartholomew 73 TF 3395
Covenham St. Mary 73 TF 3394
Coventry 50 SP 3379
Coventry Airport 50 SP 3574
Coventry Canal (Warw.) 60 SP 3196
Coventry Canal (Warw.) 50 SP 3786
Cove Point 92 NR 7107
Coverack 19 SW 7818
Coverdale 78 SE 0682
Coverham 78 SE 1086
Cover Head Bents 78 SD 9978
Covesea Skerries 120 NJ 1971
Covington 52 TL 0570
Cowan Bridge 77 SD 6476
Cowbeech 29 TQ 6114
Cowbit 63 TF 2618
Cowbridge 41 SS 9974
Cowden 29 TQ 4640
Cowdenbeath 102 NT 1691
Cowdenburn 95 NT 2052
Cowden Station 29 TQ 4741
Cowes 27 SZ 4995
Cowesby 85 SE 4689
Cowes Roads 27 SZ 4997
Cowfold 28 TQ 2122
Cowgask Burn 108 NN 9419
Cow Green Resr. 83 NY 7930
Cowick 79 SE 6521
Cowie 101 NS 8389
Cowie Water 119 NO 7687
Cowley (Devon) 21 SX 9095
Cowley (Glos.) 46 SO 9614
Cowley (Gtr London) 36 TQ 0582
Cowley (Oxon.) 47 SP 5404
Cowling (N Yorks.) 78 SD 9743
Cowling (N Yorks.) 79 SE 2387
Cowlinge 54 TL 7154
Cowm Resr. 69 SD 8819
Cowpen Bewley 85 NZ 4824
Cowplain 27 SU 7011
Cow Ridge 85 SE 5496
Cowshill 83 NY 8540
Cowstrandburn 102 NT 0390
Coxbank 59 SJ 6541
Coxbench 60 SK 3743
Cox Common 55 TM 4082
Coxheath 29 TQ 7451
Coxhoe 84 NZ 3235
Coxley 33 ST 5343
Coxwold 79 SE 5377
Coychurch 41 SS 9379
Coyles of Muick, The (mt.) 118 NO 3291
Coylton 93 NS 4119
Coylumbridge 117 NH 9110
Coynach 118 NJ 4405
Coynachie 121 NJ 4934
Craach Mhòr 100 NN 0514
Crabadon 21 SX 7555
Crabbs Cross 50 SP 0464
Crab Rocks 81 TA 1974
Crabtree 28 TQ 2225
Crabtree Green 58 SJ 3344
Crackenthorpe 83 NY 6622
Crackington Haven 20 SX 1496
Crackleybank 59 SJ 7611
Crackpot 84 SD 9796
Cracoe 78 SD 9760
Cradley 49 SO 7347
Crafthole 20 SX 3654
Cragabus 98 NR 3345
Cragdale Moor 78 SD 9202
Cragg 78 SE 0023
Craggan (Grampn.) 117 NJ 0226
Craggan (Strath.) 100 NS 2699
Craggie 134 NC 8719
Craggie Water 134 NC 8819
Craghead 84 NZ 2150
Crag Hill 77 SD 7083
Crag Lough 90 NY 7667
Crai 41 SN 8924
Craibstone (Grampn.) 121 NJ 4959
Craibstone (Grampn.) 119 NJ 8611
Craichie 109 NO 5047
Craig (Dumf. and Galwy.) 88 NX 6875
Craig (Highld.) 126 NH 0349
Craigairie Fell 86 NX 2373
Craiganour Forest 107 NN 6064
Craiganour Lodge 107 NN 6159
Craig Castle 121 NJ 4724
Craigcefnparc 40 SN 6703
Craigdallie 108 NO 2428
Craigdam 121 NJ 8430
Craigdarroch 88 NS 6306
Craig Ddrwg 67 SH 6532
Craigearn 119 NJ 7214
Craigellachie (Grampn.) 120 NJ 2844
Craigellachie (Highld.) 117 NH 8811
Craigend 108 NO 1120
Craigendoran 100 NS 3181
Craigendunton Resr. 93 NS 5245
Craigenlee Fell 86 NX 0157
Craigens 98 NR 2967
Craig Fell 86 NX 1761
Craiggiecat 119 NO 8592
Craig Goch Resr. 57 SN 8969
Craig Gyfynys 67 SH 6838
Craighall 108 NO 1748
Craighat 101 NS 4984
Craig Hill 107 NN 8045
Craighoar Hill 88 NT 0002
Craighouse 98 NR 5267
Craigie (Grampn.) 119 NJ 9119
Craigie (Strath.) 93 NS 4232
Craigie (Tays.) 108 NO 1143
Craigievar Castle (ant.) 119 NJ 5609
Craiglee 87 NX 4796
Craigleith (is.) 103 NT 5586
Craiglich 119 NJ 5305
Craiglockhart 103 NT 2270
Craig Lodge 100 NS 0077
Craiglowrie 87 NX 5467
Craigluscar Hill 102 NT 0690
Craigmahandle 118 NO 4891
Craigmaid 89 NT 0717
Craigmaud 121 NJ 8858
Craigmillar 103 NT 2871
Craig nan Caisean 107 NN 7760
Craignane 88 NS 5804
Craignant 58 SJ 2535
Craignarget Hill 86 NX 2652
Craignelder 87 NX 5070
Craigneuk (Strath.) 94 NS 7656
Craigneuk (Strath.) 101 NS 7764
Craignish Castle 99 NM 7701
Craignish Point 99 NR 7599
Craignure 105 NM 7236
Craignure Bay 105 NM 7137
Craigo 109 NO 6864
Craig of Bunzeach 118 NJ 3609
Craig of Dalfro 119 NO 6789
Craigow 102 NO 0806
Craig Rhiwarth 57 SJ 0527
Craig River 123 NG 7864
Craig Rossie 108 NN 9812
Craig Rostan 100 NN 3404
Craigrothie 103 NO 3710
Craigruie 107 NN 5020
Craigston Castle 121 NJ 7655
Craigton (Grampn.) 119 NJ 8301
Craigton (Highld.) 128 NH 6296
Craigton (Tays.) 108 NO 3250
Craigton (Tays.) 109 NO 5138
Craigtown 134 NC 8856
Craig Twrch 43 SN 6649
Craig Veann 117 NJ 1011
Craigvinean Forest 108 NN 9745
Craig-y-cae 57 SH 7022
Craig y Llyn 41 SN 9103
Craig-y-nos 41 SN 8315
Craig yr Hyrddod 67 SH 8237
Craik 89 NT 3408
Craik Cross Hill 89 NT 3004
Craik Forest 89 NT 3309
Craik Moor 90 NT 8118
Crail 103 NO 6107
Crailing 96 NT 6824
Crailinghall 96 NT 6921
Crailzie Hill 95 NT 1945
Crakehall 84 SE 2490
Cramalt 95 NT 1922
Crambe 80 SE 7364
Cramlington 91 NZ 2776
Crammag Head 86 NX 0834
Cramond 102 NT 1876
Cramond Bridge 102 NT 1775
Cramond Island 103 NT 1978
Cranage 69 SJ 7568
Cranberry 59 SJ 8236
Cranborne 26 SU 0513
Cranborne Chase 26 ST 9417
Cranbourne 36 SU 9272
Cranbrook 30 TQ 7735
Cranbrook Common 30 TQ 7938
Crane Islands 18 SW 6344
Cranfield 52 SP 9542
Cranfield Airfield 52 SP 9543
Cranford 37 TQ 1077
Cranford St. Andrew 52 SP 9277
Cranford St. John 52 SP 9276
Cranham (Essex) 37 TQ 5787
Cranham (Glos.) 46 SO 8912
Crank 69 SJ 5099
Cranleigh 28 TQ 0638
Cranmore (I. of W.) 26 SZ 3990
Cranmore (Somer.) 33 ST 6843
Cranna 121 NJ 6352
Crannach 121 NJ 4954
Cranoe 61 SP 7695
Cransford 55 TM 3164
Cranshaws 96 NT 6961
Cranshaws Hill 103 NT 6781
Cranstackie (mt.) 132 NC 3555
Cranstal 76 NX 4602
Crantock 19 SW 7860
Cranwell 62 TF 0349
Cranwich 64 TL 7795
Cranworth 64 TF 9804
Crapstone 20 SX 5067
Crarae 100 NR 9897
Craro Island 92 NR 6247
Crask Inn 133 NC 5224
Craskins 118 NJ 5105
Crask of Aigas 128 NH 4642
Craster 91 NU 2519
Cratfield 55 TM 3175
Crathes 119 NO 7596
Crathes Castle (ant.) 119 NO 7396
Crathie (Grampn.) 117 NO 2695
Crathie (Highld.) 116 NN 5893
Crathorne 85 NZ 4407
Craufurdland Castle (ant.) 93 NS 4540
Craven Arms 48 SO 4382
Crawcrook 91 NZ 1363
Crawford 88 NS 9520
Crawfordjohn 95 NS 8823
Crawick 88 NS 7710
Crawick Water 88 NS 8014
Crawley (Hants.) 26 SU 4234
Crawley (Oxon.) 47 SP 3312
Crawley (W Susx) 28 TQ 2636
Crawley Down 29 TQ 3237
Crawleyside 84 NY 9940
Crawshawbooth 78 SD 8125
Crawton 119 NO 8779
Crawton Bay 119 NO 8779
Cray (N Yorks.) 78 SD 9479
Crayford 37 TQ 5175
Crayke 79 SE 5670
Crays Hill 38 TQ 7192
Cray's Pond 36 SU 6380
Creachan Mòr 100 NS 1891
Creach Beinn (Island of Mull) 105 NM 6427
Creach Bheinn (Highld.) 111 NM 8757
Creach Bheinn (Island of Mull) 105 NM 4228
Creach Bheinn (Strath.) 106 NN 0242
Creach Bheinn Lodge 105 NM 6425
Creacombe 23 SS 8119
Creag a' Chaorainn 126 NH 0043
Creag a' Chlachain 116 NH 6533
Creag a'Lain 123 NG 4658
Creagan 106 NM 9744
Creagan a' Chaise 117 NJ 1024
Creagan an Eich 100 NN 1003
Creag an Doil Bheag 117 NO 1598
Creag an Eunan 118 NJ 3819
Creagan Glas 128 NC 6701
Creag an Lòin 116 NH 6901
Creagan Mòr 116 NN 6180
Creagantairbh Mòr 99 NM 8401
Creag an t-Sithein 108 NO 0365
Creag a' Phuill 100 NN 1005
Creag Beinn nan Eun 107 NN 7213
Creag Bhalg 117 NO 0991
Creag Bhàn (Highld.) 111 NM 7884
Creag Bhàn (Strath.) 92 NR 6450
Creag Dhubh (Highld.) 115 NN 3282
Creag Dhubh (Highld.) 116 NN 6897
Creag Dhubh (Tays.) 108 NO 0261
Creag Fhraoch 131 NB 5142
Creag Gharbh 107 NN 6332
Creag Island 105 NM 8337
Creag Leacach 117 NO 1574
Creag Liath (Highld.) 129 NH 7295
Creag Liath (Highld.) 117 NJ 0031
Creag Loch nan Dearcag 127 NH 3356
Creag Loisgte 127 NH 3695
Creag Meagaidh 116 NN 4187
Creag Mholach 100 NS 0993
Creag Mhòr (Central) 107 NN 5134
Creag Mhòr (Highld.) 133 NC 6924
Creag Mhòr (Highld.) 116 NN 4997
Creag Mhòr (Isle of Lewis) 131 NB 1741
Creag Mhòr (Strath.) 105 NM 8202
Creag Mhòr (Strath.) 100 NR 9273
Creag Mhòr (Tays.) 107 NN 3936
Creag na h-Iolaire (Highld.) 133 NC 6728
Creag na h-Iolaire (Highld.) 127 NH 1398
Creag na h-Iolaire (Highld.) 127 NH 1749
Creag nam Bodach 116 NN 7596
Creag nam Fiadh 134 NC 8323
Creag nam Mial 108 NO 0554
Creag-nan-Eun Forest 116 NH 4519
Creag nan Gabhar 117 NO 1584
Creag nan Gall 117 NO 2691
Creagorry 124 NF 7948
Creag Riabhach 132 NC 2763
Creag Riabhach na Greighe 133 NC 6120
Creag Scalabsdale 134 NC 9624
Creaguaineach Lodge 106 NN 3069
Creag Uchdag 107 NN 7032
Creaton 51 SP 7071
Creca 89 NY 2270
Credenhill 45 SO 4543
Crediton 21 SS 8300
Creech St. Michael 24 ST 2725
Creed 19 SW 9347
Creedy Park 23 SS 0301
Creekmouth 37 TQ 4581
Creeting St. Mary 55 TM 0956
Creeton 62 TF 0120
Creetown 87 NX 4758
Creggans 100 NN 0802
Cregneish 76 SC 1967
Cregrina 44 SO 1252
Creich (Fife) 108 NO 3221
Creich (Island of Mull) 104 NM 3124
Creigh Hill 108 NO 2759
Creigiau 41 ST 0881
Cressage 59 SJ 5904
Cresselly 42 SN 0606
Cressing 38 TL 7920
Cresswell (Dyfed) 42 SN 0506
Cresswell (Northum.) 91 NZ 2993
Cresswell (Staffs.) 60 SJ 9739
Creswell 71 SK 5274
Cretingham 55 TM 2260
Cretshengan 99 NR 7167
Creuch Hill 100 NS 2668
Crewe (Ches.) 59 SJ 4253
Crewe (Ches.) 59 SJ 7055
Crewe Hall 59 SJ 7353
Crew Green 58 SJ 3215
Crewkerne 25 ST 4409
Crews Hill 37 TL 3000
Crianlarich 107 NN 3825
Cribba Head 18 SW 4022
Cribbie (pt.) 140 HU 1562
Cribin Fawr 57 SH 8014
Crib Law 96 NT 5259
Cribyn 43 SN 5251
Criccieth 66 SH 4938
Crich 60 SK 3554
Crichie 121 NJ 9544
Crichton 103 NT 3862
Crick (Gwent) 33 ST 4890
Crick (Northants.) 51 SP 5872
Crickadarn 44 SO 0942
Cricket St. Thomas 24 ST 3708
Crickheath 58 SJ 2923
Crickhowell 41 SO 2118
Cricklade 46 SU 0993
Cridling Stubbs 79 SE 5221
Crieff 108 NN 8621
Criffel 88 NX 9561
Crigdon Hill 90 NT 8604
Criggion 58 SJ 2915
Crigglestone 71 SE 3116
Crimond 121 NK 0556
Crimonmogate 121 NK 0458
Crimplesham 64 TF 6503
Crim Rocks 18 SV 8009
Crinaglack 116 NH 4240
Crinan 99 NR 7894
Crinan Canal 99 NR 8391
Cringate Law 101 NS 6888
Cringleford 65 TG 1905
Crinow 42 SN 1214
Crionaig (mt.) 125 NB 2906
Cripplesease 18 SW 5036
Cripp's Corner 30 TQ 7821
Croachy 116 NH 6527
Croasdale Fell 77 SD 6857
Crockenhill 37 TQ 5067
Crockernwell 21 SX 7592
Crockerton 33 ST 8642
Crocketford or Ninemile Bar 88 NX 8272
Crockey Hill 79 SE 6246
Crockham Hill 29 TQ 4450
Crockleford Heath 54 TM 0426
Crockness 136 ND 3192
Croeserw 41 SS 8695
Croesgoch 42 SM 8330
Croesor 67 SH 6344
Croesyceiliog (Gwent) 45 ST 3196
Croesyceiliog 43 SN 4016
Croes-y-mwyalch 32 ST 3092
Croft (Ches.) 69 SJ 6393
Croft (Leic.) 61 SP 5195
Croft (Lincs.) 73 TF 5162
Croft Ambrey (ant.) 48 SO 4466
Croftamie 101 NS 4786
Croftgarbh 107 NN 7246
Croft Head 89 NT 1505
Croft Marsh 73 TF 5460
Crofton 71 SE 3717
Croft-on-Tees 84 NZ 2909
Crofts of Benachielt 135 ND 1838
Crofts of Blackburn 121 NJ 5334
Crofts of Haddo 121 NJ 8337
Crofts of Inverthernie 121 NJ 7343
Crofts of Meikle Ardo 121 NJ 8541
Crofts of Savoch 121 NK 0459
Crofts of Shanquhar 121 NJ 5435
Crofty 40 SS 5295
Crogary Mòr (mt.) 124 NF 8673
Crogary na Hoe 124 NF 9772
Crogen 67 SJ 0036
Croggan 105 NM 7027
Croglin 83 NY 5747
Croglin Water 83 NY 5646
Cròic-bheinn 123 NG 7652
Croick 128 NH 4591
Croir 131 NB 1539
Croit Bheinn 111 NM 8177
Cròm Allt 116 NH 5404
Crom Allt (Highld.) 127 NC 2506
Cromalt Hills 127 NC 2205
Cromar (dist.) 118 NJ 4703
Cromarty 129 NH 7867
Cromarty Bay 129 NH 7466
Cromarty Firth 128 NH 6667
Cromblet 121 NJ 7734
Cromdale 117 NJ 0728
Cromer (Herts.) 53 TL 2928
Cromer (Norf.) 65 TG 2142
Cromer Point 81 TA 0392
Cromford 60 SK 2956
Cromhall 33 ST 6990
Cromhall Common 33 ST 6989
Cromlet (mt.) 101 NN 7811
Crom Loch 127 NH 3982
Cromore 131 NB 4021
Cromra 116 NN 5489
Cromwell 72 SK 7961
Cronberry 94 NS 6022
Crondall 35 SU 7948
Cronkley Fell 83 NY 8427
Cronk Sumark (ant.) 76 SC 3893
Cronk, The 76 SC 3495
Cronk-y-Voddy 76 SC 3086
Cronton 69 SJ 4988
Crook (Cumbr.) 83 SD 4694
Crook (Durham) 84 NZ 1635
Crookedshaws Hill 97 NT 8024
Crookfoot Resr. 85 NZ 4331
Crookham (Berks.) 35 SU 5364
Crookham (Northum.) 97 NT 9138
Crookham Village 35 SU 7952
Crookhouse 96 NT 7626
Crook Inn 95 NT 1026
Crooklands 77 SD 5383
Crook of Devon 102 NO 0301
Croome Court 49 SO 8844
Cropredy 51 SP 4646
Cropston 61 SK 5511
Cropston Resr. 61 SK 5410
Cropthorne 50 SO 9944
Cropton 80 SE 7589
Cropwell Bishop 61 SK 6835
Cropwell Butler 61 SK 6837
Crosbie 93 NS 2150
Crosby (Cumbr.) 82 NY 0738
Crosby (I. of M.) 76 SC 3279
Crosby (Lincs.) 74 SE 8711
Crosby (Mers.) 68 SJ 3099
Crosby Channel 68 SJ 2799
Crosby Court 85 SE 3992
Crosby Garrett 83 NY 7309
Crosby Ravensworth 83 NY 6214
Crosby Ravensworth Fell 83 NY 6010
Croscombe 33 ST 5844
Cross (Isle of Lewis) 131 NB 5061
Cross (Somerset) 32 ST 4154
Crossaig 92 NR 8351
Crossaig Glen 92 NR 8152
Crossapol 104 NL 9943
Crossapol Bay 110 NM 1352
Cross Ash 45 SO 4019
Crossbost 131 NB 3924
Crosscanonby 82 NY 0739
Crossdale Street 65 TG 2239
Crossdougal 112 NF 7520
Cross Drain 62 TF 1514
Crossens 68 SD 3719
Cross Fell 83 NY 6834
Crossford (Fife) 102 NT 0686
Crossford (Strath.) 95 NS 8246
Crossgates (Fife) 102 NT 1488
Crossgates (Powys) 57 SO 0865
Crossgill 77 SD 5562
Cross Green (Devon) 20 SX 3888
Cross Green (Suff.) 54 TL 9952
Cross Hands 43 SN 5612
Cross Hill (Borders) 89 NT 2507
Crosshill (Fife) 102 NT 1796
Crosshill (Strath.) 93 NS 3206
Crosshouse (Strath.) 93 NS 3938
Cross Houses (Shrops.) 59 SJ 5307
Crossings 90 NY 5177
Cross in Hand 29 TQ 5621
Cross Inn (Dyfed) 43 SN 3957
Cross Inn (Dyfed) 56 SN 5464
Cross Inn (Mid Glam.) 41 ST 0582
Crosskeys (Gwent) 41 ST 2292
Crosskeys (Strath.) 100 NS 3385
Crosskirk 135 ND 0370
Cross Lanes (Clwyd) 58 SJ 3746
Crosslanes (N Yorks.) 79 SE 5264
Crosslanes (Shrops.) 58 SJ 3218
Cross Law 97 NT 8767
Crosslee 89 NT 3018
Crossmichael 88 NX 7267
Crossmoor 77 SD 4438
Cross of Jackston 121 NJ 7432
Crossraguel Abbey (ant.) 93 NS 2708
Crossroads 119 NO 7594
Cross Sands 131 NB 4962
Cross Water of Luce 86 NX 1867
Crossway 45 SO 4419
Crossway Green 49 SO 8368
Crosswell 42 SN 1236
Crosswood Resr. 95 NT 0557
Crosthwaite 83 SD 4491
Croston 69 SD 4818
Crostwick 65 TG 2515
Crostwight 65 TG 3329
Crouch Hill 25 ST 7010
Croughton 47 SP 5433
Crovie 121 NJ 8065
Crowan 18 SW 6434
Crowborough 29 TQ 5130
Crowcombe 24 ST 1336
Crowdecote 70 SK 1065
Crowdundle Beck 83 NY 6631
Crowdy Reservoir 20 SX 1483
Crowfield (Northants.) 51 SP 6141
Crowfield (Suff.) 55 TM 1557
Crow Hill 45 SO 6326
Crowhurst (E Susx) 29 TQ 7512
Crowhurst (Surrey) 29 TQ 3947
Crowland 63 TF 2310
Crowlas 18 SW 5133
Crowle (Here. and Worc.) 49 SO 9256
Crowle (Humbs.) 74 SE 7713
Crowlin Islands 123 NG 6934
Crowlista 130 NB 0433
Crowmarsh Gifford 36 SU 6189
Crownhill 20 SX 4857
Crownthorpe 65 TG 0803
Crow Rock 42 SR 8894
Crow Sound 18 SV 9312
Crowthorne 36 SU 8464
Crowthorn School 69 SD 7418
Crowton 69 SJ 5774
Croxall 60 SK 1913
Croxdale 84 NZ 2636
Croxden 60 SK 0639
Croxley Green 36 TQ 0795
Croxton (Cambs.) 53 TL 2459
Croxton (Humbs.) 75 TA 0912
Croxton (Norf.) 54 TL 8786
Croxton (Staffs.) 59 SJ 7832
Croxton Kerrial 62 SK 8329
Croxton Park 62 SK 8227
Croy (Highld.) 129 NH 7949
Croy (Strath.) 101 NS 7275
Croyde 22 SS 4439
Croyde Bay 22 SS 4239
Croydon (Cambs.) 53 TL 3149
Croydon (Gtr London) 37 TQ 3365
Croydon Hill 23 SS 9739
Cruach a'Bhuie 100 NS 1693
Cruachan 100 NN 3507
Cruachan Beinn a'Chearcaill 122 NG 3546
Cruachan Druim na Croise 111 NM 4549
Cruach an Eachlaich 105 NM 8606
Cruach an Locha 99 NR 7865
Cruach an Lochain 100 NS 0493

Cruachan Min 105 NM 4421
Cruachan Odhar 104 NM 3846
Cruachan Reservoir 106 NN 0828
Cruach an Tailleir 99 NR 7469
Cruach an Uillt Fheàrna 99 NR 6290
Cruach a'Phubuill 99 NR 8270
Cruach Brenfield 99 NR 8283
Cruach Chuilceachan 100 NR 9887
Cruach Ionnastail 99 NR 6491
Cruach Lagain 99 NR 7466
Cruach Lusach 99 NR 7883
Cruach Maolachy 100 NM 8914
Cruach Mhic Fhionnlaidh 100 NM 9402
Cruach Mhic-Gougain 92 NR 7550
Cruach Mhòr 100 NN 0514
Cruach nam Fiadh (Strath.) 99 NR 8085
Cruach nam Fiadh (Strath.) 92 NR 8256
Cruach nan Caorach 100 NR 9980
Cruach nan Capull (Strath.) 100 NN 1405
Cruach nan Capull (Strath.) 100 NS 0797
Cruach nan Capull (Strath.) 100 NS 0979
Cruach nan Cuilean 100 NS 0484
Cruach nan Gabhar 92 NR 7542
Cruach nan Tarbh 100 NR 9782
Cruach na Seilcheig 99 NR 6898
Cruach Rarey 105 NM 8116
Cruach Scarba 105 NM 6904
Cruach Tairbeirt 100 NN 3105
Crùban Beag 116 NN 6692
Crubenmore Lodge 116 NN 6791
Cruckmeole 58 SJ 4309
Cruckton 58 SJ 4210
Crucymel (ant.) 41 SO 2220
Cruden Bay 121 NK 0936
Crudgington 59 SJ 6317
Crudwell 34 ST 9592
Crûg 48 SO 1872
Crugmeer 19 SW 9076
Cruib (mt.) 91 NR 5684
Cruick Water 109 NO 5462
Cruinn a'Bheinn 101 NN 3605
Cruinn Bheinn 101 NN 4312
Cruivie Castle (ant.) 109 NO 4122
Crulivig 131 NB 1733
Crumlin 41 ST 2198
Crummock Water 82 NY 1519
Crumpton Hill 89 NY 3491
Crundale (Dyfed) 42 SM 9718
Crundale (Kent) 31 TR 0749
Crunwear 43 SN 1810
Cruwys Morchard 23 SS 8712
Crux Easton 34 SU 4256
Cruys (mt.) 118 NO 4275
Crwbin 43 SN 4713
Crychan Forest 44 SN 8540
Crymmych 43 SN 1833
Crynant 41 SN 7905
Crystal Palace 37 TQ 3470
Cuaig 123 NG 7057
Cubbington 50 SP 3368
Cubert 19 SW 7857
Cublington 36 SP 8422
Cuckfield 29 TQ 3024
Cucklington 25 ST 7527
Cuckmere River 29 TQ 5408
Cuckney 71 SK 5671
Cudden Point 18 SW 5427
Cuddesdon 47 SP 5902
Cuddington (Bucks.) 36 SP 7311
Cuddington (Ches.) 69 SJ 5971
Cuddington Heath 58 SJ 4646
Cuddy Hill 77 SD 4937
Cudham 37 TQ 4459
Cudliptown 21 SX 5278
Cudworth (Somer.) 24 ST 3810
Cudworth (S Yorks.) 71 SE 3808
Cuffley 37 TL 3002
Cuiashader 131 NB 5458
Cuilags (mt.) 136 HY 2003
Cuil Bay 106 NM 9755
Cuillin Hills 123 NG 4422
Culachy Forest 115 NN 3999
Culardoch (mt.) 117 NO 1998
Cùl Beag (mt.) 127 NC 1408
Culbin Forest 129 NH 9862
Culblean Hill 118 NJ 3901
Culbo 128 NH 6360
Culbokie 128 NH 6059
Culbone Hill 23 SS 8247
Culburnie 128 NH 4941
Culcabock 128 NH 6844
Culcharry 129 NH 8650
Cùl Doirlinn 111 NM 6672
Culdrain 121 NJ 5133
Culduie 123 NG 7140
Culford 54 TL 8370
Culgaith 83 NY 6129
Culham 47 SU 5095
Culkein 132 NC 0333
Culkerton 46 ST 9296
Cullachie 117 NH 9720
Cullaloe Resr. 102 NT 1887
Cullen 121 NJ 5166
Cullen Bay 121 NJ 5068
Cullercoats 91 NZ 3571
Cullerlie 119 NJ 7603
Cullicudden 128 NH 6564
Culligran Falls 115 NH 3640
Cullingworth 78 SE 0636
Cullipool 105 NM 7313
Cullisse 129 NH 8275
Cullivoe 143 HP 5402
Culloch 107 NN 7818
Culloden Forest 129 NH 7647
Culloden Muir 129 NH 7345
Cullompton 24 ST 0207
Culmaily 129 NH 8099
Culmark Hill 88 NX 6489
Culmington 48 SO 4982
Cul Mòr (mt.) 132 NC 1611
Culmstock 24 ST 1013
Culm Valley 24 ST 1013
Culnacraig 127 NC 0603
Culrain 128 NH 5794
Culross 102 NS 9885
Culroy 93 NS 3114
Culsh (Grampn.) 121 NJ 8848
Culsh (Grampn.) 118 NO 3497
Culswick 140 HU 2745
Culter Cleuch Shank (mt.) 95 NT 0422
Cultercullen 121 NJ 9124
Culter Fell 95 NT 0529
Culter Water 95 NT 0329
Culter Waterhead Resr. 95 NT 0427
Cult Hill 102 NT 0295
Cults (Grampn.) 121 NJ 5331
Cults (Grampn.) 119 NJ 8903
Culver Cliff 27 SZ 6385
Culverstone Green 30 TQ 6363
Culverthorpe 62 TF 0240
Culworth 51 SP 5447
Culzean Bay 93 NS 2311
Culzean Castle 93 NS 2310
Culzie Lodge 128 NH 5171
Cumb 143 HU 5292
Cumbernauld 101 NS 7676
Cumberworth 73 TF 5073
Cumbrian Mountains 82 NY 2716
Cuminestown 121 NJ 8050
Cummersdale 83 NY 3952
Cummertrees 89 NY 1366
Cummingstown 129 NJ 1368
Cumnock 88 NS 5619
Cumnor 47 SP 4604
Cumrew 83 NY 5450
Cumrew 83 NY 5550
Cumwhinton 83 NY 4552
Cumwhitton 83 NY 5052
Cundall (N Yorks.) 79 SE 4272
Cunndal (Isle of Lewis) 131 NB 5065
Cunnigill Hill 141 HU 4367
Cunninghame (dist.) 93 NS 4047
Cunninghamhead 93 NS 3741
Cunningsburgh (dist.) 141 HU 4130
Cunnister 143 HU 5296
Cupar 103 NO 3714
Cupar Muir 103 NO 3613
Curbar 71 SK 2574
Curbridge (Hants.) 27 SU 5211
Curbridge (Oxon.) 47 SP 3208
Curdridge 27 SU 5313
Curdworth 50 SP 1892
Curland 24 ST 2716
Curragh's, The 76 SC 3694
Currarie 86 NX 1690
Currarie Port 86 NX 0577
Currie 102 NT 1867
Curr, The (mt.) 97 NT 8523
Curry Mallet 24 ST 3221
Curry Rivel 24 ST 3824
Curtisden Green 29 TQ 7440
Curtisknowle 21 SX 7353
Cury 18 SW 6721
Cushat Law 90 NT 9213
Cushnie 121 NJ 7962
Cushuish 24 ST 1930
Cusop 45 SO 2341
Cut Hill 21 SX 5982
Cutiau 57 SH 6317
Cutnall Green 49 SO 8768
Cutsdean 46 SP 0830
Cutthorpe 71 SK 3473
Cutts 141 HU 4038
Cuxham 36 SU 6695
Cuxton 30 TQ 7166
Cuxwold 75 TA 1701
Cwm (Clwyd) 67 SJ 0677
Cwm (Gwent) 41 SO 1805
Cwm (W Glam.) 40 SS 6895
Cwmafan 41 SS 7892
Cwmaman 41 SS 9999
Cwmbach (Dyfed) 43 SN 2525
Cwmbach (Mid Glam.) 41 SO 0201
Cwmbelan 57 SN 9481
Cwmbran 45 ST 2894
Cwmcarn 41 ST 2293
Cwmcarvan 45 SO 4707
Cwm Ceulan 57 SN 6890
Cwm-Cewydd 57 SH 8713
Cwmcoy 43 SN 2941
Cwm Croes 57 SH 8825
Cwm Cynllwyd 57 SH 8827
Cwmdare 41 SN 9803
Cwmdu (Dyfed) 43 SN 6330
Cwmdu (Powys) 41 SO 1823
Cwmduad 43 SN 3731
Cwm Einion 57 SN 6994
Cwmfelin Boeth 43 SN 1919
Cwmfelinfach 41 ST 1891
Cwmfelin Mynach 43 SN 2324
Cwmffrwd 43 SN 4217
Cwmgwrach 41 SN 8605
Cwm Irfon 44 SN 8549
Cwmisfael 43 SN 4915
Cwm-Llinau 57 SH 8407
Cwmllynfell 41 SN 7413
Cwm Owen 44 SO 0144
Cwmparc 41 SS 9496
Cwmpengraig 43 SN 3436
Cwm Prysor 67 SH 7536
Cwmsychpant 43 SN 4746
Cwmtillery 41 SO 2106
Cwmtudu 43 SN 3557
Cwm-y-glo 66 SH 5562
Cwmyoy 45 SO 2923
Cwmystwyth 57 SN 7873
Cwrt-newydd 43 SN 4847
Cwrt-y-gollen 45 SO 2317
Cyffylliog 67 SJ 0557
Cymer Abbey (ant.) 57 SH 7219
Cymmer (Mid Glam.) 41 ST 0290
Cymmer (W Glam.) 41 SS 8696
Cymyran Bay 66 SH 2974
Cynfall Falls 67 SH 7041
Cynghordy 44 SN 8139
Cynwyd 67 SJ 0541
Cynwyl Elfed 43 SN 3727
Cyrn-y-Brain (mt.) 58 SJ 2149

D

Daaey 143 HU 6094
Dacre (Cumbr.) 83 NY 4526
Dacre (N Yorks.) 78 SE 1960
Dacre Banks 78 SE 1961
Daddry Shield 84 NY 8937
Dadford 51 SP 6638
Dadlington 60 SP 4098
Daer Resr. 88 NS 9707
Dafen 40 SN 5201
Daffy Green 64 TF 9609
Dagenham 37 TQ 5084
Daglingworth 46 SO 9905
Dagnall 36 SP 9916
Daill 98 NR 3662
Dailly 93 NS 2701
Dairsie or Osnaburgh 109 NO 4117
Dalavich 100 NM 9612
Dalbeattie 88 NX 8361
Dalbeattie Forest 87 NX 8557
Dalbeg 131 NB 2345
Dalbeg Bay 131 NB 2246
Dalblair 88 NS 6419
Dalbog 109 NO 5871
Dalby 76 SC 2178
Dalby Point 76 SC 2178
Dalcapon 108 NN 9755
Dalchalloch 107 NN 7264
Dalchenna 100 NN 0706
Dalchork 133 NC 5710
Dalchreichart 115 NH 2912
Dalchruin 107 NN 7116
Dalcross 129 NH 7748
Dalderby 73 TF 2465
Dale (Derby.) 60 SK 4338
Dale (Dyfed) 42 SM 8005
Dale (Shetld.) 140 HU 1852
Dale Dike Resr. 71 SK 2391
Dale Head 83 NY 4316
Dalelia 111 NM 7369
Dale Point 42 SM 8205
Dales Head Dike 73 TF 1463
Dales Voe (Shetld.) 143 HU 4270
Dales Voe (Shetld.) 141 HU 4545
Dalgarven 93 NS 2945
Dalgety Bay 102 NT 1783
Dalgig 93 NS 5512
Dalginross 107 NN 7721
Dalguise 108 NN 9947
Dalhalvaig 134 NC 8954
Dalham 54 TL 7261
Daliburgh 112 NF 7421
Dalinlongart Hill 100 NS 1481
Dalkeith 103 NT 3367
Dall 107 NN 5956
Dallas 129 NJ 1252
Dallas Forest 129 NJ 1253
Dall Burn 107 NN 5654
Dalleagles 88 NS 5710
Dalle Crucis Abbey (ant.) 58 SJ 2044
Dallinghoo 55 TM 2654
Dallington 29 TQ 6519
Dallowgill Moor 78 SE 1770
Dalmacallan Forest 88 NX 8087
Dalmally 106 NN 1527
Dalmary 101 NS 5195
Dalmellington 93 NS 4705
Dalmeny 102 NT 1477
Dalmeny House 102 NT 1678
Dalmigavie 116 NH 7419
Dalmigavie Lodge 116 NH 7523
Dalmore (Highld.) 128 NH 6668
Dalmore (Isle of Lewis) 131 NB 2244
Dalmunzie Hotel 108 NO 0971
Dalnabreck 111 NM 7069
Dalnacardoch Forest 116 NN 6775
Dalnacardoch Lodge 107 NN 7270
Dalnaglar Castle 108 NO 1464
Dalnamein Forest 116 NN 7777
Dalnaspidal Lodge 107 NN 6472
Dalnavie 128 NH 6473
Dalnawillan Lodge 135 ND 0240
Dalness 106 NN 1751
Dalnessie 133 NC 6315
Da Logat 140 HT 9541
Dalqueich 102 NO 0704
Dalquhairn 86 NX 3296
Dalquharran Castle 93 NS 2702
Dalreavoch 129 NC 7508
Dalry 93 NS 2949
Dalrymple 93 NS 3514
Dalserf 94 NS 7950
Dalston 83 NY 3750
Dalswinton 88 NX 9385
Dalton (Dumf. and Galwy.) 89 NY 1173
Dalton (Lancs.) 69 SD 4907
Dalton (Northum.) 90 NY 9158
Dalton (Northum.) 91 NZ 1172
Dalton (N Yorks.) 84 NZ 1108
Dalton (N Yorks.) 79 SE 4376
Dalton (N Yorks.) 71 SK 4593
Dalton-in-Furness 76 SD 2374
Dalton-le-Dale 85 NZ 4047
Dalton-on-Tees 84 NZ 2908
Dalton Piercy 85 NZ 4631
Dalveich 107 NN 6124
Dalvina Lodge 133 NC 6944
Dalwhat Water 88 NX 7194
Dalwhinnie 116 NN 6384
Dalwood 24 ST 2400
Damerham 26 SU 1015
Damflask Resr. 71 SK 2791
Damgate 65 TG 3909
Damnaglaur 86 NX 1235
Dam of Hoxa 136 ND 4294
Damsay 136 HY 3913
Danbury 38 TL 7805
Danby 80 NZ 7009
Danby Low Moor 85 NZ 7110
Danby Wiske 84 SE 3398
Dandaleith 120 NJ 2845
Danderhall 103 NT 3069
Danebridge 70 SJ 9665
Danebury (ant.) 26 SU 3237
Dane End 37 TL 3321
Danehill 29 TQ 4027
Dane Hills 61 SK 5605
Danesborough (ant.) 52 SP 9234
Dane's Brook 23 SS 8331
Danes' Dyke (ant.) 81 TA 2172
Danskine 103 NT 5667
Darden Lough 90 NY 9795
Daren-felen 41 SO 2212
Darenth 37 TQ 5671
Daresbury 69 SJ 5782
Darfield 71 SE 4104
Dargate 31 TR 0861
Darite 19 SX 2569
Darlaston 60 SO 9796
Darleith House 100 NS 3480
Darlingscote 50 SP 2342
Darlington 84 NZ 2914
Darliston 59 SJ 5833
Darlochan 92 NR 6723
Darlton 72 SK 7773
Darnaw (mt.) 87 NX 5176
Darnaway Forest 129 NH 9751
Darnbrook Fell 78 SD 8872
Darowen 57 SH 8302
Darra 121 NJ 7447
Darras Hall 91 NZ 1571
Darrington 71 SE 4919
Darsham 55 TM 4170
Dartford 37 TQ 5474
Dartington 21 SX 7862
Dartmeet 21 SX 6773
Dartmoor Forest 21 SX 6180
Dartmouth 21 SX 8751
Darton 71 SE 3110
Darvel 94 NS 5637
Darwell Resr. 29 TQ 7121
Darwen 77 SD 6922
Da Scrodhurdins 140 HT 9339
Datchet 36 SU 9876
Datchworth 37 TL 2619
Daugh of Cairnborrow 121 NJ 4542
Daugh of Carron 117 NJ 2339
Daugh of Invermarkie 121 NJ 4141
Daugh of Kinermony 120 NJ 2441
Dauntsey 34 ST 9882
Davenham 69 SJ 6570
Daventry 51 SP 5762
Daventry Resr. 51 SP 5763
Davidstow 20 SX 1587
Davington 89 NT 2302
Daviot (Grampn.) 121 NJ 7528
Daviot (Highld.) 116 NH 7239
Davoch of Grange 121 NJ 4951
Dawes Heath 38 TQ 8188
Dawley 59 SJ 6807
Dawlish 21 SX 9676
Dawlish Warren 21 SX 9778
Dawn 67 SH 8672
Dawpool Bank (sbk.) 68 SJ 2281
Dawsmere 63 TF 4430
Daylesford 47 SP 2425
Ddyle 57 SO 0575
Deadh Choimhead 106 NM 9428
Deadwater 90 NY 6096
Deal 31 TR 3752
Deal Hall 39 TR 0097
Dean (Cumbr.) 82 NY 0725
Dean (Devon) 21 SX 7364
Dean (Hants.) 27 SU 5619
Dean (Somer.) 33 ST 6743
Deanburnhaugh 89 NT 3911
Deane 35 SU 5450
Dean Hill 26 SU 2526
Deanich Lodge 127 NH 3683
Deanland 26 ST 9918
Dean Prior 21 SX 7363
Dean Row 69 SJ 8781
Deans 102 NT 0268
Deanscale 82 NY 0926
Deanshanger 51 SP 7639
Deanston 101 NN 7101
Dean Water 109 NO 3548
Dearg Abhainn 106 NM 9739
Dearham 82 NY 0736
Dearne 71 SE 4505
Deasker (is.) 124 NF 6466
Debach 55 TM 2454
Debden 53 TL 5533
Debden Green 53 TL 5832
Debenham 55 TM 1763
Dechmont 102 NT 0370
Deddington 47 SP 4631
Dedham 54 TM 0533
Dedridge 102 NT 0566
Deene 52 SP 9492
Deenethorpe 52 SP 9592
Deepcar 71 SK 2897
Deepcut 35 SU 9057
Deepdale (Cumbr.) 77 SD 7284
Deep Dale (Durham) 84 NY 9615
Deeping Fen 62 TF 1916
Deeping Gate 62 TF 1509
Deeping St. James 62 TF 1609
Deeping St. Nicholas 62 TF 2115
Deeps, The (chan.) 141 HU 3241
Deerhill 121 NJ 4556
Deerhurst 46 SO 8729
Deer Law 95 NT 2225
Deerlee Knowe 90 NT 7208
Deerness 137 HY 5606
Deer's Hill 121 NJ 8045
Deer Sound 137 HY 5307
Defford 49 SO 9143
Defynnog 41 SN 9227
Deganwy 67 SH 7779
Deighton (N Yorks.) 85 NZ 3801
Deighton (N Yorks.) 79 SE 6244
Deil's Caldron 107 NN 7623
Deil's Heid, The (pt.) 109 NO 6741
Deil's or Celtic Dike (ant.) 88 NS 7011
Deiniolen 66 SH 5863
Delabole 20 SX 0683
Delamere 69 SJ 5668
Delamere Forest 69 SJ 5570
Delamere Station 69 SJ 5570
De Lank River 19 SX 1175
Delfrigs 121 NJ 9721
Delgatie Castle 121 NJ 7550
Delgaty Forest 121 NJ 7748
Dell 131 NB 4861
Delliefure 117 NJ 0731
Dell Lodge 117 NJ 0119
Dell River 131 NB 5058
Delnadamph Lodge 117 NJ 2208
Delny Dock 129 NH 7569
Delph 70 SD 9807
Delph Bank 63 TF 3721
Delph Resr. 69 SD 6916
Delph, The 54 TL 7080
Delvine 108 NO 1240
Dembleby 62 TF 0437
Denbigh 67 SJ 0566
Denbury 21 SX 8268
Denby 60 SK 3946
Denby Dale 71 SE 2208
Denchworth 34 SU 3891
Dene Mouth 85 NZ 4640
Denend 121 NJ 6038
Denford 52 SP 9976
Denge Beach 31 TR 0717
Denge Marsh 31 TR 0419
Dengie 39 TL 9801
Dengie Flat (sbk.) 39 TM 0404
Denham (Bucks.) 36 TQ 0386
Denham (Suff.) 54 TL 7561
Denham (Suff.) 55 TM 1974
Denham Aerodrome 36 TQ 0288
Denham Castle 54 TL 7462
Denham Green 36 TQ 0388
Denhead (Fife) 103 NO 4613
Denhead (Grampn.) 121 NJ 9952
Denhead of Arbirlot 109 NO 5742
Denhead of Gray 109 NO 3431
Denholm 90 NT 5718
Denholme 78 SE 0633
Denmead 27 SU 6511
Denmore 119 NJ 9411
Denne Park 28 TQ 1729
Dennington 55 TM 2866
Dennis Head 139 HY 7855
Denny 101 NS 8182
Dennyloanhead 101 NS 8180
Denny Lodge 26 SU 3305
Denside 119 NO 8095
Densole 31 TR 2141
Denston 54 TL 7652
Denstone 60 SK 0940
Dent 77 SD 7087
Dentdale 77 SD 7286
Den, The 93 NS 3251
Denton (Cambs.) 52 TL 1487
Denton (Durham) 84 NZ 2118
Denton (E Susx) 29 TQ 4502
Denton (Gtr Mches.) 69 SJ 9295
Denton (Kent) 31 TR 2146
Denton (Lincs.) 62 SK 8632
Denton (Norf.) 55 TM 2888
Denton (Northants.) 52 SP 8357
Denton (N Yorks.) 78 SE 1448
Denton (Oxon.) 47 SP 5902
Denton Fell 90 NY 6162
Denton Resr. 62 SK 8633
Denver 64 TF 6101
Denwick (Northum.) 91 NU 2014
Den Wick (Orkney) 137 HY 5709
Deopham 64 TG 0400
Deopham Green 64 TM 0499
Depden Green 54 TL 7756
Deptford (Gtr London) 37 TQ 3676
Deptford (Wilts.) 34 SU 0038
Derby 60 SK 3435
Derbyhaven 76 SC 2867
Dere Street (Durham) (ant.) 84 NZ 2120
Dere Street (Northum.) (ant.) 90 NY 9179
Dere Street (Northum.) (ant.) 84 NZ 0757
Dere Street (N Yorks.) (ant.) 79 SE 4363
Dergoals 86 NX 2459
Deri 41 SO 1202
Dernaglar Loch 86 NX 2658
Derringstone 31 TR 2049
Derrington 59 SJ 8822
Derry Burn 117 NO 0396
Derry Cairngorm 117 NO 0198
Derryguaig 105 NM 4835
Derry Hill 34 ST 9670
Derrythorpe 74 SE 8208
Dersalloch Hill 93 NS 4204
Dersingham 64 TF 6830
Dervaig 111 NM 4351
Derventio Roman Fort (ant.) 82 NY 1031
Derwen 67 SJ 0650
Derwent Fells 82 NY 2218
Derwent Reservoir (Derby. - S Yorks.) 70 SK 1790
Derwent Reservoir (Durham - Northum.) 84 NZ 0152
Derwent Water 82 NY 2621
Desborough 52 SP 8083
Desford 61 SK 4703
Deskry Water 118 NJ 3807
Detchant 97 NU 0836
Dethenydd (dist.) 57 SO 0082
Detling 30 TQ 7958
Deuchar Hill 109 NO 4662
Deuchar Law 95 NT 2829
Deuchary Hill 108 NO 0348
Deuddwr 58 SJ 2317
Deva (ant.) 68 SJ 4066
Devauden 45 ST 4899
Devilla Forest 102 NS 9588
Devil's Beef Tub 89 NT 0713
Devil's Bridge 57 SN 7477
Devil's Causeway (Northum.) (ant.) 97 NU 0046
Devil's Causeway (Northum.) (ant.) 97 NU 0426
Devil's Causeway (Northum.) (ant.) 91 NU 1203
Devil's Causeway (Northum.) (ant.) 91 NZ 0478
Devil's Ditch (ant.) 54 TL 6062
Devil's Dyke (Norf.) (ant.) 64 TF 7408
Devil's Dyke (W Susx) (ant.) 28 TQ 2611
Devil's Elbow 117 NO 1476
Devil's Point, The (mt.) 117 NN 9795
Devil's Water 84 NY 9356
Devizes 34 SU 0061
Devoke Water 82 SD 1596
Devonport 20 SX 4554
Devonside 102 NS 9296
Devoran 19 SW 7939
Dewi Fawr 43 SN 3023
Dewlish 25 SY 7798
Dewsall Court 45 SO 4833
Dewsbury 79 SE 2422
Dhoon 76 SC 4586
Dhoor 76 SC 4396
Dhowin 76 NX 4101
Dial Post 28 TQ 1519
Diaval (mt.) 131 NB 4552
Dibden 26 SU 3908
Dibden Purlieu 26 SU 4106
Dibyn Du (mt.) 57 SN 7865
Dickleburgh 55 TM 1682
Didbrook 46 SP 0531
Didcot 35 SU 5290
Diddington 52 TL 1965
Diddlebury 48 SO 5085
Didley 45 SO 4432
Didmarton 33 ST 8287
Didsbury 69 SJ 8490
Didworthy 21 SX 6862
Diebidale Forest 128 NH 4584
Diebidale River 128 NH 4383
Diffwys 57 SH 6523
Digby 62 TF 0754
Diggle 70 SE 0008
Dighty Water 109 NO 4232
Dihewyd 43 SN 4855
Dilham 65 TG 3325
Dilhorne 60 SJ 9743
Dilston 91 NY 9763
Dilton Marsh 33 ST 8449
Dilwyn 45 SO 4154
Dinam 67 SJ 0033
Dinas (Dyfed) 42 SN 0139
Dinas (Dyfed) 43 SN 2730
Dinas (Gwyn.) 66 SH 2736
Dinas Head 42 SN 0041
Dinas-Mawddwy 57 SH 8514
Dinas Powys 41 ST 1571
Dinchope 48 SO 4583
Dinder 33 ST 5744
Dinedor 45 SO 5336
Din Fell 89 NY 4696
Dingestow 45 SO 4115
Dingley 51 SP 7687
Dingwall 128 NH 5458
Din Lligwy (ant.) 66 SH 5085
Dinnet 118 NO 4698
Dinnings Hill 89 NY 2297
Dinnington (Somer.) 24 ST 4012
Dinnington (S Yorks.) 71 SK 5386
Dinnington (Tyne and Wear) 91 NZ 2073
Dinorben (ant.) 67 SH 9575
Dinorwic 66 SH 5961
Dinorwig (ant.) 66 SH 5565
Dinsdale Station 85 NZ 3413
Dinton 26 SU 0131
Dinwoodie Mains 89 NY 1090
Dinworthy 22 SS 3015
Diollaid Mhòr 92 NR 7739
Dippen 92 NR 7937
Dippen Hall 35 SU 8146
Dippin 92 NS 0422
Dippin Head 92 NS 0522
Dipple (Grampn.) 121 NJ 3258
Dipple (Strath.) 93 NS 2002
Diptford 21 SX 7256
Dipton 84 NZ 1554
Dirleton 103 NT 5183
Dirrie More 127 NH 2475
Dirrington Great Law 96 NT 6954
Dirrington Little Law 96 NT 6853
Discoed 48 SO 2764
Diseworth 61 SK 4524
Dishes 137 HY 6523
Dishforth 79 SE 3873
Disley 70 SJ 9784
Diss 55 TM 1179
Disserth 44 SO 0458
Distington 82 NY 0023
Ditcheat 25 ST 6236
Ditchingham 55 TM 3391
Ditchling 29 TQ 3215
Ditchling Beacon 29 TQ 3313
Dittisham 21 SX 8655
Ditton (Ches.) 69 SJ 4986
Ditton (Kent) 30 TQ 7158
Ditton Green 54 TL 6658
Ditton Priors 49 SO 6089
Dixton (Glos.) 46 SO 9830
Dixton (Gwent) 45 SO 5114
Dizzard Point 20 SX 1699
Dobwalls 19 SX 2165
Doccombe 21 SX 7786
Dochfour House 116 NH 6039
Dochgarroch 116 NH 6140
Dochrie Hill 102 NO 0808
Docking 64 TF 7637
Docklow 45 SO 5657
Dockray 83 NY 3921
Doctor's Gate (ant.) 70 SK 0794
Dodburn 89 NT 4707
Dodd Fell 78 SD 8484
Dodd Hill 88 NX 5697
Doddinghurst 38 TQ 5998
Doddington (Cambs.) 53 TL 4090
Doddington (Kent) 30 TQ 9357
Doddington (Lincs.) 72 SK 8970
Doddington (Northum.) 97 NU 0032
Doddington (Salop) 49 SO 6176
Doddiscombsleigh 21 SX 8586
Dodford (Here. and Worc.) 49 SO 9273
Dodford (Northants.) 51 SP 6160
Dodington (Avon) 33 ST 7579
Dodleston 68 SJ 3661
Dodman Point 19 SX 0039
Dodworth 71 SE 3105
Doe Lea 71 SK 4566
Dog Bank (sbk.) 108 NO 3025
Dogdyke 62 TF 2055
Dogmersfield 35 SU 7852

Dog Village 21 SX 9896
Doire Bhuidhe 92 NR 9249
Doire Tana (mt.) 115 NH 2128
Doirlinn Head 112 NL 6299
Dolanog 57 SJ 0612
Dolau 48 SO 1367
Dolbenmaen 66 SH 5043
Dolebury (ant.) 33 ST 4458
Doles Wood 34 SU 3751
Dolfach 57 SN 9077
Dol-fôr (Powys) 57 SH 8006
Dolfor (Powys) 57 SO 1087
Dolgarrog 67 SH 7766
Dolgellau 57 SH 7217
Dol-gran 43 SN 4634
Doll 129 NC 8803
Dollar 102 NS 9697
Dollar Law 95 NT 1727
Dolleycanney 45 SO 1849
Dolphinholme 77 SD 5153
Dolphinton 95 NT 1046
Dolton 23 SS 5712
Dolwar Hall 57 SJ 0715
Dolwen (Clwyd) 67 SH 8874
Dolwen (Powys) 57 SH 9707
Dolwyddelan 67 SH 7352
Dolyhir 45 SO 2458
Domgay 58 SJ 2819
Doncaster 71 SE 5803
Donhead St. Andrew 25 ST 9124
Donhead St. Mary 25 ST 9024
Donibristle 102 NT 1688
Donington 62 TF 2135
Donington on Bain 73 TF 2382
Donisthorpe 60 SK 3114
Donkey Town 36 SU 9460
Donna Nook 75 TF 4399
Donnington (Berks.) 35 SU 4668
Donnington (Glos.) 47 SP 1928
Donnington (Here. and Worc.) 46 SO 7034
Donnington (Shrops.) 59 SJ 5807
Donnington (Shrops.) 59 SJ 7114
Donnington (W Susx) 27 SU 8502
Donyatt 24 ST 3313
Doolie Ness 109 NO 8370
Doonfoot 93 NS 3218
Doonholm 93 NS 3317
Doonie Point 119 NO 9090
Doon of May 86 NX 2951
Dorback Burn (Grampn.) 129 NH 9943
Dorback Burn (Highld.) 117 NJ 0517
Dorback Lodge 117 NJ 0716
Dorchester (Dorset) 25 SY 6990
Dorchester (Oxon.) 47 SU 5794
Dordon 60 SK 2600
Dore 71 SK 3081
Dore Holm 142 HU 2176
Dores 116 NH 5934
Dorking 28 TQ 1649
Dormansland 29 TQ 4042
Dormanstown 85 NZ 5823
Dormington 45 SO 5840
Dorney 36 SU 9379
Dornie 114 NG 8826
Dornoch 129 NH 7989
Dornoch Firth 129 NH 8488
Dornoch Sands 129 NH 7887
Dornock (Dumf. and Galwy.) 89 NY 2366
Dorrery 135 ND 0754
Dorridge 50 SP 1774
Dorrington (Lincs.) 62 TF 0752
Dorrington (Shrops.) 59 SJ 4703
Dorsington 50 SP 1349
Dorstone 45 SO 3142
Dorton 36 SP 6714
Dorusduain 114 NG 9822
Dosthill 60 SP 2199
Doublebois 19 SX 1964
Dougarie 92 NR 8837
Dougarie Point 92 NR 8737
Dough Crag 91 NY 9794
Doughton 33 ST 8791
Douglas (I. of M.) 76 SC 3070
Douglas (Strath.) 95 NS 8330
Douglas and Angus 109 NO 4332
Douglas Bay 76 SC 3976
Douglas Burn 95 NT 2628
Douglas Head 76 SC 3974
Douglastown 109 NO 4147
Douglas Water (Strath.) 100 NN 0106
Douglas Water (Strath.) 95 NS 8330
Douglas Water (Strath.) 95 NS 8736
Doulting 33 ST 6443
Dounan Bay 86 NW 9668
Dounby 136 HY 2920
Doune (Highld.) 128 NC 4400
Doune (Tays.) 101 NN 7201
Doune Hill 100 NS 2896
Douneside 118 NJ 4806
Dounie 128 NH 5690
Dounreay Experimental Reactor Establishment 134 NC 9867
Dour Hill 90 NT 7902
Dousland 21 SX 5368
Dove Dale 60 SK 1452
Dove Holes 70 SK 0778
Dovenby 82 NY 0933
Dover 31 TR 3141
Dover Beck 71 SK 4963
Doverdale 49 SO 8566
Doveridge 60 SK 1134
Dove Stone Reservoir 70 SE 0103
Dovey Valley 57 SH 7401
Dowally 108 NO 0047
Dow Crag 82 NY 8419
Dowdeswell 46 SO 9919
Dowhill 93 NS 2003
Dowland 23 SS 5610
Dowlish Wake 24 ST 3712
Down Ampney 46 SU 1097
Downan Point 86 NX 0680
Downderry 20 SX 3153
Downe 37 TQ 4361
Downend (Berks.) 35 SU 4775
Downend (I.of W.) 27 SZ 5387
Downfield 109 NO 3833
Downgate 20 SX 3772
Downham (Essex) 38 TQ 7395
Downham (Lancs.) 78 SD 7844
Downham (Northum.) 97 NT 8633
Downham Market 64 TF 6003
Down Hatherley 46 SO 8622
Downhead 33 ST 6845
Downholme 84 SE 1197
Downies 119 NO 9294
Downing 68 SJ 1578
Downley 36 SU 8495
Downs 41 ST 1174
Downside Abbey 33 ST 6550
Downs, The (roadstead) 31 TR 4252
Down St. Mary 23 SS 7404
Downton (Hants.) 26 SZ 2693
Downton (Wilts.) 26 SU 1721
Downton on the Rock 48 SO 4273
Dowsby 62 TF 1129
Dowsdale 63 TF 2810
Dowthwaitehead 83 NY 3720
Doxey 59 SJ 9023
Doxford 97 NU 1823
Doynton 33 ST 7173
Dozmary Pool 19 SX 1974
Draethen 41 ST 2287
Draffan 94 NS 7945
Drakeland Corner 21 SX 5758
Drake Law 95 NS 9021
Drakemyre 93 NS 2850
Drakes Broughton 49 SO 9248
Drake's Island 20 SX 4652
Draughton (Northants.) 51 SP 7676
Draughton (N Yorks.) 78 SE 0352
Drax 79 SE 6726
Draycote 51 SP 4469
Draycote Water 51 SP 4570
Draycott (Derby) 61 SK 4433
Draycott (Glos.) 50 SP 1836
Draycott (Somer.) 33 ST 4750
Draycott in the Clay 60 SK 1528
Draycott in the Moors 60 SJ 9840
Drayton (Hants.) 27 SU 6605
Drayton (Here. and Worc.) 49 SO 9076
Drayton (Leic.) 52 SP 8392
Drayton (Norf.) 65 TG 1713
Drayton (Oxon.) 50 SP 4241
Drayton (Oxon.) 47 SU 4794
Drayton (Somer.) 24 ST 4024
Drayton Bassett 60 SK 1900
Drayton Parslow 52 SP 8428
Drayton St. Leonard 47 SU 5996
Drefach (Dyfed) 43 SN 3538
Drefach (Dyfed) 43 SN 5045
Drefach (Dyfed) 43 SN 5213
Dreghorn 93 NS 3538
Drem 103 NT 5079
Dreswick Point 76 SC 2865
Drewsteignton 21 SX 7391
Driby 73 TF 3874
Driesh (mt.) 117 NO 2773
Driffield 46 SU 0799
Drift 18 SW 4328
Drift Reservoir 18 SW 4329
Drigg 82 SD 0698
Drighlington 79 SE 2229
Drimnin 111 NM 5553
Drimnin House 111 NM 5554
Drimpton 24 ST 4104
Drimsynie 100 NN 1901
Drinishader 125 NG 1794
Drinkstone 54 TL 9561
Drinkstone Green 54 TL 9660
Drinkstone Hill 89 NT 4818
Drip Moss 101 NS 7595
Drochaid Lusa 123 NG 7024
Drochil Castle (ant.) 95 NT 1643
Drointon 60 SK 0226
Droitwich 49 SO 8962
Dron 108 NO 1415
Dronfield 71 SK 3578
Dronfield Woodhouse 71 SK 3278
Drongan 93 NS 4418
Dronger (pt.) 139 HZ 2074
Drongs, The (is.) 142 HU 2675
Dronley 109 NO 3435
Drosgl 67 SH 6668
Drosgol 57 SN 7587
Droxford 27 SU 6018
Droylsden 69 SJ 9098
Druid 67 SJ 0343
Druidale 76 SC 3688
Druidston 42 SM 8716
Druimarbin 106 NN 0861
Druimavuic 106 NN 0044
Druimdrishaig 99 NR 7370
Druim Fada (Highld.) 114 NG 8808
Druim Fada (Highld.) 115 NN 0781
Druim Fada (Island of Mull) 105 NM 6422
Druim Fiaclach 111 NM 7979
Druim Gleann Laoigh 115 NN 0685
Druimkinnerras 116 NH 4639
Druim Leathad nam Fias 106 NM 9669
Druim na Dubh Ghlaic 105 NM 7608
Druim na Leitire 123 NG 8022
Druim nan Cliar 133 NC 5157
Druimyeon Bay 92 NR 6550
Drum (Grampn.) 121 NJ 8946
Drum (Gwyn.) 67 SH 7169
Drum (Tays.) 102 NO 0400
Drumadoon Bay 92 NR 8927
Drumadoon Point 92 NR 8828
Drumashie Moor 116 NH 6136
Drumbeg 132 NC 1232
Drumblade 121 NJ 5840
Drumblair House 121 NJ 6343
Drumbuie (Dumf. and Galwy.) 88 NX 5682
Drumbuie (Highld.) 123 NG 7730
Drumburgh 89 NY 2659
Drum Castle 119 NJ 7900
Drumchapel 101 NS 5270
Drumchardine 128 NH 5644
Drumclog 94 NS 6339
Drum-ddu (Powys) 44 SN 9744
Drum-ddu (Powys) 44 SN 9760
Drumderg 108 NO 1754
Drumeldrie 103 NO 4403
Drumelzier 95 NT 1333
Drumfearn 123 NG 6715
Drumgask 116 NN 6193
Drumgley 109 NO 4250
Drumguish 116 NN 7999
Drumhead 119 NO 6092
Drum Hollistan (dist.) 134 NC 9264
Drumin 117 NJ 1830
Drumine Forest 129 NJ 0250
Drumlamford House 86 NX 2876
Drumlamford Loch 86 NX 2777
Drumlanrig Castle 88 NX 8599
Drumlassie 119 NJ 6405
Drumlemble 92 NR 6619
Drumlithie 119 NO 7880
Drummin 116 NN 4695
Drummond Castle 107 NN 8418
Drummond Hill 107 NN 7646
Drummore 86 NX 1336
Drummossie Muir (dist.) 129 NH 7343
Drummuir Castle 121 NJ 3744
Drumnadrochit 116 NH 5029
Drumnagorrach 121 NJ 5252
Drum of Clashmore (mt.) 101 NS 4897
Drum Peithnant 57 SN 7785
Drumphaill 86 NX 2262
Drumrash 88 NX 6871
Drumrunie 127 NC 1605
Drumrunie Forest 132 NC 1710
Drums 121 NJ 9822
Drumsallie 114 NM 9578
Drumshang 93 NS 2513
Drumsturdy 109 NO 4935
Drumtochty Castle 119 NO 6979
Drumtochty Forest 119 NO 7078
Drumtroddan 86 NX 3645
Drumuie 123 NG 4546
Drumuillie 117 NH 9420
Drumvaich 101 NN 6803
Drumwhindle 121 NJ 9236
Drum yr Eira 44 SN 8557
Drunkendub 109 NO 6646
Druridge Bay 91 NZ 2897
Drury 68 SJ 2964
Drybeck 83 NY 6615
Drybridge (Grampn.) 121 NJ 4362
Drybridge (Strath.) 93 NS 3536
Drybrook 46 SO 6416
Dryburgh Abbey (ant.) 96 NT 5931
Dry Burn 96 NT 7074
Dryden Fell 89 NT 4008
Dry Doddington 62 SK 8446
Dry Drayton 53 TL 3862
Dryfe Water 89 NY 1588
Drygarn Fawr 44 SN 8658
Dryhope 95 NT 2624
Drymen 101 NS 4788
Drymuir 121 NJ 9146
Drynoch 123 NG 4031
Duart Bay 105 NM 7335
Duart Point 105 NM 7535
Dubford 121 NJ 7963
Dubh Artach 104 NM 1203
Dubh Chreag 99 NR 7970
Dubh Eas 106 NN 2920
Dubh Eilean 98 NR 3388
Dubh-fheith 105 NM 7014
Dubh Ghleann 117 NO 0698
Dubh Lighe 114 NM 9482
Dubh Loch (Grampn.) 117 NO 2382
Dubh Loch (Highld.) 123 NG 8470
Dubh Loch (Highld.) 126 NG 9876
Dubh Loch (Strath.) 100 NN 1111
Dubh Sgeir (Muck) 111 NM 4278
Dubh Sgeir (Strath.) 105 NM 7625
Dubmill Point 82 NY 0745
Dubris (ant.) 31 TR 3141
Dubton 109 NO 5652
Dubwath 82 NY 1931
Duchally 132 NC 3816
Duchal Moor 100 NS 2866
Duchray Hill or Mealna Letter 108 NO 1667
Duchray Water 101 NS 4699
Duckington 59 SJ 4851
Ducklington 47 SP 3507
Duck's Cross 52 TL 1156
Duddenhoe End 53 TL 4636
Duddingston 103 NT 2972
Duddington 62 SK 9800
Duddo 97 NT 9342
Duddon 69 SJ 5164
Duddon Bridge 76 SD 1988
Duddon Sands 76 SD 1675
Dudleston Heath 58 SJ 3636
Dudley 91 NZ 2673
Dudley 49 SO 9390
Dudwell Mountain 42 SM 9023
Duff House 121 NJ 6963
Duffield 60 SK 3443
Duffryn (S Glam.) 41 ST 2985
Duffryn (W Glam.) 41 SS 8495
Dufftown 121 NJ 3240
Duffus 129 NJ 1668
Duffus Castle (ant.) 129 NJ 1867
Dufton 83 NY 6925
Dufton Fell 83 NY 7628
Duggleby 81 SE 8766
Duggleby Howe (ant.) 81 SE 8866
Duhonw 44 SO 0248
Duich Lots 98 NR 3354
Duich River 98 NR 3154
Duirinish 123 NG 7831
Duisk River 86 NX 2184
Duisky 114 NN 0176
Dukestown 41 SO 1410
Dukinfield 69 SJ 9497
Dulais 43 SN 7804
Dulas (Gwyn.) 66 SH 4789
Dulas (Powys) 44 SN 9452
Dulas Bay 66 SH 4989
Dulcote 33 ST 5644
Dulford 24 ST 0606
Dull 107 NN 8049
Dullan Water 117 NJ 2935
Dullatur 101 NS 7476
Dullingham 54 TL 6357
Dulnain Bridge 117 NH 9924
Duloe (Beds.) 52 TL 1560
Duloe (Corn.) 19 SX 2358
Dulsie 129 NH 9341
Dulverton 33 SS 9127
Dulwich 37 TQ 3373
Dulyn Reservoir 67 SH 7066
Dumbarton 101 NS 4075
Dumbarton Muir 101 NS 4579
Dumbleton 46 SP 0135
Dumcrieff 89 NT 1003
Dumfries 88 NX 9775
Dumgoyne 101 NS 5283
Dummer 35 SU 5845
Dumyat 101 NS 8397
Dun (St. Kilda or Hirta) (is.) 124 NF 1097
Dun (Strath.) (ant.) 92 NR 6206
Dun (Tays.) 109 NO 6659
Dunadd (ant.) 99 NR 8393
Dunagoil Bay 93 NS 0853
Dunain House 128 NH 6242
Dunalastair 107 NN 7159
Dunalastair Water 107 NN 7058
Dunan (Isle of Skye) 123 NG 5827
Dunan (Strath.) 100 NS 1571
Dunans 100 NS 0491
Dunball 32 ST 3140
Dunbar 96 NT 6878
Dunbar Common 103 NT 6469
Dunbeath 135 ND 1629
Dunbeath Bay 135 ND 1628
Dunbeath Castle 135 ND 1528
Dunbeath Water 135 ND 0733
Dunbeg 105 NM 8734
Dun Bhruichlinn (ant.) 98 NR 3663
Dunblane 101 NN 7801
Dunbog 108 NO 2817
Dun Borve (ant.) 124 NG 0393
Dun Caan 123 NG 5739
Duncangill Head 95 NT 0025
Duncansby Head 135 ND 4073
Duncanston (Grampn.) 121 NJ 5826
Duncanston (Highld.) 128 NH 5956
Dunchurch 51 SP 4871
Dun Corr-bhile 100 NN 1010
Duncote 51 SP 6750
Duncow 88 NX 9683
Duncrievie 102 NO 1309
Dun Crutagain 105 NM 7813
Duncton 28 SU 9516
Dun da Ghaoithe 105 NM 6736
Dundas Castle (ant.) 102 NT 1176
Dundas House 136 ND 4485
Dundee 109 NO 4030
Dundee Airport 109 NO 3729
Dunderave Point 100 NN 1409
Dundeugh Forest 88 NX 5690
Dundon 25 ST 4732
Dundonald 93 NS 3634
Dundonnell 127 NH 0987
Dundonnell Forest 127 NH 1181
Dundonnell House 127 NH 1185
Dundonnell River 127 NH 1279
Dundraw 82 NY 2149
Dundreggan 115 NH 3114
Dundreggan Forest 115 NH 3615
Dundrennan 87 NX 7447
Dundry 33 ST 5566
Dundry Hill 33 ST 5766
Dùn Dubh 100 NR 8995
Dundurn 107 NN 7023
Duneaton Water 88 NS 8420
Dunecht 119 NJ 7509
Dunfallandy House 108 NN 9456
Dunfermline 102 NT 0987
Dunford Bridge 70 SE 1602
Dungavel Hill 95 NS 9430
Dungeness 31 TR 0917
Dungeon Banks (sbk.) 68 SJ 4480
Dungeon Ghyll Force 82 NY 2706
Dùn Grugaig (Highld.) (ant.) 123 NG 8515
Dùn Grugaig (Island of Skye) (ant.) 123 NG 5312
Dunham-on-the-Hill 69 SJ 4772
Dunham on Trent 72 SK 8174
Dunhampton 49 SO 8466
Dunham Town 69 SJ 7488
Dunholme 72 TF 0279
Dunino 103 NO 5311
Dunion Hill 90 NT 6219
Dunipace 101 NS 8083
Dunira 107 NN 7323
Dunkeld 108 NO 0242
Dunkeld House 108 NO 0142
Dunkery Hill 23 SS 9042
Dunkeswell 24 ST 1407
Dunkeswell Airport 24 ST 1307
Dunkirk 31 TR 0758
Dun Knowe 89 NT 3517
Dunk's Green 29 TQ 6152
Dunlappie 109 NO 5967
Dun Law (Borders) 96 NT 3749
Dun Law (Strath.) 88 NS 9113
Dun Leacainn 100 NN 0301
Dunley 49 SO 7869
Dunlop 93 NS 4049
Dunmaglass Lodge 116 NH 5922
Dunmail Raise 82 NY 3212
Dunmoor Hill 90 NT 9618
Dùn Mòr (Strath.) 100 NS 0480
Dùn Mòr (Tiree) (ant.) 110 NM 0449
Dunmore (Central.) 102 NS 8989
Dunmore (Strath.) 99 NR 7961
Dùn Mòr Ghil 98 NR 2744
Dunnerdale 82 SD 1991
Dunnet 135 ND 2171
Dunnet Bay 135 ND 1970
Dunnet Head 135 ND 2076
Dunnet Hill 135 ND 1973
Dunnichen 109 NO 5048
Dunninald Castle 109 NO 7054
Dunning 102 NO 0114
Dunnington (Humbs.) 81 TA 1551
Dunnington (N Yorks.) 79 SE 6652
Dunnington (Warw.) 50 SP 0653
Dunnockshaw 78 SD 8127
Dunnose 27 SZ 5778
Dùn Nosebridge (ant.) 98 NR 3760
Dunnottar Castle (ant.) 119 NO 8883
Dunollie 105 NM 8532
Dunoon 100 NS 1777
Dunragit 86 NX 1557
Dun Rig 95 NT 2531
Dùn Ringill (ant.) 123 NG 5617
Dunrobin Castle (ant.) 129 NC 8500
Duns 97 NT 7853
Dunsby 62 TF 1026
Dùn Scaich (ant.) 123 NG 5912
Dunscore 88 NX 8684
Dunscroft 71 SE 6409
Dunsden Green 36 SU 7477
Dunsfold 28 TQ 0036
Dunsford 21 SX 8089
Dunshelt 103 NO 2410
Dunshillock 121 NJ 9848
Dunsinnan 108 NO 1632
Dunskeath Ness 129 NH 7869
Dunskeig Bay 92 NR 7356
Dunskey Castle (ant.) 86 NX 0053
Dunslair Heights 95 NT 2843
Dunsland Cross Station 22 SS 4002
Dunsley 85 NZ 8511
Dunsmore 36 SP 8605
Dunsop Bridge 77 SD 6550
Dunstable 36 TL 0221
Dunstaffnage Castle (ant.) 106 NM 8834
Dunstall 60 SK 1920
Dunstall Green 54 TL 7460
Dunstan 91 NU 2419
Dunstanburgh Castle (ant.) 97 NU 2521
Dunster 23 SS 9943
Duns Tew 47 SP 4528
Dunston (Lincs.) 72 TF 0663
Dunston (Norf.) 65 TG 2302
Dunston (Staffs.) 59 SJ 9217
Dunston (Tyne and Wear) 91 NZ 2263
Dunsville 71 SE 6407
Dunswell 74 TA 0735
Dunsyre 95 NT 0748
Dunterton 20 SX 3779
Duntisbourne Abbots 46 SO 9707
Duntisbourne Leer 46 SO 9707
Duntisbourne Rouse 46 SO 9805
Duntish 25 ST 6906
Duntocher 101 NS 4972
Dunton (Beds.) 53 TL 2344
Dunton (Bucks.) 36 SP 8224
Dunton (Norf.) 64 TF 8730
Dunton Bassett 51 SP 5490
Dunton Green 29 TQ 5157
Dunton Wayletts 38 TQ 6590
Duntreath Castle 101 NS 5381
Duntroon Castle (ant.) 99 NR 7995
Dunure 93 NS 2515
Dunvant 40 SS 5993
Dunvegan 122 NG 2547
Dunvegan Head 122 NG 1756
Dunwan Dam 93 NS 5549
Dunwich 55 TM 4770
Dunyvaig Castle (ant.) 98 NR 4045
Durdar 83 NY 4051
Dure Down 23 SS 7541
Durham 84 NZ 2742
Durisdeer 88 NS 8903
Durleigh 24 ST 2736
Durleigh Resr. 24 ST 2736
Durley (Hants.) 27 SU 5115
Durley (Wilts.) 34 SU 2364
Durley Street 27 SU 5217
Durlston Bay 26 SZ 0477
Durlston Head 26 SZ 0377
Durnamuck 126 NH 0192
Durness 132 NC 4067
Durn Hill 121 NJ 5763
Durno 121 NJ 7128
Durnovaria (ant.) 25 SY 6990
Durobrivae (ant.) 62 TL 1297
Durovernum (ant.) 31 TR 1557
Durran 135 ND 1863
Durrington (Wilts.) 34 SU 1544
Durrington (W Susx) 28 TQ 1105
Durris Forest 119 NO 7993
Dursley 46 ST 7597
Durston 24 ST 2828
Durweston 25 ST 8508
Dury 141 HU 4560
Dury Voe 141 HU 4862
Dusk Water 93 NS 3248
Duslic (is.) 132 NC 2676
Duston 51 SP 7261
Dutchman Bank 67 SH 6578
Dutchman's Cap or Bac Mòr 104 NM 2438
Dutch River 74 SE 7021
Duthil 117 NH 9324
Duthil Burn 117 NH 9225
Dutlas 48 SO 2077
Duton Hill 54 TL 6026
Dutton 69 SJ 5779
Duxford 53 TL 4846
Dwarfie Stane (ant.) 136 HY 2400
Dwygyfylchi 67 SH 7377
Dwyran 66 SH 4465
Dyce 119 NJ 8812
Dye House 90 NY 9358
Dye Water 103 NT 6458
Dyffryn 41 SS 8593
Dyffryn Ardudwy 56 SH 5822
Dyffryn Ceidrych 40 SN 7025
Dyffryn Cellwen 41 SN 8509
Dyffryn Crawnon 41 SO 1218
Dyffryn Tywi 43 SN 6624
Dyke (Devon) 22 SS 3123
Dyke (Grampn.) 129 NH 9858
Dyke (Lincs.) 62 TF 1022
Dykehead (Central) 101 NS 5997
Dykehead (Strath.) 102 NS 8759
Dykehead (Tays.) 109 NO 3860
Dykends 108 NO 2557
Dylife 57 SN 8594
Dymchurch 31 TR 1029
Dymock 46 SO 6931
Dyne, The (ant.) 35 SU 6356
Dynevor Castle 43 SN 6122
Dyrham 33 ST 7375
Dyrham Park (ant.) 33 ST 7475
Dyrysgol (Gwyn.) (mt.) 57 SH 8328
Dyrysgol (Powys) (mt.) 57 SN 9474
Dysart 103 NT 3093
Dyserth 67 SJ 0579

E

Eachkamish 124 NF 7959
Eagan 126 NH 0144
Eagland Hill 77 SD 4345
Eagle 72 SK 8767
Eaglescliffe 85 NZ 4215
Eaglesfield (Cumbr.) 82 NY 0928
Eaglesfield (Dumf. and Galwy.) 89 NY 2374
Eaglesham 94 NS 5751
Eag na Maoile (is.) 110 NM 2765
Eairy 76 SC 2977
Eakring 71 SK 6762
Ealand 74 SE 7811
Ealing 37 TQ 1781
Eamont Bridge 83 NY 5228
Earadale Point 92 NR 5917
Earby 78 SD 9046
Earcroft 77 SD 6824
Eardington 49 SO 7290
Eardisland 45 SO 4158
Eardisley 45 SO 3149
Eardiston (Here. and Worc.) 49 SO 6968
Eardiston (Shrops.) 58 SJ 3725
Earith 53 TL 3875
Earle 97 NT 9826
Earlestown 69 SJ 5795
Earlham 65 TG 1908
Earlish 122 NG 3861
Earls Barton 52 SP 8563
Earlsburn Resrs. 101 NS 7089
Earls Colne 54 TL 8528
Earl's Croome 49 SO 8642
Earlsdon 50 SP 3177
Earl Seat 78 SE 0658
Earlsferry 103 NO 4800
Earlsford 121 NJ 8334
Earl's Green 54 TM 0366
Earlshall (ant.) 109 NO 4621
Earl's Hill 101 NS 7188
Earl Shilton 61 SP 4697
Earl Soham 55 TM 2363
Earl's Seat (Central) (mt.) 101 NS 5783
Earl's Seat (Northum.) 90 NY 7192
Earl Sterndale 70 SK 0967
Earlston (Borders) 96 NT 5738
Earlston (Strath.) 93 NS 4035
Earl Stonham 55 TM 1158
Earlstoun 88 NX 6183
Earlstoun Loch 88 NX 6182
Earlswood (Gwent) 45 ST 4595
Earlswood (Warw.) 50 SP 1174
Earnley 27 SZ 8096
Earn Water 93 NS 5353
Earsary 112 NL 7099
Earsdon 91 NZ 3272
Earshaig 89 NT 0402
Earsham 55 TM 3289
Earshaw Hill 89 NY 3582
Earswick 79 SE 6157
Eartham 28 SU 9309
Eas a'Ghaill 106 NN 2126
Easaval (mt.) 112 NF 7715
Easby 85 NZ 5708
Eascairt Point 92 NR 8453
Eas Daimh 107 NN 4345
Easdale (Strath.) 105 NM 7317
Easdale (Strath.) (is.) 105 NM 7316
Easebourne 27 SU 8922
Easedale Tarn 82 NY 3008
Easenhall 51 SP 4679
Easington (Bucks.) 36 SP 6810
Easington (Cleve.) 85 NZ 7418
Easington (Durham) 85 NZ 4143
Easington (Humbs.) 75 TA 3919
Easington (Northum.) 97 NU 1234
Easington (Oxon.) 36 SU 6697
Easington Fell 77 SD 7248
Easington Lane 85 NZ 3646
Easingwold 79 SE 5269
Easole Street 31 TR 2652
Eassie and Nevay 108 NO 3345
East Aberthaw 41 ST 0367
East Allington 21 SX 7648
East Anstey 23 SS 8626
East Ashling 27 SU 8207
East Auchronie 119 NJ 8109
East Barming 29 TQ 7254
East Barnet 37 TQ 2794
East Barsham 64 TF 9133
East Baugh Fell 83 SD 7491
East Beckham 65 TG 1640
East Bedfont 36 TQ 0574
East Benula Forest 115 NH 1431
East Bergholt 54 TM 0734
East Bilney 64 TF 9519
East Blatchington 29 TQ 4800
East Boldre 26 SU 3700
East Bolton Moor 84 SE 0194
Eastbourne 29 TV 6199
East Brent 32 ST 3452
East Bridge 55 TM 4566
East Bridgford 61 SK 6943
East Buckland 23 SS 6731
East Budleigh 24 SY 0684
East Burra (is.) 141 HU 3832
East Burrafirth 141 HU 3658
East Burton 25 SY 8386
Eastbury (Berks.) 34 SU 3477
Eastbury (Gtr London) 36 TQ 0991
East Cairnbeg 119 NO 7076
East Calder 102 NT 0867
East Carleton (Norf.) 65 TG 1802
East Carlton (Northants.) 52 SP 8389
East Chaldon or Chaldon Herring 25 SY 7983
East Challow 34 SU 3988
East Chiltington 29 TQ 3715
East Chisenbury 34 SU 1352

Eastchurch 31 TQ 9871
East Clandon 28 TQ 0651
East Claydon 51 SP 7325
Eastcombe (Glos.) 46 SO 8804
East Combe (Somer.) 24 ST 1631
Eastcote (Gtr London) 37 TQ 1188
Eastcote (W Mids) 50 SP 1979
Eastcott (Corn.) 22 SS 2515
Eastcott (Wilts.) 34 SU 0255
East Cottingwith 74 SE 7042
East Coulston 34 ST 9454
Eastcourt 34 ST 9792
East Cowes 27 SZ 5095
East Cowton 84 NZ 3103
East Cramlinton 91 NZ 2876
East Creech 25 SY 9282
East Croftmore 117 NH 9519
East Dart River 21 SX 6676
East Dean (E Susx) 29 TV 5596
East Dean (Hants.) 26 SU 2726
East Dean (W Susx) 27 SU 9013
East Dereham 64 TF 9913
East Down 23 SS 5941
East Drayton 72 SK 7775
East End (Avon) 33 ST 4770
East End (Dorset) 26 SY 9998
East End (Hants.) 34 SU 4161
East End (Hants.) 26 SZ 3697
East End (Herts.) 53 TL 4527
East End (Kent) 30 TQ 8335
East End (Oxon.) 47 SP 3914
Easter Ardross 128 NH 6373
Easter Balloch 118 NO 3480
Easter Balmoral 117 NO 2693
Easter Boleskine 116 NH 5122
Easter Compton 33 ST 5782
Easter Davoch 118 NJ 4607
Easter Fearn 128 NH 6486
Easter Fearn Burn 128 NH 6384
Easter Galcantray 129 NH 8148
Eastergate 28 SU 9405
Easter Kinkell 128 NH 5755
Easter Lednathie 108 NO 3363
Easter Moniack 128 NH 5543
Easter Muckovie 129 NH 7044
Eastern Green 50 SP 2780
Eastern Isles 18 SV 9514
Easter Ord 119 NJ 8304
Easter Ross (dist.) 128 NH 5878
Easter Rova Head 141 HU 4745
Easter Skeld 141 HU 3044
Easterton 34 SU 0154
Eastertown 32 ST 3454
Easter Whyntie 121 NJ 6264
East Farleigh 29 TQ 7353
East Farndon 51 SP 7185
East Fen 64 TF 4255
East Fenton 97 NT 5179
East Ferry 74 SK 8199
Eastfield (N Yorks.) 81 TA 0484
Eastfield (Strath.) 101 NS 7574
Eastfield (Strath.) 102 NS 8964
Eastfield Hall 91 NU 2206
East Garston 34 SU 3676
Eastgate (Durham) 84 NY 9538
Eastgate (Norf.) 65 TG 1423
East Ginge 35 SU 4486
East Glenquoich Forest 115 NH 1003
East Glen River 62 TF 0426
East Goscote 61 SK 6413
East Grafton 34 SU 2560
East Grimstead 26 SU 2227
East Grinstead 29 TQ 3938
East Guldeford 30 TQ 9321
East Haddon 51 SP 6668
East Hagbourne 35 SU 5388
East Halton 75 TA 1419
East Halton Skitter 75 TA 1423
East Ham (Essex) 37 TQ 4283
Eastham (Mers.) 68 SJ 3580
Easthampstead 36 SU 8667
Eastham Sands 68 SJ 3980
East Hanney 34 SU 4192
East Hanningfield 38 TL 7601
East Hardwick 71 SE 4618
East Harling 54 TL 9986
East Harlsey 85 SE 4299
East Harptree 33 ST 5655
East Hartford 91 NZ 2679
East Harting 27 SU 7919
East Hatley 53 TL 2850
East Hauxwell 84 SE 1693
East Haven 109 NO 5836
East Heckington 62 TF 1944
East Hedleyhope 84 NZ 1540
East Hendred 35 SU 4588
East Heslerton 81 SE 9276
East Hoathly 29 TQ 5216
Easthope 59 SO 5695
Easthorpe 38 TL 9121
East Horrington 33 ST 5846
East Horsley 28 TQ 0952
East Hoyle Bank (sbk.) 68 SJ 2090
East Huntspill 32 ST 3444
East Hyde 37 TL 1317
East Ilsley 35 SU 4981
Eastington (Glos.) 46 SO 7705
Eastington (Glos.) 47 SP 1213
East Kame (mt.) 141 HU 4257
East Kennett 34 SU 1167
East Keswick 79 SE 3544
East Kilbride 94 NS 6354
East Kirkby 73 TF 3362
East Knighton 25 SY 8185
East Knoyle 25 ST 8830
East Lambrook 25 ST 4319
East Lamington 129 NH 7577
East Langdon 31 TR 3346
East Langton 51 SP 7292
East Langwell 129 NC 7206
East Lavington 28 SU 9416
East Layton 84 NZ 1609
Eastleach Martin 47 SP 2005
Eastleach Turville 47 SP 1905
East Leake 61 SK 5526
East Leigh (Devon) 23 SS 6905
Eastleigh (Hants.) 27 SU 4518
East Lexham 64 TF 8617
East Lilburn 97 NU 0423
Eastling 31 TQ 9656
East Linga (is.) 141 HU 6162
East Linton 103 NT 5977
East Liss 27 SU 7827
East Loch Roag 131 NB 1837
East Loch Tarbert (Isle of Lewis) 125 NG 1896
East Loch Tarbert (Strath.) 99 NR 8769
East Lochussie 128 NH 5056
East Lound 74 SK 7899
East Lulworth 25 SY 8581
East Mains 119 NO 6797
East Malling 29 TQ 7057
East March 109 NO 4436
East Marden 27 SU 8014
East Markham 72 SK 7472
East Marsh 43 SN 2808
East Marton 78 SD 9050
East Meon 27 SU 6822
East Mersea 39 TM 0414
East Midlands Airport 61 SK 4525
East Molesey 37 TQ 1568
East Monar Forest 127 NH 1842
East Moor 71 SK 2870
East Morden 25 SY 9194
East Morton 78 SE 1042
Eastney 27 SZ 6698
Eastnor 49 SO 7337
East Norton 61 SK 7800
East Oakley 35 SU 5749
Eastoft 74 SE 8016
East Ogwell 21 SX 8370
Easton (Cambs.) 52 TL 1371
Easton (Cumbr.) 89 NY 4372
Easton (Devon) 21 SX 7288
Easton (Dorset) 25 SY 6871
Easton (Hants.) 27 SU 5132
Easton (I.of W.) 26 SZ 3485
Easton (Lincs.) 62 SK 9226
Easton (Norf.) 65 TG 1311
Easton (Somer.) 33 ST 5147
Easton (Suff.) 55 TM 2858
Easton Grey 33 ST 8787
Easton Hill 34 SU 2059
Easton-in-Gordano 33 ST 5175
Easton Maudit 52 SP 8858
Easton on the Hill 62 TF 0004
Easton Royal 34 SU 2060
East Ord 97 NT 9851
East Panson 20 SX 3692
East Peckham 29 TQ 6649
East Pennard 25 ST 5937
East Portlemouth 21 SX 7438
East Prawle 21 SX 7736
East Preston 28 TQ 0702
East Putford 22 SS 3616
East Quantoxhead 32 ST 1343
East Rainton 84 NZ 3347
East Ravendale 75 TF 2399
East Raynham 64 TF 8825
Eastrea 63 TL 2997
East Retford 72 SK 7080
East Rhidorroch Lodge 127 NH 2393
Eastriggs 89 NY 2465
Eastrington 74 SE 7929
East Road 31 TR 1123
East Rudham 64 TF 8228
East Runton 65 TG 1942
East Ruston 65 TG 3427
Eastry 31 TR 3155
East Saltoun 103 NT 4767
East Sleekburn 91 NZ 2785
East Stoke (Dorset) 25 SY 8787
East Stoke (Notts.) 61 SK 7549
East Stour 25 ST 8022
East Stourmouth 31 TR 2662
East Stour River 31 TR 0837
East Stratton 35 SU 5440
East Studdal 31 TR 3149
East Taphouse 19 SX 1863
East Tarbert Bay 92 NR 6552
East Thirston 91 NZ 1999
East Tilbury 38 TQ 6878
East Tisted 27 SU 7032
East Torrington 73 TF 1483
East Tuddenham 65 TG 0811
East Tytherley 26 SU 2929
East Tytherton 34 ST 9674
East Village 23 SS 8405
Eastville 73 TF 4057
East Voe of Quarff 141 HU 4335
East Wall 59 SO 5293
East Walton 64 TF 7416
East Wear Bay 31 TR 2537
Eastwell 61 SK 7728
East Wellow 26 SU 3020
Eastwell Park 31 TR 0147
East Wemyss 103 NT 3396
East Whitburn 102 NS 9665
Eastwick 37 TL 4311
East Wickham 37 TQ 4576
East Williamston 42 SN 0905
East Winch 64 TF 6916
East Wittering 27 SZ 7996
East Witton 78 SE 1486
Eastwood (Essex) 38 TQ 8588
Eastwood (Notts.) 61 SK 4646
Eastwood (W Yorks.) 78 SD 9625
East Woodhay 34 SU 4061
East Worldham 35 SU 7538
East Wretham 54 TL 9190
East Yell 143 HU 5284
Eathorpe 50 SP 3969
Eaton (Ches.) 69 SJ 5763
Eaton (Ches.) 69 SJ 8765
Eaton (Leic.) 61 SK 7929
Eaton (Norf.) 65 TG 2006
Eaton (Notts.) 72 SK 7077
Eaton (Oxon.) 47 SP 4403
Eaton (Shrops.) 48 SO 3789
Eaton (Shrops.) 48 SO 4989
Eaton Bishop 45 SO 4439
Eaton Bray 36 SP 9720
Eaton Constantine 59 SJ 5906
Eaton Hall 68 SJ 4160
Eaton Socon 52 TL 1658
Eaton upon Tern 59 SJ 6523
Eaval (mt.) 124 NF 8960
Ebberston 81 SE 8983
Ebbesborne Wake 26 ST 9824
Ebbw River 41 ST 2489
Ebbw Vale (Gwent) 41 SO 1609
Ebbw Vale (Gwent) 41 ST 2094
Ebchester 84 NZ 1055
Ebford 21 SX 9887
Ebrington 50 SP 1840
Eburacum (ant.) 79 SE 6052
Ecchinswell 35 SU 5060
Ecclaw 96 NT 7568
Ecclefechan 89 NY 1974
Eccles (Borders) 96 NT 7641
Eccles (Gtr Mches.) 69 SJ 7798
Eccles (Kent) 30 TQ 7260
Ecclesfield 71 SK 3393
Ecclesgreig 109 NO 7365
Eccleshall 59 SJ 8329
Ecclesmachan 102 NT 0573
Eccles Road 54 TM 0190
Eccleston (Ches.) 68 SJ 4162
Eccleston (Lancs.) 69 SD 5216
Eccleston (Mers.) 69 SJ 4895
Eccup 79 SE 2842
Eccup Reservoir 79 SE 2941
Echnaloch Bay 136 ND 4797
Echt 119 NJ 7305
Eckford 96 NT 7125
Eckington (Derby.) 71 SK 4379
Eckington (Here. and Worc.) 49 SO 9241
Ecton 52 SP 8263
Edale 70 SK 1285
Edale Cross (mt.) 70 SK 0886
Eday 138 HY 5634
Eday Sound 138 HY 5833
Edburton 28 TQ 2311
Edderton 129 NH 7184
Eddisbury Hill 69 SJ 5569
Eddleston 95 NT 2447
Eddleston Water 95 NT 2346
Eddrachillis Bay 132 NC 1336
Eddystone Rocks 20 SX 3833
Edenbridge 29 TQ 4446
Edendon Water 116 NN 7176
Edenfield 69 SD 8019
Edenhall 83 NY 5632
Edenham 62 TF 0621
Edenhope Hill 48 SO 2688
Eden Mouth 109 NO 5021
Eden Park 37 TQ 3868
Edensor 71 SK 2469
Edentaggart 100 NS 3394
Edenthorpe 71 SE 6206
Eden Water 96 NT 6345
Ederline 105 NM 8702
Edern 66 SH 2739
Edgarhope Wood 96 NT 5549
Edgbaston 50 SP 0684
Edgcott 36 SP 6722
Edge 58 SJ 3908
Edgebolton 59 SJ 5721
Edge End 45 SO 5913
Edgefield 65 TG 0934
Edgefield Street 65 TG 0933
Edge Hill 50 SP 3747
Edgelaw Resr. 103 NT 3058
Edgeworth 46 SO 9406
Edgmond 59 SJ 7119
Edgmond Marsh 59 SJ 7120
Edgton 48 SO 3885
Edgware 37 TQ 2091
Edgworth 69 SD 7416
Edinample 107 NN 6022
Edinbane 122 NG 3451
Edinburgh 103 NT 2674
Edinburgh Airport 102 NT 1573
Edingale 60 SK 2112
Edinglight House 121 NJ 5155
Edingley 61 SK 6655
Edingthorpe 65 TG 3132
Edington (Somer.) 32 ST 3939
Edington (Wilts.) 33 ST 9252
Edithmead 32 ST 3249
Edith Weston 62 SK 9205
Edlesborough 36 SP 9719
Edlingham 91 NU 1108
Edlington 73 TF 2371
Edmondsham 26 SU 0611
Edmondsley 84 NZ 2348
Edmondthorpe 62 SK 8517
Edmonstone 137 HY 5220
Edmonton 37 TQ 3493
Edmundbyers 84 NZ 0150
Ednam 96 NT 7337
Edradour House 108 NN 9558
Edradynate 108 NN 8852
Edrom 97 NT 8255
Edstaston 59 SJ 5131
Edstone 50 SP 1761
Edvin Loach 49 SO 6658
Edwalton 61 SK 5935
Edwardstone 54 TL 9442
Edwinsford 43 SN 6334
Edwinstowe 71 SK 6266
Edworth 53 TL 2241
Edwyn Ralph 49 SO 6457
Edzell 109 NO 5968
Eela Water 142 HU 3378
Efail Isaf 41 ST 0884
Efailnewydd 66 SH 3536
Efenechtyd 58 SJ 1155
Effingham 28 TQ 1253
Effingham Junction Station 28 TQ 1055
Effirth 141 HU 3152
Efford 23 SS 8901
Egerton (Gtr Mches.) 69 SD 7014
Egerton (Kent) 30 TQ 9047
Egerton Forstal 30 TQ 8946
Egga Field (mt.) 142 HU 3289
Eggardon Hill 25 SY 5494
Eggerness Point 87 NX 4946
Eggesford Station 23 SS 6811
Eggington 52 SP 9525
Egginton 60 SK 2628
Egglescliffe 85 NZ 4213
Eggleston 84 NZ 0023
Eggleston Common 84 NZ 0128
Egglestone Abbey (ant.) 84 NZ 0615
Egham 36 TQ 0171
Egilsay (Orkney) (is.) 136 HY 4729
Egilsay (Shetld.) (is.) 142 HU 3169
Egleton 62 SK 8707
Eglingham 91 NU 1019
Egloshayle 19 SX 0071
Egloskerry 20 SX 2786
Eglwysbach 67 SH 8070
Eglwys-Brewis 41 ST 0168
Eglwyseg Mountain 58 SJ 2347
Eglwys Nunydd Resr. 41 SS 7985
Eglwyswrw 42 SN 1438
Egmanton 72 SK 7368
Egremont 82 NY 0110
Egton 80 NZ 8006
Egton Bridge 80 NZ 8005
Egton High Moor 80 NZ 7701
Eididh nan Clach Geala (mt.) 127 NH 2584
Eigg (is.) 111 NM 4786
Eigg, The (pt.) 143 HU 4495
Eight Ash Green 54 TL 9425
Eignaig 105 NM 7944
Eigneig Bheag (pt.) 124 NF 9260
Eigneig Mhòr (pt.) 124 NF 9361
Eil 117 NH 8217
Eilanreach 123 NG 8017
Eildon Hills 96 NT 5432
Eileach an Naoimh 105 NM 6409
Eilean a' Bhreitheimh 132 NC 1339
Eilean a'Chalmain 104 NM 3017
Eilean a'Chladaich 98 NR 3392
Eileanach Lodge 128 NH 5468
Eilean a'Chùirn 98 NR 4749
Eilean a' Ghaill 111 NM 6282
Eilean Annraidh 104 NM 2926
Eilean an Ròin Mòr 132 NC 1758
Eilean an Tighe 125 NG 4297
Eilean an t-Snidhe 111 NM 6381
Eilean Aoidhe 100 NR 9367
Eilean Balnagowan 106 NM 9554
Eilean Beag (Highld.) 123 NG 6836
Eilean Beag (Islay) 98 NR 2774
Eilean Bhride 98 NR 4547
Eilean Chaluim Chille 131 NB 3821
Eilean Chathastail 111 NM 4883
Eilean Choraidh 133 NC 4258
Eilean Chrona 132 NC 0633
Eilean Clùimhrig 133 NC 4666
Eilean Craobhach 98 NR 4649
Eilean Creagach 122 NG 2965
Eilean Dallaig 112 NF 6908
Eilean Darach 127 NH 1087
Eilean Dioghlum 104 NM 3542
Eilean Dubh (Highld.) 126 NB 9703
Eilean Dubh (Strath.) 105 NM 8338
Eilean Dubh (Strath.) 105 NM 8742
Eilean Dubh (Strath.) 99 NR 7187
Eilean Dubh Cruinn 105 NM 4433
Eilean Dubh Mòr 105 NM 6910
Eilean Duin 105 NM 7821
Eilean Fladday 123 NG 5851
Eilean Flodigarry 123 NG 4771
Eilean Furadh Mòr 126 NG 7993
Eilean Garbh (Gigha Island) 92 NR 6554
Eilean Garbh (Island of Rona) 123 NG 6056
Eilean Ghaoideamal 98 NR 3687
Eilean Glas (Isle of Lewis) 125 NG 2494
Eilean Grianain 92 NR 8142
Eilean Heast 123 NG 6415
Eilean Hoan 133 NC 4467
Eilean Horrisdale 123 NG 7874
Eilean Ighe 111 NM 6388
Eilean Imersay 98 NR 4346
Eilean Iosal 122 NG 2865
Eilean Iubhard 131 NB 3809
Eilean Kearstay 131 NB 1933
Eilean Leathan 98 NR 3290
Eilean Loain 99 NR 7585
Eilean Loch Oscair 105 NM 8645
Eilean Mhic Chrion 105 NM 8003
Eilean Mhuire 125 NG 4398
Eilean Mór (Coll, Strath.) 110 NM 2765
Eilean Mór (Highld.) 132 NC 0517
Eilean Mór (Highld.) 123 NG 6934
Eilean Mór (Island of Skye) 122 NG 3557
Eilean Mór (Strath.) 99 NR 6675
Eilean Mór (Strath.) (is.) 106 NM 8834
Eilean Mór a' Bhàigh 125 NB 2600
Eilean Mullagrach 132 NB 9511
Eilean Musdile 105 NM 7835
Eilean na Bà 123 NG 6938
Eilean na Creiche 104 NM 3837
Eilean na h-Airde 123 NG 5211
Eilean na h-Aon Chaorach 104 NM 2520
Eilean nam Muc 104 NM 2819
Eilean nan Caorach 106 NM 9046
Eilean nan Coinean 99 NR 7186
Eilean nan Each 111 NM 3981
Eilean nan Gamhna 105 NM 8130
Eilean nan Gobhar 111 NM 6979
Eilean nan Ròn (Colonsay) 98 NR 3386
Eilean nan Ròn (Highld.) 133 NC 6365
Eilean Ona 105 NM 7602
Eilean Orasaidh 131 NB 4121
Eilean Ornsay 110 NM 2255
Eilean Ràrsaidh 123 NG 8111
Eilean Righ 99 NM 8001
Eilean Ruairidh Mór 126 NG 8973
Eilean Shona 111 NM 6474
Eilean Sùbhainn 126 NG 9272
Eilean Thòraidh 131 NB 4220
Eilean Thuilm 111 NM 4891
Eilean Tigh 123 NG 6053
Eilean Treadhrach 98 NR 3788
Eilean Trodday 125 NG 4478
Eishken 131 NB 3211
Eitshal (mt.) 131 NB 3030
Elan Village 57 SN 9365
Elberton (Avon) 33 ST 6088
Elburton (Devon) 21 SX 5353
Elchies Forest 120 NJ 2246
Elcho 108 NO 1620
Elcombe 34 SU 1280
Eldernell 63 TL 3298
Eldersfield 46 SO 7931
Elderslie 101 NS 4462
Eldrable Hill 134 NC 9816
Eldrick Hill 86 NX 3693
Eldrig Fell 86 NX 2568
Eldroth 78 SD 7665
Eldwick 78 SE 1240
Elford (Northum.) 97 NU 1830
Elford (Staffs.) 60 SK 1810
Elgin 120 NJ 2162
Elgol 123 NG 5214
Elham 31 TR 1744
Elibank and Traquair Forest 96 NT 3635
Elie 103 NO 4900
Elim 66 SH 3584
Eling 26 SU 3612
Elishader 123 NG 5065
Elishaw 90 NY 8694
Elkesley 72 SK 6875
Elkstone 46 SO 9612
Elland 78 SE 1020
Ellary 99 NR 7476
Ellastone 60 SK 1143
Ellemford 96 NT 7360
Ellenhall 59 SJ 8426
Ellen's Green 28 TQ 1035
Ellen's Isle 101 NN 4808
Eller Beck (N Yorks.) 78 SD 9854
Ellerbeck (N Yorks.) 85 SE 4396
Ellerby (N Yorks.) 85 NZ 7914
Ellerdine Heath 59 SJ 6121
Elleric 106 NN 0348
Ellerker 74 SE 9229
Ellerton (Humbs.) 74 SE 7039
Ellerton (Shrops.) 59 SJ 7126
Ellesborough 36 SP 8306
Ellesmere 58 SJ 3934
Ellesmere Port 68 SJ 4077
Ellingham (Norf.) 55 TM 3592
Ellingham (Northum.) 97 NU 1725
Ellingstring 78 SE 1783
Ellington (Cambs.) 52 TL 1671
Ellington (Northum.) 91 NZ 2792
Elliot Water 109 NO 5841
Ellis Crag 90 NT 7401
Ellisfield 35 SU 6345
Ellister 98 NR 1852
Ellistown 60 SK 4311
Ellon 121 NJ 9530
Ellough 55 TM 4486
Elloughton 74 SE 9428
Ellwood 45 SO 5808
Elm 63 TF 4607
Elmbridge 49 SO 8967
Elmdon (Essex) 53 TL 4639
Elmdon (W Mids) 50 SP 1783
Elmdon Heath 50 SP 1580
Elmesthorpe 61 SP 4696
Elmhurst 60 SK 1112
Elmley Castle 50 SO 9841
Elmley Island 30 TQ 9468
Elmley Lovett 49 SO 8669
Elmore 46 SO 7715
Elmore Back 46 SO 7716
Elm Park 37 TQ 5385
Elmscott 22 SS 2321
Elmsett 54 TM 0546
Elmstead Market 39 TM 0624
Elmsted Court 31 TR 1145
Elmstone 31 TR 2660
Elmstone Hardwicke 46 SO 9226
Elmswell 54 TL 9964
Elmton 71 SK 5073
Elphin 132 NC 2111
Elphinstone 103 NT 3970
Elrick 119 NJ 8206
Elrick Burn 116 NH 6811
Elrig 86 NX 3247
Elsdon 90 NY 9393
Elsecar 71 SE 3800
Elsenham 53 TL 5425
Elsfield 47 SP 5409
Elsham 74 TA 0312
Elsick House 119 NO 8894
Elsing 64 TG 0516
Elslack 78 SD 9349
Els Ness 139 HY 6738
Elsrickle 95 NT 0643
Elstead (Surrey) 28 SU 9043
Elsted (W Susx) 27 SU 8119
Elston 61 SK 7548
Elstone 23 SS 6716
Elstow 52 TL 0547
Elstree 37 TQ 1895
Elstree Aerodrome 37 TQ 1596
Elstronwick 75 TA 2232
Elswick 77 SD 4138
Elsworth 53 TL 3163
Elterwater 82 NY 3204
Eltham 37 TQ 4274
Eltisley 53 TL 2759
Elton (Cambs.) 62 TL 0893
Elton (Ches.) 68 SJ 4575
Elton (Cleve.) 85 NZ 4017
Elton (Derby.) 71 SK 2261
Elton (Glos.) 46 SO 6914
Elton (Here. and Worc.) 48 SO 4571
Elton (Notts.) 61 SK 7638
Elvanfoot 88 NS 9517
Elvan Water 88 NS 9216
Elvaston 60 SK 4132
Elveden 54 TL 8279
Elvingston 103 NT 4674
Elvington (Kent) 31 TR 2750
Elvington (N Yorks.) 74 SE 6947
Elwick (Cleve.) 85 NZ 4532
Elwick (Northum.) 97 NU 1136
Elworth 69 SJ 7361
Elworthy 24 ST 0835
Ely (Cambs.) 53 TL 5380
Ely (S Glam.) 41 ST 1476
Ely River 41 ST 0185
Ely Valley 41 ST 0579
Emberton 52 SP 8849
Emblehope Moor 90 NY 7395
Embleton (Cumbr.) 82 NY 1630
Embleton (Northum.) 97 NU 2322
Embleton Bay 97 NU 2423
Embo 129 NH 8192
Emborough 33 ST 6151
Embsay 78 SE 0053
Embsay Moor 78 SE 0056
Embsay Resr. 78 SE 0054
Emery Down 26 SU 2808
Emley 71 SE 2413
Emmer Green 36 SU 7177
Emmington 36 SP 7402
Emneth 63 TF 4807
Emneth Hungate 63 TF 5107
Empingham 62 SK 9408
Empshott 27 SU 7731
Emsworth 27 SU 7405
Emsworth Channel 27 SU 7403
Enaclete 131 NB 1228
Enard Bay 132 NC 0416
Enborne 34 SU 4365
Enchmarsh 59 SO 4996
Enderby 61 SP 5399
End Moor 77 SD 5584
Endon 59 SJ 9253
Endrick Water 101 NS 6087
Enfield 37 TQ 3296
Enfield Chase 37 TQ 2998
Enford 34 SU 1351
Enford Down 34 SU 1049
Engine Common 33 ST 6984
Englefield 36 SU 6272
Englefield Green 36 SU 9870
English Bicknor 45 SO 5815
Englishcombe 33 ST 7162
English Frankton 58 SJ 4529
English Stones (pt.) 33 ST 5285
Enham-Alamein 34 SU 3648
Enmore 24 ST 2335
Ennerdale Bridge 82 NY 0615
Ennerdale Fell 82 NY 1313
Ennerdale Water 82 NY 1015
Enoch 88 NS 8801
Enochdhu 108 NO 0662
Enoch Hill 88 NS 5606
Ensay (Harris) 124 NF 9786
Ensay (Island of Mull) 104 NM 3648
Ensbury 26 SZ 0896
Ensdon 58 SJ 4016
Ensis 23 SS 5626
Enstone 47 SP 3724
Enterkinfoot 88 NS 8504
Entwistle Station 69 SD 7217
Enville 49 SO 8286
Enyas Hill 136 HY 4020
Eochar 124 NF 7846
Eoligarry 112 NF 7007
Eorabus 104 NM 3823
Eoropie 131 NB 5165
Eorsa (is.) 105 NM 4837
Epperstone 61 SK 6548
Epping 37 TL 4602
Epping Forest 37 TQ 4197
Epping Green (Essex) 37 TL 4305
Epping Green (Herts.) 37 TL 2906
Epping Upland 37 TL 4404
Eppleby 84 NZ 1713
Epsom 37 TQ 2160
Epsom Downs Station 37 TQ 2259
Epwell 50 SP 3540
Epworth 74 SE 7803
Erbistock 58 SJ 3541
Erbusaig 123 NG 7629
Erchless Castle 115 NH 4040
Erchless Forest 128 NH 4145
Erdington 50 SP 1291
Eredine 100 NM 9609
Eredine Forest (Strath.) 100 NM 9507
Eredine Forest (Strath.) 100 NN 0012
Eriboll 133 NC 4356
Ericstane 89 NT 0710
Eridge Green 29 TQ 5535
Eridge Station 29 TQ 5434
Erines 99 NR 8575
Erisgeir 104 NM 3832
Eriska (dist.) 106 NM 8943
Eriskay 112 NF 7910
Eriswell 54 TL 7278
Erith 37 TQ 5177
Erlestoke 34 ST 9853
Ermine Street (Cambs.) (ant.) 62 TL 1593
Ermine Street (Cambs.) (ant.) 53 TL 2667
Ermine Street (Herts.) (ant.) 37 TL 3720
Ermine Street (Lincs.) (ant.) 72 SK 9685
Ermington 21 SX 6353
Ermin Way (ant.) 46 SO 9611
Ernan Water 117 NJ 2712
Erne Stack 141 HU 3067
Erpingham 65 TG 1931
Erraid (is.) 104 NM 2919
Errochty Water 107 NN 7663
Errogie 116 NH 5622
Errol 108 NO 2522
Errwood Resr. 70 SK 0175
Erskine 101 NS 4670
Erskine Bridge 101 NS 4672
Ervie 86 NX 0067
Erwarton 55 TM 2234
Erwood 44 SO 0943
Eryholme 84 NZ 3208
Eryrys 68 SJ 2057
Esclusham Mountain 58 SJ 2550
Escrick 79 SE 6243
Esgair Ambor 44 SN 7559
Esgair Berfa 57 SH 6309
Esgair Cerrig 44 SN 7556
Esgair Cwmowen 57 SJ 0100
Esgair Ddu 57 SH 8710
Esgair Fraith 44 SN 7057
Esgair Garthen 57 SN 8364
Esgairgeiliog 57 SH 7605
Esgair Llethr 44 SN 7254
Esgair Llyn-du 57 SN 7661
Esgairnantau 48 SO 1762
Esgair Priciau 57 SH 9304
Esgair Ychion 57 SN 8480

Esgair y Maesnant 57 SN 8386
Esh 84 NZ 1944
Esha Ness 142 HU 2279
Esher 37 TQ 1464
Eshott 91 NZ 2097
Eshton 78 SD 9356
Esh Winning 84 NZ 1942
Eskadale 116 NH 4539
Eskbank 103 NT 3266
Eskdale (Cumbr.) 82 NY 1800
Eskdale (Dumf. and Galwy.) 89 NY 3489
Esk Dale (N Yorks.) 80 NZ 7407
Eskdale Green 82 NY 1400
Eskdalemuir 89 NY 2597
Eskdalemuir Forest 89 NT 2503
Eskielawn (mt.) 108 NO 2766
Esknish 98 NR 3664
Espley Hall 91 NZ 1790
Esprick 77 SD 4035
Essendine 62 TF 0412
Essendon 37 TL 2708
Essich 116 NH 6539
Essington 60 SJ 9603
Esslemont 121 NJ 9329
Esthwaite Water 82 SD 3596
Eston 85 NZ 5518
Etal 97 NT 9339
Etchilhampton 34 SU 0460
Etchingham 29 TQ 7126
Etchinghill (Kent) 31 TR 1639
Etchinghill (Staffs.) 60 SK 0218
Ethie Castle 109 NO 6846
Eton 36 SU 9678
Etteridge 116 NN 6892
Ettington 50 SP 2649
Etton (Humbs.) 74 SE 9743
Etton (Northants.) 62 TF 1306
Ettrick 89 NT 2714
Ettrick Bay 100 NS 0365
Ettrickbridge 96 NT 3824
Ettrick Forest 96 NT 3724
Ettrick Pen 89 NT 1907
Ettrick Water 89 NT 3118
Etwall 60 SK 2732
Euchan Water 88 NS 7206
Euston 54 TL 8978
Euston Station 37 TQ 2982
Euximoor Fen 63 TL 4799
Euxton 69 SD 5518
Evanton 128 NH 6066
Evedon 62 TF 0947
Evelix 129 NH 7691
Evenjobb 48 SO 2662
Evenley 47 SP 5834
Evenlode 47 SP 2229
Eventide Home 119 NJ 9618
Evenwood 84 NZ 1524
Everbay 137 HY 6724
Evercreech 33 ST 6438
Everdon 51 SP 5957
Everingham 74 SE 8042
Everleigh 34 SU 1953
Everley 81 SE 9789
Eversholt 52 SP 9933
Evershot 25 ST 5704
Eversley 36 SU 7762
Eversley Cross 36 SU 7961
Everton (Beds.) 52 TL 2051
Everton (Hants.) 26 SZ 2993
Everton (Notts.) 72 SK 6891
Evertown 89 NY 3576
Evesbatch 49 SO 6848
Evesham 50 SP 0344
Evington 61 SK 6203
Ewden Village 71 SK 2796
Ewe Hill 95 NT 0540
Ewelairs Hill 89 NT 1602
Ewell 37 TQ 2262
Ewell Minnis 31 TR 2643
Ewelme 36 SU 6491
Ewen 46 SU 0097
Ewenny 41 SS 9077
Ewerby 62 TF 1247
Ewes 89 NY 3690
Eweslees Knowe 89 NT 3201
Ewesley 91 NZ 0592
Ewes Water 89 NY 3791
Ewhurst (Surrey) 28 TQ 0940
Ewhurst Green 30 TQ 7924
Ewloe 68 SJ 3066
Eworthy 20 SX 4494
Ewshot 35 SU 8149
Ewyas Harold 45 SO 3828
Exbourne 23 SS 6002
Exbury 26 SU 4200
Exebridge 23 SS 9324
Exelby 79 SE 2986
Exeter 21 SX 9292
Exeter Airport 21 SX 9993
Exe Valley 23 SS 9415
Exford 23 SS 8538
Exhall 50 SP 1055
Exminster 21 SX 9487
Exmoor Forest 23 SS 7642
Exmouth 21 SY 0080
Exnaboe 141 HU 3912
Exning 54 TL 6265
Exton (Devon) 21 SX 9886
Exton (Hants.) 27 SU 6121
Exton (Leic.) 62 SK 9211
Exton (Somer.) 23 SS 9233
Eyam 70 SK 2176
Ey Burn 117 NO 0886
Eydon 51 SP 5450
Eye (Here. and Worc.) 48 SO 4963
Eye (Northants.) 63 TF 2202
Eye (Suffolk) 55 TM 1473
Eye Brook 61 SK 7602
Eyebrook Resr. 62 SP 8595
Eyebroughy (pt.) 103 NT 4986
Eyemouth 97 NT 9464
Eye Peninsula 131 NB 5332
Eye Water 97 NT 8263
Eyeworth 53 TL 2545
Eyhorne Street 30 TQ 8354
Eyke 55 TM 3151
Eynesbury 52 TL 1859
Eynhallow (is.) 136 HY 3529
Eynhallow Sound 136 HY 3827
Eynort 122 NG 3826
Eynort River 122 NG 3727
Eynsford 37 TQ 5365
Eynsham 47 SP 4309
Eype 25 SY 4491
Eyre 123 NG 4152
Eyre Point 123 NG 5834
Eythorne 31 TR 2849
Eyton (Here. and Worc.) 48 SO 4761
Eyton (Salop) 48 SO 3687
Eyton upon the Weald Moors 59 SJ 6414

F

Faan Hill 142 HU 3480
Faccombe 34 SU 3857
Faceby 85 NZ 4903
Faddiley 59 SJ 5752
Fadmoor 85 SE 6789
Faifley 101 NS 5073
Failand 33 ST 5272
Failford 93 NS 4526
Failsworth 69 SD 9002
Fairbourne 56 SH 6113
Fairburn 79 SE 4727
Fairfield 49 SO 9475
Fairford 47 SP 1501
Fairham Brook 61 SK 5531
Fair Isle 139 HZ 2172
Fairlie 93 NS 2155
Fairlie Roads 93 NS 1753
Fairlight 30 TQ 8612
Fairmile 24 SY 0997
Fairmilehead 103 NT 2567
Fairnington House 96 NT 6427
Fair Oak (Hants.) 27 SU 4918
Fairoak (Staffs.) 59 SJ 7632
Fairoaks Airport 36 TQ 0062
Fairseat 30 TQ 6261
Fair Snape Fell 77 SD 5947
Fairstead (Essex) 38 TL 7616
Fairwarp 29 TQ 4626
Fairy Cross 22 SS 4024
Fairy Glen 67 SH 8054
Faither, The (pt.) 142 HU 2585
Fakenham 64 TF 9229
Fala 103 NT 4361
Fala Dam 103 NT 4261
Falahill 96 NT 3956
Fala Moor 103 NT 4258
Faldingworth 72 TF 0684
Falfield 46 ST 6893
Falkenham 55 TM 2939
Falkirk 102 NS 8880
Falkland 103 NO 2507
Falla 90 NT 7013
Fallin 101 NS 8391
Fall of Glomach 114 NH 0325
Fall of Warness (chan.) 137 HY 5427
Fallowlees Burn 91 NY 9992
Falls of Acharn 107 NN 7543
Falls of Bruar The 107 NN 8267
Falls of Cruachan 106 NN 0727
Falls of Falloch 106 NN 3420
Falls of Garbh Allt 117 NO 2089
Falls of Keltie 108 NN 8625
Falls of Lochay 107 NN 5434
Falls of Lora 106 NM 9134
Falls of Moness 108 NN 8547
Falls of Rogie 128 NH 4458
Falls of Tummel 108 NN 9159
Falmer 29 TQ 3508
Falmouth 19 SW 8032
Falmouth Bay 19 SW 8130
Falstone 90 NY 7287
Fambridge Station 38 TQ 8597
Fanagmore 132 NC 1750
Fan Fawr 41 SN 9619
Fangdale Beck 85 SE 5694
Fangfoss 80 SE 7653
Fan-Gihirych 41 SN 8819
Fan Hill 57 SN 9388
Fan Hir (mt.) 41 SN 8220
Fan Llia 41 SN 9318
Fanmore 105 NM 4244
Fanna Hill 90 NT 5603
Fannich Forest 127 NH 1968
Fannich Lodge 127 NH 2166
Fannyside Lochs 101 NS 8073
Fans 96 NT 6140
Fara (is.) 136 ND 3295
Faraclett Head 138 HY 4433
Faraid Head 132 NC 3971
Faray 138 HY 5336
Farcet 62 TL 2094
Farcet Fen 53 TL 2392
Far Cotton 51 SP 7458
Farden 48 SO 5770
Fareham 27 SU 5806
Farewell 60 SK 0811
Farigaig Forest 116 NH 5221
Faringdon 47 SU 2895
Farington 77 SD 5425
Farlam 90 NY 5558
Farland Head 93 NS 1748
Farlary 129 NC 7606
Farleigh 37 TQ 3660
Farleigh Hungerford 33 ST 7957
Farleigh Wallop 35 SU 6246
Farlesthorpe 73 TF 4774
Farleton 77 SD 5380
Farley (Shrops.) 58 SJ 3808
Farley (Staffs.) 60 SK 0644
Farley (Wilts.) 26 SU 2229
Farley Green 28 TQ 0645
Farley Hill 36 SU 7564
Farley Mount 26 SU 3928
Farleys End 46 SO 7615
Farlington 79 SE 6167
Farlow 40 SO 6380
Farmborough 33 ST 6560
Farmcote 46 SP 0629
Farmers 43 SN 6444
Farmington 47 SP 1315
Farmoor 47 SP 4407
Farmoor Resr. 47 SP 4406
Farmtown 121 NJ 5051
Farnborough (Berks.) 34 SU 4381
Farnborough (Gtr London) 37 TQ 4464
Farnborough (Hants.) 35 SU 8753
Farnborough (Warw.) 50 SP 4349
Farncombe 28 SU 9755
Farndale 80 SE 6895
Farndale Moor 85 NZ 6500
Farndish 52 SP 9263
Farndon (Ches.) 58 SJ 4154
Farndon (Notts.) 61 SK 7651
Farne Islands 97 NU 2337
Farnell 109 NO 6255
Farnham (Dorset) 26 ST 9514
Farnham (Essex) 37 TL 4724
Farnham (N Yorks.) 79 SE 3460
Farnham (Suff.) 55 TM 3660
Farnham (Surrey) 35 SU 8446
Farnham Common 36 SU 9584
Farnham Green 53 TL 4625
Farnham Royal 36 SU 9682
Farningham 37 TQ 5566
Farnley 78 SE 2147
Farnley Tyas 70 SE 1612
Farnsfield 61 SK 6456
Farnworth (Ches.) 69 SJ 5187
Farnworth (Gtr Mches.) 69 SD 7305
Farquhar's Point 111 NM 6272
Farr (Highld.) 134 NC 7163
Farr (Highld.) 116 NH 6833
Farr (Highld.) 117 NH 8203
Farragon Hill 107 NN 8455
Farr Bay 133 NC 7063
Farr House 116 NH 6831
Farringdon 24 SY 0191
Farrington Gurney 33 ST 6255
Farrmheall (mt.) 132 NC 3058
Farr Point 134 NC 7164
Farsley 78 SE 2135
Farthinghoe 51 SP 5339
Farthingstone 51 SP 6155
Farway 24 SY 1895
Fascadale 111 NM 5070
Faseny Water 103 NT 6162
Fasheilach 118 NO 3485
Fashven (mt.) 132 NC 3167
Faslane Bay 100 NS 2489
Fasnacloich 106 NN 0247
Fasnakyle 115 NH 3128
Fasnakyle Forest 115 NH 2630
Fasque 119 NO 6475
Fassfern 114 NN 0278
Fast Castle (ant.) 97 NT 8671
Fastheugh Hill 96 NT 3927
Fatfield 84 NZ 3053
Fathan Glinne 107 NN 4917
Fattahead 121 NJ 6657
Faugh 83 NY 5155
Fauldhouse 102 NS 9260
Faulkbourne 38 TL 7917
Faulkland 33 ST 7354
Fauls 59 SJ 5933
Faversham 31 TR 0161
Favillar 117 NJ 2734
Fawfieldhead 70 SK 0763
Fawkham Green 37 TQ 5865
Fawler 47 SP 3717
Fawley (Berks.) 34 SU 3981
Fawley (Bucks.) 36 SU 7586
Fawley (Hants.) 27 SU 4503
Fawley Chapel 45 SO 5829
Faw Side (mt.) 89 NY 3596
Faxfleet 74 SE 8624
Faygate 28 TQ 2134
Fazeley 60 SK 2001
Feadda Ness 141 HU 5438
Feall Bay 110 NM 1354
Fearby 78 SE 1981
Feardar Burn 117 NO 1995
Fearnan 107 NN 7244
Fearnbeg 123 NG 7359
Fearnhead 69 SJ 6290
Fearn Lodge 128 NH 6387
Fearnmore 123 NG 7260
Fearnoch Forest 106 NM 9631
Fearn Station 129 NH 8178
Featherbed Top 70 SK 0892
Featherstone (Staffs.) 59 SJ 9305
Featherstone (W Yorks.) 79 SE 4222
Featherstone Castle 90 NY 6761
Feckenham 50 SP 0061
Fedderate 121 NJ 8949
Feering 38 TL 8720
Feetham 84 SD 9898
Feinne-bheinn Mhór 133 NC 4346
Féith a'Chaoruinn 133 NC 5522
Féith Gaineimh Mhór 134 NC 9332
Féith Talagain 116 NN 5497
Feizor 78 SD 7968
Felbridge 29 TQ 3739
Felbrigg 65 TG 2039
Felcourt 29 TQ 3841
Felden 36 TL 0404
Felindre (Dyfed) 40 SN 7027
Felindre (Powys) 48 SO 1681
Felindre (W Glam.) 40 SN 6302
Felinfach 41 SO 0933
Felinfoel 40 SN 5202
Felingwm Uchaf 43 SN 5024
Felixkirk 79 SE 4684
Felixstowe 55 TM 3034
Felkington 97 NT 9444
Felling 91 NZ 2762
Fell of Barhullion 86 NX 3742
Fell of Carleton 86 NX 4037
Fell of Fleet 88 NX 5670
Fell Side 82 NY 3037
Fell Top 77 SD 5751
Felmersham 52 SP 9957
Felmingham 65 TG 2529
Felpham 28 SZ 9599
Felsham 54 TL 9457
Felsted 38 TL 6720
Feltham 37 TQ 1072
Felthorpe 65 TG 1618
Felton (Avon) 33 ST 5165
Felton (Here. and Worc.) 45 SO 5748
Felton (Northum.) 91 NU 1800
Felton Butler 58 SJ 3917
Feltwell 54 TL 7190
Feltwell Anchor 54 TL 6789
Fence 78 SD 8237
Fencote 84 SE 2893
Fender Burn 108 NN 9169
Fendike Corner 73 TF 4560
Fen Ditton 53 TL 4860
Fen Drayton 53 TL 3468
Fen End 50 SP 2274
Feniscowles 77 SD 6425
Feniton 24 SY 1199
Fenn's Moss 59 SJ 4937
Fenny Bentley 60 SK 1750
Fenny Bridges 24 SY 1198
Fenny Compton 50 SP 4152
Fenny Drayton 60 SP 3597
Fenny Stratford 52 SP 8834
Fen Road (ant.) 63 TL 4698
Fenrother 91 NZ 1792
Fenstanton 53 TL 3168
Fenton (Cambs.) 53 TL 3279
Fenton (Lincs.) 72 SK 8476
Fenton (Lincs.) 62 SK 8750
Fenton (Staffs.) 59 SJ 8944
Fenwick (Northum.) 97 NU 0639
Fenwick (Northum.) 91 NZ 0572
Fenwick (Strath.) 93 NS 4643
Fenwick (S Yorks.) 71 SE 5916
Fenwick Water 93 NS 4541
Feochaig 92 NR 7613
Feochan Bheag 106 NM 8824
Feock 19 SW 8238
Feolin Ferry 98 NR 4469
Feriniquarrie 122 NG 1750
Fern 109 NO 4861
Ferndale 41 SS 9997
Ferndown 26 SU 0700
Ferness 129 NH 9645
Fernham 34 SU 2991
Fernhill Heath 49 SO 8659
Fernhurst 27 SU 9028
Fernie 108 NO 3115
Ferniehirst Castle (ant.) 90 NT 6517
Fernilea 122 NG 3634
Fernilee 70 SK 0178
Fernilee Resr. 70 SK 0176
Fernworthy Reservoir 21 SX 6684
Ferrensby 79 SE 3660
Ferring 28 TQ 0902
Ferrybridge 79 SE 4824
Ferryden 109 NO 7156
Ferryhill 84 NZ 2832
Ferryside 43 SN 3610
Fersfield 54 TM 0682
Fersit 115 NN 3577
Fers Ness 138 HY 5334
Fersness Bay 138 HY 5434
Fersness Hill 138 HY 5332
Feshiebridge 117 NH 8504
Fetcham 28 TQ 1555
Fethaland 143 HU 3793
Fetlar (is.) 143 HU 6291
Fetterangus 121 NJ 9850
Fettercairn 119 NO 6573
Fetteresso Forest 119 NO 7786
Fewston 78 SE 1954
Fewston Resr. 78 SE 1754
Ffairfach 43 SN 6220
Ffestiniog 67 SH 7042
Fforest 43 SN 5804
Fforest Fach (Powys) 41 SN 9027
Fforest-fach (Powys) 48 SO 1867
Fforest-fach (W Glam.) 40 SS 6396
Fforest Fawr 41 SN 9018
Ffostrasol 43 SN 3747
Ffridd 57 SH 9603
Ffridd Faldwyn (ant.) 58 SO 2196
Ffridd Fawr 67 SJ 0560
Ffridd-uchaf 66 SH 5751
Ffrith 58 SJ 2855
Ffrwdgrech 41 SO 0227
Ffynnonddrain 43 SN 4021
Ffynnongroew 68 SJ 1382
Ffynnon Llugwy Reservoir 67 SH 6962
Fiag Lodge (ruin) 133 NC 4528
Fiarach (mt.) 106 NN 3425
Fiaray 112 NF 7010
Fiavig Bàgh 130 NB 0335
Fidden 104 NM 3021
Fiddes 119 NO 8181
Fiddington (Glos.) 46 SO 9231
Fiddington (Somer.) 32 ST 2140
Fiddlers Hamlet 37 TL 4701
Fidra (is.) 103 NT 5186
Field 60 SK 0233
Field Broughton 77 SD 3881
Field Dalling 64 TG 0039
Field Head 61 SK 4909
Fifehead Magdalen 25 ST 7721
Fifehead Neville 25 ST 7610
Fife Ness 103 NO 6309
Fifield (Berks.) 36 SU 9076
Fifield (Oxon.) 47 SP 2318
Figheidean 34 SU 1547
Figsbury Ring (ant.) 26 SU 1833
Filby 65 TG 4613
Filey 81 TA 1180
Filey Bay 81 TA 1378
Filgrave 52 SP 8748
Filkins 47 SP 2304
Filla (is.) 143 HU 6668
Filleigh (Devon) 23 SS 6628
Filleigh (Devon) 23 SS 7410
Fill Geo 143 HP 5708
Fillingham 72 SK 9485
Fillongley 50 SP 2787
Filton 33 ST 6079
Filton Airfield 33 ST 5880
Fimber 81 SE 8960
Finalty Hill 117 NO 2074
Finavon 109 NO 4957
Finavon Castle 109 NO 4956
Finbracks (mt.) 109 NO 4070
Finchale Priory (ant.) 84 NZ 2947
Fincham 64 TF 6806
Finchampstead 36 SU 7963
Fincharn 100 NM 9003
Finchdean 27 SU 7312
Finchingfield 54 TL 6832
Finchley 37 TQ 2890
Findern 60 SK 3030
Findhorn 129 NJ 0464
Findhorn Bay 129 NJ 0462
Findhorn Bridge 116 NH 8027
Findhu Glen 107 NN 7115
Findochty 121 NJ 4667
Findo Gask 108 NO 0020
Findon (Grampn.) 119 NO 9397
Findon (W Susx) 28 TQ 1208
Findon Forest 128 NH 6458
Findon Mains 128 NH 6060
Findon Ness 119 NO 9497
Findrack House 119 NJ 6004
Finedon 52 SP 9272
Fingal's Cave 104 NM 3234
Fingal Street 55 TM 2169
Fingask 121 NJ 7827
Fingask Castle 108 NO 2227
Fingest 36 SU 7791
Finghall 84 SE 1889
Fingland 88 NS 7517
Fingland Fell 89 NY 1495
Finglen Burn 107 NN 6734
Finglen Rig 95 NT 1332
Fingringhoe 39 TM 0220
Finiskaig 111 NM 8694
Finlarig 107 NN 5733
Finlas Water 100 NS 3389
Finlaystone House 101 NS 3673
Finmere 51 SP 6333
Finnart 107 NN 5157
Finnarts Bay 86 NX 0472
Finningham 54 TM 0669
Finningly 71 SK 6699
Finnygaud 121 NJ 6054
Finsbay 125 NG 0786
Finsbury 37 TQ 3282
Finsthwaite 77 SD 3687
Finstock 47 SP 3516
Finstown 136 HY 3513
Fintry (Central) 101 NS 6186
Fintry (Grampn.) 121 NJ 7554
Fionn Bheinn 127 NH 1462
Fionn Bheinn Mhór 127 NC 3704
Fionn Lighe 114 NM 9682
Fionn Loch (Highld.) 132 NC 1317
Fionn Loch (Highld.) 126 NG 9578
Fionn Loch Mór 132 NC 3323
Fionnphort (Island of Mull) 104 NM 2923
Fionn Phort (Strath.) 100 NR 9065
Firbank 83 SD 6294
Firbeck 71 SK 5688
Fire Beacon Point 20 SX 1092
Firgrove 69 SD 9113
Firle Beacon 29 TQ 4806
Firsby 73 TF 4563
Firth 143 HU 4473
Firth of Clyde 93 NS 1354
Firth of Forth 103 NT 3786
Firth of Lorn 105 NM 7221
Firth of Tay 109 NO 3727
Firths Voe 143 HU 4474
Firth, The 141 HU 3450
Fir Tree 84 NZ 1334
Fishbourne (I. of W.) 27 SZ 5592
Fishbourne (W Susx) 27 SU 8304
Fishburn 85 NZ 3632
Fishcross 102 NS 8995
Fisherfield Forest 126 NH 0080
Fisherford 121 NJ 6635
Fisher's Pond 27 SU 4820
Fisherstreet 28 SU 9531
Fisher Tarn Reservoir 83 SD 5592
Fisherton (Highld.) 129 NH 7451
Fisherton (Strath.) 93 NS 2717
Fishguard 42 SM 9637
Fishguard Bay 42 SM 9839
Fish Holm 143 HU 4774
Fishlake 71 SE 6513
Fishnish Bay 105 NM 6442
Fishpool 69 SD 8009
Fishtoft 63 TF 3642
Fishtoft Drove 63 TF 3148
Fishtown of Usan 109 NO 7254
Fishwick 97 NT 9151
Fiskavaig 122 NG 3234
Fiskerton (Lincs.) 72 TF 0472
Fiskerton (Notts.) 61 SK 7351
Fistral Bay 19 SW 7862
Fitful Head 141 HU 3413
Fittleton 34 SU 1449
Fittleworth 28 TQ 0119
Fitton End 63 TF 4312
Fitty Hill 138 HY 4244
Fitz 58 SJ 4417
Fitzhead 24 ST 1228
Fitzwilliam 71 SE 4115
Fiunary 105 NM 6246
Fiunary Forest 105 NM 6447
Five Ashes 29 TQ 5525
Fivehead 24 ST 3522
Five Oak Green 29 TQ 6445
Five Oaks 28 TQ 0928
Five Penny Borve 131 NB 4056
Five Penny Ness 131 NB 5364
Five Roads 43 SN 4905
Five Sisters 114 NG 9617
Flackwell Heath 36 SU 8890
Fladbury 50 SO 9946
Fladda (is.) 104 NM 2943
Fladdabister 141 HU 4332
Fladda-chùain (is.) 125 NG 3681
Flag Fen 63 TL 2894
Flagg 70 SK 1368
Flamborough 81 TA 2270
Flamborough Head 81 TA 2570
Flamstead 36 TL 0814
Flanders Moss (Central) 101 NS 5595
Flanders Moss (Central) 101 NS 6398
Flannan Isles 130 NA 7146
Flansham 28 SU 9601
Flasby 78 SD 9456
Flash 70 SK 0267
Flashader 122 NG 3553
Flashes, The (pt.) 85 NZ 6125
Flat Holm (is.) 41 ST 2265
Flatt, The 90 NY 5678
Flaunden 36 TL 0100
Flawborough 61 SK 7842
Flawith 79 SE 4865
Flax Bourton 33 ST 5069
Flaxby 79 SE 3957
Flaxley 46 SO 6915
Flaxpool 24 ST 1435
Flaxton 79 SE 6762
Fleam Dyke (ant.) 53 TL 5553
Fleckney 61 SP 6493
Flecknoe 51 SP 5163
Fleet (Hants.) 35 SU 8054
Fleet (Lincs.) 63 TF 3823
Fleet Bay 87 NX 5651
Fleet Hargate 63 TF 3925
Fleetwood 77 SD 3247
Flemingston 41 ST 0170
Flemington 101 NS 6559
Flempton 54 TL 8169
Fleshwick Bay 76 SC 2071
Fletching 29 TQ 4323
Flexford 28 SU 9350
Flimby 82 NY 0233
Flimwell 29 TQ 7131
Flint 68 SJ 2472
Flintham 61 SK 7446
Flint Mountain 68 SJ 2369
Flinton 75 TA 2136
Flitcham 64 TF 7226
Flitton 52 TL 0536
Flitwick 52 TL 0335
Flixborough 74 SE 8715
Flixton (Gtr Mches.) 69 SJ 7494
Flixton (N Yorks.) 81 TA 0479
Flixton (Suff.) 55 TM 3186
Float Bay 86 NX 0647
Flockton 71 SE 2314
Flodabay 125 NG 0988
Floday (Isle of Lewis) 131 NB 1033
Floday (Isle of Lewis) 131 NB 1241
Flodda (is.) 124 NF 8455
Flodday (Barra) 112 NF 7502
Flodday (W Isles) 112 NL 8192
Floddaybeg 124 NF 9158
Floddaymore 124 NF 9157
Flodden 97 NT 9235
Flodigarry 123 NG 4671
Flookburgh 77 SD 3675
Floors Castle 96 NT 7134
Flordon 65 TM 1897
Flore 51 SP 6460
Flossnan 122 NG 2337
Flotta (Orkney) (is.) 136 ND 3593
Flotta (Shetld.) (is.) 141 HU 3746
Flotterton 91 NT 9902
Flowerdale Forest 126 NG 8867
Flowton 55 TM 0847
Flushing (Corn.) 19 SW 8034
Flushing (Grampn.) 121 NK 0546
Flyford Flavell 50 SO 9754
Fobbing 38 TQ 7183
Fochabers 121 NJ 3458
Fochno 57 SN 6493
Fochriw 41 SO 1005
Fockerby 74 SE 8410
Fodder Fen 53 TL 5287
Fodderletter 117 NJ 1421
Fodderty 128 NH 5159
Foel 57 SH 9911
Foel-cwmcerwyn 42 SN 0931
Foel-drych 42 SN 1630
Foeleryr 42 SN 0632
Foel Fenlli (ant.) 68 SJ 1660
Foel Figenau 57 SH 9128
Foel Fraith 41 SN 7517
Foel-Fras 67 SH 6968
Foel Fynyddau 41 SS 7893
Foel Goch 67 SH 9542
Foel Gurig 57 SN 9279
Foel Rhiwlas 58 SJ 2032
Foel Rhudd 57 SH 8924
Foel Wen 67 SJ 0933
Foel-y-ffridd 57 SH 8312
Foel y Geifr 57 SH 9327
Foffarty 109 NO 4145
Foggathorpe 74 SE 7537
Fogla Skerry 140 HU 1461
Fogo 96 NT 7749
Foinaven (mt.) 132 NC 3149
Foindle 132 NC 1948
Folda 108 NO 1964
Fole 60 SK 0437
Foleshill 50 SP 3582
Folke 25 ST 6513
Folkestone 31 TR 2336
Folkingham 62 TF 0733
Folkington 29 TQ 5604
Folksworth 52 TL 1490
Folkton 81 TA 0579
Folla Rule 121 NJ 7333
Follifoot 79 SE 3452
Folly Gate 21 SX 5797
Fontburn Resr. 91 NZ 0493
Fonthill Bishop 26 ST 9332
Fonthill Gifford 25 ST 9231
Fontmell Magna 25 ST 8616
Fontwell 28 SU 9407
Foolow 70 SK 1976
Foots Cray 37 TQ 4770
Foot, The 137 HY 5316
Fora Ness (Shetld.) 141 HU 3517
Fora Ness (Shetld.) 143 HU 4571
Forcett 84 NZ 1712
Ford (Bucks.) 36 SP 7709
Ford (Devon) 21 SX 7840
Ford (Glos.) 46 SP 0829
Ford (Mers.) 68 SJ 3598

Ford (Northum.)	97	NT	9437
Ford (Shrops.)	58	SJ	4113
Ford (Staffs.)	60	SK	0654
Ford (Strath.)	105	NM	8603
Ford (Wilts.)	33	ST	8475
Ford (W Susx)	28	TQ	0003
Fordcombe	29	TQ	5240
Forde Abbey (ant.)	24	ST	3505
Fordell	102	NT	1588
Fordell Castle (ant.)	102	NT	1485
Forden	58	SJ	2201
Ford End	38	TL	6716
Forder Green	21	SX	7867
Fordham (Cambs.)	54	TL	6370
Fordham (Essex)	54	TL	9228
Fordham (Norf.)	64	TL	6199
Fordham Abbey	54	TL	6369
Fordingbridge	26	SU	1413
Fordon	81	TA	0475
Fordoun	119	NO	7475
Fordstreet (Essex)	54	TL	9227
Ford Street (Somer.)	24	ST	1518
Fordwells	47	SP	3013
Fordwich	31	TR	1859
Fordyce	121	NJ	5563
Fore Holm	141	HU	3544
Foreland (pt.)	27	SZ	6687
Foreland House	98	NR	2664
Foreland Point	23	SS	7551
Foreland, The, or Handfast Point	26	SZ	0582
Foremark	60	SK	3326
Foremark Resr	60	SK	3324
Foreness Point	31	TR	3871
Forest	84	NY	8629
Forestburn Gate	91	NZ	0696
Forestfield	102	NS	8566
Forest Gate	37	TQ	4085
Forest Green	28	TQ	1241
Forest Hall	83	NY	5401
Forest Head	83	NY	5857
Forest Hill	47	SP	5807
Forest Lodge (Highld.)	117	NJ	0216
Forest Lodge (Strath.)	106	NN	2742
Forest Lodge (Tays.)	117	NN	9274
Forest Mill	102	NS	9594
Forest Moor	79	SE	2256
Forest of Ae	88	NX	9991
Forest of Alyth	108	NO	1755
Forest of Atholl	116	NN	7973
Forest of Bere	27	SU	6711
Forest of Birse	119	NO	5291
Forest of Bowland	77	SD	6455
Forest of Clunie	108	NO	0850
Forest of Dean	45	SO	6310
Forest of Deer	121	NJ	9750
Forest of Glenartney	107	NN	6818
Forest of Glenavon	117	NJ	1005
Forest of Glen Tanar	118	NO	4995
Forest of Harris	130	NB	0609
Forest of Mamlorn	107	NN	4034
Forest of Mar	117	NO	0292
Forest of Pendle, The	78	SD	8239
Forest of Rossendale	78	SD	8424
Forest of Trawden, The	78	SD	9437
Forest Row	29	TQ	4235
Forestside	27	SU	7512
Forest Town	71	SK	5662
Forfar	109	NO	4550
Forgandenny	108	NO	0818
Forgie	121	NJ	3954
Forglen House	121	NJ	6952
Formartine (dist.)	121	NJ	8729
Formby	68	SD	2907
Formby Hills	68	SD	2708
Forncett End	65	TM	1493
Forncett St. Mary	65	TM	1694
Forncett St. Peter	65	TM	1693
Forneth	108	NO	0945
Fornham All Saints	54	TL	8367
Fornham St. Martin	54	TL	8566
Forres	129	NJ	0358
Forrestburn Resr.	102	NS	8765
Forrest Lodge	87	NX	5586
Forret Hill	109	NO	3920
Forsbrook	60	SJ	9641
Forse	135	ND	2234
Forse House	135	ND	2135
Forsie	135	ND	0463
Forsinain	134	NC	9149
Forsinain Burn	134	NC	9247
Forsinard	134	NC	8842
Forsnaval (mt.)	130	NB	0635
Forss House	135	ND	0369
Forss Water	135	ND	0360
Forston	25	SY	6695
Fort Augustus	115	NH	3709
Forter	108	NO	1864
Forteviot	108	NO	0517
Fort George	129	NH	7656
Forth	95	NS	9453
Forthampton	46	SO	8532
Forth and Clyde Canal	101	NS	6674
Forth Bridge	102	NT	1379
Forth Road Bridge	102	NT	1279
Fortingall	107	NN	7447
Forton (Lancs.)	77	SD	4851
Forton (Shrops.)	58	SJ	4216
Forton (Somer.)	24	ST	3306
Forton (Staffs.)	59	SJ	7521
Fortree	121	NJ	9640
Fortrie	121	NJ	6645
Fortrose	129	NH	7256
Fortuneswell	25	SY	6873
Fort William	115	NN	1074
Forty Foot or Vermuden's Drain	53	TL	3888
Forty Hill	37	TQ	3398
Forvie Ness or Hackley Head	121	NK	0226
Forward Green	55	TM	1059
Fosbury	34	SU	3157
Fosdyke	63	TF	3133
Foss	107	NN	7958
Fossdyke Navigation	72	SK	9274
Fossebridge	46	SP	0811
Foss Way (Devon - Somer.) (ant.)	24	ST	3102
Foss Way (Glos. - Wilts.) (ant.)	46	ST	9394
Foss Way (Lincs.) (ant.)	72	SK	9064
Foss Way (Somer.) (ant.)	25	ST	4920
Foss Way (Somer.) (ant.)	33	ST	6345
Foss Way (Warw.) (ant.)	50	SP	3358
Foss Way (Wilts.) (ant.)	33	ST	8277
Foss-y-ffin	43	SN	4460
Foster Street	37	TL	4909
Foston (Derby.)	60	SK	1831
Foston (Lincs.)	62	SK	8542
Foston (N Yorks.)	80	SE	6965
Foston Beck	62	SK	8739
Foston on the Wolds	81	TA	1055
Fotherby	73	TF	3191
Fotheringhay	62	TL	0593
Fothringham Hill	109	NO	4645
Foubister	136	HY	5104
Foula (is.)	140	HT	9638
Foulden (Borders)	97	NT	9355
Foulden (Norf.)	64	TL	7699
Foulholme Sands	75	TA	1920
Foulis Castle	128	NH	5864
Foul Mile	29	TQ	6215
Foulmire Heights	90	NY	5794
Foulnaze (sbk)	77	SD	3124
Foulness	65	TG	2441
Foulness Island	39	TR	0192
Foulness Point	39	TR	0495
Foulness Sands	39	TR	0997
Foulney Island	76	SD	2463
Foulridge	78	SD	8942
Foulsham	64	TG	0324
Fountainhall	96	NT	4349
Fountains Abbey (ant.)	79	SE	2768
Fountains Fell	78	SD	8671
Four Ashes	54	TM	0070
Four Crosses (Powys)	57	SJ	0508
Four Crosses (Powys)	58	SJ	2718
Four Crosses (Staffs.)	60	SJ	9509
Four Elms	29	TQ	4648
Four Forks	24	ST	2336
Four Gotes	63	TF	4516
Four Lanes	18	SW	6838
Fourlanes End	69	SJ	8059
Fourman Hill	121	NJ	5745
Four Marks	27	SU	6634
Four Mile Bridge	66	SH	2778
Four Oaks (E Susx)	30	TQ	8624
Four Oaks (W Mids)	60	SP	1198
Four Oaks (W Mids)	50	SP	2480
Fourpenny	129	NH	8094
Fourstones	90	NY	8967
Four Throws	30	TQ	7729
Fovant	26	SU	0028
Foveran	121	NJ	9824
Foveran Burn	121	NJ	9323
Fowberry Tower	97	NU	0429
Fowey	19	SX	1251
Fowlis	108	NO	3133
Fowlis Wester	108	NN	9223
Fowlmere	53	TL	4245
Fownhope	45	SO	5734
Foxcote Reservoir	51	SP	7136
Foxdale	76	SC	2878
Foxearth	54	TL	8344
Foxfield	76	SD	2085
Foxham	34	ST	9777
Foxhole (Corn.)	19	SW	9654
Foxholes (N Yorks.)	81	TA	0173
Fox Lane	35	SU	8557
Foxley (Norf.)	64	TG	0321
Foxley (Wilts.)	33	ST	8985
Foxt	60	SK	0348
Foxton (Cambs.)	53	TL	4148
Foxton (Leic.)	51	SP	7090
Foxup	78	SD	8676
Foxwist Green	69	SJ	6168
Foy	45	SO	5928
Foyers	116	NH	4921
Fraddon	19	SW	9158
Fradley	60	SK	1513
Fradswell	60	SJ	9831
Fraisthorpe	81	TA	1561
Framfield	29	TQ	4920
Framingham Earl	65	TG	2702
Framingham Pigot	65	TG	2703
Framlingham	55	TM	2863
Frampton (Dorset)	25	SY	6294
Frampton (Lincs.)	63	TF	3239
Frampton Cotterell	33	ST	6582
Frampton Mansell	46	SO	9202
Frampton on Severn	46	SO	7407
Frampton West End	63	TF	3040
Framsden	55	TM	1959
Framwellgate Moor	84	NZ	2644
Franche	49	SO	8178
Frankby	68	SJ	2486
Frankley	50	SO	9980
Frank Lockwood's Island	105	NM	6219
Frankton	50	SP	4270
Frant	29	TQ	5835
Fraochaidh	106	NN	0251
Fraserburgh	121	NJ	9966
Fraserburgh Bay	121	NK	0165
Frating Green	39	TM	0923
Fratton	27	SU	6600
Freathy	20	SX	3952
Freckenham	54	TL	6672
Freckleton	77	SD	4228
Fredden Hill	97	NT	9526
Freeby	61	SK	8020
Freeland	47	SP	4112
Freester	141	HU	4553
Freethorpe	65	TG	4105
Freethorpe Common	65	TG	4004
Freevater Forest	127	NH	3588
Freiston	63	TF	3743
Fremington	22	SS	5132
Frenchay	33	ST	6377
Frenchbeer	21	SX	6785
Freni-fawr	43	SN	2035
Frensham	35	SU	8441
Fresgoe	134	NC	9566
Freshfield	68	SD	2807
Freshford	33	ST	7860
Freshwater	26	SZ	3487
Freshwater Bay	26	SZ	3485
Freshwater West	42	SR	8899
Fressingfield	55	TM	2677
Freston	55	TM	1739
Freswick	135	ND	3667
Freswick Bay	135	ND	3867
Fretherne	46	SO	7309
Frettenham	65	TG	2417
Freuchie	103	NO	2806
Friar's Gate	29	TQ	4933
Friday Bridge	63	TF	4605
Fridaythorpe	81	SE	8759
Friern Barnet	37	TQ	2892
Friesland	110	NM	1853
Friesthorpe	72	TF	0683
Frieth	36	SU	7990
Frilford	47	SU	4497
Frilsham	35	SU	5373
Frimley	36	SU	8758
Frindsbury	30	TQ	7369
Fring	64	TF	7334
Fringford	47	SP	6028
Frinsted	30	TQ	8957
Frinton-on-Sea	39	TM	2319
Friockheim	109	NO	5949
Frisby on the Wreake	61	SK	6917
Friskney	63	TF	4555
Friskney Flats (sbk.)	63	TF	4851
Friston (E Susx)	29	TV	5498
Friston (Suff.)	55	TM	4160
Fritchley	60	SK	3553
Fritham	26	SU	2413
Frith Bank	63	TF	3147
Frith Common	49	SO	6969
Frithelstock	22	SS	4619
Frithville	63	TF	3250
Frittenden	30	TQ	8141
Fritton (Norf.)	65	TG	4700
Fritton (Norf.)	65	TM	2293
Fritwell	47	SP	5229
Frizington	82	NY	0316
Frocester	46	SO	7803
Frodesley	59	SJ	5101
Frodsham	69	SJ	5177
Froggatt	71	SK	2476
Froghall	60	SK	0247
Frogmore	36	SU	8360
Frogmore House	36	SU	9775
Frolesworth	51	SP	5090
Frome	33	ST	7747
Fromes Hill	49	SO	6846
Frome St. Quintin	25	ST	5902
Fron (Gwyn.)	66	SH	3539
Fron (Powys)	58	SJ	2203
Fron (Powys)	57	SO	0865
Fron Cysyllte	58	SJ	2741
Fron-goch	67	SH	9039
Frosterley	84	NZ	0237
Frosty Hill	118	NJ	4510
Froxfield	34	SU	2967
Froxfield Green	27	SU	7025
Fruid Reservoir	93	NS	1019
Fryerning	38	TL	6400
Fryton	80	SE	6875
Fuar Bheinn	111	NM	8556
Fuar Larach (mt.)	92	NR	8154
Fuday	112	NF	7308
Fugla Ness (Shetld.)	142	HU	3091
Fugla Ness (Shetld.)	142	HU	3674
Fugla Ness (West Burra)	141	HU	3635
Fugla Stack	141	HU	3529
Fugla Water	143	HU	5172
Fuiay	112	NF	7402
Fulbeck	62	SK	9450
Fulbourn	53	TL	5256
Fulbrook	47	SP	2513
Fulford (N Yorks.)	79	SE	6149
Fulford (Somer.)	24	ST	2129
Fulford (Staffs.)	59	SJ	9438
Fulham	37	TQ	2576
Fulking	28	TQ	2411
Fuller's Moor	59	SJ	4953
Fuller Street	38	TL	7415
Fullerton	34	SU	3739
Fulletby	73	TF	2973
Full Sutton	80	SE	7455
Fullwood	93	NS	4450
Fulmer	36	SU	9985
Fulmodeston	64	TF	9931
Fulnetby	73	TF	0979
Fulstow	73	TF	3297
Fulwell	91	NZ	3959
Fulwood (Lancs.)	77	SD	5331
Fulwood (S Yorks.)	71	SK	3085
Funlack Burn	116	NH	7833
Funtington	27	SU	7908
Funtley	27	SU	5607
Funzie	143	HU	6690
Funzie Bay	143	HU	6689
Furnace	100	NN	0200
Furness Abbey (ant.)	76	SD	2271
Furness Fells	82	NY	2900
Furneux Pelham	53	TL	4327
Furzehill	23	SS	7245
Fyfett	24	ST	2314
Fyfield (Essex)	37	TL	5707
Fyfield (Glos.)	47	SP	2003
Fyfield (Hants.)	34	SU	2946
Fyfield (Oxon.)	47	SU	4298
Fyfield (Wilts.)	34	SU	1468
Fylingdales Moor	81	SE	9199
Fylingthorpe	81	NZ	9405
Fyvie	121	NJ	7637

G

Gablon	129	NH	7191
Gabroc Hill	93	NS	4551
Gaddesby	61	SK	6813
Gadie Burn	121	NJ	6424
Gaer	41	SO	1721
Gaer-fawr	45	ST	4498
Gaerllwyd	45	ST	4496
Gaerwen	66	SH	4871
Gagingwell	47	SP	4025
Gaick Forest	116	NN	7584
Gaick Lodge	116	NN	7584
Gailey	59	SJ	9110
Gainford	84	NZ	1716
Gainsborough	72	SK	8189
Gainsford End	54	TL	7235
Gairbeinn	116	NN	4698
Gairich (mt.)	114	NN	0299
Gairletter Point	100	NS	1984
Gairloch	123	NG	8076
Gairlochy	115	NN	1784
Gairney Bank	102	NT	1299
Gairnshiel Lodge	117	NJ	2900
Gairsay	136	HY	4422
Gairsay Sound	136	HY	4424
Gairy Craig	87	NX	5490
Gairy Hill	136	ND	4685
Gaitnip Hill	136	HY	4505
Gaitsgill	83	NY	3946
Gala Lane	87	NX	4792
Galashiels	96	NT	4936
Gala Water	96	NT	4152
Galby	61	SK	6901
Galgate	77	SD	4855
Galhampton	25	ST	6329
Gallanach (Coll, Strath.)	110	NM	2160
Gallanach (Strath.)	105	NM	8226
Gallan Head	130	NB	0539
Gallatown	103	NT	2994
Galley Common	50	SP	3192
Galleyend	38	TL	7103
Galloway (dist.)	87	NX	4867
Gallowfauld	109	NO	4342
Gallow Hill (Dumf. and Galwy.)	89	NT	0806
Gallow Hill (Tays.)	109	NO	3841
Gallrope Bank (sbk.)	129	NH	7885
Galltair	123	NG	8120
Galmisdale	111	NM	4883
Galmpton (Devon)	21	SX	6940
Galmpton (Devon)	21	SX	8856
Galphay	79	SE	2572
Galson	131	NB	4358
Galston	93	NS	5036
Galtachean (is.)	125	NG	3998
Galtrigill	122	NG	1854
Galt, The (pt.)	136	HY	4821
Gamallt (Dyfed)	44	SN	7756
Gamallt (Powys)	57	SN	9570
Gamblesby	83	NY	6039
Gamhna Gigha	92	NR	6854
Gamlingay	53	TL	2452
Gamrie	121	NJ	7962
Gamrie Bay	121	NJ	7965
Gamriw	57	SN	9461
Gamston (Notts.)	61	SK	6037
Gamston (Notts.)	72	SK	7076
Gana Hill	88	NS	9500
Ganarew	45	SO	5216
Ganavan	105	NM	8632
Ganllwyd	57	SH	7224
Gannochy	109	NO	5970
Ganstead	75	TA	1434
Ganthorpe	80	SE	6870
Ganton	81	SE	9877
Ganu Mór	132	NC	3150
Gaodhail	105	NM	6038
Gaor Bheinn or Gulvain	114	NM	9987
Garadhban Forest	101	NS	4790
Garbat	128	NH	4167
Garbat Forest	128	NH	4368
Garbh-allt (Highld.)	134	NC	7738
Garbhallt (Strath.)	100	NS	0295
Garbh Bheinn (Highld.)	106	NM	9062
Garbh Bheinn (Highld.)	106	NN	1659
Garbh-bheinn (Island of Skye)	123	NG	5323
Garbh Eileach	105	NM	6612
Garbh Eilean (Island of Rona)	123	NG	6153
Garbh Eilean (Shiant Islands)	125	NG	4198
Garbh Ghaoir	107	NN	4356
Garbh-mheall Mór	116	NN	7292
Garbh Phort	104	NM	3325
Garbh Rèisa	99	NR	7597
Garbh Shlios	105	NM	7542
Garbh Thorr	92	NR	9335
Garboldisham	54	TM	0081
Gardenstown	121	NJ	7964
Garderhouse	141	HU	3347
Gardie House	141	HU	4842
Gareg Lâs	41	SN	7720
Gare Hill	33	ST	7840
Gare Loch	100	NS	2486
Garelochhead	100	NS	2491
Garenin	131	NB	1944
Garford	47	SU	4296
Garforth	79	SE	4033
Garf Water	95	NS	9032
Gargrave	78	SD	9354
Gargunnock	101	NS	7094
Gargunnock Hills	101	NS	6891
Garioch (dist.)	121	NJ	7024
Garleffin Fell	86	NX	3598
Garleton Hills	103	NT	5076
Garlick Hill	87	NX	4372
Garlies Castle (ant.)	87	NX	4269
Garlieston	87	NX	4746
Garlogie	119	NJ	7805
Garmond	121	NJ	8052
Garmony	105	NM	6740
Garmouth	121	NJ	3364
Garmsley Camp (ant.)	49	SO	6162
Garmus Taing	142	HU	3594
Garn	66	SH	2734
Garnant	40	SN	6813
Garn Boduan (ant.)	66	SH	3139
Garn Caws	41	SO	1317
Garn Ddu	41	SO	0212
Garn-Dolbenmaen	66	SH	4944
Garnedd-goch	66	SH	5149
Garnett Bridge	83	SD	5299
Garnkirk	101	NS	6768
Garn Prys	67	SH	8848
Garpol Water	88	NT	0103
Garrabost	131	NB	5133
Garragie Lodge	116	NH	5211
Garraron	105	NM	8008
Garras	18	SW	7023
Garreg	66	SH	6141
Garreg Bank	58	SJ	2811
Garreg-ddu Resr.	57	SN	9165
Garrick	101	NN	8412
Garrigill	83	NY	7441
Garrisdale Point	110	NG	2005
Garrison, The	18	SV	8910
Garroch	88	NX	5981
Garroch Head	93	NS	0951
Garron Point	119	NO	8987
Garros	123	NG	4963
Garrow	107	NN	8240
Garrow Tor	19	SX	1478
Garrynamonie	112	NF	7416
Garsdale	83	SD	7389
Garsdale Head	83	SD	7992
Garsdon	34	ST	9687
Garshall Green	60	SJ	9633
Garsington	47	SP	5802
Garso Wick	139	HY	7755
Garstang	77	SD	4945
Garston	68	SJ	4083
Garswood	69	SJ	5599
Gartbreck	98	NR	2858
Gartcosh	101	NS	6968
Garth (Clwyd)	58	SJ	2542
Garth (I. of M.)	76	SC	3177
Garth (Mid Glam.)	41	SS	8690
Garth (Powys)	44	SN	9549
Garth (Shetld.)	140	HU	2157
Garthbrengy	41	SO	0433
Gartheli	43	SN	5956
Garth Head	136	ND	3188
Garthmyl	58	SO	1999
Garthorpe (Humbs.)	74	SE	8419
Garthorpe (Leic.)	62	SK	8320
Garths Ness	141	HU	3611
Garths, The	143	HP	6615
Garths Voe	143	HU	4073
Gartmore	101	NS	5297
Gartmore House	101	NS	5297
Gartnagrenach	99	NR	7959
Gartness (Central)	101	NS	5086
Gartness (Strath.)	101	NS	7864
Gartocharn	101	NS	4286
Garton	75	TA	2635
Garton-on-the-Wolds	81	SE	9859
Gartymore	135	ND	0114
Garvald	103	NT	5870
Garvard	98	NR	3691
Garvary Burn	134	NC	7222
Garve	127	NH	3961
Garvellachs (is.)	105	NM	6511
Garveston	64	TG	0207
Garvock	100	NS	2571
Garwall Hill	86	NX	3483
Garway	45	SO	4522
Garynahine	131	NB	2331
Gasay	124	NF	8443
Gaskan	111	NM	8072
Gasker (is.)	130	NA	8711
Gastard	33	ST	8868
Gasthorpe	54	TL	9780
Gatcombe	27	SZ	4885
Gatebeck	77	SD	5485
Gate Burton	72	SK	8382
Gateforth	79	SE	5528
Gatehead	93	NS	3936
Gate Helmsley	80	SE	6955
Gateholm Island	42	SM	7707
Gatehouse	90	NY	7988
Gatehouse of Fleet	87	NX	5956
Gatelawbridge	88	NX	9096
Gateley	64	TF	9624
Gatenby	79	SE	3287
Gatescarth Pass	83	NY	4709
Gateshead	91	NZ	2562
Gatesheath	69	SJ	4760
Gateside (Fife)	102	NO	1809
Gateside (Strath.)	93	NS	3653
Gateside (Tays.)	109	NO	3749
Gateside (Tays.)	109	NO	4344
Gathurst	69	SD	5307
Gatley	69	SJ	8387
Gat Sand	63	TF	4738
Gattonside	96	NT	5435
Gatwick Airport - London	28	TQ	2740
Gauldry	109	NO	3723
Gauls	108	NO	0734
Gaunt's Common	26	SU	0205
Gautby	73	TF	1772
Gavinton	96	NT	7652
Gawber	71	SE	3207
Gawcott	51	SP	6831
Gawdy Hall (ant.)	55	TM	2485
Gawsworth	69	SJ	8869
Gawthorpe Hall (ant.)	78	SD	8033
Gawthrop	77	SD	6987
Gawthwaite	77	SD	2784
Gaydon	50	SP	3654
Gayhurst	52	SP	8446
Gayle Moor	78	SD	8082
Gayles	84	NZ	1207
Gay Street	28	TQ	0820
Gayton (Mers.)	68	SJ	2680
Gayton (Norf.)	64	TF	7219
Gayton (Northants.)	51	SP	7054
Gayton (Staffs.)	60	SJ	9728
Gayton le Marsh	73	TF	4284
Gayton Sands	68	SJ	2478
Gayton Thorpe	64	TF	7418
Gaywood	64	TF	6320
Gazeley	54	TL	7264
Geal Charn (Grampn.)	117	NJ	2810
Geal Charn (Highld.)	117	NJ	0812
Geal Charn (Highld.)	115	NN	1594
Geal Charn (Highld.)	116	NN	5081
Geal Charn (Highld.)	116	NN	5698
Geal Charn (Highld.)	116	NN	5978
Geal-charn Mór	117	NH	8312
Geallaig Hill	117	NO	2998
Gealldruig Mhór (is.)	130	HW	8131
Geanies House	129	NH	8979
Gearr Garry	115	NH	0801
Geary	122	NG	2661
Geddes House	129	NH	8852
Gedding	54	TL	9457
Geddington	52	SP	8983
Gedintailor	123	NG	5235
Gedney	63	TF	4024
Gedney Broadgate	63	TF	4022
Gedney Drove End	63	TF	4629
Gedney Dyke	63	TF	4126
Gedney Hill	63	TF	3311
Gedney Marsh	63	TF	4329
Gee Cross	70	SJ	9593
Geifas (mt.)	57	SN	8172
Geilston	100	NS	3477
Geise	135	ND	1064
Geldeston	55	TM	3891
Geldie Burn	117	NN	9687
Gell	67	SH	8569
Gelligaer	41	ST	1397
Gelli-gaer Common	41	ST	1298
Gelli Gynan	58	SJ	1854
Gellilydan	67	SH	6839
Gellioedd	67	SH	9344
Gelly	42	SN	0819
Gellyburn	108	NO	0939
Gellywen	43	SN	2723
Gelston	88	NX	7758
Geltsdale Middle	83	NY	6052
Genie Fea (mt.)	136	ND	2494
Genoch Mains	86	NX	1356
Gentlemens' Cave	138	HY	3948
Gentleshaw	60	SK	0511
Geocrab	125	NG	1190
Geodh'a' Bhrideoin	133	NC	4867
Geodha Daraich	122	NG	3719
Geodha Mór (Highld.)	127	NC	0802
Geodha Mór (Island of Skye)	122	NG	2039
Geodha na Crich	131	NB	1538
Geodha nan Calman	131	NB	1339
Geodha nan Each	122	NG	1554
Geodha Nasavig	130	NB	0336
Geodha Ruadh	132	NC	2368
Geodha Ruadh na Fola	132	NC	2471
Geo Dubh	125	NB	2200
Geo Luon	137	HY	5429
Geo of Hellia	136	HY	1904
Geo of Markamouth	143	HP	4701
Geo of Odderaber	138	HY	4954
Geo of the Ujn	141	HU	4118
Geo of Vigon	143	HP	4704
Geordie's Hill	89	NY	4396
Georgeham	22	SS	4639
Georgemas Junction Station	135	ND	1559
George Nympton	23	SS	7023
Georgetown	101	NS	4567
Georgia	18	SW	4836
Georth	136	HY	3625
Germansweek	20	SX	4394
Germoe	18	SW	5829
Gerrans	19	SW	8735
Gerrans Bay	19	SW	8937
Gerrards Cross	36	TQ	0088
Geshader	131	NB	1131
Gestingthorpe	54	TL	8138
Geuffordd	58	SJ	2114
Geufron	57	SN	8885
Geur Rubha	111	NG	5501
Ghlas-bheinn	132	NC	3161
Giant's Leg (pt.)	141	HU	5135
Giant, The (ant.)	25	ST	6601
Gibbet Hill	27	SU	9035
Gibbon Hill	84	SE	0096
Gibraltar	73	TF	5558
Gidea Park	37	TQ	5390
Gidleigh	21	SX	6788
Gifford	103	NT	5368
Gigalum Island	92	NR	6445
Giggleswick	78	SD	8163
Gigha Island	92	NR	6449
Gighay	112	NF	7604
Gilberdyke	74	SE	8329
Gilchriston	103	NT	4865
Gilcrux	82	NY	1138
Gilderdale Forest	83	NY	6644
Gildersome	79	SE	2429
Gildingwells	71	SK	5585
Gileston	41	ST	0167
Gilfach Goch	41	SS	9890
Gilfachrheda	43	SN	4058
Gilgarran	82	NY	0323
Gilkicker Point	27	SZ	6097
Gillamoor	80	SE	6890
Gillaval Glas (mt.)	125	NB	1402
Gill Burn	135	ND	3368
Gillies Hill	101	NS	7791
Gilling East	79	SE	6176
Gillingham (Dorset)	25	ST	8026
Gillingham (Kent)	30	TQ	7768
Gillingham (Norf.)	55	TM	4191
Gilling West	84	NZ	1805
Gill of Garth	136	HY	4707
Gillow Heath	69	SJ	8858
Gills	135	ND	3172
Gills Bay	135	ND	3373
Gilmanscleuch	96	NT	3321
Gilmerton (Lothian)	103	NT	2968
Gilmerton (Tays.)	108	NN	8823
Gilmorton	51	SP	5787
Gilsay	124	NG	0279
Gilsland	90	NY	6366
Gilsland Spa	90	NY	6367
Gilston	96	NT	4456
Giltar Point	42	SS	1298
Giltarump (is.)	140	HU	2742
Gilwern	45	SO	2414
Gilwern Hill	44	SO	0958
Gimingham	65	TG	2836
Ginst Point	43	SN	3207
Gipping	54	TM	0763
Gipsey Bridge	63	TF	2850
Girdle Fell	90	NT	7001
Girdle Ness	119	NJ	9705
Girlsta	141	HU	4250
Girnock Burn	118	NO	3191
Girsby	85	NZ	3508
Girthon	87	NX	6053
Girtley Hill	100	NS	2361
Girton (Cambs.)	53	TL	4262
Girton (Notts.)	72	SK	8266
Girvan	86	NX	1897
Gisborough Moor	85	NZ	6213

Gisburn 78 SD 8248
Gisla River 131 NB 1126
Gisleham 55 TM 5188
Gislingham 54 TM 0771
Gissing 55 TM 1485
Gittisham 24 SY 1398
Giùr-bheinn 98 NR 3772
Glackossian 116 NH 5938
Gladestry 45 SO 2355
Gladhouse Reservoir 96 NT 2953
Gladsmuir 103 NT 4573
Glais 40 SN 7000
Glais Bheinn 105 NM 7143
Glaisdale (N Yorks.) 80 NZ 7603
Glaisdale (N Yorks.) 80 NZ 7705
Glaisdale Moor 80 NZ 7101
Glaisdale Rigg 80 NZ 7404
Glamaig (mt.) 123 NG 5129
Glam Burn 123 NG 5542
Glame 123 NG 5542
Glamis 109 NO 3846
Glamis Castle (ant.) 109 NO 3848
Glanaber Terrace 67 SH 7547
Glanaman 40 SN 6713
Glan-Conwy 67 SH 8352
Glandford 64 TG 0441
Glandwr (Dyfed) 43 SN 1928
Glandŵr (Gwent) 41 SO 2101
Glangrwyne 45 SO 2316
Glan-Mule 48 SO 1690
Glanrhyd 42 SN 1442
Glanton 91 NU 0714
Glanton Pyke 91 NU 0514
Glanvilles Wootton 25 ST 6708
Glan-y-don 68 SJ 1679
Glan-yr-afon (Clwyd-Gwyn.) 67 SJ 0242
Glan-yr-afon (Gwyn.) 67 SH 9141
Glapthorn 52 TL 0290
Glapwell 71 SK 4766
Glaramara 82 NY 2410
Glas-allt Shiel 117 NO 2782
Glas Bheinn (Highld.) 132 NC 2526
Glas Bheinn (Highld.) 123 NG 9043
Glas Bheinn (Highld.) 115 NN 1397
Glas Bheinn (Highld.) 106 NN 2564
Glas Bheinn (Islay) 98 NR 4259
Glas Bheinn (Jura) 98 NR 5069
Glas Bheinn Mhòr 123 NG 5525
Glasbury 45 SO 1739
Glas-charn 111 NM 8483
Glascoed 45 SO 3301
Glascorrie 118 NO 3997
Glascote 60 SK 2203
Glascwm 44 SO 1553
Glascwm Hill 44 SO 1552
Glasdrum 106 NN 0046
Glas Eilean (Highld.) 111 NG 7000
Glas Eilean (Highld.) 123 NG 8425
Glas Eilean (Jura) 98 NR 4465
Glas-eileanan 124 NF 8641
Glasfryn 67 SH 9150
Glasfynydd Forest 41 SN 8524
Glasgow 101 NS 5865
Glasgow Airport 101 NS 4766
Glasha Burn 127 NH 3792
Glasinfryn 66 SH 5868
Glaslaw 119 NO 8584
Glas-leac Beag (is.) 126 NB 9205
Glas-leac Mòr (is.) 132 NB 9509
Glas-loch Mòr 133 NC 6619
Glaslyn 57 SN 8294
Glas Maol (mt.) 117 NO 1676
Glas Mheall Mòr 116 NN 6876
Glasnakille 123 NG 5313
Glaspwll 57 SN 7397
Glassburn 115 NH 3634
Glasserton 87 NX 4238
Glassford 94 NS 7247
Glasshouse Hill 46 SO 7020
Glasshouses 78 SE 1764
Glasslaw 121 NJ 8659
Glasslie 103 NO 2305
Glasson (Cumbr.) 89 NY 2560
Glasson (Lancs.) 77 SD 4455
Glassonby 83 NY 5738
Glasterlaw 109 NO 6051
Glaston 62 SK 8900
Glastonbury 33 ST 4938
Glas Tulaichean 117 NO 0576
Glatton 52 TL 1586
Glazebury 69 SJ 6796
Glazeley 49 SO 7088
Gleadless Townend 71 SK 3883
Gleadsmoss 69 SJ 8469
Gleann a'Chilleine 107 NN 7336
Gleann a'Choilich 115 NH 0926
Gleann Airigh 100 NR 9195
Gleann an Dubh-Lochain 111 NG 8100
Gleann an Fhiodh 106 NN 0855
Gleann Aoistail 98 NR 6085
Gleann Astaile 98 NR 4871
Gleann Beag 127 NH 3383
Gleann Bhruthadail 131 NB 3343
Gleann Camgharaidh 114 NM 9988
Gleann Casaig 101 NN 5410
Gleann Cia-aig 115 NN 1891
Gleann Còsaidh 114 NG 9402
Gleann Da-Eig 107 NN 6045
Gleann Da-ghob 107 NN 6945
Gleann Diridh 117 NN 8775
Gleann Dubh (Highld.) 132 NC 2721
Gleann Dubh (Highld.) 132 NC 3033
Gleann Dubh (Highld.) 111 NM 7353
Gleann Dubh Lighe 114 NM 9582
Gleann Duibhe 107 NN 4655
Gleann Feàrnach 108 NO 0368
Gleann Fhiodhaig 127 NH 1448
Gleann Fionnlighe 114 NM 9782
Gleann Geal 111 NM 7250
Gleann Gniomhaidh 115 NH 0519
Gleann Goibhre 128 NH 4247
Gleann Leireag 132 NC 1730
Gleann Leòra 98 NR 4254
Gleann Màma 111 NM 7485
Gleann Meadhonach 111 NG 5904
Gleann Mèinich 127 NH 2553
Gleann Mòr (Highld.) 127 NH 4085
Gleann Mòr (South Uist) 112 NF 8125
Gleann Mòr (Tays.) 117 NN 9475
Gleann Mòr Barvas 131 NB 3845
Gleann na Guiserein 111 NG 7803
Gleann nam Fiadh 115 NH 1726
Gleann Oraid 122 NG 3330
Gleann Salach 106 NM 9738
Gleann Seilisdeir 105 NM 4730
Gleann Sithidh 115 NH 0727
Gleann Suileag 114 NN 0281
Gleann Tanagaidh 127 NH 0866
Gleann Udalain 114 NG 8831
Gleann Ullibh 98 NR 4666
Gleaston 76 SD 2570
Glemanuilt Hill 92 NR 6408
Glemsford 54 TL 8247
Glen 87 NX 5457
Glenacardoch Point 92 NR 6637
Glen Achall 127 NH 2294
Glen Affric 115 NH 1922
Glenaffric Forest 115 NH 1020
Glen Albyn or Glen Mór 116 NH 4211
Glen Aldie 129 NH 7779
Glenalla Field 86 NS 3500
Glen Almond (Tays.) 108 NN 9128
Glenalmond (Tays.) 108 NN 9627
Glen Ample 107 NN 5918
Glenan Bay 100 NR 9170
Glenancross 111 NM 6691
Glen App 86 NX 0774
Glenapp Castle 86 NX 0980
Glen Aray 100 NN 0913
Glen Arnisdale 123 NG 8709
Glenaros House 105 NM 5544
Glen Arroch 123 NG 7321
Glen Artney 107 NN 7218
Glenastle 98 NR 3044
Glen Auldyn 76 SC 4393
Glen Avon 117 NJ 1106
Glen Banchor 116 NN 6798
Glenbarr 92 NR 6736
Glen Barrisdale 114 NG 9003
Glen Barry 121 NJ 5554
Glen Batrick 98 NR 5178
Glen Beasdale 111 NM 7385
Glen Beg (Grampn.) 117 NJ 0028
Glen Beg (Highld.) 111 NM 5862
Glen Bernisdale 123 NG 4048
Glenbervie 119 NO 7680
Glenboig 101 NS 7268
Glenborrodale 111 NM 6060
Glen Bragar 131 NB 3041
Glenbranter 100 NS 1097
Glenbranter Forest 100 NS 1097
Glen Breackerie 92 NR 6511
Glenbreck 95 NT 0521
Glen Brein 116 NH 4809
Glenbrein Lodge 116 NH 4711
Glen Brerachan 108 NO 0063
Glen Brittle 123 NG 4123
Glen Brittle Forest 123 NG 4026
Glenbrittle House 123 NG 4121
Glen Bruar 117 NN 8274
Glenbuchat Lodge 118 NJ 3318
Glenbuck 94 NS 7429
Glenburn 101 NS 4761
Glencaird Hill 86 NX 3580
Glen Callater 117 NO 1883
Glencalvie Forest 128 NH 4387
Glencalvie Lodge 128 NH 4689
Glencanisp Forest 132 NC 1619
Glencanisp Lodge 132 NC 1122
Glen Cannel 105 NM 5935
Glen Cannich 115 NH 1930
Glencannich Forest 115 NH 2433
Glencaple 88 NX 9968
Glen Carron 127 NH 0852
Glencarron and Glenuig Forest 127 NH 1249
Glencarron Lodge 127 NH 0651
Glencarse 108 NO 1922
Glen Cassley 132 NC 4112
Glencassley Castle 128 NC 4407
Glenceitlein 106 NN 1447
Glen Clachaig 105 NM 5735
Glen Clova 109 NO 3570
Glencloy 92 NS 0036
Glen Cochill 108 NN 9042
Glencoe (Highld.) 106 NN 1058
Glen Coe (Highld.) 106 NN 1557
Glen Convinth 116 NH 5137
Glen Corodale 112 NF 8331
Glencorse Resr. 103 NT 2163
Glen Coul 132 NC 2829
Glencraig 102 NT 1795
Glen Creran 106 NN 0448
Glencripesdale Burn 111 NM 6658
Glen Croe 100 NN 2404
Glen Cross 131 NB 5160
Glen Dale 122 NG 1847
Glen Damff 108 NO 2567
Glendaruel 100 NR 9985
Glendaruel Forest 100 NS 0288
Glendavan House 118 NJ 4301
Glendebadel Bay 99 NR 6295
Glen Dee 117 NN 9894
Glen Dessarry 114 NM 9593
Glendevon (Tays.) 102 NN 9504
Glen Devon (Tays.) 102 NN 9804
Glendevon Forest 102 NO 0006
Glendevon Reservoirs 102 NN 9204
Glendhu Forest 132 NC 2834
Glendhu Hill 90 NY 5686
Glen Diebidale 128 NH 4482
Glen Dochart 107 NN 4828
Glen Docherty 127 NH 0559
Glendoebeg 116 NH 4109
Glendoe Forest 116 NH 4404
Glendoe Lodge 115 NH 4008
Glendoick 108 NO 2022
Glen Doll 117 NO 2570
Glendoll Forest 108 NO 2766
Glendoll Lodge 117 NO 2776
Glendon Hall 52 SP 8481
Glen Douchary 127 NH 2591
Glen Douglas 100 NS 3198
Glen Drolla 124 NF 7672
Glenduckie 108 NO 2818
Glendue Fell 83 NY 6454
Glen Duror 106 NN 0153
Glen Dye 119 NO 6384
Glendye Lodge 119 NO 6486
Glen Eagles 102 NN 9306
Gleneagles 102 NN 9308
Gleneagles Station 102 NN 9210
Glen Effock 118 NO 4478
Glenegedale 98 NR 3351
Glenegedale River 98 NR 3352
Glen Einig 127 NH 3698
Glen Elchaig 114 NG 9627
Glenelg 123 NG 8119
Glenelg Bay 123 NG 8019
Glen Ernan 118 NJ 3112
Glen Errochty 107 NN 7663
Glen Esk 119 NO 5377
Glen Etive 106 NN 1751
Glen Euchar 105 NM 8319
Glen Ey 117 NO 0985
Glen Falloch 107 NN 3622
Glenfarg (Tays.) 108 NO 1310
Glen Farg (Tays.) 102 NO 1413
Glenfarg Resr. 102 NO 1011
Glenfarquhar Lodge 119 NO 7281
Glen Fenzie 118 NJ 3202
Glen Feochan 106 NM 8924
Glenferness House 129 NH 9342
Glen Feshie 117 NN 8594
Glenfeshie Forest 117 NN 8790
Glenfeshie Lodge 117 NN 8493
Glen Fiag 133 NC 4524
Glen Fiddich 121 NJ 3234
Glen Fiddich Forest 121 NJ 3130
Glenfiddich Lodge 121 NJ 3132
Glenfield 61 SK 5306
Glen Finart 100 NS 1790
Glenfinart Forest 100 NS 1887
Glenfinart House 100 NS 1888
Glen Finglas 101 NN 5010
Glen Finglas Resr. 101 NN 5209
Glen Finlet 108 NO 2267
Glenfinnan (Highld.) 114 NM 9080
Glen Finnan (Highld.) 114 NM 9083
Glenfoot 108 NO 1715
Glen Fruin 100 NS 2888
Glen Fyne (Strath.) 106 NN 2216
Glen Fyne (Strath.) 100 NS 1173
Glenfyne Lodge 106 NN 2215
Glen Gairn 118 NO 3399
Glengap Forest 88 NX 6460
Glengarnock 93 NS 3252
Glengarrisdale Bay 99 NR 6497
Glen Garry (Highld.) 115 NH 1300
Glen Garry (Tays.) 107 NN 7568
Glengarry Forest 115 NN 2396
Glen Garvan 114 NM 9675
Glengavel Reservoir 94 NS 6634
Glengavel Water 94 NS 6535
Glen Gelder 117 NO 2689
Glen Girnaig 108 NN 9366
Glen Glass 128 NH 5668
Glen Gloy 115 NN 2790
Glen Golly 133 NC 4243
Glen Golly River 132 NC 4144
Glengorm Castle 111 NM 4357
Glen Gour 106 NM 9463
Glengrasco 123 NG 4444
Glen Grudie 126 NG 9665
Glen Harris 110 NM 3696
Glenhead Fm. 108 NO 2562
Glenhoul 88 NX 6087
Glen House 96 NT 2932
Glen Hurich 111 NM 8469
Glen Iorsa 92 NR 9239
Gleniron Fell 86 NX 1962
Glenkens, The (dist.) 88 NX 5887
Glenkerry 89 NT 2710
Glen Kin 100 NS 1279
Glenkindie 118 NJ 4313
Glen Kingie 114 NN 0397
Glen Kinglas (Strath.) 100 NN 2109
Glen Kinglass (Strath.) 106 NN 1435
Glen Kyllachy 116 NH 7225
Glenlatterach 120 NJ 1954
Glenlatterach Resr 120 NJ 1953
Glen Lean 100 NS 0982
Glen Lednock 107 NN 7327
Glenlee (Dumf. and Galwy.) 88 NX 6080
Glen Lee (Tays.) 118 NO 3781
Glenlichorn 101 NN 7912
Glen Liver 106 NN 0835
Glenlivet 117 NJ 1929
Glenlivet 117 NJ 2126
Glen Loch 108 NN 9872
Glen Lochay 107 NN 4936
Glen Lochy 106 NN 2428
Glen Logie 108 NO 3168
Glen Lonan 106 NM 9427
Glenlood Hill 95 NT 0828
Glen Loth 134 NC 9312
Glen Loy 115 NN 1084
Glen Loyne 115 NH 1404
Glenluce 86 NX 1957
Glen Lui 117 NO 0492
Glen Luss 100 NS 3394
Glen Lussa 92 NR 7426
Glenlussa Water 92 NR 7226
Glen Lyon 107 NN 5646
Glenlyon House 107 NN 7347
Glenmaid Moor 88 NX 9689
Glen Mallie 115 NN 0887
Glen Mark 118 NO 3684
Glen Markie (Highld.) 116 NH 5708
Glen Markie (Highld.) 116 NN 5898
Glen Massan 100 NS 1286
Glenmavis 101 NS 7467
Glenmaye 76 SC 2380
Glen Mazeran 116 NH 7121
Glen More (Highld.) 114 NG 8818
Glen More (Highld.) 117 NH 9809
Glen More (Island of Mull) 105 NM 6029
Glenmore (Island of Skye) 123 NG 4340
Glenmore (Strath.) 105 NM 8412
Glenmore Loch 117 NJ 0833
Glenmore Lodge 117 NH 9709
Glenmore River 123 NG 8519
Glen Moriston 115 NH 2411
Glen Mòr or Glen Albyn 116 NH 4211
Glenmorven Cottage 111 NM 5651
Glenmoy 109 NO 4064
Glenmuck Height 95 NT 0724
Glen Muick 118 NO 3187
Glenmuir 94 NS 6321
Glenmuirshaw 88 NS 6920
Glenmuir Water 88 NS 6719
Glen Nant 106 NN 0128
Glen Nevis 106 NN 1468
Glen Nevis House 106 NN 1272
Glen Noe 106 NN 0633
Glen of Artloch Croft 121 NJ 4839
Glen of Coachford 121 NJ 4646
Glen of Rothes 120 NJ 2454
Glen Ogle 107 NN 5726
Glen Orchy 106 NN 2433
Glen Orrin 127 NH 3449
Glen Oykel 132 NC 3111
Glen Parva 61 SP 5798
Glen Pean 114 NM 9490
Glen Prosen 108 NO 2967
Glenprosen Village 108 NO 3265
Glen Quaich 108 NN 8638
Glenquiech 109 NO 4261
Glen Quoich 114 NH 0206
Glenquoich Forest 114 NH 0304
Glenridding 83 NY 3817
Glenrigh Forest 106 NN 0663
Glen Rinnes 117 NJ 2834
Glenrisdell 99 NR 8658
Glen Rosa 92 NR 9838
Glen Rossal 128 NC 4604
Glenrothes 103 NO 2600
Glen Roy 115 NN 3088
Glensanda 105 NM 8246
Glen Sannox 92 NR 9844
Glensaugh 119 NO 6778
Glensax Burn 95 NT 2634
Glen Scaddle 106 NM 9667
Glen Shee (Tays.) 119 NN 9735
Glenshee (Tays.) 108 NN 9834
Glen Shee (Tays.) 108 NO 1362
Glenshero Lodge 116 NN 5493
Glen Shiel 114 NG 9614
Glenshieldaig Forest 123 NG 8349
Glenshiel Forest 114 NG 9413
Glen Shira 100 NN 1314
Glenshirra Forest 116 NN 4793
Glenside 131 NB 3615
Glen Sletdale 134 NC 9112
Glen Sligachan 123 NG 4927
Glensluain 100 NS 0999
Glens of Foudland 121 NJ 6034
Glen Spean 115 NN 3479
Glenstockadale 86 NX 0061
Glen Stockdale 106 NM 9549
Glen Strae 106 NN 1531
Glen Strathfarrar 115 NH 2938
Glen Strathfarrar Forest 115 NH 2339
Glenstriven 100 NS 0878
Glen Tanar 118 NO 4594
Glen Tanar House 118 NO 4795
Glen Tarbert 106 NM 8960
Glen Tarff 115 NH 3902
Glen Tarken 107 NN 6626
Glen Tarsan 100 NS 0785
Glententmont Height 89 NY 2986
Glentham 72 TF 0090
Glen Tig 86 NX 1382
Glen Tilt 108 NN 9172
Glen Tolsta 131 NB 5244
Glentoo Loch 88 NX 7062
Glen Torridon 126 NG 9456
Glentress 95 NT 2839
Glentress Forest 95 NT 2841
Glen Tromie 116 NN 7694
Glentromie Lodge 116 NN 7796
Glen Trool 86 NX 4080
Glen Trool 86 NX 4180
Glentrool Forest 86 NX 3581
Glentrool Village 86 NX 3578
Glentrosdale Bay 99 NM 6700
Glen Truim 116 NN 6789
Glentruim House 116 NN 6895
Glen Turret 107 NN 8226
Glentworth 72 SK 9488
Glenuig Bay 111 NM 6778
Glen Ure 106 NN 0647
Glen Urquhart 116 NH 4430
Glenurquhart Forest 116 NH 4428
Glen Varragill 123 NG 4837
Glen Village 102 NS 8878
Glen Vine 76 SC 3378
Glen Water 94 NS 5739
Glenwhappen Rig 95 NT 0625
Gleouraich (mt.) 115 NH 0405
Glespin 94 NS 8028
Gletness 141 HU 4651
Glevum (ant.) 46 SO 8318
Glewstone 45 SO 5522
Glimps Holm 136 ND 4799
Glinton 62 TF 1506
Glog Hill 48 SO 2169
Glooston 61 SP 7596
Glossop 70 SK 0393
Gloster Hill 91 NU 2504
Gloucester 46 SO 8318
Gloucester and Sharpness Canal 46 SO 7305
Gloucester & Cheltenham (Staverton) Airport 46 SO 8821
Gloup 143 HP 5004
Gloup Holm 143 HP 4806
Gloup Ness 143 HP 5005
Glusburn 78 SE 0344
Gluss 143 HU 3477
Gluss Isle 143 HU 3778
Gluss Voe 142 HU 3678
Gluss Water 142 HU 2581
Glutt Lodge 134 NC 9936
Glutt Water 134 NC 9935
Glyder Fawr (mt.) 67 SH 6457
Glympton 47 SP 4221
Glynarthen 43 SN 3148
Glyn Ceiriog 58 SJ 2038
Glyncorrwg 41 SS 8799
Glyn-Cywarch 66 SH 6034
Glynde 29 TQ 4509
Glyndebourne 29 TQ 4510
Glyn Dyfrdwy 58 SJ 1542
Glyn-Neath 41 SN 8806
Glynogwr 41 SS 9587
Glyntaff 41 ST 0889
Glyn Tarell 41 SN 9823
Glynteg 43 SN 3637
Glyntrefnant 57 SN 9192
Gnosall 59 SJ 8220
Gnosall Heath 59 SJ 8220
Goadby 61 SP 7598
Goadby Marwood 61 SK 7826
Goatacre 34 SU 0176
Goat Fell 92 NR 9941
Goathill 25 ST 6717
Goathland 80 NZ 8301
Goathland Moor 80 SE 8597
Goathurst 24 ST 2534
Gob a' Chuaille 126 NG 8496
Gob Aird an Tolmachain 125 NB 0904
Gob Dubh 99 NR 6385
Gobernuisgach Lodge 133 NC 4341
Goblin's Cave 101 NN 4807
Gob na h-Airde Mòire 130 NB 0117
Gob na h-Oa 122 NG 3134
Gob na Hoe 122 NG 1954
Gob na Milaid 131 NB 4211
Gobowen 58 SJ 3033
Gob Rubh' Uisenis 125 NB 3503
Gob Shilldinish 131 NB 4631
Gob y Deigan 76 SC 2887
Gòdag (is.) 111 NM 4181
Godalming 28 SU 9743
Godington 51 SP 6327
Godmanchester 53 TL 2470
Godmanstone 25 SY 6697
Godmersham 31 TR 0650
Godney 33 ST 4842
Godolphin Cross 18 SW 6031
Godre'r-graig 41 SN 7507
Godrevy Island 18 SW 5743
Godshill (Hants.) 26 SU 1714
Godshill (I. of W.) 27 SZ 5281
Godstone 29 TQ 3551
Godstone Station 29 TQ 3648
Goetre 45 SO 3205
Goff's Oak 37 TL 3202
Gogar 102 NT 1672
Goginan 57 SN 6981
Gog Magog Hills 53 TL 4954
Golan 66 SH 5242
Golant 19 SX 1254
Golberdon 20 SX 3271
Golborne 69 SJ 6097
Golcar 70 SE 0915
Goldcliff 32 ST 3683
Golden Cross 29 TQ 5312
Golden Green 29 TQ 6348
Golden Grove 43 SN 5919
Goldenhill 59 SJ 8553
Golden Pot 35 SU 7143
Golden Valley (Glos.) 46 SO 9022
Golden Valley (Here. and Worc.) 45 SO 3537
Golders Green 37 TQ 2488
Goldhanger 38 TL 9009
Golding 58 SJ 5403
Goldsborough (N Yorks.) 79 SE 3856
Goldsborough (N Yorks.) 85 NZ 8314
Goldsithney 18 SW 5430
Goldthorpe 71 SE 4604
Gollanfield 129 NH 8053
Golspie 129 NH 8399
Golspie Burn 129 NC 8103
Golval 134 NC 8962
Gomersal 78 SE 2026
Gometra (is.) 104 NM 3640
Gomshall 28 TQ 0847
Gonalston 61 SK 6847
Gon Firth (Shetld.) 141 HU 3662
Gonfirth (Shetld.) 141 HU 3761
Goodber Common 77 SD 6263
Good Easter 38 TL 6212
Gooderstone 64 TF 7602
Goodie Water 101 NN 6200
Goodleigh 23 SS 5934
Goodmanham 74 SE 8842
Goodnestone (Kent) 31 TR 0461
Goodnestone (Kent) 31 TR 2554
Goodrich 45 SO 5719
Goodrington 21 SX 8958
Goodwick 42 SM 9438
Goodwin Sands 31 TR 4555
Goodwood House 27 SU 8808
Goodworth Clatford 34 SU 3642
Goodyers End 50 SP 3385
Goole 74 SE 7423
Goole Fields 74 SE 7519
Goonbell 18 SW 7249
Goonhavern 19 SW 7953
Goonhilly Downs 18 SW 7120
Gooseham 22 SS 2316
Goosetrey 69 SJ 7769
Goosey 34 SU 3591
Goosnargh 77 SD 5536
Gop Hill 67 SJ 0880
Gordon 96 NT 6443
Gordonbush 134 NC 8409
Gordonstoun 129 NJ 1868
Gordonstown (Grampn.) 121 NJ 5656
Gordonstown (Grampn.) 121 NJ 7138
Gorebridge 103 NT 3461
Gorefield 63 TF 4112
Gore Sand 32 ST 2851
Goring 35 SU 6080
Goring-by-Sea 28 TQ 1102
Gorleston on Sea 65 TG 5203
Gorley 26 SU 1511
Gorllwyn 44 SN 9159
Gorm Loch 132 NC 2144
Gorm-loch Beag 133 NC 7027
Gorm Loch Mòr (Highld.) 132 NC 3124
Gorm-loch Mòr (Highld.) 134 NC 7123
Gorple Resrs. 78 SD 9231
Gorpley Resr. 78 SD 9123
Gorrachie 121 NJ 7358
Gorran Haven 19 SX 0141
Gors 57 SN 6277
Gorsedd 68 SJ 1476
Gorsedd Brân 67 SH 9760
Gorseinon 40 SS 5998
Gorseness 136 HY 4119
Gors-goch 57 SN 9393
Gorslas 43 SN 5713
Gorsley 46 SO 6826
Gorslydan 48 SO 1276
Gorstan 127 NH 3862
Gorsty Common 45 SO 4537
Gortantaoid 98 NR 3373
Gortantaoid Point 98 NR 3374
Gorton 69 SJ 8996
Gosbeck 55 TM 1555
Gosberton 63 TF 2331
Goseland Hill 95 NT 0735
Gosfield 54 TL 7829
Gosford Bay 103 NT 4478
Gosford House 103 NT 4578
Gosforth (Cumbr.) 82 NY 0603
Gosforth (Tyne and Wear) 91 NZ 2467
Gosmore 52 TL 1927
Gosport 27 SZ 6199
Gossabrough 143 HU 5383
Gossa Water (Shetld.) 141 HU 3045
Gossa Water (Shetld.) 141 HU 4360
Gossa Water (Yell) 143 HU 4899
Goswick 97 NU 0545
Gote o'Tram (pt.) 135 ND 3648
Gotham 61 SK 5330
Gotherington 46 SO 9629
Gott 141 HU 4345
Gott Bay 104 NM 0546
Goudhurst 29 TQ 7337
Goulceby 73 TF 2579
Gourdas 121 NJ 7741
Gourdon 109 NO 8270
Gourock 100 NS 2477
Gouthwaite Reservoir 78 SE 1368
Govan 101 NS 5464
Goveton 21 SX 7546
Govig 130 NB 0109
Gowanhill 121 NK 0363
Gowdall 79 SE 6122
Gower (Highld.) 128 NH 5057
Gower (W Glam.) 40 SS 5290
Gowerton 40 SS 5896
Gowkhall 102 NT 0589
Goxhill (Humbs.) 75 TA 1021
Goxhill (Humbs.) 75 TA 1844
Goyle Hill 119 NO 6881
Goyt's Moss 70 SK 0072
Graddon Moor 22 SS 4602
Graemsay 136 HY 2505
Graffham (W Susx) 28 SU 9216
Grafham (Cambs.) 52 TL 1669
Grafham Water 52 TL 1566
Grafton (Here. and Worc.) 45 SO 4937
Grafton (Here. and Worc.) 48 SO 5761
Grafton (N Yorks.) 79 SE 4163
Grafton (Oxon.) 47 SP 2600
Grafton Flyford 50 SO 9655
Grafton Regis 51 SP 7546
Grafton Underwood 52 SP 9280
Grafty Green 30 TQ 8748
Graianrhyd 58 SJ 2156
Graig (Clwyd) 67 SJ 0872
Graig (Gwyn.) 67 SH 8071
Graig Fawr 43 SN 6207
Graig-fechan 68 SJ 1454
Graig Goch 57 SH 7108
Graig Penllyn 41 SS 9777
Graig Wen 67 SH 7339
Grain 30 TQ 8876
Grainsby 75 TF 2799
Grainthorpe 73 TF 3896
Graizelound 74 SK 7798
Grampian Mountains (Central - Tays.) 107 NN 4151
Grampian Mountains (Grampn.) 117 NJ 2402
Grampound 19 SW 9348
Grampound Road 19 SW 9150
Gramsdale 124 NF 8255
Granborough 51 SP 7625
Granby 61 SK 7536
Grandborough 51 SP 4866
Grandtully 108 NN 9152
Grandtully Castle 108 NN 8951
Grandtully Hill 108 NN 9147
Grand Union Canal (Bucks.) 36 SP 9220
Grand Union Canal (Warw.) 50 SP 2466
Grange (Cumbr.) 82 NY 2517
Grange (Mers.) 68 SJ 2286
Grange (N Yorks.) 85 SE 5796
Grange (Tays.) 108 NO 2725
Grange Crossroads 121 NJ 4754
Grange Fell 89 NY 2481
Grange Hall 129 NJ 0660
Grange Heath 25 SY 9083
Grange Hill 37 TQ 4492
Grange Moor 71 SE 2216
Grangemouth 102 NS 9281
Grange of Lindores 108 NO 2516
Grange-over-Sands 77 SD 4077
Grangepans 102 NT 0282
Grange, The 27 SU 5636
Grangetown 85 NZ 5420
Grange Villa 84 NZ 2352
Granish 117 NH 8914
Gransmoor 81 TA 1259
Granston 42 SM 8934
Grantchester 53 TL 4355
Grantham 62 SK 9135
Grantham Canal 61 SK 7431
Grantley 79 SE 2369
Grantlodge 119 NJ 7017
Granton (Dumf. and Galwy.) 89 NT 0709
Granton (Lothian) 103 NT 2277
Grantown-on-Spey 117 NJ 0327
Grantshouse 97 NT 8065

Grappenhall	69	SJ 6385
Grasby	74	TA 0804
Grasmere (Cumbr.)	82	NY 3307
Grasmere (Cumbr.)	82	NY 3406
Grasscroft	70	SD 9804
Grassendale	68	SJ 3985
Grassholme	84	NY 9221
Grassholme Resr.	84	NY 9422
Grassington	78	SE 0064
Grassmoor	71	SK 4067
Grass Point	105	NM 7430
Grassthorpe	72	SK 7967
Grassy Cletts	136	ND 2887
Grateley	34	SU 2741
Gratwich	60	SK 0231
Graveley (Cambs.)	53	TL 2564
Graveley (Herts.)	53	TL 2328
Gravelly Hill	50	SP 1090
Gravels	58	SJ 3300
Graveney	31	TR 0562
Gravesend	30	TQ 6473
Gravir	131	NB 3815
Grayingham	72	SK 9395
Grayrigg	83	SD 5797
Grays	30	TQ 6177
Grayshott	27	SU 8735
Grayswood	28	SU 9234
Graythorp	85	NZ 5227
Grazeley	36	SU 6966
Grèabhal (mt.)	124	NG 0089
Grean	112	NF 6703
Greanamul (Barra)	112	NF 7305
Greanamul (W Isles)	112	NL 6289
Greanamul Deas	124	NF 8848
Greasbrough	71	SK 4195
Greasby	68	SJ 2587
Great Abington	53	TL 5348
Great Addington	52	SP 9575
Great Alne	50	SP 1159
Great Altcar	68	SD 3206
Great Amwell	37	TL 3712
Great Asby	83	NY 6813
Great Ashfield	54	TM 0068
Great Ayton	85	NZ 5510
Great Baddow	38	TL 7204
Great Bardfield	54	TL 6730
Great Barford	52	TL 1352
Great Barr	60	SP 0495
Great Barrington	47	SP 2013
Great Barrow	68	SJ 4668
Great Barton	54	TL 8967
Great Barugh	80	SE 7478
Great Bavington	91	NY 9880
Great Bedwyn	34	SU 2764
Great Bentley	39	TM 1121
Great Bernera (is.)	131	NB 1635
Great Billing	52	SP 8162
Great Bircham	64	TF 7632
Great Blakenham	55	TM 1150
Great Bolas	59	SJ 6421
Great Bookham	28	TQ 1454
Great Borne (mt.)	82	NY 1216
Great Bosullow	18	SW 4133
Great Bourton	51	SP 4545
Great Bowden	51	SP 7488
Great Bradley	54	TL 6753
Great Braxted	38	TL 8614
Great Bricett	54	TM 0350
Great Brickhill	52	SP 9030
Great Bridgeford	59	SJ 8827
Great Brington	51	SP 6665
Great Bromley	55	TM 0826
Great Broughton	85	NZ 5406
Great Budworth	69	SJ 6677
Great Burbo Bank (sbk.)	68	SJ 2597
Great Burdon	84	NZ 3116
Great Burstead	38	TQ 6892
Great Busby	85	NZ 5105
Great Calva	82	NY 2831
Great Canfield	38	TL 5917
Great Carlton	73	TF 4185
Great Casterton	62	TF 0009
Great Chart	31	TQ 9842
Great Chatwell	59	SJ 7914
Great Chesterford	53	TL 5042
Great Cheverell	34	ST 9858
Great Chishill	53	TL 4238
Great Clacton	39	TM 1716
Great Coates	75	TA 2310
Great Comberton	50	SO 9542
Great Corby	83	NY 4754
Great Cornard	54	TL 8840
Great Coxwell	47	SU 2693
Great Cransley	52	SP 8376
Great Cressingham	64	TF 8501
Great Crosby	68	SJ 3199
Great Cubley	60	SK 1637
Great Cumbrae Island	93	NS 1656
Great Dalby	61	SK 7414
Great Dodd (mt.)	82	NY 3420
Great Doddington	52	SP 8864
Great Driffield	81	TA 0257
Great Dunham	64	TF 8714
Great Dunmow	38	TL 6221
Great Durnford	34	SU 1338
Great Easton (Essex)	54	TL 6125
Great Easton (Leic.)	62	SP 8493
Great Eau	73	TF 4485
Great Eccleston	77	SD 4240
Great Edstone	80	SE 7084
Great Ellingham	64	TM 0196
Great Elm	33	ST 7449
Great End (mt.)	82	NY 2208
Great Eversden	53	TL 3653
Great Fen	54	TL 5978
Great Finborough	54	TM 0157
Greatford	62	TF 0811
Great Fransham	64	TF 8913
Great Gable	82	NY 2110
Great Gaddesden	36	TL 0211
Great Gidding	52	TL 1183
Great Givendale	80	SE 8153
Great Glemham	55	TM 3361
Great Glen	61	SP 6597
Great Gonerby	62	SK 8938
Great Gransden	53	TL 2756
Great Green (Norf.)	55	TM 2789
Great Green (Suff.)	54	TL 9155
Great Habton	80	SE 7576
Great Hallingbury	37	TL 5119
Greatham (Cleve.)	85	NZ 4927
Greatham (Hants.)	27	SU 7730
Greatham (W Susx)	28	TQ 0415
Great Hampden	36	SP 8402
Great Harrowden	52	SP 8871
Great Harwood	77	SD 7332
Great Haseley	36	SP 6401
Great Hatfield	75	TA 1842
Great Haw (mt.)	78	SE 0779
Great Haywood	60	SJ 9922
Great Heck	71	SE 5920
Great Henny	54	TL 8738
Great Hill	88	NX 9492
Great Hinton	33	ST 9058
Great Hockham	54	TL 9592
Great Holland	39	TM 2119
Great Horkesley	54	TL 9731
Great Hormead	53	TL 4030
Great Horwood	51	SP 7731
Great Houghton (Northants.)	51	SP 7958
Great Houghton (S Yorks.)	71	SE 4206
Great Hucklow	70	SK 1777
Great Kelk	81	TA 1058
Great Kingshill	36	SU 8798
Great Lake (Notts.)	71	SK 5773
Great Lake (N Yorks.)	80	SE 7170
Great Langton	84	SE 2996
Great Law	96	NT 4041
Great Leighs	38	TL 7317
Great Limber	75	TA 1308
Great Linford	52	SP 8542
Great Livermere	54	TL 8871
Great Longstone	70	SK 1971
Great Lumley	84	NZ 2949
Great Lyth	58	SJ 4507
Great Malvern	49	SO 7845
Great Maplestead	54	TL 8034
Great Marton	77	SD 3335
Great Massingham	64	TF 7922
Great Mew Stone (is.)	20	SX 5047
Great Milton	36	SP 6302
Great Missenden	36	SP 8901
Great Mis Tor	21	SX 5676
Great Mitton	77	SD 7138
Great Mongeham	31	TR 3451
Greatmoor Hill	89	NT 4800
Great Moulton	55	TM 1690
Great Musgrave	83	NY 7613
Great Ness	58	SJ 3918
Great Oakley (Essex)	55	TM 1927
Great Oakley (Northants.)	52	SP 8686
Great Offley	52	TL 1427
Great Ormes Head	67	SH 7584
Great Ormside	83	NY 7017
Great Orton	82	NY 3254
Great Oxendon	51	SP 7383
Great Palgrave	64	TF 8312
Great Parndon	37	TL 4308
Great Paxton	52	TL 2164
Great Pinseat (mt.)	84	NY 9702
Great Plumstead	65	TG 2910
Great Ponton	62	SK 9230
Great Postland	63	TF 2612
Great Preston	79	SE 4029
Great Raveley	53	TL 2581
Great Ridge	25	ST 9236
Great Rissington	47	SP 1917
Great Rollright	47	SP 3231
Great Ryburgh	64	TF 9527
Great Ryle	91	NU 0212
Great Saling	54	TL 7025
Great Salkeld	83	NY 5536
Great Sampford	54	TL 6435
Great Sankey	69	SJ 5688
Great Saxham	54	TL 7862
Great Shefford	34	SU 3875
Great Shelford	53	TL 4652
Great Shunner Fell	83	SD 8497
Great Shutter Rock	22	SS 1343
Great Smeaton	85	NZ 3404
Great Snoring	64	TF 9434
Great Somerford	34	ST 9682
Great Stainton	84	NZ 3322
Great Stambridge	38	TQ 8991
Great Staughton	52	TL 1264
Great Steeping	73	TF 4364
Great Stonar	31	TR 3359
Greatstone-on-Sea	31	TR 0822
Great Stour	31	TR 0651
Great Strickland	83	NY 5522
Great Stukeley	53	TL 2275
Great Sturton	73	TF 2176
Great Swinburne	90	NY 9375
Great Tew	47	SP 3929
Great Tey	54	TL 8925
Great Torrington	22	SS 4919
Great Tosson	91	NU 0300
Great Totham (Essex)	38	TL 8511
Great Totham (Essex)	38	TL 8613
Great Wakering	38	TQ 9487
Great Waldingfield	54	TL 9143
Great Walsingham	64	TF 9437
Great Waltham	38	TL 6913
Great Warley	37	TQ 5890
Great Washbourne	46	SO 9834
Great Welnetham	54	TL 8759
Great Wenham	54	TM 0738
Great Whernside (mt.)	78	SE 0074
Great Whittington	91	NZ 0070
Great Wigborough	39	TL 9615
Great Wilbraham	53	TL 5557
Great Wishford	26	SU 0835
Great Witcombe	46	SO 9014
Great Witley	49	SO 7566
Great Wolford	47	SP 2434
Greatworth	51	SP 5542
Great Wratting	54	TL 6848
Great Wyrley	60	SJ 9907
Great Wytheford	59	SJ 5719
Great Yarmouth	65	TG 5207
Great Yeldham	54	TL 7638
Greave	104	NM 2420
Greeb Point	19	SW 8733
Greenbooth Resr.	69	SD 8515
Greenburn	102	NS 9360
Greendikes	97	NU 0628
Greenfield (Beds.)	52	TL 0534
Greenfield (Clwyd)	68	SJ 1977
Greenfield (Gtr Mches.)	70	SD 9904
Greenfield (Highld.)	115	NH 2000
Greenfield (Oxon.)	36	SU 7191
Greenford	37	TQ 1382
Greengairs	101	NS 7870
Greenham	35	SU 4865
Green Hammerton	79	SE 4656
Greenhaugh	90	NY 7987
Green Head (Hoy, Orkney)	136	ND 3099
Greenhead (Northum.)	90	NY 6665
Greenhill (Central)	101	NS 8278
Greenhill (Gtr London)	37	TQ 1688
Green Hill (Northum.)	84	NY 8647
Greenhill (S Yorks.)	71	SK 3481
Green Hill (Wilts.)	34	SU 0686
Greenhithe	30	TQ 5974
Greenholm	94	NS 5637
Greenholme	83	NY 5905
Greenhouse	96	NT 5523
Greenhow Hill	78	SE 1164
Greenigo	136	HY 4107
Greenland	135	ND 2367
Green Law (Borders)	90	NT 6304
Greenlaw (Borders)	96	NT 7145
Greenlee Lough	90	NY 7669
Greenli Ness	137	HY 6221
Greenloaning	101	NN 8307
Green Lowther	88	NS 8911
Green Mount	69	SD 7714
Greenock	100	NS 2776
Greenodd	77	SD 3182
Green Ore	33	ST 5749
Green Road Station	76	SD 1984
Green Scar	42	SM 7922
Greenside	91	NZ 1362
Greensidehill	91	NT 9716
Greenside Reservoir	101	NS 4775
Greensides (mt.)	86	NX 2889
Greenskairs	121	NJ 7863
Greens Norton	51	SP 6649
Greenstead Green	54	TL 8227
Greensted	37	TL 5302
Greenstone Point	126	NG 8598
Green Street	37	TQ 1998
Green Street Green	37	TQ 4563
Green, The (Cumbr.)	76	SD 1784
Green, The (Wilts.)	25	ST 8731
Greenwich	37	TQ 4077
Greet	46	SP 0230
Greeta River or River Creed	131	NB 3632
Greete	48	SO 5770
Greetham (Leic.)	62	SK 9214
Greetham (Lincs.)	73	TF 3070
Greetland	78	SE 0821
Greg Ness	119	NJ 9704
Gregson Lane	77	SD 5926
Greian Head	112	NF 6404
Greinton	24	ST 4136
Gremista	141	HU 4643
Grendon (Northants.)	52	SP 8760
Grendon (Warw.)	60	SP 2799
Grendon Common	60	SP 2799
Grendon Green	45	SO 5957
Grendon Underwood	36	SP 6720
Grenitote	124	NF 8275
Grenoside	71	SK 3394
Gresford	58	SJ 3454
Gresham	65	TG 1738
Greshornish	122	NG 3454
Greshornish Point	122	NG 3456
Gress	131	NB 4942
Gressenhall	64	TF 9615
Gressenhall Green	64	TF 9616
Gressingham	77	SD 5769
Gress River	131	NB 4545
Greta Bridge	84	NZ 0813
Gretna	89	NY 3167
Gretna Green	89	NY 3268
Gretton (Glos.)	46	SP 0030
Gretton (Northants.)	62	SP 8994
Gretton (Shrops.)	59	SO 5195
Grewelthorpe	79	SE 2276
Grey Cairns (ant.)	135	ND 2544
Greygarth	78	SE 1872
Grey Head	138	HY 5740
Grey Hill	86	NX 1692
Grey Mare's Tail (mt.)	89	NT 1814
Greysouthen	82	NY 0729
Greystoke	83	NY 4330
Greystone	109	NO 5343
Greywell	35	SU 7151
Gribbin Head	19	SX 0949
Gribun	105	NM 4533
Grice Ness	137	HY 6728
Griff	50	SP 3588
Griffithstown	45	ST 2999
Grif Skerry	141	HU 6362
Grigghall	83	SD 4691
Grike (mt.)	82	NY 0814
Grimeford Village	69	SD 6112
Grime's Graves (ant.)	54	TL 8189
Grimes Hill	77	SD 6286
Grimethorpe	71	SE 4109
Griminish	124	NF 7851
Griminish Point	124	NF 7276
Grimister	143	HU 4693
Grimley	49	SO 8360
Grimness (S. Ronaldsay)	136	ND 4793
Grim Ness (S.Ronaldsay)	136	ND 4992
Grimoldby	73	TF 3988
Grimsargh	77	SD 5834
Grimsay	124	NF 8656
Grimsby	75	TA 2810
Grimscote	51	SP 6553
Grimscott	22	SS 2606
Grimshader	131	NB 4025
Grimspound (ant.)	21	SX 7080
Grimsthorpe	62	TF 0423
Grimston (Leic.)	61	SK 6821
Grimston (Norf.)	64	TF 7221
Grimstone	25	SY 6393
Grimwith Resr.	78	SE 0664
Grindale	81	TA 1371
Grindle	59	SJ 7403
Grindleford	71	SK 2477
Grindleton	78	SD 7545
Grindlow	70	SK 1877
Grind of the Navir (pt.)	142	HU 2180
Grindon (Northum.)	97	NT 9144
Grindon (Staffs.)	60	SK 0854
Grindstone Law	90	NT 7607
Gringley on the Hill	72	SK 7390
Grinsdale	89	NY 3758
Grinshill	59	SJ 5223
Grinton	84	SE 0498
Griomaval (mt.)	130	NB 0122
Grisedale	83	NY 3715
Grisedale Pike	82	NY 1922
Grisedale Tarn	82	NY 3512
Grishipoll	110	NM 1959
Griskerry	141	HU 3622
Gristhorpe	81	TA 0882
Griston	64	TL 9499
Gritley	137	HY 5605
Grittenham	34	SU 0382
Grittleton	33	ST 8579
Grizebeck	76	SD 2384
Grizedale	82	SD 3394
Grizedale Forest	82	SD 3394
Groatay	124	NF 9773
Groay	124	NG 0079
Groban (mt.)	127	NH 0970
Gròb Bàgh	92	NR 6346
Grobister	137	HY 6524
Groby	61	SK 5207
Groemeshall Burn	136	HY 4704
Groes (Clwyd)	67	SJ 0064
Groes (W Glam.)	41	SS 7986
Groes-faen	41	ST 0780
Groesffordd Marli	67	SJ 0073
Groeslon	66	SH 4755
Grogport	92	NR 8044
Gronant	67	SJ 0883
Groombridge	29	TQ 5337
Grosebay	125	NG 1592
Grosmont (Gwent)	45	SO 4024
Grosmont (N Yorks.)	80	NZ 8205
Groton	54	TL 9641
Grove (Dorset)	25	SY 6972
Grove (Kent)	31	TR 2362
Grove (Notts.)	72	SK 7379
Grove (Oxon.)	34	SU 4090
Grovely Wood	26	SU 0534
Grove Park	37	TQ 4172
Grovesend	40	SN 5900
Grudie Burn	128	NC 5305
Grudie River	132	NC 3161
Gruids	128	NC 5604
Gruinard Bay	126	NG 9293
Gruinard House	126	NG 9692
Gruinard Island	126	NG 9494
Gruinard River	126	NG 9789
Gruinart	98	NR 2866
Grula	122	NG 3826
Gruline	105	NM 5440
Gruline House	105	NM 5539
Grumbla	18	SW 4029
Grumby Rock	133	NC 7010
Gruna (is.)	140	HU 2859
Grunasound	141	HU 3733
Gruna Stack	142	HU 2886
Grunay	143	HU 6971
Grundisburgh	55	TM 2251
Gruney (is.)	143	HU 3896
Grunka Hellier	143	HP 5815
Gruting	140	HU 2849
Gruting Voe	140	HU 2647
Grutness	141	HU 4009
Grut Wick	141	HU 5138
Grwyne Fechan	45	SO 2324
Gryfe Reservoirs	100	NS 2871
Gualachulain	106	NN 1145
Gualann (mt.)	101	NS 4594
Gualin House	132	NC 3056
Guallann Mhór	100	NR 9062
Guardbridge	109	NO 4519
Guarlford	49	SO 8145
Guay	108	NO 0049
Guens, The (is.)	143	HU 6568
Guestling Green	30	TQ 8513
Guestwick	64	TG 0627
Gugh	18	SV 8908
Guide Post	91	NZ 2585
Guilden Morden	53	TL 2744
Guilden Sutton	68	SJ 4468
Guildford	28	TQ 0049
Guildtown	108	NO 1331
Guillamon Island	123	NG 6327
Guilsborough	51	SP 6773
Guilsfield	58	SJ 2111
Guirasdeal	105	NM 6907
Guirdil Bay	110	NG 3101
Guisachan Forest	115	NH 2520
Guisborough	85	NZ 6115
Guiseley	78	SE 1941
Guist	64	TF 9925
Guith	138	HY 5536
Guiting Power	46	SP 0924
Gulber Wick	141	HU 4438
Gulf of Corryvreckan	99	NM 6901
Gulland Rock	19	SW 8778
Gullane	103	NT 4882
Gullane Bay	103	NT 4783
Gull Point	93	NS 1450
Gulvain or Gaor Bheinn	114	NM 9987
Gulval	18	SW 4831
Gumfreston	42	SN 1101
Gumley	51	SP 6890
Gunby (Humbs.)	74	SE 7135
Gunby (Lincs.)	62	SK 9021
Gundleton	27	SU 6133
Gunfleet Sand	39	TM 2611
Gunn	23	SS 6333
Gunna (is.)	110	NM 0951
Gunnerside	84	SD 9598
Gunnerton	90	NY 9074
Gunness	74	SE 8411
Gunnislake	20	SX 4371
Gunnista	141	HU 5043
Gunthorpe (Norf.)	64	TG 0135
Gunthorpe (Notts.)	61	SK 6744
Gunton Hall	65	TG 2234
Gunton Sta	65	TG 2535
Gunver Head	19	SW 8977
Gunwalloe Fishing Cove	18	SW 6522
Gurnard	27	SZ 4795
Gurnard Bay	27	SZ 4795
Gurnard's Head	18	SW 4338
Gurn Ddu	66	SH 4046
Gurney Slade	33	ST 6249
Gurnos	41	SN 7709
Gussage All Saints	26	SU 0010
Gussage St. Michael	26	ST 9811
Guston	31	TR 3244
Gutcher	143	HU 5498
Guthrie	109	NO 5650
Gutter Sound	136	ND 3197
Guyhirn	63	TF 3903
Guy's Head	63	TF 4825
Guy's Marsh	25	ST 8420
Guyzance	91	NU 2103
Gwaelod-y-garth	41	ST 1183
Gwaenysgor	67	SJ 0780
Gwalchmai	66	SH 3975
Gwastad	45	SO 2305
Gwastedyn Hill	57	SN 9866
Gwaun-Cae-Gurwen	40	SN 7011
Gwaunceste Hill	44	SO 1555
Gwaun Nant-ddu	41	SO 0017
Gwaynynog	67	SJ 0365
Gwbert-on-Sea	42	SN 1650
Gweek	18	SW 7026
Gwehelog	45	SO 3804
Gwenddwr	44	SO 0643
Gwendraeth (sbk.)	43	SN 3606
Gwendraeth Fâch	43	SN 4714
Gwendraeth Fawr	43	SN 5011
Gwennap	18	SW 7340
Gwennap Head	18	SW 3621
Gwenter	18	SW 7418
Gwernaffield	68	SJ 2064
Gwernesney	45	SO 4101
Gwernogle	43	SN 5234
Gwernymynydd	68	SJ 2162
Gwespyr	68	SJ 1183
Gwinear	18	SW 5937
Gwithian	18	SW 5841
Gwrhyd	44	SN 9339
Gwrych Castle	67	SH 9277
Gwyddelwern	67	SJ 0746
Gwyddgrug	43	SN 4635
Gwytherin	67	SH 8761
Gylchedd	67	SH 8644
Gypsey Race	81	TA 0970

H

Haaf Gruney (is.)	143	HU 6398
Haa, The (pt.)	141	HU 5560
Habberley (Here. and Worc.)	49	SO 8077
Habberley (Shrops.)	58	SJ 3903
Habitancum (ant.)	90	NY 8986
Habost (Isle of Lewis)	131	NB 3219
Habost (Isle of Lewis)	131	NB 5262
Habrough	75	TA 1514
Haccombe	21	SX 8970
Haceby	62	TF 0236
Hacheston	55	TM 3059
Hackenthorpe	71	SK 4183
Hackford	64	TG 0502
Hackforth	84	SE 2493
Hackland	136	HY 3920
Hacklete	131	NB 1534
Hackleton	51	SP 8055
Hackley Head or Forvie Ness	121	NK 0226
Hackness (N Yorks.)	81	SE 9690
Hackness (South Walls)	136	ND 3391
Hackney	37	TQ 3585
Hacko's Ness	137	HY 5215
Hackpen Hill (Devon)	24	ST 1112
Hackpen Hill (Wilts.)	34	SU 1274
Hacks Ness	139	HY 6134
Hackthorn	72	SK 9882
Hackthorpe	83	NY 5423
Haconby	62	TF 1025
Hadden	97	NT 7836
Haddenham (Bucks.)	36	SP 7408
Haddenham (Cambs.)	53	TL 4675
Haddington	103	NT 5174
Haddiscoe	65	TM 4497
Haddock Sands (chan.)	141	HU 3443
Haddo House	121	NJ 8634
Haddon	52	TL 1392
Haddon Hall (ant.)	71	SK 2366
Haddon Hill	23	SS 9628
Hademore	60	SK 1708
Hadfield	70	SK 0296
Hadham Cross	37	TL 4218
Hadham Ford	37	TL 4321
Hadleigh (Essex)	38	TQ 8087
Hadleigh (Suff.)	54	TM 0242
Hadley	59	SJ 6712
Hadley End	60	SK 1320
Hadlow	29	TQ 6349
Hadlow Down	29	TQ 5324
Hadnall	59	SJ 5120
Hadrian's Wall (Cumbr.) (ant.)	89	NY 2661
Hadrian's Wall (Cumbr.) (ant.)	83	NY 3757
Hadrian's Wall (Cumbr.) (ant.)	89	NY 4561
Hadrian's Wall (Northum.) (ant.)	90	NY 7167
Hadrian's Wall (Northum.) (ant.)	90	NY 8069
Hadrian's Wall (Northum.) (ant.)	91	NZ 0568
Hadstock	53	TL 5645
Hadston Carrs (pt.)	91	NU 2800
Hadyard Hill	86	NX 2799
Hadzor	49	SO 9162
Haffenden Quarter	30	TQ 8841
Hafod-Dinbych	67	SH 8953
Haggbeck	89	NY 4774
Haggerston Castle	97	NU 0443
Hagley (Here. and Worc.)	45	SO 5641
Hagley (Here. and Worc.)	49	SO 9181
Hagshaw Hill	94	NS 7831
Hagworthingham	73	TF 3469
Haigh	69	SD 6108
Haighton Green	77	SD 5634
Haile	82	NY 0308
Hailes	46	SP 0530
Hailes Castle (ant.)	103	NT 5775
Hailey (Herts.)	37	TL 3710
Hailey (Oxon.)	47	SP 3512
Hailsham	29	TQ 5909
Hail Weston	52	TL 1662
Hainault	37	TQ 4691
Hainford	65	TG 2218
Hainton	73	TF 1784
Haisborough (lightship)	65	TG 4049
Haisthorpe	81	TA 1264
Halam	61	SK 6754
Halberry Head	135	ND 3037
Halberton	23	ST 0012
Halcro	135	ND 2260
Halcro Head	136	ND 4785
Hale (Ches.)	68	SJ 4682
Hale (Gtr Mches.)	69	SJ 7786
Hale (Hants.)	26	SU 1919
Hale (Lincs.)	62	TF 1443
Hale Bank	69	SJ 4784
Halebarns	69	SJ 7985
Hales (Norf.)	65	TM 3897
Hales (Staffs.)	59	SJ 7134
Halesowen	50	SO 9683
Hales Place	31	TR 1459
Hale Street	29	TQ 6749
Halesworth	55	TM 3877
Halewood	68	SJ 4585
Halford (Shrops.)	48	SO 4383
Halford (Warw.)	50	SP 2545
Halfpenny Green	49	SO 8292
Halfpenny Green Airport	49	SO 8291
Halfway (Berks.)	34	SU 4068
Halfway (Dyfed)	43	SN 6430
Halfway (Dyfed)	41	SN 8232
Halfway House	58	SJ 3411
Halfway Houses	30	TQ 9373
Halidon Hill	97	NT 9655
Halifax	78	SE 0825
Halistra	122	NG 2459
Halket	93	NS 4252
Halkirk	135	ND 1359
Halkyn	68	SJ 2071
Halkyn Mountain	68	SJ 1971
Halladale River	134	NC 8855
Halland	29	TQ 5016
Hallaton	61	SP 7896
Hallatrow	33	ST 6356
Hallbankgate	90	NY 5859
Hall Dunnerdale	82	SD 2195
Hallen	33	ST 5479
Hall Green	50	SP 1181
Hallhills Loch	89	NY 1688
Halliburton	96	NT 6748
Halliman Skerries	120	NJ 2172
Hallin	122	NG 2558
Halling	30	TQ 7063
Hallington	91	NY 9875
Hallington Resr.	91	NY 9776
Hallival (mt.)	111	NM 3996
Hall of Clestrain	136	HY 2907
Hall of Tankerness	137	HY 5208
Hall of the Forest	48	SO 2083
Halloughton	61	SK 6851
Hallow	49	SO 8258
Hall Road Station	68	SD 3000
Hallrule	90	NT 5914
Halls	103	NT 6572
Hallsands	21	SX 8138
Hall's Green	53	TL 2728
Hall, The	143	HU 6098
Hallthwaites	76	SD 1884
Hallworthy	20	SX 1787
Hallyburton Forest	108	NO 2333
Hallyburton House	108	NO 2438
Hallyne	95	NT 1940
Halmer End	59	SJ 7949
Halmore	46	SO 6902
Halmyre Mains	95	NT 1749
Halnaker	28	SU 9108
Halsall	68	SD 3710
Halse (Northants.)	51	SP 5640
Halse (Somer.)	24	ST 1327
Halsetown	18	SW 5038
Halsham	75	TA 2627
Halsinger	22	SS 5138
Halstead (Essex)	54	TL 8130
Halstead (Kent)	37	TQ 4961
Halstead (Leic.)	61	SK 7505
Halstock	25	ST 5308
Halstow Marshes	30	TQ 7877
Haltham	73	TF 2463
Haltoft End	63	TF 3645
Halton (Bucks.)	36	SP 8710
Halton (Ches.)	69	SJ 5381
Halton (Clwyd)	58	SJ 3039
Halton (Lancs.)	77	SD 5065
Halton East	78	SE 0454
Halton Gill	78	SD 8876
Halton Holegate	73	TF 4165
Halton Lea Gate	90	NY 6558
Halton West	78	SD 8454
Haltwhistle	90	NY 7064
Halvergate	65	TG 4206
Halvergate Marshes	65	TG 4506
Halwell	21	SX 7753
Halwill	20	SX 4299
Halwill Junction	20	SS 4400
Ham (Bressay)	141	HU 4939
Ham (Foula)	140	HT 9739
Ham (Glos.)	46	ST 6898
Ham (Gtr London)	37	TQ 1672
Ham (Highld.)	135	ND 2373
Ham (Kent)	31	TR 3354
Ham (Wilts.)	34	SU 3262
Hamar (pt.)	141	HU 5136
Hamara River	122	NG 1947
Hamars Ness	143	HU 5894
Hamble	27	SU 4806

Hamble Airfield	27	SU	4707
Hambleden (Bucks.)	36	SU	7886
Hambledon (Hants.)	27	SU	6414
Hambledon (Surrey)	28	SU	9638
Hambledon Hill (ant.)	25	ST	8412
Hambleton (Lancs.)	77	SD	3742
Hambleton (N Yorks.)	79	SE	5430
Hambleton Hill	78	SE	1573
Hambleton Hills, The	79	SE	5286
Hambridge	24	ST	3921
Hambrook (Avon)	33	ST	6378
Hambrook (W Susx)	27	SU	7806
Hameldon Hill	78	SD	7928
Hameldown Tor	21	SX	7080
Hamera Head	141	HU	4862
Hameringham	73	TF	3167
Hamerton	52	TL	1379
Hametoun	140	HT	9637
Hamford Water	55	TM	2325
Ham Green (Avon)	33	ST	5575
Ham Green (Here. and Worc.)	50	SP	0063
Ham Hill (ant.)	25	ST	4816
Hamilton	94	NS	7255
Hamly Hill	136	HY	4904
Hammersmith	37	TQ	2279
Hammerwich	60	SK	0707
Hammond Beck	62	TF	2038
Hammond Street	37	TL	3304
Hammoon	25	ST	8114
Hamna Voe (Papa Stour)	140	HU	1659
Hamna Voe (Shetld.)	142	HU	2380
Hamnavoe (Shetld.)	142	HU	2381
Hamnavoe (Shetld.)	143	HU	4971
Hamnavoe (West Burra)	141	HU	3735
Hamna Voe (Yell)	143	HU	4879
Hamnavoe (Yell)	143	HU	4980
Ham of Muness	143	HP	6301
Hampden Park	29	TQ	6002
Hampnett	46	SP	0915
Hampole	71	SE	5010
Hampreston	26	SZ	0598
Hampstead	37	TQ	2485
Hampstead Norreys	35	SU	5276
Hampsthwaite	79	SE	2558
Hampton	50	SP	0243
Hampton (Gtr London)	37	TQ	1369
Hampton (Shrops.)	49	SO	7486
Hampton Bishop	45	SO	5538
Hampton Court (ant.)	37	TQ	1568
Hampton Heath	59	SJ	4949
Hampton in Arden	50	SP	2081
Hampton Lovett	49	SO	8865
Hampton Lucy	50	SP	2557
Hampton on the Hill	50	SP	2564
Hampton Poyle	47	SP	5015
Hamsey	29	TQ	4112
Hamstall Ridware	60	SK	1019
Hamstead (I. of W.)	26	SZ	3991
Hamstead (W Mids)	60	SP	0593
Hamstead Marshall	34	SU	4165
Hamsterley (Durham)	84	NZ	1131
Hamsterley (Durham)	84	NZ	1156
Hamsterley Forest	84	NZ	0328
Hamstreet (Kent)	31	TR	0034
Ham Street (Somer.)	25	ST	5534
Hamworthy	26	SY	9990
Hanbury (Here and Worc.)	50	SO	9663
Hanbury (Staffs.)	60	SK	1727
Hanchurch	59	SJ	8441
Handa Island	132	NC	1348
Handbridge	68	SJ	4164
Handcross	28	TQ	2630
Handfast Point or The Foreland	26	SZ	0582
Handforth	69	SJ	8883
Handley	68	SJ	4657
Handsacre	60	SK	0916
Handsworth (S Yorks.)	71	SK	4086
Handsworth (W Mids)	60	SP	0400
Hanford	59	SJ	8642
Hanging Langford	26	SU	0237
Hanham	33	ST	6372
Hankelow	59	SJ	6645
Hankerton	34	ST	9690
Hankham	29	TQ	6105
Hanley	59	SJ	8847
Hanley Castle	49	SO	8342
Hanley Childe	49	SO	6565
Hanley Swan	49	SO	8143
Hanley William	49	SO	6765
Hanlith	78	SD	9061
Hanmer	58	SJ	4540
Hanningfield Resr.	38	TQ	7398
Hannington (Hants.)	35	SU	5355
Hannington (Northants.)	52	SP	8171
Hannington (Wilts.)	47	SU	1793
Hannington Wick	47	SU	1795
Hanslope	51	SP	8046
Hanthorpe	62	TF	0824
Hanwell	50	SP	4343
Hanwood	58	SJ	4309
Hanworth (Gtr London)	37	TQ	1271
Hanworth (Norf.)	65	TG	1935
Happendon	95	NS	8533
Happisburgh	65	TG	3731
Happisburgh Common	65	TG	3729
Happyland Hall	84	NZ	0932
Hapsford	69	SJ	4774
Hapton (Lancs.)	78	SD	7931
Hapton (Norf.)	65	TM	1796
Harberton	21	SX	7758
Harbertonford	21	SX	7856
Harbledown	31	TR	1358
Harborne	50	SP	0384
Harborough Magna	51	SP	4779
Harbottle	90	NT	9304
Harbury	50	SP	3759
Harby (Leic.)	61	SK	7431
Harby (Notts.)	72	SK	8770
Harcombe	24	SY	1590
Harden	78	SE	0838
Hardgate	119	NJ	7801
Hardham	28	TQ	0317
Hardhorn	77	SD	3538
Hardingham	64	TG	0403
Hardingstone	51	SP	7657
Hardings Wood	59	SJ	8054
Hardington	33	ST	7452
Hardington Mandeville	25	ST	5111
Hardington Marsh	25	ST	5009
Hard Knott Pass	82	NY	2301
Hardley	26	SU	4205
Hardley Street	65	TG	3801
Hardmead	52	SP	9347
Hardrow	84	SD	8691
Hardstoft	71	SK	4463
Hardway (Hants.)	27	SU	6101
Hardway (Somer.)	25	ST	7134
Hardwick (Bucks.)	36	SP	8019
Hardwick (Cambs.)	53	TL	3758
Hardwick (Norf.)	55	TM	2290
Hardwick (Northants.)	52	SP	8569
Hardwick (Oxon.)	47	SP	3706
Hardwick (Oxon.)	47	SP	5729
Hardwicke (Glos.)	46	SO	7912
Hardwicke (Glos.)	46	SO	9127
Hardwick Hall (ant.)	71	SK	4663
Hareby	73	TF	3365
Hareden	77	SD	6350
Hare Faulds (ant.)	96	NT	5750
Harefield	36	TQ	0590
Hare Hatch	36	SU	8077
Hare Hill (Strath.)	88	NS	6509
Hare Hill (Strath.)	95	NS	9153
Harehope	91	NU	0920
Harelaw Dam	93	NS	4753
Hare Ness	119	NO	9599
Harescombe	46	SO	8410
Haresfield	46	SO	8110
Hareshaw Hill	94	NS	7629
Hare Street	53	TL	3929
Harewood	79	SE	3245
Harewood Forest	34	SU	3943
Harford	21	SX	6359
Hargrave (Ches.)	69	SJ	4862
Hargrave (Northants.)	52	TL	0370
Hargrave (Suff.)	54	TL	7759
Harker	89	NY	3960
Harkstead	55	TM	1935
Harland Hill	78	SE	0284
Harlaston	60	SK	2111
Harlaw House	121	NJ	7424
Harlaw Resr.	102	NT	1865
Harlaxton	62	SK	8832
Harlech	66	SH	5831
Harlesden	37	TQ	2383
Harleston (Devon)	21	SX	7945
Harleston (Norf.)	55	TM	2483
Harleston (Suff.)	54	TM	0160
Harlestone	51	SP	7064
Harle Syke	78	SD	8634
Harley	59	SJ	5901
Harling Road Station	54	TL	9788
Harlington	52	TL	0330
Harlosh	122	NG	2841
Harlosh Island	122	NG	2739
Harlosh Point	122	NG	2840
Harlow	37	TL	4711
Harlow Hill	91	NZ	0768
Harlthorpe	74	SE	7337
Harlton	53	TL	3852
Harman's Cross	26	SY	9880
Harmby	84	SE	1289
Harmer Green	37	TL	2516
Harmer Hill	59	SJ	4822
Harmston	72	SK	9762
Harnham	26	SU	1229
Harnhill	46	SP	0600
Harold Hill	37	TQ	5391
Haroldston West	42	SM	8615
Haroldswick (Unst)	143	HP	6312
Harold's Wick (Unst)	143	HP	6411
Harold Wood	37	TQ	5590
Harome	79	SE	6482
Harpenden	37	TL	1314
Harperleas Resr.	103	NO	2105
Harperrig Reservoir	102	NT	0961
Harper's Brook	52	SP	9286
Harpford	24	SY	0890
Harpham	81	TA	0961
Harpley (Here. and Worc.)	49	SO	6861
Harpley (Norf.)	64	TF	7826
Harpole	51	SP	6961
Harpsdale	135	ND	1256
Harpsden	36	SU	7680
Harpswell	72	SK	9389
Harpurhey	69	SD	8701
Harpur Hill	70	SK	0671
Harrabrough Head	136	ND	4190
Harrapool	123	NG	6522
Harrier	140	HT	9540
Harrietfield	108	NN	9829
Harrietsham	30	TQ	8753
Harrington (Cumbr.)	82	NX	9926
Harrington (Lincs.)	73	TF	3671
Harrington (Northants.)	51	SP	7780
Harringworth	62	SP	9197
Harris (Rhum)	110	NM	3395
Harris (W Isles) (dist.)	125	NG	1198
Harriseahead	59	SJ	8656
Harrogate	79	SE	3066
Harrold	52	SP	9456
Harrow	37	TQ	1388
Harrowbarrow	20	SX	3969
Harrowden	52	TL	0646
Harrow Hill	28	TQ	0810
Harrow on the Hill	37	TQ	1586
Harsgeir	131	NB	1040
Harston (Cambs.)	53	TL	4251
Harston (Leic.)	62	SK	8331
Hart	85	NZ	4735
Harta Corrie	123	NG	4723
Hartamul	112	NF	8311
Hartburn	91	NZ	0886
Harter Fell (Cumbr.)	83	NY	4609
Harter Fell (Cumbr.)	82	SD	2199
Hartest	54	TL	8352
Hart Fell (Dumf. and Galwy.)	89	NT	1113
Hart Fell (Dumf. and Galwy.)	89	NY	2289
Hartfield	29	TQ	4735
Hartford (Cambs.)	53	TL	2572
Hartford (Ches.)	69	SJ	6372
Hartfordbridge	35	SU	7757
Hartford End	38	TL	6817
Harthill (Ches.)	59	SJ	4955
Harthill (Lothian)	102	NS	9064
Harthill (S Yorks.)	71	SK	4980
Harthope Burn	97	NT	9623
Hartington	70	SK	1360
Hartland	22	SS	2624
Hartland Point	22	SS	2227
Hartland Quay	22	SS	2224
Hartlebury	49	SO	8470
Hartlepool	85	NZ	5032
Hartlepool Bay	85	NZ	5232
Hartley (Cumbr.)	83	NY	7808
Hartley (Kent)	30	TQ	6166
Hartley (Kent)	29	TQ	7634
Hartley (Northum.)	91	NZ	3475
Hartley Wespall	36	SU	6958
Hartley Wintney	35	SU	7756
Hartlip	30	TQ	8364
Harton (N Yorks.)	80	SE	7061
Harton (Shrops.)	48	SO	4888
Harton (Tyne and Wear)	91	NZ	3864
Hartpury	46	SO	7924
Hartshill	60	SP	3293
Hartshorne	60	SK	3221
Hartshorn Pike	90	NT	6201
Hartsop	83	NY	4013
Hartwell	51	SP	7850
Hartwood	101	NS	8459
Harvel	30	TQ	6563
Harvington	50	SP	0548
Harvington Cross	50	SP	0549
Harwell	35	SU	4989
Harwich	55	TM	2431
Harwich Harbour	55	TM	2632
Harwood (Durham)	83	NY	8133
Harwood (Gtr Mches.)	69	SD	7411
Harwood Beck	83	NY	8321
Harwood Dale	81	SE	9595
Harwood Forest	91	NY	9994
Harworth	71	SK	6291
Hascombe	28	TQ	0039
Hascosay	143	HU	5592
Hascosay Sound	143	HU	5492
Haselbech	51	SP	7177
Haselbury Plucknett	25	ST	4711
Haseley	50	SP	2368
Haselor	50	SP	1257
Hasfield	46	SO	8227
Hasguard	42	SM	8509
Haskayne	68	SD	3507
Haskeir Eagach (is.)	124	NF	5980
Haskeir Island	124	NF	6182
Hasketon	55	TM	2550
Hasland	71	SK	3969
Haslemere	27	SU	9032
Haslingden	78	SD	7823
Haslingden Grane	78	SD	7523
Haslingfield	53	TL	4052
Haslington	59	SJ	7355
Hassall	69	SJ	7657
Hassall Green	69	SJ	7758
Hassell Street	31	TR	0946
Hassendean	90	NT	5420
Hassingham	65	TG	3605
Hassocks	29	TQ	3015
Hassop	71	SK	2272
Hastigrow	135	ND	2661
Hastingleigh	31	TR	0945
Hastings	30	TQ	8009
Hastingwood	37	TL	4807
Hastoe	36	SP	9209
Haswell	85	NZ	3743
Hatch (Beds.)	52	TL	1547
Hatch (Hants.)	35	SU	6752
Hatch (Wilts.)	25	ST	9228
Hatch Beauchamp	24	ST	3020
Hatch End	37	TQ	1391
Hatching Green	37	TL	1313
Hatchmere	69	SJ	5572
Hatcliffe	75	TA	2100
Hatfield (Here. and Worc.)	45	SO	5859
Hatfield (Herts.)	37	TL	2309
Hatfield (S Yorks.)	71	SE	6609
Hatfield Aerodrome	37	TL	2009
Hatfield Broad Oak	37	TL	5416
Hatfield Chase	74	SE	7109
Hatfield Heath	37	TL	5215
Hatfield House (ant.)	37	TL	2308
Hatfield Moors	74	SE	7006
Hatfield Peverel	38	TL	7911
Hatfield Woodhouse	71	SE	6708
Hatford	47	SU	3394
Hatherden	34	SU	3450
Hatherleigh	23	SS	5404
Hathern	61	SK	5022
Hatherop	47	SP	1505
Hathersage	71	SK	2381
Hatherton (Ches.)	59	SJ	6847
Hatherton (Staffs.)	60	SJ	9610
Hatley St. George	53	TL	2851
Hatt	20	SX	3962
Hatterrall Hill	45	SO	3025
Hattingley	27	SU	6437
Hatton (Ches.)	69	SJ	5982
Hatton (Derby.)	60	SK	2130
Hatton (Grampn.)	121	NK	0537
Hatton (Gtr London)	37	TQ	1075
Hatton (Lincs.)	73	TF	1776
Hatton (Shrops.)	48	SO	4690
Hatton (Warw.)	50	SP	2367
Hatton Castle (ant.)	121	NJ	7546
Hattoncrook	121	NJ	8424
Hatton Heath	68	SJ	4561
Hatton of Fintray	119	NJ	8316
Hattons Lodge	34	SU	0688
Haugham	73	TF	3381
Haugh Head	97	NU	0026
Haughley	54	TM	0262
Haughley Green	54	TM	0364
Haugh of Glass	121	NJ	4239
Haugh of Urr	88	NX	8066
Haughs of Cromdale	117	NJ	0927
Haughton (Notts.)	71	SK	6772
Haughton (Shrops.)	58	SJ	3727
Haughton (Shrops.)	59	SJ	5516
Haughton (Shrops.)	59	SO	6795
Haughton (Staffs.)	59	SJ	8620
Haughton Common	90	NY	8172
Haughton Green	69	SJ	9393
Haughton Moss	59	SJ	5756
Haunn	104	NM	3347
Haunton	60	SK	2411
Hauxley	91	NU	2703
Hauxley Haven	91	NU	2902
Hauxton	53	TL	4351
Havant	27	SU	7106
Haven	45	SO	4054
Havengore Island	39	TQ	9788
Havenhouse Station	73	TF	5259
Havenstreet	27	SZ	5690
Haven, The	63	TF	3540
Haverfordwest	42	SM	9515
Haverhill	54	TL	6745
Haverigg	76	SD	1578
Havering-atte-Bower	37	TQ	5193
Haversham	52	SP	8343
Haverthwaite	77	SD	3483
Hawarden	68	SJ	3165
Hawarden Airport	68	SJ	3565
Hawes	84	SD	8789
Haweswater Resr.	83	NY	4814
Hawford	49	SO	8460
Hawick (Borders)	89	NT	5014
Ha Wick (Hoy, Orkney)	136	ND	2589
Hawkchurch	24	ST	3400
Hawkedon	54	TL	7952
Hawkeridge	33	ST	8653
Hawkerland	24	SY	0588
Hawkesbury	33	ST	7687
Hawkesbury Upton	33	ST	7786
Hawkes End	50	SP	2983
Hawkhill	91	NU	2212
Hawkhope	90	NY	7188
Hawkhurst	29	TQ	7630
Hawkinge	31	TR	2139
Hawkley	27	SU	7429
Hawkridge	23	SS	8630
Hawkridge Reservoir	24	ST	2036
Hawkshead	82	SD	3598
Hawksland	95	NS	8439
Hawks Ness	141	HU	4648
Hawkswick	78	SD	9570
Hawksworth (Notts.)	61	SK	7543
Hawksworth (W Yorks.)	78	SE	1641
Hawkwell	38	TQ	8691
Hawkwood Hill	94	NS	6838
Hawley (Hants.)	36	SU	8558
Hawley (Kent)	37	TQ	5571
Hawling	46	SP	0623
Hawnby	85	SE	5389
Haworth	78	SE	0337
Haworth Moor	78	SD	9935
Hawsker	81	NZ	9207
Hawstead	54	TL	8559
Hawthorn	85	NZ	4145
Hawthorn Hill	36	SU	8873
Hawthornthwaite Fell	77	SD	5752
Hawton	61	SK	7851
Haxby	79	SE	6057
Haxey	74	SK	7699
Haxton Down	34	SU	2049
Hay Bluff	45	SO	2436
Haycock	82	NY	1410
Haydock	69	SJ	5696
Haydon	25	ST	6615
Haydon Bridge	90	NY	8464
Haydon Dean	97	NT	9743
Haydon Wick	34	SU	1388
Haydown Hill	34	SU	3155
Haye	20	SX	3570
Hayes (Gtr London)	36	TQ	0980
Hayes (Gtr London)	37	TQ	4165
Hayfield	70	SK	0386
Hayhillock	109	NO	5242
Hayle	18	SW	5537
Hayling Bay	27	SZ	7198
Hayling Island	27	SU	7201
Haylot Fell	77	SD	5861
Haynes	52	TL	1042
Haynes Church End	52	TL	0841
Hay-on-Wye	45	SO	2342
Hayscastle	42	SM	8925
Hayscastle Cross	42	SM	9125
Hay Stacks	82	NY	2013
Hayton (Cumbr.)	82	NY	1041
Hayton (Cumbr.)	83	NY	5057
Hayton (Humbs.)	74	SE	8145
Hayton (Notts.)	72	SK	7284
Hayton's Bent	48	SO	5280
Haytor Vale	21	SX	7677
Haywards Heath	29	TQ	3324
Haywood Oaks	61	SK	6055
Hazelbank	95	NS	8344
Hazelbury Bryan	25	ST	7408
Hazeley	36	SU	7459
Hazel Grove	69	SJ	9287
Hazelrigg	97	NU	0533
Hazelslade	60	SK	0212
Hazelton Walls	108	NO	3321
Hazelwood	60	SK	3245
Hazlemere	36	SU	8895
Hazlerigg	91	NZ	2472
Hazleton	46	SP	0718
Heacham	64	TF	6737
Headbourne Worthy	27	SU	4831
Headcorn	30	TQ	8344
Headington	47	SP	5407
Headlam	84	NZ	1818
Headless Cross	50	SP	0365
Headley (Hants.)	35	SU	5162
Headley (Hants.)	27	SU	8236
Headley (Surrey)	28	TQ	2054
Head o' da Taing	140	HT	9739
Head of Bratta	143	HU	4799
Head of Brough	143	HU	4484
Head of Garness	121	NJ	7464
Head of Holland	136	HY	4812
Head of Hosta	143	HU	6791
Head of Lambhoga	143	HU	6287
Head of Moclett	138	HY	4949
Head of Muir	101	NS	8080
Head of Stanshi	142	HU	2180
Headon	72	SK	7476
Heads Nook	83	NY	4955
Heads of Ayr	93	NS	2818
Heage	60	SK	3650
Healabhal Bheag (mt.)	122	NG	2242
Healabhal Mhór (mt.)	122	NG	2244
Healaugh (N Yorks.)	84	SE	0198
Healaugh (N Yorks.)	79	SE	4947
Healaval (mt.)	122	NG	2464
Heald Green	69	SJ	8385
Heald Moor	78	SD	8726
Heale	23	SS	6446
Healey (Lancs.)	69	SD	8817
Healey (Northum.)	91	NZ	0158
Healey (N Yorks.)	78	SE	1780
Healeyfield	84	NZ	0648
Healing	75	TA	2110
Heamoor	18	SW	4631
Heanish	104	NM	0343
Heanor	60	SK	4346
Heanton Punchardon	22	SS	5035
Heapham	72	SK	8788
Hearnish (pt.)	124	NF	6263
Hearthstane	95	NT	1125
Heart Law	96	NT	7166
Heast	123	NG	6417
Heath (Derby.)	71	SK	4466
Heath (S Glam.)	41	ST	1779
Heath and Reach	52	SP	9228
Heathcote	70	SK	1460
Heath End (Hants.)	35	SU	5762
Heath End (Hants.)	35	SU	8550
Heather	60	SK	3910
Heathfield (Devon)	21	SX	8376
Heathfield (E Susx)	29	TQ	5821
Heathfield (Somer.)	24	ST	1526
Heathfield (Strath.)	100	NS	3262
Heathfield Moor	78	SE	1067
Heath Hayes	60	SK	0110
Heath Hill	59	SJ	7614
Heath House	32	ST	4146
Heathrow Airport - London	36	TQ	0875
Heath, The	54	TL	9043
Heathton	49	SO	8192
Heatley	69	SJ	6988
Heaton (Lancs.)	77	SD	4460
Heaton (Staffs.)	69	SJ	9462
Heaton (Tyne and Wear)	91	NZ	2665
Heaton Moor	69	SJ	8691
Heaval (mt.)	112	NL	6799
Heaverham	37	TQ	5758
Heaviley	69	SJ	9088
Hebburn	91	NZ	3265
Hebden	78	SE	0263
Hebden Bridge	78	SD	9927
Hebden Green	69	SJ	6365
Hebden Moor	78	SE	0466
Hebden Water	78	SD	9631
Hebrides or Western Isles	112	NG	0239
Hebron	91	NZ	1989
Heckfield	36	SU	7260
Heckington	62	TF	1444
Heckmondwike	78	SE	2123
Hecla (mt.)	112	NF	8234
Heddington	34	ST	9966
Heddle	136	HY	3512
Heddon-on-the-Wall	91	NZ	1366
Heddon's Mouth	23	SS	6549
Hedenham	65	TM	3193
Hedge End	27	SU	4812
Hedgehope Hill	90	NT	9419
Hedgerley	36	SU	9787
Hedging	24	ST	3029
Hedley on the Hill	91	NZ	0759
Hednesford	60	SK	0012
Hedon	75	TA	1828
Hedsor	36	SU	9086
Hegdon Hill	45	SO	5854
Heglibister	141	HU	3851
Heighington (Durham)	84	NZ	2522
Heighington (Lincs.)	72	TF	0269
Heights of Brae	128	NH	5161
Heights of Kinlochewe	127	NH	0764
Heilam	133	NC	4659
Heillia	142	HU	2684
Heishival Mór (mt.)	112	NL	6296
Heisker or Monach Islands	124	NF	6262
Heiskers (is.)	112	NL	5786
Heiton	96	NT	7130
Heldale Water	136	ND	2592
Heldon Hill	129	NJ	1257
Hele (Devon)	23	SS	5347
Hele (Devon)	23	SS	9902
Helensburgh	100	NS	2982
Helford	18	SW	7526
Helford River	18	SW	7626
Helhoughton	64	TF	8626
Helions Bumpstead	54	TL	6541
Hellabrick's Wick	140	HT	9536
Helland	19	SX	0770
Hellesdon	65	TG	1810
Helliar Holm	136	HY	4815
Hellidon	51	SP	5158
Hellifield	78	SD	8556
Helli Ness	141	HU	4628
Hellingly	29	TQ	5812
Hellington	65	TG	3103
Hellir (pt.)	143	HU	3892
Hellisay	112	NF	7504
Hellister	141	HU	3949
Hellmoor Loch	89	NT	3816
Hell's Glen	100	NN	1806
Hell's Mouth or Porth Neigwl	56	SH	2626
Helman Head	135	ND	3646
Helmdon	51	SP	5843
Helmingham	55	TM	1857
Helmsdale	135	ND	0215
Helmshore	78	SD	7821
Helmsley	79	SE	6183
Helmsley Moor	85	SE	5991
Helperby	79	SE	4369
Helperthorpe	81	SE	9570
Helpringham	62	TF	1340
Helpston	62	TF	1205
Helsby	69	SJ	4875
Helston	18	SW	6527
Helstone	20	SX	0881
Helton	83	NY	5122
Helvellyn (mt.)	82	NY	3315
Helwick (lightship)	40	SS	3281
Helwith Bridge	78	SD	8169
Hemblington	65	TG	3411
Hembury (ant.)	24	ST	1103
Hemel Hempstead	36	TL	0506
Hemingbrough	79	SE	6730
Hemingby	73	TF	2374
Hemingford Abbots	53	TL	2870
Hemingford Grey	53	TL	2970
Hemingstone	55	TM	1453
Hemington (Northants.)	52	TL	0985
Hemington (Somer.)	33	ST	7253
Hemley	55	TM	2842
Hempholme	81	TA	0850
Hempnall	65	TM	2494
Hempnall Green	65	TM	2593
Hempriggs	129	NJ	1064
Hempriggs House	135	ND	3547
Hempstead (Essex)	54	TL	6338
Hempstead (Norf.)	65	TG	4028
Hempsted (Glos.)	46	SO	8117
Hempsted (Norf.)	65	TG	1037
Hempton (Norf.)	64	TF	9129
Hempton (Oxon.)	47	SP	4431
Hemsby	65	TG	4917
Hemsby Hole	65	TG	5118
Hemswell	72	SK	9290
Hemsworth	71	SE	4213
Hemyock	24	ST	1313
Henbury (Avon)	33	ST	5478
Henbury (Ches.)	69	SJ	8873
Hendersyde Park	96	NT	7435
Hendon (Gtr London)	37	TQ	2389
Hendon (Tyne and Wear)	85	NZ	4055
Hendreys Course	102	NS	9758
Hendy	43	SN	5804
Heneglwys	66	SH	4276
Henfield	28	TQ	2116
Hen Gerrig	57	SH	9518
Hengistbury Head	26	SZ	1790
Hengoed (Mid Glam.)	41	ST	1495
Hengoed (Powys)	45	SO	2253
Hengoed (Shrops.)	58	SJ	2833
Hengrave	54	TL	8268
Hengynwydd-fawr	57	SN	9882
Henham	53	TL	5428
Heniarth	58	SJ	1108
Henley (Shrops.)	48	SO	5476
Henley (Somer.)	25	ST	4232
Henley (Suff.)	55	TM	1551
Henley (W Susx)	27	SU	8926
Henley-in-Arden	50	SP	1465
Henley-on-Thames	36	SU	7682
Henley Park	28	SU	9352
Henllan (Clwyd)	67	SJ	0268
Henllan (Dyfed)	43	SN	3540
Henllan Amgoed	43	SN	1820
Henllys	45	ST	2693
Henlow	52	TL	1738
Hennock	21	SX	8380
Henryd	67	SH	7674
Henry's Moat (Castell Hendre)	42	SN	0428
Hensall	79	SE	5923
Hensbarrow Downs	19	SW	9957
Henshaw	90	NY	7664
Henstead	55	TM	4986
Henstridge	25	ST	7219
Henstridge Marsh	25	ST	7420
Henton (Oxon.)	36	SP	7602
Henton (Somer.)	33	ST	4045
Henwick	49	SO	8354
Henwood	20	SX	2673
Heogan	141	HU	4743
Heoga Ness	143	HU	5379
Heol Senni	41	SN	9223
Heol-y-Cyw	41	SS	9484
Hepburn	97	NU	0724
Hepple	91	NT	9800
Hepscott	91	NZ	2284
Heptonstall	78	SD	9827
Heptonstall Moor	78	SD	9330
Hepworth (Suff.)	54	TL	9874
Hepworth (W Yorks.)	70	SE	1606
Herbrandston	42	SM	8707
Hereford	45	SO	5040
Hergest	45	SO	2655
Hergest Ridge	45	SO	2556
Heriot	96	NT	3952
Herma Ness	143	HP	6018
Hermaness Hill	143	HP	6017
Herman Law	89	NT	2115
Hermetray	124	NF	9874
Hermitage (Berks.)	35	SU	5072
Hermitage (Borders)	89	NY	5095
Hermitage (Dorset.)	25	ST	6306
Hermitage (Hants.)	27	SU	7505
Hermitage, The	28	TQ	2253
Hermon (Dyfed)	43	SN	2032
Hermon (Dyfed)	43	SN	3630
Hermon (Gwyn.)	66	SH	3868
Herne	31	TR	1866
Herne Bay	31	TR	1768
Herner	23	SS	5926
Herne, The	53	TL	2590
Hernhill	31	TR	0660
Herodsfoot	19	SX	2160
Herongate	38	TQ	6391
Heronsgate	36	TQ	0294
Herra, The	143	HU	4693
Herriard	35	SU	6645
Herringfleet	65	TM	4797
Herringswell	54	TL	7170
Herrington	85	NZ	3553
Herscha Hill	119	NO	7380
Hersden	31	TR	1961
Hersham	37	TQ	1164
Herstmonceux	29	TQ	6312
Herston	136	ND	4291
Herston Head	136	ND	4191
Hertford	37	TL	3212
Hertford Heath	37	TL	3511
Hertingfordbury	37	TL	3112
Hesketh Bank	77	SD	4323
Hesketh Lane	77	SD	6141
Hesket Newmarket	82	NY	3438
Heskin Green	69	SD	5315

Hesleden 85 NZ 4438
Hesleyside 90 NY 8183
Heslington 79 SE 6250
Hessay 79 SE 5253
Hessenford 20 SX 3057
Hessett 54 TL 9361
Hessle 74 TA 0326
Hestan Island 87 NX 8350
Hest Bank 77 SD 4566
Hesti Geo 140 HT 9736
Heston 37 TQ 1277
Heswall 68 SJ 2682
Hethe 47 SP 5929
Hethersett 65 TG 1505
Hethersgill 89 NY 4767
Hethpool 97 NT 8928
Hett 84 NZ 2836
Hetton 78 SD 9658
Hetton-le-Hole 85 NZ 3548
Hetty Peglers Tump 46 SO 7900
Heugh 91 NZ 0873
Heugh-Head 118 NJ 3711
Hevdadale Head 142 HU 3089
Heveningham 55 TM 3372
Hever 29 TQ 4744
Heversham 77 SD 4983
Hevingham 65 TG 2022
Hewelsfield 45 SO 5602
Hewish (Avon) 32 ST 4064
Hewish (Somer.) 24 ST 4108
Hexham 90 NY 9364
Hexhamshire Common 84 NY 8853
Hextable 37 TQ 5170
Hexton 52 TL 1030
Hexworthy 21 SX 6572
Heybridge (Essex) 38 TL 8508
Heybridge (Essex) 38 TQ 6498
Heybridge Basin 38 TL 8707
Heybrook Bay 20 SX 4948
Heydon (Cambs.) 53 TL 4340
Heydon (Norf.) 65 TG 1127
Heydon Hill 24 ST 0327
Heydour 62 TF 0039
Heyford 51 SP 6558
Heylipol 104 NL 9643
Heylor 142 HU 2881
Heysham 77 SD 4161
Heysham Lake (chan.) 77 SD 3758
Heyshott 27 SU 8918
Heytesbury 33 ST 9242
Heythrop 47 SP 3527
Heywood (Gtr Mches.) 69 SD 8510
Heywood (Wilts.) 33 ST 8753
Hibaldstow 74 SE 9702
Hickleton 71 SE 4805
Hickling (Norf.) 65 TG 4124
Hickling (Notts.) 61 SK 6929
Hickling Green 65 TG 4023
Hickling Heath 65 TG 4022
Hidcote Boyce 50 SP 1742
High Ackworth 71 SE 4317
Higham (Derby.) 71 SK 3959
Higham (Kent) 30 TQ 7171
Higham (Lancs.) 78 SD 8036
Higham (Suff.) 54 TL 7465
Higham (Suff.) 54 TM 0335
Higham Dykes 91 NZ 1375
Higham Ferrers 52 SP 9669
Higham Gobion 52 TL 1033
Higham on the Hill 60 SP 3895
Highampton 22 SS 4804
Higham Wood 29 TQ 6048
High Banton 101 NS 7480
High Beach 37 TQ 4097
High Bentham 77 SD 6669
High Bickington 23 SS 5920
High Birkwith 78 SD 8076
High Blantyre 94 NS 6756
High Bonnybridge 101 NS 8378
High Bradfield 71 SK 2692
Highbridge 32 ST 3147
Highbrook 29 TQ 3630
Highburton 70 SE 1813
Highbury 33 ST 6849
High Buston 91 NU 2308
High Callerton 91 NZ 1670
High Catton 80 SE 7153
Highclere 34 SU 4360
Highclere Castle 34 SU 4358
Highcliffe 26 SZ 2193
High Cogges 47 SP 3709
High Coniscliffe 84 NZ 2215
High Cross (Hants.) 27 SU 7126
High Cross (Herts.) 37 TL 3618
High Cross Bank 60 SK 3018
High Easter 38 TL 6214
High Ellington 78 SE 1983
Higher Ansty 25 ST 7603
Higher Ballam 77 SD 3630
High Ercall 59 SJ 5917
Higher Penwortham 77 SD 5128
Higher Sharpnose Point 22 SS 1914
Higher Tale 24 ST 0601
Higher Town 18 SV 9315
Higher Walreddon 20 SX 4771
Higher Walton (Ches.) 69 SJ 5985
Higher Walton (Lancs.) 77 SD 5727
Higher Wych 59 SJ 4943
High Etherley 84 NZ 1628
Highfield (Northum.) 90 NY 7291
Highfield (Strath.) 93 NS 3050
Highfield (Tyne and Wear) 91 NZ 1459
Highfields 53 TL 3559
High Force 84 NY 8727
High Garrett 54 TL 7726
High Grange 84 NZ 1731
High Green (Here. and Worc.) 49 SO 8745
High Green (Norf.) 65 TG 1305
High Green (S Yorks.) 71 SK 3397
Highgreen Manor 90 NY 8191
High Halden 30 TQ 9037
High Halstow 30 TQ 7875
High Ham 25 ST 4231
High Hatton 59 SJ 6024
High Hesket 83 NY 4744
High Hoyland 71 SE 2710
High Hunsley 74 SE 9535
High Hurstwood 29 TQ 4926
High Knowes 90 NT 9612
Highland Hotel, The 100 NR 9986
High Lane 49 SO 6760
High Laver 37 TL 5208
Highleadon 46 SO 7623
High Legh 69 SJ 6984
Highleigh 27 SZ 8498
Highley 49 SO 7483
High Littleton 33 ST 6458
High Lorton 82 NY 1625
High Melton 71 SE 5001
Highmoor Cross 36 SU 7084
Highmoor Hill 33 ST 4689
High Moor of Killiemore 86 NX 3660
High Murdonochee 86 NX 1674
Highnam 46 SO 7919
High Neb (mt.) 71 SK 2385
High Newton 77 SD 4082
High Newton-by-the-Sea 97 NU 2325
High Offley 59 SJ 7826
High Ongar 37 TL 5603
High Onn 59 SJ 8216
High Peak (dist.) 70 SK 1187
High Pike 82 NY 3135
High Roding 38 TL 6017
High Salvington 28 TQ 1206
High Seat (mt.) 82 NY 2818
High Shaw 84 SD 8791
High Spen 91 NZ 1359
Highsted 30 TQ 9161
High Stile 82 NY 1714
High Street (Corn.) 19 SW 9753
High Street (Cumbr.) (ant.) 83 NY 4515
High Street (Cumbr.) (mt.) 83 NY 4411
High Street (Suff.) 55 TM 4355
High Street Green 54 TM 0055
Hightae 89 NY 0979
Hightown (Ches.) 69 SJ 8762
Hightown (Mers.) 68 SD 2903
High Toynton 73 TF 2869
High Trewhitt 91 NU 0105
Highway (Corn.) 19 SX 1453
Highway (Wilts.) 34 SU 0474
High White Stones (mt.) 82 NY 2809
High Willhays (mt.) 21 SX 5789
Highworth 34 SU 2092
High Wray 83 SD 3799
High Wych 37 TL 4614
High Wycombe 36 SU 8593
Hildasay 141 HU 3540
Hildenborough 29 TQ 5648
Hildersham 53 TL 5448
Hilderstone 59 SJ 9434
Hilderthorpe 81 TA 1765
Hilgay 64 TL 6298
Hilgay Fen 63 TL 5795
Hill 46 ST 6495
Hillam 79 SE 5028
Hillbeck 83 NY 7915
Hillberry 76 SC 3879
Hillborough (Kent) 31 TR 2168
Hillborough (Norf.) 64 TF 8200
Hillbrae (Grampn.) 121 NJ 6047
Hillbrae (Grampn.) 121 NJ 7923
Hill Brow 27 SU 7926
Hilldyke 63 TF 3447
Hill End (Durham) 84 NZ 0135
Hill End (Fife) 102 NT 0495
Hillend (Fife) 102 NT 1483
Hillend Reservoir 101 NS 8367
Hillesden 51 SP 6828
Hillesley 33 ST 7689
Hillfarrance 24 ST 1624
Hillhead (Devon) 21 SX 9053
Hill Head (Hants.) 27 SU 5402
Hillhead (Strath.) 93 NS 4219
Hillhead of Auchentumb 121 NJ 9258
Hillhead of Cocklaw 121 NK 0844
Hilliard's Cross 60 SK 1412
Hilliclay 135 ND 1764
Hillingdon 36 TQ 0882
Hillington 64 TF 7225
Hillmorton 51 SP 5374
Hill Ness 143 HP 6517
Hillockhead 118 NJ 3809
Hill of Aitnoch 117 NH 9739
Hill of Alyth 108 NO 2450
Hill of Arisdale 143 HU 4984
Hill of Bakkanalee 143 HP 4903
Hill of Barra 121 NJ 8025
Hill of Beath 102 NT 1690
Hill of Berran 109 NO 4471
Hill of Camb 143 HU 5092
Hill of Cammie 119 NO 5285
Hill of Cat 118 NO 4887
Hill of Colvadale 143 HP 6105
Hill of Corsegight 121 NJ 8550
Hill of Couternach 109 NO 3566
Hill of Crooksetter 143 HU 4175
Hill of Dalsetter 143 HU 5098
Hill of Dudwick 121 NJ 9737
Hill of Edendocher 119 NO 5985
Hill of Fare 119 NJ 6803
Hill of Fearn 129 NH 8377
Hill of Finavon 109 NO 4955
Hill of Fingray 119 NO 5681
Hill of Fishrie 121 NJ 8257
Hill of Foudland 121 NJ 6033
Hill of Garbet 109 NO 4668
Hill of Glansie 109 NO 4269
Hill of Maud Crofts 121 NJ 4661
Hill of Menmuir 109 NO 5266
Hill of Miffia 136 HY 2313
Hill of Mulderie 121 NJ 3851
Hill of Nigg 129 NH 8372
Hill of Oliclett 135 ND 2946
Hill of Rangag 135 ND 1843
Hill of Reafirth 143 HU 5087
Hill of Saughs 118 NO 4485
Hill of Shurton 141 HU 4440
Hill of Skilmafilly 121 NJ 8940
Hill of Stake 100 NS 2763
Hill of the Wangie 129 NJ 1353
Hill of Three Stones 121 NJ 3422
Hill of Tillymorgan 121 NJ 6534
Hill of Tomechole 129 NJ 0649
Hill of Towie 121 NJ 3847
Hill of Trusta 119 NO 7886
Hill of Wirren 119 NO 5273
Hill Ridware 60 SK 0718
Hill Row 53 TL 4475
Hill Row Doles 53 TL 4276
Hillside (Grampn.) 119 NO 9298
Hillside (Shetld.) 141 HU 4063
Hillside (Tays.) 109 NO 7061
Hills of Cromdale 117 NJ 1126
Hillswick 142 HU 2877
Hill, The 76 SD 1783
Hill Top (Hants.) 26 SU 4002
Hill Top (W Yorks.) 71 SE 3315
Hillwell 141 HU 3714
Hilmarton 34 SU 0175
Hilperton 33 ST 8759
Hilpsford Point 76 SD 2061
Hilsea 27 SU 6503
Hilton (Cambs.) 53 TL 2966
Hilton (Cleve.) 85 NZ 4611
Hilton (Cumbr.) 83 NY 7320
Hilton (Derby.) 60 SK 2430
Hilton (Dorset) 25 ST 7802
Hilton (Durham) 84 NZ 1621
Hilton (Grampn.) 121 NJ 9434
Hilton (Shrops.) 59 SO 7795
Hilton of Cadboll 129 NH 8776
Himbleton 49 SO 9458
Himley 49 SO 8891
Hincaster 77 SD 5184
Hinchingbrooke House (ant.) 53 TL 2271
Hinckley 60 SP 4294
Hinderclay 54 TM 0276
Hinderwell 85 NZ 7916
Hindford 58 SJ 3333
Hindhead 27 SU 8736
Hindhope Law 90 NY 7797
Hindlethwaite Moor 78 SE 0680
Hindley 69 SD 6104
Hindley Green 69 SD 6403
Hindlip 49 SO 8758
Hindolveston 64 TG 0329
Hindon 25 ST 9032
Hindringham 64 TF 9836
Hingham 64 TG 0202
Hinstock 59 SJ 6926
Hintlesham 55 TM 0843
Hinton (Avon) 33 ST 7376
Hinton (Hants.) 26 SZ 2095
Hinton (Northants.) 51 SP 5352
Hinton (Shrops.) 58 SJ 4008
Hinton Ampner 27 SU 5927
Hinton Blewett 33 ST 5956
Hinton Charterhouse 33 ST 7758
Hinton-in-the-Hedges 51 SP 5537
Hinton Marsh 27 SU 5827
Hinton Martell 26 SU 0106
Hinton on the Green 50 SP 0240
Hinton Parva 34 SU 2283
Hinton St. George 25 ST 4212
Hinton St. Mary 25 ST 7816
Hinton Waldrist 47 SU 3799
Hints (Shrops.) 49 SO 6175
Hints (Staffs.) 60 SK 1503
Hinwick 52 SP 9361
Hinxhill 31 TR 0442
Hinxton 53 TL 4945
Hinxworth 53 TL 2340
Hipperholme 78 SE 1225
Hipswell Moor 84 SE 1496
Hirfynydd 41 SN 8205
Hirn 119 NJ 7300
Hirnant 57 SJ 0423
Hirst 91 NZ 2787
Hirst Courtney 79 SE 6124
Hirta or St. Kilda (is.) 124 NF 0999
Hirwaun 41 SN 9505
Hirwaun Common 41 SN 9304
Hiscott 23 SS 5426
Hisehope Resr. 84 NZ 0246
Histon 53 TL 4363
Hitcham 54 TL 9851
Hitchin 52 TL 1829
Hither Green 37 TQ 3874
Hittisleigh 21 SX 7395
Hixon 60 SK 0026
Hoaden 31 TR 2759
Hoaldalbert 45 SO 3923
Hoar Cross 60 SK 1223
Hoarwithy 45 SO 5429
Hoath 31 TR 2064
Hobarris 48 SO 3078
Hobbister 136 HY 3807
Hobhole Drain 63 TF 3647
Hobkirk 90 NT 5810
Hobland Hall 65 TG 5101
Hobson 84 NZ 1755
Hoby 61 SK 6617
Hockering 64 TG 0713
Hockerton 61 SK 7156
Hockley 38 TQ 8293
Hockley Heath 50 SP 1572
Hockliffe 52 SP 9726
Hockwold cum Wilton 54 TL 7288
Hockwold Fens 54 TL 6887
Hockworthy 24 ST 0319
Hoddesdon 37 TL 3709
Hoddlesden 77 SD 7122
Hoddom Castle (ant.) 89 NY 1573
Hodge Beck 85 SE 6294
Hodgeston 42 SS 0399
Hod Hill 25 ST 8510
Hodnet 59 SJ 6128
Hodthorpe 71 SK 5476
Hoe 64 TF 9916
Hoe Gate 27 SU 6213
Hoe Point 122 NG 1641
Hoe Rape (pt.) 122 NG 1543
Hoe, The 122 NG 1641
Hoff 83 NY 6717
Hog Fell 89 NY 3989
Hoggeston 51 SP 8025
Hogh Bay 110 NM 1657
Hog Hill 89 NY 2895
Hoghton 77 SD 6125
Hognaston 60 SK 2350
Hog's Back 28 SU 9348
Hogs Law 96 NT 5555
Hogsthorpe 73 TF 5372
Holbeach 63 TF 3625
Holbeach Bank 63 TF 3627
Holbeach Drove 63 TF 3212
Holbeach Hurn 63 TF 3927
Holbeach Marsh 63 TF 3729
Holbeach St. Johns 63 TF 3418
Holbeach St. Marks 63 TF 3731
Holbeach St. Matthew 63 TF 4132
Holbeck 71 SK 5473
Holberrow Green 50 SP 0259
Holbeton 21 SX 6150
Holborn 37 TQ 3181
Holborn Head 135 ND 1071
Holbrook (Derby.) 60 SK 3645
Holbrook (Suff.) 55 TM 1636
Holbrook Bay 55 TM 1633
Holburn 97 NU 0436
Holbury 26 SU 4303
Holcombe (Devon) 21 SX 9574
Holcombe (Somer.) 33 ST 6649
Holcombe Rogus 24 ST 0519
Holcot 51 SP 7969
Holden 78 SD 7749
Holdenby 51 SP 6967
Holderness Drain 75 TA 1135
Holdgate 48 SO 5589
Holdingham 62 TF 0547
Holehouse Hill 88 NY 0195
Hole-in-the-Wall 45 SO 6128
Hole o' Row 136 HY 2218
Hole Park 30 TQ 8332
Holes of Scraada 142 HU 2179
Holestane 88 NX 8799
Hole Stone Bay 86 NX 0646
Holford 32 ST 1541
Holker 77 SD 3577
Holkham 64 TF 8944
Holkham Bay 64 TF 8746
Hollacombe 22 SS 3702
Holland (Papa Westray) 138 HY 4851
Holland (Stronsay) 137 HY 6622
Holland Fen 63 TF 2445
Holland-on-Sea 39 TM 2016
Hollandstoun 139 HY 7553
Hollesley 55 TM 3544
Hollesley Bay 55 TM 3844
Hollinfare 69 SJ 6990
Hollingbourne 30 TQ 8455
Hollington (Derby.) 60 SK 2239
Hollington (E Susx) 30 TQ 7911
Hollington (Staffs.) 60 SK 0538
Hollingworth 70 SK 0096
Hollingworth Lake 69 SD 9314
Hollins 69 SD 8108
Hollinsclough 70 SK 0666
Hollinswood 59 SJ 6909
Hollinwood 59 SJ 5236
Holliwell Point 39 TR 0396
Hollocombe 23 SS 6311
Holloway 60 SK 3256
Hollowell 51 SP 6972
Hollowell Resr. 51 SP 6873
Holl Resr. 103 NO 2203
Hollybush (Gwent) 41 SO 1603
Hollybush (Here. and Worc.) 49 SO 7636
Hollybush (Strath.) 93 NS 3914
Holly End 63 TF 4906
Hollym 75 TA 3425
Holm (Dumf. and Galwy.) 89 NY 2498
Holm (Isle of Lewis) 131 NB 4531
Holmbury St. Mary 28 TQ 1144
Holme (Cambs.) 52 TL 1987
Holme (Cumbr.) 77 SD 5278
Holme (Notts.) 72 SK 8059
Holme (W Yorks.) 70 SE 1005
Holme Chapel 78 SD 8728
Holme Hale 64 TF 8807
Holme Island 77 SD 4278
Holme Lacy 45 SO 5535
Holme Marsh 45 SO 3354
Holme next the Sea 64 TF 7043
Holme-on-Spalding-Moor 74 SE 8138
Holme on the Wolds 74 SE 9646
Holmer 45 SO 5042
Holmer Green 36 SU 9097
Holmes Chapel 69 SJ 7667
Holmesfield 71 SK 3277
Holmeswood 68 SD 4316
Holmewood 71 SK 4365
Holmfirth 70 SE 1408
Holmhead 88 NS 5620
Holm Island 123 NG 5251
Holm of Helliness 141 HU 4628
Holm of Huip 139 HY 6231
Holm of Melby 140 HU 1958
Holm of Noss 141 HU 5539
Holm of Papa 138 HY 5052
Holm of Skaw 143 HP 6617
Holm of West Sandwick 143 HU 4389
Holmpton 75 TA 3623
Holmrook 82 SD 0799
Holmsgarth 141 HU 4642
Holms of Ire 139 HY 6446
Holm Sound 136 ND 5099
Holms Water 95 NT 0831
Holmwood Station 28 TQ 1743
Holne 21 SX 7069
Holnest 25 ST 6509
Holnicote Estate 23 SS 8944
Holoman Bay 123 NG 5439
Holsworthy 22 SS 3403
Holsworthy Beacon 22 SS 3508
Holt (Clwyd) 58 SJ 4053
Holt (Dorset) 26 SU 0203
Holt (Here. and Worc.) 49 SO 8262
Holt (Norf.) 64 TG 0738
Holt (Wilts.) 33 ST 8661
Holtby 79 SE 6754
Holt End 50 SP 0769
Holt Heath 49 SO 8163
Holton (Oxon.) 47 SP 6006
Holton (Somerset) 25 ST 6826
Holton (Suff.) 55 TM 4077
Holton cum Beckering 73 TF 1181
Holton Heath 26 SY 9491
Holton le Clay 75 TA 2802
Holton le Moor 72 TF 0797
Holton St. Mary 54 TM 0537
Holwell 25 ST 7011
Holwell (Herts.) 52 TL 1633
Holwell (Leic.) 61 SK 7323
Holwell (Oxon.) 47 SP 2309
Holwick 84 NY 9026
Holworth 25 SY 7683
Holybourne 35 SU 7341
Holy Cross 49 SO 9279
Holyhead 66 SH 2482
Holyhead Bay 66 SH 2587
Holyhead Mountain 66 SH 2182
Holy Island (Gwyn.) 66 SH 2579
Holy Island (Island of Arran) 92 NS 0630
Holy Island (Northum.) 97 NU 1342
Holy Island Sands 97 NU 1041
Holy Loch 100 NS 1780
Holymoorside 71 SK 3369
Holyport 36 SU 8977
Holystone 90 NT 9502
Holytown 101 NS 7760
Holywell (Cambs.) 53 TL 3370
Holywell (Clwyd) 68 SJ 1875
Holywell (Corn.) 18 SW 7658
Holywell (Dorset) 25 ST 5904
Holywell Bank 68 SJ 2178
Holywell Bay 18 SW 7559
Holywell Green 70 SE 0918
Holywell Lake 24 ST 1020
Holywell Row 54 TL 7077
Holywood 88 NX 9480
Homer 59 SJ 6101
Homersfield 55 TM 2885
Hom Green 45 SO 5822
Homington 26 SU 1226
Honddu 44 SO 0137
Honeyborough 42 SM 9506
Honeybourne 50 SP 1144
Honeychurch 23 SS 6202
Honey Hill 31 TR 1161
Honiley 50 SP 2472
Honing 65 TG 3227
Honingham 65 TG 1011
Honington (Lincs.) 62 SK 9443
Honington (Suff.) 54 TL 9174
Honington (Warw.) 50 SP 2642
Honister Pass 82 NY 2214
Honiton 24 ST 1600
Honley 70 SE 1311
Hooe (Devon) 20 SX 5052
Hooe (E Susx) 29 TQ 6809
Hoo Green 55 TM 2559
Hook (Dyfed) 42 SM 9811
Hook (Hants.) 35 SU 7254
Hook (Humbs.) 74 SE 7525
Hook (Surrey) 37 TQ 1764
Hook (Wilts.) 34 SU 0784
Hooke (Dorset) 25 ST 5300
Hookgate 59 SJ 7435
Hook Norton 47 SP 3533
Hookway 21 SX 8598
Hookwood 28 TQ 2643
Hoole 68 SJ 4367
Hoo Stack 141 HU 5052
Hoo St. Werburgh 30 TQ 7872
Hooton 68 SJ 3679
Hooton Levitt 71 SK 5291
Hooton Pagnell 71 SE 4808
Hooton Roberts 71 SK 4897
Hope 133 NC 4760
Hope (Clwyd) 68 SJ 3058
Hope (Derby.) 70 SK 1783
Hope (Devon) 21 SX 6740
Hope (Powys) 58 SJ 2507
Hope (Shrops.) 58 SJ 3401
Hope Bagot 48 SO 5874
Hope Bowdler 48 SO 4792
Hope House 90 NY 6880
Hopeman 129 NJ 1469
Hope Mansell 45 SO 6219
Hopesay 48 SO 3883
Hope's Nose (pt.) 21 SX 9463
Hopes Resr. 103 NT 5462
Hopes Water 103 NT 5562
Hopetoun House 102 NT 0878
Hope under Dinmore 45 SO 5052
Hopton (Norf.) 65 TG 5200
Hopton (Shrops.) 59 SJ 5926
Hopton (Staffs.) 59 SJ 9426
Hopton (Suff.) 54 TL 9979
Hopton Cangeford 48 SO 5480
Hopton Castle 48 SO 3678
Hopton Titterhill 48 SO 3577
Hopton Wafers 49 SO 6476
Hopwas 60 SK 1705
Hopwood 50 SP 0375
Horam 29 TQ 5717
Horbling 62 TF 1135
Horbury 71 SE 2918
Horden 85 NZ 4441
Horden Point 85 NZ 4443
Horderley 48 SO 4086
Hordle 26 SZ 2795
Hordley 58 SJ 3730
Horeb 43 SN 3942
Horham 55 TM 2172
Horkstow 74 SE 9818
Horley (Oxon.) 50 SP 4143
Horley (W Susx) 29 TQ 2843
Hornblotton Green 25 ST 5833
Hornby (Lancs.) 77 SD 5868
Hornby (N Yorks) 85 NZ 3605
Horncastle 73 TF 2669
Hornchurch 37 TQ 5487
Horncliffe 97 NT 9249
Horndean 27 SU 7013
Horndon on the Hill 38 TQ 6683
Horne 29 TQ 3344
Horn Hill 36 TQ 0292
Horniehaugh 109 NO 4161
Horning 65 TG 3417
Horninghold 61 SP 8097
Horninglow 60 SK 2324
Horningsea 53 TL 4962
Horningsham 33 ST 8241
Horningtoft 64 TF 9323
Hornish (pt.) 112 NF 7309
Hornish Point 124 NF 7547
Hornsby 83 NY 5150
Hornsea 75 TA 2047
Hornsea Mere 75 TA 1946
Hornsey 37 TQ 3089
Hornton 50 SP 3945
Horrabridge 20 SX 5169
Horringer 54 TL 8261
Horsanish 124 NA 9908
Horsea Island 27 SU 6304
Horse Bank (sbk.) 68 SD 3220
Horsebridge (E Susx) 29 TQ 5911
Horsebridge (Hants.) 26 SU 3430
Horse Bridge (Staffs.) 60 SJ 9553
Horsebrook 59 SJ 8810
Horsehay 59 SJ 6707
Horseheath 54 TL 6147
Horse Hope Hill 95 NT 2130
Horsehouse 78 SE 0481
Horse Island (Highld.) 126 NC 0204
Horse Island (Shetld.) 141 HU 3807
Horse Isle (Strath.) 93 NS 2142
Horseley Fen 53 TL 4083
Horseley Hill 97 NT 8362
Horsell 36 SU 9959
Horseman's Green 58 SJ 4441
Horse of Burravoe 143 HU 5381
Horse of Copinsay (is.) 137 HY 6202
Horse Sound 126 NC 0304
Horseway 53 TL 4287
Horsey 65 TG 4523
Horsey Island 39 TM 2324
Horsford 65 TG 1915
Horsforth 79 SE 2337
Horsham (Here. and Worc.) 49 SO 7357
Horsham (W Susx) 28 TQ 1730
Horsham St. Faith 65 TG 2114
Horsington (Lincs.) 73 TF 1868
Horsington (Somer.) 25 ST 7023
Horsley (Derby.) 60 SK 3744
Horsley (Glos.) 46 ST 8398
Horsley (Northum.) 90 NY 8496
Horsley (Northum.) 91 NZ 0966
Horsley Cross 55 TM 1227
Horsleycross Street 55 TM 1228
Horsleyhill 90 NT 5319
Horsley Woodhouse 60 SK 3945
Horsmonden 29 TQ 7040
Horspath 47 SP 5704
Horstead 65 TG 2619
Horsted Keynes 29 TQ 3828
Horton (Avon) 33 ST 7684
Horton (Berks.) 36 TQ 0175
Horton (Bucks.) 36 SP 9219
Horton (Dorset) 26 SU 0307
Horton (Lancs.) 78 SD 8550
Horton (Northants.) 52 SP 8254
Horton (Northum.) 97 NU 0230
Horton (Staffs.) 69 SJ 9457
Horton (W Glam.) 40 SS 4785
Horton (Wilts.) 34 SU 0463
Horton Court (ant.) 33 ST 7685
Horton-cum-Studley 47 SP 5912
Horton Green 58 SJ 4549
Horton Heath 27 SU 4916
Horton in Ribblesdale 78 SD 8172
Horton Kirby 37 TQ 5668
Horton Moor 78 SD 8274
Horwich 69 SD 6311
Horwood 22 SS 5027
Hose 61 SK 7329
Hoselaw Loch 97 NT 8031
Hoses 82 SD 2192
Hosh 108 NN 8523
Hoswick 141 HU 4123
Hotham 74 SE 8934
Hothfield 31 TQ 9644
Hoton 61 SK 5722
Hot Point 18 SW 7112
Hott Hill 89 NT 4210
Houbie 143 HU 6290
Hough 59 SJ 7151
Hougham 62 SK 8844
Hougharry 124 NF 7071
Hough Bay 104 NL 9346
Hough Green 69 SJ 4885
Hough-on-the-Hill 62 SK 9246
Hough Skerries 104 NL 9247
Houghton (Cambs.) 53 TL 2871
Houghton (Cumbr.) 89 NY 4159
Houghton (Dyfed) 42 SM 9807
Houghton (Hants.) 26 SU 3331
Houghton (W Susx) 28 TQ 0111
Houghton Conquest 52 TL 0441
Houghton House (ant.) 52 TL 0339
Houghton-le-Spring 85 NZ 3450
Houghton on the Hill 61 SK 6703
Houghton Regis 36 TL 0224
Houghton St. Giles 64 TF 9235
Houlsyke 80 NZ 7308
Hound Green 36 SU 7259
Houndslow 96 NT 6347
Houndwood 97 NT 8464
Hounslow 37 TQ 1276
Housa Water 140 HU 2844
Housay 143 HU 6771
Housedon Hill 97 NT 9032
House of Aquahorthies 121 NJ 7220
House of Daviot 116 NH 7240
House of Glenmuick 118 NO 3794
Housetter 142 HU 3684
Houss Ness 141 HU 3729
Houston 101 NS 4067
Houstry 135 ND 1534
Houton Head 136 HY 3003
Hove 29 TQ 2805
Hoveringham 61 SK 6946
Hoveton 65 TG 3018
Hovingham 79 SE 6675
How 83 NY 5056
Howardian Hills 79 SE 6472
Howat's Hill 89 NY 2279

How Caple 45 SO 6030
Howden 74 SE 7428
Howden-le-Wear 84 NZ 1633
Howden Moors 70 SK 1697
Howden Reservoir 70 SK 1693
Howe (Highld.) 135 ND 3062
Howe (Norf.) 65 TM 2799
Howe Green 38 TL 7403
Howell 62 TF 1346
Howe of Alford (dist.) 119 NJ 5716
Howe of Fife (dist.) 103 NO 2910
Howe of Teuchar 121 NJ 7947
Howequoy Head 136 HY 4601
Howe Street (Essex) 38 TL 6914
Howe Street (Essex) 54 TL 6934
Howe, The 76 SC 1967
Howe, The 77 SD 4588
Howey 44 SO 0558
Howgate 95 NT 2457
Howgate Hill 95 NS 9134
Howgill Fells 83 SD 6799
Howick 91 NU 2517
Howick Haven 91 NU 2616
Howlaws 96 NT 7242
Howle 59 SJ 6823
Howlett End 53 TL 5834
Howmore 112 NF 7636
Hownam 90 NT 7719
Hownam Law 97 NT 7921
Hownam Mains 90 NT 7820
How Of The Mearns (dist.) 119 NO 6974
Howsgarth 139 HY 6539
Howsham (Humbs.) 74 TA 0404
Howsham (N Yorks.) 80 SE 7362
How Stean Beck 78 SE 0572
Howton 45 SO 4129
Howtown 83 NY 4419
Howwood 101 NS 3960
Hoxa 136 ND 4193
Hoxne 55 TM 1876
Hoy (Orkney) (is.) 136 ND 2596
Hoy (Shetld.) (is.) 141 HU 3744
Hoylake 68 SJ 2189
Hoyland Nether 71 SE 3600
Hoyland Swaine 71 SE 2604
Hoy Sound 136 HY 2407
Hubbert's Bridge 63 TF 2643
Huby 79 SE 5665
Hucclecote 46 SO 8717
Hucking 30 TQ 8358
Hucknall 61 SK 5349
Hucknall Airfield 61 SK 5347
Huddersfield 70 SE 1416
Huddington 49 SO 9457
Hudscott 23 SS 6424
Hudswell 84 NZ 1400
Huggate 81 SE 8855
Hughenden Valley 36 SU 8695
Hughley 59 SO 5697
Hugh Town 18 SV 9010
Hugmore 58 SJ 3752
Huip Ness 139 HY 6430
Huip Sound 139 HY 6330
Huish (Devon) 23 SS 5311
Huish (Wilts.) 34 SU 1463
Huish Champflower 24 ST 0429
Huish Episcopi 25 ST 4226
Hulcott 36 SP 8516
Hule Moss 96 NT 7149
Hulland 60 SK 2447
Hullavington 33 ST 8982
Hullbridge 38 TQ 8194
Hulme End 70 SK 1059
Hulme Walfield 69 SJ 8465
Hulne Park 91 NU 1514
Hulne Priory (ant.) 91 NU 1615
Hulver Street 55 TM 4686
Humber (lightship) 75 TA 5712
Humber Court 45 SO 5356
Humberside Airport 75 TA 0911
Humberston 75 TA 3105
Humberstone 61 SK 6206
Humbie 103 NT 4562
Humbleton (Humbs.) 75 TA 2234
Humbleton (Northum.) 97 NT 9728
Hume 96 NT 7041
Humla (is.) 110 NG 1900
Humphrey Head Point 77 SD 3973
Humshaugh 90 NY 9171
Huna 135 ND 3573
Huncoat 78 SD 7730
Huncote 61 SP 5197
Hunda (is.) 136 ND 4396
Hundalee 90 NT 6418
Hunderthwaite 84 NY 9821
Hunderthwaite Moor 84 NY 9119
Hundleby 73 TF 3966
Hundleshope Heights 95 NT 2433
Hundleton 42 SM 9600
Hundon 54 TL 7348
Hundred Acres 27 SU 5911
Hundred End 77 SD 4122
Hundred Foot Drain or New Bedford River 53 TL 4987
Hundred Foot Washes, The (chan.) 53 TL 4988
Hundred Stream 65 TG 4521
Hundred, The 48 SO 5264
Huney (is.) 143 HP 6406
Hungarton 61 SK 6807
Hungerford (Berks.) 34 SU 3368
Hungerford (Hants.) 26 SU 1612
Hungerford Newtown 34 SU 3571
Hungry Law 90 NT 7406
Hunmanby 81 TA 0977
Hunningham 50 SP 3768
Hunsbury 51 SP 7358
Hunsdon 37 TL 4114
Hunsingore 79 SE 4253
Hunsonby 83 NY 5835
Hunspow 135 ND 2172
Hunstanton 64 TF 6741
Hunstanworth 84 NY 9449
Hunston (Suff.) 54 TL 9768
Hunston (W Susx) 27 SU 8601
Hunstrete 33 ST 6462
Hunt End 50 SP 0364
Hunter's Quay 100 NS 1879
Hunterston House 93 NS 1951
Hunthill Lodge 109 NO 4771
Hunt House 80 SE 8198
Huntingdon 53 TL 2371
Huntingfield 55 TM 3374
Huntington (Here. and Worc.) 45 SO 2553
Huntington (Lothian) 103 NT 4875
Huntington (N Yorks.) 79 SE 6156
Huntington (Staffs.) 60 SJ 9713
Huntingtower 108 NO 0725
Hunt Law 103 NT 5758
Huntley 46 SO 7219
Huntly 121 NJ 5339
Hunton (Kent) 29 TQ 7149
Hunton (N Yorks.) 84 SE 1892
Hunt's Cross 68 SJ 4385
Huntsham 24 ST 0020
Huntspill 32 ST 3045
Huntspill Level 32 ST 3144
Huntworth 24 ST 3134
Hunwick 84 NZ 1832
Hunworth 64 TG 0635
Hurdsfield 69 SJ 9274
Hurgin 48 SO 2379
Hurley (Berks.) 36 SU 8283
Hurley (Warw.) 60 SP 2495
Hurlford 93 NS 4536
Hurliness 136 ND 2889
Hurn 26 SZ 1296
Hursley 26 SU 4225
Hurst (Berks.) 36 SU 7972
Hurst (Gtr Mches.) 69 SD 9400
Hurst (N Yorks.) 84 NZ 0402
Hurstbourne Priors 34 SU 4346
Hurstbourne Tarrant 34 SU 3853
Hurst Castle (ant.) 26 SZ 3189
Hurst Green (E Susx) 29 TQ 7327
Hurst Green (Lancs.) 77 SD 6838
Hurst Green (Surrey) 29 TQ 3951
Hurstpierpoint 29 TQ 2816
Hurstway Common 45 SO 2949
Hurstwood Resr. 78 SD 8931
Hurtwood 28 TQ 0743
Hurworth Burn Resr. 85 NZ 4033
Hurworth-on-Tees 84 NZ 3010
Hury 84 NY 9619
Hury Resr. 84 NY 9619
Husbands Bosworth 51 SP 6484
Husborne Crawley 52 SP 9535
Hushinish 130 NA 9811
Hushinish Bay 130 NA 9911
Hushinish Point 130 NA 9811
Husival Mór (mt.) 130 NB 0211
Huskeiran (is.) 124 NF 5764
Husthwaite 79 SE 5175
Hutcherleigh 21 SX 7850
Hutchwaite 71 SK 4659
Huttoft 73 TF 5176
Hutton (Avon) 32 ST 3458
Hutton (Borders) 97 NT 9053
Hutton (Cumbr.) 83 NY 4326
Hutton (Essex) 38 TQ 6394
Hutton (Lancs.) 77 SD 4926
Hutton (N Yorks.) 80 SE 7667
Hutton Bonville 84 NZ 3300
Hutton Buscel 81 SE 9784
Hutton Conyers 79 SE 3273
Hutton Cranswick 81 TA 0252
Hutton End 83 NY 4538
Hutton Henry 85 NZ 4236
Hutton-le-Hole 80 SE 7090
Hutton Magna 84 NZ 1212
Hutton Roof (Cumbr.) 83 NY 3734
Hutton Roof (Cumbr.) 77 SD 5777
Hutton Rudby 85 NZ 4606
Hutton Sessay 79 SE 4776
Hutton Wandesley 79 SE 5050
Huxley 69 SJ 5061
Huxter (Shetld.) 141 HU 3950
Huxter (Whalsay) 141 HU 5662
Huyton-with-Roby 68 SJ 4391
Hycemoor 82 SD 0989
Hyde (Glos.) 46 SO 8801
Hyde (Gtr Mches.) 69 SJ 9294
Hyde Heath 36 SP 9300
Hyde Park 37 TQ 2780
Hydestile 28 SU 9740
Hydro 76 SC 4596
Hynish 104 NL 9839
Hynish Bay 104 NM 0042
Hyssington 58 SO 3194
Hythe (Hants.) 26 SU 4207
Hythe (Kent) 31 TR 1635
Hythe End 36 TQ 0172
Hythie 121 NK 0051

I

Ibberton 26 ST 7807
Ible 71 SK 2457
Ibsley 26 SU 1509
Ibstock 60 SK 4010
Ibstone 36 SU 7593
Ibthorpe 34 SU 3753
Ibworth 35 SU 5654
Ickburgh 64 TL 8195
Ickenham 36 TQ 0786
Ickford 36 SP 6407
Ickham 31 TR 2258
Ickleford 52 TL 1831
Icklesham 30 TQ 8816
Ickleton 53 TL 4943
Icklingham 54 TL 7772
Icknield Way (ant.) 53 TL 2836
Ickwell Green 52 TL 1545
Icomb 47 SP 2122
Idbury 47 SP 2320
Iddesleigh 23 SS 5608
Ide 21 SX 8990
Ideford 21 SX 8977
Ide Hill 29 TQ 4851
Iden 30 TQ 9123
Iden Green 30 TQ 8031
Idlicote 50 SP 2844
Idmiston 26 SU 1937
Idridgehay 60 SK 2849
Idrigill 122 NG 3863
Idrigill Point 122 NG 2536
Idstone 34 SU 2584
Idvies 109 NO 5347
Ifield (W Susx) 28 TQ 2537
Ifield or Singlewell (Kent) 30 TQ 6471
Ifold 28 TQ 0231
Iford 29 TQ 4007
Ifton Heath 58 SJ 3236
Ightfield 59 SJ 5938
Ightham 29 TQ 5956
Ightham Mote (ant.) 29 TQ 5753
Iken 55 TM 4155
Ilam 60 SK 1351
Ilchester 25 ST 5222
Ilderton 97 NU 0121
Ilford 37 TQ 4586
Ilfracombe 22 SS 5147
Ilkeston 61 SK 4642
Ilketshall St. Andrew 55 TM 3887
Ilketshall St. Lawrence 55 TM 3883
Ilketshall St. Margaret 55 TM 3485
Ilkley 78 SE 1147
Ilkley Moor 78 SE 1145
Illeray 124 NF 7863
Illey 50 SO 9881
Illingworth 78 SE 0728
Illogan 18 SW 6643
Illston on the Hill 61 SP 7099
Ilmer 36 SP 7605
Ilmington 50 SP 2143
Ilminster 24 ST 3614
Ilsington 21 SX 7876
Ilston 40 SS 5590
Ilton (N Yorks.) 78 SE 1878
Ilton (Somer.) 24 ST 3517
Imachar 92 NR 8640
Imber 34 ST 9648
Immingham 75 TA 1714
Impington 53 TL 4463
Ince 68 SJ 4476
Ince Banks (sbk.) 68 SJ 4478
Ince Blundell 68 SD 3203
Ince-in-Makerfield 69 SD 5903
Inchbae Forest 127 NH 3878
Inchbae Lodge 127 NH 4069
Inchbare 109 NO 6065
Inchberry 121 NJ 3155
Inchcailloch 101 NS 4190
Inchcape or Bell Rock 109 NO 7626
Inchcolm 102 NT 1882
Inchfad 101 NS 3990
Inch Garvie 102 NT 1379
Inchgrundle 118 NO 4179
Inchina 126 NG 9690
Inchinnan 101 NS 4768
Inchkeith 103 NT 2982
Inch Kenneth 105 NM 4335
Inchlaggan 115 NH 1801
Inchlonaig 101 NS 3893
Inchmarnock 100 NS 0159
Inchmickery 103 NT 2080
Inchmurrin 101 NS 3786
Inchnacardoch Forest 115 NH 3508
Inchnadamph 132 NC 2521
Inchnadamph Forest 132 NC 2821
Inchnadamph National Nature Reserve 132 NC 2619
Inchture 108 NO 2728
Inchyra 108 NO 1820
Indian Queens 19 SW 9158
Inerval 98 NR 3241
Ingale Skerry 137 HY 6719
Inga Ness 138 HY 4144
Inganess Bay 136 HY 4709
Ingatestone 38 TQ 6499
Ingbirchworth 71 SE 2205
Ingbirchworth Resr. 70 SE 2106
Ingestre 60 SJ 9724
Ingham (Lincs.) 72 SK 9483
Ingham (Norf.) 65 TG 3825
Ingham (Suff.) 54 TL 8570
Ingleborough Hill 77 SD 7474
Ingleby Arncliffe 85 NZ 4400
Ingleby Greenhow 85 NZ 5806
Inglesbatch 33 ST 7061
Inglesham 47 SU 2098
Ingleton (Durham) 84 NZ 1720
Ingleton (N Yorks.) 77 SD 6972
Inglewhite 77 SD 5439
Inglewood Forest 83 NY 4738
Inglismaldie Forest 109 NO 6567
Ingliston 102 NT 1472
Ingmire Hall 83 SD 6391
Ingoe 91 NZ 0374
Ingoldisthorpe 64 TF 6832
Ingoldmells 73 TF 5668
Ingoldmells Point 73 TF 5768
Ingoldsby 62 TF 0030
Ingram 91 NU 0116
Ingrave 38 TQ 6292
Ings 83 SD 4498
Ingst 33 ST 5887
Ingworth 65 TG 1929
Inishail 106 NN 0924
Inkberrow 50 SP 0157
Inkhorn 121 NJ 9239
Inkpen 34 SU 3564
Inkstack 135 ND 2570
Innellan 100 NS 1469
Innerdouny Hill 102 NO 0307
Innerhadden 107 NN 6757
Innerhadden Burn 107 NN 6655
Inner Hebrides 110 NM 1288
Innerleithen 96 NT 3336
Innerleven 103 NO 3700
Innermessan 86 NX 0863
Inner Sound (Highld.) 123 NG 6443
Inner Sound (Northum.) 97 NU 2035
Innerwell Port 87 NX 4849
Innerwick (Lothian) 96 NT 7273
Innerwick (Tays.) 107 NN 5947
Innimore Bay 105 NM 7141
Innis Chonain 106 NN 1025
Inns Holm 141 HU 3620
Insch 121 NJ 6327
Insh 116 NH 8101
Inshes House 128 NH 6943
Insh Island 105 NM 7319
Inshore 132 NC 3269
Inshriach Forest 117 NH 8302
Inskip 77 SD 4537
Instow 22 SS 4730
Inver (Grampn.) 117 NO 2393
Inver (Highld.) 129 NH 8682
Inver (Tays.) 108 NO 0142
Inverailort 111 NM 7681
Inveralligin 123 NG 8457
Inverallochy 121 NK 0464
Inveramsay 121 NJ 7424
Inveran 128 NH 5797
Inveraray 100 NN 0908
Inverarish 123 NG 5535
Inverarity 109 NO 4444
Inverarnan 106 NN 3118
Inverasdale 126 NG 8286
Inverbervie 109 NO 8372
Inverbroom Lodge 127 NH 1003
Inverbrough 116 NH 8130
Invercassley 128 NC 4602
Invercauld House 117 NO 1792
Inverchaolain Glen 100 NS 1076
Invercharnan 106 NN 1448
Invercharron House 128 NH 5991
Inverchoran 127 NH 2650
Inver Cottage 98 NR 4471
Invercreran 106 NN 0147
Inver Dalavil 111 NG 5705
Inverdruie 117 NH 9010
Inverebrie 121 NJ 9233
Invereck 100 NS 1486
Inverernan House 117 NJ 3210
Invereshie House 117 NH 8405
Inveresk 103 NT 3471
Inverey 117 NO 0889
Inverfarigaig 116 NH 5224
Invergarry 115 NH 3101
Invergeldie 107 NN 7427
Invergeldie Burn 107 NN 7529
Inverghiusachan Point 106 NN 0940
Invergloy House 115 NN 2288
Invergordon 129 NH 7168
Invergowrie 109 NO 3430
Inverguseran 111 NG 7407
Inverharroch 121 NJ 3831
Inverie 111 NG 7600
Inverie Bay 111 NM 7599
Inverinan 106 NM 9917
Inverinan Forest 106 NM 9816
Inverinate 114 NG 9122
Inverkeilor 109 NO 6649
Inverkeithing 102 NT 1383
Inverkeithing Bay 102 NT 1481
Inverkeithny 121 NJ 6246
Inverkip 100 NS 2071
Inverkirkaig 132 NC 0719
Inverlael 127 NH 1885
Inverlael Forest 127 NH 2286
Inverliever Forest 100 NM 9409
Inverliever Lodge 100 NM 8905
Inverlochlarig 107 NN 4318
Inverlochy Castle 115 NN 1376
Inver Mallie 115 NN 1388
Invermark Lodge 118 NO 4380
Invermoriston 116 NH 4117
Invernaver 133 NC 7060
Inverneill House 99 NR 8481
Inverness 128 NH 6645
Inverness Airport 129 NH 7752
Invernoaden 100 NS 1197
Inveroran Hotel 106 NN 2741
Inverpattack Lodge 116 NN 5590
Inverpolly Forest 132 NC 1111
Inverpolly Lodge 132 NC 0614
Inverpolly National Nature Reserve 132 NC 1412
Inverquharity 109 NO 4057
Inverquhomery 121 NK 0246
Inverroy 115 NN 2581
Inversanda Bay 106 NM 9559
Inverscaddle Bay 106 NN 0367
Invershin 128 NH 5796
Inversnaid Hotel 100 NN 3308
Inveruglie 121 NK 0947
Inveruglas 100 NN 3109
Inveruglas Water 100 NN 2810
Inverurie 121 NJ 7721
Invervar 107 NN 6648
Inverwick Forest 115 NH 3413
Invery House 119 NO 6993
Inwardleigh 21 SX 5599
Inworth 38 TL 8717
Inzie Head 121 NK 0662
Iona (is.) 104 NM 2723
Iorcail 110 NG 2706
Iping 27 SU 8522
Ipplepen 21 SX 8366
Ipsden 36 SU 6385
Ipstones 60 SK 0249
Ipswich 55 TM 1744
Ipswich Airport 55 TM 1941
Irby 68 SJ 2584
Irby in the Marsh 73 TF 4763
Irby upon Humber 75 TA 1904
Irchester 52 SP 9265
Ireby (Cumbr.) 82 NY 2338
Ireby (Lancs.) 77 SD 6575
Ireland (Orkney) 136 HY 3009
Ireland (Shetld.) 141 HU 3722
Ireleth 76 SD 2277
Ireshopeburn 84 NY 8638
Ireshope Moor 83 NY 8436
Irfon (Powys) 44 SN 8355
Irfon (Powys) 44 SN 9749
Irish Law (mt.) 100 NS 2559
Irlam 69 SJ 7194
Irnham 62 TF 0226
Iron Acton 33 ST 6783
Iron-Bridge 59 SJ 6703
Iron Cross 50 SP 0552
Ironside 121 NJ 8852
Ironville 60 SK 4351
Irstead 65 TG 3620
Irthington 89 NY 4961
Irthlingborough 52 SP 9470
Irton 81 TA 0084
Irvine 93 NS 3239
Irvine Bay 93 NS 2837
Isauld 134 NC 9765
Isay 125 NB 1002
Isay Island 122 NG 2157
Isbister (Orkney) 136 HY 2623
Isbister (Orkney) 136 HY 4018
Isbister (Shetld.) 143 HU 3790
Isbister (Whalsay) 141 HU 5763
Isca (ant.) 21 SX 9292
Isca Roman Fort (ant.) 32 ST 3390
Isfield 29 TQ 4417
Isham 52 SP 8873
Island Davarr 92 NR 7520
Island Macaskin 99 NR 7899
Island of Arran 92 NR 9637
Island of Bute 100 NS 0566
Island of Danna 99 NR 6978
Island of Mull 105 NM 6235
Island of Raasay 123 NG 5740
Island of Rona 123 NG 6258
Island of Skye 123 NG 4333
Island of Stroma 135 ND 3677
Islands of Fleet 87 NX 5749
Islawr-dref 57 SH 6815
Islay (is.) 98 NR 3960
Islay (Port Ellen) Aerodrome 98 NR 3251
Islay House 98 NR 3362
Isle Abbotts 24 ST 3520
Isle Brewers 24 ST 3621
Isleham 54 TL 6474
Isleham Fen 54 TL 6276
Isle Martin 127 NH 0999
Isle of Axholme (dist.) 74 SE 7905
Isle of Dogs 37 TQ 3778
Isle of Ewe 126 NG 8588
Isle of Fethaland 143 HU 3794
Isle of Grain 30 TQ 8676
Isle of Harty 31 TR 0267
Isle of Lewis 131 NB 3138
Isle of Man 76 SC 3281
Isle of Man (Ronaldsway) Airport 76 SC 2868
Isle of May 103 NT 6599
Isle of Nibon 142 HU 3073
Isle of Noss 141 HU 5440
Isle of Oxney 30 TQ 9128
Isle of Portland 25 SY 6972
Isle of Purbeck 26 SY 9681
Isle of Sheppey 31 TQ 9669
Isle of Stenness 142 HU 2076
Isle of Thanet 31 TR 3267
Isle of Walney 76 SD 1767
Isle of West Burrafirth 140 HU 2558
Isle of Whithorn 87 NX 4736
Isle of Wight 27 SZ 4987
Isleornsay 123 NG 6912
Isle Ristol 132 NB 9711
Islesburgh 142 HU 3369
Isles of Scilly 18 SV 9211
Isleworth 37 TQ 1675
Isley Walton 60 SK 4225
Islington 37 TQ 3085
Islip (Northants.) 52 SP 9879
Islip (Oxon.) 47 SP 5214
Islivig 130 NA 9927
Istead Rise 30 TQ 6369
Itchen Abbas 27 SU 5332
Itchen Stoke 27 SU 5532
Itchingfield 28 TQ 1328
Itchington 33 ST 6586
Itteringham 65 TG 1430
Itton 21 SX 6898
Itton Common 45 ST 4896
Ivegill 83 NY 4143
Ivelet 84 SD 9398
Iver 36 TQ 0381
Iver Heath 36 TQ 0283
Iveston 84 NZ 1350
Ivinghoe 36 SP 9416
Ivinghoe Aston 36 SP 9518
Ivington 45 SO 4756
Ivington Green 45 SO 4656
Ivybridge 21 SX 6356
Ivychurch 31 TR 0227
Ivy Hatch 29 TQ 5854
Iwade 30 TQ 9067
Iwerne Courtney or Shroton 25 ST 8512
Iwerne Minster 25 ST 8614
Ixworth 54 TL 9370
Ixworth Thorpe 54 TL 9172

J

Jack Hill 78 SE 1951
Jackstown 121 NJ 7531
Jackton 94 NS 5953
Jacobstow (Corn.) 20 SX 1995
Jacobstowe (Devon) 23 SS 5801
Jameston 22 SS 0599
Jamestown (Dumf. and Galwy.) 89 NY 2996
Jamestown (Highld.) 128 NH 4756
Jamestown (Strath.) 101 NS 3981
Jamieson's Point 86 NX 0371
Jarrow 91 NZ 3265
Jawcraig 101 NS 8475
Jaw Resr. 101 NS 4975
Jayes Park 28 TQ 1440
Jaywick 39 TM 1513
Jedburgh 90 NT 6520
Jed Water 90 NT 6712
Jeffreyston 42 SN 0906
Jemimaville 129 NH 7165
Jervaulx Abbey (ant.) 78 SE 1785
Jevington 29 TQ 5601
Johnby 83 NY 4333
John o' Groats 135 ND 3872
Johnshaven 109 NO 7966
Johnston (Dyfed) 42 SM 9310
Johnstone (Strath.) 101 NS 4263
Johnstonebridge 89 NY 1091
Johnston's Point 92 NR 7713
Jordans 36 SU 9791
Jordanston 42 SM 9132
Jumbles Resr. 69 SD 7314
Jump 71 SE 3701
Junction 70 SD 9710
Juniper Green 103 NT 2068
Jura (is.) 98 NR 5683
Jura Forest 98 NR 5072
Jura House 98 NR 4863
Jurby Aerodrome 76 SC 3698
Jurby East 76 SC 3899
Jurby Head 76 SC 3498
Jurby West 76 SC 3598

K

Kaber 83 NY 7911
Kaim Dam 100 NS 3462
Kaimes (Lothian) 103 NT 2767
Kaim Hill 93 NS 2253
Kale Water 97 NT 7822
Kalnakill 123 NG 6954
Kame of Corrigall (mt.) 136 HY 3320
Kame of Flouravoug (pt.) 143 HP 5916
Kame of Hoy (pt.) 136 HY 1904
Kame of Sandwick 143 HU 4787
Kames (Strath.) 105 NM 8211
Kames (Strath.) 100 NR 9771
Kames (Strath.) 94 NS 6926
Kames Bay 100 NS 0767
Kame, The (pt.) 140 HT 9340
Kea 19 SW 8042
Keadby 74 SE 8311
Keal 73 TF 3763
Keal Coates 73 TF 3661
Kearsley 69 SD 7504
Kearstay 130 NA 9617
Kearstwick 77 SD 6079
Kearton 84 SD 9999
Kearvaig 132 NC 2972
Kearvaig River 132 NC 2871
Keasden 77 SD 7266
Keava (is.) 131 NB 1935
Kebister Ness 141 HU 4746
Kebock Head 131 NB 4214
Keddington (Lincs.) 73 TF 3300
Kedington (Suff.) 54 TL 7046
Kedleston 60 SK 2941
Keelby 75 TA 1610
Keele 59 SJ 8045
Keeley Green 52 TL 0046
Keel Head 97 NU 1343
Keelylang Hill 136 HY 3710
Keen, The (pt.) 141 HU 5057
Keeston 42 SM 9019
Keevil 33 ST 9157
Kegworth 61 SK 4826
Kehelland 18 SW 6241
Keig 119 NJ 6119
Keighley 78 SE 0641
Keighley Moor 78 SD 9939
Keilarsbrae 102 NS 8993
Keillhill 121 NJ 7259
Keillmore 99 NR 6880
Keillor 108 NO 2640
Keillour 108 NN 9725
Keillour Forest 108 NN 9422
Keills Cross 99 NR 6880
Keil Point 92 NR 6707
Keils 98 NR 5268
Keinton Mandeville 25 ST 5430
Keir Hills 88 NX 8491
Keir Mill 88 NX 8593
Keisby 62 TF 0328
Keiss 135 ND 3461
Keith 121 NJ 4350
Keith Hall 121 NJ 7821
Keithock 109 NO 6063
Kelbrook 78 SD 9044
Kelburn (ant.) 93 NS 2156
Kelby 62 TF 0041
Keld (Cumbr.) 83 NY 5514
Keld (N Yorks.) 84 NY 8901
Keldholme 80 SE 7086
Keld, The (chan.) 139 HY 6032
Keldy Castle 80 SE 7791
Kelfield 79 SE 5938
Kelham 61 SK 7755
Kelk Beck 81 TA 0958
Kellan 105 NM 5240
Kellas (Grampn.) 129 NJ 1654
Kellas (Tays.) 109 NO 4535
Kellaton 21 SX 8039
Kelleth 83 NY 6605
Kellie Castle (ant) 109 NO 6040
Kellie Law 103 NO 5106
Kelling 65 TG 0942
Kellington 79 SE 5524
Kelloe 85 NZ 3435
Kello Water 88 NS 6908
Kelly 20 SX 3981
Kelly Bray 20 SX 3571
Kelmarsh 51 SP 7379
Kelmscot 47 SU 2499
Kelsale 55 TM 3865
Kelsall 69 SJ 5268
Kelsey Head 18 SW 7660
Kelshall 53 TL 3236
Kelso 96 NT 7333
Kelstern 73 TF 2590
Kelston 33 ST 6966
Keltie Water 101 NN 6311
Keltney Burn (Tays.) 107 NN 7651
Keltneyburn (Tays.) 107 NN 7749
Kelton or Rhonehouse Hill 88 NX 7459
Kelty 102 NT 1494
Kelty Water 101 NS 4995
Kelvedon 38 TL 8618
Kelvedon Hatch 37 TQ 5698

Kelynack 18 SW 3729
Kemback 109 NO 4115
Kemberton 59 SJ 7204
Kemble 46 ST 9897
Kemerton 49 SO 9437
Kemeys Commander 45 SO 3405
Kemnay 119 NJ 7315
Kemnay Forest 119 NJ 7418
Kempley 46 SO 6729
Kempock Point 100 NS 2478
Kempsey 49 SO 8549
Kempsford 47 SU 1596
Kempston 52 TL 0347
Kempston Hardwick 52 TL 0244
Kempton 48 SO 3582
Kemp Town 29 TQ 3303
Kemsing 37 TQ 5558
Kenardington 31 TQ 9732
Kenchester 45 SO 4343
Kencot 47 SP 2504
Kendal 83 SD 5192
Kenderchurch 45 SO 4028
Kendoon Loch 88 NX 6090
Kenfig 41 SS 8081
Kenfig Burrows 41 SS 7981
Kenfig Hill 41 SS 8483
Kengharair Farm 105 NM 4348
Kenilworth 50 SP 2872
Kenknock 107 NN 4636
Kenley (Gtr London) 37 TQ 3259
Kenley (Shrops.) 59 SJ 5600
Kenmore (Highld.) 123 NG 7557
Kenmore (Tays.) 107 NN 7745
Kenmure Castle (ant.) 88 NX 6376
Kenn (Avon) 32 ST 4168
Kenn (Devon) 21 SX 9285
Kennacraig 99 NR 8262
Kenna Craig 99 NR 8267
Kennedy's Pass 86 NX 1493
Kennerleigh 23 SS 8107
Kennet 102 NS 9291
Kennet and Avon Canal (Wilts.) 33 ST 8761
Kennet and Avon Canal (Wilts.) 34 SU 2363
Kennethmont 121 NJ 5328
Kennett 54 TL 6968
Kennford 21 SX 9186
Kennick Resr. 21 SX 8084
Kenninghall 54 TM 0386
Kennington (Kent) 31 TR 0245
Kennington (Oxon.) 47 SP 5202
Kennoway 103 NO 3402
Kenny Hill 54 TL 6680
Kennythorpe 80 SE 7865
Kenovay 104 NL 9946
Kensaleyre 123 NG 4251
Kensington 37 TQ 2579
Kensworth 36 TL 0318
Kensworth Common 36 TL 0317
Kentallen 106 NN 0057
Kentchurch 45 SO 4125
Kentchurch Court (ant.) 45 SO 4225
Kentford 54 TL 7066
Kentisbeare 24 ST 0608
Kentisbury 23 SS 6144
Kentmere 83 NY 4504
Kentmere Reservoir 83 NY 4408
Kent Oil Refinery 30 TQ 8674
Kenton (Devon) 21 SX 9583
Kenton (Suff.) 55 TM 1965
Kentra 111 NM 6568
Kentra Bay 111 NM 6468
Kents Bank 77 SD 3975
Kent's Green 46 SO 7423
Kent's Oak 26 SU 3224
Kentwell Hall (ant.) 54 TL 8647
Kenwick 58 SJ 4230
Kenwyn 19 SW 8145
Kenyon 69 SJ 6295
Keoldale 132 NC 3866
Keose 131 NB 3521
Keppanach 106 NN 0262
Keppoch 114 NG 9621
Kepwick 85 SE 4690
Keresley 50 SP 3182
Kerloch (mt.) 119 NO 6987
Kerne Bridge 45 SO 5819
Kerran Hill 92 NR 7313
Kerrera (is.) 105 NM 8128
Kerridge 69 SJ 9376
Kerris 18 SW 4427
Kerry 48 SO 1490
Kerrycroy 100 NS 1061
Kerry Hill 48 SO 1386
Kerrysdale 123 NG 8273
Kerry's Gate 45 SO 3933
Kersall 72 SK 7162
Kersey 54 TM 0044
Kershader 131 NB 3420
Kershope Burn 89 NY 5083
Kershopefoot 89 NY 4782
Kershope Forest 90 NY 5181
Kersoe 50 SO 9939
Kerswell 24 ST 0806
Kerswell Green 49 SO 8646
Kesgrave 55 TM 2245
Kessingland 55 TM 5286
Kestle Mill 19 SW 8459
Keston 37 TQ 4164
Keswick (Cumbr.) 82 NY 2723
Keswick (Norf.) 65 TG 2004
Keswick (Norf.) 65 TG 3533
Ketligill Head 142 HU 2784
Kettering 52 SP 8778
Ketteringham 65 TG 1503
Kettins 108 NO 2338
Kettla Ness 141 HU 3428
Kettlebaston 54 TL 9650
Kettlebridge 103 NO 3007
Kettlebrook 60 SK 2103
Kettleburgh 55 TM 2660
Kettleness 85 NZ 8315
Kettleshulme 70 SJ 9879
Kettlesing Bottom 79 SE 2257
Kettlestone 64 TF 9631
Kettlethorpe 72 SK 8475
Kettletoft 139 HY 6538
Kettletoft Bay 139 HY 6638
Kettlewell 78 SD 9772
Ketton 62 SK 9704
Kew 37 TQ 1877
Kewstoke 32 ST 3363
Kex Beck 78 SE 0953
Kexbrough 71 SE 3009
Kexby (Lincs.) 72 SK 8785
Kexby (N Yorks.) 80 SE 7050
Key Green 69 SJ 8963
Keyham 61 SK 6606
Keyhaven 26 SZ 3091
Keyingham 75 TA 2425
Keymer 29 TQ 3115
Keynsham 33 ST 6568
Keysley Down 25 ST 8634
Keysoe 52 TL 0763
Keysoe Row 52 TL 0861
Keyston 52 TL 0475
Keyworth 61 SK 6130
Kibblesworth 84 NZ 2456
Kibworth Beauchamp 61 SP 6893
Kibworth Harcourt 61 SP 6894
Kidbrooke 37 TQ 4076
Kiddemore Green 59 SJ 8509
Kidderminster 49 SO 8376
Kiddington 47 SP 4122
Kidlington 47 SP 4913
Kidmore End 36 SU 6979
Kidsgrove 59 SJ 8354
Kidstones 78 SD 9581
Kidwelly 43 SN 4106
Kielder 90 NY 6293
Kielder Burn 90 NY 6494
Kielder Castle 90 NY 6393
Kielder Forest 90 NY 6591
Kielderhead Moor 90 NT 6600
Kielder Reservoir 90 NY 6689
Kiells 98 NR 4168
Kierfea Hill 138 HY 4132
Kierfiold House 136 HY 2518
Kiessimul Castle (ant.) 112 NL 6697
Kilbarchan 101 NS 4063
Kilbeg 111 NG 6506
Kilberry 99 NR 7164
Kilberry Head 99 NR 7064
Kilbirnie 93 NS 3154
Kilbirnie Loch 93 NS 3354
Kilblaan Burn 100 NN 1413
Kilbrannan Sound 92 NR 8441
Kilbraur Hill 129 NC 8208
Kilbride (Island of Skye) 123 NG 5820
Kilbride (South Uist) 112 NF 7614
Kilbride (Strath.) 105 NM 8525
Kilbride Bay 100 NR 9666
Kilbride Point 122 NG 3766
Kilbryde Castle (ant.) 101 NN 7503
Kilburn (Derby.) 60 SK 3845
Kilburn (N Yorks.) 79 SE 5179
Kilby 61 SP 6295
Kilcadzow 95 NS 8848
Kilchamaig 99 NR 8061
Kilchattan (Bute) 93 NS 1054
Kilchattan (Colonsay) 98 NR 3795
Kilchattan Bay 93 NS 1055
Kilchenzie 92 NR 6725
Kilcheran 105 NM 8238
Kilchiaran 98 NR 2060
Kilchiaran Bay 98 NR 1960
Kilchoan 111 NM 4963
Kilchoan Bay 111 NM 4762
Kilchoman 98 NR 2163
Kilchrenan 106 NN 0322
Kilchurn Castle (ant.) 106 NN 1327
Kilconquhar 103 NO 4802
Kilconquhar Loch 103 NO 4801
Kilcot 46 SO 6925
Kilcoy 128 NH 5751
Kilcoy Forest 128 NH 6355
Kilcreggan 100 NS 2380
Kildale 85 NZ 6009
Kildalloig 92 NR 7518
Kildalton Castle 98 NR 4347
Kildalton Cross (ant.) 98 NR 4650
Kildary 129 NH 7775
Kildavanan 100 NS 0266
Kildermorie Forest 128 NH 4678
Kildermorie Lodge 128 NH 5177
Kildonan (Island of Arran) 92 NS 0321
Kildonan Burn 134 NC 9122
Kildonan Lodge 134 NC 9022
Kildonnan 111 NM 4885
Kildrummy 118 NJ 4617
Kildwick 78 SE 0145
Kilennan River 98 NR 3657
Kilfinan 100 NR 9378
Kilfinan Bay 100 NR 9178
Kilfinichen Bay 105 NM 4827
Kilfinnan 115 NN 2795
Kilgetty 42 SN 1207
Kilgwrrwg Common 45 ST 4797
Kilham (Humbs.) 81 TA 0564
Kilham (Northum.) 97 NT 8832
Kili Holm 138 HY 4732
Kilkenneth 104 NL 9444
Kilkerran 93 NS 3003
Kilkhampton 22 SS 2511
Killamarsh 71 SK 4680
Killay 40 SS 6092
Killchianaig 99 NR 6486
Killean 92 NR 6944
Killearn 101 NS 5286
Killegray 124 NF 9783
Killen 128 NH 6758
Killerby 84 NZ 1919
Killichonan 107 NN 5458
Killichonan Burn 107 NN 5660
Killichronan 105 NM 5441
Killiechonate 115 NN 2481
Killiechonate Forest 115 NN 2074
Killiecrankie 108 NN 9162
Killiemor 105 NM 4939
Killilan 114 NG 9430
Killilan Forest 114 NH 0333
Killimster 135 ND 3156
Killin 107 NN 5732
Killinallan 98 NR 3171
Killinghall 79 SE 2858
Killingholme 75 TA 1416
Killington 77 SD 6188
Killington Resr. 83 SD 5991
Killin Lodge 116 NH 5209
Killochan (ant.) 86 NS 2200
Killochyett 96 NT 4545
Killocraw 92 NR 6630
Killundine 111 NM 5849
Kilmacolm 100 NS 3569
Kilmahumaig 99 NR 7893
Kilmalieu 106 NM 8955
Kilmaluag 123 NG 4374
Kilmaluag Bay 123 NG 4475
Kilmannan Resr. 101 NS 4978
Kilmany 109 NO 3821
Kilmarie 123 NG 5417
Kilmarnock 93 NS 4237
Kilmaron Castle 109 NO 3516
Kilmartin 99 NR 8398
Kilmar Tor 19 SX 2574
Kilmaurs 93 NS 4141
Kilmein Hill 93 NS 4510
Kilmelfort 105 NM 8413
Kilmeny 98 NR 3865
Kilmersdon 33 ST 6952
Kilmeston 27 SU 5825
Kilmichael Forest 100 NR 9095
Kilmichael Glassary 99 NR 8593
Kilmichael of Inverlussa 99 NR 7785
Kilmington (Devon) 24 SY 2798
Kilmington (Wilts.) 25 ST 7736
Kilmorack 128 NH 4944
Kilmore (Island of Skye) 111 NG 6507
Kilmore (Strath.) 106 NM 8824
Kilmory (Highld.) 111 NM 5270
Kilmory (Island of Arran) 92 NR 9621
Kilmory (Rhum) 110 NG 3503
Kilmory (Strath.) 99 NR 7075
Kilmory Bay 99 NR 6974
Kilmory Castle 99 NR 8686
Kilmory Glen 110 NG 3602
Kilmory Lodge 105 NM 7105
Kilmory Water 92 NR 9622
Kilmuir (Highld.) 128 NH 6749
Kilmuir (Highld.) 129 NH 7573
Kilmuir (Island of Skye) 122 NG 2547
Kilmun 100 NS 1781
Kilnave 98 NR 2871
Kilndown 29 TQ 7035
Kilnhurst 71 SK 4697
Kilninian 105 NM 3945
Kilninver 105 NM 8221
Kiln Pit Hill 84 NZ 0454
Kilnsea 75 TA 4015
Kilnsey 78 SD 9767
Kilnwick 81 SE 9949
Kiloran 98 NR 3996
Kiloran Bay 98 NR 3999
Kilpatrick 92 NR 9027
Kilpatrick Hills 101 NS 4776
Kilpeck 45 SO 4430
Kilpheder 112 NF 7419
Kilphedir 134 NC 9818
Kilpin 74 SE 7726
Kilravock Castle 129 NH 8149
Kilrenny 103 NO 5705
Kilsby 51 SP 5671
Kilspindie 108 NO 2225
Kilstay Bay 86 NX 1338
Kilsyth 101 NS 7178
Kilsyth Hills 101 NS 6980
Kiltarlity 128 NH 5041
Kilton 32 ST 1644
Kilt Rock 123 NG 5066
Kilvaxter 122 NG 3869
Kilve 32 ST 1443
Kilvington 61 SK 7942
Kilwinning 93 NS 3043
Kimberley (Norf.) 64 TG 0704
Kimberley (Notts.) 61 SK 4944
Kimberley House 65 TG 0904
Kimble 36 SP 8206
Kimblesworth 84 NZ 2547
Kimble Wick 36 SP 8007
Kimbolton (Cambs.) 52 TL 0967
Kimbolton (Here. and Worc.) 48 SO 5261
Kimcote 51 SP 5886
Kimmeridge 25 SY 9179
Kimmerston 97 NT 9535
Kimpton (Hants.) 34 SU 2746
Kimpton (Herts.) 37 TL 1718
Kinbrace 134 NC 8631
Kinbrace Burn 134 NC 8828
Kinbuck 101 NN 7905
Kincaple 109 NO 4518
Kincardine (Fife) 102 NS 9387
Kincardine (Highld.) 128 NH 6089
Kincardine Castle (Tays.) 102 NN 9411
Kincardine O'Neil 119 NO 5999
Kinclaven 108 NO 1538
Kincorth 119 NJ 9303
Kincorth House 129 NJ 0161
Kincraig 117 NH 8305
Kincraigie 108 NN 9849
Kindallachan 108 NN 9950
Kinder Reservoir 70 SK 0588
Kinder Scout (mt.) 70 SK 0888
Kineton (Glos.) 46 SP 0926
Kineton (Warw.) 50 SP 3351
Kinfauns 108 NO 1622
Kinfauns Forest 108 NO 1923
Kingairloch 111 NM 8553
Kingairloch House 111 NM 8353
Kingarth 93 NS 0956
Kingcoed 45 SO 4205
Kingham 47 SP 2523
Kingholm Quay 88 NX 9773
Kinghorn 103 NT 2686
Kinglassie 103 NT 2298
Kingoodie 108 NO 3329
King Orry's Grave (ant.) 76 SC 4485
Kingsand 20 SX 4350
Kingsbarns 103 NO 5912
Kingsbridge (Devon) 21 SX 7344
Kingsbridge (Somer.) 23 SS 9837
King's Bromley 60 SK 1216
Kingsburgh 123 NG 3955
Kingsbury (Gtr London) 37 TQ 1989
Kingsbury (Warw.) 60 SP 2196
Kingsbury Episcopi 25 ST 4320
Kings Caple 45 SO 5628
King's Cave 129 NH 8371
Kingsclere 35 SU 5258
King's Cliffe 62 TL 0097
Kingscote 46 ST 8196
Kingscott 23 SS 5318
King's Coughton 50 SP 0858
Kingscross 92 NS 0428
Kingscross Point 92 NS 0528
King's Cross Station 37 TQ 3083
King's Delph 63 TL 2595
Kingsdon 25 ST 5126
Kingsdown 31 TR 3748
Kingseat 102 NT 1290
Kingsey 36 SP 7406
Kingsfold 28 TQ 1636
Kingsford 49 SO 8281
King's Forest of Geltsdale 83 NY 5853
Kingsforth 74 TA 0219
Kingshall Street 54 TL 9161
King's Heath 50 SP 0781
Kingshouse 107 NN 5620
Kingskerswell 21 SX 8767
Kingskettle 103 NO 3008
Kingsland 48 SO 4461
Kings Langley 36 TL 0702
Kingsley (Ches.) 69 SJ 5474
Kingsley (Hants.) 35 SU 7838
Kingsley (Staffs.) 60 SK 0047
Kingsley Green 35 SU 8930
King's Lynn 64 TF 6220
Kings Meaburn 83 NY 6221
Kings Muir (Borders) 95 NT 2539
Kingsmuir (Fife) 103 NO 5409
Kingsmuir (Tays.) 109 NO 4849
Kingsnorth (Kent) 30 TQ 8072
Kingsnorth (Kent) 31 TR 0039
King's Norton (Leic.) 61 SK 6800
King's Norton (W Mids) 50 SP 0579
King's Nympton 23 SS 6819
King's Pyon 45 SO 4350
Kings Ripton 53 TL 2576
King's Seat (mt.) 108 NO 2333
King's Seat Hill 102 NS 9399
King's Sedge Moor 25 ST 4433
King's Somborne 26 SU 3631
King's Stag 25 ST 7210
King's Stanley 46 SO 8103
Kings Sutton 51 SP 4936
Kingstanding 60 SP 0794
Kingsteignton 21 SX 8773
King Sterndale 70 SK 0972
Kingsthorne 45 SO 4932
Kingsthorpe 52 SP 7563
Kingston (Cambs.) 53 TL 3455
Kingston (Devon) 21 SX 6347
Kingston (Dorset) 25 ST 7509
Kingston (Dorset) 26 SY 9579
Kingston (Grampn.) 121 NJ 3365
Kingston (Hants.) 26 SU 1401
Kingston (I. of W.) 27 SZ 4781
Kingston (Kent) 31 TR 1951
Kingston (Lothian) 103 NT 5482
Kingston Bagpuize 47 SU 4098
Kingston Blount 36 SU 7399
Kingston by Sea 28 TQ 2205
Kingston Deverill 25 ST 8436
Kingstone (Here. and Worc.) 45 SO 4235
Kingstone (Somer.) 24 ST 3713
Kingstone (Staffs.) 60 SK 0629
Kingston Lisle 34 SU 3287
Kingston near Lewes 29 TQ 3908
Kingston on Soar 61 SK 5027
Kingston Russell 25 SY 5891
Kingston Seymour 32 ST 3966
Kingston St. Mary 24 ST 2229
Kingston upon Hull 75 TA 0929
Kingston upon Thames 37 TQ 1869
Kingstown 89 NY 3959
King Street (Ches.) (ant.) 69 SJ 6969
King Street (Northants.) (ant.) 62 TF 1108
King's Walden 37 TL 1623
Kingswear 21 SX 8851
Kingswells 119 NJ 8606
Kingswinford 49 SO 8888
Kings Wood 30 TQ 8351
Kingswood (Avon) 33 ST 6473
Kingswood (Bucks.) 36 SP 6819
Kingswood (Glos.) 33 ST 7491
Kingswood (Powys) 58 SJ 2402
Kingswood (Surrey) 28 TQ 2455
Kingswood (Warw.) 50 SP 1871
Kingswood Common 45 SO 2854
Kings Worthy 27 SU 4932
Kington (Here. and Worc.) 45 SO 2956
Kington (Here. and Worc.) 50 SO 9955
Kington Langley 33 ST 9276
Kington Magna 25 ST 7622
Kington St. Michael 33 ST 9077
Kingussie 116 NH 7500
King Water 90 NY 5365
Kingweston 25 ST 5230
Kinharrachie 121 NJ 9231
Kininvie House 121 NJ 3144
Kinkell Bridge 108 NN 9316
Kinkell Church (ant.) 119 NJ 7819
Kinknockie 109 NO 5315
Kinknockie 121 NK 0041
Kinlet 49 SO 7280
Kinloch (Fife) 103 NO 2812
Kinloch (Highld.) 132 NC 3434
Kinloch (Island of Skye) 123 NG 6917
Kinloch (Tays.) 108 NO 1444
Kinloch (Tays.) 108 NO 2644
Kinlochard 101 NN 4502
Kinlochbervie 132 NC 2156
Kinloch Castle 111 NM 4099
Kinlocheil 114 NM 9779
Kinlochewe 126 NH 0261
Kinlochewe Forest 127 NH 0766
Kinloch Glen 110 NG 3800
Kinloch Hourn 114 NG 9407
Kinlochleven 106 NN 1861
Kinloch Lodge 133 NC 5552
Kinlochluichart Forest 127 NH 2769
Kinlochmore 106 NN 1962
Kinloch Rannoch 107 NN 6658
Kinloch River 133 NC 5450
Kinlochspelve 105 NM 6525
Kinloss 129 NJ 0661
Kinmel Bay 67 SH 9881
Kinmount House 89 NY 1368
Kinmuck 119 NJ 8119
Kinmundy 119 NJ 8817
Kinnadie 121 NJ 9643
Kinnaird 108 NO 2428
Kinnaird Castle 109 NO 6357
Kinnaird Head 121 NJ 9967
Kinneff 119 NO 8574
Kinneil House (ant.) 102 NS 9880
Kinnelhead 88 NT 0201
Kinnell 109 NO 6050
Kinnel Water 89 NY 0690
Kinnerley 58 SJ 3321
Kinnersley (Here. and Worc.) 45 SO 3449
Kinnersley (Here. and Worc.) 49 SO 8743
Kinnerton (Ches.) 68 SJ 3361
Kinnerton (Powys) 48 SO 2463
Kinnesswood 102 NO 1702
Kinninvie 84 NZ 0521
Kinniside Common 82 NY 0810
Kinnordy 109 NO 3654
Kinnoull Hill 108 NO 1322
Kinoulton 61 SK 6730
Kinpurney Hill 108 NO 3241
Kinrive Hill 128 NH 6875
Kinross 102 NO 1102
Kinrossie 108 NO 1832
Kinsham 48 SO 3664
Kinsley 71 SE 4114
Kinson 26 SZ 0696
Kintail Forest 114 NG 9917
Kintarvie 131 NB 2317
Kintbury 34 SU 3866
Kintessack 129 NJ 0060
Kintillo 108 NO 1317
Kintocher 119 NJ 5709
Kintore 119 NJ 7916
Kintour 98 NR 4551
Kintra 98 NR 3248
Kintra River 98 NR 3249
Kintyre (dist.) 100 NR 7540
Kinuachdrach 99 NR 7098
Kinuachdrach Harbour 99 NR 7098
Kinveachy 117 NH 9118
Kinver 49 SO 8483
Kippax 79 SE 4030
Kippax Park 79 SE 4228
Kippen 101 NS 6594
Kippenross House 101 NN 7800
Kippford or Scaur 87 NX 8355
Kirbister (Orkney) 136 HY 3607
Kirbister (Stronsay) 137 HY 6823
Kirbuster 136 HY 2825
Kirby Bedon 65 TG 2705
Kirby Bellars 61 SK 7117
Kirby Cane 65 TM 3794
Kirby Cross 55 TM 2120
Kirby Grindalythe 81 SE 9067
Kirby Hall (ant.) 62 SP 9293
Kirby Hill (N Yorks.) 84 NZ 1306
Kirby Hill (N Yorks.) 79 SE 3868
Kirby Knowle 79 SE 4687
Kirby-le-Soken 39 TM 2222
Kirby Mills 80 SE 7185
Kirby Misperton 80 SE 7779
Kirby Muxloe 61 SK 5104
Kirby Row 55 TM 3792
Kirby Sigston 85 SE 4194
Kirby Underdale 80 SE 8158
Kirby Wiske 79 SE 3784
Kirdford 28 TQ 0226
Kirivick 131 NB 2041
Kirk 135 ND 2859
Kirkabister 141 HU 4938
Kirkaig Point 132 NC 0521
Kirkandrews on Eden 89 NY 3558
Kirkbampton 82 NY 3056
Kirkbean 88 NX 9859
Kirk Bramwith 71 SE 6111
Kirkbride 82 NY 2356
Kirkbuddo 109 NO 5043
Kirkburn (Highld.) 135 ND 3164
Kirkburn (Humbs.) 81 SE 9855
Kirkburton 70 SE 1912
Kirkby (Lincs.) 72 TF 0692
Kirkby (Mers.) 68 SJ 4098
Kirkby (N Yorks.) 85 NZ 5306
Kirkby Fell 78 SD 8664
Kirkby Fleetham 84 SE 2894
Kirkby Green 72 TF 0857
Kirkby in Ashfield 61 SK 4956
Kirkby Industrial Estate 68 SJ 4398
Kirkby-in-Furness 76 SD 2282
Kirkby la Thorpe 62 TF 0946
Kirkby Lonsdale 77 SD 6178
Kirkby Malham 78 SD 8960
Kirkby Mallory 61 SK 4500
Kirkby Malzeard 79 SE 2374
Kirkbymoorside 80 SE 6986
Kirkby on Bain 73 TF 2362
Kirkby Overblow 79 SE 3249
Kirkby Stephen 83 NY 7708
Kirkby Thore 83 NY 6325
Kirkby Underwood 62 TF 0727
Kirkcaldy 103 NT 2791
Kirkcambeck 90 NY 5368
Kirkcarswell 87 NX 7549
Kirkcolm 86 NX 0268
Kirk Connel (Dumf. and Galwy.) 88 NS 7312
Kirk Connel (Dumf. and Galwy.) (ant.) 89 NY 2575
Kirkconnell (Dumf. and Galwy.) 88 NX 9767
Kirkcowan 86 NX 3260
Kirkcudbright 87 NX 6851
Kirkcudbright Bay 87 NX 6644
Kirk Deighton 79 SE 3950
Kirk Ella 74 TA 0129
Kirk Fell 82 NY 1910
Kirkfieldbank 95 NS 8643
Kirkgunzeon 88 NX 8666
Kirk Hallam 61 SK 4540
Kirkham (Lancs.) 77 SD 4231
Kirkham (N Yorks.) 80 SE 7365
Kirkhamgate 79 SE 2922
Kirk Hammerton 79 SE 4655
Kirkharle 91 NZ 0182
Kirkheaton (Northum.) 91 NZ 0177
Kirkheaton (W Yorks.) 70 SE 1817
Kirkhill (Highld.) 128 NH 5545
Kirkhill (Tays.) 109 NO 6860
Kirkhope (Borders) 96 NT 3823
Kirk Hope (South Walls) 136 ND 3490
Kirkhouse 96 NT 3233
Kirkhouse Point 136 ND 4790
Kirkibost (Island of Skye) 123 NG 5518
Kirkibost (Isle of Lewis) 131 NB 1834
Kirkibost Island 124 NF 7564
Kirkinch 108 NO 3144
Kirkinner 87 NX 4251
Kirkintilloch 101 NS 6573
Kirk Ireton 60 SK 2650
Kirkland (Cumbr.) 82 NY 0718
Kirkland (Cumbr.) 83 NY 6432
Kirkland (Dumf. and Galwy.) 88 NS 7214
Kirkland (Dumf. and Galwy.) 88 NX 8090
Kirkland Hill 88 NS 7215
Kirk Langley 60 SK 2838
Kirkleatham 85 NZ 5921
Kirklevington 85 NZ 4309
Kirkley 55 TM 5491
Kirklington (Notts.) 71 SK 6757
Kirklington (N Yorks.) 79 SE 3181
Kirklinton 89 NY 4366
Kirkliston 102 NT 1274
Kirkmaiden 86 NX 1236
Kirk Merrington 84 NZ 2631
Kirk Michael (I. of M.) 76 SC 3190
Kirkmichael (Strath.) 93 NS 3408
Kirkmichael (Tays.) 108 NO 0860
Kirkmond le Mire 73 TF 1892
Kirkmuirhill 94 NS 7943
Kirknewton (Lothian) 102 NT 1166
Kirknewton (Northum.) 97 NT 9130
Kirkney Water 121 NJ 4830
Kirk of Shotts 101 NS 8462
Kirkoswald (Cumbr.) 83 NY 5541
Kirkoswald (Strath.) 93 NS 2407
Kirkpatrick Durham 88 NX 7870
Kirkpatrick-Fleming 89 NY 2770
Kirk Sandall 71 SE 6007
Kirksanton 76 SD 1380
Kirk Smeaton 71 SE 5116
Kirkstall 79 SE 2635
Kirkstile (Grampn.) 121 NJ 5235
Kirkstone Pass 83 NY 4008
Kirk Taing 138 HY 5633
Kirkton (Borders) 90 NT 5413
Kirkton (Dumf. and Galwy.) 88 NX 9781
Kirkton (Fife) 109 NO 3625
Kirkton (Grampn.) 119 NJ 6112
Kirkton (Grampn.) 121 NJ 6425
Kirkton (Grampn.) 121 NJ 6950
Kirkton (Grampn.) 121 NJ 8243
Kirkton (Highld.) 121 NK 1050
Kirkton (Highld.) 126 NG 9141
Kirkton (Highld.) 129 NH 7998
Kirkton (Strath.) 88 NS 9320
Kirkton (Tays.) 108 NN 9618
Kirkton (Tays.) 109 NO 4246
Kirkton Head 121 NK 1250
Kirkton Manor 95 NT 2137
Kirkton of Airlie 108 NO 3151
Kirkton of Auchterhouse 108 NO 3338
Kirkton of Barevan 129 NH 8347
Kirkton of Collace 108 NO 1931
Kirkton of Craig 109 NO 7055
Kirkton of Culsalmond 121 NJ 6432
Kirkton of Durris 119 NO 7796
Kirkton of Glenbuchat 118 NJ 3715
Kirkton of Glenisla 108 NO 2160
Kirkton of Kingoldrum 108 NO 3354
Kirkton of Largo 103 NO 4203
Kirkton of Lethendy 108 NO 1241
Kirkton of Logie Buchan 121 NJ 9829
Kirkton of Maryculter 119 NO 8599
Kirkton of Menmuir 109 NO 5364
Kirkton of Monikie 109 NO 5138
Kirkton of Rayne 121 NJ 6930
Kirkton of Skene 119 NJ 8007
Kirkton of Strathmartine 109 NO 3735
Kirkton of Tealing 109 NO 4037
Kirktown 121 NK 0952
Kirktown of Alvah 121 NJ 6760
Kirktown of Auchterless 121 NJ 7141
Kirktown of Bourtie 121 NJ 8024
Kirktown of Deskford 121 NJ 5061
Kirktown of Fetteresso 119 NO 8585
Kirkwall 136 HY 4410
Kirkwall Airport 136 HY 4808
Kirkwhelpington 91 NY 9984
Kirk Yetholm 97 NT 8227
Kirmington 75 TA 1011
Kirn 100 NS 1878
Kirriemuir 109 NO 3854
Kirriereoch Hill 87 NX 4287
Kirroughtree Forest 87 NX 4473
Kirstead Green 65 TM 2997
Kirtlebridge 89 NY 2372
Kirtle Water 89 NY 2577
Kirtling 54 TL 6857
Kirtling Green 54 TL 6855
Kirtlington 47 SP 4919
Kirtomy 134 NC 7463
Kirtomy Point 134 NC 7566
Kirton (Highld.) 123 NG 8227
Kirton (Lincs.) 63 TF 3038
Kirton (Notts.) 72 SK 6869
Kirton (Suff.) 55 TM 2739
Kirton End 63 TF 2840
Kirton Holme 63 TF 2642
Kirton in Lindsey 74 SK 9398
Kishorn Island 123 NG 8037
Kislingbury 51 SP 6959
Kites Hardwick 51 SP 4668
Kit Hill 20 SX 3771

Kithurst Hill 28 TQ 0712
Kit's Coty House (ant.) 30 TQ 7461
Kittybrewster 119 NJ 9208
Kitwood 27 SU 6633
Kiveton Park 71 SK 4982
Klibreck 133 NC 5834
Klibreck Burn 133 NC 5832
Knaith 72 SK 8284
Knap Corner 25 ST 8023
Knapdale (dist.) 99 NR 8176
Knapdale Forest 99 NR 7890
Knaphill 36 SU 9658
Knap of Howar (ant.) 138 HY 4851
Knap of Trowieglen 136 ND 2398
Knapp (Somer.) 24 ST 3025
Knapp (Tays.) 108 NO 2831
Knaps Longpeak (Pt.) 22 SS 2018
Knapton (Norf.) 65 TG 3034
Knapton (N Yorks.) 79 SE 5652
Knapton (N Yorks.) 81 SE 8775
Knapwell 53 TL 3362
Knaresborough 79 SE 3557
Knarsdale 83 NY 6753
Knaven 121 NJ 8943
Knayton 79 SE 4188
Knayton 79 SE 4387
Knebworth 37 TL 2520
Kneesall 72 SK 7064
Kneesworth 53 TL 3444
Kneeton 61 SK 7146
Knelston 40 SS 4689
Knightacott 23 SS 6439
Knightcote 50 SP 3954
Knighton (Devon) 21 SX 5249
Knighton (Leic.) 61 SK 6001
Knighton (Powys) 48 SO 2872
Knighton (Staffs.) 59 SJ 7240
Knighton (Staffs.) 59 SJ 7427
Knighton Down 34 SU 1245
Knightwick 49 SO 7355
Knill 45 SO 2960
Knipe, The (mt.) 88 NS 6410
Knipton 62 SK 8231
Knipton Reservoir 62 SK 8130
Knitsley 84 NZ 1148
Kniveton 60 SK 2050
Knock (Cumbr.) 83 NY 6826
Knock (Grampn.) 121 NJ 5452
Knock (Island of Mull) 105 NM 5438
Knock (Isle of Lewis) 131 NB 4931
Knockally 135 ND 1428
Knockan 132 NC 2110
Knockandhu 117 NJ 2123
Knockando 120 NJ 1941
Knockando House 120 NJ 2042
Knockandy Hill 121 NJ 5431
Knockangle Point 98 NR 3151
Knockbain 128 NH 6255
Knock Bay 111 NG 6708
Knockbrex 87 NX 5849
Knock Castle 100 NS 1963
Knockcoid 86 NX 0168
Knockdaw Hill 86 NX 1688
Knockdee 135 ND 1761
Knockdhu 86 NX 1483
Knockdolian 86 NX 1184
Knockdolian Castle 86 NX 1285
Knockdow 100 NS 1070
Knockendon Resr. 93 NS 2452
Knockenkelly 92 NS 0426
Knockentiber 93 NS 3939
Knockespock House 121 NJ 5424
Knockfin Heights 134 NC 9134
Knock Head 121 NJ 6565
Knock Hill (Fife) 102 NT 0593
Knock Hill (Grampn.) 121 NJ 5355
Knockholt 37 TQ 4058
Knockholt Pound 37 TQ 4859
Knockie Lodge 116 NH 4413
Knockin 58 SJ 3322
Knockinlochie 86 NX 2889
Knockintorran 124 NF 7367
Knock Moss 86 NX 2057
Knocknaha 92 NR 6817
Knocknain 86 NW 9764
Knocknevis 87 NX 5474
Knock of Balmyle 108 NO 1156
Knock of Braemoray 129 NJ 0141
Knockrome 98 NR 5571
Knocksharry 76 SC 2785
Knock, The 89 NY 2291
Knodishall 55 TM 4261
Knole (ant.) 29 TQ 5354
Knolls Green 69 SJ 8079
Knolton 58 SJ 3738
Knook 34 ST 9341
Knossington 61 SK 8008
Knott 82 NY 2932
Knott End-on-Sea 77 SD 3548
Knotting 52 TL 0063
Knottingley 79 SE 5023
Knotty Green 36 SU 9392
Knowbury 48 SO 5774
Knowe 86 NX 3171
Knowehead 88 NX 6090
Knowesgate 91 NY 9885
Knowes Hill 96 NT 4338
Knoweside 93 NS 2512
Knowetownhead 90 NT 5418
Knowle (Avon) 33 ST 6170
Knowle (Devon) 22 SS 4938
Knowle (Devon) 23 SS 7801
Knowle (W Mids) 50 SP 1876
Knowl Green 77 SD 6337
Knowl Hill 36 SU 8279
Knowlton 31 TR 2853
Knowsley 68 SJ 4396
Knowsley Hall 68 SJ 4494
Knowstone 23 SS 8223
Knox Hill 109 NO 8171
Knox Knowe 90 NT 6502
Knoydart (dist.) 111 NG 8301
Knucklas 48 SO 2574
Knutsford 69 SJ 7578
Knypersley 59 SJ 8856
Kokoarrah (pt.) 82 SD 0496
Kuggar 18 SW 7216
Kyle (dist.) 93 NS 5022
Kyleakin (Highld.) 123 NG 7526
Kyle Akin (Highld.) 123 NG 7527
Kylechorky Lodge 115 NH 4029
Kyle Forest 93 NS 4911
Kyle of Durness 132 NC 3765
Kyle of Lochalsh 123 NG 7527
Kyle of Sutherland 128 NH 5795
Kyle of Tongue 133 NC 5757
Kylerhea (Highld.) 123 NG 7820
Kyle Rhea (Highld.) 123 NG 7922
Kyles Lodge 124 NF 9987
Kylesmorar 111 NM 8093
Kyles of Bute (Strath.) 100 NR 9969
Kyles of Bute (Strath.) 100 NS 0473
Kyles Stockinish 125 NG 1391
Kylestrome 132 NC 2234
Kyllachy House 116 NH 7825
Kyloe 97 NU 0540
Kyloe Hills 97 NU 0439
Kynance Cove 18 SW 6813
Kynnersley 59 SJ 6716
Kype Muir 94 NS 7138
Kype Water 94 NS 7439
Kyre Park 49 SO 6263

L

Labost 131 NB 2749
Lacastal 131 NB 4240
Laceby 75 TA 2106
Lacey Green 36 SP 8200
Lach Dennis 69 SJ 7071
Lachlan Bay 100 NS 0095
Lackalee 125 NG 1292
Lackford 54 TL 7970
Lacock 33 ST 9168
Ladbroke 50 SP 4158
Ladder Burn 118 NO 4185
Ladder Hills 117 NJ 2718
Laddingford 29 TQ 6948
Laddus Fens 63 TF 4701
Lade Bank 63 TF 3954
Ladhar Bheinn 111 NG 8204
Ladock 19 SW 8950
Ladybank (Fife) 103 NO 3009
Ladybank (Strath.) 93 NS 2102
Ladybower Resr. 70 SK 1888
Lady Isle 93 NS 2729
Ladykirk 97 NT 8847
Ladyland Moor 100 NS 3059
Ladylea Hill 118 NJ 3416
Ladysford 121 NJ 9060
Lady's Holm 141 HU 3709
Ladyside Height 96 NT 3647
Lael Forest 127 NH 1982
Lagars Geo 141 HU 4422
Lagavulin 98 NR 4045
Lagg (Island of Arran) 92 NR 9521
Lagg (Jura) 98 NR 5978
Laggan (Highld.) 115 NN 2997
Laggan (Highld.) 116 NN 6194
Laggan (Islay) 98 NR 2855
Laggan (Strath.) 86 NX 2582
Laggan Bay (Island of Mull) 105 NM 4440
Laggan Bay (Islay) 98 NR 2951
Laggan Deer Forest 105 NM 6221
Laggan Lodge 105 NM 6223
Laggan Point 98 NR 2755
Laggantalluch Head 86 NX 0836
Lagganulva 105 NM 4541
Laid 132 NC 4159
Laide 126 NG 8991
Laiken Forest 129 NH 9052
Laindon 38 TQ 6889
Lair 126 NH 0148
Lairg 128 NC 5806
Lairg Lodge 128 NC 5707
Lairg Station 128 NC 5803
Lairig a'Mhuic 107 NN 5749
Lairig Breisleich 107 NN 5641
Lairig Ghru 117 NH 9603
Lairig Leacach 106 NN 2972
Lair of Aldararie (mt.) 118 NO 3177
Laival a Tuath (mt.) 130 NB 0224
Lake 34 SU 1239
Lake Cottage 86 NX 0948
Lakenham 65 TG 2307
Lakenheath 54 TL 7182
Lakenheath Station 54 TL 7286
Lakenheath Warren 54 TL 7581
Lake of Menteith 101 NS 5699
Lakesend 63 TL 5196
Lakeside 77 SD 3787
Lake Vyrnwy 57 SH 9821
Laleham 36 TQ 0568
Laleston 41 SS 8779
Lamachan Hill 87 NX 4376
Lamahip (mt.) 119 NO 5592
Lamaload Resr. 70 SJ 9775
Lamarsh 54 TL 8935
Lamas 65 TG 2423
Lamba (is.) 143 HU 3881
Lamba Ness 143 HP 6715
Lamba Taing 141 HU 4326
Lamba Water 141 HU 3856
Lamberhurst 29 TQ 6735
Lamberton 97 NT 9657
Lamberton Beach 97 NT 9758
Lambeth 37 TQ 3078
Lambfell Moar 76 SC 2984
Lambgarth Head 141 HU 4550
Lamb Head 137 HY 6921
Lamb Hoga 143 HU 6088
Lambhoga Head 141 HU 4013
Lamb Holm 136 HY 4800
Lamblair Hill 90 NT 5701
Lambley (Northum.) 90 NY 6758
Lambley (Notts.) 61 SK 6245
Lambourn 34 SU 3278
Lambourn Downs 34 SU 3481
Lambourne End 37 TQ 4894
Lambrigg Fell 83 SD 5893
Lambs Green 28 TQ 2136
Lambston 42 SM 9016
Lamerton 20 SX 4476
Lamesley 84 NZ 2557
Lamford Hill 87 NX 5398
Lamh Dearg 108 NO 1163
Lamington (Highld.) 129 NH 7577
Lamington (Strath.) 95 NS 9730
Lamlash 92 NS 0231
Lamlash Bay 92 NS 0330
Lammer Law 103 NT 5261
Lammermuir 96 NT 7258
Lammermuir Hills 103 NT 5863
Lamonby 83 NY 4135
Lamorna 18 SW 4524
Lamorran 19 SW 8741
Lampeter 43 SN 5748
Lampeter-Velfrey 42 SN 1514
Lamphey 42 SN 0100
Lamplugh 82 NY 0820
Lamport 51 SP 7574
Lamyatt 25 ST 6535
Lana 20 SX 3496
Lanark 95 NS 8843
Lancaster 77 SD 4761
Lancaster Canal 77 SD 5041
Lanchester 84 NZ 1647
Landbeach 53 TL 4765
Landcross 22 SS 4524
Landerberry 119 NJ 7404
Landford 26 SU 2519
Landford Manor 26 SU 2620
Landimore 40 SS 4693
Landkey 23 SS 5931
Landore 40 SS 6595
Landrake 20 SX 3760
Landscove 21 SX 7766
Land's End (pt.) 18 SW 3425
Land's End (St. Just) Aerodrome 18 SW 3728
Landshipping 42 SN 0211
Landulph 20 SX 4261
Landwade 54 TL 6268
Landywood 60 SJ 9806
Laneast 20 SX 2283
Lane End 36 SU 8091
Lane Green 59 SJ 8802
Laneham 72 SK 8076
Lanercost Priory (ant.) 90 NY 5563
Laneshaw Bridge 78 SD 9240
Laneshaw Resr. 78 SD 9441
Langa (is.) 141 HU 3739
Langar 61 SK 7234
Langaton Point 135 ND 3579
Langay 124 NG 0181
Langbank 101 NS 3873
Langbar 78 SE 0951
Langcliffe 78 SD 8264
Lang Clodie Wick 142 HU 3088
Lang Craig 109 NO 7048
Langdale End 81 SE 9391
Langdale Fell 83 NY 6400
Langdale Pikes (mt.) 82 NY 2707
Langdon Beck 83 NY 8521
Langdon Common 83 NY 8532
Langdon Hills 38 TQ 6786
Langdyke 103 NO 3304
Langenhoe 39 TM 0018
Langford (Beds.) 52 TL 1841
Langford (Devon) 24 ST 0203
Langford (Essex) 38 TL 8408
Langford (Notts.) 72 SK 8258
Langford (Oxon.) 47 SP 2402
Langford Budville 24 ST 1122
Langford End 52 TL 1654
Langford Grounds 32 ST 3568
Langham (Essex) 54 TM 0233
Langham (Leic.) 62 SK 8411
Langham (Norf.) 64 TG 0041
Langham (Suff.) 54 TL 9769
Lang Head 142 HU 3070
Langho 77 SD 7034
Langholm 89 NY 3684
Langlee Crags 97 NT 9721
Langleeford 97 NT 9521
Langley (Berks.) 36 TQ 0078
Langley (Ches.) 69 SJ 9471
Langley (Essex) 53 TL 4435
Langley (Hants.) 27 SU 4400
Langley (Herts.) 37 TL 2122
Langley (Kent) 30 TQ 8051
Langley (Warw.) 50 SP 1962
Langley (W Susx) 27 SU 8029
Langley Burrell 33 ST 9275
Langley Hill 46 SP 0028
Langley Marsh 24 ST 0729
Langley Park 84 NZ 2144
Langley Street 65 TG 3601
Langness 76 SC 2966
Langney 29 TQ 6302
Langney Point 29 TQ 6401
Langold 71 SK 5887
Langore 20 SX 3086
Langport 25 ST 4226
Langrick 63 TF 2648
Langridge 33 ST 7369
Langrigg 82 NY 1645
Langrish 27 SU 7023
Langsett 70 SE 2100
Langsett Reservoir 70 SE 2000
Langshaw 96 NT 5139
Langskaill 138 HY 4342
Langstone 27 SU 7104
Langstone Harbour 27 SU 6901
Langstrothdale Chase (dist.) 78 SD 8879
Langthorne 84 SE 2491
Langthorpe 79 SE 3867
Langthwaite 84 NZ 0002
Langtoft (Humbs.) 81 TA 0166
Langtoft (Lincs.) 62 TF 1212
Langton (Durham) 84 NZ 1719
Langton (Lincs.) 73 TF 2368
Langton (Lincs.) 73 TF 3970
Langton (N Yorks.) 80 SE 7967
Langton by Wragby 73 TF 1476
Langton Green 29 TQ 5439
Langton Herring 25 SY 6182
Langton Matravers 26 SY 9978
Langtree 22 SS 4415
Langwathby 83 NY 5733
Langwell Forest 135 ND 0325
Langwell House 135 ND 1122
Langwell Lodge 127 NC 1702
Langwell Water 135 ND 0324
Langwood Fen 53 TL 4385
Langworth 72 TF 0676
Lanherne or Vale of Mawgan 19 SW 8964
Lanhydrock House 19 SX 0863
Lanivet 19 SX 0364
Lank Rigg 82 NY 0912
Lanlivery 19 SX 0759
Lanlluest 48 SO 1874
Lanner 18 SW 7139
Lanreath 19 SX 1756
Lanrick Castle 101 NN 6803
Lansallos 19 SX 1751
Lanton (Borders) 96 NT 6221
Lanton (Northum.) 97 NT 9231
Lanyar Taing 143 HU 3893
Lapford 23 SS 7308
Laphroaig 98 NR 3845
Lapley 59 SJ 8713
Lapworth 50 SP 1671
Larachbeg 105 NM 0940
Larbert 102 NS 8582
Larg Hill 86 NX 4175
Largie 121 NJ 6131
Largie Castle 92 NR 7046
Largiemore 100 NR 9486
Largo Bay 103 NO 4201
Largo Law 103 NO 4204
Largoward 103 NO 4607
Largs 100 NS 2058
Largs Bay 100 NS 1959
Largybeg 92 NS 0423
Largybeg Point 92 NS 0523
Largymore 92 NS 0424
Larig Hill 117 NJ 0840
Larkfield 100 NS 2376
Larkhall 94 NS 7651
Larkhill 34 SU 1243
Larling 54 TL 9889
Larriston 90 NY 5494
Larriston Fells 90 NY 5792
Lartington 84 NZ 0117
Lary 118 NJ 3300
Lasham 35 SU 6742
Lashy Sound 138 HY 5938
Lassodie 102 NT 1292
Lastingham 80 SE 7290
Latchingdon 38 TL 8800
Latchley 20 SX 4173
Lately Common 69 SJ 6797
Lathbury 52 SP 8745
Latheron 135 ND 1933
Latheronwheel 135 ND 1932
Latheronwheel House 135 ND 1832
Lathones 103 NO 4708
Latimer 36 TQ 0099
Latrigg 82 NY 2824
Latteridge 33 ST 6684
Lattiford 25 ST 6926
Latton 46 SU 0995
Lauchintilly 119 NJ 7412
Laudale House 111 NM 7459
Lauder 96 NT 5347
Lauder Common 96 NT 5046
Lauderdale 96 NT 5746
Laugharne 43 SN 3011
Laugharne Sands 43 SN 3006
Laughterton 72 SK 8375
Laughton (E Susx) 29 TQ 4913
Laughton (Leic.) 51 SP 6589
Laughton (Lincs.) 72 SK 8497
Laughton en le Morthen 71 SK 5188
Launcells 22 SS 2405
Launceston 20 SX 3384
Launde Abbey 61 SK 7904
Launton 47 SP 6022
Laurencekirk 109 NO 7171
Laurieston 88 NX 6864
Laurieston Forest 88 NX 6564
Lauriston Castle 109 NO 7666
Lavan Sands 67 SH 6375
Lavant 27 SU 8608
Lavendon 52 SP 9153
Lavenham 54 TL 9149
Laverhay 89 NY 1498
Lavernock Point 41 ST 1868
Laverstock 26 SU 1530
Laverstoke 35 SU 4948
Laverton (Glos.) 46 SP 0735
Laverton (N Yorks.) 79 SE 2273
Laverton (Somer.) 33 ST 7753
Law 95 NS 8252
Lawers (Tays.) 107 NN 6739
Lawers (Tays.) 107 NN 7923
Lawers Burn 107 NN 6742
Lawford 55 TM 0830
Lawhitton 20 SX 3582
Lawkland 78 SD 7766
Law Kneis 89 NT 2912
Lawley 59 SJ 6608
Lawnhead 59 SJ 8224
Lawrenny 42 SN 0107
Lawshall 54 TL 8654
Lawton 45 SO 4459
Laxa Burn 143 HU 4988
Laxadale Lochs 125 NB 1801
Laxay 131 NB 3321
Laxdale 131 NB 4234
Laxey 76 SC 4384
Laxey Bay 76 SC 4481
Laxey Head 76 SC 4483
Laxfield 55 TM 2972
Laxfirth (Shetld.) 141 HU 4346
Lax Firth (Shetld.) 141 HU 4447
Laxford Bridge 132 NC 2347
Laxo 141 HU 4463
Laxobigging 143 HU 4173
Laxton (Humbs.) 74 SE 7825
Laxton (Northants.) 62 SP 9496
Laxton (Notts.) 72 SK 7266
Layaval (mt.) 112 NF 7723
Laycock 78 SE 0340
Layer Breton 38 TL 9417
Layer de la Haye 39 TL 9620
Layham 54 TM 0340
Laytham 74 SE 7439
Lazenby 85 NZ 5719
Lazonby 83 NY 5439
Lea (Derby.) 71 SK 3357
Lea (Here. and Worc.) 46 SO 6521
Lea (Lincs.) 72 SK 8286
Lea (Shrops.) 58 SJ 4108
Lea (Shrops.) 48 SO 3589
Lea (Wilts.) 34 ST 9586
Leacann Doire Bainneir (mt.) 115 NN 2994
Leac Dhonn 126 NH 0199
Leac Eskadale 125 NG 2399
Leachie Hill 119 NO 7385
Leachkin 128 NH 6344
Leac nam Faoileann 123 NG 4214
Leac Shoilleir 111 NM 6165
Leac Tressirnish 123 NG 5257
Leadburn 95 NT 2355
Leadenham 62 SK 9452
Leaden Roding 38 TL 5913
Leader Water 96 NT 5151
Leadgate (Cumbr.) 83 NY 7043
Leadgate (Durham) 84 NZ 1251
Leadhills 88 NS 8814
Leafield 47 SP 3115
Lea Green 69 SJ 6561
Leake Common Side 63 TF 3952
Leake Hurn's End 63 TF 4248
Lealholm 80 NZ 7607
Lealholm Moor 80 NZ 7509
Lealt (Island of Skye) 123 NG 5060
Lealt (Jura) 99 NR 6690
Lealt Burn 99 NR 6691
Lealt River 123 NG 4960
Lea Marston 60 SP 2093
Leamington Hastings 51 SP 4467
Leanachan Forest 115 NN 1977
Leanoch Burn 129 NJ 1851
Leap Hill (Borders) 89 NT 5001
Leap Hill (Northum.) 90 NT 7207
Leap Moor 100 NS 2269
Leargybreck 98 NR 5371
Learin 98 NR 3548
Learmouth 97 NT 8537
Leasgill 77 SD 4984
Leasingham 62 TF 0548
Leask 121 NK 0232
Lea Taing (pt.) 137 HY 5410
Leatherhead 28 TQ 1656
Leathley 79 SE 2346
Leaton 58 SJ 4618
Lea Town 77 SD 4930
Leaveland 31 TQ 9854
Leavening 80 SE 7863
Leavesden Airport 36 TL 0900
Leaves Green 37 TQ 4162
Lea Yeat 78 SD 7587
Lebberston 81 TA 0882
Lechlade 47 SU 2199
Lecht Road 117 NJ 2413
Leck Beck 77 SD 6376
Leck Fell 77 SD 6678
Leckford 26 SU 3737
Leckfurin 133 NC 7059
Leckgruinart 98 NR 2769
Leckhampstead (Berks.) 34 SU 4375
Leckhampstead (Bucks.) 51 SP 7237
Leckhampton 46 SO 9419
Leckie (ant.) 101 NS 6894
Leckmelm 127 NH 1690
Leckwith 41 ST 1574
Leconfield 74 TA 0143
Leconfield Aerodrome 74 TA 0343
Ledaig 106 NM 9037
Ledaig Point 106 NM 9034
Ledbeg River 132 NC 2413
Ledburn 36 SP 9022
Ledbury 49 SO 7037
Ledcharrie 107 NN 5027
Ledgemoor 45 SO 4150
Ledgowan Forest 127 NH 1256
Ledicot 48 SO 4162
Ledmore 132 NC 2412
Ledsham (Ches.) 68 SJ 3574
Ledsham (W Yorks.) 79 SE 4529
Ledston 79 SE 4328
Ledwell 47 SP 4128
Lee (Devon) 22 SS 4846
Lee (Hants.) 26 SU 3517
Lee (Island of Mull) 105 NM 4022
Lee (Lancs.) 77 SD 5655
Lee (Shrops.) 58 SJ 4032
Leebotten 141 HU 4324
Leebotwood 59 SO 4798
Lee Brockhurst 59 SJ 5426
Leece 76 SD 2469
Lee Clump 36 SP 9004
Leeds (Kent) 30 TQ 8253
Leeds (W Yorks.) 79 SE 3034
Leeds and Bradford Airport 79 SE 2241
Leeds and Liverpool Canal 78 SE 1338
Leedstown 18 SW 6034
Lee Fell 77 SD 5657
Leek 60 SJ 9856
Leek Wootton 50 SP 2868
Lee Mill 21 SX 5955
Leeming 84 SE 2989
Leeming Bar 84 SE 2889
Lee Moor 21 SX 5862
Lee-on-the-Solent 27 SU 5600
Lee Pen 96 NT 3238
Lees (Derby.) 60 SK 2637
Lees (Gtr Mches) 70 SD 9504
Lees Scar Lighthouse 82 NY 0952
Leeswood 68 SJ 2759
Lee, The 36 SP 8904
Leet Water 97 NT 8043
Leez Lodge Lakes 38 TL 7118
Legbourne 73 TF 3684
Legerwood 96 NT 5843
Legsby 73 TF 1385
Leicester 61 SK 5904
Leicester East Aerodrome 61 SK 6602
Leicester Forest East 61 SK 5203
Leigh (Dorset) 25 ST 6108
Leigh (Gtr Mches) 69 SJ 6899
Leigh (Here. and Worc.) 49 SO 7853
Leigh (Kent) 29 TQ 5546
Leigh (Shrops.) 58 SJ 3303
Leigh (Surrey) 28 TQ 2246
Leigh (Wilts.) 34 SU 0692
Leigh Beck 38 TQ 8182
Leigh Common 25 ST 7329
Leigh Delamere 33 ST 8879
Leigh Green 30 TQ 8933
Leigh-on-Sea 38 TQ 8385
Leigh Sinton 49 SO 7750
Leighterton 33 ST 8290
Leigh, The 46 SO 8725
Leighton (Powys) 58 SJ 2405
Leighton (Shrops.) 59 SJ 6105
Leighton (Somer.) 33 ST 7043
Leighton Bromswold 52 TL 1175
Leighton Buzzard 52 SP 9225
Leighton Resr. 78 SE 1578
Leigh upon Mendip 33 ST 6847
Leigh Woods 33 ST 5572
Leim 92 NR 6346
Leinthall Earls 48 SO 4467
Leinthall Starkes 48 SO 4369
Leintwardine 48 SO 4074
Leire 51 SP 5290
Leirinmore 133 NC 4267
Leishmore 115 NH 3940
Leiston 55 TM 4462
Leiston Abbey (ant.) 55 TM 4464
Leitfie 108 NO 2545
Leith 103 NT 2676
Leithen Water 96 NT 3043
Leith Hall 121 NJ 5429
Leith Hill 28 TQ 1342
Leitholm 97 NT 7944
Leithope Forest 90 NT 7408
Lelant 18 SW 5437
Lelley 75 TA 2032
Lem Hill 49 SO 7274
Lemmington Hall 91 NU 1211
Lempitlaw 97 NT 7832
Lemreway 131 NB 3811
Lendalfoot 86 NX 1390
Lendrick 101 NN 5506
Lendrick Hill 102 NO 0103
Lenham 30 TQ 8952
Lenham Heath 30 TQ 9249
Lenie 116 NH 5127
Lennel 97 NT 8540
Lennoxtown 101 NS 6277
Lenton 62 TF 0230
Lentram House 128 NH 5745
Lenwade 65 TG 0918
Leny House 101 NN 6108
Lenzie 101 NS 6571
Leoch 109 NO 3636
Leochel Cushnie 119 NJ 5210
Leominster 45 SO 4959
Leonach Burn 117 NH 9236
Leonard Stanley 46 SO 8003
Leosaval (mt.) 130 NB 0309
Lepe 27 SZ 4498
Leperstone Resr. 100 NS 3571
Lephin 122 NG 1749
Lephinmore 100 NR 9892
Leppington 80 SE 7661
Lepton 70 SE 2015
Lerryn 19 SX 1356
Lerwick (Shetld.) 141 HU 4741
Ler Wick (Yell) 143 HU 4492
Lesbury 91 NU 2311
Leslie (Fife) 103 NO 2401
Leslie (Grampn.) 121 NJ 5924
Lesmahagow 95 NS 8139
Lesnewth 20 SX 1390
Lessendrum 121 NJ 5741
Lessingham 65 TG 3928
Lessonhall 82 NY 2250
Leswalt 86 NX 0263
Letchmore Heath 37 TQ 1597
Letchworth 52 TL 2132
Letcombe Bassett 34 SU 3785
Letcombe Regis 34 SU 3786
Letham (Fife) 103 NO 3014
Letham (Tays.) 109 NO 5248
Letham Grange 109 NO 6245
Lethenty 121 NJ 8041
Letheringham 55 TM 2757
Letheringsett 64 TG 0638
Letocetum (ant.) 60 SK 0906
Lettaford 21 SX 7084
Letterewe 126 NG 9571
Letterewe Forest 126 NG 9772
Letterfearn 114 NG 8823
Lettermore 105 NM 4948
Letters 127 NH 1687
Letterston 42 SM 9429
Lettoch (Grampn.) 117 NJ 0932
Lettoch (Highld.) 117 NJ 0219
Letton (Here. and Worc.) 45 SO 3346
Letton (Here. and Worc.) 48 SO 3770
Letton Hall 64 TF 9705
Letton Lake 45 SO 3547
Letty Green 37 TL 2810
Letwell 71 SK 5587
Leuchar Burn 119 NJ 7804
Leuchars 109 NO 4521
Leuchars Airport 109 NO 4620
Leuchars House 120 NJ 2564
Leuchars Junction Station 109 NO 4420
Leum Uilleim 106 NN 3364
Leurbost 131 NB 3725
Levedale 59 SJ 8916
Leven (Fife) 103 NO 3700
Leven (Humbs.) 75 TA 1045
Levenish (is.) 124 NF 1396
Levens 77 SD 4886
Levenshulme 69 SJ 8794
Levenwick 141 HU 4021
Levenwick Ness 141 HU 4121
Leverburgh 124 NG 0186
Leverington 63 TF 4411
Levers Water 82 SD 2799
Leverton 63 TF 3947
Levington 55 TM 2339

Levisham 80 SE 8390
Levishie Forest 115 NH 3919
Lew 47 SP 3206
Lewannick 20 SX 2780
Lewdown 20 SX 4486
Lewes 29 TQ 4110
Leweston 42 SM 9422
Lewisham 37 TQ 3674
Lewiston 116 NH 5029
Lewknor 36 SU 7197
Leworthy 23 SS 6638
Lews Castle 131 NB 4133
Lewtrenchard 20 SX 4586
Ley (Corn.) 19 SX 1766
Ley (Grampn.) 119 NJ 5312
Leybourne 30 TQ 6858
Leyburn 84 SE 1190
Leycett 59 SJ 7846
Leyland 77 SD 5421
Leylodge 119 NJ 7713
Leys (Grampn.) 121 NK 0052
Leys (Tays.) 108 NO 2537
Leys Castle 128 NH 6841
Leysdown on Sea 31 TR 0370
Leysmill 109 NO 6047
Leys of Cossans 109 NO 3749
Leysters 48 SO 5563
Leyton 37 TQ 3886
Lezant 20 SX 3378
Lhanbryde 120 NJ 2761
Lhen, The 76 NX 3801
Liathach (mt.) 126 NG 9257
Liath Eilean 100 NR 8883
Libbers Hill 143 HP 5813
Libberton 95 NS 9943
Liberton 103 NT 2769
Lichfield 60 SK 1209
Lickey 50 SO 9975
Lickey End 50 SO 9772
Lickfold 28 SU 9225
Licklyhead Castle 121 NJ 6223
Liddel 136 ND 4683
Liddel Water 89 NY 4478
Liddesdale (Dumf. and Galwy.) 89 NY 4787
Liddesdale (Highld.) 111 NM 7859
Liddington 34 SU 2081
Liddington Castle (ant.) 34 SU 2079
Lidgate 54 TL 7258
Lidlington 52 SP 9939
Lidstone 47 SP 3524
Liernish 124 NF 8758
Lieurary (dist.) 135 ND 0762
Liff 108 NO 3332
Lifton 20 SX 3885
Ligger or Perran Bay 18 SW 7256
Lighthazles 70 SE 0220
Lighthorne 50 SP 3355
Lightwater 36 SU 9262
Lightwood 59 SJ 9041
Lightwood Green 58 SJ 3840
Likisto 125 NG 1292
Lilbourne 51 SP 5677
Lilburn Tower 97 NU 0224
Lilford Hall (ant.) 52 TL 0284
Lilleshall 59 SJ 7315
Lilley 52 TL 1226
Lilliesleaf 96 NT 5325
Lillingstone Dayrell 51 SP 7039
Lillingstone Lovell 51 SP 7140
Lillington 25 ST 6212
Lilly Loch 101 NS 8267
Lilstock 32 ST 1644
Limbrick 69 SD 6016
Limefield 69 SD 8012
Limekilnburn 94 NS 7050
Limekilns 102 NT 0783
Limerigg 102 NS 8570
Limington 25 ST 5422
Limmerhaugh 94 NS 6126
Limpenhoe 65 TG 3903
Limpley Stoke 33 ST 7760
Limpsfield 29 TQ 4152
Linacre Resrs 71 SK 3372
Linby 61 SK 5350
Linchmere 27 SU 8630
Lincluden College (ant.) 88 NX 9678
Lincoln 72 SK 9771
Lincomb 49 SO 8268
Lincombe 21 SX 7458
Lindale 77 SD 4180
Lindal in Furness 76 SD 2575
Lindean 96 NT 4931
Lindfield 29 TQ 3425
Lindford 27 SU 8136
Lindisfarne (ant.) 97 NU 1343
Lindley Wood Resr 78 SE 2149
Lindores 108 NO 2616
Lindores Loch 108 NO 2616
Lindridge 49 SO 6769
Lindsell 54 TL 6427
Lindsey 54 TL 9744
Linfern Lock 86 NX 3697
Linford (Essex) 38 TQ 6779
Linford (Hants.) 26 SU 1707
Linga (Hildasay) (is.) 141 HU 3639
Linga (Shetld.) (is.) 141 HU 3563
Linga (Shetld.) (is.) 143 HU 4673
Linga (Yell) (is.) 143 HU 5598
Lingague 76 SC 2172
Linga Holm 137 HY 6127
Lingarabay Island 125 NG 0684
Linga Sound (Stronsay) 137 HY 6228
Linga Sound (Whalsay) 141 HU 5464
Lingay (Harris, W Isles) 124 NG 0178
Lingay (North Uist) 124 NF 8778
Lingay (South Uist) 112 NF 7511
Lingay (W Isles) 112 NL 6089
Lingdale 85 NZ 6716
Lingen 48 SO 3667
Lingfield 29 TQ 3943
Linglie Hill 96 NT 4530
Lingmell 82 NY 2007
Ling Ness 141 HU 4954
Lingwood 65 TG 3609
Linhouse Water 102 NT 0662
Liniclate 124 NF 7949
Linicro 123 NG 3967
Linkenholt 34 SU 3657
Linkinhorne 20 SX 3173
Linklater 136 ND 4587
Linklet Bay 139 HY 7754
Linksness (Hoy, Shetld.) 136 HY 2403
Linksness (Orkney) 137 HY 5210
Links Ness (Stronsay) 137 HY 6129
Linktown 103 NT 2790
Linley 58 SO 3593
Linley Green 49 SO 6953
Linley Hill 58 SO 3594
Linlithgow 102 NS 9977
Linlithgow Bridge 102 NS 9877
Linney 42 SR 8996
Linney Head 42 SR 8896
Linn of Dee 117 NO 0589
Linshader (Isle of Lewis) 131 NB 2032
Linshiels 90 NT 8906
Linsidemore 128 NH 5499
Linslade 52 SP 9125
Linstead Parva 55 TM 3377
Linstock 89 NY 4258
Linthwaite 70 SE 0913
Lintlaw 97 NT 8258
Lintmill 121 NJ 5165
Linton (Borders) 96 NT 7726
Linton (Cambs.) 53 TL 5646
Linton (Derby.) 60 SK 2716
Linton (Here. and Worc.) 46 SO 6625
Linton (Kent) 29 TQ 7549
Linton (N Yorks.) 78 SD 9962
Linton Hill 97 NT 7827
Linton-on-Ouse 79 SE 4960
Linwood (Hants.) 26 SU 1809
Linwood (Lincs.) 73 TF 1186
Linwood (Strath.) 101 NS 4464
Lionel 131 NB 5363
Liphook 27 SU 8431
Liscombe 23 SS 8732
Lisgear Mhór 130 HW 8133
Liskeard 19 SX 2564
Lismore 105 NM 8441
Liss 27 SU 7727
Lisset 81 TA 1458
Liss Forest 27 SU 7929
Lissington 73 TF 1083
Lisvane 41 ST 1983
Litcham 64 TF 8817
Litchborough 51 SP 6354
Litchfield 35 SU 4553
Litherland 68 SJ 3397
Litlington (Cambs.) 53 TL 3142
Litlington (E Susx) 29 TQ 5201
Little Abington 53 TL 5349
Little Addington 52 SP 9573
Little Alne 50 SP 1361
Little Aston 60 SK 0900
Little Atherfield 27 SZ 4680
Little Ayre (Hoy, Orkney) 136 ND 3091
Little-ayre (Muckle Roe) 141 HU 3262
Little Ayton 85 NZ 5710
Little Baddow 38 TL 7807
Little Badminton 33 ST 8084
Little Ballinluig 108 NN 9152
Little Bardfield 54 TL 6530
Little Barford 52 TL 1857
Little Barningham 65 TG 1333
Little Barrington 47 SP 2012
Little Barugh 80 SE 7579
Little Bedwyn 34 SU 2966
Little Bentley 55 TM 1125
Little Berkhamsted 37 TL 2907
Little Bernera (is.) 131 NB 1441
Little Billing 51 SP 8061
Little Birch 45 SO 5031
Little Blakenham 55 TM 1048
Littleborough (Gtr Mches) 69 SD 9316
Littleborough (Notts.) 72 SK 8282
Littlebourne 31 TR 2057
Little Bowden 51 SP 7487
Little Bradley 54 TL 6852
Little Brampton 48 SO 3681
Little Brechin 109 NO 5862
Littlebredy 25 SY 5888
Little Brickhill 52 SP 9032
Little Brington 51 SP 6663
Little Bromley 55 TM 0928
Little Budworth 69 SJ 5965
Little Burstead 38 TQ 6691
Littlebury 53 TL 5139
Littlebury Green 53 TL 4938
Little Bytham 62 TF 0118
Little Carlton 73 TF 3985
Little Casterton 62 TF 0109
Little Cawthorpe 73 TF 3583
Little Chalfont 36 SU 9997
Little Chart 30 TQ 9245
Little Chesterford 53 TL 5141
Little Cheverell 34 ST 9853
Little Chishill 53 TL 4237
Little Clacton 39 TM 1618
Little Colonsay (is.) 104 NM 3736
Little Comberton 50 SO 9643
Little Common 29 TQ 7107
Little Compton 47 SP 2530
Littlecote (ant.) 34 SU 3070
Little Cowarne 45 SO 6051
Little Coxwell 47 SU 2893
Little Cressingham 64 TF 8600
Little Cumbrae Island 93 NS 1451
Little Dalby 61 SK 7714
Littledale 77 SD 5761
Little Dart River 23 SS 7814
Littledean 46 SO 6713
Little Dens 121 NK 0744
Little Dewchurch 45 SO 5231
Little Don or The Porter River 71 SK 2399
Little Downham 53 TL 5284
Little Dunham 64 TF 8613
Little Dunkeld 108 NO 0242
Little Dunmow 38 TL 6521
Little Easton 38 TL 6023
Little Eaton 60 SK 3641
Little Ellingham 64 TM 0099
Little End 37 TL 5400
Little Eversden 53 TL 3752
Little Fakenham 54 TL 9076
Little Faringdon 47 SP 2201
Little Fen 53 TL 5868
Little Fenton 79 SE 5135
Littleferry 129 NH 8095
Little Fransham 64 TF 9011
Little Gaddesden 36 SP 9913
Little Garway 45 SO 4424
Little Gidding 52 TL 1382
Little Glemham 55 TM 3458
Little Gransden 53 TL 2755
Little Gruinard 126 NG 9489
Little Gruinard River 126 NG 9486
Little Hadham 37 TL 4422
Little Haldon (dist.) 21 SX 9176
Little Hallingbury 37 TL 5017
Littleham (Devon) 22 SS 4323
Littleham (Devon) 24 SY 0281
Little Hampden 36 SP 8603
Littlehampton 28 TQ 0202
Little Harrowden 52 SP 8771
Little Hartmidden (mt.) 94 NS 6032
Little Haseley 36 SP 6400
Little Hautbois 65 TG 2521
Little Haven 42 SM 8513
Little Hay 60 SK 1202
Little Haywood 60 SK 0021
Littlehempston 21 SX 8162
Little Hereford 48 SO 5568
Little Hill 48 SO 1267
Little Holm 143 HU 4086
Little Horkesley 54 TL 9531
Little Horsted 29 TQ 4718
Little Horwood 51 SP 7930
Little Houghton (Northants.) 51 SP 8059
Littlehoughton (Northum.) 91 NU 2316
Little Hucklow 70 SK 1678
Little Hulton 69 SD 7103
Little John's Haven 119 NO 8574
Little Kingshill 36 SU 8999
Little Langdale 82 NY 3103
Little Langford 26 SU 0436
Little Laver 37 TL 5409
Little Leigh 69 SJ 6175
Little Leighs 38 TL 7116
Little Lever 69 SD 7507
Little Loch Broom 126 NH 0292
Little Loch Roag 131 NB 1327
Little London (E Susx) 29 TQ 5420
Little London (Hants.) 34 SU 3749
Little London (Hants.) 36 SU 6259
Little London (Lincs.) 63 TF 2321
Little Longstone 70 SK 1871
Little Lynturk 119 NJ 5712
Little Malvern 49 SO 7741
Little Maplestead 54 TL 8233
Little Marcle 49 SO 6736
Little Marlow 36 SU 8788
Little Massingham 64 TF 7924
Little Melton 65 TG 1506
Little Mill (Gwent) 45 SO 3102
Littlemill (Highld.) 129 NH 9150
Littlemill (Strath.) 93 NS 4515
Little Milton 36 SP 6100
Little Minch, The 125 NG 0560
Little Minch, The (chan.) 122 NG 0661
Little Missenden 36 SU 9298
Littlemore 47 SP 5302
Little Ness (I. of M.) 76 SC 3673
Little Ness (Shrops.) 58 SJ 4019
Little Newcastle 42 SM 9829
Little Newsham 84 NZ 1217
Little Oakley (Essex) 55 TM 2229
Little Oakley (Northants.) 52 SP 8985
Little Ormes Head 67 SH 8182
Little Orton 82 NY 3555
Little Ouse River 54 TL 8387
Littleover 60 SK 3234
Little Paxton 52 TL 1862
Little Petherick 19 SW 9172
Little Pitlurg 121 NJ 4245
Little Plumstead 65 TG 3112
Littleport 53 TL 5686
Little Rack Wick 136 ND 2392
Little Rahane 100 NS 2386
Little Raveley 53 TL 2579
Little Ribston 79 SE 3853
Little Rissington 47 SP 1819
Little River 135 ND 1548
Little Roe (is.) 143 HU 4079
Little Ross 87 NX 6543
Little Ryburgh 64 TF 9628
Little Ryle 91 NU 0211
Little Salkeld 83 NY 5636
Little Sampford 54 TL 6533
Little Saxham 54 TL 7963
Little Scatwell 127 NH 3756
Little Shelford 53 TL 4551
Little Shillay 124 NF 8790
Little Skerry 143 HU 6371
Little Smeaton 71 SE 5219
Little Snoring 64 TF 9532
Little Somerford 34 ST 9684
Little Stainton 85 NZ 3420
Little Stanney 68 SJ 4173
Little Staughton 52 TL 1062
Little Steeping 73 TF 4362
Littlestone-on-Sea 31 TR 0824
Little Stonham 55 TM 1160
Little Stretton (Leic.) 61 SK 6600
Little Stretton (Shrops.) 48 SO 4491
Little Strickland 83 NY 5619
Little Stukeley 52 TL 2075
Little Tew 47 SP 3828
Little Thetford 53 TL 5376
Littlethorpe 79 SE 3269
Little Thurrock 30 TQ 6477
Littleton (Ches.) 68 SJ 4366
Littleton (Hants.) 27 SU 4532
Littleton (Somer.) 25 ST 4830
Littleton (Surrey) 36 TQ 0768
Littleton (Tays.) 108 NO 2633
Littleton Down 34 ST 9751
Littleton Drew 33 ST 8280
Littleton-on-Severn 33 ST 5990
Littleton Pannell 34 ST 9954
Little Torrington 22 SS 4816
Little Totham 38 TL 8812
Little Town (Cumbr.) 82 NY 2319
Littletown (Durham) 84 NZ 3343
Little Wakering 38 TQ 9388
Little Walden 53 TL 5441
Little Waldingfield 54 TL 9245
Little Walsingham 64 TF 9336
Little Waltham 38 TL 7012
Little Warley 38 TQ 6090
Little Water 121 NJ 8441
Little Weighton 74 SE 9833
Little Welnetham 54 TL 8859
Little Wenlock 59 SJ 6406
Little Whernside 78 SE 0277
Little Whittingham Green 55 TM 2877
Littlewick Green 36 SU 8379
Little Wilbraham 53 TL 5458
Little Witley 49 SO 7863
Little Wittenham 47 SU 5693
Little Wolford 47 SP 2635
Littleworth (Here. and Worc.) 49 SO 8850
Littleworth (Oxon.) 47 SU 3197
Littleworth (Staffs.) 60 SK 0111
Little Wyrley 60 SK 0105
Little Wyvis (mt.) 128 NH 4364
Little Yeldham 54 TL 7739
Litton (Derby.) 70 SK 1674
Litton (N Yorks.) 78 SD 9074
Litton (Somer.) 33 ST 5954
Litton Cheney 25 SY 5490
Littondale 78 SD 9172
Liundale 98 NR 5478
Liuthaid (mt.) 131 NB 1713
Liverpool 68 SJ 3591
Liverpool Airport 68 SJ 4183
Liverpool Bay 68 SJ 1599
Liverpool Street Station 37 TQ 3381
Liversedge 78 SE 2024
Liverton 85 NZ 7115
Livingston 102 NT 0568
Livingston Village 102 NT 0366
Lixwm 68 SJ 1671
Lizard 18 SW 6912
Lizard Point 18 SW 6911
Llanaber 56 SH 6018
Llanaelhaearn 66 SH 3844
Llanafan 57 SN 6872
Llanafan-fechan 44 SN 9650
Llanallgo 66 SH 5085
Llanarmon 66 SH 4239
Llanarmon Dyffryn Ceiriog 58 SJ 1532
Llanarmon-yn-Ial 58 SJ 1856
Llanarth (Dyfed) 43 SN 4257
Llanarth (Gwent) 45 SO 3711
Llanarthney 43 SN 5320
Llanasa 67 SJ 1081
Llanbabo 66 SH 3786
Llanbadarn Fawr 56 SN 6080
Llanbadarn Fynydd 57 SO 0977
Llanbadarn-y-garreg 44 SO 1148
Llanbadrig 66 SH 3794
Llanbeder 32 ST 3890
Llanbedr (Gwyn.) 56 SH 5826
Llanbedr (Powys) 44 SO 1346
Llanbedr (Powys) 45 SO 2320
Llanbedr-Dyffryn-Clwyd 68 SJ 1459
Llanbedrgoch 66 SH 5180
Llanbedr Hill 44 SO 1348
Llanbedrog 66 SH 3231
Llanbedr-y-cennin 67 SH 7569
Llanberis 66 SH 5760
Llanbister 57 SO 1073
Llanbister Road Station 48 SO 1771
Llanblethian 41 SS 9873
Llanboidy 43 SN 2123
Llanbradach 41 ST 1490
Llanbrynmair 57 SH 9002
Llancarfan 41 ST 0570
Llancayo 45 SO 3603
Llancynfelyn 57 SN 6492
Llandaff 41 ST 1578
Llandanwg 56 SH 5728
Llandawke 43 SN 2811
Llanddaniel Fab 66 SH 4970
Llanddarog 43 SN 5016
Llanddeiniol 56 SN 5672
Llanddeiniolen 66 SH 5465
Llandderfel 67 SH 9837
Llanddeusant (Dyfed) 41 SN 7724
Llanddeusant (Gwyn.) 66 SH 3485
Llanddew 41 SO 0530
Llanddewi 40 SS 4689
Llanddewi Brefi 43 SN 6655
Llanddewi'r Cwm 44 SO 0348
Llanddewi Rhydderch 45 SO 3412
Llanddewi Velfrey 42 SN 1417
Llanddewi Ystradenni 57 SO 1068
Llanddoged 67 SH 8063
Llanddona 66 SH 5779
Llanddowror 43 SN 2514
Llanddulas 67 SH 9078
Llanddwyn Island 66 SH 3862
Llanddyfnan 66 SH 5078
Llandefaelog 43 SN 4111
Llandefaelog Fach 41 SO 0332
Llandefaelog-tre'r-graig 41 SO 1230
Llandefalle 41 SO 1135
Llandefalle Hill 44 SO 0637
Llandegai 66 SH 5970
Llandegfan 66 SH 5674
Llandegfedd Resr. 45 ST 3299
Llandegla 58 SJ 1952
Llandegley 48 SO 1363
Llandegley Rhos 44 SO 1360
Llandegveth 45 ST 3395
Llandeilo 43 SN 6322
Llandeilo Graban 44 SO 0944
Llandeilo Hill 44 SO 0946
Llandeilo'r Fan 41 SN 8934
Llandeloy 42 SM 8526
Llandenny 45 SO 4104
Llandevenny 32 ST 4186
Llandinabo 45 SO 5128
Llandinam 57 SO 0288
Llandissilio 42 SN 1221
Llandogo 45 SO 5204
Llandough (S Glam.) 41 SS 9972
Llandough (S Glam.) 41 ST 1673
Llandovery 41 SN 7634
Llandow 41 SS 9473
Llandre (Dyfed) 57 SN 6286
Llandre (Dyfed) 43 SN 6641
Llandrillo 67 SJ 0337
Llandrillo-yn-Rhos 67 SH 8380
Llandrindod Wells 57 SO 0561
Llandrinio 58 SJ 2917
Llandudno 67 SH 7782
Llandudno Junction 67 SH 7977
Llandwrog 66 SH 4556
Llandybie 43 SN 6215
Llandyfan 43 SN 6417
Llandyfriog 43 SN 3241
Llandyfrydog 66 SH 4485
Llandygwydd 43 SN 2443
Llandyrnog 67 SJ 1064
Llandyssil 58 SO 1995
Llandysul 43 SN 4140
Llanegryn 56 SH 5905
Llanegwad 43 SN 5121
Llanelian-yn-Rhos 67 SH 8376
Llanelidan 67 SJ 1050
Llanelieu 41 SO 1834
Llanellen 45 SO 3010
Llanelli (Dyfed) 40 SN 5000
Llanelltyd 57 SH 7119
Llanelly (Gwent) 45 SO 2314
Llanelwedd 44 SO 0451
Llanenddwyn 56 SH 5823
Llanengan 56 SH 2927
Llanerchymedd 66 SH 4183
Llanerfyl 57 SJ 0309
Llanfachraeth 66 SH 3182
Llanfachreth 57 SH 7522
Llanfaelog 66 SH 3373
Llanfaes 66 SH 6077
Llanfaethlu 66 SH 3186
Llanfaglan 66 SH 4760
Llanfair 66 SH 5729
Llanfair Caereinion 57 SJ 1006
Llanfair Clydogau 43 SN 6251
Llanfair Dyffryn Clwyd 58 SJ 1355
Llanfairfechan 67 SH 6874
Llanfair-green 45 SO 3919
Llanfair-Nant-Gwyn 42 SN 1637
Llanfairpwllgwyngyll 66 SH 5371
Llanfair Talhaiarn 67 SH 9269
Llanfair Waterdine 48 SO 2476
Llanfairynghornwy 66 SH 3290
Llanfair-yn-Neubwll 66 SH 3077
Llanfallteg 42 SN 1520
Llanfallteg West 42 SN 1519
Llanfaredd 44 SO 0651
Llanfechain 58 SJ 1820
Llanfechell 66 SH 3691
Llanfendigaid 56 SH 5605
Llanferres 68 SJ 1860
Llanfflewyn 66 SH 3689
Llanfihangel ar-Arth 43 SN 4539
Llanfihangel Crucorney 45 SO 3220
Llanfihangel Glyn Myfyr 67 SH 9849
Llanfihangel Nant Bran 41 SN 9434
Llanfihangel-nant-Melan 45 SO 1758
Llanfihangel Rhydithon 48 SO 1466
Llanfihangel Rogiet 33 ST 4487
Llanfihangel-Tal-y-llyn 41 SO 1128
Llanfihangel uwch-Gwili 43 SN 4822
Llanfihangel-y-Creuddyn 57 SN 6676
Llanfihangel-yng-Ngwynfa 57 SJ 0817
Llanfihangel-y-pennant (Gwyn.) 66 SH 5245
Llanfihangel-y-Pennant (Gwyn.) 57 SH 6708
Llanfihangel Ystum Llywern 45 SO 4313
Llanfihangel-y-traethau 66 SH 5935
Llanfilo 41 SO 1133
Llanfoist 45 SO 2813
Llanfor 67 SH 9336
Llanfrechfa 45 ST 3193
Llanfrothen 67 SH 6241
Llanfrynach 41 SO 0726
Llanfwrog (Clwyd) 68 SJ 1157
Llanfwrog (Gwyn.) 66 SH 3083
Llanfyllin 58 SJ 1419
Llanfynydd (Clwyd) 58 SJ 2756
Llanfynydd (Dyfed) 43 SN 5527
Llanfyrnach 43 SN 2231
Llangadfan 57 SJ 0010
Llangadog 40 SN 7028
Llangadwaladr (Clwyd) 58 SJ 1730
Llangadwaladr (Gwyn.) 66 SH 3869
Llangaffo 66 SH 4468
Llangain 43 SN 3815
Llangammarch Wells 44 SN 9347
Llangan 41 SS 9577
Llangarron 45 SO 5221
Llangasty-Talyllyn 41 SO 1426
Llangathen 43 SN 5822
Llangattock 41 SO 2117
Llangattock Lingoed 45 SO 3620
Llangattock-Vibon-Avel 45 SO 4515
Llangedwyn 58 SJ 1824
Llangefni 66 SH 4575
Llangeinor 41 SS 9187
Llangeitho 43 SN 6159
Llangeler 43 SN 3739
Llangelynin 56 SH 5707
Llangendeirne 43 SN 4514
Llangennech 40 SN 5601
Llangennith 40 SS 4291
Llangenny 45 SO 2418
Llangernyw 67 SH 8767
Llangian 56 SH 2928
Llangiwg 40 SN 7205
Llanglydwen 43 SN 1826
Llangoed 66 SH 6079
Llangoed Castle (ant.) 44 SO 1140
Llangoedmor 43 SN 2045
Llangollen 58 SJ 2141
Llangollen Canal (Ches.) 59 SJ 5847
Llangollen Canal (Clwyd) 58 SJ 2342
Llangolman 42 SN 1127
Llangorse 41 SO 1327
Llangorse Lake 41 SO 1326
Llangorwen 56 SN 6084
Llangovan 45 SO 4505
Llangower 67 SH 9032
Llangranog 43 SN 3154
Llangristiolus 66 SH 4373
Llangrove 45 SO 5219
Llangua 45 SO 3926
Llangunllo 48 SO 2171
Llangunnor 43 SN 4219
Llangurig 57 SN 9080
Llangwm (Clwyd) 67 SH 9644
Llangwm (Dyfed) 42 SM 9909
Llangwm (Gwent) 45 SO 4200
Llangwnadl 66 SH 2033
Llangwyfan 68 SJ 1266
Llangwyllog 66 SH 4379
Llangwyryfon 56 SN 5970
Llangybi (Dyfed) 43 SN 6053
Llangybi (Gwent) 45 ST 3796
Llangybi (Gwyn.) 66 SH 4240
Llangyfelach 40 SS 6499
Llangynhafal 68 SJ 1263
Llangynidr 41 SO 1519
Llangynin 43 SN 2519
Llangynog (Dyfed) 43 SN 3316
Llangynog (Powys) 57 SJ 0526
Llanhamlach 41 SO 0926
Llanharan 41 ST 0083
Llanharry 41 ST 0080
Llanhennock 32 ST 3592
Llanhilleth 41 SO 2101
Llanidloes 57 SN 9584
Llanieston 66 SH 2633
Llanigon 45 SO 2139
Llanilar 57 SN 6275
Llanilid 41 SS 9781
Llanishen (Gwent) 45 SO 4703
Llanishen (S Glam.) 41 ST 1781
Llaniwared 57 SN 8977
Llanllechid 67 SH 6268
Llanlleonfel 44 SN 9350
Llanllowell 45 ST 3998
Llanllugan 57 SJ 0402
Llanllwch 43 SN 3818
Llanllwchaiarn 48 SO 1192
Llanllyfni 66 SH 4651
Llanmadoc 40 SS 4493
Llanmaes 41 SS 9869
Llanmartin 32 ST 3989
Llanmerewig 58 SO 1593
Llanmihangel 41 SS 9771
Llanmorlais 40 SS 5294
Llannefydd 67 SH 9770
Llannerch Hall 67 SJ 0572
Llannon 43 SN 5408
Llannor 66 SH 3537
Llanon 56 SN 5167
Llanpumsaint 43 SN 4129
Llanreithan 42 SM 8628
Llanrhaeadr 67 SJ 0763
Llanrhaeadr-ym-Mochnant 58 SJ 1226
Llanrhain 42 SM 8131
Llanrhidian 40 SS 4992
Llanrhidian Sands 40 SS 4895
Llanrhos 67 SH 7880
Llanrhyddlad 66 SH 3389
Llanrhystud 56 SN 5369
Llanrothal 45 SO 4618
Llanrug 66 SH 5363
Llanrwst 67 SH 7961
Llansadurnen 43 SN 2810
Llansadwrn (Dyfed) 40 SN 6931
Llansadwrn (Gwyn.) 66 SH 5575
Llansaint 43 SN 3808
Llansamlet 40 SS 6997
Llansannan 67 SH 9365
Llansannor 41 SS 9977
Llansantffraed 41 SO 1223
Llansantffraed-Cwmdeuddwr 57 SN 9667
Llansantffraed-in-Elvel 44 SO 0954
Llansantffraid 56 SN 5167
Llansantffraid Glan Conwy 67 SH 8075
Llansantffraid-ym-Mechain 58 SJ 2220
Llansawel 43 SN 6136
Llansilin 58 SJ 2028
Llansoy 45 SO 4402
Llanspyddid 41 SO 0328
Llanstadwell 42 SM 9505
Llanstephan (Dyfed) 43 SN 3511
Llanstephan (Powys) 44 SO 1142
Llanthony 45 SO 2827
Llantilio-Crossenny 45 SO 3914
Llantilio Pertholey 45 SO 3116
Llantrisant (Gwent) 45 ST 3996
Llantrisant (Mid Glam.) 41 ST 0483
Llantrithyd 41 ST 0472
Llantwit Fardre 41 ST 0785
Llantwit Major 41 SS 9768
Llantysilio Hall 58 SJ 1943
Llantysilio Mountain 58 SJ 1545
Llanuwchllyn 67 SH 8730
Llanvaches 33 ST 4391
Llanvair-Discoed 33 ST 4492
Llanvapley 45 SO 3614
Llanvetherine 45 SO 3617
Llanveynoe 45 SO 3031
Llanvihangel Gobion 45 SO 3409
Llanwarne 45 SO 5028
Llanwddyn 57 SJ 0219
Llan-wen Hill 48 SO 3069
Llanwenog 43 SN 4945
Llanwern 32 ST 3688
Llanwinio 43 SN 2626
Llanwnda (Dyfed) 42 SM 9339
Llanwnda (Gwyn.) 66 SH 4758
Llanwnen 43 SN 5347
Llanwnog 57 SO 0293
Llanwrda 40 SN 7131
Llanwrin 57 SH 7803
Llanwrthwl 57 SN 9763
Llanwrtyd 44 SN 8647
Llanwrtyd Wells 44 SN 8746
Llanwyddelan 57 SJ 0801
Llanyblodwel 58 SJ 2322
Llanybri 43 SN 3312
Llanybyther 43 SN 5244
Llanycefn 42 SN 0923

Llanychaer	42	SM	9835
Llanycrwys	43	SN	6445
Llanymawddwy	57	SH	9019
Llanymynech	58	SJ	2620
Llanynghenedl	66	SH	3181
Llanynys	67	SJ	1062
Llanyre	57	SO	0462
Llanystumdwy	66	SH	4738
Llanywern	41	SO	1028
Llawhaden	42	SN	0717
Llawllech (mt.)	57	SH	6321
Llawnt	58	SJ	2430
Llawr-y-dre	56	SH	2728
Llawryglyn	57	SN	9291
Llay	58	SJ	3255
Llechcynfarwy	66	SH	3881
Llechfaen	41	SO	0828
Llechryd (Dyfed)	43	SN	2243
Llechryd (Mid Glam.)	41	SO	1009
Llechrydau	58	SJ	2234
Lledrod (Clwyd)	58	SJ	2229
Lledrod (Dyfed)	57	SN	6470
Lleyn Peninsula	66	SH	3237
Llidiadnenog	43	SN	5437
Llidiardau	66	SH	1929
Llithfaen	66	SH	3543
Lliw Resrs.	43	SN	6505
Llong	68	SJ	2562
Llowes	45	SO	1941
Llwydcoed	41	SN	9905
Llwydiarth	57	SJ	0315
Llwyn	48	SO	2880
Llwyncelyn	43	SN	4459
Llwyndafydd	43	SN	3755
Llwynderw	58	SJ	2004
Llŵyndyrys	66	SH	3741
Llwyngwril	56	SH	5909
Llwynhendy	40	SS	5599
Llwynmawr	58	SJ	2236
Llŵyn-on Resr.	41	SO	0011
Llwynypia	41	SS	9993
Llyn Alaw	66	SH	3986
Llyn Aled	67	SH	9157
Llyn Alwen	67	SH	8956
Llyn Arennig-Fawr	67	SH	8437
Llyn Berwyn	44	SN	7456
Llyn Bodlyn	57	SH	6423
Llyn Brân	67	SH	9659
Llyn Brianne	44	SN	8050
Llyn Celyn	67	SH	8640
Llynclys	58	SJ	2924
Llyn Clywedog	57	SN	8989
Llyn Coch-hwyad	57	SH	9211
Llyn Conwy	67	SH	7746
Llyn Coron	66	SH	3770
Llyn Cowlyd Resr.	67	SH	7262
Llyn Crafnant Resr.	67	SH	7461
Llyn Cwellyn	66	SH	5554
Llyn Cwmystradllyn	66	SH	5644
Llyn Dinas	66	SH	6149
Llyn Dulyn Resr.	67	SH	7066
Llyn-dŵr Hill	57	SO	0583
Llyn Eigiau Resr.	67	SH	7065
Llyn Elsi Resr.	67	SH	7855
Llynfaes	66	SH	4178
Llyn Frogwy	66	SH	4477
Llyn Gwyddior	57	SH	9307
Llyn Gwynant	67	SH	6452
Llyn Helyg	68	SJ	1177
Llyn Hywel	57	SH	6626
Llyn Llydaw	67	SH	6254
Llyn Llywenan	66	SH	3481
Llyn Mawr	57	SO	0097
Llyn Nantle Uchat	66	SH	5153
Llyn Ogwen	67	SH	6560
Llyn Padarn	66	SH	5761
Llyn Peris	66	SH	5959
Llyn Syfydrin	57	SN	7284
Llyn Tegid or Bala Lake	67	SH	9033
Llyn Teifi	57	SN	7867
Llyny Fan Fawr	41	SN	8321
Llynytarw	57	SO	0297
Llysfaen	67	SH	8977
Llyswen	44	SO	1337
Llysworney	41	SS	9674
Llys-y-frân	42	SN	0424
Llys-y-frân Resr.	42	SN	0425
Llywel	41	SN	8630
Loadpot Hill	83	NY	4518
Loan	102	NS	9575
Loanend	97	NT	9450
Loanhead	103	NT	2765
Loans	93	NS	3431
Lòba Sgeir	130	HW	8031
Lochaber (dist.)	115	NN	1492
Lochaber Loch	88	NX	9270
Loch a' Bhaid-luachraich	126	NG	8986
Loch a'Bhealaich (Highld.)	133	NC	6026
Loch a' Bhealaich (Highld.)	123	NG	8664
Loch a' Bhealaich (Highld.)	114	NH	0221
Loch a' Bhealaich Bheithe	107	NN	5171
Loch a' Bhràige	123	NG	6261
Loch a' Bhraoin	127	NH	1374
Loch a'Bhùrra	99	NR	6696
Loch a' Chàirn Bhàin	132	NC	1934
Loch Achall	127	NH	1795
Loch Achanalt	127	NH	2761
Loch a' Chaorainn	128	NH	4678
Loch a'Chaoruinn	99	NR	7866
Loch Achilty	128	NH	4356
Loch Achnamoine	134	NC	8132
Loch a'Chnuic Bhric	98	NR	4473
Loch a' Choire	111	NM	8452
Loch a' Choire Mhóir	127	NH	3088
Loch Achonachie	128	NH	4354
Loch a' Chraeaich	123	NG	7657
Loch a' Chràthaich	115	NH	3621
Loch Achray	101	NN	5106
Loch a' Chroisg	127	NH	1258
Loch Affric	115	NH	1522
Loch a' Gharbh-bhaid Mór	132	NC	2748
Loch a'Gheòidh	99	NR	6695
Loch a' Ghlinne	130	NB	0212
Loch a' Ghorm-choire	133	NC	4433
Loch a' Ghriama	132	NC	3926
Loch Ailort (Highld.)	111	NM	7379
Lochailort (Highld.)	111	NM	7682
Loch Ailsh	132	NC	3110
Loch Ainort	123	NG	5528
Loch Airdeglais	105	NM	6228
Loch Airigh na Beinne	132	NC	3266
Loch Airigh na h-Airde	131	NB	2123
Loch Akran	134	NC	9260
Loch a' Laip	124	NF	8647
Lochaline (Highld.)	105	NM	6744
Loch Aline (Highld.)	105	NM	6845
Loch Alsh	123	NG	8125
Loch Alvie	117	NH	8609
Loch a' Mhuilinn	135	ND	0142
Loch a' Mhuillidh	115	NH	2738
Lochan a' Chairn	128	NH	5184
Loch an Aircill	98	NR	5076
Loch an Alltan Fheàrna	134	NC	7533
Lochan Breaclaich	107	NN	6231
Lochan Burn	88	NT	0000
Loch an Daimh (Highld.)	127	NH	2794
Loch an Daimh (Tays.)	107	NN	4846
Loch an Dherue	133	NC	5448
Loch an Doire Dhuibh	132	NC	1310
Loch an Draing	126	NG	7790
Lochan Dubh nan Geodh	135	ND	0248
Loch an Dùin	116	NN	7279
Loch an Easain Uaine	132	NC	3246
Loch an Eircill	132	NC	3027
Loch an Eoin	126	NG	9251
Lochan Fada	126	NH	0271
Lochan Gaineamhach	106	NN	3053
Loch an Iasaich	114	NG	9535
Loch an Laoigh	126	NH	0241
Loch an Leathaid Bhuain	132	NC	2736
Loch an Leothaid	132	NC	1729
Lochan na Bi	106	NN	3031
Lochan na h-Achlaise	106	NN	3147
Lochan na h-Earba	116	NN	4883
Lochan na Làirige	107	NN	5940
Loch an Ruathair	134	NC	8636
Lochans	86	NX	0656
Lochan Shira	106	NN	1720
Lochan Sron Mór	106	NN	1619
Loch an Tachdaidh	115	NH	0937
Lochan Thulachan	135	ND	1041
Loch an t-Seilich	116	NN	7586
Loch a'Phuill	104	NL	9542
Loch Arail	99	NR	8179
Locharbriggs	88	NX	9980
Loch Ard	101	NN	4601
Loch Ard Forest	101	NS	4898
Loch Arichlinie	134	NC	8435
Loch Arienas	111	NM	6851
Loch Arkaig	115	NN	0891
Loch Arklet Reservoir	101	NN	3708
Lochar Moss	89	NY	0371
Loch Arnish`	123	NG	5848
Loch Arthur	88	NX	9069
Lochar Water	88	NY	0178
Loch Ascaig	134	NC	8425
Loch a' Sguirr	123	NG	5952
Loch Ashie	116	NH	6334
Loch Assapol	105	NM	4020
Loch Assynt	132	NC	2024
Lochassynt Lodge	132	NC	1726
Loch a Tuath or Broad Bay	131	NB	5037
Loch Aulasary	124	NF	9474
Loch Avich (Strath.)	100	NM	9314
Loch Avon	117	NJ	0102
Loch Awe (Highld.)	132	NC	2415
Loch Awe (Strath.)	100	NM	9610
Lochawe (Strath.)	106	NN	1227
Loch Bà (Island of Mull)	105	NM	5637
Loch Ba (Strath.)	106	NN	3250
Loch Bad a' Chreamh	126	NG	8180
Loch Bad a' Ghaill	132	NC	0710
Loch Badanloch	134	NC	7734
Loch Bad an Sgalaig	123	NG	8571
Loch Baligill	134	NC	8562
Loch Ballygrant	98	NR	4066
Loch Bay	122	NG	2655
Loch Beanie	108	NO	1668
Loch Beannach (Highld.)	132	NC	1326
Loch Beannach (Highld.)	133	NC	6012
Loch Beannacharain	127	NH	2351
Loch Beannacharan	115	NH	3039
Loch Bee	124	NF	7743
Loch Beinn a' Mheadhoin	115	NH	2224
Loch Beinn Uraraidh	98	NR	4053
Loch Benachally	108	NO	0750
Loch Benisval	131	NB	0819
Loch Beoraid	111	NM	8285
Loch Bhac	107	NN	8262
Loch Bharcasaig	122	NG	2542
Loch Bhrodainn	116	NN	7483
Loch Bhrollum	125	NB	3103
Loch Blàir	115	NN	0594
Loch Bodavat	130	NB	0619
Lochboisdale (South Uist)	112	NF	7919
Loch Boisdale (South Uist)	112	NF	8018
Loch Boltachan	107	NN	6926
Loch Borralan	132	NC	2610
Loch Borralie	132	NC	3867
Loch Bracadale	122	NG	2837
Loch Bradan Reservoir	87	NX	4297
Loch Bràigh an Achaidh	123	NG	7440
Loch Brandy	118	NO	3375
Loch Breac	135	ND	0637
Loch Breachacha	110	NM	1853
Loch Breivat	131	NB	3345
Loch Brittle	123	NG	4019
Loch Broom (Highld.)	127	NH	1392
Loch Broom (Tays.)	108	NO	0158
Loch Brora	129	NC	8508
Loch Bruicheach	116	NH	4536
Loch Buidhe	128	NH	6698
Loch Buidhe Mór	134	NC	7758
Loch Buie (Strath.)	105	NM	5922
Lochbuie (Strath.)	105	NM	6125
Loch Builg	117	NJ	1803
Loch Calavie	115	NH	0538
Loch Calder	135	ND	0760
Loch Callater	117	NO	1883
Loch Caluim	135	ND	0251
Loch Cam	98	NR	3466
Loch Caoldair	116	NN	6189
Loch Caolisport	99	NR	7374
Loch Caravat	124	NF	8461
Loch Carloway	131	NB	1842
Lochcarnan	124	NF	8043
Loch Càrnan	124	NF	8243
Loch Caroy	122	NG	2941
Loch Carron (Highld.)	123	NG	8735
Lochcarron (Highld.)	114	NG	8939
Loch Ceann Dibig	125	NG	1597
Loch Chaolartan	130	NB	0624
Loch Chaorunn Reservoir	99	NR	8371
Loch Choire	133	NC	6228
Loch Choire Forest	133	NC	6229
Loch Choire Lodge	133	NC	6530
Loch Chon	101	NN	4205
Loch Ciaran	92	NR	7754
Loch Claidh	125	NB	2702
Loch Clàir (Highld.)	123	NG	7771
Loch Clair (Highld.)	126	NH	0057
Loch Clash	132	NC	2156
Loch Cliad	110	NM	2058
Loch Cluanie	115	NH	1409
Loch Coire na Saighe Duibhe	133	NC	4436
Loch Coirigerod	131	NB	1721
Loch Con	107	NN	6867
Loch Connan	122	NG	3843
Loch Connell	86	NX	0168
Loch Coruisk	123	NG	4820
Lochcote Resr.	102	NS	9874
Loch Coulin	126	NH	0155
Loch Coulside	133	NC	5843
Loch Coulter Reservoir	101	NS	7686
Loch Coultrie	123	NG	8546
Loch Cracail Mór	128	NC	6202
Loch Craggie (Highld.)	127	NC	3205
Loch Craggie (Highld.)	133	NC	6152
Loch Craggie (Highld.)	128	NC	6207
Lochcraig Head	89	NT	1617
Loch Craignish	99	NM	7800
Lochcraig Reservoir	93	NS	5351
Loch Cravadale	130	NB	0114
Loch Creran	106	NM	9442
Loch Crinan	99	NR	7795
Loch Cròcach (Highld)	132	NC	1027
Loch Cròcach (Highld.)	132	NC	1939
Loch Cròcach (Highld.)	133	NC	4249
Loch Cròcach (Highld)	134	NC	8043
Loch Crò Criosdaig	131	NB	0820
Loch Crunachdan	116	NN	5492
Loch Cruoshie	115	NH	0536
Loch Cuaich	116	NN	6987
Loch Culag	132	NC	0921
Loch Dallas	129	NJ	0947
Loch Damh	123	NG	8650
Loch Davan	118	NJ	4400
Loch Dee	87	NX	4678
Loch Derculich	108	NN	8655
Loch Derry	86	NX	2573
Lochdhu Hotel	135	ND	0144
Loch Diabaigas Airde	123	NG	8159
Loch Dionard	132	NC	3549
Loch Dochard	106	NN	2141
Loch Dochart	107	NN	4025
Lochdochart House	107	NN	4327
Loch Doilet	111	NM	8067
Loch Doine	107	NN	4719
Loch Don	105	NM	7332
Lochdon	105	NM	7333
Loch Doon	87	NX	4997
Loch Doon Hill	86	NX	1068
Loch Dornal	86	NX	2976
Loch Droma	127	NH	2675
Loch Druidibeg	112	NF	7937
Loch Druim a'Chliabhain	134	NC	8041
Loch Drunkie	101	NN	5404
Loch Duagrich	123	NG	3939
Loch Dubh	135	ND	0536
Loch Dubh a' Chuail	132	NC	3428
Loch Dùghaill (Highld.)	132	NC	1852
Loch Dùghaill (Highld.)	126	NH	0047
Loch Duich	114	NG	9121
Loch Dungeon	87	NX	5284
Loch Duntelchaig	116	NH	6231
Loch Dunvegan	122	NG	2153
Lochead	99	NR	7778
Loch Earn	107	NN	6423
Lochearnhead	107	NN	5823
Loch Eatharna	110	NM	2256
Loch Eck	100	NS	1391
Loch Eck Forest	100	NS	1494
Lochee	109	NO	3631
Loch Eigheach	107	NN	4557
Loch Eil	114	NN	0277
Loch Eilde Beag	106	NN	2565
Loch Eilde Mór	106	NN	2364
Loch Eileanach (Highld.)	133	NC	5940
Loch Eileanach (Highld.)	135	ND	0747
Locheil Forest	115	NN	0788
Locheilside Station	114	NM	9978
Loch Eilt	111	NM	8182
Loch Einich	117	NN	9198
Loch Eishort	123	NG	6114
Lochenbreck Loch	88	NX	6465
Lochend (Highld.)	135	ND	2668
Lochend (Highld.)	116	NH	5937
Loch Enoch	87	NX	4485
Locheport (North Uist)	124	NF	8563
Loch Eport (North Uist)	124	NF	8863
Locherben	88	NX	9597
Loch Eriboll	133	NC	4360
Loch Ericht	107	NN	5371
Loch Ericht Forest	116	NN	5981
Loch Erisort	131	NB	3420
Loch Errochty	107	NN	6965
Locher Water	101	NS	3663
Loch Esk	117	NO	2379
Loch Etchachan	117	NJ	0000
Loch Etive	106	NN	0434
Loch Ewe	126	NG	8387
Loch Eye	129	NH	8379
Loch Eynort (Island of Skye)	122	NG	3624
Loch Eynort (South Uist)	112	NF	8026
Loch Fad	100	NS	0661
Loch Fada (Colonsay)	98	NR	3895
Loch Fada (Highld.)	126	NG	9186
Loch Fada (Island of Skye)	123	NG	4949
Loch Fada (North Uist)	124	NF	8770
Loch Fannich	127	NH	2165
Loch Faskally	108	NN	9258
Loch Féith an Leòthaid	132	NC	1822
Loch Fell	89	NT	1704
Loch Feochan	105	NM	8423
Loch Fiag	133	NC	4429
Loch Fiart	105	NM	8037
Loch Finlaggan	98	NR	3867
Loch Finlas	87	NX	4598
Loch Finsbay	125	NG	0886
Loch Fitty	102	NT	1291
Loch Fleet	129	NH	7896
Loch Flodabay	125	NG	1087
Lochfoot	88	NX	8973
Loch Freuchie	108	NN	8637
Loch Frisa	105	NM	4848
Loch Fuaroil	131	NB	1224
Loch Fuaron	105	NM	5826
Loch Fyne	100	NR	9591
Loch Gaineamhach (Highld.)	133	NC	5824
Loch Gaineamhach (Highld.)	123	NG	7553
Loch Gaineamhach (Strath.)	100	NM	9100
Lochgair	100	NR	9290
Loch Gairloch	123	NG	7676
Loch Garasdale	92	NR	7651
Loch Garbhaig	126	NH	0070
Loch Garry (Highld.)	115	NH	2302
Loch Garry (Tays.)	107	NN	6270
Loch Garten	117	NH	9718
Lochgarthside	116	NH	5219
Loch Garve	128	NH	4159
Lochgelly	102	NT	1893
Loch Gelly	103	NT	2092
Loch Ghuilbinn	116	NN	4174
Loch Gilp	99	NR	8584
Lochgilphead	99	NR	8687
Loch Glascarnoch	127	NH	3172
Loch Glashan	100	NR	9193
Loch Glass	128	NH	5172
Loch Glencoul	132	NC	2531
Loch Glendhu	132	NC	2633
Loch Glow	102	NT	0895
Loch Goil	100	NS	1996
Lochgoilhead	100	NN	1901
Lochgoin Reservoir	93	NS	5447
Loch Gorm	98	NR	2365
Loch Gowan	127	NH	1455
Loch Grannoch	87	NX	5469
Loch Greshornish	122	NG	3454
Loch Grosebay	125	NG	1691
Loch Gruinart	98	NR	2870
Loch Grunavat	131	NB	0827
Loch Haluim	133	NC	5545
Loch Harport	122	NG	3734
Loch Harrow	87	NX	5286
Loch Heilen	135	ND	2568
Loch Hempriggs	135	ND	3447
Loch Heouravay	124	NF	8250
Loch Heron	86	NX	2764
Lochhill	120	NJ	2964
Loch Hoil	108	NN	8643
Loch Hope	133	NC	4654
Loch Hourn	123	NG	8309
Loch Humphrey	101	NS	4576
Loch Huna	124	NF	8166
Loch Hunish	123	NG	4076
Loch Inchard	132	NC	2454
Lochinch Castle	86	NX	1061
Loch Indaal	98	NR	2758
Lochindorb	117	NH	9736
Lochindorb Lodge	117	NH	9635
Loch Insh	117	NH	8304
Loch Inshore	132	NC	3369
Lochinvar	88	NX	6585
Loch Inver (Highld.)	132	NC	0721
Lochinver (Highld.)	132	NC	0922
Loch Iubhair	107	NN	4226
Loch Kanaird	127	NH	1099
Loch Katrine	101	NN	4409
Loch Keisgaig	132	NC	2668
Loch Ken	88	NX	6474
Loch Kennard	108	NN	9046
Loch Kernsary	126	NG	8880
Loch Kildonan	112	NF	7327
Loch Killin	116	NH	5210
Loch Kinardochy	107	NN	7755
Loch Kindar	88	NX	9664
Loch Kinnabus	98	NR	3042
Loch Kinord	118	NO	4499
Loch Kirkaig	132	NC	0719
Loch Kishorn	123	NG	8138
Loch Knockie	116	NH	4513
Loch Laggan	116	NN	4886
Loch Laidon	107	NN	3854
Lochlane	107	NN	8320
Loch Langass	124	NF	8464
Loch Langavat (Harris, W Isles)	124	NG	0489
Loch Langavat (Isle of Lewis)	131	NB	1718
Loch Langavat (Isle of Lewis)	131	NB	5254
Loch Laro	128	NH	6099
Loch Laxavat Ard	131	NB	2438
Loch Laxford	132	NC	2049
Loch Leacann	100	NM	9903
Loch Leathan	123	NG	5051
Loch Leathaun an Sgorra	98	NR	4052
Loch Lednock Reservoir	107	NN	7129
Loch Lee	118	NO	4279
Loch Lesgamaill	98	NR	5777
Loch Leven (Highld.)	106	NN	1260
Loch Leven (Tays.)	102	NO	1401
Loch Linnhe	106	NM	9354
Loch Loch	117	NN	9874
Loch Lochy	115	NN	2390
Loch Lomond	100	NS	3598
Loch Long (Highld.)	114	NG	9029
Loch Long (Strath.)	100	NS	2292
Loch Losait	122	NG	2759
Loch Loyal	133	NC	6247
Loch Loyal Lodge	133	NC	6146
Loch Loyne	115	NH	1705
Loch Lubnaig	101	NN	5713
Lochluichart	127	NH	3262
Loch Luichart	127	NH	3661
Loch Lundie	123	NG	8049
Loch Lurgainn	127	NC	1208
Loch Lyon	107	NN	3839
Lochmaben	89	NY	0882
Lochmaben Stone	89	NY	3166
Loch Maberry	86	NX	2874
Loch Macaterick	87	NX	4491
Lochmaddy (North Uist)	124	NF	9168
Loch Maddy (North Uist)	124	NF	9368
Loch Mahaick	101	NN	7006
Loch Mannoch	88	NX	6660
Loch Maree	126	NG	9570
Loch ma Stac	115	NH	3421
Loch Meadaidh	132	NC	3964
Loch Meadie (Highld.)	133	NC	5041
Loch Meadie (Highld.)	134	NC	7560
Loch Meadie (Highld.)	135	ND	0948
Loch Meala	134	NC	7856
Loch Meallbrodden	108	NN	9125
Loch Mealt	123	NG	5065
Loch Meig	127	NH	3655
Loch Meiklie	116	NH	4330
Loch Melfort	105	NM	8012
Loch Merkland	132	NC	3831
Loch Mhairc	117	NN	8879
Loch Mhór	116	NH	5419
Loch Migdale	128	NH	6390
Loch Moan	86	NX	3485
Loch Moidart	111	NM	6472
Loch Monar	115	NH	1440
Loch Moraig	108	NN	9066
Loch Mór an Stàirr	131	NB	3938
Loch Morar	111	NM	7790
Loch More (Highld.)	132	NC	3237
Loch More (Highld.)	135	ND	0745
Lochmore Cottage	135	ND	0846
Lochmore Lodge	132	NC	2938
Loch Morie	128	NH	5376
Loch Morlich	117	NH	9609
Loch Mór na Caorach	134	NC	7654
Loch Mór Sandavat	131	NB	4952
Loch Morsgail	131	NB	1322
Loch Moy	116	NH	7734
Loch Muck	87	NS	5100
Loch Mudle	111	NM	5466
Loch Muick	117	NO	2882
Loch Mullardoch	115	NH	1931
Loch na Beinne Baine	115	NH	2819
Loch na Caoidhe	127	NH	2246
Loch na Cille	99	NR	6878
Loch na Claise Càrnaich	132	NC	2852
Loch na Claise Móire	127	NC	3805
Loch na Conaire	99	NR	6796
Loch na Craige	108	NN	8845
Loch na Creige Duibhe	132	NC	2836
Loch na Crèitheach	123	NG	5120
Loch na Dal	123	NG	7114
Loch na Fuaralaich	128	NC	4806
Loch na Gainimh (Highld.)	132	NC	1718
Loch na Gainimh (Highld.)	132	NC	2061
Lochnagar (mt.)	117	NO	2485
Loch na h-Oidhche	126	NG	8965
Loch Na Keal	105	NM	5038
Loch na Lathaich	104	NM	3623
Loch na Leitreach	114	NH	0227
Loch nam Bonnach	128	NH	4848
Loch nam Brac	132	NC	1848
Loch nam Breac	134	NC	8247
Loch nam Breac Dearga	116	NH	4522
Loch nam Falcag	131	NB	2927
Loch na Mile	98	NR	5470
Loch nan Ceall	111	NM	6486
Loch nan Clach (Highld.)	134	NC	7752
Loch nan Clach (Highld.)	105	NM	7846
Loch nan Clàr	134	NC	7535
Loch nan Eilean	131	NB	3617
Loch nan Eun	117	NO	0678
Loch nan Eun (Highld.)	123	NG	7048
Loch nan Eun (Highld.)	114	NG	.9526
Loch nan Eun (Highld.)	115	NH	3120
Loch nan Eun (Highld.)	128	NH	4648
Loch nan Geireann	124	NF	8472
Loch nan Stearnag	131	NB	3236
Loch Nant	106	NN	0024
Loch nan Torran	99	NR	7568
Loch nan Uamh	111	NM	6982
Loch na Saobhaidhe	134	NC	8047
Loch na Scaravat	131	NB	3540
Loch na Sealga	126	NH	0383
Loch na Seilg	133	NC	4951
Loch na Seilge	134	NC	9258
Loch Naver	133	NC	6136
Lochnaw Castle	86	NW	9962
Loch Nedd	132	NC	1332
Loch Neldricken	87	NX	4482
Loch Nell	106	NM	8927
Lochnell House	106	NM	8838
Loch Ness	116	NH	5023
Loch Nevis	111	NM	7695
Loch Niarsco	123	NG	3947
Loch Obisary	124	NF	8961
Loch Ochiltree	86	NX	3174
Loch Odhairn	131	NB	4114
Loch of Boardhouse	136	HY	2626
Loch of Cliff	143	HP	6011
Loch of Girlsta	141	HU	4352
Loch of Harray	136	HY	2915
Loch of Hundland	136	HY	2926
Loch of Kirbister	136	HY	3608
Loch of Lintrathen	108	NO	2754
Loch of Lowes	108	NO	0544
Loch of Mey	135	ND	2773
Loch of Skaill	136	HY	2418
Loch of Skellister	141	HU	4656
Loch of Skene	119	NJ	7807
Loch of Spiggie	141	HU	3716
Loch of Stenness	136	HY	2813
Loch of Strathbeg	121	NK	0758
Loch of Strom	141	HU	4048
Loch of St. Tredwell	138	HY	4950
Loch of Swannay	136	HY	3128
Loch of the Lowes	89	NT	2319
Loch of Tingwall	141	HU	4142
Loch of Toftingall	135	ND	1852
Loch of Vaara	141	HU	3256
Loch of Vatsetter	143	HU	5389
Loch of Voxterby	140	HU	2653
Loch of Watlee	143	HP	5905
Loch of Wester	135	ND	3259
Loch of Yarrows	135	ND	3043
Loch Oich	115	NH	3201
Loch Olginey	135	ND	0857
Loch Ollay	112	NF	7531
Loch Orasay	131	NB	3928
Loch Ordie	108	NO	0350
Loch Ore	102	NT	1695
Lochore	102	NT	1796
Loch Osgaig	132	NC	0412
Loch Ossian	107	NN	3967
Loch Pattack	116	NN	5479
Loch Poit na h-I	104	NM	3122
Loch Poll	132	NC	1030
Loch Pooltiel	122	NG	1650
Loch Quien	100	NS	0659
Loch Quoich	114	NH	0102
Loch Rangag	135	ND	1741
Loch Rannoch	107	NN	5857
Loch Ranza (Island of Arran)	92	NR	9251
Lochranza (Island of Arran)	92	NR	9350
Loch Resort	130	NB	0617
Loch Riddon	100	NS	0076
Loch Riecawr	87	NX	4393
Loch Righ Mór	98	NR	5185
Loch Rimsdale	134	NC	7335
Loch Roag	131	NB	1233
Loch Ronald	86	NX	2664
Lochrosque Forest	127	NH	2162
Loch Ruard	135	ND	1443
Loch Rumsdale	134	NC	9641
Loch Rusky	101	NN	6103
Loch Ruthven	116	NH	6127
Lochrutton Loch	88	NX	8972
Loch Ryan	86	NX	0565
Loch Sand	135	ND	0940
Loch Scadavay (North Uist)	124	NF	8568
Loch Scadavay (North Uist)	124	NF	8766
Loch Scammadale	106	NM	8820
Loch Scarmclate	135	ND	1859
Loch Scaslavat	130	NB	0231
Loch Scavaig	123	NG	5015
Loch Scoly	108	NN	9147
Loch Scresort	111	NM	4199
Loch Scridain	105	NM	4625
Loch Scye	135	ND	0055
Loch Seaforth	125	NB	2106
Loch Sealg or Loch Shell	131	NB	3410
Loch Sgamhain	127	NH	1052
Loch Sgeireach Mór	131	NB	4945
Loch Sgibacleit	131	NB	3116
Loch Sguabain	105	NM	6230
Loch Sguod	126	NG	8187
Loch Shanndabhat	131	NB	3413
Loch Shell or Loch Sealg	131	NB	3410
Loch Shiel	111	NM	8072
Loch Shieldaig	123	NG	8055
Loch Shin	133	NC	4816
Loch Shira	100	NN	1009
Loch Shurrery	135	ND	0455
Lochside (Grampn.)	109	NO	7464
Lochside (Highld.)	133	NC	4758
Lochside (Highld.)	134	NC	8735
Loch Sionascaig	132	NC	1113
Loch Skealtar	124	NF	8968
Loch Skeen	89	NT	1716
Loch Skerrow	88	NX	6068
Loch Skiach	108	NN	9547
Lochskipport (South Uist)	112	NF	8238
Loch Skipport (South Uist)	112	NF	8438
Loch Slapin	123	NG	5718
Loch Sletill	134	NC	9547
Loch Sligachan	123	NG	5132
Loch Sloy	100	NN	2811
Loch Smigeadail	98	NR	3875
Loch Smuaisaval	131	NB	2030
Loch Snigisclett	112	NF	8025
Loch Snizort	122	NG	3261
Loch Snizort Beag	123	NG	3954
Lochs of Beosetter	141	HU	4943
Lochs of Lumbister	143	HU	4896
Loch Spallander Resr.	93	NS	3908
Loch Spelve	105	NM	6927
Loch Spey	116	NN	4293
Loch Spynie	120	NJ	2366
Loch Stack	132	NC	3042
Lochstack Lodge	132	NC	2643
Loch Staosnaig	98	NR	3993
Loch Steisevat	124	NG	0187
Loch Stornoway	99	NR	7260
Loch Strandavat	131	NB	2519
Loch Strathy	134	NC	7747
Loch Striven	100	NS	0776
Loch Stulaval	112	NF	7922
Loch Suainaval	130	NB	0629
Loch Sunart	111	NM	7262
Loch Sween	99	NR	7382
Loch Syre	133	NC	6644
Loch Tamanavay	130	NB	0220
Loch Tanna	92	NR	9242
Loch Tarbert	98	NR	5481
Loch Tarff	116	NH	4210
Loch Tay	107	NN	6838
Loch Teacuis	111	NM	6355
Loch Tealasavay	130	NB	0218
Loch Teàrnait	105	NM	7446
Loch Thom	100	NS	2572
Loch Thota Bridein	131	NB	3327
Loch Tollaidh	126	NG	8478
Lochton	119	NO	7592
Loch Torridon	123	NG	7560
Loch Tralaig	105	NM	8716
Loch Trealaval	131	NB	2723
Loch Treig	106	NN	3372
Loch Trollamarig	125	NB	2201
Loch Tromlee	106	NN	0425
Loch Trool	86	NX	4179
Loch Truderscaig	134	NC	7132
Loch Tuath	105	NM	3943
Loch Tuim Ghlais	134	NC	9852
Loch Tulla	106	NN	2942
Loch Tummel	107	NN	8259
Loch Tungavat	131	NB	1628
Loch Turret Reservoir	107	NN	8028
Loch Uisg	105	NM	6325
Lochuisge (Highld.)	111	NM	7955
Loch Uisge (Highld.)	111	NM	8054
Loch Uiskevagh	124	NF	8551
Loch Uraval	131	NB	3032

Loch Urigill 132 NC 2409
Loch Urr 88 NX 7584
Loch Urrahag 131 NB 3247
Loch Ussie 128 NH 5057
Loch Vaich 127 NH 3477
Loch Valigan 108 NN 9769
Loch Valley 87 NX 4481
Loch Venachar 101 NN 5705
Loch Veyatie 132 NC 1813
Loch Voil 107 NN 5019
Loch Vrotachan 117 NO 1278
Loch Walton 101 NS 6686
Loch Watten 135 ND 2256
Loch Whinyeon 88 NX 6260
Lochwinnoch 100 NS 3558
Lochwood (Dumf. and Galwy.) 89 NY 0896
Lochwood (Strath.) 101 NS 6966
Lock Awe (Argyll.) 100 NM 9610
Lockengate 19 SX 0361
Lockerbie 89 NY 1381
Lockeridge 34 SU 1467
Lockerley 26 SU 2925
Lockerley Hall 26 SU 2928
Locking 32 ST 3659
Lockington (Humbs.) 74 SE 9947
Lockington (Leic.) 61 SK 4628
Lockleywood 59 SJ 6828
Lockmaddy 124 NF 9168
Locks Heath 27 SU 5207
Lockton 80 SE 8489
Lockwood Beck Resr. 85 NZ 6713
Loddington (Leic.) 61 SK 7802
Loddington (Northants.) 52 SP 8178
Loddiswell 21 SX 7148
Loddon 65 TM 3698
Lode 53 TL 5362
Loder Head 141 HU 5243
Loders 25 SY 4994
Lodsworth 28 SU 9223
Loe, The 18 SW 6425
Loft Hill 90 NT 8513
Lofthouse (N Yorks.) 78 SE 1073
Lofthouse (W Yorks.) 79 SE 3325
Loftus 85 NZ 7118
Logan 88 NS 5820
Loganlea Resr. 103 NT 1962
Logan Mains 86 NX 0942
Logan Rock 18 SW 3523
Logan Water 94 NS 7537
Loggerheads 59 SJ 7336
Loggie 127 NH 1490
Logie (Fife) 109 NO 4020
Logie (Grampn.) 121 NK 0356
Logie (Tays.) 109 NO 6963
Logiealmond (dist.) 108 NN 9731
Logiealmond Lodge 108 NN 9531
Logie Coldstone 118 NJ 4304
Logie Head 121 NJ 5267
Logie Hill 129 NH 7776
Logie Newton 121 NJ 6638
Logie Pert 109 NO 6664
Logierait 108 NN 9752
Login 42 SN 1623
Lolworth 53 TL 3664
Lomond Hills 103 NO 2106
Lonbain 123 NG 6852
Londesborough 74 SE 8645
Londinium (ant.) 37 TQ 3079
London 37 TQ 3079
London Airport (Eday) 138 HY 5634
London Airport (Gatwick) 28 TQ 2740
London Airport (Heathrow) 36 TQ 0875
London Bridge Station 37 TQ 3280
London Colney 37 TL 1603
Londonderry 79 SE 3087
Londonthorpe 62 SK 9537
Londubh 126 NG 8680
Lonemore 129 NH 7688
Longa Island 126 NG 7377
Longannet Point 102 NS 9485
Long Ashton 33 ST 5470
Longay 123 NG 6531
Long Bennington 62 SK 8344
Longbenton 91 NZ 2668
Longborough 47 SP 1729
Long Bredy 25 SY 5690
Longbridge (Warw.) 50 SP 2662
Longbridge (W Mids.) 50 SP 0178
Longbridge Deverill 33 ST 8640
Long Buckby 51 SP 6267
Longburton 25 ST 6412
Long Clawson 61 SK 7227
Longcliffe 60 SK 2255
Long Common 27 SU 5014
Long Compton (Staffs.) 59 SJ 8522
Long Compton (Warw.) 47 SP 2832
Longcot 34 SU 2790
Long Crag 91 NU 0606
Long Craig 109 NO 7254
Long Crendon 36 SP 6908
Long Crichel 26 ST 9710
Longcroft 101 NS 7979
Longden 58 SJ 4306
Longdendale 70 SK 0397
Long Ditton 37 TQ 1666
Longdon (Here. and Worc.) 49 SO 8336
Longdon (Staffs.) 60 SK 0714
Longdon on Tern 59 SJ 6215
Longdown 21 SX 8691
Longdowns 18 SW 7434
Long Drax 79 SE 6528
Long Duckmanton 71 SK 4371
Long Eaton 61 SK 4933
Long Fell 88 NX 9064
Longfield 30 TQ 6068
Longford (Derby.) 60 SK 2137
Longford (Glos.) 46 SO 8320
Longford (Gtr London) 36 TQ 0576
Longford (Shrops.) 59 SJ 6433
Longford (Shrops.) 59 SJ 7218
Longford (W Mids.) 50 SP 3583
Longford Castle (ant.) 26 SU 1626
Longforgan 108 NO 3129
Longformacus 96 NT 6957
Longframlington 91 NU 1201
Long Geo 136 HY 4404
Long Gill 78 SD 7858
Longham (Dorset) 26 SZ 0697
Longham (Norf.) 64 TF 9415
Long Hanborough 47 SP 4114
Long Haven 121 NK 1240
Long Hermiston 102 NT 1770
Longhirst 91 NZ 2289
Long Holcombe 23 SS 7636
Longhope (Glos.) 46 SO 6819
Longhope (Hoy, Orkney) (chan.) 136 ND 3191
Longhorsley 91 NZ 1494
Longhoughton 91 NU 2414
Long Itchington 50 SP 4165
Long Lawford 51 SP 4775
Longleat House (ant.) 33 ST 8042
Longley Green 49 SO 7350
Long Load 25 ST 4623
Long Loch (Strath.) 93 NS 4752
Long Loch (Tays.) 108 NO 2938
Longmanhill 121 NJ 7462
Longman Point 128 NH 6747
Long Man, The (ant.) 29 TQ 5403
Long Marston (Herts.) 36 SP 8915
Long Marston (N Yorks.) 79 SE 4951
Long Marston (Warw.) 50 SP 1548
Long Marton 83 NY 6624
Long Melford 54 TL 8646
Longmoor Camp 27 SU 7930
Longmorn 120 NJ 2358
Long Mountain 58 SJ 2808
Long Mynd, The (mt.) 58 SO 4093
Long Newnton (Glos.) 33 ST 9092
Longnewton (Borders) 96 NT 5827
Longnewton (Cleve.) 85 NZ 3816
Longnewton Forest 96 NT 6227
Longney 46 SO 7612
Longniddry 103 NT 4476
Longnor (Shrops.) 59 SJ 4800
Longnor (Staffs.) 70 SK 0864
Long Nose Spit 31 TR 3771
Longparish 34 SU 4344
Long Preston 78 SD 8357
Longridge (Lancs.) 77 SD 6037
Longridge (Lothian) 102 NS 9462
Longridge Fell 77 SD 6540
Longridge Towers 97 NT 9549
Longriggend 101 NS 8270
Long Riston 75 TA 1242
Long Sand 63 TF 5548
Longsdon 60 SJ 9554
Longships 18 SW 3225
Longside 121 NK 0347
Longsleddale 83 NY 4902
Longslow 59 SJ 6535
Longstanton 53 TL 3966
Longstock 26 SU 3536
Longstone Wells 23 SS 7633
Long Stowe 53 TL 3054
Long Stratton 55 TM 1992
Long Street 51 SP 7947
Long Sutton (Hants.) 35 SU 7347
Long Sutton (Lincs.) 63 TF 4322
Long Sutton (Somer.) 25 ST 4625
Long Taing 143 HU 3785
Longthorpe 62 TL 1698
Longton (Lancs.) 77 SD 4725
Longton (Staffs.) 59 SJ 9043
Longtown (Cumbr.) 89 NY 3768
Longtown (Here. and Worc.) 45 SO 3228
Long Valley 35 SU 8351
Longville in the Dale 59 SO 5393
Long Whatton 61 SK 4723
Longwick 36 SP 7805
Long Wittenham 47 SU 5493
Longwitton 91 NZ 0788
Longwood House 27 SU 5324
Longwood Warren 27 SU 5226
Longworth 47 SU 3899
Longyester 103 NT 5465
Lòn Liath 111 NM 6590
Lonmore 122 NG 2646
Looe 19 SX 2553
Looe Bay 20 SX 2753
Looe or St. George's Island 19 SX 2551
Loose 29 TQ 7552
Loosley Row 36 SP 8100
Lootcherbrae 121 NJ 6054
Lopcombe Corner 26 SU 2435
Lopen 25 ST 4214
Lop Ness 139 HY 7643
Loppington 58 SJ 4629
Lorbottle 91 NU 0306
Lorbottle Hall 91 NU 0407
Lord Arthur's Cairn 118 NJ 5019
Lord's Seat (mt.) 82 NY 2026
Lorn (dist.) 106 NN 0735
Lornty 108 NO 1746
Lornty Burn 108 NO 1048
Lorton 82 NY 1625
Lorton Vale 82 NY 1526
Loscoe 60 SK 4247
Lossie Forest 120 NJ 2767
Lossiemouth 120 NJ 2370
Lossit 98 NR 1856
Lossit Bay 98 NR 1755
Lossit Point 98 NR 1756
Lostock Gralam 69 SJ 6874
Lostock Junction 69 SD 6708
Lostwithiel 19 SX 1059
Lothbeg 134 NC 9410
Lothbeg Point 134 NC 9609
Lothersdale 78 SD 9545
Lothmore 134 NC 9611
Lotus Hill 88 NX 9067
Loudoun Hill 94 NS 6037
Loudwater 36 SU 8990
Loughborough 61 SK 5319
Loughor 40 SS 5898
Loughton (Bucks.) 52 SP 8337
Loughton (Essex) 37 TQ 4296
Loughton (Shrops.) 49 SO 6183
Lound (Lincs.) 62 TF 0618
Lound (Notts.) 72 SK 6986
Lound (Suff.) 65 TM 5099
Lount 60 SK 3819
Louth 73 TF 3287
Love Clough 78 SD 8126
Lover 26 SU 2120
Loversall 71 SK 5798
Loves Green 38 TL 6404
Loveston 42 SN 0808
Lovington 25 ST 5931
Low Bentham 77 SD 6469
Low Bradfield 71 SK 2691
Low Bradley 78 SE 0048
Low Braithwaite 83 NY 4242
Lowbridge House 83 NY 5301
Low Brunton 90 NY 9269
Low Burnham 74 SE 7702
Lowca 82 NX 9821
Low Catton 80 SE 7053
Low Coniscliffe 84 NZ 2514
Low Crosby 89 NY 4459
Lowdham 61 SK 6646
Low Dinsdale 85 NZ 3411
Low Eggborough 79 SE 5522
Lower Aisholt 24 ST 2035
Lower Assendon 36 SU 7484
Lower Basildon 35 SU 6078
Lower Beeding 28 TQ 2227
Lower Benefield 52 SP 9888
Lower Boddington 51 SP 4752
Lower Bullingham 45 SO 5038
Lower Cam 46 SO 7401
Lower Chapel 41 SO 0235
Lower Chute 34 SU 3153
Lower Cwmtwrch 41 SN 7710
Lower Darwen 77 SD 6824
Lower Diabaig 123 NG 7960
Lower Down 48 SO 3384
Lower Dunsforth 79 SE 4464
Lower Farringdon 27 SU 7035
Lower Frankton 58 SJ 3732
Lower Froyle 35 SU 7544
Lower Gledfield 128 NH 5990
Lower Green 64 TF 9837
Lower Halstow 30 TQ 8567
Lower Hardres 31 TR 1453
Lower Heyford 47 SP 4824
Lower Higham 30 TQ 7172
Lower Hope, The (chan.) 30 TQ 7077
Lower Hordley 58 SJ 3929
Lower Icknield Way (ant.) 36 SP 8912
Lower Killeyan 98 NR 2743
Lower Langford 33 ST 4660
Lower Largo 103 NO 4102
Lower Lemington 47 SP 2134
Lower Lye 48 SO 4067
Lower Machen 41 ST 2288
Lower Maes-coed 45 SO 3431
Lower Moor 50 SO 9847
Lower Nazeing 37 TL 3906
Lower Penarth 41 ST 1869
Lower Penn 59 SO 8696
Lower Pennington 26 SZ 3193
Lower Peover 69 SJ 7474
Lower Quinton 50 SP 1847
Lower Sharpnose Point 22 SS 1912
Lower Shelton 52 SP 9942
Lower Shiplake 36 SU 7779
Lower Shuckburgh 51 SP 4862
Lower Slaughter 47 SP 1622
Lower Stanton St. Quintin 33 ST 9180
Lower Sundon 52 TL 0526
Lower Swanwick 27 SU 4909
Lower Swell 47 SP 1725
Lower Tamar Lake 22 SS 2910
Lower Thurlton 65 TM 4299
Lower Tysoe 50 SP 3445
Lower Upham 27 SU 5219
Lower Vexford 24 ST 1135
Lower Weare 32 ST 4053
Lower Wield 35 SU 6340
Lower Winchendon or Nether Winchendon 36 SP 7312
Lower Woodend 36 SU 8088
Lower Woodford 26 SU 1235
Lowesby 61 SK 7207
Lowestoft 65 TM 5493
Lowestoft End 65 TM 5394
Loweswater 82 NY 1421
Loweswater Fell 82 NY 1319
Low Gate 90 NY 9064
Lowgill (Cumbr.) 83 SD 6297
Lowgill (Lancs.) 77 SD 6564
Low Ham 25 ST 4329
Low Hartsop 83 NY 4013
Low Hesket 83 NY 4646
Low Hesleyhurst 91 NZ 0997
Lowick (Cumbr.) 77 SD 2985
Lowick (Northants.) 52 SP 9781
Lowick (Northum.) 97 NU 0139
Lowlandman's Bay 98 NR 5672
Low Mill 85 SE 6795
Low Moor 77 SD 7241
Lownie Moor 109 NO 4848
Lowood 96 NT 5235
Low Redford 84 NZ 0731
Low Row (Cumbr.) 90 NY 5863
Low Row (N Yorks.) 84 SD 9897
Lowsonford 50 SP 1867
Lowther Castle 83 NY 5223
Lowther College 67 SH 9975
Lowther Hill 88 NS 8810
Lowther Hills 88 NS 8910
Lowthorpe 81 TA 0860
Lowton 69 SJ 6197
Lowton Common 69 SJ 6397
Low Torry 102 NT 0086
Low Waters 94 NS 7353
Low Worsall 85 NZ 3909
Loxbeare 23 SS 9116
Loxhill 28 TQ 0037
Loxhore 23 SS 6138
Loxley 50 SP 2553
Loxton 32 ST 3755
Loxwood 28 TQ 0431
Lubcroy 127 NC 3501
Lubenham 51 SP 7087
Lùb Score 123 NG 3973
Luccombe 23 SS 9144
Luccombe Chine 27 SZ 5879
Luccombe Village 27 SZ 5880
Luce Bay 86 NX 2244
Luce Sands 86 NX 1453
Lucker 97 NU 1530
Luckett 20 SX 3873
Luckington 33 ST 8383
Lucklawhill 109 NO 4222
Luckwell Bridge 23 SS 9038
Lucton 48 SO 4364
Ludag 112 NF 7714
Ludborough 73 TF 2995
Ludchurch 42 SN 1411
Luddenden 78 SE 0425
Luddenham Court 31 TQ 9963
Luddesdown 30 TQ 6766
Luddington 74 SE 8216
Lude House 108 NN 8865
Ludford (Lincs.) 73 TF 1989
Ludford (Shrops.) 48 SO 5173
Ludgershall (Bucks.) 36 SP 6617
Ludgershall (Wilts.) 34 SU 2650
Ludgvan 18 SW 5033
Ludham 65 TG 3818
Ludlow 48 SO 5175
Ludwell 25 ST 9122
Ludworth 85 NZ 3641
Luffincott 20 SX 3394
Lugar 94 NS 5821
Lugar Water 93 NS 5022
Lugate Water 96 NT 4145
Luggate Burn 103 NT 6074
Luggiebank 101 NS 7672
Lugton 93 NS 4152
Lugton Water 93 NS 3848
Luguvalium (ant.) 83 NY 3955
Lugwardine 45 SO 5441
Luib 123 NG 5627
Luing (is.) 105 NM 7410
Luinga Bheag (is.) 111 NM 6187
Luinga Mhór (is) 111 NM 6086
Luinne Bheinn 111 NG 8600
Luirsay Dubh 112 NF 8640
Luithaid 131 NB 1713
Lui Water 117 NO 0592
Lulham 45 SO 4041
Lullingstone Castle 37 TQ 5364
Lullington (Derby.) 60 SK 2513
Lullington (Somer.) 33 ST 7851
Lulsgate Bottom 33 ST 5065
Lulsley 49 SO 7455
Lulworth Cove 25 SY 8279
Lumb 78 SE 0221
Lumby 79 SE 4830
Lumley Moor Resr. 79 SE 2270
Lumloch 101 NS 6369
Lumphanan 119 NJ 5804
Lumphinnans 102 NT 1692
Lumsdaine 97 NT 8769
Lumsden 121 NJ 4722
Lunan 109 NO 6851
Lunan Bay 109 NO 7051
Lunan Burn 108 NO 1542
Lunanhead 109 NO 4752
Lunan Water 109 NO 6149
Luncarty 108 NO 0929
Lund (Humbs.) 81 SE 9648
Lund (N Yorks.) 79 SE 6532
Lund (Unst) 143 HP 5703
Lunda Wick 143 HP 5604
Lunderston Bay 100 NS 1873
Lundie (Highld.) 115 NH 1410
Lundie (Tays.) 108 NO 2836
Lundin Links 103 NO 4002
Lundy 22 SS 1443
Lune Forest 83 NY 8323
Lune Moor 84 NY 9023
Lunga (Island of Mull) (is.) 104 NM 2741
Lunga (Strath.) (is.) 105 NM 7008
Lunga Hotel 105 NM 7906
Lunna 143 HU 4869
Lunna Holm 143 HU 5274
Lunnasting (dist.) 141 HU 4865
Lunning 141 HU 5066
Lunning Sound 141 HU 5165
Lunsford's Cross 29 TQ 7210
Lunt 68 SD 3401
Luntley 45 SO 3955
Luppitt 24 ST 1606
Lupton 77 SD 5581
Lupton Beck 77 SD 5580
Lurgashall 28 SU 9326
Lurg Hill 121 NJ 5057
Lurg Mhór (mt.) 115 NH 0640
Lurgmore 116 NH 5937
Lusby 73 TF 3367
Luskentyre 125 NG 0699
Lusragan Burn 106 NM 9031
Luss 100 NS 3592
Lussa Loch 92 NR 7130
Lussa Point 99 NR 6486
Lussa River (Island of Mull) 105 NM 6531
Lussa River (Jura) 99 NR 6292
Lusta 122 NG 2756
Lustleigh 21 SX 7881
Luston 48 SO 4863
Luthermuir 109 NO 6568
Luther Water 109 NO 6870
Luthrie 108 NO 3219
Luton (Beds.) 36 TL 0821
Luton (Devon) 21 SX 9076
Luton (Kent) 30 TQ 7766
Luton Airport 37 TL 1221
Lutterworth 51 SP 5484
Lutton (Devon) 21 SX 5959
Lutton (Lincs.) 63 TF 4325
Lutton (Northants.) 52 TL 1187
Luxborough 23 SS 9738
Luxhay Reservoir 24 ST 2017
Luxulyan 19 SX 0458
Lybster 135 ND 2435
Lydbury North 48 SO 3486
Lydcott 23 SS 6936
Lydd 31 TR 0421
Lydd Airport 31 TR 0621
Lydden 31 TR 2645
Lyddington 62 SP 8797
Lydd-on-Sea 31 TR 0819
Lydeard St. Lawrence 24 ST 1232
Lydford (Devon) 20 SX 5084
Lydford (Somer.) 25 ST 5731
Lydgate 78 SD 9225
Lydham 48 SO 3391
Lydiard Millicent 34 SU 0986
Lydiate 68 SD 3604
Lydlinch 25 ST 7413
Lydney 45 SO 6203
Lydney Sand 45 ST 6399
Lydstep 42 SS 0898
Lye 49 SO 9284
Lye Green 36 SP 9703
Lyford 47 SU 3994
Lymbridge Green 31 TR 1243
Lyme Park (ant.) 70 SJ 9682
Lyme Regis 24 SY 3492
Lyminge 31 TR 1641
Lyminge Forest 31 TR 1545
Lymington 26 SZ 3295
Lymington River 26 SU 3102
Lyminster 28 TQ 0204
Lymm 69 SJ 6786
Lymore 26 SZ 2992
Lympne 31 TR 1235
Lympsham 32 ST 3454
Lympstone 21 SX 9984
Lynaberack 116 NN 7694
Lynchat 116 NH 7801
Lyn Cwmdulyn Reservoir 66 SH 4949
Lyndale House 122 NG 3654
Lyndale Point 122 NG 3657
Lyndhurst 26 SU 2907
Lyndhurst Road Station 26 SU 3309
Lyndon 62 SK 9004
Lyne 36 TQ 0166
Lyneal 58 SJ 4433
Lyneham (Oxon.) 47 SP 2720
Lyneham (Wilts.) 34 SU 0179
Lyne House 28 TQ 1938
Lynemouth 91 NZ 2991
Lyne of Gorthleck 116 NH 5420
Lyne of Skene 119 NJ 7610
Lyness 136 ND 3094
Lyne Water 95 NT 1645
Lyng (Norf.) 64 TG 0617
Lyng (Somer.) 24 ST 3328
Lynmouth 23 SS 7249
Lynn Deeps (chan.) 63 TF 5846
Lynn of Lorn 105 NM 8639
Lynsted 30 TQ 9461
Lynton 23 SS 7149
Lyon's Gate 25 ST 6605
Lyonshall 45 SO 3356
Lype Hill 23 SS 9537
Lyrawa Burn 136 ND 2699
Lyrie Geo 136 ND 2096
Lytchett Matravers 26 SY 9495
Lytchett Minster 26 SY 9593
Lyth 135 ND 2763
Lytham 77 SD 3727
Lytham St. Anne's 77 SD 3427
Lythe 85 NZ 8413
Lythes 136 ND 4589

M

Maaey Riabhach 124 NF 8850
Maaruig 125 NB 1906
Maa Water 141 HU 3755
Mabe Burnthouse 18 SW 7634
Mabie 88 NX 9570
Mablethorpe 73 TF 5085
Macaterick 87 NX 4390
Macclesfield 69 SJ 9173
Macclesfield Canal (Ches.) 69 SJ 9166
Macclesfield Canal (Ches.) 69 SJ 9482
Macclesfield Forest 70 SJ 9772
Macduff 121 NJ 7064
Macduff's Castle (ant.) 103 NT 3497
Machany Water 107 NN 8415
Macharioch 92 NR 7309
Machars, The (dist.) 86 NX 3753
Machen 41 ST 2189
Machir Bay 98 NR 1962
Machrie Bay 92 NR 8834
Machrie Water 92 NR 9334
Machrihanish 92 NR 6220
Machrihanish Airfield 92 NR 6622
Machrihanish Bay 92 NR 6423
Machrihanish Water 92 NR 6520
Machynlleth 57 SH 7401
Mackworth 60 SK 3137
Maclean's Nose 111 NM 5361
Macleod's Maidens (is.) 122 NG 2436
Macleod's Tables (mt.) 122 NG 2243
Macmerry 103 NT 4372
Madadh Gruamach (is.) 124 NF 9566
Madderty 108 NN 9522
Maddiston 102 NS 9476
Madehurst 28 SU 9810
Madeley (Shrops.) 59 SJ 6904
Madeley (Staffs.) 59 SJ 7744
Madingley 53 TL 3960
Madley 45 SO 4138
Madresfield 49 SO 8047
Madron 18 SW 4532
Mad Wharf (sbk.) 68 SD 2607
Maelienydd 48 SO 1271
Maenclochog 42 SN 0827
Maendy 41 ST 0176
Mae Ness 138 HY 4831
Maentwrog 67 SH 6640
Maer 59 SJ 7938
Maerdy (Clwyd) 67 SJ 0144
Maerdy (Mid Glam.) 41 SS 9798
Maesbrook 58 SJ 3121
Maesbury Marsh 58 SJ 3125
Maes-glas 32 ST 2985
Maesgwynne 43 SN 2024
Maeshafn 68 SJ 2061
Maes Howe (ant.) 136 HY 3112
Maesllyn 43 SN 3644
Maesmynis 44 SO 0148
Maesteg 41 SS 8591
Maesybont 43 SN 5616
Maesycwmmer 41 ST 1594
Maesyrchen Mountain 58 SJ 1846
Magdalen Laver 37 TL 5108
Maggieknockater 121 NJ 3145
Magham Down 29 TQ 6111
Maghannan 131 NB 0821
Maghull 68 SD 3702
Magor 33 ST 4287
Maiden Bradley 33 ST 8038
Maiden Castle (ant.) 25 SY 6688
Maidencombe 21 SX 9268
Maidenhead 36 SU 8881
Maidenhead Bay 93 NS 2008
Maiden Island 105 NM 8432
Maiden Law 84 NZ 1749
Maiden Newton 25 SY 5997
Maidenpap (Dumf. and Galwy.) (mt.) 88 NX 8961
Maiden Pap (Highld.) (mt.) 135 ND 0429
Maiden Paps (Borders) (mt.) 89 NT 5002
Maidens 93 NS 2107
Maiden Stone (ant.) 121 NJ 7024
Maiden Way (Cumbr.) (ant.) 83 NY 6535
Maiden Way (Northum.) (ant.) 83 NY 6756
Maidenwell 19 SX 1470
Maidford 51 SP 6052
Maids Moreton 51 SP 7035
Maidstone 29 TQ 7656
Maidwell 51 SP 7477
Mail 141 HU 4228
Mainland (Orkney) 136 HY 3711
Mainland (Shetld.) 141 HU 4051
Mains 116 NH 4239
Mains of Ardestie 109 NO 5034
Mains of Balhall 109 NO 5163
Mains of Ballindarg 109 NO 4051
Mains of Dalvey 117 NJ 1132
Mains of Dillavaird 119 NO 7481
Mains of Drum 119 NO 8099
Mains of Melgund 109 NO 5456
Mains of Thornton 109 NO 6871
Mainstone 48 SO 2687
Main Water of Luce 86 NX 1468
Maisemore 46 SO 8121
Maisgeir (is.) 104 NM 3539
Malasgair (mt.) 131 NB 3017
Malborough 21 SX 7039
Malcolm's Head 139 HZ 1970
Malcolm's Point 105 NM 4918
Maldon 38 TL 8506
Malham 78 SD 9062
Malham Tarn 78 SD 8966
Mallaig 111 NM 6796
Mallart River 133 NC 6737
Mallerstang Common 83 SD 7798
Mallowdale Fell 77 SD 6159
Malltraeth Bay 66 SH 3764
Malltraeth Marsh 66 SH 4471
Malltraeth Sands 66 SH 4066
Mallwyd 57 SH 8612
Malmesbury 34 ST 9387
Malpas (Ches.) 59 SJ 4847
Malpas (Cornwall) 19 SW 8442
Malpas (S Glam.) 32 ST 3091
Maltby (Cleve.) 85 NZ 4613
Maltby (S Yorks.) 71 SK 5392
Maltby le Marsh 73 TF 4681
Maltman's Hill 30 TQ 9043
Malton 80 SE 7871
Malvern Hills 49 SO 7641
Malvern Link 49 SO 7848
Malvern Wells 49 SO 7742
Màm an Staing 123 NG 7813
Mamble 49 SO 6871
Mam na Gualainn 106 NN 1162
Mamore Forest 106 NN 1765
Màm Sodhail 115 NH 1225
Màm Suim 117 NJ 0109
Mam Tor (ant.) 70 SK 1283
Manaccan 18 SW 7625
Manacle Point 19 SW 8121
Manacles, The (pt.) 19 SW 8120
Manafon 58 SJ 1102
Man and his man or Bawden Rocks 18 SW 6953
Manar House 119 NJ 7319
Manaton 21 SX 7481
Manby 73 TF 3986
Mancetter 60 SP 3196
Manchester 69 SJ 8397
Manchester Airport 69 SJ 8184
Manchester Ship Canal 69 SJ 6989
Mancot 68 SJ 3267
Mandally 115 NH 2900
Manea 53 TL 4789
Manfield 84 NZ 2213
Mangaster 142 HU 3270
Mangersta 130 NB 0131
Mangotsfield 33 ST 6676
Manish (Harris, W Isles) 125 NG 1089
Manish (Scarp) 130 NA 9513
Manish Point (Island of Raasay) 123 NG 5648
Manish Point (North Uist) 124 NF 7173
Mankinholes 78 SD 9523
Manley 69 SJ 5071
Manmoel 41 SO 1703
Mannal 104 NL 9840
Manningford Bohune 34 SU 1357
Manningford Bruce 34 SU 1359
Manning's Heath 28 TQ 2028
Mannington 26 SU 0605
Manningtree 55 TM 1031
Mannofield 119 NJ 9104
Manorbier 42 SS 0698
Manorhill 96 NT 6632
Manorowen 42 SM 9336
Manor Water 95 NT 2031
Man o' Scord (mt.) 142 HU 3283
Manquhill Hill 88 NX 6694
Mansell Gamage 45 SO 3944
Mansell Lacy 45 SO 4245
Mansergh 77 SD 6082
Mansfield (Notts.) 71 SK 5361
Mansfield (Strath.) 88 NS 6214
Mansfield Woodhouse 71 SK 5363

Mansie's Berg (pt.) ....141 HU 5341
Mansriggs ....77 SD 2880
Manston ....25 ST 8115
Manston Aerodrome ....31 TR 3366
Manthorpe ....62 TF 0616
Manton (Humbs.) ....74 SE 9302
Manton (Leic.) ....62 SK 8704
Manton (Wilts.) ....34 SU 1768
Mantyn Dyke (ant.) ....48 SO 2090
Manuden ....53 TL 4926
Maoile Lunndaidh (mt.) ....127 NH 1345
Maol Breac ....106 NN 2515
Maol Buidhe ....98 NR 2945
Maol Chean-dearg ....126 NG 9249
Maol Chinn-dearg ....115 NH 0407
Maol nan Damh ....99 NR 6288
Maovally (mt.) ....132 NC 3721
Maplebeck ....72 SK 7160
Maple Cross ....36 TQ 0392
Mapledurham ....36 SU 6776
Mapledurwell ....35 SU 6851
Maplehurst ....28 TQ 1924
Mapleton ....73 SK 1648
Maplin Sands ....39 TR 0388
Mapperley ....60 SK 4343
Mapperton ....25 SY 5099
Mappleborough Green ....50 SP 0866
Mappleton ....75 TA 2244
Mappowder ....25 ST 7105
Maragay Mòr ....124 NF 8952
Marazion ....18 SW 5130
Marbury ....59 SJ 5545
March ....63 TL 4197
Marcham ....47 SU 4596
Marchamley ....59 SJ 5929
Marchbankwood ....89 NY 0899
March Ghyll Resr. ....78 SE 1251
Marchington ....73 SK 1330
Marchington Woodlands ....60 SK 1128
Marchnant ....57 SN 7470
Marchwiel ....58 SJ 3547
Marchwood ....26 SU 3809
Marcross ....41 SS 9269
Mardale Common ....83 NY 4811
Marden (Here. and Worc.) ....45 SO 5247
Marden (Kent) ....29 TQ 7444
Marden (Wilts.) ....34 SU 0857
Mardy ....45 SO 3016
Mare Fen ....53 TL 5488
Marefield ....61 SK 7408
Mareham le Fen ....73 TF 2761
Mareham on the Hill ....73 TF 2867
Maresfield ....29 TQ 4624
Mare Tail (sbk.) ....63 TF 4437
Marfleet ....75 TA 1329
Margam ....41 SS 7887
Margam Burrows ....41 SS 7785
Margaret Marsh ....25 ST 8218
Margaret Roding ....38 TL 5912
Margaretting ....38 TL 6601
Margate ....31 TR 3670
Marg na Craige ....116 NN 6297
Margnaheglish ....92 NS 0331
Marham ....64 TF 7110
Marhamchurch ....22 SS 2203
Marholm ....62 TF 1402
Marian-glas ....68 SH 5084
Mariansleigh ....23 SS 7422
Marishader ....123 NG 4963
Maristow ....20 SX 4764
Mark ....32 ST 3747
Marka Ber ....137 HY 5907
Markbeech ....29 TQ 4842
Markby ....73 TF 4878
Mark Causeway ....32 ST 3547
Mark Cross ....29 TQ 5831
Market Bosworth ....60 SK 4003
Market Deeping ....62 TF 1310
Market Drayton ....59 SJ 6734
Market Harborough ....51 SP 7387
Markethill ....108 NO 2239
Market Lavington ....34 SU 0154
Market Overton ....62 SK 8816
Market Rasen ....72 TF 1089
Market Stainton ....73 TF 2279
Market Weighton ....74 SE 8741
Market Weston ....54 TL 9877
Markfield ....60 SK 4810
Markham ....41 SO 1600
Markinch ....103 NO 2901
Markington ....79 SE 2864
Marksbury ....33 ST 6662
Marks Tey ....54 TL 9123
Markwell ....20 SX 3658
Markyate ....36 TL 0616
Marlborough ....34 SU 1869
Marlborough Downs ....34 SU 1574
Marlcliff ....50 SP 0950
Marldon ....21 SX 8663
Marlesford ....55 TM 3258
Marley Green ....59 SJ 5745
Marlingford ....65 TG 1208
Marloes ....42 SM 7908
Marlow ....36 SU 8587
Marlpit Hill ....29 TQ 4447
Marnhull ....25 ST 7718
Marnoch (Grampn.) ....121 NJ 5950
Marnoch (Strath.) ....101 NS 7168
Marple ....79 SJ 9588
Marr ....71 SE 5105
Marrick ....84 SE 0798
Marrister ....141 HU 5464
Marrival (mt.) ....124 NF 8070
Marros ....43 SN 2008
Marsco (mt.) ....123 NG 5025
Marsden (Gtr Mches.) ....78 SE 0411
Marsden Bay ....91 NZ 4065
Marsett ....78 SD 9086
Marsh ....24 ST 2410
Marshalls Heath ....37 TL 1515
Marsham ....65 TG 1924
Marshaw ....77 SD 5853
Marsh Baldon ....47 SU 5699
Marshborough ....31 TR 2958
Marshbrook ....58 SO 4389
Marshchapel ....75 TF 3598
Marshfield (Avon) ....33 ST 7773
Marshfield (Gwent) ....32 ST 2582
Marshgate ....20 SX 1592
Marsh Gibbon ....36 SP 6423
Marsh Green (Devon) ....24 ST 0093
Marsh Green (Kent) ....29 TQ 4344
Marsh Green (Shrops.) ....59 SJ 6014
Marshland (Humbs.) ....74 SE 7820
Marshland (Norf.) ....63 TF 5412
Marshland Fen ....63 TF 5407
Marshland St. James ....63 TF 5108
Marshside ....76 SD 3419
Marske ....84 NZ 1000
Marske-by-the-Sea ....91 NZ 6322
Marston (Ches.) ....59 SJ 6474
Marston (Here. and Worc.) ....45 SO 3657
Marston (Lincs.) ....62 SK 8943
Marston (Oxon.) ....47 SP 5208
Marston (Staffs.) ....59 SJ 8314
Marston (Staffs.) ....59 SJ 9227
Marston (Warw.) ....60 SP 2095

Marston (Wilts.) ....34 ST 9656
Marston Green ....50 SP 1685
Marston Magna ....25 ST 5922
Marston Meysey ....47 SU 1297
Marston Montgomery ....60 SK 1338
Marston Moor ....79 SE 4853
Marston Moretaine ....52 SP 9941
Marston on Dove ....60 SK 2329
Marston St. Lawrence ....51 SP 5342
Marston Stannett ....45 SO 5655
Marston Trussell ....51 SP 6986
Marstow ....45 SO 5519
Marsworth ....36 SP 9214
Marten ....34 SU 2860
Marthall ....69 SJ 8076
Martham ....65 TG 4518
Martin (Hants.) ....26 SU 0719
Martin (Lincs.) ....73 TF 1259
Martindale ....83 NY 4218
Martindale Common ....83 NY 4417
Martin Dales ....73 TF 1761
Martin Drove End ....26 SU 0420
Martinhoe ....23 SS 6648
Martin Hussingtree ....49 SO 8860
Martinscroft ....69 SJ 6589
Martinstown ....25 SY 6488
Martlesham ....55 TM 2547
Martlesham Heath ....55 TM 2545
Martletwy ....42 SN 0310
Martley ....49 SO 7559
Martnaham Loch ....93 NS 3917
Martock ....25 ST 4619
Marton (Ches.) ....69 SJ 8468
Marton (Cleve.) ....85 NZ 5115
Marton (Lincs.) ....72 SK 8381
Marton (N Yorks.) ....79 SE 4162
Marton (N Yorks.) ....80 SE 7383
Marton (Shrops.) ....58 SJ 2802
Marton (Warw.) ....50 SP 4069
Marton Abbey ....79 SE 5869
Marvig ....131 NB 4119
Mar Wick (Orkney) ....136 HY 2224
Marwick (Orkney) ....136 HY 2325
Marwick Head ....136 HY 2225
Marwood ....23 SS 5437
Marybank ....128 NH 4753
Maryburgh ....128 NH 5456
Marygold ....97 NT 8160
Maryhill ....121 NJ 8245
Marykirk ....109 NO 6865
Marylebone ....69 SD 5807
Marylebone ....37 TQ 2881
Marypark ....117 NJ 1938
Maryport (Cumbr.) ....82 NY 0336
Maryport (Dumf. and Galwy.) ....86 NX 1434
Maryport Bay ....86 NX 1434
Marystow ....20 SX 4382
Mary Tavy ....20 SX 5079
Maryton (Grampn.) ....119 NO 6856
Marywell (Grampn.) ....119 NO 5896
Marywell (Tays.) ....109 NO 6544
Masham ....79 SE 2280
Masham Moor ....78 SE 1079
Mashbury ....38 TL 6511
Mason ....91 NZ 2073
Massacamber (pt.) ....124 NF 9382
Massingham Heath ....64 TF 7620
Mastrick ....119 NJ 9007
Matching ....37 TL 5212
Matching Green ....37 TL 5311
Matching Tye ....37 TL 5111
Matfen ....91 NZ 0371
Matfield ....29 TQ 6541
Mathern ....33 ST 5291
Mathon ....49 SO 7345
Mathry ....42 SM 8832
Matlaske ....65 TG 1534
Matlock ....71 SK 3060
Matlock Bath ....71 SK 2958
Matson ....46 SO 8316
Matterdale End ....83 NY 3923
Mattersey ....72 SK 6889
Matthew's Port ....93 NS 1903
Mattingley ....35 SU 7357
Mattishall ....64 TG 0510
Mattishall Burgh ....64 TG 0511
Mauchline ....93 NS 4927
Maud ....121 NJ 9247
Maugersbury ....47 SP 1925
Maughold ....76 SC 4991
Maughold Head ....76 SC 4991
Maulden ....52 TL 0538
Maulds Meaburn ....83 NY 6216
Maunby ....79 SE 3486
Maund Bryan ....45 SO 5550
Mautby ....65 TG 4712
Mavesyn Ridware ....60 SK 0817
Mavis Enderby ....73 TF 3666
Mavis Grind ....142 HU 3469
Mawbray ....82 NY 0846
Mawdesley ....76 SD 4914
Mawgan ....18 SW 7024
Mawgan Porth ....19 SW 8467
Maw Green ....60 SP 0197
Mawla ....18 SW 6945
Mawnan ....19 SW 7827
Mawnan Smith ....18 SW 7728
Maxey ....62 TF 1208
Maxstoke ....50 SP 2386
Maxton ....96 NT 6129
Maxwellheugh ....96 NT 7333
Maxwellston ....86 NS 2600
Mayar (mt.) ....117 NO 2373
Maybole ....103 NS 3009
Mayfield ....73 SK 1445
Mayfield (E Susx) ....29 TQ 5827
Mayfield (Staffs.) ....60 SK 1545
Mayford ....28 SU 9956
May Hill ....46 SO 6921
Mayland ....39 TL 9101
Maypole ....45 SO 4716
Maypole Green ....65 TM 4195
Maywick ....141 HU 3724
McArthur's Head ....98 NR 4659
McFarlane's Rock ....122 NG 3031
McFarquhar's Cave ....129 NH 7965
Meadie Burn ....133 NC 5038
Meadle ....36 SP 8005
Meadowtown ....58 SJ 3101
Mealasta ....130 NA 0122
Mealasta Island ....130 NA 9721
Meal Bank ....83 SD 5495
Mealdarroch Point ....100 NR 8868
Mealfuarvonie ....116 NH 4522
Mealisval (mt.) ....130 NB 0227
Meall a' Bhata ....133 NG 6326
Meall a' Bhreacraibh ....116 NH 7935
Meall a' Bhuachaille ....117 NH 9811
Meall a' Chàise ....105 NM 7517
Meall a' Chaorainn ....127 NH 1360
Meallach Mhòr ....116 NN 7791
Meall a' Choire Bhuidhe ....108 NO 0671
Meall a' Chrasgaidh ....127 NH 1873
Meall a' Chràthaich ....115 NH 3622
Meall a' Churain ....107 NN 4632
Meall a' Ghrianain ....127 NH 3677
Meall a' Mhadaidh ....107 NN 5925
Meall a' Mhuic ....107 NN 5750
Meall an Aonach ....132 NC 5316
Meall an Arbhair ....98 NR 3990
Meallan Buidhe (Highld.) ....115 NH 1337
Meallan Buidhe (Highld.) ....127 NH 3344

Meall an Damhain ....111 NM 7259
Meall an Doirein ....123 NG 8575
Meall an Fhuarain (Highld.) ....127 NC 2802
Meall an Fhuarain (Highld.) ....133 NC 5130
Meall an Fhuarain (Island of Skye)
                                  123 NG 4535
Meall an Inbhire ....124 NM 4656
Meallan Liath ....133 NC 5150
Meallan Liath Beag ....134 NC 8815
Meallan Liath Coire Mhic Dhughaill
                                  132 NC 3539
Meall Liath Mòr ....133 NC 6517
Meall an t-Seallaidh ....107 NN 5423
Meall an t-Sithe ....127 NH 1376
Meall an Tuirc ....128 NH 5471
Meall a' Phiobaire ....133 NC 6915
Meall a' Phubuill ....114 NN 0385
Meall Bhenneit ....128 NN 5483
Meall Blàir ....115 NN 0795
Meall Buidhe (Highld.) ....116 NN 8095
Meall Buidhe (Highld.) ....111 NM 8498
Meall Buidhe (Strath.) ....92 NR 7332
Meall Buidhe (Tays.) ....107 NN 4245
Meall Buidhe (Tays.) ....107 NN 4949
Meall Caia ....101 NN 5012
Meall Cruaidh ....116 NN 5780
Meall Cruinn ....108 NN 4547
Meall Dearg ....108 NN 8841
Meall Dheirgidh ....128 NH 4794
Meall Dubh (Argyll.) ....100 NS 0789
Meall Dubh (Highld.) ....127 NH 2089
Meall Dubh (Highld.) ....115 NH 2407
Meall Fuar-mhonaidh ....116 NH 4522
Meall Gainmheich ....101 NN 5109
Meall Garbh (Strath.) ....106 NN 1636
Meall Garbh (Tays.) ....107 NN 6443
Meall Geal ....131 NB 5660
Meall Ghaordaidh ....107 NN 5139
Meall Gorm (Grampn.) ....117 NO 1894
Meall Gorm (Highld.) ....123 NG 7840
Meall Gorm (Highld.) ....127 NH 2269
Meall Leacachain ....127 NH 2477
Meall Liath ....116 NN 2296
Meall Loch Airigh Alasdair ....123 NG 7436
Meall Luaidhe ....107 NN 5843
Meall Luidh Mòr ....116 NN 4179
Meall Meadhonach ....132 NC 4162
Meall Mhic Iomhair ....128 NH 3167
Meall Mòr (Highld.) ....128 NH 5174
Meall Mòr (Highld.) ....116 NH 7335
Meall Mòr (Highld.) ....106 NN 1056
Meall Mòr (Highld.) (is.) ....127 NC 1237
Meall Moraig ....128 NH 6694
Meall na Caorach ....135 ND 0927
Meall na Drochaide ....128 NH 5069
Meall na h-Aisre ....116 NH 5061
Meall na h-Uamha ....123 NG 5332
Meall na h-Uamha ....123 NG 7765
Meall na Leitreach ....107 NN 6470
Meall nam Bràdhan ....127 NH 2690
Meall na Mèine ....126 NG 9081
Meall nan Fuaran ....116 NH 6297
Meall nan Caorach ....116 NH 4735
Meall nan Caorach (Tayside) ....108 NN 9234
Meall nan Con (Highld.) ....133 NC 5830
Meall nan Con (Highld.) ....111 NM 5068
Meall nan Creag Leac ....111 NM 8674
Meall nan Each ....111 NM 6364
Meall nan Ruadhag ....106 NN 2957
Meall nan Tarmachan ....107 NN 5838
Meall nan Tighearn ....106 NN 2323
Meall na Speireig ....128 NH 4966
Meall na Suiramach ....123 NG 4469
Meall Odhar (Strath.) ....106 NM 9416
Meall Odhar (Tays.) ....107 NN 6414
Meall Odhar (Tays.) ....107 NN 6639
Meall Reamhar (Strath.) ....108 NR 8370
Meall Reamhar (Tays.) ....107 NN 6721
Meall Reamhar (Tays.) ....108 NN 8670
Meall Reamhar (Tays.) ....108 NN 8732
Meall Reamhar (Tays.) ....108 NO 0356
Meall Tairneachan ....107 NN 8054
Meall Tarsuinn ....108 NN 8729
Meall Taurnie ....107 NN 4838
Meall Uaine ....108 NO 1167
Mealna Letter or Duchray Hill .....108 NO 1667
Meal nan Damh ....92 NN 9146
Mealsgate ....82 NY 2141
Mearbeck ....78 SD 8160
Meare ....33 ST 4541
Mears Ashby ....51 SP 8366
Measham ....60 SK 3312
Meathop ....77 SD 4380
Meaul (mt.) ....87 NX 5091
Meavaig ....130 TA 0939
Meavag ....125 NG 1596
Meavaig ....125 NB 0905
Meavaig River ....125 NB 0908
Meavy ....135 SX 5407
Medbourne ....61 SP 7993
Medburn ....91 NZ 1370
Meddon ....22 SS 2717
Meden Vale ....54 SK 5869
Medmenham ....36 SU 8084
Medstead ....66 SU 6537
Meerbrook ....70 SJ 9860
Meer End ....50 SP 2474
Meesden ....53 TL 4432
Meeth ....23 SS 5408
Meggat Water ....89 NY 2996
Meggernie Castle ....107 NN 5546
Meggethead ....95 NT 1621
Megget Reservoir (under constn.)
                                   95 NT 1922
Meg's Craig ....109 NO 6844
Meidrim ....39 SN 2820
Meifod ....58 SJ 1513
Meigle ....108 NO 2844
Meigle Hill ....96 NT 4636
Meikle Black Law ....108 NT 8268
Meikle Carewe Hill ....119 NO 8291
Meikle Conval ....117 NJ 2937
Meikle Craigs ....93 NS 3228
Meikle Earnock ....94 NS 7253
Meikle Float ....86 NX 0748
Meikle Hard Hill ....88 NX 9363
Meikle Hill ....129 NJ 1450
Meikleour ....108 NO 1539
Meikle Says Law ....103 NT 5861
Meikle Strath ....109 NO 6471
Meikle Tarty ....121 NJ 9928
Meikle Wartle ....121 NJ 7230
Meinciau ....43 SN 4810
Meir ....59 SJ 9342
Meirheim ....111 NM 8287
Melbecks Moor ....84 NY 9400
Melbost ....131 NB 4632
Melbost Sands ....131 NB 4535
Melbourn (Cambs.) ....53 TL 3844
Melbourne (Derby.) ....60 SK 3825
Melbourne (Humbs.) ....74 SE 7543
Melbury ....22 SS 3719
Melbury Bubb ....25 ST 5906
Melbury Osmond ....25 ST 5707
Melbury Sampford ....25 ST 5705
Melby House ....140 HU 1857
Melchbourne ....52 TL 0265
Melcombe Bingham ....25 ST 7602
Meldon (Devon) ....21 SX 5592
Meldon (Northum.) ....91 NZ 1284

Meldon Reservoir ....21 SX 5691
Meldreth ....53 TL 3746
Meldrum House ....121 NJ 8129
Melfort ....105 NM 8314
Melgarve ....116 NN 4695
Meliden ....67 SJ 0580
Melin-y-coed ....67 SH 8201
Melincourt ....41 SN 8402
Melin-y-ddôl ....57 SJ 0807
Melin-y-grug ....57 SJ 0507
Melin-y-wig ....67 SJ 0448
Melkinthorpe ....83 NY 5525
Melkridge ....90 NY 7363
Melksham ....33 ST 9063
Melldalloch ....100 NR 9375
Mellerstain Ho. ....96 NT 6439
Mell Head ....135 ND 3476
Mellguards ....90 NY 7444
Mell Fell ....83 NY 4024
Melling (Lancs.) ....77 SD 5970
Melling (Mers.) ....68 SD 3800
Mellis ....55 TM 0974
Mellon Charles ....126 NG 8491
Mellon Udrigle ....126 NG 8895
Mellor (Gtr Mches.) ....79 SJ 9888
Mellor (Lancs.) ....77 SD 6530
Mellor Brook ....77 SD 6331
Mells ....33 ST 7249
Melmerby (Cumbr.) ....83 NY 6137
Melmerby (N Yorks.) ....78 SE 0785
Melmerby (N Yorks.) ....79 SE 3376
Melness ....133 NC 5862
Melon Green ....54 TL 8653
Melplash ....25 SY 4797
Melrose ....96 NT 5433
Melsetter ....136 ND 2689
Melsonby ....84 NZ 1908
Meltham ....70 SE 0910
Melton ....55 TM 2850
Meltonby ....80 SE 7952
Melton Constable ....64 TG 0433
Melton Mowbray ....61 SK 7518
Melton Ross ....74 TA 0610
Melvaig ....126 NG 7486
Melverley ....58 SJ 3316
Melvich ....134 NC 8864
Melvich Bay ....134 NC 8865
Membury ....24 ST 2703
Memsie ....121 NJ 9762
Memus ....108 NO 4258
Menabilly ....19 SX 0951
Menai Bridge ....66 SH 5572
Menai Strait ....66 SH 5471
Mendham ....55 TM 2783
Mendick Hill ....95 NT 1250
Mendip Forest ....33 ST 4954
Mendip Hills ....33 ST 5255
Mendlesham ....55 TM 1065
Mendlesham Green ....55 TM 0963
Menheniot ....20 SX 2862
Mennock ....88 NS 8008
Menston ....78 SE 1743
Menstrie ....102 NS 8596
Menteith Hills ....101 NN 5502
Mentmore ....36 SP 9019
Meòir Langwell ....128 NH 4298
Meole Brace ....59 SJ 4811
Meon Hill ....50 SP 1745
Meonstoke ....118 SU 6119
Meon Valley ....27 SU 5915
Meopham ....38 TQ 6466
Meopham Station ....38 TQ 6467
Mepal ....53 TL 4481
Meppershall ....52 TL 1336
Merbach ....45 SO 3045
Mere (Ches.) ....69 SJ 7281
Mere (Wilts.) ....25 ST 8132
Mere Brow ....76 SD 4118
Mereclough ....78 SD 8730
Mere Green ....50 SP 1298
Mere, The ....58 SJ 4134
Mereworth ....29 TQ 6553
Mereworth Castle ....29 TQ 6653
Mergie ....119 NU 7988
Meriden ....50 SP 2482
Merkadale ....122 NG 3831
Merkland ....86 NX 2491
Merkland Lodge ....132 NC 4029
Merkland Point ....92 NS 0339
Merlin's Bridge ....42 SM 9414
Merrick ....87 NX 4285
Merrington ....58 SJ 4621
Merriott ....24 ST 4412
Merrivale ....21 SX 5475
Merrymeet ....20 SX 2766
Merse (dist.) ....97 NT 8247
Mersea Flats (sbk.) ....39 TM 0513
Mersea Island ....39 TM 0314
Mersehead Sands ....88 NX 9153
Mersham ....31 TR 0539
Merstham ....37 TQ 2953
Merston ....27 SU 8903
Merstone ....27 SZ 5285
Merther ....19 SW 8644
Merthyr ....43 SN 3520
Merthyr Cynog ....44 SN 9837
Merthyr Dyfan ....41 ST 1169
Merthyr Mawr ....41 SS 8877
Merthyr Tydfil ....41 SO 0406
Merthyr Vale ....41 ST 0899
Merton (Devon) ....23 SS 5212
Merton (Gtr London) ....37 TQ 2569
Merton (Norf.) ....64 TL 9098
Merton (Oxon.) ....47 SP 5717
Mervinslaw ....90 NT 6713
Meshaw ....23 SS 7519
Messing ....38 TL 8918
Messingham ....74 SE 8904
Metfield ....55 TM 2980
Metheringham ....72 TF 0661
Methil ....103 NT 3699
Methley ....79 SE 3826
Methlick ....121 NJ 8537
Methven ....108 NO 0225
Methwold ....64 TL 7394
Methwold Fens ....63 TL 6593
Methwold Hythe ....64 TL 7195
Mettingham ....55 TM 3689
Mevagissey ....19 SX 0144
Mevagissey Bay ....19 SX 0246
New Stone ....17 SX 4149
Mexborough ....124 NF 4799
Mey ....135 ND 2872
Meysey Hampton ....34 SU 1199
Miavaig ....131 NB 0834
Michaelchurch ....45 SO 5125
Michaelchurch Escley ....45 SO 3134
Michaelchurch-on-Arrow ....45 SO 2450
Michaelston-le-Pit ....41 ST 1573
Michaelston-y-Fedw ....32 ST 2484
Michaelstow ....20 SX 0778
Micheldever ....35 SU 5138
Micheldever Forest ....35 SU 5741
Micheldever Station ....35 SU 5142
Micheldever Wood ....27 SU 5337
Michelmersh ....26 SU 3426
Mickfield ....55 TM 1361
Micklebring ....71 SK 5194
Mickle Fell ....83 NY 8024
Micklefield ....29 TQ 1753
Mickleover ....60 SK 3034

Mickleton (Durham) ....84 NY 9623
Mickleton (Glos.) ....50 SP 1543
Mickle Trafford ....68 SJ 4469
Mickley ....28 SE 2576
Mickley Square ....91 NZ 0761
Mid Ardlaw ....121 NJ 9464
Mid Barrow (lightship) ....39 TR 1992
Mid Beltie ....119 NJ 6200
Midbea ....138 HY 4444
Mid Beltie ....119 NJ 6200
Midberg (pt.) ....143 HU 5988
Middle Assendon ....36 SU 7385
Middle Aston ....47 SP 4726
Middle Barton ....47 SP 4326
Middlebere Heath ....26 SY 9484
Middlebie ....89 NY 2176
Middle Claydon ....51 SP 7125
Middle Drums ....109 NO 5957
Middle Fell ....83 NY 7444
Middle Fen ....53 TL 5679
Middlefield Law ....94 NS 6730
Middle Grounds (sbk) ....32 ST 3577
Middleham ....78 SE 1287
Middle Hambleton ....62 SK 9007
Middlehope ....48 SO 4988
Middle Level Main Drain ....63 TF 5506
Middle Littleton ....50 SP 0747
Middle Maes-coed ....45 SO 3334
Middlemarsh ....25 ST 6707
Middle Mill ....42 SM 8025
Middle Moor (Cambs.) ....53 TL 2589
Middle Moor (Northum.) ....97 NU 1423
Middle Mouse (is.) ....66 SH 3895
Middle Muir ....95 NS 8425
Middlemuir Farm ....121 NJ 9420
Middle Rasen ....72 TF 0889
Middle Rigg ....102 NO 0608
Middlesbrough ....85 NZ 4920
Middle Shield Park ....90 NY 6070
Middlesmoor ....78 SE 0974
Middlestone Moor ....84 NZ 2532
Middlestown ....71 SE 2617
Middleton (Cumbr.) ....77 SD 6286
Middleton (Derby.) ....70 SK 1963
Middleton (Derby.) ....60 SK 2755
Middleton (Essex) ....54 TL 8639
Middleton (Grampn.) ....119 NJ 8419
Middleton (Gtr Mches.) ....69 SD 8606
Middleton (Hants.) ....34 SU 4243
Middleton (Here. and Worc.) ....48 SO 5469
Middleton (Lancs.) ....77 SD 4258
Middleton (Lothian) ....96 NT 3657
Middleton (Norf.) ....64 TF 6616
Middleton (Northants.) ....52 SP 8489
Middleton (Northum.) ....97 NU 0024
Middleton (Northum.) ....97 NU 1035
Middleton (Northum.) ....91 NZ 0585
Middleton (N Yorks.) ....80 SE 7885
Middleton (N Yorks. - W Yorks.) ....78 SE 1249
Middleton (Shrops.) ....58 SJ 3128
Middleton (Shrops.) ....48 SO 2999
Middleton (Shrops.) ....48 SO 5377
Middleton (Suff.) ....55 TM 4267
Middleton (Tays.) ....102 NO 1206
Middleton (Tays.) ....108 NO 1447
Middleton (Tays.) ....104 NN 9443
Middleton (Tiree) ....104 NL 9443
Middleton (Warw.) ....60 SP 1798
Middleton (W Yorks.) ....79 SE 3027
Middleton Cheney ....51 SP 4941
Middleton Common ....84 NY 9630
Middleton Green ....60 SJ 9935
Middle Tongue (mt.) ....78 SD 9181
Middleton Hall ....97 NT 9825
Middleton in Teesdale ....84 NY 9425
Middleton-on-Sea ....28 SU 9800
Middleton on the Hill ....48 SO 5464
Middleton-on-the-Wolds ....81 SE 9449
Middleton Priors ....49 SO 6290
Middleton Scriven ....49 SO 0707
Middleton St. George ....85 NZ 3412
Middleton Stoney ....47 SP 5323
Middleton Tyas ....84 NZ 2205
Middletown ....58 SJ 3012
Middle Tysoe ....50 SP 3344
Middle Wallop ....26 SU 2937
Middlewich ....69 SJ 7066
Middle Winterslow ....26 SU 2432
Middle Witchampton ....121 NK 6356
Middle Woodford ....26 SU 1136
Middlewood Green ....55 TM 0961
Middlewood Station ....69 SJ 9484
Middleyard ....93 NS 5132
Midelroy ....24 ST 3733
Middridge ....84 NZ 2526
Midfield ....133 NC 5864
Midge Hall ....77 SD 5123
Midgeholme ....90 NY 6458
Midgham ....35 SU 5567
Midgley ....78 SE 0226
Mid Hill (Dumf. and Galwy.) ....88 NX 6907
Mid Hill (Urkney) ....136 IIY 3324
Midhope Moors ....70 SK 2098
Midhopestones ....71 SK 2399
Midhurst ....27 SU 8821
Mid Kame (mt.) ....141 HU 4158
Midland Ness ....136 HY 3203
Midlem ....96 NT 5227
Midmar Forest ....119 NJ 7104
Mid Moile (mt.) ....86 NX 0972
Mid Sannox ....92 NS 0145
Midsomer Norton ....33 ST 6654
Mid Thundergay ....92 NR 8846
Midtown ....126 NG 8285
Midtown of Buchromb ....121 NJ 4144
Mid Urchany ....129 NH 8849
Midville ....73 TF 3857
Mid Yell ....143 HU 5190
Mid Yell Voe ....143 HU 5191
Miefield ....88 NX 6559
Migneint ....67 SH 7642
Migvie ....118 NJ 4306
Milborne Port ....25 ST 6718
Milborne St. Andrew ....25 SY 7997
Milborne Wick ....25 ST 6620
Milbourne ....91 NZ 1175
Milburn (Cumbr.) ....83 NY 6529
Milburn Forest ....83 NY 7132
Milburn Geo ....141 HU 4012
Milbury Heath ....33 ST 6690
Milcombe ....47 SP 4134
Milden ....54 TL 9546
Mildenhall (Suff.) ....54 TL 7074
Mildenhall (Wilts.) ....34 SU 2069
Mildenhall Fen ....53 TL 6382
Milebrook ....48 SO 3172
Milebush ....30 TQ 7546
Mile Elm ....34 ST 9968
Mile End ....54 TL 9827
Mileham ....64 TF 9119
Mile Hill ....108 NO 3157
Milesmark ....102 NT 0688
Milfield ....97 NT 9333
Milford (Derby.) ....60 SK 3445
Milford (Staffs.) ....60 SJ 9721
Milford (Surrey) ....28 SU 9442
Milford Haven (Dyfed) ....42 SM 9006
Milford Haven (Dyfed) (chan.) ......42 SM 8804
Milford on Sea ....26 SZ 2891
Milk Hill ....34 SU 1064
Milkieston Rings ....95 NT 2545
Milkwall ....45 SO 5809
Milland ....27 SU 8228

Milland Marsh	27	SU 8326
Mill Bank	78	SE 0321
Mill Bay (Eday)	138	HY 5735
Mill Bay (Hoy, Orkney)	136	ND 3095
Mill Bay (Stronsay)	137	HY 6626
Millbounds	138	HY 5635
Millbreck	121	NK 0045
Millbridge	35	SU 8542
Millbridge (Orkney)	136	HY 3222
Millbrook (Beds.)	52	TL 0138
Millbrook (Corn.)	20	SX 4252
Millbrook (Hants.)	26	SU 4012
Millbrook Station	52	TL 0040
Mill Buie (Grampn.) (mt.)	129	NJ 0950
Millbuie (Highld.)	128	NH 6460
Millburn (Strath.)	93	NS 4429
Millburn Geo (Bressay)	141	HU 5239
Millburn Geo (Shetld.)	141	HU 4012
Millden Lodge	119	NO 5478
Milldens	109	NO 5450
Milldoe (mt.)	136	HY 3520
Mill End (Bucks.)	36	SU 7885
Mill End (Herts.)	53	TL 3332
Miller Corner	30	TQ 8223
Millerhill	103	NT 3269
Miller's Bay	99	NR 7067
Miller's Dale	70	SK 1373
Milleur Point	86	NX 0273
Millfire	87	NX 5084
Mill Green (Essex)	38	TL 6400
Mill Green (Shrops.)	59	SJ 6727
Millheugh	94	NS 7551
Mill Hill	37	TQ 2292
Millholme	83	SD 5690
Mill House (Cumbr.)	82	NY 3637
Millhouse (Strath.)	100	NR 9570
Millikenpark	101	NS 4162
Millington	80	SE 8351
Milljoan Hill	86	NX 1176
Mill Lane	35	SU 7850
Millmeece	59	SJ 8333
Mill of Kingoodie	121	NJ 8425
Millom	76	SD 1780
Millport	93	NS 1655
Mill Rig	94	NS 6334
Mill Side	77	SD 4484
Millstone Edge	89	NT 4300
Millstone Hill (Grampn.)	121	NJ 4256
Millstone Hill (Grampn.)	121	NJ 6720
Millstone Point	92	NR 9950
Mill Street	64	TG 0118
Millthrop	83	SD 6691
Milltimber	119	NJ 8501
Millton of Corsindae	119	NJ 6809
Millton of Murtle	119	NJ 8702
Milltown (Derby.)	71	SK 3561
Milltown (Dumf. and Galwy.)	89	NY 3375
Milltown (Grampn.)	118	NJ 4616
Milltown (Grampn.)	121	NJ 5447
Milltown of Aberdalgie	108	NO 0720
Milltown of Auchindoun	121	NJ 3540
Milltown of Campfield	119	NJ 6400
Milltown of Craigston	121	NJ 7655
Milltown of Edinvillie	117	NJ 2639
Milltown of Towie	118	NJ 4612
Milnathort	102	NO 1204
Milne Height	89	NY 1597
Milngavie	101	NS 5574
Milnrow	69	SD 9212
Milnthorpe	77	SD 4981
Milovaig	122	NG 1550
Milray Hill	88	NS 5905
Milson	49	SO 6372
Milsted	30	TQ 9058
Milston	34	SU 1645
Milton (Cambs.)	53	TL 4762
Milton (Central)	101	NN 5001
Milton (Central)	101	NS 4490
Milton (Cumbr.)	90	NY 5560
Milton (Dumf. and Galwy.)	86	NX 2154
Milton (Dumf. and Galwy.)	88	NX 8470
Milton (Grampian)	117	NJ 1719
Milton (Grampn.)	121	NJ 5163
Milton (Highld.)	135	ND 3451
Milton (Highld.)	127	NH 3055
Milton (Highld.)	116	NH 4930
Milton (Highld.)	128	NH 5749
Milton (Highld.)	129	NH 7674
Milton (Highld.)	129	NH 9553
Milton (Oxon.)	47	SP 4535
Milton (Oxon.)	35	SU 4892
Milton (Strath.)	101	NS 4274
Milton (Tays.)	108	NN 9138
Milton (Tays.)	109	NO 3843
Milton Abbas	25	ST 8001
Milton Abbot	20	SX 4079
Milton Bridge	103	NT 2363
Milton Bryan	52	SP 9730
Milton Burn	108	NN 9532
Milton Clevedon	25	ST 6637
Milton Coldwells	121	NJ 9538
Milton Combe	20	SX 4866
Milton Damerel	22	SS 3810
Miltonduff	129	NJ 1760
Milton Ernest	52	TL 0156
Milton Green	68	SJ 4558
Milton Hill	35	SU 4790
Miltonise	86	NX 2073
Milton Keynes	52	SP 8636
Milton Keynes Village	52	SP 8939
Milton Lilbourne	34	SU 1860
Milton Loch	88	NX 8371
Milton Malsor	51	SP 7355
Milton Morenish	107	NN 6135
Milton Ness	109	NO 7664
Milton of Auchinhove	119	NJ 5503
Milton of Balgonie	103	NO 3100
Milton of Campsie	101	NS 6576
Milton of Cushnie	118	NJ 5111
Milton of Gollanfield	129	NH 7852
Milton of Lesmore	121	NJ 4628
Milton of Noth	121	NJ 5028
Milton of Potterton	119	NJ 9415
Milton of Tullich	118	NO 3897
Milton on Stour	25	ST 7928
Milton Point	86	NX 3146
Milton Regis	30	TQ 9064
Milton-under-Wychwood	47	SP 2618
Milverton	24	ST 1225
Milwich	60	SJ 9632
Milwr	68	SJ 1974
Minard	100	NR 9796
Minard Castle	100	NR 9794
Minard Forest	100	NR 9395
Minard Point	105	NM 8123
Minchinhampton	46	SO 8600
Minch Moor	96	NT 3633
Mindrum	97	NT 8432
Minehead	23	SS 9746
Minera	58	SJ 2651
Minety	34	SU 0290
Minffordd	66	SH 5938
Mingary	112	NF 7426
Mingay	122	NG 2257
Minginish (dist.)	123	NG 4224
Mingulay	112	NL 5683
Mingulay Bay	112	NL 5783
Miningsby	73	TF 3264
Minions	20	SX 2671
Minishant	93	NS 3314
Minley Manor	35	SU 8157
Minnes	121	NJ 9423
Minnigaff	86	NX 4166
Minnonie	121	NJ 7760
Minnygap Height	88	NY 0296
Minskip	79	SE 3864
Minstead	26	SU 2811
Minster (Kent)	30	TQ 9573
Minster (Kent)	31	TR 3164
Minsteracres	84	NZ 0255
Minsterley	58	SJ 3705
Minster Lovell	47	SP 3111
Minsterworth	46	SO 7717
Minterne Magna	25	ST 6504
Minting	73	TF 1873
Mintlaw	121	NK 0048
Minto	90	NT 5620
Minto Hills	90	NT 5520
Minton	48	SO 4290
Minwear	42	SN 0413
Minworth	50	SP 1592
Mio Ness (Housay)	143	HU 6670
Mio Ness (Shetld.)	143	HU 4279
Mirbister	136	HY 3019
Mireland	135	ND 3160
Mirfield	70	SE 2019
Mirkady Point	137	HY 5306
Misbister Geo	136	ND 3388
Miserden	46	SO 9308
Mishnish (dist.)	111	NM 4654
Miskin	41	ST 0481
Misson	72	SK 6895
Misterton (Leic.)	51	SP 5584
Misterton (Notts.)	72	SK 7694
Misterton (Somer.)	25	ST 4508
Mistley	55	TM 1231
Mistylaw Muir	100	NS 3061
Mitcham	37	TQ 2868
Mitcheldean	46	SO 6618
Mitchell	19	SW 8554
Mitchel Troy	45	SO 4910
Mitcheltroy Common	45	SO 4909
Mitford	91	NZ 1786
Mithian	18	SW 7450
Mitton	59	SJ 8815
Mixbury	47	SP 6033
Mixon	70	SK 0457
Mobberley	69	SJ 7880
Moccas	45	SO 3542
Mochdre (Clwyd)	67	SH 8278
Mochdre (Powys)	57	SO 0788
Mochrum	86	NX 3446
Mochrum Fell	86	NX 3050
Mochrum Loch	86	NX 3053
Mockbeggar Wharf (sbk.)	68	SJ 2692
Mockerkin	82	NY 0823
Modbury	21	SX 6551
Moddershall	59	SJ 9236
Moel-ddu	66	SH 5744
Moel Fammau	68	SJ 1562
Moel Feity	41	SN 8323
Moel Fferna	58	SJ 1139
Moelfre (Clwyd)	58	SJ 1828
Moelfre (Dyfed)	43	SN 3236
Moelfre (Gwyn.)	66	SH 5186
Moelfre (Gwyn.)	57	SH 6224
Moelfre (Powys)	57	SN 8498
Moelfre Isaf	67	SH 9473
Moelfre Uchaf	67	SH 8971
Moel Garegog	58	SJ 2152
Moel Hebog	66	SH 5646
Moel hirradug (ant.)	67	SJ 0678
Moel Hywel	57	SN 9971
Moel Llyfnant	67	SH 8035
Moel Llyn	67	SH 8957
Moel Llys-y-coed	68	SJ 1465
Moel Morfydd	58	SJ 1445
Moel Penamnen	67	SH 7148
Moel Seisiog	67	SH 8557
Moel Ton-mawr	41	SS 8387
Moel Tryfan	66	SH 5155
Moel Wnion	67	SH 6469
Moelwyn Mawr	67	SH 6544
Moel y Feidiog	67	SH 7732
Moel y Gaer (ant.)	68	SJ 1461
Moel-y-Llyn (Dyfed)	57	SN 7191
Moel-y-Llyn (Powys)	57	SH 9414
Moel-y-mor	43	SN 4146
Moel Ysgyfarnogod	67	SH 6534
Moffat	89	NT 0805
Moffat Water	89	NT 1205
Mogerhanger	52	TL 1349
Moidart (dist.)	111	NM 7673
Moine House	133	NC 5160
Moine Mhór	99	NR 8292
Moira	60	SK 3216
Molash	31	TR 0251
Mol a' Tuath	112	NF 8535
Mol-chlach	123	NG 4513
Mold	68	SJ 2363
Molehill Green	37	TL 5624
Molescroft	74	TA 0140
Molesworth	52	TL 0775
Molland	23	SS 8028
Molland Common	23	SS 8130
Mollington (Ches.)	68	SJ 3870
Mollington (Northants.)	50	SP 4347
Mollinsburn	101	NS 7171
Mol Truisg	125	NB 3505
Mon	129	NC 8201
Monach or Heisker Islands	124	NF 6262
Monachty	56	SN 5062
Monachyle Glen	107	NN 4721
Monachylemore	107	NN 4719
Monadhliath Mountains	116	NH 6710
Monadh Mór	117	NN 9394
Monamenach	108	NO 1770
Monar Lodge	115	NH 2040
Monaughty Forest	129	NJ 1358
Monawee (mt.)	118	NO 4080
Monboddo	119	NO 7478
Moncreiffe Hill	108	NO 1319
Mondynes	119	NO 7879
Monewden	55	TM 2358
Moneydie	108	NO 0629
Money Head	86	NX 0448
Mongour (mt.)	119	NO 7589
Moniaive	88	NX 7791
Monifieth	109	NO 4932
Monike Resr.	109	NO 5038
Monikie	109	NO 4938
Monikie Burn	109	NO 5437
Monikie Reservoir	109	NO 5138
Monimail	103	NO 2914
Monington	42	SN 1344
Monivey	138	HY 4048
Monken Hadley	37	TQ 2497
Monk Fryston	79	SE 5029
Monkhopton	59	SO 6293
Monkland	45	SO 4557
Monkleigh	22	SS 4520
Monknash	41	SS 9270
Monkokehampton	23	SS 5805
Monks Eleigh	54	TL 9647
Monk's Heath	69	SJ 8574
Monk Sherborne	35	SU 6056
Monkshill	121	NJ 7941
Monks House Rocks	97	NU 2033
Monkside (mt.)	90	NY 6894
Monksilver	24	ST 0737
Monks Kirby	51	SP 4683
Monk Soham	55	TM 2165
Monkstone Point	42	SN 1403
Monkswood	45	SO 3403
Monkton (Devon)	24	ST 1803
Monkton (Kent)	31	TR 2865
Monkton (Strath.)	93	NS 3527
Monkton (Tyne and Wear)	91	NZ 3463
Monkton Combe	33	ST 7761
Monkton Deverill	25	ST 8537
Monkton Farleigh	33	ST 8065
Monkton Heathfield	24	ST 2526
Monkton Up Wimborne	26	SU 0113
Monkwood	27	SU 6730
Monmouth	45	SO 5113
Monnington on Wye	45	SO 3743
Monreith	86	NX 3641
Monreith Bay	86	NX 3540
Monreith Mains	86	NX 3643
Montacute	25	ST 4916
Montacute House	25	ST 4917
Montcoffer House	121	NJ 6861
Montford	58	SJ 4114
Montgarrie	119	NJ 5717
Montgomery	58	SO 2296
Montgreenan	93	NS 3343
Montrave	103	NO 3706
Montreathmont Forest	109	NO 5655
Montreathmont Moor	109	NO 5854
Montrose	109	NO 7157
Montrose Basin	109	NO 6957
Monxton	34	SU 3144
Monyash	70	SK 1566
Monymusk	119	NJ 6815
Monynut Edge	96	NT 6968
Monynut Water	96	NT 6967
Monzie	108	NN 8725
Moonen Bay	122	NG 1346
Moonzie	108	NO 3317
Moorby	73	TF 2964
Moorcot	45	SO 3555
Moor Crichel	26	ST 9908
Moordown	26	SZ 0994
Moore	69	SJ 5584
Moorends	74	SE 6915
Moor Fea (mt.)	136	ND 1999
Moorfoot Hills	96	NT 3452
Moorhall	71	SK 3175
Moorhampton	45	SO 3846
Moorhouse (Cumbr.)	82	NY 3356
Moorhouse (Notts.)	72	SK 7566
Moorland or Northmoor Green	24	ST 3332
Moorlinch	24	ST 3936
Moor Loch	102	NS 9488
Moor Monkton	79	SE 5056
Moor Nook	77	SD 6537
Moor Park	101	NS 4792
Moorsholm	85	NZ 6814
Moorside	70	SD 9507
Moors River	26	SZ 1099
Moor, The	29	TQ 7529
Moortown (Hants.)	26	SZ 4283
Moortown (Lincs.)	74	TF 0699
Moota Hill	82	NY 1436
Morar	111	NM 6892
Moray Firth	129	NH 9467
Morborne	52	TL 1391
Morchard Bishop	23	SS 7607
Morchard Road Station	23	SS 7405
Morcombelake	24	SY 4093
Morcott	62	SK 9200
Morda	58	SJ 2827
Morden (Dorset)	25	SY 9195
Morden (Gtr London)	37	TQ 2567
Mordiford	45	SO 5637
Mordon	84	NZ 3326
More	48	SO 3491
Morebath	23	SS 9525
Morebattle	96	NT 7724
Morecambe	77	SD 4364
Morecambe Bay	78	SD 3567
Morefield	127	NH 1195
Moreleigh	21	SX 7652
Morenish	107	NN 6035
Moresby	82	NX 9821
Moresby Park	84	NY 9919
Morestead	27	SU 5125
Moreton (Dorset)	25	SY 8089
Moreton (Essex)	37	TL 5307
Moreton (Mers.)	68	SJ 2689
Moreton (Oxon.)	36	SP 6904
Moreton (Staffs)	59	SJ 7917
Moreton Corbet	59	SJ 5523
Moretonhampstead	21	SX 7586
Moreton-in-Marsh	47	SP 2032
Moreton Jeffries	45	SO 6048
Moreton Morrell	50	SP 3155
Moreton on Lugg	45	SO 5045
Moreton Pinkney	51	SP 5749
Moreton Say	59	SJ 6234
Moreton's Leam (ant.)	63	TL 3099
Moreton Valence	46	SO 7809
Morfa Bychan	66	SH 5437
Morfa Dyffryn	56	SH 5624
Morfa Glas	41	SN 8606
Morfa Harlech	66	SH 5733
Morfa Nefyn	66	SH 2840
Morgan's Hill	34	SU 0367
Morgan's Vale	26	SU 1921
Morland	83	NY 6022
Morley (Derby.)	60	SK 3941
Morley (Durham)	84	NZ 1227
Morley (W Yorks.)	79	SE 2627
Morley Green	69	SJ 8282
Morley St. Botolph	64	TM 0799
Mormond Hill	121	NJ 9657
Morningside	103	NT 2471
Morningthorpe	55	TM 2192
Mornish (dist.)	110	NM 3853
Morpeth	91	NZ 2085
Morphie	109	NO 7164
Morrey	60	SK 1218
Morris Fen	63	TF 2906
Morriston	40	SS 6698
Morsgail Forest	131	NB 1217
Morston	64	TG 0043
Morte Bay	22	SS 4343
Mortehoe	22	SS 4545
Morte Point	22	SS 4445
Mortimer	36	SU 6564
Mortimer's Cross	48	SO 4263
Mortimer's Deep	102	NT 1883
Mortimer West End	36	SU 6363
Mortlake	37	TQ 2075
Mortlich (mt.)	119	NJ 5301
Morton (Avon)	33	ST 6491
Morton (Derby.)	71	SK 4060
Morton (Lincs.)	72	SK 8091
Morton (Lincs.)	62	TF 0924
Morton (Norf.)	65	TG 1217
Morton (Shrops.)	58	SJ 2824
Morton Bagot	50	SP 1164
Morton-on-Swale	84	SE 3292
Morton Resr.	102	NT 0763
Moruisg (mt.)	127	NH 1050
Morvah	18	SW 4035
Morval	19	SX 2556
Morven (Grampn.) (mt.)	118	NJ 3704
Morven (Highld.) (mt.)	135	ND 0028
Morvern (dist.)	111	NM 6754
Morvich	129	NC 7500
Morvich	114	NG 9621
Morville	59	SO 6694
Morwenstow	22	SS 2015
Morwick Hall	91	NU 2303
Mosbrough	71	SK 4281
Moscow	93	NS 4840
Mosedale	82	NY 3532
Moseley (Here. and Worc.)	49	SO 8159
Moseley (W Mids)	50	SP 0883
Moss (Clwyd)	58	SJ 3052
Moss (Highld.)	111	NM 6868
Moss (S Yorks.)	71	SE 5914
Moss (Tiree)	104	NL 9644
Mossat	118	NJ 4719
Moss Bank (Cumbr.)	69	SJ 5198
Mossbank (Shetld.)	143	HU 4575
Moss Bay	82	NX 9727
Mossburnford	90	NT 6616
Mossdale	88	NX 6571
Mossdale Moor	83	SD 8190
Mossend	101	NS 7460
Mossgiel	93	NS 4828
Moss Hill	118	NJ 3117
Mosside	109	NO 4252
Mossley	70	SD 9702
Moss Moor	70	SE 0014
Moss of Barmuckity	120	NJ 2461
Moss of Cruden	121	NK 0540
Mosspaul Hotel	89	NY 4099
Moss Side	77	SD 3830
Mosston	109	NO 5444
Mosterton	25	ST 4505
Mostyn	68	SJ 1680
Mostyn Bank (sbk.)	68	SJ 1482
Motcombe	25	ST 8425
Mote House	30	TQ 7855
Mote of Dinning (ant.)	88	NX 8890
Mote of Druchtag (ant.)	86	NX 3547
Mote of Urr (ant.)	88	NX 8164
Motherwell	94	NS 7557
Mottingham	37	TQ 4272
Mottisfont	26	SU 3226
Mottistone	26	SZ 4083
Mottram in Logdendale	70	SJ 9995
Mottram St Andrew	69	SJ 8778
Moudy Mea (mt.)	84	NY 8711
Mouldsworth	69	SJ 5171
Moulin	108	NN 9459
Moul of Eswick	141	HU 4953
Moulsecoomb	29	TQ 3307
Moulsford	35	SU 5984
Moulsoe	52	SP 9041
Moulton (Ches.)	69	SJ 6569
Moulton (Lincs.)	63	TF 3023
Moulton (Northants.)	51	SP 7866
Moulton (N Yorks.)	84	NZ 2303
Moulton (Suff.)	54	TL 6964
Moulton Chapel	63	TF 2918
Moulton Seas End	63	TF 3227
Mound Rock	129	NH 7798
Mounie Castle	121	NJ 7628
Mount (Corn.)	19	SW 7856
Mount (Corn.)	19	SX 1467
Mountain Ash	41	ST 0498
Mountain Cross	95	NT 1446
Mountain Water	42	SM 9224
Mount Battock	119	NO 5484
Mountbenger	96	NT 3125
Mount Blair	108	NO 1662
Mount Bures	54	TL 9032
Mount Caburn (ant.)	29	TQ 4409
Mount Canisp	129	NH 7970
Mount Eagle	128	NH 6458
Mount Edgcumbe	20	SX 4353
Mountfield	29	TQ 7320
Mountgerald	128	NH 5661
Mount Grace Priory (ant.)	85	SE 4498
Mount Harry	29	TQ 3812
Mount Hawke	18	SW 7147
Mount Hill	108	NO 3216
Mountjoy	19	SW 8760
Mount Keen	118	NO 4086
Mountnessing	38	TQ 6297
Mount of Haddoch	121	NJ 4128
Mounton	45	ST 5193
Mount Pleasant	55	TM 5077
Mount's Bay	18	SW 5128
Mount Shade	119	NO 6286
Mountsorrel	61	SK 5814
Mount Stuart (Dumf. and Galwy.)	88	NS 7519
Mountstuart (Strath.)	100	NS 1059
Mount, The	95	NT 1457
Mousa (is.)	141	HU 4624
Mousa Sound	141	HU 4424
Mousehole	18	SW 4626
Mouse Water	95	NS 9045
Mouswald	89	NY 0672
Mouth of The Humber	75	TA 3708
Mouth of The Severn	32	ST 3476
Mow Cop	69	SJ 8557
Mowhaugh	90	NT 8120
Mowsley	51	SP 6489
Mowtie	119	NO 8388
Moy	116	NN 4282
Moy Burn	116	NH 7837
Moy Forest	116	NN 4284
Moy Hall	116	NH 7635
Moy House	129	NJ 0159
Moyles Court	26	SU 1608
Moylgrove	42	SN 1244
Moy Lodge	116	NN 4483
Mozie Law	90	NT 8315
Muasdale	92	NR 6840
Muchalls	119	NO 9091
Much Birch	45	SO 5030
Much Cowarne	45	SO 6147
Much Dewchurch	45	SO 4831
Muchelney	25	ST 4224
Much Hadham	37	TL 4319
Much Hoole	77	SD 4723
Muchlarnick	19	SX 2156
Much Marcle	46	SO 6533
Muchrachd	115	NH 2833
Much Wenlock	59	SO 6199
Muck (is.)	111	NM 4179
Muckfoot	86	NX 2185
Mucking	38	TQ 6881
Muckle Burn (Central)	101	NN 7707
Muckle Burn (Highld.)	129	NH 9451
Muckle Cairn	118	NO 3776
Muckle Flugga (is.)	143	HP 6019
Muckle Green Holm	137	HY 5227
Muckle Holm	143	HU 4088
Muckle Ossa (is.)	142	HU 2285
Muckle Roe (is.)	141	HU 3165
Muckle Skerry	143	HU 6273
Muckle Skerry (Orkney)	135	ND 4678
Mucklestone	59	SJ 7237
Muckleton	59	SJ 5821
Muckletown	121	NJ 5621
Muckle Water	138	HY 3930
Muckton	73	TF 3781
Mudale	133	NC 5336
Muddiford	23	SS 5638
Mudeford	26	SZ 1892
Mudford	25	ST 5719
Mudgley	33	ST 4445
Mudlee Bracks (mt)	118	NO 5185
Mugdock	101	NS 5576
Mugdock Reservoir	101	NS 5576
Mugeary	123	NG 4438
Mugginton	60	SK 2843
Muggleswick	84	NZ 0450
Muggleswick Common	84	NZ 0247
Muie	128	NC 6704
Muir	117	NO 0689
Muirden	121	NJ 7053
Muirdrum	109	NO 5637
Muirhead (Fife)	103	NO 2805
Muirhead (Strath.)	101	NS 6869
Muirhead (Tays.)	109	NO 3434
Muirhead Resr.	93	NS 2556
Muirhouses	102	NT 0180
Muirkirk	94	NS 6927
Muirneag (mt.)	131	NB 4748
Muir of Dinnet	118	NO 4498
Muir of Fairburn	128	NH 4753
Muir of Fowlis	119	NJ 5612
Muir of Lochs	120	NJ 3062
Muir of Orchill	102	NN 8612
Muir of Ord	128	NH 5250
Muir of the Clans	129	NH 8352
Muir of Thorn	108	NO 0737
Muir Park Resr.	101	NS 4892
Muirshearlich	115	NN 1380
Muirskie	119	NO 8295
Muirtack (Grampn.)	121	NJ 8146
Muirtack (Grampn.)	121	NJ 9937
Muirton	129	NH 7463
Muirton of Ardblair	108	NO 1743
Muirton of Ballochy	109	NO 6462
Muirtown	102	NN 9211
Muiryfold	121	NJ 7651
Muker	84	SD 9198
Mulbarton	65	TG 1901
Mulben	121	NJ 3450
Muldoanich (is.)	112	NL 6893
Mulgrave Castle	85	NZ 8412
Mulindry	98	NR 3659
Mullach Clach a' Bhlàir	117	NN 8892
Mullach Coire a' Chuir	100	NN 1703
Mullach Coire Mhic Fhearchair (mt.)	127	NH 0574
Mullach Fraoch-choire	115	NH 0917
Mullach Mór (mt.)	110	NG 3801
Mullach na Càrn	123	NG 6029
Mullach nan Coirean	106	NN 1266
Mullach na Reidheachd (mt.)	131	NB 0914
Mull Aerodrome	105	NM 5943
Mullardoch House	115	NH 2331
Mull Head (Orkney)	137	HY 5909
Mull Head (Papa Westray)	138	HY 4955
Mullion	18	SW 6719
Mullion Cove	18	SW 6617
Mullion Island	18	SW 6517
Mull of Cara	92	NR 6343
Mull of Galloway	86	NX 1530
Mull of Kintyre	92	NR 5907
Mull of Logan	86	NX 0742
Mull of Miljoan	86	NX 2796
Mull Of Oa	98	NR 2641
Mullwharchar	87	NX 4586
Mumbles Head	40	SS 6387
Mumbles, The	40	SS 6287
Mumby	73	TF 5174
Muncaster Castle	82	SD 1096
Munderfield Row	49	SO 6451
Munderfield Stocks	49	SO 6550
Mundesley	65	TG 3136
Mundford	64	TL 8093
Mundham (Norf.)	65	TM 3298
Mundham (W. Susx)	27	SU 8701
Mundon	38	TL 8702
Mundurno	119	NJ 9413
Munerigie	115	NH 2602
Mu Ness (Shetld.)	140	HU 1652
Mu Ness (Unst)	143	HP 6301
Muness Castle (ant.)	143	HP 6201
Mungasdale	126	NG 9693
Mungrisdale	82	NY 3630
Munlochy	128	NH 6453
Munlochy Bay	128	NH 6752
Munnoch Resr.	93	NS 2547
Munsley	49	SO 6640
Munslow	48	SO 5187
Murbie Stacks	141	HU 3062
Murch	41	ST 1670
Murcott	47	SP 5815
Murkle	135	ND 1668
Mùrlaggan	115	NN 3181
Murlaggan (Highld.)	114	NN 0192
Murra	136	HY 2104
Murrow	63	TF 3707
Mursley	52	SP 8128
Murthill	109	NO 4657
Murthly	108	NO 0938
Murton (Cumbr.)	83	NY 7221
Murton (Durham)	85	NZ 3947
Murton (Northum.)	97	NT 9748
Murton (N Yorks.)	79	SE 6452
Murton Fell (Cumbr.)	82	NY 0918
Murton Fell (Cumbr.)	83	NY 7524
Musbury	24	SY 2794
Muscoates	80	SE 6880
Muskna Field (mt.)	141	HU 4032
Musselburgh	103	NT 3472
Muston (Leic.)	62	SK 8237
Muston (N Yorks.)	81	TA 0979
Mustow Green	49	SO 8774
Mutford	55	TM 4888
Muthill	108	NN 8616
Mutterton	24	ST 0304
Mwdwl Eithin	67	SH 8268
Mybster	135	ND 1652
Myddfai	41	SN 7730
Myddle	58	SJ 4623
Mydroilyn	43	SN 4555
Mylor Bridge	19	SW 8036
Mynachlog-ddu	42	SN 1430
Myndd Bach (Gwyn.)	67	SH 7431
Myndtown	48	SO 3889
Mynydd Aberyscir	41	SN 9832
Mynydd Allt-y-grug	41	SN 7507
Mynydd Bach (Dyfed)	56	SN 6066
Mynydd Bach (Dyfed)	57	SN 7070
Mynydd-bâch (Gwent)	45	ST 4894
Mynydd Baedon	41	SS 8785
Mynydd Bodrochwyn	67	SH 9372
Mynydd Bryn-llech	67	SH 8231
Mynydd Bwlch-y-Groes	41	SN 8635
Mynydd Caerau	41	SS 8894
Mynydd Caregog	42	SN 0436
Mynydd Ceiswyn	57	SH 7613
Mynydd Cenin	66	SH 4544
Mynydd Cerrig	43	SN 5013
Mynydd Clogau	57	SO 0399
Mynydd Cribau	67	SH 7555
Mynydd Dinas	41	SS 7691
Mynydd Dolgoed	57	SH 7813
Mynydd Eglwysilan	41	ST 1192
Mynydd Eppynt	44	SN 9644
Mynydd Figyn	43	SN 5830
Mynydd Garnclochdy	45	SO 2905
Mynydd Garn-fach	43	SN 6506
Mynydd Hiraethog	67	SH 9455
Mynydd Illtyd	41	SN 9626
Mynydd Llandegai	66	SH 6065
Mynydd Llangattock	41	SO 1815
Mynydd Llangorse	41	SO 1627
Mynydd Llangynidr	41	SO 1214
Mynydd Llanllwni	43	SN -5037
Mynydd Llanwenarth	45	SO 2717
Mynydd Llanybyther	43	SN 5339
Mynydd Llysiau	41	SO 2028
Mynydd Maen	45	ST 2597
Mynydd Maes-teg	41	SS 9690
Mynydd Mallaen	44	SN 7344
Mynydd Marchywell	41	SN 7705

Mynydd Margam 41 SS 8188
Mynyddmelyn 42 SN 0236
Mynydd Merddin 45 SO 3428
Mynydd Merthyr 41 ST 0599
Mynydd Myddfai 41 SN 8029
Mynydd Pen-bre 43 SN 4503
Mynydd Pencarreg 43 SN 5743
Mynydd Pennant 57 SH 6610
Mynydd Pen-y-fal 45 SO 2619
Mynydd Perfedd 67 SH 6262
Mynydd Preseli 42 SN 1032
Mynydd Resolfen 41 SN 8603
Mynydd Rhiw-Saeson 57 SH 9006
Mynydd Sylen 43 SN 5108
Mynydd Tan-y-coed 57 SH 6604
Mynydd Tarw 58 SJ 1132
Mynydd Trawsnant 44 SN 8249
Mynydd Troed 41 SO 1728
Mynydd Waun Fawr 57 SJ 0105
Mynydd y Betws 40 SN 6710
Mynydd y Cemais 57 SH 8707
Mynydd y Drum 41 SN 8109
Mynydd y Gadfa 57 SH 9914
Mynydd y Gaer 41 SS 9585
Mynydd-y-Garreg 43 SN 4409
Mynydd-y-glog 41 SN 9808
Mynydd y Gwair 43 SN 6607
Mynytho 66 SH 3031
Myrebird 119 NO 7498
Mytchett 35 SU 8855
Mytholm 78 SD 9827
Mytholmroyd 78 SE 0125
Myton-on-Swale 79 SE 4366

N

Naast 126 NG 8283
Naburn 79 SE 5945
Nackington 31 TR 1554
Nacton 55 TM 2240
Na Cuiltean (is.) 98 NR 5464
Naden Resrs. 69 SD 8516
Na Dromannan 127 NC 2101
Nafferton 81 TA 0559
Na Gamhnaichean (is.) 123 NG 4312
Nailsea 33 ST 4670
Nailstone 60 SK 4107
Nailsworth 46 ST 8499
Nairn 129 NH 8856
Nancegollan 18 SW 6632
Nancledra 18 SW 4936
Nanhoron 66 SH 2831
Nannau 57 SH 7420
Nannerch 68 SJ 1669
Nanpantan 61 SK 5017
Nanpean 19 SW 9556
Nant Bran 41 SN 9533
Nantclwyd Hall 58 SJ 1151
Nant Cynnen 43 SN 3522
Nant-ddu 41 SO 0015
Nanternis 43 SN 3756
Nant Ffrancon 67 SH 6363
Nantgaredig 43 SN 4921
Nantgarw 41 ST 1285
Nant-glâs 57 SN 9965
Nantglyn 67 SJ 0061
Nantgwynant 66 SH 6049
Nantlle 66 SH 5053
Nantmawr 58 SJ 2424
Nantmel 57 SO 0366
Nantmor 66 SH 6046
Nant Peris 66 SH 6058
Nantstallon 19 SX 0367
Nantwich 59 SJ 6552
Nant-y-derry 45 SO 3306
Nantyffyllon 41 SS 8492
Nantyglo 41 SO 1911
Nant-y-moch Resr. 57 SN 7587
Nant-y-moel 41 SS 9393
Nant yr Eira 57 SH 9505
Naphill 36 SU 8496
Nappa 78 SD 8553
Napton on the Hill 51 SP 4661
Narachan Burn 92 NR 7548
Narberth 42 SN 1114
Narborough (Leic.) 61 SP 5497
Narborough (Norf.) 64 TF 7413
Nare Head 19 SW 9136
Nare Point 18 SW 7925
Narrows of Raasay 123 NG 5435
Nasareth 66 SH 4749
Naseby 51 SP 6878
Naseby Field 51 SP 6879
Naseby Resr. 51 SP 6677
Nash (Bucks.) 51 SP 7734
Nash (Gwent) 32 ST 3483
Nash (Here. and Worc.) 48 SO 3062
Nash (Shrops.) 49 SO 6071
Nash Lee 36 SP 8408
Nash Point 41 SS 9168
Nassington 62 TL 0696
Nass, The (sbk.) 39 TM 0011
Nasty 37 TL 3624
Nateby (Cumbr.) 83 NY 7706
Nateby (Lancs.) 77 SD 4644
National Exhibition Centre 50 SP 1883
Natland 83 SD 5289
Naughton 54 TM 0249
Naunton (Glos.) 46 SP 1123
Naunton (Here. and Worc.) 49 SO 8739
Naunton Beauchamp 50 SO 9652
Navax Point 18 SW 5943
Nave Island 98 NR 2875
Navenby 72 SK 9857
Naver Forest 133 NC 6938
Navestock Heath 37 TQ 5397
Navestock Side 37 TQ 5697
Navio (ant.) 70 SK 1882
Naworth Castle (ant.) 90 NY 5662
Nawton 79 SE 6584
Nayland 54 TL 9734
Nazeing 37 TL 4106
Naze, The (pt.) 39 TM 2624
Neacroft 26 SZ 1897
Neal's Green 50 SP 3384
Neap 141 HU 5058
Neap of Skea 143 HU 3783
Near Cotton 60 SK 0646
Neasham 84 NZ 3210
Neath 41 SS 7597
Neatishead 65 TG 3421
Neaty Burn 127 NH 3542
Neave or Coomb Island 133 NC 6664
Neban Point 136 HY 2113
Neblonga (pt.) 136 HY 2111
Nebo (Dyfed) 56 SN 5465
Nebo (Gwyn.) 66 SH 4750
Nebo (Gwyn.) 67 SH 8356
Necton 64 TF 8709
Nedd 132 NC 1332
Nedging Tye 54 TM 0149
Needham 55 TM 2281
Needham Market 55 TM 0855
Needingworth 53 TL 3472
Needles, The (pt.) 26 SZ 2984
Needs Law 90 NT 6002
Needs Oar Point 27 SZ 4498
Needwood Forest 60 SK 1524
Neegirth (pt.) 143 HU 5171
Neen Savage 49 SO 6777
Neen Sollars 49 SO 6572
Neenton 49 SO 6487
Nefyn 66 SH 3040
Neidpath Castle (ant.) 95 NT 2340
Neil's Helly (pt.) 138 HY 5054
Neilston 93 NS 4657
Neilston Pad (mt.) 93 NS 4755
Neist 122 NG 1247
Nelson (Lancs.) 78 SD 8737
Nelson (Mid Glam.) 41 ST 1195
Nelson Village 91 NZ 2577
Nemphlar 95 NS 8544
Nempnett Thrubwell 33 ST 5360
Nenthead 83 NY 7743
Nenthorn 96 NT 6837
Nercwys 68 SJ 2260
Nereabolls 98 NR 2255
Nerston 94 NS 6457
Nesbit 97 NT 9833
Ness (Ches.) 68 SJ 3075
Ness (Isle of Lewis) (dist.) 131 NB 5261
Ness (N Yorks.) 80 SE 6878
Nesscliffe 58 SJ 3819
Ness Glen 93 NS 4701
Ness Head 135 ND 3866
Ness of Boray 136 HY 4371
Ness of Brough 139 HY 6542
Ness of Burravoe 143 HU 3890
Ness of Gossabrough 143 HU 5383
Ness of Hillswick 142 HU 2775
Ness of Houlland (Shetld.) 143 HU 3788
Ness of Houlland (Yell) 143 HP 5205
Ness of Ireland 141 HU 3723
Ness of Olnesfirth 142 HU 3076
Ness of Ork 137 HY 5422
Ness of Ramnageo 143 HU 6299
Ness of Sound (Shetld.) 141 HU 4638
Ness of Sound (Yell) 143 HU 4482
Ness of Trebister 141 HU 4538
Ness Point or North Cheek 81 NZ 9506
Ness, The (Orkney) 137 HY 5408
Ness, The (South Havra) 141 HU 3626
Ness, The (Stronsay) 139 HY 6630
Neston (Ches.) 68 SJ 2877
Neston (Wilts.) 33 ST 8667
Nether Alderley 69 SJ 8476
Netheravon 34 SU 1448
Nether Blainslie 96 NT 5443
Netherbrae 121 NJ 7959
Nether Broughton 61 SK 6925
Netherburn 94 NS 7947
Nether Burrow 77 SD 6174
Netherbury 25 SY 4799
Netherby 89 NY 3971
Nether Cerne 25 SY 6698
Nether Compton 25 ST 5907
Nether Crimond 121 NJ 8222
Nether Dallachy 121 NJ 3663
Netherend 45 SO 5900
Nether Exe 21 SS 9300
Netherfield 29 TQ 7018
Netherhampton 26 SU 1029
Nether Handwick 109 NO 3641
Nether Haugh 71 SK 4196
Nether Howecleuch 89 NT 0312
Nether Kellet 77 SD 5067
Nether Kinmundy 121 NK 0444
Nether Kirkton 93 NS 4757
Nether Langwith 71 SK 5371
Netherlaw 87 NX 7445
Netherley 119 NO 8593
Nethermill 89 NY 0487
Nethermuir 121 NJ 9143
Nether Padley 71 SK 2478
Netherplace 93 NS 5155
Nether Poppleton 79 SE 5654
Nether Row 82 NY 3237
Netherseal 60 SK 2813
Nether Silton 85 SE 4592
Nether Stowey 32 ST 1939
Netherthird 88 NS 5818
Netherthong 70 SE 1309
Netherthorpe Airfield 71 SK 5480
Netherton (Central) 101 NS 5579
Netherton (Devon) 21 SX 8971
Netherton (Here. and Worc.) 50 SO 9941
Netherton (Mers.) 68 SD 3500
Netherton (Northum.) 97 NT 9807
Netherton (Tays.) 108 NO 1452
Netherton (Tays.) 109 NO 5457
Netherton (W Yorks.) 71 SE 2716
Nethertown (Cumbr.) 82 NX 9807
Nethertown (Island of Stroma) 135 ND 3578
Nether Urquhart 102 NO 1808
Nether Wallop 26 SU 3036
Nether Wasdale 82 NY 1204
Nether Whitacre 60 SP 2393
Nether Winchendon or Lower Winchendon 36 SP 7312
Netherwitton 91 NZ 1090
Netherwood 94 NS 6528
Nether Worton 47 SP 4230
Nethy Bridge 117 NJ 0020
Netley 27 SU 4508
Netley Marsh 26 SU 3312
Nettlebed 36 SU 7086
Nettlebridge 33 ST 6448
Nettlecombe 25 SY 5195
Nettleden 36 TL 0210
Nettle Geo 137 HY 5319
Nettleham 72 TF 0075
Nettle Hill 83 NY 7107
Nettlestead 29 TQ 6852
Nettlestead Green 29 TQ 6850
Nettlestone 27 SZ 6290
Nettlestone Point 27 SZ 6391
Nettleton (Lincs.) 75 TA 1000
Nettleton (Wilts.) 33 ST 8178
Neuadd Reservoirs 41 SO 0218
Neuk, The 119 NO 7397
Nevendon 38 TQ 7390
Nevern 42 SN 0840
Nevis Forest 106 NN 1271
Nev of Stuis (pt.) 143 HU 4697
Nev, The (Shetld.) (pt.) 140 HU 2643
Nev, The (Shetld.) (pt.) 141 HU 3414
Nev, The (Unst) (pt.) 143 HP 6611
Nev, The (Westray) (pt.) 138 HY 4452
New Abbey 88 NX 9665
New Aberdour 121 NJ 8863
New Addington 37 TQ 3863
New Alresford 27 SU 5832
New Alyth 108 NO 2447
Newark (Northants.) 62 TF 2100
Newark (Sanday, Orkney) 139 HY 7242
Newark Bay (Orkney) 137 HY 5703
Newark Bay (S. Ronaldsay) 136 ND 4689
Newark Castle (Borders) (ant.) 96 NT 4229
Newark Castle (Strath.) (ant.) 93 NS 3217
Newark Castle (Strath.) (ant.) 93 NS 3274
Newark-on-Trent 61 SK 7953
New Arley 50 SP 2989
Newarthill 101 NS 7859
New Ash Green 30 TQ 6065
Newbald 74 SE 9136
New Bedford River or Hundred Foot Drain 53 TL 4987
New Bewick 91 NU 0620
Newbiggin (Cumbr.) 83 NY 4729
Newbiggin (Cumbr.) 83 NY 5649
Newbiggin (Cumbr.) 83 NY 6228
Newbiggin (Cumbr.) 76 SD 2669
Newbiggin (Durham) 84 NY 9127
Newbiggin (N Yorks.) 84 SD 9591
Newbiggin (N Yorks.) 78 SD 9985
Newbiggin-by-the-Sea 91 NZ 3187
Newbiggin Common 84 NY 9131
Newbigging (Strath.) 95 NT 0145
Newbigging (Tays.) 108 NO 2841
Newbigging (Tays.) 109 NO 4237
Newbigging (Tays.) 109 NO 4936
Newbiggin on Lune 83 NY 7005
Newbold (Derby.) 71 SK 3773
Newbold (Leic.) 60 SK 4018
Newbold on Avon 51 SP 4877
Newbold-on-Stour 50 SP 2446
Newbold Pacey 50 SP 2957
Newbold Verdon 61 SK 4403
New Bolingbroke 73 TF 3058
Newborough (Gwyn.) 66 SH 4265
Newborough (Northants.) 62 TF 2006
Newborough (Staffs.) 60 SK 1325
Newborough Warren 66 SH 4063
Newbottle 51 SP 5236
Newbourn 55 TM 2743
New Brancepeth 84 NZ 2241
Newbridge (Clwyd) 58 SJ 2841
Newbridge (Corn.) 18 SW 4231
Newbridge (Gwent) 41 ST 2197
Newbridge (Hants.) 26 SU 2915
Newbridge (I. of W.) 26 SZ 4187
Newbridge (Lothian) 102 NT 1272
Newbridge-on-Usk 45 ST 3894
Newbridge on Wye 44 SO 0158
New Brighton 68 SJ 3093
New Brinsley 61 SK 4550
Newbrough 90 NY 8767
New Buckenham 55 TM 0890
Newburgh (Fife) 108 NO 2318
Newburgh (Grampn.) 121 NJ 9925
Newburgh (Lancs.) 69 SD 4810
Newburgh Bar 121 NK 0023
Newburgh Priory 79 SE 5476
Newburn 91 NZ 1765
Newbury 35 SU 4666
Newby (Cumbr.) 83 NY 5921
Newby (N Yorks.) 85 NZ 5012
Newby (N Yorks.) 77 SD 7269
Newby Bridge 77 SD 3686
Newby East 89 NY 4758
Newby Hall (ant.) 79 SE 3467
Newby Moss 77 SD 7472
New Byth 121 NJ 8254
Newby West 82 NY 3653
Newby Wiske 79 SE 3687
Newcastle (Gwent) 45 SO 4417
Newcastle (Shrops.) 48 SO 2482
Newcastle Airport 91 NZ 1971
Newcastle Emlyn 43 SN 3040
Newcastleton 89 NY 4887
Newcastleton Forest 90 NY 5287
Newcastle-under-Lyme 59 SJ 8445
Newcastle upon Tyne 91 NZ 2464
Newchapel (Dyfed) 43 SN 2239
Newchapel (Staffs.) 59 SJ 8654
Newchapel (Surrey) 29 TQ 3642
Newchurch (Dyfed) 43 SN 3724
Newchurch (Gwent) 45 ST 4597
Newchurch (I. of W.) 27 SZ 5585
Newchurch (Kent) 31 TR 0531
Newchurch (Powys) 45 SO 2150
Newchurch in Pendle 78 SD 8239
New Clipstone 71 SK 5863
New Costessey 65 TG 1710
Newcott 24 ST 2309
New Cross 57 SN 6376
New Cumnock 88 NS 6113
New Deer 121 NJ 8846
Newdigate 28 TQ 2042
New Duston 51 SP 7162
New Earswick 79 SE 6155
New Edlington 71 SK 5399
New Ellerby 75 TA 1639
Newell Green 36 SU 8771
New Eltham 37 TQ 4573
New End 50 SP 0560
Newenden 30 TQ 8327
Newent 46 SO 7226
New Farnley 79 SE 2431
New Ferry 68 SJ 3385
Newfield (Durham) 84 NZ 2033
Newfield (Highld.) 129 NH 7877
New Forest 26 SU 2806
New Fryston 79 SE 4526
Newgale 42 SM 8422
New Galloway 88 NX 6377
Newgate 64 TG 0443
Newgate Street 37 TL 3005
New Gilston 103 NO 4207
Newgord 143 HP 5706
New Grimsby 18 SV 8815
New Grounds 46 SO 7204
Newhall 95 NT 1750
Newhall (Ches.) 59 SJ 6045
Newhall (Derby.) 60 SK 2821
Newhall House (Highld.) 128 NH 6965
Newham (Northum.) 97 NU 1728
Newham Hall 97 NU 1729
New Hartley 91 NZ 3076
Newhaven 29 TQ 4401
New Hedges 42 SN 1302
Newhey 69 SD 9311
New Holland 74 TA 0724
Newholm 85 NZ 8610
New Horton Grange 91 NZ 1975
New Houghton (Derby.) 71 SK 4965
New Houghton (Norf.) 64 TF 7827
Newhouse 101 NS 7961
New Houses 78 SD 8073
New Hutton 83 SD 5691
New Hythe 30 TQ 7159
Newick 29 TQ 4121
Newington (Kent) 30 TQ 8665
Newington (Kent) 31 TR 1737
Newington (Oxon.) 36 SU 6196
New Inn (Gwent) 45 SO 4800
New Inn (Gwent) 45 ST 3099
New Inn (N Yorks.) 78 SD 8072
New Invention 48 SO 2976
New Kelso 126 NG 9442
New Lanark 95 NS 8742
Newland (Glos.) 45 SO 5509
Newland (Here. and Worc.) 49 SO 7948
Newland (N Yorks.) 74 SE 6824
Newlandrig 103 NT 3662
Newlands (Borders) 90 NY 5194
Newlands (Grampn.) 120 NJ 3051
Newlands (Northum.) 84 NZ 0955
Newlands of Fleenas Wood 129 NH 9146
Newlands of Geise 135 ND 0865
Newlands Pass 82 NY 1917
New Lane 68 SD 4212
New Leake 73 TF 4057
New Leeds 121 NJ 9954
New Longton 77 SD 5125
New Luce 86 NX 1764
Newlyn 18 SW 4628
Newlyn Downs 19 SW 8354
Newmachar 119 NJ 8819
Newmains 95 NS 8256
New Mains of Ury 119 NO 8787
New Malden 37 TQ 2166
Newmarket (Isle of Lewis) 131 NB 4235
Newmarket (Suff.) 54 TL 6463
Newmarket Heath 54 TL 6363
New Marske 85 NZ 6220
New Marton 58 SJ 3334
Newmill (Borders) 89 NT 4510
New Mill (Corn.) 18 SW 4534
Newmill (Grampn.) 121 NJ 4352
New Mill (Herts.) 36 SP 9212
New Mill (W Yorks.) 70 SE 1608
Newmill Farm 119 NO 7883
Newmill of Inshewan 109 NO 4260
New Mills (Corn.) 19 SW 8952
New Mills (Derby.) 70 SK 0085
New Mills (Gwent) 45 SO 5107
New Mills (Powys) 57 SJ 0901
Newmiln 108 NO 1230
Newmilns 93 NS 5337
New Milton 26 SZ 2495
New Moat 42 SN 0625
Newnham (Glos.) 46 SO 6911
Newnham (Hants.) 35 SU 7054
Newnham (Herts.) 53 TL 2437
Newnham (Kent) 30 TQ 9557
Newnham (Northants.) 51 SP 5859
Newnham Bridge 49 SO 6469
New Park 26 SU 2904
New Pitsligo 121 NJ 8855
New Polzeath 19 SW 9379
Newport (Devon) 23 SS 5631
Newport (Dyfed) 42 SN 0639
Newport (Essex) 53 TL 5234
Newport (Glos.) 46 ST 7097
Newport (Gwent) 32 ST 3187
Newport (Highld.) 135 ND 1224
Newport (Humbs.) 74 SE 8530
Newport (I. of W.) 27 SZ 4989
Newport (Norf.) 65 TG 5017
Newport (Shrops.) 59 SJ 7419
Newport Bay 42 SN 0340
Newport-on-Tay 109 NO 4228
Newport Pagnell 52 SP 8743
Newpound Common 28 TQ 0627
New Prestwick 93 NS 3424
Newquay (Corn.) 19 SW 8161
New Quay (Dyfed) 43 SN 3859
Newquay Bay 19 SW 8162
New Rackheath 65 TG 2812
New Radnor 48 SO 2161
New River (Cambs.) 53 TL 5869
New River (Lincs.) 63 TF 2518
New River Ancholme 74 SE 9717
New Romney 31 TR 0624
New Rossington 71 SK 6198
New Sauchie 102 NS 8993
New Scone 108 NO 1325
Newseat (Grampn.) 121 NJ 7033
Newseat (Grampn.) 121 NK 0749
Newsham (Northum.) 91 NZ 3079
Newsham (N Yorks.) 84 NZ 1010
Newsholme (Humbs.) 74 SE 7229
Newsholme (Lancs.) 78 SD 8451
New Silksworth 85 NZ 3853
Newstead (Borders) 96 NT 5634
Newstead (Northum.) 97 NU 1526
Newstead (Notts.) 61 SK 5252
New Stevenston 101 NS 7659
Newthorpe 79 SE 4632
Newtimber Place 28 TQ 2613
New Tolsta 131 NB 5348
Newton (Borders) 90 NT 6020
Newton (Cambs.) 63 TF 4314
Newton (Cambs.) 53 TL 4349
Newton (Ches.) 69 SJ 5059
Newton (Ches.) 69 SJ 5274
Newton (Cumbr.) 76 SD 2371
Newton (Dumf. and Galwy.) 89 NY 1194
Newton (Grampn.) 129 NJ 1663
Newton (Hants.) 26 SU 2322
Newton (Here. and Worc.) 45 SO 3433
Newton (Here. and Worc.) 45 SO 5054
Newton (Highld.) 132 NC 2331
Newton (Highld.) 135 ND 3449
Newton (Highld.) 129 NH 7448
Newton (Highld.) 129 NH 7766
Newton (Lancs.) 77 SD 4431
Newton (Lancs.) 77 SD 5974
Newton (Lancs.) 77 SD 6950
Newton (Lincs.) 62 TF 0436
Newton (Lothian) 102 NT 0877
Newton (Mid Glam.) 41 SS 8377
Newton (Norf.) 64 TF 8315
Newton (Northants.) 52 SP 8883
Newton (North Uist) 124 NF 8977
Newton (Northum.) 91 NZ 0364
Newton (Notts.) 61 SK 6841
Newton (S Glam.) 32 ST 2478
Newton (Staffs.) 60 SK 0325
Newton (Strath.) 100 NS 0498
Newton (Strath.) 101 NS 6560
Newton (Strath.) 95 NS 9331
Newton (Suff.) 54 TL 9140
Newton (Warw.) 51 SP 5378
Newton (W Glam.) 40 SS 6088
Newton (W Yorks.) 79 SE 4427
Newton Abbot 21 SX 8671
Newton Arlosh 82 NY 1955
Newton Aycliffe 84 NZ 2824
Newton Bewley 85 NZ 4626
Newton Blossomville 52 SP 9251
Newton Bromswold 52 SP 9966
Newton Burgoland 60 SK 3609
Newton by Toft 72 TF 0487
Newton Dale 80 SE 8191
Newton Ferrers 21 SX 5447
Newtonferry 124 NF 8978
Newton Flotman 65 TM 2198
Newtongarry Croft 121 NJ 5735
Newtongrange 103 NT 3364
Newton Harcourt 61 SP 6397
Newton Heath 26 SZ 0084
Newtonhill 119 NO 9193
Newton House 121 NJ 6629
Newton Kyme 79 SE 4644
Newton-le-Willows (Mers.) 69 SJ 5894
Newton-le-Willows (N Yorks.) 84 SE 2189
Newton Longville 52 SP 8431
Newton Mearns 93 NS 5456
Newtonmill 109 NO 6064
Newtonmore 116 NN 7199
Newton Mountain 42 SM 9807
Newton of Balcanquhal 102 NO 1510
Newton-on-Ouse 79 SE 5059
Newton-on-Rawcliffe 80 SE 8090
Newton-on-the-Moor 91 NU 1605
Newton on Trent 72 SK 8374
Newton or St. Mary's Haven 97 NU 2424
Newton Poppleford 24 SY 0889
Newton Purcell 51 SP 6230
Newton Regis 60 SK 2707
Newton Reigny 83 NY 4731
Newton Solney 60 SK 2825
Newton Stacey 34 SU 4040
Newton St. Cyres 21 SX 8797
Newton Stewart 86 NX 4165
Newton St. Faith 65 TG 2117
Newton St. Loe 33 ST 7064
Newton St. Petrock 22 SS 4112
Newton Toney 34 SU 2140
Newton Tors 97 NT 9026
Newton Tracey 23 SS 5226
Newton under Roseberry 85 NZ 5613
Newton upon Derwent 80 SE 7149
Newton Valence 27 SU 7232
Newtown (Ches.) 59 SJ 6247
Newtown (Ches.) 70 SJ 9784
Newtown (Cumbr.) 89 NY 5062
Newtown (Dorset) 26 SZ 0393
Newtown (Hants.) 26 SU 2710
Newtown (Hants.) 26 SU 3023
Newtown (Hants.) 35 SU 4763
Newtown (Hants.) 27 SU 6013
Newtown (Here. and Worc.) 45 SO 6145
Newtown (Highld.) 115 NH 3504
Newtown (I. of M.) 76 SC 3273
Newtown (I. of W.) 26 SZ 4290
New Town (Lothian) 103 NT 4470
Newtown (Northum.) 97 NT 9731
Newtown (Northum.) 97 NU 0300
Newtown (Northum.) 97 NU 0425
Newtown (Powys) 57 SO 1091
Newtown (Shrops.) 58 SJ 4831
Newtown (Staffs.) 69 SJ 9060
Newtown (Wilts.) 25 ST 9128
Newtown Bay 26 SZ 4192
Newtown-in-St. Martin 18 SW 7323
Newtown Linford 61 SK 5110
Newtown St. Boswells 96 NT 5731
New Tredegar 41 SO 1403
New Tupton 71 SK 3966
Newtyle 108 NO 2941
Newtyle Forest 129 NJ 0552
Newtyle Hill 108 NO 0541
New Ulva 99 NR 7080
New Waltham 75 TA 2804
New Wimpole 53 TL 3450
New Winton 103 NT 4271
New Yatt 47 SP 3713
New York (Lincs.) 63 TF 2455
New York (Tyne and Wear) 91 NZ 3270
Neyland 42 SM 9605
Niarbyl Bay 76 SC 2176
Nibley 33 ST 6882
Nibon 142 HU 3073
Nicholashayne 24 ST 1015
Nicholaston 40 SS 5188
Nidd 79 SE 3060
Nidderdale 78 SE 0974
Nigg (Grampn.) 119 NJ 9402
Nigg (Highld.) 129 NH 8071
Nigg Bay (Grampn.) 119 NJ 9604
Nigg Bay (Highld.) 129 NH 7771
Nightcott 23 SS 8925
Nikka Vord (mt.) 143 HP 6210
Nilig 67 SJ 0254
Nine Ashes 38 TL 5902
Ninebanks 83 NY 7853
Nine Barrow Down 26 SZ 0081
Ninemile Bar or Crocketford 88 NX 8272
Ninfield 29 TQ 7012
Ningwood 26 SZ 3989
Nisbet 96 NT 6725
Nithsdale 88 NX 8991
Niton 27 SZ 5076
Nitshill 101 NS 5160
Noak Hill 37 TQ 5493
Nobottle 51 SP 6763
Nocton 72 TF 0564
Noddsdale Water 100 NS 2163
Noke 47 SP 5413
Noltland Castle (ant.) 138 HY 4348
Nolton 42 SM 8718
No Man's Heath (Ches.) 59 SJ 5148
No Man's Heath (Warw.) 60 SK 2709
Nomansland (Devon) 23 SS 8313
Nomansland (Wilts.) 26 SU 2517
Noneley 59 SJ 4727
No Ness 141 HU 4421
Nonington 31 TR 2552
Nook 89 NY 4679
Nookton Fell 84 NY 9148
Noonsbrough 140 HU 2957
Noose, The (sbk.) 46 SO 7107
Noranside Institution (Borstal) 109 NO 4761
Noran Water 109 NO 4860
Norbury (Ches.) 59 SJ 5547
Norbury (Derby.) 60 SK 1242
Norbury (Shrops.) 58 SO 3693
Norbury (Staffs.) 59 SJ 7823
Norbury Camp (ant.) 46 SO 9815
Nordelph 63 TF 5501
Norden (Dorset) 26 SY 9483
Norden (Gtr Mches.) 69 SD 8514
Nordley 59 SO 6998
Norham 97 NT 9047
Norley 69 SJ 5672
Norleywood 26 SZ 3597
Normanby (Humbs.) 74 SE 8716
Normanby (N Yorks.) 80 SE 7381
Normanby-by-Spittal 72 TF 0088
Normanby le Wold 73 TF 1294
Norman Cross 52 TL 1691
Normandy 28 SU 9251
Norman's Green 24 ST 0503
Norman's Law 108 NO 3020
Normanton (Derby.) 60 SK 3433
Normanton (Lincs.) 61 SK 9446
Normanton (Notts.) 61 SK 7054
Normanton (W Yorks.) 79 SE 3822
Normanton le Heath 60 SK 3712
Normanton on Soar 61 SK 5123
Normanton-on-the-Wolds 61 SK 6232
Normanton on Trent 72 SK 7868
Normoss 77 SD 3437
Norrington Common 33 ST 8864
Norris Hill 60 SK 3216
Northallerton 85 SE 3793
Northam (Devon) 22 SS 4429
Northam (Hants.) 26 SU 4312
Northampton 51 SP 7561
Northampton (Sywell) Aerodrome 52 SP 8268
North Ascot 36 SU 9069
North Ashton 69 SD 5600
North Aston 47 SP 4728
Northaw 37 TL 2802
North Baddesley 26 SU 3920
North Ballachulish 106 NN 0560
North Barrow 25 ST 6029
North Barrule (mt.) 76 SC 4491
North Barsham 64 TF 9135
North Bay (Barra) 112 NF 7202
North Bay (Hoy, Orkney) 136 ND 2890
North Bay (Sanday, Orkney) 139 HY 6543
North Benfleet 38 TQ 7590
North Berwick 103 NT 5485
North Berwick Law 103 NT 5584
North Birny Fell 89 NY 4791
North Boarhunt 27 SU 6010
Northborough 62 TF 1508
Northbourne 31 TR 3352
North Bovey 21 SX 7483
North Bradley 33 ST 8554
North Brentor 20 SX 4781
North Buckland 22 SS 4740
North Burlingham 65 TG 3610
North Burnt Hill 100 NS 2665
North Cadbury 25 ST 6327
North Cairn 86 NW 9770
North Carlton 72 SK 9477
North Carr (lightship) 103 NO 6612
North Cave 74 SE 8832
North Cerney 46 SP 0208
Northchapel 28 SU 9529
North Charford 26 SU 1919

North Charlton 97 NU 1622
North Cheek or Ness Point 81 NZ 9506
Northchurch 36 SP 9708
North Cliffe 74 SE 8737
North Clifton 72 SK 8272
Northcote Manor 23 SS 6218
North Cotes 75 TA 3400
Northcott 20 SX 3392
North Cove 55 TM 4689
North Cowton 84 NZ 2803
North Crawley 52 SP 9244
North Cray 37 TQ 4972
North Creake 64 TF 8538
North Curry 24 ST 3125
North Dalton 81 SE 9352
North Dawn 136 HY 4803
North Deep 108 NO 2219
North Deighton 79 SE 3851
North Downs (Hants.) 27 SU 8207
North Downs (Kent) 30 TQ 6763
North Drove Drain 62 TF 1817
North Duffield 74 SE 6837
Northdyke 136 HY 2320
North Elkington 73 TF 2890
North Elmham 64 TF 9820
North End (Avon) 32 ST 4167
Northend (Avon) 33 ST 7867
North End (Berks.) 34 SU 4063
Northend (Bucks.) 36 SU 7392
North End (Hants.) 27 SU 6502
Northend (Warw.) 50 SP 3852
North End (W Susx) 28 TQ 1209
North Erradale 126 NG 7481
North Esk Resr. 102 NT 1558
Northey Island 38 TL 8706
North Fearns 123 NG 5935
North Fen (Cambs.) 63 TF 2909
North Fen (Cambs.) 53 TL 5169
North Ferriby 74 SE 9826
Northfield (Borders) 97 NT 9167
Northfield (Grampn.) 119 NJ 9008
Northfield (W Mids.) 50 SP 0179
Northfleet 30 TQ 6274
North Foreland 31 TR 4069
North Frodingham 81 TA 1053
North Glen Sannox 92 NR 9746
North Green 55 TM 2288
North Greetwell 72 TF 0173
North Grimston 80 SE 8467
North Harris (dist.) 125 NB 1207
North Haven (Fair Isle) 139 HZ 2272
North Haven (Grampn.) 121 NK 1138
North Havra (is.) 141 HU 3642
North Hayling 27 SU 7203
North Head (Highld.) 135 ND 3851
North Head (Swona) 136 ND 3985
North Heasley 23 SS 7333
North Heath 28 TQ 0621
North Hill (Corn.) 20 SX 2776
North Hill (Papa Westray) 138 HY 4954
North Hill (Somer.) 23 SS 9347
North Hill (Westray) 138 HY 4048
North Hinksey Village 47 SP 4806
North Holms 143 HP 5611
North Holmwood 28 TQ 1646
North Huish 21 SX 7156
North Hykeham 72 SK 9465
Northiam 30 TQ 8324
Northill (Beds.) 52 TL 1446
Northington 27 SU 5637
North Kelsey 74 TA 0401
North Kelsey Beck 74 TA 0102
North Kessock 128 NH 6548
North Kilvington 79 SE 4285
North Kilworth 51 SP 6183
North Kingennie 109 NO 4736
North Kyme 62 TF 1452
North Lancing 28 TQ 1805
Northlands 63 TF 3453
Northleach 46 SP 1114
North Lee (Bucks.) 36 SP 8309
North Lee (North Uist) (mt.) 124 NF 9366
Northleigh (Devon) 24 SY 1995
North Leigh (Oxon.) 47 SP 3813
North Leverton with Habblesthorpe 72 SK 7882
Northlew 20 SX 5099
North Littleton 50 SP 0847
North Loch 139 HY 7545
North Lopham 54 TM 0383
North Luffenham 62 SK 9303
North Marden 27 SU 8015
North Marston 36 SP 7722
North Medwin 95 NT 0149
North Middleton 103 NT 3559
North Molton 23 SS 7329
Northmoor 47 SP 4202
Northmoor Green or Moorland 24 ST 3332
North Morar (dist.) 111 NM 7892
North Moreton 35 SU 5689
Northmuir 109 NO 3855
North Muskham 72 SK 7958
North Neaps 143 HP 4805
North Ness 140 HU 1861
North Nesting (dist.) 141 HU 4559
North Nevi (pt.) 137 HY 6101
North Newbald 74 SE 9136
North Newington 50 SP 4139
North Newnton 34 SU 1257
North Newton 24 ST 2931
North Nibley 46 ST 7396
North Oakley 35 SU 5354
North Ockendon 38 TQ 5984
Northolt 37 TQ 1285
Northop 68 SJ 2468
Northop Hall 68 SJ 2767
North Ormsby 73 TF 2893
Northorpe (Lincs.) 72 SK 8996
Northorpe (Lincs.) 62 TF 0917
North Otterington 85 SE 3589
Northover 25 ST 5223
North Owersby 72 TF 0594
Northowram 78 SE 1127
North Perrott 25 ST 4709
North Petherton 24 ST 2832
North Petherwin 20 SX 2889
North Pickenham 64 TF 8606
North Piddle 50 SO 9654
North Poorton 25 SY 5197
Northpunds 141 HU 4022
North Queensferry 102 NT 1380
Northrepps 65 TG 2439
North Rigton 79 SE 2749
North Rode 69 SJ 8866
North Roe 142 HU 3689
North Roe (dist.) 142 HU 3487
North Ronaldsay 139 HY 7654
North Ronaldsay Aerodrome 139 HY 7653
North Ronaldsay Firth 139 HY 7549
North Runcton 64 TF 6416
North Sandwick 143 HU 5496
North Scale 76 SD 1769
North Scarle 72 SK 8466
North Seaton 91 NZ 2986
North Shian 106 NM 9143
North Shields 91 NZ 3468
North Shoebury 38 TQ 9286
North Shore 77 SD 3037
North Side 63 TL 2799
North Somercotes 73 TF 4296
North Sound, The 138 HY 5845
North Stack (pt.) 66 SH 2183
North Stainley 79 SE 2876
North Stainmore 83 NY 8215
North Stane 143 HP 6613
North Stifford 38 TQ 6080
North Stoke (Avon) 33 ST 7068
North Stoke (Oxon.) 36 SU 6186
North Stoke (W Susx) 28 TQ 0211
North Street 27 SU 6433
North Sunderland 97 NU 2131
North Sutor (pt.) 129 NH 8168
North Taing (Auskerry) 137 HY 6716
North Taing (Stronsay) 137 HY 6225
North Tamerton 20 SX 3197
North Tawton 23 SS 6601
North Third Resr. 101 NS 7588
North Thoresby 75 TF 2998
North Tidworth 34 SU 2248
North Tolsta 131 NB 5347
Northton 124 NF 9989
Northtown 136 ND 4797
North Tuddenham 64 TG 0413
North Ugie Water 121 NJ 9553
North Uist (is.) 124 NF 8370
Northwaa 139 HY 7544
North Walsham 65 TG 2730
North Waltham 35 SU 5546
North Warnborough 35 SU 7351
North Water Bridge 109 NO 6566
North Watten 135 ND 2458
Northway 46 SO 9234
North Weald Basset 37 TL 4904
North West Passage 18 SV 8411
North West Point 22 SS 1347
North Wharf (sbk.) 77 SD 3149
North Whilborough 21 SX 8766
Northwich 69 SJ 6573
Northwick (Avon) 33 ST 5586
North Wick (Avon) 33 ST 5865
North Widcombe 33 ST 5758
North Willingham 73 TF 1688
North Wingfield 71 SK 4064
North Witham 62 SK 9221
Northwold 64 TL 7596
Northwood (Gtr London) 37 TQ 1090
Northwood (I. of W.) 27 SZ 4992
Northwood (Shrops.) 58 SJ 4633
Northwood Green 46 SO 7216
North Wootton (Dorset) 25 ST 6614
North Wootton (Norf.) 64 TF 6424
North Wootton (Somer.) 33 ST 5641
North Wraxall 33 ST 8174
North Yardhope 90 NT 9201
North York Moors 80 SE 7398
North Yorkshire Moors Railway 80 SE 8495
Norton (Ches.) 69 SJ 5581
Norton (Cleve.) 85 NZ 4421
Norton (Glos.) 46 SO 8624
Norton (Here. and Worc.) 49 SO 8750
Norton (Here. and Worc.) 50 SP 0447
Norton (Herts.) 53 TL 2234
Norton (I. of W.) 26 SZ 3489
Norton (Northants.) 51 SP 6063
Norton (Notts.) 71 SK 5772
Norton (N Yorks.) 80 SE 7971
Norton (N Yorks.) 71 SK 3581
Norton (Powys) 48 SO 3067
Norton (Shrops.) 59 SJ 5609
Norton (Shrops.) 59 SJ 7200
Norton (Shrops.) 48 SO 4581
Norton (Suff.) 54 TL 9565
Norton (S Yorks.) 71 SE 5415
Norton (Wilts.) 33 ST 8884
Norton (W Susx) 28 SU 9306
Norton Bavant 33 ST 9043
Norton Bridge 59 SJ 8730
Norton Canes 60 SK 0108
Norton Canon 45 SO 3847
Norton Disney 72 SK 8859
Norton Ferris 25 ST 7936
Norton Fitzwarren 24 ST 1925
Norton Green 26 SZ 3388
Norton Hawkfield 33 ST 5964
Norton Heath 38 TL 6004
Norton in Hales 59 SJ 7038
Norton-in-the-Moors 59 SJ 8951
Norton-Juxta-Twycross 60 SK 3207
Norton-le-Clay 79 SE 4071
Norton Lindsey 50 SP 2263
Norton Malreward 33 ST 6064
Norton Mandeville 37 TL 5804
Norton Marshes 65 TG 4200
Norton St. Philip 33 ST 7755
Norton Subcourse 65 TM 4098
Norton sub Hamdon 25 ST 4615
Norwell 72 SK 7661
Norwell Woodhouse 72 SK 7462
Norwich 65 TG 2308
Norwich Airport 65 TG 2213
Norwick (Unst) 143 HP 6514
Nor Wick (Unst) 143 HP 6614
Norwood Green 37 TQ 1378
Norwood Hill 28 TQ 2443
Noseley 61 SP 7398
Noss Head 135 ND 3854
Noss Mayo 21 SX 5447
Nosterfield 79 SE 2780
Nostie 123 NG 8527
Notgrove 46 SP 1020
Nottage 41 SS 8278
Nottingham 61 SK 5741
Nottingham Airport 61 SK 6236
Notton (Wilts.) 33 ST 9169
Notton (W Yorks.) 71 SE 3413
Nounsley 38 TL 7910
Noup Head 138 HY 3950
Noup of Noss 141 HU 5539
Noup, The (pt.) 143 HP 6318
Noutard's Green 49 SO 7966
Novar House 128 NH 6167
Nox 58 SJ 4010
Nuffield 36 SU 6687
Nunburnholme 80 SE 8548
Nuneaton 50 SP 3592
Nuneham Courtenay 47 SU 5599
Nun Monkton 79 SE 5057
Nunney 33 ST 7345
Nunnington 79 SE 6679
Nunnykirk 91 NZ 0892
Nunthorpe 85 NZ 5313
Nunton (Benbecula) 124 NF 7653
Nunton (Wilts.) 26 SU 1525
Nunwick 90 NY 8774
Nursling 26 SU 3615
Nursted 27 SU 7621
Nutbery Hill 94 NS 7433
Nutbourne 28 TQ 0718
Nutfield 29 TQ 3150
Nuthall 61 SK 5144
Nuthampstead 53 TL 4134
Nuthurst 28 TQ 1926
Nutley 29 TQ 4427
Nutwell 71 SE 6303
Nybster 135 ND 3663
Nyetimber 27 SZ 8998
Nyewood 27 SU 8021
Nyland Hill 33 ST 4550
Nymet Rowland 23 SS 7108
Nymet Tracey 21 SS 7200
Nympsfield 46 SO 8000
Nynehead 24 ST 1422
Nyton 28 SU 9305

O

Oadby 61 SK 6200
Oad Street 30 TQ 8762
Oakamoor 60 SK 0544
Oakbank 102 NT 0866
Oakdale 41 ST 1898
Oake 24 ST 1525
Oaken 59 SJ 8502
Oakenclough 77 SD 5447
Oakengates 59 SJ 7010
Oakenshaw (Durham) 84 NZ 2036
Oakenshaw (W Yorks.) 78 SE 1727
Oakford (Devon) 23 SS 9021
Oakford (Dyfed) 43 SN 4557
Oakgrove 69 SJ 9169
Oakham 62 SK 8509
Oakhanger 27 SU 7635
Oakhill 33 ST 6347
Oakington 53 TL 4164
Oaklands 67 SH 8158
Oakle Street 46 SO 7517
Oakley (Beds.) 52 TL 0153
Oakley (Bucks.) 36 SP 6412
Oakley (Fife) 102 NT 0289
Oakley (Hants.) 35 SU 5650
Oakley (Suff.) 55 TM 1678
Oakley Green 36 SU 9376
Oakley Park 57 SN 9886
Oakridge 46 SO 9103
Oaks 58 SJ 4204
Oaksey 46 ST 9893
Oakthorpe 60 SK 3213
Oakwoodhill 28 TQ 1337
Oakworth 78 SE 0238
Oare (Kent) 31 TR 0062
Oare (Somer.) 23 SS 8047
Oare (Wilts.) 34 SU 1563
Oasby 62 TF 0039
Oa, The (dist.) 98 NR 3144
Oathlaw 109 NO 4756
Oban 105 NM 8630
Oban Bay 105 NM 8530
Obney 108 NO 0336
Obney Hills 108 NO 0238
Oborne 25 ST 6518
Occlestone Green 69 SJ 6962
Occold 55 TM 1570
Ochertyre 107 NN 8323
Ochil Hills 102 NO 0509
Ochiltree 93 NS 5121
Ochtermuthill 107 NN 8216
Ockbrook 60 SK 4235
Ockham 28 TQ 0756
Ockle 111 NM 5570
Ockle Point 111 NM 5471
Ockley 28 TQ 1640
Ockran Head 142 HU 2484
Ocle Pychard 45 SO 5946
Odcombe 25 ST 5015
Odda's Chapel (ant.) 46 SO 8629
Oddingley 49 SO 9159
Oddington (Glos.) 47 SP 2225
Oddington (Oxon.) 47 SP 5514
Odell 52 SP 9658
Odie 137 HY 6229
Odiham 35 SU 7350
Odin Bay 137 HY 6824
Odness 137 HY 6926
Odstock 26 SU 1426
Odstock Down 26 SU 1324
Odstone 60 SK 3907
Offa's Dyke (Clwyd) (ant.) 67 SJ 1079
Offa's Dyke (Clwyd) (ant.) 58 SJ 2948
Offa's Dyke (Here. and Worc.) (ant.) 45 SO 2959
Offa's Dyke (Salop) (ant.) 48 SO 2578
Offchurch 50 SP 3565
Offenham 50 SP 0546
Offham (E Susx) 29 TQ 4012
Offham (Kent) 29 TQ 6557
Offord Cluny 53 TL 2267
Offord D'Arcy 53 TL 2266
Offton 54 TM 0649
Offwell 24 SY 1999
Ogbourne Maizey 34 SU 1871
Ogbourne St. Andrew 34 SU 1872
Ogbourne St. George 34 SU 2074
Ogbury (ant.) 34 SU 1438
Ogden Reservoir (Lancs.) 78 SD 7622
Ogden Reservoir (Lancs.) 78 SD 8140
Ogil 109 NO 4561
Ogle 91 NZ 1378
Ogmore 41 SS 8877
Ogmore-by-Sea 41 SS 8674
Ogmore Forest 41 SS 9489
Ogmore Vale 41 SS 9490
Ogston Reservoir 71 SK 3760
Oh Me Edge 90 NY 7099
Oigh-sgeir 110 NM 1596
Oisgill Bay 122 NG 1349
Oitir Fhiadhaich 124 NF 7465
Oitir Mhòr (Barra) 112 NF 7306
Oitir Mhòr (Benbecula) 124 NF 8157
Okeford Fitzpaine 25 ST 8010
Okehampton 21 SX 5895
Okehampton Camp 21 SX 5893
Okement Hill 21 SX 6087
Okraquoy 141 HU 4331
Olantigh 31 TR 0648
Old 51 SP 7873
Old Aberdeen 119 NJ 9408
Old Alresford 27 SU 5834
Oldany Island 132 NC 0834
Old Bedford River 53 TL 4888
Oldberrow 50 SP 1165
Old Bewick 97 NU 0621
Old Bolingbroke 73 TF 3564
Oldborough 23 SS 7706
Old Brampton 71 SK 3371
Old Bridge of Urr 88 NX 7767
Old Buckenham 54 TM 0691
Old Burghclere 35 SU 4657
Oldbury (Shrops.) 49 SO 7092
Oldbury (Warw.) 60 SP 3194
Oldbury (W Mids.) 50 SO 9889
Oldbury Castle (ant.) 34 SU 0469
Oldbury-on-Severn 33 ST 6092
Oldbury on the Hill 33 ST 8089
Oldbury Sands 45 ST 5793
Old Byland 79 SE 5486
Oldcastle 45 SO 3224
Old Castle Head 42 SS 0796
Old Castleton 90 NY 5190
Oldchapel Hill 57 SN 9780
Old Cleeve 32 ST 0342
Old Clipstone 71 SK 6064
Oldcoates 71 SK 5888
Old Colwyn 67 SH 8678
Old Croft River 63 TL 4996
Old Dailly 86 NX 2299
Old Dalby 61 SK 6723
Old Deer 121 NJ 9747
Old Denaby 71 SK 4899
Old Ellerby 75 TA 1637
Old Felixstowe 55 TM 3135
Oldfield 49 SO 8464
Old Fletton 62 TL 1997
Oldford 33 ST 7849
Old Hall, The (Humbs.) 75 TA 2717
Oldham 69 SD 9305
Oldhamstocks 96 NT 7470
Old Head 136 ND 4683
Old Heath 39 TM 0122
Old Howe 81 TA 1156
Oldhurst 53 TL 3077
Old Hutton 77 SD 5688
Old Kea 19 SW 8441
Old Kilpatrick 101 NS 4673
Old Knebworth 37 TL 2320
Oldland 33 ST 6771
Old Leake 63 TF 4050
Old Lynn Channel 63 TF 5234
Old Malton 80 SE 7972
Old Man of Coniston, The 82 SD 2797
Old Man of Hoy (mt.) 136 HY 1700
Old Man of Storr (mt.) 123 NG 5054
Oldmeldrum 121 NJ 8027
Old Milverton 50 SP 2967
Old Monkland 101 NS 7163
Old Montsale 39 TR 0097
Old Newton 54 TM 0662
Old Oswestry (ant.) 58 SJ 2931
Oldpark 59 SJ 6909
Old Peak or South Cheek 81 NZ 9802
Old Philpstoun 102 NT 0577
Old Radnor 45 SO 2559
Old Rayne 121 NJ 6728
Old River Ancholme 74 SE 9615
Old River Don 74 SE 7613
Old Romney 31 TR 0325
Old Sarum (ant.) 26 SU 1332
Old Scone 108 NO 1226
Oldshoremore 132 NC 2059
Old Soar Manor (ant.) 29 TQ 6254
Old Sodbury 33 ST 7581
Old Somerby 62 SK 9633
Old South (sbk.) 63 TF 4735
Oldstead 79 SE 5280
Old Town (Cumbr.) 77 SD 6082
Old Town (Northum.) 90 NY 8891
Oldtown of Ord 121 NJ 6259
Old Warden 52 TL 1343
Oldways End 23 SS 8624
Old Weston 52 TL 0977
Old West River or River Great Ouse 53 TL 4671
Oldwhat 121 NJ 8551
Old Winchester Hill (ant.) 27 SU 6420
Old Windsor 36 SU 9874
Old Wives Lees 31 TR 0755
Olgrinmore 135 ND 0955
Oliver 95 NT 0924
Oliver's Battery 27 SU 4527
Ollaberry 142 HU 3680
Ollach 123 NG 5136
Ollerton (Ches.) 69 SJ 7776
Ollerton (Notts.) 71 SK 6567
Ollerton (Shrops.) 59 SJ 6425
Ollinsgarth (pt.) 141 HU 4430
Ollisdal Geo 122 NG 2138
Olna Firth 141 HU 3864
Olney 52 SP 8851
Olrig House 135 ND 1866
Olton 50 SP 1282
Olveston 33 ST 6087
Ombersley 49 SO 8463
Ompton 72 SK 6865
Onchan 76 SC 4078
Onchan Head 76 SC 4077
Onecote 60 SK 0555
Ongar Hill 63 TF 5724
Ongar Street 48 SO 3967
Onibury 48 SO 4579
Onich 106 NN 0261
Onllwyn 41 SN 8310
Onneley 59 SJ 7542
Onslow Village 28 SU 9849
Opinan (Highld.) 123 NG 7472
Opinan (Highld.) 126 NG 8796
Opsay 124 NF 9876
Orbost 122 NG 2543
Orby 73 TF 4967
Orby Marsh 73 TF 5266
Orchard 25 ST 8216
Orchardleigh House 33 ST 7750
Orchard Portman 24 ST 2421
Orcheston 34 SU 0545
Orcheston Down 34 SU 0747
Orcop 45 SO 4726
Orcop Hill 45 SO 4628
Ord 123 NG 6113
Ordhead 119 NJ 6610
Ordie Burn 108 NO 0534
Ordiequish 121 NJ 3357
Ord River 123 NG 6212
Ords, The 141 HU 3413
Ord, The (pt.) 141 HU 4936
Ore 30 TQ 8311
Ore Bay 136 ND 3094
Oreham Common 28 TQ 2214
Oreton 49 SO 6580
Oreval (mt.) 131 NB 0809
Orfasay 143 HU 4977
Orford (Ches.) 69 SJ 6090
Orford (Suff.) 55 TM 4250
Orford Ness 55 TM 4549
Orgreave 60 SK 1415
Orinsay 131 NB 3612
Orka Voe 143 HU 4077
Orknagable (pt.) 143 HP 5713
Orkney Islands 136 HY 4821
Orlestone 31 TR 0034
Orleton (Here. and Worc.) 48 SO 4967
Orleton (Here. and Worc.) 49 SO 6967
Orlingbury 52 SP 8572
Ormesby 85 NZ 5317
Ormesby St. Margaret 65 TG 4915
Ormesby St. Michael 65 TG 4814
Ormiclate Castle 112 NF 7331
Ormiscaig 126 NG 8590
Ormiston 103 NT 4169
Ormsaigmore 111 NM 4763
Ormsary House 99 NR 7372
Ormskirk 68 SD 4107
Ornish Island 112 NF 8538
Oronsay 123 NG 7112
Oronsay (Colonsay) (is.) 98 NR 3588
Oronsay (Highld.) 111 NM 5959
Oronsay (Island of Skye) 122 NG 3136
Oronsay (North Uist) 124 NF 8475
Orosay (Barra) 112 NF 7106
Orosay (South Uist) 112 NF 7217
Orphir 136 HY 3404
Orpington 37 TQ 4665
Orrell 69 SD 5203
Orrin Falls 128 NH 4751
Orrin Reservoir 127 NH 3850
Orrisdale Head 76 SC 3192
Orroland 87 NX 7746
Orsay 98 NR 1651
Orsett 38 TQ 6481
Orslow 59 SJ 8015
Orston 61 SK 7741
Orton (Cumbr.) 83 NY 6208
Orton (Northants.) 51 SP 8079
Orton Longueville 62 TL 1696
Orton-on-the-Hill 60 SK 3004
Orton Waterville 62 TL 1596
Orval (mt.) 110 NM 3399
Orwell 53 TL 3650
Osbaldeston 77 SD 6431
Osbaston 60 SK 4204
Osborne Bay 27 SZ 5395
Osborne House 27 SZ 5194
Osbournby 62 TF 0638
Oscroft 69 SJ 5066
Ose 122 NG 3141
Osea Island 38 TL 9106
Osgathorpe 60 SK 4219
Osgodby (Lincs.) 72 TF 0792
Osgodby (N Yorks.) 79 SE 6433
Osgodby (N Yorks.) 81 TA 0585
Oskaig 123 NG 5438
Oskamull 105 NM 4540
Osmaston 60 SK 1944
Osmington 25 SY 7282
Osmington Mills 25 SY 7381
Osmotherley 85 SE 4597
Osnaburgh or Dairsie 109 NO 4117
Ospisdale 129 NH 7189
Ospringe 31 TQ 9960
Ossett 71 SE 2720
Ossington 72 SK 7564
Ostend 38 TQ 9397
Osterley Park 37 TQ 1577
Oswaldkirk 79 SE 6279
Oswaldtwistle 77 SD 7327
Oswestry 58 SJ 2829
Otford 29 TQ 5359
Otham 30 TQ 7954
Othery 24 ST 3831
Othona (ant.) 39 TM 0308
Otley (Suff.) 55 TM 2055
Otley (W Yorks.) 78 SE 2045
Ot Moor 47 SP 5614
Otterbourne 27 SU 4522
Otterburn (Northum.) 90 NY 8893
Otterburn (N Yorks.) 78 SD 8857
Otterburn Camp 90 NY 8995
Otterden Place 30 TQ 9454
Otter Ferry 100 NR 9384
Otterham 20 SX 1690
Ottershaw 36 TQ 0264
Otters Wick (Sanday, Orkney) 139 HY 6944
Otterswick (Yell) 143 HU 5185
Otters Wick (Yell) 143 HU 5285
Otterton 24 SY 0785
Ottery St. Mary 24 SY 0995
Ottringham 75 TA 2624
Oughtershaw 78 SD 8781
Oughtibridge 71 SK 3093
Oulston 79 SE 5474
Oulton (Cumbr.) 82 NY 2551
Oulton (Norf.) 65 TG 1328
Oulton (Staffs.) 59 SJ 9035
Oulton (Suff.) 65 TM 5194
Oulton (W Yorks.) 79 SE 3627
Oulton Broad 55 TM 5292
Oulton Street 65 TG 1527
Oundle 52 TL 0488
Ousby 83 NY 6134
Ousdale 135 ND 0620
Ousden 54 TL 7359
Ouseburn 79 SE 4461
Ousefleet 74 SE 8223
Ouse Ness 138 HY 4549
Ouston 84 NZ 2554
Outer Hebrides 124 NG 0085
Outertown 136 HY 2310
Out Gate 82 SD 3599
Outhgill 83 NY 7801
Outlane 70 SE 0817
Out Newton 75 TA 3822
Out Rawcliffe 77 SD 4041
Outshore Point 136 HY 2222
Out Skerries 143 HU 6771
Out Stack 143 HP 6120
Outward Bound Mountain School (Cumbr.) 82 NY 1400
Outward Bound Mountain School (Cumbr.) 83 NY 4021
Outwell 63 TF 5104
Outwood (Surrey) 29 TQ 3246
Outwood (W Yorks.) 79 SE 3223
Oval, The 33 ST 7363
Ovenden 78 SE 0727
Over (Avon) 33 ST 5882
Over (Cambs.) 53 TL 3770
Overbister 139 HY 6840
Overbury 50 SO 9537
Overcombe 25 SY 6982
Over Haddon 70 SK 2066
Over Kellet 77 SD 5169
Over Kiddington 47 SP 4122
Over Norton 47 SP 3128
Overseal 60 SK 2915
Over Silton 85 SE 4593
Overstone 51 SP 8066
Overstrand 65 TG 2440
Overton (Clwyd) 58 SJ 3741
Overton (Dumf. and Galwy.) 88 NX 9864
Overton (Grampn.) 119 NJ 8714
Overton (Hants.) 35 SU 5149
Overton (Lancs.) 77 SD 4357
Overton (Shrops.) 48 SO 4972
Overton Green 69 SJ 7960
Overtown 95 NS 8052
Over Wallop 34 SU 2838
Over Water 82 NY 2535
Over Whitacre 50 SP 2591
Oving (Bucks.) 36 SP 7821
Oving (W Susx) 27 SU 9005
Ovingdean 29 TQ 3503
Ovingham 91 NZ 0863
Ovington (Durham) 84 NZ 1314
Ovington (Essex) 54 TL 7742
Ovington (Hants.) 27 SU 5631
Ovington (Norf.) 64 TF 9202
Ovington (Northum.) 91 NZ 0663
Ower 26 SU 3216
Owermoigne 25 SY 7685
Owlswick 36 SP 7906
Owmby-by-Spittal 72 TF 0087
Owslebury 27 SU 5123
Owston 61 SK 7708
Owston Ferry 74 SE 8000
Owstwick 75 TA 2732
Owthorpe 61 SK 6733
Oxborough 64 TF 7401
Oxcars 103 NT 2081
Oxenfoord Castle 103 NT 3865
Oxenholme 83 SD 5390
Oxenhope 78 SE 0334
Oxen Park 77 SD 3187
Oxenton 46 SO 9531
Oxenwood 34 SU 3059
Oxford 47 SP 5305
Oxford Airport 47 SP 4615
Oxford Canal 51 SP 4837
Ox Hill (Dumf. and Galwy.) 88 NS 7200
Oxhill (Warw.) 50 SP 3145
Oxley 59 SJ 9002
Oxley's Green 29 TQ 6921
Oxna (is.) 141 HU 3537
Oxnam 90 NT 7018
Oxnam Water 90 NT 7017
Oxshott 37 TQ 1460
Oxspring 71 SE 2601
Oxted 29 TQ 3852
Oxton (Borders) 96 NT 4953
Oxton (Notts.) 61 SK 6351
Oxwich 40 SS 4986
Oxwich Bay 40 SS 5386
Oxwick 64 TF 9125

Oykel Bridge 127 NC 3800
Oyne 121 NJ 6725

P

Pabay (Highld.) 123 NG 6727
Pabay Mòr 131 NB 1037
Pabbay (North Uist) 124 NF 8887
Pabbay (W Isles) 112 NL 6087
Packington 60 SK 3614
Padanaram 109 NO 4251
Padbury 51 SP 7130
Paddaburn Moor 90 NY 6378
Paddington 37 TQ 2482
Paddington Station 37 TQ 2681
Paddlesworth 31 TR 1939
Paddockhaugh 120 NJ 2058
Paddock Wood 29 TQ 6645
Paddolgreen 59 SJ 5032
Padeswood 68 SJ 2761
Padiham 78 SD 7933
Padon Hill 90 NY 8292
Padstow 19 SW 9175
Padstow Bay 19 SW 9179
Pagham 27 SZ 8897
Pagie Hill 95 NS 8528
Paglesham Churchend 38 TQ 9292
Paglesham Eastend 38 TQ 9492
Paible (North Uist) 124 NF 7367
Paible (Taransay) 124 NG 0299
Paignton 21 SX 8960
Pailton 51 SP 4781
Painscastle 45 SO 1646
Painshawfield 91 NZ 0660
Painswick 46 SO 8609
Pairc or Park (dist.) 131 NB 3112
Paisley 101 NS 4864
Pakefield 55 TM 5390
Pakenham 54 TL 9267
Pale 67 SH 9836
Palestine 34 SU 2640
Paley Street 36 SU 8776
Palgowan 86 NX 3783
Palgrave 55 TM 1178
Pallinsburn House 97 NT 8939
Palmerstown 41 ST 1369
Palnackie 87 NX 8257
Palnure 87 NX 4563
Palnure Burn 87 NX 4668
Palterton 71 SK 4768
Pamber End 36 SU 6158
Pamber Green 36 SU 6059
Pamber Heath 36 SU 6262
Pamphill 26 ST 9900
Pampisford 53 TL 4948
Pan 136 ND 3794
Panbride 109 NO 5635
Pancrasweek 22 SS 2905
Pandy (Clwyd) 58 SJ 1935
Pandy (Gwent) 45 SO 3322
Pandy (Powys) 57 SH 9004
Pandy Tudur 67 SH 8564
Panfield 54 TL 7325
Pangbourne 36 SU 6376
Pan Hope 136 ND 3794
Pannal 79 SE 3051
Pannanich Hill 118 NO 3994
Panorama Walk 57 SH 6216
Panshanger Aerodrome 37 TL 2712
Pant 58 SJ 2722
Pant-glas (Gwyn.) 66 SH 4747
Pant Glas (Powys) 57 SN 7798
Pantglas Hall 43 SN 5425
Pantgwyn 43 SN 2446
Pant Mawr 57 SN 8482
Panton 73 TF 1778
Pant-pastynog 67 SJ 0461
Pantperthog 57 SH 7504
Pant Sychbant 41 SN 9809
Pant-y-dŵr 57 SN 9875
Pant-y-ffridd 58 SJ 1502
Pantyffynnon 43 SN 6210
Panxworth 65 TG 3413
Papa (is.) 141 HU 3637
Papa Little (is.) 141 HU 3361
Papa Sound 138 HY 4752
Papa Stour (is.) 140 HU 1660
Papa Stronsay 137 HY 6629
Papa Westray 138 HY 4952
Papa Westray Aerodrome 138 HY 4852
Papcastle 82 NY 1131
Papil Ness 143 HP 5404
Papley 136 ND 4691
Pap of Glencoe (mt.) 106 NN 1259
Papple 103 NT 5972
Papplewick 61 SK 5451
Paps of Jura (mt.) 98 NR 4974
Papworth Everard 53 TL 2862
Papworth St. Agnes 53 TL 2664
Par 19 SX 0653
Parbold 69 SD 4911
Parbrook 25 ST 5736
Parcllyn 43 SN 2451
Pardshaw 82 NY 0924
Parham 55 TM 3060
Parham House (ant.) 28 TQ 0514
Park (Grampn.) 119 NO 7798
Park (Strath.) 106 NM 9340
Park Corner 36 SU 6988
Parkend (Glos.) 45 SO 6108
Park End (Northum.) 90 NY 8775
Parkeston 55 TM 2332
Parkgate (Ches.) 68 SJ 2778
Parkgate (Ches.) 69 SJ 7874
Parkgate (Dumf. and Galwy.) 88 NY 0288
Park Gate (Hants.) 27 SU 5108
Parkgate (Surrey) 28 TQ 2043
Parkham 22 SS 3821
Parkham Ash 22 SS 3620
Park Head 19 SW 8370
Parkhill House 119 NJ 8914
Parkhouse 45 SO 5002
Parkhurst 27 SZ 4991
Parkhurst Forest 27 SZ 4790
Parkneuk 119 NO 7976
Park or Pairc (Isle of Lewis) (dist.) 131 NB 3112
Parkstone 26 SZ 0491
Parley Common 26 SZ 0999
Parley Cross 26 SZ 0898
Parracombe 23 SS 6744
Parrog 42 SN 0439
Parson Drove 63 TF 3708
Partick 101 NS 5567
Partington 69 SJ 7191
Partney 73 TF 4168
Parton (Cumbr.) 82 NX 9720
Parton (Dumf. and Galwy.) 88 NX 6970
Partridge Green 28 TQ 1919
Parwich 60 SK 1854
Parys Mountain 66 SH 4390
Passenham 51 SP 7839
Pass of Aberglaslyn 66 SH 5946
Pass of Brander 106 NN 0627
Pass of Drumochter 116 NN 6376
Pass of Killiecrankie 108 NN 9162
Pass of Leny 101 NN 5908
Pass of Llanberis 67 SH 6355
Pass of Melfort 105 NM 8315
Paston 65 TG 3235
Patcham 29 TQ 3009
Patching 28 TQ 0806
Patchole 23 SS 6142
Patchway 33 ST 6082
Pateley Bridge 78 SE 1565
Pateley Moor 78 SE 1967
Pathhead (Fife) 103 NT 2892
Pathhead (Grampn.) 109 NO 7363
Pathhead (Lothian) 103 NT 3964
Pathhead (Strath.) 88 NS 6114
Path of Condie 102 NO 0711
Patmore Heath 53 TL 4526
Patna 93 NS 4110
Patney 34 SU 0758
Patrick 76 SC 2482
Patrick Brompton 84 SE 2290
Patrington 75 TA 3122
Patrixbourne 31 TR 1855
Patshull Hall 59 SJ 8001
Patterdale 83 NY 3915
Patterton Station 93 NS 5357
Pattingham 59 SO 8299
Pattishall 51 SP 6654
Patton Bridge 83 SD 5597
Paul 18 SW 4627
Paulerspury 51 SP 7145
Paull 75 TA 1626
Paull Holme Sands 75 TA 1823
Paulton 33 ST 6456
Pauperhaugh 91 NZ 1099
Pavenham 52 SP 9955
Pawlaw Pike 84 NZ 0032
Pawlett 32 ST 2942
Pawston 97 NT 8532
Paxford 50 SP 1837
Paxhill Park 29 TQ 3626
Paxton 97 NT 9352
Payhembury 24 ST 0801
Paythorne 78 SD 8251
Peacehaven 29 TQ 4101
Peachley 49 SO 8057
Peak Dale 70 SK 0976
Peak Forest 70 SK 1179
Peakirk 62 TF 1606
Peanmeanach 111 NM 7180
Pearsie 109 NO 3659
Peasedown St. John 33 ST 7057
Peasemore 35 SU 4576
Peasenhall 55 TM 3569
Peaslake 28 TQ 0844
Peasmarsh 30 TQ 8822
Peaston 103 NT 4265
Peaston Bank 103 NT 4466
Peathill (Grampn.) 121 NJ 9365
Peat Hill (Tays.) 109 NO 5067
Peat Inn 103 NO 4509
Peatling Magna 51 SP 5992
Peatling Parva 51 SP 5889
Peaton 48 SO 5385
Pebmarsh 54 TL 8533
Pebworth 50 SP 1347
Pecket Well 78 SD 9929
Peckforton 59 SJ 5356
Peckleton 61 SK 4701
Peddars Way (ant.) 64 TF 8312
Pedmore 49 SO 9182
Pedwell 25 ST 4236
Peebles 95 NT 2540
Peel 76 SC 2484
Peel Fell 90 NY 6299
Peffer Burn 103 NT 5778
Pegal Burn 136 ND 2798
Pegswood 91 NZ 2287
Pegwell Bay 31 TR 3563
Peinchorran 123 NG 5233
Peinlich 123 NG 4158
Pelaw 91 NZ 2962
Peldon 39 TL 9816
Pelsall 60 SK 0103
Pelton 84 NZ 2553
Pelutho 82 NY 1249
Pelynt 19 SX 2055
Pembrey 40 SN 4201
Pembridge 45 SO 3858
Pembroke 42 SM 9901
Pembroke Dock 42 SM 9603
Pembury 29 TQ 6240
Penallt 45 SO 5210
Pen Allt-mawr 41 SO 2024
Penally 42 SS 1199
Penant 56 SN 5163
Penare 19 SW 9940
Penarth 41 ST 1871
Pen-bont Rhydybeddau 57 SN 6783
Pen Brush 42 SM 8839
Penbryn 43 SN 2952
Penbwchdy 42 SM 8737
Pencader 43 SN 4436
Pen Caer 42 SM 9140
Pencaitland 103 NT 4468
Pencarreg 43 SN 5345
Pencarreg-gopa 57 SN 7294
Pencarrow Head 19 SX 1450
Pencelli 41 SO 0925
Pen Cerrig-calch 41 SO 2122
Penclawdd 40 SS 5495
Penclegyr (Dyfed) 42 SM 7629
Penclegyr (Dyfed) 42 SM 8032
Pencoed (Mid Glam.) 41 SS 9581
Pen Coed (Powys.) 57 SH 9808
Pencombe 45 SO 5952
Pencoyd 45 SO 5126
Pencraig (Here. and Worc.) 45 SO 5621
Pencraig (Powys) 57 SJ 0427
Pendeen 18 SW 3834
Pendeen Watch (pt.) 18 SW 3736
Pendennis Point 18 SW 8231
Penderry Hill 86 NX 0675
Penderyn 41 SN 9408
Penderyn Resr. 41 SN 9407
Pen Dinas (ant.) 56 SN 5880
Pendine 43 SN 2308
Pendine Sands 43 SN 2706
Pendlebury 69 SD 7802
Pendle Hill 78 SD 7941
Pendleton 78 SD 7539
Pendock 46 SO 7832
Pendoggett 19 SX 0279
Pendoylan 41 ST 0576
Penegoes 57 SH 7701
Pen-ffordd 42 SN 0722
Penge 37 TQ 3570
Pengorffwysfa 66 SH 4692
Pengwern 67 SJ 0176
Pen Gwyllt-meirch 45 SO 2524
Penhale Point 18 SW 7559
Penhale Sands 18 SW 7656
Penhalvean 18 SW 7037
Penhill 78 SE 0486
Penhow 33 ST 4290
Penhurst 29 TQ 6916
Peniarth 56 SH 6105
Penicuik 103 NT 2359
Peniel Heugh 96 NT 6526
Penifiler 123 NG 4841
Peninver 92 NR 7524
Pen-isa'r-cwm 57 SJ 0018
Penisa'r Waun 66 SH 5564
Penistone 71 SE 2402
Penjerrick 18 SW 7730
Penketh 69 SJ 5687
Penkill 86 NX 2398
Penkill Burn 87 NX 4369
Penkridge 59 SJ 9214
Penlee Point 20 SX 4448
Penley 58 SJ 4039
Penllechwen 42 SM 7429
Penllergaer 40 SS 6199
Pen Llithrig-y-wrâch 67 SH 7162
Pen-llyn (Gwyn.) 66 SH 3482
Penllyn (S Glam.) 41 SS 9776
Penmachno 67 SH 7950
Penmaen 40 SS 5288
Penmaenmawr 67 SH 7176
Penmaenpool 57 SH 6918
Penmaen Swatch 67 SH 6577
Penmark 41 ST 0568
Pen Milan 41 SN 9923
Penmon 67 SH 6381
Penmorfa 66 SH 5440
Penmynydd 66 SH 5174
Penn 36 SU 9193
Pennal 57 SH 6900
Pennan 121 NJ 8465
Pennan Head 121 NJ 8565
Pennant 57 SN 8897
Pennant-Melangell 57 SJ 0226
Pennard 40 SS 5688
Pennerley 58 SO 3599
Pennines, The 78 SE 0077
Penninghame Forest 86 NX 3568
Pennington 76 SD 2577
Penn Street 36 SU 9296
Penny Bridge 77 SD 3082
Pennycross 105 NM 5025
Pennygown 105 NM 6042
Pennymoor 23 SS 8611
Penparc 43 SN 2148
Penparcau 56 SN 5980
Penperlleni 45 SO 3204
Penpillick 19 SX 0756
Penpol 19 SW 8139
Penpoll 19 SX 1454
Penpont (Dumf. and Galwy.) 88 NX 8494
Penpont (Powys) 41 SN 9728
Pen Pumlumon-Arwystli 57 SN 8187
Penrherber 43 SN 2839
Penrhiwceiber 41 ST 0597
Pen Rhiw-clochdy 44 SN 7552
Penrhiwllan 43 SN 3742
Penrhiwpal 43 SN 3445
Pen-rhos (Gwent) 45 SO 4111
Penrhos (Gwyn.) 66 SH 2781
Penrhos (Gwyn.) 66 SH 3433
Penrhos (Powys) 41 SN 8011
Penrhyn Bay 67 SH 8281
Penrhyn Castle (ant.) 66 SH 6071
Penrhyncoch 57 SN 6484
Penrhyndeudraeth 66 SH 6139
Penrhyn Mawr (Gwyn.) 66 SH 1632
Penrhyn Mawr (Gwyn.) 66 SH 2080
Penrhyn-side 67 SH 8181
Penrice 40 SS 4988
Penrith 83 NY 5130
Penrose 19 SW 8770
Penruddock 83 NY 4227
Penryn 18 SW 7834
Pensarn (Clwyd) 67 SH 9478
Pen-Sarn (Gwyn.) 66 SH 4344
Pen-Sarn (Gwyn.) 56 SH 5728
Pensax 49 SO 7269
Pensby 68 SJ 2683
Penselwood 25 ST 7531
Pensford 33 ST 6163
Penshaw 84 NZ 3253
Penshurst 29 TQ 5243
Penshurst Place (ant.) 29 TQ 5243
Penshurst Station 29 TQ 5246
Pensilva 20 SX 2969
Pentewan 19 SX 0147
Pentir 66 SH 5767
Pentire 19 SW 7961
Pentire Point 19 SW 9280
Pentland Firth 136 ND 3082
Pentland Hills 102 NT 1459
Pentland Skerries 135 ND 4777
Pentney 64 TF 7213
Penton Mewsey 34 SU 3247
Pentraeth 66 SH 5278
Pentre (Clwyd) 67 SJ 0862
Pentre (Clwyd) 58 SJ 1334
Pentre (Clwyd) 58 SJ 2840
Pentre (Powys) 57 SO 0686
Pentre (Powys) 48 SO 2466
Pentre (Shrops.) 58 SJ 3617
Pentrebach (Mid Glam.) 41 SO 0604
Pentre-bâch (Powys) 41 SN 9033
Pentrebeirdd 58 SJ 1913
Pentre Berw 66 SH 4772
Pentre-celyn (Clwyd) 58 SJ 1453
Pentre-celyn (Powys) 57 SH 8806
Pentre-cwrt 43 SN 3938
Pentre-Dolau-Honddu 44 SN 9943
Pentredwr 58 SJ 1946
Pentre-dwr 40 SS 6996
Pentrefelin 66 SH 5239
Pentrefelin 67 SH 8074
Pentrefoelas 67 SH 8751
Pentregat 43 SN 3551
Pentre-Gwenlais 43 SN 6116
Pentre Halkyn 68 SJ 2072
Pentre'r-felin 41 SN 9130
Pentre'r-tafarn-y-fedw 67 SH 8162
Pentre ty gwyn 41 SN 8135
Pentrich 60 SK 3852
Pentridge 26 SU 0317
Pentridge Hill 26 SU 0416
Pen Trum-gwr 57 SH 6503
Pen-twyn (Gwent) 45 SO 5209
Pentwyn (S Glam.) 41 ST 2081
Pentwyn Resr. 41 SO 0515
Pentyrch 41 ST 1082
Penuwch 43 SN 5962
Penwhapple Resr. 86 NX 2697
Penwhirn Resr. 86 NX 1269
Penwithick 19 SX 0256
Penybanc 43 SN 6124
Pen y Bedw 67 SH 7747
Pen-y-bont (Clwyd) 58 SJ 2123
Penybont (Powys) 48 SO 1164
Penybontfawr 57 SJ 0824
Pen-y-bryn 57 SH 6919
Pen-y-bwlch 57 SN 7763
Penycae (Clwyd) 58 SJ 2745
Pen-y-cae (Powys) 41 SN 8413
Pen-y-cae-mawr 45 ST 4195
Pen-y-cefn 68 SJ 1175
Pen-ychain 66 SH 4335
Pen y Cil 56 SH 1523
Pen-y-clawdd 45 SO 4508
Penycloddiau (ant.) 68 SJ 1267
Pen-y-coedcae 41 ST 0587
Pen y crug (ant.) 41 SO 0230
Penyffordd 68 SJ 3061
Pen y Ffridd Gownwy 57 SH 9717
Pen-y-garn 43 SN 5731
Penygarnedd 57 SJ 1023
Pen-y-garreg Resr. 57 SN 9067
Pen-y-Ghent (mt.) 78 SD 8373
Pen-y-Gogarth 67 SH 7584
Penygraig 41 SS 9991
Penygroes (Dyfed) 43 SN 5813
Penygroes (Gwyn.) 66 SH 4753
Pen y Gurnos 44 SN 7751
Pen y Manllwyn 41 SO 2131
Penysarn 66 SH 4690
Penywaun 41 SN 9704
Penzance 18 SW 4730
Peopleton 49 SO 9350
Peover Heath 69 SJ 7973
Peper Harow 28 SU 9344
Peplow 59 SJ 6324
Percie 119 NO 5991
Percyhorner 121 NJ 9565
Perivale 37 TQ 1682
Perranarworthal 18 SW 7738
Perran or Ligger Bay 18 SW 7256
Perranporth 18 SW 7554
Perranuthnoe 18 SW 5329
Perranzabuloe 18 SW 7752
Perry 52 TL 1466
Perry Barr 50 SP 0791
Perry Green 37 TL 4317
Pershore 49 SO 9446
Pert 109 NO 6565
Pertenhall 52 TL 0865
Perth 108 NO 1123
Perth Aerodrome 108 NO 1528
Perthy 58 SJ 3633
Perton 59 SO 8598
Peter Black Sand 64 TF 6231
Peterborough 62 TL 1999
Peterborough Airport (Conington) 52 TL 1887
Peterburn 126 NG 7483
Peterchurch 45 SO 3438
Peterculter 119 NJ 8400
Peterhead 121 NK 1346
Peterhead Bay 121 NK 1345
Peter Hill 119 NO 5788
Peterlee 85 NZ 4440
Petersfield 27 SU 7423
Peters Green 37 TL 1419
Peter's Hill 118 NJ 3600
Peters Marland 22 SS 4713
Peterstone Wentlooge 32 ST 2680
Peterston-super-Ely 41 ST 0876
Peterstow 45 SO 5624
Peter Tavy 20 SX 5177
Petertown 136 HY 3105
Petham 31 TR 1251
Petrockstow 22 SS 5109
Pett 30 TQ 8714
Pettaugh 55 TM 1659
Pettinain 95 NS 9542
Pettistree 55 TM 2954
Petton (Devon) 23 ST 0024
Petton (Shrops.) 58 SJ 4326
Petty 121 NJ 7636
Pettycur 103 NT 2686
Pettymuk 121 NJ 9024
Petworth 28 SU 9721
Petworth House (ant.) 28 SU 9721
Pevensey 29 TQ 6405
Pevensey Bay 29 TQ 6603
Pevensey Levels 29 TQ 6307
Peveril Castle (ant.) 70 SK 1482
Peveril Point 26 SZ 0378
Pewsey Down 34 SU 1656
Philham 22 SS 2522
Philiphaugh 96 NT 4427
Philip Law 90 NT 7210
Phillack 18 SW 5539
Philleigh 19 SW 8639
Philpstoun 102 NT 0577
Phoenix Green 35 SU 7655
Pibble Hill 87 NX 5360
Pica 82 NY 0222
Piccotts End 36 TL 0509
Pickering 80 SE 7983
Picket Piece 34 SU 3947
Picket Post 26 SU 1905
Pickhill 79 SE 3483
Picklescott 58 SO 4399
Pickmere 69 SJ 6876
Pickwell (Devon) 22 SS 4540
Pickwell (Leic.) 61 SK 7811
Pickworth (Leic.) 62 SK 9913
Pickworth (Lincs.) 62 TF 0433
Picton (Ches.) 68 SJ 4371
Picton (N Yorks.) 85 NZ 4107
Piddinghoe 29 TQ 4303
Piddington (Northants.) 51 SP 8054
Piddington (Oxon.) 36 SP 6317
Piddlehinton 25 SY 7197
Piddletrenthide 25 SY 7099
Pidley 53 TL 3377
Pidley Fen 53 TL 3480
Piel Bar (pt.) 76 SD 2361
Piel Island 76 SD 2363
Piercebridge 84 NZ 2115
Pierowall 138 HY 4348
Pigdon 91 NZ 1588
Pike Fell 89 NY 4193
Pikehall 70 SK 1959
Pike Hill 89 NT 3505
Pike Hill Moss 80 NZ 7600
Pikeston Fell 84 NZ 0432
Pike, The 89 NT 4904
Pikey Hill 120 NJ 2151
Pilgrims Hatch 37 TQ 5895
Pilgrims' Way (ant.) 30 TQ 6561
Pilham 72 SK 8693
Pill 33 ST 5275
Pillar (mt.) 82 NY 1712
Pillar Bank (sbk.) 100 NS 3475
Pillaton 20 SX 3664
Pillerton Hersey 50 SP 2948
Pillerton Priors 50 SP 2947
Pilleth 48 SO 2568
Pilley 71 SE 3300
Pilling 77 SD 4048
Pilling Lane 77 SD 3749
Pilning 33 ST 5585
Pilsbury 70 SK 1163
Pilsdon 24 SY 4199
Pilsdon Pen 24 ST 4101
Pilsley (Derby.) 71 SK 2471
Pilsley (Derby.) 71 SK 4262
Pilton (Leic.) 62 SK 9102
Pilton (Northants.) 52 TL 0284
Pilton (Somer.) 33 ST 5940
Pimperne 25 ST 9009
Pimperne Down 25 ST 8910
Pinchbeck 63 TF 2425
Pinchbeck West 63 TF 2024
Pinderachy (mt.) 109 NO 4565
Pindonnan Craigs 88 NX 2787
Pinfold 68 SD 3811
Pinhoe 21 SX 9694
Pinkworthy Pond 23 SS 7242
Pinminnoch Burn 86 NX 0356
Pinmore 86 NX 2092
Pinner 37 TQ 1289
Pinvin 50 SO 9548
Pinwherry 86 NX 1987
Pinwherry Hill 86 NX 1885
Pinxton 61 SK 4555
Pipe and Lyde 45 SO 5044
Pipe Gate 59 SJ 7340
Piperhill 129 NH 8651
Pipewell 52 SP 8385
Pippacott 23 SS 5237
Pirbright 28 SU 9455
Pirnmill 92 NR 8744
Pirton (Here. and Worc.) 49 SO 8847
Pirton (Herts.) 52 TL 1431
Pishill 36 SU 7289
Pistyll 66 SH 3242
Pitagowan 107 NN 8266
Pitblae 121 NJ 9865
Pitcairlie Hill 108 NO 2115
Pitcairngreen 108 NO 0627
Pitcaple 121 NJ 7225
Pitchcombe 46 SO 8408
Pitchcott 36 SP 7720
Pitchford 59 SJ 5303
Pitch Green 36 SP 7703
Pitch Place 28 SU 9752
Pitcombe 25 ST 6732
Pitcox 103 NT 6475
Pitcur 108 NO 2536
Pitfichie 119 NJ 6716
Pitfichie Forest 119 NJ 6415
Pitforthie 119 NO 8079
Pitfour Castle 108 NO 1921
Pitgrudy 129 NH 7991
Pitkennedy 109 NO 5454
Pitkevy 103 NO 2403
Pitlessie 103 NO 3309
Pitlochry 108 NN 9458
Pitmain 116 NH 7400
Pitmedden 121 NJ 8927
Pitmedden Forest 103 NO 2114
Pitmedden House 121 NJ 8828
Pitminster 24 ST 2119
Pitmuies 109 NO 5649
Pitmunie 119 NJ 6615
Pitney 25 ST 4428
Pitroddie 108 NO 2224
Pitscottie 103 NO 4113
Pitsea 38 TQ 7488
Pitsford 51 SP 7568
Pitsford Reservoir 51 SP 7669
Pitstone 36 SP 9415
Pitt Down 26 SU 4128
Pittendreich 120 NJ 1961
Pittentrail 129 NC 7202
Pittenweem 103 NO 5402
Pittington 84 NZ 3245
Pittodrie 121 NJ 6924
Pitton 26 SU 2131
Pixey Green 55 TM 2475
Place Newton 81 SE 8872
Pladda (Island of Arran) (is.) 92 NS 0219
Pladda Island 105 NM 8337
Plains 101 NS 7966
Plaish 59 SO 5296
Plaistow 28 TQ 0030
Plaitford 26 SU 2719
Plâs 43 SN 4827
Plas Gogerddan 57 SN 6283
Plas Gwynant 67 SH 6250
Plas Isaf 67 SJ 0442
Plâs Llwyd 67 SH 9979
Plas Llwyngwern 57 SH 7504
Plas Llysyn 57 SN 9597
Plas Nantyr 58 SJ 1537
Plastow Green 35 SU 5361
Plas-yn-Cefn 67 SJ 0171
Platt 29 TQ 6257
Plawsworth 84 NZ 2647
Plaxtol 29 TQ 6053
Playden 30 TQ 9121
Playford 55 TM 2148
Play Hatch 36 SU 7376
Playing Place 19 SW 8141
Plealey 58 SJ 4206
Plean 101 NS 8387
Pleasington 77 SD 6425
Pleasley 71 SK 5064
Plenmeller 90 NY 7162
Plenmeller Common 90 NY 7361
Pleshey 38 TL 6614
Plock of Kyle (pt.) 123 NG 7527
Plockton 123 NG 8033
Plockton Aerodrome 123 NG 7933
Plocrapool Point 125 NG 1893
Ploughfield 45 SO 3841
Plover Hill 78 SD 8575
Plowden 48 SO 3888
Ploxgreen 58 SJ 3604
Pluckley 30 TQ 9245
Pluckley Station 30 TQ 9243
Plumbland 82 NY 1438
Plumley 69 SJ 7275
Plumpton (E Susx) 29 TQ 3613
Plumpton (Lancs.) 77 SD 3732
Plumpton Green 29 TQ 3616
Plumpton Head 83 NY 5035
Plumpton Wall 83 NY 4937
Plumstead 65 TG 1335
Plumtree 61 SK 6133
Plungar 61 SK 7633
Pluscarden 129 NJ 1455
Pluscarden Priory 129 NJ 1457
Plush 25 ST 7102
Plwmp 43 SN 3652
Plymouth 20 SX 4755
Plymouth Airport 20 SX 5060
Plymouth Breakwater 20 SX 4750
Plympton 21 SX 5356
Plymstock 20 SX 5152
Plymtree 24 ST 0502
Plynlimon (Pumlumon Fawr) (mt.) 57 SN 7885
Pocan Smoo (pt.) 133 NC 4267
Pockley 79 SE 6385
Pocklington 80 SE 8048
Pocklington Canal 74 SE 7445
Pock Stones Moor 78 SE 1060
Pode Hole 62 TF 2122
Podimore 25 ST 5424
Podington 52 SP 9462
Podmore 59 SJ 7835
Pods Brook 54 TL 7126
Point Clear 39 TM 0915
Point Lynas 66 SH 4793
Point of Ardnamurchan 111 NM 4167
Point of Ayr (Clwyd) 68 SJ 1285
Point of Ayre (I. of M.) 76 NX 4605
Point of Ayre (Orkney) 137 HY 5904
Point of Backaquoy 136 HY 3915
Point of Cairndoon 86 NX 3738
Point of Fethaland 143 HU 3795
Point of Howana Geo 136 HY 2220
Point of Huro 138 HY 4938
Point of Knap 99 NR 6972
Point of Neven 138 HY 4939
Point of Oxan 136 HY 2406
Point of Sinsoss 139 HY 7856
Point of Sleat 111 NM 5699
Point of Stoer 132 NC 0235
Point of the Graand 136 HY 4726
Pointon 62 TF 1131
Pokesdown 26 SZ 1292
Polapit Tamar 20 SX 3389
Polbae 86 NX 2873
Polbain 132 NB 9910
Polbathic 20 SX 3456
Polbeth 102 NT 0364
Polchar 117 NH 8909
Poldean 89 NT 1000
Poldhu Point 18 SW 6519
Poldorais (chan) 123 NG 4771
Polebrook 52 TL 0687
Polegate 29 TQ 5805
Pole Hill (Highld.) 133 NC 6441

Pole Hill (Tays.) 108 NO 1926
Pole of Itlaw, The 121 NJ 6856
Polesworth 60 SK 2602
Polglass 126 NC 0307
Polgooth 19 SW 9950
Poling 28 TQ 0405
Polkerris 19 SX 0952
Polla 132 NC 3854
Pollachar 112 NF 7414
Pollagach Burn 118 NO 3992
Poll Gainmhich (roadstead) 131 NB 1343
Pollington 71 SE 6119
Polliwilline Bay 92 NR 7409
Poll na h-Ealaidh 122 NG 3759
Polloch 111 NM 7968
Pollokshaws 101 NS 5560
Pollokshields 101 NS 5663
Polmaddie Hill 86 NX 3391
Polmassick 19 SW 9745
Polnessan 93 NS 4111
Polperro 19 SX 2051
Polruan 19 SX 1250
Polsham 33 ST 5142
Polskeoch 88 NS 6802
Polstead 54 TL 9938
Poltalloch 99 NR 8196
Poltimore 21 SX 9696
Polton 103 NT 2964
Polwarth 96 NT 7450
Polyphant 20 SX 2682
Polzeath 19 SW 9378
Pondersbridge 53 TL 2691
Ponders End 37 TQ 3695
Ponsanooth 18 SW 7336
Ponsworthy 21 SX 7073
Pontamman 43 SN 6312
Pontantwn 43 SN 4412
Pontardawe 40 SN 7204
Pontardulais 43 SN 5903
Pontarsais 43 SN 4428
Pont Cwm Pydew 67 SJ 0031
Pont Cyfyng 67 SH 7357
Pontefract 79 SE 4522
Ponteland 91 NZ 1672
Ponterwyd 57 SN 7481
Pontesbury 58 SJ 3905
Pontfadog 58 SJ 2338
Pontfaen (Dyfed) 42 SN 0234
Pont-faen (Powys) 41 SN 9934
Pont-Henri 43 SN 4709
Ponthirwaun 43 SN 2645
Pontllanfraith 41 ST 1895
Pontlliw 40 SN 6101
Pontlottyn 41 SO 1206
Pontlyfni 66 SH 4352
Pont Nêdd Fechan 41 SN 9007
Pont Pentryal 67 SJ 0351
Pont Pen-y-benglog 67 SH 6460
Pontrhydfendigaid 57 SN 7366
Pont Rhyd-y-cyff 41 SS 8788
Pont-rhyd-y-fen 41 SS 7994
Pontrhydygroes 57 SN 7472
Pontrilas 45 SO 3927
Pontrobert 58 SJ 1112
Pont-rug 66 SH 5163
Ponts Green 29 TQ 6717
Pontshaen 43 SN 4346
Pontshill 45 SO 6321
Pontsticill 41 SO 0511
Pontsticill Resr. 41 SO 0513
Pontyates 43 SN 4708
Pontyberem 43 SN 4911
Pontybodkin 68 SJ 2759
Pontyclun 41 ST 0381
Pontycymer 41 SS 9091
Pontymister 32 ST 2490
Pont-y-pant 67 SH 7554
Pontypool 45 SO 2701
Pontypridd 41 ST 0690
Pontywaun 41 ST 2293
Pooksgreen 26 SU 3710
Pool (W Yorks.) 79 SE 2445
Poole (Dorset) 26 SZ 0190
Poole Bay 26 SZ 1089
Poole Harbour 26 SZ 0189
Poole Keynes 46 ST 9995
Poolewe 126 NG 8580
Pooley Bridge 83 NY 4724
Poolhill (Glos.) 46 SO 7329
Pool Hill (Powys) 48 SO 1775
Pool of Virkie 141 HU 3911
Pool o'Muckart 102 NO 0001
Pool Quay 58 SJ 2512
Popham 35 SU 5543
Popham's Eau (ant.) 63 TF 5300
Poplar 37 TQ 3781
Porchfield 27 SZ 4491
Porin 127 NH 3155
Poringland 65 TG 2701
Porkellis 18 SW 6933
Porlock 23 SS 8846
Porlock Bay 23 SS 8848
Port a'Bhata (Colonsay) 98 NR 4195
Port a'Bhata (Ulva) 105 NM 4237
Port a'Bhorrain 92 NR 6635
Port a'Chaisteil An Stuadh 105 NM 8246
Portachoillan 92 NR 7557
Port a' Ghàraidh 123 NG 8017
Port Allen 87 NX 4741
Port Allt a' Mhuilinn 134 NC 8167
Port Alsaig 98 NR 3048
Port a'Mhadaidh 100 NR 9269
Port a' Mhurain 110 NM 1251
Port an Eas 98 NR 2840
Port an Fhearainn 123 NG 6159
Port Ann 100 NR 9086
Port an Obain 98 NR 3994
Port an Righ 129 NH 8573
Port Appin 106 NM 9045
Port Askaig 98 NR 4369
Portavadie 100 NR 9369
Port Bàn 111 NM 5170
Port Bannatyne 100 NS 0867
Port Bharrapol 104 NL 9342
Port Bun a' Ghlinne 131 NB 5244
Portbury 33 ST 4975
Port Cam 123 NG 7731
Port Carlisle 89 NY 2461
Port Castle Bay 86 NX 4136
Port Ceann a'Gharraidh 98 NR 4298
Port Charlotte 98 NR 2558
Portchester 27 SU 6105
Port Cill Maluaig 99 NR 7270
Portclair Forest 115 NH 3815
Port Corbert 92 NR 6528
Port Cornaa 76 SC 4787
Port Dinorwic 66 SH 5267
Port Doir' a'Chrorain 98 NR 5875
Port Driseach 100 NR 9973
Port Ellen 98 NR 3645
Port Elphinstone 119 NJ 7719
Portencross 93 NS 1748
Port Erin 76 SC 1969
Porter or Little Don River, The 71 SK 2399
Port Erradale 126 NG 7381
Portesham 25 SY 6085
Port e Vullen 76 SC 4793
Port-Eynon 40 SS 4685
Port-Eynon Bay 40 SS 4884
Port-Eynon Point 40 SS 4784
Portfield Gate 42 SM 9115
Portgate 20 SX 4185
Portgaverne 19 SX 0080
Port Glasgow 100 NS 3274
Port Gleann na Gaoidh 98 NR 2153
Portgordon 121 NJ 3964
Portgower 135 ND 0013
Port Groudle 76 SC 4278
Porth 41 ST 0291
Porthallow 19 SW 7923
Porthcawl 41 SS 8176
Porth Colmon 66 SH 1934
Porthcothan Bay 19 SW 8572
Porthcurno 18 SW 3822
Porth Dinllaen 66 SH 2741
Port Henderson 123 NG 7573
Porth-gain 42 SM 8132
Porthkerry 41 ST 0866
Porthleven 18 SW 6225
Porthmadog 66 SH 5638
Porth-mawr or Whitesand Bay 42 SM 7227
Porthmeor 18 SW 4337
Porth Navas 18 SW 7428
Porth Neigwl or Hell's Mouth 56 SH 2626
Portholland 19 SW 9541
Porthor 66 SH 1630
Porthoustock 19 SW 8021
Porthpean 19 SX 0350
Porth Resr. 19 SW 8662
Porthtowan 18 SW 6847
Porthyrhyd (Dyfed) 43 SN 5115
Porthyrhyd (Dyfed) 44 SN 7137
Porth Ysglaig 66 SH 2137
Portincaple 100 NS 2393
Portington 74 SE 7830
Portinnisherrich 100 NM 9711
Port Isaac 19 SW 9980
Port Isaac Bay 19 SX 0181
Portishead 33 ST 4676
Port Kemin 86 NX 1231
Portknockie 121 NJ 4868
Portland Grounds (sbk.) 33 ST 4283
Portland Harbour 25 SY 6876
Port Leathan 100 NR 9176
Portlethen 119 NO 9396
Portloe 19 SW 9339
Port Logan 86 NX 0940
Port Logan or Port Nessock Bay 86 NX 0941
Portmahomack 129 NH 9184
Port Mary 87 NX 7545
Port Mean 92 NR 6407
Portmeirion 66 SH 5937
Portmellon 19 SX 0143
Port Mine 110 NM 1254
Port Mooar 76 SC 4890
Port Mór (Gigha Island) 92 NR 6654
Port Mòr (Muck) 111 NM 4279
Port Mór (Strath.) 99 NR 7161
Port Mór (Tiree) 104 NL 9343
Portmore (Hants) 26 SZ 3397
Portmore Loch 95 NT 2650
Port Mór na Carraig 98 NR 2355
Port Mulgrave 85 NZ 7917
Port na Birlinne 98 NR 5265
Port na Croise 105 NM 4326
Portnacroish 106 NM 9247
Port na Cuilce 98 NM 4100
Port na Cullaidh 123 NG 5113
Port na Feannaiche 92 NR 9122
Portnaguran 131 NB 5536
Portnahaven 98 NR 1652
Port na h-Eather 110 NM 2053
Portnalong 122 NG 3434
Port nam Bothaig 131 NB 5446
Port nam Partan 110 NM 3452
Port na Muice Duibhe 105 NM 7023
Portnancon 133 NC 4260
Port nan Crullach 105 NM 7226
Port nan Laogh 99 NR 6792
Portneora 123 NG 7732
Port Nessock or Port Logan Bay 86 NX 0941
Portobello (Dumf. and Galwy.) 86 NW 9666
Portobello (Lothian) 103 NT 3073
Port of Menteith 101 NN 5801
Port of Ness 131 NB 5363
Port of Spittal Bay 86 NX 0152
Porton 26 SU 1836
Portpatrick 86 NX 0054
Portquin 19 SW 9780
Port Quin Bay 19 SW 9480
Port Ramsay 106 NM 8845
Portreath 18 SW 6545
Portree 123 NG 4843
Port Righ 92 NR 8237
Portrye 100 NS 1758
Portscatho 19 SW 8735
Ports Down 27 SU 6406
Portsea 27 SU 6300
Portsea Island 27 SU 6501
Portskerra 134 NC 8765
Portskewett 33 ST 4988
Port Skigersta 131 NB 5562
Portslade 28 TQ 2506
Portslade-by-Sea 28 TQ 2604
Portsmouth 27 SU 6501
Portsmouth Harbour 27 SU 6202
Port Snoig 104 NL 9638
Port Soderick 76 SC 3472
Portsoy 121 NJ 5865
Port St. Mary 76 SC 2067
Port Sunlight 68 SJ 3483
Portswood 26 SU 4314
Port Talbot 41 SS 7690
Portuairk 111 NM 4468
Port Vasgo 133 NC 5865
Portvoller 131 NB 5636
Portvoller Bay 131 NB 5636
Portway (Warw.) 50 SP 0872
Portway, The (Shrops.) (Ant.) 58 SO 4295
Port Wemyss 98 NR 1751
Port William 86 NX 3343
Portwrinkle 20 SX 3553
Portyerrock Bay 87 NX 4839
Poslingford 54 TL 7648
Possingworth Park 29 TQ 5420
Postbridge 21 SX 6579
Postcombe 36 SU 7099
Postling 31 TR 1439
Post Rocks 98 NR 4079
Postwick 65 TG 2907
Potarch 119 NO 6097
Potrail Water 88 NS 9308
Potsgrove 52 SP 9529
Potten End 36 TL 0108
Potterhanworth 72 TF 0566
Potter Heigham 65 TG 4119
Potteries, The 59 SJ 8744
Potterne 34 ST 9958
Potterne Wick 34 ST 9957
Potters Bar 37 TL 2501
Potter's Cross 49 SO 8484
Potterspury 51 SP 7543
Potter Street 37 TL 4608
Potto 85 NZ 4703
Potton 53 TL 2249
Potton Island 38 TQ 9591
Pott Row 64 TF 7021
Pott Shrigley 69 SJ 9479
Poughill (Corn.) 22 SS 2207
Poughill (Devon) 23 SS 8508
Poulshot 34 ST 9659
Poulton 46 SP 1001
Poulton-le-Fylde 77 SD 3439
Pound Bank 49 SO 7373
Pound Hill 29 TQ 2937
Poundon 51 SP 6425
Poundsgate 21 SX 7072
Poundstock 20 SX 2099
Pow Burn (Central) 102 NS 8886
Powburn (Northum.) 91 NU 0616
Powderham 21 SX 9784
Powerstock 25 SY 5196
Powfoot 89 NY 1465
Powick 49 SO 8351
Powis Castle (ant.) 58 SJ 2106
Powmill 102 NT 0197
Pow Water 108 NN 9723
Poxwell 25 SY 7484
Poyle 36 TQ 0376
Poynings 28 TQ 2612
Poyntington 25 ST 6419
Poynton 69 SJ 9283
Poynton Green 59 SJ 5618
Poys Street 55 TM 3570
Poystreet Green 54 TL 9858
Praa Sands 18 SW 5828
Prail Castle 109 NO 6946
Pratt's Bottom 37 TQ 4762
Prawle Point 21 SX 7735
Praze-an-Beeble 18 SW 6336
Precipice Walk (mt.) 57 SH 7321
Predannack Wollas 18 SW 6616
Prees 59 SJ 5533
Preesall 77 SD 3646
Prees Green 59 SJ 5631
Preesgweene 58 SJ 3135
Prees Higher Heath 59 SJ 5636
Prendwick 91 NU 0012
Pren-gwyn 43 SN 4244
Prenteg 66 SH 5841
Prenton 68 SJ 3184
Prescot (Mers.) 68 SJ 4692
Prescott (Shrops.) 58 SJ 4221
Preshaw House 27 SU 5723
Press Castle 97 NT 8765
Pressen 97 NT 8335
Pressendye 118 NJ 4909
Prestatyn 67 SJ 0682
Prestbury (Ches.) 69 SJ 8976
Prestbury (Glos.) 46 SO 9724
Presteigne 48 SO 3164
Presthope 59 SO 5897
Prestleigh 33 ST 6340
Preston (Borders) 97 NT 7957
Preston (Devon) 21 SX 8574
Preston (Dorset) 25 SY 7082
Preston (E Susx) 29 TQ 3107
Preston (Glos.) 46 SO 6734
Preston (Glos.) 46 SP 0400
Preston (Herts.) 37 TL 1724
Preston (Humbs.) 75 TA 1830
Preston (Kent) 31 TR 2561
Preston (Lancs.) 77 SD 5329
Preston (Leic.) 62 SK 8602
Preston (Lothian) 103 NT 5977
Preston (Northum.) 97 NU 1825
Preston (Wilts.) 34 SU 0377
Preston Bagot 50 SP 1766
Preston Bissett 51 SP 6530
Preston Brockhurst 59 SJ 5324
Preston Brook 69 SJ 5680
Preston Candover 35 SU 6041
Preston Capes 51 SP 5754
Preston Gubbals 59 SJ 4819
Preston Hill 97 NT 9223
Preston Law 95 NT 2535
Preston on Stour 50 SP 2049
Preston on Wye 45 SO 3842
Prestonpans 103 NT 3874
Preston St. Mary 54 TL 9450
Preston-under-Scar 84 SE 0791
Preston upon the Weald Moors 59 SJ 6815
Preston Wynne 45 SO 5646
Prestwich 69 SD 8103
Prestwick (Northum.) 91 NZ 1872
Prestwick (Strath.) 93 NS 3525
Prestwick Scotland Airport 93 NS 3626
Prestwood 36 SP 8700
Price Town 41 SS 9392
Prickeny Hill 93 NS 5405
Prickwillow 54 TL 5982
Priddy 33 ST 5250
Priesthope Hill 96 NT 3539
Priest Hutton 77 SD 5273
Priest Island 126 NB 9202
Priestside Bank (sbk.) 89 NY 1164
Priestweston 58 SO 2997
Primethorpe 61 SP 5293
Primrose Green 64 TG 0616
Primrose Hill (Cambs.) 53 TL 3889
Prince Charles's Cave (Island of Skye) 123 NG 5112
Prince Charles's Cave (Island of Skye) 123 NG 5148
Prince Charlie's Cave (Highld.) 107 NN 4968
Prince's Cave 112 NF 8331
Princes Risborough 36 SP 8003
Princethorpe 50 SP 3970
Princetown 21 SX 5873
Prinknash Park (ant.) 46 SO 8713
Prior Muir 103 NO 5213
Prior Park 82 SD 1490
Priors Hardwick 51 SP 4756
Priors Marston 51 SP 4857
Priory, The 27 SZ 6390
Priory Wood 45 SO 2545
Priston 33 ST 6960
Prittlewell 38 TQ 8787
Privett 27 SU 6726
Probus 19 SW 8947
Proncy 129 NH 7792
Prudhoe 91 NZ 0962
Ptarmigan Lodge 100 NN 3500
Puckeridge 37 TL 3823
Puckington 24 ST 3718
Pucklechurch 33 ST 6976
Puckpool Point 27 SZ 6192
Puddington (Ches.) 68 SJ 3273
Puddington (Devon) 23 SS 8310
Puddledock 54 TM 0592
Puddletown 25 SY 7594
Pudleston 45 SO 5659
Pudsey 79 SE 2232
Puffin Island 67 SH 6481
Pulborough 28 TQ 0418
Puldrite Skerry 136 HY 4318
Puleston 59 SJ 7322
Pulford 68 SJ 3758
Pulham 25 ST 7008
Pulham Market 55 TM 1986
Pulham St. Mary 55 TM 2185
Pulloxhill 52 TL 0634
Pulpit Rock 100 NN 3414
Pulverbatch 58 SJ 4202
Pumsaint 43 SN 6540
Puncheston 42 SN 0029
Puncknowle 25 SY 5388
Pund Head 140 HU 1655
Punnett's Town 29 TQ 6220
Purbeck Hills 25 SY 9081
Purbrook 27 SU 6707
Purfleet 37 TQ 5578
Puriton 32 ST 3241
Purleigh 38 TL 8301
Purley (Berks.) 36 SU 6676
Purley (Gtr London) 37 TQ 3161
Purlogue 48 SO 2877
Purls Bridge 53 TL 4787
Purse Caundle 25 ST 6917
Purslow 48 SO 3680
Purston Jaglin 71 SE 4319
Purton (Glos.) 46 SO 6605
Purton (Glos.) 46 SO 6904
Purton (Wilts.) 34 SU 0887
Purton Stoke 34 SU 0890
Purves Hall 96 NT 7644
Pury End 51 SP 7045
Pusey 47 SU 3596
Putley 49 SO 6437
Putney 37 TQ 2274
Puttenham (Herts.) 36 SP 8814
Puttenham (Surrey) 28 SU 9347
Puxton 32 ST 4063
Pwll 40 SN 4801
Pwllcrochan 42 SM 9202
Pwlldefaid 56 SH 1526
Pwlldu Head 40 SS 5786
Pwllheli 66 SH 3735
Pwllmeyric 33 ST 5192
Pwll-y-glaw 41 SS 7993
Pwllygranant 42 SN 1147
Pyecombe 29 TQ 2912
Pye Corner 32 ST 3485
Pykestone Hill 95 NT 1731
Pyle (I. of W.) 27 SZ 4879
Pyle (Mid Glam.) 41 SS 8282
Pylle 33 ST 6038
Pymore 53 TL 4986
Pyrford 36 TQ 0458
Pyrton 36 SU 6895
Pytchley 52 SP 8574
Pyworthy 22 SS 3102

Q

Quabbs 48 SO 2080
Quadring 63 TF 2233
Quainton 36 SP 7419
Quandale 138 HY 3632
Quanter Ness 136 HY 4114
Quantock Forest 24 ST 1736
Quantock Hills 24 ST 1537
Quarff 141 HU 4135
Quarley 34 SU 2743
Quarndon 60 SK 3340
Quarrier's Homes 101 NS 3666
Quarrington 62 TF 0544
Quarrington Hill 84 NZ 3337
Quarrybank (Ches.) 69 SJ 5465
Quarry Bank (W Mids.) 49 SO 9386
Quarry Head 121 NJ 9065
Quarryhill 129 NH 7481
Quarry, The 46 ST 7399
Quarrywood 129 NJ 1864
Quarter 94 NS 7251
Quarter Fell 86 NX 1969
Quatford 49 SO 7390
Quatt 49 SO 7588
Quebec 84 NZ 1743
Quedgeley 46 SO 8114
Queen Adelaide 53 TL 5681
Queenborough 30 TQ 9471
Queen Camel 25 ST 5924
Queen Charlton 33 ST 6366
Queensberry (mt.) 88 NX 9899
Queensbury 78 SE 1030
Queen's Cairn 128 NH 4672
Queensferry (Clwyd) 68 SJ 3168
Queensferry (Lothian) 102 NT 1278
Queen's Forest, The 117 NH 9710
Queen's Ground 64 TL 6793
Queenside Muir 100 NS 2864
Queen's View 108 NN 8560
Queenzieburn 101 NS 6977
Quendale 141 HU 3713
Quendon 53 TL 5130
Queniborough 61 SK 6412
Quenington 47 SP 1404
Quernmore 77 SD 5160
Quethiock 20 SX 3164
Quey Firth 142 HU 3682
Quholm 136 HY 2412
Quidenham 54 TM 0287
Quidhampton (Hants.) 35 SU 5150
Quidhampton (Wilts.) 26 SU 1030
Quien Hill 100 NS 0559
Quies 19 SW 8376
Quilquox 121 NJ 9038
Quilva Taing 140 HU 1757
Quinag (mt.) 132 NC 2028
Quindry 136 ND 4392
Quine's Hill 76 SC 3473
Quinish (Island of Mull) (dist.) 111 NM 4254
Quinish (Pabbay) (is.) 124 NF 8886
Quinish Point 111 NM 4056
Quintin Knowe 88 NS 6508
Quinton 51 SP 7754
Quoditch 20 SX 4097
Quoig 107 NN 8222
Quorndon (Quorn) 61 SK 5616
Quothquan 95 NS 9939
Quoyloo 136 HY 2420
Quoy Ness 139 HY 6236
Quoys 143 HP 6112

R

Raasay House 123 NG 5436
Rabbit Islands 133 NC 6063
Raby 68 SJ 3179
Raby Castle (ant.) 84 NZ 1321
Rachub 67 SH 6268
Rackenford 23 SS 8418
Rackham 28 TQ 0514
Rackheath 65 TG 2814
Racks 89 NY 0374
Rackwick (Hoy, Orkney) 136 ND 1999
Rack Wick (Hoy, Orkney) 136 ND 2098
Rackwick (Westray) 138 HY 4449
Rack Wick (Westray) 138 HY 4450
Rack Wick (Westray) 138 HY 5042
Radcliffe (Gtr Mches) 69 SD 7806
Radcliffe (Northum.) 91 NU 2602
Radcliffe on Trent 61 SK 6439
Radclive 51 SP 6734
Radcot 47 SU 2899
Raddery 129 NH 7159
Radernie 103 NO 4609
Radford Semele 50 SP 3464
Radlett 37 TL 1600
Radley 47 SU 5398
Radnage 36 SU 7897
Radnor Forest 48 SO 1864
Radstock 33 ST 6854
Radstone 51 SP 5840
Radway 50 SP 3648
Radway Green 59 SJ 7754
Radwell 53 TL 2335
Radwinter 54 TL 6037
Radyr 41 ST 1380
Raera 105 NM 8320
Raerinish Point 131 NB 4224
Raes Knowes 89 NY 2882
Rafford 129 NJ 0656
Ragdale 61 SK 6619
Raglan 45 SO 4107
Ragnall 72 SK 8073
Rainberg Mór 98 NR 5687
Rainford 69 SD 4700
Rainham (Gtr London) 37 TQ 5282
Rainham (Kent) 30 TQ 8165
Rainhill 69 SJ 4990
Rainhill Stoops 69 SJ 5090
Rainow 70 SJ 9575
Rainton 79 SE 3775
Rainworth 71 SK 5958
Raisbeck 83 NY 6407
Rait 108 NO 2226
Raithby (Lincs.) 73 TF 3084
Raithby (Lincs.) 73 TF 3767
Raitts Burn 116 NH 7604
Rake 27 SU 8027
Rake Law 88 NS 8717
Ralfland Forest 83 NY 5413
Ramasaig 122 NG 1644
Rame (Corn.) 18 SW 7233
Rame (Corn.) 20 SX 4249
Rame Head 20 SX 4148
Ram Lane 31 TQ 9646
Ramna Stacks 143 HU 3797
Rampisham 25 ST 5502
Rampside 76 SD 2366
Rampton (Cambs.) 53 TL 4268
Rampton (Notts.) 72 SK 7978
Ramsbottom 69 SD 7916
Ramsbury 34 SU 2771
Ramscraigs 135 ND 1427
Ramsdean 27 SU 7021
Ramsdell 35 SU 5957
Ramsden 47 SP 3515
Ramsden Bellhouse 38 TQ 7194
Ramsden Heath 38 TQ 7195
Ramsey (Cambs.) 53 TL 2885
Ramsey (Essex) 55 TM 2130
Ramsey (I. of M.) 76 SC 4594
Ramsey Bay 76 SC 4796
Ramseycleuch 89 NT 2714
Ramsey Forty Foot 53 TL 3187
Ramsey Hollow 53 TL 3186
Ramsey Island (Dyfed) 42 SM 7023
Ramsey Island (Essex) 39 TL 9605
Ramsey Knowe 89 NT 2516
Ramsey Mereside 53 TL 2889
Ramsey Sound 42 SM 7124
Ramsey St. Mary's 53 TL 2588
Ramsgate 31 TR 3865
Ramsgate Municipal Airport 31 TR 3767
Ramsgill 78 SE 1170
Ramshorn 60 SK 0845
Rams Ness 143 HU 6087
Ranachan Hill 92 NR 6825
Ranby 71 SK 6480
Rand 73 TF 1078
Randwick 46 SO 8206
Ranfurly 101 NS 3865
Rangemore 60 SK 1822
Rangeworthy 33 ST 6886
Ranish 131 NB 4024
Rankinston 93 NS 4514
Rannoch Forest 107 NN 4565
Rannoch Moor 107 NN 3852
Rannoch River 105 NM 7046
Rannoch Station 107 NN 4257
Ranskill 71 SK 6587
Ranson Moor 63 TL 3893
Ranton 59 SJ 8524
Ranworth 65 TG 3514
Rapness 138 HY 5141
Rapness Sound 138 HY 5138
Rappach (dist.) 127 NC 2401
Rappach Water 127 NH 3098
Rascarrel 87 NX 7948
Rascarrel Bay 87 NX 8047
Raskelf 79 SE 4971
Rassau 41 SO 1411
Rastrick 78 SE 1321
Ratagan 114 NG 9220
Ratagan Forest 114 NG 8919
Ratby 61 SK 5105
Ratcliffe Culey 60 SP 3299
Ratcliffe on the Wreake 61 SK 6314
Rathen 121 NK 0060
Rathillet 109 NO 3620
Rathmell 78 SD 8059
Ratho 102 NT 1370
Ratho Station 102 NT 1372
Rathven 121 NJ 4465
Rat Island 22 SS 1443
Ratley 50 SP 3847
Ratlinghope 58 SO 4096
Rattar 135 ND 2672
Ratten Row 77 SD 4241
Rattery 21 SX 7361
Rattlesden 54 TL 9758
Rattray 108 NO 1745
Rattray Head 121 NK 1057
Rauceby 62 TF 0146
Rauceby Station 62 TF 0344
Raughton Head 83 NY 3745
Raunds 52 SP 9972
Ravenfield 71 SK 4895
Ravenglass 82 SD 0896
Raveningham 65 TM 3996
Ravenscar 81 NZ 9801
Ravensdale 76 SC 3592
Ravensden 52 TL 0754
Ravenshead 61 SK 5654
Ravens Knowe 90 NT 7806
Ravensmoor 59 SJ 6250
Ravensthorpe (Northants.) 51 SP 6670
Ravensthorpe (W Yorks.) 71 SE 2220
Ravensthorpe Resr. 51 SP 6770
Ravenstone (Bucks.) 52 SP 8450
Ravenstone (Leic.) 60 SK 4013
Ravenstonedale 83 NY 7203
Ravenstonedale Common 83 NY 6900
Ravenstown 77 SD 3574
Ravenstruther 95 NS 9245
Ravensworth 84 NZ 1407
Raw 81 NZ 9305
Rawcliffe (Humbs.) 74 SE 6822
Rawcliffe (N Yorks.) 79 SE 5855
Rawcliffe Bridge 74 SE 6921
Rawmarsh 71 SK 4396
Rawreth 38 TQ 7793
Rawridge 24 ST 2006
Rawtenstall 78 SD 8122
Rayburn Lake 91 NZ 1192
Raydon 54 TM 0438
Raylees 90 NY 9291
Rayleigh 38 TQ 8090
Rayne 38 TL 7222
Ray Sand 39 TM 0500
Rea Brook 49 SO 6586
Reach 53 TL 5666
Read 78 SD 7634
Reading 36 SU 7272
Reading Street 30 TQ 9230
Read's Island 74 SE 9622
Reagill 83 NY 6017
Rearquhar 129 NH 7492
Rearsby 61 SK 6514
Rease Heath 59 SJ 6454
Reaster 135 ND 2565
Reawick 141 HU 3244

Reay 134 NC 9664
Reay Forest 132 NC 2939
Reculver 31 TR 2269
Redberth 42 SN 0804
Redbourn 37 TL 1012
Redbourne 74 SK 9699
Redbrook 45 SO 5310
Redbrook Street 30 TQ 9336
Redburn (Highld.) 128 NH 5767
Redburn (Highld.) 129 NH 9447
Redcar 85 NZ 6024
Redcastle (Highld.) 128 NH 5849
Redcastle (Tays.) 109 NO 6850
Redcleuch Edge (mt.) 89 NT 3410
Redcliff Bay 33 ST 4475
Red Dial 82 NY 2545
Redding 102 NS 9178
Reddingmuirhead 102 NS 9177
Reddish 69 SJ 8993
Redditch 50 SP 0468
Red Down 20 SX 2685
Rede 54 TL 8055
Redenhall 55 TM 2684
Redesdale 90 NY 8396
Redesdale Camp 90 NY 8298
Redesdale Forest 90 NT 7601
Redesmouth 90 NY 8681
Redford 109 NO 5644
Redfordgreen 89 NT 3615
Redgrave 54 TM 0478
Red Head (Eday) 138 HY 5640
Red Head (Stroma) 135 ND 3477
Red Head (Tays.) 109 NO 7047
Redheugh 109 NO 4463
Redhill (Avon) 33 ST 4962
Redhill (Grampn.) 121 NJ 6837
Redhill (Grampn.) 119 NJ 7704
Red Hill (Powys) 44 SO 1550
Redhill (Surrey) 29 TQ 2850
Redhill Aerodrome & Heliport 29 TQ 3047
Redhythe Point 121 NJ 5767
Redisham 55 TM 4084
Redland (Avon) 33 ST 5875
Redland (Orkney) 136 HY 3724
Redlingfield 55 TM 1871
Red Lion Hill 57 SO 0577
Redlynch (Somer.) 25 ST 6933
Redlynch (Wilts.) 26 SU 2020
Redmarley D'Abitot 46 SO 7531
Redmarshall 85 NZ 3821
Redmile 61 SK 7935
Redmire 84 SE 0491
Redmire Moor 84 SE 0593
Redmires Dam 78 SD 9327
Redmires Reservoirs 71 SK 2685
Redmoor 19 SX 0761
Redmyre Loch 108 NO 2733
Rednal 58 SJ 3628
Red Nev (pt.) 138 HY 4145
Redpath 96 NT 5835
Red Pike 82 NY 1615
Red Point (Highld.) 134 NC 9265
Redpoint (Highld.) 123 NG 7369
Red Rock 69 SD 5809
Red Roses 43 SN 2012
Red Row 91 NZ 2599
Redruth 18 SW 6941
Redshin Cove 97 NU 0150
Red Street 59 SJ 8251
Red Wharf Bay (Gwyn.) 66 SH 5281
Red Wharf Bay (Gwyn.) 66 SH 5480
Redwick (Avon) 33 ST 5485
Redwick (Gwent) 32 ST 4184
Redworth 84 NZ 2423
Reed 53 TL 3636
Reedham 65 TG 4201
Reedness 74 SE 7922
Reed Point 96 NT 7772
Reef 131 NB 1134
Reeker Pike 90 NY 6682
Reepham (Lincs.) 72 TF 0373
Reepham (Norf.) 65 TG 1023
Reeth 84 SE 0499
Regaby 76 SC 4397
Regents Park 37 TQ 2882
Regoul 129 NH 8851
Réidh Eilean 104 NM 2426
Reiff 132 NB 9614
Reigate 28 TQ 2550
Reighton 81 TA 1275
Reighton Sands 81 TA 1476
Rèisa an t-Sruith 99 NR 7399
Rèisa Mhic Phaidean 99 NM 7400
Reisgill Burn 135 ND 2238
Reiss 135 ND 3354
Rejerrah 19 SW 8055
Relubbus 18 SW 5632
Relugas 129 NH 9948
Remenham 36 SU 7784
Remenham Hill 36 SU 7883
Remony 107 NN 7644
Rempstone 61 SK 5724
Remuil Hill 92 NR 6212
Rendcomb 46 SP 0109
Rendham 55 TM 3564
Rendlesham Forest 55 TM 3449
Renfrew 101 NS 4967
Renhold 52 TL 0953
Renishaw 71 SK 4477
Renish Point 124 NG 0481
Rennington 91 NU 2118
Renton 101 NS 3878
Renwick 83 NY 5943
Repps 65 TG 4116
Repton 60 SK 3026
Rerwick Head 137 HY 5411
Rescobie 109 NO 5152
Resipole 111 NM 7264
Resolis 128 NH 6765
Resolven 41 SN 8202
Rest and be thankful 100 NN 2307
Reston 97 NT 8861
Reswallie 109 NO 5051
Retew 19 SW 9256
Rettendon 38 TQ 7698
Rettendon Place 38 TQ 7796
Revesby 73 TF 2961
Rewe 21 SX 9499
Reydon 55 TM 4977
Reymerston 64 TG 0206
Reynalton 42 SN 0909
Reynoldston 40 SS 4890
Rhaeadr Cynfal 67 SH 7041
Rhandirmwyn 44 SN 7843
Rhayader 57 SN 9668
Rhedyn 66 SH 3032
Rheindown 128 NH 5147
Rhemore 111 NM 5750
Rhenigidale 125 NB 2201
Rhes-y-cae 68 SJ 1870
Rhewl (Clwyd) 67 SJ 1060
Rhewl (Clwyd) 58 SJ 1744
Rhian 133 NC 5616
Rhicarn 132 NC 0825
Rhiconich 132 NC 2552
Rhicullen 128 NH 6971
Rhidorroch Forest 127 NH 2497
Rhidorroch House 127 NH 1795
Rhidorroch River 127 NH 2294
Rhifail 134 NC 7249
Rhigos 41 SN 9205
Rhilean Burn 117 NH 8937
Rhilochan 129 NC 7407
Rhinns of Kells (mt.) 87 NX 5083
Rhinog Fawr (mt.) 57 SH 6428
Rhins, The (dist.) 86 NX 0454
Rhiroy 127 NH 1589
Rhiwbryfdir 67 SH 6946
Rhiwderin 32 ST 2587
Rhiwlas (Clwyd) 58 SJ 1931
Rhiwlas (Gwyn.) 66 SH 5765
Rhiwlas (Gwyn.) 67 SH 9237
Rhobell Fawr 57 SH 7825
Rhodesia 71 SK 5680
Rhodes Minnis 31 TR 1542
Rhôd-mâd 56 SN 5974
Rhondda 41 SS 9696
Rhondda Fach 41 SS 9996
Rhondda Fawr 41 SS 9993
Rhonehouse or Kelton Hill 88 NX 7459
Rhoose 41 ST 0666
Rhôs (Dyfed) 43 SN 3835
Rhos (W Glam.) 40 SN 7303
Rhoscolyn 66 SH 2675
Rhoscrowther 42 SM 9002
Rhos Dirion 41 SO 2133
Rhosesmor 68 SJ 2168
Rhos-fawr 66 SH 3838
Rhosgadfan 66 SH 5057
Rhosgoch (Gwyn.) 66 SH 4189
Rhosgoch (Powys) 45 SO 1847
Rhoslan 66 SH 4841
Rhoslefain 56 SH 5705
Rhosllanerchrugog 58 SJ 2946
Rhosmeirch 66 SH 4677
Rhosneigr 66 SH 3172
Rhosnesni 58 SJ 3451
Rhos-on-Sea 67 SH 8480
Rhossili 40 SS 4188
Rhossili Bay 40 SS 3990
Rhosson 42 SM 7225
Rhostryfan 66 SH 4958
Rhostyllen 58 SJ 3148
Rhosybol 66 SH 4288
Rhos-y-gwaliau 67 SH 9434
Rhos-y-llan 66 SH 2337
Rhos-y-mawn 67 SH 8566
Rhu (Kintyre) 99 NR 8364
Rhu (Strath.) 100 NS 2783
Rhuallt 67 SJ 0774
Rhuddlan 67 SJ 0277
Rhue 127 NH 0997
Rhulen 44 SO 1350
Rhum (is.) 110 NM 3798
Rhunahaorine 92 NR 7048
Rhu Nòa 126 NH 0064
Rhyd (Gwyn.) 67 SH 6341
Rhyd (Powys) 57 SH 9700
Rhydargaeau 43 SN 4326
Rhydcymerau 43 SN 5738
Rhydd 49 SO 8345
Rhyd-Ddu 66 SH 5652
Rhyddhywel 57 SO 0279
Rhydding 41 SS 7498
Rhyd Galed 44 SN 7142
Rhydlewis 43 SN 3447
Rhydlios 66 SH 1830
Rhydlydan 67 SH 8950
Rhydowen 43 SN 4445
Rhydrosser 56 SN 5667
Rhydtalog 58 SJ 2354
Rhŷd-y-clafdy 66 SH 3235
Rhydycroesau 58 SJ 2330
Rhydyfelin (Dyfed) 56 SN 5979
Rhydyfelin (Mid Glam.) 41 ST 0988
Rhyd-y-fro 40 SN 7105
Rhydymain 57 SH 7922
Rhyd-y-meirch 45 SO 3107
Rhydymwyn 68 SJ 2066
Rhyd-yr-onnen 56 SH 6102
Rhyl 67 SJ 0181
Rhymney 41 SO 1107
Rhymney River 41 ST 2283
Rhymney Valley 41 ST 1491
Rhyn 58 SJ 3136
Rhynd 108 NO 1520
Rhynie (Grampn.) 121 NJ 4927
Rhynie (Highld.) 129 NH 8578
Ribbesford 49 SO 7874
Ribblehead 78 SD 7879
Ribblesdale 78 SD 8059
Ribbleton 77 SD 5630
Ribchester 77 SD 6435
Ribigill 133 NC 5854
Riby 75 TA 1807
Riccall 79 SE 6237
Riccarton 93 NS 4235
Richards Castle 48 SO 4969
Richmond 84 NZ 1701
Richmond (Surrey) 37 TQ 1874
Richmond Park 37 TQ 1972
Rickarton 119 NO 8188
Rickets Head 42 SM 8519
Rickinghall 54 TM 0475
Rickling 53 TL 4931
Rickmansworth 36 TQ 0594
Riddell 96 NT 5124
Riddlecombe 23 SS 6013
Riddlesden 78 SE 0742
Ridge (Dorset) 26 SY 9386
Ridge (Herts.) 37 TL 2100
Ridge (Wilts.) 26 ST 9531
Ridgehill (Avon) 33 ST 5362
Ridge Hill (Here. and Worc.) 45 SO 5035
Ridge Lane 60 SP 2994
Ridge Way (Berks.) (ant.) 35 SU 5381
Ridge Way (Oxon.) (ant.) 34 SU 3484
Ridge Way (Wilts.) (ant.) 34 SU 0151
Ridge Way (Wilts.) (ant.) 34 SU 1168
Ridgeway Cross 49 SO 7147
Ridgewell 54 TL 7340
Ridgewood 29 TQ 4719
Ridgmont 52 SP 9736
Riding Mill 91 NZ 0161
Ridlees Cairn 90 NT 8404
Ridlington (Leic.) 62 SK 8402
Ridlington (Norf.) 65 TG 3430
Ridsdale 90 NY 9084
Riechip 108 NO 0647
Riemore Lodge 108 NO 0449
Riereach Burn 129 NH 8445
Rievaulx 79 SE 5785
Rigg 89 NY 2966
Riggend 101 NS 7670
Riggs Moor 78 SE 0373
Rigg, The 90 NY 6484
Rigmaden Park 77 SD 6184
Rig of the Shalloch 86 NX 3892
Rigside 95 NS 8734
Rileyhill 60 SK 1115
Rilla Mill 20 SX 2973
Rillington 80 SE 8574
Rimington 78 SD 8045
Rimpton 25 ST 6021
Rimsdale Burn 134 NC 7440
Rimswell 75 TA 3128
Rinaston 42 SM 9825
Ringford 87 NX 6857
Ringland 65 TG 1313
Ringmer 29 TQ 4412
Ringmore 21 SX 6545
Ringorm 120 NJ 2644
Ring's End 63 TF 3902
Ringsfield 55 TM 4088
Ringsfield Corner 55 TM 4187
Ringshall (Bucks.) 36 SP 9814
Ringshall (Suff.) 54 TM 0452
Ringshall Stocks 54 TM 0551
Ringstead (Norf.) 64 TF 7040
Ringstead (Northants.) 52 SP 9875
Ringstead Bay 25 SY 7579
Ringwood 26 SU 1405
Ringwood Forest 26 SU 1108
Ringwould 31 TR 3648
Rinmore 118 NJ 4117
Rinn Druim Tallig 131 NB 3150
Rinnigill 136 ND 3193
Rinns of Islay 98 NR 2056
Rinns Point 98 NR 1751
Rinn Thorbhais 104 NL 9340
Rinsey 18 SW 5927
Ripe 29 TQ 5010
Ripley (Derby.) 60 SK 3950
Ripley (Hants.) 26 SZ 1698
Ripley (N Yorks.) 79 SE 2860
Ripley (Surrey) 28 TQ 0556
Riplingham 74 SE 9631
Ripon 79 SE 3171
Rippingale 62 TF 0927
Ripple (Here. and Worc.) 49 SO 8737
Ripple (Kent) 31 TR 3550
Ripponden 70 SE 0319
Rippon Tor 21 SX 7475
Rireavach 126 NH 0295
Risabus 98 NR 3143
Risbury 45 SO 5455
Risby (Humbs.) 74 SE 9214
Risby (Suff.) 54 TL 7966
Risca 32 ST 2391
Rise 75 TA 1541
Risegate 62 TF 2029
Rise Hill 77 SD 7388
Riseley (Beds.) 52 TL 0463
Riseley (Berks.) 36 SU 7263
Risga 111 NM 6159
Rishangles 55 TM 1568
Rishton 77 SD 7229
Rishworth 70 SE 0317
Rishworth Moor 70 SD 9917
Risley 69 SJ 6592
Risley 61 SK 4635
Risplith 79 SE 2467
Rispond 133 NC 4565
Rivar 34 SU 3161
Rivenhall End 38 TL 8316
River Add 99 NR 8192
River Adur 28 TQ 2118
River Affric (Highld.) 115 NH 0920
River Affric (Highld.) 115 NH 2627
River Aire 79 SE 3630
River Alde 55 TM 2967
River Allen (Corn.) 19 SX 0678
River Allen (Dorset) 26 SU 0006
River Allen (Northum.) 90 NY 7962
River Almond (Tays.) 107 NN 7833
River Almond (Tays.) 108 NO 0228
River Aln 91 NU 1214
River Alne 50 SP 1562
River Alport 70 SK 1292
River Alt 68 SD 3105
River Alun 42 SM 7627
River Alwin 90 NT 9110
River Alyn 58 SJ 3656
River Amber 71 SK 3463
River Anker 60 SK 2305
River Annan (Dumf. and Galwy.) 89 NT 0901
River Annan (Dumf. and Galwy.) 89 NY 1176
River Ant 65 TG 3617
River Applecross 123 NG 7448
River Ardle 108 NO 1054
River Arnol 131 NB 3045
River Arrow (Here. and Worc.) 45 SO 4058
River Arrow (Warw.) 50 SP 0861
River Arun 28 TQ 0422
River Ash 37 TL 4216
River Ashop 70 SK 1389
River Attadale 114 NG 9337
River Averon 128 NH 6372
River Avon (Avon) 33 ST 5476
River Avon (Avon) 33 ST 6966
River Avon (Central) 102 NS 8773
River Avon (Devon) 21 SX 7157
River Avon (Grampn.) 117 NJ 1614
River Avon (Warw.) 50 SP 2659
River Avon (Wilts.) 26 SU 1301
River Awe 106 NN 0229
River Axe (Dorset.) 24 ST 3303
River Axe (Somer.) 33 ST 4647
River Ayr 94 NS 5826
River Bà 106 NN 2648
River Bain 73 TF 2473
River Bank 53 TL 5368
River Barle 23 SS 8829
River Barrisdale 114 NG 8803
River Beauly 128 NH 4641
River Bellart 105 NM 4448
River Beult 30 TQ 7747
River Blackwater 38 TL 8322
River Bladnoch 86 NX 3657
River Bleng 82 NY 0804
River Blithe 60 SK 0424
River Blyth (Northum.) 91 NZ 1877
River Blyth (Suff.) 55 TM 4376
River Blythe (Warw.) 50 SP 2184
River Bogie 121 NJ 5234
River Bollin 69 SJ 7785
River Borgie 133 NC 6655
River Bourne 34 SU 2038
River Bovey 21 SX 7583
River Braan 108 NN 9438
River Brain 38 TL 7918
River Bran 127 NH 2160
River Brant 62 SK 9356
River Brathay 82 NY 3102
River Bray 23 SS 6932
River Breamish 90 NT 9515
River Brede 30 TQ 8217
River Brent 54 TM 0145
River Brit 25 SY 4795
River Brittle 123 NG 4023
River Brock 77 SD 5140
River Broom 127 NH 1881
River Brora 133 NC 6613
River Brue (Somer.) 32 ST 4044
River Brue (Somer.) 25 ST 6032
River Bure 65 TG 2521
River Calder (Cumbr.) 82 NY 0609
River Calder (Highld.) 116 NN 6698
River Calder (Lancs.) 77 SD 5346
River Calder (Lancs.) 78 SD 7833
River Calder (Strath.) 100 NS 3162
River Calder (W Yorks.) 71 SE 2620
River Cale 25 ST 7422
River Cam (Cambs.) 53 TL 5268
River Camel 19 SX 0168
River Cam or Granta (Essex) 53 TL 5231
River Cam or Rhee (Cambs.) 53 TL 3648
River Can 38 TL 6807
River Cannich 115 NH 2833
River Carey 20 SX 3687
River Carron (Central) 101 NS 6584
River Carron (Central) 101 NS 7684
River Carron (Highld.) 126 NG 9442
River Carron (Highld.) 128 NH 4890
River Cary 25 ST 4530
River Cassley 132 NC 4012
River Ceiriog 58 SJ 2237
River Char 24 SY 3996
River Chater 62 SK 8303
River Chelmer 38 TL 6520
River Chelmer 38 TL 7709
River Cherwell (Northants.) 51 SP 4947
River Cherwell (Oxon.) 47 SP 5212
River Chess 36 TQ 0695
River Chet 65 TM 3799
River Churn 46 SP 0108
River Churnet 60 SK 0147
River Claw 20 SX 3498
River Clun 48 SO 3976
River Clwyd 67 SJ 0276
River Clyde (Strath.) 94 NS 7753
River Clyde (Strath.) 95 NS 9933
River Clyst 21 SX 9998
River Clywedog 67 SJ 0962
River Cocker 82 NY 1228
River Coiltie 116 NH 4426
River Cole (Oxon.) 47 SU 2195
River Cole (W Mids.) 50 SP 1587
River Coll 131 NB 4540
River Coln 47 SP 1305
River Colne 54 TL 9327
River Conder 77 SD 4958
River Conon (Highld.) 128 NH 4255
River Conon (Isle of Skye) 123 NG 4163
River Cononish 106 NN 3228
River Conwy (Gwyn.) 67 SH 7769
River Conwy (Gwyn.) 67 SH 8145
River Coquet 91 NZ 1599
River Corfe 26 SY 9685
River Corve 48 SO 5286
River Coulin 126 NH 0254
River Coupall 106 NN 2054
River Cover 78 SE 1186
River Cree 86 NX 3184
River Creed or Greeta River 131 NB 3632
River Crouch 38 TQ 8095
River Culm 24 ST 0207
River Cur 100 NN 1000
River Dalch 23 SS 7510
River Dane (Ches.) 69 SJ 6868
River Dane (Staffs.) 69 SJ 9463
River Dart 21 SX 7565
River Darwen 77 SD 6129
River Dean 69 SJ 8781
River Dearne 71 SE 3408
River Deben 55 TM 2061
River Dee (Clwyd) 58 SJ 3543
River Dee (Cumbr.) 77 SD 6788
River Dee (Dumf. and Galwy.) 88 NX 7463
River Dee (Grampn.) 117 NN 9991
River Dee (Grampn.) 118 NO 3396
River Dee (Grampn.) 119 NO 8298
River Dee or Black Water of Dee 88 NX 5973
River Deer 20 SS 3200
River Delph 53 TL 5090
River Derwent (Cumbr.) 82 NY 2312
River Derwent (Derby.) 71 SK 2564
River Derwent (Derby.) 60 SK 4333
River Derwent (Durham-Northum.) 84 NZ 0350
River Derwent (Humbs. - N Yorks.) 74 SE 7035
River Derwent (N Yorks.) 80 SE 8578
River Dessarry 114 NM 9393
River Deveron (Grampn.) 121 NJ 4439
River Deveron (Grampn.) 121 NJ 6247
River Devon (Central) 102 NS 9497
River Devon (Notts.) 61 SK 7847
River Dibb 78 SE 0563
River Dionard 132 NC 3357
River Divie 120 NJ 0344
River Dochart 107 NN 5430
River Doe 115 NH 1914
River Don (Grampn.) 117 NJ 2707
River Don (Grampn.) 119 NJ 6519
River Don (S Yorks.) 71 SK 4696
River Doon 93 NS 4308
River Dorn 47 SP 4420
River Douchary 127 NH 2490
River Douglas 68 SD 4619
River Dove (Derby.) 60 SK 1132
River Dove (N Yorks.) 85 SE 6793
River Dove (Staffs.) 70 SK 1163
River Dove (Suff.) 55 TM 1370
River Dovey (Afon Dyfi) 57 SN 6395
River Drolsay 98 NR 3366
River Druie 117 NH 9011
River Drynoch 123 NG 4330
River Duddon 82 SD 2398
River Dudwell 29 TQ 6824
River Dulnain 117 NH 8419
River Dyke 134 NC 8547
River E 116 NH 5413
River Eamont 83 NY 4725
River Earn (Tays.) 107 NN 7821
River Earn (Tays.) 108 NO 1318
River East Allen 83 NY 8354
River Eau 72 SK 9097
River Ebble 26 SU 1126
River Eden (Cumbr.) 89 NY 3462
River Eden (Cumbr.) 83 NY 5342
River Eden (Cumbr.) 83 NY 5830
River Eden (Fife) 103 NO 3209
River Eden (Kent) 29 TQ 4645
River Ehen 82 NY 0213
River Eidart 117 NN 9193
River Einig 127 NH 3799
River Elchaig 114 NG 9628
River Ellen 82 NY 1541
River Elwy 67 SH 9972
River Enrick 115 NH 3526
River Erewash 61 SK 4743
River Ericht 107 NN 5161
River Erme 21 SX 6355
River Erradale 123 NG 7669
River Esk (Cumbr.) 89 NY 3289
River Esk (Cumbr.) 82 SD 1297
River Esk (Lothian) 103 NT 3470
River Esk (N Yorks.) 80 NZ 7407
River Eskin 116 NH 6110
River Esragan 106 NM 9835
River Etherow 70 SJ 9791
River Evelix 129 NH 7293
River Evenlode 47 SP 3220
River Ewe 126 NG 8679
River Exe (Devon) 23 SS 9409
River Exe (Devon) 21 SX 9882
River Eye 62 SK 8118
River Fal 19 SW 9246
River Falloch 107 NN 3723
River Farigaig 116 NH 5625
River Farrar 115 NH 3339
River Feehlin 116 NH 5012
River Feshie 117 NN 8590
River Fiag 133 NC 4524
River Fiddich 121 NJ 3232
River Findhorn 117 NH 8839
River Finnan 114 NM 9182
River Fleet 129 NC 7301
River Forsa 105 NM 6041
River Forth 101 NS 6496
River Foulness 74 SE 7839
River Fowey 19 SX 0962
River Foyers 116 NH 4917
River Freshney 75 TA 2308
River Frome (Avon) 33 ST 6376
River Frome (Dorset) 25 SY 7490
River Frome (Here. and Worc.) 49 SO 6544
River Frome (Somer.) 33 ST 7643
River Fyne 106 NN 2215
River Gairn 117 NJ 2501
River Garnock 93 NS 3050
River Garry (Highld.) 115 NH 1400
River Garry (Tays.) 107 NN 7668
River Gaur 107 NN 4857
River Gele 67 SH 9476
River Gelt 83 NY 5654
River Gilpin 77 SD 4687
River Gipping 55 TM 1152
River Glass (Highld.) 115 NH 3734
River Glass (Highld.) 128 NH 5666
River Glass (I. of M.) 76 SC 3680
River Glaven 64 TG 0440
River Glen (Lincs.) 62 TF 0711
River Glen (Lincs.) 63 TF 2427
River Glen (Northum.) 97 NT 9030
River Glenderamackin 82 NY 3426
River Gloy 115 NN 2588
River Glyme 47 SP 4418
River Gour 106 NM 9364
River Gowy 69 SJ 4864
River Granta 53 TL 5051
River Granta or Cam 53 TL 5231
River Great Ouse (Bucks.) 51 SP 5936
River Great Ouse (Bucks.) 52 SP 8646
River Great Ouse (Cambs.) 54 TL 5990
River Great Ouse or Old West River (Cambs.) 53 TL 4671
River Greta (Cumbr.) 82 NY 2924
River Greta (Durham) 84 NZ 0511
River Greta (Lancs.) 77 SD 6271
River Grudie (Highld.) 126 NG 9666
River Grudie (Highld.) 127 NH 2964
River Gryfe 101 NS 3666
River Gwash 62 SK 8906
River Hamble 27 SU 5214
River Hart 36 SU 7659
River Haultin 123 NG 4451
River Hayle 18 SW 5632
Riverhead 29 TQ 5156
River Helmsdale 134 NC 8925
River Hepste 41 SN 9612
River Hertford 81 TA 0281
River Hindburn 77 SD 6366
River Hinnisdal 123 NG 4158
River Hiz 52 TL 1833
River Hodder 77 SD 7050
River Hope 133 NC 4760
River Hull 74 TA 0646
River Humber 75 TA 2316
River Hurich 111 NM 8267
River Idle 72 SK 7497
River Inny 20 SX 2383
River Inver 132 NC 1123
River Irt 82 NY 1000
River Irthing 90 NY 6469
River Irvine 93 NS 4737
River Irwell 69 SD 7913
River Isbourne 46 SP 0334
River Isis or Thames (Oxon.) 47 SP 4302
River Isis or Thames (Wilts.) 47 SU 1596
River Isla (Grampn.) 121 NJ 4046
River Isla (Tays.) 108 NO 1738
River Isla (Tays.) 117 NO 1974
River Isla (Tays.) 108 NO 2357
River Isle 24 ST 3722
River Itchen (Hants.) 27 SU 4616
River Itchen (Warw.) 50 SP 4062
River Ithon 57 SO 1066
River Ivel 52 TL 1938
River Kanaird 127 NC 1602
River Keekle 82 NY 0118
River Keer 77 SD 5472
River Kelvin 101 NS 6775
River Kenn (Avon) 33 ST 4269
River Kenn (Devon.) 21 SX 9385
River Kennet (Berks.) 35 SU 5366
River Kennet (Wilts.) 34 SU 2369
River Kennett (Cambs.) 54 TL 6969
River Kent (Cumbr.) 83 NY 4502
River Kent (Cumbr.) 77 SD 5086
River Kerry 123 NG 8371
River Kiachnish 106 NN 0969
River Killin 116 NH 5308
River Kingie 114 NN 0197
River Kirkaig 132 NC 1018
River Knaik 101 NN 8012
River Kym 52 TL 1066
River Lael 127 NH 2284
River Laggan 98 NR 3156
River Làir 126 NG 9850
River Lambourn 34 SU 4370
River Lark 54 TL 6476
River Laver 78 SE 2072
River Laxay 131 NB 3022
River Laxdale 131 NB 3935
River Laxford 132 NC 2545
River Leach 47 SP 1708
River Leadon 46 SO 7628
River Leam 51 SP 4568
River Lea or Lee (Gtr London) 37 TQ 3695
River Lea or Lee (Herts.) 37 TL 2609
River Lednock 107 NN 7625
River Leen 61 SK 5450
River Lee or Lea (Gtr London) 37 TQ 3695
River Lee or Lea (Herts.) 37 TL 2609
River Len 30 TQ 8054
River Leven (Fife) 103 NO 2601
River Leven (Highld.) 106 NN 2160
River Leven (N Yorks.) 85 NZ 4906
River Leven (Strath.) 101 NS 3976
River Lew 23 SS 5301
River Liever 100 NM 8907
River Ling 114 NG 9834
River Livet 117 NJ 2523
River Liza 82 NY 1313
River Loanan 132 NC 2418
River Lochay 107 NN 5037
River Lochy (Highld.) 115 NN 1581
River Lochy (Strath.) 106 NN 2629
River Loddon 36 SU 7568
River Lodon 45 SO 6152
River Lossie (Grampn.) 129 NJ 1045
River Lossie (Grampn.) 120 NJ 2564
River Lostock 69 SD 5119
River Loughor 43 SN 6007
River Lovat or Ouzel 52 SP 8831
River Lowther 83 NY 5120
River Loxley 71 SK 2989
River Loy 115 NN 1183
River Loyne 115 NH 0706
River Lugg (Here. and Worc.) 45 SO 5251
River Lugg (Powys) 48 SO 3264
River Luineag 117 NH 9209
River Lune (Cumbr.) 83 NY 6105
River Lune (Durham) 84 NY 8720
River Lune (Lancs.) 77 SD 3653
River Lune (Lancs.) 77 SD 6075
River Lydden 25 ST 7208
River Lyne 89 NY 4871
River Lynher 20 SX 3663
River Lyon 107 NN 6147
River Lyvennet 83 NY 6122
River Mallie 115 NN 0687
River Manifold 60 SK 1054
River Mashie 116 NN 5787
River Maun 71 SK 6166

River Mease 60 SK 2711
River Meden 71 SK 5565
River Medina 27 SZ 5094
River Medway 29 TQ 6446
River Meig 127 NH 3655
River Meoble 111 NM 7986
River Meon 27 SU 5407
River Mersey (Gtr Mches.) 69 SJ 8092
River Mersey (Mers.) 68 SJ 3684
River Misbourne 36 SU 9696
River Mite 82 SD 0998
River Moidart 111 NM 7471
River Mole (Devon) 23 SS 7327
River Mole (Surrey) 37 TQ 1263
River Mole (Surrey) 28 TQ 2347
River Monnow (Afon Mynwy) 45 SO 4716
River Moriston 115 NH 3414
River Mudale 133 NC 5135
River Muick 118 NO 3389
River Nadder 26 SU 0130
River Nairn 129 NH 7947
River Nar 64 TF 6812
River Naver 134 NC 7255
River Neath 41 SN 9013
River Neb 76 SC 2883
River Nene (Cambs.) 63 TL 2398
River Nene (Northants.) 51 SP 5959
River Nene (Northants.) 52 TL 0385
River Nene (Old Course) (Cambs.) 53 TL 3291
River Ness 116 NH 6139
River Nethan 94 NS 7835
River Nethy 117 NJ 0214
River Nevis 106 NN 1370
River Nidd 79 SE 3357
River Nith 88 NS 7012
River Noe 70 SK 1485
River North Esk (Lothian) 103 NT 2158
River North Esk (Tays.) 118 NO 5078
River North Tyne 90 NY 6887
River Ock 47 SU 4095
River Oich 115 NH 3405
River Okement 23 SS 5901
River Orchy 106 NN 2534
River Ore (Fife) 103 NT 2796
River Ore (Suff.) 55 TM 3845
River Orrin 128 NH 4250
River Orwell 55 TM 2138
River Ose 122 NG 3442
River Ossian 107 NN 4172
River Otter 24 SY 0996
River Ottery 20 SX 2788
River Oude 105 NM 8415
River Ouse (E Susx) 29 TQ 4208
River Ouse (Norf.) 64 TF 5903
River Ouse (N Yorks.) 79 SE 4959
River Ouzel or Lovat 52 SP 8831
River Oykel 127 NC 3503
River Pang 36 SU 6173
River Pant 54 TL 6631
River Parrett (Somer.) 32 ST 2842
River Parrett (Somer.) 24 ST 3928
River Pattack 116 NN 5483
River Pean 114 NM 9290
River Penk 59 SJ 8905
River Perry 58 SJ 3828
River Petteril 83 NY 4839
River Piddle or Trent 25 SY 8392
River Plym 21 SX 5464
River Polly 132 NC 0812
River Pont 91 NZ 1676
River Poulter 71 SK 6475
River Quaich 107 NN 7939
River Quin 53 TL 3927
River Ray (Oxon.) 47 SP 5917
River Ray (Wilts.) 34 SU 1191
River Rea 49 SO 6673
River Rede 90 NY 7899
River Rha 123 NG 4065
River Rhee or Cam 53 TL 3647
River Rhiw 58 SJ 1102
River Rib 37 TL 3818
River Ribble 77 SD 6434
River Riccal 79 SE 6382
River Roach 38 TQ 9592
River Roch 69 SD 8712
River Roden 59 SJ 5915
River Roding 37 TQ 4294
River Romesdal 123 NG 4354
River Rother (E Susx) 29 TQ 6125
River Rother (Hants.) 27 SU 7625
River Rother (W Susx) 28 SU 9420
River Roy 115 NN 3088
River Rue 100 NS 0188
River Runie 127 NC 1302
River Rye 79 SE 5784
River Ryton 71 SK 6185
River Sand 126 NG 7779
River Sark 89 NY 3273
River Scaddle 106 NM 9567
River Seaton 20 SX 2959
River Sence (Leic.) 60 SK 3503
River Sence (Leic.) 61 SP 5997
River Seph 85 SE 5691
River Seven 80 SE 7380
River Severn (Avon) 33 ST 5992
River Severn (Here. and Worc.) 49 SO 8448
River Severn (Powys) 58 SJ 2612
River Severn (Powys) 57 SO 0890
River Severn (Shrops.) 59 SJ 6901
River Sgitheach 128 NH 5765
River Sheaf 71 SK 3282
River Shiel 114 NG 9813
River Shin 128 NH 5798
River Shira 106 NN 1518
River Skerne 84 NZ 3026
River Skinsdale 134 NC 7518
River Skirfare 78 SD 8875
River Slea 62 TF 1149
River Sligachan 123 NG 4927
River Snizort 123 NG 4244
River Soar (Leic.) 61 SP 5599
River Soar (Notts.) 61 SK 4925
River Solva 42 SM 8527
River Sorn 98 NR 3563
River South Esk (Lothian) 103 NT 3262
River South Esk (Tays.) 109 NO 3471
River South Tyne 83 NY 6854
River Sow 59 SJ 8628
River Sowe 50 SP 3777
River Spean 115 NN 2481
River Spey (Grampn.) 120 NJ 3050
River Spey (Highld.) 117 NH 9315
River Spey (Highld.) 116 NN 5094
River Sprint 83 NY 4903
River Stiffkey 64 TF 9233
River Stinchar 86 NX 2291
River Stort 53 TL 4829
River Stour (Dorset) 25 ST 7619
River Stour (Dorset) 26 SZ 1096
River Stour (Essex) 54 TL 9233
River Stour (Here. and Worc.) 49 SO 8278
River Stour (Kent) 31 TR 2763
River Stour (Warw.) 50 SP 2249
River Strae 106 NN 1833
River Strathy 134 NC 8051
River Swale 84 SE 2796
River Swere 47 SP 4733
River Swift 51 SP 5283
River Taff 41 ST 1578
River Tale 24 ST 0702
River Tamar 20 SX 3682
River Tame (Gtr Mches.) 69 SJ 9092
River Tame (Staffs.) 60 SK 1807
River Tame (Warw.) 50 SP 2091
River Tarbert 106 NM 9259
River Tarff 115 NH 3805
River Tavy 20 SX 4765
River Taw (Devon) 23 SS 6614
River Tawe (W Glam.) 40 SS 6799
River Tay (Tays.) 108 NO 1138
River Tay (Tays.) 108 NO 1221
River Tees (Cumbr. - Durham) 83 NY 7733
River Tees (Durham - N Yorks.) 84 NZ 2711
River Teign 21 SX 7689
River Teith 101 NN 6306
River Teme (Here. and Worc.) 49 SO 7067
River Teme (Shrops.) 48 SO 3073
River Ter 38 TL 7714
River Tern 59 SJ 7037
River Test 26 SU 3637
River Teviot 96 NT 6424
River Thames (Essex - Kent) 37 TQ 5577
River Thames (Oxon.) 35 SU 5985
River Thames or Isis (Oxon.) 47 SP 4302
River Thames or Isis (Wilts.) 47 SU 1596
River Thet 54 TL 9584
River Thrushel 20 SX 4789
River Thurne 65 TG 4017
River Thurso 135 ND 1055
River Tiddy 20 SX 3064
River Til (Beds.) 52 TL 0268
River Till (Lincs.) 72 SK 9077
River Till (Northum.) 97 NT 9533
River Tillingham 30 TQ 8720
River Tilt 117 NN 9575
River Tirry 133 NC 5318
River Tone 24 ST 3227
River Torne 71 SE 6502
River Torridge 23 SS 5509
River Torridon 126 NG 9255
River Toscaig 123 NG 7438
River Tove 51 SP 7746
River Traligill 132 NC 2720
River Trent (Humbs.) 74 SE 8619
River Trent (Notts.) 61 SK 6239
River Trent (Staffs.) 59 SJ 9231
River Trent or Piddle (Dorset) 25 SY 8392
River Tromie 116 NN 7694
River Truim 116 NN 6485
River Tud 65 TG 0812
River Tummel (Tays.) 107 NN 7459
River Tummel (Tays.) 108 NN 9555
River Turret 115 NN 3394
River Tweed (Borders) 95 NT 0722
River Tweed (Borders) 96 NT 4235
River Tweed (Borders) 96 NT 7737
River Tyne (Lothian) 103 NT 5474
River Tyne (Northum.) 91 NZ 0361
River Ugie 121 NK 0849
River Ure (N Yorks.) 78 SE 2085
River Ure (N Yorks.) 79 SE 4662
River Urie 121 NJ 6629
River Usk 45 SO 2515
River Ver 37 TL 1209
River Waldon 22 SS 3610
River Wampool 82 NY 2454
River Wansbeck 91 NZ 1285
River Washburn 78 SE 1458
River Waveney 55 TM 2381
River Waver 82 NY 1850
River Wear 84 NZ 1134
River Weaver 69 SJ 5877
River Welland (Lincs.) 63 TF 2828
River Welland (Northants.) 62 SP 8894
River Wenning 77 SD 7167
River Wensum 64 TG 0518
River Went 71 SE 5917
River West Allen 83 NY 7854
River Wey (Hants.) 35 SU 7742
River Wey (Surrey) 28 TQ 0557
River Wharfe 78 SE 0262
River Wheelock 69 SJ 7063
River Whitelake 33 ST 5340
River Windrush 47 SP 1817
River Winster 77 SD 4185
River Wiske 85 SE 3497
River Wissey 64 TF 8401
River Witham (Lincs.) 62 SK 9328
River Witham (Lincs.) 72 SK 9463
River Witham (Lincs.) 63 TF 2548
River Wolf 20 SX 4290
River Worfe 59 SO 7698
River Worth 78 SE 0137
River Wreake 61 SK 6616
River Wye (Afon Gwy) (Here. and Worc.) 45 SO 3045
River Wye (Derby.) 70 SK 2069
River Wylye 26 SU 0536
River Wyre 77 SD 4341
River Wyre 77 SD 5553
River Yar 27 SZ 6186
River Yare 65 TG 1108
River Yarrow 69 SD 5117
River Yarty 24 ST 2505
River Yealm 21 SX 6056
River Yeo (Avon) 33 ST 4463
River Yeo (Devon) 23 SS 7306
River Yeo (Devon) 23 SS 7726
River Yeo (Somer.) 25 ST 5223
River Ythan 121 NJ 8636
Rivington 69 SD 6214
Riv, The (sbk.) 139 HY 6847
Rivvalee (pt.) 143 HP 4805
Roade 51 SP 7551
Roadmeetings 95 NS 8649
Roadside 135 ND 1560
Roadside of Kinneff 119 NO 8476
Road, The (chan.) 18 SV 8912
Roadwater 32 ST 0238
Roag 122 NG 2744
Roa Island 76 SD 2364
Roana Bay 137 HY 5905
Roan Fell 89 NY 4592
Roan Head 136 ND 3896
Roath 41 ST 1978
Roberton (Borders) 89 NT 4314
Roberton (Strath.) 95 NS 9428
Roberton Law 95 NS 9129
Robertsbridge 29 TQ 7323
Roberttown 78 SE 1922
Robeston Cross 42 SM 8809
Robeston Wathen 42 SN 0815
Robin Hood's Bay 81 NZ 9505
Roborough 23 SS 5717
Rob Roy's Cave 100 NN 3310
Rob Roy's House 106 NN 1516
Roby Mill 69 SD 5106
Rocester 60 SK 1039
Roch 42 SM 8821
Rochdale 69 SD 8913
Rochdale Canal (Gtr Mches.) 70 SD 9518
Rochdale Canal (W Yorks.) 69 SD 9420
Roche 19 SW 9860
Roche Abbey (ant.) 71 SK 5489
Rochester (Kent) 30 TQ 7467
Rochester (Northum.) 90 NY 8397
Rochester Airport 30 TQ 7464
Rochford (Essex) 38 TQ 8790
Rochford (Here. and Worc.) 49 SO 6268
Rock (Corn.) 19 SW 9475
Rock (Here. and Worc.) 49 SO 7371
Rock (Northum.) 91 NU 2020
Rockbeare 24 SY 0195
Rockbourne 26 SU 1118
Rockbourne Down 26 SU 1020
Rockcliffe (Cumbr.) 89 NY 3561
Rockcliffe (Dumf. and Galwy.) 87 NX 8553
Rocken End 27 SZ 4875
Rock Ferry 68 SJ 3386
Rockfield (Gwent) 45 SO 4814
Rockfield (Highld.) 129 NH 9282
Rockham Bay 22 SS 4546
Rockhampton 46 ST 6593
Rockingham 52 SP 8691
Rockingham Forest 52 SP 9490
Rockland All Saints 64 TL 9896
Rockland St. Mary 65 TG 3104
Rockland St. Peter 64 TL 9897
Rockley 34 SU 1571
Rockwell End 36 SU 7988
Rodbourne 34 ST 9383
Rodd 48 SO 3162
Roddam 91 NU 0220
Rodden 25 SY 6184
Rode 33 ST 8053
Rode Heath (Ches.) 59 SJ 8056
Rodeheath (Ches.) 69 SJ 8766
Rodel 124 NG 0483
Roden 59 SJ 5716
Rodhuish 32 ST 0139
Rodings, The (dist.) 37 TL 5813
Rodington 59 SJ 5814
Rodley 46 SO 7411
Rodmarton 46 ST 9397
Rodmell 29 TQ 4106
Rodmersham 30 TQ 9261
Rodney Stoke 33 ST 4849
Rodono Hotel 95 NT 2321
Rodsley 60 SK 2040
Roecliffe 79 SE 3765
Roehampton 37 TQ 2373
Roe Ness 141 HU 3242
Roer Water 142 HU 3386
Roesound 141 HU 3465
Roewen 67 SH 7571
Roffey 28 TQ 1931
Rogan's Seat (mt.) 84 NY 9203
Rogart 129 NC 7303
Rogart Halt 129 NC 7202
Rogate 27 SU 8023
Roger Sand 63 TF 4841
Rogerstone 32 ST 2688
Rogerton 94 NS 6256
Rogiet 33 ST 4587
Roineabhal (mt.) 124 NG 0486
Roineval (Island of Skye) (mt.) 123 NG 4135
Roineval (Isle of Lewis) (mt.) 131 NB 2321
Roinn a' Bhuic 131 NB 4057
Rois-Bheinn 111 NM 7577
Roker 91 NZ 4059
Rollesby 65 TG 4415
Rolleston (Leic.) 61 SK 7300
Rolleston (Notts.) 61 SK 7452
Rolleston (Staffs.) 60 SK 2327
Rolston 75 TA 2145
Rolvenden 30 TQ 8431
Rolvenden Layne 30 TQ 8530
Romaldkirk 84 NY 9921
Romanby 85 SE 3693
Roman Gold Mines (ant.) 44 SN 6740
Romannobridge 95 NT 1547
Roman Ridge (ant.) 79 SE 4235
Roman River 39 TL 9920
Roman Road (ant.) 45 SO 4137
Romansleigh 23 SS 7220
Roman Steps 67 SH 6530
Rombalds Moor 78 SE 0845
Romford 37 TQ 5188
Romiley 69 SJ 9390
Romney Marsh 31 TR 0430
Romney Sands 31 TR 0823
Romsey 26 SU 3521
Romsley (Here. and Worc.) 50 SO 9679
Romsley (Shrops.) 49 SO 7883
Rona (is.) 130 HW 8132
Ronachan House 92 NR 7455
Ronachan Point 92 NR 7455
Ronague 76 SC 2472
Ronas Hill 142 HU 3083
Ronas Voe 142 HU 2881
Rona, The (chan.) 141 HU 3260
Ronay 124 NF 8955
Roneval (South Uist) (mt.) 112 NF 8114
Rooken Edge 90 NY 7895
Rookhope 84 NY 9342
Rookley 27 SZ 5084
Rooks Bridge 32 ST 3752
Roos 75 TA 2830
Roosebeck 76 SD 2568
Roos Wick 139 HY 6545
Rootpark 95 NS 9554
Ropley 27 SU 6431
Ropley Dean 27 SU 6331
Ropsley 62 SK 9834
Rora 121 NK 0650
Rora Head 136 ND 1799
Rora Moss 121 NK 0451
Rorandle 119 NJ 6518
Rorrington 58 SJ 3000
Rosall Point 77 SD 3147
Rosarie Forest 121 NJ 3548
Rose 18 SW 7754
Roseacre 77 SD 4336
Rose Ash 23 SS 7821
Rosebank 95 NS 8049
Rosebery Resr. 96 NT 3056
Rosebrough 97 NU 1326
Rose Cottage 111 NM 5369
Rosedale 80 SE 7295
Rosedale Abbey 80 SE 7296
Rosedale Moor 80 SE 7199
Roseden 97 NU 0321
Rosefield 129 NH 8552
Rosehaugh House 128 NH 6755
Rosehearty 121 NJ 9367
Rosehill 59 SJ 6630
Roseisle 129 NJ 1367
Roseisle Forest 129 NJ 1266
Rosemarket 42 SM 9508
Rosemarkie 129 NH 7357
Rosemarkie Bay 129 NH 7457
Rosemary Lane 24 ST 1514
Rosemount (Strath.) 93 NS 3729
Rosemount (Tays.) 108 NO 2043
Rosemullion Head 19 SW 7928
Rosenannon 19 SW 9566
Rose Ness 137 ND 5298
Rosewell 103 NT 2862
Roseworthy 18 SW 6139
Rosgill 83 NY 5316
Roshven 111 NM 7078
Rosinish (is.) 112 NL 6187
Roskhill 122 NG 2745
Rosley 82 NY 3245
Roslin 103 NT 2663
Rosliston 60 SK 2416
Rosneath 100 NS 2583
Rosneath Point 100 NS 2780
Ross (Dumf. and Galwy.) 87 NX 6444
Ross (Northum.) 97 NU 1336
Ross (Tays.) 107 NN 7621
Rossdhu House 101 NS 3689
Rossett 68 SJ 3657
Rossie Farm School 109 NO 6653
Rossie Moor 109 NO 6554
Rossie Ochill 102 NO 0812
Rossie Priory 108 NO 2830
Rossington 71 SK 6298
Rossinish 124 NF 8653
Rosskeen 128 NH 6869
Rossland 101 NS 4370
Ross of Mull (dist.) 105 NM 3919
Ross-on-Wye 45 SO 6024
Ross Priory 101 NS 4187
Roster 135 ND 2639
Rostherne 69 SJ 7483
Rosthwaite 82 NY 2514
Roston 60 SK 1241
Rosyth 102 NT 1183
Rothbury 91 NU 0601
Rothbury Forest 91 NU 0600
Rotherby 61 SK 6716
Rotherfield 29 TQ 5529
Rotherfield Greys 36 SU 7282
Rotherfield Peppard 36 SU 7081
Rotherham 71 SK 4492
Rother Levels 30 TQ 8725
Rothersthorpe 51 SP 7156
Rotherwick 35 SU 7156
Rothes 120 NJ 2749
Rothesay 100 NS 0864
Rothesay Bay 100 NS 0865
Rothiebrisbane 121 NJ 7437
Rothiemurchus 117 NH 9206
Rothienorman 121 NJ 7235
Rothiesholm 137 HY 6123
Rothiesholm Head 137 HY 6021
Rothley 61 SK 5812
Rothley Lakes 91 NZ 0490
Rothmaise 121 NJ 6832
Rothwell (Lincs.) 75 TF 1599
Rothwell (Northants.) 52 SP 8181
Rothwell (W Yorks.) 79 SE 3428
Rotsea 81 TA 0651
Rottal 109 NO 3769
Rottingdean 29 TQ 3702
Rottington 82 NX 9613
Roud 27 SZ 5280
Rougham 64 TF 8320
Rougham Green 54 TL 9061
Roughburn 115 NN 3781
Rough Close 59 SJ 9239
Rough Common 31 TR 1359
Rough Hill 93 NS 5445
Rough Island 87 NX 8453
Roughlee 78 SD 8440
Roughley 60 SP 1399
Rough Pike 90 NY 6285
Roughrigg Resr. 101 NS 8164
Roughsike 90 NY 5275
Roughton (Lincs.) 73 TF 2364
Roughton (Norf.) 65 TG 2136
Roughton (Shrops.) 59 SO 7594
Rough Tor (Corn.) 19 SX 1480
Rough Tor (Devon) 21 SX 6079
Rough Tower 55 TM 3928
Round Fell 87 NX 5372
Roundhay 79 SE 3235
Round Hill (Cumbr.) 83 NY 7336
Round Hill (Grampn.) 121 NJ 3427
Round Hill (N Yorks.) 78 SE 1253
Roundhill Resr. 78 SE 1476
Round Island 18 SV 9017
Round Loch of the Dungeon 87 NX 4684
Roundstreet Common 28 TQ 0528
Roundway 34 SU 0163
Roundway Hill 34 SU 0164
Rounton 85 NZ 4103
Rousay 138 HY 4030
Rousay Sound 136 HY 4529
Rousdon 24 SY 2990
Rous Lench 50 SP 0153
Routenburn 100 NS 1961
Routh 74 TA 0842
Row (Corn.) 19 SX 0976
Row (Cumbr.) 83 SD 4589
Rowallan Castle (ant.) 93 NS 4342
Rowanburn 89 NY 4177
Rowardennan Forest 101 NS 3896
Rowardennan Lodge 101 NS 3699
Rowde 34 ST 9762
Rowe Ditch (ant.) 45 SO 3859
Rowfoot 90 NY 6860
Row Head 136 HY 2218
Rowhedge 39 TM 0221
Rowhook 28 TQ 1234
Rowington 50 SP 2069
Rowland 70 SK 2072
Rowland's Castle 27 SU 7310
Rowland's Gill 91 NZ 1658
Rowledge 35 SU 8243
Rowley (Devon) 23 SS 7219
Rowley (Humbs.) 74 SE 9732
Rowley (Shrops.) 58 SJ 3006
Rowley Regis 50 SO 9787
Rowlstone 45 SO 3727
Rowly 28 TQ 0441
Rowney Green 50 SP 0471
Rownhams 26 SU 3816
Rowsham 36 SP 8518
Rowsley 71 SK 2566
Rowston 62 TF 0856
Rowton (Ches.) 68 SJ 4464
Rowton (Shrops.) 59 SJ 6119
Rowton Castle (ant.) 58 SJ 3712
Roxburgh 96 NT 6930
Roxby (Humbs.) 74 SE 9217
Roxby (N Yorks.) 85 NZ 7616
Roxby Beck 85 NZ 7415
Roxby High Moor 85 NZ 7512
Roxton 52 TL 1554
Roxwell 38 TL 6408
Royal British Legion Village 29 TQ 7257
Royal Forest 106 NN 2053
Royal Greenwich Observatory 29 TQ 6410
Royal Leamington Spa 50 SP 3166
Royal Military Canal 31 TR 0133
Royal Sovereign (lightship) 29 TV 7393
Royal Tunbridge Wells 29 TQ 5839
Roybridge 115 NN 2781
Roydon (Essex) 37 TL 4009
Roydon (Norf.) 64 TF 7022
Roydon (Norf.) 55 TM 0980
Royl Field (mt.) 141 HU 3928
Royston (Herts.) 53 TL 3541
Royston (S Yorks.) 71 SE 3611
Royton 69 SD 9207
Ruabon 58 SJ 3043
Ruabon Mountain 58 SJ 2446
Ruadh Sgeir 99 NR 7292
Ruadh-stac Mór 126 NG 9561
Ruaig 104 NM 0647
Ruan Lanihorne 19 SW 8942
Ruan Minor 18 SW 7115
Ruardean 45 SO 6117
Ruardean Woodside 45 SO 6216
Rubers Law 90 NT 5715
Rubery 50 SO 9777
Rubha a Ghraineig 110 NM 1555
Rubha Aird Druimcrich 111 NM 5772
Rubha Airigh Bheirg 92 NR 8848
Rubha a'Mhail 98 NR 4872
Rubha a'Mharaiche 92 NR 5812
Rubha an Aird 110 NM 3855
Rubha an Daraich 123 NG 7909
Rubha an Dùine 124 NF 9771
Rubha an Fhasaidh 111 NM 4487
Rubha an Ridire 105 NM 7340
Rubha Ard Slisneach 123 NG 7409
Rubha Ardvule 112 NF 7029
Rubha Beag 126 NG 8897
Rubh' a'Bhacain 99 NR 7096
Rubh' a' Bhaid Bheithe 106 NN 0259
Rubh' a' Bhàigh Uaine 131 NB 4229
Rubh' a' Bhaile Fo Thuath 124 NF 9087
Rubh' a' Bhaird 125 NB 3101
Rubha Bhilidh 112 NF 8632
Rubh' a' Bhinnein 110 NM 2263
Rubh' a' Bhiogair 131 NB 3451
Rubha Bhlanisgaidh 131 NB 3755
Rubha Bhocaig 125 NG 1891
Rubha Bhoisnis 124 NF 8880
Rubha Bholsa 98 NR 3778
Rubha Bhrollum 125 NB 3202
Rubha Bolum 112 NF 8328
Rubha Buidhe 123 NG 7812
Rubha Cam nan Gall 124 NF 8847
Rubha Caol 131 NB 2447
Rubha Carrach 111 NM 4670
Rubh' a'Chàirn Bhàin 92 NR 6653
Rubh' a'Chamais 98 NR 5978
Rubh' a'Chaoil 104 NM 3346
Rubha Charn nan Cearc 111 NG 5503
Rubha Chlachan 92 NR 6106
Rubh' a'Chnaip 105 NM 7810
Rubh' a' Choin 132 NC 0314
Rubha Chràiginis 104 NL 9245
Rubh' a'Chrois-aoinidh 98 NR 5080
Rubha Chuaig 123 NG 6959
Rubha Còigeach 132 NB 9818
Rubha Crago 125 NG 2397
Rubha Creagan Dubha 92 NR 9352
Rubha Dubh (Colonsay) 98 NR 3991
Rubha Dubh (Island of Mull) 105 NM 5621
Rubha Dubh (Tiree) 104 NM 0948
Rubha Dubh Tighary 124 NF 7072
Rubha Dùin Bhàin 92 NR 5914
Rubha Fàsachd 110 NM 1652
Rubha Garbh àird 105 NM 8736
Rubha Garbh-ard 99 NR 7896
Rubh'a'Geodha 98 NR 4399
Rubha Ghlamraidh 98 NR 1758
Rubha Hellisdale 112 NF 8430
Rubha Hogh 110 NM 1759
Rubha Hunish 125 NG 4077
Rubha Iosal 131 NB 4216
Rubh' Aird an Fheidh 111 NM 6375
Rubh' Aird an t-Sionnaich 132 NC 1443
Rubh' Aird-mhicheil 112 NF 7233
Rubh' Aird na Sgitheich 98 NR 4779
Rubha Lamanais 98 NR 2068
Rubha Langanes 110 NG 2406
Rubha Leacach 124 NB 0107
Rubha Leathan 100 NR 9261
Rubha Leathann 131 NB 3654
Rubha Leumair 132 NC 0426
Rubha Màs a' Chnuic 124 NF 9794
Rubha Meall na Hoe 112 NF 8217
Rubh a'Mhail 98 NR 4279
Rubha Mhic Gille-mhicheil 124 NF 9363
Rubh' a' Mhill Dheirg 132 NC 0228
Rubh' a' Mhucard 132 NC 1637
Rubha Mór (Barra) 112 NL 6997
Rubha Mór (Coll, Strath.) 110 NM 2464
Rubha Mór (Highld.) 132 NB 9814
Rubha Mór (Highld.) 126 NG 8696
Rubha Mór (Highld.) 106 NM 9655
Rubha Mór (Island of Mull) 105 NM 5844
Rubha Mór (Islay) 98 NR 2948
Rubha na Brèige 132 NC 0519
Rubha na Crannaig 111 NM 4984
Rubha na Creige Móire (Isle of Lewis) 131 NB 4217
Rubha na Creige Móire (South Uist) 112 NF 8320
Rubha na Faing 98 NR 1553
Rubha na Faing Móire 111 NM 6477
Rubha na Fearn 123 NG 7261
Rubha na Gainmhich 98 NR 4346
Rubha na Greine 131 NB 5633
Rubha na h-Airde 99 NR 7083
Rubha na h-Airde Glaise 123 NG 5145
Rubha na h-Airde Uinnsinn 111 NM 8752
Rubha na h-Aiseig 123 NG 4476
Rubha na h-Easgainne 123 NG 5211
Rubha na h-Ordaig 112 NF 8414
Rubha na h-Uamha 105 NM 4028
Rubha na h-Uamha-sàile 98 NR 6094
Rubha na' Leac 123 NG 5938
Rubha na Leacaig 132 NC 2055
Rubha nam Bàirneach 131 NB 5531
Rubha nam Bàrr 99 NR 7491
Rubha nam Bràithrean 105 NM 4317
Rubha nam Brathairean 123 NG 5262
Rubha na Mèise Bàine 98 NR 3341
Rubha nam Faoilean 105 NM 6704
Rubha nam Maol Móra 104 NM 3316
Rubha nam Meirleach 110 NM 3691
Rubha nam Plèac 124 NF 9467
Rubha nan Cearc 104 NM 3225
Rubha nan Clach 122 NG 3033
Rubha nan Còsan 132 NC 0734
Rubha nan Crann 98 NR 6181
Rubha nan Eun 112 NF 7307
Rubha nan Gall (Island of Mull) 111 NM 5056
Rubha nan Gall (Ulva) 105 NM 4141
Rubha nan Leacan 98 NR 3140
Rubha nan Oirean 110 NM 3551
Rubha nan Sàsan 126 NG 8192
Rubha nan Sgarbh (Highld.) 129 NH 7087
Rubha nan Sgarbh (Strath.) 92 NR 8033
Rubha nan Totag 124 NB 0303
Rubha nan Tri Chlach 111 NM 4989
Rubha na Rodagrich 124 NF 8953
Rubha na Roinne 111 NG 4200
Rubha na Seann Charraige 104 NM 0445
Rubha na Stròine 104 NM 3642
Rubha na Tràille 98 NR 5162
Rubh' an Dùnain (Island of Skye) 122 NG 3816
Rubh' an Dùnain (Isle of Lewis) 131 NB 2448
Rubha Nead a' Gheòidh 104 NM 0946
Rubh' an Fhir Léithe 132 NC 1863
Rubh' an Teampuill 124 NF 9791
Rubh' an Tòrra Mhóir 123 NG 5333
Rubh' an t-Sàilein 98 NR 5082
Rubh' an t-Suibhein 104 NM 3645
Rubh 'Aoineadh Mhéinis 105 NM 6521
Rubha Port Bhiosd 104 NL 9648
Rubha Port na Caranean 111 NM 4298
Rubha Port Scolpaig 124 NF 7068
Rubha Quidnish 125 NG 1086
Rubha Raonuill 111 NM 7399
Rubha Raouill 124 NF 7166
Rubh' Ardalanish 104 NM 3516
Rubh' Ard na Bà 126 NG 8584
Rubha Réidh 126 NG 7391
Rubha Righinn 105 NM 7002
Rubh' Arisaig 111 NM 6184
Rubha Rodha 132 NC 0523
Rubha Romagi 124 NG 0396
Rubha Rossel 112 NF 8734
Rubha Ruadh (Highld.) 132 NC 1651
Rubha Ruadh (Highld.) 111 NG 8208
Rubha Seanach 105 NM 8025
Rubha Sgeirigin 124 NF 9998
Rubha Sgorr an t-Snidhe 110 NM 3493

Rubha Shamhnan Insir 110 NG 3704
Rubha Suisnish 123 NG 5815
Rubha Thormaid 133 NC 5467
Rubha Tràigh an Dùin 104 NM 0343
Rubh' Dubh 131 NB 5229
Rubh Fiart 105 NM 7835
Ru Chorachan 122 NG 3761
Ruckcroft 83 NY 5344
Ruckinge 31 TR 0233
Ruckland 77 TF 3378
Ruckley 59 SJ 5300
Ruddington 61 SK 5733
Ruddons Point 103 NO 4500
Rudge 33 ST 8252
Rudgeway 33 ST 6286
Rudgwick 28 TQ 0934
Rudhall 45 SO 6225
Rudland Rigg 85 SE 6495
Rudloe 33 ST 8470
Rudry 41 ST 1986
Rudston 81 TA 0967
Rudyard 70 SJ 9557
Rudyard Resr. 70 SJ 9459
Rue Point 76 NX 4003
Rueval (mt.) 124 NF 8253
Rufford 68 SD 4515
Rufforth 79 SE 5251
Rufus Stone (ant.) 26 SU 2612
Rugby 51 SP 5075
Rugeley 60 SK 0418
Ruilick 128 NH 5046
Ruinsival (mt.) 110 NM 3594
Ruisgarry 124 NF 9282
Ruishton 24 ST 2624
Ruislip 36 TQ 0987
Ruislip Common 36 TQ 0789
Rumble (is.) 141 HU 6060
Rumbling Bridge 102 NT 0199
Rumblings (is.) 143 HP 6019
Rumburgh 55 TM 3581
Rumford 19 SW 8970
Rumley Point 136 ND 4894
Rumney 41 ST 2179
Rumps Point 19 SW 9381
Rumsdale Water 134 NC 9840
Rumster Forest 135 ND 2038
Runcorn 69 SJ 5182
Runcton 27 SU 8802
Runcton Holme 64 TF 6109
Runfold 35 SU 8747
Runhall 64 TG 0507
Runham 65 TG 4610
Runnel Stone 18 SW 3720
Runnington 24 ST 1121
Runswick 85 NZ 8016
Runtaleave 108 NO 2867
Runwell 38 TQ 7494
Ruperra Castle 41 ST 2186
Rushall (Here. and Worc.) 46 SO 6434
Rushall (Norf.) 55 TM 1982
Rushall (Wilts.) 34 SU 1255
Rushall (W Mids.) 60 SK 0201
Rushbrooke 54 TL 8961
Rushbury 48 SO 5191
Rushden (Herts.) 53 TL 3031
Rushden (Northants.) 52 SP 9566
Rushford 54 TL 9281
Rush Green 37 TQ 5187
Rushlake Green 29 TQ 6218
Rushmere 55 TM 4987
Rushmere St. Andrew 55 TM 2046
Rushmoor 35 SU 8740
Rushmore House 26 ST 9518
Rushock 49 SO 8871
Rusholme 69 SJ 8494
Rushton (Ches.) 69 SJ 5863
Rushton (Northants.) 52 SP 8483
Rushton (Shrops.) 59 SJ 6008
Rushton Spencer 69 SJ 9363
Rushwick 49 SO 8353
Rushyford 84 NZ 2828
Rushy Knowe 90 NY 9299
Rusk Holm 138 HY 5136
Ruskie 101 NN 6200
Ruskington 62 TF 0850
Rusland 77 SD 3488
Rusper 28 TQ 2037
Ruspidge 46 SO 6512
Russaness Hill 141 HU 3749
Russell's Water 36 SU 7089
Rustington 28 TQ 0502
Ruston Parva 81 TA 0661
Ruswarp 87 NZ 8809
Rutherford 98 NT 6530
Rutherglen 101 NS 6161
Ruthernbridge 19 SX 0166
Ruthin 68 SJ 1257
Ruthrieston 119 NJ 9204
Ruthven (Grampn.) 121 NJ 5046
Ruthven (Highld.) 116 NH 8133
Ruthven (Tays.) 108 NO 2848
Ruthven Barracks 116 NN 7699
Ruthven House 108 NO 3048
Ruthvoes 19 SW 9360
Ruthwell 89 NY 1067
Rutland Water 62 SK 9307
Rutupiae (ant.) 31 TR 3060
Ruyton-XI-Towns 58 SJ 3922
Ryal 91 NZ 0174
Ryal Fold 77 SD 6621
Ryall 24 SY 4094
Ryarsh 30 TQ 6659
Rydal 82 NY 3606
Rydal Fell 82 NY 3609
Rydal Water 82 NY 3606
Ryde 27 SZ 5992
Ryde Roads 27 SZ 5894
Ryder's Hill 21 SX 6569
Rye 30 TQ 9220
Rye Bay 31 TQ 9617
Rye Dale 79 SE 5982
Rye Foreign 30 TQ 8822
Rye Harbour 30 TQ 9419
Rye Water 93 NS 2752
Ryhall 62 TF 0311
Ryhill 71 SE 3814
Ryhope 85 NZ 4152
Ryknild Street (Derby.) (ant.) 60 SK 2930
Ryknild Street (Derby.) (ant.) 60 SK 3848
Ryknild Street (Warw.) (ant.) 50 SP 0762
Rylstone 78 SD 9758
Ryme Intrinseca 25 ST 5810
Rysa Little (is.) 136 ND 3197
Ryther 79 SE 5539
Ryton (Glos.) 46 SO 7232
Ryton (N Yorks.) 80 SE 7975
Ryton (Shrops.) 59 SJ 7502
Ryton (Tyne and Wear) 91 NZ 1564
Ryton-on-Dunsmore 50 SP 3874

S

Sabden 78 SD 7737
Sabden Brook 78 SD 7535
Sàbhal Beag 132 NC 3742
Sacombe 37 TL 3419
Sacquoy Head 138 HY 3835
Sacriston 84 NZ 2447
Sadberge 85 NZ 3416
Saddell 92 NR 7832
Saddell Bay 92 NR 7931
Saddell Glen 92 NR 7832
Saddington 51 SP 6591
Saddington Resr. 51 SP 6691
Saddleback or Blencathra (ant.) 82 NY 3227
Saddle Bow 64 TF 6015
Saddle Hill 129 NH 7843
Saddle, The (Highld.) (mt.) 114 NG 9313
Saddle, The (Strath.) (mt.) 100 NS 2296
Saddleworth Moor 70 SE 0305
Saddle Yoke 89 NT 1412
Sadgill 83 NY 4805
Sae Breck (mt.) 142 HU 2178
Saffron Walden 53 TL 5438
Saham Toney 64 TF 9002
Saighton 68 SJ 4462
Sail Chalmadale 92 NR 9139
Sàil Mhòr (mt.) 126 NH 0388
St. Abbs 97 NT 9167
St. Abb's Head 97 NT 9169
St. Agnes (Corn.) 18 SW 7150
St. Agnes (Is. of Sc.) (is.) 18 SV 8807
St. Agnes Head 18 SW 6951
St. Albans 37 TL 1507
St. Alban's or St. Aldhelm's Head 26 SY 9675
St. Aldhelm's or St. Alban's Head 26 SY 9675
St. Allen 19 SW 8250
St. Andrews 103 NO 5016
St. Andrews Bay 109 NO 5318
St. Andrews Major 41 ST 1471
St. Anne's (Lancs.) 77 SD 3129
St. Ann's (Dumf. and Galwy.) 89 NY 0793
St. Ann's Chapel (Corn.) 20 SX 4170
St. Ann's Chapel (Devon) 21 SX 6647
St. Ann's Head 42 SM 8002
St. Anthony-in-Meneage 18 SW 7725
St. Arvans 45 ST 5196
St. Asaph (Lanelwy) 67 SJ 0374
St. Athan 41 ST 0168
St. Austell 19 SX 0152
St. Austell Bay 19 SX 0650
St. Baldred's Boat (pt.) 103 NT 6184
St. Baldred's Cradle (pt.) 103 NT 6381
St. Bees 82 NX 9611
St. Bees Head 82 NX 9314
St. Blazey 19 SX 0654
St. Boswells 96 NT 5930
St. Breock 19 SW 9771
St. Breock Downs 19 SW 9668
St. Breward 19 SX 0977
St. Briavels 45 SO 5504
St. Brides 42 SM 8010
St. Brides Bay 42 SM 7917
St. Bride's Major 41 SS 8974
St. Brides Netherwent 33 ST 4289
St. Brides-super-Ely 41 ST 1078
St. Bride's Wentlooge 32 ST 2982
St. Budeaux 20 SX 4558
St. Buryan 18 SW 4025
St. Catherines 100 NN 1207
St. Catherine's Bay 137 HY 6226
St. Catherine's Dub (pt.) 121 NK 0428
St. Catherine's Point 27 SZ 4975
St. Clears 43 SN 2716
St. Cleer 19 SX 2468
St. Clement 19 SW 8443
St. Clement's Isle 18 SW 4726
St. Clether 20 SX 2084
St. Colmac 100 NS 0467
St. Colme House 102 NT 1884
St. Columb Major 19 SW 9163
St. Columb Minor 19 SW 8362
St. Columb Road 19 SW 9059
St. Combs 121 NK 0563
St. Cross South Elmham 55 TM 2984
St. Cyrus 109 NO 7464
St. David's (Dyfed) 42 SM 7525
St. Davids (Fife) 102 NT 1582
St. David's (Tays.) 108 NN 9420
St. David's Head 42 SM 7228
St. Day 18 SW 7242
St. Dennis 19 SW 9558
St. Devereux 45 SO 4431
St. Dogmaels 42 SN 1646
St. Dogwells 42 SM 9728
St. Dominick 20 SX 3967
St. Donats 41 SS 9368
St. Endellion 19 SW 9978
St. Enoder 19 SW 8956
St. Erme 19 SW 8449
St. Erth 18 SW 5435
St. Erth Praze 18 SW 5735
St. Ervan 19 SW 8870
St. Eval 19 SW 8769
St. Ewe 19 SW 9745
St. Fagans 41 ST 1177
St. Fergus 121 NK 0951
St. Fergus Moss 121 NK 0553
St. Fillans 107 NN 6924
St. Florence 42 SN 0801
St. Gennys 20 SX 1497
St. George (Clwyd) 67 SH 9775
St. George's (S Glam.) 41 ST 0976
St. George's or Looe Island 19 SX 2551
St. Germans 20 SX 3557
St. Giles in the Wood 23 SS 5318
St. Giles-on-the-Heath 20 SX 3590
St. Govan's Head 42 SR 9792
St. Gwynno Forest 41 ST 0396
St. Harmon 57 SN 9872
St. Helena 65 TG 1816
St. Helen Auckland 84 NZ 1826
St. Helens (I. of W.) 27 SZ 6288
St. Helen's (Is. of Sc.) (is.) 18 SV 9017
St. Helens (Mers.) 69 SJ 5095
St. Hilary (Corn.) 18 SW 5531
St. Hilary (S Glam.) 41 ST 0173
St. Illtyd 41 SO 2102
St. Ippollitts 52 TL 1927
St. Ishmael's 42 SM 8307
St. Issey 19 SW 9271
St. Ive (Corn.) 20 SX 3167
St. Ives (Cambs.) 53 TL 3171
St. Ives (Corn.) 18 SW 5140
St. Ives (Dorset) 26 SU 1203
St. Ives Bay 18 SW 5441
St. James South Elmham 55 TM 3281
St. John (Corn.) 20 SX 4053
St. John's (Durham) 84 NZ 0634
St. Johns (Here. and Worc.) 49 SO 8453
St. John's (I. of M.) 76 SC 2781
St. John's Beck 82 NY 3123
St. John's Chapel 84 NY 8837
St. John's Fen End 63 TF 5311
St. John's Head 136 HY 1803
St. John's Highway 63 TF 5314
St. John's Loch 135 ND 2272
St. John's Point 135 ND 3175
St. John's Town of Dalry 88 NX 6281
St. Jude's 76 SC 3996
St. Just 18 SW 3631
St. Just in Roseland 19 SW 8435
St. Katherines 121 NJ 7834
St. Keverne 18 SW 7821
St. Kew 19 SX 0276
St. Kew Highway 19 SX 0375
St. Keyne 19 SX 2460
St. Kilda or Hirta (is.) 124 NF 0999
St. Lawrence (Corn.) 19 SX 0466
Saintbury 50 SP 1139
Saint Hill 29 TQ 3835
St. Lawrence (Essex) 39 TL 9604
St. Lawrence (I. of W.) 27 SZ 5476
St. Leonards (Bucks.) 36 SP 9006
St. Leonards (Dorset) 26 SU 1002
St. Leonards (E Susx) 30 TQ 8009
St. Leonard's Forest 28 TQ 2231
St. Levan 18 SW 3722
St. Lythans 41 ST 1073
St. Mabyn 19 SX 0373
St. Magnus Bay 142 HU 2568
St. Magnus's Church (ant.) 138 HY 4630
St. Margarets 45 SO 3534
St. Margaret's at Cliffe 31 TR 3644
St. Margaret's Bay 31 TR 3744
St. Margaret's Hope (Fife) 102 NT 1181
St. Margaret's Hope (S. Ronaldsay) 136 ND 4493
St. Margaret South Elmham 55 TM 3183
St. Mark's 76 SC 2974
St. Martin 18 SW 7324
St. Martin (Corn.) 19 SX 2555
St. Martin's (Is. of Sc.) 18 SV 9215
St. Martin's (Shrops.) 58 SJ 3236
St. Martins (Tays.) 108 NO 1530
St. Mary Bourne 34 SU 4250
St. Mary Church 41 ST 0071
St. Mary Cray 37 TQ 4767
St. Mary Hill 41 SS 9678
St. Mary Hoo 30 TQ 8076
St. Mary in the Marsh 31 TR 0628
St. Mary's (Is. of Sc.) (is.) 18 SV 9111
St. Mary's (Orkney) 136 HY 4701
St. Mary's Bay 31 TR 0927
St. Mary's Grove 33 ST 4769
St. Mary's Isle 87 NX 6749
St. Mary's Loch 95 NT 2422
St. Mary's Marshes 38 TQ 8078
St. Mary's or Bait Island 91 NZ 3575
St. Mary's or Newton Haven 97 NU 2424
St. Mary's Sound 18 SV 8909
St. Mawes 19 SW 8433
St. Mawgan 19 SW 8765
St. Mellion 20 SX 3865
St. Mellons 41 ST 2281
St. Merryn 19 SW 8874
St. Mewan 19 SW 9951
St. Michael Caerhays 19 SW 9642
St. Michael Penkevil 19 SW 8542
St. Michaels (Here. and Worc.) 48 SO 5765
St. Michaels (Kent) 30 TQ 8835
St. Michael's Island 76 SC 2967
St. Michael's Mount 18 SW 5130
St. Michael's on Wyre 77 SD 4640
St. Michael South Elmham 55 TM 3483
St. Minver 19 SW 9677
St. Monance 103 NO 5201
St. Neot (Corn.) 19 SX 1867
St. Neots (Cambs.) 52 TL 1860
St. Newlyn East 19 SW 8356
St. Nicholas (Dyfed) 42 SM 9035
St. Nicholas (S Glam.) 41 ST 0874
St. Nicholas at Wade 31 TR 2666
St. Ninians 101 NS 7991
St. Ninian's Cave 87 NX 4236
St. Ninian's Chapel 87 NX 4836
St. Ninian's Isle 141 HU 3621
St. Ninian's Point 100 NS 0361
St. Osyth 39 TM 1215
St. Osyth Marsh 39 TM 1113
St. Owen's Cross 45 SO 5324
St. Pancras Station 37 TQ 2982
St. Patrick's Isle 76 SC 2484
St. Pauls Cray 37 TQ 4768
St. Paul's Walden 37 TL 1922
St. Peter's 31 TR 3668
St. Peter's Flat (sbk.) 39 TM 0408
St. Petrox 42 SR 9797
St. Pinnock 19 SX 2063
St. Quivox 93 NS 3723
St. Radegund's Abbey 31 TR 2471
St. Serf's Island 102 NO 1500
St. Stephen (Corn.) 19 SW 9453
St. Stephens (Corn.) 20 SX 3285
St. Stephen's (Corn.) 20 SX 4158
St. Teath 19 SX 0680
St. Tudwal's Islands 56 SH 3425
St. Tudwal's Road 56 SH 3328
St. Tudy 19 SX 0676
St. Twynnells 42 SR 9597
St. Vigeans 109 NO 6443
St. Wenn 19 SW 9664
St. Weonards 45 SO 4924
St. Winnow 19 SX 1157
S Airde Beinn 111 NM 4753
Salachan Glen 106 NM 9852
Salcey Forest 51 SP 7951
Salcombe 21 SX 7338
Salcombe Regis 24 SY 1488
Salcott 38 TL 9413
Sale 69 SJ 7990
Saleby 73 TF 4578
Sale Green 49 SO 9358
Salehurst 29 TQ 7424
Salem (Dyfed) 43 SN 6226
Salem (Dyfed) 57 SN 6684
Salem (Gwyn.) 66 SH 5456
Salen (Highld.) 111 NM 6864
Salen (Island of Mull) 105 NM 5743
Salen Forest (Strath.) 105 NM 5347
Salen Forest (Strath.) 105 NM 6739
Salesbury 77 SD 6732
Sales Point 39 TM 0209
Salford (Beds.) 52 SP 9339
Salford (Gtr Mches.) 69 SJ 7796
Salford (Oxon.) 47 SP 2828
Salford Priors 50 SP 0751
Salfords 29 TQ 2846
Salhouse 65 TG 3114
Saligo Bay 98 NR 2066
Saline 102 NT 0292
Salisbury 26 SU 1429
Salisbury Plain 34 SU 0645
Sallachan Point 106 NM 9961
Sallachy (Highld.) 128 NC 5408
Sallachy (Highld.) 114 NG 9130
Salle 65 TG 1024
Salmonby 73 TF 3273
Salmond's Muir 109 NO 5837
Salperton 46 SP 0720
Salph End 52 TL 0752
Salsburgh 101 NS 8262
Salt 60 SJ 9527
Saltash 20 SX 4259
Saltburn 129 NH 7269
Saltburn-by-the-Sea 85 NZ 6621
Saltby 62 SK 8426
Saltcoats 93 NS 2441
Saltdean 29 TQ 3802
Salter 77 SD 6073
Salterforth 78 SD 8845
Saltergate 80 SE 8594
Salter's Bank (sbk.) 77 SD 3126
Saltersbrook Bridge 70 SE 1300
Salterswall 69 SJ 6267
Saltfleet 73 TF 4593
Saltfleetby All Saints 73 TF 4590
Saltfleetby St. Clements 73 TF 4591
Saltfleetby St. Peter 73 TF 4389
Saltford 33 ST 6867
Salthaugh Grange 75 TA 2321
Salthouse 64 TG 0743
Salt Island 66 SH 2583
Saltmarshe 74 SE 7824
Saltney 68 SJ 3864
Saltom Bay 82 NX 9515
Salton 80 SE 7180
Salt Scar 85 NZ 6126
Saltwick 91 NZ 1780
Saltwick Bay 81 NZ 9211
Saltwood 31 TR 1536
Salum 104 NM 0648
Salwarpe 49 SO 8762
Salwayash 25 SY 4596
Salwick Station 77 SD 4632
Samala 124 NF 7962
Samalaman Island 111 NM 6678
Samalan Island 105 NM 4536
Sambourne 50 SP 0561
Sambrook 59 SJ 7124
Samlesbury 77 SD 5829
Samlesbury Aerodrome 77 SD 6230
Samlesbury Bottoms 77 SD 6229
Sampford Arundel 24 ST 1018
Sampford Brett 32 ST 0940
Sampford Courtenay 23 SS 6301
Sampford Peverell 24 ST 0314
Sampford Spiney 21 SX 5372
Samphrey (is.) 143 HU 4676
Samson (is.) 18 SV 8712
Samuelston 103 NT 4870
Sanaigmore 98 NR 2370
Sancreed 18 SW 4029
Sancton 74 SE 8939
Sand 141 HU 3447
Sandaig 111 NG 7102
Sandaig Bay 111 NG 7101
Sandaig Islands 123 NG 7614
Sanda Island 92 NR 7204
Sanda Stour (is.) 141 HU 3441
Sanday (Highld.) 110 NG 2704
Sanday (Orkney) 139 HY 6841
Sanday Aerodrome 139 HY 6740
Sanday Sound 139 HY 6634
Sandbach 69 SJ 7560
Sandbank 100 NS 1580
Sandbanks 26 SZ 0487
Sand Bay 32 ST 3264
Sandend 121 NJ 5566
Sandend Bay 121 NJ 5666
Sanderstead 37 TQ 3461
Sandford (Avon) 32 ST 4159
Sandford (Cumbr.) 83 NY 7216
Sandford (Devon) 23 SS 8202
Sandford (Dorset) 25 SY 9289
Sandford (Strath.) 94 NS 7143
Sandford Bay 121 NK 1243
Sandfordhill 121 NK 1141
Sandford-on-Thames 47 SP 5301
Sandford Orcas 25 ST 6220
Sandford St. Martin 47 SP 4226
Sandgarth 137 HY 5215
Sandgate 31 TR 2035
Sandgreen 87 NX 5752
Sandhaven 121 NJ 9667
Sandhead 86 NX 0949
Sandhoe 91 NY 9766
Sandholme (Humbs.) 74 SE 8230
Sandholme (Lincs.) 63 TF 3337
Sandhurst (Berks.) 36 SU 8361
Sandhurst (Glos.) 46 SO 8223
Sandhurst (Kent) 30 TQ 8028
Sandhutton (N Yorks.) 79 SE 3881
Sand Hutton (N Yorks.) 80 SE 6958
Sandiacre 61 SK 4736
Sandilands 73 TF 5280
Sandiway 69 SJ 6070
Sandleheath 26 SU 1214
Sandleigh 47 SP 4501
Sandling 30 TQ 7558
Sandness 140 HU 1957
Sandness Hill 140 HU 1955
Sandon (Essex) 38 TL 7404
Sandon (Herts.) 53 TL 3234
Sandon (Staffs.) 59 SJ 9429
Sandown 27 SZ 5984
Sandown Airport 27 SZ 5784
Sandown Bay 27 SZ 6083
Sandplace 19 SX 2457
Sand Point 32 ST 3165
Sandray 112 NL 6491
Sandridge 37 TL 1710
Sandringham 64 TF 6928
Sandsend 85 NZ 8512
Sand Side 76 SD 2282
Sandside Bay (Highld.) 134 NC 9666
Sandside Bay (Orkney) 137 HY 5900
Sandside Burn 134 NC 9661
Sandside House 134 NC 9565
Sands of Forvie 121 NK 0126
Sands of Nigg 129 NH 7670
Sandsound 141 HU 3548
Sandsound Voe 141 HU 3548
Sandtoft 74 SE 7408
Sand Water (Shetld.) 141 HU 4154
Sand Water (Shetld.) 143 HU 4274
Sandwich 31 TR 3358
Sandwich Bay 31 TR 3759
Sandwich Flats (sbk.) 31 TR 3560
Sandwick (Cumbr.) 83 NY 4219
Sandwick (Isle of Lewis) 131 NB 4432
Sandwick (Shetld.) 141 HU 4323
Sand Wick (Shetld.) 141 HU 4324
Sandwick (Shetld.) (dist.) 141 HU 3924
Sandwick (South Uist) 124 NF 8343
Sand Wick (S. Ronaldsay) 136 ND 4388
Sandwick (S. Ronaldsay) 136 ND 4389
Sand Wick (Unst) 143 HP 6202
Sandwith 82 NX 9714
Sandwood Loch 132 NC 2364
Sandy 52 TL 1649
Sandycroft 68 SJ 3366
Sandy Edge 90 NT 5201
Sandygate 76 SC 3797
Sandy Lane 34 ST 9668
Sangobeg 133 NC 4266
Sanna 111 NM 4469
Sanna Bay 111 NM 4368
Sanna Point 111 NM 4370
Sannox Bay 92 NS 0145
Sanquhar 88 NS 7809
Santon 74 SE 9312
Santon Bridge 82 NY 1001
Santon Downham 54 TL 8187
Santon Head 76 SC 3370
Sapcote 51 SP 4893
Sapey Common 49 SO 7064
Sapiston 54 TL 9175
Sapperton (Glos.) 46 SO 9403
Sapperton (Lincs.) 62 TF 0133
Saracen's Head 63 TF 3427
Sarclet 135 ND 3443
Sarclet Head 135 ND 3543
Sarisbury 27 SU 5008
Sarkfoot Point 89 NY 3264
Sarn (Mid Glam.) 41 SS 9083
Sarn (Powys) 48 SO 2090
Sarnau (Dyfed) 43 SN 3151
Sarnau (Dyfed) 43 SN 3318
Sarnau (Gwyn.) 67 SH 9739
Sarnau (Powys) 58 SJ 2315
Sarn-bâch 56 SH 3026
Sarnesfield 45 SO 3750
Sarn Helen (Dyfed) (ant.) 43 SN 6449
Sarn Helen (Gwyn.) (ant.) 67 SH 7229
Sarn Meyllteyrn 66 SH 2432
Saron (Dyfed) 43 SN 3738
Saron (Dyfed) 43 SN 6012
Sarratt 36 TQ 0499
Sarre 31 TR 2565
Sarsden 47 SP 2822
Sarsgrum 132 NC 3764
Satley 84 NZ 1143
Satterleigh 23 SS 6622
Satterthwaite 82 SD 3392
Sauchar Point 103 NT 4999
Sauchen 119 NJ 7010
Saucher 108 NO 1933
Sauchieburn 109 NO 6669
Sauchie Law 89 NT 2910
Sauchrie 93 NS 3014
Saughall 68 SJ 3669
Saugh Hill 86 NX 2197
Saughtree 90 NY 5696
Saughtree Fell 90 NY 5599
Saul 46 SO 7409
Saundby 72 SK 7888
Saundersfoot 42 SN 1304
Saundersfoot Station 42 SN 1206
Saunderton 36 SP 7901
Saunderton Station 36 SU 8198
Saunton 22 SS 4537
Sausthorpe 73 TF 3869
Saval 128 NC 5908
Savary 105 NM 6346
Savernake Forest 34 SU 2266
Saviskaill Bay 138 HY 4133
Saviskaill Head 138 HY 4035
Sawbridgeworth 37 TL 4814
Sawdon 81 SE 9485
Sawley (Derby.) 61 SK 4731
Sawley (Lancs.) 78 SD 7746
Sawley (N Yorks.) 79 SE 2467
Sawrey 82 SD 3695
Sawston 53 TL 4849
Sawtry 52 TL 1683
Saxa Vord (mt.) 143 HP 6316
Saxby (Leic.) 62 SK 8220
Saxby (Lincs.) 72 TF 0086
Saxby All Saints 74 SE 9816
Saxelbye 61 SK 6921
Saxilby 72 SK 8875
Saxlingham 64 TG 0239
Saxlingham Nethergate 65 TM 2397
Saxmundham 55 TM 3863
Saxondale 61 SK 6840
Saxon Street 54 TL 6859
Saxtead 55 TM 2665
Saxtead Green 55 TM 2564
Saxthorpe 65 TG 1130
Saxton 79 SE 4736
Sayers Common 28 TQ 2618
Scabbacombe Head 21 SX 9251
Scabra Head 138 HY 3631
Scackleton 79 SE 6472
Scadabay 125 NG 1792
Scad Head 136 HY 2900
Sca Fell 82 NY 2006
Scafell Pikes 82 NY 2107
Scaftworth 71 SK 6691
Scagglethorpe 80 SE 8372
Scaladale River 131 NB 1709
Scalasaig 98 NR 3894
Scalby 81 TA 0090
Scalby Ness Rocks 81 TA 0391
Scald Law 103 NT 1961
Scaldwell 51 SP 7672
Scaleby 89 NY 4563
Scaleby Hill 89 NY 4363
Scale Houses 83 NY 5845
Scales (Cumbr.) 82 NY 3426
Scales (Cumbr.) 77 SD 2772
Scales Moor 77 SD 7176
Scalford 61 SK 7624
Scaling 85 NZ 7413
Scaling Resr. 85 NZ 7412
Scalla Field (mt.) 141 HU 3857
Scallastle 105 NM 6938
Scallastle Bay 105 NM 6939
Scalloway 141 HU 4039
Scalpay (Harris, W Isles) 125 NG 2395
Scalpay (Island of Skye) 123 NG 6030
Scalpay House 123 NG 6328
Scalpsie Bay 100 NS 0558
Scalp, The (mt.) 121 NJ 3636
Scamblesby 73 TF 2778
Scammonden Resr. 70 SE 0416
Scamodale 111 NM 8473
Scampston 80 SE 8575
Scampton 72 SK 9479
Scapa 136 HY 4309
Scapa Bay 136 HY 4307
Scapa Flow (roadstead) 136 ND 3899
Scar 139 HY 6745
Scaraben (mt.) 135 ND 0626
Scarastavore 124 NG 0092
Scaravay 124 NG 0177
Scarba 105 NM 7004
Scarborough 81 TA 0388
Scarcliffe 71 SK 4968
Scarcroft 79 SE 3540
Scardroy 127 NH 2151
Scares (is.) 86 NX 2634
Scarff 142 HU 2480
Scarfskerry 135 ND 2673
Scarfskerry Point 135 ND 2674
Scargill 84 NZ 0510
Scargill High Moor 84 NZ 0009
Scargill Resr. 79 SE 2353
Scar Hill 118 NJ 4801
Scar House Reservoir 78 SE 0576
Scarinish 104 NM 0444
Scarisbrick 68 SD 3713
Scarning 64 TF 9512
Scarp (is.) 130 NA 9715
Scarrington 61 SK 7341
Scars, The 91 NZ 2993
Scarth Gap Pass 82 NY 1813
Scarth Hill 68 SD 4206
Scartho 75 TA 2606
Scarva Taing 137 HY 5708
Scar Water 88 NX 8195
Scarweather (lightship) 40 SS 6574
Scat Ness 141 HU 3809
Scatsta 143 HU 3972
Scaur Hill 95 NS 8830
Scaur or Kippford 87 NX 8355
Scawby 74 SE 9605
Scawton 79 SE 5483
Scayne's Hill 29 TQ 3723
Scethrog 41 SO 1025
Schiehallion (mt.) 107 NN 7154
Schil, The 97 NT 8722
Scholar Green 69 SJ 8357
Scholes (W Yorks.) 70 SE 1507
Scholes (W Yorks.) 71 SE 3736
Schooner Point 110 NM 3090
Scleddau 42 SM 9434
Scoat Fell 82 NY 1511
Scock Ness 138 HY 4532
Scole 55 TM 1579
Scolpaig 124 NF 7275
Scolton 42 SM 9922
Scolty 119 NO 6793
Sconce (pt.) 26 SZ 3389

Scone Palace 108 NO 1126
Sconser 123 NG 5232
Scoor 105 NM 4119
Scootmore Forest 117 NJ 1638
Scopwick 72 TF 0658
Scoraig 126 NH 0096
Scorborough 74 TA 0145
Score Head 141 HU 5145
Score Horan 122 NG 2859
Scorrier 18 SW 7244
Scorton (Lancs.) 77 SD 5048
Scorton (N Yorks.) 84 NZ 2400
Sco Ruston 65 TG 2821
Scotasay 125 NG 1897
Scotby 83 NY 4455
Scotch Corner 84 NZ 2104
Scotforth 77 SD 4759
Scothern 72 TF 0377
Scotland Gate 91 NZ 2584
Scotlandwell 102 NO 1801
Scotney Castle 29 TQ 6835
Scotsburn 129 NH 7275
Scotscalder Station 135 ND 0956
Scotscraig 109 NO 4428
Scots' Gap 91 NZ 0486
Scotston 108 NN 9042
Scotston Hill 100 NR 9090
Scotstown 111 NM 8263
Scotstown Head 121 NK 1151
Scottarie Burn 129 NC 7907
Scottas 111 NG 7500
Scotter 74 SE 8800
Scotterthorpe 74 SE 8701
Scotton (Lincs.) 74 SK 8899
Scotton (N Yorks.) 84 SE 1895
Scotton (N Yorks.) 79 SE 3259
Scottow 65 TG 2623
Scoughall 103 NT 6183
Scoulag Point 100 NS 1160
Scoulton 64 TF 9800
Scoured Rig 96 NT 5851
Scourie 132 NC 1544
Scourie Bay 132 NC 1445
Scousburgh 141 HU 3717
Scout Hill 77 SD 5682
Scrabster 135 ND 0970
Scrainwood 91 NT 9909
Scrane End 63 TF 3841
Scraptoft 61 SK 6405
Scratby 65 TG 5115
Scratchbury (ant.) 33 ST 9144
Scrayingham 80 SE 7360
Screapadal 123 NG 5844
Scredington 62 TF 0940
Screel Hill 87 NX 7855
Screes, The 82 NY 1503
Scremby 73 TF 4467
Scremerston 97 NU 0049
Screveton 61 SK 7343
Scriven 79 SE 3458
Scrooby 71 SK 6590
Scropton 60 SK 1930
Scrub Hill 63 TF 2355
Scruton 84 SE 2992
Sculthorpe 64 TF 8931
Scunthorpe 74 SE 8910
Scurdie Ness 109 NO 7356
Scurrival Point 112 NF 6909
Scuthvie Bay 139 HY 7744
Seaborough 25 ST 4205
Seacombe 68 SJ 3190
Seacombe Cliff 26 SY 9876
Seacroft 73 TF 5660
Seafield 102 NT 0066
Seafield Tower (ant.) 103 NT 2788
Seaford 29 TV 4899
Seaforth 68 SJ 3297
Seaforth Head 131 NB 2916
Seaforth Island 131 NB 2010
Sea Geo 136 ND 4995
Seagrave 61 SK 6117
Seaham 85 NZ 4149
Seahouses 97 NU 2132
Seal 29 TQ 5556
Sealand 68 SJ 3568
Sealky Head 135 ND 3852
Seal Sand (Norf.) 63 TF 5635
Seal Sands (Cleve.) 85 NZ 5224
Seal Skerry (Eday) 138 HY 5331
Seal Skerry (N. Ronaldsay) 139 HY 7856
Seamer (N Yorks.) 85 NZ 4910
Seamer (N Yorks.) 81 TA 0183
Seamill 93 NS 2047
Seana Bhraigh 127 NH 2887
Seana Chamas 126 NG 7484
Sea of the Hebrides 112 NF 9209
Sea Palling 65 TG 4327
Searby 74 TA 0605
Seasalter 31 TR 0864
Seascale 82 NY 0301
Seatallan (mt.) 82 NY 1308
Seathorne 73 TF 5666
Seathwaite (Cumbr.) 82 NY 2312
Seathwaite (Cumbr.) 82 SD 2296
Seathwaite Tarn 82 SD 2598
Seaton (Corn.) 20 SX 3054
Seaton (Cumbr.) 82 NY 0130
Seaton (Devon) 24 SY 2490
Seaton (Durham) 85 NZ 4049
Seaton (Humbs.) 75 TA 1646
Seaton (Leic.) 62 SP 9098
Seaton (Northum.) 91 NZ 3276
Seaton Bay 24 SY 2489
Seaton Burn 91 NZ 2374
Seaton Carew 85 NZ 5229
Seaton Delaval 91 NZ 3075
Seaton Ross 74 SE 7741
Seaton Sluice 91 NZ 3376
Seat Sandal (mt.) 82 NY 3411
Seave Green 85 NZ 5600
Seaview 27 SZ 6291
Seavington St. Mary 24 ST 3914
Seavington St. Michael 24 ST 4015
Sebastapol 45 ST 2999
Sebergham 82 NY 3541
Seckington 60 SK 2607
Sedbergh 83 SD 6592
Sedbury 45 ST 5493
Sedbusk 84 SD 8891
Sedgeberrow 50 SP 0238
Sedgebrook 62 SK 8537
Sedgefield 85 NZ 3528
Sedgeford 64 TF 7136
Sedgehill 25 ST 8627
Sedgemoor Battle (ant.) 24 ST 3535
Sedgley 59 SO 9193
Sedgwick 77 SD 5186
Sedlescombe 30 TQ 7818
Seend 34 ST 9460
Seend Cleeve 33 ST 9260
Seer Green 36 SU 9691
Seething 65 TM 3197
Sefton 68 SD 3500
Seggie Burn 141 HU 4364
Seghill 91 NZ 2874
Segsbury (ant.) 34 SU 3884
Seighford 59 SJ 8725
Seil 105 NM 7618
Seilebost 125 NG 0696
Seilebost River 125 NG 0695
Seil Sound 105 NM 7715
Seisdon 59 SO 8394
Selattyn 58 SJ 2633
Selborne 27 SU 7433
Selby 79 SE 6132
Selby Canal 79 SE 5829
Selcoth Burn 89 NT 1406
Selham 28 SU 9320
Seli Voe 140 HU 2848
Selker Bay 76 SD 0788
Selkirk 96 NT 4728
Sellack 45 SO 5627
Sellafield Station 82 NY 0203
Sellafirth 143 HU 5297
Sellindge 31 TR 0938
Selling 31 TR 0356
Sells Green 34 ST 9462
Selly Oak 50 SP 0482
Selmeston 29 TQ 5007
Selsdon 37 TQ 3562
Selset Reservoir 84 NY 9121
Selsey 27 SZ 8593
Selsey Bill (pt.) 27 SZ 8592
Selsfield Common 29 TQ 3434
Selston 61 SK 4553
Selworthy 23 SS 9146
Selworthy Beacon 23 SS 9148
Semblister 141 HU 3350
Semer 54 TL 9946
Semer Water 78 SD 9287
Semington 33 ST 8960
Semley 25 ST 8926
Send 28 TQ 0155
Senghenydd 41 ST 1191
Sennen 18 SW 3525
Sennen Cove 18 SW 3425
Sennybridge 41 SN 9228
Seolait Mhic Neacail (roadstead) 124 NF 9676
Sessay 79 SE 4575
Setchey 64 TF 6313
Setley 26 SU 3000
Seton House 103 NT 4175
Setter (Bressay) 141 HU 5141
Setter (Shetld.) 141 HU 3954
Setter Hill 141 HU 4043
Settiscarth 136 HY 3618
Settle 78 SD 8263
Settrington 80 SE 8370
Sevenhampton (Glos.) 46 SP 0321
Sevenhampton (Wilts.) 34 SU 2090
Seven Kings 37 TQ 4586
Sevenoaks 29 TQ 5355
Sevenoaks Weald 29 TQ 5351
Seven Sisters 41 SN 8108
Seven Stones 18 SW 0424
Severn Beach 33 ST 5384
Severn Road Bridge 33 ST 5590
Severn Stoke 49 SO 8544
Severn Tunnel 33 ST 5286
Severn Tunnel Junction Station 33 ST 4787
Severn Valley Railway 49 SO 7585
Sevington 31 TR 0340
Sewards End 53 TL 5738
Sewerby 81 TA 2068
Seworgan 18 SW 7030
Sewstern 62 SK 8821
Sezincote 47 SP 1731
Sgairail 98 NR 3575
Sgaoth Aird (mt.) 125 NB 1603
Sgarbh Breac 98 NR 4076
Sgarbh Dubh 98 NR 3675
Sgeir a' Chàil 124 NF 9679
Sgeir a' Mhàim-ard 111 NM 4193
Sgeir a' Mhill 112 NF 8312
Sgeir Dhearg 123 NG 6332
Sgeir Dhoirbh 104 NM 2811
Sgeir Eskernish 111 NM 4484
Sgeir Fiavig Tarras 130 NB 0235
Sgeir Ghlas 123 NG 7366
Sgeir Leathann 131 NB 5041
Sgeir Liath (Barra) 112 NF 6503
Sgeir Liath (Isle of Lewis) 124 NG 0093
Sgeir Mhòr (Highld.) 111 NM 6693
Sgeir Mhór (Island of Skye) 123 NG 4943
Sgeir na Eireann 123 NG 4872
Sgeir na Faoilinn 105 NM 4130
Sgeir nam Biast 122 NG 2356
Sgeir nam Maol 125 NG 3981
Sgeir nan Gabhar 105 NM 6805
Sgeir nan Gall 132 NC 0835
Sgeir na Trian 123 NG 7364
Sgeir Orival 124 NF 7377
Sgeir Thraid 123 NG 6233
Sgiath Bhuidhe 107 NN 4639
Sgòrach Breac 123 NG 6513
Sgorach Mór 100 NS 0985
Sgòran Dubh Mór 117 NH 9000
Sgor Gaibhre 107 NN 4467
Sgòr Gaoith (Highld.) 117 NN 9098
Sgòr Gaoithe (Highld.) 117 NJ 0721
Sgor Mór (Grampn.) 117 NO 0091
Sgor Mór (Grampn.) 117 NO 1182
Sgor na h-Ulaidh 106 NN 1151
Sgorr an Tarmachain 111 NM 8471
Sgorr Craobh a' Chaorainn 114 NM 8976
Sgorr Mhór 110 NM 3099
Sgorr na Diollaid 115 NH 2836
Sgorr Reidh 110 NM 3197
Sgorr Ruadh 126 NG 9550
Sgreadan Hill 92 NR 7429
Sgribhis-bheinn 132 NC 3171
Sguinean nan Creagan Briste 131 NB 5553
Sgùman Còinntich 114 NG 9730
Sgurr a' Chaorachain (Highld.) 123 NG 7842
Sgurr a' Chaorachain (Highld.) 127 NH 0844
Sgurr a' Choire-bheithe 114 NG 8901
Sgurr a' Choire Ghlais 127 NH 2542
Sgurr a' Gharaidh 126 NG 8844
Sgurr a' Ghlas Leathaid 127 NH 2456
Sgurr a' Ghreadaidh 123 NG 4423
Sgurr Alasdair 123 NG 4520
Sgurr a'Mhàim 106 NN 1666
Sgurr a' Mhaoraich 114 NG 9806
Sgurr a' Mhuilinn 127 NH 2655
Sgurr an Airgid 114 NG 9422
Sgurr an Eilein Ghuibhais 111 NM 7297
Sgurr an Lochain 100 NN 0010
Sgurr an Ursainn 111 NM 8786
Sgurr an Utha 114 NM 8883
Sgurr Breac 111 NM 8492
Sgurr Coire Choineachain 111 NG 7801
Sgurr Coire nan Gobhar 111 NM 7996
Sgurr Dearg 105 NM 6634
Sgurr Dhomhnuill 106 NM 8867
Sgurr Dhomhuill Mór 111 NM 7476
Sgurr Dubh 126 NG 9855
Sgurr Fhuaran 114 NG 9716
Sgurr Marcasaidh 127 NH 3559
Sgurr Mhic Bharraich 114 NG 9117
Sgurr Mhurlagain 114 NN 0194
Sgurr Mór (Highld.) 127 NH 2071
Sgurr Mór (Highld.) 114 NM 9697
Sgurr na Ciche 114 NM 9096
Sgurr na Coinnich 123 NG 7622
Sgurr na Feartaig 127 NH 0545
Sgurr na h-Eanchainne 106 NM 9965
Sgurr na h-Iolaire 123 NG 6109
Sgurr na Lapaich (Highld.) 115 NH 1524
Sgurr na Lapaich (Highld.) 115 NH 1635
Sgurr nan Caorach 111 NG 5802
Sgurr nan Ceathreamhnan 115 NH 0522
Sgurr nan Coireachan 114 NM 9087
Sgurr nan Conbhairean 115 NH 1213
Sgurr nan Eag 123 NG 4519
Sgurr nan Gillean (Island of Skye) 123 NG 4725
Sgurr nan Gillean (Rhum) 110 NM 3893
Sgurr na Ruaidhe 127 NH 2842
Sgurr na Sgine 114 NG 9411
Sgurr na Stri 123 NG 5119
Sgurr Thuilm 114 NM 9488
Shabbington 36 SP 6606
Shackerstone 60 SK 3706
Shackleford 28 SU 9345
Shader 131 NB 3854
Shadforth 85 NZ 3441
Shadingfield 55 TM 4383
Shadoxhurst 31 TQ 9737
Shaftesbury 25 ST 8622
Shafton 71 SE 3810
Shaggie Burn 108 NN 8727
Shalbourne 34 SU 3163
Shalcombe 26 SZ 3985
Shalden 35 SU 6941
Shaldon 21 SX 9272
Shalfleet 26 SZ 4189
Shalford (Essex) 54 TL 7229
Shalford (Surrey) 28 TQ 0047
Shalford Green 54 TL 7127
Shallowford 23 SS 7144
Shalstone 51 SP 6436
Shambles (lightship) 25 SY 7668
Shamley Green 28 TQ 0344
Shandon 100 NS 2586
Shandwick 129 NH 8575
Shangton 61 SP 7196
Shanklin 27 SZ 5881
Shanklin Chine 27 SZ 5880
Shap 83 NY 5615
Shap Fells 83 NY 5309
Shapinsay 136 HY 5018
Shapinsay Sound 137 HY 5213
Shapwick (Dorset) 26 ST 9301
Shapwick (Somer.) 24 ST 4137
Shardlow 60 SK 4330
Shareshill 59 SJ 9406
Sharkham Point 21 SX 9354
Sharlston 71 SE 3818
Sharnbrook 52 SP 9959
Sharnford 51 SP 4891
Sharoe Green 77 SD 5332
Sharow 79 SE 3271
Sharpenhoe 52 TL 0630
Sharperton 90 NT 9503
Sharpham House 21 SX 8257
Sharpness 46 SO 6702
Sharpthorne 29 TQ 3732
Sharrington 64 TG 0337
Shatterford 49 SO 7980
Shaugh Prior 21 SX 5463
Shavington 59 SJ 6951
Shavington Park 59 SJ 6338
Shaw (Berks.) 35 SU 4768
Shaw (Gtr Mches.) 69 SD 9308
Shaw (Wilts.) 33 ST 8865
Shawbost 131 NB 2646
Shawbury 59 SJ 5521
Shawdon Hall 91 NU 0914
Shawell 51 SP 5480
Shawford 27 SU 4624
Shawforth 69 SD 8920
Shawhead 88 NX 8675
Shaw Hill 88 NX 5871
Shaw Mills 79 SE 2562
Shaws Under Loch 89 NT 3919
Shawwood 93 NS 5325
Shear Cross 33 ST 8642
Shearsby 51 SP 6291
Sheaval (mt.) 112 NF 7627
Shebbear 22 SS 4309
Shebdon 59 SJ 7525
Shebster 135 ND 0164
Shedfield 27 SU 5512
Sheen 70 SK 1161
Sheep Island (Cumbr.) 76 SD 2163
Sheep Island (Dyfed) 42 SM 8401
Sheep Island (Strath.) 92 NR 7305
Sheep Rock 139 HZ 2271
Sheepscombe 46 SO 8910
Sheepstor 21 SX 5567
Sheepwash 22 SS 4806
Sheepy Magna 60 SK 3201
Sheepy Parva 60 SK 3301
Sheering 37 TL 5013
Sheerness 30 TQ 9274
Sheet 27 SU 7524
Sheffield 71 SK 3587
Sheffield Bottom 36 SU 6469
Sheffield Park Station 29 TQ 4023
Shefford 52 TL 1439
Sheinton 59 SJ 6104
Shelderton 48 SO 4077
Sheldon (Derby.) 70 SK 1768
Sheldon (Devon) 24 ST 1208
Sheldon (W Mids.) 50 SP 1584
Sheldwich 31 TR 0156
Shelf 78 SE 1228
Shelfanger 55 TM 1083
Shelfield 60 SK 0302
Shelford 61 SK 6642
Shellag Point 76 SC 4699
Shellbrook Hill 58 SJ 3439
Shelley 70 SE 2011
Shellingford 47 SU 3193
Shell Ness 31 TR 0567
Shellow Bowells 38 TL 6108
Shell Top (mt.) 21 SX 5963
Shelsley Beauchamp 49 SO 7362
Shelsley Walsh 49 SO 7263
Shelter Stone 117 NJ 0001
Shelton (Beds.) 52 TL 0368
Shelton (Norf.) 55 TM 2191
Shelton (Notts.) 61 SK 7744
Shelton Green 55 TM 2390
Shelve 58 SO 3399
Shelwick 45 SO 5243
Shenfield 38 TQ 6094
Shenington 50 SP 3642
Shenley 37 TL 1900
Shenley Brook End 52 SP 8335
Shenleybury 37 TL 1802
Shenley Church End 52 SP 8336
Shenmore 45 SO 3938
Shenstone (Here. and Worc.) 49 SO 8673
Shenstone (Staffs.) 60 SK 1004
Shenton 60 SK 3800
Shenval 117 NJ 2129
Shepherd's Green 36 SU 7183
Shepherdswell or Sibertswold 31 TR 2548
Shepley 70 SE 1909
Shepperdine 45 ST 6195
Shepperton 36 TQ 0867
Shepreth 53 TL 3947
Shepshed 61 SK 4719
Shepton Beauchamp 24 ST 4016
Shepton Mallet 33 ST 6143
Shepton Montague 25 ST 6731
Shepway 30 TQ 7753
Sheraton 85 NZ 4334
Sherborne (Dorset) 25 ST 6316
Sherborne (Glos.) 47 SP 1714
Sherborne St. John 35 SU 6155
Sherbourne 50 SP 2661
Sherburn (Durham) 84 NZ 3142
Sherburn (N Yorks.) 81 SE 9577
Sherburn in Elmet 79 SE 4933
Shere 28 TQ 0747
Shereford 64 TF 8829
Sherfield English 26 SU 2922
Sherfield on Loddon 35 SU 6757
Sherford 21 SX 7744
Sheriffhales 59 SJ 7512
Sheriff Hutton 79 SE 6566
Sheriff Muir 101 NN 8303
Sheringham 65 TG 1543
Sherington 52 SP 8846
Shernborne 64 TF 7132
Sherrington 34 ST 9638
Sherston 33 ST 8585
Sherwood Forest 71 SK 6060
Sherwood Green 23 SS 5520
Sheshader 131 NB 5534
Shetland Islands 141 HU 4258
Shettleston 101 NS 6464
Shevington 69 SD 5408
Shevington Moor 69 SD 5410
Sheviock 20 SX 3655
Shevock, The 121 NJ 6127
Shian Bay 98 NR 5287
Shian River 98 NR 5386
Shiant Islands 125 NG 4298
Shiel Bridge 114 NG 9318
Shieldaig (Highld.) 123 NG 7973
Shieldaig (Highld.) 123 NG 8153
Shieldaig Forest 123 NG 8564
Shieldhill (Central) 102 NS 8976
Shieldhill (Strath.) (ant.) 95 NT 0040
Shielfoot 111 NM 6670
Shiel Hill (Dumf. and Galwy.) 88 NS 7604
Shiel Hill (Strath.) 86 NX 1981
Shielhill (Tays.) 109 NO 4257
Shiel Muir 121 NJ 4761
Shifnal 59 SJ 7407
Shilbottle 91 NU 1908
Shildon 84 NZ 2226
Shillay (Monach Islands) 124 NF 5962
Shillay (Pabbay, North Uist) 124 NF 8891
Shillingford (Devon) 23 SS 9723
Shillingford (Oxon.) 35 SU 5992
Shillingford St. George 21 SX 9087
Shillingstone 25 ST 8211
Shillington 52 TL 1234
Shillmoor (Northum.) 90 NT 8807
Shill Moor (Northum.) 90 NT 9415
Shiltenish 131 NB 2819
Shilton (Oxon.) 47 SP 2608
Shilton (Warw.) 50 SP 4084
Shimpling (Norf.) 55 TM 1583
Shimpling (Suff.) 54 TL 8551
Shimpling Street 54 TL 8652
Shiney Row 84 NZ 3252
Shinfield 36 SU 7368
Shin Forest 128 NC 5601
Shining Tor 70 SJ 9973
Shinnel Water 88 NX 7696
Shinness 133 NC 5314
Shinness Lodge 133 NC 5314
Shin, The (mt.) 89 NY 2889
Shipbourne 29 TQ 5952
Shipdham 64 TF 9607
Shipham 33 ST 4457
Shiphay 21 SX 8965
Shiplake 36 SU 7678
Shipley (Shrops.) 59 SO 8095
Shipley (W Susx) 28 TQ 1422
Shipley (W Yorks.) 78 SE 1337
Shipmeadow 55 TM 3789
Shippea Hill Station 54 TL 6484
Shippon 47 SU 4898
Shipston on Stour 50 SP 2540
Shipton (Glos.) 46 SP 0318
Shipton (N Yorks.) 79 SE 5558
Shipton (Shrops.) 48 SO 5591
Shipton Bellinger 34 SU 2345
Shipton Gorge 25 SY 4991
Shipton Green 27 SU 8000
Shipton Moyne 33 ST 8889
Shipton-on-Cherwell 47 SP 4716
Shiptonthorpe 74 SE 8543
Shipton-under-Wychwood 47 SP 2717
Shipwash (lightship) 55 TM 5344
Shirburn 36 SU 6995
Shirdley Hill 68 SD 3612
Shirebrook 71 SK 5267
Shirehampton 33 ST 5276
Shiremoor 91 NZ 3171
Shirenewton 45 ST 4793
Shire Oak 60 SK 0504
Shireoaks 71 SK 5581
Shirland 71 SK 3958
Shirlaw Pike 91 NU 1003
Shirley (Derby.) 60 SK 2141
Shirley (Hants.) 26 SU 4114
Shirley (W Mids.) 50 SP 1277
Shirley Moor 30 TQ 9232
Shirl Heath 45 SO 4359
Shirrell Heath 27 SU 5714
Shirwell 23 SS 5937
Shiskine 92 NR 9129
Shobdon 48 SO 3961
Shobdon Aerodrome 48 SO 3161
Shobrooke 21 SS 8600
Shochie Burn 108 NO 0231
Shocklach 58 SJ 4348
Shoeburyness (Essex) 38 TQ 9384
Shoebury Ness (Essex) (pt.) 38 TQ 9383
Sholden 31 TR 3552
Sholing 27 SU 4511
Shooting House Hill 76 SD 2581
Shop (Corn.) 22 SS 2214
Shop (Corn.) 19 SW 8773
Shopland Hall 38 TQ 8988
Shoreditch 37 TQ 3284
Shoreham 37 TQ 5261
Shoreham-by-Sea 28 TQ 2105
Shoresdean 97 NT 9546
Shoreswood 97 NT 9446
Shoretown 128 NH 6161
Shorncote 46 SU 0296
Shorne 30 TQ 6970
Short Cross 58 SJ 2605
Shortgate 29 TQ 4915
Short Heath (Leic.) 60 SK 3014
Short Heath (W Mids.) 50 SP 0992
Shortlanesend 19 SW 8047
Shortless 93 NS 4335
Shorwell 27 SZ 4582
Shoscombe 33 ST 7156
Shotesham 65 TM 2599
Shotgate 38 TQ 7692
Shotley 55 TM 2335
Shotley Bridge 84 NZ 0752
Shotley Gate 55 TM 2433
Shottenden 31 TR 0454
Shottermill 27 SU 8732
Shottery 50 SP 1854
Shotteswell 50 SP 4245
Shottisham 55 TM 3144
Shottle 60 SK 3149
Shotton (Clwyd) 68 SJ 3069
Shotton (Durham) 85 NZ 4139
Shotton (Northum.) 97 NT 8430
Shotton Colliery 85 NZ 3941
Shotts 102 NS 8760
Shotwick 68 SJ 3371
Shoughlaige-e-Caine 76 SC 3187
Shouldham 64 TF 6708
Shouldham Thorpe 64 TF 6607
Shoulsbarrow Common 23 SS 7040
Shoulton 49 SO 8058
Shrawardine 58 SJ 3915
Shrawley 49 SO 8064
Shrewley 50 SP 2167
Shrewsbury 59 SJ 4912
Shrewton 34 SU 0643
Shripney 28 SU 9302
Shrivenham 34 SU 2489
Shropham 64 TL 9893
Shropshire Union Canal 69 SJ 5160
Shroton or Iwerne Courtney 25 ST 8512
Shrub End 39 TL 9723
Shucknall 45 SO 5842
Shudy Camps 54 TL 6244
Shulishader 131 NB 5334
Shuna (Strath.) (is.) 105 NM 7508
Shuna Island (Strath.) 106 NM 9148
Shuna Point 105 NM 7606
Shuna Sound 105 NM 7508
Shurdington 46 SO 9118
Shurlock Row 36 SU 8374
Shurrery 135 ND 0458
Shurrery Lodge 135 ND 0356
Shurton 32 ST 2044
Shustoke 50 SP 2290
Shute 24 SY 2597
Shut End 49 SO 9089
Shutford 50 SP 3840
Shuthonger 46 SO 8935
Shutlanger 51 SP 7249
Shuttington 60 SK 2505
Shuttlewood 71 SK 4672
Sibbertoft 51 SP 6782
Sibdon Carwood 48 SO 4083
Sibertswold or Shepherdswell 31 TR 2548
Sibford Ferris 50 SP 3537
Sibford Gower 50 SP 3537
Sible Hedingham 54 TL 7734
Siblyback Lake Reservoir 19 SX 2370
Sibsey 63 TF 3551
Sibson (Cambs.) 62 TL 0997
Sibson (Leic.) 60 SK 3500
Sibthorpe 61 SK 7645
Siccar Point 97 NT 8170
Sicklesmere 54 TL 8760
Sicklinghall 79 SE 3548
Sidbury (Devon) 24 SY 1491
Sidbury (Shrops.) 49 SO 6885
Sidbury (Wilts.) (ant.) 34 SU 2150
Sidcup 37 TQ 4672
Siddington (Ches.) 69 SJ 8470
Siddington (Glos.) 46 SU 0399
Sidestrand 65 TG 2539
Sidford 24 SY 1390
Sidhean Achadh nan Eun (mt.) 133 NC 6311
Sidhean Mór (mt.) 111 NM 7286
Sidhean Raireag (mt.) 127 NH 3491
Sidh Mór (mt.) 100 NM 9100
Sidinish 124 NF 8763
Sidlaw Hills 108 NO 3138
Sidlesham 27 SZ 8599
Sidley 29 TQ 7409
Sidmouth 24 SY 1287
Siefton 48 SO 4883
Sigford 21 SX 7773
Siggar Ness 141 HU 3411
Sigglesthorne 75 TA 1545
Sighty Crag 90 NY 6081
Sike Moor 78 SD 8178
Silbury Hill 34 SU 0968
Silchester 36 SU 6462
Sileby 61 SK 6015
Silecroft 76 SD 1281
Silian 43 SN 5751
Silkstone Common 71 SE 2904
Silksworth 85 NZ 3752
Silk Willoughby 62 TF 0542
Silloth 82 NY 1153
Sills 90 NT 8200
Sillyearn 121 NJ 5254
Silpho 81 SE 9692
Silsden 78 SE 0446
Silsoe 52 TL 0835
Silverburn 103 NT 2060
Silverdale (Lancs.) 77 SD 4674
Silverdale (Staffs.) 59 SJ 8146
Silver End (Essex) 38 TL 8019
Silverford 121 NJ 7764
Silverley's Green 55 TM 2976
Silverstone 51 SP 6644
Silverton 23 SS 9502
Sil Wick (Shetld.) 140 HU 2941
Silwick (Shetld.) 140 HU 2942
Simonburn 90 NY 8773
Simon Fell 78 SD 7574
Simonsbath 23 SS 7739
Simonstone 78 SD 7734
Simprim 97 NT 8545
Simpson 52 SP 8836
Simpson Cross 42 SM 8919
Sim's Hill 102 NN 9907
Sinclair's Bay 135 ND 3656
Sinclairston 93 NS 4716
Sinderby 79 SE 3481
Sinderhope 83 NY 8452
Sindlesham 36 SU 7769
Singleton (Lancs.) 77 SD 3838
Singleton (W Susx) 27 SU 8713
Singlewell or Ifield 30 TQ 6471
Sinnahard 118 NJ 4713
Sinnington 80 SE 7485
Sinton Green 49 SO 8160
Siòr Loch 106 NM 9622
Sipson 36 TQ 0877
Sirhowy 41 SO 1410
Sirhowy River 41 SO 1507
Sirhowy Valley 41 ST 1791
Sissinghurst 30 TQ 7937
Sisters, The (mt.) 106 NN 1556
Siston 33 ST 6875
Sithean an Airgid (mt.) 131 NB 2513
Sithean na Raplaich 111 NM 6351
Sithney 18 SW 6329
Sittaford Tor 21 SX 6383
Sittenham 128 NH 6574
Sittingbourne 30 TQ 9163
Six Ashes 49 SO 6988
Sixhills 73 TF 1787
Six Mile Bottom 53 TL 5756
Sixpenny Handley 26 ST 9917
Sixteen Foot Drain 63 TL 4593
Sizewell 55 TM 4762
Skail 134 NC 7146
Skaill (Orkney) 136 HY 2318
Skaill (Orkney) 137 HY 5806
Skara Brae (ant.) 136 HY 2318
Skares 93 NS 5217
Skarpigarth 140 HU 1949
Skateraw 96 NT 7375
Skaw (Unst) 143 HP 6516
Skaw (Whalsay) 141 HU 5966
Skaw Taing 141 HU 6066
Skea 138 HY 2930
Skeabost 123 NG 4148
Skeabrae 136 HY 2720
Skea Skerries 138 HY 4440
Skeeby 84 NZ 1902
Skeffington 61 SK 7402
Skeffling 75 TA 3619
Skegby 71 SK 4961

Skegness	73	TF 5663
Skegness (Ingoldmells) Aerodrome	73	TF 5667
Skelberry	141	HU 3916
Skelbo	129	NH 7995
Skelda Ness	141	HU 3041
Skelda Voe	141	HU 3144
Skeldyke	63	TF 3337
Skelfhill Pen	89	NT 4403
Skellingthorpe	72	SK 9272
Skellister	141	HU 4654
Skellow	71	SE 5310
Skelly Rock	119	NJ 9614
Skelmanthorpe	71	SE 2210
Skelmersdale	68	SD 4605
Skelmonae	121	NJ 8839
Skelmorlie	100	NS 1967
Skelmorlie Castle (ant.)	100	NS 1965
Skelmuir	121	NJ 9842
Skelpick	134	NC 7256
Skelpick Burn	134	NC 7355
Skelton (Cleve.)	85	NZ 6518
Skelton (Cumbr.)	83	NY 4335
Skelton (N Yorks.)	84	NZ 0900
Skelton (N Yorks.)	79	SE 3568
Skelton (N Yorks.)	79	SE 5656
Skelwick (Westray)	138	HY 4845
Skel Wick (Westray)	138	HY 4945
Skelwith Bridge	82	NY 3503
Skendleby	73	TF 4369
Skene House	119	NJ 7609
Skenfrith	45	SO 4520
Skerne	81	TA 0455
Skeroblingarry	92	NR 7026
Skerray	133	NC 6563
Skerries, The (is.)	66	SH 2694
Skerry of Eshaness	142	HU 2076
Skervuile Lighthouse	98	NR 6071
Sketty	40	SS 6293
Skewen	40	SS 7297
Skewsby	79	SE 6270
Skeyton	65	TG 2425
Skiag Bridge	132	NC 2324
Skibo Castle	129	NH 7389
Skidbrooke	73	TF 4393
Skidby	74	TA 0133
Skiddaw (mt.)	82	NY 2629
Skiddaw Forest	82	NY 2629
Skigersta	131	NB 5461
Skilgate	23	SS 9827
Skillington	62	SK 8925
Skinburness	82	NY 1255
Skinflats	102	NS 9083
Skinidin	122	NG 2247
Skinningrove	85	NZ 7119
Skipness	92	NR 8957
Skipness Bay	92	NR 9057
Skipness Point	92	NR 9157
Skipsea	81	TA 1655
Skipton	78	SD 9851
Skipton-on-Swale	79	SE 3679
Skipwith	79	SE 6538
Skirling	95	NT 0739
Skirmett	36	SU 7789
Skirpenbeck	80	SE 7457
Skirwith (Cumbr.)	83	NY 6132
Skirwith (N Yorks.)	77	SD 7073
Skirza	135	ND 3868
Skirza Head	135	ND 3968
Skokholm Island	42	SM 7305
Skomer Island	42	SM 7209
Skroo (pt.)	139	HZ 2274
Skuda Sound	143	HU 6099
Skulamus	123	NG 6722
Skullomie	133	NC 6161
Skye of Curr	117	NH 9924
Slack	78	SD 9828
Slackhall	70	SK 0781
Slackhead	121	NJ 4063
Slacks of Cairnbanno (mt.)	121	NJ 8446
Slad	46	SO 8707
Slade	22	SS 5046
Slade Green	37	TQ 5276
Slaggan Bay	126	NG 8394
Slaggyford	83	NY 6752
Slaidburn	77	SD 7152
Slaithwaite	70	SE 0714
Slaley	84	NY 9757
Slamannan	102	NS 8573
Slapton (Bucks.)	36	SP 9320
Slapton (Devon)	21	SX 8244
Slapton (Northants.)	51	SP 6346
Slate, The	92	NR 6316
Slattocks	69	SD 8808
Slaugham	28	TQ 2528
Slawston	61	SP 7794
Sleach Water	135	ND 0145
Sleaford (Hants.)	27	SU 8037
Sleaford (Lincs.)	62	TF 0645
Sleagill	83	NY 5919
Sleapford	59	SJ 6315
Sledge Green	46	SO 8134
Sledmere	81	SE 9364
Sleightholme	84	NY 9510
Sleightholme Moor	84	NY 9208
Sleights	80	NZ 8607
Slepe	25	SY 9293
Sletill Hill	134	NC 9246
Sliabh Gaoil	99	NR 8174
Slickly	135	ND 2966
Sliddery	92	NR 9322
Sliddery Water	92	NR 9525
Slidderywater Foot	92	NR 9321
Slieau Dhoo (mt.)	76	SC 3589
Slieau Ruy (mt.)	76	SC 3282
Sliemore	117	NJ 0320
Sligachan Hotel	123	NG 4829
Slimbridge	46	SO 7303
Slindon (Staffs.)	59	SJ 8232
Slindon (W Susx)	28	SU 9608
Slinfold	28	TQ 1131
Slingsby	80	SE 6974
Slioch (Grampn.)	121	NJ 5638
Slioch (Highld.) (mt.)	126	NH 0069
Slios Garbh	111	NM 8284
Slip End	36	TL 0818
Slipton	52	SP 9479
Slitrig Water	90	NT 5110
Slochd	117	NH 8424
Slockavullin	99	NR 8297
Sloc nam Feàrna	99	NR 8674
Sloley	65	TG 2924
Sloothby	73	TF 4970
Slouchnawen Bay	86	NW 9563
Slough	36	SU 9779
Slugaide Glas	98	NR 2846
Slymaback (mt.)	101	NN 7510
Slyne	77	SD 4765
Sma' Glen	108	NN 9029
Smailholm	96	NT 6436
Smallbridge	69	SD 9114
Smallburgh	65	TG 3324
Smallburn (Grampn.)	121	NK 0141
Smallburn (Strath.)	94	NS 6827
Small Dole	28	TQ 2112
Small Downs, The (roadstead)	31	TR 3957
Smalley	60	SK 4044
Smallfield	29	TQ 3243
Small Hythe	30	TQ 8930
Small Isles	98	NR 5468
Smallridge	24	ST 3001
Smardale	83	NY 7308

Smarden	30	TQ 8842
Smasha Hill	89	NT 4417
Smeatharpe	24	ST 1910
Smeeth	31	TR 0739
Smeeton Westerby	51	SP 6792
Smerclate	112	NF 7415
Smerral	135	ND 1733
Smethwick	50	SP 0288
Smiddy Shaw Resr.	84	NZ 0446
Smigel Burn	134	NC 9057
Smirisary	111	NM 6477
Smisby	60	SK 3419
Smithey Fen	53	TL 4570
Smithfield	89	NY 4465
Smithincott	24	ST 0611
Smith Sound	18	SV 8706
Smithton	129	NH 7145
Snaefell	76	SC 3988
Snaigow House	108	NO 0843
Snailbeach	58	SJ 3702
Snailwell	54	TL 6467
Snainton	81	SE 9182
Snaip Hill	95	NT 0232
Snaith	79	SE 6422
Snape	55	TM 3958
Snape (N Yorks.)	79	SE 2684
Snape (Suff.)	55	TM 3959
Snap, The (pt.)	143	HU 6587
Snarestone	60	SK 3409
Snarford	72	TF 0482
Snargate	31	TQ 9928
Snarravoe	143	HP 5602
Snave	31	TR 0130
Snead	48	SO 3191
Sneaton	81	NZ 8907
Sneatonthorpe	81	NZ 9006
Snelland	72	TF 0780
Snelston	60	SK 1543
Snettisham	64	TF 6834
Sneug, The (mt.)	140	HT 9439
Sneuk Head	136	ND 2095
Snilesworth Moor	85	SE 5396
Snishival	112	NF 7534
Snitter	91	NU 0203
Snitterby	72	SK 9894
Snitterfield	50	SP 2159
Snitton	48	SO 5575
Snodhill	45	SO 3140
Snodland	30	TQ 7061
Snook Point	97	NU 2425
Snowdon (mt.)	66	SH 6054
Snowhope Hill	84	NY 9434
Snowshill	46	SP 0933
Soa (Coll, Strath.) (is.)	110	NM 1551
Soa (Tiree) (is.)	104	NM 0746
Soa Island	104	NM 2419
Soay (Island of Skye)	123	NG 4414
Soay (St. Kilda or Hirta)	124	NA 0601
Soay Mór	125	NB 0605
Soay Sound	123	NG 4416
Soberton	27	SU 6016
Soberton Heath	27	SU 6014
Socach Burn	100	NR 8899
Socach, The (mt.)	117	NJ 2714
Soham	54	TL 5973
Soham Mere	53	TL 5773
Soldon Cross	22	SS 3210
Soldridge	27	SU 6534
Solent, The (chan.)	27	SZ 4797
Sole Street	30	TQ 6567
Sole Street	31	TR 0949
Solihull	50	SP 1479
Sollas	124	NF 8174
Sollers Dilwyn	45	SO 4255
Sollers Hope	45	SO 6033
Sollom	68	SD 4518
Solva	42	SM 8024
Solway Firth	82	NY 0050
Solway Moss	89	NY 3369
Somerby	61	SK 7710
Somercotes	60	SK 4253
Somerford Keynes	46	SU 0195
Somerley	27	SZ 8198
Somerleyton	65	TM 4897
Somersall Herbert	60	SK 1335
Somersby	73	TF 3472
Somersham (Cambs.)	53	TL 3677
Somersham (Suff.)	55	TM 0848
Somersham High North Fen	53	TL 3581
Somerton (Norf.)	65	TG 4719
Somerton (Oxon.)	47	SP 4928
Somerton (Somer.)	25	ST 4828
Sompting	28	TQ 1605
Sonachan Hotel	111	NM 4566
Sonning	36	SU 7575
Sonning Common	36	SU 7080
Soonhope Burn	96	NT 5356
Sopley	26	SZ 1596
Sopworth	33	ST 8286
Sorbie	87	NX 4346
Sor Brook	51	SP 4437
Sordale	135	ND 1462
Sorisdale	110	NM 2763
Sorn	93	NS 5526
Sornhill	93	NS 5134
Soroba Hill	105	NM 7905
Sortat	135	ND 2863
Sotby	73	TF 2078
Sots Hole	73	TF 1164
Sotterly	55	TM 4584
Soudley	59	SJ 7228
Soughton (Sychdyn)	68	SJ 2466
Soulbury	52	SP 8827
Soulby	83	NY 7410
Souldern	47	SP 5231
Souldrop	52	SP 9861
Soulseat Loch	86	NX 1058
Sound (Shetld.)	141	HU 3850
Sound (Shetld.)	141	HU 4640
Sound Gruney (is.)	143	HU 5796
Sound of Arisaig	111	NM 6580
Sound of Barra	112	NF 7510
Sound of Berneray (North Uist)	124	NF 9079
Sound of Berneray (W Isles)	112	NL 5581
Sound of Bute	92	NS 0154
Sound of Canna	110	NG 3002
Sound of Eigg	111	NM 4482
Sound of Eriskay	112	NF 7913
Sound of Faray	138	HY 5437
Sound of Fiaray	112	NF 6909
Sound of Fuday	112	NF 7108
Sound of Gigha	92	NR 6747
Sound of Handa	132	NC 1547
Sound of Harris	124	NF 9681
Sound of Hellisay	112	NF 7503
Sound of Hoxa	136	ND 3893
Sound of Insh	105	NM 7318
Sound of Iona	104	NM 2822
Sound of Islay	98	NR 4369
Sound of Jura	99	NR 6480
Sound of Kerrera	105	NM 8328
Sound of Luing	105	NM 7209
Sound of Mingulay	112	NL 5885
Sound of Monach	124	NF 6865
Sound of Mull	105	NM 5945
Sound of Pabbay (North Uist)	124	NF 8984
Sound of Pabbay (W Isles)	112	NL 6289
Sound of Papa	140	HU 1758
Sound of Pladda	92	NS 0220
Sound of Raasay	123	NG 5654
Sound of Rhum	111	NM 4390

Sound of Sandray	112	NL 6393
Sound of Shiant	125	NB 3701
Sound of Shillay	124	NF 8890
Sound of Shuna	106	NM 9248
Sound of Sleat	111	NG 6804
Sound of Spuir	124	NF 8685
Sound of Taransay	124	NB 0500
Sound of Ulva	105	NM 4538
Sound of Vatersay	112	NL 6297
Sound, The	20	SX 4752
Soundwell	33	ST 6574
Source of River Thames	46	ST 9898
Source of River Wye	57	SN 8087
Sourhope	90	NT 8420
Sourin	138	HY 4331
Sourton	21	SX 5390
Soutergate	76	SD 2281
Souter Head	119	NJ 9601
Souterrain (ant)	109	NO 4137
South Achinduin	105	NM 8139
South Acre	64	TF 8014
Southall	37	TQ 1280
South Allington	21	SX 7938
South Alloa	102	NS 8791
Southam (Glos.)	46	SO 9725
Southam (Warw.)	50	SP 4161
South Ambersham	28	SU 9120
Southampton	26	SU 4212
Southampton Airport	27	SU 4516
Southampton Water	27	SU 4506
South Bank	85	NZ 5220
South Barrow	25	ST 6027
South Barrule (mt.)	76	SC 2576
South Bay	139	HY 7552
South Benfleet	38	TQ 7785
Southborough	29	TQ 5842
Southbourne (Dorset)	26	SZ 1491
Southbourne (W Susx)	27	SU 7705
South Brent	21	SX 6960
Southburgh	64	TG 0004
South Burlingham	65	TG 3708
South Burn	136	ND 2299
South Cadbury	25	ST 6325
South Cairn	86	NW 9768
South Carlton	72	SK 9476
South Cave	74	SE 9231
South Cerney	46	SU 0497
South Channel (Humbs.)	74	SE 9521
South Channel (Kent)	31	TR 3272
South Chard	24	ST 3205
South Charlton	91	NU 1620
South Cheek or Old Peak	81	NZ 9802
Southchurch	38	TQ 9186
South Cliffe	74	SE 8736
South Clifton	72	SK 8270
Southcott	21	SX 5495
South Cove	55	TM 5081
South Creake	64	TF 8536
South Croxton	61	SK 6810
South Dalton	74	SE 9645
South Darenth	37	TQ 5669
South Deep	108	NO 2318
South District	63	TL 5298
South Downs	29	TQ 3707
South Drove Drain	62	TF 2013
South Duffield	79	SE 6733
Southease	29	TQ 4205
South Elkington	73	TF 2900
South Elmsall	71	SE 4711
Southend (Berks.)	35	SU 5970
South End (Cumbr.)	76	SD 2063
Southend (Strath.)	92	NR 6908
Southend Municipal Airport	38	TQ 8789
Southend-on-Sea	38	TQ 8885
Southerndown	41	SS 8874
Southerness	82	NX 9754
Southerness Point	82	NX 9754
South Erradale	123	NG 7471
Southery	64	TL 6294
Southery Fens	64	TL 6093
South Fambridge	38	TQ 8694
South Fawley	34	SU 3979
South Ferriby	74	SE 9820
Southfield Reservoir	71	SE 6519
Southfleet	30	TQ 6171
South Foreland	31	TR 3643
South Forty Foot Drain	62	TF 1633
South Galson River	131	NB 4555
South Garth	143	HU 5499
South Garvan	114	NM 9977
Southgate (Gtr London)	37	TQ 3093
Southgate (Norf.)	64	TF 6833
Southgate (Norf.)	65	TG 1324
Southgate (W Glam.)	40	SS 5587
South Goodwin (lightship)	31	TR 4342
South Green	38	TQ 6893
South Hall	100	NS 0672
South Hanningfield	38	TQ 7497
South Harbour	139	HZ 2069
South Harris (dist.)	125	NG 0893
South Harris Forest	125	NG 1098
South Harting	27	SU 7819
South Havra (is.)	141	HU 3627
South Hayling	27	SZ 7299
South Head (Highld.)	135	ND 3749
South Head (Shetld.)	142	HU 2382
South Heath	36	SP 9102
South Heighton	29	TQ 4503
South Hetton	85	NZ 3745
South Hiendley	71	SE 3812
South Hill	20	SX 3272
South Hole	22	SS 2219
South Holland Main Drain	63	TF 3718
South Holms	143	HP 5710
South Holmwood	28	TQ 1745
South Hornchurch	37	TQ 5283
South Hylton	85	NZ 3556
Southill	52	TL 1442
South Isle of Gletness	141	HU 4750
South Kelsey	74	TF 0398
South Kilvington	79	SE 4283
South Kilworth	51	SP 6082
South Kirkby	71	SE 4410
South Kirkton	119	NJ 7405
South Kyme	62	TF 1749
South Kyme Fen	62	TF 1748
South Lancing	28	TQ 1804
South Lee (mt.)	124	NF 9165
Southleigh (Devon)	24	SY 2093
South Leigh (Oxon.)	47	SP 3908
South Leverton	72	SK 7881
South Littleton	50	SP 0746
South Lochboisdale	112	NF 7817
South Lopham	54	TM 0481
South Luffenham	62	SK 9402
South Mains	109	NO 6948
South Malling	29	TQ 4211
South Marston	34	SU 1987
South Medwin	95	NT 0445
South Milford	79	SE 4931
South Milton	21	SX 7042
South Mimms	37	TL 2200
Southminster	38	TQ 9599
South Molton	23	SS 7125
South Moor	84	NZ 1952
South Morar (dist.)	111	NM 7588
South Moreton	35	SU 5688
South Muskham	72	SK 7957
South Ness	140	HT 9636
South Nesting	141	HU 4554
South Nesting Bay	141	HU 4956
South Nevi (pt.)	137	HY 6000

South Newington	47	SP 4033
South Newton	26	SU 0834
South Normanton	61	SK 4456
South Norwood	37	TQ 3468
South Nutfield	29	TQ 3048
South Ockendon	38	TQ 5982
Southoe	52	TL 1864
Southolt	55	TM 1968
South Ormsby	73	TF 3675
Southorpe	62	TF 0803
South Otterington	79	SE 3787
Southowram	78	SE 1123
South Oxhey	37	TQ 1193
South Perrott	25	ST 4706
South Petherton	25	ST 4316
South Petherwin	20	SX 3182
South Pickenham	64	TF 8504
South Pool	21	SX 7740
Southport	68	SD 3316
Southport Birkdale Sands (aerodrome)	68	SD 3116
South Queich	102	NO 0303
South Radworthy	23	SS 7432
South Raynham	64	TF 8723
Southrepps	65	TG 2536
South Reston	73	TF 4082
Southrey	73	TF 1366
South Ronaldsay	136	ND 4590
Southrop	47	SP 1903
Southrope	35	SU 6744
South Runcton	64	TF 6308
South Scarle	72	SK 8463
Southsea	27	SZ 6498
South Shian	106	NM 9042
South Shields	91	NZ 3667
South Shore	77	SD 3033
South Skirlaugh	75	TA 1439
South Somercotes	73	TF 4193
South Sound	143	HU 5390
South Stack (pt.)	66	SH 2082
South Stainley	79	SE 3063
South Stoke (Avon)	33	ST 7461
South Stoke (Oxon.)	35	SU 6083
South Stoke (W Susx)	28	TQ 0210
South Street	29	TQ 3918
South Tawton	21	SX 6594
South Thoresby	73	TF 4077
South Tidworth	34	SU 2347
Southtown (Burray)	136	ND 4895
South Town (Hants.)	27	SU 6536
South Ugie Water	121	NJ 9846
South Uist (is.)	112	NF 7829
South View	141	HU 3842
Southwaite	83	NY 4445
South Walls (is.)	136	ND 3189
South Walsham	65	TG 3613
South Ward (mt.)	141	HU 3264
South Warnborough	35	SU 7247
Southwater	28	TQ 1526
Southway	33	ST 5142
South Weald	37	TQ 5793
Southwell (Dorset)	25	SY 6870
Southwell (Notts.)	61	SK 7053
South Weston	36	SU 7098
South Wheatley	20	SX 2492
Southwick (Hants.)	27	SU 6208
Southwick (Northants.)	52	TL 0192
South Wick (Shetld.)	142	HU 3191
Southwick (Tyne and Wear)	91	NZ 3758
Southwick (Wilts.)	33	ST 8354
Southwick (W Susx)	28	TQ 2405
South Widcombe	33	ST 5756
South Wigston	61	SP 5898
South Willingham	73	TF 1983
South Wingfield	60	SK 3755
South Witham	62	SK 9219
Southwold	55	TM 5076
South Wonston	27	SU 4635
Southwood (Norf.)	65	TG 3905
Southwood (Somer.)	25	ST 5533
South Woodham Ferrers	38	TQ 8097
South Wootton	64	TF 6422
South Wraxall	33	ST 8364
South Zeal	21	SX 6593
Soutra Mains	103	NT 4559
Soval Lodge	131	NB 3424
Sowerby (N Yorks.)	79	SE 4381
Sowerby (W Yorks.)	78	SE 0423
Sowerby Bridge	78	SE 0523
Sowerby Row	83	NY 3940
Sow of Athol, The	116	NN 6274
Sow, The (pt.)	136	HY 1802
Sowton	21	SX 9792
Soyea Island	132	NC 0421
Soyland Moor	70	SD 9819
Spa Common	65	TG 2930
Spadeadam Fm.	90	NY 5870
Spadeadam Forest	90	NY 6272
Spade Mill Resrs.	77	SD 6137
Spalding	63	TF 2422
Spaldington	74	SE 7533
Spaldwick	52	TL 1272
Spalford	72	SK 8369
Spango Hill	88	NS 8118
Spanish Head	76	SC 1865
Sparham	64	TG 0619
Spark Bridge	77	SD 3084
Sparkford	25	ST 6026
Sparkwell	21	SX 5757
Sparrowpit	70	SK 0980
Sparsholt (Hants.)	26	SU 4331
Sparsholt (Oxon.)	34	SU 3487
Spartleton Edge	103	NT 6565
Spaunton	80	SE 7289
Spaunton Moor	80	SE 7194
Spaxton	24	ST 2236
Spean Bridge	115	NN 2281
Spear Head	135	ND 0971
Speen (Berks.)	35	SU 4568
Speen (Bucks.)	36	SU 8499
Speeton	81	TA 1574
Speinne Mór	111	NM 4949
Speke	68	SJ 4383
Speldhurst	29	TQ 5541
Spellbrook	37	TL 4817
Spelsbury	47	SP 3421
Spencers Wood	36	SU 7166
Spennithorne	84	SE 1489
Spennymoor	84	NZ 2533
Spetchley	49	SO 8953
Spettisbury	25	ST 9002
Spexhall	55	TM 3780
Spey Bay	121	NJ 3866
Speymouth Forest	121	NJ 3657
Spilsby	73	TF 4066
Spindlestone	97	NU 1533
Spinningdale	128	NH 6789
Spirthill	34	ST 9975
Spital Burn	119	NO 6583
Spithead (roadstead)	27	SZ 6396
Spithurst	29	TQ 4217
Spittal (Dyfed)	42	SM 9723
Spittal (Highld)	135	ND 1654
Spittal (Lothian)	103	NT 4677
Spittal (Northum.)	97	NU 0051
Spittalfield	108	NO 1040
Spittal of Glenmuick	118	NO 3184
Spittal of Glenshee	108	NO 1069
Spixworth	65	TG 2415
Spofforth	79	SE 3650
Spondon	60	SK 3935
Spo Ness (Westray)	138	HY 4846

Spooner Row	65	TM 0997
Spoo Ness (Unst)	143	HP 5607
Sporle	64	TF 8411
Spott	103	NT 6775
Spratton	51	SP 7170
Spreakley	35	SU 8341
Spreyton	21	SX 6996
Spridlington	72	TF 0084
Springburn	101	NS 5968
Springfield (Fife)	103	NO 3411
Springfield (Grampn.)	129	NJ 0459
Springfield (W Mids.)	50	SP 1082
Springfield Resr.	95	NS 9052
Springholm	88	NX 8070
Springkell	89	NY 2575
Spring Mill Resr.	69	SD 8717
Springside	93	NS 3639
Springthorpe	72	SK 8789
Sproatley	75	TA 1934
Sproston Green	69	SJ 7367
Sprotbrough	71	SE 5302
Sproughton	55	TM 1244
Sprouston	96	NT 7535
Sprowston	65	TG 2412
Sproxton (Leic.)	62	SK 8524
Sproxton (N Yorks.)	79	SE 6181
Spuir (is.)	124	NF 8584
Spurn (lightship)	75	TA 4709
Spur Ness	139	HY 6033
Spurness Sound	139	HY 6132
Spurn Head (pt.)	75	TA 3910
Spurstow	59	SJ 5556
Spur, The	135	ND 1669
Spùt Rolla	107	NN 7328
Spynie Palace (ant.)	120	NJ 2365
Srath a'Chràisg	133	NC 5424
Srath Beag	132	NC 3853
Srath Dionard	132	NC 3254
Srath Lungard	126	NG 9165
Srath nan Lòn	127	NC 2300
Srath nan Lùb	100	NS 0691
Srath na Seilge	133	NC 7018
Srianach	131	NB 4010
Sròn Ach' a' Bhacaidh (mt.)	128	NH 6198
Sròn a' Chleirich	116	NN 7877
Sròn a' Choire Ghairbh	115	NN 2294
Sròn a' Gheodha Dhuibh	126	NG 7792
Sròn Bheag (Highld.)	111	NM 4662
Sròn Bheag (Tays.)	107	NN 5262
Sròn Mhór	107	NN 6526
Sròn na Carra	123	NG 7473
Sròn na Cléite	126	NG 7389
Sròn na h-Iolaire	110	NM 3891
Sronphadruig Lodge	116	NN 7178
Sròn Romul (mt.)	130	NA 9615
Sròn Ruadh	131	NB 4636
Sròn Rubha na Gaoithe	134	NC 9911
Stab Hill	86	NX 1472
Staca Leathann	130	NA 9828
Stac a' Mheadais	122	NG 3325
Stac an Aoineidh	104	NM 2522
Stac an Tuill	122	NG 3521
Stack Clò Kearvaig (pt.)	132	NC 2973
Stackhouse	78	SD 8165
Stack Islands	112	NF 7807
Stack o' da Noup	141	HU 3516
Stack of Billyageo	141	HU 4421
Stack of Birrier	143	HU 6394
Stack of the Brough	141	HU 4015
Stackpole	42	SR 9896
Stackpole Head	42	SR 9994
Stack Rocks	42	SM 8113
Stack Skerry	132	HX 5617
Stacks of Duncansby	135	ND 4071
Stacksteads	78	SD 8421
Stac na Cathaig	116	NH 6430
Stac Pollaidh (mt.)	132	NC 1010
Stac Shuardail	131	NB 4830
Staddiscombe	20	SX 5151
Staddlethorpe	74	SE 8426
Stadhampton	47	SU 6098
Staffa (is.)	104	NM 3235
Staffield	83	NY 5442
Staffin	123	NG 4967
Staffin Bay	123	NG 4869
Staffin Island	123	NG 4969
Stafford	59	SJ 9223
Staffordshire and Worcestershire Canal	49	SO 8689
Stagsden	52	SP 9849
Stainburn	79	SE 2448
Stainby	62	SK 9022
Staincross	71	SE 3210
Stain Dale	80	SE 8690
Staindrop	84	NZ 1220
Staines	36	TQ 0471
Stainfield (Lincs.)	62	TF 0724
Stainfield (Lincs.)	73	TF 1173
Stainforth (N Yorks.)	78	SD 8267
Stainforth (S Yorks.)	71	SE 6411
Stainforth and Keadby Canal	74	SE 7311
Staining	77	SD 3435
Stainland	70	SE 0719
Stainmore Forest	84	NY 9411
Stainsacre	81	NZ 9108
Stainton (Cleve.)	85	NZ 4714
Stainton (Cumbr.)	83	NY 4827
Stainton (Cumbr.)	77	SD 5285
Stainton (Durham)	84	NZ 0718
Stainton (N Yorks.)	84	SE 1096
Stainton (S Yorks.)	71	SK 5593
Stainton by Langworth	72	TF 0577
Staintondale	81	SE 9898
Stainton Fell	82	SD 1594
Stainton le Vale	73	TF 1794
Stainton with Adgarley	76	SD 2472
Stair (Cumbr.)	82	NY 2321
Stair (Strath.)	93	NS 4323
Staithes	85	NZ 7818
Stakeford	91	NZ 2785
Stake Pass	82	NY 2608
Stake Pool	77	SD 4148
Stalbridge	25	ST 7317
Stalbridge Weston	25	ST 7216
Stalham	65	TG 3725
Stalham Green	65	TG 3824
Stalisfield Green	31	TQ 9652
Stallingborough	75	TA 2011
Stalling Busk	78	SD 9185
Stalmine	77	SD 3745
Stalybridge	70	SJ 9698
Stambourne	54	TL 7238
Stamford	62	TF 0207
Stamford Bridge	80	SE 7155
Stamfordham	91	NZ 0772
Stanborough	37	TL 2210
Stanbridge (Beds.)	36	SP 9623
Stanbridge (Dorset)	26	SU 0003
Stand	101	NS 7668
Standard (mt.)	86	NX 3085
Standburn	102	NS 9274
Standeford	59	SJ 9107
Standen	30	TQ 8539
Standford	27	SU 8134
Standish	69	SD 5609
Standlake	47	SP 3902
Standon (Hants.)	26	SU 4227
Standon (Herts.)	37	TL 3922
Standon (Staffs.)	59	SJ 8134
Stane	102	NS 8859
Stanegate (Cumbr.) (ant.)	89	NY 4660
Stanegate (Northum.) (ant.)	90	NY 7868

Stane Street (Essex) (ant.) 37 TL 5421
Stane Street (Surrey) (ant.) 28 TQ 1439
Stanfield 64 TF 9320
Stanford (Beds.) 52 TL 1641
Stanford (Kent) 31 TR 1238
Stanford Bishop 49 SO 6851
Stanford Bridge 49 SO 7165
Stanford Dingley 35 SU 5771
Stanford in the Vale 47 SU 3493
Stanford le Hope 38 TQ 6882
Stanford on Avon 51 SP 5878
Stanford on Soar 61 SK 5422
Stanford on Teme 49 SO 7065
Stanford Rivers 37 TL 5301
Stanger Head 138 HY 5142
Stanghow 85 NZ 6715
Stanhoe 64 TF 8036
Stanhope 95 NT 1229
Stanhope 84 NY 9939
Stanhope Common 84 NY 9642
Stanion 52 SP 9187
Stanley (Derby.) 60 SK 4140
Stanley (Durham) 84 NZ 1953
Stanley (Staffs.) 59 SJ 9252
Stanley (Tays.) 108 NO 1033
Stanley (W Yorks.) 79 SE 3422
Stanley Force 82 SD 1699
Stanmer 29 TQ 3309
Stanmore (Berks.) 35 SU 4778
Stanmore (Gtr London) 37 TQ 1692
Stannery Knowe 93 NS 4912
Stannington (Northum.) 91 NZ 2179
Stannington (S Yorks.) 71 SK 2988
Stansbatch 48 SO 3461
Stansfield 54 TL 7852
Stansore Point 27 SZ 4698
Stanstead 54 TL 8449
Stanstead Abbotts 37 TL 3811
Stansted 30 TQ 6062
Stansted Airport 37 TL 5422
Stansted House 27 SU 7610
Stansted Mountfitchet 37 TL 5124
Stanton (Glos.) 46 SP 0634
Stanton (Northum.) 91 NZ 1390
Stanton (Staffs.) 60 SK 1246
Stanton (Suff.) 54 TL 9673
Stanton by Bridge 60 SK 3627
Stanton by Dale 61 SK 4637
Stanton Drew 33 ST 5963
Stanton Fitzwarren 34 SU 1790
Stanton Harcourt 47 SP 4105
Stanton Hill 71 SK 4860
Stanton in Peak 71 SK 2464
Stanton Lacy 48 SO 4978
Stanton Long 48 SO 5690
Stanton-on-the-Wolds 61 SK 6330
Stanton Prior 33 ST 6762
Stanton St. Bernard 34 SU 0962
Stanton St. John 47 SP 5709
Stanton St. Quintin 33 ST 9079
Stanton Street 54 TL 9566
Stanton under Bardon 61 SK 4610
Stanton upon Hine Heath 59 SJ 5624
Stanton Wick 33 ST 6162
Stanwardine in the Fields 58 SJ 4124
Stanway (Essex) 38 TL 9324
Stanway (Glos.) 46 SP 0532
Stanwell 36 TQ 0574
Stanwell Moor 36 TQ 0474
Stanwick 52 SP 9871
Stanydale 140 HU 2850
Stape 80 SE 7993
Stapehill 26 SU 0500
Stapeley 59 SJ 6749
Staple 31 TR 2756
Staplecross 30 TQ 7822
Staplefield 28 TQ 2728
Staple Fitzpaine 24 ST 2618
Stapleford (Cambs.) 53 TL 4751
Stapleford (Herts.) 37 TL 3117
Stapleford (Leic.) 61 SK 8018
Stapleford (Lincs.) 72 SK 8757
Stapleford (Notts.) 61 SK 4837
Stapleford (Wilts.) 26 SU 0637
Stapleford Abbotts 37 TQ 5095
Stapleford Aerodrome 37 TQ 4996
Stapleford Tawney 37 TQ 5098
Staplegrove 24 ST 2126
Staple Hill 24 ST 2416
Staplehurst 30 TQ 7843
Staplers 27 SZ 5189
Staple Sound 97 NU 2236
Stapleton (Avon) 33 ST 6175
Stapleton (Cumbr.) 89 NY 5071
Stapleton (Here. and Worc.) 48 SO 3265
Stapleton (Leic.) 60 SP 4398
Stapleton (N Yorks.) 84 NZ 2612
Stapleton (Shrops.) 58 SJ 4604
Stapleton (Somer.) 25 ST 4621
Stapley 24 ST 1813
Staploe 52 TL 1460
Star (Dyfed) 43 SN 2435
Star (Fife) 103 NO 3103
Star (Somer.) 33 ST 4358
Starbotton 78 SD 9574
Starcross 21 SX 9781
Stare Dam 108 NO 0438
Starston 55 TM 2384
Start Bay 21 SX 8444
Startforth 84 NZ 0416
Startley 34 ST 9482
Start Point (Corn.) 20 SX 0485
Start Point (Devon) 21 SX 8337
Start Point (Sanday, Orkney) 139 HY 7843
Startup Hill 95 NS 9729
Stathe 24 ST 3728
Stathern 61 SK 7731
Station Town 85 NZ 4036
Stattic Point 126 NG 9796
Staughton Highway 52 TL 1364
Staunton (Glos.) 45 SO 5412
Staunton (Glos.) 46 SO 7929
Staunton Harold Hall 60 SK 3721
Staunton Harold Reservoir 60 SK 3723
Staunton on Arrow 45 SO 3660
Staunton on Wye 45 SO 3645
Stava Ness 141 HU 5060
Staveley (Cumbr.) 83 SD 4698
Staveley (Derby.) 71 SK 4374
Staveley (N Yorks.) 79 SE 3662
Staveley-in-Cartmel 77 SD 3886
Staverton (Devon) 21 SX 7964
Staverton (Glos.) 46 SO 8923
Staverton (Northants.) 51 SP 5461
Staverton (Wilts.) 33 ST 8560
Stawell 32 ST 3638
Staxigoe 135 ND 3852
Staxton 81 TA 0179
Staylittle 57 SN 8892
Staythorpe 61 SK 7554
Stean 78 SE 0873
Stean Moor 78 SE 0770
Stearsby 79 SE 6171
Steart 32 ST 2745
Stebbing 38 TL 6624
Stedham 27 SU 8622
Steele Road 90 NY 5292
Steel's Knowe 102 NN 9607
Steen's Bridge 45 SO 5457
Steep 27 SU 7525
Steep Holm (is.) 32 ST 2260
Steeping River 73 TF 4661
Steeple (Dorset) 25 SY 9080
Steeple (Essex) 38 TL 9303
Steeple Ashton 33 ST 9056
Steeple Aston 47 SP 4725
Steeple Barton 47 SP 4424
Steeple Bumpstead 54 TL 6741
Steeple Claydon 51 SP 7027
Steeple Gidding 52 TL 1381
Steeple Langford 26 SU 0337
Steeple Morden 53 TL 2842
Steer Rig 97 NT 8524
Steeton 78 SE 0344
Steilston Hill 88 NX 8782
Steinacleit (ant.) 131 NB 3954
Steinmanhill 121 NJ 7642
Steisay 124 NF 8544
Stelling Minnis 31 TR 1446
Stemster 135 ND 1862
Stemster Hill 135 ND 1941
Stemster House 135 ND 1860
Stenalees 19 SX 0157
Stenbury Down 27 SZ 5378
Stenhousemuir 102 NS 8682
Stenhouse Resr. 103 NT 2187
Stenness 142 HU 2177
Stenton 103 NT 6274
Stepney 37 TQ 3581
Steppingley 52 TL 0135
Stepps 101 NS 6668
Sternfield 55 TM 3861
Stert 34 SU 0259
Stert Flats (sbk.) 32 ST 2647
Stetchworth 54 TL 6458
Stevenage 53 TL 2325
Stevenston 93 NS 2642
Steventon (Hants.) 35 SU 5547
Steventon (Oxon.) 35 SU 4691
Stevington 52 SP 9853
Stewartby 52 TL 0242
Stewarton 93 NS 4246
Stewkley 52 SP 8525
Stewton 73 TF 3687
Stey Fell 87 NX 5560
Steyning 28 TQ 1711
Steynton 42 SM 9108
Stibb 22 SS 2210
Stibbard 64 TF 9828
Stibb Cross 22 SS 4314
Stibb Green 34 SU 2262
Stibbington 62 TL 0898
Stichill 96 NT 7138
Sticker 19 SW 9750
Stickford 73 TF 3560
Sticklepath 21 SX 6394
Stickle Pike 82 SD 2192
Stickle Tarn 82 NY 2907
Stickney 63 TF 3456
Stiffkey 64 TF 9743
Stifford's Bridge 49 SO 7348
Stilligarry 112 NF 7638
Stillingfleet 79 SE 5940
Stillington (Cleve. - Durham) 85 NZ 3723
Stillington (N Yorks.) 79 SE 5867
Stilton 52 TL 1689
Stinchcombe 46 ST 7298
Stinsford 25 SY 7191
Stiperstones 58 SO 3699
Stirchley 59 SJ 6906
Stirkoke House 135 ND 3150
Stirling 101 NS 7993
Stisted 38 TL 8024
Stithians 18 SW 7336
Stivichall 50 SP 3376
Stixwould 73 TF 1765
Stoak 68 SJ 4273
Stob a'Choin 107 NN 4115
Stob a'Ghrianain 115 NN 0882
Stob an Aonaich Mhóir 107 NN 5469
Stob an Eas 100 NN 1807
Stob an t-Sluichd 117 NJ 1102
Stob Binnein 107 NN 4322
Stob Choire Claurigh 115 NN 2673
Stob Coir' an Albannaich 106 NN 1644
Stob Coire a' Chearcaill 106 NN 0172
Stob Coire Easain (Highld.) 106 NN 2372
Stob Coire Easain (Highld.) 106 NN 3072
Stob Dubh 106 NN 1648
Stob Ghabhar 106 NN 2345
Stobieside 94 NS 6239
Stob Law 95 NT 2333
Stob na Cruaiche 107 NN 3657
Stobo 95 NT 1837
Stoborough 25 SY 9286
Stoborough Green 25 SY 9184
Stock 38 TQ 6998
Stockay 124 NF 6663
Stockbridge 26 SU 3535
Stockbriggs 94 NS 7936
Stockbury 30 TQ 8461
Stockcross 34 SU 4368
Stockdalewath 83 NY 3845
Stockerston 62 SP 8397
Stock Gaylard House 25 ST 7212
Stock Green 50 SO 9859
Stockingford 50 SP 3391
Stocking Pelham 53 TL 4529
Stockinish Island 125 NG 1389
Stockland 24 ST 2404
Stockland Bristol 32 ST 2443
Stockleigh English 23 SS 8406
Stockleigh Pomeroy 23 SS 8703
Stockley 34 SU 0067
Stockport 69 SJ 8989
Stocksbridge 71 SK 2798
Stocksfield 91 NZ 0561
Stocks Resr. 77 SD 7256
Stockton (Here. and Worc.) 48 SO 5161
Stockton (Norf.) 65 TM 3894
Stockton (Shrops.) 59 SO 7299
Stockton (Warw.) 50 SP 4363
Stockton (Wilts.) 34 ST 9738
Stockton Heath 69 SJ 6185
Stockton-on-Tees 85 NZ 4419
Stockton on Teme 49 SO 7167
Stockton on the Forest 79 SE 6556
Stockwith 72 SK 7994
Stock Wood 50 SP 0058
Stodmarsh 31 TR 2160
Stody 64 TG 0535
Stoer 132 NC 0328
Stoford (Somer.) 25 ST 5613
Stoford (Wilts.) 26 SU 0835
Stogumber 24 ST 0937
Stogursey 32 ST 2042
Stoke (Devon) 22 SS 2324
Stoke (Hants.) 34 SU 4051
Stoke (Hants.) 27 SU 7202
Stoke (Kent) 30 TQ 8275
Stoke Abbott 25 ST 4500
Stoke Albany 51 SP 8088
Stoke Ash 55 TM 1170
Stoke Bardolph 61 SK 6441
Stoke Bliss 49 SO 6562
Stoke Bruerne 51 SP 7450
Stoke by Clare 54 TL 7443
Stoke-by-Nayland 54 TL 9836
Stoke Canon 21 SX 9397
Stoke Charity 35 SU 4839
Stoke Climsland 20 SX 3574
Stoke D'Abernon 37 TQ 1259
Stoke Doyle 52 TL 0286
Stoke Dry 62 SP 8597
Stoke Ferry 64 TF 7000
Stoke Fleming 21 SX 8648
Stokeford 25 SY 8787
Stoke Gabriel 21 SX 8457
Stoke Gifford 33 ST 6280
Stoke Golding 60 SP 3997
Stoke Goldington 52 SP 8348
Stokeham 72 SK 7876
Stoke Hammond 52 SP 8829
Stoke Holy Cross 65 TG 2301
Stokeinteignhead 21 SX 9170
Stoke Lacy 45 SO 6149
Stoke Lyne 47 SP 5628
Stoke Mandeville 36 SP 8310
Stokenchurch 36 SU 7596
Stoke Newington 37 TQ 3286
Stokenham 21 SX 8042
Stoke on Tern 59 SJ 6327
Stoke-on-Trent 59 SJ 8745
Stoke Orchard 46 SO 9128
Stoke Poges 36 SU 9884
Stoke Point 21 SX 5645
Stoke Prior (Here. and Worc.) 45 SO 5256
Stoke Prior (Here. and Worc.) 49 SO 9467
Stoke Rivers 23 SS 6335
Stoke Rochford 62 SK 9127
Stoke Row 36 SU 6883
Stokesay 48 SO 4381
Stokes Bay 27 SZ 5897
Stokesby 65 TG 4310
Stokesley 85 NZ 5208
Stoke St. Gregory 24 ST 3426
Stoke St. Mary 24 ST 2622
Stoke St. Michael 33 ST 6646
Stoke St. Milborough 48 SO 5682
Stoke sub Hamdon 25 ST 4717
Stoke Talmage 36 SU 6799
Stoke Trister 25 ST 7328
Stolford 32 ST 2245
Stondon Massey 37 TL 5800
Stone (Bucks.) 36 SP 7812
Stone (Glos.) 46 ST 6895
Stone (Here. and Worc.) 49 SO 8675
Stone (Kent) 37 TQ 5774
Stone (Staffs.) 59 SJ 9034
Stone Allerton 32 ST 3950
Ston Easton 33 ST 6253
Stonebroom 71 SK 4159
Stonechrubie 132 NC 2419
Stone Cross 29 TQ 6104
Stonefield 94 NS 6957
Stonefield Castle Hotel 99 NR 8671
Stonegate 29 TQ 6628
Stonegate Crofts 121 NK 0339
Stonegrave 79 SE 6577
Stonehaugh 90 NY 7976
Stonehaven 119 NO 8685
Stonehenge (ant.) 34 SU 1242
Stone House (Cumbr.) 78 SD 7785
Stonehouse (Glos.) 46 SO 8005
Stonehouse (Northum.) 90 NY 6958
Stonehouse (Strath.) 94 NS 7546
Stone-in-Oxney 30 TQ 9427
Stoneleigh 50 SP 3272
Stonely 52 TL 1067
Stonesby 62 SK 8224
Stonesdale Moor 84 NY 8804
Stonesfield 47 SP 3917
Stones Green 55 TM 1626
Stoneside Hill 82 SD 1489
Stone Street (Kent) (ant.) 31 TR 1350
Stone Street (Suff.) (ant.) 55 TM 3686
Stoneybridge 112 NF 7433
Stoneyburn 102 NS 9762
Stoney Cross 26 SU 2511
Stoneygate 61 SK 6102
Stoneyhills 38 TQ 9497
Stoneykirk 86 NX 0853
Stoney Middleton. 71 SK 2275
Stoney Stanton 61 SP 4894
Stoney Stratton 33 ST 6539
Stoney Stretton 58 SJ 3809
Stoneywood 119 NJ 8910
Stonga Banks 142 HU 2985
Stonganess 143 HP 5402
Stonham Aspal 55 TM 1359
Stonnall 60 SK 0603
Stonor 36 SU 7388
Stonton Wyville 61 SP 7395
Stonybreck 139 HZ 2071
Stonyfield 128 NH 6973
Stonyhurst College 77 SD 6838
Stony Stratford 51 SP 7840
Stood Hill 88 NS 8512
Stoodleigh 23 SS 9218
Stoodleigh Beacon 23 SS 8818
Stopham 28 TQ 0219
Stopsley 37 TL 1023
Storeton 68 SJ 3084
Stornoway 131 NB 4233
Stornoway Aerodrome 131 NB 4533
Storridge 49 SO 7448
Storrington 28 TQ 0814
Storrs 83 SD 3994
Storr, The (mt.) 123 NG 4954
Storth 77 SD 4780
Stotfold 52 TL 2136
Stottesdon 49 SO 6782
Stoughton (Leic.) 61 SK 6402
Stoughton (Surrey) 28 SU 9851
Stoughton (W Susx) 27 SU 8011
Stoul 111 NM 7594
Stoulton 49 SO 9049
Stourbridge 49 SO 8984
Stourbrough Hill 140 HU 2152
Stourhead 25 ST 7734
Stourpaine 25 ST 8509
Stourport-on-Severn 49 SO 8171
Stour Provost 25 ST 7921
Stour Row 25 ST 8220
Stourton (Here. and Worc.) 49 SO 8585
Stourton (Warw.) 50 SP 2936
Stourton (Wilts.) 25 ST 7733
Stourton Caundle 25 ST 7114
Stove 139 HY 6035
Stoven 55 TM 4481
Stow (Borders) 96 NT 4644
Stow (Lincs.) 72 SK 8781
Stow Bardolph 64 TF 6205
Stow Bardolph Fen 63 TF 5603
Stow Bedon 64 TL 9596
Stowbridge 64 TF 6007
Stow cum Quy 53 TL 5260
Stowe (Shrops.) 48 SO 3173
Stowe-by-Chartley 60 SK 0027
Stowell 25 ST 6822
Stowe School 51 SP 6737
Stowford 20 SX 4386
Stowlangtoft 54 TL 9568
Stow Longa 52 TL 1171
Stow Maries 38 TQ 8399
Stowmarket 54 TM 0458
Stow-on-the-Wold 47 SP 1925
Stowting 31 TR 1241
Stowupland 54 TM 0659
Straad 100 NS 0462
Strachan 119 NO 6792
Strachur 100 NN 0901
Strachur Bay 100 NN 0801
Stradbroke 55 TM 2373
Stradishall 54 TL 7452
Stradsett 64 TF 6605
Stragglethorpe 62 SK 9152
Strait of Dover 31 TR 3828
Straiton (Lothian) 103 NT 2766
Straiton (Strath.) 93 NS 3804
Straloch (Grampn.) 121 NJ 8621
Straloch (Tays.) 108 NO 0463
Stramshall 60 SK 0735
Strandburgh Ness 143 HU 6793
Strangend Currick 83 NY 8443
Stranraer 86 NX 0660
Strata Florida 57 SN 7465
Stratfield Mortimer 36 SU 6764
Stratfield Saye 36 SU 6961
Stratfield Turgis 36 SU 6959
Stratford St. Andrew 55 TM 3560
Stratford St. Mary 54 TM 0434
Stratford Tony 26 SU 0926
Stratford-upon-Avon 50 SP 2055
Stratford-upon-Avon Canal 50 SP 1764
Strath 126 NG 7978
Strathaird 123 NG 5419
Strathallan 101 NN 8307
Strathallan Castle 108 NN 9115
Strathan (Highld.) 132 NC 0821
Strathan (Highld.) 114 NM 9891
Strath an Lòin 133 NC 4416
Strathaven 94 NS 7044
Strath Avon 117 NJ 1525
Strath Beag 127 NH 1087
Strath Beg 134 NC 8531
Strath Blane (Central) 101 NS 5381
Strathblane (Central) 101 NS 5679
Strathblane Hills 101 NS 5581
Strath Bogie (Grampn.) 121 NJ 5237
Strathbogie (Grampn.) (dist.) 121 NJ 4937
Strathbraan 108 NN 9739
Strath Bran 127 NH 2460
Strath Brora 134 NC 7609
Strath Burn 135 ND 2450
Strathcarron (Highld.) 126 NG 9442
Strathcarron (Highld.) 128 NH 5591
Strathcoil 105 NM 6830
Strathconon 127 NH 4055
Strathconon Forest 127 NH 2347
Strath Cuileannach 128 NH 4393
Strathdearn 116 NH 7724
Strathdon 118 NJ 3513
Strath Dores 116 NH 6137
Strath Eachaig 100 NS 1484
Strath Earn 108 NN 8818
Stratherrick 116 NH 5017
Strath Fillan 107 NN 3628
Strath Finella 119 NO 6879
Strathfinella Hill 119 NO 6978
Strath Fleet 128 NC 6702
Strath Gartney 101 NN 4610
Strathgarve Forest 128 NH 4163
Strathglass 115 NH 3734
Strathgryfe 100 NS 3270
Strath Halladale 134 NC 8953
Strathhardle 108 NO 1153
Strath Isla 121 NJ 4451
Strath Kanaird (Highld.) 127 NC 1400
Strath Kanaird (Highld) 127 NC 1501
Strathkinness 109 NO 4516
Strathlachlan Forest 100 NS 0093
Strath Lungard 126 NG 9264
Strath Mashie 116 NN 5891
Strathmashie House 116 NN 5891
Strath Melness Burn 133 NC 5663
Strathmiglo 103 NO 2109
Strath More (Highld.) 133 NC 4545
Strath More (Highld.) 127 NH 1882
Strathmore (Tays.) (dist.) 109 NO 4353
Strathmore Lodge 135 ND 1047
Strathmore River 133 NC 4546
Strath Mulzie 127 NH 3193
Strathnairn 116 NH 6832
Strathnairn Forest 116 NH 6930
Strath nan Lùb 100 NS 0792
Strath na Sealga 127 NH 0680
Strathnasheallag Forest 127 NH 0483
Strathnaver 134 NC 7148
Strath of Appin 106 NM 9545
Strath of Kildonan or Strath Ullie 134 NC 8923
Strath of Orchy 106 NN 1627
Strathord Forest 108 NO 0631
Strath Oykel 128 NC 4300
Strathpeffer 128 NH 4858
Strath Rannoch (Highld.) 127 NH 3872
Strathrannoch (Highld.) 127 NH 3874
Strath Rory 128 NH 6976
Strath Rusdale 128 NH 5777
Strath Sgitheach 128 NH 5263
Strath Shinary 132 NC 2561
Strath Skinsdale 134 NC 7518
Strathspey 117 NJ 1536
Strath Stack 132 NC 2740
Strath Suardal 123 NG 6221
Strath Tay 108 NO 0043
Strath Tirry 133 NC 5319
Strath Ullie or Strath of Kildonan 134 NC 8923
Strath Vagastie 133 NC 5430
Strath Vaich 127 NH 3572
Strathvaich Forest 127 NH 3276
Strathvaich Lodge 127 NH 3474
Strathwhillan 92 NS 0235
Strathy 134 NC 8465
Strathy Bay 134 NC 8366
Strathy Forest (Highld.) 134 NC 8256
Strathy Forest (Highld.) 134 NC 8262
Strathy Point 134 NC 8269
Strathyre 107 NN 5617
Strathyre Forest 107 NN 5718
Stratton (Corn.) 22 SS 2306
Stratton (Dorset) 25 SY 6593
Stratton (Glos.) 46 SP 0103
Stratton Audley 47 SP 6026
Stratton-on-the-Fosse 33 ST 6550
Stratton St. Margaret 34 SU 1787
Stratton St. Michael 65 TM 2093
Stratton Strawless 65 TG 2220
Stravanan Bay 92 NS 0755
Stravithie 103 NO 5311
Strawarren Fell 86 NX 1679
Streat 29 TQ 3515
Streatham 37 TQ 2972
Streatlam Castle 84 NZ 0819
Streatley (Beds.) 52 TL 0728
Streatley (Berks.) 35 SU 5980
Streens 117 NH 8638
Street (Lancs.) 77 SD 5252
Street (N Yorks.) 80 NZ 7304
Street (Somer.) 25 ST 4836
Street End 27 SZ 8599
Streethay 60 SK 1410
Streetly 60 SP 0898
Strefford 48 SO 4485
Strem Ness 140 HT 9741
Strensall 79 SE 6360
Strensham 49 SO 9040
Stretcholt 32 ST 2943
Strete 21 SX 8447
Stretford 69 SJ 7894
Stretford Court 45 SO 4455
Strethall 53 TL 4939
Stretham 53 TL 5174
Strettington 27 SU 8807
Stretton (Ches.) 58 SJ 4452
Stretton (Ches.) 69 SJ 6182
Stretton (Derby.) 71 SK 3961
Stretton (Leic.) 62 SK 9415
Stretton (Staffs.) 59 SJ 8811
Stretton (Staffs.) 60 SK 2526
Stretton en le Field 60 SK 3012
Stretton Grandison 45 SO 6344
Stretton Heath 58 SJ 3610
Stretton-on-Dunsmore 50 SP 4072
Stretton-on-Fosse 50 SP 2238
Stretton under Fosse 51 SP 4581
Stretton Westwood 59 SO 5998
Strichen 121 NJ 9455
Strines Resr. 71 SK 2290
Stringston 32 ST 1742
String, The 136 HY 4714
Strixton 52 SP 9061
Stroan Loch 88 NX 6470
Stroat 45 ST 5798
Stròc-bheinn 123 NG 4539
Stroin Vuigh (pt.) 76 SC 2174
Stromeferry 123 NG 8634
Stromemore 123 NG 8635
Strom Ness (Muckle Roe) 140 HU 2965
Strom Ness (N. Ronaldsay) 139 HY 7651
Stromness (Orkney) 136 HY 2509
Strom Ness (Vaila) 140 HU 2245
Stromness Taing 136 HY 4425
Stronabo 115 NN 2084
Stronachlachar 101 NN 4010
Stronchreggan 106 NN 0772
Stronchrubie 132 NC 2419
Stronchullin Hill 100 NS 1686
Strond 124 NG 0384
Strone (Highld.) 116 NH 5228
Strone (Highld.) 115 NN 1481
Strone (Strath.) 100 NS 1880
Strone Glen 92 NR 6310
Stronend (mt.) 101 NS 6289
Strone Point (Strath.) 100 NS 0771
Strone Point (Strath.) 100 NS 1980
Strone Water 92 NR 6310
Stronmilchan 106 NN 1528
Stronsay 137 HY 6525
Stronsay Aerodrome 137 HY 6329
Stronsay Firth 137 HY 5722
Strontian 111 NM 8161
Strontian River 111 NM 8363
Stronuich Reservoir 107 NN 5042
Strood 30 TQ 7369
Stroud (Glos.) 46 SO 8504
Stroud (Hants.) 27 SU 7223
Struan 122 NG 3438
Struan Station 107 NN 8065
Strubby 73 TF 4582
Struie (mt.) 128 NH 6584
Strumble Head 42 SM 8941
Strumpshaw 65 TG 3507
Strutherhill 94 NS 7650
Struy 115 NH 4039
Struy Forest 115 NH 3737
Stuartfield 121 NJ 9745
Stubbington 27 SU 5503
Stubbins 69 SD 7918
Stubhampton 25 ST 9113
Stub Place 82 SD 0890
Stubton 62 SK 8748
Stuchd an Lochain 107 NN 4844
Stuckgowan 100 NN 3202
Stuckton 26 SU 1613
Stuc Scardan 100 NN 1114
Studham 36 TL 0215
Studland 26 SZ 0382
Studland Bay 26 SZ 0584
Studley (Warw.) 50 SP 0763
Studley (Wilts.) 34 ST 9671
Studley Roger 79 SE 2970
Stulaval (Isle of Lewis) (mt.) 131 NB 1312
Stulaval (South Uist) (mt.) 112 NF 8024
Stuley 112 NF 8323
Stump Cross 53 TL 5044
Stuntney 53 TL 5578
Sturbridge 59 SJ 8330
Sturdy Hill 119 NO 5977
Sturgate Airport 72 SK 8888
Sturmer 54 TL 6944
Sturminster Common 25 ST 7812
Sturminster Marshall 26 SY 9499
Sturminster Newton 25 ST 7813
Sturry 31 TR 1760
Sturton by Stow 72 SK 8980
Sturton le Steeple 72 SK 7884
Stuston 55 TM 1378
Stutton (N Yorks.) 79 SE 4741
Stutton (Suff.) 55 TM 1434
Styal 69 SJ 8383
Sty Head 82 NY 2109
Sty Wick 139 HY 6838
Suainaval (mt.) 130 NB 0730
Succoth 121 NJ 4235
Suckley 49 SO 7151
Suckley Hills 49 SO 7352
Sudborough 52 SP 9682
Sudbourne 55 TM 4153
Sudbrook 33 ST 5087
Sudbrooke 72 TF 0276
Sudbury (Derby.) 60 SK 1631
Sudbury (Suff.) 54 TL 8741
Suddie 128 NH 6654
Sudeley Castle (ant.) 46 SP 0327
Sudgrove 46 SO 9307
Sueno's Stone (ant.) 129 NJ 0459
Suffield 65 TG 2332
Sugar Loaf 45 SO 2718
Sugnall 59 SJ 7930
Suidh'a'Mhinn 123 NG 4068
Suidhe Ghuirmain (mt.) 115 NH 3826
Suie Hill 121 NJ 5523
Suilven (mt.) 132 NC 1517
Suisgill Burn 134 NC 8925
Suisnish Hill 123 NG 5634
Sula Sgeir (is.) 130 HW 6230
Sulby 76 SC 3994
Sulby Reservoir 51 SP 6581
Sulby River 76 SC 3890
Sule Skerry 132 HX 6224
Sulgrave 51 SP 5545
Sulham 36 SU 6474
Sulhamstead 36 SU 6368
Sullington 28 TQ 0913
Sullom 142 HU 3573
Sullom Voe 143 HU 3773
Sully 41 ST 1568
Sully Island 41 ST 1667
Sulma Water 140 HU 2555
Sumburgh 141 HU 4009
Sumburgh Airport 141 HU 3910
Sumburgh Head 141 HU 4007
Sumburgh Roost (chan.) 141 HU 4006
Summer Bridge 78 SE 1962
Summercourt 19 SW 8856
Summer Down 33 ST 9148
Summer Isles 126 NB 9706
Summerleaze 33 ST 4284
Summerseat 69 SD 7914
Summit 69 SD 9418
Sunadale 92 NR 8145
Sunart (dist.) 111 NM 7966
Sunbury 37 TQ 1069
Sunderland (Cumbr.) 82 NY 1735
Sunderland (Tyne and Wear) 85 NZ 3957
Sunderland Airport 91 NZ 3458
Sunderland Bank (sbk.) 77 SD 3956

Sunderland Bridge 84 NZ 2637
Sunderland Point 77 SD 4255
Sundhope 96 NT 3324
Sundon Park 52 TL 0525
Sundridge 29 TQ 4854
Sundrum (ant.) 93 NS 4121
Sunk (lightship) 39 TM 4623
Sunk Island 75 TA 2619
Sunk Island Sands 75 TA 3016
Sunk Sand 39 TM 3000
Sunningdale 36 SU 9567
Sunninghill 36 SU 9367
Sunningwell 47 SP 4900
Sunniside (Durham) 84 NZ 1438
Sunniside (Tyne and Wear) 91 NZ 2159
Sunny Bank 82 SD 2992
Sunnylaw 101 NS 7998
Sunnyside 29 TQ 3937
Surbiton 37 TQ 1867
Surfleet 63 TF 2528
Surfleet Seas End 63 TF 2628
Surlingham 65 TG 3106
Surrey Hill 36 SU 8863
Sursay 124 NF 9576
Sustead 65 TG 1837
Susworth 74 SE 8302
Sutcombe 22 SS 3411
Suton 65 TM 0999
Sutors of Cromarty 129 NH 8067
Sutterton 63 TF 2835
Sutton (Beds.) 53 TL 2247
Sutton (Cambs.) 53 TL 4479
Sutton (Gtr London) 37 TQ 2463
Sutton (Kent) 31 TR 3349
Sutton (Norf.) 65 TG 3823
Sutton (Northants.) 62 TL 0998
Sutton (Notts.) 71 SK 6784
Sutton (Notts.) 61 SK 7637
Sutton (Oxon.) 47 SP 4106
Sutton (Shrops.) 59 SJ 6631
Sutton (Shrops.) 48 SO 5082
Sutton (Shrops.) 49 SO 7286
Sutton (Staffs.) 59 SJ 7622
Sutton (Suff.) 55 TM 3046
Sutton (Surrey) 28 TQ 1046
Sutton (W Susx) 28 SU 9715
Sutton at Hone 37 TQ 5570
Sutton Bassett 51 SP 7790
Sutton Benger 34 ST 9478
Sutton Bingham Resr. 25 ST 5410
Sutton Bonington 61 SK 5025
Sutton Bridge 63 TF 4821
Sutton Cheney 60 SK 4100
Sutton Coldfield 60 SP 1296
Sutton Courtenay 47 SU 5093
Sutton Crosses 63 TF 4321
Sutton Grange 79 SE 2874
Sutton Hoo Tumuli (ant.) 55 TM 2849
Sutton Howgrave 79 SE 3179
Sutton in Ashfield 71 SK 5058
Sutton-in-Craven 78 SE 0044
Sutton Lane Ends 69 SJ 9270
Sutton Leach 69 SJ 5393
Sutton Maddock 59 SJ 7201
Sutton Mallet 24 ST 3736
Sutton Mandeville 26 ST 9828
Sutton Montis 25 ST 6224
Sutton-on-Hull 75 TA 1132
Sutton on Sea 73 TF 5282
Sutton-on-the-Forest 79 SE 5864
Sutton on the Hill 60 SK 2333
Sutton on Trent 72 SK 7965
Sutton Park 60 SP 0996
Sutton Scotney 35 SU 4539
Sutton St. Edmund 63 TF 3613
Sutton St. James 63 TF 3918
Sutton St. Nicholas 45 SO 5345
Sutton-under-Brailes 50 SP 2937
Sutton-under-Whitestonecliffe 79 SE 4882
Sutton upon Derwent 74 SE 7046
Sutton Valence 30 TQ 8148
Sutton Veny 33 ST 9041
Sutton Waldron 25 ST 8615
Sutton Walls (ant.) 45 SO 5246
Sutton Weaver 69 SJ 5479
Swaby 73 TF 3877
Swadlincote 60 SK 3019
Swaffham 64 TF 8109
Swaffham Bulbeck 53 TL 5562
Swaffham Prior 53 TL 5764
Swafield 65 TG 2832
Swainbost 131 NB 5162
Swainby 85 NZ 4701
Swainshill 45 SO 4641
Swainsthorpe 65 TG 2101
Swainswick 33 ST 7568
Swalcliffe 50 SP 3738
Swalecliffe 31 TR 1367
Swaledale 84 SD 9598
Swale, The 31 TQ 9866
Swallow 75 TA 1703
Swallowcliffe 26 ST 9626
Swallow Falls 67 SH 7657
Swallowfield 36 SU 7264
Swanage 26 SZ 0278
Swanage Bay 26 SZ 0480
Swanbister Bay 136 HY 3604
Swanbister House 136 HY 3505
Swanbourne 51 SP 8027
Swanland 74 SE 9927
Swanley 37 TQ 5168
Swanmore 27 SU 5815
Swannington (Leic.) 60 SK 4116
Swannington (Norf.) 65 TG 1319
Swanscombe 30 TQ 6074
Swansea 40 SS 6593
Swansea Airport 40 SS 5691
Swansea Bay 40 SS 6888
Swansea Valley 41 SN 7506
Swanton Abbott 65 TG 2625
Swanton Morley 64 TG 0117
Swanton Novers 64 TG 0132
Swanwick (Derby.) 71 SK 4053
Swanwick (Hants.) 27 SU 5109
Swarbacks Head 140 HU 2861
Swarbacks Minn (chan.) 141 HU 3161
Swarby 62 TF 0440
Swardeston 65 TG 2002
Swarf, The 139 HY 6737
Swarkestone 60 SK 3728
Swarland 91 NU 1601
Swarland Estate 91 NU 1603
Swartz Geo 139 HZ 2170
Swaton 62 TF 1337
Swatte Fell 89 NT 1110
Swavesey 53 TL 3669
Sway 26 SZ 2798
Swayfield 62 SK 9822
Swaythling 26 SU 4315
Sweetheart Abbey 88 NX 9566
Sweethope Hill 96 NT 6939
Sweethope Loughs 90 NY 9482
Swefling 55 TM 3463
Swepstone 60 SK 3610
Swerford 47 SP 3731
Swettenham 69 SJ 8067
Sweyn Holm 136 HY 4522
Swffyd 41 ST 2198
Swilland 55 TM 1853
Swillington 79 SE 3830
Swimbridge 23 SS 6230
Swinbrook 47 SP 2812
Swindale Beck 83 NY 5112
Swinden Resrs. 78 SD 8933
Swinderby 72 SK 8662
Swindon (Glos.) 46 SO 9325
Swindon (Staffs.) 49 SO 8690
Swindon (Wilts.) 34 SU 1484
Swine 75 TA 1335
Swinefleet 74 SE 7621
Swineshead (Beds.) 52 TL 0565
Swineshead (Lincs.) 63 TF 2340
Swineshead Bridge 62 TF 2142
Swiney 135 ND 2335
Swinford (Leic.) 51 SP 5679
Swinford (Oxon.) 47 SP 4408
Swingfield Minnis 31 TR 2142
Swinhill 94 NS 7748
Swinhoe 97 NU 2028
Swinhope 73 TF 2196
Swining 141 HU 4566
Swining Voe 141 HU 4667
Swinister 143 HU 4472
Swinithwaite 84 SE 0489
Swinscoe 60 SK 1347
Swinside Hall 90 NT 7216
Swinstead 62 TF 0122
Swinsty Resr. 78 SE 1953
Swinton (Borders) 97 NT 8447
Swinton (Gtr Mches.) 69 SD 7701
Swinton (N Yorks.) 78 SE 2179
Swinton (N Yorks.) 80 SE 7573
Swinton (S Yorks.) 71 SK 4499
Swintonmill 97 NT 8145
Switha (is.) 136 ND 3690
Switha Sound 136 ND 3591
Swithland 61 SK 5413
Swithland Resr. 61 SK 5513
Swona (is.) 136 ND 3884
Swordale 128 NH 5765
Swordland 111 NM 7891
Swordly 134 NC 7363
Sworton Heath 69 SJ 6784
Swyddffynnon 57 SN 6966
Swynnerton 59 SJ 8435
Swyre 25 SY 5288
Syde 46 SO 9411
Sydenham (Gtr London) 37 TQ 3571
Sydenham (Oxon.) 36 SP 7301
Sydenham Damerel 20 SX 4075
Syderstone 64 TF 8332
Sydling St. Nicholas 25 SY 6399
Sydmonton 35 SU 4857
Syerston 61 SK 7447
Syke 69 SD 8915
Sykehouse 71 SE 6216
Sykes 78 SD 6251
Sykes Fell 77 SD 6048
Sylen 43 SN 5107
Symbister 141 HU 5362
Symington (Strath.) 93 NS 3831
Symington (Strath.) 95 NS 9935
Symondsbury 25 SY 4493
Symonds Yat 45 SO 5516
Synod Inn 43 SN 4054
Syre 133 NC 6843
Syreford 46 SP 0320
Syresham 51 SP 6241
Syston (Leic.) 61 SK 6211
Syston (Lincs.) 62 SK 9240
Sytchampton 49 SO 8466
Sythe Harbour 124 NB 0203
Sywell 52 SP 8267
Sywell Resr. 52 SP 8365

T

Taberon Law 95 NT 1428
Tabhaidh Mhor (is.) 131 NB 4222
Tackley 47 SP 4720
Tacolneston 65 TM 1395
Tadcaster 79 SE 4843
Tadden 26 ST 9801
Taddington 70 SK 1471
Tadley 35 SU 6060
Tadlow 53 TL 2847
Tadmarton 50 SP 3937
Tadworth 28 TQ 2356
Tafarnaubach 41 SO 1110
Tafarn-y-Gelyn 68 SJ 1861
Taf Fechan 41 SO 0317
Taff's Well 41 ST 1283
Taff Vale 41 ST 0892
Tafolog 57 SH 8902
Tafolwern 57 SH 8902
Tafts Ness 139 HY 7647
Tahay 124 NF 9675
Tai-bach (Clwyd) 58 SJ 1528
Taibach (W Glam.) 41 SS 7789
Tailor's Leap (mt.) 106 NN 0027
Tain (Highld.) 135 ND 2266
Tain (Highld.) 129 NH 7782
Taing of Kelswick 143 HU 4969
Taing of Maywick 141 HU 3725
Taing, The (Orkney) 136 HY 4225
Taing, The (Shetld.) 141 HU 4011
Tai'n Lôn 66 SH 4450
Tai'r Bull 41 SN 9926
Tairlaw Ring 86 NX 4098
Takeley 37 TL 5521
Talachddu 41 SO 0733
Talacre 67 SJ 1083
Talaton 24 SY 0699
Talbenny 42 SM 8412
Talerddig 57 SH 9300
Talgarreg 43 SN 4251
Talgarth 41 SO 1534
Talhenbont (ant.) 66 SH 4639
Taliesin 57 SN 6591
Talisker 122 NG 3230
Talisker Bay 122 NG 3030
Talke 59 SJ 8253
Talkin 83 NY 5557
Talkin Tarn 90 NY 5458
Talla Bheith Forest 107 NN 5567
Talladale 126 NG 9270
Talla Linnfoots 89 NT 1320
Talland Bay 19 SX 2251
Tallantire 82 NY 1035
Talla Resr. 95 NT 1121
Talley 43 SN 6332
Tallington 62 TF 0908
Talmine 133 NC 5862
Talog 43 SN 3325
Talsarn 43 SN 5456
Talsarnau 66 SH 6135
Talskiddy 19 SW 9165
Talwrn 66 SH 4876
Talybont (Dyfed) 57 SN 6589
Tal-y-bont (Gwyn.) 57 SH 5921
Tal-y-Bont (Gwyn.) 67 SH 7668
Talybont (Powys) 41 SO 1122
Talybont Reservoir 41 SO 0919
Tal-y-cafn 67 SH 7971
Tal y Fan 67 SH 7272
Tal-y-llyn (Gwyn.) 57 SH 7109
Talyllyn (Powys) 41 SO 1127
Talysarn 66 SH 4852
Talywern 57 SH 8200
Tamerton Foliot 20 SX 4761
Tamworth 60 SK 2004
Tandridge 29 TQ 3750
Tanera Beg (is.) 126 NB 9607
Tanera Mór (is.) 126 NB 9807
Tanfield 84 NZ 1855
Tangasdale 112 NF 6500
Tang Head (Highld.) 135 ND 2774
Tang Head (Highld.) 135 ND 3561
Tangley 34 SU 3352
Tangmere 27 SU 9006
Tangwick 142 HU 2377
Tangy Loch 92 NR 6927
Tan Hill (Durham-N Yorks.) 84 NY 8906
Tan Hill (Wilts.) 34 SU 0864
Tankerness 136 HY 5108
Tankersley 71 SK 3499
Tannach 135 ND 3247
Tannadice 109 NO 4758
Tannington 55 TM 2467
Tansley 71 SK 3259
Tansor 52 TL 0590
Tantallon Castle (ant.) 103 NT 5985
Tan, The 93 NS 1553
Tantobie 84 NZ 1754
Tanton 85 NZ 5210
Tanworth in Arden 50 SP 1170
Tan-y-fron 67 SH 9564
Tanygrisiau 67 SH 6845
Tan-y-groes 43 SN 2849
Tan-y-pistyll 67 SJ 0729
Taob 136 HY 5005
Tapeley 22 SS 4729
Taplow 36 SU 9182
Tap o' Noth (mt.) 121 NJ 4829
Tarain (mt.) 130 NB 0427
Taran Mór (mt.) 130 NB 0315
Taransay 124 NB 0201
Taransay Glorigs 124 NA 9606
Tarbat House 129 NH 7773
Tarbat Ness 129 NH 9487
Tarbert (Harris, W Isles) 125 NB 1500
Tarbert (Jura) 98 NR 6082
Tarbert (Strath.) 92 NR 6551
Tarbert (Strath.) 99 NR 8668
Tarbet (Highld.) 132 NC 1648
Tarbet (Highld.) 111 NM 7992
Tarbet (Strath.) 100 NN 3104
Tarbock Green 68 SJ 4687
Tarbolton 93 NS 4327
Tarbrax 95 NT 0255
Tarfessock (mt.) 86 NX 4088
Tarfside 118 NO 4979
Tarf Tail (pt.) 130 NB 3783
Tarf Water (Dumf. and Galwy.) 86 NX 2662
Tarf Water (Tays.) 117 NN 9080
Tarland 118 NJ 4804
Tarleton 68 SD 4420
Tarlogie 129 NH 7583
Tarlscough 68 SD 4313
Tarlshof (ant.) 141 HU 3909
Tarlton 46 ST 9599
Tarnbrook 77 SD 5855
Tarner Island 122 NG 2938
Tarporley 69 SJ 5562
Tarr 24 ST 1030
Tarrant Crawford 25 ST 9203
Tarrant Gunville 25 ST 9212
Tarrant Hinton 26 ST 9310
Tarrant Keynston 25 ST 9204
Tarrant Launceston 26 ST 9409
Tarrant Monkton 26 ST 9408
Tarrant Rawston 26 ST 9306
Tarrant Rushton 26 ST 9305
Tarras Water 89 NY 4086
Tarrenhendre 57 SH 6804
Tarring Neville 29 TQ 4404
Tarrington 45 SO 6140
Tarsappie 108 NO 1220
Tarskavaig 123 NG 5810
Tarskavaig Point 123 NG 5709
Tarty Burn 121 NJ 9325
Tarves 121 NJ 8631
Tarvie (Highld.) (dist.) 128 NH 4258
Tarvie (Tays.) 108 NO 0164
Tarvin 69 SJ 4867
Tasburgh 65 TM 2095
Tasley 59 SO 6994
Taston 47 SP 3521
Tatenhill 60 SK 2022
Tatham 77 SD 6069
Tatham Fells 77 SD 6763
Tathwell 73 TF 3282
Tatsfield 29 TQ 4156
Tattenhall 69 SJ 4858
Tattenham Corner Station 37 TQ 2258
Tatterford 64 TF 8628
Tattersett 64 TF 8429
Tattershall 73 TF 2157
Tattershall Bridge 62 TF 1956
Tattershall Thorpe 73 TF 2159
Tattingstone 55 TM 1337
Tatton Hall 69 SJ 7481
Tauchers 121 NJ 3749
Taunton 24 ST 2324
Taverham 65 TG 1513
Tavernspite 43 SN 1812
Tavistock 20 SX 4774
Tavool House 105 NM 4327
Taw Green 21 SX 6597
Tawstock 23 SS 5529
Taxal 70 SK 0079
Tay Bridge 109 NO 3827
Tayinloan 92 NR 6945
Taylorgill Force 82 NY 2211
Taymouth Castle 107 NN 7846
Taynish 99 NR 7283
Taynton (Glos.) 46 SO 7221
Taynton (Oxon.) 47 SP 2313
Taynuilt 106 NN 0031
Tayport 109 NO 4528
Tay Road Bridge 109 NO 4129
Tayvallich 99 NR 7386
Teahaval (mt.) 131 NB 1629
Tealby 73 TF 1590
Tean 18 SV 9016
Teanamachar 124 NF 7762
Teangue 111 NG 6608
Teatle Water 106 NN 1324
Tebay 83 NY 6104
Tebworth 52 SP 9926
Tedburn St. Mary 21 SX 8194
Teddington (Glos.) 46 SO 9632
Teddington (Gtr London) 37 TQ 1671
Tedstone Delamere 49 SO 6958
Tedstone Wafre 49 SO 6759
Tees Bay 85 NZ 5727
Teesdale 84 NY 9227
Tees-side Airport 85 NZ 3813
Teeton 51 SP 6970
Teffont Evias 26 ST 9831
Teffont Magna 26 ST 9832
Tegryn 43 SN 2233
Teigh 62 SK 8616
Teigngrace 21 SX 8474
Teignmouth 21 SX 9473
Teindland 120 NJ 2755
Teindland Forest 120 NJ 2956
Telegraph Hill 97 NT 8570
Telford 59 SJ 6909
Tellisford 33 ST 8055
Telscombe 29 TQ 4003
Templand 89 NY 0886
Temple (Corn.) 19 SX 1473
Temple (Lothian) 103 NT 3158
Temple (Strath.) 101 NS 5469
Temple Bar 43 SN 5354
Temple Bruer 62 TF 0053
Temple Cloud 33 ST 6157
Templecombe 25 ST 7022
Temple Ewell 31 TR 2844
Temple Grafton 50 SP 1254
Temple Guiting 46 SP 0928
Temple Hirst 79 SE 6025
Temple Newsam (ant.) 79 SE 3532
Temple Normanton 71 SK 4167
Temple Sowerby 83 NY 6127
Templeton (Devon) 23 SS 8813
Templeton (Dyfed) 42 SN 1111
Tempsford 52 TL 1653
Tenbury Wells 49 SO 5968
Tenby 42 SN 1300
Tendring 39 TM 1424
Ten Mile Bank 64 TL 6097
Tenston 136 HY 2716
Tenterden 30 TQ 8833
Tentsmuir Forest 109 NO 4825
Terally Point 86 NX 1240
Terling 38 TL 7715
Ternhill 59 SJ 6332
Terregles 88 NX 9377
Terrington 79 SE 6670
Terrington Marsh 63 TF 5423
Terrington St. Clement 63 TF 5520
Terrington St. John 63 TF 5416
Teston 29 TQ 7053
Testwood 26 SU 3514
Tetbury 46 ST 8993
Tetbury Upton 46 ST 8795
Tetchill 58 SJ 3832
Tetcott 20 SX 3396
Tetford 73 TF 3374
Tetney 75 TA 3101
Tetney Lock 75 TA 3402
Tetsworth 36 SP 6802
Tettenhall 59 SO 8899
Teuchan 121 NK 0839
Teversal 71 SK 4661
Teversham 53 TL 4958
Teviot Dale 89 NT 4815
Teviothead 89 NT 4005
Tewin 37 TL 2714
Tewkesbury 46 SO 8933
Tewsgill Hill 95 NS 9523
Texa 98 NR 3943
Teynham 31 TQ 9663
Thakeham 28 TQ 1017
Thame 36 SP 7006
Thames Ditton 37 TQ 1567
Thames Haven 38 TQ 7581
Thamesmead 37 TQ 4779
Thaneston 119 NO 6374
Thanington 31 TR 1356
Thankerton 95 NS 9737
Tharston 65 TM 1894
Thatcham 35 SU 5167
Thatto Heath 69 SJ 5093
Thaxted 54 TL 6131
Theakston 79 SE 3085
Thealby 74 SE 8917
Theale (Berks.) 36 SU 6371
Theale (Somer.) 33 ST 4646
Thearne 74 TA 0736
Theberton 55 TM 4365
Thedden Grange 35 SU 6839
Theddingworth 51 SP 6685
Theddlethorpe All Saints 73 TF 4688
Theddlethorpe St. Helen 73 TF 4788
Thelbridge Barton 23 SS 7812
Thelnetham 54 TM 0178
Thelwall 69 SJ 6587
Themelthorpe 64 TG 0524
Thenford 51 SP 5141
Therfield 53 TL 3337
Thetford 54 TL 8783
Thetford Warren 54 TL 8383
Theydon Bois 37 TQ 4598
Thickwood 33 ST 8272
Thieves Holm 136 HY 4614
Thimbleby (Lincs.) 73 TF 2369
Thimbleby (N Yorks.) 85 SE 4495
Thirkleby 79 SE 4778
Thirlby 79 SE 4884
Thirlestane 96 NT 5647
Thirlestane Castle 96 NT 5347
Thirlmere 82 NY 3116
Thirl, The (pt.) 135 ND 1873
Thirlwall Castle (ant.) 90 NY 6566
Thirlwall Common 90 NY 6669
Thirn 79 SE 2185
Thirsk 79 SE 4282
Thirstane Hill 88 NS 8709
Thistleton 62 SK 9118
Thistley Green 54 TL 6776
Thixendale 80 SE 8461
Thockrington 90 NY 9579
Tholomas Drove 63 TF 4006
Tholthorpe 79 SE 4766
Thomas Chapel 42 SN 1008
Thomastown 121 NJ 5737
Thompson 64 TL 9296
Thomshill 120 NJ 2157
Thong 30 TQ 6770
Thoralby 78 SE 0086
Thoresby 71 SK 6371
Thoresway 73 TF 1696
Thorganby (Lincs.) 73 TF 2097
Thorganby (N Yorks.) 74 SE 6841
Thorgill 80 SE 7096
Thorington 55 TM 4274
Thorington Street 54 TM 0135
Thorlby 78 SD 9652
Thorley 37 TL 4719
Thormanby 79 SE 4974
Thornaby-on-Tees 85 NZ 4518
Thornage 64 TG 0436
Thornborough (Bucks.) 51 SP 7433
Thornborough (N Yorks.) 79 SE 2979
Thornbury (Avon) 33 ST 6390
Thornbury (Devon) 22 SS 4008
Thornbury (Here. and Worc.) 45 SO 6159
Thornby 51 SP 6675
Thorncliffe 70 SK 0158
Thorncombe 24 ST 3703
Thorncombe Street 28 TQ 0042
Thorndon 55 TM 1469
Thorne 74 SE 6813
Thorne Moors or Waste 74 SE 7315
Thorner 79 SE 3740
Thorness Bay 27 SZ 4493
Thorne St. Margaret 24 ST 0920
Thorne Waste or Moors 74 SE 7315
Thorney (Cambs.) 63 TF 2804
Thorney (Notts.) 72 SK 8572
Thorney Hill 26 SZ 2099
Thorney Island 27 SU 7503
Thornfalcon 24 ST 2723
Thornford 25 ST 6013
Thorngumbald 75 TA 2026
Thornham 64 TF 7343
Thornham Magna 55 TM 1071
Thornham Parva 55 TM 1072
Thornhaugh 62 TF 0600
Thornhill (Central) 101 NS 6699
Thornhill (Derby.) 70 SK 1983
Thornhill (Dumf. and Galwy.) 88 NX 8795
Thornhill (Hants.) 27 SU 4612
Thornhill (Mid Glam.) 41 ST 1584
Thornhill (W Yorks.) 71 SE 2418
Thornicombe 25 ST 8703
Thornley (Durham) 84 NZ 1137
Thornley (Durham) 85 NZ 3639
Thornliebank 101 NS 5459
Thorns 54 TL 7455
Thornthwaite (Cumbr.) 82 NY 2225
Thornthwaite (N Yorks.) 78 SE 1858
Thornton (Bucks.) 51 SP 7535
Thornton (Fife) 103 NT 2897
Thornton (Humbs.) 74 SE 7545
Thornton (Lancs.) 77 SD 3342
Thornton (Leic.) 61 SK 4607
Thornton (Lincs.) 73 TF 2467
Thornton (Mers.) 68 SD 3300
Thornton (Northum.) 97 NT 9547
Thornton (Tays.) 109 NO 3946
Thornton (W Yorks.) 78 SE 1032
Thornton Beck 80 SE 8381
Thornton Castle 109 NO 6871
Thornton Curtis 74 TA 0817
Thornton Dale 80 SE 8383
Thorntonhall 94 NS 5955
Thornton Hough 68 SJ 3080
Thornton-in-Craven 78 SD 9048
Thornton Junction 103 NT 3097
Thornton-le-Beans 85 SE 3990
Thornton-le-Clay 80 SE 6865
Thornton le Moor (Lincs.) 72 TF 0496
Thornton-le-Moor (N Yorks.) 79 SE 3988
Thornton-le-Moors 68 SJ 4474
Thorntonloch 96 NT 7574
Thornton Moor Reservoir 78 SE 0334
Thorntonpark 97 NT 9448
Thornton Resr. (Leic.) 61 SK 4707
Thornton Resr. (N Yorks.) 78 SE 1888
Thornton Rust 78 SD 9788
Thornton Steward 78 SE 1787
Thornton Watlass 79 SE 2385
Thornwood Common 37 TL 4705
Thorny Hill 87 NX 5388
Thornyhive Bay 119 NO 8882
Thoroton 61 SK 7642
Thorp Arch 79 SE 4346
Thorpe (Derby.) 60 SK 1550
Thorpe (Lincs.) 73 TF 4982
Thorpe (Norf.) 65 TM 4398
Thorpe (Notts.) 61 SK 7649
Thorpe (N Yorks.) 78 SE 0161
Thorpe (Surrey) 36 TQ 0268
Thorpe Abbotts 55 TM 1979
Thorpe Acre 61 SK 5120
Thorpe Arnold 61 SK 7620
Thorpe Audlin 71 SE 4715
Thorpe Bassett 80 SE 8573
Thorpe Bay 38 TQ 9284
Thorpe by Water 62 SP 8996
Thorpe Constantine 60 SK 2608
Thorpe End Garden Village 65 TG 2811
Thorpe Green 54 TL 9354
Thorpe Hall 79 SE 5776
Thorpe Hesley 71 SK 3796
Thorpe in Balne 71 SE 5910
Thorpe Langton 51 SP 7492
Thorpe Larches 85 NZ 3826
Thorpe le Fallows 72 SK 9180
Thorpe-le-Soken 39 TM 1822
Thorpe Malsor 52 SP 8379
Thorpe Mandeville 51 SP 5345
Thorpe Market 65 TG 2436
Thorpe Morieux 54 TL 9453
Thorpeness 55 TM 4759
Thorpe on the Hill 72 SK 9065
Thorpe Salvin 71 SK 5281
Thorpe Satchville 61 SK 7311
Thorpe St. Andrew 65 TG 2609
Thorpe St. Peter 73 TF 4861
Thorpe Thewless 85 NZ 4023
Thorpe Underwood 79 SE 4658
Thorpe Waterville 52 TL 0281
Thorpe Willoughby 79 SE 5731
Thorrington 39 TM 0920
Thorverton 23 SS 9202
Thrandeston 55 TM 1176
Thrapston 52 SP 9978
Threapland 78 SD 9860
Threapwood 58 SJ 4345
Threave Castle (ant.) 88 NX 7362
Three Bridges 29 TQ 2837
Three Cocks 45 SO 1737
Three Crosses 40 SS 5794
Three Holes 63 TF 5000
Three Hundreds of Aylesbury, The (dist.) 36 SP 8607
Threekingham 62 TF 0836
Three Leg Cross 29 TQ 6831
Three Legged Cross 26 SU 0806
Three Mile Cross 36 SU 7168
Threemilestone 19 SW 7844
Three Pikes (mt.) 83 NY 8334
Three Sisters, The (mt.) 106 NN 1556
Threipmuir Reservoir 102 NT 1764
Threlkeld 82 NY 3225
Threshfield 78 SD 9963
Thrigby 65 TG 4512
Thringarth 84 NY 9323
Thringstone 60 SK 4217
Thrintoft 84 SE 3293
Thriplow 53 TL 4446
Throcking 53 TL 3330
Throckley 91 NZ 1567
Throckmorton 50 SO 9749
Throphill 91 NZ 1385
Thropton 91 NU 0202
Throsk 102 NS 8690
Throwleigh 21 SX 6690
Throwley 31 TQ 9955
Thrumpton 61 SK 5131
Thrumster 135 ND 3345
Thrunton 91 NU 0810
Thrunton Wood 91 NU 0709
Thrupp (Glos.) 46 SO 8603
Thrupp (Oxon.) 47 SP 4715
Thruscross Resr. 78 SE 1557
Thrushelton 20 SX 4487
Thrushgill 77 SD 6462
Thrussington 61 SK 6416
Thruxton (Hants.) 34 SU 2845
Thruxton (Here. and Worc.) 45 SO 4334
Thruxton Aerodrome 34 SU 2845
Thrybergh 71 SK 4694
Thundersley 38 TQ 7788
Thurcaston 61 SK 5610
Thurcroft 71 SK 4988
Thurgarton (Norf.) 65 TG 1835
Thurgarton (Notts.) 61 SK 6949
Thurgoland 71 SE 2801
Thurlaston (Leic.) 61 SP 5099
Thurlaston (Warw.) 51 SP 4671
Thurlby (Lincs.) 72 SK 9061
Thurlby (Lincs.) 62 TF 1017
Thurleigh 52 TL 0558
Thurlestone 21 SX 6742
Thurlow 54 TL 6750
Thurloxton 24 ST 2729
Thurlstone 71 SE 2303
Thurlton 65 TM 4198
Thurmaston 61 SK 6109
Thurnby 61 SK 6404
Thurne 65 TG 4015
Thurnham (Kent) 30 TQ 8057

Thurnham (Lancs.) 77 SD 4554
Thurning (Norf.) 64 TG 0729
Thurning (Northants.) 52 TL 0883
Thurnscoe 71 SE 4605
Thursby 82 NY 3250
Thursford 64 TF 9833
Thursley 35 SU 9039
Thurso 135 ND 1168
Thurso Bay 135 ND 1169
Thurstaston 68 SJ 2483
Thurston 54 TL 9365
Thurstonfield 82 NY 3156
Thurstonland 70 SE 1610
Thurton 65 TG 3200
Thurvaston 60 SK 2437
Thuxton 64 TG 0307
Thwaite (N Yorks.) 84 SD 8998
Thwaite (Suff.) 55 TM 1168
Thwaite St. Mary 65 TM 3395
Thwing 81 TA 0570
Tianavaig Bay 123 NG 5138
Tibbermore 108 NO 0523
Tibberton (Glos.) 46 SO 7521
Tibberton (Here. and Worc.) 49 SO 9057
Tibberton (Shrops.) 59 SJ 6720
Tibbie Sheils Inn 89 NT 2320
Tibenham 55 TM 1389
Tibshelf 71 SK 4360
Tibthorpe 81 SE 9555
Ticehurst 29 TQ 6930
Tichborne 27 SU 5630
Tickencote 62 SK 9809
Tickenham 33 ST 4571
Tick Fen 53 TL 3384
Tickhill 71 SK 5993
Ticklerton 48 SO 4890
Ticknall 60 SK 3524
Tickton 74 TA 0641
Tidbury Ring (ant.) 35 SU 4642
Tidcombe 34 SU 2858
Tiddington (Oxon.) 36 SP 6404
Tiddington (Warw.) 50 SP 2256
Tidebrook 29 TQ 6130
Tideford 20 SX 3459
Tidenham 45 ST 5596
Tidenham Chase 45 ST 5598
Tideswell 70 SK 1575
Tidmarsh 36 SU 6374
Tidmington 50 SP 2538
Tidpit 26 SU 0718
Tiers Cross 42 SM 9010
Tiffield 51 SP 6951
Tifty 121 NJ 7740
Tigerton 109 NO 5364
Tigharry 124 NF 7171
Tigh na Blair 107 NN 7716
Tighnabruaich 100 NR 9772
Tighnafiline 126 NG 8789
Tighvein (mt.) 92 NR 9927
Tigley 21 SX 7560
Tilbrook 52 TL 0769
Tilbury 30 TQ 6376
Tile Cross 50 SP 1687
Tile Hill 50 SP 2777
Tilehurst 36 SU 6673
Tilford 35 SU 8743
Tillathrowie 121 NJ 4634
Tillicoultry 102 NS 9197
Tillingham 39 TL 9903
Tillington (Here. and Worc.) 45 SO 4645
Tillington (W Susx) 28 SU 9621
Tillington Common 45 SO 4546
Tillyarblet 109 NO 5267
Tillycorthie 121 NJ 9123
Tillydrine House 119 NO 6098
Tillyfourie 119 NJ 6412
Tillygarmond 119 NO 6393
Tillygreig 121 NJ 8823
Tilly Whim Caves 26 SZ 0377
Tilmanstone 31 TR 3051
Tilney All Saints 63 TF 5618
Tilney High End 63 TF 5617
Tilney St. Lawrence 63 TF 5414
Tilshead 34 SU 0347
Tilstock 59 SJ 5337
Tilston 58 SJ 4551
Tilstone Fearnall 69 SJ 5660
Tilsworth 36 SP 9724
Tilton on the Hill 61 SK 7405
Timberland 73 TF 1158
Timberland Delph 73 TF 1559
Timbersbrook 69 SJ 8962
Timberscombe 23 SS 9542
Timble 78 SE 1752
Timperley 69 SJ 7988
Timsbury (Avon) 33 ST 6658
Timsbury (Hants.) 26 SU 3424
Timsgarry 130 NB 0533
Timworth Green 54 TL 8669
Tincleton 25 SY 7691
Tindale 90 NY 6159
Tindale Fells 83 NY 6157
Tindale Tarn 90 NY 6058
Tind, The (pt.) 143 HU 6790
Tingewick 51 SP 6533
Tingley 79 SE 2826
Tingrith 52 TL 0032
Tinhay 20 SX 4085
Tinnis Castle (ant.) 95 NT 1434
Tinnis Hill 89 NY 4385
Tinshill 79 SE 2540
Tinsley 71 SK 3990
Tintagel 20 SX 0588
Tintagel Head 20 SX 0489
Tintern Abbey (ant.) 45 SO 5300
Tintern Parva 45 SO 5200
Tintinhull 25 ST 5019
Tinto 95 NS 9534
Tinto Hills 95 NS 9534
Tintwistle 70 SK 0297
Tinwald 88 NY 0081
Tinwell 62 TF 0006
Tipperty 121 NJ 9627
Tipperweir (mt.) 119 NO 6885
Tipton 50 SO 9592
Tipton St. John 24 SY 0991
Tiptree 38 TL 8916
Tirabad 44 SN 8741
Tiree (is.) 104 NM 0045
Tiree Aerodrome 104 NM 0045
Tirfergus Hill 92 NR 6617
Tirga Mòr (mt.) 130 NB 0511
Tirley 46 SO 8328
Tirphil 41 SO 1303
Tir Rhiwiog 57 SH 9216
Tirril 83 NY 5026
Tir y mynach 57 SH 9302
Tisbury 26 ST 9429
Tissington 60 SK 1752
Titchberry 22 SS 2427
Titchfield 27 SU 5305
Titchmarsh 52 TL 0279
Titchwell 64 TF 7543
Tithby 61 SK 6936
Titley 45 SO 3260
Titlington 91 NU 1015
Tittensor 59 SJ 8738
Titterstone Clee Hill 49 SO 5978
Tittesworth Resr. 70 SJ 9959
Tittleshall 64 TF 8920
Tiumpan Head 131 NB 5737
Tiverton (Ches.) 69 SJ 5560
Tiverton (Devon) 23 SS 9512
Tiverton Junction Station 24 ST 0311
Tivetshall St. Margaret 55 TM 1787
Tivetshall St. Mary 55 TM 1686
Tixall 60 SJ 9722
Tixover 62 SK 9700
Toab (Orkney) 136 HY 5106
Toab (Shetld.) 141 HU 3811
Toa Galson 131 NB 4560
Tobermory 111 NM 5055
Toberonochy 105 NM 7408
Tobson 131 NB 1438
Tocher 121 NJ 6932
Tockenham 34 SU 0379
Tockenham Wick 34 SU 0381
Tockholes 77 SD 6623
Tockington 33 ST 6186
Tockwith 79 SE 4652
Todber 25 ST 7919
Toddington (Beds.) 52 TL 0129
Toddington (Glos.) 46 SP 0432
Toddun (mt.) 125 NB 2102
Todenham 50 SP 2436
Todhead Point 119 NO 8676
Tod Hill 92 NR 7212
Todhills 89 NY 3663
Tod Law 94 NS 7735
Todmorden 78 SD 9324
Todwick 71 SK 4984
Toe Head 124 NF 9594
Toes (is.) 42 SR 8994
Toft (Cambs.) 53 TL 3655
Toft (Ches.) 69 SJ 7676
Toft (Lincs.) 62 TF 0617
Toft Monks 65 TM 4295
Toft Newton Resr. 72 TF 0488
Toft next Newton 72 TF 0488
Toftrees 64 TF 8927
Toft Sand 63 TF 4441
Tofts Voe 143 HU 4375
Toftwood 64 TF 9811
Togston 91 NU 2401
Tokavaig 123 NG 6011
Tokers Green 36 SU 7077
Tolland 24 ST 1032
Tollard Royal 26 ST 9417
Toll Creagach 115 NH 1928
Toller Fratrum 25 SY 5797
Toller Porcorum 25 SY 5697
Tollerton (Notts.) 61 SK 6134
Tollerton (N Yorks.) 79 SE 5164
Tollesbury 38 TL 9510
Tolleshunt D'Arcy 38 TL 9312
Tolleshunt Major 38 TL 9011
Toll of Birness 121 NK 0034
Tollomuick Forest 127 NH 3380
Tolmount 117 NO 2079
Tolob 141 HU 3811
Tolpuddle 25 SY 7994
Tolquhon Castle (ant.) 121 NJ 8728
Tolsta Chaolais 131 NB 1938
Tolsta Head 131 NB 5647
Tolworth 37 TQ 1965
Tom a'Choinich 115 NH 1627
Tom an t-Saighdeir 106 NM 9715
Tom ant-Suidhe Mhóir 117 NJ 1018
Tomatin 116 NH 8028
Tom Bailgeann (mt.) 116 NH 5829
Tombane Burn 108 NN 9241
Tombreck 116 NH 6934
Tomchrasky 115 NH 2512
Tomdoun 115 NH 1501
Tomich (Highld.) 115 NH 3127
Tomich (Highld.) 128 NH 5348
Tomich (Highld.) 129 NH 7071
Tomintoul (Grampn.) 117 NJ 1618
Tomintoul (Grampn.) 117 NO 1490
Tomlachlan Burn 117 NH 9337
Tom na h-Iolaire 100 NR 9485
Tomnaven 121 NJ 4033
Tomnavoulin 117 NJ 2026
Tomont End 100 NS 1759
Tom's Cairn 119 NO 6194
Tomsléibhe 105 NM 6137
Tom Soilleir 105 NM 8409
Tomtain (mt.) 101 NS 7181
Tonbridge 29 TQ 5845
Tondu 41 SS 8984
Tong (Isle of Lewis) 131 NB 4536
Tong (Shrops.) 59 SJ 7907
Tonga 143 HP 5814
Tonge 60 SK 4123
Tongham 35 SU 8848
Tongland 87 NX 6953
Tongue 133 NC 5957
Tongue (lightship) 39 TR 3485
Tongue Bay 133 NC 6061
Tongue House 133 NC 5958
Tongwynlais 41 ST 1581
Tòn Mhór 98 NR 2371
Tonna 41 SS 7798
Ton-Teg 41 ST 0986
Tòn Tire (pt.) 105 NM 6019
Tonwell 37 TL 3317
Tonypandy 41 SS 9992
Tonyrefail 41 ST 0188
Toot Baldon 47 SP 5600
Toot Hill (Essex) 37 TL 5102
Toot Hill (Hants.) 26 SU 3718
Topcliffe 79 SE 3976
Topcroft 65 TM 2693
Topcroft Street 55 TM 2692
Toppesfield 54 TL 7337
Toppings 69 SD 7213
Topsham 21 SX 9788
Torbay 21 SX 8962
Tor Bay 21 SX 9259
Torbeg 92 NR 8929
Torboll Farm 129 NH 7598
Torbreck Burn 128 NC 6907
Torbryan 21 SX 8266
Torcastle 115 NN 1378
Torcross 21 SX 8242
Tore 128 NH 6052
Tore Hill 117 NH 9817
Torfichen Hill 96 NT 3353
Torhousemuir 86 NX 3957
Torksey 72 SK 8378
Torlum (Benbecula) 124 NF 7850
Torlum (Tays.) 107 NN 8219
Torlum Wood 107 NN 8218
Torlundy 115 NN 1477
Tormarton 33 ST 7678
Tormisdale 98 NR 1958
Tormitchell 86 NX 2394
Tormore 92 NR 8932
Tornsdale 135 ND 1350
Tornagrain 129 NH 7649
Tornahaish 117 NJ 2908
Tornashean Forest 118 NJ 3710
Tornaveen 119 NJ 6106
Torness (Highld.) 116 NH 5727
Tor Ness (Hoy, Orkney) 136 ND 2588
Tor Ness (N. Ronaldsay) 139 HY 7555
Tor Ness (Orkney) 136 HY 4219
Tor Ness (Stronsay) 137 HY 6520
Torogay 124 NF 9178
Torosay Castle 105 NM 7335
Torpantau 41 SO 0418
Torpenhow 82 NY 2039
Torphichen 102 NS 9672
Torphins 119 NJ 6202
Torpoint 20 SX 4355
Torquay 21 SX 9164
Torquhan 96 NT 4447
Torrachilty Forest 128 NH 4455
Torran (Island of Raasay) 123 NG 5949
Torran (Strath.) 105 NM 8704
Torrance 101 NS 6174
Torran Rocks 104 NM 2713
Torran Tùrach (mt.) 100 NS 0070
Torran Water 135 ND 0554
Torrent Walk 57 SH 7518
Torridon 126 NG 9056
Torridon Forest 126 NG 9158
Torridon House 123 NG 8757
Torrie Forest 101 NN 6403
Torrin 123 NG 5720
Torrisdale (Highld.) 133 NC 6761
Torris Dale (Strath.) 92 NR 7737
Torrisdale Bay 133 NC 6863
Torrisdale Castle 92 NR 7936
Torrisdale Water 92 NR 7636
Torrish 134 NC 9718
Torrisholme 77 SD 4464
Torr Meadhonach 92 NR 9551
Torr Mòr 93 NS 1053
Torr Nead an Eoin 92 NR 9549
Torroble 128 NC 5904
Torrs Warren 86 NX 1455
Torr, The 92 NR 9225
Torry (Grampn.) 121 NJ 4339
Torry (Grampn.) 119 NJ 9404
Torry Bay 102 NT 0185
Torryburn 102 NT 0286
Torrylin 92 NR 9621
Torrylinwater Foot 92 NR 9520
Torsay Island 105 NM 7613
Torside Reservoir 70 SK 0698
Torterston 121 NK 0747
Torthorwald 89 NY 0378
Tortington 28 TQ 0005
Tortworth 33 ST 6992
Torvaig 123 NG 4944
Torver 82 SD 2894
Torwood 101 NS 8484
Torworth 71 SK 6586
Toscaig 123 NG 7138
Toseland 53 TL 2362
Tosside 78 SD 7655
Tosside Beck 78 SD 7853
Tosson Hill 91 NZ 0098
Tostock 54 TL 9563
Totaig 122 NG 2050
Tote 123 NG 4149
Totegan 134 NC 8268
Totland 26 SZ 3286
Totland Bay 26 SZ 3186
Totley 71 SK 3179
Totnes 21 SX 8060
Toton 61 SK 5034
Totronald 110 NM 1656
Totscore 122 NG 3866
Tottenham 37 TQ 3491
Tottenhill 64 TF 6310
Totteridge 37 TQ 2494
Totternhoe 36 SP 9921
Tottiford Resr. 21 SX 8183
Tottington 69 SD 7712
Totton 26 SU 3513
Touch Hills 101 NS 7291
Tournaig 126 NG 8783
Toux (Grampn.) 121 NJ 5458
Toux (Grampn.) 121 NJ 9850
Tovil 29 TQ 7554
Toward 100 NS 1368
Toward Point 100 NS 1367
Towcester 51 SP 6948
Towednack 18 SW 4838
Tower Hill Station 20 SX 3690
Tower Point 42 SM 7911
Towersey 36 SP 7305
Towie 118 NJ 4412
Towiemore 121 NJ 3945
Tow Law 84 NZ 1139
Towneley Hall (ant.) 78 SD 8530
Town End (Cambs.) 63 TL 4195
Town End (Cumbr.) 77 SD 4483
Townhead 87 NX 6946
Townhead of Greenlaw 88 NX 7465
Townhill 102 NT 1089
Townshend 18 SW 5932
Town Yetholm 97 NT 8228
Towthorpe 79 SE 6258
Towton 79 SE 4839
Towy Forest 44 SN 8350
Towyn (Clwyd) 67 SH 9779
Towyn (Gwyn.) 56 SH 5800
Toynton All Saints 73 TF 3964
Toynton Fen Side 73 TF 3961
Toynton St. Peter 73 TF 4063
Toy's Hill 29 TQ 4751
Trabboch 93 NS 4321
Trabbochburn 93 NS 4621
Traboe 18 SW 7421
Tradespark (Highld.) 129 NH 8656
Tradespark (Orkney) 136 HY 4408
Traeth Bach 66 SH 5735
Trafford Park 69 SJ 7996
Trahenna Hill 95 NT 1337
Traigh House 111 NM 6590
Traigh Mhór 112 NF 7005
Trallong 41 SN 9629
Tranent 103 NT 4072
Trannon 57 SN 9096
Trantlemore 134 NC 8853
Tranwell 91 NZ 1883
Trapp 43 SN 6519
Traprain 103 NT 5975
Traprain Law (ant.) 103 NT 5874
Traquair 96 NT 3334
Trawden 78 SD 9138
Trawsallt 57 SN 7870
Trawsfynydd 67 SH 7035
Trawsfynydd Lake (Resr.) 67 SH 6936
Trealaval (mt.) 131 NB 2623
Trealaw 41 SS 9992
Treales 77 SD 4432
Trearddur Bay 66 SH 2478
Treaslane 123 NG 3953
Trebartha 20 SX 2677
Trebetherick 19 SW 9377
Treborough 23 ST 0036
Trebudannon 19 SW 8961
Treburley 20 SX 3477
Trecastle 41 SN 8729
Trecwn 42 SM 9632
Trecynon 41 SN 9903
Tredavoe 18 SW 4528
Tre-ddiog 42 SM 8928
Tredegar 41 SO 1409
Tredington 50 SP 2543
Tredinnick 19 SW 9270
Tredomen 41 SO 1231
Tredrizzick 19 SW 9577
Tredunnock 45 ST 3795
Treen 18 SW 3923
Treeton 71 SK 4387
Trefdraeth 66 SH 4070
Trefeca 41 SO 1431
Trefeglwys 57 SN 9690
Trefenter 56 SN 6068
Treffgarne 42 SM 9523
Treffynnon 42 SM 8428
Trefil 41 SO 1212
Trefilan 43 SN 5457
Trefnanney 58 SJ 2015
Trefnant 67 SJ 0570
Trefonen 58 SJ 2526
Trefor 66 SH 3779
Treforest Industrial Estate 41 ST 1186
Trefriw 67 SH 7763
Tregadillett 20 SX 2983
Tregaian 66 SH 4579
Tregaron 44 SN 6759
Tregarth 66 SH 6067
Tregeare 20 SX 2486
Tregeare Rounds (ant.) 19 SX 0379
Tregeiriog 58 SJ 1733
Tregele 66 SH 3592
Tregidden 18 SW 7523
Treglemais 42 SM 8229
Tregole 20 SX 1998
Tregonetha 19 SW 9563
Tregoney 19 SW 9244
Tregonning Hill 18 SW 6029
Tregoyd 45 SO 1937
Tre-groes 43 SN 4044
Tregurrian 19 SW 8465
Tregynon 57 SO 0999
Trehafod 41 ST 0491
Treharris 41 ST 1097
Treherbert 41 SS 9398
Treknow 20 SX 0586
Trelan 18 SW 7418
Trelawnyd 67 SJ 0879
Trelech 43 SN 2830
Trelech a'r Betws 43 SN 3026
Treleddyd-fawr 42 SM 7528
Trelewis 41 ST 1197
Treligga 20 SX 0584
Trelights 19 SW 9879
Trelill 19 SX 0477
Trelissick 19 SW 8339
Trelleck 45 SO 5005
Trelleck Grange 45 SO 4901
Trelogan 68 SJ 1180
Trelowarren (ant.) 18 SW 7124
Trelystan 58 SJ 2603
Tremadog 66 SH 5640
Tremadog Bay 66 SH 5234
Tremail 20 SX 1686
Tremain 43 SN 2348
Tremaine 20 SX 2388
Tremar 19 SX 2568
Trematon 20 SX 3959
Tremeirchion 67 SJ 0773
Trenance 19 SW 8567
Trenarren 19 SX 0348
Trench 59 SJ 6913
Trenchford Resr. 21 SX 8082
Trendrine Hill 18 SW 4838
Treneglos 20 SX 2088
Trenewan 19 SX 1753
Trent 25 ST 5918
Trent and Mersey Canal (Ches.) 69 SJ 7263
Trent and Mersey Canal (Derby.) 60 SK 3529
Trentham 59 SJ 8640
Trentishoe 23 SS 6448
Trent Valley 60 SK 0120
Treoes 41 SS 9478
Treorchy 41 SS 9596
Tre'r Ceiri (ant.) 66 SH 3744
Tre'r-ddôl 57 SN 6592
Tre'r gaer (Tregare) 45 SO 4110
Tresaith 43 SN 2751
Tresco 18 SV 8914
Trescott 59 SO 8497
Trescowe 18 SW 5731
Tresham 33 ST 7991
Treshnish Isles 104 NM 2741
Treshnish Point 104 NM 3348
Tresillian 19 SW 8646
Tresinwen 42 SM 9040
Tresmeer 20 SX 2387
Tres Ness 139 HY 7137
Tressait 107 NN 8160
Tresta (Fetlar) 143 HU 6190
Tresta (Shetld.) 141 HU 3651
Treswell 72 SK 7779
Trethewey 18 SW 3823
Trethomas 41 ST 1889
Trethurgy 19 SX 0355
Tretio 42 SM 7829
Tretire 45 SO 5124
Tretower 41 SO 1821
Tretower Court (ant.) 41 SO 1821
Treuddyn 68 SJ 2458
Trevalga 20 SX 0889
Trevanson 19 SW 9772
Trevarren 19 SW 9160
Trevarrick 19 SW 9843
Trevellas 18 SW 7452
Treverva 18 SW 7631
Trevethin 45 SO 2802
Trevigro 20 SX 3369
Trevine 42 SM 8432
Treviscoe 19 SW 9455
Trevone 19 SW 8975
Trevor 66 SH 3746
Trevose Head 19 SW 8576
Trewarmett 20 SX 0686
Trewarthenick 19 SW 9044
Trewassa 20 SX 1486
Trewavas Head 18 SW 5926
Trewellard 18 SW 3733
Trewen 20 SX 2583
Trewent Point 42 SS 0297
Trewidland 19 SX 2560
Trewint 20 SX 1897
Trewithian 19 SW 8737
Trewoon 19 SW 9952
Treyarnon Bay 19 SW 8673
Treyford 27 SU 8218
Triangular Lodge (ant.) 52 SP 8383
Trichrug 40 SN 7023
Trickett's Cross 26 SU 0801
Trigon Hill 25 SY 8989
Trimdon 85 NZ 3634
Trimdon Colliery 85 NZ 3835
Trimdon Grange 85 NZ 3735
Trimingham 65 TG 2738
Trimley St. Martin 55 TM 2737
Trimley St. Mary 55 TM 2737
Trimpley 49 SO 7978
Trimpley Resr. 49 SO 7779
Trimsaran 43 SN 4504
Trimstone 22 SS 5043
Trinant 41 SO 2000
Tring 36 SP 9211
Trinity 109 NO 6061
Trislaig 115 NN 0874
Trispen 19 SW 8450
Tritlington 91 NZ 2092
Triuirebheinn 112 NF 8121
Trochry 108 NN 9740
Troedyraur 43 SN 3245
Troedyrhiw 41 SO 0702
Trofarth 67 SH 8571
Troisgeach (mt.) 106 NN 2819
Trondra (is.) 141 HU 3936
Troon (Corn.) 18 SW 6638
Troon (Strath.) 93 NS 3230
Trossachs, The (dist.) 101 NN 4907
Troston 54 TL 8972
Troswick Ness 141 HU 4117
Trotternish (dist.) 123 NG 4552
Trottiscliffe 30 TQ 6460
Trotton 27 SU 8322
Troughend Common 90 NY 8490
Troup Head 121 NJ 8267
Troutbeck 83 NY 4103
Troutbeck Bridge 83 NY 4000
Trowbridge 33 ST 8557
Trow Green 45 SO 5706
Trowie Glen 136 ND 2499
Trowle Common 33 ST 8358
Trows 96 NT 6932
Trowse Newton 65 TG 2406
Trudoxhill 33 ST 7443
Trull 24 ST 2122
Truman 41 SN 7420
Trumau (mt.) 57 SN 8567
Trum Gelli 57 SH 6501
Trumisgarry 124 NF 8674
Trumland House 136 HY 4227
Trumpan 122 NG 2261
Trumpet 49 SO 6539
Trumpington 53 TL 4455
Trunch 65 TG 2834
Trundle, The (ant.) 27 SU 8711
Truro 19 SW 8244
Trusham 21 SX 8582
Trusley 60 SK 2535
Trusthorpe 73 TF 5183
Trwyn Cilan 56 SH 2923
Trwyn Llanbedrog (pt.) 66 SH 3330
Trwyn Maen Dylan 66 SH 4252
Trwyn-y-bwa 42 SN 0542
Trwyn y Gorlech 66 SH 3445
Trwyn yr Wylfa 56 SH 3224
Trysull 59 SO 8494
Tuarie Burn 134 NC 8120
Tubney 47 SU 4498
Tuckenhay 21 SX 8156
Tuddenham (Suff.) 54 TL 7371
Tuddenham (Suff.) 55 TM 1948
Tudeley 29 TQ 6245
Tudhoe 84 NZ 2635
Tudhope Hill 89 NY 4399
Tudweiloig 66 SH 2336
Tuffley 46 SO 8315
Tugby 61 SK 7601
Tugford 48 SO 5587
Tulach Hill 108 NN 8664
Tulliallan Castle 102 NS 9388
Tulliallan Forest 102 NS 9588
Tullibody 102 NS 8595
Tullibole Castle (ant.) 102 NO 0500
Tullich (Highld.) 129 NH 8576
Tullich (Strath.) 106 NN 0815
Tullich Hill 100 NN 7036
Tullich Muir 129 NH 7373
Tulliemet 108 NN 9952
Tulliemet House 108 NN 9954
Tulloch (Grampn.) 109 NO 7671
Tulloch (Highld.) 128 NH 6192
Tulloch (Highld.) (dist.) 117 NH 9914
Tulloch Castle 128 NH 5460
Tullochcoy 117 NO 2394
Tullochgorm 100 NR 9695
Tulloch Station 115 NN 3580
Tulloes 109 NO 5145
Tullo Hill 109 NO 4964
Tullybannocher 107 NN 7521
Tullybeagles Lodge 108 NO 0136
Tullybothy Craigs 103 NO 6310
Tullyfergus 108 NO 2149
Tullymurdoch 108 NO 1952
Tullynessle 119 NJ 5519
Tulm Bay 123 NG 4075
Tumble 43 SN 5411
Tumby 73 TF 2359
Tumby Woodside 73 TF 2657
Tummel Bridge 107 NN 7659
Tummer Hill Scar 76 SD 1767
Tumpa, The (mt.) 41 SO 2235
Tungadal River 123 NG 4238
Tunstall (Humbs.) 75 TA 3032
Tunstall (Kent) 30 TQ 8961
Tunstall (Lancs.) 77 SD 6073
Tunstall (Norf.) 65 TG 4107
Tunstall (N Yorks.) 84 SE 2195
Tunstall (Staffs.) 59 SJ 8551
Tunstall (Suff.) 55 TM 3655
Tunstall Forest 55 TM 3854
Tunstall Resr. 84 NZ 0641
Tunstead 65 TG 2921
Tunworth 35 SU 6748
Tupsley 45 SO 5340
Turgis Green 35 SU 6959
Turin 109 NO 5352
Turin Hill 109 NO 5153
Turkdean 46 SP 1017
Tur Langton 61 SP 7194
Turls Head 142 HU 2886
Turnastone 45 SO 3536
Turnberry 93 NS 2005
Turnberry Bay 93 NS 1905
Turnditch 60 SK 2946
Turner's Hill 29 TQ 3435
Turners Puddle 25 SY 8293
Turnworth 25 ST 8107
Turra Field Aerodrome 143 HU 6191
Turriff 121 NJ 7249
Turton Bottoms 69 SD 7315
Turton Moor 69 SD 6818
Turves 63 TL 3396
Turvey 52 SP 9452
Turville 36 SU 7691
Turville Heath 36 SU 7391
Turweston 51 SP 6037
Tushielaw Inn 89 NT 3017
Tusker Rock 41 SS 8474
Tutbury 60 SK 2129
Tutnall 50 SO 9870
Tutshill 45 ST 5394
Tuttington 65 TG 2227
Tuxford 72 SK 7370
Twa Havens 121 NK 1036
Twatt (Orkney) 136 HY 2624
Twatt (Shetld.) 141 HU 3253
Twechar 101 NS 6975
Tweedmouth 97 NT 9952
Tweedsmuir 95 NT 1024
Tweed's Well (Source of River Tweed) 89 NT 0514
Twelveheads 18 SW 7642
Twenty 62 TF 1520
Twenty Foot River 63 TL 3397
Twerton 33 ST 7263
Twickenham 37 TQ 1473
Twigworth 46 SO 8421
Twineham 28 TQ 2519
Twiness 138 HY 4941
Twinhoe 33 ST 7359
Twinlaw Cairns (ant.) 96 NT 6254
Twinstead 54 TL 8637
Twinyess 139 HY 7452
Twiss Green 69 SJ 6595
Twitchen (Devon) 23 SS 7830
Twitchen (Shrops.) 48 SO 3679
Twizell House 97 NU 1328
Twmpa 41 SO 2235
Two Bridges 21 SX 6075
Two Dales 71 SK 2762
Two Gates 60 SK 2101

Twopenny Knowe 94 NS 6332
Twr-gwyn (ant.) 57 SN 9195
Twycross 60 SK 3305
Twyford (Berks.) 36 SU 7975
Twyford (Bucks.) 51 SP 6626
Twyford (Hants.) 27 SU 4724
Twyford (Leic.) 61 SK 7210
Twyford (Norf.) 64 TG 0124
Twyford Common 45 SO 5135
Twyn-du 41 SO 0820
Twynholm 87 NX 6654
Twyning 49 SO 8936
Twyning Green 49 SO 9037
Twynllanan 41 SN 7524
Twyn Rhyd-car 44 SN 9642
Twyn-y-Sheriff 45 SO 4005
Twywell 52 SP 9578
Tyberton 45 SO 3739
Tyburn 50 SP 1490
Tycroes 43 SN 6010
Ty Croes Station 66 SH 3472
Tycrwyn 57 SJ 1018
Tydd Gote 63 TF 4518
Tydd St. Giles 63 TF 4216
Tydd St. Giles Fen 63 TF 3914
Tydd St. Mary 63 TF 4418
Ty-hen 66 SH 1731
Tyldesley 69 SD 6902
Tyler Hill 31 TR 1460
Tylers Green 36 SU 9094
Tylorstown 41 ST 0195
Tylwch 57 SN 9780
Ty-mawr 67 SH 9047
Ty-nant (Clwyd) 67 SH 9944
Ty-nant (Gwyn.) 57 SH 9026
Tyndrum 106 NN 3330
Tyndwr Hall 58 SJ 2241
Tyneham 25 SY 8880
Tynehead 103 NT 3959
Tyne Mouth (Lothian) 103 NT 6480
Tynemouth (Tyne and Wear) 91 NZ 3468
Tyne Water 103 NT 3863
Tynewydd 41 SS 9399
Tyninghame 103 NT 6179
Tynribbie 106 NM 9446
Tynron 88 NX 8093
Tyn-y-ffridd 58 SJ 1230
Tyn-y-graig 44 SO 0149
Ty'n-y-groes 67 SH 7771
Tyrebagger Hill 119 NJ 8412
Ty Rhiw 41 ST 1283
Tyringham 52 SP 8547
Tythegston 41 SS 8578
Tytherington (Avon) 33 ST 6788
Tytherington (Ches.) 69 SJ 9175
Tytherington (Somer.) 33 ST 7744
Tytherington (Wilts.) 33 ST 9140
Tytherleigh 24 ST 3203
Ty-uchaf 57 SH 9900
Tywardreath 19 SX 0854
Tywyn 56 SH 5901
Tywyn 67 SH 7878
Tywyn Trewan 66 SH 3175

U

Uachdar 124 NF 7955
Uags 123 NG 7235
Uair, The 134 NC 8252
Uamh Bheag 101 NN 6911
Ubbeston Green 55 TM 3271
Ubley 33 ST 5257
Uchd a' Chlàrsair 116 NN 8181
Uckerby 84 NZ 2402
Uckfield 29 TQ 4721
Uckington 46 SO 9224
Udairn 123 NG 5142
Udale Bay 129 NH 7166
Uddingston 101 NS 6960
Uddington 95 NS 8633
Udimore 30 TQ 8718
Udny Green 121 NJ 8726
Udstonhead 94 NS 7047
Uffcott 34 SU 1277
Uffculme 24 ST 0612
Uffington (Lincs.) 62 TF 0608
Uffington (Oxon.) 34 SU 3089
Uffington (Shrops.) 59 SJ 5313
Uffington Castle (ant.) 34 SU 2986
Ufford (Northants.) 62 TF 0904
Ufford (Suff.) 55 TM 2953
Ufton 50 SP 3762
Ufton Nervet 36 SU 6367
Ugadale 92 NR 7828
Ugadale Point 92 NR 7828
Ugborough 21 SX 6755
Ugborough Beacon 21 SX 6659
Ugborough Moor 21 SX 6462
Uggeshall 55 TM 4580
Ugglebarnby 81 NZ 8707
Ugley 53 TL 5128
Ugley Green 53 TL 5227
Ugthorpe 85 NZ 7911
Uig (Island of Skye) 122 NG 1952
Uig (Island of Skye) 123 NG 3963
Uig Bay 122 NG 3862
Uigshader 123 NG 4246
Uinessan (is.) 112 NL 6695
Uisenis (mt.) 125 NB 3306
Uisge Labhair 107 NN 4370
Uisge Misgeach 115 NH 1837
Uisge Toll a' Mhadaidh 126 NG 9784
Uisgnaval Mór (mt.) 125 NB 1208
Uisken 104 NM 3819
Ukna Skerry 141 HU 3531
Ulbster 135 ND 3241
Ulceby (Humbs.) 75 TA 1014
Ulceby (Lincs.) 73 TF 4272
Ulcombe 30 TQ 8449
Uldale 82 NY 2536
Uldale Head (mt.) 83 NY 6300
Uldale House 83 SD 7396
Uley 46 ST 7898
Ulfhart Point 123 NG 4716
Ulgham 91 NZ 2392
Ulladale River 130 NB 0714
Ullapool 127 NH 1294
Ullapool River 127 NH 1495
Ullaval (mt.) 131 NB 0811
Ullenhall 50 SP 1267
Ullenwood 46 SO 9416
Ulleskelf 79 SE 5140
Ullesthorpe 51 SP 5087
Ulley 71 SK 4687
Ullingswick 45 SO 5950
Ullinish 122 NG 3238
Ullock 82 NY 0724
Ullscarf 82 NY 2912
Ullswater 83 NY 4220
Ulpha 82 SD 1993
Ulpha Fell 82 SD 1695
Ulpha Park 82 SD 1990
Ulrome 81 TA 1656
Ulsta 143 HU 4680
Ulva (is.) 105 NM 4040
Ulva House 105 NM 4439
Ulverston 77 SD 2878
Ulzieside 88 NS 7708
Umberleigh 23 SS 6023
Unapool 132 NC 2332
Underbarrow 83 SD 4692
Undercliff, The (I. of W.) 26 SZ 3883
Undercliff, The (I. of W.) 27 SZ 5375
Underhoull 143 HP 5704
Underriver 29 TQ 5552
Underwood (Gwent) 32 ST 3889
Underwood (Notts.) 61 SK 4750
Undy 33 ST 4386
Unifirth 140 HU 2856
Union Canal 102 NT 1171
Union Cottage 119 NO 8290
Union Mills 76 SC 3578
Unst (is.) 143 HP 6009
Unstone 71 SK 3777
Unthank 83 NY 4536
Upavon 34 SU 1354
Up Cerne 25 ST 6502
Upchurch 30 TQ 8467
Upcott 45 SO 3250
Upend 54 TL 7058
Up Exe 23 SS 9302
Uphall 102 NT 0571
Uphall Station 102 NT 0670
Upham (Devon) 23 SS 8808
Upham (Hants.) 27 SU 5320
Up Hatherley 46 SO 9120
Uphill (Avon) 32 ST 3158
Up Hill (Kent) 31 TR 2140
Up Holland 69 SD 5105
Uplawmoor 93 NS 4355
Upleadon 46 SO 7527
Upleatham 85 NZ 6319
Uplees 31 TQ 9964
Uplowman 24 ST 0115
Uplyme 24 SY 3293
Upminster 37 TQ 5686
Up Nately 35 SU 6951
Upnor 30 TQ 7470
Upottery 24 ST 2007
Upparl 27 SU 7717
Upper Affcot 48 SO 4486
Upper Ardchronie 128 NH 6188
Upper Arley 49 SO 7680
Upper Astrop 51 SP 5137
Upper Basildon 35 SU 5976
Upper Beeding 28 TQ 1910
Upper Benefield 52 SP 9789
Upper Boddington 51 SP 4853
Upper Borth 56 SN 6088
Upper Breinton 45 SO 4640
Upper Broughton 61 SK 6826
Upper Brow Top 77 SD 5258
Upper Bucklebury 35 SU 5368
Upper Burnhaugh 119 NO 8394
Upper Caldecote 52 TL 1645
Upper Chapel 44 SO 0040
Upper Chute 34 SU 2953
Upper Clatford 34 SU 3543
Upper Clynnog 66 SH 4746
Upper Cokeham 28 TQ 1605
Upper Coll 131 NB 4539
Upper Cwmtwrch 41 SN 7611
Upper Dallachy 121 NJ 3662
Upper Dean 52 TL 0467
Upper Denby 71 SE 2207
Upper Derraid 117 NJ 0233
Upper Dicker 29 TQ 5510
Upper Elkstone 70 SK 0559
Upper End 70 SK 0876
Upper Ethie 129 NH 7663
Upper Farringdon 27 SU 7135
Upper Framilode 46 SO 7510
Upper Froyle 35 SU 7542
Upper Glenfintaig 115 NN 2588
Upper Gravenhurst 52 TL 1136
Upper Green 34 SU 3663
Upper Hackney 71 SK 2961
Upper Hale 35 SU 0440
Upper Hambleton 62 SK 8907
Upper Hardres Court 31 TR 1550
Upper Hartfield 29 TQ 4634
Upper Heath 48 SO 5685
Upper Helmsley 80 SE 6956
Upper Heyford 47 SP 4926
Upper Hill 45 SO 4753
Upper Hopton 70 SE 1918
Upper Hulme 70 SK 0160
Upper Icknield Way (ant.) 36 SP 9212
Upper Inglesham 34 SU 2096
Upper Killay 40 SS 5892
Upper Knockando 129 NJ 1843
Upper Lambourn 34 SU 3180
Upper Langwith 71 SK 5169
Upper Lochton 119 NO 6997
Upper Loch Torridon 123 NG 8556
Upper Longdon 60 SK 0614
Upper Longwood 59 SJ 6007
Upper Lydbrook 45 SO 6015
Upper Maes-coed 45 SO 3335
Uppermill 70 SD 9906
Upper Minety 34 SU 0091
Upper North Dean 36 SU 8598
Upper Poppleton 79 SE 5554
Upper Quinton 50 SP 1746
Upper Sanday 137 HY 5303
Upper Sapey 49 SO 6863
Upper Scoulag 100 NS 1059
Upper Seagry 34 ST 9580
Upper Shelton 52 SP 9943
Upper Sheringham 65 TG 1441
Upper Skelmorlie 100 NS 1968
Upper Slaughter 47 SP 1523
Upper Soudley 46 SO 6610
Upper Stondon 52 TL 1535
Upper Stowe 51 SP 6456
Upper Street (Hants.) 26 SU 1418
Upper Street (Norf.) 65 TG 3516
Upper Sundon 52 TL 0527
Upper Swell 47 SP 1726
Upper Tamar Lake Reservoir 22 SS 2811
Upper Tean 60 SK 0139
Upperthong 70 SE 1208
Upper Tillyrie 102 NO 1006
Upperton 28 SU 9522
Upper Tooting 37 TQ 2772
Upper Town (Avon) 33 ST 5265
Uppertown (Island of Stroma) 135 ND 3576
Upper Tysoe 50 SP 3343
Upper Upham 34 SU 2277
Upper Wardington 51 SP 4946
Upper Weald 51 SP 8037
Upper Weedon 51 SP 6258
Upper Wield 35 SU 6238
Upper Winchendon 36 SP 7414
Upper Woodford 26 SU 1237
Uppingham 62 SP 8699
Uppington 59 SJ 5909
Upsall 79 SE 4587
Upshire 37 TL 4100
Up Somborne 26 SU 3932
Upstreet 31 TR 2262
Up Sydling 25 ST 6201
Upton (Berks.) 36 SU 9879
Upton (Bucks.) 36 SP 7711
Upton (Cambs.) 52 TL 1778
Upton (Ches.) 68 SJ 4069
Upton (Dorset) 25 SY 9893
Upton (Hants.) 34 SU 3555
Upton (Hants.) 26 SU 3716
Upton (Leic.) 60 SP 3699
Upton (Lincs.) 72 SK 8686
Upton (Mers.) 68 SJ 2687
Upton (Norf.) 65 TG 3912
Upton (Northants.) 51 SP 7160
Upton (Northants.) 62 TF 1000
Upton (Notts.) 61 SK 7354
Upton (Notts.) 72 SK 7476
Upton (Oxon.) 35 SU 5186
Upton (Somer.) 23 SS 9928
Upton (W Yorks.) 71 SE 4713
Upton Bishop 46 SO 6427
Upton Cheyney 33 ST 6969
Upton Cressett 49 SO 6592
Upton Cross 20 SX 2872
Upton Grey 35 SU 6948
Upton Hellions 23 SS 8303
Upton Lovell 34 ST 9440
Upton Magna 59 SJ 5512
Upton Noble 33 ST 7139
Upton Pyne 21 SX 9197
Upton Scudamore 33 ST 8647
Upton Snodsbury 49 SO 9454
Upton St. Leonards 46 SO 8615
Upton upon Severn 49 SO 8540
Upton Warren 49 SO 9267
Upwaltham 28 SU 9413
Upware 53 TL 5370
Upwell 63 TF 5002
Upwell Fen (Cambs.) 63 TL 4795
Upwell Fen (Norf.) 63 TL 5499
Upwey 25 SY 6684
Upwood 53 TL 2582
Uradale 141 HU 4137
Ura Firth (Shetld.) 142 HU 2977
Urafirth (Shetld.) 142 HU 3078
Urchal 129 NH 7544
Urchfont 34 SU 0356
Urdimarsh 45 SO 5249
Ure 142 HU 2280
Urgha 125 NG 1799
Urie Lingey 143 HU 5995
Urie Ness 143 HU 5994
Urishay Common 45 SO 3137
Urit Hill 94 NS 7626
Urlar Burn 107 NN 8345
Urlay Nook 85 NZ 4014
Urmston 69 SJ 7695
Urquhart 120 NJ 2863
Urquhart Bay 116 NH 5229
Urquhart Castle (ant.) 116 NH 5328
Urra 85 NZ 5702
Urrall Fell 86 NX 2870
Urray 128 NH 5053
Urray Forest 128 NH 4850
Urr Water 88 NX 7670
Urswick 76 SD 2674
Urvaig (pt.) 110 NM 0850
Ushaw Moor 84 NZ 2342
Usinish 112 NF 8635
Usk 45 SO 3701
Uskie Geo 140 HU 2047
Usk Resr. 41 SN 8128
Usselby 73 TF 0993
Usta Ness 141 HU 3841
Usway Burn 90 NT 8713
Utley 78 SE 0542
Uton 21 SX 8298
Utterby 73 TF 3093
Uttoxeter 60 SK 0933
Uwchmynydd (Gwyn.) 56 SH 1425
Uwch-mynydd (Gwyn) 57 SH 6419
Uxbridge 36 TQ 0583
Uyea (Shetld.) (is.) 142 HU 3192
Uyea (Unst) (is.) 143 HU 6098
Uyeasound (Unst) 143 HP 5901
Uyea Sound (Unst) 143 HU 5899
Uynarey (is.) 143 HU 4480
Uzmaston 42 SM 9714

V

Vacsay 131 NB 1136
Vaila (is.) 140 HU 2346
Vaila Hall 140 HU 2246
Vaila Sound 140 HU 2347
Vaitam (is.) 124 NF 9380
Vale of Belvoir 61 SK 7838
Vale of Berkeley 46 ST 6897
Vale of Catmose 62 SK 8709
Vale of Clwyd 67 SJ 0668
Vale of Conwy 67 SH 7867
Vale of Evesham 50 SP 0943
Vale of Gloucester 46 SO 8421
Vale of Mawgan or Lanherne 19 SW 8964
Vale of Neath 41 SN 8303
Vale of Pewsey 34 SU 1259
Vale of Taunton Deane 24 ST 1727
Vale of White Horse 34 SU 3291
Valla Field (dist.) 143 HP 5807
Vallay (Harris, W Isles) 124 NG 0582
Vallay (North Uist) 124 NF 7776
Vallay Strand 124 NF 7875
Valley 66 SH 2979
Valley Airfield 66 SH 3075
Valleyfield 102 NT 0086
Valsgarth 143 HP 6413
Valtos (Island of Skye) 123 NG 5163
Valtos (Isle of Lewis) 131 NB 0936
Vange 38 TQ 7287
Vardre 40 SN 6902
Varne (lightship) 31 TR 3020
Varragill River 123 NG 4737
Varteg 45 SO 2506
Vatersay (W Isles) 112 NL 6394
Vatersay (W Isles) 112 NL 6396
Vatersay Bay 112 NL 6495
Vatisker Point 131 NB 4939
Vatten 122 NG 2843
Vaul 104 NM 0448
Vaul Bay 110 NM 0549
Vauld, The 45 SO 5349
Vaynol Hall 66 SH 5369
Vaynor 41 SO 0410
Vaynor Park 58 SJ 1700
Veantrow Bay 136 HY 5020
Veensgarth 141 HU 4244
Veilish Point 124 NF 8178
Velindre (Dyfed) 43 SN 1039
Velindre (Dyfed) 43 SN 3538
Velindre (Powys) 45 SO 1836
Vellan Head 18 SW 6615
Vementry (is.) 140 HU 2960
Veness (Eday) 137 HY 5729
Ve Ness (Orkney) 136 HY 3705
Venford Resr. 21 SX 6870
Vennington 58 SJ 3309
Venn Ottery 24 SY 0791
Venta (Gwent) (ant.) 33 ST 4790
Venta (Hants.) (ant.) 27 SU 4829
Ventnor 27 SZ 5677
Vercovicium (ant.) 90 NY 7868
Vere, The 143 HP 6403
Vermuden's or Forty Foot Drain 53 TL 3888
Vernham Dean 34 SU 3356
Vernham Street 34 SU 3457
Vernolds Common 48 SO 4780
Verran Island 112 NF 7234
Verulamium (ant.) 37 TL 1307
Verwig 43 SN 1849
Verwood 26 SU 0908
Veryan 19 SW 9139
Veryan Bay 19 SW 9640
Ve Skerries 140 HU 1065
Vestra Fiold (mt.) 136 HY 2322
Vicarage 24 SY 2088
Vickerstown 76 SD 1868
Victoria 19 SW 9961
Victoria Station 37 TQ 2979
Vidlin 141 HU 4765
Vidlin Voe 141 HU 4866
Viewing Hill 83 NY 7833
Viewpark 101 NS 7161
Villavin 23 SS 5816
Vindovala (ant.) 91 NZ 1067
Vinehall Street 29 TQ 7520
Vine's Cross 29 TQ 5917
Virda Field (mt.) 140 HU 1561
Virginia Water 36 SU 9967
Virginstow 20 SX 3792
Virley Channel 39 TM 0011
Viroconium (ant.) 59 SJ 5608
Vobster 33 ST 7048
Voe (Shetld.) 142 HU 3381
Voe (Shetld.) 141 HU 4015
Voe (Shetld.) 141 HU 4063
Voe of Cullingsburgh 141 HU 5242
Voe of Dale 140 HU 1752
Voe of Snarraness 140 HU 2356
Vord Hill 143 HU 6293
Vorogay 124 NF 7864
Vowchurch 45 SO 3636
Voxter 143 HU 3770
Voy 136 HY 2515
Vuia Beag (is.) 131 NB 1233
Vuia Mór (is.) 131 NB 1234

W

Waberthwaite 82 SD 1093
Wackerfield 84 NZ 1522
Wacton 55 TM 1891
Wadbister Voe 141 HU 4450
Wadborough 49 SO 8947
Waddesdon 36 SP 7416
Waddingham 72 SK 9896
Waddington (Lancs.) 77 SD 7243
Waddington (Lincs.) 72 SK 9764
Wadebridge 19 SW 9972
Wadeford 24 ST 3110
Wadenhoe 52 TL 0083
Wadesmill 37 TL 3517
Wadhurst 29 TQ 6431
Wadshelf 71 SK 3171
Wadsworth Moor 78 SD 9634
Wadworth 71 SK 5697
Waen Fach 58 SJ 2017
Wag 135 ND 0126
Wainfleet All Saints 73 TF 4959
Wainfleet Bank 73 TF 4759
Wainfleet Sand 63 TF 5455
Wainhope 90 NY 6793
Wainhouse Corner 20 SX 1895
Wainscott 30 TQ 7471
Wainstalls 78 SE 0428
Waitby 83 NY 7507
Wakefield 71 SE 3320
Wakerley 62 SP 9599
Wakes Colne 54 TL 8928
Walberswick 55 TM 4974
Walberton 28 SU 9705
Walbury Hill 34 SU 3761
Walcot (Lincs.) 62 TF 0535
Walcot (Shrops.) 59 SJ 5912
Walcot (Shrops.) 48 SO 3485
Walcot (Warw.) 50 SP 1258
Walcote 51 SP 5683
Walcott (Lincs.) 62 TF 1256
Walcott (Norf.) 65 TG 3632
Walden 78 SE 0082
Walden Head 78 SD 9880
Walden Stubbs 71 SE 5516
Waldersey 63 TF 4304
Waldershare Park 31 TR 2948
Walderslade 30 TQ 7563
Walderton 27 SU 7910
Walditch 25 SY 4892
Waldridge 84 NZ 2549
Waldringfield 55 TM 2744
Waldron 29 TQ 5419
Wales 71 SK 4782
Walesby (Lincs.) 73 TF 1392
Walesby (Notts.) 72 SK 6870
Walford (Here. and Worc.) 48 SO 3872
Walford (Here. and Worc.) 45 SO 5820
Walford (Shrops.) 58 SJ 4320
Walgherton 59 SJ 6948
Walgrave 51 SP 8071
Walkden 69 SD 7303
Walker 91 NZ 2864
Walkerburn 96 NT 3637
Walker Fold 77 SD 6742
Walkeringham 72 SK 7692
Walkerith 72 SK 7892
Walkern 53 TL 2926
Walker's Green 45 SO 5248
Walkerton 103 NO 2301
Walkerwood Resr. 70 SJ 9999
Walkhampton 21 SX 5369
Walkington 74 SE 9936
Walk Mill 78 SD 8629
Wall (Northum.) 90 NY 9168
Wall (Staffs.) 60 SK 0906
Wallace's Hill 96 NT 3035
Wallacetown 93 NS 3422
Walland Marsh 31 TQ 9922
Wallasey 68 SJ 2992
Wall Bank 48 SO 5092
Wallbury (ant.) 37 TL 4918
Wallend 30 TQ 8775
Waller's Haven 29 TQ 6607
Wall Hill 87 NX 7244
Wall Hills (ant.) 45 SO 6359
Walling Fen 74 SE 8829
Wallingford 35 SU 6089
Wallington (Gtr London) 37 TQ 2863
Wallington (Hants.) 27 SU 5806
Wallington (Herts.) 53 TL 2933
Wallington Hall (ant.) 64 TF 6207
Wallis 42 SN 0125
Walliswood 28 TQ 1138
Walls 140 HU 2449
Wallsend 91 NZ 2766
Walls, The (ant.) 59 SO 7896
Wallyford 103 NT 3671
Walmer 31 TR 3750
Walmer Bridge 77 SD 4724
Walmersley 69 SD 8013
Walmley 50 SP 1393
Walney Airfield 76 SD 1770
Walpole 55 TM 3674
Walpole Highway 63 TF 5113
Walpole St. Andrew 63 TF 5017
Walpole St. Peter 63 TF 5016
Walsall 60 SP 0198
Walsall Wood 60 SK 0403
Walsden 78 SD 9322
Walsgrave on Sowe 50 SP 3781
Walsham le Willows 54 TM 0071
Walshaw Dean Resrs. 78 SD 9634
Walsoken 63 TF 4710
Walston 95 NT 0545
Walter's Ash 36 SU 8398
Walterstone 45 SO 3425
Waltham (Humbs.) 75 TA 2503
Waltham (Kent) 31 TR 1148
Waltham Abbey 37 TL 3800
Waltham Chase 27 SU 5614
Waltham on the Wolds 61 SK 8025
Waltham St. Lawrence 36 SU 8276
Walthamstow 37 TQ 3788
Walton (Bucks.) 52 SP 8936
Walton (Cumbr.) 90 NY 5264
Walton (Derby.) 71 SK 3569
Walton (Leic.) 51 SP 5987
Walton (Powys) 45 SO 2559
Walton (Shrops.) 59 SJ 5818
Walton (Somer.) 25 ST 4636
Walton (Suff.) 55 TM 2935
Walton (Warw.) 50 SP 2853
Walton (W Yorks.) 71 SE 3516
Walton (W Yorks.) 79 SE 4447
Walton Cardiff 46 SO 9032
Walton East 42 SN 0123
Walton Highway 63 TF 4912
Walton-in-Gordano 33 ST 4273
Walton-le-Dale 77 SD 5627
Walton-on-Thames 37 TQ 1066
Walton-on-the-Hill (Staffs.) 60 SJ 9520
Walton on the Hill (Surrey) 28 TQ 2255
Walton-on-the-Naze 39 TM 2521
Walton on the Wolds 61 SK 5919
Walton-on-Trent 60 SK 2118
Walton West 42 SM 8713
Walworth 84 NZ 2218
Walwyn's Castle 42 SM 8711
Wambrook 24 ST 2907
Wamphray Water 89 NY 1398
Wanborough 34 SU 2082
Wandlebury (ant.) 53 TL 4953
Wandsworth 37 TQ 2673
Wangford 55 TM 4679
Wangford Fen 54 TL 7483
Wangford Warren 54 TL 7782
Wanlip 61 SK 5910
Wanlockhead 88 NS 8712
Wansdyke (Avon) (ant.) 33 ST 6763
Wansdyke (Wilts.) (ant.) 34 SU 1264
Wansford (Cambs.) 62 TL 0799
Wansford (Humbs.) 81 TA 0656
Wanstead 37 TQ 4087
Wanstrow 33 ST 7141
Wanswell 46 SO 6801
Wantage 34 SU 4087
Wapley 33 ST 7179
Wappenbury 50 SP 3769
Wappenham 51 SP 6245
Warbleton 29 TQ 6018
Warborough 47 SU 6093
Warboys 53 TL 3080
Warbstow 20 SX 2090
Warburton 69 SJ 7089
Warcop 83 NY 7415
Warcop Fell 83 NY 7920
Warden 31 TR 0271
Warden Point 31 TR 0272
Ward Green 54 TM 0564
Ward Hill (Eday) 138 HY 5530
Ward Hill (Hoy, Orkney) 136 HY 2202
Ward Hill (Orkney) 136 HY 3308
Ward Hill (S. Ronaldsay) 136 ND 4588
Wardington 51 SP 4946
Wardlaw Hill 94 NS 6822
Wardle (Ches.) 69 SJ 6057
Wardle (Gtr Mches.) 69 SD 9116
Wardley 62 SK 8300
Wardlow 70 SK 1874
Ward of Bressay (mt.) 141 HU 5038
Ward of Culswick (mt.) 140 HU 2645
Ward of Redland (mt.) 136 HY 3617
Ward of Scousburgh (mt.) 141 HU 3818
Ward of Veester (mt.) 141 HU 4126
War Down 27 SU 7218
Ward's Stone 77 SD 5858
Wardy Hill 53 TL 4782
Ware 37 TL 3614
Wareham 25 SY 9287
Wareham Forest 25 SY 8892
Warehorne 31 TQ 9832
Warenford 97 NU 1328
Waren Mill 97 NU 1534
Warenton 97 NU 1030
Wareside 37 TL 3915
Waresley 53 TL 2454
Warfield 36 SU 8872
Wargrave 36 SU 7878
Warham 64 TF 9441
Wark (Northum.) 97 NT 8238
Wark (Northum.) 90 NY 8576
Wark Forest 90 NY 7478
Warkleigh 23 SS 6422
Warks Burn 90 NY 8077
Warkton 52 SP 8980
Warkworth 91 NU 2406
Warlaby 85 SE 3591
Warland 69 SD 9419
Warland Resr. 78 SD 9521
Warleggan 19 SX 1569
Warley Moor Resr. 78 SE 0331
Warlingham 37 TQ 3658
Warmfield 71 SE 3720
Warmingham 69 SJ 7161
Warmington (Northants.) 52 TL 0791
Warmington (Warw.) 50 SP 4147
Warminster 33 ST 8644
Warmsworth 71 SE 5400
Warmwell 25 SY 7585
Warndon 49 SO 8856
War Ness 137 HY 5528
Warnford 27 SU 6223
Warnham 28 TQ 1533
Warninglid 28 TQ 2526
Warren (Ches.) 69 SJ 8870
Warren (Dyfed) 42 SR 9397
Warren Row 36 SU 8180
Warren Street 30 TQ 9253
Warrington (Bucks.) 52 SP 8954
Warrington (Ches.) 69 SJ 6088
Warsash 27 SU 4905
Warslow 70 SK 0858
Warsop 71 SK 5667
Warter 81 SE 8750
Warth Hill (Cumbr.) 77 SD 5684
Warth Hill (Highld.) 135 ND 3770
Warthill 79 SE 6755
Wart Holm 138 HY 4838
Wartling 29 TQ 6509
Wartnaby 61 SK 7123
Warton (Lancs.) 77 SD 4028
Warton (Lancs.) 77 SD 4972
Warton (Northum.) 91 NU 0002
Warton (Warw.) 60 SK 2803
Warton Aerodrome 77 SD 4127
Warton Sands 77 SD 4472
Wart, The (Sanday, Orkney) (mt.) 139 HY 6337
Wart, The (S. Ronaldsay) (mt.) 136 ND 4393
Warwick (Cumbr.) 83 NY 4656
Warwick (Warw.) 50 SP 2865
Warwick Bridge 83 NY 4756
Wasbister 138 HY 3932
Wasdale Head (mt.) 82 NY 1808
Washaway 19 SX 0369
Washbourne 21 SX 7954
Washfield 23 SS 9315

Washfold 84 NZ 0502
Washford 32 ST 0441
Washford Pyne 23 SS 8111
Washingborough 72 TF 0170
Washington (Tyne and Wear) 84 NZ 3356
Washington (W Susx) 28 TQ 1212
Wash, The (Dyfed) (pt.) 42 SR 9194
Wash, The (Lincs. - Norf.) 63 TF 5342
Wasing 35 SU 5764
Waskerley 84 NZ 0545
Waskerley Resr. 84 NZ 0244
Wasperton 50 SP 2659
Wass 79 SE 5579
Wass Wick 136 HY 4122
Waste or Thorne Moors 74 SE 7315
Wast Water 82 NY 1505
Watchet 32 ST 0743
Watchfield (Oxon.) 34 SU 2490
Watchfield (Somer.) 32 ST 3446
Watchgate 83 SD 5399
Watch Hill (Borders - Dumf. and Galwy.) 89 NY 4390
Watch Hill (Cumbr.) 83 NY 6246
Watch Water Resr. 96 NT 6556
Watendlath 82 NY 2615
Water 78 SD 8425
Waterbeach 53 TL 4965
Waterbeck 89 NY 2477
Waterden 64 TF 8835
Water End (Herts.) 36 TL 0310
Water End (Herts.) 37 TL 2304
Waterfall 60 SK 0851
Waterfoot (Lancs.) 78 SD 8321
Waterfoot (Strath.) 94 NS 5654
Waterford 37 TL 3114
Watergate Bay 19 SW 8264
Watergrove Resr. 69 SD 9017
Waterhead (Cumbr.) 83 NY 3703
Waterhead (Strath.) 93 NS 5411
Waterhead Hill 88 NS 5700
Waterhead Moor 100 NS 2562
Waterheads 95 NT 2451
Waterhouses (Durham) 84 NZ 1841
Waterhouses (Staffs.) 60 SK 0850
Wateringbury 29 TQ 6853
Wateringhouse 136 ND 3090
Waterloo (Dorset) 26 SZ 0194
Waterloo (Mers.) 68 SJ 3297
Waterloo (Norf.) 65 TG 2219
Waterloo (Strath.) 95 NS 8153
Waterloo (Tays.) 108 NO 0636
Waterloo Station 37 TQ 3179
Waterlooville 27 SU 6809
Water Meetings 88 NS 9513
Watermillock 83 NY 4322
Water Newton 62 TL 1097
Waternish (dist.) 122 NG 2658
Waternish Point 122 NG 2367
Water of Ae 88 NY 0186
Water of Ailnack 117 NJ 1314
Water of App 86 NX 0774
Water of Aven 119 NO 5988
Water of Buchat 118 NJ 3517
Water of Caiplich 117 NJ 0709
Water of Charr 119 NO 6180
Water of Coyle 93 NS 4613
Water of Deugh 93 NS 5502
Water of Dye 119 NO 6485
Water of Feugh 119 NO 6191
Water of Girvan 93 NS 3004
Water of Ken 88 NX 6494
Water of Leith 102 NT 1163
Water of Luce 86 NX 1762
Water of Mark 118 NO 3883
Water of May 102 NO 0309
Water of Milk 89 NY 1681
Water of Minnoch 86 NX 3684
Water of Nevis 106 NN 1668
Water of Nochty 118 NJ 3115
Water of Ruchill 107 NN 7217
Water of Saughs 118 NO 4274
Water of Tanar 118 NO 4392
Water of Tarf 118 NO 4883
Water of Tig 86 NX 1382
Water of Tulla 106 NN 3546
Water of Unich 118 NO 3478
Water Orton 50 SP 1791
Waterperry 36 SP 6206
Waterrow 24 ST 0525
Watersfield 28 TQ 0115
Waterside (Strath.) 93 NS 4308
Waterside (Strath.) 93 NS 4843
Waterside (Strath.) 101 NS 5160
Waterside (Strath.) 101 NS 6773
Water Sound 136 ND 4695
Waterstein Head 122 NG 1447
Waterstock 36 SP 6305
Waterston 42 SM 9306
Water Stratford 51 SP 6534
Waters Upton 59 SJ 6319
Water Yeat 82 SD 2889
Watford (Herts.) 37 TQ 1196
Watford (Northants.) 51 SP 6069
Wath (N Yorks.) 78 SE 1467
Wath (N Yorks.) 79 SE 3277
Wath Upon Dearne 71 SE 4300
Watling Street (Gtr London) (ant.) 37 TQ 1792
Watling Street (Herts.) (ant.) 37 TL 1110
Watling Street (Leic.) (ant.) 51 SP 4490
Watling Street (Staffs.) (ant.) 59 SJ 8311
Watlington (Norf.) 64 TF 6211
Watlington (Oxon.) 36 SU 6994
Watnall 61 SK 4946
Wat's Dyke (ant.) 58 SJ 3144
Wats Ness 140 HU 1750
Watten 135 ND 2454
Wattisfield 54 TM 0174
Wattisham 54 TM 0151
Watton (Humbs.) 81 TA 0150
Watton (Norf.) 64 TF 9100
Watton at Stone 37 TL 3019
Watton Beck 81 TA 0349
Wattston 101 NS 7770
Wattstown 41 ST 0194
Watty Bell's Cairn 90 NT 8901
Wauchope Forest 90 NT 6104
Waulkmill Bay 136 HY 3806
Waunarlwydd 40 SS 6095
Waun Fâch 41 SO 2129
Waunfawr 66 SH 5259
Waun Lysiog 41 SO 0215
Waun-oer 57 SH 7814
Wavendon 52 SP 9137
Waverley Abbey (ant.) 35 SU 8645
Waverton (Ches.) 68 SJ 4663
Waverton (Cumbr.) 82 NY 2247
Wawne 74 TA 0836
Waxham 65 TG 4326
Waxholme 75 TA 3229
Wayford 24 ST 4006
Wayland's Smithy (ant.) 34 SU 2885
Way Village 23 SS 8810
Wealdstone 37 TQ 1689
Weald, The (dist.) 31 TQ 6035
Weardale 84 NY 8838
Weare 32 ST 4152
Weare Giffard 22 SS 4721
Weasenham All Saints 64 TF 8421
Weasenham St. Peter 64 TF 8522
Weather Ness 138 HY 5240
Weaverham 69 SJ 6173
Weaver Hills 60 SK 0946
Weaver's Point 124 NF 9569
Weaverthorpe 81 SE 9670
Webheath 50 SP 0266
Weddel Sound 136 ND 3394
Wedder Dod (mt.) 88 NS 8215
Wedder Holm 143 HU 6197
Wedderlairs 121 NJ 8532
Wedder Law 88 NS 9302
Weddington 60 SP 3693
Wedhampton 34 SU 0557
Wedholme Flow 82 NY 2252
Wedmore 33 ST 4347
Wednesbury 60 SP 0095
Wednesfield 59 SJ 9400
Weedon 36 SP 8118
Weedon Bec 51 SP 6259
Weedon Lois 51 SP 6047
Weeford 60 SK 1404
Week 23 SS 7316
Weekley 52 SP 8880
Week St. Mary 20 SX 2397
Weeley 39 TM 1422
Weeley Heath 39 TM 1520
Weem 107 NN 8449
Weem Hill 107 NN 8251
Weeping Cross 59 SJ 9421
Wee Queensberry (mt.) 88 NX 9897
Weeting 54 TL 7788
Weeton (Lancs.) 77 SD 3834
Weeton (W Yorks.) 79 SE 2846
Weets Hill 78 SD 8544
Weetwood Hall 97 NU 0129
Weir 78 SD 8724
Weir Dike 74 SE 9714
Weir Wood Reservoir 29 TQ 3934
Weisdale (dist.) 141 HU 3953
Weisdale Voe 141 HU 3848
Welbeck Abbey 71 SK 5674
Welborne 64 TG 0610
Welbourn 62 SK 9654
Welburn 80 SE 7168
Welbury 85 NZ 3902
Welby 62 SK 9738
Welches Dam 53 TL 4786
Welcombe 22 SS 2218
Weldon 52 SP 9289
Weldon Bridge 91 NZ 1398
Welford (Berks.) 34 SU 4073
Welford (Northants.) 51 SP 6480
Welford-on-Avon 50 SP 1552
Welham 51 SP 7692
Welham Green 37 TL 2305
Well (Hants.) 35 SU 7646
Well (Lincs.) 73 TF 4473
Well (N Yorks.) 79 SE 2682
Welland 49 SO 7940
Wellesbourne 50 SP 2755
Wellgrain Dod (mt.) 88 NS 9018
Well Hill (Dumf. and Galwy.) 88 NS 9106
Well Hill (Kent) 37 TQ 4963
Welling 37 TQ 4575
Wellingborough 52 SP 8968
Wellingham 64 TF 8722
Wellingore 62 SK 9856
Wellington (Here. and Worc.) 45 SO 4948
Wellington (Shrops.) 59 SJ 6411
Wellington (Somer.) 24 ST 1320
Wellington Heath 49 SO 7140
Well of Kildinguie 137 HY 6527
Wellow (Avon) 33 ST 7358
Wellow (I. of W.) 26 SZ 3887
Wellow (Notts.) 71 SK 6666
Wells 33 ST 5445
Wellsborough 60 SK 3602
Wells-Next-The-Sea 64 TF 9143
Wells of Ythan 121 NJ 6338
Wellwood 102 NT 0888
Welney 63 TL 5294
Welshampton 58 SJ 4334
Welsh Bicknor 45 SO 5917
Welsh Channel 67 SJ 0985
Welsh End 59 SJ 5035
Welsh Frankton 58 SJ 3633
Welsh Grounds (sbk.) 33 ST 4582
Welsh Hook 42 SM 9327
Welsh Newton 45 SO 4918
Welshpool (Trallwng) 58 SJ 2207
Welsh St. Donats 41 ST 0276
Welton (Cumbr.) 82 NY 3544
Welton (Humbs.) 74 SE 9527
Welton (Lincs.) 72 TF 0079
Welton (Northants.) 51 SP 5865
Welton le Marsh 73 TF 4768
Welton le Wold 73 TF 2787
Welwick 75 TA 3421
Welwyn 37 TL 2316
Welwyn Garden City 37 TL 2412
Wem 59 SJ 5129
Wembdon 32 ST 2837
Wembley 37 TQ 1985
Wembury 20 SX 5148
Wembury Bay 20 SX 5147
Wembworthy 23 SS 6609
Wemyss Bay 100 NS 1869
Wenallt 67 SH 9842
Wendens Ambo 53 TL 5136
Wendlebury 47 SP 5519
Wendling 64 TF 9213
Wendover 36 SP 8708
Wendron 18 SW 6731
Wendy 53 TL 3247
Wenhaston 55 TM 4275
Wenlock Edge (mt.) 48 SO 5089
Wennington (Cambs.) 53 TL 2379
Wennington (Essex) 37 TQ 5381
Wennington (Lancs.) 77 SD 6169
Wensley (Derby.) 71 SK 2661
Wensley (N Yorks.) 84 SE 0989
Wensleydale 78 SD 9988
Wentbridge 71 SE 4817
Wentnor 48 SO 3892
Wentwood 45 ST 4194
Wentworth (Cambs.) 53 TL 4878
Wentworth (S Yorks.) 71 SK 3898
Wentworth Castle 71 SE 3103
Wenvoe 41 ST 1272
Weobley 45 SO 4051
Weobley Marsh 45 SO 4151
Wereham 64 TF 6801
Wergs 59 SJ 8601
Wernrheolydd 45 SO 3913
Werrington (Devon) 20 SX 3287
Werrington (Northants.) 62 TF 1703
Werrington (Staffs.) 60 SJ 9647
Wervin 68 SJ 4171
Wesham 77 SD 4132
Wessington 71 SK 3757
West Acre 64 TF 7715
West Allerdean 97 NT 9646
West Alvington 21 SX 7243
West Anstey 23 SS 8527
West Ashby 73 TF 2672
West Ashling 27 SU 8007
West Ashton 33 ST 8755
West Auckland 84 NZ 1826
West Bagborough 24 ST 1633
West Barns 103 NT 6578
West Barsham 64 TF 9033
West Baugh Fell 83 SD 7295
West Bay (Dorset) 25 SY 4690
West Bay (Dorset) 25 SY 6773
West Beckham 65 TG 1339
Westbere 31 TR 1961
West Bergholt 54 TL 9527
West Bexington 25 SY 5386
West Bilney 64 TF 7115
West Blatchington 28 TQ 2706
Westborough 62 SK 8544
Westbourne (Dorset) 26 SZ 0690
Westbourne (W Susx) 27 SU 7507
West Bradford 77 SD 7444
West Bradley 25 ST 5536
West Bretton 71 SE 2813
West Bridgford 61 SK 5837
West Bromwich 50 SP 0091
West Buckland (Devon) 23 SS 6531
West Buckland (Somer.) 24 ST 1720
West Burra (is.) 141 HU 3632
West Burrafirth 140 HU 2657
West Burton (N Yorks.) 78 SE 0186
West Burton (W Susx) 28 TQ 0014
Westbury (Bucks.) 51 SP 6235
Westbury (Shrops.) 58 SJ 3509
Westbury (Wilts.) 33 ST 8751
Westbury Leigh 33 ST 8649
Westbury-on-Severn 46 SO 7114
Westbury-sub-Mendip 33 ST 5049
Westby 77 SD 3731
West Caister 65 TG 5011
West Calder 102 NT 0163
West Camel 25 ST 5724
West Challow 34 SU 3688
West Charleton 21 SX 7542
West Chelborough 25 ST 5405
West Chevington 91 NZ 2297
West Chiltington 28 TQ 0918
West Clandon 28 TQ 0452
West Cliffe 31 TR 3445
Westcliff-on-Sea 38 TQ 8685
West Clyne 129 NC 8906
West Coker 25 ST 5113
Westcombe 33 ST 6739
West Compton (Dorset) 25 SY 5694
West Compton (Somer.) 33 ST 5942
Westcote 47 SP 2120
Westcott (Bucks.) 36 SP 7117
Westcott (Devon) 24 ST 0104
Westcott (Surrey) 28 TQ 1348
Westcott Barton 47 SP 4224
West Cross 40 SS 6189
West Curry 20 SX 2893
West Curthwaite 82 NY 3248
West Dart River 21 SX 6373
Westdean (E Susx) 29 TV 5299
West Dean (Wilts.) 26 SU 2526
West Dean (W Susx) 27 SU 8512
West Deeping 62 TF 1009
West Derby 68 SJ 3993
West Dereham 64 TF 6500
West Ditchburn 91 NU 1320
West Down (Devon) 22 SS 5142
West Down (Wilts.) 34 SU 0548
West Drayton (Gtr London) 36 TQ 0679
West Drayton (Notts.) 72 SK 7074
West End (Avon) 33 ST 4469
West End (Beds.) 52 SP 9853
West End (Hants.) 27 SU 4614
West End (Norf.) 65 TG 4911
West End (N Yorks.) 78 SE 1457
West End (Oxon.) 47 SP 4204
West End (Surrey) 36 SU 9461
West End Green 36 SU 6661
Westenhanger (ant.) 31 TR 1237
Wester Culbeuchly Crofts 121 NJ 6562
Westerdale (Highld.) 135 ND 1251
Westerdale (N Yorks.) 85 NZ 6605
Westerdale Moor 85 NZ 6502
Wester Denoon 109 NO 3543
Wester Fearn Burn 128 NH 5985
Westerfield (Shetld.) 141 HU 3551
Westerfield (Suff.) 55 TM 1747
Wester Fintray 119 NJ 8116
Westergate 28 SU 9305
Wester Gruinards 128 NH 5292
Westerham 29 TQ 4454
Wester Hoevdi (pt.) 140 HT 9338
Wester Lealty 128 NH 6073
Westerleigh 33 ST 6979
Wester Lonvine 129 NH 7172
Western Cleddau 42 SM 9418
Wester Newburn 103 NO 4405
Westernhope Moor 84 NY 9233
Western Isles or Hebrides 124 NG 0040
Western Isles or Hebrides 112 NG 0239
Western Rocks 18 SV 8406
Wester Ross (dist.) 127 NH 0562
Wester Skeld 140 HU 2943
Westerton 109 NO 6654
Wester Wick (Shetld.) 140 HU 2842
Westerwick (Shetld.) 140 HU 2843
West Farleigh 29 TQ 7152
West Fell 83 NY 6602
West Felton 58 SJ 3425
West Fen (Cambs.) 53 TL 5182
West Fen (Isle of Ely) (Cambs.) 63 TL 3698
West Fen (Lincs.) 63 TF 3053
Westfield (E Susx) 30 TQ 8115
Westfield (Highld.) 135 ND 0564
Westfield (Lothian) 102 NS 9372
Westfield (Norf.) 64 TF 9909
West Firle 29 TQ 4707
West Fleetham 97 NU 1928
Westgate (Durham) 84 NY 9038
Westgate (Humbs.) 74 SE 7707
Westgate (Norf.) 64 TF 9740
Westgate on Sea 31 TR 3270
West Gerinish 124 NF 7741
West Ginge 34 SU 4386
West Glen River 62 TF 0022
West Grafton 34 SU 2460
West Green 35 SU 7456
West Grimstead 26 SU 2026
West Grinstead 28 TQ 1721
West Haddlesey 79 SE 5526
West Haddon 51 SP 6371
West Hagbourne 35 SU 5187
Westhall (Cumbr.) 90 NY 5667
Westhall (Grampn.) (ant.) 121 NJ 6726
Westhall (Suff.) 55 TM 4280
West Hallam 60 SK 4341
West Halton 74 SE 9020
Westham (E Susx) 29 TQ 6404
West Ham (Gtr London) 37 TQ 4081
Westham (Somer.) 32 ST 4046
Westhampnett 27 SU 8706
West Handley 71 SK 3977
West Hanney 34 SU 4092
West Hanningfield 38 TQ 7399
West Hardwick 71 SE 4118
West Harptree 33 ST 5556
West Hatch 24 ST 2820
Westhay 33 ST 4342
Westhead 68 SD 4407
West Heath 35 SU 8556
West Helmsdale 135 ND 0114
West Hendred 35 SU 4488
West Heslerton 81 SE 9175
Westhide 45 SO 5844
Westhill 119 NJ 8307
West Hill 24 SY 0694
West Hoathly 29 TQ 3632
West Holme 25 SY 8885
Westhope (Here. and Worc.) 45 SO 4651
Westhope (Shrops.) 48 SO 4786
West Horndon 38 TQ 6288
Westhorpe (Lincs.) 62 TF 2131
Westhorpe (Suff.) 54 TM 0469
West Horrington 33 ST 5747
West Horsley 28 TQ 0753
West Hougham 31 TR 2640
Westhoughton 69 SD 6505
Westhouse 77 SD 6673
Westhouses 71 SK 4257
West Hoyle Bank (sbk.) 67 SJ 1088
Westhumble 28 TQ 1652
West Hyde 36 TQ 0391
West Ilsley 35 SU 4682
Westing 143 HP 5705
West Itchenor 27 SU 7900
West Kame (mt.) 141 HU 3959
West Kennet 34 SU 1167
West Kilbride 93 NS 2048
West Kingsdown 37 TQ 5762
West Kington 33 ST 8077
West Kirby 68 SJ 2186
West Knighton 25 SY 7387
West Knock 118 NO 4775
West Knoyle 25 ST 8532
Westlake 21 SX 6253
West Langdon 31 TR 3247
West Langwell 133 NC 6909
West Lavington (Wilts.) 34 SU 0052
West Lavington (W Susx) 27 SU 8920
West Lavington Down 34 ST 9949
West Layton 84 NZ 1409
West Leake 61 SK 5226
Westleigh (Devon) 22 SS 4628
Westleigh (Devon) 24 ST 0517
Westleton 55 TM 4469
West Lexham 64 TF 8417
Westley (Shrops.) 58 SJ 3507
Westley (Suff.) 54 TL 8264
Westley Waterless 54 TL 6256
West Lilling 79 SE 6465
West Linga (is.) 141 HU 5364
Westlington 36 SP 7610
West Linton (Borders) 95 NT 1551
Westlinton (Cumbr.) 89 NY 3964
West Littleton 33 ST 7575
West Loch Roag 131 NB 0939
West Loch Tarbert (Harris, W Isles) 125 NB 0803
West Loch Tarbert (Strath.) 99 NR 8062
West Lomond (mt.) 103 NO 1906
West Lulworth 25 SY 8280
West Lutton 81 SE 9269
West Lynn 64 TF 6120
West Mains 95 NS 9550
West Malling 29 TQ 6857
West Malvern 49 SO 7646
West Marden 27 SU 7613
West Markham 72 SK 7272
Westmarsh 31 TR 2761
West Marton 78 SD 8850
West Meon 27 SU 6424
West Mersea 39 TM 0112
Westmeston 29 TQ 3313
Westmill 53 TL 3627
West Milton 25 SY 5096
Westminster 37 TQ 2979
West Monar Forest 127 NH 0842
West Monkton 24 ST 2528
West Moors 26 SU 0802
West Moulie Geo 140 HU 2940
West Mouse (is.) 66 SH 3094
Westmuir (Tays.) 109 NO 3652
West Muir (Tays.) 109 NO 5661
West Ness (Fife) 103 NO 6106
Westness (Rousay) 136 HY 3829
Westnewton (Cumbr.) 82 NY 1344
West Newton (Humbs.) 75 TA 1037
West Newton (Norf.) 64 TF 6927
West Norwood 37 TQ 3171
West Ogwell 21 SX 8170
Weston (Avon) 33 ST 7266
Weston (Berks.) 34 SU 3973
Weston (Ches.) 69 SJ 5080
Weston (Ches.) 59 SJ 7252
Weston (Dorset) 25 SY 6870
Weston (Hants.) 27 SU 7221
Weston (Herts.) 53 TL 2630
Weston (Lincs.) 63 TF 2925
Weston (Northants.) 51 SP 5847
Weston (Notts.) 72 SK 7767
Weston (Shrops.) 59 SJ 5628
Weston (Shrops.) 59 SO 5993
Weston (Staffs.) 60 SJ 9727
Weston (W Yorks.) 78 SE 1747
Weston Airport 32 ST 3460
Weston Bay 32 ST 3060
Weston Beggard 45 SO 5841
Weston by Welland 51 SP 7791
Weston Colville 54 TL 6153
Weston Favell 51 SP 7862
Weston Green 54 TL 6252
Weston Heath 59 SJ 7813
Weston Hill 48 SO 5582
Weston Hills 63 TF 2821
Westoning 52 TL 0332
Weston-in-Gordano 33 ST 4474
Weston Jones 59 SJ 7524
Weston Longville 65 TG 1116
Weston Lullingfields 58 SJ 4224
Weston-on-the-Green 47 SP 5318
Weston-on-Trent 60 SK 4027
Weston Patrick 35 SU 6946
Weston Rhyn 58 SJ 2835
Weston Subedge 50 SP 1240
Weston-super-Mare 32 ST 3261
Weston Turville 36 SP 8511
Weston-under-Lizard 59 SJ 8010
Weston under Penyard 45 SO 6323
Weston under Wetherley 50 SP 3569
Weston Underwood (Bucks.) 52 SP 8650
Weston Underwood (Derby.) 60 SK 2942
Westonzoyland 24 ST 3534
West Overton 34 SU 1367
Westow 80 SE 7565
West Parley 26 SZ 0997
West Peckham 29 TQ 6452
West Pennard 33 ST 5438
West Pentire 18 SW 7760
Westport 24 ST 3819
West Putford 22 SS 3515
West Quantoxhead 32 ST 1141
West Rainton 84 NZ 3246
West Rasen 72 TF 0589
Westray 138 HY 4546
Westray Aerodrome 138 HY 4652
Westray Firth 138 HY 4437
West Raynham 64 TF 8725
West Reef 104 NM 2313
Westrigg 102 NS 9067
West Road 31 TR 0016
West Row 54 TL 6775
West Rudham 64 TF 8127
West Runton 65 TG 1842
Westruther 96 NT 6349
Westry 63 TL 3998
West Saltoun 103 NT 4667
West Sandwick 143 HU 4588
West Scar 85 NZ 5926
West Scrafton 78 SE 0783
West Sedge Moor 24 ST 3525
Westside 138 HY 3730
West Somerset Railway 24 ST 1435
West Stafford 25 SY 7289
West Stoke 27 SU 8208
West Stonesdale 84 NY 8802
West Stoughton 32 ST 4149
West Stour 25 ST 7822
West Stourmouth 31 TR 2562
West Stow 54 TL 8170
West Stowell 34 SU 1362
West Street 30 TQ 9054
West Tanfield 79 SE 2778
West Tarbert 99 NR 8467
West Tarbert Bay 92 NR 6453
West Thorney 27 SU 7602
West Thurrock 37 TQ 5877
West Tilbury 30 TQ 6677
West Tisted 27 SU 6429
West Tofts 108 NO 1134
West Torrington 73 TF 1381
West Town 33 ST 4767
West Tytherley 26 SU 2730
West Tytherton 34 ST 9474
West Voe 141 HU 3630
West Voe of Sumburgh 141 HU 3909
West Walton 63 TF 4713
Westward 82 NY 2744
Westward Ho! 22 SS 4329
West Water 109 NO 5170
West Water Resr. 95 NT 1152
Westwell (Kent) 31 TQ 9947
Westwell (Oxon.) 47 SP 2210
Westwell Leacon 31 TQ 9647
West Wellow 26 SU 2818
West Wemyss 103 NT 3294
West Wick (Avon) 32 ST 3661
Westwick (Cambs.) 53 TL 4265
Westwick (Norf.) 65 TG 2727
West Wickham (Cambs.) 54 TL 6149
West Wickham (Gtr London) 37 TQ 3866
West Winch 64 TF 6316
West Winterslow 26 SU 2232
West Wittering 27 SZ 7999
West Witton 78 SE 0688
Westwood (Devon) 24 SY 0199
Westwood (Wilts.) 33 ST 8158
West Woodburn 90 NY 8986
West Woodhay 34 SU 3962
West Woodlands 33 ST 7743
Westwoodside 74 SK 7499
West Worldham 27 SU 7436
West Wratting 54 TL 6052
West Wycombe 36 SU 8394
West Yell 143 HU 4582
Wetheral 83 NY 4654
Wetherby 79 SE 4048
Wether Cairn 90 NT 9411
Wetherden 54 TM 0062
Wether Fell 78 SD 8786
Wether Hill (Dumf. and Galwy.) 88 NX 6994
Wether Hill (Grampn.) 88 NX 7087
Wether Hill (Tays.) 102 NN 9205
Wetheringsett 55 TM 1266
Wether Lair (mt.) 90 NY 7096
Wether Law 95 NT 1948
Wethersfield 54 TL 7131
Wethersta 141 HU 3665
Wetherup Street 55 TM 1464
Wetley Rocks 60 SJ 9649
Wet Sleddale Resr. 83 NY 5511
Wettenhall 69 SJ 6261
Wetton 60 SK 1055
Wetwang 81 SE 9359
Wetwood 59 SJ 7733
Wexcombe 34 SU 2758
Weybourne 65 TG 1143
Weybread 55 TM 2480
Weybridge 36 TQ 0764
Weydale 135 ND 1464
Weyhill 34 SU 3146
Weymouth 25 SY 6778
Weymouth Bay 25 SY 6980
Whaddon (Bucks.) 51 SP 8034
Whaddon (Cambs.) 53 TL 3546
Whaddon (Glos.) 46 SO 8313
Whaddon (Wilts.) 26 SU 1926
Whaddon Chase 51 SP 7932
Whale 83 NY 5221
Whale Chine 27 SZ 4678
Whale Firth 143 HU 4694
Whale Geo 143 HU 4493
Whale Island 27 SU 6302
Whaley 71 SK 5171
Whaley Bridge 70 SK 0181
Whaligoe 135 ND 3240
Whalley 77 SD 7335
Whalsay 141 HU 5663
Whalton 91 NZ 1281
Whalwick Taing 142 HU 2381
Wham 78 SD 7762
Whaness 136 HY 2502
Whaplode 63 TF 3224
Whaplode Drove 63 TF 3113
Whaplode Fen 63 TF 3220
Whaplode River 63 TF 3429
Wharfe 78 SD 7869
Wharfedale 78 SE 0653
Wharles 77 SD 4435
Wharncliffe Side 71 SK 2994
Wharram le Street 80 SE 8666
Wharton (Ches.) 69 SJ 6666
Wharton (Here. and Worc.) 45 SO 5055
Whashton 84 NZ 1406
Whatcombe 25 ST 8301
Whatcote 50 SP 2944
Whatfield 54 TM 0246
Whatley 33 ST 7347
Whatlington 29 TQ 7618
Whatstandwell 60 SK 3354
Whatton 61 SK 7439
Whauphill 86 NX 4049
Whaw 84 NY 9804
Wheatacre 65 TM 4594
Wheathampstead 37 TL 1713
Wheatley (Hants.) 35 SU 7840
Wheatley (Notts.) 72 SK 7685
Wheatley (Oxon.) 47 SP 5905
Wheatley Hill 85 NZ 3839
Wheatley Lane 78 SD 8337
Wheaton Aston 59 SJ 8412
Wheat Stack 97 NT 8670
Wheddon Cross 23 SS 9238
Wheedlemont 121 NJ 4726
Wheeldale Moor 80 SE 7997
Wheelerstreet 28 SU 9440
Wheelock 69 SJ 7458
Wheelton 77 SD 6021
Whelen 109 NO 3670
Wheldrake 79 SE 6744
Whelford 47 SU 1698
Whelpley Hill 36 TL 0004
Whenby 79 SE 6369
Whepstead 54 TL 8358
Whernside (mt.) 77 SD 7381
Wherstead 55 TM 1540
Wherwell 34 SU 3840
Wheston 70 SK 1376
Whetsted 29 TQ 6546
Whetstone 61 SP 5597
Whicham 76 SD 1382
Whichford 47 SP 3134
Whickham 91 NZ 2061
Whiddon Down 21 SX 6992

Whigstreet 109 NO 4844
Whillan Beck 82 NY 1701
Whilton 51 SP 6364
Whimple 24 SY 0497
Whimpwell Green 65 TG 3829
Whinburgh 64 TG 0009
Whinfell Beacon 83 NY 5700
Whinlatter Pass 82 NY 1924
Whinnyfold 121 NK 0733
Whins Brow 77 SD 6353
Whippingham 27 SZ 5193
Whipsnade 36 TL 0117
Whipsnade Park Zoo 36 TL 0017
Whipton 21 SX 9493
Whissendine 62 SK 8214
Whissonsett 64 TF 9123
Whistley Green 36 SU 7974
Whiston (Mers.) 69 SJ 4791
Whiston (Northants.) 52 SP 8560
Whiston (Staffs.) 59 SJ 8914
Whiston (Staffs.) 60 SK 0347
Whiston (S Yorks.) 71 SK 4489
Whitaloo Point 136 HY 2628
Whitbeck 76 SD 1184
Whitbourne 49 SO 7156
Whitburn (Lothian) 102 NS 9464
Whitburn (Tyne and Wear) 91 NZ 4061
Whitby (Ches.) 68 SJ 4075
Whitby (N Yorks.) 81 NZ 8911
Whitchurch (Avon) 33 ST 6167
Whitchurch (Bucks.) 36 SP 8020
Whitchurch (Devon) 20 SX 4972
Whitchurch (Dyfed) 42 SM 8025
Whitchurch (Hants.) 35 SU 4648
Whitchurch (Here. and Worc.) 45 SO 5417
Whitchurch (Oxon.) 36 SU 6377
Whitchurch (S Glam.) 41 ST 1680
Whitchurch (Shrops.) 59 SJ 5441
Whitchurch Canonicorum 24 SY 3995
Whitchurch Hill 36 SU 6478
Whitcott Keysett 48 SO 2782
Whiteacen 120 NJ 2646
Whiteadder Resr. 103 NT 6563
Whiteadder Water (Borders) 97 NT 8555
Whiteadder Water (Lothian) 103 NT 6267
Whiteash Hill Wood 121 NJ 3657
Whitebrook 45 SO 5306
Whitecairns 119 NJ 9218
White Cart Water 101 NS 5263
White Castle (ant.) 45 SO 3716
White Caterthun (mt.) 109 NO 5465
White Chapel 77 SD 5542
Whitechurch 42 SN 1436
Whitecliff Bay 27 SZ 6485
White Coomb 89 NT 1614
White Coppice 69 SD 6119
Whitecraig (Lothian) 103 NT 3570
Whitecraig (Strath.) (mt.) 95 NT 0753
Whitecroft 45 SO 6106
Whitecross 102 NS 9676
White Esk 89 NY 2499
Whiteface 129 NH 7089
Whitefarland Point 92 NR 8642
Whitefauld Hill 88 NY 0293
White Fen 53 TL 3492
Whitefield (Gtr Mches.) 69 SD 8006
Whitefield (Tays.) 108 NO 1734
Whitefield Loch 86 NX 2355
Whiteford 121 NJ 7126
Whiteford Point 40 SS 4496
Whitehall 137 HY 6528
Whitehaugh Forest 121 NJ 5822
Whitehaven 82 NX 9718
White Hill (Borders) 90 NT 5211
White Hill (Grampn.) 119 NO 5388
Whitehill (Hants.) 27 SU 7934
White Hill (Lancs.) 77 SD 6758
White Hill (Strath.) 93 NS 2656
White Hill (Strath.) 88 NS 8519
White Hill (Tays.) 109 NO 4072
Whitehills 121 NJ 6565
White Hope Edge 89 NY 3397
Whitehope Law 96 NT 3344
Whitehorse Hill 34 SU 2986
Whitehouse (Grampn.) 119 NJ 6214
Whitehouse (Strath.) 99 NR 8161
White Island 18 SV 9217
Whitekirk 103 NT 5981
White Knowes 88 NS 6104
White Lackington 25 SY 7198
White Ladies Aston 49 SO 9252
White Law 97 NT 8526
Whitelaw Hill (Borders) 95 NT 1935
Whitelaw Hill (Lothian) 103 NT 5771
Whitelee Hill 93 NS 5442
Whiteley Village 36 TQ 0962
White Loch 86 NX 1060
White Lyne 90 NY 5373
Whitemans Green 29 TQ 3025
White Meldon 95 NT 2242
Whitemill Bay 139 HY 6946
Whitemill Point 139 HY 7046
Whitemire 129 NH 9754
Whitemoor 19 SW 9757
Whitemoor Reservoir 78 SD 8743
White Mounth 117 NO 2384
White Ness (Kent) 31 TR 4070
White Ness (Shetld.) 141 HU 3844
Whiteness (Shetld.) (dist.) 141 HU 4147
Whiteness Head 129 NH 8058
Whiteness Sands 129 NH 8386
Whiteness Voe 141 HU 3943
Whiten Head or An Ceann Geal 133 NC 4968
White Notley 38 TL 7818
Whiteparish 26 SU 2423
White Preston 90 NY 5977
Whiterashes 121 NJ 8523
White Roding or White Roothing 37 TL 5613
White Roothing or White Roding 37 TL 5613
Whiterow 135 ND 3548
Whitesand Bay (Corn.) 18 SW 3427
Whitesand Bay or Porth-mawr (Dyfed) 42 SM 7227
White Sands 68 SJ 2771
White Shank (mt.) 89 NT 2006
White Sheet Castle (ant.) 25 ST 8034
White Sheet Hill (Wilts.) 25 ST 8034
White Sheet Hill (Wilts.) 26 ST 9424
Whiteshill 46 SO 8307
Whiteshoot Hill 26 SU 2833
Whiteside (Lothian) 102 NS 9667
Whiteside (Northum.) 90 NY 7069
Whitesmith 29 TQ 5214
Whitestaunton 24 ST 2810
Whitestone 21 SX 8694
Whitestone Hill 90 NT 8014
White Top of Culreoch 88 NX 5963
White Waltham 36 SU 8577
Whiteway 46 SO 9110
Whiteway House 21 SX 8783
Whitewell 77 SD 6546
Whiteworks 21 SX 6071
Whitewreath 120 NJ 2356
Whitfell 82 SD 1592
Whitfield (Glos.) 33 ST 6791
Whitfield (Kent) 31 TR 3146
Whitfield (Northants.) 51 SP 6039
Whitfield (Northum.) 90 NY 7758
Whitfield Moor 83 NY 7454
Whitford 68 SJ 1477
Whitgift 74 SE 8022
Whitgreave 59 SJ 8928
Whithorn 87 NX 4440
Whiting Bay (Island of Arran) 92 NS 0425
Whiting Bay (Island of Arran) 92 NS 0526
Whitland 43 SN 1916
Whitletts 93 NS 3622
Whitley (Berks.) 36 SU 7170
Whitley (Ches.) 69 SJ 6178
Whitley (N Yorks.) 79 SE 5521
Whitley Bay 91 NZ 3572
Whitley Chapel 84 NY 9257
Whitley Row 29 TQ 5052
Whitlock's End 50 SP 1076
Whitminster 46 SO 7708
Whit Moor 77 SD 5864
Whitmore 59 SJ 8041
Whitnage 24 ST 0215
Whitnash 50 SP 3263
Whitney 45 SO 2647
Whitrigg (Cumbr.) 82 NY 2038
Whitrigg (Cumbr.) 82 NY 2257
Whitsand Bay 20 SX 3751
Whitsbury 26 SU 1218
Whitsome 97 NT 8650
Whitson 32 ST 3783
Whitstable 31 TR 1166
Whitstone 20 SX 2698
Whittingham 91 NU 0611
Whittingslow 48 SO 4288
Whittington (Derby.) 71 SK 3975
Whittington (Glos.) 46 SP 0120
Whittington (Here. and Worc.) 49 SO 8582
Whittington (Here. and Worc.) 49 SO 8752
Whittington (Lancs.) 77 SD 5976
Whittington (Norf) 64 TL 7199
Whittington (Shrops.) 58 SJ 3230
Whittington (Staffs.) 60 SK 1508
Whittlebury 51 SP 6943
Whittle-le-Woods 77 SD 5822
Whittlesey 63 TL 2797
Whittlesey Mere 53 TL 2290
Whittlesford 53 TL 4748
Whittlewood Forest 51 SP 7243
Whitton (Cleve.) 85 NZ 3822
Whitton (Humbs.) 74 SE 9024
Whitton (Northum.) 91 NU 0501
Whitton (Powys) 48 SO 2667
Whitton (Shrops.) 48 SO 5772
Whitton (Suff.) 55 TM 1447
Whittonditch 34 SU 2872
Whittonstall 84 NZ 0757
Whitwell (Derby.) 71 SK 5276
Whitwell (Herts.) 37 TL 1821
Whitwell (I. of W.) 27 SZ 5277
Whitwell (Leic.) 62 SK 9208
Whitwell (N Yorks.) 84 SE 2899
Whitwell-on-the-Hill 80 SE 7265
Whitwick 60 SK 4316
Whitwood 79 SE 4124
Whitworth 69 SD 8818
Whixall 59 SJ 5034
Whixley 79 SE 4457
Whorlton (Durham) 84 NZ 1014
Whorlton (N Yorks.) 85 NZ 4802
Whorlton Moor 85 SE 4998
Whygate 90 NY 7675
Whyle 45 SO 5560
Whyteleafe 37 TQ 3358
Wiay (Benbecula) 124 NF 8746
Wiay (Island of Skye) 122 NG 2936
Wibdon 45 ST 5797
Wibtoft 51 SP 4787
Wichenford 49 SO 7860
Wichling 30 TQ 9256
Wick (Avon) 33 ST 0972
Wick (Dorset) 26 SZ 1591
Wick (Here. and Worc.) 50 SO 9645
Wick (Highld.) 135 ND 3650
Wick (S Glam.) 41 SS 9272
Wick (Shetld.) 141 HU 4439
Wick (Unst) 143 HP 5603
Wick (Wilts.) 26 SU 1621
Wick (W Susx) 28 TQ 0203
Wick Airport 135 ND 3652
Wick Bay 135 ND 3750
Wick Down 26 SU 1321
Wicken (Cambs.) 53 TL 5770
Wicken (Northants.) 51 SP 7439
Wicken Bonhunt 53 TL 5033
Wickenby 72 TF 0882
Wickenby Airport 73 TF 1081
Wickersley 71 SK 4891
Wickford 38 TQ 7593
Wickham (Berks.) 34 SU 3971
Wickham (Hants.) 27 SU 5711
Wickham Bishops 38 TL 8412
Wickhambreaux 31 TR 2158
Wickhambrook 54 TL 7454
Wickhamford 50 SP 0642
Wickham Market 55 TM 3056
Wickhampton 65 TG 4205
Wickham Skeith 55 TM 0969
Wickham St. Paul 54 TL 8336
Wickham Street (Suff.) 54 TL 7554
Wickham Street (Suff.) 55 TM 0869
Wick Hill 36 SU 8064
Wicklewood 64 TG 0702
Wickmere 65 TG 1633
Wick of Breakon 143 HP 5205
Wick of Gruting 143 HU 6592
Wick of Mucklabrek 140 HT 9438
Wick of Sandsayre 141 HU 4325
Wick of Shunni 141 HU 3515
Wick of Tresta 143 HU 6388
Wick River 135 ND 2953
Wick St. Lawrence 32 ST 3665
Wickwar 33 ST 7288
Widdale Fell 78 SD 8088
Widdington 53 TL 5331
Widdop Resr. 78 SD 9332
Widdrington 91 NZ 2595
Widdrington Station 91 NZ 2494
Widdybank Fell 83 NY 8230
Widecombe In the Moor 21 SX 7176
Wide Firth 136 HY 4316
Wideford Hill 136 HY 4111
Widegates 20 SX 2857
Widemouth Bay 22 SS 2002
Wide Open 91 NZ 2472
Widewall 136 ND 4391
Widewall Bay 136 ND 4292
Widford (Essex) 38 TL 6905
Widford (Herts.) 37 TL 4115
Widmerpool 61 SK 6327
Widnes 69 SJ 5185
Wife Geo 135 ND 3969
Wigan 69 SD 5805
Wiggaton 24 SY 1093
Wiggenhall St. Germans 64 TF 5914
Wiggenhall St. Mary Magdalen 64 TF 5911
Wiggenhall St. Mary the Virgin 63 TF 5814
Wiggington (N Yorks.) 79 SE 5958
Wigginton (Herts.) 36 SP 9410
Wigginton (Oxon.) 47 SP 3833
Wigginton (Staffs.) 60 SK 2106
Wigglesworth 78 SD 8056
Wiggonby 82 NY 2953
Wiggonholt 28 TQ 0616
Wighill 79 SE 4746
Wighton 64 TF 9339
Wigmore (Here. and Worc.) 48 SO 4169
Wigmore (Kent) 30 TQ 8063
Wigsley 72 SK 8570
Wigsthorpe 52 TL 0482
Wigston 61 SP 6099
Wig, The (roadstead) 86 NX 0467
Wigtoft 63 TF 2636
Wigton 82 NY 2548
Wigtown 87 NX 4355
Wigtown Bay 87 NX 5249
Wigtown Sands 87 NX 4556
Wilbarston 52 SP 8188
Wilberfoss 80 SE 7350
Wilburton 53 TL 4875
Wilby (Norf.) 54 TM 0389
Wilby (Northants.) 52 SP 8666
Wilby (Suff.) 55 TM 2472
Wilcot 34 SU 1461
Wildboarclough 70 SJ 9868
Wilden 52 TL 0955
Wildhern 34 SU 3550
Wildmore Fen 63 TF 2551
Wildsworth 72 SK 8097
Wiley Sike 90 NY 6369
Wilford 61 SK 5637
Wilkesley 59 SJ 6241
Wilkhaven 129 NH 9486
Wilkieston 102 NT 1168
Willand 24 ST 0310
Willaston (Ches.) 68 SJ 3277
Willaston (Ches.) 59 SJ 6752
Willen 52 SP 8741
Willenhall (W Mids.) 60 SO 9698
Willenhall (W Mids.) 50 SP 3676
Willerby (Humbs.) 74 TA 0230
Willerby (N Yorks.) 81 TA 0079
Willersey 50 SP 1039
Willersley 45 SO 3147
Willesborough 31 TR 0441
Willesden 37 TQ 2284
Willett 24 ST 1033
Willey (Shrops.) 59 SO 6799
Willey (Warw.) 51 SP 4984
William Law 96 NT 4839
Williamscot 51 SP 4745
Willian 53 TL 2230
Willimontswick 90 NY 7763
Willingale 38 TL 5907
Willingdon 29 TQ 5902
Willingdon Hill 29 TQ 5600
Willingham (Cambs.) 53 TL 4070
Willingham by Stow 72 SK 8784
Willington (Beds.) 52 TL 1150
Willington (Derby.) 60 SK 2928
Willington (Durham) 84 NZ 1935
Willington (Tyne and Wear) 91 NZ 3167
Willington (Warw.) 50 SP 2638
Willington Corner 69 SJ 5367
Willitoft 74 SE 7434
Williton 32 ST 0740
Willoughby (Lincs.) 73 TF 4772
Willoughby (Warw.) 51 SP 5167
Willoughby-on-the-Wolds 61 SK 6325
Willoughby Waterleys 51 SP 5792
Willoughton 72 SK 9293
Willy Howe (ant.) 81 TA 0672
Wilmcote 50 SP 1658
Wilmington (Devon) 24 SY 2199
Wilmington (E Susx) 29 TQ 5404
Wilmington (Kent) 37 TQ 5372
Wilmslow 69 SJ 8480
Wilnecote 60 SK 2201
Wilpshire 77 SD 6832
Wilsden 78 SE 0935
Wilsford (Lincs.) 62 TF 0043
Wilsford (Wilts.) 34 SU 1057
Wilsford (Wilts.) 34 SU 1339
Wilsill 78 SE 1864
Wilson 60 SK 4024
Wilson's Pike 90 NY 5589
Wilstead 52 TL 0643
Wilsthorpe 62 TF 0913
Wilstone 36 SP 9014
Wilstone Reservoir 36 SP 9013
Wilton (Cleve.) 85 NZ 5819
Wilton (N Yorks.) 80 SE 8582
Wilton (Wilts.) 26 SU 0931
Wilton (Wilts.) 34 SU 2661
Wilton Dean 89 NT 4914
Wilton House (ant.) 26 SU 0831
Wimbish 54 TL 5936
Wimbish Green 54 TL 6035
Wimbleball Reservoir 23 SS 9730
Wimbledon 37 TQ 2470
Wimbledon Park 37 TQ 2472
Wimblington 53 TL 4192
Wimblington Fen 53 TL 4589
Wimborne Minster 26 SZ 0199
Wimborne St. Giles 26 SU 0212
Wimbotsham 64 TF 6205
Wimpole Hall (ant.) 53 TL 3351
Wimpstone 50 SP 2148
Wincanton 25 ST 7128
Wincham 69 SJ 6675
Winchburgh 102 NT 0874
Winchcombe 46 SP 0228
Winchelsea 30 TQ 9017
Winchelsea Beach 30 TQ 9115
Winchester 27 SU 4829
Winchfield 35 SU 7654
Winchmore Hill (Bucks.) 36 SU 9394
Winchmore Hill (Gtr London) 37 TQ 3195
Wincle 70 SJ 9565
Windbury Point 22 SS 2926
Windermere (Cumbr.) 83 SD 3995
Windermere (Cumbr.) 83 SD 4198
Winderton 50 SP 3240
Windleden Reservoirs 70 SE 1501
Windlesham 36 SU 9363
Windlestraw Law 96 NT 3743
Windley 60 SK 3045
Windmill Hill (E Susx) 29 TQ 6412
Windmill Hill (Somer.) 24 ST 3116
Windrush 47 SP 1913
Windsor 36 SU 9676
Windsor Forest 36 SU 9373
Windsor Great Park 36 SU 9572
Wind Wick 136 ND 4587
Windy Crag 90 NT 7705
Windygates 103 NO 3400
Windy Gyle 90 NT 8614
Windyheads Hill 121 NJ 8561
Windy Hill 100 NS 0469
Windy Standard (Dumf. and Galwy.) (mt.) 88 NS 6101
Windy Standard (Strath.) (mt.) 93 NS 5204
Wineham 28 TQ 2320
Winestead 75 TA 2924
Winfarthing 55 TM 1085
Winford 33 ST 5364
Winforton 45 SO 2947
Winfrith Newburgh 25 SY 8084
Wing (Bucks.) 36 SP 8822
Wing (Leic.) 62 SK 8903
Wingate (Durham) 85 NZ 4036
Wingates (Gtr Mches.) 69 SD 6507
Wingates (Northum.) 91 NZ 0995
Wingerworth 71 SK 3867
Wingfield (Beds.) 52 SP 9926
Wingfield (Suff.) 55 TM 2276
Wingfield (Wilts.) 33 ST 8256
Wingham 31 TR 2457
Wingrave 36 SP 8719
Win Green 25 ST 9220
Winkburn 72 SK 7158
Winkfield 36 SU 9072
Winkfield Row 36 SU 9071
Winkhill 60 SK 0651
Winklebury (ant.) 26 ST 9521
Winkleigh 23 SS 6308
Winksley 79 SE 2471
Winless 135 ND 3054
Winmarleigh 77 SD 4748
Winna Ness 143 HU 6098
Winnersh 36 SU 7870
Winscales 82 NY 0226
Winscar Resr. 70 SE 1502
Winscombe 32 ST 4157
Winsford (Ches.) 69 SJ 6566
Winsford (Somer.) 23 SS 9034
Winsford Hill 23 SS 8734
Winsham 24 ST 3706
Winshill 60 SK 2623
Winskill 83 NY 5835
Winslade 35 SU 6547
Winsley 33 ST 7960
Winslow 51 SP 7627
Winson 46 SP 0908
Winster (Cumbr.) 83 SD 4193
Winster (Derby.) 71 SK 2460
Winston (Durham) 84 NZ 1416
Winston (Suff.) 55 TM 1861
Winstone 46 SO 9609
Winswell 22 SS 4913
Winterborne Abbas 25 SY 6190
Winterborne Clenston 25 ST 8302
Winterborne Herringston 25 SY 6887
Winterborne Houghton 25 ST 8104
Winterborne Kingston 25 SY 8697
Winterborne Monkton (Dorset) 25 SY 6787
Winterborne Steepleton 25 SY 6289
Winterborne Stickland 25 ST 8304
Winterborne Whitechurch 25 SY 8399
Winterborne Zelston 25 SY 8997
Winterbourne 33 ST 6480
Winterbourne Bassett 34 SU 1074
Winterbourne Dauntsey 26 SU 1734
Winterbourne Earls 26 SU 1633
Winterbourne Gunner 26 SU 1735
Winterbourne Monkton (Wilts.) 34 SU 0972
Winterbourne Stoke 34 SU 0740
Winterburn 78 SD 9358
Winterburn Resr. 78 SD 9460
Wintercleuch Fell 88 NS 9910
Winter Hill 69 SD 6514
Winterhope Reservoir 89 NY 2782
Winteringham 74 SE 9222
Winterley 69 SJ 7457
Wintersett 71 SE 3815
Winterton 74 SE 9218
Winterton-on-Sea 65 TG 4919
Winthorpe (Lincs.) 73 TF 5665
Winthorpe (Notts.) 62 SK 8156
Winton (Cumbr.) 83 NY 7810
Winton (Dorset) 26 SZ 0894
Winton Fell 83 NY 8307
Wintringham 81 SE 8873
Winwick (Cambs.) 52 TL 1080
Winwick (Ches.) 69 SJ 6092
Winwick (Northants.) 51 SP 6273
Wirksworth 60 SK 2854
Wirral 68 SJ 3181
Wirswall 59 SJ 5444
Wisbech 63 TF 4609
Wisbech St. Mary 63 TF 4208
Wisborough Green 28 TQ 0526
Wiseton 72 SK 7189
Wishaw (Strath.) 94 NS 7954
Wishaw (Warw.) 60 SP 1794
Wisp Hill 89 NY 3899
Wispington 73 TF 2071
Wissett 55 TM 3679
Wiss, The (mt.) 89 NT 2620
Wistanstow 48 SO 4385
Wistanswick 59 SJ 6629
Wistaston 59 SJ 6853
Wiston (Dyfed) 42 SN 0218
Wiston (Strath.) 95 NS 9531
Wiston (W Susx) 28 TQ 1512
Wistow (Cambs.) 53 TL 2781
Wistow (N Yorks.) 79 SE 5835
Wiswell 77 SD 7437
Witcham 53 TL 4680
Witchampton 26 ST 9806
Witchford 53 TL 5078
Witham 38 TL 8114
Witham Friary 33 ST 7440
Witham on the Hill 62 TF 0516
Withens Clough Resr. 78 SD 9822
Witherenden Hill 29 TQ 6426
Witheridge 23 SS 8014
Witherley 60 SP 3297
Withern 73 TF 4382
Withernsea 75 TA 3328
Withernwick 75 TA 1940
Withersdale Street 55 TM 2781
Withersfield 54 TL 6547
Witherslack 77 SD 4384
Witherslack Hall 77 SD 4386
Withiel 19 SW 9965
Withiel Florey 23 SS 9832
Withi Gill (mt.) 136 ND 2496
Withington (Ches.) 69 SJ 8170
Withington (Glos.) 46 SP 0315
Withington (Gtr Mches.) 69 SJ 8392
Withington (Here. and Worc.) 45 SO 5643
Withington (Shrops.) 59 SJ 5713
Withington Green 59 SJ 8031
Withleigh 23 SS 9012
Withnell 77 SD 6322
Withybrook 50 SP 4384
Withy Bush Aerodrome 42 SM 9519
Withycombe 32 ST 0141
Withyham 29 TQ 4935
Withypool 23 SS 8435
Withypool Common 23 SS 8135
Witley 28 SU 9439
Witnesham 55 TM 1850
Witney 47 SP 3509
Wittering 62 TF 0502
Wittersham 30 TQ 8927
Witton 65 TG 3331
Witton Gilbert 84 NZ 2345
Witton-le-Wear 84 NZ 1431
Witton Park 84 NZ 1730
Wiveliscombe 24 ST 0827
Wivelsfield 29 TQ 3420
Wivelsfield Green 29 TQ 3519
Wivelsfield Station 29 TQ 3219
Wivenhoe 39 TM 0321
Wivenhoe Cross 39 TM 0423
Wiveton 64 TG 0343
Wix 55 TM 1628
Wixford 50 SP 0854
Wixoe 54 TL 7142
Woburn 52 SP 9433
Woburn Abbey 52 SP 9632
Woburn Sands 52 SP 9235
Woden Law 90 NT 7612
Wokefield Park 36 SU 6765
Woking 36 TQ 0058
Wokingham 36 SU 8068
Wold Fell 78 SD 7885
Woldingham 29 TQ 3755
Wold Newton (Humbs.) 81 TA 0473
Wold Newton (Humbs.) 73 TF 2496
Wolds, The (Humbs.) 81 SE 9762
Wolds, The (Lincs.) (dist.) 64 TF 2585
Wolferlow 49 SO 6661
Wolferton 64 TF 6528
Wolfhill 108 NO 1533
Wolfhole Crag 77 SD 6257
Wolf Rock 18 SW 2612
Wolf's Castle 42 SM 9627
Wolfsdale 42 SM 9321
Woll 96 NT 4622
Wollaston (Northants.) 52 SP 9062
Wollaston (Shrops.) 58 SJ 3212
Wollerton 59 SJ 6229
Wolsingham 84 NZ 0737
Wolsingham Park Moor 84 NZ 0340
Wolston 50 SP 4175
Wolvercote 47 SP 4809
Wolverhampton 59 SO 9198
Wolverley (Here. and Worc.) 49 SO 8279
Wolverley (Shrops.) 58 SJ 4631
Wolverton (Bucks.) 52 SP 8141
Wolverton (Hants.) 35 SU 5557
Wolverton (Warw.) 50 SP 2062
Wolvey 50 SP 4387
Wolviston 85 NZ 4525
Wombleton 79 SE 6683
Wombourne 59 SO 8793
Wombwell 71 SE 3902
Womenswold 31 TR 2250
Womersley 71 SE 5319
Wonastow 45 SO 4811
Wonersh 28 TQ 0145
Wonston 35 SU 4739
Wooburn 36 SU 9187
Wooburn Green 36 SU 9188
Woodale 78 SE 0279
Woodbastwick 65 TG 3315
Woodbeck 72 SK 7777
Woodborough (Notts.) 61 SK 6347
Woodborough (Wilts.) 34 SU 1059
Woodbridge 55 TM 2749
Woodbury 21 SY 0087
Woodbury Hill (ant.) 49 SO 7464
Woodbury Salterton 24 SY 0189
Woodchester 46 SO 8302
Woodchurch 30 TQ 9434
Woodcote (Oxon.) 36 SU 6481
Woodcote (Shrops.) 59 SJ 7715
Woodcroft 45 ST 5495
Wood Dalling 65 TG 0927
Woodditton 54 TL 6559
Woodeaton 47 SP 5311
Woodend (Cumbr.) 82 SD 1696
Wood End (Herts.) 53 TL 3225
Woodend (Northants.) 51 SP 6149
Wood End (Warw.) 50 SP 1071
Wood End (Warw.) 60 SP 2498
Woodend (W Susx) 27 SU 8108
Wood Enderby 73 TF 2764
Woodfalls 26 SU 1920
Woodford (Corn.) 22 SS 2113
Woodford (Devon) 21 SX 7950
Woodford (Gtr London) 37 TQ 4090
Woodford (Gtr Mches.) 69 SJ 8982
Woodford (Northants.) 52 SP 9676
Woodford (Wilts.) 26 SU 1130
Woodford Aerodrome 69 SJ 8982
Woodford Bridge 37 TQ 4291
Woodford Green 37 TQ 4192
Woodford Halse 51 SP 5452
Woodgate (Here. and Worc.) 50 SO 9666
Woodgate (Norf.) 64 TG 0215
Woodgate (W Mids.) 50 SO 9982
Woodgate (W Susx) 28 SU 9304
Wood Green (Gtr London) 37 TQ 3191
Woodgreen (Hants.) 26 SU 1717
Woodhall 84 SD 9790
Woodhall Loch 88 NX 6867
Woodhall Spa 73 TF 1963
Woodham 36 TQ 0261
Woodham Ferrers 38 TQ 7999
Woodham Mortimer 38 TL 8205
Woodham Walter 38 TL 8006
Woodhaven 109 NO 4127
Woodhead (Grampn.) 121 NJ 7938
Woodhead (Grampn.) 121 NJ 9061
Woodhenge (ant.) 34 SU 1543
Woodhill 49 SO 7384
Woodhorn 91 NZ 2988
Woodhouse (Leic.) 61 SK 5315
Woodhouse (S Yorks.) 71 SK 4184
Woodhouse Eaves 61 SK 5214
Woodhouselee 103 NT 2364
Woodhurst 53 TL 3176
Woodingdean 29 TQ 3605
Woodland (Devon) 21 SX 7968
Woodland (Durham) 84 NZ 0726
Woodland Bay 86 NX 1795
Woodland Fell (Cumbr.) 82 SD 2589
Woodland Fell (Durham) 84 NZ 0326
Woodlands 58 SJ 3253
Woodlands (Dorset) 26 SU 0508
Woodlands (Grampn.) 119 NO 7895
Woodlands (Hants.) 26 SU 3111
Woodlands Park 36 SU 8578
Woodleigh 21 SX 7348
Woodlesford 79 SE 3629
Woodley 36 SU 7973
Woodmancote (Glos.) 46 SP 0008
Woodmancote (W Susx) 27 SU 7707
Woodmancott 35 SU 5642
Woodmansey 74 TA 0537
Woodmansterne 37 TQ 2760
Woodminton 26 SU 0122
Woodnesborough 31 TR 3156
Woodnewton 62 TL 0394
Wood Norton 64 TG 0128
Wood of Ordiequish 121 NJ 3555
Woodplumpton 77 SD 4934
Woodrising 64 TF 9803
Woodseaves (Shrops.) 59 SJ 6830
Woodseaves (Staffs.) 59 SJ 7925
Woodsend 34 SU 2275
Woodsetts 71 SK 5483
Woodsford 25 SY 7690
Woodside (Berks.) 36 SU 9371
Woodside (Herts.) 37 TL 2506
Woodside (Tays.) 108 NO 2037
Woodstock 47 SP 4416
Wood Street 28 SU 9551
Woodthorpe (Derby.) 71 SK 4574
Woodthorpe (Leic.) 61 SK 5417
Woodton 65 TM 2894
Woodtown 22 SS 4926
Woodville 60 SK 3119
Woodwalton 52 TL 2180
Wood Wick 136 HY 3923
Woodyates 26 SU 0219
Woody Bay 23 SS 6849
Woofferton 48 SO 5168
Wookey 33 ST 5145
Wookey Hole 33 ST 5347
Wool 25 SY 8486
Woolacombe 22 SS 4543
Woolaston 45 ST 5999
Woolavington 32 ST 3441
Woolbeding 27 SU 8722
Wooler 97 NT 9928
Woolfardisworthy (Devon) 22 SS 3321
Woolfardisworthy (Devon) 23 SS 8208

Name	Page	Grid Ref
Woolfords Cottages	95	NT 0057
Woolhampton	35	SU 5766
Woolhope	45	SO 6135
Woollage Green	31	TR 2449
Woolland	25	ST 7706
Woolley (Cambs.)	52	TL 1474
Woolley (W Yorks.)	71	SE 3113
Woolley House	34	SU 4179
Woolmer Green	37	TL 2518
Woolpit	54	TL 9762
Woolscott	51	SP 4968
Woolsington	91	NZ 1969
Woolstaston	58	SO 4498
Woolsthorpe	62	SK 8334
Woolston (Ches.)	69	SJ 6589
Woolston (Devon)	21	SX 7141
Woolston (Hants.)	27	SU 4410
Woolston (Shrops.)	58	SJ 3224
Woolston (Shrops.)	48	SO 4287
Woolstone (Bucks.)	52	SP 8738
Woolstone (Oxon.)	34	SU 2987
Woolston Green	21	SX 7766
Wooltack Point	42	SM 7509
Woolton	68	SJ 4286
Woolton Hill	34	SU 4261
Woolverstone	55	TM 1838
Woolverton	33	ST 7853
Woolwich	37	TQ 4478
Wooperton	91	NU 0420
Woore	59	SJ 7242
Wootton (Beds.)	52	TL 0045
Wootton (Hants.)	26	SZ 2498
Wootton (Humbs.)	74	TA 0815
Wootton (Kent)	31	TR 2246
Wootton (Northants.)	51	SP 7656
Wootton (Oxon.)	47	SP 4319
Wootton (Oxon.)	47	SP 4701
Wootton (Staffs.)	59	SJ 8227
Wootton (Staffs.)	60	SK 1045
Wootton Bassett	34	SU 0682
Wootton Bridge	27	SZ 5491
Wootton Common	27	SZ 5390
Wootton Courtenay	23	SS 9343
Wootton Fitzpaine	24	SY 3695
Wootton Rivers	34	SU 1962
Wootton St. Lawrence	35	SU 5953
Wootton Wawen	50	SP 1563
Worbarrow Bay	25	SY 8579
Worcester	49	SO 8555
Worcester and Birmingham Canal	49	SO 9465
Worcester Park	37	TQ 2266
Wordsley	49	SO 8887
Worfield	59	SO 7595
Work	136	HY 4713
Workington	82	NX 9928
Worksop	71	SK 5879
Worlaby	74	TA 0113
World's End (Berks.)	35	SU 4876
World's End (Clwyd)	58	SJ 2347
Worle	32	ST 3562
Worlebury (ant.)	32	ST 3262
Worleston	59	SJ 6856
Worlingham	55	TM 4489
Worlington (Devon)	23	SS 7713
Worlington (Suff.)	54	TL 6973
Worlingworth	54	TM 2368
Wormbridge	45	SO 4230
Wormegay	64	TF 6611
Wormelow Tump	45	SO 4930
Wormhill	70	SK 1274
Wormiehills	109	NO 6239
Wormingford	54	TL 9332
Worminghall	36	SP 6408
Wormington	50	SP 0336
Worminster	33	ST 5742
Wormit	109	NO 3925
Wormleighton	51	SP 4453
Wormley	37	TL 3605
Wormley West End	37	TL 3306
Worms Head	40	SS 3887
Wormshill	30	TQ 8857
Wormsley	45	SO 4248
Worplesdon	28	SU 9753
Worrall	71	SK 3092
Worsbrough	71	SE 3503
Worsley	69	SD 7400
Worstead	65	TG 3026
Worsthorne	78	SD 8732
Worston	78	SD 7642
Worswell	21	SX 5347
Worth (Kent)	31	TR 3356
Worth (W Susx)	29	TQ 3036
Worth Abbey	29	TQ 3134
Wortham	54	TM 0777
Worthen	58	SJ 3204
Worthenbury	58	SJ 4146
Worthing (Norf.)	64	TF 9919
Worthing (W Susx)	28	TQ 1402
Worthington	60	SK 4020
Worth Matravers	26	SY 9777
Worthy Down	27	SU 4635
Wortley	71	SK 3099
Worton	34	ST 9757
Wortwell	55	TM 2784
Wotherton	58	SJ 2800
Wotter	21	SX 5561
Wotton	28	TQ 1348
Wotton Under Edge	46	ST 7593
Wotton Underwood	36	SP 6815
Woughton on the Green	52	SP 8737
Wouldham	30	TQ 7164
Wrabness	55	TM 1731
Wragby	73	TF 1378
Wrakendike (ant.)	91	NZ 3162
Wramplingham	65	TG 1106
Wrangham	121	NJ 6331
Wrangle	63	TF 4250
Wrangway	24	ST 1217
Wrantage	24	ST 3022
Wrawby	74	TA 0108
Wraxall (Avon)	33	ST 4872
Wraxall (Somer.)	25	ST 5936
Wray	77	SD 6067
Wray Castle	83	NY 3700
Wraysbury	36	TQ 0173
Wrea Green	77	SD 3931
Wreay (Cumbr.)	83	NY 4349
Wreay (Cumbr.)	83	NY 4423
Wrekenton	91	NZ 2758
Wrekin, The	59	SJ 6208
Wrelton	80	SE 7686
Wrenbury	59	SJ 5947
Wreningham	65	TM 1699
Wrentham	55	TM 4982
Wressle	74	SE 7031
Wrestlingworth	53	TL 2547
Wretton	64	TF 6800
Wrexham	58	SJ 3349
Wrexham Industrial Estate	58	SJ 3849
Wribbenhall	49	SO 7975
Wrightington Bar	69	SD 5313
Wrightington Hall (ant.)	69	SD 5310
Wrinehill	59	SJ 7546
Wrington	33	ST 4662
Writtle	38	TL 6606
Wrockwardine	59	SJ 6212
Wroot	74	SE 7102
Wrotham	30	TQ 6159
Wrotham Heath	30	TQ 6258
Wrotham Park	37	TQ 2599
Wroughton	34	SU 1480
Wroxall (I. of W.)	27	SZ 5579
Wroxall (Warw.)	50	SP 2271
Wroxeter	59	SJ 5608
Wroxham	65	TG 3017
Wroxton	50	SP 4141
Wryde Croft	63	TF 3107
Wrynose Pass	82	NY 2702
Wyaston	60	SK 1842
Wyberton	63	TF 3240
Wyboston	52	TL 1656
Wybunbury	59	SJ 6949
Wychbold	49	SO 9166
Wych Cross	29	TQ 4231
Wyche	49	SO 7643
Wyck	35	SU 7539
Wyck Rissington	47	SP 1821
Wycombe Marsh	36	SU 8992
Wyddial	53	TL 3731
Wye	31	TR 0546
Wyke (Dorset.)	25	ST 7926
Wyke (Shrops.)	59	SJ 6402
Wyke (W Yorks.)	78	SE 1526
Wykeham (N Yorks.)	80	SE 8175
Wykeham (N Yorks.)	81	SE 9683
Wyke Regis	25	SY 6677
Wyke, The (N Yorks.) (pt.)	81	TA 0983
Wyke, The (Shrops.)	59	SJ 7306
Wykey	58	SJ 3925
Wylam	91	NZ 1164
Wylde Green	60	SP 1293
Wylfa Power Sta.	66	SH 3594
Wylye	26	SU 0037
Wylye Valley	26	SU 0037
Wymering	27	SU 6405
Wymeswold	61	SK 6023
Wymington	52	SP 9564
Wymondham (Leic.)	62	SK 8518
Wymondham (Norf.)	65	TG 1101
Wymondley	52	TL 2128
Wyndburgh Hill	90	NT 5504
Wyndham	41	SS 9391
Wynford Eagle	25	SY 5895
Wyre	136	HY 4426
Wyre Forest	49	SO 7576
Wyre Piddle	50	SO 9647
Wyresdale Tower (ruin)	77	SD 6054
Wyre Sound	136	HY 4226
Wysall	61	SK 6027
Wytch Heath	26	SY 9784
Wythall	49	SP 0775
Wytham	47	SP 4708
Wythburn Fells	82	NY 3212
Wyverstone	54	TM 0468
Wyverstone Street	54	TM 0367
Wyvis Lodge	128	NH 4873

Y

Name	Page	Grid Ref
Yaddlethorpe	74	SE 8806
Yafford	27	SZ 4581
Yafforth	85	SE 3494
Yair Hill Forest	96	NT 4333
Yalding	29	TQ 7050
Yantlet Dredged Channel	38	TQ 9180
Yanworth	46	SP 0713
Yapham	80	SE 7851
Yapton	28	SU 9703
Yarburgh	73	TF 3493
Yarcombe	24	ST 2408
Yardley	50	SP 1385
Yardley Chase	52	SP 8455
Yardley Gobion	51	SP 7644
Yardley Hastings	52	SP 8656
Yardro	45	SO 2258
Yarkhill	45	SO 6042
Yarlet	59	SJ 9129
Yarlington	25	ST 6529
Yarm	85	NZ 4111
Yarmouth	26	SZ 3589
Yarmouth Roads	65	TG 5507
Yarnbury Castle (ant.)	34	SU 0340
Yarnfield	59	SJ 8632
Yarnscombe	23	SS 5523
Yarnton	47	SP 4711
Yarpole	48	SO 4665
Yarrow	96	NT 3527
Yarrow Feus	96	NT 3325
Yarrow Water	96	NT 3728
Yarsop	45	SO 4047
Yarwell	62	TL 0697
Yate	33	ST 7082
Yateley	36	SU 8160
Yatesbury	34	SU 0671
Yattendon	35	SU 5474
Yatton (Avon)	33	ST 4265
Yatton (Here. and Worc.)	48	SO 4367
Yatton Keynell	33	ST 8676
Yaverland	27	SZ 6185
Yaxham	64	TG 0010
Yaxley (Cambs.)	52	TL 1892
Yaxley (Suff.)	55	TM 1173
Yazor	45	SO 4046
Y Bwlchwrcau	41	SS 8188
Y Clogydd	57	SJ 0628
Y Cribau (mt.)	67	SH 6753
Y Drum	44	SN 7358
Yeading	37	TQ 1182
Yeadon	78	SE 2040
Yealand Conyers	77	SD 5074
Yealand Redmayne	77	SD 5075
Yealmpton	21	SX 5751
Yearsley	79	SE 5874
Yeaton	58	SJ 4319
Yeaveley	60	SK 1840
Yeavering Bell	97	NT 9329
Yedingham	81	SE 8979
Yelden	52	TL 0167
Yelford	47	SP 3504
Yell (is.)	143	HU 4890
Yelling	53	TL 2562
Yell Sound	143	HU 4087
Yelvertoft	51	SP 5975
Yelverton (Devon)	21	SX 5267
Yelverton (Norf.)	65	TG 2901
Yenston	25	ST 7120
Yeoford	21	SX 7898
Yeolmbridge	20	SX 3187
Yeoman Wharf (sbk.)	77	SD 3563
Yeovil	25	ST 5515
Yeovil Airfield	25	ST 5315
Yeovil Junction Station	25	ST 5713
Yeovil Marsh	25	ST 5418
Yeovilton	25	ST 5422
Yerbeston	42	SN 0609
Yesnaby	136	HY 2215
Yester Castle	103	NT 5566
Yester Ho.	103	NT 5467
Yes Tor	21	SX 5890
Yetlington	91	NU 0209
Yetminster	25	ST 5910
Yettington	24	SY 0585
Yetts o'Muckhart	102	NO 0001
Y Fan	57	SN 9487
Y Ffor	66	SH 3939
Y Foel	57	SN 8484
Y Gaer (Powys) (ant.)	41	SO 0029
Y Gaer (S Glam.) (ant.)	41	ST 0674
Y Gamlas	66	SH 3432
Y Garn	57	SH 7023
Y Gribin	57	SH 8417
Yieldshields	95	NS 8750
Yiewsley	36	TQ 0680
Y Llethr	57	SH 6625
Ynysboeth	41	ST 0696
Ynysddu	41	ST 1892
Ynysdeullyn	42	SM 8434
Ynys Dulas	66	SH 5090
Ynys Gwylan-fawr	56	SH 1824
Ynyshir	41	ST 0292
Ynyslas	56	SN 6092
Ynys-Lochtyn (pt.)	43	SN 3155
Ynysybwl	41	ST 0594
Yockenthwaite	78	SD 9079
Yockleton	58	SJ 3910
Yokefleet	74	SE 8124
Yoker	101	NS 5168
Yonder Bognie	121	NJ 5946
York	79	SE 6052
Yorkletts	31	TR 0963
Yorkley	45	SO 6306
Yorton	59	SJ 4923
Youlgreave	70	SK 2164
Youlstone	22	SS 2715
Youlthorpe	80	SE 7655
Youlton	79	SE 4863
Young's End	38	TL 7319
Yoxall	60	SK 1419
Yoxford	55	TM 3968
Y Pigwn	41	SN 8131
Yr Allt (Dyfed)	57	SN 8376
Yr Allt (Powys)	41	SN 9129
Yr Aran	66	SH 6051
Yr Arddu	67	SH 6751
Yr Eifl (mt.)	66	SH 3544
Y Rhiw	56	SH 2228
Ysbyty Ifan	67	SH 8448
Ysbyty Ystwyth	57	SN 7371
Ysceifiog	58	SJ 1571
Ysgubor-y-coed	57	SN 6895
Ysgyryd Fawr	45	SO 3318
Ystalyfera	41	SN 7608
Ystrad	41	SS 9796
Ystrad Aeron	43	SN 5256
Ystradfellte	41	SN 9313
Ystradfellte Resr.	41	SN 9413
Ystradffin	44	SN 7846
Ystradgynlais	41	SN 7910
Ystrad Meurig	57	SN 7067
Ystrad Mynach	41	ST 1493
Ystradowen (Dyfed)	41	SN 7512
Ystradowen (S Glam.)	41	ST 0177
Ythanbank	121	NJ 9034
Ythsie	121	NJ 8830

Z

Name	Page	Grid Ref
Zeal Monachorum	23	SS 7103
Zeals	25	ST 7731
Zelah	19	SW 8051
Zennor	18	SW 4538
Zone Point	19	SW 8431